Measurement in Economics

Measurement in Economics

Theory and Applications of Economic Indices

Edited by
Wolfgang Eichhorn

In Cooperation with
W. Erwin Diewert, Susanne Fuchs-Seliger
Helmut Funke, Wilhelm Gehrig, Andreas Pfingsten
Klaus Spremann, Frank Stehling, Joachim Voeller

With 44 Figures

Springer-Verlag Berlin Heidelberg GmbH

Professor Dr. Wolfgang Eichhorn
Institut für Wirtschaftstheorie
und Operations Research
Universität Karlsruhe
7500 Karlsruhe, FRG

ISBN 978-3-642-52483-7 ISBN 978-3-642-52481-3 (eBook)
DOI 10.1007/978-3-642-52481-3

CIP-Kurztitelaufnahme der Deutschen Bibliothek
Measurement in economics:
theory and applications of economic indices
ed. by. Wolfgang Eichhorn.
In cooperation with W. Erwin Diewert ... –

NE: Eichhorn, Wolfgang [Hrsg.]; Diewert, Walter E. [Mitverf.]

Ursprünglich erschienen bei Physica-Verlag Heidelberg 1988

Cover: Erich Kirchner, Heidelberg

7100/7130-543210

Preface

In the last ten years, the literature on theory and applications of economic indices and, in general, on measurement in economics has grown rapidly. Since this literature is scattered through many international journals, it is difficult to get an adequate picture of the present state of the art. Therefore it is desirable that from time to time books should appear which offer an overview of significant new results on the subject.

This book offers such material. It contains 51 articles by 62 authors. Each paper has been reviewed by two referees. As a consequence, the articles in this book are revised versions or, in many cases, revised revisions of the original papers.

The book is divided into nine parts. Part I contains four papers on the "Equation of Measurement", a functional equation which plays an important role in the theory of measurement in economics and elsewhere. The authors give solutions of important special cases and methods for solving this equation.

There are nine papers on price measurement in Part II. The topics range from statistical, economic, factorial and probabilistic approaches to price index theory to problems of international comparisons.

Turning to efficiency measurement in production structures, Part III consists of five contributions involving an axiomatic approach, tests for aggregation bias, and a proposal concerning efficiency measures for multiplant firms.

Part IV contains seven articles on various topics which have in common that preferences or utility play a role in them.

The next parts deal with the measurement of quality (Part V) and that of inequality (Part VI). The two papers on 'quality' represent first steps towards the measurement of environmental quality and of the noxiousness of substances. The six papers on 'inequality' are devoted to axiomatization, aggregation and decomposition in inequality and concentration measurement and to questions like retrieving the Lorenz curve from sparse data or constructing an index of bequest behavior.

Part VII consists of six articles on taxation. It takes advantage of definitions and results in Part VI. Progressive taxation, a common feature in these contributions, can be defined through the decrease of income inequality before and after income taxation.

Aggregation is the topic of the six papers in Part VIII. It contains in addition to historical remarks results on consistent aggregation of market demand and on general equilibrium models. Furthermore, the notions 'efficiency' (see Part III) and 'separability' are considered in connection with problems of aggregation.

The concluding Part IX consists of six econometric studies on productivity measurement, cost functions, allocation inefficiencies, key sector indices, and testing of integrability conditions, with applications to the economies of the U.S.A., Japan and Germany.

I take the opportunity to gratefully acknowledge the financial support of the Stiftung Volkswagenwerk which made the symposium on *Measurement in Economics* at the University of Karlsruhe (July 14-21, 1985) possible at which first discussions of several topics of this book took place. To all contributors, referees and to my friends W.Erwin Diewert, Susanne Fuchs-Seliger, Helmut Funke, Wilhelm Gehrig, Andreas Pfingsten, Klaus Spremann, Frank Stehling, and Joachim Voeller, who helped in editing this book, I express my warmest thanks. Many thanks are also due to Mrs. Ingeborg Kast for her untiring technical work in putting this book together.

Karlsruhe, September 1987 Wolfgang Eichhorn

Table of Contents

Part III Efficiency

Part IV Preferences

Part V Quality

Part VI Inequality

Part VII Taxation

Part VIII Aggregation

Part I Methodology and Methods

'Cheaper by the Dozen': Twelve Functional Equations and their Applications to the 'Laws of Science' and to Measurement in Economics

J. Aczél
University of Waterloo
Waterloo, Ont., Canada
N2L 3G1

1. SOLUTION OF THE FUNCTIONAL EQUATIONS AND THE GENERAL FORM OF THE LAWS OF SCIENCE WITHOUT DIMENSIONAL CONSTANTS

Dimensional analysis (e.g. in Physics) is based on the recognition that the laws (formulae) of Science should remain unchanged under a change of ('ratio') scales - if there are no dimensional constants. In that case (homogeneous) linear transformations of the independent variables generate similar transformations of the dependent variable:

SUMMARY AND INTRODUCTION

This research started with questions from Fred Roberts (Rutgers Univ., NJ) concerning the solutions of 12 functional equations serving to determine the general forms of the 'laws of science without dimensional constants', where (homogeneous) linear and/or affine (inhomogeneous linear) transformations are applied to the independent and dependent variables, the same or partially the same transformation to each independent variable, or independent transformations. The solutions of all these equations are enumerated (and proofs of half a dozen given) in part 1 and applied to laws of science.

Wolfgang Eichhorn (Univ. Karlsruhe) called my attention to the occurrence of similar equations in production and utility theories, theories of price levels and indices and in the theory of (economic) inequality. Part 2 deals with these.

$$x_{n+1} = u(x_1,\ldots,x_n);\quad u(r_1x_1,\ldots,r_nx_n) = R(r_1,\ldots,r_n)u(x_1,\ldots,x_n)$$

$$[\text{cf. (4E) below}];\quad u: \mathbb{R}_+^n \to \mathbb{R}_+ = \{x \mid x > 0\};$$

$$r_1,\ldots,r_n > 0,\quad R(r_1,\ldots,r_n) > 0,\quad x_1,\ldots,x_n > 0.$$

Not all scales are ratio scales, for instance temperature scales are not (consider e.g. conversion from Celsius to Fahrenheit scales; also, it makes sense, without units, that an object is twice as long as another, but not that it is twice as warm). Some quantities, like temperature, have 'interval scales': they change by affine

Measurement in Economics
ed. by W. Eichhorn

(inhomogeneous linear) transformations $x_i \mapsto r_i x_i + p_i$. In psychophysics, psychology, economics, etc., when the independent variables have interval scales, the dependent variable may have interval or ratio scale and vice-versa (Luce 1964), or a combination of the two may occur for the independent variables or other scales for independent and/or dependent variables. (We do not deal with the latter cases here; L. Paganoni works on the combination cases; for logarithmic scales, see Aczél, Roberts and Rosenbaum 1986.)

In general, if $\mathcal{T}_i$ is the set of admissible transformations for x_i $(i=1,\ldots,n)$ and $x_{n+1} = u(x_1,\ldots,x_n)$, the problem is to determine the general form of the function u ('law of science'), if we know the $\mathcal{T}_i$. If there are no 'dimensional constants', which enter the relation and cancel the effects of (some) transformations, then admissible transformations in the independent variables should lead to an admissible transformation of the dependent variable: For all $T_i \in \mathcal{T}_i$ $(i=1,\ldots,n)$, there is a $T_{n+1} = F(T_1,\ldots,T_n) \in \mathcal{T}_{n+1}$ such that $u(T_1(x_1),\ldots,T_n(x_n)) = F(T_1,\ldots,T_n)(u(x_1,\ldots,x_n))$. In our cases, the $\mathcal{T}_i$ will be sets of (homogeneous) linear or affine (inhomogeneous linear) transformations.

Another generalization may be needed. The admissible transformations in the different independent variables may not be chosen independently. [For instance, in the price index $\sum_{j=1}^{m} p_j / \sum_{j=1}^{m} p_{j,0}$ the change of (ratio) scale (say, to a different currency) has to be the same for all prices]. Eight of the following twelve cases will be such. [In cases of interval scales with $x_i \mapsto r_i x_i + p_i$, the r_i may be the same ('same unit') or the p_i ('same zero') or both.] This will allow more general laws u.

We determine all u, where the dependent and independent variables have ratio or interval scales and the transformations may or may not apply independently. (We again do not deal with mixed cases here.)

We use a vector notation $\underline{x} = (x_1,\ldots,x_n)$. Scalars are not underlined, but can be added to or multiplied by vectors in the following way: $r\underline{x} + p = (rx_1 + p,\ldots,rx_n + p)$, etc. Else, addition, multiplication, inequalities, etc. for vectors are meant componentwise.

The results are contained in the following table (for more details, see Aczél, Roberts and Rosenbaum 1986). "Regular" means, say, bounded on an open n-dimensional interval I.

	Scale Type of Independent Variables	Scale Type of Dependent Variable	Functional Equation (E)	General Solutions (S)	Regular Solutions
1	Same ratio scale $T_i(x_i)=rx_i$ $(i=1,\dots,n)$ $x_i > 0,\ r > 0$	Interval scale $T_{n+1}(x_{n+1})=Rx_{n+1}+P;$ $R > 0$	$[u(rx_1,\dots,rx_n) = R(r)u(x_1,\dots,x_n)+P(r)];$ $u(r\underline{x})=R(r)u(\underline{x})+P(r);$ $u: \mathbb{R}_+^n \to \mathbb{R},\ \underline{x} > \underline{0},$ $r > 0,\ R(r) > 0$	1. $u(\underline{x})=u(x_1,\dots,x_n) = M(x_1)f(\frac{x_2}{x_1},\dots,\frac{x_n}{x_1})+b;$ f arb. function b arb. constant $M > 0,\ M(rs)=M(r)M(S)$ — . — OR 2. $u(\underline{x})=u(x_1,\dots,x_n)= f(\frac{x_2}{x_1},\dots,\frac{x_n}{x_1})+L(x_1);$ f arb., $L(rs)=L(r)+L(s).$ (If $n=1$, f = const.)	$f \equiv 0$ on the interval $I/I_1=\{(\frac{x_2}{x_1},\dots,\frac{x_n}{x_1}) \mid (x_1,x_2,\dots,x_n) \in I\}$ OR f regular on $\mathbb{R}^{n-1}$ (bounded on I/I_1) and $M(r) = r^c$, c arb. const. — . — f regular on $\mathbb{R}^{n-1}$, $L(r) = c \log r$, c arb. const.
2	Same ratio scale $T_i(x_i) = rx_i$ $(i=1,\dots,n)$, $x_i > 0,\ r > 0$	Ratio Scale $T_{n+1}(x_{n+1})=Rx_{n+1};$ $x_{n+1} > 0,\ R > 0$	$u(r\underline{x}) = R(r)u(\underline{x});$ $u: \mathbb{R}_+^n \to \mathbb{R}_+,\ \underline{x} > \underline{0}$ $r > 0,\ R(r) > 0,$ $u(\underline{x}) > 0$ $M(rs) = M(r)M(s)$	$u(\underline{x})=u(x_1,\dots,x_n) = M(x_1)f(\frac{x_2}{x_1},\dots,\frac{x_n}{x_1});$ $f > 0$ arb., $M > 0.$ (If $n=1$, f=const. > 0.)	f regular on $\mathbb{R}^{n-1}$ $M(r) = r^c$ c arb. const.

	Scale Type of Independent Variables	Scale Type of Dependent Variable	Functional Equation (E)	General Solutions (S)	Regular Solutions
3(*)	Independent ratio scale $T_i(x_i)=r_i x_i;\ x_i > 0,$ $r_i > 0\quad (i=1,\dots,n)$	Interval scale $T_{n+1}(x_{n+1})=Rx_{n+1}+P;$ $R > 0$	$[u(r_1x_1,\dots,r_nx_n) =$ $R(r_1,\dots,r_n)u(x_1,\dots,x_n)+$ $P(r_1,\dots,r_n)];$ $u(\underline{r}\,\underline{x})=R(\underline{r})u(\underline{x})+P(\underline{r});$ $u: \mathbb{R}_+^n \to \mathbb{R},\ \underline{x} > \underline{0},$ $\underline{r} > \underline{0},\ R(\underline{r}) > 0$	1. $u(\underline{x})=u(x_1,\dots,x_n) =$ $aM(\underline{x})+b=a\prod_{i=1}^{n} M_i(x_i)+b;$ $M>0,\ M(\underline{x}\,\underline{y})= M(\underline{x})M(\underline{y}),$ $M_i(x_iy_i)=M_i(x_i)M_i(y_i)$ $(i=1,\dots,n);$ a,b arb. constants OR 2. $u(\underline{x})=L(\underline{x})+b =$ $\sum_{i=1}^{n} L_i(x_i)+b;$ $L(\underline{x}\,\underline{y}) = L(\underline{x})+L(\underline{y}),$ $L_i(x_iy_i)=L_i(x_i) +$ $L_i(y_i)\ (i=1,\dots,n);$ b arb. constant	$u(x_1,\dots,x_n) =$ $a\prod_{i=1}^{n} x_i^{c_i} + b;$ $a,b;c_1,\dots,c_n$ arb. constants $u(x_1,\dots,x_n) =$ $\sum_{i=1}^{n} c_i \log x_i+b;$ $b,c_1,\dots,c_n$ arb. constants
4(*)	Independent ratio scale $T_i(x_i) = r_ix_i;\ x_i > 0,$ $r_i > 0\quad (i=1,\dots,n)$	Ratio scale $T_{n+1}(x_{n+1})=Rx_{n+1};$ $x_{n+1} > 0,\ R > 0$	$u(\underline{r}\,\underline{x}) = R(\underline{r})u(\underline{x});$ $u: \mathbb{R}_+^n \to \mathbb{R}_+,\ \underline{x} > 0,\ \underline{r} > 0,$ $R(\underline{r}) > 0,\ u(\underline{x}) > \underline{0}$	$u(\underline{x})=aM(\underline{x})=a\prod_{i=1}^{n} M_i(x_i);$ $a > 0,\ M > 0,$ $M(\underline{x}\,\underline{y})=M(\underline{x})M(\underline{y}),$ $M_i(x_iy_i)=M_i(x_i)M_i(y_i)$ $(i=1,\dots,n)$	$u(x_1,\dots,x_n) =$ $a\prod_{i=1}^{n} x_i^{c_i}$ $a,c_1,\dots,c_n$ arb. constants, $a > 0$

	Scale Type of Independent Variables	Scale Type of Dependent Variables	Functional Equation (E)	General Solutions (S)	Regular Solutions
5	Same interval scale $T_i(x_i)=rx_i+p$ $(i=1,\dots,n)$; $r>0$	Interval scale $T_{n+1}(x_{n+1})=Rx_{n+1}+p$; $R>0$	$[u(rx_1+p)\dots,rx_n+p) =$ $R(r,p)u(x_1,\dots,x_n) +$ $P(r,p)]$; $R(r,p)>0$ $u(r\underline{x}+p)=R(r,p)u(\underline{x})+P(r,p)$; $u: \mathbb{R}^n \to \mathbb{R}$, $r>0$	1. $u(\underline{x})=u(x_1,\dots,x_n) = \begin{cases} S(\underline{x})f(\frac{1}{S(\underline{x})}[\underline{x}-A(\underline{x})])+ \\ aA(\underline{x})+b & \text{if } S(\underline{x}) \neq 0, \\ ax+b & \text{if } S(\underline{x}) = 0 \end{cases}$ (i.e. $x_1=\dots=x_n=x$) $(A(\underline{x}) = \frac{x_1+\dots+x_n}{n}$, $S(\underline{x})=\sqrt{\sum_{i=1}^{n}[x_i-A(\underline{x})]^2})$, f arb., a,b arb. constant	f regular on V; for continuous solutions: f continuous on V; $V=\{\underline{y} \mid \lVert\underline{y}\rVert=\sqrt{y_1^2+\dots+y_n^2}=1;$ $\underline{y} \perp \underline{1}\}$
				— : —	— · —
				OR 2. $u(\underline{x})=u(x_1,\dots,x_n) = \begin{cases} M[S(\underline{x})]f(\frac{1}{S(\underline{x})}[\underline{x}-A(\underline{x})]) \\ +b & \text{if } S(\underline{x}) \neq 0 \\ b & \text{if } S(\underline{x}) = 0 \end{cases}$ $M(rs)=M(r)M(s)$, $M>0$ f arb., b arb. const. (If n=1, $u(x)=ax+b$.)	$f \equiv 0$ on $I(V)$ (see Remark at the end of the table) OR f regular on V and $M(s)=s^c$, $c \in \mathbb{R}$ constant; for continuous solutions: $f \equiv 0$ on V OR f continuous on V, and $M(s)=s^c$ with $c>0$.

	Scale Type of Independent Variables	Scale Type of Dependent Variable	Functional Equation (E)	General Solutions (S)	Regular Solutions
6	Same interval scale $T_i(x_i) = rx_i + p$ $(i=1,\dots,n)$; $r > 0$	Ratio scale $T_{n+1}(x_{n+1})=Rx_{n+1}$; $x_{n+1} > 0$, $R > 0$	$u(r\underline{x}+p)=R(r,p)u(\underline{x})$; $u: \mathbb{R}^n \to \mathbb{R}_+$, $r > 0$, $R(r,p) > 0$, $u(\underline{x}) > 0$	$u(\underline{x}) = \begin{cases} f(\frac{1}{S(\underline{x})}[\underline{x}-A(\underline{x})])+b & \text{if } S(\underline{x}) \neq 0, \\ b & \text{if } S(\underline{x}) = 0 \end{cases}$ $b > 0$, $f > -b$ arbitrary (If $n=1$, u = const.>0.)	f regular on V; for continuous solutions $f \equiv 0$ on V
7	Interval scales, same zero, independent units $T_i(x_i)=r_ix_i+p$; $r_i > 0$ $(i=1,\dots,n)$	Interval scale $T_{n+1}(x_{n+1})=Rx_{n+1}+P$; $R > 0$	$[u(r_1x_1+p,\dots,r_nx_n+p) =$ $R(r_1,\dots,r_n,p)u(x_1,\dots,x_n)$ $+ P(r_1,\dots,r_n,p)]$; $u(\underline{r}\ \underline{x}+p)=R(\underline{r},p)u(\underline{x}) +$ $P(\underline{r},p)$; $u: \mathbb{R}^n \to \mathbb{R}$, $\underline{r} > 0$, $R > 0$	$u(\underline{x})=ax_j+b$ for some $j \in \{1,\dots,n\}$, a,b arb. constants	all solutions are (very) regular
8	Interval scales, same zero, independent units $T_i(x_i) = r_ix_i+p$; $r_i > 0$ $(i=1,\dots,n)$	Ratio scale $T_{n+1}(x_{n+1}) = Rx_{n+1}$; $x_{n+1} > 0$, $R > 0$	$u(\underline{r}\ \underline{x}+p)=R(\underline{r},p)u(\underline{x})$; $u: \mathbb{R}^n \to \mathbb{R}_+$, $\underline{r} > \underline{0}$, $R(\underline{r},p) > 0$, $u(\underline{x}) > 0$	u constant > 0	all solutions regular

	Scale Type of Independent Variables	Scale Type of Dependent Variable	Functional Equation (E)	General Solutions (S)	Regular Solutions
9	Interval scales, same unit, independent zeros $T_i(x_i)=rx_i+p_i$ $(i=1,\dots,n)$; $r>0$	Interval scale $T_{n+1}(x_{n+1})=Rx_{n+1}+P$; $R>0$	$[u(rx_1+p_1,\dots,rx_n+p_n) =$ $R(r,p_1,\dots,p_n)u(x_1,\dots,x_n)$ $+ P(r,p_1,\dots,p_n)$; $R(r,p_1,\dots,p_n) > 0]$; $u(r\underline{x}+\underline{p})=R(r,\underline{p})u(\underline{x})+P(r,\underline{p})$; $u\colon \mathbb{R}^n \to \mathbb{R}$, $r>0$, $R(r,\underline{p}) > 0$	$u(\underline{x}) = u(x_1,\dots,x_n) =$ $\sum_{i=1}^{n} a_i x_i + b$; $a_1,\dots,a_n,b$ arb. constants	all solutions are (very) regular
10	Interval scales, same unit, independent zeros $T_i(x_i) = rx_i+p_i$ $(i=1,\dots,n)$; $r>0$	Ratio scale $T_{n+1}(x_{n+1})=Rx_{n+1}$; $x_{n+1}>0$, $R>0$	$u(r\underline{x}+\underline{p})=R(r,\underline{p})u(\underline{x})$; $u\colon \mathbb{R}^n \to \mathbb{R}_+$; $r>0$, $R(r,\underline{p})>0$, $u(\underline{x})>0$	u constant > 0	all solutions regular
11(*)	Independent interval scales $T_i(x_i)=r_ix_i+p_i$, $r_i>0$ $(i=1,\dots,n)$	Interval scale $T_{n+1}(x_{n+1})=Rx_{n+1}+P$; $R>0$	$[u(r_1x_1+p_1,\dots,r_nx_n+p_n) =$ $R(r_1,\dots,r_n,p_1,\dots,p_n)\cdot$ $\cdot u(x_1,\dots,x_n) +$ $P(r_1,\dots,r_n,p_1,\dots,p_n)$; $r_1,\dots,r_n>0$, $R>0]$; $u(\underline{r}\,\underline{x}+\underline{p})=R(\underline{r},\underline{p})u(\underline{x}) +$ $P(\underline{r},\underline{p})$; $u\colon \mathbb{R}^n \to \mathbb{R}$, $\underline{r} > \underline{0}$, $R(\underline{r},\underline{p}) > 0$	$u(\underline{x})=u(x_1,\dots,x_n) =$ ax_j+b, for one $j \in \{1,\dots,n\}$, a,b constants	all solutions regular

	Scale Type of Independent Variables	Scale Type of Dependent Variable	Functional Equation (E)	General Solutions (S)	Regular Solutions
12(*)	Independent interval scales $T_i(x_i) = r_i x_i + p_i$, $r_i > 0$, $(i=1,\dots,n)$	Ratio scale $T_{n+1}(x_{n+1}) = Rx_{n+1}$; $x_{n+1} > 0$, $R > 0$	$u(\underline{r}\ \underline{x}+\underline{p}) = R(\underline{r},\underline{p})u(\underline{x})$; $u: \mathbb{R}^n \to R_+$, $\underline{r} > \underline{0}$, $R(\underline{r},\underline{p}) > 0$, $u(\underline{x}) > 0$	u constant > 0	all solutions regular

Remark: "Regular" (on $\mathbb{R}^n$) means bounded on an open n-dimensional interval I. "Regular on $\mathbb{R}^{n-1}$" means (in the cases 1 and 2) bounded on $I/I_1 = \{(\frac{x_2}{x_1},\dots,\frac{x_n}{x_1}) \mid (x_1,\dots,x_n) \in I\}$. In cases 5 and 6 "regular on V" means bounded on $I(V) = \{\frac{1}{\|\underline{x}-A(\underline{x})\|}(\underline{x}-A(\underline{x})) \mid \underline{x}-A(\underline{x}) \neq 0,\ \underline{x} \in I\}$. - In the cases 2, 4, 6 (and also for the solutions (1S2), (3S2), (5S1)) "bounded" in the definition of "regular" may be replaced by "bounded from above".

(*) The continuous solutions in cases 3, 4, 11, and 12 have previously been obtained by Luce [1964]. The 'regular' solutions (bounded from above on an interval) have been found in case 4 by Mohr [1951].

Implications: Clearly $(2n-1) \Rightarrow (2n)$ $(n=1,2,3,4,5,6)$.

Further implications are in the following Figure:

```
(1)  -->  (3)
 |         |
 v         v
(5)  -->  (7)
 |         ‖
 v         v
(9)  ==>  (11)
```

(I consider the double arrow ⟹ implications more useful than the single arrow → ones.)

Note that the functional equations contain two (u,R) or three (u,R,P) unknown functions. While we are interested only (or mainly) in u, the others can be readily determined by substituting the solution u into the equation, as we will see also in the following proofs (for the rest of the cases see also Aczél, Roberts and Rosenbaum 1986).

Examples of Proofs. Case 1. Put into

$$u(r\underline{x}) = R(r)u(\underline{x})+P(r), \tag{1E}$$

$\underline{x} = \underline{1}$ and subtract from (1E) to get

$$v(r\underline{x}) = R(r)v(\underline{x})+v(r) \tag{13}$$

with the notation

$$v(\underline{x}) := u(\underline{x})-u(\underline{1}). \tag{14}$$

Repeated use of (13) $(v[(rs)\underline{x}] = v[r(s\underline{x})])$ gives $R(rs) = R(r)R(s)$ except if v is constant. So u = const., or $R(r) = M(r)$, where M is multiplicative: $M(rs) = M(r)M(s)$, and

$$v(r\underline{x}) = M(r)v(\underline{x})+v(r), \tag{13'}$$

in particular,

$$v(rs) = M(r)v(s)+v(r). \tag{13"}$$

There are two subcases: (a) $M(r) \not\equiv 1$, i.e. $\exists s_0: M(s_0) \neq 1$. Putting (13") into $v(rs) = v(sr)$, then $s = s_0$ and $a := v(s_0)/[M(s_0)-1]$, we get $v(r) = a[M(r)-1]$ so that (13') becomes, with

$$w(\underline{x}) := v(\underline{x})-a, \tag{15}$$

the equation $w(r\underline{x}) = M(r)w(\underline{x})$. Therefore

$$w(x_1,\dots,x_n) = w[x_1(\frac{1}{x_1}\underline{x}] = M(x_1)w(1,\frac{x_2}{x_1},\dots,\frac{x_n}{x_1})$$
$$= M(x_1)f(\frac{x_2}{x_1},\dots,\frac{x_n}{x_1}).$$

With (15) and (14) we have

$$u(\underline{x}) = u(x_1,x_2,\dots,x_n) = M(x_1)f(\frac{x_2}{x_1},\dots,\frac{x_n}{x_1})+b \quad [M(rs)=M(r)M(s)] \tag{1S1}$$

which indeed satisfies (1E): $u(r\underline{x}) = M(r)M(x_1)f(\frac{x_2}{x_1},\ldots,\frac{x_n}{x_1})+b = M(r)u(\underline{x})+b[1-M(r)]$, so

$$R(r) = M(r) \quad \text{and} \quad P(r) = b[1-M(r)]. \quad \square \tag{16}$$

Subcase (b): $M(r) \equiv 1$, so (13") goes over into $v(rs) = v(r)+v(s)$, that is,

$v(r) = L(r)$ is 'logarithmic': $L(rs) = L(r)+L(s)$,

and, from (13'), $v(r\underline{x}) = v(\underline{x})+L(r)$ and thus

$$v(x_1,x_2,\ldots,x_n) = v[x_1(\frac{1}{x_1}\underline{x})] = v(1,\frac{x_2}{x_1},\ldots,\frac{x_n}{x_1})+L(x_1).$$

With (14) and with $f(t_2,\ldots,t_n) = v(1,t_2,\ldots,t_n)+u(1)$, we get

$$u(\underline{x}) = f(\frac{x_2}{x_1},\ldots,\frac{x_n}{x_1})+L(x_1), \quad [L(rs) = L(r)+L(s)], \tag{1S2}$$

which also satisfies (1E): $u(r\underline{x}) = f(\frac{x_2}{x_1},\ldots,\frac{x_n}{x_1})+L(x_1)+L(r)$, so

$$R(r) = 1, \quad P(r) = L(r). \quad \square \tag{17}$$

Case 2 differs from case 1 in that $P(r) = 0$ and $u(x) > 0$. So, in subcase (a), by (16), $b = 0$ (since $M(r) \neq 1$) and, in subcase (b), from (17), $L(r) \equiv 0$. Both give

$$u(\underline{x}) = M(x_1)f(\frac{x_2}{x_1},\ldots,\frac{x_n}{x_1}) \quad (f > 0 \text{ since } M > 0) \quad \square \tag{2S}$$

[The constant solution is contained in (1S1), (1S2) and (2S).]

Proof in Case 9. Put into

$$u(r\underline{x}+\underline{p}) = R(r,\underline{p})u(\underline{x})+P(r,\underline{p}), \tag{9E}$$

$\underline{x} = \underline{0}$ (which is now in the domain) and subtract from (9E) to get

$$w(r\underline{x}+p) = R(r,\underline{p})w(\underline{x})+w(\underline{p}) \tag{18}$$

with

$$w(\underline{x}) := u(\underline{x})-u(\underline{0}), \quad \text{so} \quad w(\underline{0}) = \underline{0}. \tag{19}$$

Repeated use of (18) $[w(rs\underline{x}+(r\underline{q}+\underline{p})) = w(r(s\underline{x}+\underline{q})+\underline{p})]$ gives

$$R(rs,r\underline{q}+\underline{p}) = R(r,\underline{p})R(s,\underline{q}), \text{ if } w \text{ and thus } u \text{ not constant.} \tag{20}$$

Defining $M(r) := R(r,\underline{0})$, $E(\underline{p}) := R(1,\underline{p})$, we get that M is multiplicative and E is 'exponential':

$$M(rs) = M(r)M(s) \tag{21}$$

and

$$E(\underline{p}+\underline{q}) = E(\underline{p})E(\underline{q}). \tag{21'}$$

Further,

$$R(s,\underline{p}) = R(1,\underline{p})R(s,\underline{0}) = M(s)E(\underline{p}) \tag{22}$$

and

$$M(r)E(r\underline{q}) = R(r,r\underline{q}) = R(r,\underline{0})R(1,\underline{q}) = M(r)E(\underline{q}).$$

So $E(r\underline{q}) = E(\underline{q})$ $(M(r) > 0)$, in particular $E(2\underline{q}) = E(\underline{q})$. But, from (21'), $E(2\underline{q}) = E(\underline{q})^2$, therefore $E(\underline{q}) = 1$ (since $E(\underline{q}) > 0$) and, by (22), $R(s,\underline{p}) = M(s)$. So (18) becomes

$$w(r\underline{x}+\underline{p}) = M(r)w(\underline{x})+w(\underline{p}).$$

In particular (since, see (19), $w(\underline{0}) = \underline{0}$ and, from (21), $M(1) = 1$),

$$w(r\underline{x}) = M(r)w(\underline{x}) \tag{23}$$

and

$$w(\underline{x}+\underline{p}) = w(\underline{x})+w(\underline{p}). \tag{23'}$$

Therefore $M(r+s)w(\underline{x}) = w[(r+s)\underline{x}] = w(r\underline{x}+s\underline{x}) = w(r\underline{x})+w(s\underline{x}) = (M(r)+M(s))w(\underline{x})$, so, if $w(\underline{x}) \neq 0$ (u not constant), then

$$M(r+s) = M(r)+M(s).$$

This and (21) imply (see e.g. Aczél 1966), $M(r) = r$ ($M(r) \equiv 0$ is excluded), so, from (23),

$$w(r\underline{x}) = rw(\underline{x}) \tag{23"}$$

(for $r > 0$, but the extension to all real r is easy). Together with (23') this means that w is <u>linear</u>, thus

$$w(x_1,\ldots,x_n) = w(\sum_{i=1}^{n} x_i\underline{e}_i) = \sum_{i=1}^{n} w(\underline{e}_i)x_i = \sum_{i=1}^{n} a_ix_i$$

and we have from (19)

$$u(\underline{x}) = u(x_1,\ldots,x_n) = \sum_{i=1}^{n} a_i x_i + b \qquad (9S)$$

(which contains also $u = b$ const.).

This indeed satisfies (9E): $u(r\underline{x}+\underline{p}) = \sum_{i=1}^{n} a_i(rx_i+p_i)+b = ru(\underline{x})+b(1-r) + \sum_{i=1}^{n} a_i p_i$. So now

$$R(r,\underline{p}) = r, \quad P(r,\underline{p}) = b(1-r) + \sum_{i=1}^{n} a_i p_i. \quad \square \qquad (24)$$

Case 10 differs from case 9 in that $P(r,\underline{p}) = 0$, $u(\underline{x}) > 0$. From the former, $b = a_1 = \ldots = a_n = 0$, i.e. $u(\underline{x}) = 0$, which contradicts the latter inequality. But u = const. (now > 0) is still a solution (10S).

The results in cases 7, 8 imply those in cases 11 and 12: If (11E) [(12E)] is satisfied then (7E) [(8E)] follows (with $r_1 = \ldots = r_n = r$). So u can't be of a more general form. $\square$

For the remaining proofs see Aczél, Roberts and Rosenbaum 1986. Among generalizations on which, as mentioned before, L. Paganoni works, is the (relatively easy) replacement of the scalar or vector (that is, diagonal matrix) multipliers (r and $\underline{r}$) of $\underline{x}$ by arbitrary matrices.

2. APPLICATIONS TO MEASUREMENT IN ECONOMICS

In production and utility theory the equations

$$u(\underline{r}\,\underline{x}) = R(\underline{r})u(\underline{x})$$

or

$$u(r\,\underline{x}) = R(r)u(\underline{x})$$

($\underline{x},\underline{r} \in \mathbb{R}_+^n$, $r \in \mathbb{R}_+$) come up. These are the equations (4E) and (2E), respectively, with the solutions (4S) and (2S). (The R turn out to be arbitrary multiplicative functions of several variables or of one variable, respectively.)

In the theory of price indices we encounter the equation

$$u(rx_1^0,\ldots,rx_m^0,rx_1,\ldots,rx_m) = u(x_1^0,\ldots,x_m^0,x_1,\ldots,x_m).$$

With $n = 2m$, $u(\underline{x}) = u(x_1^0,\ldots,x_m^0,x_1,\ldots,x_m)$ this is the case $R(r) \equiv 1$ of (2E) with $M(x_1) \equiv 1$ in the solution (2S). (Note, however, that in the theory of price indices further properties of u

are required).

In the <u>theory of price levels</u> we have the equations

$$u(r\,\underline{x}) = ru(\underline{x}) \quad (r \in \mathbb{R}_+) \quad \text{and} \quad u(\underline{x}+\underline{p}) = u(\underline{x}) + u(\underline{p}). \tag{25}$$

Together they give $u(r\,\underline{x}+p) = ru(\underline{x}) + u(\underline{p})$, a particular case of (9E). However, we have solved above [see (23'), (23")] exactly this pair of equations and found (without any regularity condition) as general solution

$$u(\underline{x}) = u(x_1,\ldots,x_n) = \sum_{i=1}^{n} a_i x_i.$$

Finally, in the <u>theory of measures of (economic) inequality</u>, the question whether the equation reflecting the <u>conservative</u> point of view

$$u(r\,\underline{x}) = u(\underline{x}) \quad (r \in \mathbb{R}_+) \tag{26}$$

(the inequality does not change if all incomes increase by the same factor) and that corresponding to more <u>socialistic</u> views

$$u(\underline{x}+p) = u(\underline{x}) \quad [u(x_1+p,\ldots,x_n+p) = u(x_1,\ldots,x_n)] \quad (p \in \mathbb{R}) \tag{27}$$

(the inequality remains unchanged when the incomes change by the same added (or subtracted) amount) can be both satisfied by the <u>same</u> inequality measure (with also symmetry of $u(x_1,\ldots,x_n)$ thrown in for good measure) can be answered <u>in the positive</u> via case 6: Equations (26) and (27) can be united into

$$u(r\,\underline{x}+p) = u(\underline{x}),$$

a particular case of (6E). The corresponding subcase of (6S) can also be obtained immediately from (26) and (27), which even indicates how (6S), (5S1) and (5S2) are obtained and also how the continuity statements are proved.

Put into (27) $p = -A(\underline{x}) = -\dfrac{x_1+\ldots+x_n}{n}$ and into (26) $r = S(\underline{x})^{-1} = [(x_1-A(\underline{x}))^2+\ldots+(x_n-A(\underline{x}))^2]^{-1/2}$ $(S(\underline{x}) = \|\underline{x}-A(\underline{x})\|)$ to get

$$u(\underline{x}) = u(x_1,\ldots,x_n) = u(x_1-A(\underline{x}),\ldots,x_n-A(\underline{x})) = u\left(\frac{x_1-A(\underline{x})}{S(\underline{x})},\ldots,\frac{x_n-A(\underline{x})}{S(\underline{x})}\right).$$

But one sees immediately that

$$u(\underline{x}) = f\left(\frac{\underline{x}-A(\underline{x})}{\|\underline{x}-A(\underline{x})\|}\right) = f\left(\frac{x_1-A(\underline{x})}{S(\underline{x})},\ldots,\frac{x_n-A(\underline{x})}{S(\underline{x})}\right) \tag{28}$$

with arbitrary f (symmetric if u is to be symmetric) <u>always</u>

satisfies (26) and (27). (For $x_1 = \ldots = x_n = x$, here excluded, $u(x,\ldots,x) = \text{const.}$, see (29) below.) So there are plenty of common symmetric solutions. But are there any nonconstant continuous ones?

The answer is negative (cf. Eichhorn-Gehrig 1982) and the proof is typical of how we obtain the last column of 5 and 6. First we note that (28) fails if $S(\underline{x}) = 0$, that is, $x_1 = \ldots = x_n = x$. Then (27) gives with $p = -x$

$$u(x,\ldots,x) = u(0,\ldots,0) = b = \text{const.} \tag{29}$$

In order that u be continuous, first f has to be continuous, second (28) has to go over into (29) as $S(\underline{x}) = \|\underline{x}-A(\underline{x})\| \to 0$. This means

$$\lim_{\|z\|\to 0} f\left(\frac{z}{\|z\|}\right) = b.$$

Note from (28) that f is defined only for unit vectors (orthogonal to the vector $(1,1,\ldots,1) = \underline{1}$.) We assert that it is identically equal to b. Indeed, let $\underline{e}$ be an arbitrary unit vector and $\underline{z} = t\underline{e}$. Then $\|\underline{z}\| = t$ and

$$b = \lim_{t\to 0} f\left(\frac{t\underline{e}}{t}\right) = f(\underline{e}), \quad \text{so} \quad u(\underline{x}) \equiv b. \quad \square$$

As a last example we mention the "centrist inequality measure" of Kolm [1976] for which he requires (in our notations) that

$$I_c(r(\underline{x}+s)-s) = rI_c(\underline{x}) \quad (\underline{x} > \underline{0},\ r(\underline{x}+s)-s > \underline{0},\ r > 0) \tag{30}$$

(s constant) should hold. As L. Paganoni observed, with $\underline{y} = \underline{x} + \underline{s}$,

$$u(\underline{y}) := I_c(\underline{y}-s), \tag{31}$$

equation (30) goes over into

$$u(r\underline{y}) = ru(\underline{y}), \tag{32}$$

which is the particular case $R(r) = r$ of (2E).

While the solution is contained in (2S), in the present context it may be of advantage to obtain it in the following way. We write

$$\bar{x} = A(\underline{x}) = \frac{x_1+\ldots+x_n}{n}$$

and put into (32) $r = 1/\bar{y}$ in order to get.

$$u(\underline{y}) = \bar{y}u(\frac{1}{\bar{y}}\underline{y}).$$

With (31) this gives

$$I_c(\underline{x}) = (\bar{x}+s)u(\frac{1}{\bar{x}+s}(\underline{x}+s)). \tag{33}$$

By substitution one sees that (33) satisfies (30) whatever u is, so the general solution of (30) is (33) with arbitrary u.

If I_c is supposed to be positive and/or symmetric, so is u. If $I_c(x) = I_c(x,x,\dots,x) = 0$ then $u(\underline{1}) = u(1,1,\dots,1) = 0$.

REFERENCES

Aczél, J., Lectures on Functional Equations and Their Applications. Academic Press, New York-London, 1966.

Aczél, J., Roberts, F.S. and Rosenbaum, Z., On scientific laws without dimensional constants. J. Math. Anal. Appl. 119 (1986), 389-416.

Eichhorn, W. and Gehrig, W., Measurement of inequality in economics. In Modern Applied Mathematics - Optimization and Operations Research, North Holland, Amsterdam-New York, 1982, pp. 657-693.

Kolm, S.C., Unequal inequalities, I. J. Econom. Theory 12 (1976), 416-442.

Luce, R.D., A generalization of a theorem of dimensional analysis. J. Math. Psychol. 1 (1964), 278-284.

Mohr, E., Bemerkung zur Dimensionsanalysis. Math. Nachr. 6 (1951), 145-153.

The Equation of Measurement

Wolfgang Eichhorn and Winfried Gleissner
Institut für Wirtschaftstheorie
und Operations Research
Universität Karlsruhe
D-7500 Karlsruhe 1
Federal Republic of Germany

INTRODUCTION

The twelve functional equations dealt with in the preceding contribution [Acz1] by Aczél (see also [ARR]) are all special cases of the functional equation

$$u(Ax+p) = R(A,p)u(x)+P(A,p), \tag{1}$$

where $u: X \to V$ is an unknown function from a nonempty subset X of a real vector space U into a real vector space V, where the nonempty subsets $Y \ni p$ and $S \ni A$ of $L(U)$ (the algebra of linear operators of U into itself) are such that

$$(Ax+p) \in X \text{ for all } x \in X,\ p \in Y,\ A \in S \subseteq L(U),$$

and where $R: S \times Y \to \mathbb{R}$ (the real numbers) and $P: S \times Y \to V$ are "given functions."

With the notation

$$R(A,p) =: \alpha \quad \text{and} \quad P(A,p) =: \beta$$

equation (1) becomes

$$u(Ax+p) = \alpha u(x)+\beta . \tag{2}$$

The form (2) shows why Paganoni (under certain assumptions on the function R and the set S; see [Pag1],[Pag2]) calls equation (1) a "functional equation concerning affine transformations."

We propose here to call equation (1) the *equation of measurement*. Reasons for this proposal become already clear by all what is written in [Acz1] and [ARR] about the "laws of science", dimensional analysis, scales, and applications to measurement in economics. Furthermore, almost all contributions to this volume on measurement in economics contain equations or systems of equations that are special cases of equation (1). In what follows we add further motivation to our proposal. Our examples stem from the theories of measurement of prices, inequa-

Measurement in Economics
ed. by W. Eichhorn

lity, aggregation, and utility.

1. PRICE MEASUREMENT

At the 1976 Karlsruhe Seminar on Theory and Applications of Economic Indices the first author has defined a (statistical) price index as a function

$$u:\mathbb{R}^n_{++}\to\mathbb{R}_{++},\quad x\to u(x),$$

where $\mathbb{R}_{++}$ denoted the positive real numbers,

$n=4k$, k a natural number,

$x=(x_1,\dots,x_k,x_{k+1},\dots,x_{2k},x_{2k+1},\dots,x_{3k},x_{3k+1},\dots,x_{4k})\in\mathbb{R}^n_{++}$,

$(x_1,\dots,x_k)$ the vector of the quantities of k goods in a base period, $(x_{2k+1},\dots,x_{3k})$ the vector of the quantities of the same goods in a comparison period, $(x_{k+1},\dots,x_{2k})$ and $(x_{3k+1},\dots,x_{4k})$ the vectors of the prices of these goods in the respective periods,

if this function satisfies the axioms of monotonicity, linear homogeneity, identity, price dimensionality, and commensurability; see [Eic1].

It turns out that the (statistical) price indices are those which satisfy the monotonicity axiom and the following system of special cases of equation (1).

In what follows, any row vector occuring as an argument of a function is supposed to be transposed into a column vector.

Define the (sets S of) 4k×4k matrices

$$A_1:=\begin{pmatrix} 1 & & & & & & & & & \\ & \ddots & & & & & & & 0 & \\ & & 1 & & & & & & & \\ & & & 1 & & & & & & \\ & & & & \ddots & & & & & \\ & & & & & 1 & & & & \\ & & & & & & 1 & & & \\ & & & & & & & \ddots & & \\ & 0 & & & & & & & 1 & \\ & & & & & & & & & \lambda \\ & & & & & & & & & \ddots \\ & & & & & & & & & & \lambda \end{pmatrix},\quad A_2:=\begin{pmatrix} 1 & & & & & & & & & \\ & \ddots & & & & & & 0 & \\ & & 1 & & & & & & \\ & & & 1 & & & & & \\ & & & & \ddots & & & & \\ & & & & & 1 & & & \\ & & & & & & 1 & & \\ & & & & & & & \ddots & \\ & & & & & & & & 1 \\ & 0 & & & 1 & & & & & 0 \\ & & & & & \ddots & & & & & \ddots \\ & & & & & & 1 & & & & & 0 \end{pmatrix},$$

$$A_3 := \begin{pmatrix} 1 & & & & & & & & & \\ & \ddots & & & & & & & \mathbf{0} & \\ & & 1 & & & & & & & \\ & & & \lambda & & & & & & \\ & & & & \ddots & & & & & \\ & & & & & \lambda & & & & \\ & & & & & & 1 & & & \\ & & & & & & & \ddots & & \\ & \mathbf{0} & & & & & & & 1 & \\ & & & & & & & & & \lambda \\ & & & & & & & & & & \ddots \\ & & & & & & & & & & & \lambda \end{pmatrix}, \quad A_4 := \begin{pmatrix} \lambda_1^{-1} & & & & & & & & & & & \\ & \ddots & & & & & & & & \mathbf{0} & & \\ & & \lambda_k^{-1} & & & & & & & & & \\ & & & \lambda_1 & & & & & & & & \\ & & & & \ddots & & & & & & & \\ & & & & & \lambda_k & & & & & & \\ & & & & & & \lambda_1^{-1} & & & & & \\ & & & & & & & \ddots & & & & \\ & \mathbf{0} & & & & & & & \lambda_k^{-1} & & & \\ & & & & & & & & & \lambda_1 & & \\ & & & & & & & & & & \ddots & \\ & & & & & & & & & & & \lambda_k \end{pmatrix},$$

where $\lambda \varepsilon \mathbb{R}_{++}$, $\lambda_\kappa \varepsilon \mathbb{R}_{++}$ ($\kappa=1,\ldots,k$). Then the above-mentioned special cases of equation (1) are

$$u(A_1x) = \lambda u(x), \tag{3}$$
$$u(A_2x) = 1, \tag{4}$$
$$u(A_3x) = u(x), \tag{5}$$
$$u(A_4x) = u(x), \tag{6}$$

i.e., the axioms of linear homogeneity, identity, price dimensionality and commensurability, respectively. Note that $R(A,p)=\lambda$, $P(A,p)\equiv 0$ in case (3), $R(A,p)\equiv 0$, $P(A,p)\equiv 1$ in case (4), $R(A,p)\equiv 1$, $P(A,p)\equiv 0$ in cases (5) and (6).

It should be emphasized here that the general solution of the system (3), (4), (5), (6) together with the monotonicity axiom, i.e., the set of all (statistical) price indices, is not known.

Since the sets S_i of matrices A_i ($i=1,2,3,4$) are '*small*' subsets of $L(\mathbb{R}^n)$ (the set of all real $n\times n$ matrices), the sets of solutions of each of the equations (3), (4), (5), (6) are '*large*'.

2. INEQUALITY MEASUREMENT

An inequality measure (say, of incomes $x=(x_1,\ldots,x_n)$)

$$u: \mathbb{R}_+^n \to \mathbb{R}, \quad x \to u(x) \tag{7}$$

should always satisfy Dalton's (see [Dalt] "principle of transfers" and should be *symmetric*, i.e.,

$$u(A_5x) = u(x) \tag{8}$$

for all $x\varepsilon\mathbb{R}_+^n$ and all $A_5\varepsilon S_5$, the set of the $n\times n$ permutation matrices. Pfingsten introduced inequality measures that additionally satisfy, for a fixed $\mu\varepsilon[0,1]$, the equation

$$u(x+\tau(\mu x+(1-\mu)e)) = u(x) \quad (e:=(1,\ldots 1) \tag{9}$$

for all $x \in \mathbb{R}^n_+ \setminus \{0\}$ and all $\tau \in \mathbb{R}$ such that

$$(x+\tau(\mu x+(1-\mu)e)) \in \mathbb{R}^n_+ \setminus \{\underline{0}\}. \tag{10}$$

Note that for x fixed, (10) is a ray in $\mathbb{R}^n_+$ along which u is constant. Note further that this ray is 'the more parallel', intuitively speaking, to the ray ξe (of equal incomes, say) the closer μ is to 0, and that for $\mu=0$ and $\mu=1$ we get

$$u(x+\tau e) = u(x) \tag{11}$$

and

$$u(\lambda x) = u(x), \quad \lambda \in \mathbb{R}_{++}, \tag{12}$$

that is, in the context of the measurement of inequality of incomes, leftists' and rightists' equation, respectively. Obviously, equations (11) and (12) represent extreme positions as compared with the intermediate position (9), $0<\mu<1$; see, in this connection, Kolm, Pfingsten, Aczél, and Eichhorn, i.e., [Kolm], [Pfi1], [Pfi2], [Acz1], [Acz2] [Eic2].

We notice that equations (8), (9), (11), (12) are all special cases of equation (1). For instance, equation (9) can be written as

$$u(A_6 x+\tau(1-\mu)e) = u(x)$$

which is equation (1) specialized to

$A=A_6:=(1+\tau\mu)I$, I= unit matrix, $p=\tau(1-\mu)e$,

$R(A,x) \equiv 1, \quad P(A,p) \equiv 0$.

The general solution of the system of equations (8), (11), (12) can be found in [Acz1], [Acz2] or [EiGe], whereas that of the system of equations (8) and (9) is contained in [Acz2] or [Eic2]. In [Eic2] all Schur-convex functions (7) satisfying (9) are also determined. A function (7) is called *Schur-convex* if

$$u(A_7 x) \leqq u(x) \tag{13}$$

for all $x \in \mathbb{R}^n_+$ and all $A_7 \in S_7$, the set of the *doubly stochastic* $n \times n$ *matrices*. The elements of these matrices are nonnegative real numbers, and the sum of the elements in each row as well as in each column equals one.

In this connection the well-known fact is noteworthy that a function (7) is Schur-convex if and only if it satisfies the above-mentioned principle of Dalton and is symmetric.

Inequality (13) shows that in measurement theory not only equations of the form (1), but also inequalities of the form (1), where = is replaced by $\leqq$, play an important role.

3. AGGREGATION

The problem of aggregation in production theory, say, is: Determine all systems of functions

$$F:\mathbb{R}_+^M\to\mathbb{R}_+,\quad f_1:\mathbb{R}_+^M\to\mathbb{R}_+,\ldots,f_j:\mathbb{R}_+^M\to\mathbb{R}_+,$$
$$G:\mathbb{R}_+^J\to\mathbb{R}_+,\quad g_1:\mathbb{R}_+^J\to\mathbb{R}_+,\ldots,g_M:\mathbb{R}_+^J\to\mathbb{R}_+$$

for which the functional equation

$$F(g_1(|x_1),\ldots,g_M(|x_M)) = G(f_1(\underline{x}_1),\ldots,f_J(\underline{x}_J)) \tag{14}$$

is identically satisfied in all variables. Equation (14) in which

$$|x_m \text{ denotes the vector } \begin{pmatrix} x_{1m} \\ \cdot \\ \cdot \\ \cdot \\ x_{Jm} \end{pmatrix} \qquad (m=1,\ldots,M)$$

and

$$\underline{x}_j \text{ denotes the vector } (x_{j1},\ldots,x_{jM}) \quad (j=1,\ldots,J)$$

can be illustrated by means of the following scheme (see van Daal and Merkies [DaMe]):

$$\begin{array}{ccccccc}
x_{11}, & \ldots, & x_{1m}, & \ldots, & x_{1M} & \overset{f_1}{\to} & y_1 \\
\cdot & & \cdot & & \cdot & & \cdot \\
\cdot & & \cdot & & \cdot & & \cdot \\
\cdot & & \cdot & & \cdot & & \cdot \\
x_{j1}, & \ldots, & x_{jm}, & \ldots, & x_{jM} & \overset{f_j}{\to} & y_j \\
\cdot & & \cdot & & \cdot & & \cdot \\
\cdot & & \cdot & & \cdot & & \cdot \\
\cdot & & \cdot & & \cdot & & \cdot \\
x_{J1}, & \ldots, & x_{Jm}, & \ldots, & x_{JM} & \overset{f_J}{\to} & y_J \\
\downarrow g_1 & & \downarrow g_m & & \downarrow g_M & & \downarrow G \\
x_1, & \ldots, & x_m, & \ldots, & x_M & \overset{F}{\to} & y\ .
\end{array}$$

If the inputs are that much disaggregated that the m-th input is qualitatively identical in all J production sectors, then x_m is the *sum* of the elements of the vector $|x_m$ (m=1,...,M).

If the output of each of the J production sectors is the monetary value y_j of the goods produced in the respective sector j, then

$$G(f_1(\underline{x}_1),\dots,f_J(\underline{x}_J)) = f_1(\underline{x}_1)+\dots+f_J(\underline{x}_J).$$

Hence, the following special case of equation (14) has to be solved:

$$F(\underline{x}_1+\dots+\underline{x}_J) = f_1(\underline{x}_1)+\dots+f_J(\underline{x}_J). \qquad (15)$$

Writing $\underline{x}_1=:\underline{x}$, $\underline{x}_2=:\underline{p}$, $F=:u$ and putting $\underline{x}_3=\dots=x_J=\underline{0}$ we get

$$u(\underline{x}+\underline{p}) = f_1(\underline{x})+f_2(\underline{p})+c \qquad (c:=f_3(\underline{0})+\dots+f_J(\underline{0})). \qquad (16)$$

This becomes

$$u(\underline{x}+\underline{p}) = u(\underline{x})+f_2(\underline{p})-d \qquad (d:=f_2(\underline{0})), \qquad (17)$$

since from (16) with $\underline{p}=\underline{0}$ we get $f_1(\underline{x})=u(\underline{x})-d-c$.

We have shown that the problem of aggregation leads, at least in an important special case, to the problem of solving an equation which is our equation (1) in the case

$$A=I= \text{unit matrix},\quad R(A,p)\equiv 1,\quad P(A,p)=f_2(p)-d.$$

It is well known that a system of regular (e.g., locally monotonic) functions $F,f_1,\dots,f_J$ satisfy (15) if an only if

$$F(\underline{x})=\underline{a}\underline{x}+b=a_1x_1+\dots+a_Mx_M+b,$$
$$f_1(\underline{x})=\underline{a}\underline{x}+b_1,\dots,f_J(\underline{x})=\underline{a}\underline{x}+b_J$$
$$(a_1,\dots,a_M,b_1,\dots,b_J,b=b_1+\dots+b_J \text{ real constants};$$

see [Acz3] or [Eic3].

4. UTILITY

Let $u:\mathbb{R}^n_+\to\mathbb{R}$ be a continuous nonconstant cardinal utility function. We call it *scale-invariant for equal utility differences if*

$$u(Tx)-u(Ty) = u(Tx')-u(Ty') \qquad (18)$$

holds for every quadruple of commodity vectors $x,y,x',y'\in\mathbb{R}^n_+$ satisfying

$$u(x)-u(y) = u(x')-u(y'). \qquad (19)$$

Here

$$T=\begin{pmatrix} t_1 & & 0 \\ & t_2 & \\ & & \ddots \\ 0 & & & t_n \end{pmatrix}, \qquad t_1,t_2,\dots,t_n \in \mathbb{R}_{++}.$$

This means that any changes in the units of the commodities leave the utility differences constant.

In what follows we show that the implication (19)=>(18) yields the functional equation

$$u(Tx) = R(T)u(x)+P(T) \qquad (20)$$

which is a special case of equation (1), namely case 3 in Aczél's contribution [Acz1].

The implication (19) => (18) is equivalent to the functional equation

$$u(Tx)-u(Ty) = F(u(x)-u(y),T), \qquad (21)$$

where $x,y \in \mathbb{R}^n_+$, $t_1,\dots,t_n \in \mathbb{R}_{++}$. So also

$$u(Ty)-u(Tz) = F(u(y)-u(z),T) \qquad (22)$$

and

$$u(Tx)-u(Tz) = F(u(x)-u(z),T).$$

Adding (22) to (21) we get

$$u(Tx)-u(Tz) = F(u(x)-u(y),T)+F(u(y)-u(z),T).$$

The right hand sides of the last two equations have to be equal. Since u is continuous and nonconstant,

$$u(x)-u(y)=:X, \quad u(y)-u(z)=:Y, \quad u(x)-u(z)=X+Y$$

lie in a proper interval $I \subseteq \mathbb{R}$ which contains 0. So we have

$$F(X+Y,T) = F(X,T)+F(Y,T) \qquad (X,Y,X+Y \in I,\ T \text{ as above}). \qquad (23)$$

With u also F is continuous (in all variables). For T fixed (and disregarded) equation (23) becomes the *Cauchy functional equation*

$$F(X+Y) = F(X)+F(Y) \qquad (24)$$

on the hexagon $H:=\{(X,Y)\,|\,X \in I, Y \in I, X+Y \in I \subseteq \mathbb{R}\}$.

By using arguments as can be found in Aczél's papers [Acz4], [Acz5] one can show that for $F:I\to\mathbb{R}$ satisfying (24) on H there exists a unique extension f to $\mathbb{R}$ so that

$$f(\xi+\eta) = f(\xi)+f(\eta) \tag{25}$$

for all $\xi\in\mathbb{R}$, $\eta\in\mathbb{R}$. It is well known that the general continuous solution of the Cauchy functional equation (25) is $f(\xi)=R\xi$ (R is an arbitrary constant). So the general continuous solution of (23) is

$$F(X,T) = R(T)X \qquad (X\in I,\ T \text{ as above})$$

(the 'constant' R may depend upon T). Putting this into (21) we get

$$u(Tx)-u(Ty) = R(T)(u(x)-u(y)).$$

With $y=y_o$ fixed and $P(T):= u(Ty_o)-R(T)u(y_o)$ this becomes (20). We have proven our assertion that the implication (19) => (18) yields equation (20). The continuous solutions of (20) as well as its general solution can be found in this volume (see [Acz1], [EiGl]). So *all continuous (cardinal) utility functions which are scale-invariant for equal utility differences are the following ones:*

$$u(x_1,\dots,x_n) = c_1\log x_1+\dots+c_n\log x_n+b$$

$(b,c_1,\dots,c_n$ arbitrary constants) and

$$u(x_1,\dots,x_n) = a x_1^{c_1} x_2^{c_2}\dots x_n^{c_n}+b$$

$(a,b,c_1,\dots,c_n$ arbitrary constants).

This result sligthly generalizes results obtained by Aczél and Young on scale-invariant equal sacrifice utility functions $u:\mathbb{R}_+\to\mathbb{R}$ in taxation; see [Acz5], [You1], [You2].

REFERENCES

[Acz1] Aczél J.: 'Cheaper by the Dozen': Twelve Functional Equations and Their Applications to the 'Laws of Science' and to Measurement in Economics. This volume.

[Acz2] Aczél J.: A Short Course on Functional Equations Based Upon Recent Applications to the Social and Behavioral Sciences. Dordrecht, Boston, Lancaster, Tokyo 1987.

[Acz3] Aczél J.: Lectures on Functional Equations and Their Applications. New York, San Francisco, London 1966.

[Acz4] Aczél J.: Diamonds Are not the Cauchy Extensionist's Best Friend. C.R.Math.Rep.Acad.Sci.Canada 5 (1983), 259-264.

[Acz5] Aczél J.: Scale-Invariant Equal Sacrifice in Taxation and Conditional Functional Equations. Aequationes Mathematicae 32 (1987), 336-349.

[ARR] Aczél J., Roberts F.S., Rosenbaum Z.: On Scientific Laws Without Dimensional Constants. Journal of Mathematical Analysis and Applications 119 (1986), 389-416.

[DaMe] van Daal J., Merkies A.H.Q.M.: The Problem of Aggregation of Individual Economic Relations; Consistency and Representativity in a Historical Perspective. This Volume.

[Dalt] Dalton H.: The Measurement of the Inequality of Incomes. Economic Journal 30 (1920), 348-361.

[Eic1] Eichhorn W.: What is an Economic Index? An Attempt of an Answer. In: Theory and Applications of Economic Indices, edited by W. Eichhorn, R.Henn, O.Opitz, R.W.Shephard. Würzburg, Wien 1978, 3-42.

[Eic2] Eichhorn W.: On a Class of Inequality Measures. Forthcoming in: Social Choice and Welfare.

[Eic3] Eichhorn W.: Functional Equations in Economics. Reading, London, Amsterdam, Sydney, Tokyo 1978.

[EiGe] Eichhorn W., Gehrig W.: Measurement of Inequality in Economics. In: Modern Applied Mathematics, Optimization and Operations Research, edited by B.Korte. Amsterdam, New York, Oxford 1982, 657-693.

[EiGl] Eichhorn W., Gleissner W.: The Solutions of Important Special Cases of the Equation of Measurement. This volume.

[Kolm] Kolm S.C.: Unequal Inequalities, I. Journal of Economic Theory 12 (1976), 416-442.

[Pag1] Paganoni L.: On a Functional Equation with Applications to Measurement in Economics. This volume.

[Pag2] Paganoni L.: On a Functional Equation Concerning Affine Transformations. Forthcoming in: Journal of Mathematical Analysis and Applications.

[Pfi1] Pfingsten A.: The Measurement of Tax Progression. (Studies in Contemporary Economics, 20). Berlin, Heidelberg, New York, Tokyo 1986.

[Pfi2] Pfingsten A.: Distributionally-Neutral Tax Changes for Different Inequality Concepts. Journal of Public Economics 30 (1986), 385-393.

[You1] Young H.P.: Equal Sacrifice in Taxation. This Volume.

[You2] Young H.P.: Progressive Taxation and the Equal Sacrifice Principle. Journal of Public Economics 32 (1987), 203-214.

The Solutions of Important Special Cases of the Equation of Measurement

Wolfgang Eichhorn und Winfried Gleissner
Institut für Wirtschaftstheorie
und Operations Research
Universität Karlsruhe
D-7500 Karlsruhe 1
Federal Republic of Germany

INTRODUCTION

The preceding contribution by Aczél [Acz2] (see also [ARR]) treats the equation

$$u(Ax+p) = R(A,p)u(x)+P(A,p), \qquad (1)$$

where $A \in S \leq T_n(\mathbb{R})$ (S a certain subring of $T_n(\mathbb{R})$, the full matrix ring over the real numbers $\mathbb{R}$), and $x,p \in \mathbb{R}^n$, or $x \in \mathbb{R}^n_+$, $(Ax+p) \in \mathbb{R}^n_+$. In our preceding contribution we called (a slightly more general form of) this functional equation the equation of measurement. To represent the results in a more detailed manner we introduce the following functions.

$$\mathrm{diag} : \mathbb{R}^n \to T_n(\mathbb{R}); \quad \mathrm{diag} : \begin{pmatrix} x_1 \\ \vdots \\ x_n \end{pmatrix} \to \begin{pmatrix} x_1 & & 0 \\ & \ddots & \\ 0 & & x_n \end{pmatrix},$$

$$d : \mathbb{R} \to T_n(\mathbb{R}); \quad d : r \to \begin{pmatrix} r & & 0 \\ & \ddots & \\ 0 & & r \end{pmatrix},$$

$$v : \mathbb{R} \to \mathbb{R}^n; \quad v : r \to \begin{pmatrix} r \\ \vdots \\ r \end{pmatrix}.$$

With these notations $d(r) = \mathrm{diag}(v(r))$ for $r \in \mathbb{R}$.

Aczél/Roberts/Rosenbaum [ARR] and Aczél [Acz2] present detailed tables of the functions u solving equation (1), where $A \in \mathrm{diag}(I^n)$ or $A \in d(I)$, $p \in I^n$ or $p \in v(I)$, $I=\mathbb{R}$ or $I=\mathbb{R}_+$. They consider all possible combinations of these basic cases. They are not interested in the form of the functions R and

Measurement in Economics
ed. by W. Eichhorn

P, even so they are contained in the proofs as by-products. [ARR] also do not deal explicitly with the more general case, where A is an arbitrary element of an arbitrary subalgebra of $T_n(\mathbb{R})$. In his contribution [Pag1] following the present paper, Paganoni (see also [Pag2]) generalizes these results to the case, where $u:X\to V$, $X\subseteq U$, U and V real vector spaces, A an element of an arbitrary subalgebra B of the algebra of linear operators of U into itself, and where p is an element of a positive cone C of U. He phrases the solutions of the above equation for the "given functions" $R:B\times C\to\mathbb{R}-\{0\}$, $P:B\times C\to V$ and the unknown function $u:X\to V$ in terms of the solutions of Cauchy's functional equations on B and C, respectively. To an expert in this field his results are sufficient to derive the exact form of the functions u, R, and P. He does not offer detailed solutions, however. Nevertheless, for economists or statisticians, who are not too mathematically minded, a detailed tableau of the solutions u, R, P of important special cases of equation (1) may be of interest. In what follows, we present this tableau. We have already shown in our preceding contribution that the special cases to be considered in what follows play an important role in the theory of measurement in economics.

1. PRELIMINARIES

Let $M|\mathrm{diag}(\mathbb{R}^n)$ be the restriction of $M:T_n(\mathbb{R})\to\mathbb{R}$ to the diagonal matrices. For $A,B\in T_n(\mathbb{R})$ the following equations are of general interest:

$$M_n^{(1)}(AB) = M_n^{(1)}(A)\,M_n^{(1)}(B),$$

$$M_n^{(2)}(AB) = M_n^{(2)}(A)\,M_n^{(2)}(B), \quad \text{where } M_n^{(2)} = M_n^{(1)}|\mathrm{diag}(\mathbb{R}^n),$$

$$M_n^{(3)}(AB) = M_n^{(3)}(A)\,M_n^{(3)}(B) \quad \text{where } M_n^{(3)} = M_n^{(1)}|d(\mathbb{R})$$

and

$$L_n^{(1)}(AB) = L_n^{(1)}(A) + L_n^{(1)}(B),$$

$$L_n^{(2)}(AB) = L_n^{(2)}(A) + L_n^{(2)}(B), \quad \text{where } L_n^{(2)} = L_n^{(1)}|\mathrm{diag}(\mathbb{R}^n),$$

$$L_n^{(3)}(AB) = L_n^{(3)}(A) + L_n^{(3)}(B), \quad \text{where } L_n^{(3)} = L_n^{(1)}|d(\mathbb{R}^n).$$

Note that $M_1^{(1)} = M_1^{(2)} = M_1^{(3)} =: M_1$, $L_1^{(1)} = L_1^{(2)} = L_1^{(3)} =: L_1$.

Theorem 1. a) For $A:\mathbb{R}\to\mathbb{R}$ the Cauchy functional equation

$$A(x+y) = A(x)+A(y), \quad x,y\in\mathbb{R}$$

has the following solutions

$$A(x)=cx, \text{ where } c=A(1)\in\mathbb{R}, \text{ if } A \text{ is continuous,}$$

and if A is not necessarily continuous

$$A(x) = \sum_{i=1}^{n} r_i A(s_i),$$

where

$$x = \sum_{i=1}^{n} r_i s_i,$$

and the s_i are a Hamel basis of the additive group $\mathbb{R}$ over the rational numbers Q.

b) The multiplicative functional equation

$$M(xy) = M(x)M(y), \qquad M:\mathbb{R}\to\mathbb{R}$$

has the following continuous solutions

$$M = 1, \ M = 0.$$

The solutions $M(x) = \text{sign}(x)|x|^c$, and $M(x) = \text{abs}(\text{sign}(x))|x|^c$ are continuous for $c > 0$ and continuous for $x \neq 0$, and $c \leq 0$. Furthermore, M has the following general solution (without continuity supposition)

$$M(x) = \frac{\prod_{i=1}^{n} M(p_i)}{\prod_{i=1}^{m} M(q_i)} \prod_{i=1}^{l} M(s_i),$$

where

$$x = \frac{\prod_{i=1}^{n} p_i}{\prod_{i=1}^{m} q_i} \prod_{i=1}^{l} s_i,$$

and the s_i are a Hamel basis of the multiplicative group $\mathbb{R}^*$ of the real numbers without 0.

c) From b) one derives the solutions of the functional equation of the logarithm:

$$L(xy) = L(x)+L(y), \qquad L:\mathbb{R}_+\to\mathbb{R}.$$

Proof: see [Acz1].

Theorem 2. a) Let l_i be the eigenvalues of $A\in T_n(\mathbb{R})$. As A is real, there are k complex eigenvalues $l_1,\dots,l_k$ and n-k real ones $l_{k+1},\dots,l_n$.

Then

$$M_n^{(1)}(A) = M_n^{(1)}(\det A) = \Pi_{i=1}^{k} M_1(|l_i|)\ \Pi_{i=k+1}^{n} M_1(l_i),$$

$$M_n^{(2)}(A) = \Pi_{i=1}^{n} M_{1,i}(x_i)$$

with $x=(x_1,\dots,x_n)\varepsilon\mathbb{R}^n$, and

$$M_n^{(3)}(A) = M_n^{(3)}(d(r)) = M_1(r) \text{ for } r\varepsilon\mathbb{R}.$$

b) Let $T_n^{*+}(\mathbb{R})$ denote the multiplicative subgroup of $T_n(\mathbb{R})$ which has either positive or complex eigenvalues only. Then we have with the same notation as in a),

$$L_n^{(1)}(A) = \sum_{i=1}^{k} L_1(|l_i|)+\sum_{i=k+1}^{n} L_1(l_i),$$

$$L_n^{(2)}(\mathrm{diag}(x)) = \sum_{i=1}^{n} L_{1,i}(x_i),\ x = (x_1,\dots,x_n)\varepsilon\mathbb{R}^n.$$

$$L_n^{(3)}(d(r)) = L_1(r), \qquad r\varepsilon\mathbb{R}.$$

c) If $M_n^{(2)}$ is also additive, then

$$M_n^{(2)}(A) = M_n^{(2)}(\mathrm{diag}(x)) = x_i$$

for some i, and $x\varepsilon\mathbb{R}^n$.

Proof: The proofs of a) and b) can be found in [Acz1]. Only c) shall be proven.

As M is additive,

$$M(\mathrm{diag}(p+q)) = M(\mathrm{diag}(p))+M(\mathrm{diag}(q)),$$

i.e., $M|\mathrm{diag}(\mathbb{R}^n)$ is additive. If $M(\mathbb{1}) = 0$, where $\mathbb{1}$ = unit matrix, then $M = 0$. If $M(\mathbb{1}) \neq 0$, $M(\mathbb{1}) = 1$ must hold, and

$$M(\mathrm{diag}(k,\dots,k)) = k.$$

$x = (x_1,\dots,x_n) \geqq 0$ implies with $\mathrm{diag}(x) = \mathrm{diag}(h)\mathrm{diag}(h)$

$$M(\mathrm{diag}(x)) = M(\mathrm{diag}(h)\mathrm{diag}(h)) \geqq 0.$$

For a sequence $x^{(i)}$, which converges to 0,

$$\lim M(\mathrm{diag}(x^{(i)}) = 0.$$

There exists a subsequence $x^{(k)}$ such that

$$x^{(k)} \leqq (1/k,\ldots,1/k) \ , \text{ and } 1/k \geq M(\mathrm{diag}(x^{(k)}) \geqq 0 .$$

Therefore M is continuous. As an additive and continuous function M is of the form

$$M(\mathrm{diag}(x)) = \sum_{n=1}^{k} a_k x_k .$$

Setting $x=e_k$, where e_k is the k-th unit vector, one obtains $a_k = 0$ or $a_k = 1$. As $M \neq 0$, at least one $a_k \neq 0$. If more than one $a_k \neq 0$, one deduces from

$$\mathrm{diag}(e_i+e_k) = \mathrm{diag}(e_i+e_k)\mathrm{diag}(e_i+e_k)$$

the contradiction

$$2 = M(\mathrm{diag}(e_i+e_k)) = M(\mathrm{diag}(e_i+e_k))M(\mathrm{diag}(e_i+e_k)) = 4.$$

Hence all except one $a_k = 0$. This holds if $M = M^{(1)}$ or $M = M^{(2)}$. If $M = M^{(1)}$, and $a_1 = 1$, the following holds:

$$1 = M^{(1)}(\mathrm{diag}(e_1)) = M^{(1)}(\mathrm{diag}(e_2)) = 0.$$

Hence $M^{(1)} = 0$, and $M^{(2)}(\mathrm{diag}(x)) = x_i$ for some i.

2. THE SOLUTIONS

We omit the proofs of the following Theorems 3 to 6, since they can be done using the same arguments as in [ARR]. In the following theorems we often use the generally accepted notation where c either denotes the element $c \in \mathbb{R}$ or the constant function with value $c \in \mathbb{R}$.

Theorem 3. The functional equation

$$u(Ax+p) = R(A,p)u(x)+P(A,p)$$

with $u:\mathbb{R}^n \to \mathbb{R}$, $R,P: T_n(\mathbb{R}) \times \mathbb{R}^n \to \mathbb{R}$ has the following solutions:

$u = \text{const} = c$, R arbitrary, $P(A,p) = c(1-R(A,p))$.

For $u \neq$ const the following holds:

a) $A \in T_n(\mathbb{R})$, $p \in \mathbb{R}^n$:

There are no nonconstant solutions for u.

b) $A\varepsilon\,\mathrm{diag}(\mathbb{R}^n)$, $p\varepsilon\mathbb{R}^n$:
$u(x) = ax_k-b$, $R(A,p) = a_k$, $P(A,p) = b(a_k-1)+ap_k$ for some k.

c) $A\varepsilon d(\mathbb{R})$, $p\varepsilon\mathbb{R}^n$:

$$u(x) = a\sum_{k=1}^{n} M_{n,k}(x_k) - b,$$

$$R(A,p) = R(d(r),p) = r$$

$$P(A,p) = b(r-1)+a\sum_{k=1}^{n} M_{n,k}(p_k).$$

d) $A\varepsilon T_n(\mathbb{R})$, $p\varepsilon v(\mathbb{R})$:

There are no nonconstant solutions.

e) $A\varepsilon\,\mathrm{diag}(\mathbb{R}^n)$, $p\varepsilon v(\mathbb{R})$:
$u(x) = ax_k-b$, $R(A,p) = a_k$, $P(A,p) = b(a_k-1)+ap_k$ for some k.

f) $A\varepsilon d(\mathbb{R})$, $p\varepsilon v(\mathbb{R})$:
$f:\mathbb{R}^n \to \mathbb{R}$ arbitrary, then $u(x) = f((x-m(x)e)/\sigma(x))$, $R = 1$, $P = c\varepsilon\mathbb{R}$, where $m(x)$ denotes the mean and $\sigma(x)$ the variance of $x\varepsilon\mathbb{R}^n$, $e = (1,\dots,1)\varepsilon\mathbb{R}^n$.

For $A = d(r)$ and $p = v(s)$ we have

$$R(A,p) = r,$$

$$P(A,p) = b(r-1)+as.$$

If $x\varepsilon v(\mathbb{R})$

$$u(x) = am(x)-b,$$

and if $x\varepsilon v(\mathbb{R})$, $f:\mathbb{R}^n\to\mathbb{R}$ arbitrary

$$u(x) = \sigma(x)f((x-m(x))/\sigma(x))+b\sigma(x)+am(x)-b.$$

Now the case $P = 0$ shall be considered.

Theorem 4. The equation

$$u(Ax+p) = R(A,p)u(x)$$

has the follwing solutions:

$R:T_n(\mathbb{R})\times\mathbb{R}^n\to\mathbb{R}$ arbitrary, $u = 0$,

$R = \mathrm{const} = 1$, $u = \mathrm{const} \neq 0$

for $A\epsilon T_n(\mathbb{R})$ and $p\epsilon\mathbb{R}^n$, $A\epsilon\ \mathrm{diag}(\mathbb{R}^n)$ and $p\epsilon\mathbb{R}^n$,
$A\epsilon d(\mathbb{R})$ and $p\epsilon\mathbb{R}^n$, $A\epsilon T_n(\mathbb{R})$ and $p\epsilon v(\mathbb{R})$, $A\epsilon\ \mathrm{diag}(\mathbb{R}^n)$ and $p\epsilon v(\mathbb{R})$.
For $A\epsilon d(\mathbb{R})$ and $p\epsilon v(\mathbb{R})$ we distinguish the following cases:

$n = 1$: $u = \mathrm{const}$, $R = 1$.
$n = 2$: $u|v(\mathbb{R}) = \mathrm{const} \neq 0$,

$$R = 1, \quad u(x) = \begin{cases} k, & \sigma(x) \neq 0 \\ k', & \sigma(x) = 0, \end{cases}$$

$u|v(\mathbb{R}) = 0$,

$$R = M_2^{(3)}, \quad u(x) = \begin{cases} M_1(x_1-x_2)k, & \sigma(x) \neq 0 \\ 0, & \sigma(x) = 0. \end{cases}$$

$n > 2$: $u|v(\mathbb{R}) = \mathrm{const} \neq 0$

$$R = 1, \quad u(x) = \begin{cases} f((x-v(m(x)))/\sigma(x)), & \sigma(x) \neq 0 \\ \mathrm{const}, & \sigma(x) = 0, \end{cases}$$

$u|v(\mathbb{R}) = 0$

$$R = M_n^{(3)}, \quad u(x) = \begin{cases} M_n^{(3)}(d(\sigma(x)))f((x-v(m(x)))/\sigma(x)), & \sigma(x) \neq 0 \\ 0, & \sigma(x) = 0. \end{cases}$$

$m(x)$ denotes the mean and $\sigma(x)$ the variance of the vector $x\epsilon\mathbb{R}^n$, with $f:\mathbb{R}^n\to\mathbb{R}$ arbitrary.

Theorem 5. The functional equation

$$u(Ax) = R(A)u(x)+P(A)$$

with $u:\mathbb{R}^n\to\mathbb{R}$, and $P,R: T_n(\mathbb{R})\to\mathbb{R}$ has the following solutions.

$$u = \mathrm{const} = c, \quad R \text{ arbitrary}, \quad P(A) = c(1-R(A)).$$

If $u \neq \mathrm{const}$, one distinguishes the following three cases.

a) $A\epsilon T_n(\mathbb{R})$

$u \neq \mathrm{const}$ and $R = M_n^{(1)} = 1$

$$P(A) = L_n^{(1)}(A), \quad u(x) = c+L_n^{(1)}(\mathrm{diag}(x))$$

$u \neq \mathrm{const}$ and $R = M_n^{(1)} \neq 1$

$$P(A) = c_0(M_n^{(1)}(A)-1), \quad u(x) = cM_n^{(1)}(\mathrm{diag}(x))+d,$$

with c_0, c, $d\epsilon\mathbb{R}$.

b) $A \in \mathrm{diag}(\mathbb{R}^n)$

$u \neq$ const and $R = M_n^{(2)} = 1$

$$P(A) = L_n^{(2)}(A), \quad u(x) = c + L_n^{(2)}(\mathrm{diag}(x))$$

$u \neq$ const and $R = M_n^{(2)} \neq 1$

$$P(A) = c_0(M_n^{(2)}(A) - 1), \quad u(x) = cM_n^{(2)}(\mathrm{diag}(x)) + d,$$

with c_0, c, $d \in \mathbb{R}$.

c) $A \in d(\mathbb{R})$

$u \neq$ const and $R = M_n^{(3)} = 1$

$$P(A) = L_n^{(3)}(A),$$

$$u(x) = f\left(\frac{x_1}{x_i}, \ldots, \frac{x_{i-1}}{x_i}, \frac{x_{i+1}}{x_i}, \ldots, \frac{x_n}{x_i}\right) + L_n^{(3)}(d(x_i))$$

with

$$f: \mathbb{R}^{n-1} \to \mathbb{R} \text{ arbitrary and } x_i \neq 0.$$

If $n = 1$, $u(x) = L_1(x_1)$.

$u \neq$ const and $R = M_n^{(3)} \neq 1$

$$P(A) = c_0(M_n^{(3)}(A) - 1),$$

$$u(x) = M_n^{(3)}(d(x_i))f\left(\frac{x_1}{x_i}, \ldots, \frac{x_{i-1}}{x_i}, \frac{x_{i+1}}{x_i}, \ldots, \frac{x_n}{x_i}\right) + c$$

with

$$f: \mathbb{R}_{n-1} \to \mathbb{R} \text{ arbitrary and } x_i \neq 0,\ c,\ c_0 \in \mathbb{R}.$$

If $n = 1$, $u(x) = M_1(x_1) + c$.

Theorem 6. The functional equation

$$u(Ax) = R(A)u(x)$$

has the following solutions.

$$u = 0, \ R \text{ arbitrary},$$
$$u = \text{const} \neq 0, \ R = 1,$$

a) $A \varepsilon T_n(\mathbb{R})$

$$R(A) = M_n^{(3)}(A), \quad u(x) = cR(\mathrm{diag}(x)), \text{ with } c \varepsilon \mathbb{R},$$

b) $A \varepsilon \ \mathrm{diag}(\mathbb{R}^n)$

$$R(A) = M_n^{(2)}(A), \quad u(x) = cR(\mathrm{diag}(x)), \text{ with } c \varepsilon \mathbb{R},$$

c) $A \varepsilon d(\mathbb{R})$

$$R(d(r)) = M_1(r)$$

$$u(x) = M_n^{(1)}(x_i) f\left(\frac{x_1}{x_i}, \ldots, \frac{x_{i-1}}{x_i}, \frac{x_{i+1}}{x_i}, \ldots, \frac{x_n}{x_i}\right)$$

with $f: \mathbb{R}^{n-1} \to \mathbb{R}$ arbitrary.

REFERENCES

[Acz1] Aczél J.: Lectures on Functional Equations and Their Applications. New York, San Francisco, London 1966.

[Acz2] Aczél J.: 'Cheaper by the Dozen': Twelve Functional Equations and Their Applications to the 'Laws of Science' and to Measurement in Economics. This volume.

[ARR] Aczél J., Roberts F.S., Rosenbaum Z.: On Scientific Laws Without Dimensional Constants. Journal of Mathematical Analysis and Applications 119 (1986), 389-416.

[EiG1] Eichhorn W., Gleissner W.: The Equation of Measurement. This volume.

[Pag1] Paganoni L.: On a Functional Equation with Applications to Measurement in Economics. This volume.

[Pag2] Paganoni L.: On a Functional Equation Concerning Affince Transformations. Forthcoming in Journal of Mathematical Analysis and Applications.

On a Functional Equation with Applications to Measurement in Economics

LUIGI PAGANONI
Dipartimento di Matematica
Università di Milano
20133 Milano, Italia

1. Several problems in Economics (Production Theory, Utility Theory, Theory of Prices, etc...), in particular those concerning indices (Price Indices, Inequalities Measures, etc...) lead (see [2]) to functional equations of the form

$$u(Rx+p) = \alpha(R,p)u(x) + \beta(R,p) \quad . \tag{1}$$

Equations of this form appear also in the "dimensional analysis" ([1] , [3] , [4]) and some special cases concerning the "law of science without dimensional constants" have been recently solved (see [1]).

the aim of this paper is to give the solutions of (1) in a generality which makes it possible to use them in many applications. Here we only present the results; the detailed proofs can be found in [5] . At the end of the paper we will show some simple examples of these applications.

2. In this paper we always assume that :

X is a subset of $\mathbb{R}^n$, P is a positive cone in $\mathbb{R}^n$ (i.e. $P+P \subset P$; $\lambda P \subset P$, $\lambda \geq 0$), $\mathfrak{R}$ is a subset of $L(\mathbb{R}^n)$ (the algebra of linear operators of $\mathbb{R}^n$ into itself) such that

Measurement in Economics
ed. by W. Eichhorn

$$X + P \subset X$$

$$R(X) \subset X \quad , \quad \forall R \in \mathcal{R}$$

$$RS \in \mathcal{R} \quad , \quad \forall R,S \in \mathcal{R}$$

$$\text{if } P \neq \{0\} \text{ , then } \lambda I \in \mathcal{R} \quad , \forall \lambda > 0 \quad .$$

We consider the functional equation (1) with $x \in X$, $p \in P$, $R \in \mathcal{R}$; $\alpha : \mathcal{R} \times P \to \mathbb{R} \setminus \{0\}$ and $\beta : \mathcal{R} \times P \to \mathbb{R}$ are given functions, $u : X \to \mathbb{R}$ is the unknown function.

If (1) admits the constant solution $u(x) = c_0$, it is obvious that α and β have to satisfy the condition

$$\beta(R,p) = c_0(1 - \alpha(R,p)) \quad .$$

It is possible to show more generally that, if (1) has a non trivial solution, then α and β have to be of a very special form. Indeed we have the following

THEOREM 1. *If* u *is a non constant solution of* (1), *then the functions* α *and* β *have one of the two following forms :*

i) $\alpha(R,p) = M(R)$ *where* M *is a multiplicative function* (*i.e.* $M(RS) = M(R)M(S) \quad , \forall R,S \in \mathcal{R}$);

$\beta(R,p) = \Psi(R)$ *where* Ψ *satisfies the equation*

$$\Psi(RS) = M(R)\Psi(S) + \Psi(R) \quad , \forall R,S \in \mathcal{R} \quad .$$

ii) $\alpha(R,p) = M^*(R)$ *where* M^* *is a multiplicative function which satisfies the equation* $M^*(\lambda I) = \lambda \quad , \quad \forall \lambda > 0$;

$\beta(R,p) = b(M^*(R) - 1) + A(p)$ *where* $b \in \mathbb{R}$ *and* $A \neq 0$ *is a positively homogeneous additive function.*

REMARK. If $P = \{0\}$, we can have only case i) .

Therefore the only functional equations of the form (1) which may have a non constant solution are the following ones :

(2) $u(Rx+p) = M(R)u(x) + \Psi(R)$

(3) $u(Rx+p) = M^*(R)u(x) + b(M^*(R)-1) + A(p)$, $A \not\equiv 0$,

where $M, M^*, \Psi, A, b,$ are described in Theorem 1.

Now we want to present the form of the general solution of the functional equations (2) and (3) and, to do this, we have to make some new assumptions.

From now on we assume that :

(4) for every $R \in \mathcal{R}$ there exists R^{-1}, and $R^{-1} \in \mathcal{R}$.

(5) if W is the subspace of $\mathbb{R}^n$ generated by all vectors $\{Rp\}$ with $R \in \mathcal{R}$ and $p \in P$, then there exists a supplementary subspace of W in $\mathbb{R}^n$, W' , which is $\mathcal{R}$-invariant (i.e. $\mathbb{R}^n = W \oplus W'$ and $R(W') \subset W'$, $\forall R \in \mathcal{R}$).

Now we have to introduce the following equivalence relation in W' :

$$x_1 \sim x_2 \quad \text{iff there exists} \quad R \in \mathcal{R} \quad \text{such that} \quad x_2 = Rx_1 \quad .$$

Let $\Omega \subset W'$ be a set which contains exactly one element from each equivalence class $[x]_\sim$, with $x \in (X+W) \cap W'$.

Every $x \in X$ can be uniquely represented in the form

$$x = x_1 + x_2 \quad , \quad \text{with} \quad x_1 \in W' \quad , x_2 \in W$$

Now, since $x_1 \in (X+W) \cap W'$, there exists a unique $\omega \in \Omega$ such that $x_1 = R\omega$, $R \in \mathcal{R}$. Therefore, for every $x \in X$ we can write :

$$x = R\omega + x_2$$

(Note that, while ω and x_2 are uniquely determined, R is not necessarily unique).

Finally, for every $\omega \in \Omega$, denote by $\mathcal{R}_\omega$ the subset of $\mathcal{R}$ given by

$$\mathcal{R}_\omega = \{ T \in \mathcal{R} \ : \ T\omega = \omega \}$$

Now it is possible to state the following

THEOREM 2. *Consider the functional equation*

$$\text{(2)} \qquad u(Rx+p) = M(R)u(x) + \Psi(R)$$

under the hypotheses (4),(5).

A function $u : X \to \mathbb{R}$ *is a solution of (2) if and only if there exists a function* $f : \Omega \to \mathbb{R}$ *satisfying*

$$\text{(6)} \qquad \Psi(T) = (1-M(T))f(\omega) \quad , \ \omega \in \Omega \ , \ T \in \mathcal{R}_\omega$$

such that, $\forall x \in X$ *, if* $x = R\omega + x_2$ *with* $\omega \in \Omega$ *,* $x_2 \in W$ *, then*

$$u(x) = M(R)f(\omega) + \Psi(R) \ .$$

To present a similar theorem concerning the functional equation (3) we have to introduce the following notations:

$\tilde{\mathcal{R}}$ is the subspace of $L(\mathbb{R}^n)$ generated by $\mathcal{R}$ and $\{\phi_i\}_{1\leq i\leq k}$ is a basis of $\tilde{\mathcal{R}}$;

$\tilde{P}$ is the subspace of $\mathbb{R}^n$ generated by P and $\{\eta_s\}_{1\leq s\leq l}$ is a basis of $\tilde{P}$;

$\tilde{A} : \tilde{P} \to \mathbb{R}$ is the linear extension to $\tilde{P}$ of the function A .

THEOREM 3. *Consider the functional equation*

$$\text{(3)} \qquad u(Rx+p) = M^*(R)u(x) + b(M^*(R)-1) + A(p)$$

under the hypotheses (4),(5).

A function $u : X \to \mathbb{R}$ *is a solution of (3) if and only if :*

i) there exists a linear multiplicative function $\tilde{M} : \tilde{\mathcal{R}} \to \mathbb{R}$ *, extension of* M^**, such that*

$$\text{(7)} \qquad \sum_{i=1}^{k} \sum_{s=1}^{l} a_{is}(\phi_i \eta_s) = 0 \Rightarrow \sum_{i=1}^{k} \sum_{s=1}^{l} a_{is} \tilde{M}(\phi_i)\tilde{A}(\eta_s) = 0$$

ii) there exist a real function $f : \Omega \to \mathbb{R}$ *satisfying*

$$(\tilde{M}(T)-1)f(\omega) = 0 \quad , \quad \omega \in \Omega \ , \quad T \in \mathcal{R}_\omega$$

and a real number b *such that,* $\forall x \in X$ *, if* $x = R\omega + x_2$ *with* $\omega \in \Omega$ *,* $x_2 \in W$*, then*

$$u(x) = \tilde{M}(R)f(\omega) - b + g(x_2)$$

where $g : W \to \mathbb{R}$ *is the linear function defined on the set of vectors* $\{\phi_i \eta_s\}$ *,* $1 \le i \le k$ *,* $1 \le s \le l$ *, by* $g(\phi_i \eta_s) = \tilde{M}(\phi_i)\tilde{A}(\eta_s)$ *. (the existence of the function* g *is assured by (7)).*

3. EXAMPLE 1. Consider the functional equation

(8) $\quad u(\lambda x + p) = u(x)$

with $\lambda \in \mathbb{R}^+$, $x \in \mathbb{R}^n$, $p \in \Delta_n = \{x \in \mathbb{R}^n : x_1 = x_2 = \ldots = x_n\}$.
This equation is of the form (2) with $X = \mathbb{R}^n$, $P = \Delta_n$, $\mathcal{R} = \{\lambda I\} \ \lambda > 0$, $M(R) \equiv 1$, $\Psi(R) \equiv 0$. In this case $W = \Delta_n$ and if we take $W' = W^\perp = \{ x \in \mathbb{R}^n : (x,p) = 0 \ , \ \forall p \in \Delta_n\} = \{x \in \mathbb{R}^n : \sum_{1 \le i \le n} x_i = 0\}$, then the hypotheses of Theorem 2 are fulfilled.
We can choose $\Omega = \{\omega \in W^\perp : \|\omega\| = 1\} \cup \{0\}$. Since $M \equiv 1$, (6) is trivially satisfied by every arbitrary function $f: \Omega \to \mathbb{R}$.
For every $x \in \mathbb{R}^n$, denote by $A(x)$ the vector of Δ_n given by

$$A(x) = \{ \frac{1}{n} \sum_{i=1}^n x_i , \ \ldots \ , \frac{1}{n} \sum_{i=1}^n x_i \} \ .$$

Then we have the following representation

$$x = (x - A(x)) + A(x) = \begin{cases} A(x) & \text{if } x = A(x) \\ \dfrac{x - A(x)}{\|x - A(x)\|} \|x - A(x)\| + A(x) & \text{if } x \ne A(x) \end{cases}$$

So $u(x)$ is a solution of (8) if and only if

$$u(x) = \begin{cases} f\left(\dfrac{x - A(x)}{\|x - A(x)\|}\right) & \text{if } x \neq A(x) \\ f(0) & \text{if } x = A(x) \end{cases}$$

where f is an arbitrary real function defined on Ω .

EXAMPLE 2 (From the cost of living index theory).

Consider the following functional equations

$$(9)\quad u(x_1^1/r_1,\ldots,x_n^1/r_n,x_1^2/r_1,\ldots,x_n^2/r_n,r_1x_1^3,\ldots,r_nx_n^3,r_1x_1^4,\ldots,r_nx_n^4) =$$

$$= u(x_1^1,\ldots x_n^1,x_1^2,\ldots,x_n^2,x_1^3,\ldots,x_n^3,x_1^4,\ldots,x_n^4)$$

$$(10)\quad u(x_1^1,\ldots,x_n^1,x_1^2,\ldots,x_n^2,\lambda x_1^3,\ldots,\lambda x_n^3,\lambda x_1^4,\ldots,\lambda x_n^4) =$$

$$= u(x_1^1,\ldots x_n^1,x_n^2,\ldots,x_n^2,x_1^3,\ldots,x_n^3,x_1^4,\ldots,x_n^4)$$

(9) is of the form (2) with $X = \mathbb{R}_+^{4n}$, $P = \{0\}$, $M \equiv 1$, $\Psi \equiv 0$; $\mathcal{R}$ is the set of diagonal matrices whose elements a_{ii} , $1 \leq i \leq 4n$, are given by:

$$a_{ii} = \begin{cases} 1/r_i & 1 \leq i \leq n \\ 1/r_{i-n} & n+1 \leq i \leq 2n \\ r_{i-2n} & 2n+1 \leq i \leq 3n \\ r_{i-3n} & 3n+1 \leq i \leq 4n \end{cases} \qquad r_j > 0 \ ,\ 1 \leq j \leq n \ .$$

In this case $W = \{0\}$ and $W' = \mathbb{R}^{4n}$. It is easy to see that the class Ω can be chosen in the following way

$$\Omega = \{\underline{\omega} \in \mathbb{R}_+^{4n} : \underline{\omega} = (\underline{1},\omega_2,\omega_3,\omega_4) \text{ with } \underline{1} = (1,\ldots,1) \in \Delta_n ,\ \omega_i \in \mathbb{R}_+^n, 2 \leq i \leq 4\}$$

and, for every $x \in \mathbb{R}_+^{4n}$, we have $x = R_x\omega_x$ where $R_x \in \mathcal{R}$ with $r_i = 1/x_i^1$ and $\omega_x = (1,\ldots,1,x_1^2/x_1^1,\ldots,x_n^2/x_n^1,x_1^3x_1^1,\ldots,x_n^3x_n^1,x_1^4x_1^1,\ldots,x_n^4x_n^1) \in \Omega$.

So $u : \mathbb{R}_+^{4n} \to \mathbb{R}$ is a solution of (9) if and only if, $\forall x \in \mathbb{R}_+^{4n}$,

$$u(x) = f(\omega_x)$$

where f is an arbitrary real function defined on Ω .

Similarly, for the functional equation (10) $\mathcal{R}$ is the set of diagonal matrices whose elements a_{ii}, $1 \le i \le 4n$, are given by

$$a_{ii} = \begin{cases} 1 & 1 \le i \le 2n \\ \lambda & 2n+1 \le i \le 4n \end{cases} \qquad \lambda > 0$$

and we can choose Ω in the following way

$$\Omega = \{ \omega \in \mathbb{R}_+^{4n} : \omega = (\omega_1, \omega_2, v, \omega_4), \; \|v\| = 1, \; \omega_i \in \mathbb{R}_+^n \; i = 1,2,4 \}$$

and, $\forall x \in \mathbb{R}_+^{4n}$, we have $x = R_x \omega_x$ where $R_x \in \mathcal{R}$ with $\lambda = \|x^3\|$ and $\omega_x = (x^1, x^2, x^3/\|x^3\|, x^4/\|x^4\|)$.

So $u : \mathbb{R}_+^{4n} \to \mathbb{R}$ is a solution of (10) if and only if, $\forall x \in \mathbb{R}_+^{4n}$,

$$u(x) = f(\omega_x)$$

where f is an arbitrary real function defined on Ω .

REFERENCES

[1] Aczél, J., Roberts, F.S. and Rosenbaum, Z., On scientific laws without dimensional constants. J.Math.Anal.Appl. (1986).

[2] Eichhorn, W., Functional Equations in Economics. Addison-Wesley, (1978).

[3] Luce, R.D., A generalization of a theorem of dimensional analysis. J. Math. Psychol. 1 (1964), 278-284.

[4] Mohr, E., Bemerkung zur Dimensionsanalyse. Math. Nachr. 6 (1951), 145-153.

[5] Paganoni, L., On a functional equation concerning affine transformations. To appear in the Journal of Mathematical Analysis and Applications.

Part II Prices

The Precision of Consumer Price Indices Caused by the Sampling Variability of Budget Surveys; an Example

B.M. Balk and H.M.P. Kersten*)
Department of Price Statistics
Central Bureau of Statistics
P.O. Box 959
NL-2270 AZ Voorburg

Abstract

A consumer price index number (CPI) is the result of combining data from various complex sample surveys. In the present paper we concentrate on but one aspect of the accuracy of a CPI, namely the variance due to the sampling variability of the budget survey(s) from which the weighting coefficients are derived. Using the individual budget survey data the variance of a CPI can be estimated by means of the method of balanced half samples. This method is applied to several types of CPI's and to CPI's for different groups of households.

1. Introduction

The current situation is that most official price index numbers are published without an explicit statement about their accuracy. Users of these data must satisfy themselves with the margin implied by the publication format: a price index number of 128.3, for instance, has to be read as 128.30 ± 0.05. Thus the situation has not much changed since more than twenty years ago Morgenstern (1963, pp. 188-189) remarked that "In spite of the widespread use of government price indices, there has been little done in attempting to determine the error inherent in these indices". Yet this seems to be an important issue, with relations towards other research topics. For example, it might be that much empirical research on the so-called substitution bias, or more broadly: within the framework of the economic theory of price indices, becomes futile when the statistical accuracy of the data used is taken into account. Researchers mostly use price and quantity data as if they have infinite accuracy. Actually, however, this is not the case, which might result in the conclusion that the difference between the Laspeyres and the Paasche price indices for a certain

*) The views expressed in this paper are those of the authors and do not necessarily reflect the policies of the Netherlands Central Bureau of Statistics. Computing assistance by H.A. van der Grient is gratefully acknowledged.

Measurement in Economics
ed. by W. Eichhorn

pair of years is statistically insignificant. In that case available resources should be devoted to making the index numbers more accurate rather than studying the substitution bias.

This paper presents a feasible method for estimating one component of the accuracy of a consumer price index, viz. the precision due to the sampling variability of the budget survey(s) from which the vector of weighting coefficients is obtained.[1] Emphasis is laid on the method, because the results - which are also presented - of course strongly depend on the specific situation in the country under study, in this case the Netherlands.

2. The consumer price index as a stochastic variable

We start by describing the general structure of a consumer price index (CPI for short), before discussing the various sources of stochastics (randomness). Let there be given G groups of consumer commodities. Most price indices have the following structure,

$$P^t \equiv \varphi\,(w^0, w^t, \pi^t)\,, \tag{1}$$

in which $w^u \equiv (w_1^u,\dots,w_G^u)$, $u=0,t$, is a vector of weighting coefficients adding up to 1; $\pi^t \equiv (\pi_1^t,\dots,\pi_G^t)$ is a vector of partial price indices for the commodity groups; $\pi_g^0=1$ for $g=1,\dots,G$; t denotes the comparison period (month or year) and 0 denotes the base period (usually a certain year); φ, finally, is a certain function, usually a weighted mean of the π^t.

Further specification of the CPI takes place by relating the vector(s) of weighting coefficients w (the time superscript being deleted for ease of presentation) to a certain population of households H. Usually w is 'the' average expenditure pattern of the households belonging to the set H,

$$w \equiv \Sigma_{h\in H}\, \beta^h\, w^h\,, \tag{2}$$

1) The present paper is a very condensed version of Balk and Kersten (1986), in which also the relevant literature is surveyed.

in which w^h denotes the expenditure pattern of household h, i.e. its vector of budget shares. The β^h are again weighting coefficients.

Regarding β^h, the choice is between the following two well-known candidates. The first and most usual alternative is

$$\beta_p^h \equiv e^h / \Sigma_{h\in H}\, e^h , \tag{3}$$

in which e^h denotes the total expenditure of household h. In this case we call the resulting vector w the plutocratic average expenditure pattern. The second alternative we consider is

$$\beta_d^h \equiv 1 / n(H), \tag{4}$$

where n(H) is the number of households in H. Using β_d^h we obtain the so-called democratic average expenditure pattern.

We now turn to the various sources of stochastics and error.

1. The average expenditure pattern w has to be estimated from a sample of households drawn from H. Moreover, in order to diminish the response burden for the households included in the sample, for certain commodity groups only expenditures during a certain subperiod (for instance a month) are reported. Afterwards, these subperiod expenditures are raised to yearly values.

2. In order to calculate the partial price index of a commodity group g, for each group a sample of representative products must be drawn. These representative products must be specified in detail in order to carry out an unequivocal price survey. The partial price index is then calculated as follows,

$$\pi_g^t \equiv \Sigma_{i\in g}\, \gamma_{ig}\, p_i^t / p_i^0 , \tag{5}$$

where p_i^t denotes the average price paid of product i during period t, and γ_{ig} is some weighting coefficient, if known, with $\Sigma_{i\in g}\ \gamma_{ig}=1$.

3. The average price of product i during period t is estimated by means of a sample of points-of-purchase. In general the composition of this sample and its size will vary with the specific products involved.

4. The sample of representative products is combined with a sample of points-of-time. The price of most products is surveyed once a month, but there are products that are surveyed with a higher frequency (for instance fresh fruits and vegetables: weekly) and products with a lower frequency (for instance pieces of furniture).

5. Finally, there are the inevitable measurement errors. They can be broadly distinguished as errors of observation, processing errors and procedural errors.

In the remainder we discuss a method for estimating the precision of a CPI as far as resulting from the sampling variability of the underlying budget survey. Thus we concentrate on aspect 1. Otherwise stated, in the present study we consider the partial price index numbers π_g^t as given data, without error. The sample counterpart of P will be denoted by $\underline{P}$.

The accuracy of $\underline{P}$ is the possible deviation of $\underline{P}$, calculated from a sample, with respect to P, the price index for the population. The accuracy of $\underline{P}$ is measured by its mean square error $E(\underline{P}-P)^2$, where the expectation operator E is taken over all possible samples of households from H. We have the following well-known decomposition,

$$E(\underline{P} - P)^2 = E(\underline{P} - E\underline{P})^2 + (E\underline{P} - P)^2 . \tag{6}$$

The first term on the righthand side is the variance of $\underline{P}$. It is an inverse measure of its precision. The second term on the righthand side is the square of the bias of $\underline{P}$. The latter is the balance of a multitude of factors. From sample data it is impossible to infer something about the bias of an estimator. Inference about the bias of $\underline{P}$ necessitates knowledge of P, but this is an unknown population parameter. Recourse must be taken to sensitivity analyses, for instance with methods developed by Balk (1980) and Kersten (1985). The present study is therefore restricted to calculation of the variance of $\underline{P}$.

3. The variance of consumer price indices

Our exercises are carried out on the data of the Netherlands Budget Surveys of 1980 and 1981. It should be remarked that for a number of commodity groups - on average some 25% of a household's total expenditure - only subperiod reporting is used. In the present study we used the household's expenditures on a yearly base. Thus the variance of $\underline{P}$ is caused by two indistinguishable effects: the sampling of households and the subperiod reporting of the sampled households. The number of responding households are 2859 and 2897 respectively. The survey of 1980 has been designed explicitly for producing the weighting coefficients for the Netherlands' official price indices, 1980 being the most recent base year, whereas the survey of 1981 served other purposes. This is reflected in the composition of the samples. The sample of 1981 contained fewer employees and more nonactives than that of 1980. On operational grounds we limited the number of commodity groups distinguished to 140.

Both budget surveys made use of poststratification by social group, by net income and by household size. The number of strata distinguished is 108 and 118 respectively. Let H_k denote the k-th stratum of H (k=1,...,K), thus $H=\cup_{k=1}^{K} H_k$ and $H_k \cap H_{k'}=\emptyset$. The plutocratic average expenditure pattern is estimated by

$$\underline{w}_{pg} \equiv \Sigma_{h\in\hat{H}} \nu^h e^h_g \, / \, \Sigma_{h\in\hat{H}} \nu^h e^h \quad (g=1,\ldots,G) \, , \tag{7}$$

and the democratic one by

$$\underline{w}_{dg} \equiv \left[\Sigma_{h\in\hat{H}} \nu^h e^h_g / e^h \right] / \Sigma_{h\in\hat{H}} \nu^h \quad (g=1,\ldots,G) , \tag{8}$$

where $\nu^h \equiv (n(H_k)/n(H))/(n(\hat{H}_k)/n(\hat{H}))$ for $h\in\hat{H}_k$ and $\hat{H}$ denotes a sample from H. These so-called raising factors ν^h of the households are contained in the basic data set of both budget surveys. Notice that $\Sigma_{h\in\hat{H}}\nu^h = n(\hat{H})$, the sample size.

The partial price index numbers of the 140 commodity groups for the years 1981-1982 (1980=100) are taken from the official consumer price index for the total population.

With two budget surveys and a table of partial price indices we can estimate a lot of aggregate consumer price indices. In the present study we restrict ourselves to the Laspeyres, the Paasche and the Törnqvist index, each using plutocratic average expenditure patterns. The democratic average expenditure pattern is used in conjunction with the Laspeyres index only. In case of the Laspeyres index we also compute price indices for subpopulations. For estimating the variance of an aggregate price index we used the method of balanced half samples. For the theory behind this method we refer to Wolter (1985).

According to this method, each sample stratum $\hat{H}_k$ is split randomly in two parts, say $\hat{H}_{kA}$ and $\hat{H}_{kB}$ (k=1,...,K). These parts are called half samples. The method of balanced half samples consists in the combination of these half samples over the K strata. Each particular combination α provides us with an estimator $\underline{w}_{g\alpha}$ for w_g, the population average budget share of commodity group g. It is not necessary to take all 2^K combinations of half samples. We can economize by using a Hadamard matrix, that is a square matrix of +1 and -1 of which the columns are orthogonal. In the present study we worked with a Hadamard matrix of order 160 of which the first K (K=108 and 118 respectively) rows are used. The procedure is as follows: Take a particular column α of the Hadamard matrix. If the k-th element of this column is +1 we take $\hat{H}_{kA}$, if it is -1 we take $\hat{H}_{kB}$.

In this way each combination of half samples α, $\alpha=1,\ldots,160$, provides us with an estimate of the plutocratic/democratic average expenditure pattern of 1980/1981, using the appropriate formula. These estimates can be inserted into the price index formula to obtain estimated price index numbers. More formally, let there be given the vectors $\underline{w}_\alpha^{1980}$ and $\underline{w}_\alpha^{1981}$ ($\alpha=1,\ldots,160$). Then we calculate

$$\underline{P}_\alpha^t \equiv \varphi(\underline{w}_\alpha^{1980}, \underline{w}_\alpha^{1981}, \pi^t) \qquad (\alpha=1,\ldots,160). \tag{9}$$

Thus we have 160 half sample estimates of the price index P^t. Their mean is

$$\bar{\underline{P}}^t \equiv \Sigma_{\alpha=1}^{160} \underline{P}_\alpha^t / 160, \tag{10}$$

and their standard deviation,

$$\underline{s}(\underline{P}^t) \equiv (\Sigma_{\alpha=1}^{160} (\underline{P}_\alpha^t - \bar{\underline{P}}^t)^2 / 160)^{1/2}, \tag{11}$$

can be considered as an estimator of the standard error of $\underline{P}^t$. Table 1 contains the main results. For each type of index we compare the directly estimated price index numbers, obtained by using the estimated average expenditure patterns according to formulas (7) and (8), with the means of the 160 half sample estimates. For all indices the numbers coincide within the limits of precision. It is immediately clear from table 1 that for 1981 the difference between the Laspeyres, Paasche and Törnqvist indices, each using the plutocratic average expenditure pattern, is not significant. However, the difference between both Laspeyres indices, one using the plutocratic average expenditure pattern and the other using the democratic one, is significant. The standard error of the Paasche index is rather high. This is caused by the sample design for 1981. The same fact accounts for the rather high standard error of the Törnqvist index.

In the same way as we estimated price index numbers and standard errors for the population of all households we can proceed for subpopulations. We restricted ourselves to two examples which are typical for the Netherlands' situation. Table 2 contains the results. The sample sizes are respectively

2859 (T), 476 (L) and 945 (H). It is clear that in 1981 CPI-T differs significantly from CPI-L, but the differênce between CPI-T and CPI-H is not significant. In 1982 all indices differ significantly from each other.

Table 1. Estimated price index numbers for all households and estimated standard errors (1980 = 100)

Type of index	Type of average expenditure pattern	1981 Index number	1981 Mean of half sample estimates	1981 Empirical standard error	1982 Index number	1982 Mean of half sample estimates	1982 Empirical standard error
Laspeyres	plutocratic	106.89[a)]	106.89	0.01	113.15[a)]	113.15	0.02
Laspeyres	democratic	106.99	106.99	0.02	113.41	113.41	0.03
Paasche	plutocratic	106.89	106.91	0.03			
Törnqvist	plutocratic	106.89	106.90	0.02			

a) These numbers differ from the officially published ones (106.7 and 112.8 respectively), because the official CPI incorporates in the weighting coefficients also parts of consumption which cannot be observed via a budget survey.

Table 2. Estimated Laspeyres price index numbers, using the plutocratic average expenditure pattern, and estimated standard errors (1980 = 100)

Population	1981 Index number	1981 Mean of half sample estimates	1981 Empirical standard error	1982 Index number	1982 Mean of half sample estimates	1982 Empirical standard error
All households (T)	106.89	106.89	0.01	113.15	113.15	0.02
Households of wage earners with low income (L)	106.99	106.98	0.03	113.41	113.40	0.06
Households of wage earners with high income (H)	106.88	106.88	0.02	112.99	112.98	0.03

Literature

Balk, B.M., 1980, On 'characteristicity' of price indices. In: Statistical Studies no. 26 (Staatsuitgeverij, The Hague).

Balk, B.M. and H.M.P. Kersten, 1986, On the precision of consumer price indices caused by the sampling variability of budget surveys. Journal of Economic and Social Measurement 14, pp. 19-35.

Kersten, H.M.P., 1985, Non-response assessment of a consumer price index. Journal of Business and Economic Statistics 3, pp. 336-343.

Morgenstern, O., 1963, On the accuracy of economic observations, 2nd edition (Princeton University Press, Princeton).

Wolter, K.M., 1985, Introduction to variance estimation (Springer Verlag, New York).

On the Factorial Approach to Index Number Problems, Consumption Analysis and Orthogonal Decomposition of National Income: A Review

K.S. Banerjee
Department of Mathematics and Computer Science
University of Maryland
Baltimore County, Catonsville
Maryland 21228, USA

Preliminary Remarks

Since this Review has already been published, [A1], the Review, as a whole, is withdrawn from reproduction here. However, we provide below an extended abstract of the publication and the list of references for purposes of general information concerning the topic and its developments. Additional remarks and an "Addendum to References" are also included.

Abstract

(i) Different Approaches to Index Number Problems

Ragnar Frisch [27], in his survey of general economic theory of index number problems, distinguished between two different ways in which the problem of index numbers had been approached: (ia) atomistic approach, (ib) test approach under the atomistic view point, and (ii) functional approach.

In the atomistic approach the prices and quantities are considered as two sets of independent variables. To be specific, the price index in the atomistic approach is conceived of as some sort of an estimate of the central tendency of the price ratio considered as a stochastic variable with a distribution. Such a set-up is statistical in nature. The price ratio in this approach makes no reference to quantities. In the test approach, certain tests are developed to differentiate among different index number formulae constructed heuristically without any assumption of a functional form between prices and quantities. The second category relates to the functional approach where prices and quantities are functionally related. The econimic approach comes under this category.

Samuelson and Swamy [46], in their survey and synthesis of index number problems, and Diewert [23], in his essay on the economic theory of index numbers, also recognize the same three basic

Measurement in Economics
ed. by W. Eichhorn

approaches: (i) statistical approach, (ii) test approach, and (iii) the economic or preference field approach (functional).

The developments under the different approaches follow entirely different lines of reasoning, and there is no apparent connection or link among them.

We shall discuss here a different kind of approach which, on one hand, paves the logical basis of development of some of the better known formulae, and, on the other, provides the rationale for developing index number formulae which convey the same or similar significance as economic index numbers do convey. The approach, we are going to present, accomplishes various other objectives in different directions, besides merely building up the above mentioned link. The methodology could be called statistical. Diewert [23] calls it neo-statistical. Other possible names are (i) model approach, (ii) "least squares" approach, etc. But we would prefer to call it the factorial approach, as this approach uses different models involved in the factorial experiments considered under Experimental Designs.

(ii) The Factorial Approach

In the following pages we provide a summary of the developments in different directions under what we have called the factorial approach. The factorial approach is based upon the application of simple Experimental Designs models, - models that characterize factorial experiments. Such models, it is well known, are special kinds of regression models.

The complete Review is divided into the following sections:

Section 2: The factorial approach is explained with reference to a 2^2 - factorial experiment (two factors at two levels each). Different index number formulae including Stuvel's new indexes are obtained. "True indexes" of price and quantity are presented. [11].

Section 3: Models for 2^m - factorial experiments (m factors at two levels each) are used to provide multi-dimensional indexes, indexes involving more that two factors. [9,12].

Section 4: A model for a n^2 - factorial experiment (two factors at n levels each) is used to develop multi-lateral indexes, indexes for an arbitrary number of periods time, or geographical units. [10,12].

Section 5: Factorial indexes are compared with the B.L.A.U. index numbers introduced by Theil [54], and Kloek and Dewit [39]. [10].

Section 6: A generalization of Stuvel's averaging procedure is discussed. [6].

Section 7: A connection is traced between the factorial indexes and the Divisia Integral Indexes. [14,15,16].

Section 8: An interpretation of a special pair of equations emerging from the factorial approach is presented. [14].

Section 9: The need for decomposition of national income into the price and quantity components is emphasized. [7].

Section 10: An interpretation of the factorial indexes in the light of Hicksian and Marshall-Samuelsonian, consumer surpluses is presented. [19].

Section 11: A connection is traced between factorial indexes and log-change indexes. [21,48].

Section 12: A possibility of estimating the difference in utilities in the two periods on a parametric basis is suggested.

Section 13: A comparison is made between the factorial true index of price and the two well known economic price indexes. [17].

Section 14: Concluding Remarks. [2,4,11,27,36,43,59].

(iii) Some Additional Comments

In recent years, Balk [A3] and Pfingsten [A9] have shown that the factorial true index of price can be exact only by Leontief type, fixed coefficients utility functions, in which case however L_p (Laspeyres' price index) will be equal to P_p (Paasche's price index), and the factorial true index of price will satisfy the linear homogeneity-test, as well. Although the factorial true index of price is exact in a restricted situation such as this, its value as an approximation can still be retained in other types of utility functions, its value always lying between L_p and P_p. (See Balk [A3].

An apology was offered in the preface of the monograph published, [A1], for not being able to quote all the references cited in the original papers from which the said summary monograph has been drawn. Even if it were possible to do so. those references would still not be exhaustive, and would miss some of the most important work done by other experts in this area. In fact, no work on index numbers would be considered to be complete, if no explicit mention is made about at least some of the work of Afriat [A2], Blackorby and Russell [A4], Eichhorn [A5], Eichhorn and Voeller [A6], I.Fisher [A7], Malmquist [A8], Pollak [A10], Törnquist [A11] and Ulmer [A12], whose illuminating contributions will always dominate as a permanent source of inspiration to research workers.

References

[1] Allen, R.G.D.: Index Numbers in Theory and Practice, London, The Macmillan Company (1975).

[2] Archer, C.A.: Review on the Factorial Approach Providing the True Index of Cost of Living, Journal of the Royal Statistical Society, Series A, Vol. 142, Part 1 (1979), p. 79.

[3] Balk, B.M.: Second Thoughts on Wald's Cost-of-Living Index and Frische's Double Expenditure Method, Econometrica, Vol. 49, No. 6, (1981), pp. 1553-1558.

[4] Banerjee, K.S.: A Note on the Optimal Allocation of Consumption Items in the Construction of a Cost-of-Living Index, Econometrica 24, 3 (1956), pp. 294-295.

[5] Banerjee, K.S.: Simplification of the Derivation of Wald's Formula for the Cost-of-Living Index, Econometrica, Vol. 24, No. 3 (1956), pp. 296-298.

[6] Banerjee, K.S.: A Generalization of Stuvel's Index Number Formulae, Econometrica, 27, No. 4 (1959), pp. 676-678.

[7] Banerjee, K.S.: A Factorial Approach to Construction of the Cost-of-Living Index and Its Application in Studies of Changes in National Income, Sankhyā, Series A, Vol. 23, (1961), pp. 297-303.

[8] Banerjee, K.S.: A Unified Statistical Approach to the Index Number Problem, Econometrica, Vol. 29, No. 4, (1961), pp. 591-601.

[9] Banerjee, K.S.: Index Numbers for Factorial Effects and Their Connection with a Special Kind of Irregular Fractional Plans of Factorial Experiments, Journal of the American Statistical Association, 58, (1963), pp. 497-508.

[10] Banerjee, K.S.: Best Linear Unbiased Index Numbers and Index Numbers Obtained Through a Factorial Approach, Econometrica, Vol. 31, No. 4., (1963), pp. 712-718.

[11] Banerjee, K.S.: Cost of Living Index Numbers: Practice, Precision and Theory, Marcel Dekker Inc., New York (1975).

[12] Banerjee, K.S.: On the Factorial Approach Providing the True Index of Cost of Living, Vandenhoeck & Ruprecht in Göttingen, Germany, Applied Statistics and Econometric Series, Heft 5, (First Edition, 1977; Second Edition, 1980).

[13] Banerjee, K.S.: Wald's True Index Derived Ipso Facto, Communications in Statistics, A7(8), (1978), pp. 791-798.

[14] Banerjee, K.S.: On the Factorial Approach Providing the True Index of Cost and Living: An Interpretation of a Special Pair of Equations, Communications in Statistics, A7(9), (1978), pp. 851-856. [A Correction Note appears in Communications in Statistics, A9(1), (1980), p. 115.]

[15] Banerjee, K.S.: A Note on the Divisia Indices, Statistische Hefte, Internationale Zeitschrift für Theorie und Praxis, 20. Jahrgang, Heft 3 (1979), pp. 172-175.

[16] Banerjee, K.S.: An Interpretation of the Factorial Indexes in the Light of Divisia Integral Indexes, Statistische Hefte, Internationale Zeitschrift für Theorie und Praxis, 20. Jahrgang, Heft 4, (1979), pp. 261-269.

[17] Banerjee, K.S.: A Comparison of the Constant-Utility True Index and the True Index Obtained Through the Factorial Approach, Communications in Statistics, A9(1), (1980), pp. 87-105.

[18] Banerjee, K.S.: A Review of the Factorial Approach Providing the True Index of Cost of Living, Statistische Hefte, 22. Jahrgang, No. 1, (1981) pp. 40-56.

[19] Banerjee, K.S.: On an Interpretation, Synthesis and Estimation of the Marshallian and Hicksian Consumer Surplus in the Light of the Factorial Model, Proceedings of the Statistical Association, (1981), pp. 206-210.

[20] Banerjee, K.S.: On the Existence of Infinitely, Many Ideal Log-change Index Numbers Associated with the CES Preference Ordering, Statistische Hefte, 24 (1983), pp. 141-148.

[21] Banerjee, K.S.: Some Observations on the log-change Index Numbers and Their Connection with the Factorial Indexes, Statistische Hefte, 25, (1984), pp. 143-158.

[22] Deaton, A. and Muellbauer J.: Economics and Consumer Behaviour, Cambridge University Press, 1980.

[23] Diewert, W.E.: The Economic Theory of Index Numbers: A Survey; Essays in Honour of Sir Richard Stone, Cambridge, Cambridge University Press, (1981), pp. 163-208.

[24] Divisia, F.: L'Indice Monetaire et La Theorie de la Monnaie, Revue d'Economie Politique, 39 (1925), pp. 842-861, pp. 980-1008, pp. 1121-1151.

[25] Elteto, Ö. and Köves, P.: One Index Computation Problem of International Comparisons (in Hungary), Statistische Hefte, Vol. 7, (1964).

[26] Fisher, F.M. and Shell, K.: The Economic Theory of Price Indices, Academic Press Inc., New York (1972).

[27] Frisch, R.: Annual Survey of General Economic Theory: The Problem of Index Numbers, Econometrica 4, 1 (1936), pp. 1-38.

[28] Geary, R.C.: A Note on Constant Utility Index of the Cost of Living, The Review of Economic Studies, 18 (1949-50), pp. 64-66.

[29] Geary, R.C.: A Note on the Comparison of Exchange Rates and Purchasing Power Parities Between Countries, Journal of the Royal Statistical Association, Vol. 121, Part 1, (1958).

[30] Gerardi, D.: Sul Problema Della Comparazione dei Poleri d'acquisto Dello Valute Instituto De Statistica D'ell, Universita Di Padora, Series Papers (in Italian), (1974).

[31] Gini, C.: Methods of Eliminating the Influence of Several Groups of Factors, Econometrica, 5, No. 1, (1937), pp. 56-73.

[32] Haberler, G.: Der Sinn der Indexzahlen, Tübingen (1927).

[33] Harberger, A.C.: Three Basic Postulates for Applied Welfare Economics: An Interpretative Essay, Journal of Economic Literature, Vol. 9, (1971). pp. 785-797.

[34] Hicks, J.R.: Value and Capital, 2nd Edition. Oxford University Press, (1946).

[35] Hicks, J.R.: A Revision of Demand Theory, Oxford Unversity Press, (1956).

[36] International Labor Office: Computation of Consumer Price Indices, Special Problems, Geneva (1970).

[37] Khamis, S.H.: A New System of Index Numbers for National and International Purposes, Journal of the Royal Statistical Society, Series A, (1972).

[38] Klein, L.R. and Rubin, H.: A Constant Utility Index of the Cost of Living, The Review of Economic Studies, 15 (1947-8), pp. 84-87.

[39] Kloek R. and Dewit, G.D.: Best Linear and Best Linear Umbiased Index Numbers, Econometrica, 29, No. 4, (1961), pp. 602-616.

[40] Kloek T. and Theil, H.: International Comparison of Price and Quantities Consumed, Econometrica, Vo. 33, (1965), pp. 535-556.

[41] Konüs, A.A.: The problem of the True Index of the Cost of Living, Econometrica 7, 1 (1939), pp. 10-29.

[42] McCarthy, P.J.: Sampling Considerations in the Construction of Price Indexes with Particular Reference to the United States Consumer Price Index, Govt. Price Statistics, Part 1 (1961), pp. 197-232.

[43] Mudgett, B.D.: Index Numbers, John Wiley, New York (1951).

[44] Prasad Pao, D.S.: A New System of Log-change Index Numbers for Multilateral Comparisons, Working Paper No. 9, Dept. of Economic Statistics, UNE, Armidale, Australia, (1980).

[45] Prasad Rao, D.S. and Banerjee, K.S.: A Multilateral Index Number System Based on the Factorial Approach, Statische Hefte, 27. Jahrgang, Heft 4, (1986), pp. 297-313.

[46] Samuelson, P.A. and Swamy, S.: Invariant Economic Index Numbers and Canonical Duality: Survey and Synthesis, American Economic Review, 64, (1974), pp. 566-593.

[47] Samuelson, P.A.: Foundations of Economic Analysis, Harvard University Press, Cambridge, U.S.A. (1947), Tenth Printing (1975).

[48] Sato, K.: The Ideal Log-change Index Number, Review of Economics and Statistics, 59, (1976), pp.223-228.

[49] Siegel, I.H.: The Generalized "Ideal" Index Number Formula, Journal of the American Statistical Association, 40, No. 232, (1945), p. 520.

[50] Staehle, H.: A Development of the Economic Theory of Price Index Numbers, The Review of Economic Studies, (1935), pp. 163-188.

[51] Stone, R.: Linear Expenditure Systems and Demand Analysis, Economic Journal, 64, (1954), pp. 571-527.

[52] Stuvel, G.: A New Index Number Formula, Econometrica, 26, 1, (1957), pp. 123-131.

[53] Szulc, B.: Indices for Multiregional Comparisons, Przeglad, Statystyezuy, Vol. 3 (In Polish), 1964.

[54] Theil, H.: Best Linear Index Numbers of Prices and Quantities, Econometrica, Vol. 27, No. 2, (1960), pp. 464-480.

[55] Theil, H.: More on Log-change Index Numbers, Review of Economics and Statistics, 56, (1974), pp. 552-554.

[56] Vartia, Y.: Ideal Log-change Index Numbers, Mimeo.

[57] Vartia, Y.: Ideal Log-change Index Numbers, Scandinavian Journal of Statistics, 3, (1976), pp. 121-126.

[58] Vogt, A.: Divisia Indices on Different Paths, Theory and Applications of Economic Indices, edited by Eichhorn, W., Henn, R., Opitz, O. and Shephard, R.W., Physica-Verlag, Würzburg, Wien (1978).

[59] von Hofsten, E.: Price Indixes and Quality Changes, Bokforlaget Forum AB, Stockholm (1952).

[60] Wald, A.: A New Formula for the Index of Cost of Living, Econometrica, 7, 4(1939), pp. 319-331.

[61] Wisniewski, J.K.: Extension of Fisher's Formula No. 353 to Three or More Variables, Journal of the American Statistical Association, 26, No. 173, (1931), p. 62.

Addendum to References

[A1] Banerjee, K.S.: On the Factorial Approach to Index Number Problems, Consumption Analysis and Orthogonal Decomposition of National Income: A Summary, Foreword by Professor P.A.Samuelson, Special Studies Publication 2, World Academy of Development and Cooperation, College Park, Md. 20740, U.S.A., (1985).

[A2] Afriat, S.N.: The Cost-of-Living Index. In: Essays in Mathematical Economics, In Honor of Oskar Morgenstern, ed. by M. Shubik, Princeton Univ.Press, (1967).

[A3] Balk, B.M.: A Note on the True Factorial Price Index. Statistische Hefte, 24 (1983), pp. 69-72.

[A4] Blackorby, C. and Russell, R.R.: Indices and Subindices of the Cost of Living and the Standard of Living, International Economic Review, expected in (1976).

[A5] Eichhorn, W.: Fisher's Tests Revisited, Econometrica, 44, (1976), pp. 247-256.

[A6] Eichhorn, W. and Voeller, J.: Theory of the Price Index, Springer-Verlag, Berlin-Heidelberg-New York, (1976).

[A7] Fisher, I.: The Making of Index Numbers, Houghton Mifflin, Boston, (1922).

[A8] Malmquist, S.: Index Numbers and Indifference Surfaces, Trabajos de Estadistica, 4, (1953).

[A9] Pfingsten, A.: A Note on the True Factorial Price Index - Addendum to a Note by Balk, Statistische Hefte, 26 (1985), pp. 65-69.

[A10] Pollak, R.A.: The Theory of the Cost-of-Living Index, Research Division, Office of Prices and Living Conditions, U.S.Bureau of Labor Statistics, Washington, D.C., 202/2, Research Discussion Paper No. 11, (1971).

[A11] Törnquist, L.: The Bank of Finland's Consumption Price Index, Bank of Finland Monthly Bulletin, (1936).

[A12] Ulmer, M.J.: The Economic Theory of Cost of Living Index, Columbia University Press, New York, (1948).

Test Approaches to International Comparisons

W. E. Diewert*
Department of Economics
University of British Columbia
Vancouver, B.C., Canada

1. Introduction

For many purposes, it is useful to compare the real outputs or real incomes of a number of countries or regions at a single point in time. This information may be required to allocate international aid or interregional transfer payments between member countries or regions. In this paper, we consider test approaches to the problem of providing international or interregional comparisons. For a survey of the literature on international comparisons, see Kravis [1984]. For presentations of the axiomatic or test approach for making comparisons between two countries, see Voeller [1981] and Eichhorn and Voeller [1983].

In section 2, we discuss how best to use bilateral real output indexes in order to make multilateral real output comparisons in a symmetric manner. We find that there are at least 6 plausible methods for combining the bilateral indexes into consistent multilateral indexes. In order to distinguish between these possibilities, we consider an axiomatic or test approach to multilateral quantity indexes in sections 3 and 4. Using this test approach, we are able to eliminate some of our 6 methods.

2. Multilateral Comparisons of Real Output: Preliminary Approaches

Suppose that we have collected price and (net) output data on N commodities for I regions or countries. Labour inputs and other

Measurement in Economics
ed. by W. Eichhorn

primary resource commodities. Let the positive price vector for country i be $p^i \equiv (p_1^i,\ldots,p_N^i) \gg 0_N$ and let the corresponding quantity vector be $y^i \equiv (y_1^i,\ldots,y_N^i)$ for $i = 1,\ldots,I$. If commodity n is a net input into the production sector of country i (e.g., an imported good), then $y_n^i < 0$. However, we assume that the net value of outputs is positive for each country:

$$p^i \cdot y^i \equiv \Sigma_{n=1}^N p_n^i y_n^i > 0 \qquad \text{for } i = 1,\ldots,I. \tag{1}$$

We assume that bilateral comparisons of real output can be made using an index number formula, $Q(p^j,p^i,y^j,y^i)$, which is supposed to represent the real output of country i relative to j. Microeconomic considerations[1] suggest that two good functional forms for Q are the Fisher [1922] ideal quantity index Q_F and the implicit translog quantity index $\tilde{Q}_T$ defined below by (2) and (3) respectively:

$$Q_F(p^j,p^i,y^j,y^i) \equiv [p^i \cdot y^i p^j \cdot y^i / p^i \cdot y^j p^j \cdot y^j]^{1/2} \quad ; \tag{2}$$

$$\tilde{Q}_T(p^j,p^i,y^j,y^i) \equiv p^i \cdot y^i / p^j \cdot y^j \Pi_{n=1}^N (p_n^i/p_n^j)^{(1/2)(s_n^i+s_n^j)} \tag{3}$$

where $s_n^i \equiv p_n^i y_n^i / p^i \cdot y^i$ for $i = 1,\ldots,I$ and $n = 1,\ldots,N$.

The simplest way to make consistent multilateral comparisons of real output using a bilateral quantity index Q as a building block is to use what Kravis [1984; 10] calls the star system. More explicitly, the star system works as follows. First, pick an appropriate bilateral quantity index number formula, which gives the real output of country i relative to country j, $Q(p^j,p^i,y^j,y^i)$ say. Secondly, pick a numeraire country, say $j = 1$. Then country i's share of real world private product is defined by

$$\sigma_i^j = Q(p^j,p^i,y^j,y^i)/\Sigma_{k=1}^I Q(p^j,p^k,y^j,y^k), \qquad i = 1,2,\ldots,I \tag{4}$$

where $j = 1$. Note that $\Sigma_{i=1}^I \sigma_i^j = 1$.

Of course, the problem with the star system is that the results depend on the choice of the numeraire country j; i.e., all countries are not treated in a symmetric manner in the star system. Thus we need to consider alternative methods for making multilateral comparisons.

Our first alternative method starts off with the following definition:

$$\alpha_i \equiv [\Sigma_{j=1}^{I}[Q(p^j,p^i,y^j,y^i)]^{-1}]^{-1}, \qquad i = 1,2,\ldots,I. \tag{5}$$

Country i's share of real world private product is now defined as:

$$s_i \equiv \alpha_i/\Sigma_{k=1}^{I}\alpha_k. \tag{6}$$

The intuitive interpretation of the above system for achieving multilateral comparisons of real output in a transitive and symmetric way can be grasped if we consider the case of one output good; i.e., N = 1. In this case, if Q is Q_F or $\tilde{Q}_T$ or any reasonable quantity index, (5) becomes

$$\alpha_i = y_1^i/\Sigma_{j=1}^{I}y_1^j \quad , \qquad i = 1,2,\ldots,I, \tag{7}$$

i.e., α_i becomes country i's share of total world output. In this N = 1 case, we will have $\Sigma_{k=1}^{I}\alpha_k = 1$, so that in this case, $s_i = \alpha_i$ = country i's share of world private product.

In the general N > 1 case, α_i defined by (5) defines country i's share of world product in the "metric" of country i. Since these metrics are not quite compatible in general, we make further adjustments via definitions (6) to ensure that the shares sum to one. Let us call the resulting method for making multilateral comparisons of real output, the <u>own share system</u>.

It turns out that the own share system, using the Fisher formula, is related to the Eltetö, Köves [1964] and Szulc [1964] (EKS) method for making multilateral comparisons. This can be seen as follows: using the Fisher formula, we have

$$\begin{aligned}\alpha_i &= I^{-1}[\Sigma_{j=1}^{I}I^{-1}[Q_F(p^j,p^i,y^j,y^i)]^{-1}]^{-1} \\ &\cong I^{-1}[\Pi_{j=1}^{I}Q_F(p^j,p^i,y^j,y^i)]^{1/I}\end{aligned}$$

where we have approximated the harmonic mean by a geometric mean.

Thus

$$\alpha_i/\alpha_k = s_i/s_k$$
$$\cong \Pi_{j=1}^{I} Q_F(p^j,p^i,y^j,y^i)^{1/I} / \Pi_{j=1}^{I} Q_F(p^j,p^k,y^j,y^k)^{1/I} \qquad (8)$$

= the EKS output of country i relative to k.

Thus we have provided an alternative justification for the use of the EKS method for making multilateral comparisons of real output.

Instead of using the Fisher formula Q_F in (8), Caves, Christensen and Diewert [1982a] advocated the use of the direct translog formula Q_T in place of Q_F. In the present context where some outputs can be negative, we would recommend the use of the implicit translog quantity index $\tilde{Q}_T$ in place of Q_T.

For any choice of a binary quantity index number formula Q, let us define the <u>Generalized</u> <u>EKSCCD</u> method for making multilateral quantity comparisons as follows. Define

$$\beta_i \equiv \Pi_{j=1}^{I} Q(p^j,p^i,y^j,y^i)^{i/I} \quad , \qquad i = 1,\ldots,I. \qquad (9)$$

Country i's EKSCCD share of world private product is now defined as:

$$S_i \equiv \beta_i / \Sigma_{k=1}^{I} \beta_k \,, \qquad i = 1,\ldots,I. \qquad (10)$$

We note that the own share method (6) satisfies the following <u>consistency</u> <u>in</u> <u>aggregation</u> property whereas the EKSCCD method does not: suppose any one country is split into two countries, each of which has the same price vector and one half of the original quantity vector. Then the relative outputs of the countries which are not split up should remain constant.[2]

We now consider another class of methods for making multilateral comparisons of real output.

Recall that the shares σ_i^j, i = 1,...,I, defined by (4) allowed us to partition up world product using the bilateral metric of country j. What we now propose to do is to average over these country j metrics:

$$\sigma_i(s_1,\ldots,s_I) \equiv \Sigma_{j=1}^I s_j\sigma_i^j \quad , \qquad i = 1,\ldots,I. \tag{11}$$

We still must choose the country weights s_j which occur in (11). A natural first choice would be to give each country's metric the same weight and choose <u>democratic weights</u> where $s_j \equiv 1/I$ for $j = 1,\ldots,I$. Fisher [1922; 305] recommended this method as being the very best (if it were practicable) and called it the <u>blend method</u>. However, this method seems to give tiny countries a comparitively large influence in the formation of the averages defined by (11). Moreover, the resulting method does not satisfy the consistency in aggregation (or invariance under country partitioning) property mentioned above. Thus it may be preferable to use <u>plutocratic weights</u>,[3] where $s_j \equiv p^j \cdot y^j / \Sigma_{k=1}^I p^k \cdot y^k$ is country j's share of world private product. This plutocratic averaging method satisfies the consistency in aggregation property but it has a drawback as well: the resulting shares defined by (11) are not invariant to scale changes in the prices of any one country. This is a very serious drawback, since we would not want country i's share of world real output to depend on the inflation rate in country j. A final variant for (11) would be to use <u>quantity weights</u>, where the s_j which appear in (11) are defined by (6), the own shares. The resulting method satisfies the consistency in aggregation property and is also invariant to scale changes in country prices.

In this section, we have considered six different methods for making multilateral comparisons of real output, using bilateral index number formulae based on producer theory as building blocks. The six methods were: (i) the star system, (ii) the own share system, (iii) the EKSCCD method, (iv) the democratic weights method, (v) the plutocratic weights method, and (vi) the (own share) quantity weights method. However, we have not been able to recommend any of these methods as being clearly the best. Thus in the next two sections, we shall turn to the test or axiomatic approach to index number theory and see whether this approach leads to any clear cut recommendations. In the following section, we momentarily digress and consider the axiomatic properties of bilateral index number formulae. Then in section 4, we shall look for multilateral counterparts to the bilateral properties studied in section 3.

3. Bilateral Comparisons of Real Output: The Test Approach

The test or axiomatic approach to bilateral index number theory has its origins in the work of Walsh [1901] and Fisher [1911] [1922]. More recently, the test approach has been more definitively studied by Eichhorn and Voeller [1976] [1983] and Vartia [1985]. The reason why we are devoting a section of the present paper to this well-studied topic is that the existing literature does not deal with the problems that arise from the fact that in our framework, some quantities can be negative. The existing literature on the test approach assumes that all quantities are at least nonnegative. Thus it is necessary to review existing index number tests (or axioms or properties) and see if they are sensible when some quantities can be negative.

We regard a bilateral index number formula as a function, $Q(p^1,p^2,y^1,y^2)$, of 4N variables. The N dimensional vectors p^1 and p^2 represent prices in countries 1 and 2 and the vectors y^1 and y^2 represent the net output vectors in countries 1 and 2 (if $y_n^i < 0$, then the nth good is being utilized as an input into the private production sector of country i). We shall denote the tests or properties that we would like our bilateral quantity index Q to satisfy by BT1, BT2, etc. Our first test is:

<u>BT1</u>: <u>Positivity</u>: $Q(p^1,p^2,y^1,y^2) > 0$ for $p^i \gg 0_N$, y^i such that $p^i \cdot y^i > 0$, $i = 1,2$. Moreover, Q is a continuous function.

Although the positivity test seems very reasonable, it can be verified that the Fisher ideal index Q_F does not satisfy it. (The implicit translog quantity index $\tilde{Q}_T$ does satisfy it however.) In order to have the Fisher formula satisfy a positivity test, we must strengthen BT1 to the following property:

BT1': Strong Positivity: Q is continuous and $Q(p^1,p^2,y^1,y^2) > 0$ for $p^1 \gg 0_N$, $p^2 \gg 0_N$ and y^i such that $p^j \cdot y^i > 0$ for $i,j = 1,2$.

In words, we restrict the domain of definition of Q to strictly positive price vectors and quantity vectors which have a positive inner product with both price vectors.

The following test is weaker than the usual identity test (e.g., see Eichhorn and Voeller [1976] [1983]). It is a slight modification of a test due to Vartia [1985]:

BT2: Identity: $Q(\alpha p,\beta p,y,y) = 1$ for $\alpha > 0$, $\beta > 0$.

The above test says that if the price vectors in the two countries are proportional and the quantity vectors are identical, then the output of country 2 relative to 1 should equal unity. A stronger identity test arises if we drop the hypothesis of price proportionality; i.e., $Q(p^1,p^2,y,y) = 1$ for $p^i \gg 0_N$, $p^i \cdot y > 0$ for $i = 1,2$. Q_F satisfies this stronger identity property but $\tilde{Q}_T$ does not. However both $\tilde{Q}_T$ and Q_F satisfy the weaker property BT2.

The following property (which may be found in Walsh [1901]) is a fundamental one for binary index number formulae.

BT3 Proportionality: $Q(p^1,p^2,y^1,\lambda y^2) = \lambda Q(p^1,p^2,y^1,y^2)$ for $\lambda > 0$. Thus if we double all outputs in country 2, the quantity index doubles.

If there is only one good, then it is easy to show that tests BT2 and BT3 determine the functional form for Q; i.e., if N = 1, then $Q(p^1,p^2,y^1,y^2) = y^2/y^1$ which is the output of country 2 divided by the output of country 1.

The next test is also a variant of a test due to Vartia [1985].

BT4: Strong Monetary Unit Test: $Q(\alpha p^1, \beta p^2, \gamma y^1 \gamma y^2) = Q(p^1, p^2, y^1, y^2)$ for $\alpha > 0$, $\beta > 0$ and $\gamma > 0$.

The above test says that if we simultaneously change the level in prices in each country by a (possibly different) proportional factor and we change all quantities in both countries by the same proportional factor γ, then the quantity index remains unchanged. This property implies that the quantity index does not depend on inflation rates in the two countries. Furthermore, if both countries experience output growth at the same rate, then the quantity index remains unchanged since it is supposed to represent the output of country 2 relative to that of country 1.

The following 3 tests are invariance or symmetry tests.

BT5: Commensurability (or Invariance to Scale Changes in Units): Let D be a diagonal N by N matrix with positive elements on its main diagonal. Then $Q(Dp^1, Dp^2, D^{-1}y^1, D^{-1}y^2) = Q(p^1, p^2, y^1, y^2)$ where D^{-1} denotes the inverse matrix of D.

BT6: Country Reversal (or Symmetric Treatment of Countries): $Q(p^2, p^1, y^2, y^1) = 1/Q(p^1, p^2, y^1, y^2)$.

The above test says that if we interchange the role of the countries in the index number formula Q, then the resulting value of the index equals the reciprocal of the original value of the index. It is the country counterpart to Irving Fisher's [1922] time reversal test. Test BT5 is in Fisher [1911]; however, Pierson [1896] informally suggested tests BT5 and BT6.

BT7: Commodity Reversal Test (or Symmetric Treatment of Commodities): Let P denote an N by N permutation matrix; i.e., each row and column of P contains one unit element and the remaining components are zeros. Then $Q(Pp^1, Pp^2, Py^1, Py^2) = Q(p^1, p^2, y^1, y^2)$.

This test was considered by Irving Fisher [1922; 81] and more recently by Vartia [1985].

It is straightforward to show that our two desirable bilateral index number formulae, Q_F and $\tilde{Q}_T$, that arose in our producer theory approaches to making bilateral output comparisons satisfy all of the above tests, except that Q_F does not satisfy BT1.

Some additional tests that have been considered in the bilateral context (see Eichhorn and Voeller [1976]) are:

<u>BT8</u>: <u>Strong Proportionality</u>: For $\lambda > 0$, $Q(p^1,p^2,y,\lambda y) = \lambda$;

<u>BT9</u>: <u>Montonocity</u>: For $y^2 \geq y^3$, $Q(p^1,p^2,y^1,y^2) \geq Q(p^1,p^2,y^1,y^3)$;

<u>BT10</u>: <u>Mean Value Test</u>: $\min_n\{y_n^2/y_n^1\} \leq Q(p^1,p^2,y^1,y^2) \leq \max_n\{y_n^2/y_n^1\}$ where $p^i \gg 0_N$, and $y^i \equiv [y_1^i,y_2^i,\ldots,y_N^i]$, $i = 1,2$.

The Fisher quantity index Q_F satisfies BT8 and BT9 but the implicit translog quantity index $\tilde{Q}_T$ satisfies neither. Neither Q_F nor $\tilde{Q}_T$ satisfy BT10. (If we could restrict quantities to be nonnegative, then Q_F would also satisfy BT10.)

All of the above tests seem to be intuitively desirable with the exception of BT10: when the quantity vectors y^i can have negative components, the mean value test is no longer reasonable.

To sum up this section, we have considered 10 tests or properties that we would like our bilateral quantity index Q to have. In comparing our two desirable formulae Q_F and $\tilde{Q}_T$ (derived from the viewpoint of economic theory), we found that both satisfied tests BT2 through BT7. In addition, Q_F satisfied BT8 and BT9 while $\tilde{Q}_T$ satisfied BT1. We leave it up to the reader to decide which formulae is preferable.

4. Multilateral Comparisons of Real Output: The Test Approach

We shall denote desirable properties for a multilateral system for making real output comparisons by MT1, MT2, etc. As in earlier sections, we denote the N dimensional price and net output vectors for country i by p^i and y^i for $i = 1,\ldots,I$. In order to economize on space, we now define the N by I matrices of all prices and all quantities by $p \equiv [p^1,p^2,\ldots,p^I]$ and $y \equiv [y^1,y^2,\ldots,y^I]$ respectively. A multilateral system of output indexes is a set of I functions, $S_i(p,y)$, $i = 1,\ldots,I$, where S_i is to be interpreted as country i's share of world private product.

In general, there will be domain restrictions on the $S_i(p,y)$ functions. As a minimal set of restrictions, we assume that $p^i \gg 0_N$ and $p^i \cdot y^i > 0$ for $i = 1,\ldots,I$. At times, we will also want to add additional restrictions such as $p^i \cdot y^j > 0$ for all i and j, particularly when the share functions S_i are functions of bilateral Fisher quantity indexes.

The first property we want the S_i to satisfy is a fundamental one, since it allows us to interpret the functions S_i as shares.

MT1: Share Test: $S_i(p,y) > 0$, $i = 1,\ldots,I$ and $\Sigma_{i=1}^{I} S_i(p,y) = 1$. Furthermore, the functions $S_i(p,y)$ are continuous in p,y.

The following test is an approximate counterpart to the bilateral identity test, BT2:

MT2: Weak Proportionality: Let $\alpha_i > 0$, $\beta_i > 0$ for $i = 1,\ldots,I$ with $\Sigma_{i=1}^{I}\beta_i = 1$. Let $p^1 = p^2 = \ldots = p^I$ and $y^1 = y^2 = \ldots = y^I$. Then $S_i(\alpha_1 p^1,\alpha_2 p^2,\ldots,\alpha_I p^I,\beta_1 y^1,\beta_2 y^2,\ldots,\beta_I y^I) = \beta_i$ for $i = 1,\ldots,I$.

The above property is a very fundamental one and we would expect every reasonable multilateral system to satisfy it. The test says the following: suppose that the price and quantity vectors in each country are (separately) proportional to the price and quantity vectors of all other countries. Then country i's share of world output is equal to its (common) share of world output on all N output markets. This test contains an identity test as a special case: if all output vectors are identical and all price vectors are proportional, we have

$$S_i(\alpha_1 p^1,\ldots,\alpha_I p^1, y^1,\ldots,y^I) = S_i(\alpha_1 p^1,\ldots,\alpha_I p^1, I^{-1}\Sigma_{j=1}^I y^1,\ldots, I^{-1}\Sigma_{j=1}^I y^1)$$
$$= 1/I \text{ for } i = 1,\ldots,I,$$

so that in this case, each country has an equal share of world output. Test MT2 also enables us to deduce what the functional form for $S_i(p,y)$ must be if N = 1 so that there is only one net output. In this case, we have

$$S_i(p^1,\ldots,p^I,y^1,\ldots,y^I) = S_i(1p^1,\ldots,(p^I/p^1)p^1,\beta_1\Sigma_{j=1}^I y^j,\ldots,\beta_I\Sigma_{j=1}^I y^j)$$
$$= \beta_i$$
$$\equiv y^i/\Sigma_{j=1}^I y^j \quad \text{for } i = 1,\ldots,I. \qquad (12)$$

The next multilateral test is a counterpart to the bilateral proportionality test, BT3.

<u>MT3</u>: <u>Proportionality</u>: Let $\lambda_i > 0$. Then for $i = 1,2,\ldots,I$:

$$S_j(p,y^1,\ldots,y^{i-1},\lambda_i y^i,y^{i+1},\ldots,y^I) = \lambda_i S_i(p,y)/[1+S_i(p,y)(\lambda_i-1)] \quad (13)$$
$$\text{for } j = i$$
$$= S_j(p,y)/[1+S_i(p,y)(\lambda_i-1)]$$
$$\text{for } j \neq i.$$

On the left hand side of (13), we have the country j share function after the original country i quantity vector y^i has been multiplied by the positive scalar λ_i; on the right hand side of (13), we have some algebraic expressions involving the original (before multiplication by λ_i) share functions $S_i(p,y)$. Equations (13) are supposed to hold for all I choices for the quantity vector y^i which is multiplied by the scalar λ_i.

We derived test MT3 in analogy to the N = 1 case when the share functions are defined by (12); in this case, it can be verified that equations (13) will hold.

In order to obtain a better intuititive feeling for the test MT3, one should consider the test in ratio form. Denote the left hand side of (13) by $S_j(\lambda_i)$. Then (13) implies $S_i(\lambda_i)/S_k(\lambda_i) = \lambda_i S_i(p,y)/S_k(p,y)$ for $k \neq i$ and $S_j(\lambda_i)/S_k(\lambda_i) = S_j(p,y)/S_k(p,y)$ for $j \neq i$ and $k \neq i$. These multilateral proportionality properties seem to be just as reasonable as the bilateral proportionality property BT3. Unfortunately, as we shall soon see, it proves to be very difficult to simultaneously satisfy MT3 along with other reasonable multilateral tests.

The following four tests are counterparts to the corresponding bilateral tests, BT4, BT5, BT6 and BT7.

<u>MT4</u>: <u>Monetary Unit Test</u>: Let $\alpha_i > 0$, $i = 1,\ldots,I$ and $\beta > 0$. Then

$$S_i(\alpha_1 p^1,\ldots,\alpha_I p^I,\beta y^1,\ldots,\beta y^I) = S_i(p,y), \qquad i = 1,\ldots,I.$$

This property says that inflation levels in each country and a uniform growth in outputs over all countries do not affect each country's share of world output.

<u>MT5</u>: <u>Commensurability (or Invariance to Scale Changes in Units)</u>:

Let D be a diagonal N by N matrix with positive elements on its main diagonal. Then $S_i(Dp,D^{-1}y) = S_i(p,y)$, $\qquad i = 1,\ldots,I.$

<u>MT6</u>: <u>Symmetric Treatment of Countries (Multilateral Country Reversal Test)</u>: Let Π be an I by I permutation matrix and let $S(p,y)$ be the row vector of share functions; i.e., $S(p,y) \equiv [S_1(p,y),\ldots, S_I(p,y)]$. Then $S(p,y)\Pi = S(p\Pi,y\Pi)$.

The above property says that if we evaluate our system of share functions using a permutation of the data, then the resulting share functions are the same permutation of the original share functions.

This property means that no country can be singled out to play a special role in generating the country share functions. This property is termed base country invariance in Kravis, Kenessey, Heston and Summers [1975].

MT7: Symmetric Treatment of Commodities (Commodity Reversal Test): Let P denote an N by N permutation matrix. Then $S_i(Pp,Py) = S_i(p,y)$ for $i = 1,\ldots,I$.

The next three tests have no counterparts in the bilateral context. This is due to the fact that they are consistency in aggregation tests; i.e., we ask that the system of share functions changes in a consistent manner as the number of countries I changes. In the bilateral context, it is not natural to think of changing the number of countries (which is two of course).

The following test formalizes the consistency in aggregation property that was mentioned in earlier sections.

MT8: Country Partitioning Test: Let $S_j^I \equiv S_j(p^1,\ldots,p^I,y^1,\ldots,y^I)$ for $j = 1,\ldots,I$ and let $0 < \lambda < 1$. Define $S_j^{I+1} \equiv S_i(p^1,\ldots,p^{i-1},p^i,p^{i+1},\ldots,p^I,p^i,y^1,\ldots,y^{i-1},\lambda y^i,y^{i+1},\ldots,y^I,(1-\lambda)y^i)$ for $j = 1,\ldots,I,I+1$. Then $S_j^{I+1} = S_j^I$ for $j = 1,\ldots,i-1,i+1,\ldots,I$, $S_i^{I+1} = \lambda S_i^I$ and $S_{I+1}^{I+1} = (1-\lambda)S_i$. This property is to hold no matter which country i is partitioned.

The functions S_j^I are the share functions for the initial world economy that consists of I countries. The functions S^{I+1} correspond to a new world economy, where the original country i, which had price vector p^i and quantity vector y^i, is partitioned into two countries. The new country i has price vector p^i and quantity vector λy^i where λ is a positive fraction and the separatist offshoot of the old country i is now country I + 1 with price vector p^i and quantity vector $(1-\lambda)y^i$. Test MT8 says that under these conditions the old country i share S_i^I splits into λS_i^I and $(1-\lambda)S_i^I$ and the remaining shares are unaffected by this partitioning of countries. Note that MT8 implicitly requires that the share functions can be defined for I+1 countries as well as I countries.

<u>MT9</u>: <u>Irrelevance of Tiny Countries Test</u>: Let $\lambda_i > 0$ and define $S_j^I(\lambda_i) \equiv S_j(p^1,\ldots,p^I,y^1,\ldots,y^{i-1},\lambda_i y^i,y^{i+1},\ldots,y^I)$ for $j = 1,\ldots,I$. Define $S_j^{I-1} \equiv S_j(p^1,\ldots,p^{i-1},p^{i+1},\ldots,p^I,y^1,\ldots,y^{i-1}, y^{i+1},\ldots,y^I)$ for $j = 1,\ldots,I-1$. Then $\ell im_{\lambda_i \to 0} S_j^I(\lambda_i) = S_j^{I-1}$ for $j = 1,\ldots,i-1$ and $\ell im_{\lambda_i \to 0} S_{j+1}^I(\lambda_i) = S_j^{I-1}$ for $j = i,i+1,\ldots,I-1$. This property is to hold for all choices of the disappearing country i. Note that MT9 implicitly requires that the share functions can be defined for I-1 countries and we also require the existence of the limit.

The above property may be explained in words as follows. Consider an initial world economy with I countries in it. Deflate the quantity vector for country i down to zero in a proportional manner and consider the resulting system of limiting share functions. For all countries except country i, the limiting share is equal to the corresponding share we would get if we simply deleted the data for country i and defined the resulting system of shares for the world economy consisting of only I-1 countries. Roughly speaking, MT9 says that the existence of tiny countries should not materially change the output shares of the remaining countries.

The following test is also a consistency in aggregation test, but it is not as compelling as the previous two tests.

<u>MT10</u>: <u>Strong Dependence on a Bilateral Formula</u>: Let $Q(p^i,p^j,y^i,y^j)$ be a bilateral index number formula and define the bilateral ratios $Y_{ij} \equiv Q(p^i,p^j,y^i,y^j)$, $i,j = 1,2,\ldots,I$. The share

functions $S_i(p,y)$ depend only on the bilateral ratios; i.e., we have

$$S_i(p,y) = F_i(Y_{11},Y_{12},\ldots,Y_{I-1,I},Y_{II}), \qquad i = 1,\ldots,I \tag{14}$$

for some functions of I^2 variables, F_i, $i = 1,\ldots,I$. Moreover, as the quantity vectors for all countries except i and j are deflated proportionally to zero, we have for $1 \le i < j \le I$,

$$\ell im_{\lambda\to 0} \frac{S_i(p,\lambda y^1,\ldots,\lambda y^{i-1},y^i,\lambda y^{i+1},\ldots,\lambda y^{j-1},y^j,\lambda y^{j+1},\ldots,\lambda y^I)}{S_j(p,\lambda y^1,\ldots,\lambda y^{i-1},y^i,\lambda y^{i+1},\ldots,\lambda y^{j-1},y^j,\lambda y^{j+1},\ldots,\lambda y^I)} \tag{15}$$

$$= Q(p^j,p^i,y^j,y^i).$$

A weaker version of MT10 would drop (15). An alternative weaking of MT10 would drop (14) but keep (15). The justification for this test or its weaker versions depends on how strongly one feels about the accuracy of the bilateral formula Q. If one feels strongly that Q is best for making bilateral comparisons, then property (15) is a very natural one. It says that the relative outputs for countries i and j should approach the value given by the bilateral index number formula as the outputs of all other countries shrink to zero.

Many additional multilateral tests could be devised. However, the above 10 tests are sufficient to enable us to discriminate partially between the six multilateral systems developed in section 6 above. We shall now verify which of the above tests each system satisfies.

<u>Proposition 1</u>: Suppose the bilateral quantity index $Q(p^i,p^j,y^i,y^j)$ satisfies the bilateral tests BT1 through BT7. Then: (i) the multilateral star system defined by (4) using country j as the numeraire country satisfies all of the above 10 multilateral tests except MT6, MT9 (actually the tiny country test fails only when the tiny country is chosen to be the numeraire country j) and MT10; (ii) the own share multilateral system defined by (5) and (6) satisfies all tests except MT3; (iii) the EKSCCD system defined by (9) and (10)

satisfies all tests except MT8, MT9 and MT10; (iv) the democratic weights system defined by (11) with $s_j \equiv 1/I$ satisfies all tests except MT3, MT8, MT9 and MT10; (v) the plutocratic weights system defined by (11) with $s_j \equiv p^j \cdot y^j / \Sigma_{k=1}^{I} p^k \cdot y^k$ satisfies all tests except MT3, and MT4, and (vi) the quantity weights system defined by (11) with the shares s_j defined by the own shares (6) satisfies all tests except MT3.

The above Proposition is very useful since it enables us to eliminate three of the six multilateral systems from contention if we want a country symmetric system: (i) is eliminated since it fails MT6, (iv) is eliminated since it is dominated by (ii) , (iii) and (vi), and (v) is eliminated since it is dominated by (ii) and (vi). Thus if we want our multilateral indexes to satisfy the proportionality test MT3, we should choose (iii), the EKSCCD system. If we want our indexes to have good aggregation properties and satisfy MT8 and MT9, we should choose the own share system (ii) or the own share quantity weights system (vi).

The star system is quite a reasonable one to use if there is a natural numeraire country. Thus if a single country is interested in comparing its real output with a possibly varying number of other countries, it is quite natural to give up on the symmetry test MT6, and use the star system, choosing the numeraire country to be the home country.

However, if a group of countries wish to jointly determine their relative real outputs, then it is natural to demand that the symmetric treatment of countries test MT6 hold, and thus the choice is between systems (ii) or (iii) and (vi). Note that from a numerical point of view, systems (ii) and (iii) should yield very similar results, depending on how closely various harmonic means approximate the corresponding geometric means (recall (8)).

Thus far, we have dealt with quantity indexes but not price indexes. However, once we have decided what the "correct" quantity shares $S_i(p,y)$ for each country are, we can obtain consistent country i price indexes $P_i(p,y)$ by dividing the country i nominal private product, $p^i \cdot y^i$, by the share function, $S_i(p,y)$; i.e.,

$$P_i(p,y) \equiv p^i \cdot y^i / S_i(p,y), \qquad i = 1,\ldots,I. \tag{16}$$

The resulting system of price index and share functions will have the following property:

$$\Sigma_{i=1}^{I} P_i(p,y) S_i(p,y) = \Sigma_{i=1}^{I} p^i \cdot y^i$$
$$= \text{nominal world private product.}$$

If prices p^i in each country are measured in a common currency unit such as U.S. dollars, then $P_i(p,y)$ may be interpreted as country i's <u>purchasing power parity</u>. If $P_i(p,y) > 1$, then this indicates that prices in country i are high relative to average world prices.

We conclude this chapter by noting that our analysis of the multilateral test approach to internationally comparisons is seriously incomplete. We have not shown that our ten multilateral axioms or tests are independent. Furthermore, it would be useful to introduce additional axioms to better discriminate between the six alternatives we have considered here. Finally, we have not answered the following question: is it possible to find a system of share functions that satisfies all ten multilateral tests?

FOOTNOTES

*Research support from the National Science Foundation, Grant #SES-8420937 is gratefully acknowledged. The author is indebted to W. Eichhorn, J. Van Ijzerin, Y. Vartia and a referee for helpful comments. None of the above individuals or institutions is responsible for any errors or opinions expressed in this report. This paper is a truncated version of NBER Technical Working Paper No. 53, "Microeconomic Approaches to the Theory of International Comparisons."

[1] See Diewert [1976], [1981] and Caves, Christensen and Diewert [1982b].

[2] Van Ijzeren [1983] and Hill [1984; 131] informally discuss this consistency in aggregation property when they ask whether averages of bilateral indexes should be weighted according to the "importance" of the country.

[3] The terms democratic and plutocratic are due to Prais [1959].

REFERENCES

Caves, D. W., L. R. Christensen, and W. E. Diewert. (1982a). "Multilateral Comparisons of Output, Input and Productivity using Superlative Index Numbers." Economic Journal 92, 73-86.

Caves, D. W., L. R. Christensen, and W. E. Diewert. (1982b). "The Economic Theory of Index Numbers and the Measurement of Input, Output and Productivity." Econometrica 50, 1393-1414.

Diewert, W. E. (1976). "Exact and Superlative Index Numbers." Journal of Econometrics 4, 115-145.

__________. (1981). "The Economic Theory of Index Numbers: A Survey." pp. 163-208 in Essays in the Theory and Measurement of Consumer Behavior in honour of Sir Richard Stone, A. Deaton (ed.), London: Cambridge University Press.

Eichhorn, W., and J. Voeller. (1976). Theory of the Price Index: Fisher's Test Approach and Generalizations, Lecture Notes in Economics and Mathematical Systems, Vol. 140, Berlin: Springer-Verlag.

__________. (1983). "Axiomatic Foundation of Price Indexes and Purchasing Power Parities." pp. 411-450 in Price Level Measurement, W. E. Diewert and C. Montmarquette (eds.), Ottawa: Statistics Canada.

Eltetö, O., and P. Köves. (1964). "On a Problem of Index Number Computation Relating to International Comparison." Statisztikai Szemle 42, 507-518.

Fisher, I. (1911). The Purchasing Power of Money, London: Macmillan.

__________. (1922). The Making of Index Numbers, Boston: Houghton Mifflin.

Hill, T. P. (1984). "Introduction: The Special Conference on Purchasing Power Parities." The Review of Income and Wealth 30, 125-133.

Kravis, I. B. (1984). "Comparative Studies of National Incomes and Prices." Journal of Economic Literature 22, 1-39.

Kravis, I. B., Z. Kenessey, A. Heston, and R. Summers. (1975). A System of International Comparisons of Cross Product and Purchasing Power, Baltimore: The Johns Hopkins University Press.

Pierson, N. G. (1896). "Further Considerations on Index-Numbers." Economic Journal 6, 127-131.

Prais, S. (1959). "Whose Cost-of-Living?" Review of Economic Studies 26, 126-134.

Szulc, B. (1964). "Indices for Multiregional Comparisons." Przeglad Statystyczny (Statistical Review) 3, 239-254.

Van Ijzern, J. (1983). <u>Index Numbers for Binary and Multilateral Comparison: Algebraical and Numerical Aspects</u>, Statistical Studies No. 34, The Hague: Centraal Bureau voor de Statiskiek.

Vartia, Y. O. (1985). "Defining Descriptive Price and Quantity Index Numbers: An Axiomatic Approach." Paper presented at the Fourth Karlsruhe Symposium on Measurement in Economics, University of Karlsruhe, July.

Voeller, J. (1981). "Purchasing Power Parities for International Comparisons." Discussion Paper 161, Institut für Wirtschaftstheorie und Operations Research, University of Karlsruhe, Karlsruhe, West Germany.

Walsh, C. M. (1901). <u>The Measurement of General Exchange Value</u>, New York: Macmillan.

Production-Theoretic input Price Indices and the Measurement of Real Aggregate input Use

Franklin M. Fisher*
Department of Economics
Massachusetts Institute of Technology
Cambridge, MA 02139/USA

1. Introduction

Index number theory, and the theory of price indices in particular, tends to run in terms of arithmetic properties. Such questions as whether a particular index satisfies a chain property or a reversal test are well discussed and relatively well understood. Important as such properties and such discussions are, however, they are only one side of the index number story. The other side lies in what I shall term the economic theory of index numbers: What are we trying to measure? What would we do if we had all the information possible? What, if anything, are we attempting to approximate with the index numbers computed in practice?

In the case of the theory of the individual consumer, to be sure, the economic theory of index numbers is well established. We are accustomed to regarding computed cost-of-living indices as approximations to the ratio of expenditures required to attain a given unchanging indifference curve at base and current prices. Where the analytic questions are properly asked, the theory can be extended to cast light on what to do in the presence of taste and quality change. (See, for example, Fisher and Shell 1972, Essay I.) While the aggregation problems accompanying an extension to many consumers are formidable, they present no problem of principle.

----

*I am indebted to Karl Shell for helpful conversations and to two referees for helpful comments but retain responsibility for error.

Measurement in Economics
ed. by W. Eichhorn

The situation is somewhat different when we turn to the production side of the economy and the measurement of real output and input. Here there is relatively little agreement on the analytic basis for index numbers. Indeed, the notion that what one means by aggregate real output is a Laspeyres output index is fairly widespread. Yet while anyone is free to choose his or her own meaning for words, it is still appropriate to inquire what light production theory can cast on the questions that index numbers are supposed to answer. Putting aside the question of established usage, what index numbers would one compute if one knew the technology perfectly but had to summarize prices and outputs on the one hand or factor prices and inputs on the other in a pair of aggregate measures. Only by thinking about the problem in this way can one investigate the strengths and weaknesses of actually computable indices as approximations to analytically satisfactory constructs.

More than a decade ago, Karl Shell and I began thinking along these lines (Fisher and Shell 1972, Essay II). We considered the production-theoretic foundation for output deflation and presented a number of results. The position that we took (and to which we still adhere) is that real output must be defined relative to a given technology, with points on the same production possibility frontier considered as involving the same real output. This leads to a theory of output deflation that is isomorphic to the theory of the cost-of-living index. We developed that theory on the assumption that the money output to be deflated is that of an entire closed economy but have since gone on to consider the more complex case in which inputs can be purchased by the productive unit involved (Fisher and Shell 1981).

I shall not discuss that work in detail but shall follow up a closely related subject. Upon reading a preliminary version of the output-deflation section of our book, John Muellbauer (1972) pointed out that an isomorphic theory can be built for the case of input deflation and proceeded to do so. That topic -- the deflation of inputs and the measurement of real aggregate input use -- is the subject of the present paper. Dealing with the conceptual problems involved casts light on the parallel problems of output deflation; further, there are some interesting new results to present.

2. Measuring Real Aggregate Input Use

I begin with the simplest case, that of a single firm producing one output from several inputs with a well-behaved neoclassical production function.

Any solution to the problem of measuring real aggregate input use must begin with an answer to the following question: Since we shall be reducing input vectors to index-number scalars, and since we wish to obtain a complete ordering for the resulting scalars and the input vectors to which they correspond, we must choose a set of equivalence classes for input vectors such that all vectors in the same equivalence class will be said to involve the same aggregate input. How is this to be done?

In the case of the single-output firm, the answer to this question immediately suggest itself -- the use of the isoquants of the production function to define equivalence classes. With a given technology, we will say that two input vectors corresponding to the same

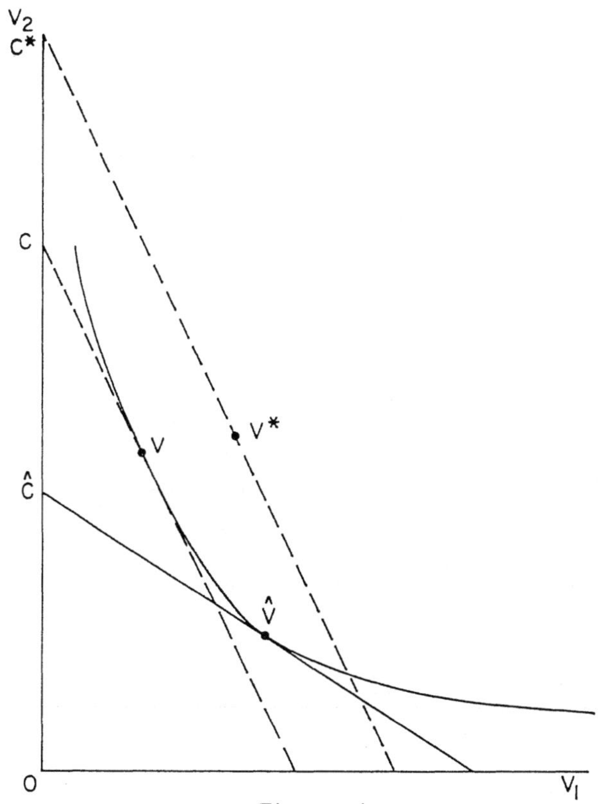

Figure 1

output involve the same aggregate input use. If factor prices change and the firm remains on the same isoquant, then any change in money input costs will be considered as a pure price phenomenon.

In Figure 1, the base-period isoquant is drawn with base-period factor prices, $\hat{w}$, represented by the solid line. Optimal input use is $\hat{v}$, and total input costs $\hat{C} = \hat{w}\hat{v}$. (For ease of notation, I omit transposition signs when writing inner products, relying on the context to make clear what is intended.) In the current period, factor prices, $\hat{w}$, are denoted by the dashed lines. Actual factor usage is v^*, and actual money costs are $C^* = wv^*$. Had factor prices been w instead of $\hat{w}$ in the base perod, the output corresponding to the base-period isoquant would have been efficiently produced with inputs v rather than $\hat{v}$, and money costs would have been C rather than $\hat{C}$. The view of input-deflation taken here is that the change in costs from $\hat{C}$ to C^* should be thought of as:

$$C^*/\hat{C} = (C^*/C)\,(C/\hat{C}), \tag{2.1}$$

with the first factor the increase in real aggregate input usage and the second reflecting price changes.

In more general terms, let the firm's cost function be $C(w, x)$, where x is output. The construction just given uses base-period output, $\hat{x}$, and calculates the deflator for money input costs as $C(w, \hat{x})/C(\hat{w}, \hat{x})$. This deflator is divided into the relative change in money input costs to give the measure of real aggregate input usage relative to the base period.

Obviously, this approach will lead to a theory largely isomorphic to that of the cost-of-living index (as well as to the Fisher-Shell theory of output deflation). In considering possible objections to the theory being advanced, therefore, it is well to consider what those same objections imply about the relatively well-established theory of the cost-of-living index. Consideration of such objections leads to insight as to what is involved in the present analysis.

The first such objection is conceptual. The procedure just described treats input vectors as identical if they can produce the same output and treats a movement to a higher-numbered isoquant as an input increase. But we are trying to build a theory of input aggregation and measurement. Is it not odd that levels of outputs become central to the theory? Moreover, different firms with different technologies facing the same set of input prices will have different factor-price deflators constructed for them.

The answer lies in consideration of the object of the enterprise. We are treating the firm as the object of interest with factor prices given from outside. Any production-theoretic view of input deflation must involve the production function of the firm. Just as the cost-of-living index describes price changes from the point of view of the individual consumer, so the production-theoretic input price index describes factor price changes from the point of view of the individual firm. The fact that different firms have different points of view, so to speak, is not a valid objection. The aggregation problem to which it points cannot be solved by choosing a firm-independent measure of input prices. To do that is merely to impose on all firms a measure not relevant to any one of them.

3. Homogeneity and Related Properties

The second objection to the approach taken here is somewhat more troublesome, at least at first glance. Suppose that input prices change but that it just so happens that the usage of every factor changes in the same proportion, so that the actual input point in the current period is on the ray through $\hat{v}$ in Figure 2. To fix ideas, suppose that the usage of every input exactly doubles. It is evident that the production-theoretic view taken here does not lead to a measure of increase in aggregate real input usage which doubles. In terms of Figure 2, real input usage will be said to increase by a factor of $C^*/C > 2$.

It is easy to see that the sense of the inequality is no accident. Because a Laspeyres price index must bound the production-theoretic input-price deflator from above, the corresponding Paasche quantity index bounds the production-theoretic aggregate input index from below. The Paasche quantity index, $C^*/(C^*/2)$, is obviously 2, however. Hence the production-theoretic index of aggregate input usage is not homogeneous of degree one in the inputs being aggregated.

This objection was made by Diewert (1983, pp. 16-26) to the parallel theory of the measurement of real output. At first glance, it seems a telling one. Careful consideration, however, reveals that its force is far less than first appears.

Suppose first that the technology is one of constant returns and that there has been no technological change between the base and the current periods. Then the isoquant through the point $2\hat{v}$ must be parallel along rays to that through $\hat{v}$. In that case, however, the situation pictured in Figure 2 cannot occur. In such circumstances, the only

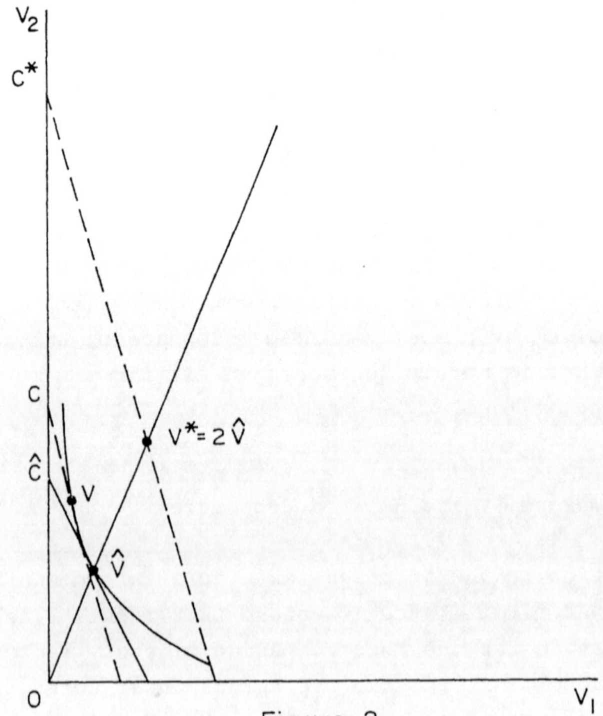

Figure 2

way that $2\hat{v}$ can be the input point for the current period is if relative input prices do not change. But if relative input prices do not change, then it is easy to see that the production-theoretic approach (like every other sensible approach in such circumstances) will lead to an input-usage index of 2.

Now suppose (still with no technical change) that the technology does not exhibit constant returns. If the isoquant map is homothetic, the situation pictured in Figure 2 still cannot occur; in more general circumstances, however, it can. Once one leaves constant returns, however, it ceases to be obvious that it is desirable for an index of aggregate input use to be homogeneous of degree one in the individual inputs. Inputs are important because they are employed in production. The measurement of aggregate input usage properly ought to be from the point of view of that employment. Without homotheticity in the underlying technology it is not at all clear why movements along a ray should play any special role in aggregate input measurement.

If this view that doubling does not mean doubling seems hard to swallow, consider the parallel issue that arises in the theory of the cost-of-living index. There is nothing about Figure 2 that could not apply to that theory with isoquants and costs being replaced by indifference curves and expenditures. Indeed, in the case of the cost-of-living index, there is relatively little interest in homothetic maps and none at all in constant returns, so situations such as Figure 2 are the rule rather than the exception. In such a context, one surely hesitates to insist that a doubling of the consumption of every commodity must mean a doubling of real income. Yet the apparent appeal of the homogeneity property is every bit as strong in the consumer context as in the production one -- precisely because that appeal rests on no consideration of the context involved or the question being asked.

This is, of course, not to say that the homogeneity property may not be an interesting one. One can perfectly well construct an input index by asking by what factor the current-period input vector must be multiplied to place it on the base period isoquant.[1] Such a construction guarantees the homogeneity property, but concentrates on movements along a ray. Once one leaves homothetic isoquant maps, it is not clear why such movements should be of special interest.

One can think of such a ray-centered construction in a different way. Instead of asking by what factor the current period input point must be multiplied to place it on the base period isoquant, ask the equivalent question: By what factor must the base period isoquant be expanded (or contracted) parallel along rays to pass through the current-period input point? Obviously, this amounts to the same thing.

Thinking about matters in this way, however, points up the difference between such an approach and the one taken here. The aggregate real input index constructed in the theory here being espoused answers the question: By what factor must the base period isoquant be expanded (or contracted) parallel along rays to become tangent to the isocost line at the new prices through the new input point? (See Figure 3.) Where the isoquant map is homothetic (and unchanging), this construction gives the same answer as does the ray-centered one. Where homotheticity is lacking (or the isoquant map changes), the answers are different.

That difference can be seen in another way. The ray-centered construction takes as its reference point the point where the ray through the current-period input point crosses the base period isoquant.

----

1. In the case of real output measurement this is what Diewert (1983, p. 18) terms the "Malmquist-Bergson-Moorsteen" approach. He gives an extensive bibliography and discussion of these matters in that context.

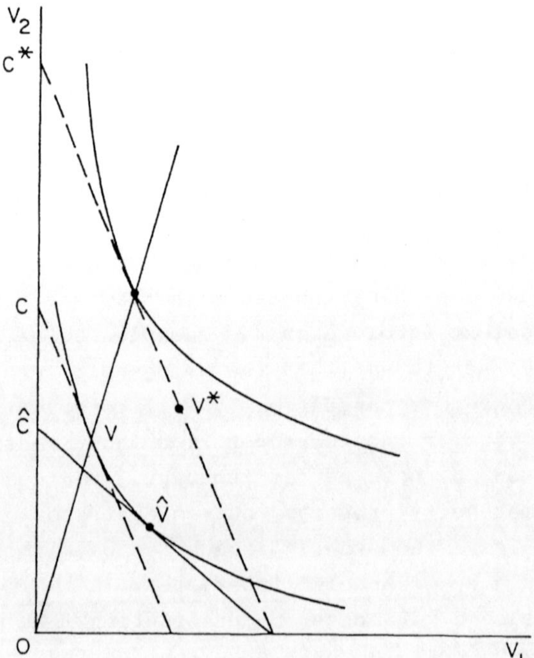

Figure 3

In effect, it begins by asking the question: What would inputs have been in the base period had the firm been restricted to the current period's input proportions? By contrast, the production-theoretic index takes as its base pont the point on the base-period isoquant where that isoquant is tangent to an isocost line corresponding to the current period's input prices. In effect, it begins by asking the question: What would inputs have been in the base period had the firm faced current period input prices? Both ways of looking at the problem are interesting, but I believe the approach taken here is much more of an economics-oriented one. Certainly it lends itself readily (as the ray-centered approach does not) to an accompanying theory of input-price deflation.

But what if technology changes between the base period and the current period? Here again the ray-centered and the production-theoretic approach will give different answers. Perhaps surprisingly, regardless of whether there is constant returns, there is a powerful case to be made that the answers of the production-theoretic approach are superior (and that case also applies to an unchanging non-homothetic technology).

The reason for this lies in the fact that every way of constructing a real input-usage index implies the construction of a corresponding input-price deflator and conversely. Hence, in considering the properties of any approach to the problem, one must consider the properties of both price and quantity indices, not merely the properties of only one of them.

Implicit in the idea that homogeneity of degree one in the input vector is a desirable property for a real input index is the view that a weaker property is even more naturally desirable: The measure of aggregate input should not change if the input vector itself does not change. Parallel to this is a similar statement about the input-price deflator: The input price deflator should not change if input prices do not change (and, we may add, should be homogeneous of degree one in those prices).

Unfortunately, one cannot have all these desirable properties at the same time. In particular:

Theorem 3.1

A. The production-theoretic input-price deflator and its associated index of real input usage are the only indices having the following properties:

1. The relative change in the index of factor prices multiplied by the relative change in the index of real input usage equals the relative change in expenditures on inputs.

2. With an unchanging technology, a movement along the base period isoquant leaves the index of real input usage unchanged.

3. The index of factor prices does not change if factor prices remain constant.

In addition, the production-theoretic input-price deflator is homogeneous of degree one in the input prices.

B. There exists no way of constructing a pair of input-price and real input-usage indices that have properties 1-3 just given and also the following property:

4. The index of real input usage does not change if inputs remain constant.

Proof. A. It is obvious that the indices resulting from the production-theoretic approach have properties 1-3. Further, the resulting input-price deflator is obviously homogeneous of degree one in the input prices. Consider Figure 1 once again. Since v and $\hat{v}$ both lie on the base-period isoquant, property 2 implies that the index of real input usage is the same at both points. Hence, by property 1, the movement in costs from $\hat{C}$ to C is entirely a price phenomenon. Since input prices (as shown by the dashed lines) are the same at v as at v*, property 3 implies that there is no price change between those two points. Hence, by property 1, the movement of money costs from C to C* is entirely a change in real input usage. This division of the movement from $\hat{C}$ to C* into monetary and real changes, however, is just that of the production-theoretic approach. (See equation (2.1).)

B. In view of part A of the theorem, it suffices to show that the production-theoretic approach does not have property 4. Consider Figure 4. Here, the technology changes between the base and the current periods, and it just so happens that input usage remains at $\hat{v}$ despite the fact that relative input prices change. (Obviously, this requires a change in the isoquant map.) The production-theoretic input-price deflator, however, will still call the change in money costs from $\hat{C}$ to C a pure price phenomenon and the change from C to C* an increase in real input usage. It follows that real input usage will be said to have changed from $\hat{v}$ to v*, violating property 4.

Lest the violation of property 4 just exemplified in the proof be considered particularly damaging, it is instructive to examine the situation in Figure 4 again to see the contradiction between property 4 and property 3 in the presence of properties 1 and 2. In Figure 4,

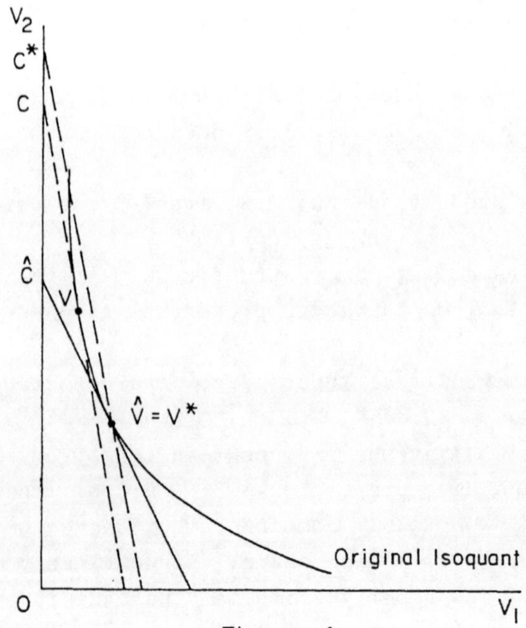

Figure 4

the prices corresponding to costs C and C^* are the same. By property 2, real input usage at v is the same as at $\hat{v}$. It follows that any approach (the ray-centered one, for example) that satisfies property 4 and has real input usage the same at v^* as at $\hat{v}$ *must* describe the change in costs from C to C^* as purely monetary to satisfy property 1. Hence any such approach will show a change in input prices between the situation corresponding to C and that corresponding to C^* even though no input price changes.

Thus, in the presence of properties 1 and 2, properties 3 and 4 are contradictory. One cannot have both an input-price index that depends only on input prices and an input-usage index that depends only on input usage, have them multiply in the obvious way, and still have movements along an isoquant represent no change in input usage. Something has to give. In the case of Paasche or Laspeyres indices, the missing property is property 2 -- equivalence along an isoquant. In the case of more sophisticated approaches, either property 3 or property 4 must be abandoned once we leave homotheticity and an unchanging technology.

Which property should be retained? That depends on what it is that one is trying to do. I take the view that input price deflation means looking at input prices from the point of view of the input-using unit -- the firm in the simplest case. Those prices are among the givens of that unit's problem, whereas the quantities of input used are functions of those prices. If we wish to form aggregates in this context, then, it is property 3 that should be retained. The resulting input-price index should depend only on the input prices; the fact that the corresponding input-usage index will depend both on prices and on quantities merely reflects the fact that quantities themselves depend on prices.

I add two points in this connection that may serve to make the argument more convincing. First, we have already seen that the tension between properties 3 and 4 does not arise until we leave the case of an unchanging homothetic isoquant map. When we leave homotheticity behind, the case in favor of an input-usage index homogeneous of degree one in the input vector stops being a convincing one. With or without a homogeneous isoquant map, however, the case in favor of an input-price index homogeneous of degree one in the input prices remains convincing. The cost function continues to have that property even when the underlying isoquant map is not homothetic.

Second, consider again the case of the cost-of-living index and interpret Figure 4 as an indifference map. Insistence on property 4 in that context leads to a case in which unchanging consumer prices (the dashed lines) imply a change in the cost-of-living index. Retention of property 3, on the other hand, does not do this but does lead to the proposition that the change from C to C* involves an increase in real income despite the fact that v and v* appear to be on the same base-period indifference curve. Once one realizes that v* must be on a higher-numbered indifference curve than v according to the current period's indifference map, that property does not seem so odd. Plainly, the same argument must apply to input (or output) deflation and measurement.

Thus, while it might be nice to have both property 3 and property 4, this is impossible in the presence of properties 1 and 2. Given that, it seems sensible to me to retain property 3 and abandon property 4.[2] Certainly, the implications of an approach that does so are well worth investigating; it is far from a fatal objection that such an approach fails to make the measurement of real input usage depend only on the input vector and fails to be homogeneous of degree one in the elements of that vector.

References

Diewert, W.E. (1983), "The Theory of the Output Price Index and the Measurement of Real Output Change." University of British Columbia, Department of Economics, Discussion Paper No. 83-10.

Fisher, F.M. and K. Shell (1972), The Economic Theory of Price Indices, New York: Academic Press.

Fisher, F.M. and K. Shell (1981), "Output Price Indices." University of Pennsylvania, Center for Analytic Research in Economics and the Social Sciences, CARESS Working Paper #81-05.

Muellbauer, J.N.J. (1972), "The Theory of True Input Price Indices." University of Warwick, Revision of Economic Research Paper 17.

----

2. A referee suggests the abandonment of property 1 instead. This seems to me to involve the abandonment of any hope of mutually consistent price and quantity aggregation.

Mean Value Properties of the Weights of Linear Price Indices

Helmut Funke
Abteilung Wirtschaftswissenschaften
Universität Ulm
Oberer Eselsberg
D-7900 Ulm

0. Introduction

Often a price index is taken as a ratio of two price levels which are linear functions of prices. For calculating the nominator a linear function is applied to the vector of the current year prices and for calculating the denominator the same function is applied to the vector of the base year prices. Usually the weights (or coefficients) of such a linear level function are interpreted as a vector of quantities which represents the so-called basket of goods. Commonly one requires this basket of goods to be some average of the two baskets of goods, the one stated for the base year and the other stated for the current year. Obviously, this requires mean value properties for the weights of a linear price index. For example, such mean value properties are fulfilled for the well-known indices of Laspeyres and Paasche in a weak sense and for the indices of Edgeworth-Marshall and Walsh in a strict sense.

The aim of this paper is to give several characterizations of mean value properties of the weights of linear price indices through general requirements for price indices. In Section I we define linear price indices and point out a close connection with the concept of additive indices of Aczél and Eichhorn (1974). Subsequently we present two sets of well-known properties. The first ones are implied by the condition of linearity for price indices. The second ones are desiderata which on the one hand are compatible with our condition of linearity but which on the other hand are not a consequence of it. Section 2 proceeds with the definition of (mainly) mean value properties of the weights of linear price indices. It will turn out, that

Measurement in Economics
ed. by W. Eichhorn

they are equivalent to the properties quoted in Section 1. Finally we point out some subsets of logically independent conditions.

1. Linearity and Additional Properties

Here a price index P is mapping

$$P : \mathbb{R}^{4n}_{++} \to R_{++}$$ [1]

that is

$$(q^o,p^o,q,p) \to P(q^o,p^o,q,p)$$

where P satisfies a certain set of properties (e.g. see Eichhorn and Voeller (1976, pp. 24,25)). More detailed: For the commodities 1,...,n the four vectors of quantities and prices stated for a base year and for the current year are mapped into the positive reals. The value of P is usually taken as the relative increase (or its reciprocal as the relative decrease) of the price level. Throughout this paper we exclusively consider linear price indices:

(P1) Linearity Property: A price index P is said to be linear if it can be represented in the form

$$P(q^o,p^o,q,p) = \frac{w(q^o,q)p}{v(q^o,q)p^o} \qquad \forall\ q^o,p^o,q,p \in \mathbb{R}^n_{++}$$

where

$$v,w : \mathbb{R}^{2n}_{++} \to \mathbb{R}^n_{++}$$

and nominator and denominator are inner products. We call v and w weight functions.

Well-known examples of such linear price indices are those of

Laspeyres: $\frac{q^op}{q^op^o}$, [2]

Paasche: $\frac{qp}{qp^o}$,

---

1) $\mathbb{R}^k_{++} := \{x \in \mathbb{R}^k \mid x_i > o \quad \text{for } i = 1,\dots,k\}$.

2) Throughout this paper we use ab for the inner product of two vectors a and b.

Edgeworth-Marshall: $\frac{(q^o+q)p}{(q^o+q)p^o}$,

Walsh: $\frac{\sum_{i=1}^{n} \sqrt{q_i^o q_i} p_i}{\sum_{i=1}^{n} \sqrt{q_i^o q_i} p_i^o}$.

Obviously, each of these price indices possesses equal weight functions, that is, $v = w$. If v and w are not equal, the related linear price index has several drawbacks, e.g. it does not fulfill the Identity Axiom (see (P6)). The reason for presenting the more general form (P1) with possibly $v \neq w$ is based on the equivalence with the

(P1*) Additivity Property: A price index P is said to be additive if it satisfsfies the following two conditions:

Additivity with respect to current prices:

$$P(q^o,p^o,q,\tilde{p}+\bar{p}) = P(q^o,p^o,q,\tilde{p}) + P(q^o,p^o,q,\bar{p}) \quad \forall\, q^o,p^o,q,\tilde{p},\bar{p} \in \mathbb{R}^n_{++} .$$

Reciprocal Additivity with respect to base year prices:

$$\frac{1}{P(q^o,\tilde{p}^o+\bar{p}^o,q,p)} = \frac{1}{P(q^o,\tilde{p}^o,q,p)} + \frac{1}{p(q^o,\bar{p}^o,q,p)} \quad \forall\, q^o,\tilde{p}^o,\bar{p}^o,q,p \in \mathbb{R}^n_{++} .$$

THEOREM 1: A price index P is linear in the sense of (P1) if and only if it is additive in the sense of (P1*).

Proof: First one applies the result of Aczél and Eichhorn (1974) for arbitrarily chosen but constant (q^o,q). P turns out to be a ratio of two linear functions with positive and constant coefficients. Secondly, as (q^o,q) is not held constant any more, the coefficients in general depend on (q^o,q), i.e., they can be regarded as (weight) functions of (q^o,q). ▌

It can be easily seen that a linear price index in the sense of (P1) always meets the following three properties:

(P2) Monotonicity Axiom:

$$P(q^o,p^o,q,p) > P(q^o,\tilde{p}^o,q,\tilde{p})$$

if $p^o \leqq \tilde{p}^o$, $p \geqq \tilde{p}$, and $(p^o,p) \neq (\tilde{p}^o,\tilde{p})$.

(P3) Linear Homogeneity Axiom:

$$P(q^o, p^o, q, \lambda p) = \lambda P(q^o, p^o, q, p) \qquad \forall \lambda \in \mathbb{R}_{++} .$$

(P4) Dimensionality Axiom:

$$P(q^o, \lambda p^o, q, \lambda p) = P(q^o, p^o, q, p) \qquad \forall \lambda \in \mathbb{R}_{++} .$$

The basic axioms (P2), (P3), and (P4) have been required by Eichhorn and Voeller (1976, pp. 24,25). But their minimal set of indespensable properties contains two more axioms namely the Identity Axiom derived from Fisher's (1922) Proportionality Test and the Commensurability Axiom that also is due to Fisher:

(P5) Identity Axiom:

$$P(q^o, p^o, q, p^o) = 1 .$$

(P6) Commensurability Axiom:

$$P(\Lambda^{-1}q^o, \Lambda p^o, \Lambda^{-1}q, \Lambda p) = P(q^o, p^o, q, p)$$

$$\text{for } \Lambda = \begin{pmatrix} \lambda_1 & & 0 \\ & \ddots & \\ 0 & & \lambda_n \end{pmatrix} \qquad \text{and for all } \lambda_1, \dots, \lambda_n \in \mathbb{R}_{++} .$$

Obviously, an index function that is linear in the sense of (P1) does not necessarily meet these two basic axioms. Therefore we require (P5) and (P6) in addition to (P1). Note that now Fisher's Circular Test cannot be fulfilled, i.e., it is not compatible with the set (P1), (P5), and (P6) of properties. [1)]

Apart from the Linearity Property (P1), the Identity Axiom (P5), and the Commensurability Axiom (P6) we consider six additional conditions from which the first three are due to Fisher (1922). It will turn out that the complete system (P1) and (P5) to (P12) is equivalent to mean value properties of the weight functions.

---

1) I'm indebted to Yrjö O. Vartia and Janos Aczél who gave hints that a linear price index may also not meet Fisher's Factor Reversal Test. In the meantime it turned out that this assertion is true if a weak regularity condition is fulfilled.

(P7) Time Reversal Test:

$$P(q^o,p^o,q,p) \cdot P(q,p,q^o,p^o) = 1 \quad .$$

(P8) Commodity Reversal Test:

$$P(\Pi q^o,\Pi p^o,\Pi q,\Pi p) = P(q^o,p^o,q,p)$$

for all permutation matrices Π on $\mathbb{R}^n$.

(P9) Gravity Centre Axiom:

For $k = 1,\dots,n$ and for all fixed p^o,p, $(q_j^o)_{j\neq k}$, $(q_j)_{j\neq k}$, the mapping d_k given by

$$d_k(q_k^o,q_k) = \left|P(q^o,p^o,q,p) - \frac{p_k}{p_k^o}\right|$$

is weakly decreasing.

(P10) Value Ratio Preserving Test:

$$P(q^o,p^o,q^o,p) = \frac{q^o p}{q^o p^o} \quad .$$

(P11) Weight Property:

$$P(q,p^o,q^o,p) = P(q^o,p^o,q,p) \quad .$$

(P12) Price Reversal Test:

$$P(q^o,p,q,p^o) \cdot P(q^o,p^o,q,p) = 1 \; .$$

Property (P7) is discussed by Eichhorn and Voeller (1976, p.31), (P8) and (P10) by Vogt (1979, pp. 64,71), (P9) by Krtscha (this volume), (P11) by Funke and Voeller (1976), and (P12) by Funke and Voeller (1979). Note that the properties (P7) and (P11) are equivalent for linear price indices which fulfill (P5). Such indices also meet (P12).

2. Mean Value Properties of the Weight Functions

The purpose of this section is to show that the conditions given in the previous section are equivalent to certain properties of the weight functions. The point is that most of these properties are mean value properties. In particular we will obtain the following conditions:

(S) Separability Property: The price index function P can be represented in the sense of (P1) where the common weight of both prices of commodity i depends only on its both quantities. This holds for all commodities, i.e.:

$$P(q^o,p^o,q,p) = \frac{\sum_{i=1}^{n} m_i(q_i^o,q_i)p_i}{\sum_{i=1}^{n} m_i(q_i^o,q_i)p_i^o} \tag{1}$$

where $m_i : \mathbb{R}^2_{++} \to \mathbb{R}_{++}$ $(i = 1,\dots,n)$ are appropriate (weight) functions.

(M1) Monotonicity Property: All weight functions of the representation (1) are weakly increasing functions:

$$m_i(\tilde{q}_i^o,\tilde{q}_i) \geq m_i(q_i^o,q_i) \quad \text{if} \quad (\tilde{q}_i^o,\tilde{q}_i) \geq (q_i^o,q_i) \quad .$$

(M2) Linear Homogeneity Property: Every weight of the representation (1) changes λ-fold if both quantities of its corresponding commodity also change λ-fold:

$$m_i(\lambda q_i^o,\lambda q_i) = \lambda m_i(q_i^o,q_i) \qquad \forall \ \lambda \in \mathbb{R}_{++} \ .$$

(M3) Standardization Property: There exists a representation of the form (1) such that

$$m_i(q_i,q_i) = q_i$$

holds.

(M4) Mean Value Property: There exists a representation of the form (1) such that every weight lies between its two arguments:

$$\min\{q_i^o,q_i\} \leq m_i(q_i^o,q_i) \leq \max\{q_i^o,q_i\} \quad .$$

(M5) Symmetry Property: The weight functions of the representation (1) are all symmetric:

$$m_i(q_i^o,q_i) = m_i(q_i,q_i^o) \ .$$

(A) Anonymity Property: The weight functions of the representation (1) are all equal:

$$m_i = m_j \qquad \forall\ i,j = 1,\dots,n .$$

Obviously, separability in the sense of (S) cannot be regarded as a proper mean value property but it is helpful in deriving the ensuing properties.

Now we derive the most important result which serves as a very helpful tool for deriving the mean value properties quoted above.

THEOREM 2: Let $n \geqq 3$ and let P be a price index function that is linear in the sense of (P1). Then P meets the Commensurability Axiom (P6) and the Gravity Centre Axiom (P9) if and only if P fulfills the Separability Property (S) where its weight functions meet the Monotonicity Property (M1) and the Linear Homogeneity Property (M2).

Proof: We only show the nontrivial direction, i.e., that the conditions (P1) (P6), and (P9) imply the properties (S), (M1), and (M2). This can be done by two steps. First, we show that

$$w_i = v_i \qquad (i = 1,\dots,n) ,$$

i.e. the Identity Axiom (P5) holds. Secondly, we derive condition

$$\text{(2)} \qquad \frac{w_r(q^o,q)}{w_s(q^o,q)} = f_{rs}(q_r^o,q_r,q_s^o,q_s) \qquad (r,s = 1,\dots,n) ,$$

that is, every ratio of two weights depends only on the four quantities of the two commodities which are directly involved. Condition (2) leads to a circularity condition of f_{rs} that implies separability (S). Then the remaining properties (M1) and (M2) can easily be shown.

Employing (P6) we obtain

$$\frac{\sum_{j=1}^{n} w_j(\Lambda^{-1}q^o,\ \Lambda^{-1}q)\lambda_j p_j}{\sum_{j=1}^{n} v_j(\Lambda^{-1}q^o,\ \Lambda^{-1}q)\lambda_j p_j^o} = \frac{\sum_{j=1}^{n} w_j(q^o,q)p_j}{\sum_{j=1}^{n} v_j(q^o,q)p_j^o}$$

where

$$\Lambda = \begin{pmatrix} \lambda_1 & & 0 \\ & \ddots & \\ 0 & & \lambda_n \end{pmatrix}, \quad \lambda_1,\dots,\lambda_n > 0 .$$

Both sides are linear functions in p and its reciprocal values are linear in p^o. Equating the coefficients of these linear functions we obtain

$$(3) \qquad \frac{w_i(\Lambda^{-1}q^o, \Lambda^{-1}q)\lambda_i}{v_j(\Lambda^{-1}q^o, \Lambda^{-1}q)\lambda_j} = \frac{w_i(q^o,q)}{v_j(q^o,q)} \qquad (i,j=1,\dots,n) .$$

By $i = j$, $(\lambda_1,\dots,\lambda_n) = (q_1^o,\dots,q_n^o)$, and

$$h_i(x_1,\dots,x_n) := \frac{v_i(1,\dots,1, x_1,\dots,x_n)}{w_i(1,\dots,1, x_1,\dots,x_n)} \qquad (x_j \in \mathbb{R}_{++}, \; i,j = 1,\dots,n)$$

equation (3) yields

$$v_i(q^o,q) = w_i(q^o,q)\, h_i\left(\frac{q_1}{q_1^o}, \dots, \frac{q_n}{q_n^o}\right) \qquad (i = 1,\dots,n) .$$

Putting this result back into equation (3) the terms with h_j cancel out, that is,

$$\frac{w_i(\Lambda^{-1}q^o, \Lambda^{-1}q)\lambda_i}{w_j(\Lambda^{-1}q^o, \Lambda^{-1}q)\lambda_j} = \frac{w_i(q^o,q)}{w_j(q^o,q)} \qquad (i,j = 1,\dots,n)$$

holds. A corresponding equations holds für v_i and v_j. The application of both equations for the representation

$$(4) \qquad \begin{cases} P(q^o,p^o,q,p) = \dfrac{\sum_{k=1}^{n} \bar{w}_k(q^o,q)p_k}{\sum_{k=1}^{n} \bar{v}_k(q^o,q)p_k^o} \\ \text{where} \\ \bar{w}_k(q^o,q) := \dfrac{w_k(q^o,q)}{w_1(q^o,q)} , \\ \bar{v}_k(q^o,q) := \dfrac{v_k(q^o,q)}{w_1(q^o,q)} \end{cases}$$

shows homogeneity in the sense of

$$
(5)\qquad \begin{cases}
\bar{w}_i(\Delta q^o,\Delta q) = \frac{\delta_i}{\delta_1}\,\bar{w}_i(q^o,q)\ , \\[2ex]
\bar{v}_i(\Delta q^o,\Delta q) = \frac{\delta_i}{\delta_1}\,\bar{v}_i(q^o,q)\ , \\
\text{where} \qquad\qquad\qquad\qquad\qquad (i = 1,\dots,n)\ . \\[2ex]
\Delta = \begin{pmatrix} \delta_1 & & 0 \\ & \ddots & \\ 0 & & \delta_n \end{pmatrix},\quad \delta_1,\dots,\delta_n > 0\ ,
\end{cases}
$$

This property is a tool for deriving $\bar{w}_i = \bar{v}_i$: For arbitrary but fixed (q^o,q) we will look for a price vector (p^o,p) such that

$$
(6)\qquad P(q^o,p^o,q,p) = \frac{p_i}{p_i^o}
$$

holds. Since the Gravity Centre Axiom (P9) holds equation (6) remains valid if we replace (q_i^o,q_i) by its δ_i-fold, namely $\delta_i(q_i^o,q_i)$, with arbitrary $\delta_i \geqq 1$. Now let

$$
\begin{aligned}
p_i^o &= p_i = 1, \\
p_j^o &= y \qquad \forall\, j \neq i, \\
p_j &= x \qquad \forall\, j \neq i,
\end{aligned}
$$

and

$$
x = \frac{\bar{v}_i(q^o,q) - \bar{w}_i(q^o,q) + y\left(\sum_{k=1}^{n} \bar{v}_k(q^o,q) - \bar{v}_i(q^o,q)\right)}{\sum_{k=1}^{n} \bar{w}_k(q^o,q) - \bar{w}_i(q^o,q)}\ ,
$$

where y is choosen such that x is positive, i.e. y has to be sufficiently large.

This construction is such that

$$(7)\quad \begin{cases} P(q^o,p^o,q,p) = \dfrac{\bar{w}_i(q^o,q) + x\left(\sum\limits_{k=1}^{n} \bar{w}_k(q^o,q) - \bar{w}_i(q^o,q)\right)}{\bar{v}_i(q^o,q) + y\left(\sum\limits_{k=1}^{n} \bar{v}_k(q^o,q) - \bar{v}_i(q^o,q)\right)} \\[2ex] \qquad = 1 = \dfrac{p_i}{p_i^o} \end{cases}$$

holds. With

$$\Delta = \begin{pmatrix} \delta_1 & & 0 \\ & \ddots & \\ 0 & & \delta_n \end{pmatrix}$$

where

$$\delta_j = 1 \qquad \forall\, j \neq i\,,$$

$$\delta_i \geq 1 \qquad \text{arbitrary}$$

we can apply the Gravity Centre Axiom (P9) to equation (7), that is

$$P(\Delta q^o, p^o, \Delta q, p) = 1\,.$$

Using condition (5) we obtain

$$1 = \frac{\sum\limits_{j=1}^{n} \delta_j\, \bar{w}_j(q^o,q)p_j}{\sum\limits_{j=1}^{n} \delta_j\, \bar{v}_j(q^o,q)p_j^o}$$

$$= \frac{\delta_i\, \bar{w}_i(q^o,q) + x\left(\sum\limits_{k=1}^{n} \bar{w}_k(q^o,q) - \bar{w}_i(q^o,q)\right)}{\delta_i\, \bar{v}_i(q^o,q) + y\left(\sum\limits_{k=1}^{n} \bar{v}_k(q^o,q) - \bar{v}_i(q^o,q)\right)}$$

Combining this result with equation (7) we see that

$$(\delta_i - 1)(\bar{w}_i(q^o,q) - \bar{v}_i(q^o,q)) = 0$$

must hold für all $\delta_i \geq 1$, that is,

$$\bar{w}_i(q^o,q) = \bar{v}_i(q^o,q)$$

is proven as well as

$$w_i(q^o,q) = v_i(q^o,q) .$$

The second step of the proof of Theorem 2 is to show equation

(2) $$\frac{w_r(q^o,q)}{w_s(q^o,q)} = f_{rs}(q_r^o,q_r,q_s^o,q_s)$$

by starting with the representation

$$P(q^o,p^o,q,p) = \frac{\sum_{j=1}^{n} w_j(q^o,q)p_j}{\sum_{j=1}^{n} w_j(q^o,q)p_j^o} .$$

Given $r,s \in \{1,\ldots,n\}$ let $(\bar{q}^o,\bar{q},x,y) \in R_{++}^{2n+2}$ be arbitrary but fixed. Furthermore let

(8) $$\begin{cases} \left.\begin{aligned} p_j &= x, \\ p_j^o &= y \end{aligned}\right\} \quad \forall\, j \neq r,s \;, \\ p_r = 2xw_s(\bar{q}^o,\bar{q}) \;, \\ p_s = xw_r(\bar{q}^o,\bar{q}) \;, \\ p_r^o = yw_s(\bar{q}^o,\bar{q}) \;, \\ p_s^o = 2yw_r(\bar{q}^o,\bar{q}) \;. \end{cases}$$

Thus we have

(9) $$P(\bar{q}^o,p^o,\bar{q},p) = \frac{x}{y} ,$$

and a sequential application of the Gravity Centre Axiom (P9) to this equation, that is, for $j \in \{1,\ldots,n\} \setminus \{r,s\}$ yields

(10) $$\begin{cases} P(q^o,p^o,q,p) = \dfrac{x}{y} \\ \forall\, (q^o,q) \in R_{++}^{2n} \quad \text{where} \quad (q_r^o,q_r,q_s^o,q_s) = (\bar{q}_r^o,\bar{q}_r,\bar{q}_s^o,\bar{q}_s) \end{cases}$$

where (p^o,p) is given by (8). Condition (10) implies

$$(11) \qquad \frac{w_r(q^o,q)}{w_s(q^o,q)} = \frac{w_r(\bar{q}^o,\bar{q})}{w_s(\bar{q}^o,\bar{q})} ,$$

that is, the ratio on the left hand side does not depend on (q^o,q) except for (q_r^o,q_r,q_s^o,q_s). Therefore we can write

$$(2) \qquad f_{rs}(q_r^o,q_r,q_s^o,q_s) = \frac{w_r(q^o,q)}{w_s(q^o,q)}$$

where f_{rs} is defined by the right hand side. This functional equation immediately leads to the circular condition

$$(12) \qquad f_{rs}(q_r^o,q_r,q_s^o,q_s)\, f_{st}(q_s^o,q_s,q_t^o,q_t) = f_{rt}(q_r^o,q_r,q_t^o,q_t) .$$

In the case of $n \geq 3$ this condition leads by means of well-known substitutions to the representation (1) claimed in Theorem 2:

$$(1) \qquad P(q^o,p^o,q,p) = \frac{\sum_{j=1}^{n} m_j(q_j^o,q_j)p_j}{\sum_{j=1}^{n} m_j(q_j^o,q_j)p_j^o} .$$

Continuing with the representation (1) of P it will be easy to show that the Commensurability Axiom (P6) implies the Linear Homogeneity Property (M2) for the m_js and that the Gravity Centre Axiom (P9) yields the Monotonicity Property (M1) for the m_js. This completes the proof of Theorem 2. ∎

<u>Remark 1:</u> Now it is easy to see that the assumptions of Theorem 2, namely (P1), (P6), and (P9), also imply the Identity Axiom (P5).

Example (E4) in the proof of Theorem 6 will show that the assumptions of Theorem 2 are not sufficient to ensure that there exists a representation of P of the form (1) where the weight functions m_j also meet the mean value properties (M3) and (M4). But this can be done by adding the Commodity Reversal Test (P8) or the Value Ratio Preserving Test (P10).

THEOREM 3: Let $n \geqq 3$ and let P be a price index function that is linear in the sense of (P1) and that meets both the Commensurability Axiom (P6) and The Gravity Centre Axiom (P9). Then P satisfies the Value Ratio Preserving Test (P10) if and only if P fulfills the Separability Property (S) where its weight functions meet the Monotonicity Property (M1), the Linear Homogeneity Property (M2), the Standardization Property (M3), and the Mean Value Property (M4).

Proof: We only show the nontrivial part of the proof. Because of (P1), (P6), and (P9) we can apply Theorem 2, that is, we can start with the representation

$$(1) \qquad P(q^o,p^o,q,p) = \frac{\sum_{j=1}^{n} m_j(q_j^o,q_j)p_j}{\sum_{j=1}^{n} m_j(q_j^o,q_j)p_j^o} .$$

Now the Value Ratio Preserving Test (P10) can be written as

$$\frac{\sum_{j=1}^{n} m_j(q_j,q_j)p_j}{\sum_{j=1}^{n} m_j(q_j,q_j)p_j^o} = \frac{\sum_{j=1}^{n} q_j p_j}{\sum_{j=1}^{n} q_j p_j^o} .$$

By means of linear independence with respect to p and to p^o this equations yields

$$\frac{m_j(q_j,q_j)}{m_i(q_i,q_i)} = \frac{q_j}{q_i} \qquad (i,j = 1,\ldots,n)$$

or

$$\frac{m_j(q_j,q_j)}{q_j} = \frac{m_i(q_i,q_i)}{q_i} \qquad (i,j = 1,\ldots,n) ,$$

respectively. The second equation shows that both ratios are independent from their variables q_j and q_i. Therefore these ratios are constant and do not depend on subscripts i and j. Thus the standardization

$$(13) \qquad \bar{m}_j(q_j^o,q_j) := \frac{m_j(q_j^o,q_j)}{m_1(1,1)}$$

allows for the representation

$$P(q^o,p^o,q,p) = \frac{\sum_{j=1}^{n} \bar{m}_j(q_j^o,q_j)p_j}{\sum_{j=1}^{n} \bar{m}_j(q_j^o,q_j)p_j^o}$$

where

$$\bar{m}_j(q_j,q_j) = q_j ,$$

that is, the Standardization Property (M3) holds. Again the properties (P6) and (P9) imply (M1) and (M2) for the $\bar{m}_j$s. The Mean Value Property (M4) is a mere consequence of (M1) and (M3). ▮

THEOREM 4: Let $n \geq 3$ and let P be a price index function that is linear in the sense of (P1) and that meets both the Commensurability Axiom (P6) and the Gravity Centre Axiom (P9). Then P satisfies the Commodity Reversal Test (P8) if and only if P fulfills the Separability Property (S) where its weight functions meet the Monotonicity Property (M1), the Linear Homogeneity Property (M2), the Standardization Property (M3), the Mean Value Property (M4), and the Anonymity Property (A).

Proof: We again show only the nontrivial part of the proof. Because of (P1), (P6), and (P9) we can start with the representation

$$(1) \qquad P(q^o,p^o,q,p) = \frac{\sum_{j=1}^{n} m_j(q_j^o,q_j)p_j}{\sum_{j=1}^{n} m_j(q_j^o,q_j)p_j^o}$$

where the weight functions m_j are linearly homogeneous. For two arbitrary but different commodities i and j we apply the Commodity Reversal Test (P8). That means, we take a permutation Π that interchanges exclusively the i-th and the j-th variable of each vector. From

$$\frac{\sum_{k\neq i,j} m_k(q_k^o,q_k)p_k + m_i(q_j^o,q_j)p_j + m_j(q_i^o,q_i)p_i}{\sum_{k\neq i,j} m_k(q_k^o,q_k)p_k^o + m_i(q_j^o,q_j)p_j^o + m_j(q_i^o,q_i)p_i^o}$$

$$= \frac{\sum_{k=1}^{n} m_k(q_k^o,q_k)p_k}{\sum_{k=1}^{n} m_k(q_k^o,q_k)p_k^o}$$

we can derive by means of linear independence

$$(14) \qquad \frac{m_j(q_j^o,q_j)}{m_i(q_j^o,q_j)} = \frac{m_i(q_i^o,q_i)}{m_j(q_i^o,q_i)} .$$

Obviously, both sides are constant and equal 1 can be seen by taking $(q_j^o,q_j) = (q_i^o,q_i)$. Therefore the Anonymity Property (A) holds.

Now the Standardization Property (M3) is given first by cancelling out the factor $m_1(1,1)$ as we have done by equation (13) in the proof of Theorem 3 and secondly by applying the linear homogeneity of the m_js or $\bar{m}_j$s, respectively. Again, the Mean Value Property (M4) is a mere consequence of the properties (M1) and (M3). ∎

Now we consider the time Reversal Test (P7) and the Weight Property (P11) and state the following theorem without its easy proof that is left to the reader:

<u>THEOREM 5:</u> Let $n \geqq 3$ and let P be a linear price index in the sense of (P1) that meets both the Commensurability Axiom (P6) and the Gravity Centre Axiom (P9). If P additionally fulfills either the Time Reversal Test (P7) or the Weight Property (P11) then it meets the Symmetry Property (M5) simultaneously with the Separability Property (S), the Monotonicity Property (M1), and the Linear Homogeneity Property (M2). Conversely, if a linear price index P meets the properties (S), (M1), (M2), and (M5), it also meets both the properties (P7) and (P11).

Finally, we state independence of our properties.

<u>THEOREM 6:</u> The Linearity Property (P1), the Commensurability Axiom (P6), the Time Reversal Test (P7), the Commodity Reversal Test (P8), and the Gravity Centre Axiom (P9) are independent conditions in the following sense: Any four of these conditions can be satisfied by a function $F: \mathbb{R}_{++}^{4n} \to \mathbb{R}_{++}$ that does not fulfill the remaining condition. This statement is also true if one replaces (P9) by the Weight Property (P11) and/or (P8) by the Value Ratio Preserving Test (P10).

Proof: The function F given by

$$
\text{(E1)}\quad
\begin{cases}
F(q^o,p^o,q,p) = \\[1ex]
\dfrac{\sum_{i=1}^{n}\left(\frac{1}{2}(q_i^o)^{f(p^o,p)} + \frac{1}{2}(q_i)^{f(p^o,p)}\right)^{\frac{1}{f(p^o,p)}} \cdot p_i}{\sum_{i=1}^{n}\left(\frac{1}{2}(q_i^o)^{f(p^o,p)} + \frac{1}{2}(q_i)^{f(p^o,p)}\right)^{\frac{1}{f(p^o,p)}} \cdot p_i^o} \\[1ex]
\text{where} \\[1ex]
f(p^o,p) = \prod_{j=1}^{n} \dfrac{p_j}{p_j^o} + \prod_{j=1}^{n} \dfrac{p_j^o}{p_j}
\end{cases}
$$

satisfies (P6) to (P11), but not (P1). The following examples (E2) to (E5) of F are of the form

$$
(1)\qquad F(q^o,p^o,q,p) = \frac{\sum_{i=1}^{n} m_i(q_i^o,q_i)p_i}{\sum_{i=1}^{n} m_i(q_i^o,q_i)p_i^o} .
$$

The function F given by (1) with

$$
\text{(E2)}\qquad m_i(q_i^o,q_i) = \min\{q_i^o,q_i\} + \sqrt{(q_i^o-q_i)^2 + 1} - 1
$$

satisfies (P7) to (P11) and (P1), but not (P6). The function F given by (1) with

$$
\text{(E3)}\qquad m_i(q_i^o,q_i) = q_i
$$

satisfies (P1), (P6), and (P8) to (P10), but neither (P7) nor (P11). The function F given by (1) with

$$
\text{(E4)}\qquad m_i(q_i^o,q_i) = i(q_i^o+q_i)
$$

satisfies (P1), (P6), (P8), (P9), and (P11), but neither (P8) nor (P10). The function F given by (1) with

(E5) $$m_i(q_i^o,q_i) = \frac{(q_i^o)^2 + (q_i)^2}{q_i^o + q_i}$$

satisfies (P1), (P6) to (P8), (P10), and (P11), but not (P9). The violation of (P9) can be seen by comparison of P(4,1,1,1,1,1,2,1) with P(4,1,1,1,2,1,2,1) . ∎

Remark 2: The examples (E2) to (E5) also show the independence of the properties (M1), (M2), (M5), and either (M3) or (A). Note that the Separability Property (S) is required by each one of the properties (M1) to (M5), and (A) by definition.

References

Aczél, J. and W. Eichhorn (1974). A Note on Additive Indices, Journal of Economic Theory 8, 525-529.

Eichhorn, W. (1978). Functional Equations in Economics (Applied Mathematics and Computation 11). Addison-Wesley Publishing Company, Reading, Mass.

Eichhorn W. and J. Voeller (1976). Theory of the Price Index (Lecture Notes in Economics and Mathematical Systems, 140). Springer Verlag, Berlin, Heidelberg, New York.

Fisher, I. (1922). The Making of Index Numbers. Houghton Mifflin Co., The Riverside Press, Cambridge, Massachusetts (3d ed., rev., 1927); reprinted by Augustus M. Kelley, New York, 1967.

Funke, H. and J. Voeller (1976). A Note on the Characterization of Fisher's "Ideal Index", in: Theory and Applications of Economic Indices (W. Eichhorn et al., eds.). Physica-Verlag, Würzburg, 177-181.

Funke, H. and J. Voeller (1979). Characterization of Fisher's "Ideal Index" by Three Reversal Tests. Statistische Hefte, 20. Jg., Heft 1, 54-60.

Krtscha, M. (1987). Axiomatic Characterization of Statistical Price Indices. This volume.

Vogt, A. (1979). Das statistische Indexproblem im Zwei-Situationen-Fall. Junis Druck + Verlag, Zürich.

Axiomatic Characterization of Statistical Price Indices

Manfred Krtscha
Institut für Mathematische Statistik
Universität Karlsruhe
D-7500 Karlsruhe
Federal Republic of Germany

1. Introduction

Our original intention was to find out the best statistical or "mechanistic" price index fitting to empirical data. At last our investigations were finished by the characterization of three known indices.

Now to the data of n selected commodities which are commonly known by a statistical bureau:

$\underline{q}^o = (q_1^o, q_2^o, \ldots, q_n^o)$ is the vector of the quantities in the base year t_o.
$\underline{p}^o = (p_1^o, p_2^o, \ldots, p_n^o)$ is the vector of the prices at t_o.
$\underline{p}^k = (p_1^k, p_2^k, \ldots, p_n^k)$ is the vector of the prices at t_k.

The data q_i^k $(i=1,2,\ldots,n)$ are commonly unknown because it is more expensive to get $\underline{q}^k$ than $\underline{p}^k$. Moreover there is no general rule by which we could determine $\underline{q}^k$. For instance we cannot expect that the quantity of a commodity always increases if its price decreases. (That may be true for one commodity, but wrong for another one.) Therefore we have to accept this given situation simplifying the index problem because only q_i^o can influence the weight of the commodity i.

Measurement in Economics
ed. by W. Eichhorn

The "index problem" is now to get the "best" price index function comparing the prices at the date t_2 with the prices at the date t_1.

We solve this problem in two steps. In the first step we demand natural properties or axioms which every good price index comparing the date t_2 with the base date t_o should satisfy.

In the second step these natural axioms will be completed by the requirement that a good price index ought to satisfy the "Circularity Axiom" if the weights of all commodities don't change. By means of this property we will finally be able to determine the index number comparing the prices at the date t_2 with the prices at the date t_1 - unchanged weights supposed. Distinguishing three possible weights we are able to characterize three different indices which are well-known. By means of these characterizations - so we think - it is easy to decide which price index function is the "best" one.

2. A Comparison of the Current Year with the Base Year

In this chapter we give a list of requirements which a good price index function

$$P_n: \begin{array}{l} \mathbb{R}^{3n}_{++} \to \mathbb{R}_+ \\ (\underline{q}^o, \underline{p}^o, \underline{p}) \mapsto P_n(\underline{q}^o, \underline{p}^o, \underline{p}) \end{array}$$

comparing the current year t with the base year t_o should satisfy.

(A_o) COMMODITY REVERSAL TEST

The order of the commodities must not influence the index number. (see I.Fisher [1968,p.63])

(A_1) PROPORTIONALITY TEST

$P_n(\underline{q}^o, \underline{p}^o, \lambda \underline{p}^o) = \lambda$ for all $\underline{q}^o, \underline{p}^o \in \mathbb{R}^n_{++}$, $\lambda \in \mathbb{R}_{++}$.

(A_2) COMMENSURABILITY TEST

$$P_n(\frac{q_1^o}{\lambda_1},\dots,\frac{q_n^o}{\lambda_n},\lambda_1 p_1^o,\dots,\lambda_n p_n^o,\lambda_1 p_1,\dots,\lambda_n p_n) = P_n(\underline{q}^o,\underline{p}^o,\underline{p}).$$

A price index must not depend on the units of the measurement of the quantities.

These basic requirements have first been formulated by I.Fisher, whereas the following two natural demands are stated by Eichhorn/Voeller [1976,p.23,24] if we ignore the dependance of $\underline{q}$.

(A_3) DIMENSIONALITY AXIOM

$P_n(\underline{q}^o,\lambda\underline{p}^o,\lambda\underline{p}) = P_n(\underline{q}^o,\underline{p}^o,\underline{p})$ for all $\lambda\in \mathbb{R}_{++}, \underline{q}^o,\underline{p}^o,\underline{p}$.

A price index must not depend on the unit of the money.

(A_4) MONOTONICITY AXIOM[1)]

a) $P_n(\underline{q}^o,\underline{p}^o,\underline{p})>P_n(\underline{q}^o,\underline{p}^o,\tilde{\underline{p}})$ for all $\underline{q}^o,\underline{p}^o,\underline{p},\tilde{\underline{p}}$ with $\underline{p}\geq\tilde{\underline{p}}$.

b) $P_n(\underline{q}^o,\underline{p}^o,\underline{p})<P_n(\underline{q}^o,\tilde{\underline{p}}^o,\underline{p})$ for all $\underline{q}^o,\underline{p}^o,\tilde{\underline{p}}^o,\underline{p}$ with $\underline{p}^o\geq\tilde{\underline{p}}^o$.

The following requirements are new, but most of them we consider as natural as the former demands.

(A_5) GRAVITY CENTRE AXIOM

$$d(q_k^o):=|P_n(\dots,q_k^o,\dots,p_k^o,\dots,p_k,\dots)-\frac{p_k}{p_k^o}|$$

must not increase if q_k^o increases.

The following idea leads us to this axiom:
A price index is something like a mean-value of the price relatives $\frac{p_i}{p_i^o}$ ($i=1,2,\dots,n$). (compare I.Fisher [1968,p.3].) If we regard the price relative $\frac{p_k}{p_k^o}$ as a "point" the "weight" of which is increased by a bigger quantity q_k^o, then the distance between the gravity centre P_n of all weighted $\frac{p_i}{p_i^o}$ and the point $\frac{p_k}{p_k^o}$ must not increase.

---

1) The notation is explained in Eichhorn [1978,p.229].

Regarding the special case $d(\bar{q}_k^o) = 0$ the axiom (A_5) implies $P_n(..,q_k^o,..,p_k^o,..,p_n,..) = \frac{p_k}{p_k^o}$ for all $q_k^o \geq \bar{q}_k^o$.

This effect inspires us to the following demand:

(A_5^*) WEAK GRAVITY CENTRE AXIOM

If $P_n(\underline{q}^o,\underline{p}^o,\underline{p}) = \frac{p_k}{p_k^o}$,

then this equation must hold for all $q_k^o > 0$.

The next two axioms come from I.Fisher's Determinateness Test.

(A_6) FIRST REDUCTION AXIOM

For $(q_{k_1}^o,\ldots,q_{k_m}^o,p_{k_1}^o,\ldots,p_{k_m}^o,p_{k_1},\ldots,p_{k_m}) \to (0,0,\ldots,0)$

$P_n(\underline{q}^o,\underline{p}^o,\underline{p})$ must converge.

Then $\lim P_n(\underline{q}^o,\underline{p}^o,\underline{p}) := P_{n-m}(\qquad)$

depends only on the quantities and prices of the other n-m commodities.

(A_7) SECOND REDUCTION AXIOM

For $(q_{k_1}^o,\ldots,q_{k_m}^o) \to (0,0,\ldots,0)$

$P_n(\underline{q}^o,\underline{p}^o,\underline{p})$ must converge, and

$\lim P_n(\underline{q}^o,\underline{p}^o,\underline{p}) =: P_{n-m}(\qquad)$

must only depend on the quantities and prices of the other n-m commodities.

If we were forced to dispense with (A_6) or (A_7) we could hardly decide because both axioms are independent requirements. Nevertheless one reduction axiom is necessary for a natural transition from P_n to P_{n-m}.

The following two axioms are requirements only in case P_{n-k} exists. Therefore we use a different notation.

(B_1) AGGREGATION AXIOM

If P_{n-m+1} exists and $p^o_{k_1} = p^o_{k_2} = \ldots = p^o_{k_m}$,

$p_{k_1} = p_{k_2} = \ldots = p_{k_m}$, then

$$P_n(\ldots, q^o_{k_1}, \ldots, q^o_{k_m}, \ldots, p^o_{k_1} \ldots, p^o_{k_m}, \ldots, p_{k_1}, \ldots, p_{k_m}, \ldots)$$

$$= P_{n-m+1}(\ldots, \sum_{i=1}^{m} q^o_{k_i}, \ldots\ldots, p^o_{k_1}, \ldots\ldots, p_{k_1}, \ldots\ldots)$$

$$\vdots$$

$$= P_{n-m+1}(\ldots\ldots, \sum_{i=1}^{m} q^o_{k_i}, \ldots\ldots, p^o_{k_m}, \ldots\ldots, p_{k_m}, \ldots).$$

That means there must be no difference if the place of the aggregated commodity is the place of commodity k_1 or $k_2, \ldots,$ or k_m in the limit P_{n-m+1} where the other m-1 commodities have vanished.

Versa vice by this new axiom a splitted commodity which in reality is only one commodity induces only one index number calculated by P_n and by P_{n-m+1}, too. Therefore this axiom prevents that an artificial splitting of one commodity changes the index number. This equivalent property is shortly formulated in the following axiom.

(B_2) SPLITTING AXIOM

If there is a sequence of index functions (P_k) (k=1,2,...,n) generated from P_n by (A_6) or (A_7), then the splitting of any commodity must not change the index number. (Of course, the splitting must not generate more than n commodities.)

Remark: If the function P_m which is generated from P_n satisfies (B_2) and Weak Gravity Centre Axiom (A_5^*), then P_m ($m<n$) has the following property: The introduction of a new commodity m+1 which happens to have a price relative exactly equal to the index number P_m does not change the index number.

The last property was accepted by I.Fisher [1968,p.115] although he didn't notice that his "ideal index" doesn't have this property.

All these axioms except of (A_6) or (A_7) we consider natural requirements. We deeply deplore that we don't know if the Laspeyres'index is the only function which satisfies all these axioms. But relinquishing only (A_6) the following functions

$$P_n(\underline{q}^o,\underline{p}^o,\underline{p}) = \left(\frac{\sum_{i=1}^{n} q_i^o p_i^o \left(\frac{p_i}{p_i^o}\right)^r}{\sum_{i=1}^{n} q_i^o p_i^o} \right)^{\frac{1}{r}} \qquad (r \geq 1)$$

satisfy all other axioms. We can also mix functions of this type so that there is a lot of functions satisfying all mentioned natural axioms (and the so-called Linear Homogeneity Axiom). Therefore we may add the natural requirement, that P_n should satisfy I.Fisher's Circularity Test , if the weights of all commodities are unchanged.

3. Circularity Axiom Supposed Unchanged Weights

If we demand Circularity Test

(C) $P_n(\underline{q}^o,\underline{p}^o,\underline{p}^1) \cdot P_n(\underline{q}^1,\underline{p}^1,\underline{p}^2) = P_n(\underline{q}^o,\underline{p}^o,\underline{p}^2)$

for all possible weights, then P_n must be a function ignoring the weights which may be different at t_o an t_1. This property we consider unnatural. However if the weights are unchanged we can forget them and insist on the circularity property as a natural demand! The remaining question is: What are the "right weights" of the commodities?

Avoiding this "philosophical problem" we suggest three possible weights:

1. the quantities q_i^o
2. the base values $q_i^o \cdot p_i^o$
3. the mixed values $q_i^o \cdot p_i$.

Therefore we have to distinguish three different circularity axioms:

(C_1) $P_n(\underline{q}^o,\underline{p}^o,\underline{p}^1)\cdot P_n(\underline{q}^o,\underline{p}^1,\underline{p}^2) = P_n(\underline{q}^o,\underline{p}^o,\underline{p}^2)$.

(C_2) $P_n(\underline{q}^o,\underline{p}^o,\underline{p}^1)\cdot P_n(\underline{q}^1,\underline{p}^1,\underline{p}^2) = P_n(\underline{q}^o,\underline{p}^o,\underline{p}^2)$

if $q_i^1\, p_i^1 = q_i^o\, p_i^o$ $(i=1,2,\ldots,n)$.

(C_3) $P_n(\underline{q}^o,\underline{p}^o,\underline{p}^1)\cdot P_n(\underline{q}^1,\underline{p}^1,\underline{p}^2) = P_n(\underline{q}^o,\underline{p}^o,\underline{p}^2)$

if $q_i^1\, p_i^2 = q_i^o\, p_i^1$ $(i=1,2,\ldots,n)$.

Each of these special circularity axioms is a very strong requirement, because the addition of only four other axioms characterizes a known index function. Moreover we have elected the other four axioms so that all five axioms are independent requirements.

4. Characterization of Three Price Indices

(4.1) Theorem:

For $n\geq 3$ the only price index function $P_n:\mathbb{R}^{3n}_{++}\to\mathbb{R}_{++}$ satisfying (A_1), (A_2), (A_6), (B_1), (C_1) is the Laspeyres' index

$$P_n(\underline{q}^o,\underline{p}^o,\underline{p}) = \frac{\sum_{i=1}^{n} q_i^o p_i}{\sum_{i=1}^{n} q_i^o p_i^o}\ .$$

(4.2) Theorem:

Axioms (A_1), (A_2), (A_6), (B_1), (C_1) are independent: Any four of them can be satisfied by a function $P_n:\mathbb{R}^{3n}_{++}\to\mathbb{R}_{++}$ that does not fulfill the remaining axiom.

The proof of theorem (4.1) and theorem (4.2) is to be found in Krtscha [1979,p.52-58].

But if you prefer (C_2) - believing that the true weights are the base values $q_i^o p_i^o$ - then there is no better price index function than $\tilde{P}_n$ given by

$$(4.3)\quad \tilde{P}_n(\underline{q}^o,\underline{p}^o,\underline{p}) = \left(\frac{p_1}{p_1^o}\right)^{\frac{q_1^o p_1^o}{\sum_{i=1}^n q_i^o p_i^o}} \left(\frac{p_2}{p_2^o}\right)^{\frac{q_2^o p_2^o}{\sum_{i=1}^n q_i^o p_i^o}} \cdots \left(\frac{p_n}{p_n^o}\right)^{\frac{q_n^o p_n^o}{\sum_{i=1}^n q_i^o p_i^o}},$$

for you can verify that $\tilde{P}_n$ satisfies (A_o), (A_1), (A_2), (A_3), (A_4a), (A_5), (A_7), (B_1), (C_2) and the Linear Homogeneity Axiom. (It's only difficult to verify (A_5).) However $\tilde{P}_n$ does not satisfy the monotonicity axiom (A_4b), and I.Fisher's Determinateness Test implying (A_6). You have to accept this bad property because of the following theorem.

(4.4) <u>Theorem:</u>

For $n \geq 3$ the only price index function $P_n : \mathbb{R}_{++}^{3n} \to \mathbb{R}_{++}$ satisfying (A_1), (A_2), (A_7), (B_1), (C_2) is $\tilde{P}_n$ given by (4.3).

Proof:

As P_n satisfies (A_2), we can write

$$P_n(\underline{q}^o,\underline{p}^o,\underline{p}) = P_n(q_1^o p_1^o,\ldots,q_n^o p_2^o,1,\ldots,1,\frac{p_1}{p_1^o},\ldots,\frac{p_n}{p_n^o})$$

$$= f_n(q_1^o p_1^o,\ldots,q_n^o p_n^o,\frac{p_1}{p_1^o},\ldots,\frac{p_n}{p_n^o}),$$

or shorter

$$(1)\quad P_n(\underline{q}^o,\underline{p}^o,\underline{p}) = f_n(x_1,\ldots,x_n,y_1,\ldots,y_n)$$

where $x_i := q_i^o p_i^o$ and $y_j := \frac{p_j}{p_j^o}$ are independent positive variables.

For constant weights x_i $(i=1,2,..,n)$ axiom (C_2) induces

$$(2)\quad f_n(x_1,\dots,x_n,\dots,\frac{p_i}{p_i^o},\dots)\cdot f_n(x_1,\dots,x_n,\dots,\frac{\bar{p}_i}{p_i},\dots)$$

$$= f_n(x_1,\dots,x_n,\dots,\frac{p_i}{p_i^o}\cdot\frac{\bar{p}_i}{p_i},\dots),$$

or

$$(2')\quad \Phi(y_1,\dots,y_n)\cdot\Phi(\bar{y}_1,\dots,\bar{y}_n) = \Phi(y_1\cdot\bar{y}_1,\cdot\ \dots,y_n\cdot\bar{y}_n).$$

where $\Phi:\mathbb{R}^n_{++}\to\mathbb{R}_{++}$ is strictly increasing,

supposed $y_i=y_1$ $(i=1,2,\dots,n)$, and $\Phi(1,\dots,1) = 1$

because of (A_1).

Comparing with Eichhorn [1978,p.67-68] one has only to consider that this special monotonicity is sufficient for excluding trivial cases and density of the graph of $y_i\mapsto\Phi(\dots,y_i,\dots)$ in $\mathbb{R}^2$.

Then the only solution of (2') is

$$(3)\quad \Phi(y_1,\dots,y_n) = y_1^{\alpha_1}\cdot y_2^{\alpha_2}\cdot\ \dots y_n^{\alpha_n},$$

where $\alpha_1,\dots,\alpha_n$ are positive constants.

Observing that $\alpha_1,\alpha_2,\dots,\alpha_n$ are only constants if $x_1,x_2,\dots,x_n$ are fixed, equation (3) implies

$$(4)\quad f_n(x_1,\dots,y_n) = y_1^{\alpha_1(x_1,\dots,x_n)}\, y_2^{\alpha_2(x_1,\dots,x_n)}\cdots y_n^{\alpha_n(x_1,\dots,x_n)}.$$

Now we have to study the consequences of (A_7) and (B_1) for the unknown functions α_i.

Applying (A_7) the limit

$$\lim_{x_i\to 0} f_n(x_1,\dots,x_n,1,\dots,1,y_i,1,\dots,1)=\lim_{x_i\to 0} y_i^{\alpha_i(x_1,\dots,x_i,\dots,x_n)}$$

must exist and not depend on p_i respectively y_i.

That is only possible if

$$(5)\quad \alpha_i(x_1,\ldots,0,\ldots,x_n):=\lim_{x_i\to 0}\alpha_i(x_1,\ldots,x_i,\ldots,x_n)=0.$$

For $j\neq i$ (A_7) again implies that

$$\lim_{x_i\to 0} f_n(x_1,\ldots,x_n,1,\ldots,1,y_j,1,\ldots,1)=\lim_{x_i\to 0} y_j^{\alpha_j(x_1,\ldots,x_i,\ldots,x_n)}$$

exists. That is only possible if

$$(6)\quad \alpha_j(x_1,\ldots,x_{i-1},0,x_{i+1},\ldots,x_n):=\lim_{x_i\to 0}\alpha_j(x_1,\ldots,x_i,\ldots,x_n)$$

exists.

For the following considerations we assume $p_i^o = p_i$ $(i=4,5,\ldots,n)$ and use Aggregation Axiom (B_1) for the case $p_2 = p_2^o$, $p_3 = p_3^o$, i.e. $y_2 = y_3$.

$$(7)\quad y_1^{\alpha_1(x_1,\ldots,x_n)}\, y_2^{\alpha_2(x_1,\ldots,x_n)+\alpha_3(x_1,\ldots,x_n)}$$

$$= y_1^{\alpha_1(x_1,x_2+x_3,0,\ldots)}\cdot y_2^{\alpha_2(x_1,x_2+x_3,0,\ldots)}$$

$$= y_1^{\alpha_1(x_1,0,x_2+x_3,\ldots)}\, y_3^{\alpha_3(x_1,0,x_1+x_3,\ldots)}$$

As equation (7) must hold for all y_1, y_2 we get the conditions

$$(8)\quad \alpha_1(x_1,x_2,\ldots,x_n)=\alpha_1(x_1,x_2+x_3,0,\ldots)=\alpha_1(x_1,0,x_2+x_3,\ldots)$$

$$(9)\quad \alpha_2(x_1,\ldots,x_n)+\alpha_3(x_1,\ldots,x_n)=\alpha_2(x_1,x_2+x_3,0,\ldots)=\alpha_3(x_1,0,x_2+x_3,\ldots).$$

Assuming the case $p_1 = p_2$, $p_1^o = p_2^o$ and the case $p_1 = p_3$, $p_1^o = p_3^o$ the requirement (B_1) implies further equations for the unknown functions $\alpha_1, \alpha_2, \alpha_3$. All these equations together with (5), (8), (9) we write by a shorter notation and get

$$(10) \quad g_1(0,x,y) = g_2(x,0,z) = g_3(x,y,0) = 0$$

$$(11) \quad g_1(x,y,z) = g_1(x,y+z,0) = g_1(x,0,y+z)$$

$$(12) \quad g_2(x,y,z) = g_2(x+z,y,0) = g_2(0,y,x+z)$$

$$(13) \quad g_3(x,y,z) = g_3(x+y,0,z) = g_3(0,x+y,z)$$

$$(14) \quad g_1(x,y,z)+g_2(x,y,z) = g_1(x+y,0,z) = g_2(0,x+y,z)$$

$$(15) \quad g_1(x,y,z)+g_3(x,y,z) = g_1(x+z,y,0) = g_3(0,y,x+z)$$

$$(16) \quad g_2(x,y,z)+g_3(x,y,z) = g_2(x,y+z,0) = g_3(x,0,y+z) .$$

The problem now is to get all functions g_1, g_2, g_3 solving the equations (10) - (16). May be that there is a shorter way for the solution, but we prefer it because two interesting functional equations are solved on this way.

Because of (11) we replace
$g_1(x,y,0)$ by $g_1(x,0,y)$.

Because of (14) we replace
$g_1(x,0,y)$ by $g_2(0,x,y)$.

Because of (12) we replace
$g_2(0,x,y)$ by $g_2(y,x,0)$.

The result of all these replacements is

$$(17) \quad g_1(x,y,0) = g_2(y,x,0) .$$

Using (11) and (12) from (17) we derive

$$(18) \quad g_1(x,y-z,z) = g_1(x,y,0) = g_2(y,x,0) = g_2(y-z,x,z) .$$

The essential result of (18) is

(19) $g_2(y,x,z) = g_1(x,y,z)$ for all $x,y,z \in \mathbb{R}_{++}$.

Analogously we prove

(20) $g_3(z,y,x) = g_1(x,y,z)$, $g_3(x,z,y) = g_2(x,y,z)$.

Because of (19) and (20) we must only solve a system of three equations for one function $g := g_1$ coming from (10), (11), (14):

(10') $g(0,y,z) = 0$

(11') $g(x,y,z) = g(x,z,y)$

(14') $g(x,y,z)+g(y,x,z) = g(x+y,0,z)$

The general solution of (10'), (11'), (14') is
$g(x,y,z) = a(x+y,z)+a(y+z,y)-a(y+z,x)+a(x+y+z,0)$
where $a(x,y) = -a(y,x)$. (see Volkmann [1985].)
Observing that by (11) the equation
$g(x,y,z) = g(x,y+z,0)$
must hold, the function a must also satisfy the equation

(21) $a(x+y,z)+a(x+z,y)+a(y+z,x) = a(x+y+z,0)$.

By equation (21) the unknown function a is completely determined by $a(t,0)$ $(t \geq 0)$. This assertion will be proved contructively step by step.

1.) $x = \frac{t}{2}$, $y = z = \frac{t}{4}$

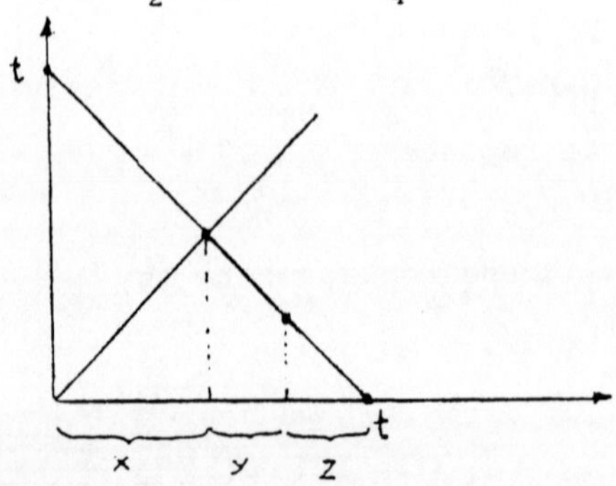

By (21) we then obtain

$a(\frac{3}{4}t, \frac{t}{4}) + a(\frac{3}{4}t, \frac{t}{4})+a(\frac{t}{2}, \frac{t}{2}) = a(t,0)$, implying

(22) $a(\frac{3}{4}t, \frac{t}{4}) = \frac{1}{2} a(t,0)$ and $a(\frac{t}{4}, \frac{3}{4}t) = -\frac{1}{2} a(t,0)$.

2.1) $x = \frac{3}{4}t, \; y = z = \frac{t}{8}$

By (21) we then obtain

$$a(\frac{7}{8}t, \frac{t}{8}) + a(\frac{7}{8}t, \frac{t}{8}) + a(\frac{t}{4}, \frac{3}{4}t) = a(t,0).$$

Inserting (22) we obtain

(23) $a(\frac{7}{8}t, \frac{t}{8}) = \frac{3}{4} a(t,0)$ and $a(\frac{t}{8}, \frac{7}{8}t) = -\frac{3}{4} a(t,0)$.

2.2) $x = \frac{1}{4}t, \; y = z = \frac{3}{8}t$

By (21) we then obtain

$$a(\frac{5}{8}t, \frac{3}{8}t) + a(\frac{5}{8}t, \frac{3}{8}t) + a(\frac{3}{4}t, \frac{1}{4}t) = a(t,0).$$

Inserting (22) we obtain

$$a(\frac{5}{8}t, \frac{3}{8}t) = \frac{1}{4} a(t,0) \text{ and } a(\frac{3}{8}t, \frac{5}{8}t) = -\frac{1}{4} a(t,0).$$

Each further step doubles the number of points $(x_i, t-x_i)$ where $a(x_i, t-x_i)$ is known.

For all $x = t \sum_{k=1}^{m} b_k (\frac{1}{2})^k$, $b_k \in \{0,1\}$

the result is

(24) $a(x,t-x) = \frac{2x-t}{t} \cdot a(t,0)$.

Moreover $\lim_{x \to t} a(x,t-x)$ must be $a(t,0)$,

otherwise $\lim_{z \to 0} g(x,y,z)$ wouldn't exist.

Because of this special continuity equation (24) must hold for all $x \in [0,t]$. Hence from (24) we obtain

(25) $a(x,y) = \frac{x-y}{x+y} a(x+y,0) =: (x-y)h(x+y)$.

Equation (25) induces

(26) $g(x,y,z) = 4xh(x+y+z)$.

Now using the original notation we obtain

(27) $\alpha_1(x_1,x_2,x_3,\ldots,x_n) = 4x_1h(x_1+x_2+x_3,x_4,\ldots,x_n)$

If we replace x_3 by x_k $(k>3)$ und repeat all considerations from equation (7) to (27) we obtain instead of (27)

(27') $\alpha_1(x_1,x_2,\ldots,x_n) = 4x_1\tilde{h}(x_1+x_2+x_k,x_3,\ldots,x_n)$.

The comparison of (27) and (27') implies

(28) $h(x_1+x_2+x_3,\ldots,x_k,\ldots) = \tilde{h}(x_1+x_2+x_k,x_3,\ldots.)$.

If x_k tends to zero in equation (28) the limit exists because of (6). The result is

(29) $h(x_1+x_2+x_3,\ldots,0,\ldots) = \tilde{h}(x_1+x_2,x_3,\ldots.)$.

Replacing x_1 by x_1+x_k from (29) we obtain

$$h(x_1+x_2+x_3+x_k,\ldots,0,\ldots.) = \tilde{h}(x_1+x_2+x_k,x_3,\ldots).$$

The repetition of this consideration finally leads us to the following result:

(30) $\alpha_1(x_1,x_2,\ldots,x_n) = 4x_1\cdot\beta(x_1+x_2+\ldots+x_n)$

Because of (19) and (20) instead of (30) we can generally write

(31) $\alpha_i(x_1,x_2,\ldots,x_n) = 4x_i\cdot\beta(x_1+x_2+\ldots+x_n)\ (i=1,2,..n)$.

Proportionality Test (A_1) finally leads us from (31) to the result

$$\alpha_i(x_1,x_2,\ldots,x_n) = \frac{x_i}{x_1+x_2+..+x_n} \qquad (i=1,2,\ldots n)$$

which completes our proof.

Remark: This proof hasn't been our first characterization of the special Cobb-Douglas index $\tilde{P}_n$. Other characterizations with more requirements have been easier than this proof, but this is our first characterization by means of independent axioms.

Theorem 4

The axioms (A_1), (A_2), (A_7), (B_1), (C_2) are independent.

Proof:

a) The function P_n given by $P_n(\underline{q}^o,\underline{p}^o,\underline{p}) = 1$ satisfies (A_2), (A_7), (B_1), (C_2), but not (A_1).

b) The function P_n given by $P_n(\underline{q}^o,\underline{p}^o,\underline{p})= \dfrac{\sum_{i=1}^{n} q_i^o p_i^o p_i}{\sum_{i=1}^{n} q_i^o p_i^o p_i^o}$

satisfies (A_1), (A_7), (B_1), (C_2), but not (A_2).

c) The function P_n given by $P_n(\underline{q}^o,\underline{p}^o,\underline{p})= \left(\frac{p_1}{p_1^o}\right)^{\frac{1}{n}} \cdot \left(\frac{p_2}{p_2^o}\right)^{\frac{1}{n}} \cdots \left(\frac{p_n}{p_n^o}\right)^{\frac{1}{n}}$

satisfies (A_1), (A_2), (B_1), (C_2), but not (A_7).

d) The function P_n given by

$$P_n(\underline{q}^o,\underline{p}^o,\underline{p})= \left(\frac{p_1}{p_1^o}\right)^{\frac{(q_1^o p_1^o)^2}{\sum_{i=1}^{n}(q_i^o p_i^o)^2}} \cdots\cdots \left(\frac{p_n}{p_n^o}\right)^{\frac{(q_n^o p_n^o)^2}{\sum_{i=1}^{n}(q_i^o p_i^o)^2}}$$

satisfies (A_1), (A_2), (A_7), (C_2), but not (B_1).

e) The Laspeyres' index does not satisfy (C_2), but all other natural axioms.

Replacing (C_2) by (C_3) leads to two theorems which correspond with theorem (4.4) and theorem (4.5).

(4.6) Theorem:

For $n \geq 3$ the only price index function $P_n : \mathbb{R}^{3n}_{++} \to \mathbb{R}_{++}$ satisfying $(A_1),(A_2),\ldots(A_7),(B_1),(C_3)$, is $\tilde{\tilde{P}}_n$ given by

$$\tilde{\tilde{P}}_n(\underline{q}^o,\underline{p}^o,\underline{p}) = \left(\frac{p_1}{p_1^o}\right)^{\frac{q_1^o p_1}{\sum_{i=1}^n q_i^o p_i}} \cdots\cdots \left(\frac{p_n}{p_n^o}\right)^{\frac{q_n^o p_n}{\sum_{i=1}^n q_i^o p_i}}$$

(4.7) Theorem:

The axioms (A_1), (A_2), (A_7), (B_1), (C_3) are independent.

The proofs of theorem (4.6) and theorem (4.7) are almost equal to the proofs of theorem (4.4) and theorem (4.5).

5. References

Eichhorn,W. and J.Voeller: Theory of the Price Index. Fisher's Test Approach and Generalization. Lecture Notes in Economics and Mathematical Systems. Vo.140, Springer Verlag, Berlin-Heidelberg-New York 1976.

Eichhorn,W.: Functional Equation in Economics. Addison- Wesley Publishing Company 1978.

Fisher,F.: The Making of Index Numbers. Houghton Mifflin, Boston 1922, third edition revised 1927. Reprinted by A.M.Kelley, New York 1968.

Krtscha,M.: Über Preisindices und deren axiomatische Charakterisierung. Dissertation Karlsruhe 1979.

Volkmann,P.: see this volume, 1985.

A System of Functional Equations Considered by Krtscha

Peter Volkmann
Mathematisches Institut I
Universität Karlsruhe
D-7500 Karlsruhe
Federal Republic of Germany

Let R be the reals, and denote $Q_2 = \{(x,y) \mid x,y \geq 0;\ x+y > 0\}$, $Q_3 = \{(x,y,z) \mid x,y,z \geq 0;\ x+y+z > 0\}$. The following theorem gives the solution of a system of functional equations considered by M.Krtscha [1].

Theorem. The solutions $g: Q_3 \longrightarrow R$ of

$$g(x,y,z) + g(y,x,z) = g(x+y,0,z) \qquad ((x,y,z) \in Q_3), \qquad (1)$$

$$g(x,y,z) = g(x,z,y) \qquad ((x,y,z) \in Q_3), \qquad (2)$$

$$g(0,y,z) = 0 \qquad ((y,z) \in Q_2) \qquad (3)$$

are

$$g(x,y,z) = a(x+y,z) + a(x+z,y) - a(y+z,x) + a(x+y+z,0), \qquad (4)$$

where $a: Q_2 \longrightarrow R$ satisfies

$$a(y,x) = -a(x,y) \qquad ((x,y) \in Q_2). \qquad (5)$$

Proof. The function $a: Q_2 \longrightarrow R$ being skew-symmetric, i.e. satisfying (5), it is easy to see that g given by (4) is a solution of (1),(2),(3).

Conversely, let now $g: Q_3 \longrightarrow R$ satisfy (1),(2),(3). Equation (1) can be written as

$$g(x,y,z) + g(y,x,z) = 2h(x+y,z) \qquad (6)$$

($h: Q_2 \longrightarrow R$ being defined by $h(x,y) = \frac{1}{2}\, g(x,0,y)$).

From (6) one gets

$$g(y,z,x) + g(z,y,x) = 2h(y+z,x), \qquad (7)$$

$$g(z,x,y) + g(x,z,y) = 2h(z+x,y). \qquad (8)$$

Measurement in Economics
ed. by W. Eichhorn

Summing (6),(8), subtracting (7), using (2), and dividing by 2 yields

$$g(x,y,z) = h(x+y,z) + h(x+z,y) - h(y+z,x) . \tag{9}$$

Condition (3) delivers $0 = h(y,z) + h(z,y) - h(y+z,0)$, i.e.

$$h(x,y) + h(y,x) = h(x+y,0) \qquad ((x,y) \in Q_2) . \tag{10}$$

Decompose

$$h(x,y) = s(x,y) + a(x,y) , \tag{11}$$

where $s(x,y) = \frac{1}{2}(h(x,y) + h(y,x))$ is symmetric and $a(x,y) = \frac{1}{2}(h(x,y) - h(y,x))$ skew-symmetric. By (10), $s(x,y)$ is a function of $x+y$, whence (11) can be written as

$$h(x,y) = f(x+y) + a(x,y) . \tag{12}$$

Substituting in (10) yields

$$2f(x+y) = f(x+y) + a(x+y,0) ,$$

i.e. $f(x+y) = a(x+y,0)$. Therefore (12) becomes

$$h(x,y) = a(x,y) + a(x+y,0).$$

Substituting in (9) gives the representation (4) of g .

References

[1] Krtscha, Manfred: Axiomatic characterization of statistical price indices. Preceding article.

Author's address: Mathematisches Institut I, Universität Karlsruhe, Postfach 6380, 7500 Karlsruhe 1, West Germany.

A Probabilistic Model for Price Levels in Discontinuous Markets

Cary Webb
Chicago State University
Department of Mathematics
Ninety-Fifth Street at King Drive
Chicago, Illinois 60628, USA

Abstract. A linear model is constructed that allows estimation of price levels in markets wherein goods are traded only irregularly. The model is tested with real estate data collected by the state of Arizona. The assumption of the model is that prices of individual properties follow independent random walks. The results presented here amplify work done by Court in 1938 and by Bailey, Muth and Nourse in 1963.

1. Introduction

Methods for computing price levels in the real estate market or any other market wherein a given good is traded only irregularly are less precise than those methods for computing price levels in other types of markets such as stocks or consumer goods. In both these markets, most goods are traded regularly, that is, goods which are perfect substitutes (e.g., shares of IBM) are traded at regular intervals (e.g., on trading days of the NYSE). Clearly similar conditions are not met in the real estate market, since any given property is usually quite distinct and is traded only irregularly.

To be sure, there are several price indexes currently used in the real estate market, for example, the mean price of new single-family houses [1], a hedonic (i.e., quality-adjusted) price index for new single-family houses [2], and the mean price of existing single-family houses [3], [4]. Of these, only the hedonic index in [2] takes account of changes through time in the set of properties traded. In particular, there is no definitive index that measures price levels of existing single-family houses.

Because of the relative lack of price information in real estate markets, the reliability of a real estate price index is necessarily less

Measurement in Economics
ed. by W. Eichhorn

than the reliability of financial indexes and of the Consumer Price Index (CPI). For this reason, one must realize that the accuracy of financial indexes and the CPI can never be duplicated in the real estate market or any market wherein a given good transacts only irregularly.

The purpose here is to establish a methodology that will produce the most accurate real estate index and to quantify the reliability of this index. The method to be developed will apply also to any other market wherein a sufficiently large subset of the goods are known to have transacted at least twice.

It may well turn out that the most accurate possible index for a particular market is not accurate enough for one of its intended purposes. In such a case, the work that we present here and elsewhere [15] will suggest the amount of additional information necessary to achieve the desired reliability.

One line of research on real estate and similar markets has produced the hedonic indexes. These were pioneered by Andrew Court in his 1938 study of automobiles [5]. More recent work on hedonic indexes is contained in [6], [7], and [8].

It is possible to derive the model developed in this paper from Court's 1938 model. Historically, however, models based on data from a minimum of two sales had a separate development. The earliest example is a chaining technique, dating from 1927 [9]. A further development of the chaining technique is contained in [10]. In 1963, Bailey, Muth, and Nourse introduced a regression model [11] which avoided the drawback of the chain method in not using information about the price level at a given time that may be contained in the returns on investments made in properties sold afterwards.

In this paper we present a regression method that is a refinement of [11] which avoids problems with heteroscedasticity. The underlying assumption that allows us to infer optimal estimates is that real estate prices follow a random walk (in discrete time). By this we mean that the return to every period is chosen from the same distribution. In other words, the random variables that are the returns of the various properties in the various periods are identical and identically distributed (i.i.d.).

2. Theory

In order to build the price index model, let P_i denote the (unobserved) market price level in period i, i = 0,1,...,n, and let w_i be the logarithm of the associated price relative, $w_i = \log(P_i/P_{i-1})$. Define w_{ij} to be the sum of the w_k's, k = i+1,...,j.

An implication of the random walk assumption is that the distributions for which the w_i's are drawn are independent and identically distributed. It is also true, for the same reason, that the distributions from which the quantities $w_{ij}(j-i)^{-1/2}$ are drawn are homoscedastic.

Suppose property 1 was bought in period i for price p_i and next sold in period j for p_j. Let $Y_{ij\ell} = \log(p_j/p_i)(j-i)^{-1/2}$. Then $Y_{ij\ell}$ is an estimate for $w_{ij}(j-i)^{-1/2}$. In other words

$$Y_{ij\ell} = (j-i)^{-1/2}(w_{i+1} + \cdots w_j) + e_\ell, \tag{1}$$

where e_ℓ is a disturbance term. When a regression is performed, it will be "weighted least squares" because of the factor $(j-i)^{-1/2}$ in equation (1).

Equation (1) can be written in the conventional form,

$$Y = b_1x_1 + \cdots + b_nx_n + e, \tag{2}$$

where Y is of the form $Y_{ij\ell}(j-i)^{-1/2}$, $b_k = w_k$, and x_k is the 'dummy' variable, $x_k = (j-i)^{-1/2}$, k = i+1,...,j, and $x_k = 0$, otherwise. The object is to estimate the coefficients b_k, k = 1,...,n.

It is important to notice in equation (2) that there is no constant term. Hence we cannot expect the residuals from the regression to total (exactly) zero. There will be evidence in the data we analyze, however, that the actual mean residual is not significantly different from zero (section 3).

Assuming individual properties follow independent random walks, the true disturbances are uncorrelated and have mean zero. It is a consequence that the least-squares estimates for the b_k's are unbiased and of minimum variance among all unbiased estimates that are linear transformations of the vector of y values. These optimality properties are direct consequences of the Gauss-Markov theorem [12].

The end results of our calculations are the values P_i/P_{i-1}, the market price relatives. It is, however, the value $\log(P_i/P_{i-1})$ that is estimated by b_i. This means that if c is the expected value of b_i the expected value of P_i/P_{i-1} is $e^{v/2}e^c$ where v is the variance of the estimator b_i. In our data (section 3), however, the factor $e^{v/2}$ is very nearly 1. (For the three data sets that were analyzed, it was 1.0012, 1.0002, and 1.0001.) The difference between using the correction factor $e^{v/2}$ and not using it, is several orders of magnitude smaller than the standard deviations of the estimates (which average .0483 for the annual series and larger for the finer series). It was, therefore, neglected.

Notwithstanding the influence of the Gauss-Markov theorem in the formulation of our model, in [15] it will become apparent there is some natural multicollinearity in the model. This is especially true, in real estate markets, whenever the time periods are one month in duration. Therefore we should not be surprised if estimates of monthly price levels are unreliable. This will be true of the data we analyze in the next section.

Suppose there are N buy-sell pairs in the data. Then there is a system of N equations of the form of equation (2). Such a system can be represented with matrices, $\mathbf{y} = \mathbf{X}\mathbf{b} + \mathbf{e}$, where $\mathbf{y}$ and $\mathbf{e}$ are N-dimensional column vectors, $\mathbf{X}$ is an N by n matrix, and $\mathbf{b}$ is an n-dimensional column vector.

There are two necessary and sufficient conditions on the data that guarantee the nonsingularity of the matrix $\mathbf{X}'\mathbf{X}$. First of all, there must be a transaction in every period for which we want to estimate a return. Second, in every period at least one of the properties must be held and not sold (i.e., in every period we must be strictly between the buying date and the selling date of one of the observed properties). We call data that satisfy these two conditions "connected". (This term has been applied to similar conditions: for a discussion see [13].)

It is not hard to see that these two conditions are necessary for non-singularity. That the conditions are also sufficient can be derived from a theorem in the theory of M-matrices [14]. This derivation is contained in section 4. We are grateful to Charles Johnson and the editors of Linear Algebra and Its Applications for this observation.

It is simple enough to modify the model to accommodate either kind of singularity. First of all, if there is no transaction in a certain period, one merely omits the corresponding variable from the model.

Of course, the regression procedure produces no estimate for the return and price level for the missing period. The estimate for the return of the preceding period includes the return of the "missing" period.

Secondly, suppose all properties purchased prior to a certain period either have been sold or are sold in that period. Then the regression procedure must be broken into two parts. The first part estimates the returns and prices up to the pivotal period. The second part estimates the other returns and prices.

The model can be illustrated with a small example (Table 1).

Table 1

Property	Period of Trade	Price
1	1	1000
1	3	1500
2	1	1200
2	2	1600
3	2	2000
3	3	2500

For these data the Y vector and the **X** matrix are the following

$$\mathbf{Y} = \begin{bmatrix} 2^{-1/2}\log(1500/1000) \\ \log(1600/1200 \\ \log(2500/2000) \end{bmatrix} = \begin{bmatrix} .2867 \\ .2877 \\ .2231 \end{bmatrix}$$

$$\mathbf{X} = \begin{bmatrix} 2^{-1/2} & 2^{-1/2} \\ 1 & 0 \\ 0 & 1 \end{bmatrix} .$$

From this it follows that the least squares estimate of $\mathbf{b} = (\mathbf{X}'\mathbf{X})^{-1}\mathbf{X}'\mathbf{Y}$ is,

$$\mathbf{b} = \begin{bmatrix} .2614 \\ .1968 \end{bmatrix} .$$

Thus, setting $P_0 = 1$, we have $P_1/P_0 = e^{.2614} = 1.30$ and $P_2/P_1 = e^{.1968} = 1.22$

A limiting case for the model is when all holding periods are one period in duration. In this case, one of the variables x_i is 1 and the remainder are 0. In other words, the rows of the $\mathbf{X}$ matrix each contain a single 1. The remaining entries are 0.

In this situation it is easy to see the matrix $\mathbf{X}'\mathbf{X}$ is diagonal. The entry in the (k,k) position is the number of properties held during the kth period. Therefore the market return for period k is the geometric mean return of the individual properties held in this period. In this sense, the market return is known without the possibility of error. The non-zero variance of the return is merely a measure of the dispersion of the yields of the individual properties. Hence it is a measure of how much we can expect the market return to vary over time.

3. Empirical Results

Our data is the set of all transactions in Cochise County, Arizona, involving single-family housing which traded at least twice in the 78-month interval from January 1971 through June 1977. This data was originally collected by the state government of Arizona. We are grateful to Roger Ibbotson for making it available to us.

In the data there are 798 properties that changed hands at least twice in different months. Of these, 662 changed hands only twice. There were 116, 17, and 3 properties that changed hands 3, 4, and 5 times, respectively. None changed hands more than 5 times. These transactions constitute a total of 957 holding periods. The mean duration of a holding period was 22.991 months.

There were no transactions recorded in December 1971 and so in estimating monthly returns, month 12 has been omitted. Therefore, the estimated return for November 1971 is really an estimate for the two-month return over November and December.

The model was used to estimate monthly, quarterly, semiannual, and annual market returns. The least-squares estimates are presented in Table 2. Included are the derived price index numbers which are also displayed graphically in Figure 1. As is usual, the price in the base period was set to 100.

The most striking feature in the four series of index numbers is the differences in their volatility. There is a distinct rise in volatility from the annual series, through the intermediate series, to the monthly series.

For each series the mean standard error was computed (Table 3). Included in this table is the mean return for each series and the ratio of mean return to mean standard error. These ratios correspond closely to what we usually refer to as a t-statistic.

It should be noted that the mean return is not exactly the mean of the b_k's because the b_k's are the estimates for the logarithms of the price relatives. If these price relatives are close to 1, then w_k is close to the return from period k-1 to period k. For our numbers, the mean return is slightly larger than the mean of the b_k's. We have chosen to display the mean returns because they have more intuitive and practical appeal.

The ratio of the mean return to mean standard error declines monotonically, as we would expect, from a value of 3.76 for the annual series to one of .17 for the monthly series. Even the semiannual series is only 1.12. Therefore, our confidence in the annual series is relatively high but in the quarterly and monthly series is low. The semiannual series merits at best only moderate confidence.

One expects R^2 to decrease as the number of explanatory variables decreases, but this is only partially true for our results (Table 4). R^2 does indeed decrease from .28 in the case of the monthly series to .20 for the quarterly series and semiannual series. But then there is an increase to .23 for the annual series. (These same observations apply to the adjusted R^2 values except that the adjusted R^2 for the annual series is greater than the other adjusted R^2's.) The explanation of this increase is that the returns for the holding periods that are contained in the same calendar year are to some extent atypical of the other returns. When these shorter holding periods are omitted, the explanatory power of the model increases. Regressions that delete presumed outliers are caried out later in the paper. They suggest we can probably expect a significant increase in accuracy by being able to identify outliers properly.

The serial correlation of each of the four series is displayed in Table 5. All but the annual series exhibits negative correlation ranging from -.3132 for the monthly series to -.5290 for the semi-annual series. The confidnece that the correlation cannot be explained by chance fluctuation in the estimates ranges from 99% for the monthly and quarterly series to 95% for the semiannual series.

The annual series, on the other hand, exhibits a positive serial correlation of .4741. There are only 5 returns in this series, however, so although that figure does suggest a certain amount of positive correlation, for this number of returns it is significant only at the less than 75% level.

A deeper understanding of the model would lead us to expect negatively correlated return estimates, even though the true returns are not correlated. This subject is explored in [15] where negative correlation is explained as part of a unified theory that contains theoretical confidence intervals for the coefficient estimates as functions only of the parameters n and N and the standard deviation of the y variables.

Since there is no constant term in the model we cannot expect the residuals to total exactly zero. The mean residual, however, is .027 with a standard deviation of .466. Therefore the mean is not significantly different from zero. This is consistent with the assumption that the true disturbances have a mean of exactly zero.

The distribution of residuals is more peaked than the normal distribution with 91% within one standard deviation of the mean. In their tails, the residuals are skewed appreciably to the right with 8% to the right of one standard deviation from the mean and only 1% to the left of one standard deviation from the mean.

Observations whose residuals are greater than 1 correspond to properties whose prices have grown 172% more than is explained by the model. 6% of the observations are in this category. If we assume for the moment that these observations are outliers because, perhaps major additions or other improvements have been made in the properties, then the right-skewness of the residuals largely disappears and their (small) positive bias also is diminished.

The coefficient estimates for the annual series together with their standard errors and t-statistics for the null-hypothesis are given in Table 6. One notes the t-statistics range from 1.81 to 8.27. Most of this variation is explained by the variation in coefficient estimates and not by the variation in standard errors all of which are in the range .052 plus or minus .012.

It is likely that much of what variation there is in the standard errors, a steady decrease from .0627 to .0397 from 1972 to 1976, can be explained by the increase in portfolio size throughout most of the interval of study. This increase is monotonic from 136 in 1972 to 352 in 1975. (There is a decrease to 278 in 1976.) The relationship between portfolio size and accuracy is investigated more thoroughly in [15].

In order to investigate the increase in accuracy from higher quality data, the Cochise data which produced the annual series were analyzed further by deleting the 42 out of 672 observations that produced residuals either greater than 1 or less than -1. (Recall, these correspond to properties that appreciated more than 172% or less than 37% of that of the market.) The rationale behind this approach is that these observations are quite likely outliers for reasons that have already been discussed.

Table 7 displays the results of applying the model to the edited data. The mean standard error is .0196 which implies a 95% confidnece of being, on average, within 4.3% of the true return in any given year. This compares with 11.2% for the unedited data. This is a significant increase in reliability.

The ending price level is 173.6. We are 95% confident that the true ending price is within $(5^{1/2})(4.3)$ = 9.6 of the true ending price level. This compares with 95% confidence of being within $(5^{1/2})(11.2)$ = 25.0 of the true ending price level with unedited data. Hence, we expect significantly more reliable results if the quality of the data can be moderately increased.

For the edited data, the mean residual is .004 with a standard deviation of .183. In other words, the mean differs only insignificantly from zero. This is strong evidence that the true disturbances have been precisely zero.

In section 2 the values of the variables x_k were specified to assure the homoschedasticity of the model. In order to confirm empirically the correctness of this specification, the market returns were estimated with an unweighted least-squares regression (which is the method employed in [11]). Compared with results from the weighted least-squares regression, (a) the mean residual increased 130%, from .027 to .062, and (b) the standard deviation of the residuals increased 18% from .466 to .550. Both of these results are indications that our estimates become poorer when the specification is changed. For the same reasons, these results are also confirmation that the i.i.d. hypothesis on returns (i.e., the random walk assumption) is appropriate.

4. Connectivity Theorem

The purpose of this section is to demonstrate the equivalence of connected data and the nonsingularity of the matrix $\mathbf{X'X}$. Our method will be to reduce the problem to a theorem in the theory of M-matrices.

The first state in the reduction is to multiply $\mathbf{X}$ on the right by the n by n+1 matrix $\mathbf{A} = (a_{ij})$ where $a_{ii} = -1$, $a_{i,i+1} = 1$, and all other entries are 0. Clearly, $\mathbf{W} = \mathbf{XA}$ has the same rank as $\mathbf{X}$. It is not hard to see the entries of $\mathbf{W}$ are, (a) $w_{k\ell} = -(j-i)^{-1/2}$ if the holding period began in period $\ell = i$ and ended in period j, (b) $w_{k\ell} = (j-i)^{-1/2}$ if the holding period began in period i and ended in period $\ell = j$, and (c) $w_{k\ell} = 0$ otherwise.

The second stage in the reduction is to multiply $\mathbf{W}$ on the left by the diagonal matrix $\mathbf{D}$ that transforms each entry of $\mathbf{W}$ of the form $-(j-i)^{-1/2}$ into -1. Clearly, the rank of $\mathbf{Z} = \mathbf{DW} = \mathbf{DXA}$ is the same as the rank of $\mathbf{W}$, hence, the same rank as $\mathbf{X}$.

Let n_{ij} be the (i,j)th entry inthe (n+1)-dimensioal square matrix, $\mathbf{Z'Z}$. It is not hard to see that if $i < j$ then n_{ij} is minus the number of observations with purchase date in period i and selling date in period j. n_{ij} is the number (without sign change) of the transactions, both "buys" and "sells", that occurred in period i. Thus, a diagonal element of $\mathbf{Z'Z}$ is the sum of the other elements in the same row (or column) with the sign changed. This means, of course, that the trace of $\mathbf{Z'Z}$ is the total number of transactions represented by the data.

In terms of Z'**Z**, the first condition of connectedness, that in every period there was at least one transaction, means every diagonal element of Z'**Z** is nonzero. The second condition of connectedness, that at all times at least one property is contained in the portfolio being observed, means that Z'**Z** is not a direct sum of two submatrices.

That Z'**Z** is an M-matrix is a consequence of (ch. 6, Theorem 4.67 in [14]), and that Z'**Z** has rank n if the data is connected is a consequence of (ch. 6, Theorem 4.16 in [14]). The converse is obviously true. Therefore we have the following theorem.

Connectivity Theorem. The **X** matrix in the price index model is of full rank if and only if the data are connected.

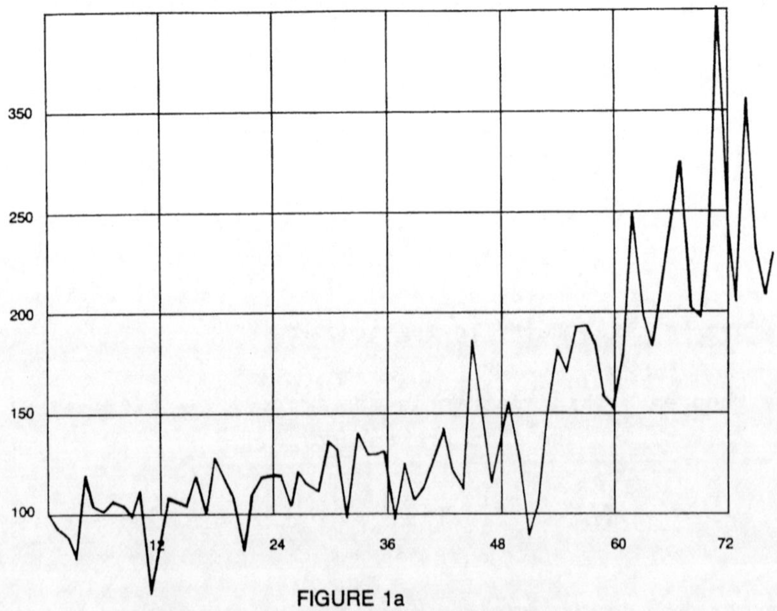

FIGURE 1a
ESTIMATES OF MONTHLY PRICE LEVELS

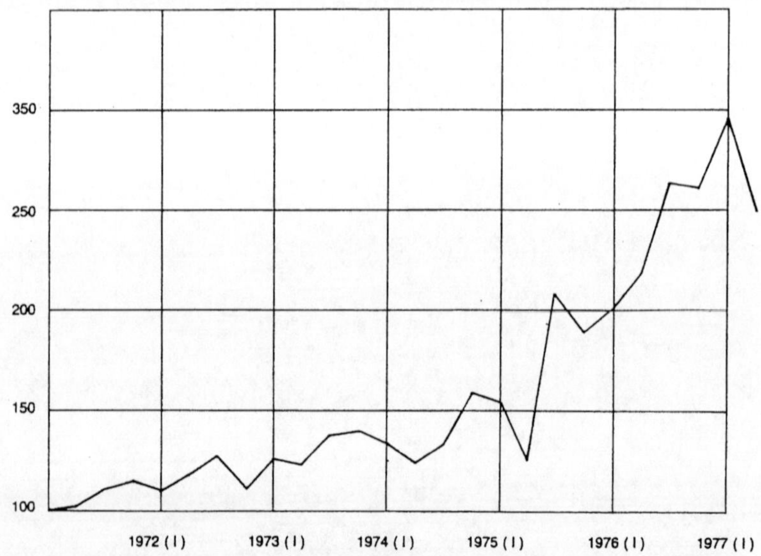

FIGURE 1b
ESTIMATES OF QUARTERLY PRICE LEVELS

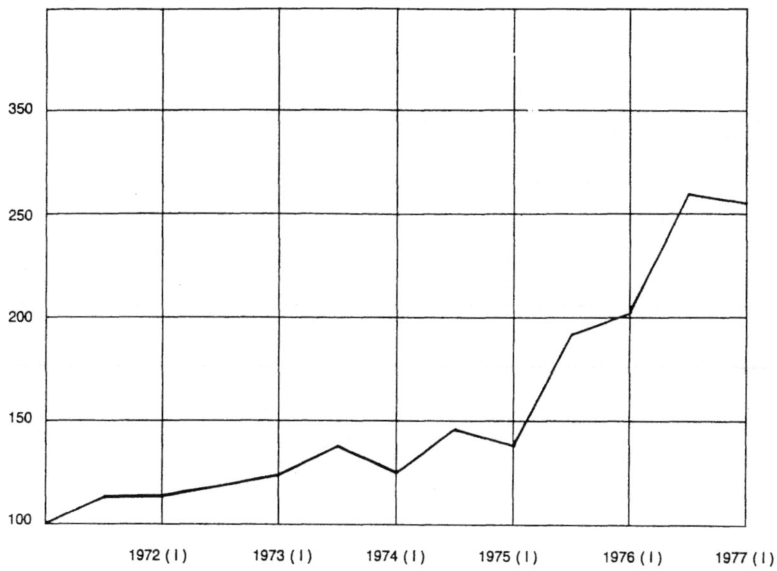

FIGURE 1c
ESTIMATES OF SEMI-ANNUAL PRICE LEVELS

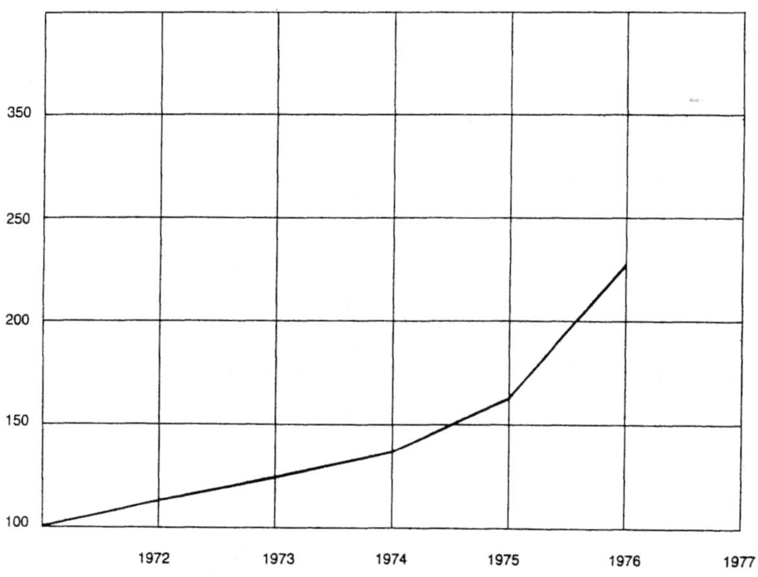

FIGURE 1d
ESTIMATES OF ANNUAL PRICE LEVELS

Table 2a

MONTHLY MARKET RETURNS AND PRICE LEVELS

Month	Return	Price
1/71	-	100.0
2/	-.0924	90.76
3/	-.0276	88.26
4/	-.1392	75.98
5/	.5898	120.79
6/	-.1393	103.97
7/	-.0261	101.26
8/	.0528	106.60
9/	-.0180	104.69
10/	-.0453	99.95
11& 12/	.1244	112.38
1/72	-.4565	61.08
2/	.7695	108.08
3/	-.0200	105.92
4/	-.0151	104.32
5/	.1431	119.24
6/	-.1522	101.09
7/	.2639	127.77
8/	-.0608	120.00
9/	-.0958	108.51
10/	-.2458	81.84
11/	.3305	108.89
12/	.0844	118.07
1/73	.0144	119.77
2/	-.0002	119.75
3/	-.1417	102.78
4/	.1701	120.27
5/	-.0472	114.58
6/	-.0252	111.69
7/	.2255	136.88
8/	-.0269	133.21
9/	-.2723	96.94
10/	.4638	141.91
11/	-.0865	129.63
12/	-.0050	128.98
1/74	.0109	130.39
2/	-.2483	98.01
3/	.2920	126.62
4/	-.1677	105.38
5/	.0767	113.47
6/	.1191	126.98
7/	.1344	144.04
8/	-.1589	121.16
9/	-.0755	112.02
10/	.6900	189.30
11/	-.1820	154.86
12/	-.2540	115.52
1/75	.1730	135.50
2/	.1566	156.72

(cont'd)

Table 2a (cont'd)

3/	-.1785	128.75
4/	-.3117	88.61
5/	.1774	104.33
6/	.4210	148.26
7/	.2376	183.47
8/	-.0732	170.04
9/	.1451	194.71
10/	.0013	194.96
11/	-.0545	184.34
12/	-.1329	159.83
1/76	-.0352	154.20
2/	.1758	181.31
3/	.4061	254.94
4/	-.2101	201.38
5/	-.0829	184.68
6/	.1373	210.02
7/	.1661	244.91
8/	.1501	281.66
9/	-.2764	203.81
10/	-.0206	199.62
11/	.1907	237.67
12/	.5446	367.11
1/77	-.3502	238.55
2/	-.1239	208.98
3/	.4822	309.76
4/	-.2431	234.46
5/	-.1071	209.36
6/	.1383	238.30

Table 2b

QUARTERLY MARKET RETURNS AND PRICE LEVELS

Quarter	Return	Price
1971 (I)		100.00
(II)	.0258	102.58
(III)	.0899	111.80
(IV)	.0312	115.29
1972 (I)	-.0437	110.25
(II)	.0750	118.51
(III)	.0822	128.85
(IV)	-.1357	110.85
1973 (I)	.1392	126.29
(II)	-.0217	123.55
(III)	.1173	138.05
(IV)	.0187	140.62
1974 (I)	-.0404	134.94
(II)	-.0775	124.49
(III)	.0720	133.46
(IV)	.1935	159.28
1975 (I)	-.0304	154.43
(II)	-.1842	125.98
(III)	.6517	208.09
(IV)	-.0835	190.72
1976 (I)	.0546	201.14
(II)	.0902	219.29
(III)	.2027	263.73
(IV)	-.0057	262.24
1977 (I)	.1297	296.24
(II)	-.1590	249.14

Table 2c

SEMI ANNUAL MARKET RETURNS AND PRICE LEVELS

Half-year		Return	Price
1971	(I)	--	100.00
	(II)	.1259	112.59
1972	(I)	.0039	113.03
	(II)	.0520	118.91
1973	(I)	.0440	124.14
	(II)	.1124	138.09
1974	(I)	-.0905	125.59
	(II)	.1624	146.01
1975	(I)	-.0498	138.75
	(II)	.3862	192.33
1976	(I)	.0524	202.42
	(II)	.2846	260.03
1977	(I)	-.0176	255.44

Table 2d

YEARLY MARKET RETURN AND PRICE LEVELS

Year	Return	Price
1971	--	100.00
1972	.1204	112.04
1973	.1182	125.29
1974	.0981	137.58
1975	.1815	162.55
1976	.3885	225.71

Table 3

ACCURACY OF INDEX NUMBERS

Price Series	Mean Return r	Mean Std. Error e	$\frac{r}{e}$
Annual	.1814	.0483	3.76
Semi-Annual	.0888	.0791	1.12
Quarterly	.0477	.1231	.39
Monthly	.0373	.2232	.17

Table 4

R^2 OF THE PRICE SERIES

Price Series	R^2	Adjusted R^2 *
Annual	.227	.222
Semi-Annual	.202	.192
Quarterly	.201	.180
Monthly	.277	.216

*For the method of adjusting, see [12].

Table 5

SERIAL CORRELATION IN THE RETURN SERIES

Series	Serial Correlation	Level of Confidence
Monthly	-.3131	99%
Quarterly	-.4882	99%
Semi-annual	-.5290	95%
Annual	.4741	Less than 75%

Table 6

RELIABILITY OF ANNUAL RETURNS

Year	Coefficient Estimate	Standard Error	t - statistic
1972	.1137	.0627	1.81
1973	.1117	.0506	2.22
1974	.0936	.0491	1.91
1975	.1668	.0398	4.19
1976	.3282	.0397	8.27
mean	.1628	.0483	3.68

Table 7

COCHISE COUNTY, 1971-76

Edited Data Set

Year	Coefficient Estimate	Standard Error	t - Statistic	Return Estimate	Price Level
1972	.1001	.0250	4.00	.1053	110.5
1973	.1101	.0201	5.48	.1164	123.4
1974	.0761	.0198	3.84	.0790	133.2
1975	.1184	.0165	7.19	.1183	148.9
1976	.1532	.0168	9.11	.1656	173.6
Mean	.1116	.0196	5.92	.1180*	---

*Geometric mean

REFERENCES

[1] US Bureau of the Census, *New One-Family Houses Sold and for Sale*, Washington, D.C.

[2] US Bureau of the Census, *Price Index of New One Family Houses*, Washington, D.C.

[3] US Bureau of the Census, *Annual Housing Survey*, Part C, Financial Characteristics of the Housing Inventory, Washington, D.C.

[4] National Association of Realtors, *Existing Home Sales*, Washington, D.C.

[5] Court, Andrew T. 1939. "Hedonic Price Indexes with Automobile Examples", *The Dynamnics of Automobile Demand* (based on a joint meeting of the American Statistical Association and the Econometric Society in Detroit, Dec. 27, 1938) New York: General Motors Corp.

[6] Griliches, Zvi 1961. "Hedonic Price Indexes for Automobiles: An Econometric Analysis of Quality Change", *The Price Statistics of the Federal Government*, General Series, no. 73, New York: National Bureau of Econometric Research.

[7] Griliches, Zvi 1965. "Hedonic Parice Indexes Revisted: some Notes on the State of the Art", University of Chicago, Center for Mathematical Studies in Business and Economics, Report no. 6802.

[8] Griliches, Zvi 1971. *Price Indexes and Quality Change*. Cambridge.

[9] Wyngarden, Herman 1927. *An Index of Local Real Estate Prices*. Ann Arbor: University of Michigan Press.

[10] Wenzlick, Roy 1952. "As I See the Fluctuations in the Selling Prices of Single-Family Residences", *Real Estate Analyst* 21:541-48.

[11] Bailey, M. J., Muth. R. F., Nourse, H. O. 1963. "A Regression Method for Real Estate Price Index Construction", *J. of Amer. Stat. Assoc.* 58:933-42.

[12] Theil, Henri 1971. *Principles of Econometrics*. New York: John Wiley.

[13] Searle, S. R. 1971. *Linear Models*. New York: John Wiley.

[14] Berman, A. and Plemmons, R. J. 1979. *Nonnegative Matrices in the Mathematical Sciences*. New York: Academic Press.

[15] Webb, C. 1981. "The Expected Accuracy of a Price Index for Discontinuous Markets", preprint.

Weighting and Additivity Problems of Multilateral Comparison

J. van Yzeren
Postbus 513
Technische Hogeschool Eindhoven
NL-5600 MB Eindhoven

1. Gradual differences, but antithesis too.

The question of weighting in multilateral comparison divides practice. On the one hand the very plausible method of Geary-Khamis uses international prices with proportional weights for countries of different size. Therefore, a big country's prices may dominate the international pattern. On the other hand Gerardi's method is neutral, as it most practically uses geometrical means. Thus, it makes for every product a purely individual international price, independent of other products or size differences of countries. Both methods lead to additivity of international values, simply as a consequence of their using international prices. Of course, this is very important in practice. It is embarrassing, however, to get different results.

But even more embarrassing seems the general obscurity of theory. In fact, this is an actual point. In particular, Hill has made an attempt to bring clarity with his well-known Report [1] that focuses on comparing the above methods. It is shown that mathematical subtleties, like using arithmetical or geometrical means, are not so important. Indeed, Hill localizes the true origin of the differences in the alternative "to weight or not" and deliberately prefers to weight. This view, however, has been thoroughly criticized by Gerardi [2].

It seems a good thing to take an overall view. Information should be found not only from international prices (= combined price patterns), but just as well from international baskets (= combined quantity patterns). In fact, the total basket method (Edgeworth-Marshall) was employed by the Economic Commission for South America for comparing price levels. This happened, however, just many years ago (1960) and meanwhile the National Accounts quest for additivity has fixed attention to those methods that quite oppositely stick to the price line. Indeed, important but nevertheless purely practical reasons have led to preference for one-sided information. Theory, however, should inform itself independently, it meets the intertwinement of the price line and the quantity line and may look askance even at additivity. It is unrealistic, of course, to expect that theory would be able to move a massive practice directly. Its realistic task, however, consists in considering whether and to what extent practice possibly goes astray.

Measurement in Economics
ed. by W. Eichhorn

2. A simple experimental model.

In order to illustrate the above, some results of the author's 1983 Report [3] are put forward. They are found from a fictitious six products model of four countries, A, B, C, D, that have different size (GDP), roughly proportionate to 5 : 25 : 1 : 1.[1] The following table presents converting parities according to the various methods. The intermediate country A is given parity 1.

	A	B	C	D	
Geary-Khamis (weighted p's)	1	1,017	10,35	2,039	
Gerardi (unweighted prices)	1	1,008	11,41	2,254	
Total basket (weighted q's)	1	0,998	12,53	2,585	E.C.L.A.
....					
Gerardi (weighted version!)	1	1,018	10,27	2,019	Hill
Geary-Khamis (de-weighted!)	1	1,006	11,63	2,304	Iklé

Apparently, with respect to the pair of Geary-Khamis and Gerardi, Total basket is quite an outlier, thus showing its antithetical background (quantity line). The additional figures under the dotted line illustrate the secondary point of weighting effects. As Hill has put forward a weighted version of Gerardi (weighted geometric means) fairly approaches to Geary-Khamis. The reverse effect is found by de-weighting Geary-Khamis (i.e. by employing the method of Iklé). This approaches to Gerardi.

Practically the same picture, but much more conceptual coherence, is obtained by going back to the author's theoretical methods [4]. The next table shows the results of their weighted versions.

		A	B	C	D	
Homogeneous	weighted	1	1,018	10,27	2,018	
Balanced	weighted	1	1,008	11,32	2,278	E.K.S.
Heterogeneous	weighted	1	0,998	12,53	2,585	Total basket

Heterogeneous is identical with the above Total basket. Balanced, numerically, corresponds to the (weighted) Eltetö-Köves-Szulc results, in this case up to all decimals! (The theoretical difference between Balanced and E.K.S. is small of third order.)

When looking more critically at both tables, it is striking that the *weighted* Balanced method agrees with Gerardi, which is an unweighted method. This observation invites to consider also the *un*weighted versions of the three methods.

---

1) For the reader who is interested in the details, all data and formulas are presented in the Appendix.

		A	B	C	D	
Homogeneous	unweighted	1	1,008	11,41	2,248	E.K.S.
Balanced	unweighted	1	1,010	11,37	2,277	E.K.S.
Heterogeneous	unweighted	1	1,012	11,33	2,306	E.K.S.

Clearly, all differences shrink very much. So it is seen that the great *opposite* deviations of Geary-Khamis and Total basket are antithetic weighting effects. Essentially, they can be identified with the well-known Laspeyres, Paasche biases (upwards respectively downwards). The Balanced and E.K.S. methods just cancel them.

3. Two theoretical hints.

a. The weighting should refer to international trade.

The above empirical results suggest to the practical eye that non-weighting is a sound thing. But whatever are the theoretical views in this matter? Are there any positive or negative points concerning non-weighting? Theory has its own specific methods. For example, it can test itself by considering extreme cases.

Thus, let be given two countries C_1, C_2, with size (GDP) Q_1, Q_2, that form a ternary system, together with the country C(s). The size of the latter, Qs, should contain the factor s ($\in R_+$) that is supposed to be present in the price-quantity vector (p,qs). In words: the price pattern is fixed and the quantity pattern is fixed, but the parameter s allows proportional changing of the quantities. So C(s) may be seen as small, but just as well as big. Apparently, when making *un*weighted international prices for the system $(C_1,C_2,C(s))$ the size differences are excluded. This implies that the three mutual price indices will be independent of s. Naturally, if s tends to 0, the ternary system $(C_1,C_2,C(s))$ should tend to the binary (C_1,C_2). But the *constant* price index for the pair C_1, C_2 in the changing system $(C_1,C_2,C(s))$, $s \downarrow 0$, generally differs from the binary price index in (C_1,C_2). Contradiction.

Hence, theory rejects non-weighting. Surely, common sense does too! But if weighting with size and non-weighting both lead to impasses, whatever perspective remains? Again, common sense suggests that price levels are related to international trade. Therefore, it may be asked whether there is any model, however rough, for estimating trade intensities in the system $(C_1,C_2,C(s))$.

In fact, there is. Suppose international trade is done by agents whose number in C_1, C_2 and C(s) is proportional to Q_1, Q_2 respectively Qs. Each country is engaged in a number of their relations and it is reasonable to put these numbers proportional to

$$Q_1(Q_2 + Qs) \; : \; Q_2(Q_1 + Qs) \; : \; Qs(Q_1 + Q_2) \; .$$

So this proportionality may stand for the trade pattern.

Now, weighting according to this pattern is consistent with extreme cases. Clearly, if $s \downarrow 0$, then the weight of C(s) vanishes. Moreover, C_1 and C_2 obtain *equal* weights, as $Q_1 Q_2 = Q_2 Q_1$. This binary result is most plausible as it points to Fisher's indices or to indices that are closely related to them.

Also the other extreme case, $s \rightarrow \infty$, leads to a very plausible result, namely, the proportionality $Q_1 : Q_2 : Q_1 + Q_2$. Thus, the disturbing idea of overwhelming dominance disappears!

However, there remain great weighting differences. For example, the above proportionality 5 : 25 : 1 : 1 turns into 135 : 175 : 31 : 31. Consequently, there remain also great differences between index numbers of the Geary-Khamis respectively Total basket type (price line versus quantity line), even if trade weights would be used. Hence, a synthetic theory should keep to some balancing method. This even turns up in the structure of formulas. Indeed, the most general form of the balanced method ([3], p. 46, [4], p. 33) inserts weights that can be interpreted as trade flows between countries, just *two* flows between every pair, all together in the equilibrium of a "trade balance".

Even the theoretical case of a big, but economically isolated country fits in this model. Indeed, binary comparison of each pair of countries then leads to direct price and quantity indices. However, all indices should be modified in order to obtain transitivity and in this process the isolated country has no influence on the other ones.

Finally, it seems useful to comment on the idea of obtaining transitivity by minimizing the deviations from binary indices. This idea is at the base of the E.K.S. method, the balanced method (see also [6]) and Gerardi's newly developed additive (IP) method [7]. The point is that this minimizing can be done in an unweighted way, but just as well in a way that inserts weights. Therefore, the whole problem of weighting remains existent if one aims at optimal adjustment by minimizing deviations.

b. Additivity can be controlled from a balanced view-point.

Balanced methods work perfectly well for inter-country price and quantity indices. Modern statistics, however, wishes to look inside the countries, at subaggregates. For that purpose the indices of the price line, i.e. quantity indices based on an international price pattern and their companion *indirect* price indices, become the practical tools that give additivity of international values. But the price line is inconsistent with the quantity line, that produces natural *direct* price indices based on an international basket. The conflict already turns up in practice, where convertor indices and price level indices are competing in parallel situations [5].

From the theoretical view-point this is a very disappointing development, for the true aim of pure index number theory consists in providing every aggregate (countries included) with a "price" and a "quantity". Of course, this is impossible without some "frictional" corrections, but these are - always theoretically - to be preferred to splitting up things into two biased systems, to the neglect of the basic intertwinement. However, is there any anticipation of such synthetic approach that goes straight amidst disturbance, maybe without immediate practical use?

Indeed there is. The true guide in this matter is elementary algebra and the appropriate example is the binary case (C_1,C_2) where, exceptionally, formulas keep to both lines. It is just a bit of standard theory.

Value index: $\Sigma p_{i2}\, q_{i2}/\Sigma p_{i1}\, q_{i1} = V.$

Price and quantity index: P, Q, indefinite yet, but $PQ = V$.

"International" price respectively quantity pattern:

$p_{i0} = \frac{1}{2}p_{i1} + \frac{1}{2}p_{i2}/P,\quad q_{i0} = \frac{1}{2}q_{i1} + \frac{1}{2}q_{i2}/Q.$

(For country 1 both the deflating and the reducing factors are 1.)

Quantity index: $\Sigma p_{i0}\, q_{i2}/\Sigma p_{i0}\, q_{i1} = Q.$

Indirect price index: $V/Q = P$.

Direct price index: $\Sigma p_{i2}\, q_{i0}/\Sigma p_{i1}\, q_{i0} = P.$

It is easily verified (use $P/Q = \Sigma p_{i2} q_{i1}/\Sigma p_{i1} q_{i2}$) that P and Q are Fisher's ideal indices. Indeed, their special feature is that the indirect price index is identical with the direct one. In other words, the price line and the quantity line do not diverge here, thanks Fisher's indices.

Explicitly, the intertwinement shows up in the *balancing principle*

for each country the cost of the international basket equals the cost of the own basket at international price,

or in terms of *balancing equations*

$$\Sigma p_{i1}\, q_{i0} = \Sigma p_{i0}\, q_{i1}\ ,\quad \Sigma p_{i2}\, q_{i0}/P = \Sigma p_{i0}\, q_{i2}/Q\ .$$

All this matter can be extended to n countries and to weighting patterns. The n balancing equations fit in with the above formulation. Their solutions are the essence of the balanced method, moreover, the E.K.S. formulas provide very accurate approximations.

However, leaving the price line for balanced methods means that there is no more additivity of international values. Something changes and the best way to understanding is to go back to the binary example.

As is well-known, the price index number of Laspeyres, $L = \Sigma p_{i2} q_{i1}/\Sigma p_{i1} q_{i1}$, and that of Paasche, $P = \Sigma p_{i2} q_{i2}/\Sigma p_{i1} q_{i2}$, generally differ and there are many reasons to consider Fisher's indices, $F = (LP)^{\frac{1}{2}}$, a deliberate improvement, anyway theoretically. Of course, algebraically, the cause for L and P going astray is to be found in the artificial, hybrid sums $\Sigma p_{i2} q_{i1}$ and $\Sigma p_{i1} q_{i2}$. Now there is a simple way to adjust these sums by dividing them by the root

$$(\Sigma p_{i2} q_{i1} \Sigma p_{i1} q_{i2} / \Sigma p_{i1} q_{i1} \Sigma p_{i2} q_{i2})^{\frac{1}{2}} = (L/P)^{\frac{1}{2}} .$$

Indeed, changing $\Sigma p_{i2} q_{i1}$, $\Sigma p_{i1} q_{i2}$ into $\Sigma p_{i2} q_{i1}/(L/P)^{\frac{1}{2}} = S$, $\Sigma p_{i1} q_{i2}/(L/P)^{\frac{1}{2}} = T$, turns L and P into $S/\Sigma p_{i1} q_{i1} = F$ respectively $\Sigma p_{i2} q_{i2}/T = F$.

Thus, a means is found to improve the hybrid sums, by taking away internal algebraic effects (owing to intercorrelation of price and quantity patterns).

The same can be done with the artificial sums over the international price and quantity patterns. For example, $\Sigma p_{i0} q_{i1}$, the international value of the C_1-basket, is subject to internal algebraic effects that can be taken away by the root

$$r = (\Sigma p_{i0} q_{i1} \Sigma p_{i1} q_{i0} / \Sigma p_{i0} q_{i0} \Sigma p_{i1} q_{i1})^{\frac{1}{2}}$$ (N.B. both p_0 and q_0 are needed.)

Thus, $\Sigma p_{i0} q_{i1}/r = S$ is freed from the biasing effects. Of course, comparative National Accounts will be interested in such "real" value estimates. The difficulty, however, is that they are only approximately additive.

In fact, let the C_1-basket split up into two subaggregates (say private and other consumption): $q_1 = q_1' + q_1''$, with real value estimates $\Sigma' p_{i0} q_{i1}/r' = S'$ respectively $\Sigma'' p_{i0} q_{i1}/r'' = S''$ (primes indicate summing over subaggregates). Obviously, $S'r' + S''r'' = \Sigma p_{i0} q_{i1} = Sr$. Hence,

$$S' \cdot \frac{r'}{r} + S'' \cdot \frac{r''}{r} = S .$$

Thus, adding should be accompanied by correcting! Every artificial sum should have its accompanying correcting root (usually near to 1). Is not it a good statistical habit to provide figures with some indication of accuracy? Even more here, there is need for some indication of deviation. (See also [6].)

Of course, all this is a nuisance in practice. On the other hand, incidental balancing computations besides customary additivity practice may give some idea about the internal effects that work in algebraic sums.

It should constantly be realized that additivity is attended with systematic deviations, owing to intrinsic one-sidedness. It is an offspring of the price line only.

4. Appendix

1° Table of data.

Fictitious prices and quantities:

product	1		2		3		4		5		6	
	p	q	p	q	p	q	p	q	p	q	p	q
country A	11	55	20	45	10	100	17	55	10	140	8	120
B	15	175	14	275	10	500	21	200	9	675	9	575
C	88	26	112	19	140	17	200	10	96	12	216	10
D	15	32	24	24	18	24	63	6	24	11	42	14

2° Table of formulas.

Products $i = 1,\ldots,N$ $(N = 6)$, Countries $j = 1,\ldots,n$ $(n = 4)$.
Prices p_{ij}, Quantities q_{ij}, Values $v_{ij} = p_{ij}q_{ij}$.
When summing over products the i's are generally omitted.

Binary comparison: countries 1 and 2.

	Price index	Quantity index
Laspeyres	$P_L = \Sigma p_2 q_1/\Sigma v_1$	$Q_L = \Sigma p_1 q_2/\Sigma v_1$
Paasche	$P_P = \Sigma v_2/\Sigma p_1 q_2$	$Q_P = \Sigma v_2/\Sigma p_2 q_1$
Fisher	$P_F = (P_L P_P)^{\frac{1}{2}}$	$Q_F = (Q_L Q_P)^{\frac{1}{2}}$

Multilateral comparison: countries $j = 1,\ldots,n$.
General relationship of price indices P_j and quantity indices Q_j:

$P_j Q_j \sim \Sigma_i v_{ij}$ ($\sim$ means: is proportionate to).

Total basket $P_j \sim \Sigma p_j(q_1 + \ldots + q_n)$

Gerardi $Q_j \sim \Sigma q_j(p_1 p_2 \cdots p_n)^{1/n}$

weighted $Q_j \sim \Sigma q_j(p_1^{Q_1} \cdot p_2^{Q_2} \cdots p_n^{Q_n})^{1/\Sigma_j Q_j}$

Geary-Khamis $Q_j \sim \Sigma_i q_{ij} p_i$ with $p_i = (\Sigma_j v_{ij}/P_j)/(\Sigma_j q_{ij})$

de-weighted $Q_j \sim \Sigma_i q_{ij} p_i$ with $p_i = (\Sigma_j v_{ij}/P_j Q_j)/(\Sigma_j q_{ij}/Q_j)$

E.K.S. $P_j \sim (P_{j1} \cdot P_{j2} \cdots P_{jn})^{1/n}$ with P_{jk} = Fisher price index

weighted $P_j \sim (P_{j1}^{Q_1} \cdots P_{jn}^{Q_n})^{1/\Sigma_j Q_j}$

➡

Van Yzeren $P_j \sim \Sigma_k g_k(\Sigma p_j q_k)/Q_k$: heterogeneous

$Q_j \sim \Sigma_k g_k(\Sigma p_k q_j)/P_k$: homogeneous g_k: weighting factors

$P_j/Q_j \sim (\Sigma_k g_k(\Sigma p_j q_k)/Q_k)/(\Sigma_k g_k(\Sigma p_k q_j)/P_k)$: balanced

unweighted: $g_k = 1$, weighted: $g_k = Q_k$

5. References

[1] Hill, P., Multilateral measurements of purchasing power and real GDP, Office for official publications of the European Communities, 1982.

[2] Gerardi, D., Review of Income and Wealth 28, 1982, p. 381-406 and Special Conference of I.A.R.I.W., september 1982.

[3] Van Yzeren, J., Index Numbers for Binary and Multilateral Comparison, The Netherlands Central Bureau of Statistics, 1983.

[4] Van Yzeren, J., Three Methods of Comparing the Purchasing Power of Currencies, The Netherlands Bureau of Statistics, 1956.

[5] Drechsler, L. and Krzeczkowska, E., Purchasing Power Parities in International Comparisons: Quantity vs. Price Changes, Review of Income and Wealth 28, 1982, p. 253-259.

[6] Kurabayashi, Y. and Sakuma, I., Reorientation of a Matrix Consistent Method for the Multilateral International Comparisons of Real Product and Prices, Discussion Paper Series, No. 66, Institute of Economic Research, Hitotsubaski University, September 1982.

[7] Gerardi, D., Comparison in Real Values of the Aggregates of ESA, Eurostat, 1983.

Part III Efficiency

On the Definition of Efficiency Measures: A Note

Georg Bol
Institut für Statistik und Mathematische Wirtschaftstheorie
Universität Karlsruhe
D 7500 Karllsruhe

In the last years a growing number of articles have been concerned with the axiomatic approach to measures of technical efficiency. The main steps in this direction were taken by Färe and Lovell [3], Färe, Lovell and Zieschang [4], Zieschang [8] and Russell [5],[6] and [7] (see also Bol [1]). In these papers properties are formulated and discussed which are desirable for "good" efficiency measures. Moreover, measures from the literature are investigated for fulfillment of these properties and new measures are constructed. In the following we will give a short but general note on the definition of efficiency measures.

Usually technical efficiency measures depend on the combination (u,x) of an output vector $u \in \mathbb{R}^m_+$ and an input vector $x \in \mathbb{R}^n_+$ to be considered and the technology which underlies that production. This technology may be expressed by an input correspondence $L: \mathbb{R}^m_+ \rightarrowtail \mathbb{R}^n_+$ (also called upper level set mapping), assigning to any $u \in \mathbb{R}^m_+$ the set L(u) of input vectors that can produce the output vector $u \in \mathbb{R}^m_+$. Letting $\mathcal{L}$ be the class of all feasable input correspondences and

$$\Gamma_L = \{u \in \mathbb{R}^m_+ \mid L(u) \neq \emptyset \text{ and } o \notin L(u)\}$$

the set of admissible output vectors, an **input efficiency measure** is defined (compare e.g. Russell [5]) as a mapping

$$E: \Gamma_L \times \mathbb{R}^m_+ \times \mathcal{L} \longrightarrow (0,1] \cup \{+\infty\}$$

with certain properties (see f.e. Färe and Lovell [3] and Russell [6]). An extended discussion of such properties is given in [2] and [5]. Using a definition of this kind does not exclude the possibility that for different input correspondences different computing methods are applied. To be more precise: It cannot be excluded -except in the case that the axioms proposed imply some kind of uniqueness- that for a pair (u,x) in the same local but different global context we get different values of technical efficiency. To be formal: For two different input correspon-

Measurement in Economics
ed. by W. Eichhorn

dences L_1 and L_2 such that $L_1(u) = L_2(u)$ for the given u it does not necessarily follow that $E(u,x,L_1) = E(u,x,L_2)$. But that contradicts the reasoning behind efficiency measures. Efficiency measures give the possibility to compare the production methods applied by individual firms. These firms may produce the same outputs with identical inputs but also be from very different production sectors. An efficiency measure must therefore be constructed in such a way that it reflects the relation between what the firm in fact does, and what could be done in a technically optimal manner. Therefore differing values in the situation above contradict the philosophy of efficiency measures.

One possible way out is to require the following axiom:
For any two input correspondences L_1 and L_2 and any pair (u,x) such that $0 \notin L_1(u) = L_2(u) \neq \emptyset$, $E(u,x,L_1) = E(u,x,L_2)$ holds.
Another possibility is the following: as pointed out, an input efficiency measure relates a combination (u,x) to a somehow better combination (u,x^*) with $x^* \in L(u)$. So only the set L(u) - as a small facet of the whole correspondence L - is considered for the evaluation of (u,x). That leads to the following definition:
Let ℓs be the set of all possible level sets, i.e.

$$\ell s = \{S \subseteq \mathbb{R}^n_+ \mid \text{there exists } L \in \ell,\ u \in \mathbb{R}^m_+ \text{: } S = L(u)\}.$$

An input efficiency measure E is defined as a mapping

$$E\colon \mathbb{R}^n_+ \times \ell s \longrightarrow (0,1] \cup \{+\infty\}$$

satisfying a list of properties. In fact there is no problem in formulating all axioms known to the author from the literature in this context. Moreover some may be formulated (and investigated) in an easier way (compare f.e. Russell [7]). Furthermore this definition coincides also with the usual construction of efficiency measures, i.e. the optimization of a function $d(x,x')$ subject to $x' \in L(u)$ (see the socalled Debreu-Farrell-measure, the Färe-Lovell-measure, etc.). For these reasons, we prefer this definition for measures of technical efficiency of inputs.

References:

1. Bol, G. (1986), On technical efficiency measures: a remark, JET 38, 380 - 385.

2. Färe, R., S.Grosskopf and C.A.K.Lovell (1985), The measurement of efficiency of production, Kluwer-Nijhoff Publishing.

3. Färe, R. and C.A.K.Lovell (1978), Measering the technical efficieny of production, JET 19, 150 - 162.

4. Färe, R., C.A.K.Lovell and K.Zieschang (1982), Measering the technical efficiency of multiple output technologies, in "Quantitative Studies in Production and Prices" (W.Eichhorn et al., Eds.), Physika-Verlag.

5. Russell, R.R. (1985a), Measures of technical efficiency, JET 35, 109 - 126.

6. Russell, R.R., (1985b), The axiomatic approach to the measurement of technical efficiency, mimeo, New York.

7. Russell, R.R., (1986), Continuity of cost and distance functions, mimeo, New York.

8. Zieschang, K.D. (1984), An extended Farrell technical efficiency measure, JET 33, 337 -356.

Efficiency Gains from Addition of Technologies: A Nonparametric Approach

Rolf Färe*
Department of Economics
Southern Illinois University
Carbondale, IL 62901
U.S.A.

1. Introduction

The theory of contestable markets, see Baumol, Panzar and Willig (1982), applies notions like (dis-)economies of scope to investigate if combining two or more firms (plants) increases efficiency. Various parametric methods have been suggested to test or estimate (dis-)economies of scope as well as the more general notion of sub/super additivity of cost functions, see e.g., Baumol, Panzar and Willig (1982) or Evans and Heckman (1984).

The purpose of this paper is to extend the primal nonparametric method introduced by Färe (1986) for calculating efficiency gains (losses) realized from the addition of technologies. In particular, a dual nonparametric cost approach is introduced. This dual method, which requires data different than the primal formulation, is compared to the primal method.

2. The Primal and Dual Measures

Following Färe (1986), suppose a firm consists of K plants and that there are J firm observations. Denote for plant k the matrix of observed inputs by X^k and the matrix of observed outputs by U^k. Then X^k is of order (J×n), J observations and n inputs and U^k is of order (J×m), J observations and m outputs.

If each plant's technology is a convex set, an inner approximation, see Afriat [1972] or Diewert and Parkan [1983], to the input requirement set for plant k is[1]

$$L(u^k) = \{x: zU^k \geqq u^k,\ zX^k \leqq x,\ z \in R^J_+,\ \sum_{j=1}^{J} z_j = 1\},\ k = 1, \ldots, K, \tag{2.1}$$

where the vector z denote the intensity level at which each observation is run. From (2.1) the sum of the input requirement sets $L(u^k)$ is defined as

$$\sum_{k=1}^{K} L(u^k) = \{x: z^kU^k \geqq u^k,\ \sum_{k=1}^{K} z^kX^k \leqq x,\ z^k \in R^J_+,\ \sum_{j=1}^{J} z^k_j = 1,\ k = 1, \ldots, K\}. \tag{2.2}$$

*I would like to thank two anonymous referees for their comments.

[1]The input requirement set $L(u) = \{\text{inputs } x \in R^n_+ \text{ capable of producing output } u \in R^m_+\}$. The mapping $L: R^m_+ \to L(u) \subseteqq R^n_+$ is called the input correspondence.

Measurement in Economics
ed. by W. Eichhorn

The input-based Farrell efficiency measure associated with the sum technology (2.2) can be calculated as the solution to the L.P. problem

$$F_i^s(u^1, \ldots, u^K, x) = \min \lambda \tag{2.3}$$

$$\text{s.t.} \quad \lambda x \geqq \sum_{k=1}^{K} z^k X^k,$$

$$z^k U^k \geqq u^k, \; k = 1, \ldots, K,$$

$$z^k \in R_+^J, \; \sum_{j=1}^{J} z_j^k = 1.$$

To compute the gains from combining the K plants, we also need to calculate the input-based Farrell efficiency measure for the combined technology. To that end, we define the combined firm as[2]

$$L(\sum_{k=1}^{K} u^k) = \{x: \sum_{k=1}^{K} zU^k \geqq \sum_{k=1}^{K} u^k, \; \sum_{k=1}^{K} zX^k \leqq x, \; z \in R_+^J, \; \sum_{j=1}^{J} z_j = 1\}. \tag{2.4}$$

The input-based Farrell efficiency measure associated with the combined technology (2.4) can be calculated as the solution to the L.P. problem

$$F_i^c(\sum_{k=1}^{K} u^k, x) = \min \lambda \tag{2.5}$$

$$\text{s.t.} \quad \lambda x \geqq \sum_{k=1}^{K} zX^k,$$

$$\sum_{k=1}^{K} zU^k \geqq \sum_{k=1}^{K} u^k,$$

$$z \in R_+^J, \; \sum_{j=1}^{J} z_j = 1,$$

The gains from combining K plants is obtained as

$$G_i(u,x) = F_i^s(u^1, \ldots, u^K, x)/F_i^c(\sum_{k=1}^{K} u^k, x), \tag{2.6}$$

where u and x are formed by the observations.

In the primal approach discussed above, observations on inputs and outputs were used to compute efficiency gains. For the dual cost approach, suppose once more that U^k, $k = 1, \ldots, K$ are given. Moreover, assume that for each plant, J observation of total costs are given. Denote by C^k, $k = 1, \ldots, K$, the vector of these costs. For plant k, form the cost technology as

$$T_k = \{(c,u): zU^k \geqq u, \; zC^k \leqq c, \; z \in R_+^J, \; \sum_{j=1}^{J} z_j = 1\}, \; k = 1, \ldots, K. \tag{2.7}$$

---

[2] An alternative, more general, way of forming the combined technology is to sum each plant observation (j,k) to each observation of the other plants and then form the inner approximation.

The cost-based Farrell efficiency measure associated with the cost sum technology, formed by (2.7), can be calculated as the solution to the L.P. problem

$$F_c^s(u^1, \ldots, u^K, c) = \min \lambda \tag{2.8}$$

$$\text{s.t.} \quad \lambda c \geqq \sum_{k=1}^{K} z^k C^k,$$

$$z^k U^k \geqq u^k, \ k = 1, \ldots, K,$$

$$z^k \in R_+^J, \ \sum_{j=1}^{J} z_j^k = 1.$$

Since C^k is a vector, $z^k C^k$ is a scalar, thus $F_c^s(u^1, \ldots, u^K, c)$ may also be calculated as follows. First solve

$$\hat{F}_c^s(u^1, \ldots, u^K) = \min \sum_{k=1}^{K} z^k C^k \tag{2.9}$$

$$\text{s.t.} \quad z^k U^k \geqq u^k, \ k = 1, \ldots, K,$$

$$z^k \in R_+^J, \ \sum_{j=1}^{J} z^k = 1,$$

then compute $F_c^s(u^1, \ldots, u^K, c) = \hat{F}_c^s(u^1, \ldots, u^K)/c$, where $\hat{F}_c^s(u^1, \ldots, u^K)$ is the potential minimum cost.

In order to compute the dual cost gains from combining K plants, we also need to compute the cost-based Farrell efficiency measure for the combined cost technology. This measure can be obtained as the solution to the L.P. problem

$$F_c^c(\sum_{k=1}^{K} u^k, c) = \min \lambda \tag{2.10}$$

$$\text{s.t.} \quad \lambda c \geqq \sum_{k=1}^{K} z C^k,$$

$$\sum_{k=1}^{K} z U^k \geqq \sum_{k=1}^{K} u^k,$$

$$z \in R_+^J, \ \sum_{j=1}^{J} z_j = 1,$$

We note that (2.10) may like (2.8) be computed in two steps.

Given $F_c^s(u^1, \ldots, u^K, c)$ and $F_c^c(\sum_{k=1}^{K} u^k, c)$, the dual cost gains from combining K plants is obtained as

$$G_c(u,c) = F_c^s(u^1, \ldots, u^K, c)/F_c^c(\sum_{k=1}^{K} u^k, c), \tag{2.11}$$

where u and c are formed by the observations.

3. Comparison of the Calculations

In order to derive conditions under which the primal and dual measures are equal, compute

$$C^c\left(\sum_{k=1}^{K} u^k, p\right) = \min px \tag{3.1}$$

$$\text{s.t.} \quad x \geq \sum_{k=1}^{K} zX^k,$$

$$\sum_{k=1}^{K} zU^k \geq \sum_{k=1}^{K} u^k,$$

$$z \in R_+^J, \quad \sum_{j=1}^{J} z_j = 1,$$

i.e., the minimal cost relative to the reference technology (2.4). Prices are taken as given and since X^k is given, observed total cost $c = px$ is known. Following Farrell, the overall measure of efficiency is $C^c(\sum_{k=1}^{K} u^k, p)/px$. This measure is decomposed into overall technical efficiency $TE^c = F_i^c(\sum_{k=1}^{K} u^k, x)$ and allocative efficiency (AE^c), thus

$$C^c\left(\sum_{k=1}^{K} u^k, p\right) = AE^c \cdot F_i^c\left(\sum_{k=1}^{K} u^k, x\right). \tag{3.2}$$

Next consider the cost minimization problem relative to the sum technology.

$$C^s(u^1, \ldots, u^K, p) = \min px \tag{3.3}$$

$$\text{s.t.} \quad x \geq \sum_{k=1}^{K} z^k X^k,$$

$$z^k U^k \geq u^k, \; k = 1, \ldots, K,$$

$$z^k \in R_+^J, \quad \sum_{j=1}^{J} z_j^k = 1.$$

Given the cost $C^s(u^1, \ldots, u^K, p)$ and observed cost c, the Farrell decomposition for $C^s(u^1, \ldots, u^K, p)/c$ is

$$C^s(u^1, \ldots, u^K, p)/c = AE^s \cdot F_i^s(u^1, \ldots, u^K, x). \tag{3.4}$$

From the quotient of (3.2) and (3.4) we obtain

$$\frac{C^s(u^1, \ldots, u^K, p)}{C^c(\sum_{k=1}^{K} u^k, p)} = \frac{AE^s}{AE^c} \cdot \frac{F_i^s(u^1, \ldots, u^K, x)}{F_i^c(\sum_{k=1}^{K} u^k, x)}, \tag{3.5}$$

Thus if $AE^c = AE^s$, $G_i(u,x) = C^s(u^1, \ldots, u^K, p)/C^c(\sum_{k=1}^{K} u^k, p)$.

To derive the relationship between $G_i(u,x)$ and $G_c(u,c)$, consider problem (3.3). If each plant faces the same input prices, from the inequality $x \geqq \sum_{k=1}^{K} z^k X^k$, by multiplying with p and summing over inputs, the following problem is derived

$$C^s(u^1, \ldots, u^K, p) = \min px \tag{3.6}$$

$$\text{s.t.} \quad px \geqq \sum_{k=1}^{K} z^k C^k$$

$$z^k U^k \geqq u^k, \; k = 1, \ldots, K,$$

$$z^k \in R^J_+, \; \sum_{j=1}^{J} z^k_j = 1,$$

or equivalently

$$C^s(u^1, \ldots, u^k, p) = \min \sum_{k=1}^{K} z^k C^k \tag{3.7}$$

$$\text{s.t.} \quad z^k U^k \geqq u^k, \; k = 1, \ldots, K,$$

$$z^k \in R^J_+, \; \sum_{j=1}^{J} z^k_j = 1.$$

It now follows from (3.7) and (2.9) that

$$C^s(u^1, \ldots, u^K, p) = \hat{F}^s_c(u^1, \ldots, u^K). \tag{3.8}$$

Repeating the last procedure for problem (3.1) it follows that

$$C^c(\sum_{k=1}^{K} u^k, p) = \hat{F}^c_c(\sum_{k=1}^{K} u^k), \tag{3.9}$$

where

$$\hat{F}^c_c(\sum_{k=1}^{K} u^k) = \min \sum_{k=1}^{K} zC^k$$

$$\text{s.t.} \quad \sum_{k=1}^{K} zU^k \geqq \sum_{k=1}^{K} u^k,$$

$$z \in R^J_+, \; \sum_{j=1}^{J} z_j = 1$$

and

$$F^c_c(\sum_{k=1}^{K} u^k, c) = \hat{F}^c_c(\sum_{k=1}^{K} u^k)/c. \tag{3.10}$$

If $AE^c = AE^s$,

$$G_i(u,x) = C^s(u^1, \ldots, u^K, p)/C^c(\sum_{k=1}^{K} u^k, p),$$

and it follows from (3.8) and (3.9) that

$$G_i(u,x) = \frac{\hat{F}_c^s(u^1, \ldots, u^K) \cdot c}{\hat{F}_c^c(\sum_{k=1}^{K} u^k) \cdot c} = \frac{F_c^s(u^1, \ldots, u^K, c)}{F_c^c(\sum_{k=1}^{K} u^k, c)} = G_c(u,c), \text{ i.e.,}$$

if each plant faces the same input prices and $AE^c = AE^s$, the primal and dual gain measures are equal.

References

Afriat, S.N., "Efficiency Estimation of Production Functions," International Economic Review, 1972, 13, 568-598.

Baumol, W., Panzar, J. and Willig, R., Contestable Markets and the Theory of Industry Structure, San Diego: Harcourt, Brace, Jovanovich, 1982.

Diewert, W.E., "Duality Approaches in Microeconomic Theory," in The Handbook of Mathematical Economics, Vol. 2, eds. Arrow, K. and Intriligator, M. Amsterdam: North-Holland Publishing Co., 1982.

Diewert, W.E. and Parkan, C., "Linear Programming Tests of Regularity Conditions for Production Functions," in Quantitative Studies on Production and Prices, eds. Eichhorn, W., Henn, R., Neumann, K. and Shephard, R.W. Würzburg: Physica-Verlag, 1983.

Evans, D. and Heckman, J., "A Test for Subadditivity of the Cost Function, an Application to the Bell System," American Economic Review, September 1984, 74, 615-623.

Färe, R., "Addition and Efficiency," The Quarterly Journal of Economics, November 1986, 861-865.

Färe, R., Grosskopf, S. and Lovell, C.A.K., The Measurement of Efficiency of Production, Boston: Kluwer-Nijhoff Publishing, 1985.

Efficiency Measures for Multiplant Firms with Limited Data

Rolf Färe and Daniel Primont
Department of Economics
Southern Illinois University
Carbondale, IL 62901
U.S.A.

0. Introduction and Summary

Measures of technical efficiency typically require data on outputs and inputs measured in physical units. However, in many applications such data may be difficult or costly to obtain. Examples of this problem include:

(a) Firms which only report financial data, i.e., outputs and inputs measured in money units.

(b) Multiproduct firms which only report total revenue for an extensive product line.

(c) Firms which only report total cost.

In this paper we suggest some ways by which these data limitations may be overcome. Attention is focussed on output-based efficiency measures of the type introduced by Farrell [1957]. In section 1 we define these measures for both single plant and multiplant firms. The problem in example (a) is then addressed. If the money revenue of each output and the money cost of each input is given we show that the technical efficiency measures can be exactly computed as long as prices don't vary over observations.

In section 2 we examine the problem in example (b). We assume that total revenue and the physical quantity of each input is given for each observation. We show that the technical efficiency measures could be exactly computed if the observed output is allocatively efficient. In section 3 it is assumed that the physical quantity of each output and the total cost is given for each observation, as in example (c). For this case it is not possible, in general, to exactly compute the technical efficiency measures. We can, however, provide upper and lower bounds. In section 4 it is assumed that only total revenue and total cost are known, i.e., examples (b) and (c) are combined. Section 5 concludes.

1. Efficiency Measures for Multiplant Firms

Suppose, initially, that each firm owns just one plant and that the available data is a set of observations (u_i, x_i), $i = 1, \ldots, k$, for k single plant firms where u_i is a vector of m outputs and x_i is a vector of n inputs. Let

Measurement in Economics
ed. by W. Eichhorn

$$M = \begin{bmatrix} u_1 \\ u_2 \\ \cdot \\ \cdot \\ \cdot \\ u_k \end{bmatrix} = \begin{bmatrix} u_{11} & u_{12} & \cdots & u_{1m} \\ \cdot & & & \\ \cdot & & & \\ \cdot & & & \\ \cdot & & & \\ u_{k1} & u_{k2} & \cdots & u_{km} \end{bmatrix}$$

be the $(k \times m)$ matrix of observed outputs and let

$$N = \begin{bmatrix} x_1 \\ x_2 \\ \cdot \\ \cdot \\ \cdot \\ x_k \end{bmatrix} = \begin{bmatrix} x_{11} & x_{12} & \cdots & x_{1n} \\ \cdot & & & \\ \cdot & & & \\ \cdot & & & \\ \cdot & & & \\ x_{k1} & x_{k2} & \cdots & x_{kn} \end{bmatrix}$$

be the $(k \times n)$ matrix of observed inputs.

Following Afriat [1972], let T^A be the free-disposal convex hull of the k output-input data points. We shall occasionally refer to T^A as the Afriat technology. Interpreting T^A as the reference technology, the efficiency of each firm (which, in this case, is synonymous with each plant) is measured by comparing the firm's productivity to T^A. Specifically, for firm i, Farrell's [1957] output-based efficiency measure is the reciprocal of the real number $\overset{*}{\theta}$ for which $(\overset{*}{\theta} u_i, x_i)$ is on the frontier of T^A. Though $\overset{*}{\theta}$ depends on u_i, x_i, M, and N, for brevity we will write $\overset{*}{\theta} = A(u_i, x_i)$. This efficiency measure is the optimal value of the linear programming problem:

$$A(u_i, x_i) := \max_{(\theta, z)} \theta \qquad (1.1)$$

$$\text{s.t.} \quad \theta u_i \leq zM,$$

$$zN \leq x_i,$$

$$z \in Z_A,$$

where $z = (z_1, z_2, \ldots, z_k)$ is a $(1 \times k)$ row vector of intensity levels and

$$Z_A = \{z \mid \sum_{j=1}^{k} z_j = 1, \ z_j \geq 0, \ j = 1, \ldots, k\}.$$

A feasible solution to (1.1) is $\theta = 1$, $z_i = 1$, $z_j = 0$, $j \neq i$. Thus, $A(u_i, x_i) \geq 1$. Firm i is efficient relative to T^A if $A(u_i, x_i) = 1$. Otherwise, it is inefficient. Let the vector $A(u_i, x_i)u_i$ be interpreted as a potential output vector for firm i relative to T^A. Then

$$A(u_i, x_i) = \frac{\| A(u_i, x_i) u_i \|}{\| u_i \|},$$

i.e., $A(u_i, x_i)$ is the ratio of Euclidean norms of the potential to the actual output vector. Farrell's output based efficiency measure is given by

$$PE(u_i, x_i) = \frac{1}{A(u_i, x_i)} .$$

Now consider the case in which firms may own more than one plant. Reinterpret the data (u_i, x_i), $i = 1, \ldots, k$ as observations of k plants. Let K be the set of plants, i.e., $K = \{1, 2, \ldots, k\}$. A partition of K is $\hat{K} = \{K^1, \ldots, K^f, \ldots, K^g\}$, where $G = \{1, 2, \ldots, f, \ldots, g\}$ is the set of firms. Thus there are g multiplant firms and we write $i \in K^f$ if firm f owns plant i.

The construction of the reference technology for efficient, multiplant firms proceeds in two steps. First, an efficient technology for each firm is constructed using each firm's plant data. To do this we adopt the procedure discussed by Koopmans [1977]. For firm f, let $\overline{K}^f$ be any nonempty subset of K^f and let $\alpha(\overline{K}^f)$ be the sum

$$\alpha(\overline{K}^f) = \sum_{i \in \overline{K}^f} (u_i, x_i).$$

Let T_f^K be the free disposal convex hull of the set of vectors $\alpha(\overline{K}^f)$ for all $\overline{K}^f \subseteq K^f$. We shall occasionally refer to T_f^K as the <u>Koopmans technology</u> for firm f.

Efficient points of T_f^K include the points $(K_f(u_i, x_i)u_i, x_i)$, $i \in K^f$, where

$$K_f(u_i, x_i) = \max_{(\theta, z^f)} \theta \tag{1.2}$$

$$\text{s.t.} \quad \theta u_i \leqq z^f M^f$$

$$z^f N^f \leqq x_i$$

$$0 \leqq z_j \leqq 1, \; z_j \geqq 0, \; j \in K^f$$

where $z^f = (z_i \colon i \in K^f)$, $M^f = (u_i \colon i \in K^f)$, and $N^f = (x_i \colon i \in K^f)$.

In the second step, an Afriat technology is constructed from the efficient points of each T_f^K, $f \in G$. As an Afriat technology for "Koopmans-efficient" firms we denote it by T^{AK} and refer to it as the Afriat-Koopmans technology.

In practice, efficient points of T^{AK} can be found by solving a single linear programming problem. Define $AK(u_i, x_i)$ by:

$$AK(u_i, x_i) = \max_{(\theta, z)} \theta \tag{1.3}$$

$$\text{s.t.} \quad \theta u_i \leqq zM$$

$$zN \leqq x_i$$

$$z \in Z_{AK}$$

where

$$Z_{AK} = \{z \,|\, 0 \leqq z_j \leqq z^f, \; j \in K^f, \; \sum_{f \in G} z^f = 1, \; z^f \geqq 0, \; f \in G\}$$

Then efficient points of T^{AK} include points $(AK(u_i, x_i)u_i, x_i)$, $i = 1, \ldots, k$.

A feasible solution to (3) is $\theta = 1$, $z_i = 1$, $z_j = 0$, $j \neq i$. Thus $AK(u_i, x_i) \geqq 1$. If (u_i, x_i) is on the efficient frontier of T^{AK} then $AK(u_i, x_i) = 1$. Interpreting $AK(u_i, x_i)u_i$ as a potential output vector for plant i relative to T^{AK}, we see that

$$AK(u_i, x_i) = \frac{\| AK(u_i, x_i)u_i \|}{\| u_i \|} .$$

At this point several ways of measuring efficiency relative to T^{AK} could be suggested (see Färe and Primont [1984]). One such measure would compare (u_i, x_i) to efficient points of T^{AK} and is given by

$$MPE(u_i, x_i) = \frac{1}{AK(u_i, x_i)} .$$

This measure can be decomposed multiplicatively. Doing so facilitates its interpretation. Let

$$PF(u_i, x_i) = \frac{A(u_i, x_i)}{AK(u_i, x_i)} . \tag{1.4}$$

Then,

$$MPE(u_i, x_i) = PE(u_i, x_i) \cdot PF(u_i, x_i),$$

recalling that $PE(u_i, x_i) = 1/A(u_i, x_i)$. The first term in the product measures the efficiency of a plant relative to T^A. The second term measures the efficiency of an Afriat-efficient plant realtive to T^{AK}. Multiplant efficiency, $MPE(u_i, x_i)$, is the product of the two and equals one only if both terms in the product equal one.

In general, all of the above measures require that the output and input data be given in physical units. This is a potential drawback if the data is only available in money units and individual prices are unknown. However, if it can be assumed that the vector of output and input prices is the same for each of the k observations then it makes no difference whether the data is measured in physical units or in money units. In the remainder of this section we formally state and demonstrate this idea.

Let q be the (m × 1) column vector of output prices and let p be the (n × 1) column vector of input prices. First consider the constraint, $\theta u_i \leq zM$. Writing out these m inequalities,

$$\theta[u_{11}, \ldots, u_{1m}] \leq [z_1, \ldots, z_k] \begin{bmatrix} u_{11} & \cdots & u_{1m} \\ \cdot & & \\ \cdot & & \\ \cdot & & \\ u_{k1} & & u_{km} \end{bmatrix} .$$

Multiply the jth inequality by q_j, the price of output j, for j = 1, ..., m, and let $r_{ij} = u_{ij}q_j$. Then

$$\theta[r_{i1}, \ldots, r_{im}] \leqq [z_1, \ldots, z_k] \begin{bmatrix} r_{11} & \cdots & r_{1m} \\ \cdot & & \\ \cdot & & \\ \cdot & & \\ r_{k1} & \cdots & r_{km} \end{bmatrix}$$

or

$$\theta r_i \leqq zR$$

where $r_i = [r_{i1}, \ldots, r_{im}]$ and R is the $(k \times m)$ matrix of the r_{ij}'s.

Similarly, let $c_{ij} = x_{ij}p_j$, $i = 1, \ldots, k$, $j = 1, \ldots, n$, where p_j is the price of input j, let $c_i = [c_{i1}, \ldots, c_{in}]$, and let C be the $(k \times n)$ matrix of the c_{ij}'s. Then the constraint $zN \leqq x_i$ is equivalent to

$$zC \leqq c_i.$$

Thus, for example, $A(u_i, x_i)$, defined by (1.1), may also be computed by:

$$A(u_i, x_i) = \max_{(\theta,z)} \theta$$

$$\text{s.t.} \quad \theta r_i \leqq zR$$

$$zC \leqq c_i$$

$$z \in Z_A.$$

A similar result holds for $AK(u_i, x_i)$.

2. Revenue-based Measures with Revenue-input Data

In this section the available data consists of k observations of total revenue, R_i, and the input vector, x_i. Let R be a $(k \times 1)$ vector of revenues. All previous notation is retained.

An efficiency measure which is "revenue-based" might be found by first solving:

$$A_R(R_i, x_i) = \max_{(\theta,z)} \theta \qquad (2.1)$$

$$\text{s.t.} \quad \theta R_i \leqq zR,$$

$$zN \leqq x_i,$$

$$z \in Z_A.$$

Since R_i and zR are scalars, (2.1) may be solved in two steps.

$$\hat{A}_R(x_i) = \max_{z} zR \qquad (2.1a)$$

$$\text{s.t.} \; zN \leqq x_i,$$

$$z \in Z_A.$$

Then,

$$A_R(R_i, x_i) = \hat{A}_R(x_i)/R_i \qquad (2.1b).$$

In the multiplant case the analogous problem is given by:

$$AK_R(R_i, x_i) = \max_{(\theta,z)} \theta \qquad (2.2)$$

$$\text{s.t.} \quad \theta R_i \leq zR, \quad zN \leq x_i, \quad z \in Z_{AK}.$$

This may also be solved in two steps, viz.,

$$\hat{AK}_R(x_i) = \max zR \tag{2.2a}$$

$$\text{s.t.} \quad zN \leq x_i, \quad z \in Z_{AK}.$$

Then,

$$AK_R(R_i, x_i) = \hat{AK}_R(x_i)/R_i \tag{2.2b}.$$

The revenue based version of $PF(u_i, x_i)$ is given by:

$$PF_R(R_i, x_i) = \frac{A_R(R_i, x_i)}{AK_R(R_i, x_i)} = \frac{\hat{A}_R(x_i)}{\hat{AK}_R(x_i)} \tag{2.3}$$

where the second equality is a consequence of (2.1b) and (2.2b).

In certain cases, all of the above revenue-based measures are equal to their corresponding output-based measures. Let q be the (k × 1) vector of the m output prices. If an observed output vector, u_i, is collinear with an output vector that maximizes revenue, $R_i = u_i q$, over all feasible output vectors given the observed input vector, x_i, then the revenue- and output-based measures coincide.

To develop this point consider:

$$RA(q, x_i) = \max_{(u,z)} uq \tag{2.4}$$

$$\text{s.t.} \quad u \leq zM, \quad zN \leq x_i, \quad z \in Z_A.$$

<u>Lemma 2.1</u>: If $q >> 0$ then

$$RA(q, x_i) = \hat{A}_R(x_i). \tag{2.5}$$

<u>Proof</u>: The solution, $(\overset{*}{u}, \overset{*}{z})$, to (2.4) must satisfy the equation system $\overset{*}{u} = \overset{*}{z}M$ since otherwise if $\overset{*}{u}_j < \overset{*}{z}M_{\cdot j}$ then for some $\bar{u}_j > \overset{*}{u}_j$ the objective function can be increased without violating the constraints. ($M_{\cdot j}$ is column j of M.) Thus

$$RA(q, x_i) = \max_z zMq,$$

$$\text{s.t.} \quad zN \leq x_i, \quad z \in Z_A.$$

Since $Mq = R$ we have:

$$RA(q, x_i) = \max_z zR$$

$$\text{s.t.} \quad zN \leq x_i, \quad z \in Z_A.$$

Thus $RA(q, x_i) = \hat{A}_R(x_i)$. Q.E.D.

In the multiplant case the revenue maximization problem becomes:

$$RAK(q, x_i) = \max_{(u,z)} uq \tag{2.6}$$

s.t. $u \leq zM$,

$zN \leq x_i$,

$z \in Z_{AK}$.

Lemma 2.2: If $q >> 0$ then

$$RAK(q,x_i) = \hat{AK}_R(x_i) \tag{2.7}$$

Proof: Same as the proof of Lemma 2.1. Q.E.D.

Let $RAM(q, x_i)$ be the set of output vectors which are solutions to (2.4) and let $RAKM(q, x_i)$ be the set of output vectors which are solutions to (2.6). Following Färe, Grosskopf, and Lovell [1985], an output vector u is allocatively efficient relative to T^A for a price vector q if there exists a scalar $\theta \geq 1$ such that $\theta u \in RAM(q, x_i)$. Similarly, an output vector u is allocatively efficient relative to T^{AK} for a price vector q if there exists a scalar $\theta \geq 1$ such that $\theta u \in RAKM(q, x_i)$.

Theorem 2.1: In general

(a) $A_R(R_i, x_i) \geq A(u_i, x_i) \geq 1$.

(b) $A_R(R_i, x_i) = A(u_i, x_i)$ if and only if u_i is allocatively efficient relative to T^A.

(c) $AK_R(R_i, x_i) \geq AK(u_i, x_i) \geq 1$.

(d) $AK_R(R_i, x_i) = AK(u_i, x_i)$ if and only if u_i is allocatively efficient relative to T^{AK}.

Proof: We will prove (a) and (b) only since the proofs of (c) and (d) are essentially the same. The feasible sets of (1.1) and (2.1) are identical except that in (1.1) we have $\theta u_i \leq zM$ and in (2.1) we have $\theta R_i \leq zR$. If (θ,z) satisfy the former constraint then $\theta u_i \leq zM \Rightarrow \theta u_i q \leq zMq \Rightarrow \theta R_i \leq zR$, i.e., (θ, z) satisfy the latter constraint. Thus $A_R(R_i, x_i) \geq A(u_i, x_i)$. Moreover, $A(u_i, x_i) \geq 1$ (see section 1). This establishes (a).

Assume now that u_i is allocatively efficient relative to T^A. Then there is a scalar $\theta \geq 1$ such that $\theta u_i \in RAM(q, x_i)$ and hence $RA(q, x_i) = \theta u_i q$. By Lemma 2.1, $RA(q, x_i) = \hat{A}_R(x_i)$ and thus, by (2.1b), $RA(q, x_i) = A_R(R_i, x_i)R_i = A_R(R_i, x_i)u_i q$. Therefore, $A_R(R_i, x_i) = \theta$ which implies that $A_R(R_i, x_i)u_i \in RAM(q, x_i)$. Thus $A_R(R_i, x_i)u_i$ is feasible in (2.4), i.e.,

$$A_R(R_i, x_i)u_i \leq \overset{*}{z}M,$$

$$\overset{*}{z}N \leq x_i,$$

$$\overset{*}{z} \in Z_A.$$

for some $\overset{*}{z}$. Hence $(A_R(R_i, x_i), \overset{*}{z})$ is feasible in (1.1) implying that $A(u_i, x_i) \geq A_R(R_i, x_i)$. This last inequality and (a) imply that $A(u_i, x_i) = A_R(R_i, x_i)$.

Conversely, suppose $A(u_i, x_i) = A_R(R_i, x_i)$. Let $(A(u_i, x_i), \overset{*}{z})$ be the optimal solution to (1.1). To be optimal it must be feasible and thus $A(u_i, x_i)u_i \leq \overset{*}{z}M$. This implies that $(A(u_i, x_i)u_i, \overset{*}{z})$ is feasible in (2.4). Moreover it is optimal since:

$$A(u_i, x_i)u_i q_i = A_R(u_i, x_i)u_i q \quad \text{(by assumption)}$$
$$= A_R(u_i, x_i)R_i \quad \text{(by definition)}$$
$$= \hat{A}_R(x_i) \quad \text{(by (2.1b))}$$
$$= RA(q, x_i). \quad \text{(by Lemma 2.1)}$$

Hence $A(u_i, x_i)u_i \in RAM(q, x_i)$ implying that u_i is allocatively efficient.

3. Output-based Measures with Output-cost Data

In this section the available data consists of k observations of the output vector, u_i, and total cost, C_i. Let p be the column vector of input prices. Then $C_i = x_i p = \sum_{j=1}^{n} x_{ij} p_j$. The column vector of total cost is $C = Np$.

An output-based measure using output-cost data in the single plant case may be found by first solving:

$$A_C(u_i, C_i) = \max_{(\theta, z)} \theta \tag{3.1}$$
$$\text{s.t.} \quad \theta u_i \leqq zM,$$
$$zC \leqq C_i$$
$$z \in Z_A.$$

For the multiplant case:

$$AK_C(u_i, C_i) = \max_{(\theta, z)} \theta \tag{3.2}$$
$$\text{s.t.} \quad \theta u_i \leqq M,$$
$$zC \leqq C_i,$$
$$z \in Z_{AK}.$$

Theorem 3.1: If $p >> 0$ then

(a) $A_C(u_i, C_i) \geqq A(u_i, x_i) \geqq 1$.

(b) $AK_C(u_i, C_i) \geqq AK(u_i, x_i) \geqq 1$.

Proof: The only difference between (1.1) and (3.1) is that the constraint $zN \leqq x_i$ in (1.1) is replaced $zC \leqq C_i$ in (3.1). If z is feasible in (1.1) then

$$zN \leqq x_i \Rightarrow zNp \leqq x_i p \quad \text{for } p >> 0$$
$$\Rightarrow zC \leqq C_i,$$

i.e., z is feasible in (3.1). However, the converse is not generally true. Hence $A_C(u_i, C_i) \geqq A(u_i, x_i)$. The fact that $A(u_i, x_i) \geqq 1$ was demonstrated in section 1. By comparing (1.3) and (3.2) the above argument also establishes (b). Q.E.D.

4. Revenue-based Measures with Revenue-cost Data

In this section the available data consists of k observations of total revenue, R_i, and total cost, C_i. As defined in sections 2 and 3, R and C are $(k \times 1)$ vectors of revenue and cost, respectively.

In the single plant case, a revenue-based measure may be found by solving:

$$A_{RC}(R_i, C_i) = \max_{(\theta,z)} \theta \qquad (4.1)$$

$$\text{s.t.} \quad \theta R_i \leqq zR,$$

$$zC \leqq C_i,$$

$$z \in Z_A.$$

For the multiplant case:

$$AK_{RC}(R_i, C_i) = \max_{(\theta,z)} \theta \qquad (4.2)$$

$$\text{s.t.} \quad \theta R_i \leqq zR,$$

$$zC \leqq C_i,$$

$$z \in Z_{AK}.$$

Theorem 4.1: If $q \gg 0$ and $p \gg 0$ then

(a) $A_{RC}(R_i, C_i) \geqq \max\{A_R(R_i, x_i), A_C(u_i, C_i)\}$
$\geqq A(u_i, x_i)$
$\geqq 1$

(b) $AK_{RC}(R_i, C_i) \geqq \max\{AK_R(R_i, x_i), AK_C(u_i, C_i)\}$
$\geqq AK(u_i, x_i)$
$\geqq 1$

Proof: To prove (a), note that the feasible set of (4.1) is no smaller than either the feasible set of (2.1) or (3.1). Thus the optimal value of (4.1) must be at least as large as the optimal value of either (2.1) or (3.1). This establishes the first inequality of (a). The other two inequalities in (a) are simply restatements of Theorem 2.1, (a) and (c), and Theorem 3.1 (a).

The proof of (b) is analogous to that of (a). Q.E.D.

5. Conclusion

More often than not, the data available to the economist does not correspond to the disaggregated input and output quantities called for in the theory. When data is, to some extent, aggregated to dollar values of groups of inputs or outputs (a likely case) our results indicate that an output-based efficiency measure computed from these aggregates will overestimate the theoretical measure of inefficiency and thus underestimate the theoretical measure of efficiency.

References

Afriat, S. 1972. Efficiency estimation of production functions. International Economic Review 13:568-598.

Färe, R., S. Grosskopf, and K. Lovell 1985. The Measurement of Efficiency of Production. Boston: Kluwer-Nijhof.

Färe, R. and D. Primont 1984. Efficiency measures for multiplant firms. Operations Research Letters 3:257-260.

Farrell, M. 1957. The measurement of productive efficiency. Journal of the Royal Statistical Society Series A General 120:253-281.

Koopmans, T. 1977. Examples of production relations based on microdata. in G.C. Harcourt, ed., The Microeconomics Foundation of Macroeconomics, London, 144-171.

Testing for Aggregation Bias in Efficiency Measurement[1]

C. A. Knox Lovell
Univ. of North Carolina
Chapel Hill, NC,
27514, USA

Asani Sarkar
Univ. of Pennsylvania
Philadelphia, PA,
19104, USA

Robin Sickles
Rice Univ.
Houston, TX,
77251, USA

1. Introduction

It is common practice to aggregate inputs prior to estimating the structure of production technology. It is of interest, therefore to have some idea of the impact of such aggregation on the resulting inferences concerning the structure of production technology. This information is of interest in its own right, and has been the subject of considerable research. However a knowledge of the effect of input aggregation on inferences concerning the structure of technology is valuable for another reason: since productive efficiency is measured relative to an estimated technology, input aggregation also influences one's inferences concerning the structure of productive efficiency.

There are two conditions under which input aggregation has no effect on efficiency measurement. If the price proportionality conditions of the Hicks aggregation theorem are satisfied, (see Diewert (1980)), then input aggregation has no effect on conventional measures of efficiency. Alternatively, as Färe and Lovell (1987) show, if production technology is homothetically separable, then again input aggregation has no effect on efficiency measurement. The purpose of this paper is to examine the Färe-Lovell result empirically.

The Färe-Lovell result is a straightforward extension of a result of Blackorby, Primont and Russell (1978). They were not concerned with efficiency measurement, but rather with alternative characterizations of a separable technology. They established an equivalence among a (well-behaved) homothetically separable production function, a separable cost function, and a separable distance function. While Färe and Lovell exploit separability of the distance function, here we exploit separability of the cost function. This property is of particular value for two reasons.

1Funding for this research was provided by a grant from the U.S. National Science Foundation. The authors would like to thank Jere Behrman and two readers for their helpful comments.

Measurement in Economics
ed. by W. Eichhorn

First, many empirical analyses of production estimate a cost function or a cost-minimizing equation system including the cost function. Second, two types of test for separability of a cost function already exist. Nonparametric tests have been devised by Diewert and Parkan (1978, 1985) and Varian (1984), while parametric tests have been proposed by Denny and Fuss (1977).

In this paper we estimate a flexible cost-minimizing equation system, and test various separability restrictions. We then use the test results to draw conclusions about the effect of input aggregation on measures of productive efficiency. The data base we use is a 1975-1977 panel containing 210 observations on agricultural plots in six villages located in Semi-Arid Tropical India. On each plot up to four variable inputs are combined with one fixed input to produce a single output. Two of the variable inputs are hired labor and family labor, and it is these two inputs we wish to aggregate. The aggregability of these two types of labor is an issue of longstanding interest in studies of agricultural production in developing areas; for a recent example see Deolalikar and Vijverberg (1983).

The paper proceeds as follows. In Section 2 we describe production technology and relate separability of the technology to input aggregation and efficiency measurement. In Section 3 we discuss hypothesis tests in the context of a translog variable cost function. In Section 4 our data and empirical results are discussed. Section 5 concludes with implications of our findings.

2. Separability, Aggregation and Efficiency

We begin by describing the technology relative to which efficiency is to be measured, both without and with input aggregation. The sensitivity of efficiency measurement to input aggregation turns on separability of the technology, as Färe and Lovell note. However they examine the symmetric notion of separability among groups of inputs, while we investigate the nonsymmetric notion of separability of one input group from its complement. Consequently the two analyses are somewhat different, although their implications for efficiency measurement are similar.

We assume that the production unit uses inputs $x = (x_1,\dots,x_n) \in R^n_+$, available at fixed prices $p = (p_1,\dots,p_n) \in R^n_{++}$, to produce a single output $u \in R_+$. Production technology is characterized by a continuous, monotonic and quasi-concave production function $\phi: R^n_+ \to R_+$. An alternative primal characterization of technology is provided by the input distance function

$$D_I(u,x) = \max \{\lambda: \phi(x/\lambda) \geq u\}, \quad [2.1]$$

where $D_I(u,x) \geq 1 \iff \phi(x) \geq u$. The subscript "I" on the distance function D and the efficiency indexes F, O and A below indicates that they are input-based functions, and serve to distinguish them from analogous output-based functions. An equivalent dual characterization of technology is provided by the cost function

$$Q(u,p) = \min \{px: D_I(u,x) \geq 1\}. \quad [2.2]$$

The ability of the production unit to conserve on input usage is measured by the Debreu (1951)-Farrell (1957) index of technical efficiency

$$F_I(u,x) = \min \{\lambda: \phi(\lambda x) \geq u\} = D_I(u,x)^{-1}. \quad [2.3]$$

The ability of the production unit to conserve on cost is measured by a cost efficiency index

$$O_I(u,x,p) = Q(u,p)/px. \quad [2.4]$$

Since cost inefficiency not attributable to technical inefficiency must be due to allocative inefficiency, an index of the latter is provided by

$$A_I(u,x,p) = O_I(u,x,p)/F_I(u,x). \quad [2.5]$$

We now partition the input vector $x \in R^n_+$ into a subvector $x^a = (x_1,\ldots,x_k) \in R^k_+$ we wish to aggregate, and a subector $x^b = (x_{k+1},\ldots,x_n) \in R^{n-k}_+$ we do not wish to aggregate. The input price vector is partitioned accordingly, so that $p = (p^a, p^b)$. We then construct a single economic quantity index $\phi^a(x^a)$ and a single economic price index $P^a(p^a)$, each homogeneous of degree +1, that satisfy $px = P^a(p^a)\phi^a(x^a) + \Sigma^n_{i=k+1}p_ix_i$. At issue is the effect this input aggregation has on the three efficiency indexes. Insight is provided by the following result.

Proposition (Blackorby, Primont and Russell (1978, Theorem 3.8, p. 94): If ϕ is continuous, monotonic, and quasi-concave, then the following structures are equivalent:

(i) x^a is homothetically separable from x^b in ϕ, so that

$$\phi(x) = \hat{\phi}(\phi^a(x^a), x^b),$$

where $\hat{\phi}$ is monotonic and ϕ^a is homothetic;

(ii) p^a is separable from (u,p^b) in Q, so that

$$Q(u,p) = \hat{Q}(u,Q^a(p^a),\ p^b);$$

(iii) x^a is separable from (u,x^b) in D_I, so that

$$D_I(u,x) = \hat{D}_I(u,\ D_I(x^a),\ x^b).$$

This result is useful for two reasons. First, recall that $D_I(u,x)^{-1} = F_I(u,x)$. Then parts (ii) and (iii) establish separability conditions under which the measurement of technical, cost and allocative efficiency, using the indexes $F_I(u,x)$, $O_I(u,x,p)$ and $A_I(u,x,p)$, is invariant with respect to input aggregation. Second, parts (i) and (ii) suggest two alternative methods for determining whether these conditions are satisfied in practice. All we have to do is estimate a production function, and test for the homothetic separability of x^a from x^b, or estimate a cost function, and test for the separability of p^a from (u,p^b). However it is also worth noting a useful service not provided by this result. It provides no guidance concerning either the direction or the magnitude of the errors in the three efficiency indexes that arise when the appropriate separability conditions are not satisfied. Direction and magnitude can only be determined after estimation, to which we now turn.

3. The Translog Variable Cost Function

We use a variable cost function to investigate the effect of input aggregation on efficiency measurement, and we use the translog functional form because of its flexibility. However as Blackorby, Primont and Russell (1977) have pointed out, the flexibility of the translog functional form does not extend to the separability property--the translog is "separability-inflexible." This is a potentially serious drawback for us, since separability is at the heart of the aggregation/efficiency question. Fortunately, Denny and Fuss have provided a solution to the problem. They have shown that the separability-inflexibility of the translog applies only when the translog is treated as an exact functional form, in which case a separable translog function must be either a translog function of (inflexible) Cobb-Douglas subaggregates, or a Cobb-Douglas function of translog subaggregates. Consequently a test of the separability hypothesis based on the translog treated as an exact functional form is in fact a test of an undesirably strong joint hypothesis of separability plus Cobb-Douglas at one level or the other. However when the translog is treated as a second-order approximation to some unknown functional form, Denny and Fuss have developed a separability test that does not impose unwarranted structure on the unknown functional form being approximated.

This suggests the following sequential procedure. Estimate a translog variable cost function. Then re-estimate, imposing the Denny-Fuss approximate separability constraints. The resulting test statistic leads us to a conclusion concerning the sensitivity of the three efficiency indexes to input aggregation. If the test statistic is not significant, re-estimate again, this time imposing the stronger exact separability constraints. The resulting test statistic tells us whether the insensitivity remains when Cobb-Douglas structure is imposed on the input price index. If this test statistic is not significant, re-estimate a third time, imposing a stronger set of constraints sufficient for separability. This test statistic tells us whether the insensitivity remains when the variable cost function is a Cobb-Douglas function of translog subaggregates. Finally, for purposes of comparison, perform the input aggregation and estimate the aggregate model.

We now illustrate this procedure with a translog variable cost function tailored specifically to meet the requirements of the empirical application to be discussed below. There we analyze a sample of production units using four variable inputs and one quasi-fixed input to produce a single output. We are interested in measuring the productive efficiency of these units, and we want to know whether measured efficiency is sensitive, and if so, how, to the aggregation of two of those variable inputs. A related issue which we do not investigate, the aggregability of quasi-fixed inputs, has been analyzed by Epstein (1983), although Epstein did not consider the implications for efficiency measurement. A four-equation system, consisting of a translog variable cost function and three variable input share functions, appropriate to this environment may be written as

$$\ln(px) = \alpha_o + \alpha_u \ln u + \alpha_H \ln H + \Sigma_{i=1}^{4} \alpha_i \ln p_i \qquad [3.1]$$
$$+ 1/2\ \alpha_{uu} (\ln u)^2 + 1/2\ \alpha_{HH} (\ln H)^2 + 1/2\ \Sigma_{i=1}^{4} \Sigma_{j=1}^{4} \alpha_{ij} \ln p_i \ln p_j$$
$$+ \Sigma_{i=1}^{4} \alpha_{iu} \ln p_i \ln u + \Sigma_{i=1}^{4} \alpha_{iH} \ln p_i \ln H,$$

and

$$S_i = \alpha_i + \Sigma_{j=1}^{4} \alpha_{ij} \ln p_j + \alpha_{iu} \ln u + \alpha_{iH} \ln H, \qquad i=1,2,3, \qquad [3.2]$$

where px is variable cost, $S_i = p_i x_i/px$ is the share of the i-th variable input in variable cost, H is the quantity of the quasi-fixed input, and all other variables are as previously defined. The condition for exact separability of ($\ln p_1$, $\ln p_2$) from Z = ($\ln p_3$, $\ln p_4$, ln u, ln H) in the translog variable cost function is

$$\nabla_Z\left(\frac{\partial \ln(px)/\partial \ln p_1}{\partial \ln(px)/\partial \ln p_2}\right) = \nabla_Z(S_1/S_2) = 0, \qquad [3.3]$$

which can be written as the system of four equations

$$(\alpha_2\alpha_{1k} - \alpha_1\alpha_{2k}) + (\alpha_{1k}\ \Sigma_{m=1}^{4}\alpha_{2m}) - \alpha_{2k}\ \Sigma_{m=1}^{4}\alpha_{1m})\ \ln p_m \qquad [3.4]$$

$$+ (\alpha_{1k}\ \alpha_{2u} - \alpha_{2k}\ \alpha_{1u})\ \ln u + (\alpha_{1k}\ \alpha_{2H} - \alpha_{2k}\ \alpha_{1H})\ \ln H = 0,$$

where k = 3, 4, u, H.

A sufficient condition for this exact separability condition to hold is

$$\alpha_{1k} = \alpha_{2k} = 0, \qquad \forall k = 3,\ 4,\ u,\ H, \qquad [3.5]$$

in which case [3.1] collapses to a Cobb-Douglas variable cost function with a translog labor price index. In this case the Allen-Uzawa partial elasticities of substitution σ_{ij} satisfy $\sigma_{1k} = \sigma_{2k} = 1$ for k = 3, 4. A necessary and sufficient condition for exact separability is

$$\alpha_1\ \alpha_{2k} - \alpha_2\ \alpha_{1k} = 0, \qquad \forall k = 1,2,3,4,u,H, \qquad [3.6]$$

or, alternatively,

$$\frac{\alpha_1}{\alpha_2} = \frac{\alpha_{11}}{\alpha_{21}} = \frac{\alpha_{12}}{\alpha_{22}} = \frac{\alpha_{13}}{\alpha_{23}} = \frac{\alpha_{14}}{\alpha_{24}} = \frac{\alpha_{1u}}{\alpha_{2u}} = \frac{\alpha_{1H}}{\alpha_{2H}}, \qquad [3.7]$$

in which case [3.1] collapses to a translog variable cost function with a Cobb-Douglas labor price index. In this case $\sigma_{1k} = \sigma_{2k}$ for k = 3, 4. Finally, the Denny-Fuss condition for approximate separability is

$$\alpha_1\ \alpha_{2k} - \alpha_2\ \alpha_{1k} = 0, \qquad \forall k = 3,4,u,H, \qquad [3.8]$$

or, alternatively,

$$\frac{\alpha_1}{\alpha_2} = \frac{\alpha_{13}}{\alpha_{23}} = \frac{\alpha_{14}}{\alpha_{24}} = \frac{\alpha_{1u}}{\alpha_{2u}} = \frac{\alpha_{1H}}{\alpha_{2H}}, \qquad [3.9]$$

in which case [3.1] is a second-order approximation to an arbitrary separable variable cost function.

The procedure just described is designed to test hypotheses concerning the sensitivity of estimates of cost and technical (and hence allocative) efficiency to input aggregation. The procedure can be carried out without actually calculating these efficiency measures. However in order to gauge the direction and magnitude of errors resulting from inappropriate aggregation, and to provide a check on results when aggregation is warranted, these efficiency measures must be calculated. One way of calculating these measures is to treat the cost function as a "full frontier." That is, the four-equation system [3.1] and [3.2] is estimated, after which the estimated cost function is shifted down until all residuals are nonnegative. The transformed residuals are interpreted as percentage deviations above minimum cost, from which measures of cost efficiency can be calculated using equation [2.4]. Next, these deviations are decomposed into technical and allocative components using the Zieschang (1983) modification of an algorithm proposed by Kopp and Diewert (1982). This algorithm operates by finding a shadow price vector for which allocative inefficiency disappears; consequently it reveals the direction, as well as the cost, of allocative inefficiency. These three efficiency measures are calculated for each production unit without and with the various separability constraints. This procedure provides empirical evidence concerning direction and magnitude of sensitivity of estimated efficiency measures to input aggregation.

4. An Empirical Application

Our data base is a micro panel of agricultural production in Semi-Arid Tropical India. The data have been collected at regular intervals since 1975 as part of the Village Level Studies of the ICRISAT Economics Program, and are described in detail by Binswanger and Jodha (1978). We have data on production activities on individual plots of land located in six villages during the period 1975-1977, for a total of 210 observations. Output is an index of cereals, pulses, vegetables and other products. The four variable inputs are family labor (x_1), hired labor (x_2), seeds (x_3) and other non-labor inputs (x_4). The quasi-fixed input is the value of the plot being cultivated. In addition, the quality of the soil is controlled for with an index of eight different soil types, and year and village dummy variables are also included. Consequently most non-input sources of output variation either are accounted for or, as in the case of climate, are unlikely to vary across plots in a given year. Finally, the ratio of the price of family labor to the price of hired labor varies widely over the sample. This precludes the exploitation of the Hicks aggregation theorem as a justification for aggregating the two types of labor, and necessitates the separability tests just described.

Estimation of the four equation system consisting of the cost equation [3.1] and three share equations [3.2] was carried out by iterated seemingly unrelated regressions (ITSUR). The translog system is linear in parameters, and a linear estimator such as ITSUR imposes minimal distributional assumptions on the underlying error structure, and hence on the structure of cost inefficiencies. The system is estimated five times: in unconstrained form, with the approximate separability restrictions [3.8] imposed, with the weak exact separability restrictions [3.6] imposed, with the strong exact separability conditions [3.5] imposed, and finally as a three-equation, three input system with a labor price aggregate. In all five systems symmetry and homogeneity restrictions are imposed. In the last system the labor price index is a share-weighted sum of the prices of family labor and hired labor.

Parameter estimates for the five systems are reported in Table 1. Estimates of first-order parameters are fairly stable across models, although estimates of second-order parameters show greater variability. The primary interest of Table 1 centers on the Wald statistics of the tests of the three sets of separability restrictions. The test statistic is distributed as chi-square with degrees of freedom equal to the number of restrictions being imposed. All three test statistics are highly significant. The critical 0.01 chi-square values with 4, 6 and 8 degrees of freedom are 13.3, 16.8 and 20.1, respectively.

The approximate separability restrictions are decisively rejected. The translog cost function [3.1] is not a quadratic approximation to an arbitrary separable cost function. Since this structure is rejected by the data, so too are the more restrictive structures implied by weak exact separability and strong exact separability. There is no technological (i.e., functional separability) justification for aggregating family labor and hired labor in this context.

Another way of demonstrating failure of the separability restrictions is to examine the behavior of Allen-Uzawa partial elasticities of substitution reported in Table 2. All three types of separability impose structure on input substitution possibilities that are not apparent in the unconstrained model. In particular, two of three instances of complementarity are eliminated by the separability restrictions.

The translog cost function is not a quadratic approximation to an arbitrary separable cost function. What does this imply for efficiency measurement? Since the various separability restrictions impose unwarranted structure on production technology, they distort the standard relative to which efficiency is being calculated. It follows from the Blackorby, Primont and Russell proposition that measures of cost, technical and allocative efficiency are not invariant to input aggregation. What does not follow from that proposition is any indication of the direction and magnitude of the distortion.

To quantify the effect of the separability restrictions on the three efficiency measures, we have calculated these three measures for every observation in the unconstrained model, the three separability-constrained models, and the aggregate labor model. This involves transforming each estimated cost function into a full cost frontier in order to calculate cost efficiency, and then applying the Kopp-Diewert-Zieschang decomposition algorithm to calculate technical and allocative efficiency.

Sample means of the three types of inefficiency appear in Table 3. Frequency distributions appear in Figures 1-5. All means are small, reflecting the fact that many non-input sources of output variation are controlled for in estimation, and lending considerable support to the "poor-but-efficient" hypothesis. Also, the mean values of technical and allocative inefficiency move in opposite directions as unwarranted separability restrictions are imposed and tightened. Both means change by fully 60% as separability restrictions warp estimated efficient production isoquants (recall the results of Table 2). Overall cost inefficiency is also affected, its mean being increased by 12%. The aggregate labor results are most similar to the approximate separability results because the labor price index is consistent with approximate, but not weak exact or strong exact, separability.

The only dimension of efficiency measurement that appears invariant to the imposition of separability restrictions and input aggregation is the direction of the allocative inefficiency. In all four disaggregated models the ratios of family labor, hired labor and seeds to other non-labor inputs is inefficiently small. In the aggregated model the ratios of labor and seeds to other non-labor inputs is inefficiently small.

The sensitivity of efficiency measurement to the imposition of unwarranted separability restrictions and to unjustified input aggregation is even greater than Table 3 and Figures 1-5 suggest. Table 3 reports mean values, and Figures 1-5 depict frequency distributions. Neither tracks specific observations through the five scenarios. Furthermore, variation in individual efficiency measures through the five scenarios is greater than variation in sample frequency distributions or sample means.

5. Conclusions

Inferences concerning the structure of technology are sensitive to input aggregation. Consequently so are inferences concerning the structure of efficiency relative to that technology. The results of Färe and Lovell, based on those of Blackorby, Primont and Russell (1978), make this clear. In this paper we have developed a framework for empirical implementation of these ideas, and applied the framework to Indian agricultural production. The principal general finding of the study is that calculations of cost, technical and allocative efficiency can be quite sensitive to the imposition of unwarranted functional separability restrictions and to input aggregation that is unjustified on functional separability grounds. This sensitivity is all the more serious if interest centers on the efficiency of particular observations rather than on the efficiency of the sample as a whole.

References

Binswanger, H.P., and N.S. Jodha (1978), "Manual of Instructions for Economic Investigators in ICRISAT's Village Level Studies," Hyderabad, India, mimeo.

Blackorby, C., D. Primont and R.R. Russell (1977), "On Testing Separability Restrictions With Flexible Functional Forms," Journal of Econometrics 5:2 (March), 195-209.

Blackorby, C., D. Primont and R.R. Russell (1978), Duality, Separability, and Functional Structure: Theory and Economic Applications. New York: North-Holland.

Debreu, G. (1951), "The Coefficient of Resource Utilization," Econometrica 19:3 (July), 273-92.

Denny, M., and M. Fuss (1977), "The Use of Approximation Analysis to Test For Separability and the Existence of Consistent Aggregates," American Economic Review 67:3 (June), 404-18.

Deolalikar, A.B., and W.P.M. Vijverberg (1983), "The Heterogeneity of Family and Hired Labor in Agricultural Production: A Test Using District-Level Data From India," Journal of Economic Development 8:2 (December), 45-69.

Diewert, W.E. (1980), "Aggregation Problems in the Measurement of Capital," in The Measurement of Capital, ed. D. Usher. Chicago:

The University of Chicago Press for The National Bureau of Economic Research.

Diewert, W.E., and C. Parkan (1978), "Tests For the Consistency of Consumer Data and Nonparametric Index Numbers," Discussion paper No. 78-27, Department of Economics, University of British Columbia.

Diewert, W.E., and C. Parkan (1985), "Tests for the Consistency of Consumer Data," Journal of Econometrics 30:1/2 (October/November), 127-47.

Epstein, L.G. (1983), "Aggregating Quasi-Fixed Factors," Scandinavian Journal of Economics 85:2, 191-205.

Färe, R., and C.A.K. Lovell (1987), "Aggregation and Efficiency," this volume.

Farrell, M.J. (1957), "The Measurement of Productive Efficiency," Journal of the Royal Statistical Society, Series A, General, 120, Part 3, 253-81.

Kopp, R.J., and W.E. Diewert (1982), "The Decomposition of Frontier Cost Function Deviations into Measures of Technical and Allocative Efficiency," Journal of Econometrics 19:2/3 (August), 319-31.

Varian, H. (1984), "The Nonparametric Approach to Production Analysis," Econometrica 52:3 (May), 579-97.

Zieschang, K.D. (1983), "A Note on the Decomposition of Cost Efficiency into Technical and Allocative Components," Journal of Econometrics 23:3 (December), 401-05.

FIGURE 1

PLOT OF INEFFICIENCY FOR UNCONSTRAINED MODEL
TOTAL ALLOCATIVE AND TECHNICAL INEFFICIENCY

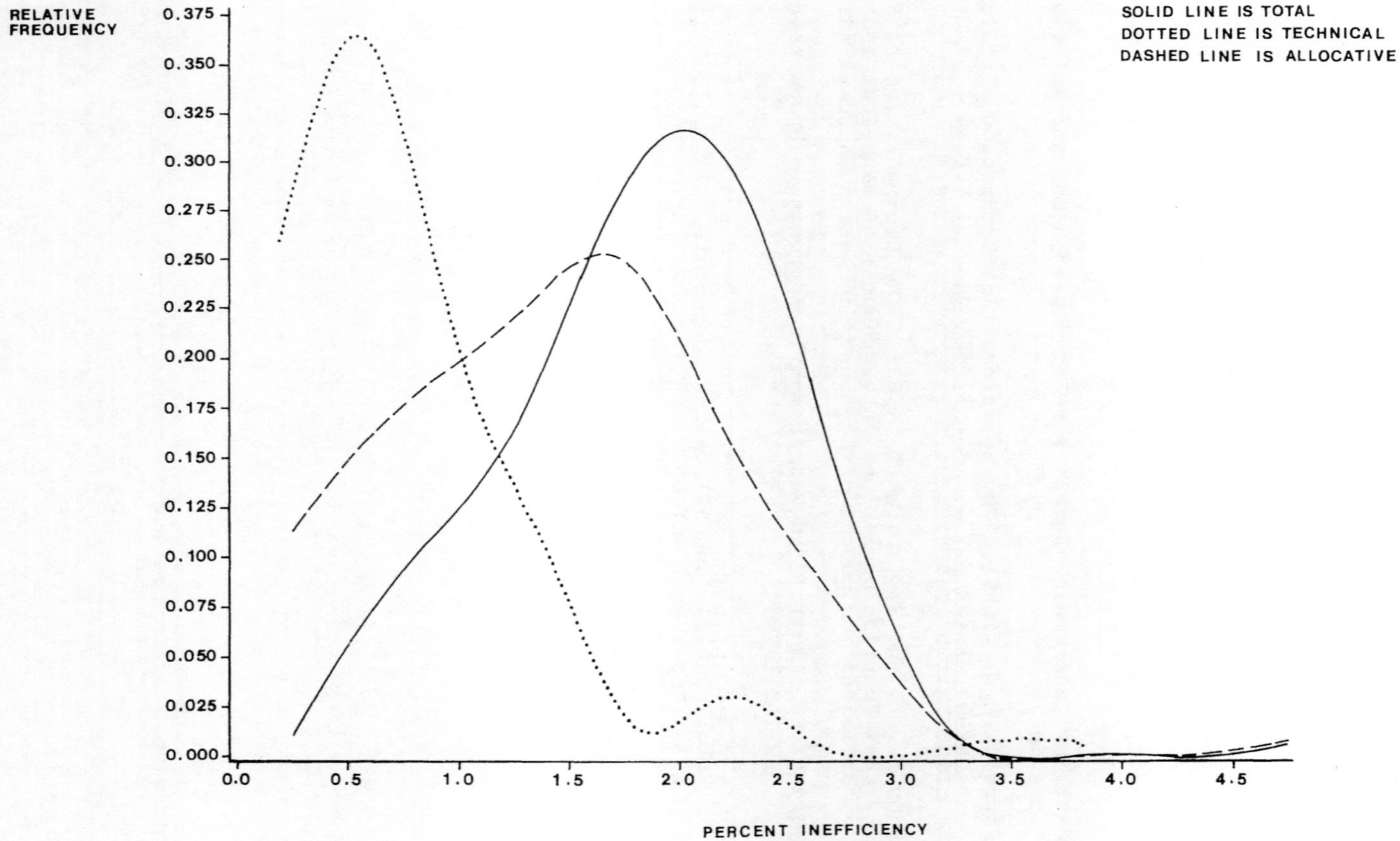

FIGURE 2

PLOT OF INEFFICIENCY FOR APPROXIMATE SEPARABILITY
TOTAL ALLOCATIVE AND TECHNICAL INEFFICIENCY

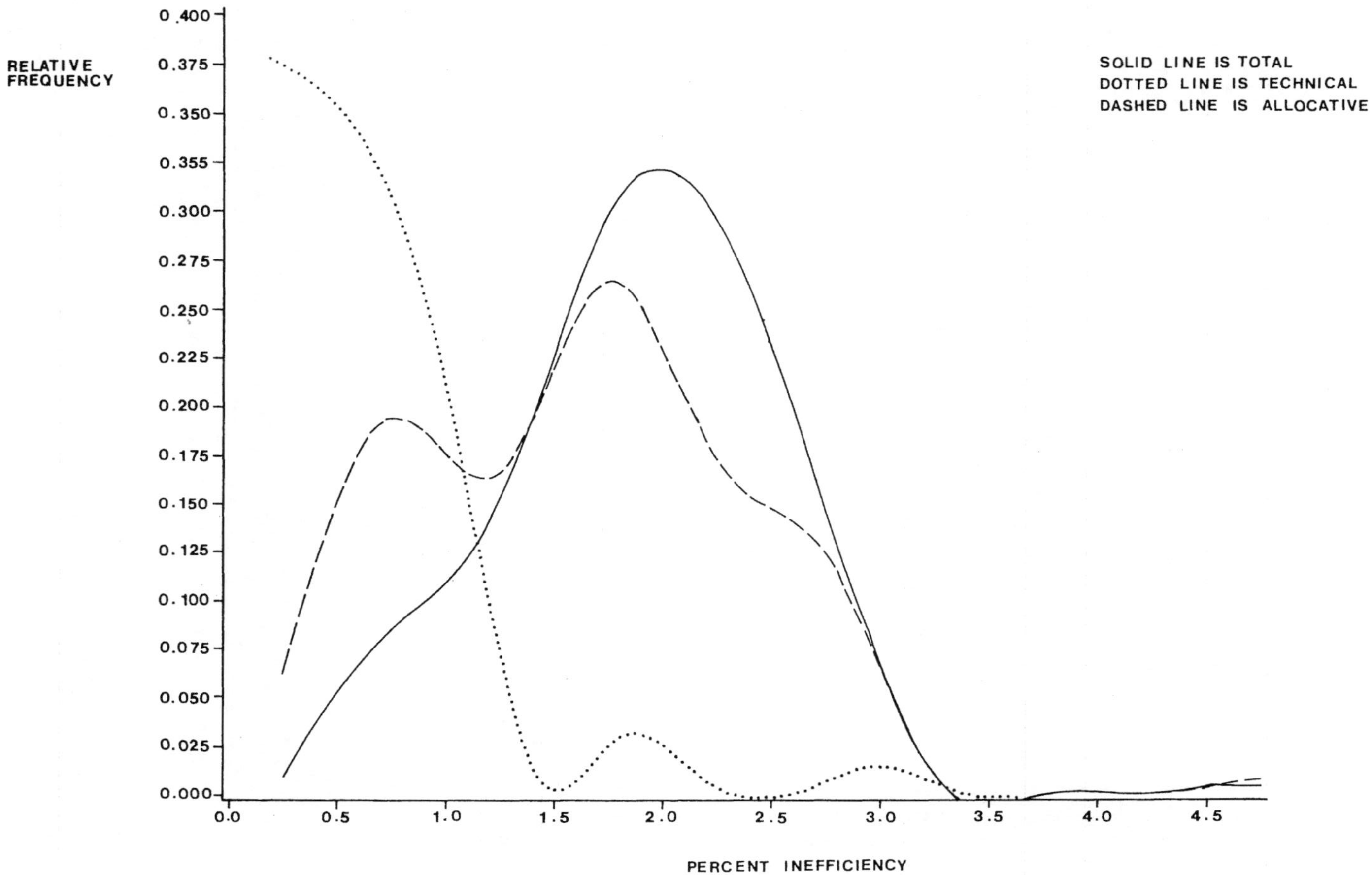

FIGURE 3

PLOT OF INEFFICIENCY FOR WEAK EXACT SEPARABILITY
TOTAL ALLOCATIVE AND TECHNICAL INEFFICIENCY

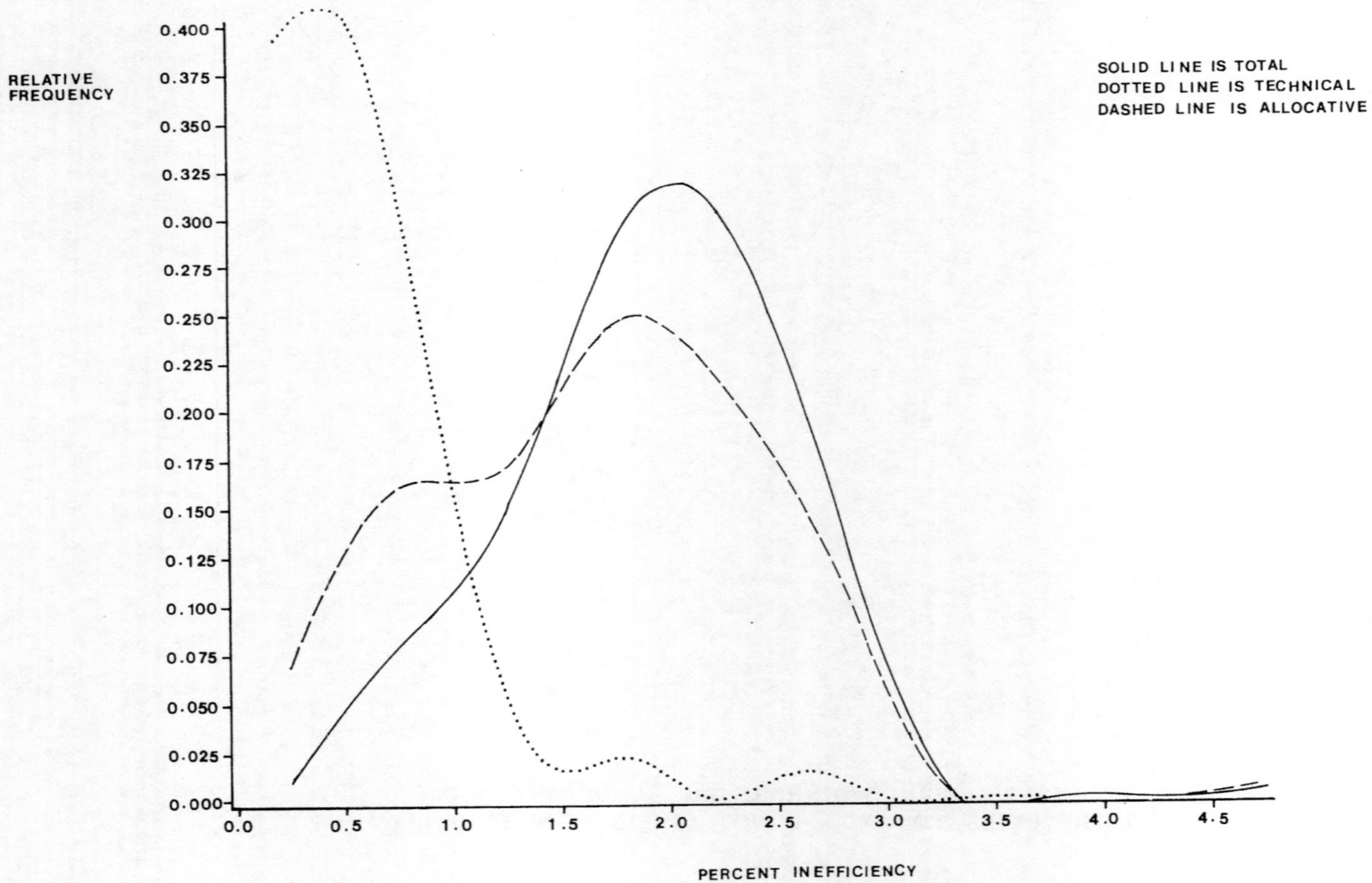

FIGURE 4

PLOT OF INEFFICIENCY FOR STRONG EXACT SEPARABILITY
TOTAL ALLOCATIVE AND TECHNICAL INEFFICIENCY

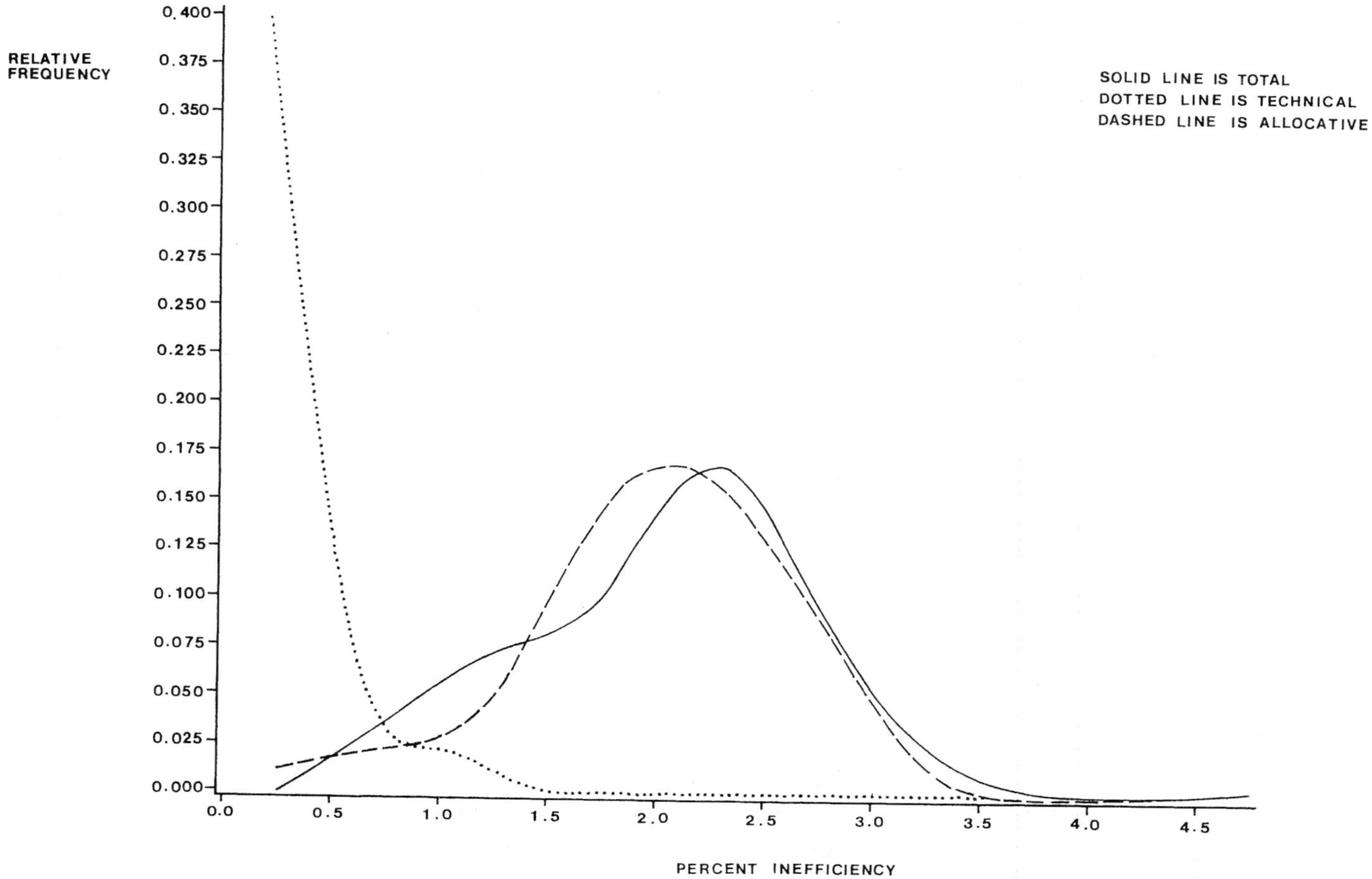

FIGURE 5

PLOT OF INEFFICIENCY FOR AGGREGRATED LABOR
TOTAL ALLOCATIVE AND TECHNICAL INEFFICIENCY

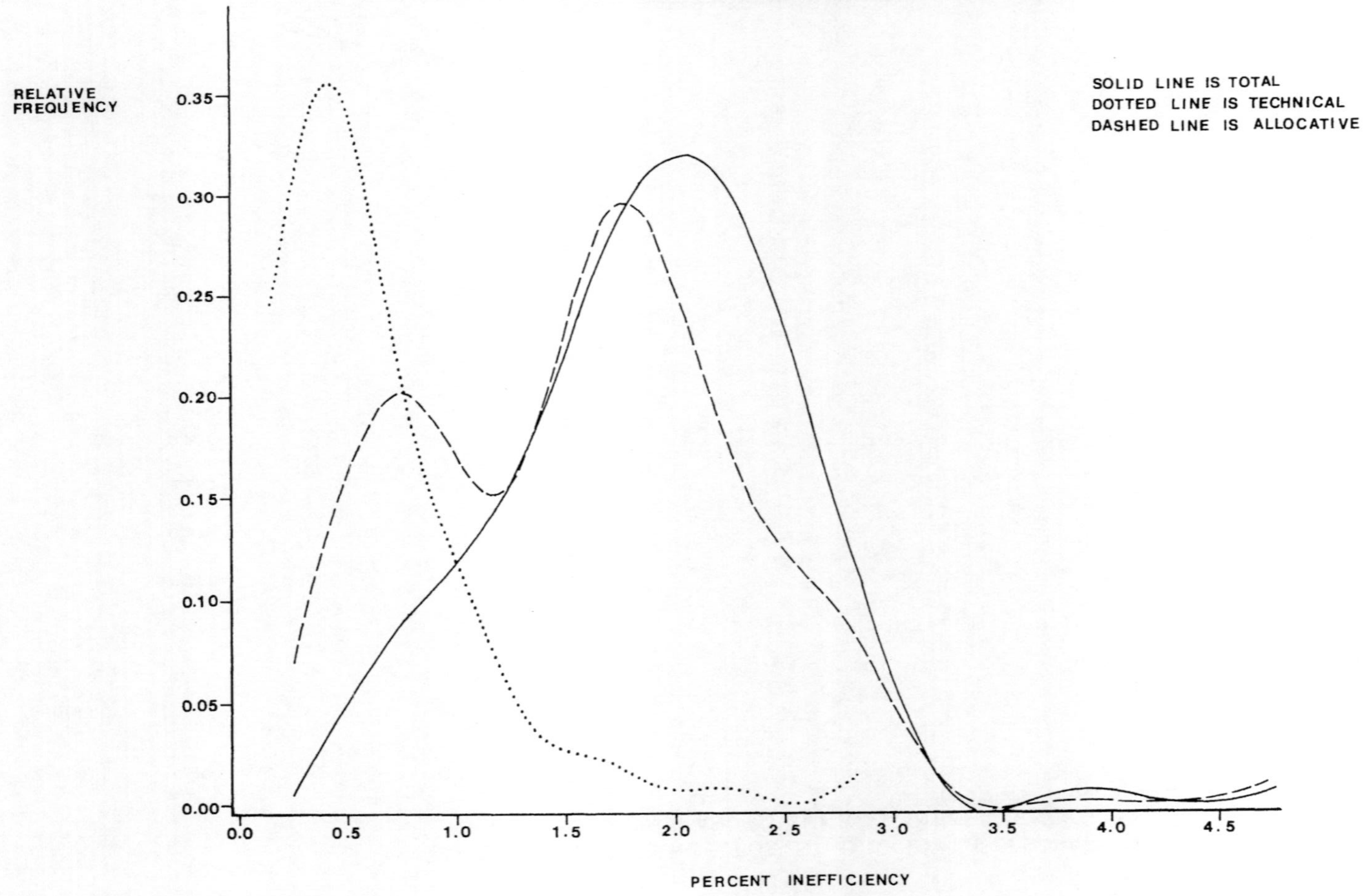

Table 1. Translog Variable Cost Functions

parameter	unconstrained model estimate	approximate separability estimate	weak exact separability estimate	strong exact separability estimate	aggregate labor estimate
α_u	0,398 (2.35)	0.346 (1.96)	0.356 (2.01)	0.393 (2.11)	0.397 (2.32)
α_H	-1.197 (-2.07)	-1.349 (-2.24)	-1.261 (-2.09)	-1.072 (-1.69)	-0.921 (-1.578)
α_1	0.739 (6.02)	0.656 (9.19)	0.621 (9.32)	0.256 (16.53)	1.252 (9.71)
α_2	0.472 (4.18)	0.564 (8.91)	0.593 (9.35)	0.256 (19.62)	
α_3	0.390 (3.85)	0.381 (4.04)	0.386 (4.09)	0.542 (6.34)	0.388 (3.94)
α_{uu}	0.041 (1.50)	0.042 (1.50)	0.042 (1.46)	0.037 (1.23)	0.040 (1.46)
α_{HH}	0.168 (2.27)	0.188 (2.45)	0.177 (2.29)	0.152 (1.87)	0.132 (1.77)
α_{11}	0.003 (0.05)			-0.023 (5.06)	0.071 (1.67)
α_{12}	-0.035 (-0.77)	0.095 (2.09)	0.016 (1.59)		
α_{13}	-0.054 (-2,57)				-0.040 (-1.93)
α_{22}	0.126 (2.38)	-0.070 (-1.52)			
α_{23}	0.019 (0.94)	-0.016 (-1.78)	-0.016 (-1.65)		
α_{33}	0.100 (4.86)	0.096 (4.98)	0.095 (4.94)	0.086 (5.06)	0.102 (5.12)
α_{1u}	-0.078 (-9.68)				-0.057 (-7.28)
α_{2u}	0.024 (3.21)	-0.027 (-7.16)	-0.026 (-6.91)		
α_{3u}	-0.015 (-2.16)	-0.015 (-2.28)	-0.015 (-2.33)	-0.023 (-3.71)	-0.016 (-2.53)
α_{1H}	0.002 (0.13)				-0.029 (-2.33)
α_{2H}	-0.030 (-2.62)	-0.013 (-2.28)	-0.014 (-2.44)		

Table 1. Translog Variable Cost Functions (continued)

parameter	unconstrained model estimate	approximate separability estimate	weak exact separability estimate	strong exact separability estimate	aggregate labor estimate
α_{3H}	-0.020	-0.020	-0.019	-0.026	-0.020
	(-1.83)	(-1.93)	(-1.92)	(-2.63)	(-1.88)
t_1	0.157	0.132	0.138	0.126	0.173
	(1.65)	(1.33)	(1.39)	(1.23)	(1.80)
t_2	0.249	0.223	0.231	0.230	0.273
	(2.63)	(2.26)	(2.33)	(2.23)	(2.84)
v_1	7.445	8.265	(7.902	7.090	6.422
	(3.22)	(3.44)	(3.28)	(2.79)	(2.75)
v_2	7.228	8.094	7.728	6.848	6.207
	(3.13)	(3.37)	(3.22)	(2.71)	(2.67)
v_3	7.305	8.204	7.838	6.911	6.276
	(3.20)	(3.46)	(3.30)	(2.76)	(2.73)
v_4	6.919	7.755	7.393	6.482	5.886
	(2.99)	(3.23)	(3.07)	(2.56)	(2.52)
v_5	7.187	7.983	7.621	6.770	6.184
	(3.10)	(3.31)	(3.16)	(2.67)	(2.65)
v_6	7.474	8.307	7.933	7.056	6.448
	(3.24)	(3.46)	(3.30)	(2.79)	(2.77)
s	0.034	0.040	0.038	0.028	0.027
	(1.05)	(1.21)	(1.13)	(0.79)	(0.84)
Wald test		58.21	137.99	175.01	

Note: t-statistics in parentheses.

Table 2. Allen-Uzawa Partial Elasticities of Substitution

	unconstrained	approximate separability	weak exact separability	strong exact separability	aggregate labor
σ_{11}	-2.917	-3.653	-2.594	-3.289	
σ_{12}	0.472	2.473	1.243	1.348	
σ_{13}	-0.055	0.653	0.685	1.0	
σ_{14}	2.212	0.859	0.791	1.0	
σ_{22}	-0.979	-4.344	-2.778	-3.226	
σ_{23}	1.359	0.669	0.685	1.0	
σ_{24}	-0.493	0.866	0.791	1.0	
σ_{33}	-1.499	-1.599	-1.620	-1.855	-1.461
σ_{34}	-0.132	-0.055	-0.086	-0.498	-0.066
σ_{44}	-1.426	-1.470	-1.328	-1.423	-1.347
σ_{LL}					-0.681
σ_{L3}					0.606
σ_{L4}					0.788

Note: σ_{ij} are evaluated at mean values of explanatory variables.

Table 3. Mean Values of Overall, Technical and Allocative Inefficiency (in %)

	unconstrained	approximate separability	weak exact separability	strong exact separability	aggregate labor
O_I	1.840	1.880	1.897	2.063	1.861
F_I	0.773	0.622	0.574	0.312	0.608
A_I	1.269	1.476	1.543	2.017	1.454

Note: O_I means based on 203 observations having positive values of output; F_I and A_I means based on 137 observations having positive values of output and all four variable inputs. Consequently $O_I \neq F_I + A_I$.

On the Axiomatic Approach to the Measurement of Technical Efficiency[1]

R. Robert Russell
Graduate School of Management
University of California
Riverside, California 92521/USA

1. Introductory Remarks

Efforts to axiomatize the measurement of technical efficiency were stimulated by the Färe/Lovell [1987] suggestion that (input) efficiency measures should satisfy three conditions:

(I) indication of efficient input vectors (the measure is equal to one if and only if the input bundle is techically efficient in the sense of Koopmans [1951]),

(M) monotonicity (increasing one input quantity while holding all other inputs and all outputs constant lowers the measure),

and

(H) homogeneity of degree minus one (e.g., doubling all input quantities while holding all outputs constant cuts the measure in half).

These criteria have been used to assess several proposed efficiency measures -- most notably,

• the Debreu [1951] / Farrell [1957] measure, E_{DF} (essentially the inverse of the Malmquist [1951] / Shephard [1970] distance function, which measures the maximum amount that an input vector can be shrunk along a ray while holding output levels constant),

• the Färe/Lovell [1978] measure, E_{FL} (the maximum sum of proportionate reductions in individual inputs in coordinate directions), and

• the Zieschang [1984] measure, E_Z (essentially an amalgam of the Debreu/Farrell and Färe/Lovell measures, shrinking input vectors along a ray to the isoquant and then shrinking in coordinate directions along the isoquant until an efficient point is reached).

[1]This research was supported by National Science Foundation Grant No. SES-8510922. I am grateful to Rolf Färe for pointing out a problem with the original version of one of my theorems. An anonymous referee made valuable suggestions about exposition.

Measurement in Economics
ed. by W. Eichhorn

Bol [1986], however, has recently shown that there does not exist a measure satisfying the three Färe/Lovell conditions for the broad class of technologies considered in this literature. Bol's result leaves wide open the issue of what combinations of desirable properties of a measure of technical efficiency are feasible. As Bol points out, in the light of his impossibility result there are two approaches to identifying properties that can be satisfied by an efficiency measure: (1) relaxation of the desired properties and (2) narrowing the class of technologies to which the efficiency measure is to be applied. In this paper, I pursue the first of these avenues of inquiry.

One way of relaxing the Färe/Lovell properties is by the elimination of conditions. Only two results along this line have held up:

R1: (H) is satisfied by E_{DF} for all technologies (Färe/Lovell [1978]), and

R2: (I) $\wedge$ (H) is satisfied by E_Z for all technologies (Zieschang [1984]).

Questions that have not been answered are the following:

Q1: Does there exist a measure satisfying (M) for all technologies?

Q2: If so, does there exist a measure satisfying (M) $\wedge$ (H) for all technologies?

Q3: Does there exist a measure satisfying (I) $\wedge$ (M) for all technologies?

Another approach is to weaken (rather than eliminate) conditions. Russell [1985] suggested the following weakening of monotonicity:

(WM) weak monotonicity (increasing one input quantity while holding other inputs and all outputs constant cannot increase the efficiency measure).

The one positive result regarding (WM) is

R3: (I) $\wedge$ (WM) is satisfied by E_{FL} for all technologies (Russell [1985]).

Since the Färe/Lovell measure fails to satisfy the homogeneity condition, the following question remains unanswered:

Q4: Does there exist a measure satisfying (WM) $\wedge$ (H)?

In this paper, I answer Q1 and Q4 (affirmatively). Q2 and Q3 remain open questions, but additional results in this paper render them (in my view) uninteresting. In particular, I consider a condition that is perhaps more fundamental than any of those identified above (or below): invariance with respect to changes in the units of measurement. This (commensurability) condition interacts profoundly with the other axioms. Most important -- and perhaps surprising -- is the result that commensurabilty (C) and monotonocity (M) are mutually inconsistent. To the extent that (C) is considered essential, this result renders Q2 and Q3 (and the affirmative answer to Q1) uninteresting.[2]

Finally, I also consider a modification of the indication condition (I). The modification, which is neither weaker nor stronger than (I), is to require the identification of <u>weakly</u> efficient input vectors (the measure is equal to 1 if and only if the input vector is weakly efficent). As might be expected, this condition interacts significantly with other conditions in producing both possibility and impossibility results.

After laying down the groundwork in Section 2, I state and prove the results in Section 3 and conclude in Section 4.

2. <u>Production Technologies and Efficiency Measures</u>

Let $\mathbf{R}^n$ be the nonnegative Euclidean n-orthant and adopt the following notations for $(z,\hat{z}) \in \mathbf{R}^{2n}$:

$$z \geqq \hat{z} \ \text{ if } \ z_i \geq \hat{z}_i \ \forall\, i,$$

$$z \geq \hat{z} \ \text{ if } \ z_i \geq \hat{z}_i \ \forall\, i \ \text{ and } \ z \neq z,$$

$$z > z \ \text{ if } \ z_i > z_i \ \forall\, i,$$

and

$$z \not> z \ \text{ if } \ z_i \geq z_i \ \text{ for some } i.$$

Also, $\underline{0}$ is the n-dimensional zero vector and $\hat{\mathbf{R}}^n_+ = \mathbf{R}^n_+ \setminus \{\underline{0}\}$.

The production technology is characterized by the upper-level-set mapping, $L: \mathbf{R}^m_+ \to \mathbf{R}^n_+$. $L(u)$ is the set of input vectors that can produce the output vector $u \in \mathbf{R}^m$. Let

$$\Gamma = \{u \in \mathbf{R}^n_+ \mid L(u) \neq \emptyset \wedge \underline{0} \notin L(u)\}$$

and define $\mathcal{L}$ as the collection of upper-level-set mappings that satisfy

---

[2] These questions may remain of interest if the relaxation of conditions is combined with the alternative avenue of inquiry -- narrowing the class of technologies to which the efficiency measure is to be applied.

(L1) $z \in L(u)$ implies $\lambda z \in L(u)\ \forall \lambda \in [1, +\infty), \forall u \in \Gamma$,

and

(L2) $L(u)$ is closed $\forall u \in \Gamma$.

An input vector $z \in L(u)$ is efficient (in the sense of Koopmans [1951]) if $z \geq \hat{z}$ implies $\hat{z} \notin L(u)$. A vector $z \in L(u)$ is weakly efficient if $z > \hat{z}$ implies $\hat{z} \notin L(u)$.

An (input) efficiency measure is a mapping $E : \Gamma \times \hat{\mathbf{R}}^n_+ \times \mathcal{L} \rightarrow (0,1] \cup \{+\infty\}$ with the property that $E(u, z, L) \in (0,1]$ if and only if $z \in L(u)$. The properties of E proposed by Färe and Lovell [1978] are

(I) $\quad E(u, z, L) = 1$ iff z is efficient,

(M) $\quad E(u, z, L) < E(u, z, L)$ if $\hat{z} \geq z$, $\hat{z} \in L(u)$, and $z \in L(u)$,

and

(H) $\quad E(u, \lambda z, L) = \lambda^{-1} E(u, z, L)\ \forall \lambda \in [D(u, z, L)^{-1}, +\infty), \forall z \in L(u)$,

where D is the distance function, defined by

$$D(u, z, L) = \max \{\lambda \in \mathbf{R}_+ \mid z/\lambda \in L(u)\}.$$

The weaker version of (M) suggested by Russell [1975] is

(WM) $\quad E(u, \hat{z}, L) \leq E(u, z, L)$ if $\hat{z} \geq z$, $\hat{z} \in L(u)$, and $z \in L(u)$.

The efficiency measures proposed by Debreu [1951] and Farrell [1957], Färe and Lovell [1978], and Zieschang [1984] are defined, for $z \in L(u)$, by

$$E_{DF}(u, z, L) = D(u, z)^{-1},$$

$$E_{FL}(u, z, L) = \min_K \{ \textstyle\sum_i \kappa_i / \sum_i \delta(z_i) \mid Kz \in L(u) \wedge \kappa_i \in [0,1]\ \forall i \},$$

and

$$E_Z(u, z, L) = E_{FL}(u, z/D(u, z, L^+) / (D(u, z, L^+)),$$

where K is the positive diagonal matrix with $\kappa = [\kappa_1, \ldots, \kappa_n]$ on the diagonal,

$$\delta(z_i) = \begin{cases} 1 \text{ if } z_i > 0, \\ 0 \text{ if } z_i = 0, \end{cases}$$

and $L^+(u) = L(u) + \mathbf{R}^n_+$ (the free-disposal hull of $L(u)$).

3. Results

The first theorem shows that, by dispensing with the homogeneity condition (H), we can salvage the indication and monotonicity conditions (I) and (M). To this end, define the efficiency measure, E_{FL}, by

$$E_{FL}^{\varepsilon}(u, z, L) = \begin{cases} \min_{\kappa} \{ \sum_i \kappa_i / n \mid K(z + \underline{\varepsilon}) \in L(u) + \{\underline{\varepsilon}\} \wedge \kappa_i \in [0,1] \, \forall i \} & \text{if } z \in L(u) \\ +\infty & \text{if } z \notin L(u), \end{cases}$$

where K is the $n \times n$ diagonal matrix with κ on the diagonal and $\underline{\varepsilon} \in \mathbf{R}^n$ is the vector with each element equal to $\varepsilon \in (0,+\infty)$. Note that, although the definition only restricts κ_i to the closed interval [0,1], the maximizing vector κ^* satisfies $\kappa^* > 0$, since $L(u) + \{\underline{\varepsilon}\}$ is contained in the interior of $\mathbf{R}^n_+$.

Thus, E_{FL}^{ε} is a modification of the Färe/Lovell measure, obtained by displacing the level set L(u) and the vector z by the factor $\underline{\varepsilon}$.[3] This displacement, which can be arbitrarily small, eliminates those cases where E_{FL} fails the monotonicity criterion, as shown by Theorem 1.

Theorem 1. E_{FL}^{ε} satisfies (I) and (M) for all $L \in \mathcal{L}$.

Proof. To prove (I), suppose the contrary: there exists an efficient $z^* \in L(u)$ such that $E_{FL}^{\varepsilon}(u, z^*, L) < 1$ or, alternatively, there exists an inefficient $z^* \in L(u)$ with $E_{FL}^{\varepsilon}(u, z^*, L) = 1$. In the first case, for some i, say j, $\kappa_j^* < 1$, where

$$\kappa^* = \arg\min_{\kappa} \{ \sum_i \kappa_i / n \mid K(z^* + \underline{\varepsilon}) \in L(u) + \{\underline{\varepsilon}\} \wedge \kappa_i \in [0,1] \, \forall i \}. \qquad \text{(a)}$$

Since $K^*(z^* + \underline{\varepsilon}) \in L(u) + \{\underline{\varepsilon}\}$, we have

$$K^*z^* \in L(u) + \{ \underline{\varepsilon} - K^*\underline{\varepsilon} \}. \qquad \text{(b)}$$

Together with $\underline{\varepsilon} - K^*\underline{\varepsilon} > 0$, (b) implies that $K^*z^* \in L(u)$. Since $\kappa^*z^* < z^*$, this contradicts the assumption that z^* is efficient.

---

[3] Note that the denominator in the maximand, $\sum_i \delta(z_i + \varepsilon)$, is identically equal to n, since $z + \underline{\varepsilon} > \underline{0}$.

In the second case, there exists a $\hat{z} \in L(u)$ such that $\hat{z}_j < z_j^*$ for some j and $\hat{z}_i = z_i^*$ for all $i \neq j$. Thus, $\hat{z} + \underline{\varepsilon} \in L(u) + \{\underline{\varepsilon}\}$. Consequently, for $\hat{\kappa}_j \leq (\hat{z}_j + \varepsilon) / (z_j^* + \varepsilon) < 1$, $\hat{K}(\hat{z} + \underline{\varepsilon}) \in L(u) + \{\underline{\varepsilon}\}$, contradicting $E_{FL}^{\varepsilon}(u, z^*, L) = 1$.

To prove (M), consider $z^* \in L(u)$ and $\hat{z} \in L(u)$ satisfying $z^* \leq \hat{z}$. As κ^*, defined in (a), is positive, $K^*(\hat{z} + \underline{\varepsilon}) \geq K^*(z^* + \underline{\varepsilon})$, and there exists a $\hat{\kappa}$ satisfying $\hat{\kappa} \leq \kappa^*$ such that $\hat{K}(\hat{z} + \underline{\varepsilon}) \in L(u) + \{\underline{\varepsilon}\}$. Hence, $E_{FL}^{\varepsilon}(u, \hat{z}, L) < E_{FL}^{\varepsilon}(u, z^*, L)$. ||

While the construction of E_{FL} provides a way of salvaging two of the three Färe/Lovell conditions,[4] it unfortunately has a perverse property that undermines its attractiveness. It is not invariant with respect to changes in the units of measurement. Essentially, this is because the shrinkage factor, κ, is proportional with respect to $\underline{\varepsilon}$ rather than the origin, $\underline{0}$. I believe sensitivity to the choice of units of measurement is a more fundamental property of efficiency measures than either (I) or (M). Let us, therefore, explore the implications of adding the following commensurability axiom:[5]

(C) If $\hat{u} = \Omega u$ and $\hat{z} = \Lambda z$, where Ω and Λ are, respectively, $m \times m$ and $n \times n$ positive diagonal matrices and $\hat{L}(\hat{u}) = \{\hat{z} \in \mathbb{R}_+^n \mid z \in L(u)\}$, then $E(\hat{u}, \hat{z}, \hat{L}) = E(u, z, L)$.

The next result shows that, not only does E_{FL}^{ε} fail to satisfy (C) but, in fact, <u>no</u> measure satisfying (M) can meet the criterion (C) for all technologies.

<u>Theorem 2</u>. There does not exist an efficiency measure E satisfying (C) and (M) for all $L \in \mathcal{L}$.

<u>Proof</u>. Consider the technology with the level set,

$$L(u^\circ) = \{z \in \mathbb{R}^n \mid z_j \geq 0 \;\wedge\; z_i \geq \tilde{z}_i > 0 \;\forall i \neq j\}$$

for some $u^\circ \in \Gamma$. It is easy to show that this level set is consistent with (L1) and (L2).

---

4 An anonymous referee notes that, while E_{FL} fails to satisfy the homogeneity condition (H), it is affinely homogeneous (to the point $\underline{\varepsilon}$). One could therefore proceed by weakening rather than jettisoning (H). In the light of the next theorem, however, this does not seem to be a promising avenue of inquiry.

5 The term is borrowed from the axiomatic treatment of price indices by Eichhorn and Voeller [1976]

For $z^\circ \in L(u^\circ)$, define $\hat{z}$ by $\hat{z}_j = \lambda z_j^\circ$, where $\lambda \in (1, +\infty)$, and $\hat{z}_i = z_i^\circ \neq 0$ for all $i \neq j$. From the definition of $L(u^\circ)$, $z^\circ \in L(u^\circ)$ implies that $\hat{z} \in L(u^\circ)$. By (C),

$$E(u^\circ, z^\circ, L) = E(u^\circ, \hat{z}, \hat{L}),$$

where $\hat{L}$ is defined by

$$\begin{aligned}\hat{L}(u^\circ) &= \{\hat{z} \in \mathbf{R}^n_+ \mid z^\circ \in L(u^\circ)\} \\ &= \{\hat{z} \in \mathbf{R}^n_+ \mid \hat{z} \in L(u^\circ)\} \\ &= L(u^\circ).\end{aligned}$$

Consequently,

$$E(u^\circ, z^\circ, L) = E(u^\circ, \hat{z}, L),$$

contradicting (M). ||

If one takes the commensurability condition (C) to be essential, it would appear that the monotonicity condition (M) should be jettisoned from the list of desirable criteria for efficiency measures. The question this raises is whether the weaker monotonicity condition (WM) is compatible with commensurability. The next theorem answers this questions affirmatively.

Theorem 3. E_{FL} satisfies (C), (I), and (WM) for all $L \in \mathcal{L}$.

Proof. The properties (I) and (WM) were established by Färe and Lovell [1978] and Russell [1985], respectively. To prove that E_{FL} satisfies (C), let

$$\kappa^* = \arg\min_K \{\textstyle\sum_i \kappa_i / \sum_i \delta(z_i) \mid Kz \in L(u) \wedge \kappa_i \in [0,1]\ \forall i\},$$

and consider

$$E(\Omega u, \Lambda z, \hat{L}) = \min_K \{\textstyle\sum_i \kappa_i / \sum_i \delta(\lambda_i z_i) \mid K\Lambda z \in \hat{L}(\Omega u) \wedge \kappa_i \in [0,1]\ \forall i\},$$

where, as in the definition of (C), Ω and Λ are positive diagonal matrices and

$$\hat{L}(\Omega u) = \{\Lambda \in \mathbf{R}^n \mid z \in L(u)\}.$$

This last identity implies that $z \in L(u)$ if and only if $\Lambda z \in \hat{L}(\Omega u)$. Hence, $Kz \in L(u)$ if and only if $K\Lambda z \in \hat{L}(\Omega u)$. Moreover, since Λ is positive, $\delta(\lambda_i z_i) = \delta(\lambda_i)\ \forall i$. Consequently,

$$E(\Omega u, \Lambda z, \hat{L}) = E(u, z, L). \quad ||$$

The next theorem shows that homogeneity (H), along with the indication condition (I), is also compatible with (C).

<u>Theorem 4.</u> E_Z satisfies (C), (I), and (H) for all $L \in \mathcal{L}$.

<u>Proof</u>. Zieschang [1984] showed that E_Z satisfies (I) and (H). To prove that E_Z satisfies (C), in the light of Theorem 3, it suffices to show that

$$D(\Omega u, \Lambda z, \hat{L}^+) = D(u, z, L^+).$$

To see that this is so, note that

$$z \in L^+(u) \Leftrightarrow \exists \hat{z} \in \mathbf{R}^n_+ \mid z - \hat{z} \in L(u)$$

$$\Leftrightarrow \exists \hat{z} \in \mathbf{R}^n_+ \mid \Lambda z - \Lambda \hat{z} \in \hat{L}(\Omega u)$$

$$\Leftrightarrow \Lambda z \in \hat{L}(\Omega u) + \mathbf{R}^n_+ = \hat{L}^+(\Omega u),$$

where the last equivalence exploits the positiveness of Λ. Consequently,

$$D(\Omega u, \Lambda z, \hat{L}^+) = \max_\alpha \{\alpha \in \mathbf{R}_+ \mid \Lambda z/\alpha \in \hat{L}^+(\Omega u)\}$$

$$= \max_\alpha \{\alpha \in \mathbf{R}_+ \mid z/\alpha \in L^+(u)\}$$

$$= D(u, z, L^+). \quad ||$$

Theorems 3 and 4 indicate that (WM) and (H) are separately compatible with (C). This raises the question of whether (WM) and (H) are jointly consistent with (C). In fact, Bol [1986] has shown that, given (I), (WM) and (H) are incompatible whether or not (C) is satisfied:

<u>Theorem 5</u>. There does not exist an E satisfying (I), (WM), and (H) for all $L \in \mathcal{L}$.

Proof of this theorem can be found in Bol [1986], although he states the result in the weaker form with (M) substituted for (WM).

Thus, in order to salvage (WM) and (H), we would have to modify (I). To this end, consider the condition

(WI) $E(u, z, L) = 1$ iff z is weakly efficient.

As it turns out, this indication condition is incompatible with homogeneity:

<u>Theorem 6</u>. There does not exist an E satisfying (WI) and (H) for all $L \in \mathcal{L}$.

<u>Proof.</u> Consider any level set with $\hat{z} \in L(u)$ where $\hat{z} \not> \underline{0}$. By (L1), $\lambda\hat{z} \in L(u)$ for $\lambda > 1$. Since $\mathbb{R}^n_+ \supseteq L(u)$, $\hat{z}$ and $\lambda\hat{z}$ are necessarily weakly efficient, so that (WI) implies $E(u, \hat{z}, L) = E(u, \lambda\hat{z}, L) = 1$. But this violates (H). ||

It is, however, possible to salvage (WM) and (H) if we weaken (WI) to

(WI°) For all $z > \underline{0}$, $E(u, z, L) = 1$ iff z is weakly efficient.

This condition has some appeal (as compared to (WI)) because input vectors on the boundary of $\mathbb{R}^n_+$ are trivially weakly efficient and, consequently, a measure satisfying (WI) provides no (indication) information about vectors on the boundary. Define the efficiency measure E^+_{DF} by

$$E^+_{DF}(u, z, L) = \begin{cases} D(u, z, L^+)^{-1} & \text{if } z \in L(u) \\ +\infty & \text{if } z \notin L(u) \end{cases}$$

where, it will be recalled, $L^+(u) = L(u) + \mathbb{R}^n_+$. This modification of the Debreu/Farrell measure is equivalent to the "weak input measure of technical efficiency" formulated by Färe and Grosskopf [1983] (see, also, Färe, Lovell, and Grosskopf [1985, pp.57-64]).

<u>Theorem 7</u>. E^+_{DF} satisfies (C), (WI°), (WM), and (H) for all $L \in \mathcal{L}$.

<u>Proof.</u> The invariance of $D(u, z, L^+)$ with respect to changes in units of measurement was shown in the proof of Theorem 4. To prove that E^+_{DF} satisfies (WI°), suppose that $z^* > \underline{0}$, z^* is weakly efficient, and $E_{DF}(u, z^*, L) < 1$. Then $z^* \in L(u)$ and $\lambda z^* \in L^+(u)$ for some $\lambda < 1$. Thus, there exists a $\hat{z} \in L(u)$ such that $\hat{z} \leq \lambda z^* < z^*$, contradicting the supposition that z^* is weakly efficient. Hence, $E_{DF}(u, z^*, L) = 1$.

Now suppose that z^* is not weakly efficient. Then there exists a $\hat{z} \in L(u)$ such that $\hat{z} < z^*$. If $\varepsilon = \min\{z_i^* - \hat{z}_i \mid i = 1, \ldots, n\}$, and $\lambda = (\|z^*\| - \varepsilon) / \|z^*\|$, then $\lambda z^* \geq \hat{z}$. Hence, $\lambda z^* \in L^+(u)$. However, as $\lambda < 1$,

$$E^+_{DF}(u, z^*, L) = D(u, z^*, L^+)^{-1} < 1,$$

completing the proof of (WI°).

Finally, the property (H) follows immediately from the first-degree homogeneity of the distance function D.||

4. Concluding Remarks.

The summary and upshot of the foregoing results are as follows:

(1) If we insist on the fundamental commensurability property (insensitivity to changes in units of measurement), (C), we can't have monotonicity (M).

(2) If we weaken monotonicity to (WM), we can have indication of efficient vectors (I) or homogeneity (H), but not both.

(3) We can have (H) as well as (WM) if we modify (I) to the weak indication condition (WI°).

(4) Consequently, in the context of the foregoing axiom systems, we must choose among

$(C) \wedge (I) \wedge (WM)$, satisfied by E_{FL},

$(C) \wedge (I) \wedge (H)$, satisfied by E_Z,

and

$(C) \wedge (WI°) \wedge (WM) \wedge (H)$, satisfied by E_{DF}.

References

Bol, G. [1986], "On Technical Efficiency Measures: A Remark," Journal of Economic Theory 38, 380-85.

Debreu, G. [1951], "The Coefficient of Resource Utilization," Econometrica 19, 273-92.

Eichhorn, W., and J. Voeller [1976], Theory of the Price Index: Fisher's Test Approach and Generalizations (Lecture Notes in Operations Research and Mathematical Systems, Vol. 140). Springer-Verlag, Berlin, Heidelberg, New York.

Färe, R., and S. Grosskopf [1983], "Measuring Congestion in Production," Zeitschrift für Nationalökonomie 43, 257-71.

Färe, R., S. Grosskopf, and C. A. K. Lovell [1985], The Measurement of Efficiency of Production, Kluwer-Nijhoff, Boston.

Färe, R., and C. A. K. Lovell [1978], "Measuring the Technical Efficiency of Production," Journal of Economic Theory 19, 150-62.

Farrell, M. J. [1957], "The Measurement of Production Efficiency," Journal of the Royal Statistical Society, Ser. A 120, 253-61.

Koopmans, T. C. [1951], "Analysis of Production as an Efficient Combination of Activities," in T. C. Koopmans, ed., Activity Analysis of Production and Allocation, Wiley, New York.

Malmquist, S. [1951], "Index Numbers and Indifference Surfaces," Trabajo de Estatistica 3, 209-42.

Russell, R. R. [1985], "Measures of Technical Efficiency," Journal of Economic Theory 35, 109-26.

Shephard, R. W. [1970], Theory of Cost and Production Functions, Princeton University Press, Princeton.

Zieschang, K. D. [1984], "An Extended Farrell Technical Efficiency Measure," Journal of Economic Theory 33, 387-96.

Part IV Preferences

On the Role of Income Compensation Functions as Money - Metric Utility Functions

S. Fuchs - Seliger
Institut für Wirtschaftstheorie und Operations Research
Universität Karlsruhe, D-7500 Karlsruhe 1
Federal Republic of Germany

In this paper income compensation functions in different models of consumer behaviour are investigated. Under appropriate conditions these functions can be used as money-metric utility functions representing consumer's preferences. Therefore it is interesting to know their properties which depend on the hypotheses of the respective models. We will see that income compensation functions find a nice field of application in index number theory.

1. Introduction

The use of income compensation functions as money - metric utility functions has become of increasing interest. Contrarily to ordinary utility functions, incpme compensation functions are in principle observable and describe consumer's preferences in amounts of money. A money - metric utility function assigns a numbering to indifference contours equal to how much income would at least be needed to reach that indifference contour if prices p^0 prevail. Therefore, if we know the income compensation function we have got a money - metric utility function which represents consumer's preferences and can be determined by observation. It was Lionel McKenzie who first introduced income compensation functions in his article "Demand theory without a utility index". He developed a model of consumer behaviour in which income compensation functions and compensated demand functions play a crucial role [9]. Later on Hurwicz and Uzawa [8] recognized the usefulness of income compensation functions in order to define a utility function generating the give demand function in integrability theory. Samuelson was the first to investigate the role of income compensation functions for complementary goods. The denotion "money - metric utility function" is also due to him [11].

In this paper we shall study income compensation functions in different models of consumer behaviour. We shall see that similar results can be deduced in the usual neoclassical approach to consumption theory, in integrability theory and in the theory of revealed preference. Moreover, the relationship between income compensation functions, economic price indices and welfare measures will be studied. We shall also see that the relation indirectly revealed preferred (R^*) is represented

Measurement in Economics
ed. by W. Eichhorn

by the income compensation function. Thus, a money - metric representation for R^* has been found.

2. Income Compensation Functions in Various Models of Consumer Behaviour

We shall start our investigation of income compensation functions recalling its definition in three different models of consumer behaviour. Given a nonempty set $X \subseteq \mathbb{R}^n_+$ of commodity bundles we can define income compensation functions according to Samuelson and Swamy [12] by

$$m(p,x^0) = \min_{x \in X} \{px \mid u(x) \geq u(x^0)\} .$$

where p is a price vector, $x^0 \in X$ is a commodity bundle, and $u: X \to \mathbb{R}_+$ a utility function. In order that the minimum always exists, X is assumed to be closed and bounded from below and u is assumed to be upper semicontinuous. Obviously, $m(p,x^0)$ is the money - income making the individual in the price situation p as happy as he was in the price - income situation (p^0,M^0), where x^0 was chosen.

The function $m(p,x^0)$ has the same meaning as the income compensation function $\mu(p;p^0,M^0)$ in integrability theory, being the solution of the following system of partial differential equations

$\dfrac{\partial M(p)}{\partial p_i} = h_i(p,M)$, given the initial value (p^0,M^0). Here h_i denotes the demand for the i'th good, and M is the income of the individual. The denotation $\mu(p;p^0,M^0)$ will be preserved in this paper in order to announce that we are concerned with the role of the income compensation function in integrability theory.

If we want to expose that we are interested in income compensation functions in the theory of revealed preference we use another notation. Here the income compensation function is defined by means of the relation "indirectly revealed preferred" (R^*) which is the transitive hull of the relation "revealed preferred" (R), defined by:

$$xRy: \iff \exists (p,M) \in \mathbb{R}^n_{++} \times \mathbb{R}_+ : x = h(p,M) \wedge x \neq y \wedge py \leq M,$$

$$xR^*y \iff xRy \vee \exists x^1,\dots x^k: xRx^1 \wedge \dots \wedge x^kRy,$$

when a demand function $h: \mathbb{R}^n_{++} \times \mathbb{R}_+ \to \mathbb{R}^n_+$ is given.

Formally, this results from the following two theorems (see Lemma 1 in [13] and Lemma 2 in [4]).

Theorem 1

Consider a continuous demand function h: $\mathbb{R}^n_{++} \to \mathbb{R}_+ \to \mathbb{R}^n_+$, with the following properties:

a) h satisfies the budget equality,

b) the range of h is $\mathbb{R}^n_{++}$ or $\mathbb{R}^n_+$,

c) h satisfies a Lipschitz condition with respect to M, i.e.: For all $p^0, p^1 \in \mathbb{R}^n_{++}$ there exists a real number $K \in \mathbb{R}_{++}$ such that for all $M', M'' \in \mathbb{R}_{++}$ and for all $p(t) = tp^0 + (1-t)p^1$, $t \in]0,1[$, we have

$$||h(p(t),M') - h(p(t),M'')|| \leqq K|M' - M''|.$$

d) $xR^*y \Rightarrow \neg(yR^*x)$, ($\neg$ means: not).

Then the following results:

$M^b < F(p^b;p^a,M^a) \Leftrightarrow h(p^a,M^a)R^*h(p^b,M^b)$,

$M^b > F(p^b;p^a,M^a) \Leftrightarrow h(p^b,M^b)R^*h(p^a,M^a)$.

If we define the relations "not revealed worse" ($\bar{R}^*$) and "revealed equivalent" (I^*) by:

$$x\bar{R}^*y: \Leftrightarrow \neg(yR^*x), \ \forall x,y \in \text{ range of h}$$

and

$$xI^*y: \Leftrightarrow x\bar{R}^*y \wedge y\bar{R}^*x, \ \forall x,y \in \text{ range of h},$$

the following corollary to Theorem 1 results (see [4], p.616).

Corollary 2

From the assumptions of Theorem 1 follows:

On every income consumption path $I(p^b)$, $p^b \in \mathbb{R}^n_{++}$, there exists only one commodity bundle revealed equivalent to some given commodity bundle $x^a = h(p^a,M^a)$, and this is $x^b = h(p^b,F(p^b;p^a,M^a))$.

Finally, another case should be mentioned: If we keep p^a and p^b constant and vary M^a, all of the commodity bundles of the income consumption paths $I(p^a)$ and $I(p^b)$ are compared with each other. We see that for every commodity bundle on $I(p^a)$ there exists an equivalent one on $I(p^b)$.

The income compensation function F: $\mathbb{R}^n_{++} \to \mathbb{R}_+$ is defined by

$$F(p;p^a,M^a) = \sup \{M | h(p^a,M^a) R^* h(p,M)\}, \text{ for } (p^a,M^a) \in \mathbb{R}^{n+1}_{++} .$$

According to $\mu(p^b;p^a,M^a)$, $F(p^b;p^a,M^a)$ can be interpreted as the income which makes the individual in the price situation p^b as happy as he has been in the price - income situation (p^a,M^a). Intuitively speaking, if we keep (p^a,M^a) constant and vary p^b, then for every income consumption path $I(p^b) = \{x | x=h(p^b,M), M \in \mathbb{R}_+\}$, $h(p^b,F(p^b;p^a,M^a))$ is the commodity bundle equivalent to (p^a,M^a) (see Figure 1).

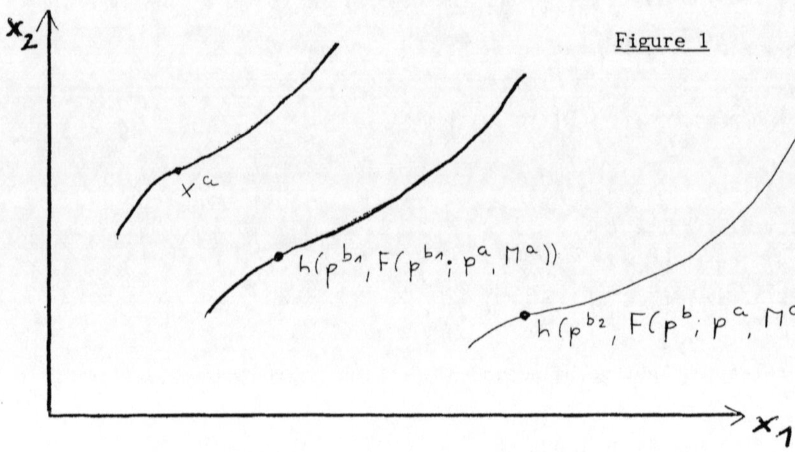

Figure 1

$h(p,F(p;p^a,M^a))$ is called the "compensated demand function". Alternatively, if we vary (p^a,M^a) and keep p constant, then for every commodity bundle $x^a = h(p^a,M^a)$ there exists one commodity bundle on the income consumption path I(p) (see Figure 2) equivalent to x^a.

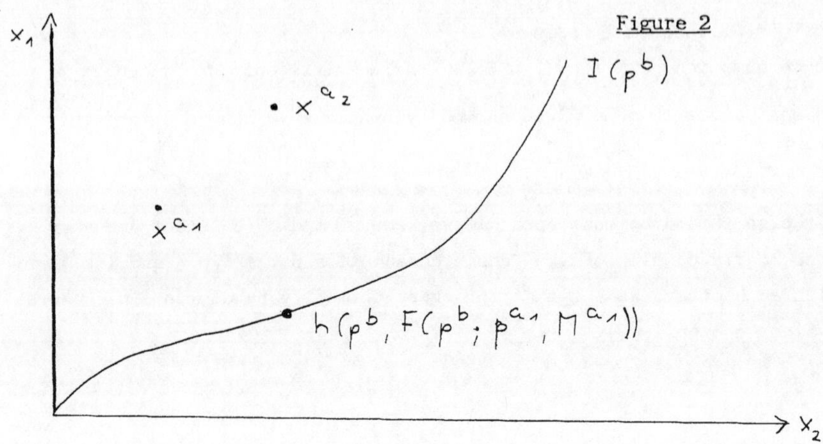

Figure 2

Note that the above analysis can be transferred to other models of consumer behaviour. In integrability theory for instance, we can also find a commodity bundle $h(p^b,\mu(p^b;p^a,M^a))$ equivalent to $h(p^a,M^a)$ on the income consumption path corresponding to p^b. In summary we can say, that $F(p^b;p^a,M^a)$, $\mu(p^b;p^a,M^a)$ and $m(p^b,x^a)$ represents the money income by which a commodity bundle on the income consumption path $I(p^b)$ is determined, which makes the individual as happy as he has been in the price - income situation (p^a,M^a), where he has chosen the commodity bundle $h(p^a,M^a)$. These different notations of the income compensation function are only used in order to emphasize which of the models of consumer behaviour is just considered.

3. Income Compensation Functions as Utility Functions

Hurwicz and Uzawa [7] recognized that McKenzie's income compensation function is a useful tool in order to establish a utility function in integrability theory generating the given demand function. In Lemma 8 they have shown that the utility function

$$U_{p^*}(x) := \mu(p^*;p,M), \ x = h(p,M), \qquad \forall \ (p,M) \in \mathbb{R}^n_{++} \times \mathbb{R}_+,$$

generates the given demand function h. They also realized that $\mu(p^*;p,M)$ can be also considered as an indirect utility function which ranks two arbitrary situations (p',M') and (p'',M'') in the following way

$$(p',M') \succ (p'',M''): \Leftrightarrow \mu(p^*;p',M') > \mu(p^*;p'',M'').$$

It has been pointed out by Samuelson [11] and commented by Varian [14], that $m(p,x^0)$ is a monotonic transformation of a utility function and is therefore itself a utility function.

We want to show now that the income compensation function can be also used as a money - metric utility function in the theory of revealed preference. Therefore, we want to show now that $F(p^0;p,M)$ represents the relation indirectly revealed preferred independently from any given price situation p^0, i.e.,

$$h(p^a,M^a)R^*h(p^b,M^b) \Leftrightarrow F(p^0;p^a,M^a)>F(p^0;p^b,M^b), \ \forall(p^a,M^a),(p^b,M^b)\in\mathbb{R}^n_{++} \times \mathbb{R}_+$$

The analysis of all the following lemmata and theorems on income compensation functions in the theory of revealed preference will be based on the conditions of

Theorem 1. This must be always remembered if the assertions are considered. Our representation theorem will be a consequence of Lemma 3 and 4.

Lemma 3

Let us consider two commodity bundles $h(p',M')$, $h(p'',M'')$ and any price situation p^0. If $F(p^0;p',M') = F(p^0;p'',M'')$ then also $F(p;p',M') = F(p;p'',M'')$ for any $p\in\mathbb{R}^n_{++}$

Proof:

By Corollary 2, $h(p',M')I^*h(p^0;F(p^0;p',M'))$ and $h(p'',M'')\ I^*h(p^0,F(p^0;p'',M''))$. Hence $h(p',M')I^*h(p'',M'')$, following from the transitivity and completeness of $\bar{R}^*$ (see [13]). Moreover, since $h(p',M')I^*h(p,F(p;p',M'))$ and $h(p'',M'')I^*h(p,F(p,p'',M''))$, $\forall\ p\in\mathbb{R}^n_{++}$, Theorem 1 implies that $F(p;p',M') = F(p;p'',M'')$.

Lemma 4

Consider $h(p',M')$, $h(p'',M'')$ and any price situation p^0. Then $F(p^0;p',M') < F(p^0;p'',M'')$ implies $F(p;p',M') < F(p;p'',M'')$, $\forall\ p \in \mathbb{R}^n_{++}$

Proof:

Application of Corollary 2 yields,

$h(p',M')I^*h(p^0,F(p^0,F(p^0,p',M'))$ and $h(p'',M'')I^*h(p^0,F(p^0;p'',M''))$.

From $F(p^0;p',M') < F(p^0;p'',M'')$ we obtain, $h(p^0,F(p^0;p'',M''))R^*h(p^0,F(p^0;p',M'))$. Thus, $h(p'',M'')R^*h(p',M')$. Combining this result with $h(p',M')I^*h(p,F(p;p',M'))$ and $h(p'',M'')I^*h(p,F(p;p'',M''))$ yields $h(p,F(p;p'',M''))R^*h(p,F(p;p',M'))$. Thus, in view of the Strong Axiom we obtain, $F(p;p'',M'') > F(p;p',M')$.

Hurwicz and Uzawa have proven similar results in integrability theory [8]. However, the proofs differ completely.

It will be demonstrated now, that $F(p^0;p,M)$ represents the relation $\bar{R}^*$. Therefore we will show that under the conditions of Theorem 1 the following equivalences hold:

Theorem 5

Assume the conditions of Theorem 1.

For any $p^0\in\mathbb{R}^n_{++}$ we have

a) $x^a\ R^*\ x^b \iff F(p^0;p^a,M^a) > F(p^0;p^b,M^b)$, where $x^{\cdot} = h(p^{\cdot},M^{\cdot})$

b) $x^a\ I^*\ x^b \iff F(p^0;p^a,M^a) = F(p^0;p^b,M^b)$.

Proof for a)

Assume $x^a R^* x^b$. Then by Corollary 2, $M^b < F(p^b;p^a,M^a)$. However, since in view of Theorem 1 we have $M^b = F(p^b;p^b,M^b)$, we obtain $F(p^b;p^b,M^b) < F(p^b;p^a,M^a)$. This together with Lemma 4 implies, $F(p^0;p^b,M^b) < F(p^0;p^a,M^a)$. Conversely, if $F(p^0;p^a,M^a) > F(p^0;p^b,M^b)$, then in view of Lemma 4, $F(p^a;p^a,M^a) > F(p^a;p^b,M^b)$. Thus by Theorem 1, $h(p^a,M^a)R^*h(p^b,M^b)$.

Proof for b)

If $x^a I^* x^b$, then by Theorem 1, $M^a \leqq F(p^a;p^b,M^b)$ and $M^b \leqq F(p^b;p^a,M^a)$. Thus $F(p^a;p^a,M^a) \leqq F(p^a;p^b,M^b)$ and $F(p^b;p^b,M^b) \leqq F(p^b;p^a,M^a)$.
From this we obtain, $F(p^0;p^a,M^a) \leqq F(p^0;p^b,M^b)$ and $F(p^0;p^b,M^b) \leqq F(p^0;p^a,M^a)$. Thus $F(p^0;p^a,M^a) = F(p^0;p^b,M^b)$. Conversely, if $F(p^0;p^a,M^a) = F(p^0;p^b,M^b)$, then according to Lemma 3, $M^a = F(p^a;p^a,p^a) = F(p^a;p^b,M^b)$. Thus, by Theorem 1, $\neg(h(p^b,M^b)\ R^*h(p^a,M^a))$ and $\neg(h(p^a,M^a)R^*h(p^b,M^b))$. The application of the definition of I^* completes our proof. q.e.d.

The following result demonstrates that the income compensation function $F(p^0;p,M)$ attributes equal values to any commodity bundle x independent from whether it is chosen in a price income situation (p^1,M^1) or (p^2,M^2).

Lemma 6

Assume the conditions of Theorem 1.
For all $(p^1,M^1),(p^2,M^2)$ we have:

$$h(p^1,M^1) = h(p^2,M^2) \Rightarrow F(p^0;p^1,M^1) = F(p^0;p^2,M^2).$$

Proof:

$h(p^1,M^1) = h(p^2,M^2)$ implies, $h(p^1,M^1)I^*h(p^2,M^2)$.
Thus, by Theorem 4, $F(p^0;p^1,M^1) = F(p^0;p^2,M^2)$. q.e.d.

We will define a real valued function by

$$u_{p^0}(x) = F(p^0;p,M),\ x = h(p,M),$$

given some $p^0 \in \mathbb{R}^n_{++}$.

Thus, by definition, $u_{p^0}(x)$ is a utility function on the range of h for $\bar{R}^*$. Hence, by application of Theorem 5, we obtain the following result:

Theorem 7

Under the assumptions of Theorem 1 the utility function u_{p^0} represents the relation $\bar{R}^*$ on the range of h, i.e.,

$$u_{p^0}(x^1) \geqq u_{p^0}(x^2) \iff x^1 \bar{R}^* x^2,$$

From the above defintion we see that U_{p^*} and u_{p^0} correspond to each other.

In the following we shall see that income compensation functions find a nice field of application in index number theory and in welfare theory.

4. An Application of Compensating Income to Economic Price Indices

Samuelson and Swamy [12] were the first to define economic price indices in neoclassical consumption theory by means of the income compensation function:

$$P_K(p^a, p^b, x^0) = \frac{m(p^b, x^0)}{m(p^a, x^0)}, \qquad m(p^a, x^0) \neq 0.$$

In the model of revealed preference we can define a Laspeyres - type cost of living index in terms of the income compensation function by

$$P_R(p^a, p^b, M^a) = \frac{F(p^b; p^a, M^a)}{M^a}, \quad M^a \neq 0 ,$$

and a Paasche - type economic price index by

$$P'_R(p^a, p^b, M^b) = \frac{M^b}{F(p^a; p^b, M^b)}$$

where $(p^a, M^a), (p^b, M^b) \in \mathbb{R}^{n+1}_{++}$ denote the price-income situations at a base time and a comparison time, respectively (see [6]).

In a similar way we can also define an economic price index in integrability theory by:

$$P_I(p^a, p^b, M^a) = \frac{\mu(p^b; p^a, M^a)}{M^a} \qquad \text{(Laspeyres - type)}$$

and

$$P_I'(p^a,p^b,M^b) = \frac{M^b}{\mu(p^a;p^b,M^b)} \qquad \text{(Paasche - type).}$$

Analogously to the proofs of the theorems in [6] it can be shown that P_I has also some well - known properties of price indices as for instance:

a) $p^{b_2} \geq p^{b_1} \Rightarrow P_I(p^a,p^{b_2},M^a) > P_I(p^a,p^{b_1},M^a)$, [1]

b) $p^{a_2} \geq p^{a_1} \Rightarrow P_I(p^{a_2},p^b,M^a) < P_I(p^{a_1},p^b,M^a)$,

c) $P_I(\lambda p^a,p^b,\lambda M^a) = \frac{1}{\lambda}P_I(p^a,p^b,M^a)$.

It will be shown here that P_I satisfies Fisher's Time Reversal and Circular Test if and only if the demand function is linear in M (i.e. $h(p,\lambda M) = \lambda\cdot h(p,M)$, $\forall\lambda\in\mathbb{R}_{++}$). Preliminarily we recall the definitions of two relations in integrability theory (see Hurwicz and Uzawa [8], and Chipman and Moore [2]):

For any $(p',M'),(p'',M'')$:

$$h(p',M')Ph(p'',M''): \Leftrightarrow \mu(p^0;p',M') > \mu(p^0;p'',M''),$$
$$h(p',M')Ih(p'',M''): \Leftrightarrow \mu(p^0;p',M') = \mu(p^0;p'',M''),$$
$$h(p',M')R'h(p'',M'') \Leftrightarrow \mu(p^0;p',M') \geqq \mu(p^0;p'',M'').$$

It will be shown next that the indirect utility function

$$V_{p^0}(p,M) = \mu(p^0;p,M), \qquad \forall(p,M) \in \mathbb{R}^{n+1}_{++},$$

is linear in M if and only if the demand function is linear in M, i.e.

$$\lambda\mu(p^0;p^a,M^a) = \mu(p^0;p^a,\lambda M^a) \Leftrightarrow \lambda h(p,M) = h(p,\lambda M),\ \forall\ \lambda \in \mathbb{R}_{++}.$$

<u>Theorem 8</u>

$V_{p^0}(p,M)$ is linear in M iff h is linear in M.

---

1) $x \geq y$, for $x,y \in \mathbb{R}^n$, means: $\Leftrightarrow x \geqq y \wedge x \neq y$

Proof:

1) Assume $h(p,\lambda M) = \lambda h(p,M)$, $\lambda \in \mathbb{R}_{++}$. In view of Lemma 1 in Chipman [1] we obtain,

$$\mu(p^0;p,\lambda M) = \lambda\mu(p^0;p,M).$$

Thus the definition of V gives

$$V_{p^0}(p,\lambda M) = \lambda V_{p^0}(p,M).$$

2) In order to prove the converse assume $V_{p^0}(p,\lambda M) = \lambda V_{p^0}(p,M)$, $\forall\lambda \in \mathbb{R}_{++}$. We shall see now, that the direct utility function U_{p^0} corresponding to V_{p^0} is linear in x. Analogously to Theorem 8 in [6] we also obtain in integrability theory:

$$\begin{aligned}
U_{p^0}(\lambda x) &= \inf\{V_{p^0}(p,M)\,|\,p\cdot\lambda x \leqq M,\ \forall(p,M)\in\mathbb{R}^{n+1}_{++}\} \\
&= \inf\{V_{p^0}(p,M)\,|\,p\cdot x \leqq \tfrac{M}{\lambda},\ \forall(p,M)\in\mathbb{R}^{n+1}_{++}\} \\
&= \inf\{\lambda V_{p^0}(p,\tfrac{M}{\lambda})\,|\,p\cdot x \leqq \tfrac{M}{\lambda},\ \forall(p,\tfrac{M}{\lambda})\in\mathbb{R}^{n+1}_{++}\} \\
&= \lambda\cdot\inf\{V_{p^0}(p,M')\,|\,p\cdot x \leqq M',\ \forall(p,M')\in\mathbb{R}^{n+1}_{++}\} \\
&= \lambda\cdot U_{p^0}(x).
\end{aligned}$$

Suppose now, h is not linear in M. Then there exists $(p^a,M^a) \in \mathbb{R}^{n+1}_{++}$ such that

$$h(p^a,M^a) \neq M^a\cdot h(p^a,1).$$

Lemma 8 in [8] implies, $U_{p^0}(h(p^a,M^a)) > U_{p^0}(M^a\cdot h(p^a,1))$.

Othersides we have,

$$\begin{aligned}
U_{p^0}(h(p^a,M^a)) &= V_{p^0}(p^a,M^a) = M^a\cdot V_{p^0}(p^a,1) \\
&= M^a\cdot U_{p^0}(h(p^a,1)) = U_{p^0}(M^a\cdot h(p^a,1)),
\end{aligned}$$

contradicting our previous result. Thus, h(p,M) is linear in M. q.e.d.

The next theorem will be concerned with the relationship of the Time Reversal and the Circular Test.

Theorem 9

The following statements are equivalent:

a) $V_{p^0}(p,M)$ is linear in M,

b) h is linear in M,

c) P_I satisfies the Time Reversal Test:

$$P_I(p^a,p^b,M^a)\cdot P_I(p^b,p^a,M^b) = 1$$

d) P_I satisfies the Circular Test:

$$P_I(p^a,p^b,M^a)\cdot P_I(p^b,p^c,M^b) = P_I(p^a,p^c,M^a)$$

$$\forall\ (p^a,M^a),(p^b,M^b) \in \mathbb{R}^{n+1}_{++},\ p^c \in \mathbb{R}^n_{++}.$$

Proof:

In view of the former results we are going to show, b) $\leftrightarrow$ c), a) $\leftrightarrow$ d). First we will show that b) $\leftrightarrow$ c). Therefore let h be linear in M. For all $(p^a,M^a),(p^b,M^b) \in \mathbb{R}^{n+1}_{++}$ we have, $h(p^a,M^a)Ih(p^b,\mu(p^b;p^a,M^a))$ and $h(p^b,M^b)Ih(p^a,\mu(p^a;p^b,M^b))$. Since R' is homothetic iff h is linear in M (see Chipman [1]), we thus obtain

$$h(p^a,1)Ih(p^b,P_I(p^a,p^b,M^a)) \sim h(p^b,\ \frac{1}{P_I(p^b,p^a,M^b)})Ih(p^a,1).$$

Hence we have

$$P_I(p^a,p^b,M^a) = \frac{1}{P_I(p^b,p^a,M^b)} = \frac{M^b}{\mu(p^a;p^b,M^b)} \qquad (1).$$

Conversely, if h(p,M) is not linear in M for all $p \in \mathbb{R}^n_{++}$, then $V_{p^0}(p,M)$ is not linear in M. Thus by definition, $\mu(p^a;p^b,M^b)$ is also not linear in M^b. Hence, the right-hand-side of (1) is not independent of M^b. Since the left-hand-side of (1) is independent of M^b, we thus obtain a contradiction.

In order to show a) $\leftrightarrow$ d), assume h is linear in M.
Obviously we have:

$h(p^a,M^a)Ih(p^b,\mu(p^b;p^a,M^a))$,
$h(p^b,M^b)Ih(p^c,\mu(p^c;p^b,M^b))$ and
$h(p^a,M^a)Ih(p^c,\mu(p^c;p^a,M^a))$.

Since linearity of h in M implies that R' is homothetic (see Chipman [1]), the above equivalences imply

$$h(p^a,1)\,I\,h\Big(p^b,\frac{\mu(p^b;p^a,M^a)}{M^a}\Big), \tag{2}$$

$$h(p^b,1)\,I\,h\Big(p^c,\frac{\mu(p^c;p^b,M^b)}{M^b}\Big) \text{ and}$$

$$h\Big(p^b,\frac{\mu(p^b;p^a,M^a)}{M^a}\Big)\,I\,h\Big(p^c,\frac{\mu(p^c;p^b,M^b)}{M^b}\cdot\frac{\mu(p^b;p^a,M^a)}{M^a}\Big). \tag{3}$$

Combining $h(p^a,1)\,I\,h\Big(p^c,\frac{\mu(p^c;p^a,M^a)}{M^a}\Big)$ with (2) and (3) yields

$$h\Big(p^c,\frac{\mu(p^c;p^a,M^a)}{M^a}\Big)\,I\,h\Big(p^c,\frac{\mu(p^c;p^b,M^b)}{M^b}\cdot\frac{\mu(p^b;p^a,M^a)}{M^a}\Big).$$

Hence

$$\frac{\mu(p^c;p^a,M^a)}{M^a} = \frac{\mu(p^c;p^b,M^b)}{M^b}\cdot\frac{\mu(p^b;p^a,M^a)}{M^a}.$$

Since the converse follows by the same arguments our proof is concluded. q.e.d.

Starting with utility functions, the same analysis can be applied in order to show that the Circular Test and the Time Reversal Test also hold in the usual neoclassical approach to consumption theory iff h is linearly homogeneous in M (see [7]).

5. An Application to Welfare Theory

Income compensation functions can be also employed in order to define welfare indices or welfare measures, as for instance compensated or equivalent variation. We can define a Paasche-type welfare index in integrability theory by

$$W'_I(p^0,M^0,p^1,M^1) = \frac{M^1}{\mu(p^1;p^0,M^0)},$$

or a Laspeyres - type welfare index by

$$W_I(p^0,M^0,p^1,M^1) = \frac{\mu(p^0;p^1,M^1)}{M^0},$$

where (p^0,M^0) and (p^1,M^1) are the price - income situations of the base time and the comparison time, respectively.

We see, that welfare has increased (decreased), if $W_I, W_I' > 1$ (< 1). Using $F(p^0;p^1,M^1)$ and $F(p^1;p^0,M^0)$ these indices can analogously be defined in the theory of revealed preference (see [6]). A similar welfare index has been defined by Pollak [10] by:

$$Q_L(p^0,u^0,u^1) = \frac{c(p^0,u^1)}{c(p^0,u^0)} \qquad \text{(Laspeyres - type)}$$

and

$$Q_P(p^1,u^0,u^1) = \frac{c(p^1,u^1)}{c(p^1,u^0)} \qquad \text{(Paasche - type)}$$

where $c(p,s)$ is the cost function of the individual, and u^0,u^1 are certain levels of utility. We see, if $Q_P, Q_L > 1$ (<1), then welfare has increased (decreased) in going from (p^0,M^0) to (p^1,M^1). In the theory of revealed preference we can define another welfare index by

$$Q_R(p^0,M^0,p^1,M^1) = \sup\ \{k|h(p^1,M^1)R^*h(p^0,kM^0)\}.$$

We see, if $k > 1$ (<1), then welfare has increased in going from (p^0,M^0) to (p^1,M^1). This welfare index is also in principle observable, since by Theorem 1 we can always decide, if $h(p^1,M^1)$ is preferred to $h(p^0,kM^0)$ or conversely.

Another welfare indicator which extends the above definition to comparison between any two price income situations (p^1,M^1) and (p^2,M^2) when (p^0,M^0) is fixed is:

$$Q_R^*(p^0,M^0,p^1,M^1,p^2,M^2) = \frac{Q_R(p^0,M^0,p^2,M^2)}{Q_R(p^0,M^0,p^1,M^1)}.$$

We see (p^1,M^1) and (p^2,M^2) are not compared directly with each other, but by their ratio to (p^0,M^0). Obviously, if $Q_R^* > 1$ (<1), then welfare has increased (decreased) in going from (p^1,M^1) to (p^2,M^2).

Based on the income compensation functions two other welfare indicators can be defined; these are the compensated variation (cv) and equivalent variation (EV).

Compensated and equivalent variation were introduced to neoclassical consumption theory by Hicks. Chipman and Moore investigated their role as welfare indicators in integrability theory. In the theory of revealed preference CV and EV are defined by:

$$CV_R(p^0,M^0,p^1) = M^0 - F(p^1;p^0,M^0), \text{ and}$$
$$EV_R(p^0,M^0,p^1) = F(p^0;p^1,M^0) - M^0.$$

Given some price situation p^0, according to Chipman and Moore [2] we will define a generalized version of CV in the theory of revealed preference by:

$$\Psi_R(p,M) = M - F(p;p^0,M^0), \ \forall (p,M) \in \mathbb{R}^{n+1}_{++}.$$

This welfare measure extends the definition of CV to the case of comparison between any two price income situations relative to (p^0,M^0). However, it will be interesting to note that - as in integrability theory - the generalized compensated variation furnishes an acceptable measure of welfare change in some special cases only.

It will be shown here that for fixed income $\bar{M} > 0$ the generalized compensated variation represents the relation indirectly revealed not worse $(\bar{R}^*)$, iff h is linear in M. The proof of this theorem has been inspired by Proposition H1 of Chipman and Moore [2], but in contrary to their approach no differentiability conditions are used here. Formally, it will be shown,

(A) $$h(p^1,\bar{M})\bar{R}^*h(p^2,\bar{M}) \Leftrightarrow \bar{M} - F(p^1;p^0,M^0) \geqq \bar{M} - F(p^2;p^0,M^0).$$

We will show that this relationship holds if and only if the equivalence

(B) $$h(p^1,M^1)\bar{R}^*h(p^2,M^2) \Leftrightarrow \frac{M^1}{F(p^1;p^0,M^0)} \geqq \frac{M^2}{F(p^2;p^0,M^0)}, \forall M^1,M^2 \in \mathbb{R}_{++}$$

holds.

<u>Lemma 10</u>

Condition (A) is satisfied if and only if (B) holds.

Proof:

Assume (A) and consider $(p^1,M^1), (p^2,M^2) \in \mathbb{R}^{n+1}_{++}$ such that $h(p^1,M^1)\bar{R}^*h(p^2,M^2)$. Since h is homogeneous of degree 0 in (p,M), we obtain:

$h(\bar{M}\cdot\frac{p^1}{M^1},\bar{M})\bar{R}^* h(\bar{M}\cdot\frac{p^2}{M^2},\bar{M})$. In view of (A) we obtain

$$h(\bar{M}\cdot\frac{p^1}{M^1},\bar{M})\bar{R}^* h(\bar{M}\cdot\frac{p^2}{M^2},\bar{M}) \iff \bar{M} - F(\frac{p^1\bar{M}}{M^1};p^0,M^0) \geqq \bar{M}-F(\frac{p^2\bar{M}}{M^2};p^0,M^0)$$

$$\iff \frac{M^1}{F(p^1;p^0,M^0)} \geqq \frac{M^2}{F(p^2;p^0,M^0)} \qquad (1)$$

following from $F(\lambda p;p^0,M^0) = \lambda F(p;p^0,M^0),\ \forall\ \lambda > 0$.
Conversely assume (1), then by reversing the steps in the arguments we obtain, $h(p^1,M^1)\bar{R}^* h(p^2,M^2)$. Thus we have shown the implication, (A) → (B). In order to prove the converse, assume (B). Hence we have,

$$h(p^1,\bar{M})\bar{R}^* h(p^2,\bar{M}) \iff \frac{\bar{M}}{F(p^1;p^0,M^0)} \geqq \frac{\bar{M}}{F(p^2;p^0,M^0)}$$

$$\iff \bar{M}-F(p^1;p^0,M^0) \geqq \bar{M}-F(p^2;p^0,M^0). \qquad \text{q.e.d}$$

From the following theorem we can conclude that if income remains unchanged, the generalized compensated variation is an acceptable indicator of welfare if and only if the demand function in homogeneous of degree one in M.

Theorem 11

Condition (A) is satisfied if and only if the demand functions are homogeneous of degree one in M.

Proof:

Let us first assume that h is homogeneous of degree one in M. Since the income compensation function represents $\bar{R}^*$, we have

$$h(p^1,M^1)\bar{R}^* h(p^2,M^2) \iff F(p^0;p^1,M^1) \geqq F(p^0;p^2,M^2). \qquad (1)$$

Since in view of Theorem 2 in [6] demand functions which are homogeneous of degree one in M satisfy the Time Reversal Test, we have

$$F(p^0;p^1,M^1) = \frac{M^1\cdot M^0}{F(p^1;p^0,M^0)} \text{ and } F(p^0;p^2,M^2) = \frac{M^2\cdot M^0}{F(p^2;p^0,M^0)}.$$

This together with (1) implies

$$h(p^1,M^1)\bar{R}^* h(p^2,M^2) \iff \frac{M^1 \cdot M^0}{F(p^1;p^0,M^0)} \geqq \frac{M^2 \cdot M^0}{F(p^1;p^0,M^0)}.$$

In order to prove the converse, assume (B) and suppose that h is not homogeneous of degree one in M. Then $h(p^a,M^a) \neq M^a \cdot h(p^a,1)$, for some M^a.
From $h(p^a,M^a)\cdot p^a = M^a = M^a \cdot h(p^a,1)\cdot p^a$, $h(p^a,M^a) R^* h(p^a,M^a \cdot h(p^a,1))$ results. In view of (A) the utility function

$$\tilde{u}(x) = \frac{M}{F(p;p^0,M^0)}, \quad x = h(p,M),$$

is a representation of $\bar{R}^*$. Therefore we have:

$$\tilde{u}(h(p^a,M^a)) > \tilde{u}(M^a \cdot h(p^a,1)). \tag{2}$$

Remember that for the commodity bundle $M^a \cdot h(p^a,1)$ a price - income situation (p^c,M^c), in which it is chosen, exists. If we consider the indirect utility function

$$\tilde{v}(p,M) = \frac{M}{F(p;p^0,M^0)}, \quad \forall\ (p,M) \in \mathbb{R}^{n+1}_{++},$$

we see that it is homogeneous of degree one in M. Analogously to Theorem 8 in [6] it can be shown,

$$\tilde{u}(x) = \inf\{v(p,M)\,|\,px \leqq M,\ \forall (p,M) \in \mathbb{R}^{n+1}_{++}\}.$$

Therefore, in view of (B), $\tilde{v}(p,M)$ is an indirect utility function corresponding to $\tilde{u}(x)$.

We can also show that $\tilde{u}(\lambda x) = \lambda \tilde{u}(x)$, $\forall\ \lambda > 0$, analogously to Theorem 8.
Using this result we obtain

$$\begin{aligned}\tilde{u}(h(p^a,M^a)) &= \tilde{v}(p^a,M^a) = M^a \cdot \tilde{v}(p^a,1)\\ &= M^a \cdot \tilde{u}(h(p^a,1)) = \tilde{u}(M^a \cdot h(p^a,1)),\end{aligned}$$

contradicting (2). By this our proof is concluded.

In this paper we have studied the role of the income compensation function in index number theory and in welfare economics. Since income compensation functions are in principle observable, we need practicable algorithms in order to determine them by data.First steps in this direction have been made by Varian ([14],[15]) and Vartia [16].

5. References

[1] Chipman, J.S., "Homothetic Preferences and Aggregation", J. Econ. Theory, 1974,8,26-38.

[2] Chipman, J.S. and J.C. Moore, "Compensating Variation, Consumer's Surplus and Welfare", The American Economic Review, 1980, 933-949.

[3] Fuchs-Seliger, S.,"Revealed Preference and the Economic Theory of Index Numbers", in W. Eichhorn et.al.eds., Theory and Applications of Economic Indices, Würzburg 1978.

[4] Fuchs-Seliger,S., "On the Continuity of Utility Functions in the Theory of Revealed Preference", International Economic Review, 1981,41,69-78.

[5] Fuchs-Seliger, S., "On Continuous Utility Functions Derived from Demand Functions", Journal of Mathematical Economics, 1983,12,19-32.

[6] Fuchs-Seliger, S. and A. Pfingsten,"Cost of Living Indices Based on Demand Functions", Zeitschrift für Nationalökonomie, 1986,1,49-64.

[7] Fuchs-Seliger,S., U. Niemeyer, A. Pfingsten, "An Analysis of Statistically - Motivated Tests in Economic Price Index Theory", in Martin Beckmann et. al. eds., Methods of OR, Anton Hain 1986, 233-244.

[8] Hurwicz, L. and H. Uzawa, "On the Integrability of Demand Functions", in J.S. Chipman et al. eds., Preferences, Utility, and Demand, New York 1971, 114-148.

[9] McKenzie, L.W.,"Demand Theory without a Utility Index", Rev. Econ. Stud., 1957, 24, 185-89.

[10] Pollak, R.A., "The Theory of Cost of Living Index", in W.E. Diewert eds., Conference on Price Measurement, Statistics Canada, Ottawa 1983, 87-163.

[11] Samuelson, P.A., "Complementarity - An Essay on the 40th Anniversary of the Hicks-Allen Revolution in Demand Theory", J.Econ.Lit., 1979, 1255-1289.

[12] Samuelson, P.A. and S. Swamy, "Invariant Economic Index Numbers and Canonical Duality, Survey and Synthesis", Amer. Econ. Rev., 1974,64,566-93.

[13] Uzawa, H., "Preferences and Rational Choice in the Theory of Consumption", in J.S. Chipman et al. eds., Preferences. Utility and Demand, New York 1971,7-28.

[14] Varian, H.R., "The Nonparametric Approach to Demand Analysis", Econometrica, 1982,50,945-973.

[15] Varian, H.R., "Non-parametric Tests of Consumer Behaviour", Rev.Econ.Stud.,1983,50,99-110.

[16] Vartia,Y.O., "Efficient Methods of Measuring Welfare Change and Compensated Income in Terms of Ordinary Demand Functions", Econometrica 1983,51,79-98.

[17] Weymark, J.,"Money-Metric Utility Functions", International Economic Review 1985, 26,219-232.

Algebra and Topology in Cardinal Utility Theory*

Gebhard Fuhrken and Marcel K. Richter**

Department of Economics
University of Minnesota
271 19th Avenue South
Minneapolis, Minnesota 55455, USA

1. INTRODUCTION

When do cardinal preferences have cardinal utilities? If D is a quaternary relation on a set X, when does there exist a "utility function" $f: X \to \mathrm{Re}$ satisfying:

$$xyDzw \Leftrightarrow f(x) - f(y) \geqq f(z) - f(w) \tag{1.1}$$

for all $x, y, z, w \in X$?

Since the right hand side of (1.1) is equivalent to $f(x) + f(w) \geqq f(z) + f(y)$, we can generalize the question by asking, When do composite preferences have additive utilities? If $\succcurlyeq$ is a $2m$-ary relation on a set X, when does there exist a "utility function" $f: X \to \mathrm{Re}$ satisfying:

$$x_1 \cdots x_m \succcurlyeq y_1 \cdots y_m \Leftrightarrow f(x_1) + \cdots + f(x_m) \geqq f(y_1) + \cdots + f(y_m) \tag{1.2}$$

for all $x_1, \ldots, x_m, y_1, \ldots, y_m \in X$?[1] Our characterization for (1.2) will therefore cover (1.1) as a special case.

*We thank Peter Wakker for helpful comments on an earlier version.

**The assistance of the National Science Foundation, Grant SES-8510620, is gratefully acknowledged.

[1]This question could be generalized further, by not requiring that the functions on the different factors of X^m all be the same. We will discuss that question elsewhere, but we want to keep the present discussion simple, emphasizing the basic ideas. Note that, as it stands, (1.2) is a representation assumed in many current theories dealing with economic choice over several time periods.

Measurement in Economics
ed. by W. Eichhorn

These are questions that have been much studied, and many answers have been given over many decades. The new answers offered here have several advantages. First, they give stronger theorems. Second, the method of proof is very fundamental and natural, and corresponds to methods used in other areas of utility theory. Third, and most important for the present paper, they are based on a Continuity Principle, separating the "proper" axioms for finite sets from the topological-archimedean axioms for arbitrary sets.

New theorems. Our theorems do not require "essentiality" or topological separability hypotheses, and we prove continuity of representations. For more detailed comparison with other work, see Section 5.

Structural Principle. Richter [13] gave a simple proof of Debreu's theorem [4] on continuous utility representation, by using an elementary characterization of the real line structure (Re,>), and by turning the underlying set *into* that real line. Here we do the analogous thing for cardinal and additive utility. We use a fundamental characterization of the additive group structure of the reals, and we turn the underlying set *into* that additive real group. Our Structural Principle is the simple observation that basing proofs on fundamental structures is a useful proof technique in algebraic measurement problems.

Continuity Principle. A natural way to approach a representation problem — for utility, cardinal utility, subjective probability, etc. — is to begin by seeking axioms that characterize the representation on finite sets. In [12] these were called **proper** axioms. By the Compactness Theorem of Elementary Logic, any model satisfying these axioms will then have a nonstandard representation; but on infinite sets there may not exist a standard one. Since the essential difference between the nonstandard models of analysis and the standard model is that the standard one is archimedean, this reduces the problem to one of finding an archimedean axiom. The Continuity Principle is simply the observation that a topological continuity hypothesis can often serve as an archimedean axiom; and the separation of finite-set criteria from the continuity axioms is often fruitful, both in understanding and in proving representability. If a continuity conclusion is desired, it will be a necessary condition as well.

The proper axioms, in a sense, characterize the "important," "essential" aspects of the representation. Unlike archimedean axioms, they are are practically meaningful in the sense that they could be violated by a finite number of observations. It is natural to separate them out and understand them first, and then ask what minimal extra assumptions are necessary and sufficient to obtain a continuous representation on nonfinite sets. We will see that, applying this two-step approach to cardinal and additive preferences, we can obtain a new result, a simpler proof, and natural assumptions that are both necessary and sufficient.

We prove here only a special case (Theorem 2) of our general result (Theorem 3). The proof for the special case is especially transparent, and illustrates very clearly the Continuity and Structural Principles that we wish to emphasize. In another paper we apply the same principles to prove Theorem 3.

Our results are closely related to Debreu [5] and to Krantz, Luce, Suppes, and Tversky [10], and our methods have some features in common with the latter. (See Section 5.)

2. PRELIMINARIES

We begin with a set X on which we have a $2m$-ary relation V that we may think of as a subset[2] of $X\times\cdots\times X = X^{2m}$. We assume m is any integer greater than or equal to 1. We seek a function $f : X \rightarrow \mathrm{Re}$ such that, for all $x_1, \ldots, x_m, y_1, \ldots, y_m \in X$,

$$x_1 \cdots x_m V y_1 \cdots y_m \iff f(x_1) + \cdots + f(x_m) \geqq f(y_1) + \cdots + f(y_m). \tag{2.1}$$

If such a function exists, we call it an **additive utility** V.

The following is a simple generalization of a result implicit in Scott [14].

Theorem 1. If X is finite, then for V to have an additive utility it is necessary and sufficient that the following conditions hold for all $x_i, y_i, x_i^j, y_i^j \in X$ and all permutations π, σ of $\{1,\ldots,m\}$, and all $n > 0$ and all permutations $\tau_1, \ldots, \tau_m$ of $\{0, 1, \ldots, n\}$:

$$x_1 \cdots x_m V y_1 \cdots y_m \quad \text{or} \quad y_1 \cdots y_m V x_1 \cdots x_m \tag{2.2a}$$

$$x_1 \cdots x_m V y_1 \cdots y_m \Rightarrow x_{\pi(1)} \cdots x_{\pi(m)} V y_{\sigma(1)} \cdots y_{\sigma(m)} \tag{2.2b}$$

$$\begin{aligned} &x_1^j \cdots x_m^j V x_1^{\tau_1(j)} \cdots x_m^{\tau_m(j)} \quad \text{for } j = 1, \ldots, n, \\ &\quad \Rightarrow x_1^{\tau_1(0)} \cdots x_m^{\tau_m(0)} V x_1^0 \cdots x_m^0. \end{aligned} \tag{2.2c}$$

Remark 1. Condition (2.2a) says that, considered as a binary relation on X^m, V is reflexive and total; it is clearly necessary. Condition (2.2b) is an obviously necessary symmetry condition: the ranking of vectors is independent of the sequencing of their components. In the context of the other axioms, an equivalent version is $x_1 \cdots x_m V x_{\pi(1)} \cdots x_{\pi(m)}$. Condition (2.2c), together with (2.2a),
says that, given any finite list of V-statements, $x_1^j \cdots x_m^j V y_1^j \cdots y_m^j$ $(j = 0,\ldots,n)$, if every element of X occurs as many times on the lefthand side in the i-th position as on the righthand side in the i-th position, then none of these V-instances represent "strict preference" — V holds in both directions. It, too, is clearly a necessary condition. In conjunction with (2.2a), it also implies that V is transitive: $x_1 \cdots x_m V y_1 \cdots y_m V z_1 \cdots z_m \Rightarrow x_1 \cdots x_m V z_1 \cdots z_m$.

Proof of Theorem 1. It is easily proved along the lines of Scott's Theorem 3.2 in [14]. ■

How much beyond (2.2) does continuous representability require when X is not finite? In the spirit of the Continuity Principle, we show that a continuity condition on V and a connectedness condition on X are sufficient. Our method of proof will be in the spirit of the Structural Principle, reducing our structure on X to an archimedean ordered group.

---

[2]For notational convenience and intuition, we use the infix notation $x_1 \cdots x_m V y_1 \cdots y_m$ rather than $V(x_1, \ldots, x_m, y_1, \ldots, y_m)$.

To extend Scott's theorem to arbitrary sets, the following definitions are useful. From the basic relation V on X, we define the binary relations $\succcurlyeq$, $\succ$, and $\approx$ on X by: for all $x,y \in X$,

$$x \succcurlyeq y \quad \Leftrightarrow \quad x \cdots x \, V \, y \cdots y \tag{2.3a}$$

$$x \succ y \quad \Leftrightarrow \quad x \succcurlyeq y \;\&\; \neg y \succcurlyeq x, \tag{2.3b}$$

$$x \approx y \quad \Leftrightarrow \quad x \succcurlyeq y \;\&\; y \succcurlyeq x. \tag{2.3c}$$

Then it is easy to prove

Proposition 1. Under the conditions (2.2), the relation $\succcurlyeq$ is reflexive, transitive, and total on X; the relation $\succ$ is transitive and asymmetric on X; and the relation $\approx$ is reflexive, symmetric, and transitive on X.

Proof. This follows immediately from Theorem 1, since the statements of the properties involve only finitely many elements. ■

It will be technically convenient to get rid of indifference, as follows. Because $\approx$ is an **equivalence relation** (i.e., reflexive, symmetric, and transitive), under the conditions (2.2), it partitions X into the **quotient set** $\mathbf{X} \equiv X/\!\approx\, = \{[x]\colon x \in X\}$, where the equivalence classes $x/\!\approx\, \equiv [x] \equiv \{y \in X\colon y \approx x\}$, for $x \in X$.

We define $>$ on $\mathbf{X}$ by: for all $\mathbf{x},\mathbf{y} \in \mathbf{X}$,

$$\mathbf{x} > \mathbf{y} \quad \Leftrightarrow \quad \exists x,y_{\; x \in \mathbf{x} \,\&\, y \in \mathbf{y}} \; x \succ y. \tag{2.4}$$

Again it is easy to prove

Proposition 2. Under the conditions (2.2), the relation $>$ is transitive, asymmetric, and total on $\mathbf{X}$.

Proof. Again this follows easily from Theorem 1. ■

So $(\mathbf{X},>)$ is a strictly ordered set. By its **order topology** we will mean the topology generated by the $>$-intervals. (Cf. [9], pp. 57-58.)

Given a topology on X, the **quotient topology** on $\mathbf{X}$ is the finest topology on $\mathbf{X}$ for which the projection map $\pi\colon X \to \mathbf{X}$ (with $\pi(x) \equiv [x]$) is continuous. (Cf. [9], p. 94; [3], p. 33 (Example 1).)[3]

We also define the $2m$-ary relation I on X by: for all $x_1, \ldots, x_m, y_1, \ldots, y_m \in X$,

$$x_1 \cdots x_m \, I \, y_1 \cdots y_m \quad \Leftrightarrow \quad x_1 \cdots x_m \, V \, y_1 \cdots y_m \;\&\; y_1 \cdots y_m \, V \, x_1 \cdots x_m. \tag{2.5}$$

[3] A subset $\mathbf{A}$ is open in $\mathbf{X}$ if and only if $\cup\mathbf{A} = \{x \in X\colon \exists \mathbf{y}_{\mathbf{y} \in \mathbf{A}}\; x \in \mathbf{y}\}$ is open in X. (Cf. [3], p. 39.)

Under conditions (2.2), V is complete (2.2a) and transitive (Remark 1), so I is an equivalence relation on X^m.

3. CONTINUOUS ADDITIVE UTILITY: SPECIAL CASE

Our existence theorem for additive utility is based on Loonstra's fundamental characterization of the ordered group of the reals. Our first result is a special case, in which the "comparability" condition (iv) is assumed. This allows a more transparent proof. This condition will be dropped in the next theorem.

Theorem 2. Suppose that $m \geqq 2$ and V is a $2m$-ary relation on X, where:

i) X is a connected topological space;

ii) V satisfies conditions (2.2);

iii) V is "sectionally continuous," i.e.,

$$\{w \in X : w x_2 \cdots x_m \, V \, y_1 \cdots y_m\}$$
$$\cdots$$
$$\{w \in X : x_1 \cdots x_m \, V \, y_1 \cdots y_{m-1} w\}$$

are closed for all $x_i, y_i \in X$;

iv) $\forall x_1, \ldots, x_m, y_1, \ldots, y_m \,{}_{x_i, y_i \in X} \; \exists \bar{z}, \hat{z}_{\bar{z}, \hat{z} \in X} \; \bar{z} x_2 \cdots x_m \, V \, y_1 \cdots y_m$ $\& \; y_1 \cdots y_m \, V \, \hat{z} x_2 \cdots x_m$.

Then there exists a continuous additive utility for V. Furthermore, there is only one additive utility for V, up to positive affine transformation.

Remark 2. By Theorem 1, condition (ii) is necessary. The continuity condition (iii) is also clearly necessary; and it would follow if we assumed (cf. Debreu [5]) that V is a closed subset of X^m. The comparability condition (iv) is made only temporarily; it will be dropped in the next theorem. We do not assume that X is separable (so we cannot drop our assumption that $m \geqq 2$). And we make no assumptions about "essentiality" of any of the components of X^m. While (i) is clearly not necessary for existence of continuous additive utility, the theorem is not valid without (i).

Proof Idea. Our intuition is extremely simple. Since we seek a representation in the real numbers, we want to base our proof on a fundamental characterization of the simplest real mathematical structure appropriate for our problem. Since addition is required, that will involve a group (or semigroup). Since ordering is required, it will involve an ordered group. So we will base our proof on a characterization of the ordered additive group of the reals.

Continuity of preference and connectedness of our underlying space allow us to define an "addition" on **X** that gives it a group structure. And **>** (see (2.4)) turns it into an ordered group.

The ordering has no gaps or jumps, in view of connectedness, so we can apply Loonstra's basic characterization of the real group as the only gapless and jumpless ordered group, to get an isomorphism that serves as an additive utility function.

There are, in fact, several ways to define a group structure on $\mathbf{X}$. The way we present here is not the shortest, but it is quite constructive and very natural. Indeed the proof sketch we have just given suggests all the details to be verified.

As a preliminary step, to carry topological notions from X to $\mathbf{X}$, we note

Proposition 3. a) Under hypotheses (iii) of Theorem 2, open sets in the order topology of $(\mathbf{X},\succ)$ are open in the quotient topology.

b) Under hypotheses (i) and (iii), $(\mathbf{X},\succ)$ is connected in its order topology.

Proof of Proposition 3. The proof of (a) follows easily from the definitions. The proof of (b) follows from (a). ■

Proof of Theorem 2. If $X = \varnothing$, the existence of a continuous additive utility is immediate, so we can assume that X is nonempty. Then we can pick an arbitrary element $e \in X$; and $\mathbf{0} \equiv [e]$ will play the role of zero in $\mathbf{X}$.

a) First we turn $\mathbf{X}$ into an ordered abelian group. We define an addition operator $+$ by: for all $\mathbf{x},\mathbf{y},\mathbf{z} \in \mathbf{X}$,

$$\mathbf{x}+\mathbf{y}=\mathbf{z} \iff \exists x,y,z_{x\in\mathbf{x}\ \&\ y\in\mathbf{y}\ \&\ z\in\mathbf{z}}\ xye \cdots e\ I\ ze \cdots e. \tag{3.1}$$

This is a natural definition since, if there is an additive utility f for V, then this says exactly $f(x)+f(y)=f(z)$. Of course this is a valid definition of an operator only if we know:

$$\forall \mathbf{x},\mathbf{y}_{\mathbf{x},\mathbf{y}\in\mathbf{X}}\ \exists \mathbf{z}_{\mathbf{z}\in\mathbf{X}}\ \mathbf{x}+\mathbf{y}=\mathbf{z} \tag{3.2a}$$

$$\forall \mathbf{x},\mathbf{y},\mathbf{z},\bar{\mathbf{z}}_{\mathbf{x},\mathbf{y},\mathbf{z},\bar{\mathbf{z}}\in\mathbf{X}}\ [\,\mathbf{x}+\mathbf{y}=\mathbf{z}\ \&\ \mathbf{x}+\mathbf{y}=\bar{\mathbf{z}} \ \Rightarrow\ \mathbf{z}=\bar{\mathbf{z}}\,]. \tag{3.2b}$$

But condition (3.2b) is easy to verify from the basic definitions and Theorem 1. And condition (3.2a) follows from hypothesis (iv), since, for any $x \in \mathbf{x}$ and $y \in \mathbf{y}$, neither of the sets

$$\begin{aligned} A &\equiv \{z \in X\colon ze \cdots e\ V\ xye \cdots e\} \\ B &\equiv \{z \in X\colon xye \cdots e\ V\ ze \cdots e\} \end{aligned} \tag{3.3}$$

is empty. And by hypothesis (iii), they are each closed. Since their union is all of X, connectedness of X implies that they have an element z in common:

$$ze \cdots e\ I\ xye \cdots e, \quad \text{i.e.,} \quad \mathbf{z} \equiv \mathbf{x}+\mathbf{y}. \tag{3.4}$$

It is now easy to prove that $(\mathbf{X},\mathbf{0},+,\succ)$ is a totally ordered commutative group:

$$\forall \mathbf{x},\mathbf{y}_{\mathbf{x},\mathbf{y}\in\mathbf{X}}\ \mathbf{x}+\mathbf{y}=\mathbf{y}+\mathbf{x} \tag{3.5a}$$

$$\forall \mathbf{x},\mathbf{y},\mathbf{z}_{\mathbf{x},\mathbf{y},\mathbf{z}\in\mathbf{X}}\ (\mathbf{x}+\mathbf{y})+\mathbf{z}=\mathbf{x}+(\mathbf{y}+\mathbf{z}) \tag{3.5b}$$

$$\forall \mathbf{x}_{\mathbf{x}\in\mathbf{X}}\ \mathbf{x}+\mathbf{0}=\mathbf{x} \tag{3.5c}$$

$$\forall \mathbf{x}_{\mathbf{x}\in\mathbf{X}}\exists \mathbf{y}_{\mathbf{y}\in\mathbf{X}}\ \mathbf{y}+\mathbf{x}=\mathbf{0} \tag{3.5d}$$

$$\forall \mathbf{x},\mathbf{y},\mathbf{z}_{\mathbf{x},\mathbf{y},\mathbf{z}\in\mathbf{X}}\ [\,\mathbf{x}>\mathbf{y}\ \Rightarrow\ \mathbf{x}+\mathbf{z}>\mathbf{y}+\mathbf{z}\,], \tag{3.5e}$$

where **>** is a linear ordering (see Proposition 2). In fact all these except (3.5d) follow directly from Theorem 1. To prove (3.5d) is to prove that, for any $x \in X$, there exists a $y \in X$ such that $yxe \cdots e\, I\, e \cdots e$. But, if there did not exist such a y, then the nonempty (by hypothesis (iv)) closed (by hypothesis (iii)) sets $\{y \in X : yxe \cdots e\, V\, e \cdots e\}$ and $\{y \in X : e \cdots e\, V\, yxe \cdots e\}$ would partition X, contradicting its connectedness (i). So $(\mathbf{X},\mathbf{0},+,>)$ is a totally ordered commutative group.

If $(\mathbf{X},\mathbf{0},+,>)$ is the trivial group, i.e. if $\mathbf{X}=\{\mathbf{0}\}$, then clearly the constant functions are precisely the continuous additive utilities for V, and the proof is done. So in the remainder we assume that the group is nontrivial.

b) Next we show that $(\mathbf{X},\mathbf{0},+,>)$ is "continuously" ordered, hence isomorphic to the additive real group $(\mathrm{Re},0,+,>)$. Indeed, the ordering has two special properties:[4]

> has no gap (3.6a)

> has no jump. (3.6b)

For if there were a gap or a jump, then **X** would be disconnected in its order topology, contradicting Proposition 3b.

So $(\mathbf{X},\mathbf{0},+,>)$ is a totally ordered commutative group with no **>**-gaps and no **>**-jumps. Then a basic characterization by Loonstra [11] asserts there is an isomorphism g from $(\mathbf{X},\mathbf{0},+,>)$ onto $(\mathrm{Re},0,+,>)$.

c) Next we show that this isomorphism yields the required utility function.

We define $f(x) \equiv g([x])$, for each $x \in X$. I.e.,

$$f \equiv g \circ \pi. \tag{3.7}$$

We note that f is continuous. For, as an isomorphism, g is clearly continuous in the order topology. By Proposition 3a, it is continuous in the quotient topology also. Since π is continuous in the quotient topology, f is therefore continuous.

[4] A **gap** is a partition of **X** into nonempty disjoint subsets **A** and **B** such that $\mathbf{x}>\mathbf{y}$ for all $\mathbf{x}\in\mathbf{A}$ and $\mathbf{y}\in\mathbf{B}$, with **A** having no **>**-least element and **B** having no greatest element. A **jump** means the same thing, but with **A** having a least element and **B** having a greatest element.

It is easy to show that f is an additive utility for V. Suppose $x_1 \cdots x_m V y_1 \cdots y_m$; we must show that

$$\sum_{i=1}^{m} f(x_i) \geqq \sum_{i=1}^{m} f(y_i). \tag{3.8}$$

By repeated application of (3.2a), we can obtain $z_1, \ldots, z_{m-2}$ satisfying

$$x_1 x_2 e \cdots e \, I \, z_1 e \cdots e \tag{3.9}$$

$$z_1 x_3 e \cdots e \, I \, z_2 e \cdots e$$

$$\cdots$$

$$z_{m-2} x_m e \cdots e \, I \, z_{m-1} e \cdots e.$$

so Theorem 1 implies

$$x_1 \cdots x_m \, I \, z_{m-2} e \cdots e. \tag{3.10a}$$

Similarly we obtain $w_{m-2} \in X$ such that

$$y_1 \cdots y_m \, I \, w_{m-2} e \cdots e. \tag{3.10b}$$

Therefore

$$z_{m-2} e \cdots e \, I \, x_1 \cdots x_m \, V \, y_1 \cdots y_m \, I \, w_{m-2} e \cdots e, \tag{3.11}$$

so by Theorem 1, $z_{m-2} \succcurlyeq w_{m-2}$, hence

$$\sum_{i=1}^{m} f(x_i) = \sum_{i=1}^{m} g([x_i]) = g([x_1] + \cdots + [x_m]) = g([z_{m-2}])$$
$$\geqq g([w_{m-2}]) = g([y_1] + \cdots + [y_m]) = \sum_{i=1}^{m} g([y_i]) = \sum_{i=1}^{m} f(y_i), \tag{3.12}$$

so (3.8) holds.

Conversely, suppose that

$$\sum_{i=1}^{m} f(x_i) \geqq \sum_{i=1}^{m} f(y_i); \tag{3.13}$$

we must show that

$$x_1 \cdots x_m \, V \, y_1 \cdots y_m. \tag{3.14}$$

With z_{m-2} and w_{m-2} as in (3.10), we have

$$g([z_{m-2}]) = f(z_{m-2}) = \sum_{i=1}^{m} f(x_i) \geqq \sum_{i=1}^{m} f(y_i) = f(w_{m-2}) = g([w_{m-2}]), \tag{3.15}$$

so $z_{m-2} \succcurlyeq w_{m-e}$, hence (by (3.13) and Theorem 1)

$$x_1 \cdots x_m I z_{m-2} e \cdots e V w_{m-2} e \cdots e I y_1 \cdots y_m. \tag{3.16}$$

Therefore (3.14) holds, and f is an additive utility for V.

d) Finally, we prove that additive utilities for V are unique up to positive affine transformations. Suppose that f_1 and f_2 are additive utilities for V. We want to show that there exist real $\alpha \geqq 0$ and β such that

$$f_2 = \alpha f_1 + \beta. \tag{3.17}$$

Defining $\tilde{f}_i \equiv f_i - f_i(e)$, we have $\tilde{f}_i(0) = 0$. Clearly we can define g_i: $\mathbf{X} \to \text{Re}$ by:

$$g_i(\mathbf{x}) \equiv f\,(x) \tag{3.18}$$

for any $x \in \mathbf{x}$. It is easy to verify that each g_i is an order isomorphism of the ordered group $(\mathbf{X},+,\mathbf{0},\mathbf{>})$ into the ordered group $(\text{Re},+,0,>)$. So we can define

$$\phi \equiv g_2 \circ g_1^{-1} : \text{Range}(g_1) \to \text{Re}, \tag{3.19}$$

and see that it is an order isomorphism from the image of g_1 onto the image of g_2. By a fundamental theorem of Hion ([8], [6]), any two order isomorphic nontrivial ordered subgroups, A and B, of the real group are nonnegative multiples of each other: there exists a real $\alpha \geqq 0$ such that for all $r \in A$,

$$\phi(r) = \alpha r. \tag{3.20}$$

In our case, then, there exists an $\alpha \geqq 0$ such that for all r in the range of g_1, $\phi(r) = \alpha r$. So, for any $x \in \mathbf{X}$,

$$\tilde{f}_2(x) = g_2(\mathbf{x}) = g_2(g_1^{-1}(g_1(\mathbf{x}))) = \phi(g_1(\mathbf{x})) = \alpha g_1(\mathbf{x}) = \alpha \tilde{f}_1(x), \tag{3.21}$$

where $\mathbf{x} = [x]$. Then $f_2(x) = \alpha f_1(x) + \beta$, where $\beta \equiv \alpha f_2(e) - f_1(e)$. So (3.17) holds. ∎.

Remark 3. Although our connectedness and continuity hypotheses (i) and (iii) were phrased in terms of the topology of X, they could clearly have been weakened to statements about any topology as fine as the order topology of $(\mathbf{X},\mathbf{>})$.

4. CONTINUOUS CARDINAL UTILITY: GENERAL CASE

The next theorem indicates that the comparability hypothesis (iv) in Theorem 2 is superfluous.

Theorem 3. Suppose that $m \geqq 2$ and V is a $2m$-ary relation on X, where

i) X is a connected topological space.

Then the following conditions are necessary and sufficient for V to admit a continuous additive utility:

ii) V satisfies conditions (2.2);

iii) V is "sectionally continuous," i.e.,

$$\{w \in X : wx_2 \cdots x_m V y_1 \cdots y_m\}$$
$$\cdots$$
$$\{w \in X : x_1 \cdots x_m V y_1 \cdots y_{m-1} w\}$$

are closed for all $x_i, y_i \in X$.

Furthermore, under (ii) and (iii), all additive utilities are the same, up to positive affine transformations.

Our proof of Theorem 3 is given in [7].

5. HISTORICAL NOTES

We will not survey here the long history of cardinal utility and additive utility theories. (Cf. [10].) Instead, we highlight a few of the major differences between the present paper and the two closest works, Debreu [5] and Krantz, Luce, Suppes, and Tversky [10]. A more detailed comparison is contained in our paper [7], in which Theorem 3 is proved.

Debreu ([5] Theorem 1) proves a result similar to our Theorem 3, for the special case $m = 2$. He assumes the underlying space X is topologically separable, (so that he can make use of his ordinal utility result [4]). Our results do not require separability.

The proofs are very different: Debreu's existence proof is based on a topological theorem of Blaschke ([1]; cf. [2] and [15]), while ours is based on the Hölder-Loonstra characterization of the real ordered group.

Krantz, Luce, Suppes, and Tversky's Theorem 6.15(iii) extends Debreu's Theorem 1 to handle any number of factors $m \geqq 2$. (See also their Theorem 4.2.) They do not make a clear separation between proper axioms and archimedean ones: Omitting their archimedean axiom ("every strictly bounded standard sequence is finite") does not yield a characterization for finite sets, since their "restricted solvability" axioms are not necessary for existence of additive utility. In this theorem, they avoid topological hypotheses. This has advantages and disadvantages: they do not assume connectedness of X or continuity of V; but of course they cannot obtain continuity of additive utility. Their theorem, like ours, avoids separability assumptions. In contrast to our approach, "essentiality" hypotheses are imposed for $m > 2$.

While [10] does not give an explicit proof of Theorem 6.15(iii) (see Exercise 36), most of the related theorems are ultimately based on a generalization (Theorem 2.4) of Hölder's classical theorem characterizing groups isomorphically imbeddable in the real group. It may be helpful to note that our special hypothesis (iv) in Theorem 2, together with our continuity and connectedness hypotheses, allows us to prove the "unrestricted solvability" condition of [10], p. 256, Definition 5.

Finally, our debt to Scott's finite-set axiomatization [14] is obvious. His paper is a gem of clarity, and the proof is quite straightforward. We should point out however, that while we made use of his particular axioms, we could apply our Structural and Continuity Principles to any finite-set axiomatization.

REFERENCES

[1] Blaschke, W.
Topologische Fragen der Differentialgeometrie. I.
Mathematische Zeitschrift, 28:150-157, 1928.

[2] Blaschke, W. and G. Bol.
Geometrie der Gewebe.
Springer, Berlin, 1938.

[3] Bourbaki, Nicolas.
Elements of Mathematics. General Topology, Part 1.
Addison-Wesley, Reading, Massachusetts, 1966.

[4] Debreu, Gérard,
Representation of a Preference Ordering by a Numerical Function,
pp. 159-165 in *Decision Processes*, R. M. Thrall, C. H. Coombs and R. L. Davis, editors.
Wiley, New York, 1954.

[5] Debreu, Gérard,
Topological Methods in Cardinal Utility Theory,
in *Mathematical Methods in the Social Sciences, 1959*, Kenneth J. Arrow, Samuel Karlin and Patrick Suppes, editors.
Stanford University Press, Stanford, 1960. Chapter 2.

[6] Fuchs, L.
Partially Ordered Algebraic Systems.
Pergamon Press, Oxford, 1963.

[7] Fuhrken, Gebhard and Marcel K. Richter.
Additive Measurement Theory.
Department of Economics, University of Minnesota, 1987.

[8] Hion, Ya. V.
Archimedean Ordered Rings (Russian).
Uspekhi Mat. Nauk, 9(4):237-242, 1954.

[9] Kelley, John L.
General Topology.
American Book-Van Nostrand-Reinhold, New York, 1955.

[10] Krantz, David H., R. Duncan Luce, Patrick Suppes and Amos Tversky.
Foundations of Measurement.
Academic Press, New York, 1971.

[11] Loonstra, F.
Ordered Groups.
Koninklijke Akademie Wetenschappen Te Amsterdam, 49:41-46, 1946.
Proceedings (Nederlandsche)

[12] Richter, Marcel K.
Rational Choice and Polynomial Measurement Models.
Journal of Mathematical Psychology, 12:99-113, 1975.

[13] Richter, Marcel K.
Continuous and Semi-Continuous Utility.
International Economic Review, 21:293-299, 1980.

[14] Scott, Dana.
Measurement Structures and Linear Inequalities.
Journal of Mathematical Psychology, 1:233-247, 1964.

[15] Thomsen, G.
Un teorema topologico sulle schiere di curve e una carattizzazione geometrica delle superficie isotermo-asintotiche.
Bolletino della Unione Matematica Italiana, 6:80-85, 1927.

Binary Inversions and Transitive Majorities*

Wulf Gaertner
Department of Economics
University of Osnabrück
D - 4500 Osnabrück

1. Introduction

A little more than two hundred years ago, in 1785, Marie Jean Antoine Nicolas Caritat, better known as "Marquis de Condorcet", published his "Essai sur l'application de l'analyse à la probabilité des décisions rendues à la pluralité des voix". With some justification Condorcet can be considered as one of the founders of social choice theory. In his work Condorcet discussed, among other things, the case of consistent majority voting and - what is perhaps more interesting - the situation where majority voting generates a set of inconsistent propositions. The proposed resolution scheme for the latter case, however, was fairly vague, at least for voting procedures with more than three candidates. Actually, Condorcet never followed the idea of restricting preference profiles.

It was not before the middle of this century that Arrow (1951, 1963), Black (1948, 1958), Fishburn (1973), Inada (1964, 1969), Sen (1966) and Sen and Pattanaik (1969), among others, proposed sufficient as well as necessary and sufficient domain conditions such that the rule of simple majority decision generates transitive social preferences. All these conditions are exclusion conditions; in other words, certain individual orderings are not allowed to be held by any member of society. Some of these conditions, such as "single peakedness" or "limited agreement" or "value restriction", can be viewed as conditions which require a certain degree of unanimity or social harmony, others such as "antagonistic preferences" convey just the opposite idea whereas requirements such as "dichotomy" or "extremal restriction" do not lend themselves to an easy, straightforward interpretation.

For Arrow the requirement that the social preference relation which is

*) Part of this work was done while I was a Visiting Fellow at All Souls College, Oxford. The splendid atmosphere in the college is gratefully remembered. Thanks are also due to Deutsche Forschungsgemeinschaft for financial support. Helpful comments by Nick Baigent from the Murphy Institute in New Orleans and two anonymous referees are gratefully acknowledged.

Measurement in Economics
ed. by W. Eichhorn

generated out of a set of individual orderings be transitive is nothing else but the postulate that choice-making for society as a whole reflect the same degree of rationality that is required for individual decision making. As a matter of fact, transitivity is automatically satisfied by Bergson's (1938) concept of a social welfare function where real numbers are assigned to alternative social states. However, a real-valued function is more than one needs if the purpose is to be able to choose among various social alternatives.

Slutsky (1977) on the one hand, and Gaertner (1977) and Gaertner and Heinecke (1978) on the other independently proposed a necessary and sufficient condition for social transitivity under simple majority voting that referred to artificially constructed societies and not to the originally given ones. While we still think that the issue of transitivity is best studied with reference to these constructed societies with their reduced preference profiles, we have to admit that neither Slutsky's exclusion condition (1977, p. 215 and p. 221) nor Gaertner and Heinecke's condition of "cyclically mixed preferences" (1978, p. 175) were stated in a "totally uncomplicated manner". This is a pity, for both Slutsky's and Gaertner and Heinecke's condition (which are, of course, equivalent [1]) subsume quite a few of the standard domain conditions discussed in the literature.

In this paper yet a different view is put forward. It rests upon the concept of "a similarity of attitudes towards social alternatives" (Arrow, 1963, p. 69) or, as we will describe it here, upon the notion of "preference proximity" within a given set of individual orderings. Our concept of proximity is characterized by "a path or chain of binary inversions" of adjacent alternatives. In order to give the reader a rough idea already at this early point, consider the following two profiles of individual preferences:

(1)	1:	x	y	z	(2)	1:	z	x	y
	1:	y	z	x		1:	z	y	x
	1:	z	x	y		1:	y	z	x

In both profiles, each individual ordering listed is held by exactly

---

1) Except for the fact, we should add, that Slutsky simultaneously studied the aspect of dominance.

one person. The profiles can be depicted as in the following graphs:

(1)

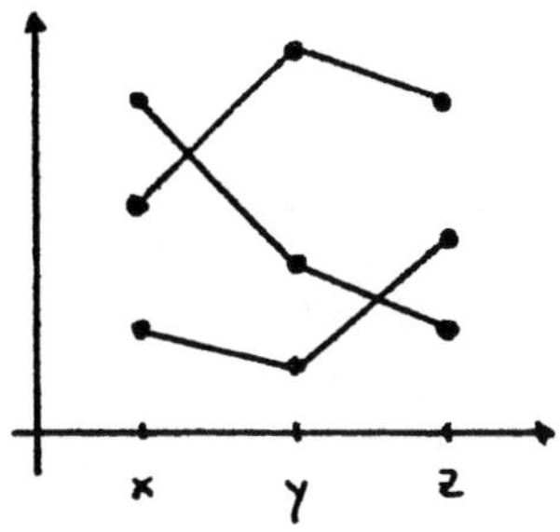

(2)

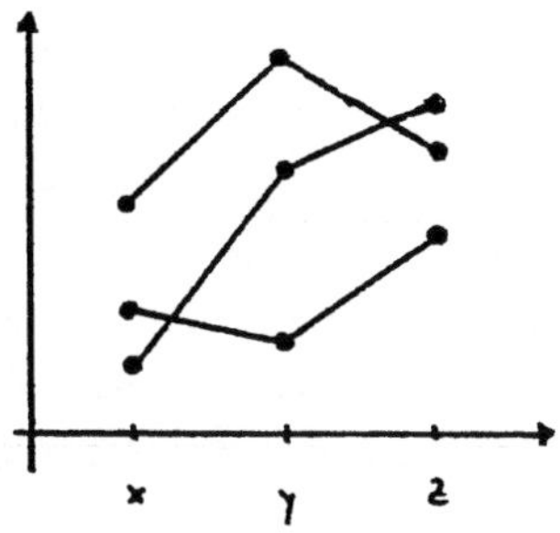

While both graphs look very much the same, the simple majority decision rule generates a preference cycle for profile (1) but produces a transitive social relation for profile (2). For the latter profile there exists a path of binary inversions of neighbouring alternatives from the first ordering to the last ordering; for profile (1) such a path which could, of course, start anywhere within the profile does not exist. Clearly, profile (2) satisfies two well-known domain conditions, viz. value restriction and limited agreement but the reader will remember that both conditions are not sufficient for the existence of transitive majorities without an additional requirement. The profile

(3) 1: x y z
    1: y z x

satisfies both value restriction and limited agreement. Transitivity of the social preference relation is not given, however. In line with our new perspective, we can state that there does not exist a binary inversion taking us in one step from the first to the second ordering (or vice versa).

The structure of the paper is as follows. Section 2 introduces a minimal amount of notation and states a few useful definitions. Section 3 outlines the process of changing an originally given preference profile into a reduced profile which is equivalent to the original one in terms of majorities. Section 4 presents the property of binary inversion and provides a characterization of all logically possible reduced strict preference profiles. Section 5 states and proves the theorem we are looking for while section 6 relates the binary inversion property to some of the well-known domain conditions. We conclude with some final remarks in section 7.

2. Notation and Definitions

Let there be a finite number of individuals forming a society S and let A be a finite set of social alternatives. R_i is individual i's preference ordering (i.e. a reflexive, complete and transitive relation) on the set of alternatives, P_i and I_i denote his strict preference and indifference respectively, derived from R_i in the customary way. All individuals in S are assumed to be "concerned" for a given set of alternatives which means that the individuals are not indifferent between every pair of elements in the set.

We now wish to make explicit which notion of necessary condition is used in this paper. As we are interested in finding qualitative (or structural) properties of reduced preference profiles the dominance property which is, as already mentioned, studied in Slutsky's contribution, is of no great interest for us. Clearly, if one individual ordering occurs more frequently in a given profile than all the other orderings together, social transitivity is guaranteed. And this holds for any logically possible profile of voters' preferences. We will use the concept of necessity in the sense in which it was used by Inada, Pattanaik, Sen, and others who were interested in structural properties of original preference profiles, focusing only on types of permissible preference orderings and not on numbers of individuals holding the various orderings (for a definition of necessary condition in this sense, see Sen and Pattanaik (1969, p. 181)).

Let N(xPy) denote the number of voters for whom $x \; P_i \; y$ where $x, y \in A$. Then the simple majority relation is defined as follows:
$\forall \, x,y \in A : x \, R \, y \leftrightarrow [N(xPy) \geq N(yPx)]$. The vector
$(N(xPy) - N(yPx), N(xPz) - N(zPx), N(yPz) - N(zPy))$ will be called majority vector of the underlying preference profile Π. Under the method of majority decision the majority vector determines the collective preference relation R. From R strict collective preference P and social indifference I can be defined in the same way as for individual relations. Clearly, two preference profiles characterized by the same majority vector yield the same social preference relation. For our analysis, these two profiles will be considered as equivalent.

In the following it proves quite useful to define the following cycles (or groups) of individual orderings for a given triple x, y, z from A: [2)]

C^+:

type 1: $x \ R_i \ y \ R_i \ z$

type 2: $y \ R_i \ z \ R_i \ x$

type 3: $z \ R_i \ x \ R_i \ y$

C^-:

type 1: $z \ R_i \ y \ R_i \ x$

type 2: $x \ R_i \ z \ R_i \ y$

type 3: $y \ R_i \ x \ R_i \ z$.

We will call C^+ and C^- the clockwise and the counter-clockwise R-cycle respectively. The idea to do so originates from Saposnik (1975). The corresponding P-cycles of strict preference are generated from C^+ and C^- by substituting P-P orderings for R-R orderings everywhere. Similarly, the P-I cycle (with one strict preference and one indifference in each individual ordering) and the I-P cycle (indifference first, then strict preference) are obtained from C^+ and C^- by replacing the R-R orderings everywhere by P-I orderings and I-P orderings respectively.

Consider a preference profile consisting of only two individual orderings. We wish to say that these two orderings are inverse to each other if the majority vector of this profile is (0,0,0). The orderings $x \ P_i \ y \ P_i \ z$ and $z \ P_j \ y \ P_j \ x$ with $i,j \in S$, for example, yield the majority vector (0,0,0); so do the orderings $x \ P_i \ y \ I_i \ z$ and $z \ I_j \ y \ P_j \ x$. In both cases, therefore, we say that the individual orderings are inverse.

More interestingly, the majority vector (0,0,0) is also obtained in the situation of a complete P-I cycle; by this we mean a P-I cycle where each of the three possible P-I orderings is held by exactly one individual. The same result is, of course, obtained for a complete I-P cycle.

3. From Original Profiles to Equivalent Strict Preference Profiles

We now propose to transform the preference profile Π of a given (original) society into another more tractable one, denoted Π^*. This process of simplification (reduction procedure) is performed by eliminating and/or combining certain orderings (or sets of orderings) of Π in

2) As transitivity is a property defined on triples, all conditions will be formulated as conditions on triples of alternatives.

such a way that the majority vector is left unchanged, the number of types of orderings in Π^*, however, being considerably diminished (if a reduction is at all possible). The following types of simplifications will be distinguished:

ρ_1: elimination of all pairs of individual P-I and I-P orderings which are inverse to each other;

ρ_2: elimination of all complete P-I cycles and I-P cycles;

ρ_3: transformation of all remaining individual P-I orderings and I-P orderings into strict preference orderings P-P. As an example, the ordering x P z I y, which occurs n_i-times, let's say, is transformed into the two strict orderings x P z P y and x P y P z, each occurring $\frac{n_i}{2}$ - times. Analogously, the ordering y I x P z, which occurs, let's say, n_j-times, will be transformed into y P x P z and x P y P z, each occurring $\frac{n_j}{2}$ - times.

ρ_4: elimination of all pairs of individual strict orderings which are inverse.

We wish to postulate that all four types of reductions are always performed in the given order. The preference profile Π of an original society S is said to have obtained its reduced equivalent strict preference profile Π^* if and only if all four reductions have been executed, i.e. if

$$\rho_i\ (\Pi^*) = \Pi^*\ ,\ i \in \{1,2,3,4\}.$$

Let N_j (K_j) be the number of individuals in Π^* who hold the type j ordering of C^+ (C^-) in its strict form P-P. Then profile Π^* is characterized by the following simple property:

$$(\alpha)\quad \forall\ j \in \{1,2,3\}: N_j > 0 \rightarrow K_j = 0.$$

We now arrive at our first important result.

Proposition 1: The logically possible set of reduced profiles

Π^* comprises exactly 6 different elements. [3]

The proof which uses the four types of reductions ρ_1 to ρ_4, is left to the reader. To simplify our argumentation, we introduce the following symbols for the six logically possible profiles Π^*.

$\Pi^*_{0,0}$: no strict orderings at all;

$\Pi^*_{1,0}$: strict individual orderings of one type occur;

$\Pi^*_{2,0}$: strict individual orderings of two types occur;

$\Pi^*_{3,0}$: strict individual orderings of all three types occur;

$\Pi^*_{1,1}$: strict orderings of one type from C^+ and one type from C^- occur;

$\Pi^*_{2,1}$: strict orderings of two types from C^+ and one type from C^- occur.

4. Preference Proximity in the Sense of Binary Inversions

As already indicated in the introduction, we wish to work with a notion of nearness or proximity of individual preferences which uses the idea of binary inversions of adjacent alternatives. Given any set of individual orderings making up society's preference profile, we construct the reduced equivalent strict preference profile and ask whether it is possible to find a path which links all remaining orderings in the following sense: Moving from any one type of ordering to the next requires one and only one inversion of adjacent alternatives. Repeating this operation step by step leads from the first picked to the last type of individual orderings thus completing the reduced preference profile. Let us depict this procedure with the help of the following profile:

---

3) It can easily be shown that for our purposes we need not distinguish between profiles Π^* which have the property of being identical up to a permutation of alternatives. This means that henceforth we need not, for example, look at $\Pi^*_{0,2}$ and $\Pi^*_{1,2}$ when we have already considered $\Pi^*_{2,0}$ and $\Pi^*_{2,1}$.

(4)

x y z

x z y

z x y

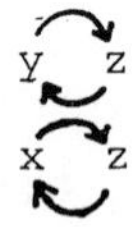

To remind the reader, such a path could not be found for profile (1) above which exhibits a latin square.

We are now in a position to define what we call the binary inversion property.

The Property of Binary Inversion (BIP). The reduced equivalent strict preference profile of a given society is said to satisfy the binary inversion property, if this profile is such that

(a) it contains no individual orderings at all;
(b) it contains orderings of just one type;
(c) for the case that it contains at least two types of orderings, the following requirement holds:

$$(N_1 + N_2 + N_3) \cdot (K_1 + K_2 + K_3) > 0 .$$

While clauses (a) and (b) describe trivial cases, clause (c) essentially captures the idea of a path composed of binary inversions. Remember that property (α) from p. 6 is satisfied by reduced equivalent strict preference profiles.

Our next step is to give a characterization of all reduced equivalent strict preference profiles Π^* that are logically possible.

Proposition 2:

(1) Profiles $\Pi^*_{0,0}$, $\Pi^*_{1,0}$, $\Pi^*_{1,1}$, and $\Pi^*_{2,1}$ satisfy BIP;

(2) Profiles $\Pi^*_{2,0}$ and $\Pi^*_{3,0}$ violate BIP.

Proof. (1) That profiles $\Pi^*_{0,0}$ and $\Pi^*_{1,0}$ satisfy BIP, follows trivially from clauses (a) and (b) in its definition. Due to property (α) the proof for $\Pi^*_{1,1}$ can be subsumed under the proof for $\Pi^*_{2,1}$.

As for $\Pi^*_{2,1}$, there are three different situations to consider:

(a)	x	y	z	(b)	x	y	z	(c)	y	z	x
	x	z	y		y	x	z		z	y	x
	z	x	y		y	z	x		z	x	y

For all three cases, there exists a path of binary inversions (actually, the orderings have been arranged in such a way that the path leads from the top to the bottom (or vice versa)).

(2) That profiles $\Pi^*_{2,0}$ and $\Pi^*_{3,0}$ do not satisfy BIP has already been observed in our introduction. It also follows immediately from the requirement under clause (c) in the definition of BIP. This completes the proof.

5. The Theorem

We now state and prove our theorem.

Theorem. The method of simple majority decision generates a transitive social relation for a given preference profile Π if and only if its reduced equivalent strict preference profile Π^* satisfies the binary inversion property for every triple of alternatives.

Proof. What we have to do in the following is to examine the two groups of reduced profiles (1) and (2) from Proposition 2.

Sufficiency. For profiles $\Pi^*_{0,0}$ and $\Pi^*_{1,0}$ the assertion is trivial. There is either complete social indifference or the social relation coincides with the only remaining strict preference ordering.

We directly prove the transitivity of the social relation for $\Pi^*_{2,1}$ which may occur in the following form:

$$\begin{array}{lllll} N_1 & : & x & y & z \\ K_3 & : & y & x & z \\ N_2 & : & y & z & x\,. \end{array}$$

Let us assume that $N_1 > 0$, $K_3 > 0$, and $N_2 \geq 0$. Clearly the assumption

$N_2 \geq 0$ enables us to integrate the case of profile $\Pi^*_{1,1}$ into our proof. As already stated before, this profile satisfies BIP. The majority vector is $(N_1-(K_3 + N_2),\ N_1 + K_3 - N_2,\ N_1 + K_3 + N_2)$. Due to our assumptions we immediately get y P z under the majority rule. If in addition y P x and x P z hold, transitivity is obvious. Therefore, we have to look at the following cases:

(a) x R y under majority decision,

(b) z R x under majority decision.

(a) x R y means that $N_1-(K_3 + N_2) \geq 0$. Since $K_3 > 0$ by assumption, it follows that $N_1 + K_3 - N_2 > 0$. This, however, is equivalent to x P z.

(b) z R x is equivalent to $N_1 + K_3 - N_2 \leq 0$. Again, due to $K_3 > 0$, it follows that $N_1 - K_3 - N_2 < 0$. This is equivalent to y P x.

Thus, we have demonstrated

(a) $x R y \rightarrow x P z$ and (b) $z R x \rightarrow y P x$.

The proof of sufficiency is complete. The reader should verify for himself that the particular form of the reduced profile $\Pi^*_{2,1}$ which we have assumed implies no loss of generality.

Necessity. We confine ourselves to an investigation of $\Pi^*_{2,0}$. Consider a situation where N_i individuals have the ordering $y P_i z P_i x$ and N_j $(N_j = N_i)$ persons hold the ordering $z P_j x P_j y$. Under the method of majority decision we obtain $x I y \wedge y I z \wedge z P x$ which is clearly intransitive.

This completes the proof of the theorem.

For profiles $\Pi^*_{2,0}$ and $\Pi^*_{3,0}$ transitivity only holds if we introduce additional quantitative assumptions. In the above case, for example, the requirement $N_i \neq N_j$ makes one preference ordering strictly dominant. Thus we have an odd number of individuals whose Π^*-orderings are value-restricted (value-restriction and an odd number of voters are sufficient conditions for social transitivity). For profile $\Pi^*_{3,0}$ a similar dominance condition can easily be given such that the social preference relation is transitive.

6. Logical Relationships

We have just given a necessary and sufficient condition for transitivity of the majority rule that refers to reduced equivalent strict preference profiles. For original unreduced profiles the condition of extremal restriction has been found to be of particular importance.

The Property of Extremal Restriction (ER). For all a, all b, and all c which can assume one of the values x, y, and z:
$[\exists i: a\ P_i\ b \wedge b\ P_i\ c \rightarrow \forall j: (c\ P_j\ a \rightarrow c\ P_j\ b \wedge b\ P_j\ a)]$.

This means that if for some R_i, a is preferred to b and b is preferred to c, then for all R_j such that c is preferred to a, c is also preferred to b and b is preferred to a.

Property ER proves to be both necessary and sufficient for transitivity of the social preference relation when applied to original preference profiles. We now wish to examine the logical relationship between condition ER and condition BIP.

Proposition 3: If the original profile Π fulfils extremal restriction, then the reduced profile Π^* necessarily satisfies BIP.

Proof. Assume that profile Π satisfies extremal restriction for every triple (x,y,z) of alternatives. We now have to distinguish the following cases:

(a) Profile Π only comprises individual orderings over triples (x,y,z) with at least one indifference (this is Inada's (1964) case of dichotomous preferences). Operations ρ_1 and ρ_2 reduce the profile to at most three P-I and I-P orderings. It is easily verified that ρ_3 and ρ_4 always lead to a reduced strict preference profile Π^* that satisfies BIP.

(b) Suppose that a strict individual ordering exists. Without loss of generality we can assume that $x\ P_i\ y\ P_i\ z$ occurs. By the definition of extremal restriction we then have
$\forall j\ (j \neq i) : (z\ P_j\ x \rightarrow z\ P_j\ y\ P_j\ x)$. Various situations now have to be examined:

(α) $\exists j : z\ P_j\ x$. Then $z\ P_j\ y\ P_j\ x$ according to the restriction and $\forall k\ (k \neq j) : (x\ P_k\ z \rightarrow x\ P_k\ y\ P_k\ z)$. Obviously the following four individual orderings are admissible (with n_1, n_2, n_3, n_4 giving the number of persons holding the four orderings):

$$\begin{aligned} n_1 &: x\ P\ y\ P\ z \\ n_2 &: y\ P\ z\ I\ x \\ n_3 &: z\ I\ x\ P\ y \\ n_4 &: z\ P\ y\ P\ x\ . \end{aligned}$$

Whether $\frac{n_3}{2} \gtreqless \frac{n_2}{2}$, the reduction process always yields a profile Π^* that satisfies BIP.

(β) $\sim (\exists j) : z\ P_j\ x.\ \exists j : x\ P_j\ z\ P_j\ y$. We now obtain $\forall k(k \neq j) : (y\ P_k\ x \rightarrow y\ P_k\ z\ P_k\ x)$. However, $y\ P_k\ z\ P_k\ x$ does not occur, nor are $y\ P\ z\ I\ x$ and $y\ P\ x\ P\ z$ admissible in this case. Clearly, the following five orderings are admissible:

$$\begin{aligned} n_1 &: x\ P\ y\ P\ z \\ n_2 &: x\ P\ y\ I\ z \\ n_3 &: x\ I\ y\ P\ z \\ n_4 &: x\ P\ z\ P\ y \\ n_5 &: x\ I\ z\ P\ y \end{aligned}$$

Also in this case, the reduction process always leads to a profile Π^* that fulfils BIP. The same result holds true for the two remaining cases

(γ) $\sim (\exists j) : z\ P_j\ x.\ \exists j : y\ P_j\ x\ P_j\ z$

and

(δ) $\sim (\exists j) : z\ P_j\ x \vee x\ P_j\ z\ P_j\ y \vee y\ P_j\ x\ P_j\ z$.

This completes the proof. Clearly, a reduced profile Π^* that fulfils BIP does not necessarily satisfy ER (if ER were reformulated for reduced profiles). However, it is interesting to note that reduced profiles that fulfil BIP are always value-restricted and satisfy limited agreement, once these restrictions are reformulated for Π^*-profiles.

Saposnik (1975) formulated a distributional requirement, his condition of cyclical balance, which is sufficient for social transitivity under the simple majority rule. Cyclical balance requires that there be the same number of strict individual orderings constituting the clockwise strict preference cycle of C^+ and the counter-clockwise strict preference cycle of C^-. If reduction ρ_4 is applied to such a case, either all individual strict orderings are eliminated or the condition $(N_1 + N_2 + N_3) \cdot (K_1 + K_2 + K_3) > 0$ holds. Thus our binary inversion property is satisfied.

Cyclical balance is a rather interesting condition. Not only is it true that under this requirement "the number of individual rankings with at least one indifference has no bearing on the social transitivity issue" (Saposnik (1975), p. 6), but this condition is the only one having this property (see Gaertner and Heinecke, 1977). We find this feature rather unique. Consider the following preference profile:

$$\begin{aligned} 2 &: x\ P\ y\ P\ z \\ 1 &: y\ P\ z\ P\ x \\ 1 &: y\ P\ x\ P\ z \end{aligned}$$

This profile does not fulfil cyclical balance but it satisfies BIP (let us assume that it is already some reduced profile Π^*). Therefore, social transitivity holds. Now assume that two more individuals are added to this society, having the identical ordering $z\ P\ y\ I\ x$. Transitivity no longer holds. Transitivity would still hold if in the given profile Π^* three individuals had held the ordering $y\ P\ x\ P\ z$ (cyclical balance).

A sufficient condition for quasi-transitivity of the social preference relation can easily be stated by modifying the requirement under clause (c) in the definition of BIP. If $(N_1 + N_2 + N_3) \cdot (K_1 + K_2 + K_3) = 0$ with any two of the N_ℓ, $\ell \in \{1,2,3\}$, being strictly positive and the third being zero (any two of the K_ℓ being strictly positive and the third being zero), then simple majority decisions generate a quasi-transitive social relation. Also in these cases, the reduced profiles satisfy both value-restriction and limited agreement but do not, of course, fulfil BIP.

7. Concluding Remarks

Starting from the concept of preference proximity we have formulated a domain condition which proved to be necessary and sufficient for transitivity of the social relation under the majority rule. This property of binary inversion is applied in the following way: Take any given preference profile Π of a society, transform it into another profile Π^*, the reduced equivalent strict preference profile, and check whether the remaining set of individual orderings is such that a path exists linking all types of orderings by binary inversions of adjacent alternatives (BIP). If and only if this property holds, we can be sure that the social relation is fully transitive. And this result holds independent of additional distributional requirements whatsoever. The main difference to the traditional domain restrictions is that our condition focuses on artificially constructed societies. We hope, however, to have convinced the reader that for the issue of social transitivity under the method of simple majority decision, it is worthwhile to focus on reduced profiles and not on the - much more complex - original ones. As has been mentioned at the beginning of this paper, the process of reduction was proposed before but the conditions which were then formulated, apparently had the disadvantage of not being easily interpretable and transparent.

References

Arrow, K. J. (1951, 1963), Social Choice and Individual Values. New York: Wiley.

Bergson, A. (1938), A Reformulation of Certain Aspects of Welfare Economics, Quarterly Journal of Economics 52, 310-334.

Black, D. (1948), On the Rationale of Group Decision-Making, Journal of Political Economy 56, 23-34.

Black, D. (1958), The Theory of Committees and Elections. Cambridge: Cambridge University Press.

Condorcet, Marquis de (1785), Essai sur l'application de l'analyse à la probabilité des décisions rendues à la pluralité des voix, Paris.

Fishburn, P. C. (1973), The Theory of Social Choice. Princeton: Princeton University Press.

Gaertner, W. (1977), Zum Problem der Existenz von Sozialen Wohlfahrtsfunktionen im Sinne von Arrow, Zeitschrift für die gesamte Staatswissenschaft 133, 61-74.

Gaertner, W. and A. Heinecke (1977), On Two Sufficient Conditions for Transitivity of the Social Preference Relation, Zeitschrift für Nationalökonomie 37, 61-66.

Gaertner, W. and A. Heinecke (1978), Cyclically Mixed Preferences: A Necessary and Sufficient Condition for Transitivity of the Social Preference Relation, 169-185, in: Decision Theory and Social Ethics, Issues in Social Choice, ed. by. H. W. Gottinger and W. Leinfellner. Dordrecht: Reidel.

Inada, K. (1964), A Note on the Simple Majority Decision Rule, Econometrica 32, 525-531.

Inada, K. (1969), The Simple Majority Decision Rule, Econometrica 37, 490-506.

Saposnik, R. (1975), On Transitivity of the Social Preference Relation under Simple Majority Rule, J. Econ. Theory 10, 1-7.

Sen, A. K. (1966), A Possibility Theorem on Majority Decisions, Econometrica 34, 491-499.

Sen, A. K. (1970), Collective Choice and Social Welfare. San Francisco: Holden-Day, and Edinburgh: Oliver and Boyd.

Sen, A. K. and Pattanaik, P. K. (1969), Necessary and Sufficient Conditions for Rational Choice under Majority Decision, J. Econ. Theory 1, 178-202.

Slutsky, S. (1977), A Characterization of Societies with Consistent Majority Decision, Rev. of Econ. Stud. 44, 211-225.

Evaluation Techniques for Paired Ratio-Comparison Matrices in a Hierarchical Decision Model

Jairus M. Hihn
Department of Agricultural and Resource Economics
University of California
Berkeley, California 94720

Charles R. Johnson
Department of Mathematical Sciences
Clemson University
Clemson, South Carolina 29634-1907

A hierarchical decision model for the ranking of discrete alternatives has been proposed by T. Saaty. This procedure has achieved some popularity in the operations research community. Among the components of the model is the deduction of a vector of weights from a matrix of paired ratio comparisons. We consider several evaluation techniques for this purpose including the Perron-Frobenius right eigenvector which was recommended by Saaty. In the absence of any theoretical basis for choice of a particular evaluation technique, these techniques are subjected to a variety of numerical tests. Among the conclusions, there seems to be no basis for preference for the Perron-Frobenius right eigenvector. Thus, there is no reason to believe that use of the model as originally proposed is generating desirable solutions. However, a nonlinear least-squares fit, initialized with a heuristic evaluation technique, performs very well. Before reliable use can be made of the overall decision model, theoretical, numerical, and empirical development of all the components should be furthered.

1. Introduction

A general scheme for calculating a cardinal ranking (prioritization) of given alternatives with respect to their impact upon an ultimate goal has been suggested [S77],[S80],[WS]. This ranking procedure has gained attention through a variety of applications (many made by the proposer and his students but several by others [SV],[W],[Z]). This procedure is attractive as a decision or planning model in that it is easy to employ, and certain portions of the procedure have a natural intuitive appeal. It is especially appropriate for decision problems that require the

Measurement in Economics
ed. by W. Eichhorn

ranking of discrete choices and the combining of inconsistent and subjective information. Here, we are concerned with only one component of the model. Therefore, only a brief outline of the overall model is given. For a more detailed discussion see [J], [JH],[S77],[S80],[WS], or [Z].

The principle underlying this procedure is that a decision problem should be disaggregated into its most basic components for evaluation, and the evaluations should be aggregated to obtain an overall ranking, the goal of the procedure.

Assuming definition of the goal and of the alternatives, the method features the following ingredients: (1) decomposition of the ranking problem through a hierarchy (with the goal at the top, subgoals and criteria in the middle, and the alternatives at the bottom) in which each lower level involves progressively more easily compared and assessed items; (2) the specification of paired ratio comparisons of items on one level with respect to their impact upon various items, in turn, on the level above; and (3) assembly of the information into an overall vector of weights associated with the alternatives via (i) deduction of positive vectors from the ratio comparisons and (ii) aggregation of these vectors through a natural multiplicative procedure. The resulting vector of weights is then taken to be the cardinal ranking of the alternatives with respect to the goal.

It might be argued that, with a few exceptions [J],[JBW],[JH],[SW], much more attention has been paid to applying the procedure than to its theoretical development and constructive criticism (i.e., understanding its applicability and outputs and appropriately refining and augmenting its component features). The quantitative features of the procedure are contained in (3) above. With the exception of some issues for which application-dependent repairs are necessary [H],[J], the aggregation procedure [part (ii)] is a very natural and well-motivated portion of the method. Our interest here is in the key quantitative aspect [contained in (i)] in which a vector of weights is estimated from a matrix of ratio comparisons.

We call a function by which a vector of positive weights is deduced from a positive matrix of ratio comparisons an <u>evaluation technique</u>. (We note that there are applications of an evaluation technique other than in context of this prioritization procedure, e.g., construction of a vector of relative price levels from ratios of prices sampled in pairs of countries.) We define several evaluation techniques meeting a natural criterion and numerically analyze them relative to various performance criteria. Among the techniques analyzed is the one recommended in [S80] and [WS].

In addition to the analytic hierarchy process another motivation for studying evaluation techniques is the problem of constructing a utility function in a situation of inconsistent preferences. In utility theory, inconsistency is generally assumed not to exist and as a result, very little work has been done in this area. In [De] and [T], it was determined that a utility function, equivalent to an interval scale, existed when obtaining multiple observations on inconsistent paired comparisons. A difficulty is that the amount of information required makes this approach of little practical value. An evaluation technique is a practical way by which to derive a utility function under the conditions that the paired comparisons (1) be specified as ratio comparisons and (2) possibly be both cardinally and ordinally inconsistent.

Therefore an intuitive way to view the subproblem of concern in this paper is to consider how the coefficients of a linear utility function are to be constructed if all that is available is a set of paired ratio comparisons which attempt to measure the intensity of the relative preference between items. Furthermore, these comparisons are possibly both cardinally and ordinally inconsistent. The set of inconsistent paired ratio comparisons can be arranged in a matrix (the properties of which are described below) which is called a (paired) ratio-comparison matrix. The issue is how the matrix of paired ratio comparisons is to be used to construct a vector whose elements are the relative weights in a linear utility function.

2. Notation and Definitions

Given items $1,2,\ldots,n$, a pairwise-comparison matrix is an n-by-n matrix $A = (a_{ij})$ of positive entries in which a_{ij} is a ratio comparison of item i to item j. A pairwise-comparison matrix A is called reciprocal if $a_{ji} = 1/a_{ij}$ for all $i, j = 1,\ldots,n$. Note that all diagonal entries of a reciprocal matrix are equal to 1. All pairwise-comparison matrices considered here are taken to be reciprocal. (This is generally the case in applications due to information requirements.) A reciprocal pairwise-comparison matrix A in which $a_{ij}a_{jk} = a_{ik}$ for all triples i, j, k is called consistent. Otherwise, A is inconsistent. Generally, we shall be interested in inconsistent (reciprocal) pairwise-comparison matrices, to be denoted as A. We use $w = (w_1, w_2, \ldots, w_n)^T$ to denote a vector of positive weights. The superscript T denotes transposition. We say that w is normalized if the sum of its components is 1. Naturally associated with each vector of weights, w, is the consistent n-by-n matrix $X = (w_i/w_j)$. We use v to denote the vector of weights produced from A by some evaluation technique. The difference between an inconsistent matrix A and the consistent matrix X built from a particular v will be of interest and will be measured in four commonly used matrix norms. A norm N on matrices is a function from n-by-n matrices to real numbers satisfying (for matrices B, C, and scalars a):

(i) $N(B) \geq 0$, with equality iff $B = 0$;

(ii) $N(aB) = |a|\, N(B)$; and

(iii) $N(B+C) \leq N(B)+N(C)$.

Thus, N(A-X) is a natural measure of the "distance" between A and X. The four norms used are defined for $B = (b_{ij})$ by:

(i) the maximum value of absolute row sums

$$N(B) = \max_{1\leq i\leq n} \sum_{j=1}^{n} |b_{ij}| \qquad \text{(row norm);}$$

(ii) the maximum value of absolute column sums

$$N(B) = \max_{1\leq j\leq n} \sum_{i=1}^{n} |b_{ij}| \qquad \text{(column norm);}$$

(iii) the spectral norm

$$N(B) = (\max \lambda)^{\frac{1}{2}}, \quad \lambda \text{ an eigenvalue of } B^TB; \quad \text{and}$$

(iv) the euclidean (Frobenius) norm

$$N(B) = \left(\sum_{i,j} b_{ij}^2\right)^{\frac{1}{2}}.$$

3. Background

The particular evaluation technique recommended in [S80] and [WS] is the normalized Perron-Frobenius right eigenvector (to be described below) of the pairwise-comparison matrix A. The only precisely given motivation which the proposer has offered for this choice is that, *in case* A *is consistent,* the Perron-Frobenius right eigenvector technique produces a vector v such that X = A, for $X=(v_i/v_j)$. In other words, this technique produces the natural and obvious vector in the consistent case. However, this is not the only evaluation technique with this important property. There are infinitely many, including all those studied below.

There seems to be no obviously preferable evaluation technique based upon theoretical or accumulated empirical grounds. Furthermore, the desirability of the Perron-Frobenius right eigenvector was brought into question in [JBW]. Thus, it seems natural to consider other evaluation techniques and view them on the basis of other potentially desirable criteria. We strongly recommend further theoretical work on evaluation techniques, and axiomatic investigation by the authors is underway. This will be reported on elsewhere.

In view of the lack of any theoretical criteria which uniquely define an evaluation technique, it seems natural to ask that the consistent matrix built from an evaluation technique approximate the pairwise-comparison matrix as closely as possible. Since there is no clearly best notion of distance underlying the word "approximate," it also seems natural to consider the often used norms: the row norm, column norm, spectral norm, and euclidean norm, defined above. These norms provide a broad range of distance notions, and use of further norms would likely add little insight. Mathematical properties of these norms may be found in [HJ].

4. Evaluation Techniques and Theory

For a reciprocal n-by-n pairwise-comparison matrix $A = (a_{ij})$, we consider the following 16 evaluation techniques $v^{(k)}$, k=1,...,16. In each case, $v^{(k)}$ is taken to be normalized (by dividing by the sum of the components) subsequent to the stated definition. The underlined portion of the title of each technique will be used for mnemonic reference and the techniques may also be referred to by number. Subscripts on the $v^{(k)}$ refer to entries of the n-vector $v^{(k)}$.

Row geometric means (RGM): $v^{(1)}$ is defined by

$$v_i^{(1)} = \left(\prod_{j=1}^{n} a_{ij}\right)^{\frac{1}{n}} . \tag{1}$$

Row sums (RS): $v^{(2)}$ is defined by

$$v_i^{(2)} = \sum_{j=1}^{n} a_{ij} . \tag{2}$$

Inverse column sums (ICS): $v^{(3)}$ is defined by

$$v_j^{(3)} = \left(\sum_{i=1}^{n} a_{ij}\right)^{-1} . \tag{3}$$

Perron-Frobenius right eigenvector (PFRE): $v^{(4)}$ is defined by

$$Av^{(4)} = \lambda_{max}(A)\,v^{(4)}, \quad v^{(4)} > 0 \tag{4}$$

in which $\lambda_{max}(A)$ denotes the largest eigenvalue of A.

Inverse Perron-Frobenius left eigenvector (IPFLE): $v^{(5)}$ is defined by

$$w^T A = \lambda_{max}(A)\,w^T, \quad w > 0 \tag{5}$$

$$v_i^{(5)} = w_i^{-1} .$$

Perron-Frobenius eigenvector of AA^T ($PFEAA^T$): $v^{(6)}$ is defined by

$$AA^T v^{(6)} = \lambda_{max}(AA^T)\,v^{(6)}, \quad v^{(6)} > 0. \tag{6}$$

Inverse Perron-Frobenius eigenvector of A^TA ($IPFEA^TA$): $v^{(7)}$ is defined by

$$A^TAw = \lambda_{max}(A^TA)\,w, \quad w > 0 \tag{7}$$

$$v_i^{(7)} = w_i^{-1} .$$

Least-squares fit (LSF): $v^{(8)}$ is defined by

$$\min \sum_{i=1}^{n} \sum_{j=1}^{n} \left(a_{ij} - \frac{x_i}{x_j} \right)^2 , \tag{8}$$

in which the minimum is taken over positive normalized vectors x and $v^{(8)}$ is the solution. This is simply determination of the closest consistent matrix in the euclidean norm.

Arithmetic mean (AM) of RS and ICS: $v^{(9)}$ is defined by

$$v^{(9)} = \frac{1}{2} \left[v^{(2)} + v^{(3)} \right] , \tag{9}$$

in which each of $V^{(2)}$ and $v^{(3)}$ is normalized.

Geometric mean (GM) of RS and ICS: $v^{(10)}$ is defined by

$$v_i^{(10)} = \left[v_i^{(2)} \cdot v_i^{(3)} \right]^{\frac{1}{2}} . \tag{10}$$

AM of PFRE and IPFLE: $v^{(11)}$ is defined by

$$v^{(11)} = \frac{1}{2} \left[v^{(4)} + v^{(5)} \right] , \tag{11}$$

in which each of $v^{(4)}$ and $v^{(5)}$ is normalized.

GM of PFRE and IPFLE: $v^{(12)}$ is defined by

$$v_i^{(12)} = \frac{1}{2} \left[v_i^{(4)} \cdot v_i^{(5)} \right]^{\frac{1}{2}} . \tag{12}$$

AM of $PFEAA^T$ and $IPFEA^TA$: $v^{(13)}$ is defined by

$$v^{(13)} = \frac{1}{2} \left[v^{(6)} + v^{(7)} \right] , \tag{13}$$

in which each of $v^{(6)}$ and $v^{(7)}$ is normalized.

GM of $PFEAA^T$ and $IPFEA^TA$: $v^{(14)}$ is defined by

$$v_i^{(14)} = \left[v_i^{(6)} \cdot v_i^{(7)} \right]^{\frac{1}{2}} . \tag{14}$$

AM of RGM and RS: $v^{(15)}$ is defined by

$$v^{(15)} = \frac{1}{2}\left[v^{(1)} + v^{(2)}\right], \tag{15}$$

in which each of $v^{(1)}$ and $v^{(2)}$ is normalized.

GM of RGM and RS: $v^{(16)}$ is defined by

$$v_i^{(16)} = \left[v_i^{(1)} \cdot v_i^{(2)}\right]^{\frac{1}{2}}. \tag{16}$$

We note that the inverse column geometric mean analog of RGM is not listed separately as it coincides with RGM. Similarly, since AA^T and A^TA are symmetric, there is no need to distinguish between left and right eigenvectors. Otherwise, the distinction is important, as normalized left and right eigenvectors need not coincide for nonsymmetric matrices.

As is well-known and easy to verify, a pairwise-comparison matrix A is consistent if, and only if, it is of the form $A=(w_i/w_j)$ for some positive vector w. We say that an evaluation technique is consistent if it necessarily produces (a multiple of) the natural vector w whenever it is applied to a consistent matrix A. This seems to be a property that should be required of an evaluation technique. Each of the 16 techniques $v^{(1)},\ldots,v^{(16)}$ is consistent. In all cases, this is easily checked. For example, in the case of RS, $A = (w_i/w_j)$ implies

$$v_i^{(2)} = \sum_{j=1}^{n} \frac{w_i}{w_j} = w_i \sum_{j=1}^{n} \frac{1}{w_j}, \qquad \text{so that} \qquad v^{(2)} = \left(\sum_{j=1}^{n} \frac{1}{w_j}\right) w,$$

a scalar multiple of w. Also, in the case of IPFEA^{T}A, we have that $A = (w_i/w_j)$ implies

$$A^TA = \sum_{k=1}^{n} w_k^2 \left(\frac{1}{w_i\ w_j}\right) \qquad \text{and} \qquad A^TA\left(\frac{1}{w}\right) = \left(\sum_{k=1}^{n} w_k^2 \sum_{j=1}^{n} \frac{1}{w_j^2}\right)\frac{1}{w},$$

where 1/w is the vector whose i^{th} component is w_i^{-1}. Thus, $v^{(7)} = w$, and $v^{(7)}$ is consistent. Furthermore, it is clear that the componentwise arithmetic and geometric means of two consistent evaluation techniques is a consistent evaluation technique. Thus, the consistency of $v^{(9)}$ through $v^{(16)}$ follows from that of $v^{(1)}$ through $v^{(7)}$.

The evaluation technique PFRE [$v^{(4)}$] is the one advocated in [S80] and [WS]. The technique RGM has been observed elsewhere, [J], [S80], and is a minor variation upon one considered in an Oak Ridge National Laboratories report. This technique (RGM) is notable in that it is the solution to a log least-squares criterion for determining an evaluation technique [J], namely,

$$\min \sum_{i=1}^{n} \sum_{j=1}^{n} \left(\log a_{ij} - \log \frac{v_i}{v_j} \right)^2 ,$$

where the minimum is taken over positive vectors v. The formula $v^{(1)}$ turns out to be a solution to this problem, and the log least-squares criterion seems to be the only optimization criterion for an evaluation technique to which an analytically specifiable solution has been given. Unfortunately, there seems to be no particular reason to believe that the log least-squares criterion is appropriate for the evaluation technique for pairwise-comparison matrices. Another evaluation technique involving a linear least-squares specification has been suggested in [M]. This one was considered in [H] in tests similar to those presented here and it performed relatively poorly. It is also somewhat more complex to compute than $v^{(1)}$ through $v^{(7)}$ and $v^{(9)}$ through $v^{(16)}$ (save LSF). Thus, it was not included among the group tested here.

Each of $v^{(1)}$ through $v^{(7)}$ and $v^{(9)}$ through $v^{(16)}$ may be considered a heuristic evaluation technique. They all satisfy the minimally desirable property of consistency and each has perhaps some intuitive appeal. The arithmetic and geometric means tend to mediate between other techniques, which may be desirable [J], [JBW]. To achieve a desired degree of accuracy, $v^{(1)}$ through $v^{(3)}$, $v^{(9)}$, $v^{(10)}$, $v^{(15)}$, and $v^{(16)}$ require the order of n^2 calculations; whereas $v^{(6)}$, $v^{(7)}$, $v^{(13)}$, and $v^{(14)}$ require the order of n^3 calculations (all are easy to calculate). The techniques $v^{(4)}$, $v^{(5)}$, $v^{(11)}$, and $v^{(12)}$ are theoretically unbounded in the required computational complexity, but all the techniques consume comparably little machine computation effort for the sizes and types of problems typically occurring in applications.

The evaluation technique (nonlinear) LSF [$v^{(8)}$], on the other hand, is based upon the optimization of a particular (natural) criterion: how well does the consistent matrix built from the evaluation vector approximate the paired comparison data in the least-squares (euclidean) sense? This (nonlinear) least-squares specification of an evaluation technique is different from the others; for example, there is no simple formula for its computation. It must be calculated through an iterative numerical algorithm beginning at some initial vector and it is more costly to compute. Even to the extent the evaluation technique LSF is considered relatively desirable, there is still reason to consider the heuristic techniques. They are much cheaper to compute, and they provide a good initial vector for the iterative calculation of LSF. This is the motivation for one of the battery of tests (to be described below) in which each of the heuristic evaluation techniques and the arbitrary vector of ones is used as an initial vector in the calculation of LSF.

Since there is no demonstrably best specification of an evaluation technique and no clearly "best" measure of distance to use in comparing how well evaluation techniques approximate the paired-comparison data, we consider how near in various measures $X=(v_i/v_j)$ is to the pairwise-comparison matrix A for each of the evaluation techniques v. This is the reason for one of the battery of tests to be described below. If one or some of the techniques approximate well (or poorly) in all of the measures of distance, this is more conclusive than a performance in a single measure.

5. Description and Results of Tests

The purpose of the numerical experiments is to compare how well the different evaluation techniques produce a vector of weights that is in some sense best. Best is measured by the four norms described above: spectral norm, euclidean norm, row norm, and the column norm. In the numerical experiments, we simulate a set of matrices that vary with respect to size, the degree of consistency, and the number of elements of the paired ratio-comparison matrices that are assigned extreme values.

The data was generated using two different methods. In both cases, 150 4 x 4, 7 x 7, and 10 x 10 matrices were produced. The two procedures for generating the matrices will be referred to as Method 1 and Method 2.

In Method 1, a random vector was generated by setting $S_i=1/3+8/3U$ where U is a drawing from a uniform [0,1] quasi-random number generator and S_i is the ith entry of the vector S, whose entries then have a uniform distribution over the range 1/3 to 3. A consistent matrix is then constructed by

$$X = S\left[S^{(-1)}\right]^T .$$

Here, $S^{(-1)}$ denotes the component-wise inverse of the vector S. The upper triangular entries of $X=(x_{ij})$ are then perturbed to produce an inconsistent matrix by

$$a_{ij} = x_{ij}\ (1 + \alpha\ Z_{i,j}) \quad \forall\ j > i$$

$$.1 \le a_{ij} \le 10$$

$$a_{ji} = \frac{1}{a_{ij}}$$

where $Z_{i,j}$ is an observation from a normal (0,1) quasi-random number generator, a_{ij} is the i, j^{th} element of an inconsistent matrix, α is a constant which is set to 0.1 for a relatively consistent matrix, 0.3 for an inconsistent matrix, and 0.5 for a highly inconsistent matrix. The matrix A is constrained to be reciprocal. Each upper triangular element of A can be viewed as a random drawing from a truncated normal distribution with a mean of x_{ij} and a standard deviation of $\alpha \cdot x_{ij}$. The truncations and ranges were chosen to allow considerable variation without problems of numerical stability in subsequent calculations.

In Method 2, the matrices were generated in a similar manner except that the random vector S was constructed by

$$S_i = 3.0 - 2.0\sqrt{1 - 2\ U} \text{ if } U < 0.5$$

$$S_i = 3.0 + 6.0\sqrt{2.0 \cdot U - 1.0} \text{ if } U > 0.5.$$

In this case, the entries of S have a V-shaped distribution with a range of 1 to 9 and a trough at 3. (This range is consistent with several experiments [S80].) Matrices generated by Method 2 have a statistically greater number of large and small entries than those generated by Method 1.

Three experiments were performed involving the 16 evaluation techniques: computation of the average and median distance for each distinct subset of the data in the four norms, totaling the number of position changes from what appears to be the best vector, and a comparison of different initial conditions for the nonlinear least-squares algorithm. When running the experiments, the data were divided into 18 subsets. The subsets were distinguished by whether the matrices were generated by Method 1 or Method 2, the size of the matrix, and by the degree of inconsistency.

The mean and median distance in each norm were computed as summary measures of the performance of each evaluation procedure. The two summary measures provide different views of the typical performance of each evaluation procedure in that the average distance is affected more by outlying observations than the median. This can and does cause mean and median to rank the evaluation procedures differently, because the distribution is skewed.

It was found that -- because of differences in the manner distance is measured between norms -- an evaluation technique that does well in one norm may do poorly in another. For example, $PFEAA^T$ does relatively well in the column norm but is one of the worst in the row norm. Another point which was raised earlier is that the geometric or arithmetic average of two techniques which are consistent but perform poorly, such as $PFEAA^T$ and $PFEA^TA$ in the euclidean norm, may perform very well. In this case, the change is from two of the lowest ranked techniques to a clear second best.

The difference between the evaluation technique that on average corresponds to the smallest distance and the technique with the greatest is around 40 percent, while the difference between the technique with the smallest and that with the second smallest distance is usually around 10 percent. In many cases, the summary distance measures are very close. Readers interested in detailed tabulations of the results of numerical experiments may contact one of the authors.

In Table 1, 2, and 3 in the text, the average rank of each evaluation technique in each norm for both mean and median is computed. Table 1 presents the results for the 4 x 4 matrices, Table 2 for the 7 x 7 matrices, and Table 3 for the 10 x 10 matrices. It is easily seen that no one technique ranks the same for all matrices in all norms. Furthermore, except for LSF in the spectral and euclidean norms and two or three other cases, no technique consistently scores the same in any one norm. Overall, LSF ranks first more often, however, than any other evaluation technique.

While different procedures produce different relative weights, it is possible that many will produce the same ordinal ranking of elements. This can be of use if only ordinal rankings are of interest and in determining what procedures are second best.

TABLE 1

Average Rank of Evaluation Techniques Measured by Mean and Median in All Norms for 4 x 4 Matrices

Evaluation Technique	Spectral Norm Mean	Spectral Norm Median	Euclidean Norm Mean	Euclidean Norm Median	Row Norm Mean	Row Norm Median	Column Norm Mean	Column Norm Median
RGM	10.67	9.67	9.67	11.33	8.16	10.00	10.67	12.33
RS	5.50	4.17	10.17	8.00	15.00	15.17	2.33	3.33
ICS	14.50	10.17	11.83	12.33	2.50	4.50	15.00	14.33
PFRE	13.00	12.17	12.00	13.50	11.33	10.17	12.50	13.50
IPFLE	13.00	12.83	11.83	11.00	9.33	9.67	13.17	10.50
$PFEAA^T$	5.17	4.50	15.17	9.50	16.00	15.83	4.00	2.33
$PFEA^TA$	14.83	13.50	12.83	12.83	2.67	4.00	16.00	15.83
LSF	1.00	1.33	1.00	1.00	1.00	1.50	1.00	1.33
AM (RS,ICS)	8.50	10.50	4.67	6.17	6.33	6.17	8.67	8.33
GM (RS,ICS)	7.83	9.50	4.33	6.33	6.33	6.50	8.17	8.67
AM (PFRE,IPFLE)	12.00	12.17	10.00	11.17	9.17	10.50	11.50	11.50
GM (PFRE,IPFLE)	12.00	11.50	10.83	11.00	10.50	10.83	11.33	12.50
AM ($PFEAA^T$,$PFEA^TA$)	3.00	6.00	3.67	4.17	5.17	3.67	3.83	5.83
GM ($PFEAA^T$,$PFEA^TA$)	3.17	6.33	2.83	2.83	4.17	3.50	4.50	5.67
AM (RGM, RS)	6.33	5.67	6.33	7.83	13.00	12.00	5.83	5.00
GM (RGM, RS)	6.00	6.00	7.33	8.33	12.00	12.00	6.17	5.00

TABLE 2

Average Rank of Evaluation Techniques Measured by Mean and Median in All Norms for 7 x 7 Matrices

Evaluation Technique	Spectral Norm		Euclidean Norm		Row Norm		Column Norm	
	Mean	Median	Mean	Median	Mean	Median	Mean	Median
RGM	10.33	9.33	8.34	10.66	8.33	9.17	10.00	10.50
RS	3.87	2.50	10.66	8.17	15.17	15.00	3.00	4.00
ICS	8.33	9.83	14.34	12.84	3.83	5.00	15.00	15.00
PFRE	13.17	11.50	12.00	11.66	12.00	8.50	13.67	12.50
IPFLE	10.67	10.50	11.50	9.17	9.83	11.00	13.33	11.67
$PFEAA^T$	4.67	5.67	14.66	10.83	15.33	15.83	3.33	3.17
$PFEA^TA$	15.67	13.50	15.83	14.50	3.33	4.00	16.00	16.00
LSF	1.00	1.00	1.00	1.00	1.00	1.17	1.00	1.17
AM (RS,ICS)	9.83	9.83	4.00	5.50	6.83	5.00	8.00	8.00
GM (RS,ICS)	9.83	10.50	5.00	6.00	6.50	6.17	8.67	8.83
AM (PFRE,IPFLE)	9.67	11.67	9.66	12.34	10.50	10.50	11.50	12.83
GM (PFRE,IPFLE)	9.67	10.50	9.83	12.50	10.00	10.50	11.50	12.50
AM ($PFEAA^T$,$PFEA^TA$)	3.50	3.87	2.50	2.66	3.67	5.00	3.83	3.50
GM ($PFEAA^T$,$PFEA^TA$)	4.17	3.33	2.50	3.00	3.50	3.67	4.50	4.00
AM (RGM, RS)	8.67	8.00	6.83	6.50	13.50	11.33	6.83	6.66
GM (RGM, RS)	7.50	8.67	7.17	7.34	13.00	11.67	6.50	6.00

TABLE 3

Average Rank of Evaluation Techniques Measured by Mean and Median in All Norms for 10 x 10 Matrices

Evaluation Technique	Spectral Norm		Euclidean Norm		Row Norm		Column Norm	
	Mean	Median	Mean	Median	Mean	Median	Mean	Median
RGM	10.50	12.33	8.67	7.33	8.17	9.17	10.17	11.17
RS	5.33	6.00	10.17	9.00	15.00	14.66	5.00	4.50
ICS	11.17	9.67	14.00	13.33	4.83	4.00	15.00	14.67
PFRE	9.67	10.50	12.50	11.00	13.00	11.17	12.33	13.33
IPFLE	10.67	9.83	12.17	12.17	9.33	11.17	13.83	12.50
$PFEAA^T$	4.17	3.00	14.33	13.33	15.33	16.00	3.00	2.33
$PFEA^TA$	13.17	11.17	16.00	15.50	5.67	4.17	16.00	16.00
LSF	1.00	1.00	1.00	1.00	1.17	1.67	1.00	1.17
AM (RS,ICS)	10.67	10.50	4.67	6.83	6.33	6.33	8.17	7.83
GM (RS,ICS)	11.83	12.17	4.50	6.50	5.83	5.17	8.50	8.17
AM (PFRE,IPFLE)	10.83	11.00	9.83	9.66	10.33	10.33	11.50	11.33
GM (PFRE,IPFLE)	10.00	11.17	9.50	9.17	10.00	9.67	11.67	11.67
AM ($PFEAA^T$,$PFEA^TA$)	4.17	4.33	2.67	2.67	3.67	4.00	4.00	4.17
GM ($PFEAA^T$,$PFEA^TA$)	6.50	5.33	2.33	3.00	3.00	3.50	3.67	2.45
AM (RGM, RS)	7.67	7.83	6.67	7.33	12.67	12.50	6.17	6.50
GM (RGM, RS)	7.00	6.67	6.67	8.00	12.33	12.50	5.67	6.50

In order to measure the difference in the ordinal ranking of the elements between two vectors, the number of position changes was counted. Consider the following two four-element vectors and their respective ordering of elements.

Vector 1	Vector 2	Order 1	Order 2	Position Change
.4	.26	1	2	1
.2	.39	3	1	2
.25	.19	2	3	1
.15	.16	4	4	0
				Total 4

The number of positions which changed is determined by the sum of the absolute value of the differences of the orders. For example, the first element has shifted from being ranked first to being ranked second so it has changed one position whereas the second element went from third to first so it has shifted two positions. The total is divided by two so the actual place change count is two.

TABLE 4

Average Counts of Changes in the Ordinal Rankings Between the LSF Vector and Heuristic Vectors for Matrices Generated by Method 1

Evaluation Technique	4x4 Matrices			7x7 Matrices			10x10 Matrices		
	RC	IC	HI	RC	IC	HI	RC	IC	HI
RGM	.04	.20	.50	.42	1.28	1.92	.90	2.56	3.72
RS	.04	.12	.36	.28	1.04	1.78	.66	1.70	2.94
ICS	.06	.26	.36	.64	1.50	2.22	1.06	3.10	4.70
PFRE	.04	.18	.52	.42	1.34	2.30	.92	2.66	4.16
IPFLE	.04	.20	.48	.42	1.26	1.96	.86	2.66	4.34
$PFEAA^T$	.04	.18	.32	.34	.86	1.86	.56	1.74	2.64
$PFEA^TA$	.06	.26	.44	.74	1.54	2.44	1.22	3.16	4.98
AM (RS,ICS)	.04	.16	.44	.34	1.12	1.88	.80	2.18	3.38
GM (RS,ICS)	.04	.16	.42	.34	1.16	1.88	.80	2.30	3.32
AM (PFRE,IPFLE)	.04	.20	.48	.42	1.26	2.06	.90	2.52	3.92
GM (PFRE,IPFLE)	.04	.20	.48	.42	1.26	2.06	.90	2.50	3.92
AM ($PFEAA^T$,$PFEA^TA$)	.04	.12	.26	.26	.82	1.36	.58	1.54	2.62
GM ($PFEAA^T$,$PFEA^TA$)	.04	.12	.28	.26	.82	1.36	.56	1.54	2.72
AM (RGM, RS)	.04	.14	.42	.32	1.18	1.78	.72	1.92	3.12
GM (RGM, RS)	.04	.14	.42	.32	1.18	1.78	.72	1.92	3.14

TABLE 5

Average Counts of Changes in the Ordinal Rankings Between the LSF Vector and Heuristic Vectors for Matrices Generated by Method 2

Evaluation Technique	4x4 Matrices			7x7 Matrices			10x10 Matrices		
	RC	IC	HI	RC	IC	HI	RC	IC	HI
RGM	.20	.40	.58	.76	1.46	1.74	1.02	2.86	3.54
RS	.10	.28	.30	.60	1.18	1.46	.64	2.10	3.40
ICS	.12	.42	.52	.76	1.64	1.82	1.00	2.66	3.28
PFRE	.20	.40	.60	.74	1.44	1.84	1.00	2.98	4.06
IPFLE	.20	.42	.60	.76	1.54	1.76	1.02	2.96	3.70
$PFEAA^T$	.10	.30	.48	.48	1.08	1.26	.70	2.02	3.18
$PFEA^TA$	.16	.42	.52	.78	1.50	1.96	.96	2.80	3.16
AM (RS, ICS)	.14	.34	.46	.76	1.40	1.58	.96	2.72	3.54
GM (RS, ICS)	.14	.34	.46	.76	1.34	1.58	.96	2.76	3.58
AM (PFRE, IPFLE)	.20	.40	.60	.76	1.44	1.74	1.02	3.00	3.76
GM (PFRE, IPFLE)	.20	.40	.60	.76	1.44	1.74	1.02	3.02	3.72
AM ($PFEAA^T$, $PFEA^TA$)	.12	.28	.38	.60	1.14	1.44	.84	2.00	3.10
GM ($PFEAA^T$, $PFEA^TA$)	.12	.30	.42	.60	1.16	1.40	.84	2.14	3.12
AM (RGM, RS)	.14	.36	.46	.74	1.26	1.54	.84	2.48	3.54
GM (RGM, RS)	.14	.36	.46	.74	1.24	1.54	.84	2.48	3.56

<u>LEGEND</u>

RC = Relatively Consistent
IC = Inconsistent
HI = Highly Inconsistent

Tables 4 and 5 show the average number of position changes in each of the data subsets for all the heuristic vectors relative to LSF. The LSF vector was selected as the reference because, on the average, it performs better than any other of the evaluation techniques considered.

From the results printed in Tables 4 and 5, several points are quite obvious. No evaluation technique, on the average, produces the same ordering as LSF even in the most consistent cases. Also, as the degree of inconsistency increases, the number of position changes increases. Finally, as the matrices increase in size, the number of position changes increases. This is partly a result of an increase in the number of possible position changes.

The least-squares evaluation technique (LSF) requires the use of a numerical algorithm. The solution was determined by using a variation on Newton's method presented in [L]. The search was stopped when either

$$\sum_{i=1}^{n} |g^{i}| \leq (1.0 \cdot 10)^{-5} \cdot n$$

where g^i is the ith element of the gradient vector or if all elements of the solution vector changed by less than $1 \cdot 10^{-10}$ during any one iteration. All 15 heuristic evaluation techniques plus the vector of ones were used as initial conditions to (1) check for a global solution and (2) determine if a particular initial vector would significantly reduce the search. The length of the search was measured by both the average number of iterations and the average amount of cpu time actually used during the running of the algorithm. This did not include the time required to compute the initial vector, which was generally small and varied little.

TABLE 6

Average Number of Iterations for Different Initial Conditions for Inconsistent Matrices of All Sizes Generated by Method 2

Initial Vector	4 x 4 Inconsistent Matrices	7 x 7 Inconsistent Matrices	10 x 10 Inconsistent Matrices
RGM	4.86	5.90	5.66
RS	5.00	6.02	6.04
ICS	4.70	5.96	5.94
PFRE	4.82	6.10	5.78
IPFLE	4.86	6.18	5.80
$PFEAA^T$	4.98	6.54	6.46
$PFEA^TA$	4.74	6.14	6.02
Vector of Ones	7.12	9.24	11.06
AM (RS,ICS)	4.72	5.88	5.64
GM (RS,ICS)	4.66	5.72	5.70
AM (PFRE,IPFLE)	4.92	6.02	5.80
GM (PFRE,IPFLE)	4.94	6.00	5.72
AM ($PFEAA^T$,$PFEA^TA$)	4.50	5.66	5.52
GM ($PFEAA^T$,$PFEA^TA$)	4.54	5.66	5.54
AM (RGM, RS)	4.68	6.00	5.94
GM (RGM, RS)	4.68	6.00	5.96

The comparisons of different initial conditions for matrices generated by Method 1 are, for the most part, identical to the results for matrices generated by Method 2. Therefore, only some selected results are presented in Table 6.

In scanning Table 6, it can be seen that the algorithm computes the optimal LSF vector relatively quickly. Also, as seen from further calculations not summarized here, the number of iterations and cpu time increases with the degree of inconsistency and with the size of the matrix (because of the increased number of variables). Finally, any informed guess at an initial vector performs significantly better than the arbitrary guess of the vector of ones.

6. Conclusions

In addition to the few conclusions we draw here about the 16 evaluation techniques defined earlier, we hope that the computational data compiled here, as well as the list of evaluation techniques, will be useful to other users and designers of evaluation techniques. We list a few observations relative to questions which motivated this study, and other observations, of course, could be drawn from the compiled outcomes.

Among the heuristic evaluation techniques $v^{(1)}$ through $v^{(7)}$ and $v^{(9)}$ through $v^{(16)}$, overall differences in performance are not particularly great. Among the heuristics, none of them uniformly stands out. In several cases, most of them are rather closely bunched and often maximal percentage differences are modest. In several categories, one or a few of the techniques are well ahead but these are then often poor in other categories. To some extent, this reflects the fact that likely poor performers were not considered, but it probably is simply due to there being no heuristic which is superior from all points of view. Furthermore, since all techniques considered are consistent, it is not surprising that performance on nearly consistent matrices is similar. On highly inconsistent matrices, performance seems to become more random and, therefore, similar on average as well.

Not only does PFRE, the evaluation technique recommended in [S80] and [WS], not stand out among the heuristics, but also its performance, if anything, seems to be relatively poor. In fact, it is not outstanding in any category we consider. Thus, we conclude that not only is there no distinguishing theoretical basis for using PFRE but also there is no apparent numerical/empirical evidence to support its use either directly as an evaluation technique or as an initial vector in the computation of LSF. Furthermore, PFRE is likely to be more costly to compute than evaluation techniques which perform generally better. We consider it important that this conclusion be widely realized in view of the fact PFRE is strongly recommended without justification in [S80].

The evaluation technique LSF, which amounts to optimization in the euclidean norm, performs well in all norms. (Although this is not surprising due to the comparability of norms on finite dimensional spaces, it is not a priori guaranteed [HJ].) Its performance becomes more dominant with the increase in size and decrease in consistency of pairwise-comparison matrices. Overall, LSF clearly stands out as the best performing evaluation technique in this study although it is not uniformly first in all categories. Thus, we recommend LSF as a good performing technique, given no conflicting criteria associated with the application. It is, however, more costly to compute than the heuristics and the relative cost grows with matrix size and inconsistency. For the conditions likely in an application, however, the absolute cost per use is rather small and the cost relative to the heuristic is well less than a factor equal to the dimension of the problem.

In some applications, a heuristic evaluation technique may be desirable relative to LSF. For example, it may be that only a very approximate vector is sufficient or a large number of calculations may make cost a factor. Furthermore, a heuristic should be calculated to initialize the calculation of LSF. If one of the heuristics considered here is to be chosen, which one? There is little reason for distinction based upon cost and no clear-cut answer from the simulations reported here, but AM (PFEAA^T, IPFEA^TA) and GM (PFEAA^T, IPFEA^TA) are somewhat preferable among the heuristics and there is little distinction between them. We emphasize that this is not a uniform preference as these two perform poorly in some categories and others may be preferable in some applications.

Given the small cost of computing a heuristic evaluation technique, it is clear that one should be used to initialize the calculation of LSF as opposed to an ad hoc initial vector. The computation costs were often greater by 60 percent or more when the vector of ones was used, relative to initialization with the best heuristic. The two evaluation techniques, v(13) and v(14), mentioned above are generally best among the heuristics for initializing LSF, but there are no great differences among the performances of the various heuristics proposed for producing initial vectors.

References

[Da] David, H.A., The Method of Paired Comparisons, Hafner Publishing, Co., New York, 1963.

[De] Debreu, G., Stochastic Choice and Cardinal Utility, Econometrica, Vol. 26 (July 1958).

[H] Hihn, J.M., "A Hierarchical Approach to Decision Making: Economic Theory and Methodology," Ph.D. Dissertation, University of Maryland, College Park, 1980.

[HJ] Horn, R.A., and Johnson, C.R., Matrix Analysis, Cambridge University Press, New York, 1985.

[J] Johnson, C.R., "Constructive Critique of a Hierarchical Prioritization Scheme Employing Paired Comparisons," in Proceedings of the International Conference on Cybernetics and Society, IEEE, Cambridge, Mass., 1980, pp. 373-378.

[JBW] Johnson, C.R., Beine, W.B., and Wang, T.J., "Right-Left Assymmetry in an Eigenvector Ranking Procedure," J. Math. Psychology, Vol. 19 (1979), pp. 61-64.

[JH] Johnson, C.R., and Hihn, J.M., "Prioritization of Research Projects," in Transactions of the First International Conference on Energy Storage, Permagon Press, 1980, pp. 562-566.

[L] Luenburger, D.G., Introduction to Linear and Non-Linear Programming, Addison-Wesley Publishing Co., Menlo Park, California, 1973.

[M] McMeekin, G.C., "The Best Composite Priority Weights Estimator within the Framework of an Incomplete Prioritized Hierarchy," Economics Department, Case-Western Reserve University, Working Paper No. 37, 1980.

[S77] Saaty, T.L., "A Scaling Method for Priorities in Hierarchical Structures," J. Math. Psychology, Vol.15 (1977), pp. 234-281.

[S80] ________, The Analytic Hierarchy Process, McGraw-Hill, San Francisco, 1980.

[SV] Saaty, T.L. and Vargas, L.G., The Logic of Priorities: Applications in Business, Energy, Health and Transportation, Klumer Boston, Inc., Hingham, Massachusetts, 1982.

[SW] Schoemaker, P.J. and Waid, C.C., "An Experimental Comparison of Different Approaches to Determining Weights in Additive Utility Models," Management Sci., Vol. 28 (February 1982), pp. 182-196.

[T] Torgeson,W., Theory and Methods of Scaling, Wiley, NY, 1958.

[W] Wind, Y., "Marketing and Corporate Strategy," Wharton Magazine, Vol. 6, No. 4 (Summer 1982), pp. 38-45.

[WS] Wind, Y. and Saaty, T.L., "Market Applications of the Analytic Hierarchy Process," Management Sci., Vol. 26 (July 1980), pp. 641-658.

[Z] Zahedi, F., The Analytic Hierarchy Process - A Survey of the Method and its Applications, Interfaces, Vol. 16 (July-August 1986), pp. 96-108.

Note: The work of the second author was supported in part by the National Science Foundation grant DMS-8500372 and by Office of Naval Research contracts N00014-86-K-0012 and N00014-86-K-0693.

On the Effects of Bayesian Learning for a Risk-Averse Consumer

Peter Kischka
Institut für Statistik und Mathematische Wirtschaftstheorie
Universität Karlsruhe, Postfach 6980, D 7500 Karlsruhe

I Introduction

There is some discussion in the literature on the effects of potential learning on initial decisions. In 1977 Grossman, Kihlstrom and Mirman [2] considered a two stage consumption problem under uncertainty. They compare the following situations: Uncertainty can be resolved using Bayes' formula (the adaptive case) and the situation when a fixed probability distribution is used (the non-adaptive case). They assume a risk averse consumer, normal distribution and a fixed budget which has to be consumed in each period. Then initial optimal consumption always is not less in the adaptive case than in the non-adaptive case.
The assumption of a fixed budget is essential for the results in [2]. In [1], [5] contrary results are proved when the budget can be spread over two periods; in [5] Tonks showed these results for certain rates of time preferences, in [1] Cyert et al. assumed that there are transaction costs. Contrary to the result in [2], the authors in [1], [5] assume the utility function to be linear. The interpretation of these results therefore only hold for a risk neutral decision maker. Risk neutrality is a very special behavorial assumption; in general risk aversion has to be assumed.
After the discussion of his results Tonks writes ([5],p.527): "We would expect that for some risk-averse utility function similar conclusions could be drawn".

Measurement in Economics
ed: by W. Eichhorn

In this paper it is shown that the results of [2] cannot be generalized to the case of a risk averse consumer when the budget can be spread. We show that within the same model there are utility functions expressing risk aversion for which initial consumption is smaller, equal or larger in the adaptive case than in the non-adaptive case. Moreover, it follows that decreasing absolute risk aversion (see [4]) - an assumption for which there is strong empirical evidence- is not sufficient to determine whether or not consumption is larger in the adaptive case or in the non-adaptrive case (in the initial period). Consequenlty, there have to be additional assumptions in order to get a unique result like in [2].
In our example relative risk aversion of logarithmic utility functions determines the effect of adaptive learning. This is in coincidence with the result in [3], where relative risk aversion of utility functions exhibiting a linear tolerance function (i.e. the inverse of the absolute risk aversion function) determines the effect of adaptive learning in a portfolio model without intermediate consumption.
Contrary to the above mentioned papers we use a two point distribution and we make the assumption that the amount of information does not depend on the amount consumed. Such a situation occurs if a gamble can be observed whether or not one takes part or in the theory of finance where the return of a certain security is known to all investors whether or not they have this security in their own portfolio.

II The model

Similar to [2] and [5] we consider a model where successive decisions are to be made in order to maximize consumption. We use a simple gamble to illustrate the results. Other interpretations can easily be given.

Let W be initial wealth. First stage consumption is $C_o \leq W$. The amount $W-C_o$ is used to play a gamble which can be repeated. Second stage consumption C_1 is the amount after playing one or two times. The aim of the gambler is to maximize

$$U(C_o) + E(U(C_1))$$

where U is an utility function and E denotes expectation. Assume

there are only two possible results of the gamble: $x < 1$, $y > 1$. If the gamble is played with amount A, the amount the gambler receives afterwards is: rA ($r \in \{x,y\}$).
So second stage consumption C_1 can be written as

$$C_1 = H + r_2(r_1(W-C_o)-H) \quad , \qquad r_1, r_2 \in \{x,y\},$$

where H denotes the amount which is not used for playing a second time.

The true distribution of the results x,y is not known. We distinguish two cases.

Adaptive case: The gambler assumes that uncertainty concerning the gamble can be resolved by observing the result of the game. The distribution of the gamble is of the form

$$P_\gamma(x) = \gamma, \; P_\gamma(y) = 1-\gamma \quad , \; \gamma \in [0,1].$$

Instead of specifying some P_γ we assume that the gambler has some information on γ given by a distribution φ over [0,1]. The distribution for this gambler in the first period then is

(1) $$W_1(x) = \int P_\gamma(x)d\varphi(\gamma), \; W_1(y) = 1 - W_1(x).$$

By observing the result r_1 of the gamble the information given by φ can be updated using Bayes' formula to the posterior distribution $\psi(\gamma|r_1) \propto \varphi(\gamma)P_\gamma(r_1)$. For a second gamble the adaptive gambler has the distribution

(2) $$W_2(x|r_1) = \int P_\gamma(x)d\psi(\gamma|r_1), \; W_2(y|r_1) = 1 - W_2(x|r_1)$$
$$(r_1 \in \{x,y\}).$$

The non-adaptive case: The gambler uses some distribution P describing the game. P can be produced like W_1, but the gambler uses it as the true distribution therefore neglecting that r_1 can contain any information. In the non-adaptive case P is the relevant distribution for the second gamble, too.
In order to compare the two cases we assume that $P = W_1$.

After the first gamble the problem is given by

(3) $$\Phi(C_o, r_1) = \max_H E(U(R_2(r_1(W-C_o)-H) + H))$$

where in the adaptive case R_2 has the distribution $W_2(\ |r_1)$ and in the non-adaptive case the distribution P.

Before the first gamble the problem is to determine C_o by

$$(4) \qquad \max_{C_o} \{U(C_o) + E(\Phi(C_o, R_1))\},$$

where R_1 is distributed along to P in both cases.
In the following example we will specify risk-averse utility function U showing that the optimal consumption can be smaller, equal or larger in the adaptive case than in the other one.

III The example

Let initial wealth be W = 1.
For the adaptive gambler we make the assumption

$$\varphi(0) + \varphi(1) = 1, \quad \varphi(0) > 0, \ \varphi(1) > 0,$$

i.e. only the values $\gamma = 0$ or $\gamma = 1$ have positive prior probability.
Then we have (see (1))

$$(5) \qquad W_1(x) = P_o(x)\varphi(0) + P_1(x)\varphi(1) = \varphi(1), \ W_1(y) = \varphi(0).$$

This means $\varphi(1)$ is the probability of x for the adaptive gambler. For the posterior distribution we have

$$\psi(0|x) = 0 = \psi(1|y), \ \psi(1|x) = 1 = \psi(0|y)$$

and for the distribution after the first gamble therefore

$$(6) \qquad W_2(x|x) = 1 = W_2(y|y), \ W_2(x|y) = 0 = W_2(y|x).$$

In this way an extreme learning process is given. Uncertainty is fully resolved by one observation.

In the non-adaptive case we have

$$(7) \qquad P(x) = W_1(x), \ P(y) = W_1(y) \ .$$

We specify the utility function

$$(8) \qquad U(z) = \ln(z + c) \qquad (z > -c) \ .$$

U describes for any c decreasing absolute risk aversion; relative (proportional) risk aversion is increasing, constant or decreasing as $c > 0$, $c = 0$, $c < 0$ (see e.g. Pratt [4]).

Case 1) $c \geq 0$

Condition (3) is in the nonadaptive case given by

$$(9) \qquad \Phi(C_o, r_1) = \max_{0 \leq H \leq r_1(1-C_o)} \{\ln(xr_1(1-C_o) + (1-x)H + c)P(x) + \ln(yr_1(1-C_o) + (1-y)H + c)P(y)\}$$

Assuming that there is an interior solution H^* this solution fulfills:

$$(10) \quad H^* = r_1(1-C_o)\frac{xy - xP(y) - yP(x)}{(1-x)(1-y)} + \frac{c(E(R_1) - 1)}{(1-x)(1-y)}$$

Inserting H^* and because of

$$x(1-y) + xy - xP(y) + yP(x) = E(R_1) - y$$

one has in the non-adaptive case

$$(11) \quad \Phi(C_o, r_1) = \ln(r_1(1-C_o)+c) + A$$

with some constant A. Therefore the problem before gambling in this case is

$$(12) \quad \max_{0 \leqslant C_o \leqslant 1} \{\ln(C_o+c) + \ln(x(1-C_o) + c)P(x) + \ln(y(1-C_o) + c)P(y)\}$$

Since in the adaptive case the distribution for the second gamble is degenerate one has for (3)

$$(13) \quad \Phi(C_o, r_1) = \begin{cases} \ln(x(1-C_o) + c) & \text{for } r_1 = x \\ \ln(y^2(1-C_o) + c) & \phantom{\text{for }} r_1 = y \end{cases}$$

and therefore the initial problem (4) now is

$$(14) \quad \max_{0 \leqslant C_o \leqslant 1} \{\ln(C_o+c) + \ln(x(1-C_o) + c)P(x) + \ln(y^2(1-C_o) + c)P(y)\}$$

We assume that (12) and (14) have interior solutions C_o^B, C_o^A respectively. C_o^B, C_o^A fulfill first order conditions

$$(15) \quad \frac{1}{C_o^B + c} - \frac{xP(x)}{x(1-C_o^B) + c} - \frac{yP(y)}{y(1-C_o^B) + c} = 0$$

$$(16) \quad \frac{1}{C_o^A + c} - \frac{xP(x)}{x(1-C_o^A) + c} - \frac{y^2P(y)}{y^2(1-C_o^A) + c} = 0$$

Since the functions which are maximized in (12), (14) are concave, the solution C_o^B, C_o^A are unique. From (15), (16) it follows

<u>Result 1</u>

For $c = 0$ we have $C_o^A = C_o^B$

<u>Result 2</u>

For $c > 0$ we have $C_o^A < C_o^B$

Result 1 immediately can be seen. For result 2 remember $y > 1$ and therefore

$$\frac{y^2 P(y)}{y^2(1-C_o^B)P(y) + c} > \frac{yP(y)}{y(1-C_o^B)P(y) + c}.$$

From this and (15) it follows that that the derivative of the function used in (14) at C_o^B is negative. Therefore $C_o^B > C_o^A$.

Case 2) $c < 0$

In order to avoid utility $-\infty$ initial consumption has to fulfill:

$$C_o > -c \qquad (\Rightarrow \ln(C_o+c) > -\infty)$$

$$C_o < \frac{c + x}{x} \qquad (\Rightarrow x(1-C_o) > -c)$$

To get $-c < \frac{c+x}{x}$ we assume $-c < \frac{x}{1+x}$. Then (9), (13) and (12), (14) are defined in this case, too, replacing in (12), (14) the maximization area by $]-c, \frac{c+x}{x}[$. The assumption assures that in (9) there is some H such that the argument of ln is positive; if ln is not defined, utility can be assumed to be $-\infty$.

<u>Result 3</u>

If $c < 0$, $-c < \frac{x}{1+x}$ then $C_o^A > C_o^B$.

For $c < 0$, $y > 1$ one gets (C_o^A, C_o^B fulfilling (15), (16)):

$$\frac{y^2 P(y)}{y^2(1-C_o^A) + c} < \frac{yP(y)}{y(1-C_o^A) + c}$$

From this and (16) it follows that the derivative of the function used in (12) at C_o^A is negative. Therefore $C_o^A > C_o^B$.

Literature

[1] Cyert R.M., DeGroot M.H. and Hölt C.A.: Sequential Investment Decicions with Bayesian Learning
Management Science 24, 1978, 712-718

[2] Grossman, S.J.; Kihlstrom, R.E.; Mirman, L.J.: A Bayesian Approach to the Production of Information and Learning by Doing, Review Economic Studies 44, 1977, 533-548

[3] Kischka, P: Bayesian Methods in Multiperiod Financial Decision Making
to appear in: Proceedings of the Symposium on Probability Theory and Bayesian Statistics, Innsbruck 1986

[4] Pratt, J.W.: Risk Aversion in the Small and in the Large
Econometrica 32, 1964, 122-136

[5] Tonks, I.: A Bayesian Approach to the Production of Information with Linear Utility Function
Review of Economic Studies 51, 1984, 521-527

Measurement by Public Opinion Polls and Consequences for Modelling Pure Competition

Christoph Klein
Institut für Statistik
und Mathematische Wirtschaftstheorie
Universität Karlsruhe
D-7500 Karlsruhe 1

A model of a market with pure competition is presented. The rational numbers in the unit interval are interpreted as agents. Rational intervals are groups. Endowment mappings are described by Riemann integrable functions.

INTRODUCTION In 1978 D.PALLASCHKE [11] presented a model of a market with pure competition which used countably many agents and finitely additive measure theory. His motivation was to obtain a model which is better to interpret than R.J.AUMANN's model [3] and, on the other hand, which fulfills better completeness requirements than the Replica model of G.DEBREU and H.SCARF [5]. By investigating a systematic use of elementary indices, i.e. public opinion polls, the author [7] deduced from D.PALLASCHKE's model a deterministic continuous approach.

S.ROLEWICZ and the author developed in [8] and [9] a general theory of the Jordan content and the Riemann-Darboux integration. The general Jordan content corresponds canonically to the finitely additive measure theory. Moreover, the Darboux integrable functions are in a natural way a Banach space.

In this paper the deterministic, continuous model [7] is combined with the probabilistic approach of [9]. The result is a model which is based on the rational numbers of the unit interval and on limits of average means.

There are also recent studies concerning the problem of modelling pure competition: T.E.ARMSTRONG gives in [1] a good survey on new developements. Especially, T.E.ARMSTRONG and M.K.RICHTER established in [2] a very general model of pure competition which includes most of the previous, finitely additive and σ-additive approaches.

Measurement in Economics
ed. by W. Eichhorn

1. THE GENERAL MODEL

We want to observe a set N of agents of a market by public opinion polls or by statistics from a census. This kind of observation is not optimal to scrutinize an individual. It is suitable for studying groups. As we are interested in modelling pure competition it is in our opinion the appropriate mean.

In [7] we have motivated and elaborated an abstract mathematical formulation of such a kind of observation. We *sketch* in the sequel the main notations and results:

1.1 A *method of measurement* is a map $\varphi_G : N \to \{0,1\}$. N is the set of agents, $G := \{n \in N \mid \varphi_G(n) = 1\}$ is the *measured group* of agents. From the viewpoint of an agent $n \in N$ this means that he has a *property* such that the value of $\varphi_G(n)$ can be decided.

Let $\Phi := \{\varphi_i \mid i \in I\}$ a family of methods of measurement where I is an index set. Then the related groups $G(i)$, $i \in I$ generate the Boolean subalgebra $BG(\Phi)$ of the power set $\mathbb{P}(N)$ of N. Every set $A \subset N$, $A \in BG(\Phi)$ corresponds to a measurement by a *finite* combination - i.e. a Boolean polynominal - of the original methods of measurement φ_i, $i \in I$. Infinite combinations are *not* considered since no individual can answer infinitely many questions. If for $n, n' \in N$, $n \neq n'$ there is always an $A(n.n') \in BG(\Phi)$ with $n \in A(n,n')$, $n' \notin A(n,n')$ then Φ *separates* N.

1.2 An agent $n \in N$ is characterized with respect to the system Φ by his *property combination* $(\varphi_i(n))_{i\in I}$. This characterization is in general a theoretical concept because we excluded to question an individual infinitely: Indeed every agent $n \in N$ possesses a property $\varphi_i(n) \in \{0,1\}$ for every $i \in I$. Hence we can formally build $(\varphi_i(n))_{i\in I}$. However we can not determine this I-tupel by asking the agent $n \in N$. Therefore the I-tupel $(\varphi_i(n))_{i\in I}$ is a *theoretical tool* similar e.g. to how an irrational number is a purely theoretical notion. A zero-one system $(a_i)_{i\in I}$, $a_i \in \{0,1\}$ is called a *realized* property combination if there is an $n \in N$ with $(a_i)_{i\in I} = (\varphi_i(n))_{i\in I}$. If Φ separates N then the mapping $n \mapsto (\varphi_i(n))_{i\in I}$ is injective.

The set of *all possible* property combinations is $\{(a_i)_{i\in I} \mid a_i \in \{0,1\}\} = 2^I$. With respect to the product topology 2^I is well known as the compact, zero dimensional Cantor-I-cube. If $io \in I$ then we call $\bar{G}(io)$

$:= \{(a_i)_{i\in I} \mid a_i\in\{0,1\},\ a_{io} = 1\} \subset 2^I$ the *property group* with respect to io. The system $\bar{G}(i)$, $i\in I$ generates the Boolean subalgebra $\overline{BG}(\Phi)$ of $\mathbb{P}(2^I)$. The Boolean algebra $\overline{BG}(\Phi)$ corresponds to the class of all open and closed - short: *clopen* - subsets of 2^I. Hence $\overline{BG}(\Phi)$ is a neighbourhood basis system of 2^I.

If $\bar{A} \in \overline{BG}(\Phi)$ then $\bar{A}$ corresponds to a Boolean polynominal of property groups $\bar{G}(i)$. Let $A \subset N$ be the same Boolean polynominal performed with respect to the group system $G(i)$, $i\in I$. Then $\bar{A}$ contains no realized property combination iff $A = \emptyset$. Hence, by a finite combination of the considered methods of measurement we can recognize that $\bar{A}$ contains no realized property combination. Therefore we deem the system $\mathcal{Z} := \{\bar{A}\in\overline{BG}(\Phi) \mid A = \emptyset\}$ to be superfluous for a description of N by Φ.

If $\bar{A} \in \overline{BG}(\Phi)$ then $\bar{A}$ is a clopen set. Hence, $\bar{A}$ is especially an open subset of 2^I. Therefore $Z := \bigcup\{\bar{A} \mid \bar{A} \in \mathcal{Z}\}$ is open and $2^I\setminus Z$ is a compact space. In [7] we deduced that $2^I\setminus Z$ is the *Stone space of* $BG(\Phi)$ which we denote $\mathrm{Stone}(BG(\Phi))$. For the explicit, mathematical definition of the Stone space of a Boolean algebra see R.SIKORSKI [13]. The clopen sets of $\mathrm{Stone}(BG(\Phi))$ are $\{\bar{A}\setminus Z \mid \bar{A} \in \overline{BG}(\Phi)\}$ and they form a neighbourhood basis system of $\mathrm{Stone}(BG(\Phi))$. Observe, that due to our interpretation *every point and every clopen subset of* $\mathrm{Stone}(BG(\Phi))$ *have a well determind meaning*.

Let $A \in BG(\Phi)$. Then one easily recognizes that the realized property combinations corresponding to the agents $n \in A$ are dense in $\bar{A}\setminus Z$ i.e. in the related clopen set of $\mathrm{Stone}(BG(\Phi))$. Therefore, if Φ separates N then we can interpret $\mathrm{Stone}(BG(\Phi))$ as a *compactification* of N. $\bar{A}\setminus Z$ corresponds then to the *closure* $cl(A)$ of $A \subset N \subset \mathrm{Stone}(BG(\Phi))$. For concrete examples cf. [7] 1.2.

1.3 If N is finite then the fraction of a group $A \in BG(\Phi)$ is defined by (cardinality of A)/(cardinality of N). If N is infinite then we *suppose* in this general part that it is given by a non negative, normalized, finitely additive measure ν; i.e. we assume that $\nu: BG(\Phi) \to [0,1]$ fulfills $\nu(\emptyset) = 0$, $\nu(N) = 1$ and $\nu(A\cup B) = \nu(A) + \nu(B)$ if $A \cap B = \emptyset$. ν is called the *natural influence measure*. Then ν yields in a unique way a normalized, non negative Radon measure $\bar{\nu}$ on $\mathrm{Stone}(BG(\Phi))$ fulfilling $\bar{\nu}(\bar{A}\setminus Z) = \nu(A)$ for every $A \in BG(\Phi)$ (cf. [7] 1.3). Interpreting $\mathrm{Stone}(BG(\Phi))$ as a compactification of N this condition can be formulated as follows: $\bar{\nu}(cl(A)) = \nu(A)$ for every $A \in BG(\Phi)$.

We are interesred in the case of *pure competition*, i.e. the natural influence of every single agent has to be zero. This condition can be formulated as follows: For every $\varepsilon > 0$ there are finitely many groups $A(i)$, $i = 1,\ldots ,n(\varepsilon)$ in $BG(\Phi)$ with $N \subset \bigcup_{i=1}^{n(\varepsilon)} A(i)$ and $\nu(A(i)) < \varepsilon$ for every i. This formulation is equivalent to the now following condition: $\bar{\nu}$ *is atomless* (cf. [7] 1.3).

One may argue that our definition of pure competition depends on the observation process Φ. But observe that we stated that pure competition is *observed* iff $\bar{\nu}$ is atomless. This does not imply that the observation process itself is sufficiently precise to recognize pure competition. This problem will be cleared in the second part.

1.4 We are not interested in the observation of a set of agents only. We want to study a *market*. A market in its abstract formulation due to L.WALRAS and G.DEBREU is a mapping $\mathcal{E} := E \times e : N \to \mathcal{P} \times \mathbb{R}^n$. The *bounded* map $e : N \to \mathbb{R}^n$ assignes every agent his commodity bundle. The assumption that e is bounded describes the fact that the amount of a good in the whole market is bounded. Nevertheless we will motivate this assumption in part 2 by a further argument. The profile $E : N \to \mathcal{P}$ assignes every agent his preference.

Here a *preference* is a pair $(X,\succ)$. X is the consumption set i.e. a subset $X \subset \mathbb{R}^n$ which is closed, convex and bounded from below. Then $\succ$ is an open subset of $X \times X$ such that $\succ$ yields a transitive and irreflexive binary relation on X. The space $\mathcal{P}$ of all preferences is a compact metric space with respect to the topology of closed convergence. A concrete picture of the metric one obtains by the spherical projection from $\mathbb{R}^{2n+1}$ onto $\mathbb{R}^{2n}$ and the Euclidean metric of $\mathbb{R}^{2n+1}$ (cf. [7] 1.4).

We mentioned that Stone(BG(Φ)) can be interpreted as a compactification of N. Hence the question arises whether we can extend $\mathcal{E}$ to a *continuous* mapping $\bar{\mathcal{E}}$: Stone(BG(Φ)) $\to \mathcal{P} \times \mathbb{R}^n$. Analogously as in the case of the natural influence measure, this is possible if the observation Φ is precise enough. In the abstract mathematical formulation: $\mathcal{E}$ extends continuously onto Stone(BG(Φ)) iff $\mathcal{E}$ is contained in the closure of the space of $\mathcal{P} \times \mathbb{R}^n$-valued, BG($\Phi$)-simple mappings with respect to the sup. metric (cf. [7] 1.4).

1.5 In the following we will restrict ourselves in general onto monotone preferences i.e. $X = \mathbb{R}^n_+$ and $\succ \subset \mathbb{R}^n_+ \times \mathbb{R}^n_+$ fulfills the monotonicity condition: If $x_i \leq y_i$ for every i, $x \neq y$ then y is prefered to x: $(x,y) \in \succ$. A profile of monotone preferences is from our viewpoint a natural assumption with respect to the fact that a market can exist for scarce commodities only. A further reason for the above restriction is the following: The distance with respect to the closed convergence metric between two preferences can be changed strongly by adding resp. subtracting nowhere dense sets. Since such sets can not be measured or verified we deem the closed convergence metric usefull for regular open sets $\succ$ only. The monotone preferences are regular open subsets of $\mathbb{R}_+^{2n}$.

Let $\mathcal{E} = E \times e : N \to \mathcal{P}_{mo} \times \mathbb{R}_+^n$ a market where $\mathcal{P}_{mo}$ symbolizes the monotone preferences. Then $\mathcal{E}$ extends to a continuous map $\bar{\mathcal{E}}$: $\text{Stone}(\text{BG}(\Phi)) \to \mathcal{P}_{mo} \times \mathbb{R}_+^n$ iff Φ is sufficiently precise and the following condition holds: If x, $y \in \mathbb{R}_+^n$ with $x_i \leq y_i$ for every i, $x \neq y$ then there are neighbourhoods U(x) of x and V(y) of y such that $(v,u) \in E(n)$ for all n and all $u \in U(x)$, $v \in V(y)$.

The above condition is a *stability condition*. If N is finite then this condition is always fulfilled. We are working with an infinite set of agents - i.e. with an idealized set of agents. The above condition excludes problems which arise in the mathematical idealization only and which we deem to have no direct relation to reality, i.e. such problems can not be observed sufficiently by methods of measurement. The above stability concept is explained and elaborated in a more general form in [7] 1.5 and 2.3.

1.6 We want to establish a model of pure competition such that the natural influence of every agent is zero. Then the cardinality of the set of agents can not be finite. Therefore in the sequel we assume that N is a *countably infinite* set. Clearly, this is an idealization. It corresponds to the idealized assumption that the natural influence of every single agent is zero.

1.7 Let $\mathcal{E} = E \times e : N \to \mathcal{P}_{mo} \times \mathbb{R}_+^n$ a map such that e is bounded. We want to sketch here a natural procedure how a system Φ consisting of *countably* many methods of measurement can be obtained such that $\mathcal{E}$ extends continuously onto Stone(BG(Φ)) (cf. [7] 2 for details).

With respect to the mapping $e : N \to \mathbb{R}_+^n$ the idea corresponds to the approximation of the real numbers by decimal fractions: We put a grid with finite range and finite grid constant on $\mathbb{R}_+^n$. Then we approximate e(n) by the nearest grid point for every $n \in N$. Every grid corresponds to finitely many methods of measurement. We choose a sequence of grids such that the ranges tend to infinity and such that the grid constants converge against zero. These grids deliver at most countably many methods of measurement and e is approximated by them with respect to the sup. norm.

The mapping $E : N \to \mathcal{P}_{mo}$ is approximated similarly. Indeed, if a fixed grid is considered then we can obtain knowledge about the preference behaviour in all pairs of grid points by finitely many questions. Extending this information onto squares around the grid point pairs we obtain a preference resp. a profile which is based on finitely many methods of measurement. By a sequence of such grids one can approximate the profile E with respect to the sup. metric deduced from the closed convergence metric. Hence countably many methods of measurement suffice to approximate E.

Lastly it is obvious that the separability assumption can be guaranteed by adding countably many methods of measurement. Therefore, if N is countably infinite then *countably infinitely* many methods of measurement *suffice* to guarantee that $\mathcal{E}$ extends continuously onto Stone(BG(Φ)).

1.8 We want to mention a way how the natural influence measure can be observed. Since Φ consists of countably many methods of measurement the compact space Stone(BG(Φ)) is metrizable. Let $\Psi : \mathbb{N} \to N$ be an enumeration of N. Identifying N with the realized property combinations in Stone(BG(Φ)) we obtain $\{ \Psi(i) \mid i \in \mathbb{N} \}$ as a sequence in Stone(BG(Φ)). We assume that this sequence is *uniformly distributed*. This assumption corresponds to the law of large numbers (cf. [10] chapter 3, lemma 2.1). Then we can calculate the integral of a continuous function $\bar{f}$, where $\bar{f} : \text{Stone}(BG(\Phi)) \to \mathbb{R}^n_+$, as follows:

$$\int_{\text{Stone}(BG(\Phi))} \bar{f}\, d\bar{\nu} = \lim_{i\to\infty} \frac{1}{i} \sum_{k=1}^{i} \bar{f}(\Psi(k)) = \lim_{i\to\infty} \frac{1}{i} \sum_{k=1}^{i} f(\Psi(k)).$$

Remember that the characteristic function of every property group $\bar{A} \setminus Z = cl(A)$, $A \in BG(\Phi)$ is continuous for cl(A) is clopen.

We interpret an enumeration of N as a method to draw random samples. Then the above calculation of the integral is a rather natural procedure. Therefore in the following we want to consider the *natural numbers* $\mathbb{N}$ as the *set of agents*. We assume that continuous functions on

Stone(BG(Φ)) can be calculated as above.

1.9 We summarize the results of this general part. A *market* is a bounded map $\mathcal{E} : \mathbb{N} \to \mathcal{P}_{mo} \times \mathbb{R}^n_+$ fulfilling the stability property of section 1.5. This market is observed by a system Φ of countably many methods of measurement. The natural influence ν is defined on the observed groups BG(Φ) and ν can be calculated by average means. The *observation* of the market $\mathcal{E}$ is the continuous extension $\bar{\mathcal{E}}$: Stone(BG(Φ)) $\to \mathcal{P}_{mo} \times \mathbb{R}^n_+$ together with the Radon measure $\bar{\nu}$ on Stone(BG(Φ)). Stone(BG(Φ)) is considered as a compactification of $\mathbb{N}$. $\bar{\nu}$ is characterized by $\bar{\nu}(\mathrm{cl}(A)) = \nu(A)$ for every $A \in$ BG(Φ). Pure competition is observed if $\bar{\nu}$ is atomless.

Hence we have deduced from a *discrete model* a *continuous model*. Especially we explained precisely which meaning the points of Stone(BG(Φ)) have and how the observable groups are interpreted.

This general model is far from being perfect: The groups BG(Φ) depend on $\mathcal{E}$. We can not guarantee that pure competition is observed. Moreover it is still unclear which measure is representing a natural influence: Indeed until this stage of the model we assumed that there exists a finitely additive measure determining the natural influence of coalitions. We have not concretized it.

2. THE REPLICA MODEL

Let us try to sketch the main motivation for this second part. We want to establish a model for markets with pure competition. This is impossible by using markets with finitely many agents. We allow countably infinitely many agents. Hence our model will be an idealization or a kind of *completion* of the class of finite markets. The completion shall include all finite markets as special cases. Moreover it shall contain as few new markets as possible without contravening the completeness requirement. Indeed, otherwise there arises the risk to create purely mathematical problems.

We reformulate the above motivation in a somewhat opposite manner: In the first part we accepted a bounded mapping $\mathcal{E}: \mathbb{N} \to \mathcal{P}_{mo} \times \mathbb{R}^n_+$ fulfilling a stability property as a candidate for a market with pure competition. However, since in reality there exists *no* market with countably infinitely many agents the mapping $\mathcal{E}$ still remains a mathematical - i.e. an idealized - object. We want to single out of the whole class of these mathematical objects a subclass which fulfills the above described completeness and minimalization requirements, i.e. which is sufficient for our purposes. In the sequel we try to render precise the above intuition.

2.1 Let $N := \{1,\ldots,n\}$ an enumerated, finite set of agents. Then let $\mathcal{E} : N \to \mathcal{P}_{mo} \times \mathbb{R}^n_+$ a finite market. We define a *replicated market* $\mathcal{E}$: $\mathbb{N} \to \mathcal{P}_{mo} \times \mathbb{R}^n_+$ deduced from $\mathcal{E}$ as follows: We associate with every agent $i \in N$ the periodic group $G(i) := \{i+kn \mid k \in \mathbb{N}\ \{0\}\}$. We define $\mathcal{E}(j) = \mathcal{E}(i)$ for every $j \in G(i)$ and $i \in \{1,\ldots,n\}$. We restrict the observable groups onto the Boolean algebra which is generated by the groups $G(i)$. Then $\mathcal{E}$ is equivalent to $\mathcal{E}$.

We define the natural influence measure ν for $\mathcal{E}$ by the *density* d:

$$d(A) := \lim_{k\to\infty} (1/k)\Sigma_{i=1}^{k} \chi_A(i).$$

Here χ_A is the characteristic function of A and A is assumed to be an observed group. The natural influence on N is 1/n for every $i \in N$. Then $\mathcal{E}$ together with d is equivalent to $\mathcal{E}$ endowed with the natural influence. Hence a *finite market* can be interpreted as a*special case of an idealized market* defined on $\mathbb{N}$.

2.2 We describe here the system Φ of methods of measurement which will be used in our model. The methods of measurement of Φ are specified by the related groups as follows: $\Phi := \{ G(i,n) := \{ i+kn \mid k \in \mathbb{N}\ \{0\}\} \mid n \in \mathbb{N},\ 1 \le i \le n \}$. Then Φ consists of all periodic groups which appear in the above description of finite markets. The Boolean algebra $R_o := BG(\Phi)$ generated by Φ is called the *proper replica algebra* R_o. Then R_o contains all groups which are necessary to describe any finite market and R_o is a Boolean algebra which separates $\mathbb{N}$. Therefore we deem R_o to be sufficient for our purposes.

Let $p \in \mathbb{N}$ a prime number. We interpret $p^{\mathbb{N}}$ as the countably infinite product of the discrete, compact space $\{1,\ldots,p\}$. Then $p^{\mathbb{N}}$ is a compact metric space. The *Stone space* Stone(R_o) of R_o is the *product of the spaces* $p^{\mathbb{N}}$, $p \ge 2$, i.e. $\text{Stone}(R_o) = 2^{\mathbb{N}} \times 3^{\mathbb{N}} \times \ldots \times p_i^{\mathbb{N}} \times \ldots$ where p_i is running throw all primes greater than two (the proof is contained in [6]).

The density d is defined for every $A \in R_o$ and d is a normalized, non negative, finitely additive measure on R_o. The canonical restriction of d onto finite markets yields the natural fraction measure. Obviously, d on R_o fulfills the condition for pure competition of section 1.3. Indeed d extends to an atomless probability measure $\bar{d}$ on Stone(R_o). The support of $\bar{d}$ is the whole space Stone(R_o) because $\bar{d}$ coincides with the natural product measure on R_o (cf [6]). Consequently, the *density* d on R_o, resp. $\bar{d}$ on Stone(R_o), yields our *unique natural influence measure.*

By collecting all requirements derived from finite markets we could answer the open questions of part one i.e. the concretizations of Φ and ν and the guarantee that pure competition is observed.

2.3 It remains to describe the class of all mappings $\mathcal{E} : \mathbb{N} \to \mathcal{P}_{mo} \times \mathbb{R}^n_+$, resp. $\bar{\mathcal{E}}$: Stone(R_o) $\to \mathcal{P}_{mo} \times \mathbb{R}^n_+$, which we admit in our model as markets. The replicated markets resp. their continuous extensions have to be dense in the class of all admitted markets since we interpreted this class as a completition.

The replicated markets coincide with the class of all R_o-*simple* mappings from $\mathbb{N}$ into $\mathcal{P}_{mo} \times \mathbb{R}^n_+$. Here a mapping $\mathcal{E} : \mathbb{N} \to \mathcal{P}_{mo} \times \mathbb{R}^n_+$ is called R_o-simple if there is a finite, dijoint decomposition of $\mathbb{N}$ by elements A_i of R_o such that $\mathcal{E}$ is constant on every A_i. Analogously the continuous extensions of the replicated markets are *simple continuous* mappings on Stone(R_o) - i.e. $\bar{\mathcal{E}}$ is constant on cl(A_i) and cl(A_i) was clopen in the space Stone(R_o). The closure of all simple, continuous mappings from Stone(R_o) into $\mathcal{P} \times \mathbb{R}^n_+$ with respect to the sup. metric is the class of *all continuous* mappings from Stone(R_o) into $\mathcal{P} \times \mathbb{R}^n_+$ (cf. [7] and Z. SEMADENI [12] § 8.2).

We denote C(Stone(R_o), $\mathcal{P}_{mo} \times \mathbb{R}^n_+$) the class of all continuous mappings from Stone(R_o) into $\mathcal{P}_{mo} \times \mathbb{R}^n_+$. Due to the above arguments it seems to be consequent to admit every $\bar{\mathcal{E}} \in$ C(Stone(R_o), $\mathcal{P}_{mo} \times \mathbb{R}^n_+$) - resp. its restriction $\mathcal{E}$ on $\mathbb{N}$ - as a market in our model. Especially, the stability property from section 1.5 is fulfilled for these mappings. *In principle* we will use later on these mappings as the class of admitted markets. However, it is still necessary to change the viewpoint from which these continuous functions are interpreted:

2.4 Until this moment we observed a market by methods of measurement i.e. in a *deterministic* way. We want to observe a market by public opinion polls. Every public opinion poll is based on a method of measurement. However, by using a public opinion poll φ, we obtain not the group $G(\varphi)$ itself but only the fraction of $G(\varphi)$ i.e. $d(G(\varphi))$. For this reason we want to interpret in the following the model in a *probabilistic* way.

There is also an intrinsic reason to introduce probabilistic elements: The influence of a single agent $n \in \mathbb{N}$ is zero in our model due to the assumption of pure competition. If we use the sup. metric for the completion procedure then we obtain easily a contradiction to that assumption. Indeed a single agent can determine the sup. distance of two functions. We conclude that every alteration of a market on a zero influence set of agents yields no alteration of the economic situation. Hence a *market* is in a natural way an *equivalence class of mappings*. This equivalence class is determined by the class of all sets $A \subset \mathbb{N}$ with $d(A)=0$.

Observe that $d(\mathbb{N}) = 1$. If we consider $\mathbb{N}$ as a subset of $\text{Stone}(R_o)$ then $\bar{d}(\mathbb{N}) = 0$ for $\bar{d}$ is atomless. Therefore we conclude that the Lebesgue zero sets are not helpfull for our model. Instead of the Lebesgue integration we will use the Jordan content and the Riemann-Darboux integration theory. This older theory can be treated *equivalently* on any dense subset of a compact support of a Radon measure and this is required in our model (The reader who is not familiar with the Riemann integration on compact spaces is refered to [8] and [9] of S.ROLEWICZ, C.KLEIN).

A bounded map $f : \text{Stone}(R_o) \to \mathcal{P} \times \mathbb{R}^n_+$ is $\bar{d}$-Darboux integrable iff f is continuous except on a $\bar{d}$-zero set. With respect to the $\bar{d}$-ess. sup. metric the $\bar{d}$-Darboux integrable mappings are in a canonical way - i.e. by forming equivalence classes - a complete metric space denoted here $D(\text{Stone}(R_o), \bar{d}, \mathcal{P} \times \mathbb{R}^n_+)$. Its subspace generated by the simple continuous mappings can be identified isometrically with the *continuous mappings* $C(\text{Stone}(R_o), \mathcal{P} \times \mathbb{R}^n_+)$ (i.e. every equivalence class of that subspace contains a continuous representative). If g is a bounded, $\mathbb{R}^n_+$-valued, Darboux integrable function on $\text{Stone}(R_o)$ then the integral formulas of section 1.8 can be applied analogously with respect to $\bar{d}$ and d. Therefore we obtain the following result:

2.5 Let $\bar{\mathcal{E}} : \text{Stone}(R_o) \to \mathcal{P}_{mo} \times \mathbb{R}^n_+$ a continuous mapping and let $\mathcal{E}$ its restriction onto $\mathbb{N}$. We interpret $\bar{\mathcal{E}}$ as an element of the complete metric space of Darboux integrable mappings $D(\text{Stone}(R_o), \bar{d}, \mathcal{P} \times \mathbb{R}^n_+)$. Analogously $\mathcal{E}$ is interpreted as an element of the trace of $D(\text{Stone}(R_o), \bar{d}, \mathcal{P} \times \mathbb{R}^n_+)$ on $\mathbb{N}$. Then $\mathcal{E}$ is called a *market with pure competition*. $\bar{\mathcal{E}}$ is called the *observation of* $\mathcal{E}$ *by public opinion polls*.

We have introduced a model of pure competition which seems us to be well interpretable. However the space Stoné(R_o) is rather abstract and the calculus on that space is unfamiliar. Therefore we have to discuss this point in the sequel.

3. THE REPRESENTATION OF THE REPLICA MODEL

3.1 Let Ki be the compact support of a normalized, non negative Radon measure μi where $i \in \{1,2\}$. We denote $M := \wp \times \mathbb{R}^n_+$. It is well known that a homeomorphism $\Pi : K1 \to K2$ induces an isometric bijection between the complete metric spaces of continuous mappings from K1, resp. K2, into M. Analogously, if $\pi : (K1,\mu 1) \to (K2,\mu 2)$ is a *topological measure isomorphism* then π induces an isometric bijection between $D(K1,\mu 1,M)$ and $D(K2,\mu 2,M)$ (cf. [8]).

For our porposes it is sufficient to know the following: Let K1 be zero dimensional such that the clopen subsets of K1 are a neighbourhood basis system of K1. Then π is a topological measure isomorphism if π is an irreducible continuous surjection from K1 onto K2 which is measure preserving on the clopen subsets of K1 (cf. [8] for a proof).

3.2 We want to construct an irreducible continuous surjection S from Stone(R_o) into [0,1] which is measure preserving on the clopen subsets of Stone(R_o) with respect to $\bar{d}$ and the Lebesgue measure λ.

The idea how we obtain S is rather easy. Recall that Stone$(R_o) = 2^{\mathbb{N}} \times 3^{\mathbb{N}} \times 5^{\mathbb{N}} \times \;.....$. We will combine G.CANTOR's method to enumerate $\mathbb{N} \times \mathbb{N}$ and the canonical irreducible continuous surjection from $2^{\mathbb{N}}$ (analogously from $p^{\mathbb{N}}$) onto the unit interval $[0,1] : (a_1,a_2,...) \mapsto \Sigma_{i=1} a_i/2^i$.

Indeed, let $a = (a_{ij})_{i\in P, j\in\mathbb{N}} \in \text{Stone}(R_o) = \Pi_{p\in P}\, p^{\mathbb{N}}$ where P is the naturally ordered set of all primes greater than one. Then S is defined as follows: $a \mapsto a_{11}/2 + a_{12}/2\cdot 2 + a_{21}/2\cdot 2\cdot 3 + a_{31}/2\cdot 2\cdot 3\cdot 5 + a_{22}/2\cdot 2\cdot 3\cdot 5\cdot 3 + \ldots$. Observe that the indices and the product sequences are following G.CANTOR's method to enumerate $\mathbb{N} \times \mathbb{N}$. One easily verifies that S is an irreducible, continuous surjection which is measure preserving on the clopen subsets of Stone(R_o). Therefore $D(\text{Stone}(R_o),\bar{d},\wp \times \mathbb{R}^n_+)$ is *isometric* to $D([0,1],\lambda,\wp \times \mathbb{R}^n_+)$ and S does not change the monotonicity.

3.3 It remains to show that the realized property combinations $\mathbb{N} \subset$ Stone(R_o) are mapped by S onto the rational numbers of the interval[0,1)

For that purpose let us recall how a number $n \in \mathbb{N}$ generates an element $(a_{ij})_{i\in P, j\in \mathbb{N}} \in \mathrm{Stone}(R_o)$: We devide $\mathbb{N}$ into the odd and even numbers. If n is odd then $a_{11} = 0$. Otherwise $a_{11} = 1$. Let n be odd. Then the odd numbers are interpreted as $\mathbb{N}$ and once more we devide into odd and even numbers. Let n be even; then $a_{12} = 1$. We interpret the odd-even numbers as $\mathbb{N}$ and - following G.CANTOR's enumeration of $\mathbb{N} \times \mathbb{N}$ - we divide $\mathbb{N}$ into the three periodic groups $G(i)$, $i \in \{1,2,3\}$. If $n \in G(i)$ then $a_{21}=i-1$etc

One recognizes that every $n \in \mathbb{N}$ generates a sequence $(a_{ij})_{j\in P, j\in \mathbb{N}}$ with finitely many non zero coefficients. Hence n is mapped by S onto a rational number in [0,1). On the other hand, since every rational number is a quotient of two natural numbers and since a natural number is a product of finitely many primes we recognize that $\mathbb{N}$ *is one-one mapped by* S *onto the set of all rational numbers in* [0,1).

Moreover, due to the special definition of S, one recognizes that a clopen subset of $\mathrm{Stone}(R_o)$ is mapped by S onto a finite union of closed rational intervals in [0,1]. Hence a simple continuous mapping $\bar{\mathcal{E}}$ on $\mathrm{Stone}(R_o)$ is transformed by S to a Darboux mapping $\bar{\mathcal{E}}'$ on [0,1] such that the discontinuity points of $\bar{\mathcal{E}}'$ are rational. Consequently $C(\mathrm{Stone}(R_o)$, $\mathcal{P} \times \mathbb{R}^n_+$ is mapped into the class of those Darboux integrable functions on [0,1] *which possess rational discontinuity points only.*Therefore we obtain the following result:

<u>3.4</u> Let $\bar{\mathcal{E}}' : [0,1] \to \mathcal{P} \times \mathbb{R}^n_+$ a bounded Darboux integrable mapping with rational discontinuity points only. Let $\mathcal{E}'$ be the restriction of $\bar{\mathcal{E}}'$ onto the rational numbers. We interpret $\bar{\mathcal{E}}'$ as an element of the complete metric space $D([0,1],\lambda,\mathcal{P} \times \mathbb{R}^n_+)$. Analogously $\mathcal{E}'$ is interpreted as an element of the trace of $D([0,1],\lambda,\mathcal{P} \times \mathbb{R}^n_+)$ on the rational numbers. Assume that $cl(\bar{\mathcal{E}}'([0,1])) \subset \mathcal{P}_{mo} \times \mathbb{R}^n_+$. Then $\mathcal{E}'$ is called a *represented market with pure competition.* $\bar{\mathcal{E}}'$ is called the *represented observation of* $\mathcal{E}'$ *by public opinion polls.* The rational numbers are called *agents*. The rational intervals correspond to the *observed groups*.

The interpretation of the irrational numbers is more difficult in the above represented Replica model. However, we mention that S is a continuous bijection except on a set of measure zero., (cf. W.BÖGE, K.KRICKEBERG, F.PAPANGELOU [4]). We mention that represented markets have even better properties than described in the above definition. This is caused by the fact that $C(\mathrm{Stone}(R_o)$, $\mathcal{P} \times \mathbb{R}^n_+)$ is mapped *into* the class of Darboux integrable functions on [0,1]. However, we have not the place here to present the necessarily technical steps which allow a more precise description.

The goal of this contribution to the Symposium on Index Theory was to demonstrate which consequences a systematic use of elementary indices - i.e. public opinion polls - can imply. We have not the place here to develop a new general equilibrium model.

REFERENCES

[1] T.E.ARMSTRONG, Remarks Related to Finitely Additive Exchange Economies, Proc. Indianapolis 1984, Editors: C.D.ALIPRANTIS, O. BURKINSHAW,and N.J.ROTHMANN, Lecture Notes in Economics and Math. Systems 244, Berlin, Heidelberg, New York 1985

[2] T.E.ARMSTRONG, M.K.RICHTER, The Core-Walras Equivalence, Journal of Economic Theory 33 (1984) 116 - 151

[3] R.J.AUMANN, Markets with a Continuum of Traders, Econometrica 32 (1964)

[4] W.BÖGE,K.KRICKEBERG,F.PAPANGELOU, Über die dem Lebesgue'schen Maß isomorphen topologischen Maßräume, Manuscripta Math. 1 (1969)

[5] G.DEBREU, On a Theorem of Scarf, Review of Economic Studies 30 (1963) 177 - 180

[6] C.KLEIN, Atomless Economies with Countably Many Agents, Proc. of the Seminar on Game Theory Bonn-Hagen 1978, Editors: O.MOESCHLIN, D.PALLASCHKE, Amsterdam 1979, 337 - 342

[7] C.KLEIN, The Observation of a Deterministic Microeconomic Model of a Large Economy, Proc. of the Seminar on Game Theory Bonn-Hagen 1980, Editors: O.MOESCHLIN, D.PALLASCHKE, Amsterdam 1981

[8] C.KLEIN, Invariance Properties of the Banach Algebra of Darboux Integrable Functions, Proc. Karlsruhe 1983, Editors: G.HAMMER, D.PALLASCHKE, Lecture Notes in Economics and Math. Systems 226, Berlin, Heidelberg, New York 1984, 382 - 411

[9] C.KLEIN, S.ROLEWICZ, On Riemann Integration of Functions with Values in Topological Linear Spaces, Studia Math. 80 (1984) 109 - 118

[10] L.KUIPERS, H.NIEDERREITER, Uniform Distribution of Sequences, New York, London, Sydney 1974

[11] D.PALLASCHKE, Markets with Countably Many Traders, Journal of Applied Math. and Comp. 4 (1978) 201 - 212

[12] Z.SEMADENI, Banach Spaces of Continuous Functions I, Warszawa 1971

Characterizations of Quasilinear Representations and Specified Forms of These*

Peter P. WAKKER
Netherlands Central Bureau of Statistics
Department of Statistical Methods
P.O.Box 959
2270 AZ Voorburg
The Netherlands

ABSTRACT. In this paper two versions of 'equivalence independence' for binary relations on Cartesian products are introduced to characterize special kinds of representing functions. The obtained results are used to characterize quasilinear economic indexes, and several specified forms of these.

1. INTRODUCTION

Many problems from many fields of science come down to one and the same kind of mathematical problem: finding a function V of several variables to the reals that has certain desirable properties. These desirable properties can often be expressed in terms of functional equations, the mathematical theory of which is treated for instance in Aczél (1966). One example from economics is production theory, where variables are in- or outputs, and the function V is a production (efficiency) function. Another example is the theory of (statistical) price indexes. Here the variables are prices or consumed quantities of goods or services, at base or comparison times or locations, and the function V is a (statistical) price index or purchasing power parity. In the measurement of inequality the variables are the shares of total welfare, allocated to individuals, and V is a measure of inequality. In decision making under uncertainty the variables are consequences, contingent on the occurrence of some state of nature, and V describes or prescribes the decision making of an individual, facing uncertainty; e.g. V is an expected utility index.

*) The views expressed in this paper are those of the author and do not necessarily reflect the policies of the Netherlands Central Bureau of Statistics. Most of the work described here was done at the University of Nijmegen, Department of Mathematics.

Measurement in Economics
ed. by W. Eichhorn

In some fields of science it is custom to take a binary relation ('preference relation') as primitive, and to search for characterizations (i.e. properties of the preference relation, necessary and sufficient) for the existence of a representing function V with desirable properties. Other fields take V as a primitive. We shall call such a V an index. One then searches for indexes that have desirable properties.

In sections 2, 3, and 4 we give some representation theorems for preference relations. In subsection 5.1 we indicate how such theorems can be reformulated for situations where indexes, instead of preference relations, are primitives, so that characterizations of the ordinal character of the indexes result. From these characterizations we derive, in subsection 5.2, characterizations of some well-known general kinds of indexes, all in an ordinal vein. Section 6 gives some conjectures. Finally, in subsection 6.3 we indicate that our results can also be used as a starting point for deriving 'non-ordinal' results, by the addition of a, usually weak, non-ordinal condition (i.e. 'test', 'axiom', 'property').

2. BASIC DEFINITIONS AND RESULTS

In this section we give definitions and state some preparatory results. Let Γ be a non-empty connected topological space. [For topological definitions, the reader is referred to Kelley (1955). Readers, not interested in topological details may simply take Γ to be a convex subset of $\mathbb{R}^m$. Such a Γ satisfies all the topological assumptions made in this paper (e.g. in Assumption 2.3 below.)] Let $n \in \mathbb{N}$. The Cartesian product Γ^n is endowed with the product topology. Its elements are called alternatives. An alternative $x \in \Gamma^n$ has i-th coordinate x_i.

A preference relation $\succsim$ is a binary relation on Γ^n. As usual we write $x \precsim y$ for $y \succsim x$, $x \approx y$ for $[x \succsim y$ & $y \succsim x]$, $x \succ y$ or $y \prec x$ for $[x \succsim y$ & not $y \succsim x]$. The preference relation $\succsim$ is a weak order if it is complete ($x \succsim y$ or $y \succsim x$ for all $x,y \in \Gamma^n$) and transitive. If so, then $\approx$ is an equivalence relation. The preference relation $\succsim$ is continuous if $\{x \in \Gamma^n : x \succ y\}$ and $\{x \in \Gamma^n : x \prec y\}$ are open for all $y \in \Gamma^n$.

A function $V:\Gamma^n \to \mathbb{R}$ represents $\succsim$ if $[x \succsim y \Leftrightarrow V(x) \geq V(y)]$ for all $x,y \in \Gamma^n$. A representable preference relation is necessarily a weak order. In the literature a representing function is often called a 'utility function'. To settle terminology further, we call, for $A \subset \mathbb{R}$, a real-valued function $\varphi:A \to \mathbb{R}$ increasing if $\varphi(\alpha) > \varphi(\beta)$ whenever $\alpha > \beta$.

NOTATION 2.1. For $1 \leq i \leq n$, $\alpha \in \Gamma$, $x \in \Gamma^n$:

$x_{-i}\alpha$:= [x with x_i replaced by α].

DEFINITION 2.2. Coordinate (or index) i is **inessential** if $x_{-i}\alpha \approx x$ for all $\alpha\in\Gamma$, $x\in\Gamma^n$. If i is not inessential, then it is **essential**.

For weak orders $\geq$ inessential coordinates do not have influence on the 'desirability' of an alternative. They may therefore be ignored and suppressed. That we shall do. For easy reference we state:

ASSUMPTION 2.3. All coordinates are essential. Γ is a connected topological space; Γ^n is endowed with the product topology. If n=1, Γ is topologically separable.

We shall be interested only in (increasing transforms of) functions of the following kind:

DEFINITION 2.4. A function $V:\Gamma^n\to\mathbb{R}$ is **additive** if there exist $V_j:\Gamma\to\mathbb{R}$ (j=1,...,n) such that $V:x\mapsto\sum_{j=1}^{n}V_j(x_j)$.

The following property goes under many names, such as (preferential) independence, additivity, strong (strict) separability, and 'sure-thing principle'. The present name abbreviates 'independent of equal coordinates'.

DEFINITION 2.5. The binary relation $\geq$ is **coordinate independent** (CI) if for all i,x,y,α,β we have

$$[x_{-i}\alpha \geq y_{-i}\alpha] \iff [x_{-i}\beta \geq y_{-i}\beta] .$$

The idea is that, once two alternatives have the same i-th coordinate, the preference between them does not depend anymore upon this particular coordinate, be it α,β, or whatever. The idea can already be recognized in Fisher (1927, page 175).

The following theorem is mainly due to Debreu (1960). We give the slightly stronger result of Wakker (1986a, Theorem III.3.7), which supplies Krantz et al. (1971, Theorem 6.14) with continuity, thus shows that the assumption of topological separability, made in the original formulation of Debreu, can be omitted.

THEOREM 2.6 (Debreu). *Let* $n\geq3$. *Under Assumption 2.3 the following two statements are equivalent for the binary relation* $\geq$ *on* Γ^n*:*

(i) **There exists a continuous additive function on Γ^n which represents the binary relation $\geq$.**

(ii) **The binary relation $\geq$ is a continuous weak order which satisfies CI.**

□

The following property has been introduced in Wakker (1984), where an elucidation of its meaning is given. The chosen term is motivated, firstly, by the observation that under reflexivity of $\succeq$ the property implies CI (set $x=y$, $\alpha=\beta$, $\gamma=\delta$ below), and secondly by the observation that the condition adds to CI a preservation of first-order differences of utility, also independent of coordinates, which is known to imply cardinality in the presence of continuity w.r.t. a connected topology. See also Wakker (1984, section 3; 1986a, section 4.2; and 1986b, formula (3.3)) where reformulations are given in terms of a strength of preference relation, derived from the preference relation.

DEFINITION 2.7. The binary relation $\succeq$ satisfies <u>cardinal coordinate independence</u> (<u>CCI</u>) if for all $i,j,x,\ldots,\delta$ we have :

$$\begin{bmatrix} x_{-i}\alpha \preceq y_{-i}\beta & \& & v_{-j}\alpha \succeq w_{-j}\beta & \& \\ x_{-i}\gamma \succeq y_{-i}\delta & & & \end{bmatrix}$$

$$\Rightarrow \qquad [v_{-j}\gamma \succeq w_{-j}\delta]$$

The idea of the condition is that the left two preferences reveal that the *strength of preference* of α over β is not larger than that of γ over δ. Further, by this the right preference above should imply the lower preference. The following theorem is the main result in Wakker (1986a; Theorem IV.3.3). Its main application lies in decision making under uncertainty where it characterizes subjective expected utility maximization, obtaining subjective probabilities and utilities simultaneously, as Savage (1954) did. Theorem V.6.1 in Wakker (1986a) extends the result to arbitrary, possibly infinite, state spaces, i.e. to possibly infinite Cartesian products. As compared to Savage's result, this theorem replaces restrictions concerning the state space by the restriction of continuity, a restriction usually satisfied in economic contexts.

THEOREM 2.8. *Under Assumption 2.3 the following two statements are equivalent for the binary relation* $\succeq$ *on* Γ^n*:*

(i) **There exist positive $(p_j)_{j=1}^n$, summing to one, and a continuous function $U:\Gamma\to\mathbb{R}$, such that $x\mapsto\sum_{j=1}^n p_j U(x_j)$ represents the binary relation $\succeq$.**

(ii) **The binary relation $\succeq$ is a continuous CCI weak order.**

□

For contexts other than decision making under uncertainty the restriction on the p_j's in (i) above may be undesirable. For instance in production theory one would want some p_j's (those associated with inputs x_j) to be negative. In the theory of price indexes one would want the weights p_j, associated with base prices x_j, to be negative. In section 4 we shall weaken the CCI condition for $\succeq$ in (ii) exactly far enough to obtain a characterization of (i) without restrictions on the p_j's. For this we first strengthen Debreu's Theorem 2.6 to a result which uses as much as possible the equivalence relation $\approx$ instead of the preference relation $\geq$ (see Theorem 3.10 below). Because of the importance of Debreu's theorem, this result may have interest of its own.

3. CHARACTERIZING ADDITIVE REPRESENTATIONS VIA EQUIVALENCE

In this section we shall replace the CI condition in Debreu's Theorem 2.6 by a weaker condition, using the equivalence relation $\approx$ instead of the preference relation $\geq$. Since it is easier to test for equivalence $\approx$ than for 'dominance' $\geq$, this may be of use in the testing of additivity of representations and indexes.

DEFINITION 3.1. The binary relation $\geq$ is **equivalence coordinate independent** (ECI) if for all i,x,y,α,β we have

$$[x_{-i}\alpha \approx y_{-i}\alpha] \iff [x_{-i}\beta \approx y_{-i}\beta].$$

LEMMA 3.2. *If $\geq$ satisfies CI, then it satisfies ECI.*

PROOF. Let $\geq$ satisfy CI.Then $[x_{-i}\alpha \approx y_{-i}\alpha]$ iff $[x_{-i}\alpha \geq y_{-i}\alpha$ & $y_{-i}\alpha \geq x_{-i}\alpha]$, which, by twofold application of CI, holds iff $[x_{-i}\beta \geq y_{-i}\beta$ & $y_{-i}\beta \geq x_{-i}\beta]$. The latter holds iff $[x_{-i}\beta \approx y_{-i}\beta]$.

□

We shall also need the following implication of CI:

DEFINITION 3.3. The binary relation $\geq$ is **weakly separable** if, for all i,x,y,α,β, we have

$$[x_{-i}\alpha \geq x_{-i}\beta] \iff [y_{-i}\alpha \geq y_{-i}\beta].$$

LEMMA 3.4. *If $\geq$ is a weak order, then CI implies weak separability.*

PROOF. CI allows one to replace in every preference any single pair of equal coordinates, thus by repetition, any arbitrary number of pairs of equal coordinates. Weak separability allows only the replacement of (n-1)-tuples of pairs of equal coordinates.

□

The following definition is useful for weakly separable weak orders.

DEFINITION 3.5. For any $1 \le i \le n$, $\succeq_i$ is defined by

$[\alpha \succeq_i \beta]$ <=> [there exists x such that $x_{-i}\alpha \succeq x_{-i}\beta$].

One easily verifies, with $\succ_i$ the asymmetric part of $\succeq_i$, $\approx_i$ the symmetric part, $\alpha \preceq_i \beta$ iff $\beta \succeq_i \alpha$, and $\alpha \prec_i \beta$ iff $\beta \succ_i \alpha$:

LEMMA 3.6. *If the binary relation $\succeq$ is a weakly separable weak order, then every $\succeq_i$ is a weak order; further*

$[x_i \succeq_i y_i$ *for all* i] => $[x \succeq y]$

and

$[x_i \succeq_i y_i$ *for all* i & $x_i \succ_i y_i$ *for some* i] => $[x \succ y]$.

□

The following property, defined in Krantz et al. (1971), will be used in our analysis.

DEFINITION 3.7. The binary relation $\succeq$ satisfies <u>restricted solvability</u> if for all i, x, y, α, γ we have:

$[x_{-i}\alpha \succeq y \succeq x_{-i}\gamma]$ => [there exists β such that $x_{-i}\beta \approx y$].

LEMMA 3.8. *Under Assumption 2.3 a continuous weak order $\succeq$ satisfies restricted solvability.*

PROOF. See Krantz et al. (1971, section 6.12.3).

□

LEMMA 3.9. *Let the binary relation $\succeq$ be a weakly separable ECI weak order. Let Assumption 2.3 hold. Let $\succeq$ be continuous. Then $\succeq$ is CI.*

PROOF. Suppose $x_{-n}\alpha \succeq y_{-n}\alpha$. We must show that $x_{-n}\beta \succeq y_{-n}\beta$. (It is no restriction to take the i of Definition 2.5 equal to n.) Let $A := \{j<n: x_j \succ_j y_j\}$. Without loss of generality, suppose $A = \{1,\ldots,k\}$ for some $0 \le k < n$. Define $x^0 := x_{-n}\alpha$, $x^\ell := x^{\ell-1}_{-\ell}y_\ell$ for $1 \le \ell \le k$. Then, by Lemma 3.6, $x^0 \succeq x^1 \succeq \ldots \succeq x^k$. Further, since $(y_{-n}\alpha)_j \succeq_j (x^k)_j$ for all j, $y_{-n}\alpha \succeq x^k$. So $x^0 \succeq y_{-n}\alpha \succeq x^k$. Let ℓ be such that $x^{\ell-1} \succeq y_{-n}\alpha \succeq x^\ell$. By restricted solvability (Lemma 3.8) there exists z_ℓ such that $x^\ell_{-\ell}z_\ell \approx y_{-n}\alpha$. Since $(x^\ell_{-\ell}z_\ell)_n = \alpha$, by ECI we obtain $(x^\ell_{-\ell}z_\ell)_{-n}\beta \approx y_{-n}\beta$. From $x^\ell_{-\ell}x_\ell = x^{\ell-1} \succeq y_{-n}\alpha \approx x^\ell_{-\ell}z_\ell$ it follows that $x_\ell \succeq_\ell z_\ell$. Hence $(x_{-n}\beta)_j \succeq_j ((x^\ell_{-\ell}z_\ell)_{-n}\beta)_j$ for all j. By Lemma 3.6, $x_{-n}\beta \succeq (x^\ell_{-\ell}z_\ell)_{-n}\beta$.

The latter is equivalent to $y_{-n}\beta$.

□

THEOREM 3.10. *Let $n\geq 3$. Under Assumption 2.3 the following two statements are equivalent for the binary relation $\geq$ on Γ^n:*

(i) **There exists a continuous additive function on Γ^n which represents the binary relation $\geq$.**

(ii) **The binary relation $\geq$ is a continuous weakly separable weak order which satisfies ECI.**

PROOF. The implication (i) => (ii) is straightforward. The implication (ii) => (i) is by Lemma 3.9 and Theorem 2.6.

□

The characterization in Theorem 3.10 is stronger than that in Theorem 2.6 in the sense that, firstly, statement (ii) in Theorem 3.10 follows elementarily from that in Theorem 2.6 (by Lemmas 3.2 and 3.4), whereas the converse is not true without essentially invoking continuity, as the following Example shows.

EXAMPLE 3.11. Let $n\geq 3$, $\Gamma=\mathbb{R}$. Let $W : x \mapsto \sum_{j=1}^{n} x_j + \min\{x_j : 1\leq j\leq n\}$. Define $\geq$ by $[x\geq y] \Leftrightarrow [x=y \text{ or } (W(x),x_2,\ldots,x_n) >_L (W(y),y_2,\ldots,y_n)]$, with $>_L$ the lexicographic order. Since $x\approx y$ only if $x=y$, ECI is trivially satisfied. Further, for every i, $\geq_i$ is the usual ordering of real numbers, from which weak separability follows. Still, $(1,9,1,9,\ldots,9) \geq (1,5,5,9,\ldots,9)$ and $(9,9,1,9,\ldots,9) < (9,5,5,9,\ldots,9)$. This violates CI.

REMARK 3.12. In literature (see Debreu,1960, Theorem 3, or Krantz et al.,1971, Theorem 6.14) the Theorem 2.6 of Debreu in fact is formulated, more generally, for a Cartesian product $\Pi_{i=1}^{n}\Gamma_i$ of connected topological spaces Γ_i which do not have to be equal. All results of this section can also be formulated for such Cartesian products, nowhere did we use the equality of the coordinate sets.

Let us finally note that an alternative proof of Theorem 3.10 could have been obtained by simply going through all the proofs in literature contributing to Theorem 2.6, and by checking that nowhere there is made essential use of implications of CI other than weak separability or ECI. Because of the complicatedness of those proofs we chose our present way of proof.

4. EQUIVALENCE CCI

In this section we characterize representations of the form $x \mapsto \sum_{j=1}^{n} \lambda_j U(x_j)$ where U is continuous and there is no restriction on the λ_j's. Our characterization is an alternative for the one in Krantz et al. (1971, Theorem 6.15). The 'equivalence CCI' condition that we shall use is stronger than the 'standard sequence invariance' condition of Krantz et al. (1971). On the other hand, we have to impose only weak separability instead of the stronger coordinate independence, and we do not have to formulate separately the theorem for the case of two coordinates.

DEFINITION 4.1. The binary relation satisfies equivalence cardinal coordinate independence (ECCI) if for all $i,j,x,\ldots,\delta$ we have :

$$\left[\begin{array}{l} x_{-i}\alpha \approx y_{-i}\beta \quad \& \quad v_{-j}\alpha \approx w_{-j}\beta \quad \& \\ x_{-i}\gamma \approx y_{-i}\delta \end{array}\right]$$

$$\Rightarrow \qquad [v_{-j}\gamma \approx w_{-j}\delta]$$

This is as cardinal coordinate independence, with all preferences replaced by equivalences.

LEMMA 4.2. *Let $\succsim$ be ECCI. If $\approx$ is reflexive (i.e. $x \approx x$ for all x) then $\succsim$ satisfies ECI.*

PROOF. Substitute $x=y$, $\alpha=\beta$, $\gamma=\delta$ in Definition 4.1.

□

The following theorem generalizes Theorem 2.8 to the case of possibly non-positive weights. Motivation for it has been given below Theorem 2.8.

THEOREM 4.3. *Under Assumption 2.3 the following two statements are equivalent for the binary relation $\succsim$ on Γ^n:*

(i) There exist real $(\lambda_j)_{j=1}^{n}$ and a continuous function $U:\Gamma\to\mathbb{R}$, such that $x\mapsto\sum_{j=1}^{n}\lambda_j U(x_j)$ represents the binary relation $\succsim$.

(ii) The binary relation $\succsim$ is a continuous weakly separable ECCI weak order.

PROOF. The implication (i)$\Rightarrow$(ii) is straightforward. So we assume (ii) and derive (i). If $n\geq3$, then by Lemma 4.2 and Theorem 3.10 there exists an additive representation $V:x\mapsto\sum_{j=1}^{n}V_j(x_j)$ for $\succsim$. If $n\leq2$ then such a representation also exists; elaboration is omitted here, and can be found in Wakker (1986a, section IV.4). If $n=1$ we take $U=V_1$, $\lambda_1=1$, and (i) is established. So from now on we assume $n \geq 2$. ECCI gives:

$$\left[\begin{array}{l} V_i(\alpha)-V_i(\beta) = \sum_{k\neq i}[V_k(y_k)-V_k(x_k)] = V_i(\gamma)-V_i(\delta) \\ \& \ V_j(\alpha)-V_j(\beta) = \sum_{k\neq j}[V_k(w_k)-V_k(v_k)] \end{array}\right] \tag{4.1}$$
$$\Rightarrow [\ V_j(\alpha)-V_j(\beta) = V_j(\gamma)-V_j(\delta)\ ] \quad .$$

Setting $\alpha=\beta$, $x=y$, $v=w$, we have $[V_i(\gamma)=V_i(\delta)] \Rightarrow [V_j(\gamma)=V_j(\delta)]$. Hence there exists φ such that $V_j=\varphi\circ V_i$. Analogously there exists ψ such that $V_i=\psi\circ V_j$. Thus, $\varphi:V_i(\Gamma)\to V_j(\Gamma)$ is bijective. Since V_i and V_j are continuous, so is $\alpha\mapsto(V_i(\alpha),V_j(\alpha))$. Consequently the graph of φ, viz. $\{(V_i(\alpha),V_j(\alpha))\in\mathbb{R}^2:\ \alpha\in\Gamma\}$, is connected. This can be seen to imply that φ has the intermediate value property. Therefore φ, being bijective and having an interval as domain, must be continuous; it must be either increasing or decreasing.

Now let $V_i(\zeta)$ be an arbitrary element of $V_i(\Gamma)$, the domain of φ. Recall that all k are essential; hence no V_k is constant, and all $V_k(\Gamma)$ are non-degenerate intervals. Since $n\geq2$ and $V_j=\varphi\circ V_i$ with φ continuous, there exists an open interval S around $V_i(\zeta)$ so small that for all $V_i(\alpha)$, $V_i(\beta)$ in S, there are x and y for which $V_i(\alpha)-V_i(\beta) = \sum_{k\neq i}[V_k(y_k)-V_k(x_k)]$ and there are v and w for which $[\varphi(V_i(\alpha))-\varphi(V_i(\beta))] = V_j(\alpha)-V_j(\beta) = \sum_{k\neq j}[V_k(w_k)-V_k(v_k)]$. Setting $\beta=\gamma$, and finding appropriate x,y,v,w, by (4.1) we get, for all $V_i(\alpha)$, $V_i(\beta)$, $V_i(\delta)$ in S:

$$[V_i(\alpha)-V_i(\beta) = V_i(\beta)-V_i(\delta)] \Rightarrow [V_j(\alpha)-V_j(\beta) = V_j(\beta)-V_j(\delta)].$$

Thus, on S, φ satisfies Jensen's equality: $\varphi((\sigma+\tau)/2) = [\varphi(\sigma)+\varphi(\tau)]/2$. By Theorem 1 of section 2.1.4 of Aczél (1966), or by (88) of section 3.7 of Hardy, Littlewood,&Pólya (1934), φ must be affine on S. Hence it has derivative zero at all $V_i(\zeta)$. Consequently φ must be affine on $V_i(\Gamma)$.

We have shown that each V_j is an affine transform of V_1. The proof is completed by specifying U and the λ_j's as follows: For arbitrary fixed α and β in Γ with $V_1(\alpha)\neq V_1(\beta)$, set $U(.) := V_1(.)-V_1(\alpha)$ and set $\lambda_j := [V_j(\beta)-V_j(\alpha)]/[V_1(\beta)-V_1(\alpha)]$, j=1,...,n.

□

5. RESULTS FOR QUASILINEAR INDEXES

5.1. TRANSLATING RESULTS FOR PREFERENCE RELATIONS TO RESULTS FOR FUNCTIONS

We turn now to indicate how the theorems, formulated so far with a preference relation as primitive, can be reformulated in a simple way to give results when indexes are instead taken as primitives. Let $v:\Gamma\to\mathbb{R}$ be a continuous index. We may ascribe all properties, introduced before for binary relations, now to V by replacing all preferences such as $x \succsim y$ by the corresponding inequalities $V(x) \geq V(y)$, replacing all equivalences $x \approx y$ by equalities $V(x)=V(y)$, etc. For example:

DEFINITION 2.7-FOR-FUNCTIONS. The fuction V satisfies cardinal coordinate independence (CCI) if for all $i, j, x, \ldots, \delta$ we have :

$$\begin{bmatrix} V(x_{-i}\alpha) \leq V(y_{-i}\beta) & \& & V(v_{-j}\alpha) \geq V(w_{-j}\beta) & \& \\ V(x_{-i}\gamma) \geq V(y_{-i}\delta) & & & \end{bmatrix}$$

$$\Rightarrow \qquad [V(v_{-j}\gamma) \geq V(w_{-j}\delta)]$$

Compare this to Definition 2.7 of CCI for $\succsim$. We obtain new theorems, Theorem 2.6-for-functions, ..., Theorem 4.3-for-functions, from the corresponding theorems for binary relations, by replacing 'represents the binary relation $\succsim$' by 'is a continuous increasing transform of V', '$\succsim$' by 'V', 'binary relation $\succsim$' by 'function V', and 'weak order' by 'function'. These new theorems can be derived straightforwardly from the corresponding theorems for binary relations. For example:

THEOREM 2.8-FOR-FUNCTIONS. *Under Assumption 2.3 the following two statements are equivalent for the function* V *on* Γ^n*:*

(i) There exist positive $(p_j)_{j=1}^n$, summing to one, and a continuous function $U:\Gamma \to \mathbb{R}$, such that $x \mapsto \sum_{j=1}^n p_j U(x_j)$ is a continuous increasing transform of V.

(ii) The function V is a continuous CCI function.

□

When treating a continuous index V this way we use only the information of V contained in the preference relation represented by V. In other words, we are then studying the ordinal character of V. The major part of the present paper is written in this ordinal perspective. Such an ordinal approach is useful if one may, or wants to, use only ordinal information of indexes. If such ordinal information is combined with other information (for example the information that the index should be additive) then by the uniqueness results as in Debreu's Theorem 2.6 (see subsection 6.3) we may be able to determine the index up to a positive affine transformation.

5.2. QUASILINEAR INDEXES

Throughout this subsection we shall assume that $\Gamma \subset \mathbb{R}$ is an interval, and we shall study the properties of a continuous index $V:\Gamma^n \to \mathbb{R}$. The following definitions can be found in Hardy, Littlewood, &Pólya (1934), or Eichhorn (1978).

DEFINITIONS. Let $W:\Gamma^n \to \mathbb{R}$. Then W is:

(5.1) **generalized quasilinear** if there exist continuous strictly monotonic (i.e. increasing or decreasing) functions φ, $g_1,\ldots,g_n$ with appropriate domains, such that $W:x \mapsto \varphi(\sum_{j=1}^{n} g_j(x_j))$;

(5.2) **quasilinear** if there exist a real b, non-zero $\lambda_1,\ldots,\lambda_n$, and a continuous strictly monotonic U, such that $W:x \mapsto U^{-1}(\sum_{j=1}^{n} \lambda_j U(x_j)+b)$;

(5.3) a **quasilinear mean** if it is quasilinear with $b=0$, $\lambda_1>0,\ldots,\lambda_n>0$, $\sum_{j=1}^{n}\lambda_j=1$;

(5.4) a **quasiaddition** if it is quasilinear with $b=0$, $\lambda_1=\ldots=\lambda_n=1$.

(5.5) In (5.2) (see however the next sentence), (5.3) and (5.4) the adjective 'quasi' may be omitted if U is the identity function.

If in (5.2) U is the identity function, then in this paper the function W will be called <u>linear</u> only if b=0, and the term <u>affine</u> will be used for general b.

We shall show how the representation theorems of the previous sections can be used to characterize the ordinal character of the functions introduced above. We shall opt for 'additive' formulations. We might just as well have used multiplicative formulations. As an illustration, this is made explicit in (5.6.iv) below.

THEOREMS. *Let $\Gamma\subset\mathbb{R}$ be an interval, and $V:\Gamma^n\to\mathbb{R}$. Then:*

(5.6) *The following four statements are equivalent:*

(i) **V is generalized quasilinear.**

(ii) **V is continuous, strictly monotonic in each variable, and CI.**

(iii) **V is continuous, strictly monotonic in each variable, and ECI.**

(iv) **There exist continuous strictly monotonic functions ψ, $h_1,\ldots,h_n$ with appropriate domains, such that all h_j are positive and $V:x\mapsto\psi(\prod_{j=1}^{n} h_j(x_j))$.**

(5.7) *The following three statements are equivalent:*

(i) **V is a continuous increasing transform of a quasilinear mean.**

(ii) **V is continuous, increasing in each variable, and CCI.**

(iii) **V is continuous, increasing in each variable, and ECCI.**

PROOFS. First note that the strict monotonicity of V in each variable implies weak separability of $\succeq$, and essentiality of all i. Further note that in Definition 5.1 one may always assume φ to be increasing. (For if φ is decreasing, we may replace $g_1,\ldots,g_n$ by $-g_1,\ldots,-g_n$, and φ by $\bar{\varphi}$ with $\bar{\varphi}:\mu\mapsto\varphi(-\mu)$.) Thus, in (5.6), (i)<=>(ii) follows from Theorem 2.6-for-functions, and (i)<=>(iii) from

Theorem 3.10-for-functions. Finally, (i)<=>(iv) in (5.6) follows by setting $h_j=\exp(g_j)$ for all j and $\psi=\varphi\circ\log$.

Next note that the function U in Definitions (5.2), (5.3) and (5.4) may be taken to be increasing. (For if U is decreasing we may replace U by -U and b by -b.) Thus, V in (5.7)(i) is increasing in each variable, and (i)=>(ii) and (i)=>(iii) in (5.7) follow. Now we suppose (ii) or (iii) in (5.7) holds, and we derive (i) there. By Theorem 2.8-for-functions or Theorem 4.3-for-functions, there exist real λ_j, j=1,...,n and a continuous function U such that $x\mapsto\sum_{j=1}^n \lambda_j U(x_j)$ is a continuous increasing transform of V. We may assume, because of the increasingness of V in each variable, that U is increasing and that all λ_j's are positive. (If not, replace U by -U, every λ_j by $-\lambda_j$.) Clearly, V is also a continuous increasing transform of $\sum_{j=1}^n p_j U(x_j)$ where $p_j=\lambda_j/(\sum_{j=1}^n \lambda_i)$ for all j. This gives $\sum_{j=1}^n p_j=1$. The reason to replace $(\lambda_j)_{j=1}^n$ by $(p_j)_{j=1}^n$, is that $\sum_{j=1}^n p_j U(x_j)$ is in the (convex!) range of U for all x so that $U^{-1}[\sum_{j=1}^n p_j U(x_j)]$ is well defined. Now V must also be a continuous increasing transform of $U^{-1}[\sum_{j=1}^n p_j U(x_j)]$; thus (i) in (5.7) is established.

□

A complication in the proof of (ii)=>(i) and (iii)=>(i) in Theorem 5.7 above was that $U^{-1}[\sum_{j=1}^n \lambda_j U(x_j)]$ should be well defined. For characterizing quasilinear functions and quasiadditions, we shall need additional assumptions to solve the analogous complication.

DEFINITION 5.8. The function V satisfies <u>unrestricted solvability</u> if for all i,x,y there exist $\alpha,\beta\in\Gamma$ such that $V(x_{-i}\alpha) < y < V(x_{-i}\beta)$.

THEOREMS. *Let* $\Gamma\subset\mathbb{R}$ *be an interval, let* $V:\Gamma^n\to\mathbb{R}$. *Let either* Γ *be compact, or let* V *satisfy unrestricted solvability.*

(5.9). *The following two statements are equivalent:*

(i) **V is a continuous increasing transform of a quasilinear function.**

(ii) **V is continuous, stricly monotonic in each variable, and ECCI.**

(5.10). *The following three statements are equivalent:*

(i) **V is a continuous increasing transform of a quasiaddition.**

(ii) **V is continuous, increasing in each variable, CCI, and** $\alpha\neq\beta$ **exist such that** $V((\alpha,\ldots,\alpha)_{-1}\beta) = V((\alpha,\ldots,\alpha)_{-j}\beta)$ **for all j.**

(iii) **V is continuous, increasing in each variable, ECCI, and** $\alpha\neq\beta$ **exist such that, for all j,** $V((\alpha,\ldots,\alpha)_{-1}\beta) = V((\alpha,\ldots,\alpha)_{-j}\beta)$.

PROOFS. Since U in Definitions 5.2 and 5.4 can be made increasing (see previous proofs), (i)=>(ii) in (5.9) and (5.10), and (i)=>(iii) in (5.10) are immediate; these implications do not need the additional compactness or unrestricted solvability condition. Next we suppose (ii) holds in (5.9), or (ii) or (iii) in (5.10), and we derive (i). The beginning of our reasoning will apply both to 5.9 and 5.10. If n=1, we may simply set U=identity, $\lambda_1=1$ if V is increasing and $\lambda_1=-1$ if V is decreasing. So from now on we suppose n≥2. By Theorem 4.3-for-functions, V is a continuous increasing transform of $x \mapsto \sum_{j=1}^{n} \lambda_j U(x_j)$, with the λ_j's real, and U continuous. We may assume, by the strict monotonicity of V, that U is actually increasing (otherwise replace U by -U, λ_j by $-\lambda_j$ for all j) and that no λ_j is zero. If V satisfies unrestricted solvability, then, n being ≥ 2, U can be seen to be unbounded from above and below. If Γ is compact, then we can extend U to a continuous increasing $U':\mathbb{R}\to\mathbb{R}$ that is unbounded from above and below. We then write U for U'. Anyway, now $U^{-1}[\sum_{j=1}^{n} \lambda_j U(x_j)]$ is always defined. And V is a continuous increasing transform of this; thus (i) in (5.9) follows.

Finally suppose (ii) or (iii) in (5.10) holds. We derive (i). V is a continuous increasing transform of $x \mapsto [\sum_{j=1}^{n} \lambda_j U(x_j)]$ where U is increasing and unbounded from above and below as we saw above. By the strict increasingness of V in each variable, all the λ_j's are positive. The 'α,β-condition' in (ii) and (iii) implies that $\lambda_j=\lambda_1$ for all j. So V is an increasing transform of $\sum_{j=1}^{n} U(x_j)$, hence of the well-defined $U^{-1}[\sum_{j=1}^{n} \lambda_j U(x_j)]$.

□

The following example demonstrates why in Theorem 5.9 we needed an extra assumption for the implication (ii)=>(i).

EXAMPLE 5.11. Let $V(x) = \exp(x_1)-\exp(x_2)$ for all $x \in \mathbb{R}^2$. If, for some b,λ_1,λ_2,U, this V is a increasing transform of $x \mapsto \sum_{j=1}^{2} \lambda_j U(x_j) + b$, then, as is easily verified, $\lambda_1=-\lambda_2$ and there exist σ,τ such that $U = \tau + \sigma\exp$ with $\lambda_1\sigma>0$. Suppose $\lambda_1>0$. (The case of $\lambda_1<0$ is analogous, instead of $(0,x_2)$ take $(x_1,0)$ with x_1 large below.) Then $\sigma>0$, and U is bounded below, unbounded above. Further there exists x_2 so large that for $x=(0,x_2)$ the value $\sum_{j=1}^{2} \lambda_j U(x_j)+b$ is too negative to be in the range of U. Thus the inverse U^{-1} of $\sum_{j=1}^{2} \lambda_j U(x_j)+b$ cannot be defined. That is, although (ii) in Theorem 5.9 is satisfied, (i) is not.

THEOREM 5.12. *Let $\Gamma\subset\mathbb{R}$ be an interval. A necessary and sufficient condition for the function* U *in Theorems 2.8-for-functions and 4.3-for-functions to be linear, and for the omission of 'quasi' in (i) in (5.7), (5.9), (5.10), is that for all (or one) coordinates* i, *and for all $\alpha,\beta,\alpha+\varepsilon,\beta+\varepsilon$ in Γ, and all* x,y, *the implication* $[V(x_{-i}\alpha) = V(y_{-i}(\alpha+\varepsilon))] \Rightarrow [V(x_{-i}\beta) = V(y_{-i}(\beta+\varepsilon))]$ *holds.*

PROOF. Obvious for n=1. For n≥2 the necessary and sufficient condition can be seen to be equivalent to the requirement that U 'locally' satisfies $U(\alpha+\varepsilon)-U(\alpha) = U(\beta+\varepsilon)-U(\beta)$ for all α,β,ε. Since U is continuous on a convex domain, this means that U must be affine. Therefore U (and also its extension in the proof of Theorems 5.9 and 5.10) may furthermore be taken to be linear.

□

REMARK 5.13. In Theorem 5.7 we may replace the term 'quasilinear' by 'quasiarithmetic' (i.e. the λ_j's of Definition 5.3 all equal 1/n) if in (ii) and (iii) we add the same 'α,β condition' as in (5.10.ii). This characterizes (5.10(ii)) and (5.10(iii)) without compactness or unrestricted solvability restriction.

6. FURTHER RESULTS AND FUTURE RESEARCH

6.1. SPECIFIED FORMS OF QUASILINEAR INDEXES

Several indexes that have attracted interest in literature are specified forms of quasilinear indexes. We can use Theorem 5.9 or 4.3-for-functions, add to (ii) there one extra condition which is weaker than those customary in the literature, and obtain from (i) the desired specified form. For instance, if n=2, then the case where V is a continuous increasing transform of $x\mapsto U(x_1)-U(x_2)$, interpreted as an index for 'intensity of preference' of x_1 over x_2, can be characterized by adding an extra condition such as $V(\alpha,\alpha)=V(\beta,\beta)$ for all α,β (or even just for some α and β with $V(\alpha,\beta)\neq V(\beta,\beta)$). The case where V is a continuous increasing transform of $x\mapsto\sum_{j=1}^{n}\lambda^j U(x_j)$, with $0<\lambda\leq 1$, is useful in dynamic utility theory (see Koopmans, 1972), where λ is the 'discount factor'. We can characterize such a V by an additional 'weak stationarity' assumption such as: there exist α,β,γ with $V(\alpha,\ldots,\alpha) \geq V(\beta,\ldots,\beta) > V(\gamma,\ldots,\gamma)$, and $V((\gamma,\ldots,\gamma)_{-i}\beta) = V((\gamma,\ldots,\gamma)_{-(i+1)}\alpha)$ for all $i \leq n-1$.

6.2. FUTURE RESEARCH

It is a large task, not taken up in this paper, to catalogue the indexes, used in literature, which are specified forms of quasilinear functions, and to determine which non-ordinal conditions should be added in the statements, numbered (ii) or (iii) in this paper, to characterize these specified forms. Results along this line may be obtained from Aczél&Alsina (1984), Stehling (1975), Eichhorn (1978, in particular Chapter 2).

We conjecture that our 'equivalence-separability condition' ECI in Theorem 3.10 can be weakened in the spirit of Gorman (1968). He showed that coordinate independence in Theorem 2.6 of Debreu (allowing the replacement in preferences of any one pair of equal coordinates, and thus by repetition of any arbitrary number of pairs of equal coordinates), can be weakened to allow for replacement of only certain subgroups of equal coordinates; see also Murphy (1981).

Probably in Theorem 5.10 the assumption of compactness of Γ or unrestricted solvability of V could have been omitted. The demonstration of that seems to be tedious.

6.3. UNIQUENESS; ADAPTING OUR RESULTS TO NON-ORDINAL CONTEXTS

We have not formulated uniqueness results for the several functions that we derived. These follow straightforwardly from the uniqueness result obtained by Debreu (1960) and Krantz et al. (1971), who showed that the additive representation V of Theorem 2.6 is cardinal, i.e. it is unique up to a positive affine transformation.

If one wants to specify V further than (as in most of our results) unique up to a continuous increasing transformation, then our results may still be useful. This is because weak 'non-ordinal' conditions will suffice, in addition to the ordinal conditions, to give non-ordinal results. A condition such as $[V(x_{-i}\alpha)+V(y_{-i}\beta) = V(x_{-i}\beta)+V(y_{-i}\alpha)]$ will enable one to replace 'V is a continuous increasing transform of' in the theorems above by 'V is', or 'V is a positive affine transform of'. Multiplicative forms, with positive factors, are characterized by conditions such as $[V(x_{-i}\alpha) \times V(y_{-i}\beta) = [V(x_{-i}\beta) \times V(y_{-i}\alpha)]$.

Analogously one may replace ECCI by

$$[V(x_{-i}\alpha) - V(y_{-i}\beta) = V(x_{-i}\gamma) - V(y_{-i}\delta)] \Rightarrow$$
$$[V(v_{-j}\alpha) - V(w_{-j}\beta) = V(v_{-j}\gamma) - V(w_{-j}\delta)]$$

to derive cardinal additive indexes, or, for multiplicative indexes, by the condition

$$[V(x_{-i}\alpha)/V(y_{-i}\beta) = [V(x_{-i}\gamma)/V(y_{-i}\delta)] \Rightarrow$$
$$[V(v_{-j}\alpha)/V(w_{-j}\beta) = [V(v_{-j}\gamma)/V(w_{-j}\delta)] .$$

REFERENCES

Aczél,J.(1966), *'Lectures on Functional Equations and Their Applications'*. Academic Press, New York.

Aczél,J.&C.Alsina (1984), 'Characterizations of Some Classes of Quasilinear Functions with Applications to Triangular Norms and to Synthesizing Judgements', *Methods of Operations Research* 48, 3-22.

Debreu,G. (1960), 'Topological Methods in Cardinal Utility Theory'. *In* K.J.Arrow, S.Karlin, and P.Suppes (Eds., 1959), *Mathematical Methods in the Social Sciences*, 16-26, Stanford University Press, Stanford.

Eichhorn,W. (1978), *'Functional Equations in Economics'*. Addison Wesley, London.

Fisher,I. (1927), 'A Statistical Method for Measuring "Marginal Utility" and Testing the Justice of a Progressive Income Tax'. *In* J.H.Hollander (Ed.), *Economic Essays Contributed in Honor of John Bates Clark*, 157-193, MacMillan, New York.

Gorman,W.M. (1968), 'The Structure of Utility Functions', *Review of Economic Studies* 35, 367-390.

Hardy,G.H.,J.E.Littlewood,&G.Pólya (1934), *'Inequalities'*. University Press, Cambridge.

Kelley,J.L,. (1955), *'General Topology'*. Van Nostrand, London.

Koopmans,T.C. (1972), 'Representations of Preference Orderings with Independent Components of Consumption', & 'Representations of Preference Orderings over Time'. *In* C.B.McGuire&R.Radner(Eds.), *Decision and Organization*, 57-100, North-Holland, Amsterdam.

Krantz, D.H., R.D.Luce, P.Suppes, &A.Tversky (1971) (=KLST), *'Foundations of Measurement, Vol. I. (Additive and Polynomial Representations)'*. Academic Press, New York.

Murphy,F.P. (1981), 'A Note on Weak Separability', *Review of Economic Studies* 48, 671-672.

Savage, L.J. (1954), *'The Foundations of Statistics'*. Wiley, New York.

Stehling,F. (1975), 'Eine Neue Characterisierung der CD- und ACMS-Produktionsfunktionen', *Operations Research-Verfahren* 21, 222-238.

Wakker,P.P. (1984), 'Cardinal Coordinate Independence for Expected Utility', *Journal of Mathematical Psychology* 28, 110-117.

Wakker,P.P. (1986a), 'Representations of Choice Situations'. Ph.D. dissertation, University of Brabant, Department of Economics, The Netherlands.

Wakker,P.P. (1986b), 'Derived Strength of Preference Relations on Coordinates'. Report 8624, Department of Mathematics, University of Nijmegen, The Netherlands. Working Paper, May 1986, The Foerder Institute for Economic Research, Faculty of the Social Sciences, Tel-Aviv University, Ramat Aviv, Israel.

ACKNOWLEDGEMENT. The presentation of the paper improved much by detailed comments of an anonymous referee.

Part V Quality

A Measure or Index of Noxiousness

W.-D. Heller and M. Rutsch
Institut für Statistik und Mathematische Wirtschaftstheorie
Universität Karlsruhe
D-7500 Karlsruhe, F.R.G.

1. Introduction

How noxious are noxious substances? To answer this question it is not sufficient to quote the damages which are commonly attributed to, and may in fact be caused by such a substance. Rather, two important aspects are to be distinguished - and investigated in every particular case. The first feature is the toxic effect in itself; it exists, initially, only in potentiality: to a certain dose of the substance, a given organism will respond more or less violently - or not at all. The random character of the ensuing response becomes evident in the notion of a 'mean lethal dose' which, when administered to a living being, accords a 50% chance of survival. Of course, there are dosages of certain preparations which guarantee a sure result - as demonstrated historically by the death of Socrates, or the successful activity of a Lucrezia Borgia. What we have considered so far is only the toxicity aspect of a noxious substance and its stochastic nature. There is, however, another chance mechanism which precedes, as a condition, the toxic action of such a substance: this is the contingency through which it finds access to the unfortunate individual. This aspect comprises all means and factors which permit, promote or hamper the access: the distribution, mobility, accessibility, safe or unsafe guarding of a substance, or the extent of its being spread in our environment through pollution - but also the necessity or advantages of its utilisation as a medicament or a pesticide, and even its attractivity as a stimulant or narcotic. This second facet of noxiousness, like the first one, needs a stochastic representation.

Both aspects combine to the overall noxiousness of the substance or pro duct in question. We propose in this paper an 'index of noxiousness' which, in simple cases, takes both aspects into account: the toxicity properly speaking and the mode of distribution or obtrusiveness of the substance. In particular, we show how the degree in which different

Measurement in Economics
ed. by W. Eichhorn

products or preparations satisfy our needs or meet our desires influences that index of overall noxiousness.

To the authors' knowledge, no such formal amalgamation of the two sides of noxiousness has hitherto been proposed in literature. Our concept is the most natural one for simple situations such as treated in this paper. It could gain in practical applicability if developed to handle more complex structures of impairment. It should be remarked that non-substantial agents (like radiation) and dangerous activities practised by the individual himself may formally be treated exactly like "noxious substances".

To the remarks of one referee we owe some useful improvements and a few necessary corrections.

2. A model for the intake and the action of a noxious substance

2.1 We consider only one response Y and suppose that it is **quantal** (= binary): Y = 0 if a certain effect fails to appear, Y = 1 if it is produced. The toxic action of a substance can then be appropriately modelled by a dose-response relationship. Let x be the dose, i.e. the quantity absorbed (in one particular instant or over a longer period) by an individual. We set

$$p(x) := P\{Y = 1 \ ; \ x\} = G\left(\frac{\log x - \mu}{\sigma}\right) ,$$

where G is some distribution function - for example

$$G(z) = \Phi(z) \quad \text{the Gaussian distribution function,}$$

or $$G(z) = \Lambda(z) := \frac{e^z}{1 + e^z} \quad \text{the logistic distribution function.}$$

If G(0) = 0.5, the 50% effective dose, ED 50, is given by log(ED 50) = μ. We consider

$$w := \log x$$

as the **stimulus** exerted by dose x, in accordance with time-honoured psycho-physical doctrines. The ***stimulus*-response curve** will then have the typical shape of G - e.g. in the logistic case it is plotted in fig. 1 (the Gaussian curve looks very similar):

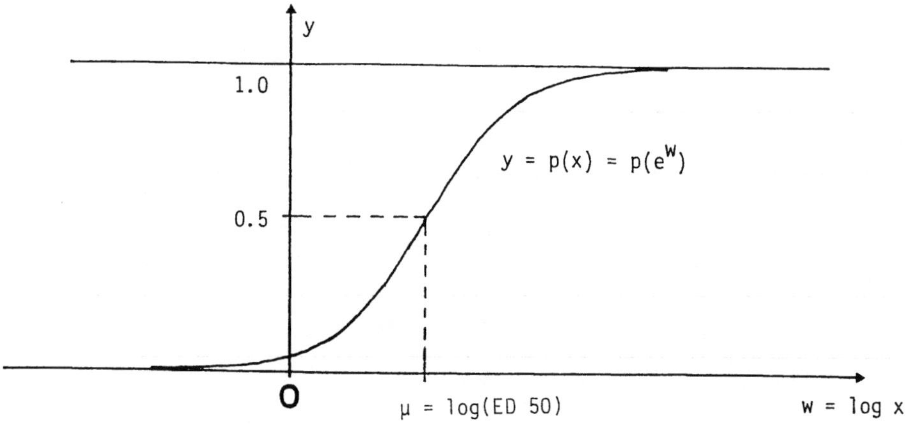

Fig. 1

A nice introduction to logistic response models is given in Sharon ANDERSON et al. [1980], chapter 9: Logit Analysis.

We can explain 'failure' and 'success' of the toxic action by means of a random variable T, distributed as $G((\log t - \mu)/\sigma)$. It represents the **tolerance** of varying subjects under varying conditions: that is the maximum amount of the substance they can stand without suffering the damage expressed by Y = 1. In fact,

$$P\{T < x\} = G\left(\frac{\log x - \mu}{\sigma}\right) = P\{Y = 1 \; ; \; x\}.$$

The curve in fig. 1 can thus be regarded as the distribution function of T, i.e. the **tolerance distribution function.**

If $G = \Phi$, $\log T$ is distributed as $N(\mu, \sigma^2)$.

2.2 The quantity of the noxious substance affecting a randomly chosen member of the population under study will now be understood to be a **random variable** X. The distribution of X may be discrete: e.g. an $X \in \text{Poisson}(\lambda)$ might denote the number of potentially dangerous 'hits' received by an arbitrary individual; if and only if this number is greater than the number T = t of hits "just tolerable" by that individual in a given period, the dreaded damage will occur!

X could also be continuous, e.g. have a *lognormal distribution*:

$$W = \log X \in N(\mu_W, \sigma_W^2) \; ,$$

which endows X with a density of the following form:

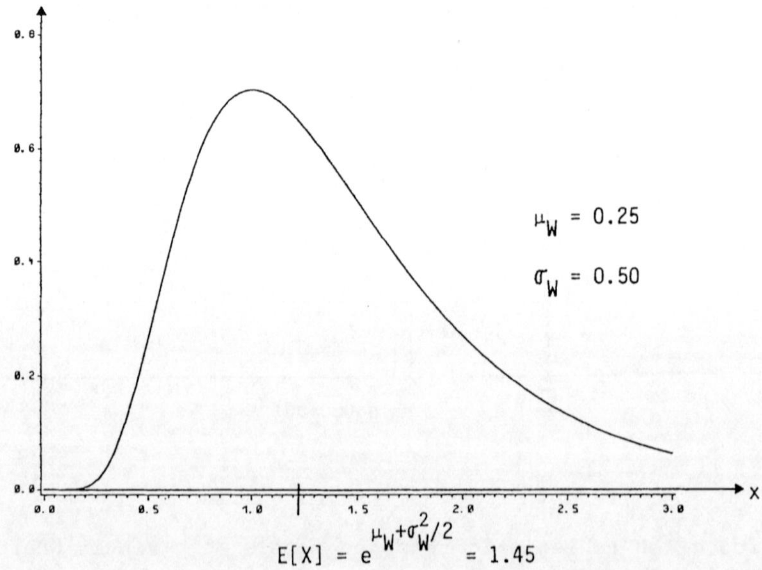

Fig. 2

In the presence of 'background response' there is a positive probability, $p(0) > 0$, for damage to occur even at dose zero: this phenomenon has appreciable consequences only when the distribution of X attaches positive probability, say f_o, to the point $x = 0$, while, for the rest, X may be a perfectly continuous variate, e.g. lognormally distributed as in the following figure:

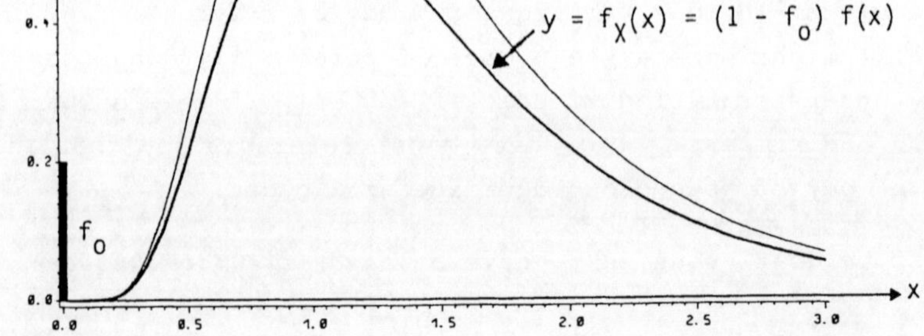

Fig. 3

2.3 With a single, quantal response as assumed in 2.1, the natural **measure of total noxiousness** is simply $P\{Y = 1\}$, i.e. the marginal probability for $Y = 1$; it is to be determined from the joint distribution of X and Y as

$$P\{Y = 1\} = \int_0^\infty p(x)\ f_X(x)\ dx\ ,$$

where $f_X(\ )$ is the density function of X (see 2.4 for the discrete case). The integral above equals the area of the hatched region in the next figure.

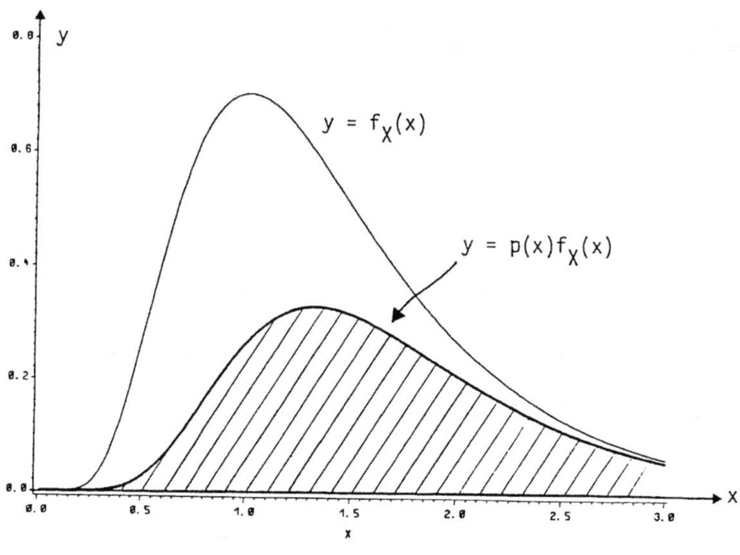

Fig. 4

In terms of the **stimulus variable** $W = \log X$ and the **tolerance variable** T,

$$P\{Y = 1\} = P\{T < X\} = P\{\log T < W\}\ .$$

With an $N(\mu_W,\ \sigma_W^2)$-distributed W and an $N(\mu,\ \sigma^2)$-distributed log T, the joint distribution of W and log T will look like in fig. 5.

If $\mu \gtreqless \mu_W$, $P\{Y = 1\} \lesseqgtr 0.5$: This holds generally when the two distributions are **symmetric** about μ_W and μ, respectively.

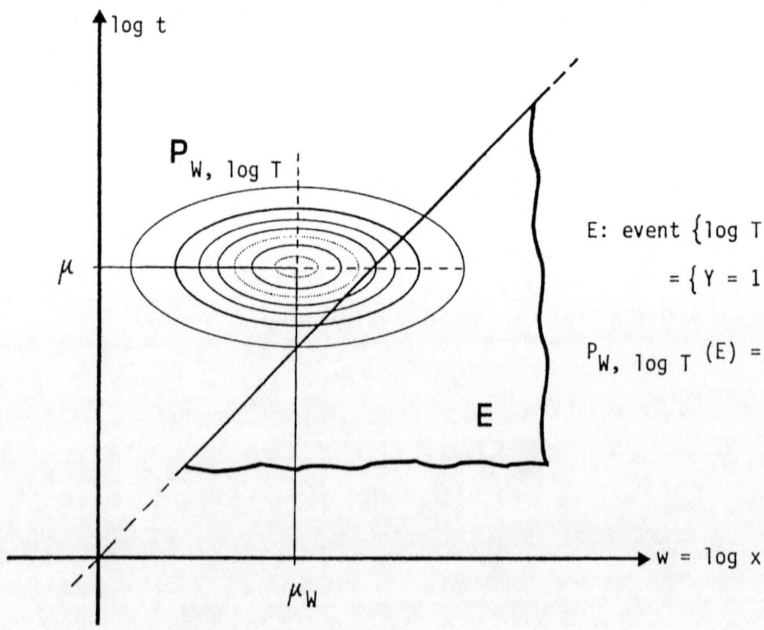

Fig. 5

2.4 The measure of noxiousness as defined in 2.3 is a single number $\in [0, 1]$ incorporating both the toxicity of the noxious substance and its presence or availability or attractivity. With a **discrete dose variable** X, capable of n different levels $x_1\ x_2\ \dots\ x_n$ only, toxicity as such is given by the vector

$$(p_1\ p_2\ \dots\ p_n) := (p(x_1)\ p(x_2)\ \dots\ p(x_n))\ ;$$

by means of the **intake probabilities** $f_i := f(x_i)$ (i = 1 2 ... n) the p_i's are algebraically merged into one real number, viz.

$$f_1p_1 + f_2p_2 + \dots + f_np_n\ ,$$

reflecting the profile of damage probabilities as well as the intake distribution. In this special form the measure of noxiousness resembles expressions employed to build index numbers. The connection with index numbers will show up when we compare the corresponding expressions for two different substances: see 3.1!

3. Comparing two or more agents

3.1 To assess the **relative noxiousness** of two different substances or preparations it will be sufficient, in the simple framework of sec. 2, to compare their measures of noxiousness - for example the expressions

$$f_1^I p_1^I + \dots + f_n^I p_n^I \quad \text{and} \quad f_1^{II} p_1^{II} + \dots + f_n^{II} p_n^{II}$$

for substances I and II, respectively, in the discrete case (see 2.4).

The situation is very similar to the comparison of the expenditures for consumption in two different countries or periods, whereby not only price differences are to be covered, but also differences or changes in the consumption pattern. An 'index of expenditures for consumption' measures the likeness or unlikeness of two expressions analogous to the ones given above, usually by forming their quotient. The measure of noxiousness defined in 2.3 being a probability, the quotient of two such measures is perhaps not the best expression of comparative noxiousness - the logit (or probit) difference might be preferred.

The primary aim of such **comparisons of noxiousness** is to find out whether an amelioration of one aspect - e.g. the reduced spreading or utilization of a harmful preparation or product - is apt to compensate a deterioration of the other - e.g. a more toxic composition of the product. With this question we shall deal in the present section.

3.2 We return to a continuous intake variable X and assume, as frequently in bioassay, that the difference in toxicity between a substance I and a substance II can be described by a fixed factor ρ_1, the **relative efficiency** of II compared with I, in the following way:

$$\forall x: \quad p^I(\rho_1 x) = p^{II}(x) \; ;$$

this means: $\rho_1 x$ of substance I is needed to obtain the same (stochastic) effect as with the amount x of substance II. ρ_1 can be interpreted as the *relative toxicity* of substance II with respect to I.

It is easy to make general statements of compensation, if at the same time there is a fixed proportionality between the intake distributions, i.e. if

$$X_I \text{ is distributed like } \rho_2 X_{II} \, ,$$

with another constant ρ_2: the latter may be understood as the *relative dosing* of substance I as compared with II. From the two assumptions it follows that

$$P\{Y_{II}=1\}=Ep^{II}(X_{II})=Ep^{I}(\rho_1 X_{II})=Ep^{I}(\frac{\rho_1}{\rho_2}X_I)\gtreqless Ep^{I}(X_I)=P\{Y_I=1\}$$

according as

$$\frac{\rho_1}{\rho_2}\gtreqless 1\ ,$$

by the monotonicity of $p^I(\ )$. Thus there is

- **exact compensation** of increased toxicity by a lesser intake iff $\rho_1=\rho_2$,
- **over-compensation** iff $\rho_2>\rho_1$, and
- **under-compensation** iff $\rho_2<\rho_1$.

All this can also be seen pictorially, starting from fig. 5. When switching from substance I to substance II, the joint distribution of $W=\log X$ and $\log T$ is shifted homothetically by the vector $(-\log\rho_2,$ $-\log\rho_1)$; so that it moves, in the third of the above-mentioned cases $(\rho_2<\rho_1)$, deeper into the half-plane $w>\log t$ - which means a higher noxiousness, or *under-compensation*.

3.3 In the case $\rho_2>\rho_1$, "over-compensation", we should like to get a quantitative idea of the improvement obtained by replacing substance I by substance II. The quantitatively expressed **reduction of noxiousness** is, however, not completely determined by ρ_1 and ρ_2: it depends also on the particular shapes of $p^I(\ )$ and $f_{X_I}(\ )$ and on their mutual position. To illustrate this fact by a very simple example, let us imagine that both substances are applied in fixed doses,

$$x_I \text{ and } x_{II}=\rho_2^{-1}x_I\ ,$$

respectively. Noxiousness would then be reduced from π_I to π_{II}, as shown in the following figure 6:

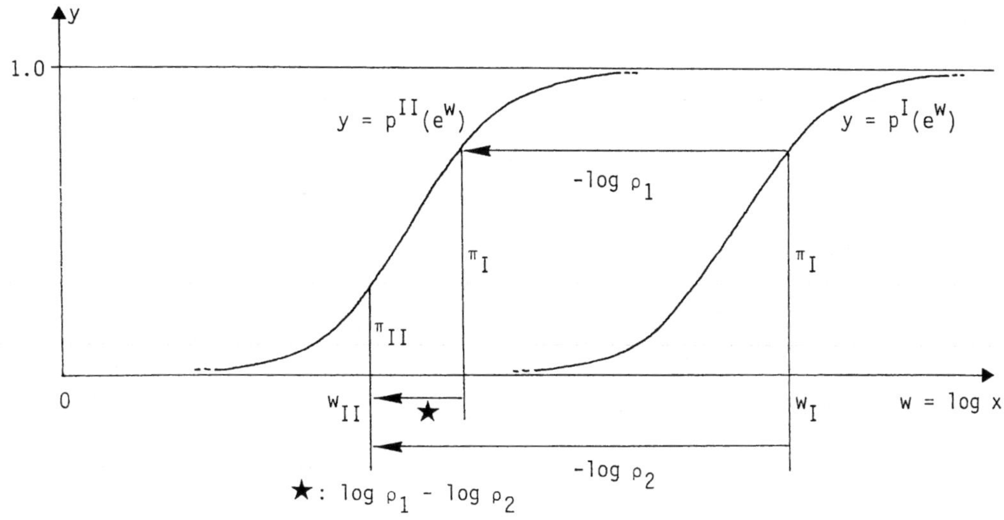

Fig. 6

This reduction, whether expressed by a difference or by a percentage (i.e. by **relative risk** under II instead of I), obviously depends on the initial position of x_I or $w_I = \log x_I$ on the abscissa axis, as to be seen in fig. 7:

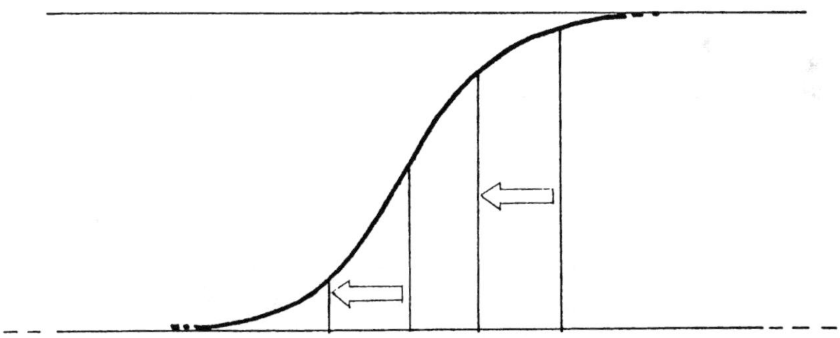

Fig. 7

On the other hand, with a **logistic** stimulus-response function, the reduction in noxiousness is **invariant** if it is expressed as a logit difference (see 3.1). "Invariant" means, that it is a function of ρ_1 and ρ_2 alone, if we consider the scale parameter σ of the logistic as fixed. This holds only for a degenerate intake distribution, $X_I = x_I$

a.s., as assumed above. For a non-degenerate distribution of the stimulus, viz. $W \in N(0, 1)$, and the special logistic stimulus-response function

$$\Lambda(w - \mu) = \frac{e^{w-\mu}}{1 + e^{w-\mu}}$$

we have calculated the measure of noxiousness for different relative positions of the two - i.e. for different values of μ. Here are some of the results:

	noxiousness		
μ	probability	logit	logit difference
2.0	0.1555	-1.6924	0.8606
1.0	0.3033	-0.8318	0.8318
0.0	0.5000	0.0000	0.8318
-1.0	0.6967	0.8318	0.8606
-2.0	0.8445	1.6924	0.9048
-3.0	0.9307	2.5972	0.9463
-4.0	0.9719	3.5435	

The easily proven symmetry of the logit values around the point 0 is evident. It is also clear that the noxiousness integral goes to 0 or 1 when μ goes to infinity or minus infinity.

3.4 Under the assumption of 3.2 the transition from substance I to substance II amounts simply to a shift of the stimulus-response function or, equivalently, to a **shift** of the stimulus distribution. In contrast, we shall now investigate how a pure **scale transformation** of the random stimulus W will affect the measure of noxiousness. To fix the problem, let us think of *a single substance*, whose dosing may be more or less tightly controlled - so that the dispersion σ_W^2 of W about its specified mean value μ_W may be smaller or greater.
It should be noted, however, that the following results cover also the case of *two substances* I and II, when these stand in a fixed relation of efficiency (as expressed in the first assumption of 3.2) and if, moreover, the mean levels μ_{W_I} and $\mu_{W_{II}}$ of the stimuli are toxically equivalent (i.e. correspond to each other under the relation mentioned).

Let

$$p(x) = p(e^w) = \frac{e^{w-1}}{1+e^{w-1}} \quad \text{and} \quad W \in N(0, \sigma_W^2).$$

We calculated

$$P_{\sigma_W}\{Y = 1\} = \frac{1}{\sigma} \int_{-\infty}^{\infty} \frac{e^{w-1}}{1 + e^{w-1}} \varphi(\frac{w}{\sigma_W}) \, dw$$

for an increasing sequence of values of σ_W and obtained:

σ_W	$P_{\sigma_W}\{Y = 1\}$
0.5	0.2794
1.0	0.3033
1.5	0.3293
2.0	0.3523
3.0	0.3868
10.0	0.4608
50.0	0.4907

For $\sigma_W \downarrow 0$ the integral goes to $p(1) = \frac{e^{-1}}{1 + e^{-1}} = \frac{1}{1 + e} = 0.2689$;

for $\sigma_W \uparrow \infty$ the integral converges to 0.5 .

Some typical situations evaluated in this way have been sketched in fig. 8.

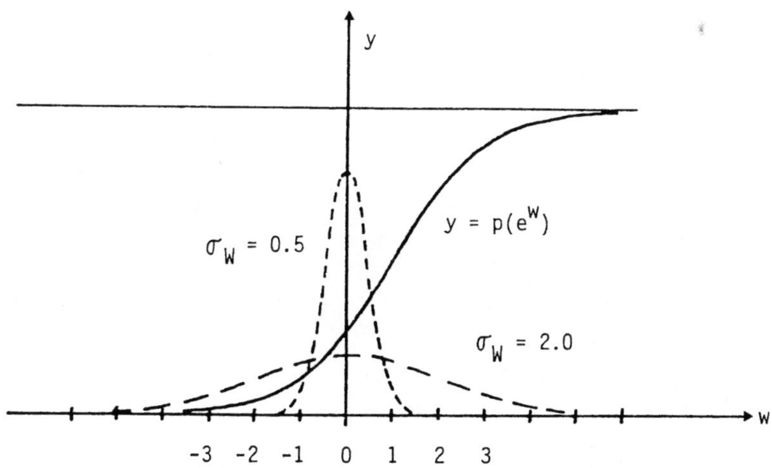

Fig. 8

4. How to explain a reduced intake of toxic substances

4.1 In many applications we can indeed observe the phenomenon investigated in sec. 3 - that is, a reduction of the doses utilized, paralleled by an increased toxicity of the product used - or the inverse process. If we know the two basic constituents of noxiousness (cf. sec. 1) for the two products well enough, the methods of sec. 3 enable us to find out whether this antithetic development of the two aspects "dosage" and "toxicity" amounts to an increase or a decrease in overall noxiousness; and to estimate, by how much the latter will change. The explanation of such an intake reduction is often very simple: one may need **less of a more toxic product** to obtain the **same positive effect** than with a less harmful product; the reasons for an increased dosage are analogous. We construct a little model which may, in certain cases, be appropriate to describe this reciprocity relation.

4.2 The two products to be compared, I and II, are supposed to contain, both, the same **useful** and the same **toxic** ingredient. Let us denote by u_I the amount of the useful ingredient, by t_I the amount of the toxic ingredients, present in one unit of product I; similarly for product II.

The quantity U of the useful substance required (or desired) at various occasions varies with the circumstances of utilization - to mention a few examples: drugs are administered in varying doses according to the weight or age of the patient or to the gravity of his or her sickness; the amount of material applied in a protective treatment of manufactured goods depends on the size of the job and the degree of protection needed; the consumption of stimulants is determined by personality, habit, mood, company etc. Thus we consider U to be a random variable, and we assume its distribution to be known.

U, in turn, determines the quantities of I or II that would be required to provide just that amount of the useful ingredient, viz.

$$X_I = u_I^{-1}U \qquad \text{and} \qquad X_{II} = u_{II}^{-1}U ,$$

respectively. They carry inevitably with them the amounts

$$t_I u_I^{-1} U \qquad \text{and} \qquad t_{II} u_{II}^{-1} U$$

of the toxic ingredient. From this we get immediately the **dosage relation**

$$X_I = u_I^{-1} u_{II} X_{II} = \rho_2 X_{II} \quad \text{where} \quad \rho_2 = u_I^{-1} u_{II} ,$$

and the **toxicity relation**

$$p^I(t_I^{-1} t_{II} x) = p^I(\rho_1 x) = p^{II}(x) \text{ where } \quad \rho_1 = t_I^{-1} t_{II}$$

- since the amounts $t_I^{-1} t_{II} x$ of product I and x of product II contain exactly the same quantum of the (same) toxin.

If we switch from I to II, the overall noxiousness decreases, remains the same, or increases according as

$$\frac{\rho_2}{\rho_1} = \frac{u_{II}}{u_I} \frac{t_I}{t_{II}} = \frac{u_{II}}{t_{II}} : \frac{u_I}{t_I} \gtreqless 1 ;$$

or equivalently, according as the **ratio of useful and toxic ingredient** increases, remains the same, or decreases.

4.3 The results of 4.2 can easily be extended to the case where the two products contain different useful and/or toxic ingredients, provided corresponding ingredients are related with one another by a fixed proportionality, as far as their (useful or toxic) efficiency is concerned - i.e. by a relation of the type considered at the beginning of 3.2.

5. Joint action of several substances

5.1 We now consider the case of a product containing several different ingredients, but in contrast to sec. 4 we suppose each ingredient to have both the toxic and the useful effect in question. Thus the ingredients may co-operate or interact in different ways - and that with respect to the positive effect as well as with respect to the negative effect. The discussion will be restricted to a composite preparation containing just <u>two</u> ingredients i = 1, 2 in fixed proportions. Let

$$x_i = q_i x \qquad (i = 1, 2)$$

be the amount of ingredient i per x units of the composite preparation. We study co-operation between ingredient 1 and 2 first in the domain of toxicity only - for the useful effect, the reasoning is exactly the same. Denote by

x_i^* : the dose of substance i, toxically equivalent, if applied alone, to x units of the composite preparation.

Then, the co-operation of substance 1 and 2 is called **additive** for the specific dose x of the preparation iff

$$\frac{x_1}{x_1^*} + \frac{x_2}{x_2^*} = 1 ;$$

this equation expresses a kind of linearity, since it states that the equi-efficient combination points $(x_1^*, 0)$, (x_1, x_2), and $(0, x_2^*)$ lie on a straight line - as represented in fig. 9.

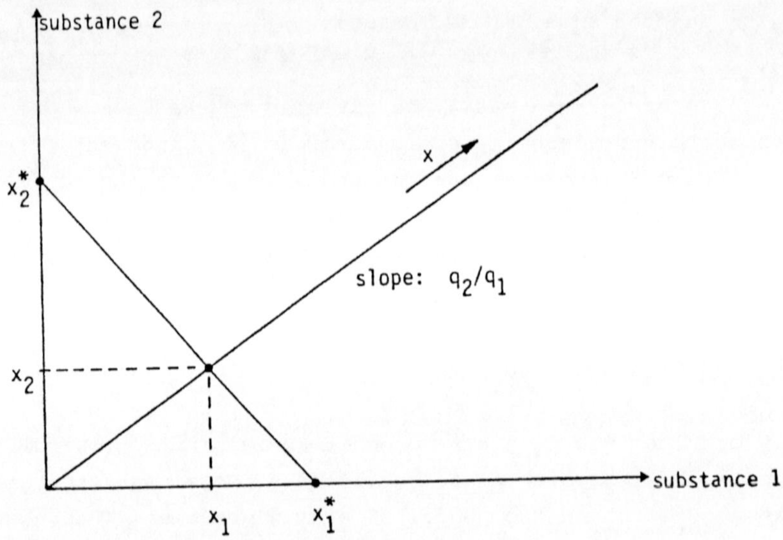

Fig. 9

Superadditive and **sub**additive co-operation are defined, respectively, by < and > instead of = in the relation above. Either state of affairs is characterized unmistakably by the constellation of the three equi-efficient points, as exhibited in fig. 10.

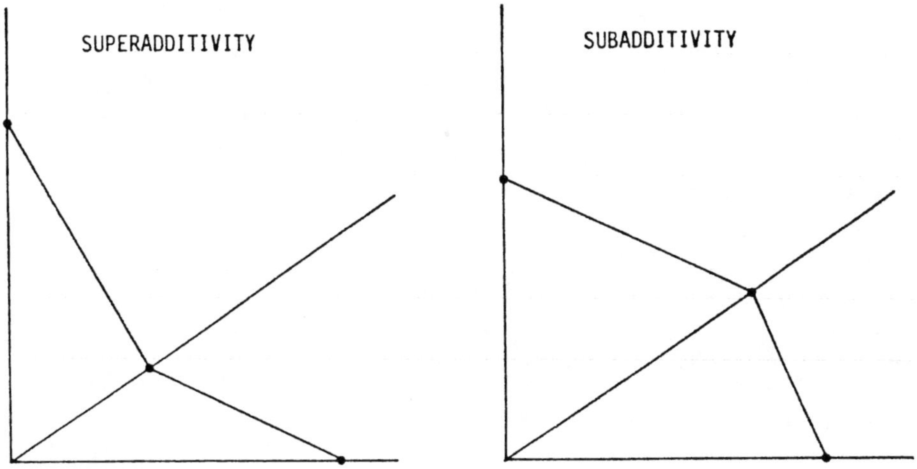

Fig. 10

5.2 Still considering the toxic effect, we now assume that both ingredients, if applied singly, act according to logistic laws:

$$p_i(x_i) = \Lambda\left(\frac{\log x_i - \mu_i}{\sigma_i}\right) \qquad (i = 1, 2).$$

We make two more assumptions:

(i) $\sigma_1 = \sigma_2 = \sigma$;

(ii) additivity of substance 1 and 2 for <u>all</u> doses x of the composite preparation.

Under these conditions the dose-response relationship **for the composite preparation** will itself be necessarily **logistic**; moreover, it is precisely determined by the laws of the components as

$$p(x) = \Lambda\left(\frac{\log x - \mu}{\sigma}\right) ,$$

where μ is a kind of mean value between μ_1 and μ_2, defined by

$$e^{-\mu} = q_1 e^{-\mu_1} + q_2 e^{-\mu_2} .$$

The configurations, depicted in the manner of fig. 9 for all the different doses x of the mixture, will automatically be *similar* to each other under assumptions (i) and (ii).

If, in violation of (ii), co-operation is **subadditive**, the response curve for the joint product will again be of the logistic type, provided the diagrams as in fig. 10 (right picture) are *similar* for all values x: Subadditivity is, then, just like additivity with the proviso that component 2, say, is replaced by a "weaker" substance! The response curve is obtained from the additive one as given above by a **shift to the right:** it will be of the form

$$p(x) = \Lambda\left(\frac{\log x - \mu - \nu}{\sigma}\right)$$

with some $\nu > 0$ whose size depends on the 'degree of subadditivity', i.e. on the angle formed by the broken lines in fig. 10.

For superadditivity, the "additivity curve" is correspondingly shifted to the left ($\nu < 0$).

If, in violation of (i), $\sigma_1 \neq \sigma_2$, response to the composite formula will, under additivity (ii), follow a **non-logistic** relationship. In fig. 11 the heavy line gives the - non-logistic! - additivity curve produced from the two logistic component curves drawn in dashed lines. Under the same similarity condition as before, subadditivity and superadditivity just shift this additivity curve to the right or to the left, respectively, by an appropriate amount - as is also indicated in fig. 11.

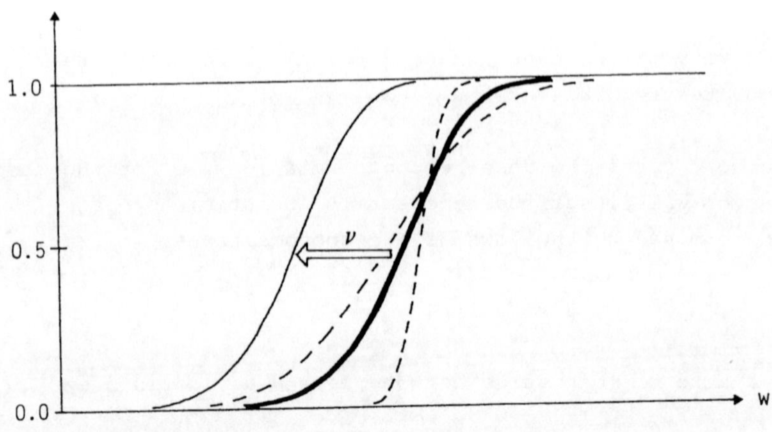

Fig. 11

The fundamental results on the co-operation of substances acting according to a probit or logit model are stated in H.D. UNKELBACH & Th. WOLF [1985]; further references are given in the same paper.

5.3 What has been said about co-operation in the toxic field carries, *mutatis mutandis*, over to the useful effect. In our context, then, the most interesting question will be: If the co-operation of the two substances is **additive** (or even subadditive) **in toxicity**, but **superadditive in their useful action**, can we expect a diminution of overall noxiousness by combining the two?

We describe the dosage of the substances 1, 2 and of the combination by the level W_1, W_2 and W of the *stimulus demanded* or required in every particular situation. We furthermore assume the distributions of W_1 and W_2 to be of the logistic type, with parameters μ_{Wi} and σ_{Wi} (i = 1, 2).

If $\sigma_{W1} = \sigma_{W2}$, the demand for the compound preparation, W, will also follow a logistic distribution function, viz.

$$F_W(w) = \Lambda\left(\frac{w - \mu_W + \nu_W}{\sigma_W}\right)$$

with some positive ν_W if we have superadditive co-operation in the domain of useful action.

Overall noxiousness of the combination will then be

$$\int \Lambda\left(\frac{\log x - \mu - \nu}{\sigma}\right) d\Lambda\left(\frac{\log x - \mu_W + \nu_W}{\sigma_W}\right),$$

with some $\nu \geq 0$ since toxic action is to be (sub-) additive.

A clearcut result **in favour of combination** can only be obtained in the rather special case

$$\mu_1 = \mu_2 \quad \text{and} \quad \mu_{W1} = \mu_{W2} :$$

in this case we have a definite advantage of the composite formula over the solitary use of either of the ingredient substances. This is demonstrated in fig. 12.

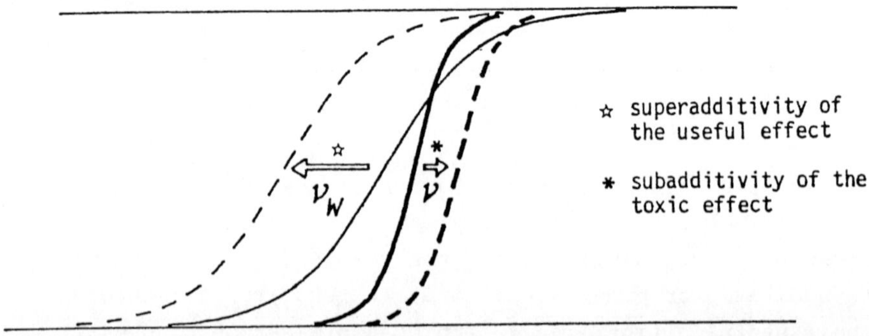

Fig. 12

Apart from this special case, however, the question remains open: With one **very poor ingredient** the combination may be worse than the better ingredient alone; on the other hand, **very strong superadditivity** might offset even a marked deficiency of one component.

6. Generalizations and other troubles

Going over the multiple limitations of our models, we notice at once the different generalizations which would be possible - and which may be desirable or necessary to deal with more complex situations. We list a few important model extensions.

(a) **Non-quantal response** - as will be present, e.g. if the damage due to the harmful substance can be classified as absent, mild, normal, or severe; or when it is measured by a quantitative variable.

(b) The possibility that **several kinds of injury** can be caused by the substance in question - they may be mutually exclusive or occur simultaneously; we might term this a **multi-dimensional response.** It can be reduced to the one-dimensional case (a) if there is a convincing trade-off between the different kinds of injury.

(c) **Over-reacting** or under-reacting (in different degrees !) to a product-change involving an increased or diminished concentration of the harmful substance in question - which means departure from the exact compensation described in sec. 4.

(d) **Heterogeneity of the population** to be investigated - with respect to the dose-response relation(s) of the individuals and/or with respect to the pattern of consumption or exposure.

Each of these generalizations involves new difficulties and further complications - requires also more comprehensive and differentiating statistical information and analysis in order to be numerically implemented with sufficient confidence. In this connection may it be remarked that we have omitted from our considerations all statistical problems, such as the estimation of the dose-response relationship or of the dose (or stimulus) distribution.

REFERENCES

[1980] Sharon ANDERSON et al.: Statistical Methods for Comparative Studies, New York etc. 1980.

[1985] H.D. UNKELBACH & Th. WOLF: Dose-Response Analysis of Combination Preparations, *Statistics in Medicine* 4(1985), p. 77-85.

Environmental Quality Indices: Problems, Concepts, Examples

Frank Stehling
Institut für Wirtschaftstheorie
und Operations Research
Universität Karlsruhe
D-7500 Karlsruhe 1
Federal Republic of Germany

1. INTRODUCTION

For a long time the environment played a subordinate role in economic theory. Even in the seventies and the beginning eighties the theory of economic growth was dominated by models using macroeconomic production functions F which connect aggregate output (e.g. GNP or GNP per capita) with only three aggregated input variables: capital K, labour L, and a variable τ being used to reflect the influence of (certain types of) technical progress:

(1.1) $$F: (K(t),L(t),\tau(t)) \to F(K(t),L(t),\tau(t)) = Y(t) \in \mathbb{R}_+;$$

see e.g. W.KRELLE(1985), P.STONEMAN(1983), J.FROHN et al.(1973, pp.33).

It is easy to show that assumption (1.1) implies that the growth rate w_Y of aggregated output is uniquely determined by the growth rates w_K, w_L, and w_τ of capital, labour, and technical progress: Let F be partially differentiable with respect to the three variables and assume that K, L, and τ are differentiable with respect to time t. Then,

$$w_Y = \frac{dY}{dt}/Y =: \frac{\dot{Y}}{Y}\ ;\ w_K = \frac{\dot{K}}{K}\ ;\ w_L = \frac{\dot{L}}{L}\quad ,$$

and (1.1) implies

(1.2) $$w_Y = s^K w_K + s^L w_L + w_\tau\ ,$$

where s^K and s^L are given by

(1.3) $$s^K := \frac{\delta F}{\delta K}\cdot\frac{K}{F}\quad ,\quad s^L := \frac{\delta F}{\delta L}\cdot\frac{L}{F}$$

and are interpreted according to the marginal productivity theory of income distribution as the relative factor shares; the rate w_τ is given by the expression

$$w_\tau := \frac{\delta F}{\delta \tau}\cdot\dot{\tau}\quad .$$

Since the growth rates w_Y, w_K, and w_L and the relative factor shares s^K and s^L can be observed (at least in principle), equation (1.2) can be used to <u>define</u> and to measure the rate w_τ of

Measurement in Economics
ed. by W. Eichhorn

technical progress as the residual term

$$(1.2') \qquad w_\tau = w_Y - s^K w_K - s^L w_L \quad ,$$

see S.KUZNETS (1971,pp.70)who did not interpret w_τ as the rate of of technical progress in contrast to J.FROHN et al.(1973,pp.33).

Of course, we know that the difference between the weighted growth rates on the right hand side of equation (1.2') is not only due to technical progress but is also due to the use of renewable and non-renewable natural resources such that in many countries high growth rates of GNP or national income (per capita) were accompanied with remarkable detoriation of the environment. The reasons for this development are obvious: The environment was regarded as a non-individual free capital and consumption good and, hence, it was used intensively, sometimes obviously too intensively such that production and traffic (as a specific form of production and consumption) had to be reduced remarkably, e.g. in Athens 1984 and 1985 and in the Ruhr-district for several days in January 1985.
It is well known that the traditional national account statistics conceal these detoriation effects completely; furthermore, all efforts for repairing and protecting the environment lead to an increase of the GNP if they are produced and sold at certain markets, and they may be - and have been - misinterpreted as an increase of welfare. Therefore, it is necessary to develop an independent monitoring system of indicators or indices which give information about the quality of the environment and its changes over time. This may serve as motivation and justification for speaking about environmental indices at a symposium on measurement in economics.

2. DEFINITION OF AND PROBLEMS WITH ENVIRONMENTAL INDICES

Referring to a useful definition of an economic index (see W. EICHHORN(1978,p.36)) the following definition of an environmental index may be suggested:

(2.1) Def.: An environmental (quality) index (EQI) measuring the environmental quality at a certain point (or in a certain region) at a certain time (or time period) t is a function

$$EQI : E \longrightarrow \mathbb{R} ,$$

which maps the set E of (all) objects which are relevant (at time t) for the environmental quality into $\mathbb{R}$ and which satisfies a system of suitable conditions.

Whereas this general concept of an environmental index may be accepted and is actually used by all scientists who ever defined an environmental index, this definition conceals the various problems in defining and using a specific index of environmental quality. Perhaps the following list of problems can give at least a partial answer to the question why there is - up to this date - no international and even in most of the countries no national consensus which environmental index should be used and whether or not such an index should be used, at all.

1. There is no consensus of what is meant by the term "environmental quality". The definition of that term is based necessarily on value judgements and is, therefore, highly subjective. It is out of question that the environmental quality (e.q.) depends on many variables. As was indicated in the above definition an ideal environmental index should be depending on all those variables which are relevant for the e.q., a requirement which hardly can be met because of practicability reasons and because of costs. But if it is required that an environmental index depends at least on the most important variables it has to be decided which variables, in fact, are the most important ones. The opinion about this may differ from person to person and - what is more serious - from time to time because of changing production processes and consumption behaviour, with new pollutants, and because of improved knowledge about the environmental damages caused by certain activities.

2. Furthermore, although in many cases an unanimous judgement can be made that a certain variable has an adverse effect on the e.q. there is often no unanimity about the intensity of this effect, see e.g. the environmental subindex function for nitrates in the air pollution index PSI in W.R.OTT (1978, p.208).

3. Each definition of e.q. must take into consideration the various aspects of this term which are, at least partially, completely different, non-comparable, and cannot be measured in a common unit. Therefore, an aggregation of all these aspects (expressed by suitably chosen variables and measured in suitably chosen units) into a single index does not seem to be adequate. For example, it does not seem reasonable to assume that a low quality of air can be compensated by a high quality of water. The best what can be reached is a definition of a system of subindices, each measuring the quality of a certain area of the environment. It is common practice to develop and use indices of

- air quality,
- water quality,
- soil quality,
- nutrition quality, including the quality of drinking water,
- human health,
- noise,
- land management,
- species diversity.

For a comprehensive list of environmental factors see R.PIKUL (1974) and for detailed environmental data S.E.JØRGENSEN(1979). By splitting up the quality of the total environment into the qualities of the different topic areas the same method is used as for measuring total social welfare or the quality of life by a system of social indicators and not by a single index, though there have been several attempts to measure the overall social welfare by a single index, see the Japanese Net-National-Welfare Concept (U.E.SIMONIS(1975)) or the approach of J.DREWNOWSKI(1974).

4. Even the attempt to define indices for a certain part of the environment causes difficulties. Again, it must be decided on which variables potentially or actually influencing the quality of this part the index should depend,and it has to be found out in which kind and intensity the variables influence this quality. As aggregates of these influences most types of environmental indices imply comparisons between the effects of different variables on the environmental quality. This can easily be demonstrated:

Let I^A be an air quality index depending on the characteristics (or factors or variables) $x_1,\ldots,x_n$ which can be regarded as different types of pollution. For a certain set of values $x^* = (x_1^*,\ldots,x_n^*)$ one may ask for that amount Δx_k of characteristic k which compensates an additional amount of one unit e_i of characteristic i such that I^A remains constant. By definition, Δx_k is implicitly defined by the equation

$$I^A(x_1^*,..,x_i^*+e_i,..,x_k^*+\Delta x_k,..,x_n^*) = I^A(x_1^*,..,x_i^*,..,x_k^*,..,x_n^*) \ .$$

As is well known from similar considerations in production theory, Δx_k is approximatively given (under the assumption of existing and non-vanishing partial derivatives) by the negative of the marginal rate of substitution between the characteristics i and k:

$$\Delta x_k \approx - MRS_{i,k}(x^*) = -\frac{\delta I^A(x^*)}{\delta x_i} \Big/ \frac{\delta I^A(x^*)}{\delta x_k} \ .$$

Hence, for all partially differentiable air quality indices with non-zero partial derivatives one can evaluate in each situation x^* which amount of - say - pollution of type k can compensate a certain additional amount of pollution of type i. In contrast to production theory where it makes sense to ask which amount of one input can be substituted by one unit of another input to produce the same output it may be objected to using the MRS concept in the theory of environmental indices because different pollutants have usually completely different effects; for example, carbone monoxide reduces the oxygen transported by the bloodstream and can, at low concentrations, reduce visual perception and alertness, whereas particulates may - depending on their size and form - cause damages of the lungs or even of other parts of the body. This shows that in spite of some shallow similarities the objective functions of traditional economic theory (e.g. real output) and of environmental theory (e.g. health) need different treatment.

Of course, there is a class of indices - again well known to economists from production theory - which does not imply the possibility of such comparisons, namely the indices of the form

$$I(x_1,\ldots,x_n) = \max\{I_1(x_1),\ldots,I_n(x_n)\} \ ,$$

where I_i is a certain subindex depending only on x_i $(i=1,...,n)$. If no relationship between the different variables is known these functions seem to be best suited as environmental indices (see W.R.OTT(1978,p.347)), but the fact that they are not strictly increasing functions of all variables may be regarded as a major disadvantage.
As a consequence, it may be recommended to avoid an aggregation of subindices of environmental quality at all and to present a complete list of all environmental observations, giving all available information in detail; but this will overtax people (and even scientists) in getting an insight in the environmental situation.

Whereas the preceding remarks point out the problems in determining which variables should influence an environmental index and of what kind this influence should be, the following additional problems arise from the measurement of such variables:

5. If a variable, e.g. a type of pollution, is found to be of strong influence on the environmental quality it may still be impossible to incorporate it in an index because there are no methods for measuring the variable in a sufficiently short time and with reasonable costs.

6. In contrast to the variables mentioned in 5., there are other variables which can and are measured by different methods; the methods can differ by the underlying concepts and/or by the techniques which are applied, and the results using those different methods can differ remarkably. To guarantee the comparability of the measurements it seems to be necessary to use unified methods at least on a national level. But because of the increasing international importance of pollution control, caused on the one hand by the transboundary effects of pollution and on the other hand by the economic interdependence and international competition, the application of unified methods on an international level is desirable.

7. The question must be answered where, when, and how often the variables should be measured. The concentration of pollutions may differ remarkably from hour to hour and from one point to another in a certain region. If the index shall give information

about the e.q. in a whole region during a certain period of time (say one day or one month) the measurements at the different time points and points of the region have to be aggregated. Several methods are known, e.g. taking averages over time and space . This approach is controversal because for some plants (e.g. trees) the maximal concentration of certain pollutants seems to be more important than an average concentration, even if reached only for a short time. For this reason, short- and long-term standards have been introduced and in some indices the percentages of observations which exceed,respectively,the short- and the long-term standards can be incorporated.
In order to get perfect information about the e.q. it would be best to have as many monitoring stations as possible and to observe the relevant variables as frequently as possible, i.e. continuously. Of course, this is a matter of cost and not each relevant variable can be measured continuously, e.g. this is not possible in the case of the biochemical oxygen demand BOD_5, telling how much oxygen in one liter of a given polluted water is needed by microorganisms in a time span of 5 days to decompose degradable organic matter. This variable needs, by definition, at least 5 days to be evaluated.
Of major importance is the question whether the emissions or the immission situation should be observed. With respect to health of human beings, animals, and plants the immission data seem to be more important than the emission data. On the other hand, in order to improve the e.q. by elaborating suitable abatement policies, it is, of course, necessary to know where the pollutants come from and, hence, the emission and the transmission processes have to be observed.

8. Finally, it has to be mentioned that because of possibly conflicting interests it will be of great importance <u>who</u> will <u>carry out</u> the measurements,in <u>which form</u> they are <u>reported</u>, <u>by whom</u> the measurements are <u>financed</u>, and <u>who is allowed</u> to obtain information about the measurements.It seems to be indispensible that only independent institutions are authorized in measuring and controlling the relevant variables in order to guarantee reliability of the environmental data reported. The form in which

the environmental data are published has to be chosen according to the persons and purposes they are intended for; e.g., in general, the public needs less detailed and more aggregated and more commented information than - say - the experts of an environmental protection organisation. At least in the long run, it is desirable that those who produce and emit the pollutants, i.e. the firms in the case of industrial emissions, have to finance the measurements. The publication of the data seems to be a problem specifically to market economies with private entrepreneurs because the pollutants of a production plant give in some cases information about the underlying production process. But since the emissions possibly have adverse effects on many people there is a great public interest in the corresponding data such that they should be made available to anybody.

Despite the various problems mentioned above there is a great need for and an increasing use of environmental indices reflecting the increasing importance of environmental conditions in the opinion of the public as well as of the local, regional, and national governments. W.R.OTT(1978,p.5) has listed the following purposes:

"- Resource Allocation: Indices may be applied to environmental decisions to assist managers in allocating funds and determining priorities.
- Ranking of Locations: Indices may be applied to assist in comparing environmental conditions at different locations or geographical areas.
- Enforcement of Standards: Indices may be applied to specific locations to determine the extent to which legislative standards and existing criteria are being met or exceeded.
- Trend Analysis: Indices may be applied to environmental data at different points in time to determine the changes of environmental quality (degradation or improvement) which have occurred over a period.
- Public Information: Indices may be used to inform the public about environmental conditions.
- Scientific Research: Indices may be applied as means for reducing a large quantity of data to a form that gives insights to the researcher conducting a study of some environmental

phenomenon."

Additionally, the following purpose should be mentioned:

- Development of new production processes and of new goods causing less adverse effects on the environment: The publication of environmental indices can lead to a greater awareness of environmental problems; thereby, the environmental burden caused by a certain good or production process may become a new and additional choice criterion for consumers and/or producers; this may be utilized by a suitable advertising.

3. INTERACTIONS BETWEEN DIFFERENT ENVIRONMENTAL INFLUENCES: THE CONCEPTS OF SYNERGISM, ANTAGONISM, AND SUPERPOSITION

The definition of an environmental index (2.1) as a function of certain variables implies that these variables have to be regarded as independent; nevertheless, several examples of interaction between different environmental influences, e.g. of different pollutants, are known. Such examples are the interaction between SO_2 and particulate matter (W.R.OTT(1978,p.18)) between SO_2 and NO_x (F.T.LAST(1983,p.112)), and very likely between SO_2 and other gases like ozone (COMMISSION OF THE EUROPEAN COMMUNITIES(1983,p.63)). In the case of SO_2 and NO_x Last observed that special plants show an additional growth effect of +17% if exposed only to (certain concentrations of) NO_x and a negative growth effect of -19% if exposed only to (certain concentrations of) SO_2, but if they are exposed simultaneously to (the same concentrations of) NO_x and SO_2 a negative growth effect of -43% is observed.

The occurrence of such interactions shows that in these situations it is not appropriate to define pollution standards or limits for single pollutants independently as it is usually done. If, for example, it has been found that a daily concentration of $75 \mu g/m^3$ of particulate matter has no severe effects on health and if the same is true for a concentration of $80 \mu g/m^3$ of SO_2 (see the National Ambient Air Quality Standards in W.R.OTT(1978,p.99)), there may be such effects on health if these concentrations are simultaneously reached. Since an enormous number of different substances is usually simultaneously present in the atmosphere, in the water and in the soil, in principle such interactions may occur quite frequently. In the following it is investigated which properties an environmental index has to have in order to describe such interactions.

Aiming at an easy interpretation it is assumed in the following that the e.q. can be described by a damage function d depending generally on n non-negative variables $x_1,\dots,x_n$, which may be interpreted as concentrations of different pollutants. If the combined effect of only two variables, say x_1 and x_2, is considered and if it is assumed that d depends only on these two variables three types of interaction are, in principle, possible which are called, respectively, synergism, antagonism, and superposition and which are usually defined in the following way (see J.W.OTT (1978,pp.330)):

It is said that, respectively, synergism, antagonism, superposition between variable 1 and variable 2 prevails at $x = (x_1,x_2)$ if the overall damage caused by the simultaneous influence of x_1 and x_2 is greater than, less than, equal to, the sum of the damages caused by the individual effects of x_1 and x_2. The usual requirement for a damage function describing a synergism is

$$(3.1) \qquad d(x_1,x_2) \underset{(=)}{\overset{>}{(<)}} d(x_1,0) + d(0,x_2) \quad ,$$

where, in the case of an antagonism, (3.1) holds with the "<"-sign and, in the case of superposition, (3.1) holds with the "="-sign.

The problem with these definitions is

- that they apply only to the case of two variables and
- that in order to identify one of the three cases the situation (x_1,x_2) has to be compared with situations where one of the variables is held on the zero-level which, even in experiments, is sometimes impossible.

Hence, it seems more useful and more natural to define these interaction phenomena in terms of (absolute) increments of the variables and the damages they cause. If the damages depend on n variables one possibility to define the three effects is the following:

(3.2) Def.: Synergism (antagonism, superposition) prevails between variable 1 and variable 2 at $x = (x_1,\dots,x_n)$ if the additional damage caused by any sufficiently small simultaneous increments $\Delta x_1 > 0$ of x_1 and $\Delta x_2 > 0$ of x_2 is greater than (less than, equal to) the sum of additional damages caused by the increments Δx_1 and Δx_2 separately. Hence, the damage function d describes this effect if and only if

$$(3.3)\quad \begin{aligned} & d(x_1+\Delta x_1, x_2+\Delta x_2, x_3,\dots,x_n) - d(x_1,x_2,x_3,\dots,x_n) \underset{(=)}{\overset{>}{(<)}} \\ & \underset{(=)}{\overset{>}{(<)}} d(x_1+\Delta x_1, x_2, x_3,\dots,x_n) - d(x_1,x_2,x_3,\dots,x_n) + \\ & + d(x_1, x_2+\Delta x_2, x_3,\dots,x_n) - d(x_1,x_2,x_3,\dots,x_n) \end{aligned}$$

for all sufficiently small $\Delta x_1 > 0$ and $\Delta x_2 > 0$.

It is said that d describes synergism (antagonism, superposition) between variable 1 and variable 2 <u>everywhere</u> if (3.3) holds <u>for all</u> $x = (x_1,\dots,x_n) \geqq 0$.

For n=2 and $d(0,0) = 0$, an evident assumption, (3.3) implies (3.1) by setting $x_1=x_2=0$ and by substitution of Δx_i by x_i; hence, the definition of synergism, antagonism, and superposition in the sense of (3.3) is stronger than that in the sense of (3.1). In the following, the concepts of synergism, antagonism, and superposition are used in the sense of definition (3.2), respectively of (3.3).

As a first result, we have

(3.4) <u>Theorem:</u> Let I be a damage function depending on the non-negative variables $x_1, x_2, \dots, x_n$; let I be partially differentiable with respect to x_1 and x_2. Then:

a) If I describes synergism (antagonism) between the first two variables everywhere, then $\frac{\delta I}{\delta x_1}$ is increasing (decreasing) in x_2 <u>and</u> $\frac{\delta I}{\delta x_2}$ is increasing (decreasing) in x_1.

Conversely, if $\frac{\delta I}{\delta x_1}$ is strictly increasing (decreasing) in x_2 <u>or</u> $\frac{\delta I}{\delta x_2}$ is strictly increasing (decreasing) in x_1, then I describes synergism (anatgonism) between x_1 and x_2 everywhere.

b) If I describes superposition between the first two variables everywhere, then $\frac{\delta I}{\delta x_1}$ does not depend on x_2 <u>and</u> $\frac{\delta I}{\delta x_2}$ does not depend on x_1.

Conversely, if $\frac{\delta I}{\delta x_1}$ does not depend on x_2 <u>or</u> $\frac{\delta I}{\delta x_2}$ does not depend on x_1, then, I describes superposition between the first two variables everywhere.

<u>Proof:</u>

a) Because of the symmetry in the definitions of synergism and antagonism it is sufficient to prove only the assertion for synergism.

From inequality (3.3) we get by rearranging terms

$$0 < I(x_1+\Delta x_1,x_2+\Delta x_2,..) - I(x_1+\Delta x_1,x_2,..) - (I(x_1,x_2+\Delta x_2,..) - I(x_1,x_2,..)) \quad ,$$

where the arguments $x_3,...,x_n$ are omitted. Dividing both sides of this inequality by $\Delta x_2>0$ and taking the limit for $\Delta x_2 \to 0$ leads to

$$0 \leqq \frac{\delta I(x_1+\Delta x_1,x_2,..)}{\delta x_2} - \frac{\delta I(x_1,x_2,..)}{\delta x_2}$$

for all sufficiently small $\Delta x_1>0$, which shows that $\frac{\delta I}{\delta x_2}$ has to increase in x_1, as asserted.

But the inequality (3.3) can also be rewritten as

$$0 < I(x_1+\Delta x_1,x_2+\Delta x_2,..) - I(x_1,x_2+\Delta x_2,..) - (I(x_1+\Delta x_1,x_2,..) - I(x_1,x_2,..)) \; .$$

Division by $\Delta x_1>0$ and taking the limit for $\Delta x_1 \to 0$ leads to

$$0 \leqq \frac{\delta I(x_1,x_2+\Delta x_2,..)}{\delta x_1} - \frac{\delta I(x_1,x_2,..)}{\delta x_1}$$

for all sufficiently small $\Delta x_2>0$, showing that $\frac{\delta I}{\delta x_1}$ has to be increasing in x_2.

Conversely, let $\frac{\delta I}{\delta x_1}$ be strictly increasing in x_2. Then, for all $\Delta x_2>0$

$$0 < \frac{\delta I(x_1,x_2+\Delta x_2,..)}{\delta x_1} - \frac{\delta I(x_1,x_2,..)}{\delta x_1} \quad ,$$

which implies for sufficiently small $\Delta x_1 > 0$ the inequality

$$0 < \frac{I(x_1+\Delta x_1, x_2+\Delta x_2, ..) - I(x_1, x_2+\Delta x_2, ..)}{\Delta x_1} - \frac{I(x_1+\Delta x_1, x_2, ..) - I(x_1, x_2, ..)}{\Delta x_1} \quad ;$$

by multiplying by $\Delta x_1 > 0$ inequality (3.3) is obtained. Assertion b) can be proved by exactly the same techniques.

An immediate consequence of this theorem is

(3.5) Corollary: Let the damage function I in theorem (3.4) be twice continuously partially differentiable with respect to the first two variables. Then:

a) $\frac{\delta^2 I}{\delta x_1 \delta x_2} = \frac{\delta^2 I}{\delta x_2 \delta x_1} \underset{(<)}{>} 0$ implies that I describes synergism (antagonism) between the first two variables everywhere; conversely, if I describes synergism (antagonism) between the first two variables everywhere then, necessarily, for all arguments

$$\frac{\delta^2 I}{\delta x_1 \delta x_2} = \frac{\delta^2 I}{\delta x_2 \delta x_1} \underset{(\leq)}{\geq} 0 \quad . \tag{3.6}$$

b) $\frac{\delta^2 I}{\delta x_1 \delta x_2} = \frac{\delta^2 I}{\delta x_2 \delta x_1} = 0$ implies that I describes superposition between the first two variables everywhere.

If more than two variables interact, synergism, antagonism, and superposition can be defined completely analogously to the case of two interacting variables. If the first three variables interact the following definitions are suggested:

(3.7) Def.: Synergism (antagonism, superposition) prevails between the variables 1, 2, and 3 at $x = (x_1, \ldots, x_n)$ if the additional damage caused by any sufficiently small simultaneous increments $\Delta x_1 > 0$, $\Delta x_2 > 0$, $\Delta x_3 > 0$ is greater than (less than, equal to) the sum of the additional damages caused by the increments Δx_1,

Δx_2, and Δx_3 separately. Hence, the damage function I describes this effect if and only if

$$
\begin{aligned}
(3.8)\qquad & I(x_1+\Delta x_1, x_2+\Delta x_2, x_3+\Delta x_3, ..) - I(x_1, x_2, x_3, ..) \overset{\geq}{(\leq)} \\
& \overset{\geq}{(\leq)} I(x_1+\Delta x_1, x_2, x_3, ..) - I(x_1, x_2, x_3, ..) + \\
& + I(x_1, x_2+\Delta x_2, x_3, ..) - I(x_1, x_2, x_3, ..) + \\
& + I(x_1, x_2, x_3+\Delta x_3, ..) - I(x_1, x_2, x_3, ..)
\end{aligned}
$$

for all sufficiently small $\Delta x_1>0$, $\Delta x_2>0$, $\Delta x_3>0$ (the arguments $x_4,...,x_n$ have been omitted).

For convenience, let us denote in the following the first three variables of the damage function I respectively by x, y, and z; let $I_x := \frac{\delta I}{\delta x}$, $I_y := \frac{\delta I}{\delta y}$, $I_z := \frac{\delta I}{\delta z}$, $I_{xx} := \frac{\delta I_x}{\delta x}$, $I_{xy} := \frac{\delta I_x}{\delta y}$ and analogously for other and higher partial derivatives. Similarly to theorem (3.4) and its corollary (3.5) we have

(3.9) <u>Theorem:</u> Let the damage function $I: \mathbb{R}^n_+ \to \mathbb{R}_{(+)}$ be three times continuously partially differentiable with respect to the first three variables. If I describes synergism (antagonism) between x, y, and z everywhere, then, necessarily, for all arguments

$$
(3.10)\qquad I_{xy} + I_{yz} + I_{zx} \overset{\geq}{(\leq)} 0 \quad .
$$

<u>Proof:</u>

Using the Taylor expansion for I, we have for $\Delta x>0$, $\Delta y>0$, $\Delta z>0$

$$
\begin{aligned}
& I(x+\Delta x, y+\Delta y, z+\Delta z, ..) - I(x,y,z,..) = \\
& = \Delta x I_x(x,y,z,..) + \Delta y I_y(x,y,z,..) + \Delta z I_z(x,y,z,..) + \\
& + \tfrac{1}{2}(\Delta x)^2 I_{xx}(...) + \tfrac{1}{2}(\Delta y)^2 I_{yy}(...) + \tfrac{1}{2}(\Delta z)^2 I_{zz}(...) + \\
& + \Delta x \Delta y I_{xy}(...) + \Delta y \Delta z I_{yz}(...) + \Delta z \Delta x I_{zx}(...) + R \ ,
\end{aligned}
$$

where $R := \frac{1}{3!}\left(\Delta x\frac{\delta}{\delta x} + \Delta y\frac{\delta}{\delta y} + \Delta z\frac{\delta}{\delta z}\right)^3 I(x+\kappa_1\Delta x, y+\kappa_2\Delta y, z+\kappa_3\Delta z, ...)$ with constants κ_1, κ_2, κ_3 satisfying $0 \leq \kappa_1, \kappa_2, \kappa_3 \leq 1$, and where the arguments of all second order derivatives are the same as those of the first order derivatives.

Correspondingly, one has

$$I(x+\Delta x,y,z,..) - I(x,y,z,..) = \Delta x I_x(...) + \frac{1}{2}(\Delta x)^2 I_{xx}(...) + R_1 ,$$

$$I(x,y+\Delta y,z,..) - I(x,y,z,..) = \Delta y I_y(...) + \frac{1}{2}(\Delta y)^2 I_{yy}(...) + R_2 ,$$

$$I(x,y,z+\Delta z,..) - I(x,y,z,..) = \Delta z I_z(...) + \frac{1}{2}(\Delta z)^2 I_{zz}(...) + R_3 ,$$

where

$$R_1 := \frac{1}{3!}(\Delta x)^3 I_{xxx}(x+\mu_1\Delta x,y,z,..) \quad \text{with} \quad 0 \leqq \mu_1 \leqq 1 ,$$

$$R_2 := \frac{1}{3!}(\Delta y)^3 I_{yyy}(x,y+\mu_2\Delta y,z,..) \quad \text{with} \quad 0 \leqq \mu_2 \leqq 1 ,$$

$$R_3 := \frac{1}{3!}(\Delta z)^3 I_{zzz}(x,y,z+\mu_3\Delta z,..) \quad \text{with} \quad 0 \leqq \mu_3 \leqq 1 .$$

Inserting these four Taylor expansions in the defining inequality (3.8) for synergism between x, y, and z leads for the special case of sufficiently small $\Delta x = \Delta y = \Delta z > 0$ to the inequality

$$0 < (\Delta x)^2 \cdot (I_{xy}(...) + I_{yz}(...) + I_{zx}(...)) + \tilde{R} - \tilde{R}_1 - \tilde{R}_2 - \tilde{R}_3 ,$$

where $\tilde{R}$, $\tilde{R}_1$, $\tilde{R}_2$, $\tilde{R}_3$ are the expressions for R, R_1, R_2, R_3 defined above but evaluated at $\Delta x = \Delta y = \Delta z$. Since

$$0 = \lim_{\Delta x \to 0} \frac{\tilde{R}}{(\Delta x)^2} = \lim_{\Delta x \to 0} \frac{\tilde{R}_1}{(\Delta x)^2} = \lim_{\Delta x \to 0} \frac{\tilde{R}_2}{(\Delta x)^2} = \lim_{\Delta x \to 0} \frac{\tilde{R}_3}{(\Delta x)^2}$$

we see that the last inequality implies that

$$0 \leqq I_{xy}(...) + I_{yz}(...) + I_{zx}(...)$$

for all arguments which is, therefore, a necessary condition for the index I to describe synergism between x, y, and z everywhere. Analogously, it can be shown that

$$0 \geqq I_{xy}(...) + I_{yz}(...) + I_{zx}(...)$$

for all arguments is a necessary condition for I to describe antagonism between x, y, and z everywhere.

It should be stressed that by definition (3.7) and, correspondingly, by inequality (3.8), synergism and antagonism have been defined in terms of the absolute increments of variables and their effects with respect to the environmental quality (expressed by a damage function). Of course, it may be suggested to define these phenomena by looking at the relative increments of variables and their relative additional effects on the e.q.. As is well known from microeconomic theory the relative effects on the function values caused by relative changes of variables are expressed by elasticities. If, for example, $f: \mathbb{R}^2 \to \mathbb{R}$ satisfies $f(x,y) \neq 0$ then the partial elasticity of f with respect to x is given, under the assumption of partial differentiability with respect to x, by the expression

$$(3.10) \qquad \eta_{f,x}(x,y) := \frac{\delta f(x,y)}{\delta x} \cdot \frac{x}{f(x,y)}$$

and gives, approximately, the percentage change of f caused by an 1 per cent increment of x.

The percentage change of f caused by a simultaneous 1 per cent change of both variables is, approximately, given by the scale elasticity of f at $\lambda = 1$, defined by

$$(3.11) \qquad \varepsilon_f(1,x,y) := \frac{\delta g(\lambda,x,y)}{\delta \lambda}\bigg|_{\lambda=1} \frac{1}{f(x,y)} ,$$

where

$$g(\lambda,x,y) := f(\lambda x,\lambda y) ,$$

see W.KRELLE(1969,p.91). In the same manner the partial elasticities and the scale elasticity of a function of more than two variables are defined.

Now, following the idea mentioned above, it may be suggested to say that (relative) synergism between the two variables x and y prevails everywhere if the percentage change of the e.q. (or the damage) caused by a simultaneous 1 per cent change of x and y is greater (in the case of antagonism: less) than the sum of the percentage changes of the e.q. (or the damage) caused by an 1 per cent change of x and y separately. For a damage function $I: \mathbb{R}_+^2 \to \mathbb{R}_{(+)}$ describing this phenomenon, that definition approach would require that the inequality

$$(3.12) \qquad \varepsilon_f(1,x,y) > \eta_{f,x}(x,y) + \eta_{f,y}(x,y)$$

holds for all $x,y \in \mathbb{R}_{(+)}$. But this is impossible because of the WICKSELL-JOHNSON-Theorem, see W.KRELLE(1969,pp.93):

(3.13) Theorem: For every function $f: \mathbb{R}^n_{(+)} \to \mathbb{R}_{(+)}$ with first order partial derivatives and with $f(x_1,\ldots,x_n) \neq 0$ for all $x = (x_1,\ldots,x_n) \in \mathbb{R}^n_{(+)}$, the following equality holds:

$$(3.14) \qquad \varepsilon_f(1,x_1,\ldots,x_n) = \sum_{i=1}^{n} \eta_{f,x_i}(x_1,\ldots,x_n) \qquad ((x_1,\ldots,x_n)\in\mathbb{R}^n_{(+)}).$$

Proof:

By definition of ε_f,

$$\varepsilon_f(1,x_1,\ldots,x_n) = \frac{\delta g(1,x_1,\ldots,x_n)}{\delta\lambda}\cdot\frac{1}{f(x_1,\ldots,x_n)} =$$

$$= \sum_{i=1}^{n} \frac{\delta f(x_1,\ldots,x_n)}{\delta x_i}\cdot\frac{x_i}{f(x_1,\ldots,x_n)} = \sum_{i=1}^{n} \eta_{f,x_i}(x_1,\ldots,x_n) .$$

This theorem shows for n=2 that the inequality (3.12) can never hold. Hence, in this case, a synergistic effect cannot be defined by this equality; of course, the same is true for general n. But even in the more realistic case, where the environmental index I depends on more than two variables not all of them being candidates for a synergistic (or an antagonistic) effect, it is not possible to define this effect by a slight modification of this inequality:

If I depends, say, on the three environmental variables x, y, and z and if x and y are candidates for a synergistic effect then, it may be suggested to compare the sum of the partial elasticities $\eta_{I,x}$ and $\eta_{I,y}$ with the partial scale elasticity $\varepsilon_{I,x,y}$ defined by

$$(3.15) \qquad \varepsilon_{I,x,y}(1,x,y,z) := \left.\frac{\delta g^{x,y}(\lambda,x,y,z)}{\delta\lambda}\right|_{\lambda=1}\cdot\frac{1}{I(x,y,z)} ,$$

where $g^{x,y}(\lambda,x,y,z) := I(\lambda x,\lambda y,z)$ for $\lambda > 0$.

But similarly to theorem (3.13) we have

(3.16) Theorem: For every function $f: \mathbb{R}^3_{(+)} \to \mathbb{R}_{(+)}$ with first order partial derivatives with respect to the first and second variable and with $f(x,y,z) \neq 0$ for all $x,y,z\in\mathbb{R}_{(+)}$, the following equation holds for all $x,y,z\in\mathbb{R}_{(+)}$:

$$(3.17) \qquad \varepsilon_{f,x,y}(1,x,y,z) = \eta_{f,x}(x,y,z) + \eta_{f,y}(x,y,z) .$$

Proof: By definition (3.15),

$$\varepsilon_{f,x,y}(1,x,y,z) = \left(\frac{\delta f(x,y,z)}{\delta x}\cdot x + \frac{\delta f(x,y,z)}{\delta y}\cdot y\right)\frac{1}{f(x,y,z)} =$$

$$= \eta_{f,x}(x,y,z) + \eta_{f,y}(x,y,z) \quad .$$

These theorems show that synergism and antagonism of environmental variables cannot be defined (at least not with the approach above) in terms of relative changes of the variables and the environmental quality (index) but have to be defined in terms of absolute changes.

4. EXAMPLES OF ENVIRONMENTAL INDICES

Just as an illustration, in the following two examples of environmental quality indices will be presented which may be not so well known to economists.

By a working group of the EPA, in 1976, an air quality index was developed which is based on the National Ambient Air Quality Standards (NAAQS) and is called Pollutant Standards Index (PSI), see W.R.OTT (1978,pp.143-190). It includes five pollutants, namely carbone monoxide, nitrogen dioxide, ozone, sulphur dioxide, and total suspended particulates, and as a sixth variable the product of sulphur dioxide and total suspended particulates, reflecting the synergistic effect between these two variables. For each of the six variables a subindex is defined; the value of the PSI for a given pollution situation is the maximum value of these subindices:

$$\text{(4.1)} \qquad PSI(x_1,\ldots,x_6) \quad := \quad \max\{I_1(x_1),\ldots,I_6(x_6)\} \quad .$$

The subindices $I_1,\ldots,I_6$ are piecewise linear and continuous functions, normalized in such a way that they take on the value 100 at the NAAQS; they reach independently the values 200, 300, 400, and 500 (the maximum value of each subindex) at concentrations (measured as certain average concentrations) which are interpreted as episode criteria points signalizing levels of increasing danger and calling for different actions to reduce air pollution:

alert level (I_i=200), warning level (I_i=300), emergency level (I_i=400), significant harm level (I_i=500). The corresponding concentrations have been promulgated by the federal government. The PSI has been adopted by several of the United States.

As an example of a water quality index let us consider the National Sanitation Foundation's Water Quality Index (NSFWQI). This index includes nine components: dissolved oxygen, fecal coliforms, pH, biochemical oxygen demand (BOD_5), nitrates, phosphates, temperature (deviation from the equilibrium temperature), turbidity, total solids. These nine variables have turned out to be, in the opinion of a certain group of experts, the most significant variables with respect to water quality. For each component a subindex has been developed, again by evaluation of expert opinion. The experts were asked to assign quality levels from 0 to 100 to different values of the individual variables and to give weights to the components indicating the relative importance of each. By taking arithmetic means of the judgements of the experts the final subindex functions I_i and the final weights w_i were found. For a calculation of the total index one has to read the subindex values from the corresponding graphs; the total index is given by the weighted linear sum of the subindices:

$$(4.2) \qquad NSFWQI^1(x_1,..,x_9) := \sum_{i=1}^{9} w_i I_i(x_i) \;;$$

but the weighted geometric mean is used as well:

$$(4.2') \qquad NSFWQI^2(x_1,..,x_9) := \prod_{i=1}^{9} I_i(x_i)^{w_i}$$

with the same weights as in (4.2). An additional procedure is used to take into account the effects of pesticides and toxic substances: The NSFWQI is automatically set to 0 if the concentration of one of these substances exceeds certain limits for which the drinking water standards are taken.
The difference between the two forms (4.2) and (4.2') is that the multiplicative form is more sensitive to extreme low values of a single subindex and that it reflects, in view of Corollary 3.5, synergistic or antagonistic effects whereas the additive form (4.2) does not.
The NSFWQI is regarded by its developers as a means for making the public aware of water quality levels (W.R.OTT(1978,p.212)).

For a detailed description of the PSI and the NSFWQI and a great variety of air and water pollution indices we refer to the book of W.R.OTT(1978).

Whereas these indices are based essentially on physical and chemical variables, the so-called biological (water quality) indices measure the impact of water quality on aquatic life: The absence, presence, density, diversity and behaviour of certain indicator organisms give information about the pollution of the water. So the German water classification is based partially on the saprobic classification systems. Whereas the former quality measurements can report the quality of a water only at a certain time point, the biological indicators are able to integrate the pollutions over time, because of the presence of the organisms in the water all over time, and, hence, they give information about all pollutions in a certain time span. For a list of indicator organisms we refer to W.BAUR(1980,pp.83).

Finally, a completely different method of measuring the water quality should be mentioned. It has turned out that drops falling down on the surface of a water cause remarkably different changes of the surface corresponding to the water quality. Thus, with a lot of experience, it may be possible to draw conclusions from the drop-pictures with respect to the pollutants and its concentrations; see W.SCHWENK(1979).

REFERENCES

W.BAUR: Gewässergüte bestimmen und beurteilen. Hamburg-Berlin, 1980

COMMISSION OF THE EUROPEAN COMMUNITIES (eds.): Acid Rain - A review of the phenomenon in the EEC and Europe. London, 1983

J.DREWNOWSKI: On Measuring and Planning the Quality of Life. The Hague-Paris, 1974

W.EICHHORN: What is an Economic Index? An Attempt of an Answer. In: W.EICHHORN/R.HENN/O.OPITZ/R.W.SHEPHARD(eds.): Theory and Applications of Economic Indices. Würzburg, 1978, 3-40

J.FROHN/R.KRENGEL/P.KUHBIER/K.H.OPPENLÄNDER/L.UHLMANN: Der technische Fortschritt in der Industrie. Berlin, 1973

S.E.JØRGENSEN(ed.): Handbook of Environmental Data and Ecological Parameters. International Society for Ecological Modelling. Vaerløse, Denmark, 1979

W.KRELLE: Produktionstheorie. Tübingen, 1969

W.KRELLE unter Mitarbeit von D.COENEN: Theorie des wirtschaftlichen Wachstums. Berlin-Heidelberg-New York, 1985

S.KUZNETS: Economic Growth of Nations. Cambridge, Mass., 1971

F.T.LAST: Direct Effects of Air Pollutions, Singly and in Mixtures, on Plants and Plant Assemblages. In: H.OTT/H.STANGL(eds.): Acid Deposition. A Challenge for Europe. Proceedings of the Symposium in Karlsruhe, 19-21 September 1983, 105-126

W.R.OTT: Environmental Indices. Theory and Practice. Ann Arbor, 1978

R.PIKUL: Development of Environmental Indices. In: J.W.PRATT(ed.): Statistical and Mathematical Aspects of Pollution Problems. New York, 1974, 103-121

W.SCHWENK: Zur Verhaltensforschung des Wassers. In: Der Aufbau, Heft 3-5, 1979 (Festschrift 100 Jahre Versuchs- und Forschungsanstalt der Stadt Wien), 132-135

U.E.SIMONIS: Netto-Wohlfahrtsindikator - ein japanischer Ansatz. In: W.ZAPF(ed.): Soziale Indikatoren.III. Frankfurt/M., 1975, 296-317

P.STONEMAN: The Economic Analysis of Technical Change. New York 1983

Part VI Inequality

How to Retrieve the Lorenz Curve from Sparse Data

Michael Braulke
Fachbereich Wirtschaftswissenschaften
Universität Osnabrück
D-4500 Osnabrück, F.R.G.

It is widely felt among empirically oriented economists that too much of the information on income distribution that is actually collected by statistical offices is lost in what is eventually published. Typically, only a few points of the Lorenz curve are made available whereas in applied work often the entire curve is required. This need to know the entire Lorenz curve arises already when the intention is merely to extract e.g. the Gini concentration ratio with a reasonable degree of accuracy, and it becomes more urgent when the informational content of such unidimensional inequality measures is to be supplemented by additional information from the Lorenz curve. For instance, calculation of the minor concentration ratio proposed by Hagerbaumer (1977), which is meant to measure the relative position of the poor, requires sufficiently reliable information on the shape of the Lorenz curve over at least the lower income deciles, whereas the derivation of Lorenz coefficients as suggested by Koo, Quan, and Rasche (1981), which may convey useful information on the contribution of certain income classes to overall inequality[1] presupposes in essence knowledge of the Lorenz curve over all its range. Finally, knowledge of the entire Lorenz curve is obviously indispensable when the extent of overlapping of income distributions of pairs of countries has to be determined as would be necessary, for example, in tests of Linder's hypothesis on intra-industry trade[2].

There are many other applications in applied work where one would prefer having the entire Lorenz curve rather than only a few points on it. The question therefore arises how one may retrieve the unknown Lorenz curve from the sparse data points which are typically available. It is the purpose of this paper to discuss three different approaches to this task and to report briefly the problems encountered in each case.

1 See also Thon (1983) and Koo, Quan, and Rasche (1983).

2 One may in fact wonder whether the poor empirical support obtained so far really speak against the validity of Linder's convincing hypothesis or rather reflect the crude approximations to the extent of income similarity between countries that had to be used due to lack of better information on income distribution. See e.g. Fortune (1979).

Measurement in Economics
ed. by W. Eichhorn

The approaches considered are (i) fitting some specified functional form to the known data points of the Lorenz curve and taking this estimate as a substitute for the unknown Lorenz curve, (ii) interpolating the known data points by a well-behaved (monotone, convex and differentiable) spline function, and finally (iii) constructing the upper and lower bounds of the band through which the true Lorenz curve must pass. The calculation of such bounds may be of interest on its own, but it will serve here essentially as a yardstick with which to judge the reliability of the other two approaches mentioned.

1. Retrieving the Lorenz Curve by Fitting Specified Functional Forms

Let p and y denote the cumulative proportions of income units and of income received. The best known functional form to represent a Lorenz curve is then presumably that of Kakwani and Podder (1976),

$$\eta = \gamma\pi^{\alpha}(\sqrt{2}-\pi)^{\beta} \quad \text{with} \quad 0<\alpha,\beta\leq 1 \quad \text{and} \quad \gamma\geq 0 \quad , \qquad (1)$$

which expresses the Lorenz curve in terms of the new coordinates $\eta=(p-y)/\sqrt{2}$ and $\pi=(p+y)/\sqrt{2}$. This specification was extensively and obviously also successfully used by Jain (1975) in her compilation of size distributions of income. From a computational point of view this representation combines the advantage of being particularly easy to estimate[3] with the disadvantage of being awkward when it comes to integrating the associated Lorenz curve over some subinterval. But what is more important, the Kakwani and Podder specification (1) has been seriously criticized by Rasche, Gaffney, Koo, and Obst (1980) on theoretical grounds for failing to comply with one of the basic properties of a Lorenz curve, i.e. to stay within the lower triangle of the unit square[4].

3 Note that after taking logarithms, (1) is linear in its parameters.

4 Indeed, it is not difficult to check that the Kakwani and Podder representation of the Lorenz curve will leave the unit square at either or both of its endpoints (0,0) and (1,1) in all but two permissible parameter constellations which are $\gamma=0$ and $\alpha=\beta=1$, $\gamma\leq 1/\sqrt{2}$. In all other cases, the derivative $d\eta/d\pi$ approaches plus or minus infinity at the two endpoints $\pi=0$ and $\pi=\sqrt{2}$, respectively, which is tantamount to a slope of -1 of the associated Lorenz curve at its two endpoints (0,0) and (1,1). Kakwani argued (1980) that this rather general defect will be of little practical importance since the Lorenz curve implied by (1) will normally possess over almost its entire range the required monotonicity. This is hardly much consolation because the essential question is how long it will take the estimated Lorenz curve to reenter the lower triangle of the unit square, and on this account, the order of magnitude involved is too often not negligible. This may not be obvious, but e.g. Jain's compilation is full of such cases. For instance, the estimates for Botswana 1971-72 imply $y<0$ for all $p\varepsilon(0,.75)$ and those for Brazil 1960 (first column) imply $p>1$ for all y in the interval (.75,1).

To avoid this flaw, Rasche et al. proposed using the generalized Pareto Lorenz curve instead,

$$y = (1-(1-p)^{\alpha})^{1/\beta} \quad \text{with} \quad 0<\alpha,\beta\leq 1 \quad , \tag{2}$$

which has all the properties (such as monotonicity and convexity) a Lorenz curve must possess. From the point of view of computational effort involved, it is perhaps comparable to Kakwani and Podder's specification (1), for it requires non-linear estimation but is somewhat easier to integrate.

As an alternative to these two specifications we will also use the functional form

$$y = \gamma p^{1/\alpha} + (1-\gamma)(1-(1-p)^{\beta}) \quad \text{with} \quad 0<\alpha,\beta\leq 1 \quad \text{and} \quad 0\leq\gamma\leq 1 \quad , \tag{3}$$

which is another generalization of the Pareto Lorenz curve, as it is simply pieced together as a convex combination of the Pareto Lorenz curve proper and its mirror image across the main diagonal of the unit square. Thus, it is clearly monotone and convex. Like the Rasche et al. specification (2), it requires non-linear estimation techniques, but unlike it, it is easily integrated[5].

2. Retrieving the Lorenz Curve by Interpolation

A priori there is little reason to believe that an actual Lorenz curve should obey one or another simple functional form. And since it is hardly any merit for a functional form to have particularly few parameters, one wonders whether or not to try retrieving the Lorenz curve by interpolation rather than through curve fitting. The simplest way of interpolation would, of course, consist of joining the known data points by linear segments. This is in no way an unusual method of interpolation - e.g. Paukert (1973) used it to calculate the Gini coefficients for his 56 country sample - but it implies identical incomes for all units within each given bracket and thus leads, as is well known, to the lowest Gini coefficient that is compatible with the data. Looking then for a smoother representation of the Lorenz curve we will require that it be continuously differentiable in addition to being monotone and convex. One should be aware, however, that differentiability in contrast to monotonicity and convexity is at best justified on intuitive grounds and constitutes no necessary attribute of a Lorenz curve.

---

5 In particular, integration of (3) does not require any inconvenient recourse to the Beta distribution, as do both the specifications (1) and (2). See Kakwani and Podder (1976) and Rasche et al. (1980).

Of the many conceivable interpolation schemes, we will consider only the quadratic spline function since with this representation differentiability, monotonicity and convexity are particularly easy to control. Let p_i (i=1,...,n) be the cumulative proportions of the population for which the associated values of the Lorenz curve, y_i, are known and define the divided differences

$$d_i = (y_{i+1}-y_i)/(p_{i+1}-p_i) \qquad i=1,\dots,n-1 \quad ,$$

i.e. the slopes of the linear segments joining the known data points. Now, the quadratic spline function is[6]

$$S(p) = (p_{i+1}-p_i)^{-2}(y_i(p_{i+1}-p)^2+2a_i(p_{i+1}-p)(p-p_i)+y_{i+1}(p-p_i)^2) \qquad (4)$$

$$\text{for} \quad p_i \leq p \leq p_{i+1} \quad \text{and} \quad i=1,\dots,n-1$$

with

$$s_{i+1} = 2d_i-s_i \qquad (5.1)$$

$$a_i = y_i+s_i(p_{i+1}-p_i)/2 \quad . \qquad (5.2)$$

Note that the s_i are the the first dervatives of the quadratic spline function S(p) at the given points p_i. From (5.1) it is evident that merely s_1, the slope at the point $p_1=0$, has to be fixed in order to make S(p) unique. Passow (1977, Theorem 2) has shown that given the conditions $d_i \geq d_{i-1}$ and choosing s_1 to satisfy $0 \leq s_1 \leq 2d_1$, the spline function S(p) will be unique and, in particular, monotone. Clearly, these conditions can always be met since all the points on a Lorenz curve must satisfy $d_i \geq d_{i-1} \geq 0$ by construction. Passow furthermore proved that S(p) will be convex if the inequalities $0 \leq s_1 \leq d_1$, $s_1 \geq 2d_1-d_2$ and $d_i-2d_{i-1}+d_{i-2} \geq 0$ for i=3,...,n-1 hold. However, these conditions are not overly helpful in the search for a particular s_1 that makes S(p) convex. Also, they can be shown to be unnecessarily strong. We therefore propose using the weaker condition[7]

$$\max(0,b_2,b_4,\dots) \leq s_1 \leq \min(b_1,b_3,b_5,\dots) \qquad (5.3)$$

$$\text{with } b_1=d_1 \quad \text{and} \quad b_i=b_{i-1}-(-1)^i(d_i-d_{i-1}) \quad \text{for} \quad i=2,\dots,n-1 \quad ,$$

which in view of (5.1) follows directly from the convexity condition

---

6 It is not difficult to check that the following representation of a quadratic spline function together with the specifications (5.1) and (5.2) is indeed an interpolation and continuously differentiable.

7 I owe this condition to Wilhelm Forst.

(implying $s_{i+1} \geq s_i$) in conjunction with the monotonicity condition (requiring $s_1 \geq 0$).

The key question is whether the permissible range of s_1 according to (5.3) is empty or not, for if it is empty, there is no quadratic spline function such as (4) that is compatible with the data and convex. Non-existence may occur for two reasons. Either there is an error in the data in that they violate the natural conditions $d_i \geq d_{i-1} \geq 0$, and then there exists, of course, no convex function at all which could accomodate these incorrect data. Or the quadratic spline (4) with its one degree of freedom is too inflexible to interpolate the given data without violating the convexity requirement in some range. Both cases occured when we tried to interpolate Paukert's data by the quadratic spline. If the failure is due to inflexibility, one might think of trying higher order splines. However, that would inevitably require a much more complex effort to control for convexity and, more importantly, this approach may not work either[8]. In the few cases where (4) actually failed, we recurred instead to McAllister and Roulier's "point insertion algorithm", a much simpler and more meaningful method that solves the convexity problem by inserting, if necessary, at most one additional (variable) knot between each pair of data points. As an additional advantage, it permits (and requires) specification of the slopes s_i at the n data points[9]. When these slopes are selected, define the variable knots

$$\bar{p}_i = (s_{i+1}p_{i+1}-s_ip_i+y_i-y_{i+1})/(s_{i+1}-s_i) \tag{6.1}$$

$$\bar{y}_i = (a_i^1(p_{i+1}-\bar{p}_i)+a_i^2(\bar{p}_i-p_i))/(p_{i+1}-p_i) \tag{6.2}$$

$$\text{with} \quad a_i^1 = y_i+s_i(\bar{p}_i-p_i)/2, \quad a_i^2 = y_{i+1}+s_{i+1}(\bar{p}_i-p_{i+1})/2 \quad .$$

McAllister and Roulier's shape-preserving quadratic spline is then given by

$$S^1(p) = (\bar{p}_i-p_i)^{-2}\{y_i(\bar{p}_i-p)^2+2a_i^1(\bar{p}_i-p)(p-p_i)+\bar{y}_i(p-p_i)^2\} \tag{7.1}$$

---

8 First of all, one may encounter data which are incompatible with a convex cubic spline even though a convex quadratic spline exists. More importantly, one may in fact construct convex data which require the shape-preserving spline to have an arbitrarily high degree. See McAllister and Roulier (1981).

9 Such information is, at times, available. When it is not, as we assume here, the slopes may be chosen more or less aribtrarily as long as they meet the natural conditions $0 \leq s_1 \leq d_1$, $d_1 \leq s_2 \leq d_2, \ldots, d_{n-1} \leq s_n \leq \infty$. However, whenever $d_i = d_{i+1}$, the Lorenz curve is necessarily linear over the corresponding interval (p_i, p_{i+2}), i.e. $S(p) = y_i + d_i(p-p_i)$ for $p_i \leq p \leq p_{i+2}$. In this case, the slopes at the two endpoints of the linear segment must be identical so that $s_i = s_{i+2} = d_i$ has to be chosen.

for $p_i \leq p \leq \bar{p}_i$,

$$S^2(p) = (p_{i+1}-\bar{p}_i)^{-2}(\bar{y}_i(p_{i+1}-p)^2+2a_i^2(p_{i+1}-p)(p-\bar{p}_i)+y_{i+1}(p-\bar{p}_i)^2) \quad (7.2)$$

for $\bar{p}_i \leq p \leq p_{i+1}$.

It is easy to check that (7) indeed interpolates the data points, observes the specified slopes, and is convex if the data are.

3. Bracketing the Lorenz Curve by Upper and Lower Bounds

Interpolating the known points on the Lorenz curve rather than fitting some simple specification such as (1) through (3) has the obvious advantage that at least the given points will be exactly hit. Yet even the interpolation form, like these simpler specifications, arbitrarily forces some specific curvature (and smoothness) on the Lorenz curve which may or may not come close to the unknown truth. Rather than relying on such a degree of arbitrariness, one may wish to extract from the known data points only that information about the Lorenz curve that can safely be trusted. This may appear to be a modest intention, but as will be demonstrated below, the resulting information is rather precise and very useful when checking the reliability of the other approaches.

Gastwirth (1972) has extensively described how to determine upper and lower bounds for the Lorenz curve, and even though his method is not entirely applicable to our problem, since we do not assume, as he does, to know the slopes of the Lorenz curve in addition to its ordinate values y_i at the n given points p_i, we will merely briefly outline the method. Consider the following figure where n=4 is assumed. Given the four points (y_i,p_i), it is obvious that the true Lorenz curve must lie somewhere inside the shaded band. This construct relies on the assumption

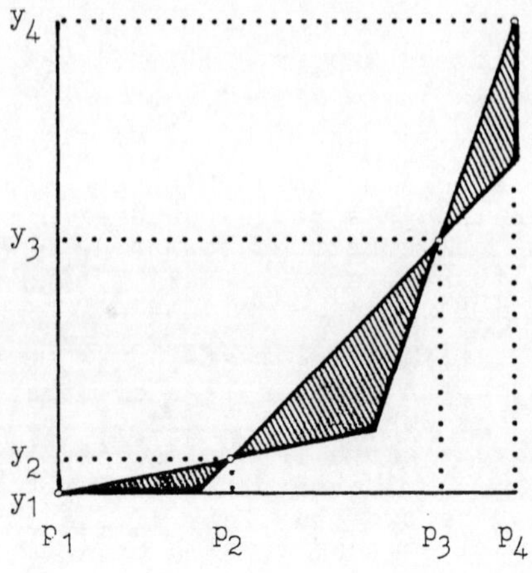

that individual incomes are non-negative and finite, and it only uses the property that units in each interval (p_i, p_{i+1}) earn at least the average income of the previous interval and at most the average income of the following interval. Normally, more than just two inner points of the Lorenz curve will be given and then the associated band will, of course, be substantially narrower and the sharpness of the bounds improve accordingly.

4. The Performance of the Three Approaches

To reach a judgement on the reliability of the three methods outlined in the previous sections, we used Paukert's data for a sample of 56 countries in which, because of an obvious data error, the data for South Africa were replaced by comparable data from Jain (1975).

Consider first the curve fitting method. In view of the fact that Paukert's data encompass just five inner points on each Lorenz curve to which our two- or three-parameter specifications have to be fitted[10], it may come as a surprise that even in terms of goodness of fit all three specifications perform poorly. The Rasche et al. specification (2) with its two parameters clearly gives the worst fit. Calculated on the basis of the entire 56-country sample, it misses the given Lorenz curve points on an average by .0086 and thus almost by a full percentage point. In relative terms, this amounts at times to enormous errors[11]. The Kakwani and Podder specification (1) and the alternative specification proposed in (3), which both have three parameters, give a somewhat better fit in that they miss on an average by only half as much as the Rasche et al. specification. In relative terms this is often still too much. One could now argue that when it comes to extract summary distribution measures these errors tend to cancel out. While this indeed seems to be the case for global measures that rely on the shape and position of the Lorenz curve over its entire range[12], this argument is certainly not

---

10 All three specifications meet the two endpoints (0,0) and (1,1) by construction.

11 In the cases of Morocco and Tunisia, for example, the Rasche et al. specification underestimates the share of the first quintile by 65 and 68 percent, respectively.

12 For instance, all estimates of the Gini concentration ratio based on the specifications (1) and (3) remained within the theoretical bounds suggested by Paukert's data. Only those derived on the basis of the Rasche et al. specification (2) failed twice, namely with respect to Morocco and Tunisia again. It should be noted that the calculation of upper and lower bounds for e.g. the Gini coefficient compatible with the given data is somewhat more involved than the simple construction of the band depicted in the figure. The lower bound is clearly given by the Gini coefficient associated with the linear connection of the given data

valid for supplementary measures such as Lorenz coefficients that may refer to smaller sections of the Lorenz curve. Here the estimates based on the fitted specifications (1) through (3) fell too often outside the range suggested by the theoretical bounds to be of any practical use.

Consider then the method of interpolating the Lorenz curve by a convex quadratic spline function. Goodness of fit is no issue, as the function will meet the given data points by construction. Furthermore, with regard to the resulting Gini concentration ratio or Lorenz coefficients estimates, this approach performs excellently since in all our calculations we did not find a single case where the estimate based on spline interpolation fell outside the range suggested by the associated theoretical upper and lower bounds.

Consider finally the method of calculating upper and lower bounds for either the Lorenz curve or associated distribution measures using parts of or the entire Lorenz curve. Unfortunately, the available data often will not, and in the case of Paukert's data, in fact do not come in a form that permits use of Gastwirth's approach to deriving upper and lower bounds for the Lorenz curve. When only cumulative income shares rather than maximum and minimum incomes for each income group are known, only the weak Lorenz curve property can be used, according to which the incomes within each group cannot be smaller than the previous group's average nor larger than the average of the following group. As a consequence, the resulting bounds are often not very sharp as is indicated by ranges that amounted on the average to about five per cent, however, at times to as much as 30 per cent of the associated lower bound. Nevertheless, these bounds were in numerous cases sharp enough to discredit the estimates on the basis of the curve fitting method as unreliable. At any rate, if they are not very sharp, rather than pretending to be precise, they reveal the lack of precision that goes along with the given data.

5. Summary

We have discussed three different ways ways of retrieving the entire Lorenz curve from a few given points, i.e. the curve fitting method, interpolation by a convex quadratic spline, and calculation of upper and lower bounds, which rests on the intrinsic properties of the Lorenz

points and thus easily derived. The upper bound, however, involves finding the piecewise linear and convex Lorenz curve that hits the data points and minimizes the area below subject to the constraint that incomes are non-negative and finite. While the procedure is straightforward, the calculatory details are too tedious to be given here.

curve. In applying these three methods to Paukert's data, it turned out that curve fitting in general and the Rasche et al. specification (2) in particular, are too unreliable to warrant practical application. Both from the computational effort involved and particularly from its impeccable performance in terms of staying within the theoretical bounds, the use of an interpolating convex quadratic spline function proved to be clearly preferable. This approach, however, still suffers from an important defect: the precision of the spline interpolation is more apparent than real since it is inevitably the result of an arbitrary selection of a specific functional form, the choice of which is guided by mathematical simplicity rather than by facts. The most dependable method thus appears to consist of calculating the upper and lower bounds for this alone guarantees that not more information is extracted from the given data than what they actually contain.

In practical application, however, one may often be willing to sacrifice at least some of the reliability for practicability and accordingly one may prefer to work with reasonable point estimates rather than with reliable but unwieldy bounds. The midpoint of the range spanned by the bounds would then constitute a possible candidate for such a point estimate and, indeed, a rather likely one. Suppose this midpoint is actually chosen. It would then make little difference whether one uses these point estimates or the computationally much simpler estimates from the spline interpolation, because in all of the calculations we made, an almost perfect correlation between these two was found.

References

Fortune, J. N., "Income Distribution and Linder's Thesis", Southern Economic Journal, Vol. 46 (1979), 158-167.

Gastwirth, J. L., "The Estimation of the Lorenz Curve and Gini Index", Review of Economics and Statistics, Vol. 54 (1972), 306-316.

Hagerbaumer, J. B., "The Gini Concentration Ratio and the Minor Concentration Ratio: A Two-Parameter Index of Inequality", Review of Economics and Statistics, Vol. 59 (1977), 377-379.

Jain, S., Size Distribution of Income, A Compilation of Data, Washington, D.C.: The World Bank, 1975.

Kakwani, N., "Functional Forms for Estimating the Lorenz Curve: A Reply", Econometrica, Vol. 48 (1980), 1063-1064.

---, and N. Podder, "Efficient Estimation of the Lorenz Curve and Associated Inequality Measures from Grouped Observations", Econometrica, Vol. 44 (1976), 137-148.

Koo, A. Y. C., N. T. Quan, and R. Rasche, "Identification of the Lorenz Curve by Lorenz Coefficient", Weltwirtschaftliches Archiv, Band 117 (1981), 125-135.

---, ---, ---, "Identification of the Lorenz Curve by Lorenz Coefficient: A Reply", Weltwirtschaftliches Archiv, Band 119 (1983), 368-369.

McAllister, D. F., and J. A. Roulier, "An Algorithm for Computing a Shape-Preserving Osculatory Quadratic Spline", ACM Transactions on Mathematical Software, Vol. 7 (1981), 331-347.

Passow, E., "Monotone Quadratic Spline Interpolation", Journal of Approximation Theory, Vol. 19 (1977), 143-147.

Paukert, F., "Income Distribution at Different Levels of Development: A Survey of Evidence", International Labour Review, Vol. 108 (1973), 97-125.

Rasche, R. H., J. Gaffney, A. Y. C. Koo, and N. Obst, "Functional Forms for Estimating the Lorenz Curve", Econometrica, Vol. 48 (1980), 1061-1062.

Thon, D., "Lorenz Curves and Lorenz Coefficients: A Sceptical Note", Weltwirtschaftliches Archiv, Band 119 (1983), 364-367.

Axiomatizations of the Entropy Numbers Equivalent Index of Industrial Concentration*

Satya R. Chakravarty, Economic Research Unit, Indian Statistical Institute, 203 Barrackpore Trunk Road, Calcutta 700 035, India

John A. Weymark, Department of Economics, University of British Columbia, Vancouver, B.C., Canada V6T 1Y2

1. Introduction

In recent years a number of axiomatizations of the Theil (1967) index of inequality have appeared in the literature.[1] The Theil inequality index has attracted considerable attention because it can be decomposed quite simply into measures which are interpreted to be indices of intragroup and intergroup inequality for population subgroups.[2] The Theil inequality index is based upon the Shannon (1948) entropy index, a measure introduced to quantify the amount of information produced by an information source. Independently, Finkelstein and Friedberg (1967), Theil (1967), and Horowitz and Horowitz (1968) proposed that Shannon's index (or an ordinal transform of Shannon's index) be used as an index of industrial concentration. Theil (1967) observed that the Shannon entropy, interpreted as an index of concentration, satisfies a simple decomposability condition analogous to the one satisfied by the Theil inequality index.

A convenient way to normalize a concentration index is to require that if n firms have equal market shares, then the index value should be equal to the actual number of firms, n. A concentration index normalized in this fashion is known as a numbers equivalent index. Numbers equivalents are inverse measures of concentration; an increase in the value of a numbers equivalent index corresponds to a reduction in concentration. In constructing a numbers equivalent measure of

* We are indebted to the Social Sciences and Humanities Research Council of Canada for research support. During the preparation of this article, Chakravarty was a visitor to the University of British Columbia.

[1] See Foster (1983) for references to this literature.

[2] See Blackorby, Donaldson, and Auersperg (1981) for a critique of this kind of decomposition.

Measurement in Economics
ed. by W. Eichhorn

concentration we are to imagine taking the actual industry output and having it produced by firms with equal market shares. The number of such firms is chosen so that this hypothetical state of affairs is judged to be equivalent to the existing distribution of output across firms.[3] Finkelstein and Friedberg's (1967) version of the entropy index of concentration is a numbers equivalent index.

In this article we are interested in axiomatizing the entropy numbers equivalent index of concentration.[4] In Section 2 we discuss a number of properties which are regarded as being intrinsic to the concept of a numbers equivalent index of concentration. In Section 3 we analyze the decomposability properties of the entropy numbers equivalent index. In Section 4 we provide three characterizations of this index. In Section 5 we discuss possible extensions of our analysis.

2. Basic Properties of Numbers Equivalents

The number of firms in an industry is indexed by $n \in N$ where N is the set of natural numbers, $N := \{1, 2, \ldots\}$. For concreteness, we suppose that a firm's size is measured by its output; the formal analysis applies equally well to any scalar measure of a firm's performance. For a fixed $n \in N$, the set of possible output distributions is $D^n := R^n_+ \backslash \{0\}$ with typical element $x = (x_1, \ldots, x_n)$ where R^n_+ is the nonnegative orthant in Euclidean n-space. The set of all possible output distributions is $D := \bigcup_{n \in N} D^n$. In this formulation, an industry consisting of n firms can include some firms that exist but are currently producing no output.

We adopt the following notation. For any function $F : D \to R$ we denote the restriction of F to D^n by F^n. For all $n \in N$, $x \in D^n$, $|x| := \sum_{i=1}^n x_i$, the sum of the components of x; $\bar{x} := |x|/n$, the mean of x; and $\tilde{x}$ is a permutation of x such that $\tilde{x}_1 \geq \tilde{x}_2 \geq \ldots \geq \tilde{x}_n$. For all $n \in N$, $x \in D^n$, the vector of output shares is $s = (s_1, \ldots, s_n) := x/|x|$. For all $n \in N$, an n-vector of ones is denoted 1^n.

The *entropy numbers equivalent index of concentration* is $E : D \to R$ defined

---

[3] In this hypothetical state, the number of firms is not required to be an integer. See Blackorby, Donaldson, and Weymark (1982) for a discussion and critique of existing methods of operationalizing this evaluation. Typically, a numbers equivalent index is constructed by inverting a direct measure of concentration and, if necessary, normalizing the resulting index so that the index value is n when n firms produce the same level of output.

[4] Subsequent to completing the research for this article we learned that Gehrig (1983) had axiomatized the Shannon concentration index in the form used by Theil (1967) and Horowitz and Horowitz (1968). Some of our results are similar to those obtained by Gehrig.

by

$$E^n(x) := \prod_{i=1}^{n} s_i^{-s_i} \tag{2.1}$$

for all $n \in N$, $x \in D^n$, with the convention that $0^0 := 1$. This measure of concentration was introduced by Finkelstein and Friedberg (1967). The *Shannon* (1948) *entropy index* $S : D \to R$ is defined by

$$S^n(x) := -\sum_{i=1}^{n} s_i \log_2(s_i) \tag{2.2}$$

for all $n \in N$, $x \in D^n$, with the convention that $0 \cdot \log_2 0 := 0$. Independently, Theil (1967) and Horowitz and Horowitz (1968) proposed that the Shannon index be used as a measure of concentration.[5] The indices E and S are both inverse measures of concentration; an increase in the value of either of these indices is interpreted to mean that concentration has decreased. These measures are ordinally equivalent to each other as $S^n(x) = \log_2 E^n(x)$ for all $n \in N$, $x \in D^n$.

There are a number of properties which are generally regarded as being intrinsic to the concept of a numbers equivalent measure of concentration; properties which should be satisfied by any numbers equivalent index, not just the entropy index E.[6] In this section we discuss a number of such properties for an arbitrary numbers equivalent measure of concentration $C : D \to R$.

As noted in the introduction, a numbers equivalent index of concentration should be normalized so that when n firms have identical outputs, the index value is n.

Normalization : For all $n \in N$, for all scalar $\lambda > 0$, $C^n(\lambda 1^n) = n$.

A numbers equivalent index has natural bounds. The index value should be bounded below by 1, taking on this value when the industry is completely concentrated. The index value should be bounded above by the actual number of firms in the industry.

Boundedness : For all $n \in N$, for all $x \in D^n$, $1 \le C^n(x) \le n$.

---

[5] Often S^n is defined only for distributions in D^n which satisfy $|x| = 1$ or $|x| \le 1$. The use of logarithms to the base 2 has its origins in Shannon's (1948) work. Of course, changing the base in (2.2) merely results in an index proportional to S.

[6] See Blackorby, Donaldson, and Weymark (1982) and Hannah and Kay (1977) for discussions of these properties.

The third property we consider is also concerned with the cardinality properties of an index. This property requires that the value of an index be increased by a factor of m if the industry is replicated m times, what we call the Replication Principle.[7] Below we demonstrate that in the presence of a decomposability axiom, the Replication Principle is equivalent to having the index normalized.

Replication Principle : For all m, $n \in N$, for all $x \in D^n$, $C^{mn}(y) = mC^n(x)$ where $y = (x, \ldots, x)$ is an m-fold replication of x.

In this article we are concerned with measures of relative concentration. For a relative index, what matters is a firm's market share rather than the absolute value of its output. Formally, we require our measure to be homogeneous of degree zero.

Homogeneity of Degree Zero : For all $n \in N$, for all $x \in D^n$, for all scalar $\lambda > 0$, $C^n(x) = C^n(\lambda x)$.

Symmetry requires that an index of concentration should be insensitive to permutations of a given output distribution among a fixed set of firms.[8]

Symmetry : For all $n \in N$, for all $x \in D^n$, if $y = Px$ where P is a permutation matrix, then $C^n(y) = C^n(x)$.

For a fixed number of firms (population), the measurement of concentration is formally equivalent to the measurement of inequality. In the present context, a Lorenz (1905) curve for an output distribution x is a graph which shows for each $t \in [0, 1]$ the cumulative proportion of output produced by the smallest $t \cdot 100$ percent of the firms.[9] For a fixed number of firms and a fixed total output, if an output distribution x has a Lorenz curve which lies closer to the diagonal than the Lorenz curve for a distribution y, x should be regarded as exhibiting less concentration than y and should be assigned a higher numbers equivalent than y. This principle can be formalized using the concept of a majorization.

[7] The Replication Principle considered by Blackorby, Donaldson, and Weymark (1982) is different from the condition discussed here.

[8] We are implicitly assuming that the index C^n is used whenever there are n firms; i.e. we are not concerned with the actual names of the firms in the industry.

[9] See Marshall and Olkin (1979) for a formal definition of a Lorenz curve.

Definition : [Hardy, Littlewood, and Pólya (1934), Marshall and Olkin (1979)]. For all $n \in N$, for all $x, y \in D^n$, y weakly majorizes x, denoted yM_wx, if and only if $|x| = |y|$ and

$$\sum_{i=1}^{k} \tilde{x}_i \leq \sum_{i=1}^{k} \tilde{y}_i \qquad k = 1, \ldots, n-1. \tag{2.3}$$

For all $n \in N$, for all $x, y \in D^n$, y strictly majorizes x, denotes yM_sx, if and only if yM_wx and not xM_wy.

For two output distributions $x, y \in D^n$ with $|x| = |y|$, y weakly majorizes x if and only if the Lorenz curve for x lies nowhere below the Lorenz curve for y and y strictly majorizes x if and only if the Lorenz curve for x lies nowhere below and somewhere strictly above the Lorenz curve for y. In terms of majorizations, the strict Lorenz criterion can be formalized as follows.[10]

Strict Lorenz Domination : For all $n \in N$, for all $x, y \in D^n$, (i) if yM_wx, then $C^n(x) \geq C^n(y)$ and (ii) if yM_sx, then $C^n(x) > C^n(y)$.

A trivial consequence of part (i) of this principle is that strict Lorenz Domination implies Symmetry.

Lemma 1 : If an index $C : D \rightarrow R$ satisfies Strict Lorenz Domination, then it also satisfies Symmetry.

Some authors, e.g. Foster (1983), Gehrig (1983, 1984), adopt axioms which are equivalent to part (ii) of Strict Lorenz Domination. Symmetry is not implied by these weaker axioms.

The fundamental differences between indices of inequality and indices of concentration manifest themselves in how the indices rank distributions involving different numbers of individuals or firms. It is generally agreed that adding an individual with no income to a population increases inequality.[11] In contrast, adding a firm which produces no output should have no affect on the degree of concentration.

[10] This principle is equivalent to requiring, for all $n \in N$, C^n to be strictly S-concave or C^n to satisfy the strict form of the Pigou (1912) – Dalton (1920) transfers principle. See Dasgupta, Sen, and Starrett (1973) or Marshall and Olkin (1979) for a discussion.

[11] According to this criterion, the standard deviation is an unsatisfactory measure of inequality.

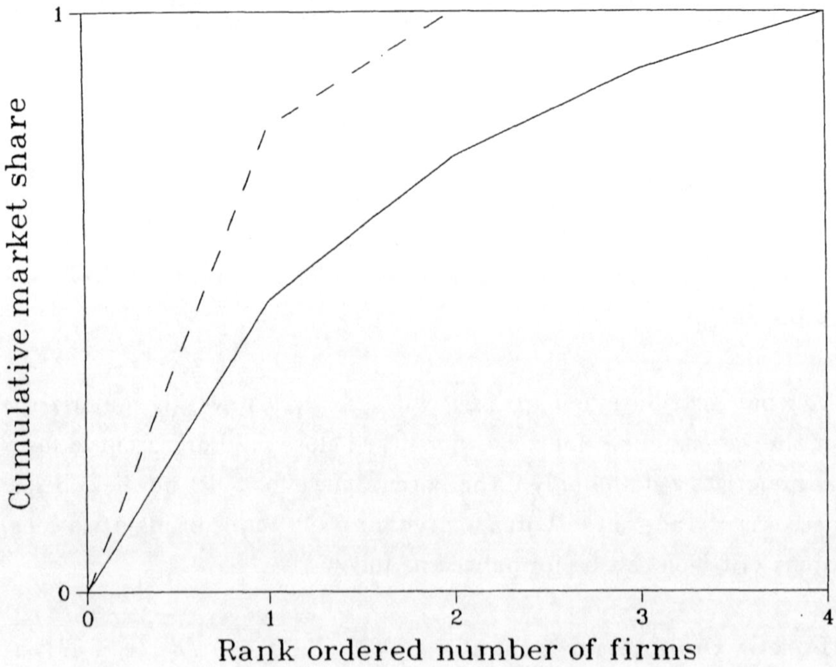

Figure 1: Concentration Curves

Zero Output Independence : For all $n \in N$, for all $x \in D^n$, $C^n(x) = C^{n+1}(0, x) = C^{n+1}(x_1, 0, x_2, \ldots, x_n) = \ldots = C^{n+1}(x, 0)$.

A concentration curve [Blair (1956)] for an output distribution x plots the cumulative market shares of output against the number of firms, with firms ranked from largest to smallest. In Figure 1 two concentration curves are depicted; the dashed line is a concentration curve for a two-firm industry and the solid line is a concentration curve for a four-firm industry. A natural extension of Strict Lorenz Domination to comparisons involving a variable number of firms is the requirement that if two distributions x and y have the same total output then (i) y is at least as concentrated as x if the concentration curve for y lies nowhere below the concentration curve for x and (ii) y is strictly more concentrated than x if the concentration curve for y lies nowhere below and somewhere strictly above the concentration curve for x.

Strict Concentration Curve Domination : For all m, $n \in N$, for all $x \in D^m$, $y \in D^n$, (i) if $y^* M_w x^*$, then $C(x) \geq C(y)$ and (ii) if $y^* M_S x^*$, then $C(x) > C(y)$ where (a) if $m = n$, $x^* = \tilde{x}$ and $y^* = \tilde{y}$, (b) if $m < n$, $x^* = (\tilde{x}, 0, \ldots, 0) \in D^n$ and $y^* = \tilde{y}$, and (c) if $m > n$, $x^* = \tilde{x}$ and $y^* = (\tilde{y}, 0, \ldots, 0) \in D^m$.

For a fixed number of firms, Strict Concentration Curve Domination is equivalent to Strict Lorenz Domination. It is straightforward to verify that Strict Lorenz Domination and Zero Output Independence are jointly equivalent to Strict Concentration Curve Domination.

Lemma 2 : [Blackorby, Donaldson, and Weymark (1982)]. An index $C : D \to R$ satisfies Strict Concentration Curve Domination if and only if it satisfies Strict Lorenz Domination and Zero Output Independence.

A common problem is obtaining accurate data on firms' outputs. It is therefore desirable that small errors in the measurement of output should have little impact on the value of a concentration index. Demanding that, for each $n \in N$, a concentration index be continuous achieves this objective.

Continuity : For all $n \in N$, C^n is a continuous function.

Combined with Zero Output Independence, Continuity also ensures that the value of a concentration index is not overly sensitive to the omission of very small firms in an industry.

3. Decomposability Axioms

It is often of interest to partition the firms in an industry into subgroups and measure the concentration within and between these groups. The entropy numbers equivalent index E has the property that it can be expressed as the product of (i) a measure of intergroup concentration and (ii) a measure of the average intragroup concentration. Specifically, the intergroup measure is the index E evaluated using the vector of subgroup total outputs and the intragroup measure is a geometric weighted average of the values obtained when the index E is applied to the output distributions of each of the subgroups, where the weight assigned to a group is the share of total output provided by that group. If there are m groups with group i containing n_i firms, the share of group i's output vector $x^i \in D^{n_i}$ in the industry output vector $x = (x^1, \ldots, x^m)$ is denoted by $s^i := |x^i|/|x|$.

Multiplicative Decomposability : For all $m \in N$ with $m \geq 2$, for all $n_1, \ldots, n_m \in N$, for all $x^i \in D^{n_i}$, $i = 1, \ldots, m$,

$$C^n(x) = C^m(|x^1|, \ldots, |x^m|) \cdot \prod_{i=1}^{m} C^{n_i}(x^i)^{s^i} \tag{3.1}$$

where $x = (x^1, \ldots, x^m)$.[12]

Corresponding to the index $C : D \to R$, we define the index $L : D \to R$ by setting

$$L^n(x) = \log_2 C^n(x) \tag{3.2}$$

for all $n \in N$ and for all $x \in D^n$. If C satisfies Multiplicative Decomposability, the analogue to (3.1) for L is

$$L^n(x) = L^m(|x^1|, \ldots, |x^m|) + \sum_{i=1}^{m} s^i L^{n_i}(x^i). \tag{3.3}$$

If L is homogeneous of degree zero, (3.3) is equivalent to

$$L^n(s) = L^m(s^1, \ldots, s^m) + \sum_{i=1}^{m} s^i L^{n_i}(\hat{s}^i) \tag{3.4}$$

where $\hat{s}^i := x^i/|x^i|$, the vector whose jth component is the share of group i's output provided by the jth firm in the group.

Theil (1967) observed that the Shannon entropy S satisfies (3.4). Gehrig (1983) used (3.4) as an axiom in his characterization of the Shannon index, applying (3.4) even if an industry subgroup produces no output. To apply (3.4) on this expanded domain, Gehrig adopts the convention that $0 \cdot L^n(0/0, \ldots, 0/0) := 0$ for all $n \in N$. By using this convention on such an expanded domain, (3.4) implies that the index L satisfies Zero Output Independence, a fact noted by Gehrig. In contrast, we do not suppose that (3.1) applies if a subgroup produces no output. As a consequence, Zero Output Independence is not implied by Multiplicative Decomposability.

[12] As defined, Multiplicative Decomposability only applies to ordered partitions of x, not to arbitrary partitions of x.

Consider replicating each of the m groups once. Adopting the Replication Principle, the numbers equivalent on the left-hand-side of (3.1) doubles. For an index satisfying (3.1) this decrease in concentration is attributed entirely to a doubling of the intergroup measure of (inverse) concentration, the first term on the right-hand-side of (3.1). There is no change in the average intragroup concentration, as measured by the weighted geometric average term in (3.1), since there are now two groups of each type with the share of each group's output in the total equal to half of the share of that type's output before the replication. For the additive decomposition shown in (3.3), such a replication also doubles the intergroup measure and leaves the intragroup measure unchanged. Unless the intragroup measure is zero, the right-hand-side of (3.3) is not doubled, leading to an inconsistency with the Replication Principle. Thus, when considering measures of concentration in their numbers equivalent form, it is appropriate to adopt the multiplicative form of decomposability in (3.1) rather than the additive form in (3.3).

In the Multiplicative Decomposability axiom, the groups in the partition need not contain the same number of firms. A weaker form of this axiom is obtained when only equal-sized partitions are considered.

Weak Multiplicative Decomposability : For all $m, n \in N$ with $m \geq 2$, for all $x^i \in D^n$, $i = 1, \ldots, m$,

$$C^{mn}(x) = C^m(|x^1|, \ldots, |x^m|) \cdot \prod_{i=1}^{m} C^n(x^i)^{s^i} \tag{3.5}$$

where $x = (x^1, \ldots, x^m)$.

In our axiomatizations of the entropy numbers equivalent index E, it is sufficient to adopt Weak Multiplicative Decomposability as one of our axioms; we do not need the full strength of Multiplicative Decomposability.

For an industry consisting of a single firm, our Normalization axiom requires that $C^1(x) = 1$ for all $x \in D^1$. By setting $n = 1$ in (3.5), we obtain the same conclusion, so Weak Multiplicative Decomposability is consistent with the Normalization axiom.

For the index L defined in (3.2), the analogue to (3.4) for Weak Multiplicative Decomposability is

$$L^{mn}(s) = L^m(s^1, \ldots, s^m) + \sum_{i=1}^{m} s^i L^n(\hat{s}^i). \tag{3.6}$$

Aczél (1984) observed that this property of the Shannon concentration index S is formally equivalent to what Aczél and Daróczy (1975) called strong additivity.

If Weak Multiplicative Decomposability is assumed, an index C is normalized if and only if it satisfies the Replication Principle.

Proposition 1 : If an index $C : D \to R$ satisfies Weak Multiplicative Decomposability, then C satisfies the Normalization axiom if and only if it satisfies the Replication Principle.

Proof : Let $y = (x, \ldots, x)$ be an m-fold replication of $x \in D^n$. From (3.5),

$$C^{mn}(y) = C^m(|x|, \ldots, |x|)C^n(x). \tag{3.7}$$

(i) If C is normalized, then $C^m(|x|, \ldots, |x|) = m$ and the Replication Principle follows from (3.7). (ii) If the Replication Principle is assumed, we have $C^{mn}(y) = mC^n(x)$. Combining this equation with (3.7) implies $C^m(|x|, \ldots, |x|) = m$ and C is normalized. ||

4. Characterization Theorems

In our axiomatizations of the entropy numbers equivalent index E, we appeal to results established in Aczél and Daróczy (1975) which involve the use of what is known as an information function.

Definition : A function $f : [0, 1] \to R$ is an information function if and only if f satisfies

$$f(1) = f(0), \tag{4.1}$$

$$f\left(\frac{1}{2}\right) = 1, \tag{4.2}$$

and

$$f(x) + (1 - x)f\left(\frac{y}{1 - x}\right) = f(y) + (1 - y)f\left(\frac{x}{1 - y}\right) \quad \text{for all } x, y \in A \tag{4.3}$$

where $A := \{(x, y) \mid x \in [0, 1), y \in [0, 1), \text{ and } x + y \leq 1\}$.

Corresponding to the index $C : D \to R$, we define a function $g : [0, 1] \to R$ by setting

$$g(t) := \log_2 C^2(1 - t,\ t) \tag{4.4}$$

for all $t \in [0, 1]$. Lemma 3 provides a set of sufficient conditions for g to be an information function.

Lemma 3 : If an index $C : D \to R$ satisfies Normalization, Symmetry, Zero Output Independence, and Weak Multiplicative Decomposability, then the function g defined in (4.4) is an information function.

Proof : That g satisfies (4.1) follows from the assumption that C satisfies Symmetry. The satisfaction of (4.2) by g is equivalent to our normalization of C^2.

The argument used to establish Proposition 2.3.3 in Aczél and Daróczy (1975) implies that for all $n \in N$ with $n \geq 3$,

$$\begin{aligned}\log_2 C^n(x) = \log_2 C^{n-1}(x_1 + x_2, x_3, \ldots, x_n) \\ + (x_1 + x_2) \log_2 C^2 \left(\frac{x_1}{x_1 + x_2}, \frac{x_2}{x_1 + x_2} \right)\end{aligned} \tag{4.5}$$

for all $x \in D^n$ such that (i) $|x| = 1$ and (ii) $x_1 + x_2 \neq 0$.[13] With these domain restrictions on x, we can apply the argument in the proof of Theorem 3.1.27 in Aczél and Daróczy (1975) with their domain restriction (3.1.30) to establish that g satisfies (4.3). ||

As noted in Section 2, intrinsic to the notion of a numbers equivalent index of concentration $C : D \to R$ is that C should be normalized and homogeneous of degree zero and should satisfy Strict Lorenz Domination (and, hence, Symmetry) and Zero Output Independence. Together with Weak Multiplicative Decomposability, these conditions uniquely characterize the entropy numbers equivalent index E.

[13] By adopting the convention that $\log_2 C^2(0/0, 0/0) := 0$ and dropping (ii), (4.5) is what Aczél and Daróczy (1975) called recursivity. With the convention that for all $n \in N$, $C^n(0, \ldots, 0) := 1$, (4.5) follows from Multiplicative Decomposability alone (but not Weak Multiplicative Decomposability) provided that the domain of applicability of Multiplicative Decomposability is expanded to permit subgroups to produce no output. Gehrig (1983) used the analogous result for (3.4) in his characterization of the Shannon index S.

Theorem 1 : An index $C : D \to R$ is the entropy numbers equivalent index of concentration E defined in (2.1) if and only if C satisfies Normalization, Homogeneity of Degree Zero, Strict Lorenz Domination, Zero Output Independence, and Weak Multiplicative Decomposability.

Proof : (i) It is straightforward to verify that E satisfies all of the properties listed in the theorem statement.

(ii) By Lemmas 1 and 3, the function g defined in (4.4) is an information function. By Strict Lorenz Domination, Zero Output Independence, and Normalization,

$$0 = g(0) = g(1) \leq g(t) \leq g\left(\frac{1}{2}\right) = 1 \tag{4.6}$$

for all $t \in [0, 1]$. Hence g is bounded. Thus by the homogeneity of C^2 and Theorem 3.3.2 in Aczél and Daróczy (1975),

$$\log_2 C^2 \equiv S^2. \tag{4.7}$$

By Lemma 3, C satisfies (4.5). Since for all $x \in D$, $x \neq (0, \ldots, 0)$, by Symmetry we can, without loss of generality, assume $x_1 \neq 0$. Since C is homogeneous of degree zero, we can then use (4.5) and the argument on the bottom of page 68 in Aczél and Daróczy (1975) to establish that for all $n \in N$, with $n \geq 2$,

$$\log_2 C^n \equiv S^n. \tag{4.8}$$

As noted above, $\log_2 C^1 \equiv S^1$, which completes the proof. ||

Lemma 2 demonstrates that Strict Concentration Curve Domination can be used instead of Strict Lorenz Domination and Zero Output Independence in Theorem 1.

Corollary 1 : An index $C : D \to R$ is the entropy numbers equivalent index of concentration E defined in (2.1) if and only if C satisfies Normalization, Homogeneity of Degree Zero, Strict Concentration Curve Domination, and Weak Multiplicative Decomposability.

While Strict Lorenz Domination appears to be a fundamental property that any numbers equivalent index should satisfy, aside from implying the index must be symmetric (Lemma 1), this condition plays only a rather minor role in the proof of Theorem 1. Theorems 2 and 3 provide alternative characterizations of the entropy numbers equivalent index which do not involve Strict Lorenz Domination as one of the axioms. In Theorem 2, Strict Lorenz Domination is replaced by Symmetry and Continuity. In Theorem 3, Strict Lorenz Domination is replaced by Symmetry and the requirement that the index be bounded.

Theorem 2 : An index $C : D \to R$ is the entropy numbers equivalent index of concentration E defined in (2.1) if and only if C satisfies Normalization, Homogeneity of Degree Zero, Symmetry, Zero Output Independence, Continuity, and Weak Multiplicative Decomposability.

Proof : The proof of Theorem 2 is identical to the proof of Theorem 1 except that continuity is used to show that g is continuous on $[0, 1]$, which by the homogeneity of C^2 and Theorem 3.2.1 in Aczél and Daróczy (1975) implies that (4.6) is satisfied. ||

Theorem 3 : An index $C : D \to R$ is the entropy numbers equivalent index of concentration E defined in (2.1) if and only if C satisfies Normalization, Homogeneity of Degree Zero, Boundedness, Symmetry, Zero Output Independence, and Weak Multiplicative Decomposability.

Proof : The proof of Theorem 3 is identical to the proof of Theorem 1 except that Boundedness directly implies that g is bounded, rather than indirectly as in the proof of Theorem 1. ||

5. Concluding Remarks

The three characterizations of the entropy numbers equivalent index E provided here are all based on axiomatizations of the Shannon entropy which involve the use of an information function. Aczél and Daróczy (1975) surveyed a number of other approaches to axiomatizing the Shannon entropy measure. Whether these alternative axiomatizations of the Shannon index can be used to provide interesting characterizations of entropy concentration indices depends on whether the axioms considered by Aczél and Daróczy (1975) have economically interesting interpretations, which at present is largely an open question.[14]

[14] Gehrig (1984) applied one of these approaches to the axiomatization of the Shannon concentration index S.

Hannah and Kay (1977) proposed a one-parameter family of numbers equivalent indices of concentration $C_\alpha : D \to R$ for $\alpha > 0$ where for all $n \in N$, all $x \in D^n$,

$$C_\alpha^n(x) := \left(\sum_{i=1}^{n} s_i^\alpha \right)^{1/(1-\alpha)}, \qquad \alpha \neq 1 \tag{5.1}$$

and

$$C_\alpha^n(x) := E^n(x), \qquad \alpha = 1. \tag{5.2}$$

When $\alpha = 2$, this index is the wellknown Herfindahl (1950) - Hirschman (1945) concentration index expressed as a numbers equivalent measure. The class of indices obtained by subjecting the Hannah-Kay measures to a logarithmic transformation are known in the information theory literature as Rényi (1961) entropies. Aczél and Daróczy (1975) considered Rényi entropies at some length. In view of the important role the Herfindahl-Hirschman index has played in the literature on measuring concentration, a worthwhile exercise would be to develop economically interesting characterizations of the Hannah-Kay class of concentration indices.

References

Aczél, J., 1984, Some recent results on information measures, a new generalization and some "real life" interpretations of the "old" and new measures, in: J. Aczél, ed., Functional Equations: History, Applications and Theory (Reidel, Dordrecht) 175–189.

Aczél, J. and Z. Daróczy, 1975, On Measures of Information and Their Characterizations (Academic Press, New York).

Blackorby, C., D. Donaldson, and M. Auersperg, 1981, A new procedure for the measurement of inequality within and among population subgroups, Canadian Journal of Economics 14, 665–685.

Blackorby, C., D. Donaldson, and J.A. Weymark, 1982, A normative approach to industrial-performance evaluation and concentration indices, European Economic Review 19, 89–121.

Blair, J.M., 1956, Statistical measures of concentration in business, Bulletin of the Oxford Institute of Statistics 18, 351–372.

Dalton, H., 1920, The measurement of inequality in incomes, Economic Journal 30, 348–361.

Dasgupta, P., A. Sen, and D. Starrett, 1973, Notes on the measurement of inequality, Journal of Economic Theory 6, 180–187.

Finkelstein, M. and R. Friedberg, 1967, The application of an entropy theory of concentration to the Clayton act, Yale Law Journal 76, 677–717.

Foster, J.E., 1983, An axiomatic characterization of the Theil measure of income inequality, Journal of Economic Theory 31, 105–121.

Gehrig, W., 1983, On a characterization of the Shannon concentration measure, Utilitas Mathematica 24, 67–85.

Gehrig, W., 1984, Two characterizations of Theil's concentration measure, in: R. Henn and D. Pallaschke, ed., Contributions to Production Theory, Natural Resources, Economic Indices and Related Topics (Verlag Anton Hain, Königstein/Ts.) 97–112.

Hannah, L. and J.A. Kay, 1977, Concentration in Modern Industry: Theory, Measurement and the U.K. Experience (Macmillan, London).

Hardy, G.H., J.E. Littlewood, and G. Pólya, 1934, Inequalities (Cambridge University Press, Cambridge).

Herfindahl, O.C., 1950, Concentration in the U.S. Steel Industry, unpublished doctoral dissertation, Columbia University, New York.

Hirschman, A.O., 1945, National Power and the Structure of Foreign Trade (University of California Press, Berkeley and Los Angeles).

Horowitz, A. and I. Horowitz, 1968, Entropy, Markov processes and competition in the brewing industry, Journal of Industrial Economics 16, 196–211.

Lorenz, M.O., 1905, Methods of measuring concentration of wealth, Journal of the American Statistical Association 9, 209–219.

Marshall, A.W. and I. Olkin, 1979, Inequalities: Theory of Majorization and Its Applications (Academic Press, New York).

Pigou, A.C., 1912, Wealth and Welfare (Macmillan, London).

Rényi, A., 1961, On measures of entropy and information, in: J. Neyman, ed., Proceedings of the Fourth Berkeley Symposium on Mathematical Statistics and Probability, Volume I (University of California Press, Berkeley and Los Angeles) 547–561.

Shannon, C.E., 1948, A mathematical theory of communication, Bell System Technical Journal 27, 379–423 and 623–656.

Theil, H., 1967, Economics and Information Theory (North-Holland, Amsterdam).

On the Decomposition of Inequality: Partitions into Nonoverlapping Sub-Groups

U. Ebert
Department of Economics
University of Bonn
D-53 Bonn 1, F.R.G.

1. Introduction*

This paper is concerned with inequality measures which are decomposable. The structure of these measures is well known. Indices which satisfy income homogeneity are decomposable if and only if they belong to the Generalized Entropy class or at least are ordinally equivalent to a member of this class (Cowell (1980), Shorrocks (1980), Cowell/Kuga (1981), Zagier (1983), Shorrocks (1984)). Thus one cannot expect any new results if one considers inequality measures which can be decomposed for every partition of the population into subgroups.

It is the objective of this paper to examine the effects of a weaker decomposition property. The measures can be decomposed for every partition of the population into two nonoverlapping subgroups, i.e., there is a poor group and a rich group. Each income of an individual who belongs to the poor group must be less than or equal to each income of an individual belonging to the rich group. In the following the structure of this class of measures will be derived.

There is no paper in literature which describes this class. Nevertheless it is known that these measures exist. Firstly, every decomposable measure fulfills the weaker decomposition property, too. Furthermore, the Gini coefficient is a member of this class. It will be proved that the indices of the Generalized Entropy class and the Gini index are the only nonoverlapping decomposable inequality measures which satisfy Dalton's principle of population and the income homogeneity as well. To

* I thank three anonymous referees for helpful comments and suggestions.

Measurement in Economics
ed. by W. Eichhorn

this extent not much new is accomplished. But if the principle of population is dropped a variety of new measures can be found as it will be shown by Theorem 3. It should be stressed that it is important to determine all these inequality measures because one often considers income brackets (and <u>not</u> the individual incomes). In that case we have a partition of the population into nonoverlapping subgroups.

In the following Section 2 the notation is defined. The properties of inequality measures which are used for a characterization are discussed in Section 3. Afterwards Section 4 will derive and present the structure of the class of all nonoverlapping decomposable inequality measures. Section 5 concludes the paper. All proofs are collected in an Appendix.

2. Notation

The size of the population or of subgroups of the population is denoted by m or n. Since we are interested in the inequality of nonoverlapping subgroups only <u>ordered</u> vectors of incomes are considered. Ω_n denotes the set of all ordered vectors of size n:

$$\Omega_n := \{x = (x_1,\dots,x_n) \in \mathbb{R}^n_+ \mid 0 \le x_1 \le \dots \le x_n\} \quad \text{for all } n \ge 1 .$$

Let $n(x)$ be the number of components of x. $\bar{x}$ denotes the average income,

i.e. $\bar{x} = \frac{1}{n(x)} \sum_{i=1}^{n(x)} x_i$. Often a subset of Ω_n plays a role:

$$\Omega^*_n := \{x \in \Omega_n \mid x_1 < \dots < x_n\}.$$

The components of $x \in \Omega^*_n$ are all distinct. Vectors of income x,y possessing an arbitrary size can be combined to a new composite vector (xy) <u>if</u> $x_{n(x)}$, the highest income of x, is less than or equal to y_1, the lowest income of y ; i.e. (xy) is an ordered vector as well. In this process of composition individual incomes may be involved; e.g. z_1 in (xz_1y). x_i, y_i, or z_k for arbitrary i, j, k <u>always</u> denote individual incomes (belonging to Ω_1 or components of vectors). Whenever in the following a composite vector (xy) is used it is understood that $x_{n(x)} \le y_1$.

Moreover we have to define inequality measures. We choose a quite general definition. Of course an inequality measure has to satisfy additional reasonable properties. These will be discussed in a moment.

<u>Definition</u>: A sequence $I = \{I_n\}_{n \ge 1}$ of functions $I_n : \Omega_n \to \mathbb{R}^1_+$ is called a measure of inequality. I_n is an index for a (sub)population of size n.

Brackets are often dropped if there can be no confusion. The same is true for the subscript n denoting the size of the population; i.e. the inequality of a composite vector (xy) is denoted by I(xy) instead of $I_{n(x)+n(y)}((xy))$. Finally the vector containing n ones is abbreviated by 1_n or 1 .

3. Basic Properties

The inequality measures discussed in this paper have to satisfy some reasonable properties. The set of attributes which characterizes the class of nonoverlapping decomposable inequality measures is introduced in this section.

Firstly, we consider the regularity conditions. The minimum requirement is the continuity of the functions I_n .

Property CONT (Continuity)

I_n is continuous for all $n \geq 1$.

This condition is rather weak, but it does not suffice for the proof proposed in the following. The indices I_n have to possess continuous first and second derivatives.

Property DIFF (Differentiability)

I_n possesses continuous first and second derivatives for all $x \in \Omega_n^*$ and $n \geq 1$.

Differentiability is not necessary for all $x \in \Omega_n$ and in fact it will not hold (e.g., the first derivatives of the Gini coefficient are not continuous for all $x \in \Omega_n$). In the proof differentiability with respect to all x_i is needed in a neighbourhood of x if the components of x are all distinct, therefore we postulate differentiability only for $x \in \Omega_n^*$.

The second property provides a normalization rule.

Property NORM (Normalization)

$I_n(x) = 0 \Leftrightarrow x = \lambda 1$ for all $\lambda > 0$, $x \in \Omega_n$, and $n \geq 1$.

It requires that an index is zero if and only if all incomes are equal. As a consequence the index is normalized, i.e. it must be zero if there is no inequality within the income distribution. Moreover the index has to be sensitive, it cannot be constant for all $x \in \Omega_n$.

Thirdly, we have to specify the decomposition property. It is a cardinal condition and identical with the property proposed by Shorrocks (1980) for arbitrary partitions of the population.

Property DECOMP (Decomposability)

There exist functions w_1 and w_2 such that

$$I(xy) = w_1((\overline{xy}),\bar{x},\bar{y},n(xy),n(x),n(y)) \cdot I(x)$$
$$+ w_2((\overline{xy}),\bar{x},\bar{y},n(xy),n(x),n(y)) \cdot I(y)$$
$$+ I(\bar{x}\, 1_{n(x)},\bar{y}\, 1_{n(y)})$$

for all $x \in \Omega_n$, $y \in \Omega_m$, such that $x_{n(x)} \le y_1$ and $n,m \ge 1$.

Consider two (nonoverlapping) subgroups. If the incomes of the first (poor) group are denoted by x, those of the second (rich) group by y, and if all incomes x_i are less than or equal to all incomes y_j, the overall inequality can be decomposed into the following two terms. One term evaluates the inequality within the subgroups, the second the inequality between these groups. Inequality within the subgroups is a weighted sum of I(x) and I(y), i.e., the respective inequality. The weights w_1 and w_2 are allowed to depend on the average income and on the size of the subgroups and of society. (It is unnecessary to include $(\overline{xy})$ and n(xy) in the arguments of w_1 and w_2, but this formulation turns out to be useful in section 4). Inequality between the groups is expressed by the term $I(\bar{x}\, 1_{n(x)},\bar{y}\, 1_{n(y)})$. Here it is supposed that each individual possesses the average income of his or her group. It is obvious how property DECOMP can be generalized to more than two nonoverlapping subgroups.

The indices considered should be invariant with respect to equal proportional changes of all incomes.

Property REL (Relative measure)

$$I_n(\lambda x) = I_n(x) \quad \text{for all } \lambda > 0,\ x \in \Omega_n, \text{ and } n \ge 1 .$$

Thus we only admit measures of relative inequality. They do not depend on the scale of income.

Finally the Pigou-Dalton principle of progressive transfers will be adopted. It belongs to the basic properties an inequality measure should satisfy (cf. e.g. Fields/Fei (1978), Eichhorn/Gehrig (1982)).

Property PT (Principle of progressive transfers)

$$I_n(y) < I_n(x)$$

for all $x,y \in \Omega_n$ such that $y_i = x_i$ for $i \ne k, l$, $k < l$,

$$y_k = x_k + \alpha, \text{ and } y_l = x_l - \alpha,\ 0 < \alpha < \min\{x_{k+1}-x_k, x_l-x_{l-1}\}, \text{ and}$$

all $n \ge 1$.

According to this principle the inequality of an income distribution is diminished if a small amount of income is redistributed from a richer to a poorer individual without affecting the ranking of incomes. The relationship between these five properties and another well known principle - namely Dalton's principle of population - will be discussed in Section 4.

4. The class of nonoverlapping decomposable inequality measures

The properties introduced above suffice to characterize the class of inequality measures which are additively decomposable for nonoverlapping subgroups. In a first step the form of the weights w_1 and w_2 is determined. We have

Proposition 1

Assume CONT, NORM, DECOMP, REL, and PT. There is a function $\theta: \mathbb{R}^1_+ \times \mathbb{N} \to \mathbb{R}^1_+$ and a positive constant β such that

$$w_1((\overline{xy}),\bar{x},\bar{y},n(xy),n(x),n(y)) = \frac{\theta(\bar{x},n(x))}{\theta((\overline{xy}),n(xy))}$$

and

$$w_2((\overline{xy}),\bar{x},\bar{y},n(xy),n(x),n(y)) = \beta^{n(x)}\cdot\frac{\theta(\bar{y},n(y))}{\theta((\overline{xy}),n(xy))}$$

for all $x \in \Omega_m$, $y \in \Omega_n$, $x_m \le y_1$, and $m,n \ge 1$.

θ is homogeneous of degree ε and unique up to the multiplication by a positive constant. $\theta(t,1)$ can be chosen arbitrarily.

The weights can be constructed by means of the function θ. They depend on the average income and the size of the respective group and on the total income and the population size. The weight of the rich group w_2 is influenced by the size of the poor group and the magnitude of a parameter β. It will be shown later that β represents a kind of social discount rate. Higher incomes have a stronger effect on inequality. In this sense an income x_i is high if there are <u>many</u> individuals j having incomes x_j less than x_i, i.e. if the rank of x_i is high. It is obvious that the normalization of θ is inessential since the weights depend on the ratio of two such functions. The inequality within a "subgroup" of <u>one</u> person equals zero. Therefore $\theta(t,1)$ can be chosen arbitrarily.

Now we introduce a new inequality measure $J = \{J_n\}_{n\ge1}$ by a modification of I_n. We consider

$$J_n(x) := \theta(\bar{x},n(x))I_n(x) \qquad \text{for all } x \in \Omega_n,\ n \ge 1 .$$

Of course J is in general not a relative measure of inequality, since it does not fulfill property REL. Nevertheless if I satisfies the properties CONT, DIFF, NORM, DECOMP, and PT then J satisfies them as well. Furthermore, if I is invariant to equal proportional change of all incomes (REL) the indices J_n are homogenous of degree ε (cf. Proposition 1).

In the next step we are able to determine the structure of the measure J exactly.

Theorem 2

Let I possess the properties CONT, DIFF, NORM, DECOMP, REL, and PT and $\theta(t,n)$ be homogeneous of degree ε.

Then there exist constants $\omega, \gamma, \delta, \rho_1, \rho_2, \ldots \in \mathbb{R}^1$ and functions $h_i : \mathbb{R}^1_+ \to \mathbb{R}^1$ such that

$$J_n(x) = \sum_{i=1}^{n} (h_i(x_i) - h_i(\bar{x})) \quad \text{for all } x \in \Omega_n,\ n \geq 1$$

where

$$h_i(t) = \beta^{i-1} h_1(t) + \omega \sum_{j=0}^{i-2} \beta^j t + \rho_i \quad \text{for all } t \geq 0,\ i \geq 2$$

and

$$h_1(t) = \begin{cases} \gamma\, t^{\varepsilon} & \text{for } \varepsilon \neq 0,1 \\ -\gamma \ln t & \text{for } \varepsilon = 0 \\ \gamma\, t \ln t + \delta t & \text{for } \varepsilon = 1 \end{cases} .$$

This theorem makes clear that the inequality measure J is an additively decomposable measure. In this respect it resembles the inequality measures belonging to the Generalized Entropy class. But there is one important difference. The indices J_n are not symmetric in the components x_i of the income vector x. In the contrary the evaluation of an income x_i depends on its position in the ordered vector x, i.e. on its rank. Moreover the relationship between the evaluation functions h_i and h_{i+1} (we have $h_{i+1}(t) = \beta\, h_i(t) + \omega t + \rho'_{i+1}$) backs up the interpretation of β given above.

Finally we obtain the following axiomatization of the class of inequality measures which are decomposable for nonoverlapping subgroups.

Theorem 3

The inequality measure $I = \{I_n\}_{n\geq 1}$ satisfies the properties CONT, DIFF, NORM, DECOMP, REL, and PT if and only if the indices I_n possess the following form (up to the multiplication by a common constant α).

$$I_n(x) = \begin{cases} \sum_{i=1}^{n} \frac{1}{\varepsilon(\varepsilon-1)} \frac{\beta^{i-1}}{\sum_{j=0}^{n-1} \beta^j} \left\{ \frac{x_i^\varepsilon}{\bar{x}^\varepsilon} - 1 \right\} & \text{for } \varepsilon \neq 0,1 \text{ and } \begin{cases} \beta \geq 1 \text{ for } \varepsilon > 1 \\ 0 < \beta \leq 1 \text{ for } \varepsilon < 1 \end{cases} \\ \sum_{i=1}^{n} \frac{\beta^{i-1}}{\sum_{j=0}^{n-1} \beta^j} \ln \frac{\bar{x}}{x_i} & \text{for } \varepsilon = 0,\ 0 < \beta \leq 1 \\ \sum_{i=1}^{n} \frac{1}{n} \frac{x_i}{\bar{x}} \ln \frac{x_i}{\bar{x}} & \text{for } \varepsilon = 1,\ \beta = 1 \\ \sum_{i=1}^{n} \frac{(\beta^{i-1} + \omega \sum_{k=0}^{i-2} \beta^k)}{\sum_{j=0}^{n-1} (\beta^j + \omega \sum_{k=0}^{j-1} \beta^k)} \left(\frac{x_i}{\bar{x}} - 1 \right) & \text{for } \varepsilon = 1,\ 1 < \beta + \omega, \text{ and } \beta > 0 \end{cases}$$

for all $x \in \Omega_n$, $n \geq 1$.

The family of measures which is characterized by the five properties proposed - namely differentiability, normalization, decomposability, relative invariance, and the strong transfer principle - is a generalization of the Generalized Entropy family. One can discriminate between different values of the parameter ε as one would expect knowing already the entropy family. Furthermore one gets new measures by choosing the parameter β different from one. If e.g. $\varepsilon > 1$ then β has to be greater or equal to one. The factor $1/(\varepsilon(\varepsilon-1))$ is positive. β^i increases with i, i.e. for higher incomes the deviation of x_i from the average income $\bar{x}$

$$\left(\frac{x_i^\varepsilon}{\bar{x}^\varepsilon} - 1 = \frac{x_i^\varepsilon - \bar{x}^\varepsilon}{\bar{x}^\varepsilon} \right)$$ is more important than for lower incomes.

Therefore β is a kind of 'social rate of discount' and the term β^i is a distributional weight. A similar interpretation can be given if $\varepsilon \leq 1$. If ε equals 1 we get a further extension in comparison with the generalized entropy class. Besides Theil's measure ($\varepsilon=1$, $\beta=1$) we obtain the Gini-coefficient ($\beta = 1$, $\omega > 0$) and a second type of measure. This is either a generalization of the Gini ($\beta > 1$, $\omega \neq 0$) or a linear discounting measure ($\beta > 1$, $\omega = 0$). It should be stressed that it is not possible to generalize Theil's measure by a factor $\beta \neq 1$. Moreover it must be noted that the normalization of all these measures is not unique. It can be changed by multiplying by a common factor $\alpha > 0$. If appropriately normalized the <u>sum</u> of Theil's measure and the Gini coefficient satisfy all properties as well.

The most important property considered in this paper is DECOMP, the decomposability of inequality measures for nonoverlapping subgroups. The consequences of this weak property of decomposition are demonstrated by Theorem 3. In a further step it is examined how DECOMP is related to Dalton's principle of population. This principle postulates that inequality is not changed if the population is replicated k-times, i.e., if for each individual having income x_i there are exactly k individuals who possess this income. Formally we have

Property DALT (Dalton's principle of population)

$$I_{n \cdot k}(x^{(k)}) = I_n(x) \quad \text{for all } k \geq 1,\ x \in \Omega_n, \text{ and } n \geq 1$$

$$\text{where } x^{(k)} = (\underbrace{x_1, \ldots, x_1}_{k}, \ldots, \underbrace{x_n, \ldots, x_n}_{k})$$

Adding this principle we get

Theorem 4

The inequality measure $I = \{I_n\}_{n \geq 1}$ satisfies the properties CONT, NORM, DIFF, DECOMP, REL, PT, and DALT if and only if the indices I_n possess the following form

$$I_n(x) = \begin{cases} \sum_{i=1}^{n} \frac{1}{n} \frac{1}{\varepsilon(\varepsilon-1)} \left[\frac{x_i^{\varepsilon}}{\bar{x}^{\varepsilon}} - 1 \right] & \text{for } \varepsilon \neq 0,1 \\ \sum_{i=1}^{n} \frac{1}{n} \ln \frac{\bar{x}}{x_i} & \text{for } \varepsilon = 0 \\ \sum_{i=1}^{n} \frac{1}{n} \frac{x_i}{\bar{x}} \ln \frac{x_i}{\bar{x}} & \text{for } \varepsilon = 1 \\ \sum_{i=1}^{n} \frac{(2i-1)}{n^2} \left(\frac{x_i}{\bar{x}} - 1\right) & \text{for } \varepsilon = 1 \end{cases}$$

Postulating the principle of population in addition we loose all measures possessing distributional weights. We are left with the Generalized Entropy class and the Gini coefficient. This result demonstrates that these two principles - decomposition into partitions with nonoverlapping subgroups and the principle of population - are quite different.

5. Conclusion

The investigations of this paper are based on the set of properties CONT,

DIFF, NORM, DECOMP, REL, and PT. Normalization NORM, income homogeneity REL, and the principle of progressive transfers PT are usual requirements for the measurement of inequality. Furthermore one cannot dispense with continuity. But one should ask oneself whether differentiability is really needed for a proof. It may be possible to drop DIFF as Shorrocks' papers (Shorrocks (1980, 1984)) suggest. The same may be true for the property of decomposition. Probably it can be weakened to a fully ordinal formulation as well. It is guessed that in both these cases the results of Theorem 3 and Theorem 4 will not be changed.

This view is supported by the results of Ebert (1987). In that paper an ordinal characterization of almost all important inequality measures is provided. Particularly an ordinal axiomatization of a part of the class of nonoverlapping decomposable inequality measures is given. It is entirely based on continuity and ordinal properties of aggregation of the underlying social welfare orderings. Thus the assumptions of this paper may be weakened by further research.

Appendix

Proof of proposition 1

A) The result for w_1 is proved by Theorem 1 in Shorrocks (1980) where symmetry is not needed for the proof. The analogous technique is applicable to the examination of w_2. Since we have no symmetry of the subgroups we obtain a function $\tau : \mathbb{R}^1_+ \times \mathbb{N} \to \mathbb{R}^1_+$ such that

$$w_2((\overline{xy}), \bar{x}, \bar{y}, n(xy), n(x), n(y)) = \frac{\tau(\bar{y}, n(y))}{\tau((\overline{xy}), n(xy))} .$$

θ and τ are unique up to the multiplication by a positive constant.

B) We consider a vector (xyz) and derive two expressions for I(xyz). In the first step we apply the property DECOMP to the vectors (xy) and z and afterwards to x and y, in the second step DECOMP is applied to x and (yz) and afterwards to y and z. Using the abbreviations

$\rho(x) := \theta(\bar{x}, n(x))$ and $\pi(x) := \tau(\bar{x}, n(x))$

we obtain

$$I(xyz) = \frac{\rho(xy)}{\rho(xyz)} \left(\frac{\rho(x)}{\rho(xy)} I(x) + \frac{\pi(y)}{\pi(xy)} I(y) + I(\bar{x}\, 1_{n(x)}, \bar{y}\, 1_{n(y)})\right.$$

$$\left. + \frac{\pi(z)}{\pi(xyz)} I(z) + I((\overline{xy})\, 1_{n(xy)}, \bar{z}\, 1_{n(z)}\right)$$

and

$$I(xyz) = \frac{\rho(x)}{\rho(xyz)} I(x) + I((x)\, 1_{n(x)},\, (\overline{yz})\, 1_{n(yz)})$$

$$+ \frac{\pi(yz)}{\pi(xyz)} \left(\frac{\rho(y)}{\rho(yz)} I(y) + \frac{\pi(z)}{\pi(yz)} I(z) + I(\bar{y}\, 1_{n(y)},\, \bar{z}\, 1_{n(z)})\right)$$

Combining these two equations we get

$$I(Y) \left\{ \frac{\rho(xy)}{\rho(xyz)} \cdot \frac{\pi(y)}{\pi(xy)} - \frac{\pi(yz)}{\pi(xyz)} \cdot \frac{\rho(y)}{\rho(yz)} \right\}$$

$$= \frac{\pi(yz)}{\pi(xyz)} I(\bar{y}\, 1_{n(y)}, \bar{z}\, 1_{n(z)}) + I(\bar{x}\, 1_{n(x)}, (\overline{yz})\, 1_{n(yz)})$$

$$- \frac{\rho(xy)}{\rho(xyz)} I(\bar{x}\, 1_{n(x)}, \bar{y}\, 1_{n(y)}) - I((\overline{xy}) 1_{n(xy)}, \bar{z}\, 1_{n(z)}) \quad .$$

A redistribution of a small amount of income within y does not change the expression within brackets and the right hand side of this equation. But because of the property PT the value of I(y) must change. Therefore we get

$$\frac{\rho(xy)}{\rho(y)} \cdot \frac{\pi(y)}{\pi(xy)} = \frac{\rho(xyz)}{\rho(yz)} \cdot \frac{\pi(yz)}{\pi(xyz)} \quad .$$

The left hand side is independent of z. This yields

$$\frac{\theta((\overline{xyz}), n(xyz))}{\tau((\overline{xyz}), n(xyz))} \cdot \frac{\tau((\overline{yz}), n(yz))}{\theta((\overline{yz}), n(yz))} = f(\bar{x}, \bar{y}, n(x), n(y)) \quad . \qquad \text{(A1)}$$

C) Now it is possible to modify y and z simultaneously without changing $(\overline{yz})$ and without affecting the left hand side of this equation. This modification means that (A1) must not depend on $\bar{y}$ and n(y). Since I fulfills REL and DECOMP the weights w_1 and w_2 satisfy

$$w_i((\overline{xy}), \bar{x}, \bar{y}, n(xy), n(x), n(y)) = w_i(\lambda(\overline{xy}), \lambda\bar{x}, \lambda\bar{y}, n(xy), n(x), n(y)), \; i=1,2.$$

This fact implies that (A1) is independent of $\bar{x}$. So we have

$$\frac{\pi(yz)}{\pi(xyz)} = g(n(x)) \frac{\rho(yz)}{\rho(xyz)} \quad .$$

From

$$\frac{\pi(z)}{\pi(xyz)} = \frac{\pi(yz)}{\pi(xyz)} \cdot \frac{\pi(z)}{\pi(yz)}$$

it follows that

$$g(n(x) + n(y)) = g(n(x)) \cdot g(n(y))$$

and

$$g(n(x)) = g(1)^{n(x)} \quad .$$

This yields $w_2 = \beta^{n(x)} w_1$ where $\beta > 0$ because of NORM and PT.

D) Choose any $m,n \in \mathbb{N}$ satisfying $1 < m < n$. Because of the properties DECOMP and REL we get

$$\frac{\theta(r,m)}{\theta(s,n)} = \frac{\theta(\lambda r,m)}{\theta(\lambda s,n)} \quad \text{for all } \lambda > 0 \text{ and } r < s.$$

Setting $r := 1$ and rearranging this equation we obtain

$$\theta(\lambda s,n) = \frac{1}{\theta(1,m)} \cdot \theta(s,n) \cdot \theta(\lambda,m) \quad .$$

For fixed m and n this is a Pexider's equation. Its solution must have the form (cf. Aczel (1966), p. 144).

$$\theta(t,m) = \alpha_m \cdot t^{\varepsilon}$$

Q.E.D.

Proof of Theorem 2

A) In a first step we use DECOMP and DIFF. Assume $n \geq 3$ and $x \in \Omega_n^*$. Applying DECOMP to the partitions of x into x_1 and $(x_2,\ldots,x_n)$ and into $(x_1,\ldots,x_{n-1})$ and x_n we obtain

$$J_n(x) = J_1(x_1) + \beta J_{n-1}(x_2,\ldots,x_n) + J_n(x_1,(\overline{x_2,\ldots,x_n})1) =: A_n \qquad (A2)$$

$$= J_{n-1}(x_1,\ldots,x_{n-1}) + \beta^{n-1} J_1(x_n) + J_n((\overline{x_1,\ldots,x_{n-1}})1,x_n) =: B_n$$

From the differentiability DIFF it follows that

$$\frac{\partial}{\partial x_n} \frac{\partial}{\partial x_1} A_n = \frac{\partial}{\partial x_1} \frac{\partial}{\partial x_n} B_n \quad ,$$

i.e., there exist two functions a_n and b_n such that

$$a_n(x_1, \frac{x_2+\ldots+x_n}{n-1}) = b_n(\frac{x_1+\ldots+x_{n-1}}{n-1},x_n)$$

This identity implies ($n \geq 3$!)

$$b_n(r,s) = b_n(r - \frac{\lambda}{n-1}, s + \lambda) \qquad \text{for } \lambda \geq 0,\ r \leq s$$

and $$\frac{\partial}{\partial x_n} \frac{\partial}{\partial x_1} A_n = b_n(0,\sum_{i=1}^{n} x_i) \quad .$$

Integrating twice we get functions f_n, g_n and ψ_n such that

$$J_n(x) = f_n(x_1,\ldots,x_{n-1}) + g_n(x_2,\ldots,x_n) - \psi_n(\bar{x}) \quad . \tag{A3}$$

B) For the moment we consider the case of $n = 3$. We define $K_n(x) := J_n(x) + \psi_n(\bar{x})$. Here we have by DECOMP

$$K_3(x) - \psi_3(\bar{x}) = J_3(x) = J_1(x_1) + \beta J_2(x_2,x_3) + J_3(x_1(\overline{x_2,x_3})1)$$

$$= \beta J_2(x_2,x_3) + K_3(x_1(\overline{x_2,x_3})1) - \psi_3(\bar{x}) \quad ,$$

and therefore

$$\beta J_2(x_2,x_3) = K_3(x_1,x_2,x_3) - K_3(x_1(\overline{x_2,x_3})1)$$

This implies

$$K_3(x) = h_1(x_1) + \tilde{h}_2(x_2,x_3) + \tilde{h}_3(x_1,(\overline{x_2,x_3}))$$

From (A3) it follows that $K_3(x) = f_3(x_1,x_2) + g_3(x_2,x_3)$. Thus $\tilde{h}_3$ must be independent of x_1 and we get

$$K_3(x) = h_1(x_1) + \hat{h}_2(x_2,x_3).$$

By considering the equation $J_3(x) = J_2(x_1,x_2) + \beta^2 J_1(x_3) + J_3((\overline{x_1,x_2})1,x_3$ we derive in the same fashion

$$K_3(x) = \hat{h}_1(x_1,x_2) + h_3(x_3) \quad .$$

Combining both decompositions of K_3 we obtain

$$K_3(x) = \sum_{i=1}^{3} h_i(x_i)$$

and since $J_3(\bar{x}1) = 0 = K_3(\bar{x}1) - \psi_3(\bar{x})$

$$J_3(x) = \sum_{i=1}^{3} (h_i(x_i) - h_i(\bar{x})). \tag{A4}$$

C) Again we consider the case of $n = 3$. Equations (A2) and (A4) imply

$$h_1(x_1) + h_2(x_2) + h_3(x_3) - \psi_3(\bar{x})$$

$$= \beta\{h_1(x_2) + h_2(x_3) - \psi_2(\overline{x_2,x_3})\}$$

$$+ h_1(x_1) + h_2(\overline{x_2,x_3}) + h_3(\overline{x_2,x_3}) - \psi_3(\bar{x}) \quad .$$

Rearranging we get

$$h_2(x_2) - \beta h_1(x_2) + h_3(x_3) - \beta h_2(x_3) =$$

$$= h_2(\overline{x_2,x_3}) + h_3(\overline{x_2,x_3}) - \beta\psi_2(\overline{x_2,x_3}) ,$$

i.e., we have a Pexider's equation

$$F(x_2) + G(x_3) = H(x_2 + x_3) .$$

According to the Corollary of Theorem 1 in Aczel (1966), p. 142, we obtain

$$F(t) = \omega \cdot t + \nu_1 , \quad G(t) = \omega \cdot t + \nu_2 ,$$

and $H(t) = \omega \cdot t + \nu_1 + \nu_2$

Therefore we deduce

$$h_2(t) - \beta h_1(t) = \omega \cdot t + \nu_1$$

and $h_3(t) - \beta h_2(t) = \omega \cdot t + \nu_2$

From this the result for h_i follows immediately.

D) J_3 can be expressed by the function $h_1(t)$. Therefore h_1 is differentiable as well and we obtain

$$\frac{\partial^2}{\partial x_1^2} J(x) = h_1''(x_1) - \frac{1}{n^2} \psi_n''(\overline{x}) = h_1''(x_1) + \alpha h_1''(\overline{x})$$

There $h_1''(t)$ is homogeneous of degree $\varepsilon - 2$. Integrating twice we get the general form of h_1.

E) Finally we have to provide a proof for $n > 3$ which is given by induction. It runs along the same lines as the proof of step B) - D) and mainly utilizes the decomposition property DECOMP.

Q.E.D.

Proof of Theorem 3

At first consider Proposition 2 and the definition of $J(x)$. Without loss of generality one can choose $\rho_i = 0$ for all $i \geq 1$. If $\varepsilon \neq 1$ we get $\omega = 0$ because of the relative invariance of $I(x)$. This property implies $\beta = 1$ for Theil's measure as well. The rest immediately follows from property PT. By the application of Theorem A.4 in Marshall/Olkin (1979) one can determine the range of β: $I_n(x)$ satisfies the Pigou-Dalton principle if and only if

$$\frac{\partial}{\partial x_i} I_n(x) \leq \frac{\partial}{\partial x_{i+1}} I_n(x)$$

for all $i = 1, \ldots, n - 1$ and $x \in \Omega_n^*$.

Q.E.D.

Proof of Theorem 4

All measures satisfying CONT, NORM, DIFF, DECOMP, and REL essentially possess the following form. There is an infinite series of constants α_i, i = 1, 2, ... and a function f such that

$$I_n(x) = \sum_{i=1}^{n} \frac{\alpha_i}{\sum_{k=1}^{n} \alpha_k} f\left(\frac{x_i}{\bar{x}}\right) .$$

The attributes of this functional form have been examined by Donaldson and Weymark (1980). They proved that the constants α_i can be expressed by $i^\delta - (i - 1)^\delta$ for some $\delta > 0$, _if_ the indices satisfy DALT in addition. From this result it follows immediately that β must equal 1.

Q.E.D.

References

Aczél, J. (1966), Lectures on Functional Equations and their Applications, Academic Press, New York.

Cowell, F.A. (1980), On the structure of additive inequality measures, Review of Economic Studies 47, 521-531.

Cowell, F.A., Kuga, D. (1981), Additivity and the entropy concept: an axiomatic approach to inequality measurement, Journal of Economic Theory 25, 131-143.

Donaldson, D., Weymark, J.A. (1980), A single-parameter generalization of the Gini Indices of inequality, Journal of Economic Theory 22, 67-86.

Ebert, U. (1987), Measurement of inequality: an attempt at unification and generalization, forthcoming in Social Choice and Welfare.

Eichhorn, W., Gehrig, W. (1982), Measurement of inequality in economics, in: B. Korte (ed.), Modern Applied Mathematics - Optimization and Operations Research, North-Holland, Amsterdam.

Fields, G., Fei, J.C.H. (1978), On inequality comparisons, Econometrica 46, 303-316.

Marshall, A.W., Olkin, I. (1979), Inequalities: Theory of Majorization and its Applications, Academic Press, New York.

Shorrocks, A.F. (1980), The class of additively decomposable inequality measures, Econometrica 48, 613-625.

Shorrocks, A.F. (1984), Inequality decomposition by population subgroups, Econometrica 52, 1369-1386.

Zagier, D. (1983), On the decomposability of the Gini coefficient and other indices of inequality, Discussion Paper 108, SFB 21, Projektgruppe "Theoretische Modelle", Universität Bonn, Bonn.

On the Shannon – Theil Concentration Measure and its Characterizations

Wilhelm Gehrig
Institut für Wirtschaftstheorie
und Operations Research der Universität Karlsruhe
Kaiserstr. 12
D-75 Karlsruhe 1

1. Introduction

The question whether a certain function is suitable to be used as a measure for the industrial concentration, is mostly answered in the following way: It is shown that the respective function satisfies certain properties that are desirable in this context. This is the usual procedure in the literature devoted to our subject. In this paper we reverse the sequence of stages in order to arrive at a senseful concentration measure. We first propose a general definition of the notion "concentration measure" which consists of a set of independent and consistent axioms and then characterize the class of functions K^n defined by

$$K^n(\underline{x}) = \gamma \cdot \sum_{i=1}^{n} x_i \log x_i \quad (\gamma>0; 0 \cdot \log 0 := 0) \tag{1.1}$$

by adding further axioms to the basic ones of the definition.
The concept of "concentration" may be very vague; the value of an axiomatic characterization is that we can take up the following position: we will use K^n (as given by (1.1) above) as a numerical measure of "concentration" if and only if our intuitive concept of "concentration" can reasonably be supposed to satisfy the axioms characterizing K^n.
We will denote (1.1) as the <u>Shannon</u> - <u>Theil</u> concentration measure; it is often also called the Shannon (see Gehrig (1983)), the Theil (see Foster (1983)) or the entropy (resp. entropy type) concentration measure (see Theil (1967), Piesch (1975) or Chakravarty and Weymark (1986)). In the appendix we give a short historical review that shall explain this variety of names for one and the same algebraic structure.
Here we only mention that K^n has its origin <u>not</u> in economics but in information theory; in fact, K^n is nothing but a negative multiple of the Shannon entropy (see Shannon (1948 a,b)), the first measure of information of general finite complete probability distributions where the $x_1,..,x_n$ are the probabilities of an experiment with outcomes

Measurement in Economics
ed. by W. Eichhorn

$A_1,\ldots,A_n$. If (1.1) is used as a measure of the industrial concentration, x_i can be interpreted as the market share of firm i.
If we want to measure the inequality of income or wealth rather than the concentration of a certain market we would not use (1.1) but a slightly modified form, namely

$$I^n(\underline{x}) = \gamma \cdot \sum_{i=1}^{n} x_i \cdot \log x_i + \log n. \tag{1.2}$$

There exist several reasons for the use of (1.2) instead of (1.1); some of them are extensively discussed in Theil (1967). The function (1.2) has been characterized by Cowell and Kuga (1981) who derive I^n out of 8 axioms. Among these axioms are some which require very strong mathematical regularity conditions, e.g. differentiability up to the third order. Such axioms, however, have no economic interpretation.

In the present paper we characterize the analogue of (1.2) for the measurement of the industrial concentration, i.e. (1.1), out of three resp. four axioms that are in the present context economically meaningful and therefore often required. Note that we do not need any additional mathematical regularity conditions.
Finally, we remark that (1.1) is often used in empirical studies of measuring industrial concentration which proves the high appreciation of K^n in the class of concentration measures (see Horowitz (1970), Buyse and Paschen (1971), or Marfels (1971,1973)).

2. Definition of Concentration Measures

A definition of the notion "concentration measure" should be given in terms of "essential" and "natural" properties, which means, roughly speaking, properties that are economically significant and independent in the sense that none of these properties is a consequence of the others. We are convinced, that the following definition satisfies these requirements:

Definition (2.1): A concentration measure is a sequence of functions

$$\{K^n \mid K^n : \Gamma^n \to \mathbb{R}\}, \Gamma^n := \{\underline{x} \in \mathbb{R}^n \mid x_i \geq 0, \sum_{j=1}^{n} x_j = 1\}$$

such that

(S) $\quad K^n(P\underline{x}) = K^n(\underline{x})$

for all permutation matrices $P \in \mathfrak{P}$[1)] and all $\underline{x} \in \Gamma^n$,

(E) $\quad K^{n+1}(\underline{x};0) = K^n(\underline{x})$

for all $\underline{x} \in \Gamma^n$,

(T) $\quad K^n(\underline{x}) > K^n(x_1,\ldots,x_i+h,\ldots,x_j-h,\ldots,x_n)$

for all $i,j\varepsilon\{1,..,n\}:x_j>x_i$, for all $h\varepsilon(0,\frac{1}{2}(x_j-x_i)]$ and for all $\underline{x}\varepsilon\Gamma^n$.

These properties are interpreted as follows:

First, the symmetry (S) reflects the principles of "equal treatment of equals" or of "horizontal equity".

Secondly, extensibility (E) states that an additional firm with zero turnover does not change concentration.

Property (T) is called the "shift-test" (see Bruckmann (1969, p.187), Giaccardi (1950, p.528) or Hall and Tideman (1967, p.164)). It states that concentration should diminish, if a firm with a higher turnover (=j) looses a certain extend (=h) to a firm with a smaller turnover (=i). In anticipation to chapter 3 we mention here, that (T), (E) and (S) imply various properties that are very meaningful in our context, such as:

(I) If a function satisfies (T), then concentration lies always between the concentration of total equality and the maximum of total inequality (i.e. if one firm has the total turnover of the market and all others nothing) (see (3.4)).

(II) According to Theil (1967, p.291) concentration should diminish if the number of firms increases while all remain of the same size; this is ensured by (T) and (E) (see (3.8)).

(III) If $\underline{x}$ and $\underline{y}$ are two vectors with the property that the Lorenz-curve of $\underline{x}$ lies inside that of $\underline{y}$, one would not hesitate ot say: "$\underline{y}$ represents more concentration than $\underline{x}$". This property follows from (T) and (S) (see (3.12)).

These are economic reasons for (T), (E) and (S). On the other hand, from the mathematical point of view, the properties (T), (E) and (S) are also well chosen since they are consistent and independent as is shown in

Theorem (2.2): Axioms (S), (E) and (T) are consistent and independent in the following sense: Any two of them can be satisfied by a function $K^n:\Gamma^n\rightarrow\mathbb{R}$ that does not fulfill the remaining axiom.

Proof: See Gehrig (1983).

3. Properties of Concentration Measures as Defined in 2.1

The first result of this section shows for symmetric functions a fundamental relationship between the shift-test (T) and the strict S-convexity [2,3].

Theorem (3.1): If, and only if, $K^n:\Gamma^n \to \mathbb{R}$ is symmetric (S) and satisfies the shift-test (T) K^n is strictly S-convex.

Proof: See Gehrig (1980, pp.50,51).

Proposition (3.2): If a function $K^n:\Gamma^n \to \mathbb{R}$ is strictly quasiconvex[5] and symmetric then it is strictly S-convex.

Proof: See Gehrig (1980, pp.52,53).

Corollary (3.3): If a function $K^n:\Gamma^n \to \mathbb{R}$ is strictly convex and symmetric then it is strictly S-convex.

Proof: A strictly convex function is strictly quasiconvex, q.e.d..

The following two results are helpful in section 4.

Theorem (3.4): If $K^n:\Gamma^n \to \mathbb{R}$ satisfies (T), then it also satisfies the "mean-value-test"

$$K^n(\frac{1}{n},\ldots,\frac{1}{n}) \leq K^n(\underline{x}) \leq \max_{P\varepsilon\mathfrak{P}} K^n(P(1,0,..,0)) \tag{3.5}$$

for all $\underline{x}\varepsilon\Gamma^n$ and all $P\varepsilon\mathfrak{P}$ with strict inequality sign if $x \neq (\frac{1}{n},\ldots,\frac{1}{n})$ or if $\underline{x}$ is not a permutation of $(1,0,..,0)$.

Proof: Let $\underline{x}\varepsilon\Gamma^n$ be arbitrary. Then

$$\underline{x} \overset{PT}{\to} \ldots\ldots \overset{PT}{\to} (\frac{1}{n},\ldots,\frac{1}{n}) \tag{3.6}$$

and

$$\underline{x} \overset{RT}{\to} \ldots\ldots \overset{RT}{\to} P(1,0,\ldots,0) \text{ for one } P\varepsilon\mathfrak{P}^{4)}, \tag{3.7}$$

where the respective sequence is empty, if either $\underline{x}=(\frac{1}{n},\ldots,\frac{1}{n})$ of $\underline{x}$ is a permutation of $(1,0,\ldots,0)$.

(3.5) follows now from (T) by (3.6) and (3.7), q.e.d..

Proposition (3.8): If $K^n:\Gamma^n \to \mathbb{R}$ satisfies (T) and (E), then the function $\psi:\mathbb{N}-\{1\}\to\mathbb{R}$, defined by

$$\psi(n) := -K^n(\frac{1}{n},\ldots,\frac{1}{n}) \qquad (n=2,3,\ldots) \tag{3.9}$$

is strictly increasing for all integers greater than one.

Proof: The extensibility (E) yields

$$K^n(\frac{1}{n},\ldots,\frac{1}{n}) = K^{n+1}(\frac{1}{n},\ldots,\frac{1}{n};0), \tag{3.10}$$

whereas (T) implies by (3.4)

$$K^{n+1}(\frac{1}{n},..,\frac{1}{n};0) > K^{n+1}(\frac{1}{n+1},\ldots,\frac{1}{n+1}). \tag{3.11}$$

Q.e.d.

Proposition (3.12): For any $\underline{x} \in \Gamma^n$, let

$$x_{(1)} \leqq x_{(2)} \leqq \ldots\ldots \leqq x_{(n)}$$

denote the components of $\underline{x}$ in increasing order, and let

$$\underline{x}\uparrow := (x_{(1)}, \ldots, x_{(n)}).$$

Let $\underline{x}, \underline{y} \in \Gamma^n$ $(\underline{x} \neq \underline{y})$ be arbitrary with

$$\sum_{i=1}^{r} x_{(i)} \geqq \sum_{i=1}^{r} y_{(i)} \qquad r=1,\ldots,n-1. \tag{3.13}$$

(3.13) is equivalent to the statement that the Lorenz-curve of $\underline{x}$ lies inside that of $\underline{y}$, briefly

$$\underline{x} \; L \; \underline{y}. \tag{3.14}$$

If K^n satisfies (T) and (S), then for all $\underline{x}, \underline{y} \in \Gamma^n$ $(\underline{x} \neq \underline{y})$ with the property (3.13) it is true that

$$K^n(\underline{y}) > K^n(x). \tag{3.15}$$

Proof: According to a well known result of Rothschild and Stiglitz (1973) condition (3.13) is equivalent with

$$\underline{y}\uparrow \overset{PT}{\rightarrow} \ldots\ldots\ldots\ldots\ldots \overset{PT}{\rightarrow} \underline{x}\uparrow \quad . \tag{3.16}$$

Since K^n satisfies (T), (3.16) implies (3.15) for $\underline{y}\uparrow$ and $\underline{x}\uparrow$. Now, (S) concludes the proof, q.e.d..

4. A First Characterization of K^n

If we want to single out one special type of concentration measure we have to add further properties to (S), (E) and (T). These additional axioms refer to a special application and must also be motivated. Especially in empirical work the question arises what type of concentration measure should be used. Clearly, the choice of one special concentration measure depends on what object the respective investigation pursues.

In this context a very important question is the following one: Which influence has the merger of firms on the concentration of the market under consideration?

We will discuss this question now in more detail: Suppose there is a market with n firms and the respective concentration $K^n(x_1,x_2,x_3,\ldots,x_n)$. Now without loss of generality, assume $x_1,x_2>0$ (in case $x_1,x_2=0$ there does not change anything) and let the first and the second firm amalgamate, so that we have a (n-1)-firm market with respective concentration $K^{n-1}(x_1+x_2,\ldots,x_n)$. It is undisputable that this fusion increases concentration, so that $K^{n-1}(x_1+x_2,x_3,\ldots,x_n) > K^n(x_1,x_2,\ldots,x_n)$, a property that is also implied by (T) and (E). On the other hand, this fusion eliminates the inner concentration between these two firms, i.e. $K^2(x_1/(x_1+x_2),x_2/(x_1+x_2))$. According to that, concentration of the new situation is equal to concentration before the merger and the intern concentration between firm 1 and firm 2 weighted with the sum of their shares (x_1+x_2), so that we have

$$\text{(F)} \qquad K^n(\underline{x}) = K^{n-1}(x_1+x_2,x_3,\ldots,x_n)+(x_1+x_2)\cdot K^2\left(\frac{x_1}{x_1+x_2},\frac{x_2}{x_1+x_2}\right) \quad (n\geq 3)$$

with the convention $0\cdot K^2(\frac{0}{0},\frac{0}{0}) := 0$.

We first note that we can omit (E) in what follows.

<u>Lemma (4.1):</u> If K^n satisfies (S) and (F), then it also satisfies (E).

<u>Proof:</u> See Aczél - Daróczy (1975, p.59).

In the proof of theorem (4.18) the function $f:[0,1]\to\mathbb{R}$ defined by

$$f(x) := K^2(x,1-x) \tag{4.2}$$

plays a certain role. Therefore we first derive some properties of f that follow from (T), (S), and (F).

<u>Lemma (4.3):</u> Let $K^n:\Gamma^n\to\mathbb{R}$ satisfy (T), (S), and (F). Then the function f as defined by (4.2) has the following properties:

(i) f satisfies the functional equation

$$f(x) + (1-x)\cdot f\left(\frac{y}{1-x}\right) = f(y) + (1-y)\cdot f\left(\frac{x}{1-y}\right) \tag{4.4}$$

for all $x,y\in[0,1)$, $x+y\in[0,1]$.

(ii) f is bounded on [0,1] with

$$f(1/2) \leq f(x) \leq \max\{f(0),f(1)\} \tag{4.5}$$

(iii) $$f(x) = f(1-x) \tag{4.6}$$

(iv) f is non-positive throughout and satisfies in addition

$$f(0) = f(1) = 0 \tag{4.7}$$

(v) f is strictly decreasing on [0,1/2] and strictly increasing on [1/2,1].

(vi) $$f \in \mathcal{C}^{\infty}([0,1]). \tag{4.8}$$

Proof:

(i) See Aczél - Daróczy (1975, p.77)

(ii) By 3.4

$$K^2(1/2),1/2) \leq K^2(x,1-x) \leq \max\{K^2(0,1),K^2(1,0)\}, \tag{4.9}$$

which means by (4.2)

$$f(1/2) \leq f(x) \leq \max\{f(0),f(1)\}. \tag{4.10}$$

(iii) An immediate consequence of (S) and (4.2).

(iv) From (R) we obtain in case n=3, setting $x_1=x_2=1/2$ and $x_3=0$

$$K^3(\tfrac{1}{2},\tfrac{1}{2},0) = K^2(1,0) + K^2(\tfrac{1}{2},\tfrac{1}{2}), \tag{4.11}$$

and by setting $x_1 = x_3 = 1/2$ and $x_2 = 0$

$$K^3(\tfrac{1}{2},0,\tfrac{1}{2}) = K^2(\tfrac{1}{2},\tfrac{1}{2}) + \tfrac{1}{2}\cdot K^2(1,0). \tag{4.12}$$

By (S), the left-hand sides of (4.11) and (4.12) are equal, and so are the right-hand sides, from where we obtain

$$K^2(1,0) = \tfrac{1}{2}\cdot K^2(1,0) \tag{4.13}$$

which is possible if and only if $K^2(1,0) = 0$. Now (iv) follows from (4.5).

(v) Direct consequence of (T) by (4.2).

(vi) From (v) we know that f is (Riemann)-integrable over every closed interval $[a,b]\subset[0,1)$. Now, let $y_0\in[0,1)$ be arbitrary, but fixed. We intergrate (4.4) over [0,b] $(0<b<1;b+y_0<1)$ in the sense of Riemann with respect to x and obtain

$$b\cdot f(y_0) = \int_0^b f(x)dx + \int_0^b (1-x)f(\tfrac{y_0}{1-x})dx - (1-y_0)\cdot\int_0^b f(\tfrac{x}{1-y_0})dx \tag{4.14}$$

From the well-known formula (see Erwe (1973, p.30))

$$\int_a^b f(x)dx = \int_{\Phi^{-1}(a)}^{\Phi^{-1}(b)} f(\Phi(t))\Phi'(t)dt \tag{4.15}$$

we obtain

$$b\cdot f(y_o) = \int_0^b f(x)dx + y_o^2 \cdot \int_{y_o}^{y_o/(1-b)} s^{-3} f(s)ds - (1-y_o)^2 \cdot \int_0^{b/(1-y_o)} f(t)\, dt. \tag{4.16}$$

The right-hand side of (4.16) is continuous in y_o (and therefore on $[0,1)$) and so is f on the left-hand side. Now, $f\in\mathcal{C}^\infty([0,1))$ follows by iteration and (4.8) by (4.6). Q.e.d..

Before we present a first characterization of K^n, we give in the class of recursive (F) and symmetric functions (S) a characterization of all functions satisfying (T).

Lemma (4.17): Let $K^n:\Gamma^n\to\mathbb{R}$ satisfy (F) and (S). Then K^n satisfies (T) if and only if $p\mapsto K^2(p,1-p)$ is strictly decreasing on $[0,1/2]$.

Proof: The "only if" part follows from (4.3) without assuming (F) or (S). As to the "if" part, we consider

$$K^n(\underline{x}) = K^{n-1}(x_1+x_2,x_3,\dots,x_n) + (x_1+x_2)K^2\left(\frac{x_1}{x_1+x_2},\frac{x_2}{x_1+x_2}\right).$$

Now, we assume without loss of generality that $0\le x_1<x_2$. We replace x_1 by $x_1+h=:x_1'$ and x_2 by $x_2-h=:x_2'$ with $h\in(0,\frac{1}{2}(x_2-x_1)]$. Then

$$x_1+x_2 = x_1'+x_2';\ \frac{1}{2} > \frac{x_1'}{x_1'+x_2'} > \frac{x_1}{x_1+x_2} \quad\text{and}\quad \frac{x_2'}{x_1'+x_2'} < \frac{x_2}{x_1+x_2}.$$

Since

$$K^2\left(\frac{x_1}{x_1+x_2},\frac{x_2}{x_1+x_2}\right) > K^2\left(\frac{x_1'}{x_1'+x_2'},\frac{x_2'}{x_1'+x_2'}\right),$$

we obtain, using (F),

$$K^n(x_1,x_2,x_3,\dots,x_n) > K^n(x_1+h,x_2-h,x_3,\dots,x_n)$$

for all $h\in(0,\frac{1}{2}(x_2-x_1)]$ $(x_2>x_1)$, i.e. K^n satisfies (T) for the pair $(i,j) = (1,2)$. The symmetry (S) then concludes the proof, q.e.d..

We are now ready to prove

Theorem (4.18): A function $K^n:\Gamma^n\to\mathbb{R}$ satisfies (T), (S) and (F) if and only if

$$K^n(\underline{x}) = \gamma\cdot\sum_{i=1}^n x_i \log x_i \tag{4.19}$$

where $\gamma>0$ is a real constant and $0\cdot\log 0 := 0$.

First Proof: That (4.19) satisfies (S) and (F) is obvious. But (4.19) also satisfies (T) since K^n is strictly S-convex (see Marshall-Olkin (1979, p.71)). This proves the "if" part.

As to the "only if" part we consider the function $\Phi:\mathbb{N}\to\mathbb{R}$ defined by

$$\Phi(n) := \begin{cases} 0 & \text{if } n=1 \\ -K^n(\frac{1}{n},\ldots,\frac{1}{n}) & \text{otherwise.} \end{cases} \tag{4.20}$$

By (F) we obtain $K^2(1,0)=0$ (see (4.13)), which means since (F) and (S) imply (E) that

$$K^n(1,0,\ldots,0) = 0 \tag{4.21}$$

From (4.21), (S) and (T) we obtain

$$K^n(\underline{x}) \begin{cases} = 0 \text{ if } \underline{x} = P(1,0,\ldots,0) \text{ for } P\varepsilon\mathcal{P} \\ < 0 \text{ otherwise.} \end{cases} \tag{4.22}$$

(4.22) says that

$$\Phi(n) \begin{cases} = 0 & \text{for } n = 1 \\ > 0 & \text{for } n \geqq 2. \end{cases} \tag{4.23}$$

But Φ satisfies in addition the inequality (see (3.8))

$$\Phi(n+1) > \Phi(n) \quad \text{for all } n\varepsilon\mathbb{N}. \tag{4.24}$$

On the other hand, it is well known that (F) and (S) yield

$$\Phi(n\cdot m) = \Phi(n) + \Phi(m) \qquad (n,m\varepsilon\mathbb{N}) \tag{4.25}$$

(see Aczél - Daróczy (1975, p.65)). From (4.24) and (4.25) we obtain (see Erdös (1946))

$$\Phi(n) = \gamma\cdot\log n \qquad (\gamma>0; n\varepsilon\mathbb{N}). \tag{4.26}$$

Using similar arguments as in Renyi (1962, p.444) it follows for all positive rationals $n\varepsilon(0,1)$ that

$$f(r) = \gamma(r\cdot\log r + (1-r)\cdot\log(1-r)), \tag{4.27}$$

from where we obtain by the regularity conditions of f

$$K^2(x,1-x) = f(x) = \gamma(x\cdot\log x + (1-x)\cdot\log(1-x)). \qquad (4.28)$$

This is (1.1) for n=2. Finally, the property (F) extends (4.28) to arbitrary n>2, q.e.d..

Second Proof: Take the functional equation

$$f(x) + (1-x)\cdot f\left(\frac{y}{1-x}\right) = f(y) + (1-y)\cdot f\left(\frac{x}{1-y}\right) \qquad (4.4)$$

and differentiate it twice, which is feasible according to

$$f\in \mathcal{C}^\infty(0,1). \qquad (4.8)$$

For details see Aczél - Daróczy (1975, pp.91-94) or Lee (1964, pp.415-418).

5. A Second Characterization of K^n

In what follows, we replace (F) by a couple of properties, namely the additivity [1)]

(A) $K^{2n}(x_1y, x_1(1-y),\dots,x_ny,x_n(1-y)) = K^n(\underline{x})+K^2(y,1-y)$

where $y\in[0,1]$

and the independence of irrelevant informations [1)]

(I) $K^n(x_1,x_2,x_3,\dots,x_n)-K^{n-1}(x_1+x_2,x_3,\dots,x_n) = H(x_1,x_2)$ (n>2),

where H is defined on the set

$$D^* := \{(x,y)\,|\,x,y\geq 0,\ x+y\leq 1\}.$$

Lemma (5.1): Let $K^n:\Gamma^n\to\mathbb{R}$ satisfy (T), (S), and (E).
Then the function H, as defined in (I), has the following properties:

(i) H satisfies (T).

(ii) H satisfies (S).

(iii) H is bounded on D^*.

(iv) $H(x,y)\begin{cases} = 0 \text{ for } x\cdot y = 0 \\ < 0 \text{ otherwise.}\end{cases}$

---

1) Notice that (I) is (F) for $H(x_1,x_2):=(x_1+x_2)\cdot K^2\left(\frac{x_1}{x_1+x_2},\frac{x_2}{x_1+x_2}\right)$. Therefore (I) is a generalization of (F). It is insofar to weak as we need an additional property in order to give a second characterization of (1.1). Such a property is given by (A).

Proof: For $x_1<x_2$ and $h\varepsilon(0,\frac{1}{2}(x_2-x_1)]$ we have in view of (T)

(i) $$H(x_1+h,x_2-h) = K^n(x_1+h,x_2-h,x_3,..,x_n)-K^{n-1}(x_1+x_2,x_3,...,x_n)$$
$$< K^n(x_1,x_2,x_3,..,x_n)-K^{n-1}(x_1+x_2,x_3,..,x_n)$$
$$= H(x_1,x_2).$$

(ii) Direct consequences of definition (2.1).

(iii) By (T), K^n and K^{n-1} are bounded on their domains, and so is H by (I).

(iv) Let $x\cdot y = 0$ (without loss of generality let $x = 0$).
Then by (E) and (S)

$$K^n(0,x_2,x_3,..,x_n) = K^{n-1}(x_2,x_3,..,x_n), \tag{5.2}$$

which implies

$$H(x,y) = 0 \qquad \text{for } x\cdot y = 0. \tag{5.3}$$

The inequality

$$H(x,y) < 0 \qquad \text{for } x\cdot y > 0 \tag{5.4}$$

is the consequence of (5.3) and (I), q.e.d..

Lemma (5.5): If K^n satisfies (S), (A) and defining

$$\Psi_y(x) := H(x\cdot y,x(1-y)) \qquad (x,y\varepsilon[0,1]), \tag{5.6}$$

then for each $x\varepsilon[0,1]$, Ψ_y is a solution of the Cauchy equation

$$\Psi_y(x_1+x_2) = \Psi_y(x_1) + \Psi_y(x_2) \tag{5.7}$$

in the domain D*.

Proof: See Forte - Daróczy (1968, pp.633,634).

Now we formulate our second main result.

Theorem (5.8): A function $K^n:\Gamma^n\to\mathbb{R}$ satisfies (T), (S), (A) and (I) if and only if K^n is of the form (4.19).

Proof: (cf. Forte - Daróczy (1968)) By (5.1), H is bounded and sign-preserving and so is Ψ_y. But then, according to (5.7),

$$\Psi_y(x) = x\cdot\Psi_y(1) \qquad (x\varepsilon[0,1]) \tag{5.9}$$

which implies by (5.6) that

$$H(x \cdot y, x \cdot (1-y)) = x \cdot H(y, 1-y) \qquad (x, y \in [0,1]). \qquad (5.10)$$

One derives that K^n satisfies (F) and now theorem (4.18) concludes the proof, q.e.d..

Appendix

In the introduction we mentioned that the mapping

$$(*) \qquad \underline{x} \mapsto \gamma \cdot \sum_{i=1}^{n} x_i \cdot \log \cdot x_i$$

is either called entropy or Shannon or Theil concentration measure. The question arises why three notations are used for one and the same algebraic structure. It can only be answered by a short historical review.

Entropy is a notion from physics. Clausius (1868) introduced it by exactly formulating the second main theorem of thermodynamics whose content was already clearly described by the french officier Carnot[6)] in 1824. (One should not confuse him with Cournot, who published his famous duopoly model 14 years later!)

Around 1880, Boltzmann, who tried to disprove the second main theorem, published his well known result $S=k \cdot \log W$, which represents the stochastic character of this theorem and now the analogy with formula (*) becomes evident.

Aczél (1984) describes different fields of research in which functions closely related to the entropy are applied.

He mentions information theory, economics, biology, ecology, psychology, detective work and political sciences.

Shannon (1948) bears the responsibility for this mutation. When he recognized that the average number of informations per signal in a code is represented by the same algebraic formula as Boltzmann's, he called this mean-value "information entropy".

Finally, Theil (1967), was the first who consequently applied formula (*) to economics.

Note: If we talk about entropy in the context of concentration measurement we always mean (*) without any relationship to the original thermodynamic content. Connections between this content and economics are described in Georgescu - Roegen (1971) and in Rifkin (1980).

List of footnotes

1) A square matrix $P=(P_{ij})$ is said to be a permutation matrix if each

row and column has one single unit and other entries are zero. We denote the set of all permutation matrices by $\mathcal{P}$.

2) An (n x x) - matrix $B=(b_{ij})$ is called <u>doubly stochastic</u> or <u>bi-stochastic</u> if

$$b_{ij} \geqq 0 \quad \text{and} \quad \sum_j b_{ij} = \sum_i b_{ij} = 1; \qquad i,j=1,\ldots,n.$$

We denote the set of all bistochastic matrices by $\mathcal{B}$. According to a theorem of Birkhoff and von Neumann (see Berge (1963, p.182)), $\mathcal{B}$ is the convex hull of $\mathcal{P}$.

3) A function $F:\Gamma^n \rightarrow \mathbb{R}$ is said to be <u>strictly S-convex</u> if

$$F(B\underline{x}) \leqq F(\underline{x})$$

for all $B \in \mathcal{B}$ and all $\underline{x} \in \Gamma^n$ with

$$F(B\underline{x}) < F(\underline{x})$$

whenever $B\underline{x}$ is <u>not</u> a permutation of $\underline{x}$. Note that the last condition is <u>not</u> equivalent to the condition that $B \notin \mathcal{B}$.

4) The notation $\underline{x}^i \overset{PT}{\rightarrow} \underline{x}^{i+1}$ means that $\underline{x}^{i+1}$ is obtained from $\underline{x}^i$ by one single <u>progressive</u> transfer.

The notation $\underline{x}^i \overset{RT}{\rightarrow} \underline{x}^{i+1}$ means that $\underline{x}^{i+1}$ is obtained from $\underline{x}^i$ by one single <u>regressive</u> transfer (i.e. a transfer from "poor" to "rich").

5) A function $F:\Gamma^n \rightarrow \mathbb{R}$ is called <u>strictly quasiconvex</u> if

$$F(\lambda\underline{x} + (1-\lambda)\underline{y}) < \max\{F(\underline{x}), F(\underline{y})\}$$

for all $\lambda \in (0,1)$ and all $\underline{x},\underline{y} \in \Gamma^n$ with $\underline{x} \neq \underline{y}$.

6) Carnot recognized that a steam engine works for the reason that one part of the system is very hot and the other part very cool.

References

J. Aczél, Some recent results on information measures, a new generalization and some "real life" interpretations of the "old" and new measures, in: J. Aczél (editor): "Functional Equations: History, Applications and Theory", D. Reidel Publ. Company, Dordrecht, Boston, Lancaster, 1984, 175-189.

J. Aczél and Z. Daróczy, "On Measures of Information and Their Characterizations", Mathematics in Science and Engineering, Vol. 115, Academic Press, New York, 1975.

C. Berge, "Topological Spaces", (English Translation, Oliver & Boyd, Edinburgh, 1963.

G. Bruckmann, Einige Bermerkungen zur statistischen Messung der Konzentration, Metrika 14, 1969, 183-213.

R. Buyse and H. Paschen, Die Konzentration in der Automobilindustrie in den Ländern der EWG, Statistische Hefte 12, 1971, 127-142 und 245-269.

S.R. Chakravarty and J.A. Weymark, Axiomatizations of the Entropy Numbers Equivalent Index of Industrial Concentration, this volume.

F.A. Cowell and K. Kuga, Additivity and the Entropy Concept: An Axiomatic Approach to Inequality Measurement, Journal of Economic Theory 25, 1981, 131-143.

P. Erdös, On the Distribution Function of Additive Functions, Ann. of. Math. 47, 1946, 1-20.

F. Erwe, "Differential- und Integralrechnung", Band 2, B.I. Hochschultaschenbücher, Bibliographisches Institut, Mannheim, Band 31, 1973.

B. Forte and Z. Daróczy, A Characterization of Shannon's Entropy. Boll. Un. Mat. Ital. [4], 1968, 631-635.

J.E. Foster, An Axiomatic Characterization of the Theil Measure of Income Inequality, Journal of Economic Theory 31, 1983, 105-121.

W. Gehrig, Zur Messung der Ungleichheit in der Wirtschaft, Inaugural Dissertation, June 1980.

W. Gehrig, On a Characterization of the Shannon Concentration Measure. Utilitas Mathematica 24, 1983, 67-85.

F. Giaccardi, Un criterio per la construzione di indici di concentrazione, Rivista Italiana di Demografia e Statistica 4, 1950, 527-538.

N. Georgescu - Roegen, "The Entropy Law and the Economic Process", Harvard University Press, Cambridge, Mass., 1971.

M. Hall and N. Tideman, Measures of Concentration, Journal of the American Statistical Association 62, 1967, 162-168.

I. Horowith, Employment Concentration in the Common Market: An Entropy Approach, Journal of the Royal Statistical Society, Series A, Vol. 133, Part 3, 1970, 463-479.

P.M. Lee, On the Axioms of Information Theory, Ann. Math. Statist. 35, 1964, 415-418.

C. Marsfels, Einige neuere Entwicklungen in der Messung der industriellen Konzentration, Metrika 17, 1971, 69-81.

C. Marsfels, Relevant Market and Concentration: The Case of the US Automobile Industry, Jahrbücher für Nationalökonomie und Statistik 187, 205-217.

A.W. Marshall and J. Olkin, "Inequalities: Theory of Majorization and Its Applications", Mathematics in Science and Engineering, Vol. 143, Academic Press, New York, 1979.

A. Renyi, "Wahrscheinlichkeitsrechnung. Mit einem Anhang über Informationstheorie", Deutscher Verlag der Wissenschaften, Berlin, 1962.

J. Rifkin, "Entropy: A New World View", The Viking Press, 1980.

M. Rothschild and J. Stiglitz, Some Further Results on the Measurement of Inequality, Journal of Economic Theory 6, 1973, 188-204.

C.E. Shannon, A Mathematical Theory of Communication, Bell System Tech. J. 27, 1948, 379-423.

C.E. Shannon, A Mathematical Theory of Communication, Bell System Tech. J. 27, 1948, 623-656.

H. Theil, "Economics and Information Theory", North Holland Publishing Company, Amsterdam, 1967.

Aggregation Issues in Inequality Measurement

Anthony F. Shorrocks

Economics Department, University of Essex,
Colchester C04 3SQ, England.

1. Introduction[1]

The elementary properties which inequality measures are usually assumed to possess admit a wide variety of specific index forms. In some circumstances, this multiplicity of potential measures does not cause any problem. For instance, if we are only interested in judging whether one distribution has more or less inequality than another, it may be the case that all the indices agree on their ranking. In most applications, however, different indices will lead to different conclusions. It is then necessary to seek criteria that will enable us to discriminate between the admissable alternatives.

One popular method of introducing further constraints on inequality measures is the explicit "ethical" link with social welfare functions developed by Kolm (1969), Atkinson (1970) and Sen (1973). But every potential inequality index can be associated with a welfare function which provides an identical ranking of any pair of distributions with a common mean and population size. So an explicit link with a social welfare function does not itself help to narrow down the choice of index.

Another way of proceeding is to consider the contexts in which inequality measures are often used, and to identify the characteristics of indices which are desirable in those circumstances. One common application of inequality measures invo-

[1] An earlier version of the paper was presented at the Fourth Karlsruhe Symposium on Measurement in Economics, and completed while I was a Visiting Fellow at the Australian National University. I am indebted to James Foster and two referees for helpful suggestions.

Measurement in Economics
ed. by W. Eichhorn

lves the relation between inequality of total income and the values obtained for population subgroups. A second type of application concerns the connection between inequality of total income and that observed for individual components of income. It is these two issues, respectively called the "subgroup aggregation issue" and the "component aggregation issue", which are the focus of attention in this paper.

For convenience, the analysis is set in the conventional context of the income inequality experienced by a population of homogenous individuals (or households) inhabiting a homogeneous environment. The paper begins with a discussion of the properties of inequality measures, and alternative ways of proceeding beyond these basic requirements. Section 3 examines the aggregation of indices across subgroups of the population, and summarises the links that have been established between aggregation relationships and the functional form of indices. Investigation of the subgroup aggregation issue leads inexorably towards the "Generalised Entropy" or "Additively Decomposable" family of inequality measures, and the analysis provided here suggests some novel and persuasive reasons for adopting these indices. In Section 4, attention is transferred to the problem of aggregating over components of income, and we again consider whether certain simple types of aggregation conditions can be used to discriminate between alternative inequality measures. Here the results are less satisfactory, and no compelling reasons emerge for concentrating on any one particular set of indices.

2. Properties of Inequality Measures

Inequality measures perform several different functions. On one level they have a purely descriptive function, capturing the degree of inequality in an appropriate way and helping to assess the significance of various contributory influences. In these applications the indices have no normative content and consequently no immediate policy relevance. In order to draw prescriptive conclusions, it is necessary to imbue the statistics with normative characteristics, by postulating a link with some representation of social objectives, commonly captured in a social welfare function.

These descriptive and prescriptive aspects of inequality values have led to different ways of approaching the construction of an inequality measure. The descriptive (or statistical) role tends to suggest an emphasis on the statistical properties of the indices, while the prescriptive (or ethical) perspective focuses on their welfare implications and policy relevance. These aspects are complementary, since "ethical" inequality measures need to have desirable "statistical" properties, just as much as "statistical" inequality measures need to be constructed with a view towards policy application. As a consequence, a large body of common ground can be developed before the statistical/ethical distinction has any relevance. This common ground covers the properties that all inequality measures may be presumed to satisfy, either because they are essential to the notion of an inequality index, or else because they are inconsequential, and hence costless to include. They will be called the "basic" properties of inequality measures. Other index characteristics may also be attractive and desirable, but their status is less compelling, and they can be discarded without abandoning the central concept of an inequality measure. These "subsidiary" properties include the points of departure between the "ethical" and "statistical" approaches.

The following notation is used in this paper. The set of all n-person (positive) income distributions is given by $\mathcal{X}_n := \{x \mid x=(x_1,\dots, x_n);\ x_i \in \mathbb{R}_{++} := (0,\infty)\}$, where x_i is the income of person i. We let $\mathcal{X} := \bigcup_{n=1}^{\infty} \mathcal{X}_n$ represent the set of all finite dimensional income distributions, and denote the mean and population size of any $x \in \mathcal{X}$ by $\mu(x)$ and $n(x)$, respectively. We will say that distribution $y \in \mathcal{X}$ is a permutation of $x \in \mathcal{X}$ if $y=\Pi x$ for some permutation matrix Π; that y is an m-replication of x if $y = (x,x,\dots,x)$ and $n(y) = m.n(x)$ for some positive integer m; and that y is obtained from x by a progressive transfer if there exist i, j such that $y_i - x_i = x_j - y_j > 0$; $y_j > x_i$; and $y_k = x_k$ for all $k \neq i,j$. Finally we will say that x is ordered if $x_{i-1} \leq x_i$ for all $i = 2,\dots, n(x)$, and use the vector $\bar{x}$ to signify the equalised version of x, defined by $n(\bar{x}) = n(x)$ and $\bar{x}_i = \mu(x)$ for all $i = 1,\dots,n(x)$.

An inequality index is normally taken to be a real valued function $I: \mathcal{X} \to \mathbb{R}$ which satisfies various conditions. The first consideration is how the index reacts to a rearrangement of some given set of incomes among different members of the population. If the individual members can be treated anonymously, as will be the case with a homogenous population, it is natural to impose the symmetry requirement:

$$I(y) = I(x) \quad \text{whenever } y \text{ is a permutation of } x. \tag{1}$$

The second consideration is how the index responds to a transfer of a fixed amount which reduces the difference between the incomes of the donor and recipient. According to the Pigou-Dalton "Principle of Transfers" any such progressive transfer must lessen the degree of inequality, so

$$I(y) < I(x) \quad \text{whenever } y \text{ is obtained from } x \text{ by a progressive transfer.} \tag{2}$$

It is this property which captures the most fundamental defining characteristic of an inequality index. If it fails to hold, it is difficult to see how the index can be a valid measure of inequality. A third requirement is the normalisation restriction

$$I(\bar{x}) = 0 \quad \text{for all } x \in \mathcal{X}, \tag{3}$$

which simply states that the index value should be zero whenever there is no income inequality. This condition has obvious appeal, and is innocuous if we accept that similar distributions generate similar inequality values, as captured by the continuity assumption

$$\text{For every } n > 0\text{: } I(x) \text{ is continuous on } \mathcal{X}_n. \tag{4}$$

This completes the list of "basic" properties, and already provides enough structure to obtain interesting results: for example, the theorem which states that if $n(x)=n(y)$ and $\mu(x)=\mu(y)$, then all inequality measures judge y to be more equal than x if and only if the Lorenz curve of y lies above that of x. But once we move away from the question of ranking distributions in very special circumstances, assumptions (1) to (4) provide little assistance. A whole host of different indices satisfy these requirements, and they will often give contradictory answers to the various questions encountered in inequality analysis. To some extent this conflict is inevitable, since an unavoidable core of subjective judgements lies at the heart of distributional issues. But practical considerations dictate that the range of inequality measures be reduced to manageable proportions, and that the normative elements be explicitly identified and understood. This is the motivation for the search for additional "subsidiary" properties, which narrow down the options, and hence assist in both theoretical and empirical applications. If this search is not undertaken, there is a tendency to continue using those measures that have been popular in the past. The index is then chosen by default, or historical accident, rather than by any assessment of its merits.

The replication invariance condition

$$I(y) = I(x) \quad \text{whenever } y \text{ is a replication of } x \tag{5}$$

is perhaps the least controversial of the "subsidiary" properties. This assumption enables comparisons to be made between populations of different sizes, or, more precisely, places some restriction on the outcome of these comparisons. Its immediate impact is modest, since statement (5) involves only exact replications of a given distribution. In conjunction with other assumptions, however, it fully constrains the way that an inequality index derived for a population with, say, n members extends to populations of a different size. The scale invariance condition

$$I(\lambda x) = I(x) \quad \text{for all } \lambda > 0 \tag{6}$$

performs a similar role, by extending the inequality comparisons to distributions with different means. This asumption is particularly useful in practical applications, since it enables us to disregard the units in which income is measured. But it also implies that inequality depends only on relative incomes, as opposed to their absolute values, and has been criticised on this score (Kolm (1976a,b)).

Note that the Lorenz curve for $x \in \mathcal{X}$ is also unchanged if all incomes are multiplied by a positive scalar, or if the distribution is replicated. Furthermore Lorenz curves are invariant to a permutation of incomes, and move towards the line of complete equality when a progressive transfer is made. So properties (1), (2), (5) and (6) are all required if the index is to provide an ordering that is identical to that given by Lorenz dominance. (See Fields and Fei (1978) and Foster (1985) for further discussion of this point.)

Although scale and replication invariance eliminate some potential indices from consideration, many still remain, and it is at this point that the "statistical" and "ethical" approaches to inequality measurement appear to diverge. The "ethical" approach pursues the relationship between inequality and social welfare, with the aim of providing inequality values with a welfare interpretation. (See, for example, Atkinson (1970), Blackorby and Donaldson (1978,1980), Blackorby *et al* (1981), Dasgupta *et al* (1973), Kolm (1969) and Sen (1973)). It may also be hoped that the welfare connection will reduce the set of admissable indices. This will be the case if the form of the social welfare function is appropriately restricted, or if inequality measures are derived from welfare functions in a particular way. Thus Atkinson (1970), for example, begins with the additive welfare function

$$W(x) = \Sigma_i \, u(x_i) \qquad u' > 0, \; u'' < 0, \tag{7}$$

and defines the inequality index

$$I(x) = 1 - \frac{x_e}{\mu(x)}, \tag{8}$$

where the "equally distributed equivalent income" x_e satisfies $W(x_e,...,x_e) = W(x)$. This construction, together with the assumption of scale invariance, leads to the single parameter Atkinson family of inequality measures.

The argument that an inequality measure should be explicitly related to a social welfare function has some force, particularly if the index is to be used to support prescriptive conclusions. It is this argument that is frequently used to justify so-called "ethical" inequality measures. However it is not the relationship between inequality and social welfare *per se* that constrains the choice of index, but rather the specific form of the welfare function, and the particular method of constructing an inequality measure from a given welfare function. These are more difficult to justify. For example, we may not necessarily wish to impose an additive structure on the social welfare function, as in (7). Nor is there any compelling reason why the inequality value should be computed from the welfare level in the way described in (8) (although it does have the advantage of allowing inequality to be interpreted as relative welfare loss). Yet it is precisely these, somewhat arbitrary, assumptions which enable the set of indices to be drastically reduced. If the statement that an $I(\cdot)$ is an "ethical" inequality index simply means that there exists a welfare function from which it may be derived, then any index satisfying assumptions (1)-(4) has "ethical" content. For the relation

$$W(x) = \mu(x)\exp[-I(x)] \tag{9}$$

provides a perfectly satisfactory way of generating a welfare function from any given inequality index, and the relation may be reversed by defining

$$I(x) = \ell n\ \mu(x) - \ell n\ x_e \tag{10}$$

where $W(x_e,\ldots,x_e) = W(x)$.[2] It follows that the "ethical" perspective itself will not help us narrow down the set of potential index forms.

An alternative approach is to consider the kinds of questions typically encountered in inequality analysis, and to see whether certain index forms have particular advantages when addressing these questions. Many of the more interesting applications of inequality measures involve an assessment of the quantitative significance of various contributory factors. It is these applications that motivate an interest in the aggregation properties of inequality indices.

3. Subgroup Aggregation

The analysis of income distributions frequently involves issues concerning the relationship between the overall inequality value and the characteristics of population subgroups. For example, we may wish to assess the degree to which total inequality is due to inequality within occupations or regions, or how much is due to differences in incomes across age or sex categories. These deceptively simple questions raise a number of conceptual and methodological problems. To begin with, the responses will typically depend on the choice of inequality measure. This particular difficulty is

[2] Note that and welfare function and inequality index pair derived in this way will be "compatible" in the sense that for all n and any $x,y \in \mathcal{X}_n$ satisfying $\mu(x)=\mu(y)$, $W(x) \geqq W(y)$ if and only if $I(x) \leqq I(y)$.

well recognised and generally unavoidable: the best that may be achieved is a set of answers corresponding to a reasonable range of inequality perceptions. Another kind of problem arises because the question posed is often ambiguous. Questions such as "How much inequality is due to income differences between males and females?" can be interpreted in various ways, and any specific index may produce several alternative answers. However, this need not be the case. The answer provided by certain forms of indices does not depend on how a given question is interpreted, and the potential confusion is therefore minimised if these inequality measures are adopted.

A third type of problem occurs even when the question is well defined and the inequality measure is selected in advance. For the results may still turn out to be nonsensical. The precise characteristics of a "sensible" answer are, to some extent, a matter of personal judgement. But certain constituents may be difficult to overlook. Consider, for instance, a population partitioned into subgroups, and suppose that a rearrangement of income within each subgroup raises the inequality level in every single group. It then seems reasonable to insist that the overall inequality value also increases, or, at the very least, does not decline. In fact any other result would appear extremely perverse. Yet this simple and sensible aggregation condition, later called the "Subgroup Consistency Axiom", is violated by a large number of inequality indices, including the Gini coefficient.[3]

One inequality measure with attractive aggregation properties is the Theil coefficient

$$I(x) = \frac{1}{n} \Sigma_i \frac{x_i}{\mu} \ell n \frac{x_i}{\mu}. \tag{11}$$

If the society is comprised of G subgroups with income distributions x^g, mean incomes $\mu_g = \mu(x^g)$ and population sizes $n_g = n(x^g)$, this index yields the exact subgroup aggregation relation

[3] For an illustration of the Gini violation, see Mookherjee and Shorrocks (1982, page 889). Other "sensible" features might include the requirement that certain factors make non-negative contributions to overall inequality. For a discussion of other aspects of inequality aggregation over subgroups see Blackorby *et al* (1981), Bourguignon (1979), Cowell (1980), Das and Parikh (1982), Ebert (1985), Kolm (1976b), Pyatt (1976) and Toyoda (1980).

$$I(x) = I(x^1,\ldots,x^G) = \Sigma_g \frac{n_g\mu_g}{n\mu} I(x^g) + I(\bar{x}^1,\ldots,\bar{x}^G). \tag{12}$$

where $n = n(x)$ and $\mu = \mu(x)$. Here the total inequality value $I(x)$ is seen to decompose into a weighted sum of the "within-group" inequality values $I(x^g)$, plus a "between-group" term which depends on the subgroup means and population sizes. A similar result holds for another index proposed by Theil (1967)

$$I(x) = \frac{1}{n} \Sigma_i [\ell n\ \mu(x) - \ell n\ x_i]. \tag{13}$$

In this case the decomposition equation is

$$I(x^1,\ldots,x^G) = \Sigma_g \frac{n_g}{n} I(x^g) + I(\bar{x}^1,\ldots,\bar{x}^G), \tag{14}$$

so the "within-group" inequality values are now weighted by the population shares, rather than the income shares found in equation (12).

The indices (11) and (13) are specific functional forms, with a limited capacity to encompass alternative inequality perceptions. However, the range of options can be extended by considering the solutions to the more general aggregation equation

$$I(x^1,\ldots,x^G) = \Sigma_g\ w_g I(x^g) + I(\bar{x}^1,\ldots,\bar{x}^G) \qquad \text{for all } x^1,\ldots,x^G \in \mathcal{X}, \tag{15}$$

where the weights w_g depend only on the set of subgroup means and sizes. Shorrocks (1980) examines this problem and shows that $I(x)$ has continuous first-order derivatives and satisfies conditions (1)-(6) and (15) if and only if it is a positive scalar multiple of an index from the family

$$E(x) = \frac{1}{nc(c-1)} \Sigma_i \left(\left(\frac{x_i}{\mu}\right)^c - 1\right) \qquad c \in \mathbb{R}. \tag{16}$$

The class of indices indicated in (16) has become known as the <u>Generalised Entropy</u> family, and includes (11) and (13) as the special cases corresponding to c=1 and c=0, respectively. (See also Cowell (1980) and Cowell and Kuga (1981). The more restrictive form of (15) given by (12) and (14) was solved by Bourguignon (1979).)

A feature shared by all the Generalised Entropy measures is the ability to provide the same answer to different interpretations of a given question. Suppose, for instance, that we are interested in the contribution made to overall inequality by inequality within subgroups. A natural response is to compute the inequality reduction which would arise if the total income of each subgroup were redistributed equally. For a two-way partition, this yields the contribution

$$C = I(x^1,x^2) - I(\bar{x}^1,\bar{x}^2). \tag{17}$$

However, another line of reasoning would calculate the contributions C_1, C_2 of inequality within each individual subgroup in a similar way, so

$$C_1 = I(x^1,x^2) - I(\bar{x}^1,x^2) \tag{18a}$$

$$C_2 = I(x^1,x^2) - I(x^1,\bar{x}^2), \tag{18b}$$

and then answer the question by summing the two components. If these two interpretations are to give consistent answers, we need to ensure that C is always the same as C_1+C_2 or, equivalently,

$$I(x^1,x^2) + I(\bar{x}^1,\bar{x}^2) = I(x^1,\bar{x}^2) + I(\bar{x}^1,x^2) \qquad \forall\ x^1,x^2 \in \mathcal{X}. \tag{19}$$

For the indices given by (16), it is easy to confirm that

$$I(x^1,\ldots,x^G) = \Sigma_g \frac{n_g}{n}\left(\frac{\mu_g}{\mu}\right)^c I(x^g) + I(\bar{x}^1,\ldots,\bar{x}^G) \tag{20}$$

and

$$C_g = \frac{n_g}{n}\left(\frac{\mu_g}{\mu}\right)^c I(x^g), \tag{21}$$

so it follows immediately that the "adding-up" condition (19) holds when Generalised Entropy indices are employed.

Generalised Entropy measures also respect changes in the subgroup inequality levels and, in this sense, ensure "sensible" answers. Imagine, for example, that we begin with the distribution x^g in subgroup g and reallocate these incomes in such a way that the new distribution y^g has the same mean and population size, but a higher inequality value. Then by (20), the overall inequality level must also rise. This implies that the Generalised Entropy indices satisfy the Subgroup Consistency Axiom:

If $n(y^g) = n(x^g)$, $\mu(y^g) = \mu(x^g)$ and $I(y^g) > I(x^g)$ for all $g=1,\ldots,G$, then

$$I(y^1,\ldots,y^G) \geqq I(x^1,\ldots,x^G). \tag{22}$$

While the Generalised Entropy Family (16) meets the demand for a flexible set of inequality measures with attractive aggregation characteristics, there remains some potential for relaxing the additive decomposition condition (15) and hence admitting other indices. There are several ways to proceed. Shorrocks (1984) replaces (15) with the more modest requirement that

$$I(x^1,x^2) = A(I(x^1),I(x^2),\mu_1,\mu_2,n_1,n_2) \qquad \text{for all } x^1,x^2 \in \mathcal{X}, \tag{23}$$

where $A(\cdot)$ is continuous in its first two arguments.[4] It is demonstrated that $I(\cdot)$ satisfies this condition and assumptions (1)-(6) if and only if it is an increasing transformation of an index drawn from the Generalised Entropy class (16). Since the distributional rankings generated by indices are invariant to positive transformations, substituting (23) for (15) does little to widen the choice of inequality measures.

Alternatively, we might wish to consider the direct consequences of the adding-up condition (19) and the Subgroup Consistency Axiom (22). If an index $I(\cdot)$ satisfies properties (1)-(4) and the adding-up condition, it turns out that $I(\cdot)$ must have the form

$$I(x) = \sum_{i=1}^{n(x)} \psi(x_i,\mu(x),n(x)) \qquad \text{for all } x \in \mathcal{X} \text{ such that } n(x) \geqq 4, \tag{24}$$

where $\psi(u,\mu,n)$ is continuous and strictly convex in u; and $\psi(\mu,\mu,n) = 0$ for all μ and n. The formal proof is lengthy and is not attempted here. It is, however, relatively easy to derive the same result in the more restrictive context of differentiable inequality measures.

Choose any population size $n \geqq 4$ and consider any distribution $x \in \mathcal{X}_n$. For any distinct positive integers $i,j \leqq n$, let the vector (x_i,x_j,x^2) be a permutation of x. Then, by symmetry (1) and the adding-up condition (19),

$$\frac{\partial I(x)}{\partial x_i} - \frac{\partial I(x)}{\partial x_j} = \operatorname*{Lt}_{\Delta\to 0} \left[\frac{I(x_i+\Delta,x_j-\Delta,x^2) - I(x_i,x_j,x^2)}{\Delta} \right]$$

---

[4] Note that $A(\cdot)$ is strictly increasing in $I(x^1)$ and $I(x^2)$ if (2) holds), so (2) and (23) imply the two group version of (22).

$$= \underset{\Delta\to 0}{\mathrm{Lt}} \left[\frac{I(x_i+\Delta, x_j-\Delta, \bar{x}^2) - I(x_i, x_j, \bar{x}^2)}{\Delta} \right]$$

$$= f(x_i, x_j, \mu(x)), \text{ say,} \tag{25}$$

since $\bar{x}^2$ depends only on x_i, x_j, $\mu(x)$ and n. From (25) we deduce

$$f(x_i, x_j, \mu(x)) + f(x_j, x_k, \mu(x)) = f(x_i, x_k, \mu(x)),$$

a Sincov equation whose solution (Aczel (1966), page 223) is given by

$$f(x_i, x_j, \mu(x)) = \phi_1(x_i, \mu(x)) - \phi_1(x_j, \mu(x)). \tag{26}$$

Defining $\phi(t,\mu) := \int_0^t \phi_1(s,\mu)ds$, $\phi_2(t,\mu) = \frac{\partial\phi(t,\mu)}{\partial\mu}$ and $J(x) = I(x) - \sum_{i=1}^{n} \phi(x_i, \mu(x))$, it follows from (25) and (26) that

$$\frac{\partial J(x)}{\partial x_i} = \frac{\partial I(x)}{\partial x_i} - \phi_1(x_i, \mu(x)) - \frac{1}{n(x)} \sum_{i=1}^{n} \phi_2(x_i, \mu(x)) = \frac{\partial J(x)}{\partial x_j} \tag{27}$$

for all $i,j \leqq n(x)$. If we now let $y(x)=(x_1,\ldots,x_{n-1},\mu(x))$ and define $H(y(x)) = J(x)$, we obtain

$$\frac{\partial J(x)}{\partial x_i} = \frac{\partial H(y)}{\partial y_i} + \frac{1}{n}\frac{\partial H(y)}{\partial y_n} \quad \text{for all } i < n; \qquad \frac{\partial J(x)}{\partial x_n} = \frac{1}{n}\frac{\partial H(y)}{\partial y_n}.$$

Hence, using (27),

$$\frac{\partial H(y)}{\partial y_i} = \frac{\partial J(x)}{\partial x_i} - \frac{\partial J(x)}{\partial x_n} = 0 \qquad \text{for all } i < n,$$

and

$$H(y) = h(y_n) = h(\mu(x)).$$

Thus

$$J(x) = I(x) - \sum_{i=1}^{n} \phi(x_i, \mu(x)) = h(\mu(x)).$$

Finally we observe that the normalisation condition (3) yields

$$h(\mu(x)) = I(\bar{x}) - \sum_{i=1}^{n} \phi(\mu(x), \mu(x)) = -n\phi(\mu(x), \mu(x)),$$

so

$$I(x) = \sum_{i=1}^{n} \psi(x_i, \mu(x)),$$

where $\psi(u,\mu) := \phi(u,\mu) - \phi(\mu,\mu)$ is continuous and strictly convex in u in order that assumptions (2) and (4) hold. Relaxing the constraints on $n(x)$ then leads to the result given in (24).

The implications of the Subgroup Consistency Axiom (22) are obtained by a rather different line of reasoning. We need only consider a two-way partition, which allows us to assume that whenever $x^1, x^2, y^1, y^2 \in \mathcal{X}$ satisfy

$$n(y^1)=n(x^1);\ n(y^2)=n(x^2);\ \mu(y^1)=\mu(x^1);\ \text{and}\ \mu(y^2)=\mu(x^2), \tag{29}$$

then

$$I(y^1) > I(x^1)\ \ \&\ \ I(y^2) > I(x^2) \ \Rightarrow\ I(y^1,y^2) \geqq I(x^1,x^2). \tag{30}$$

If $I(\cdot)$ is continuous, it must also be true that

$$I(y^1) \geqq I(x^1)\ \ \&\ \ I(y^2) \geqq I(x^2) \ \Rightarrow\ I(y^1,y^2) \geqq I(x^1,x^2),$$

and hence

$$I(y^1) = I(x^1)\ \ \&\ \ I(y^2) = I(x^2) \ \Rightarrow\ I(y^1,y^2) = I(x^1,x^2). \tag{31}$$

For any given $z \in \mathcal{X}$, let $\theta(z) := (\mu(z), n(z))$ and $\mathcal{X}(z) := \{x \in \mathcal{X} \mid \theta(x) = \theta(z)\}$. Also define $z^* := (n(z)\mu(z), 0, \ldots, 0)$ and $y(\alpha,\theta(z)) := \alpha z^* + (1-\alpha)\bar{z}$, noting that $y(\alpha,\theta(z)) \in \mathcal{X}(z)$ for all $\alpha \in [0,1)$. If $n(z) \geqq 2$, assumptions (1)-(4) imply that $h(\alpha,\theta(z)) := I(y(\alpha,\theta(z))$ is continuous and strictly increasing in $\alpha \in [0,1)$, and that $h(0,\theta(z)) = 0$. Furthermore, by assumption (2),

$$I(x) < h(1,\theta(z)) := \underset{\alpha\to 1}{\mathrm{Lt}}\ h(\alpha,\theta(z)) \qquad \text{for all } x \in \mathcal{X}(z).$$

Hence there exists $\alpha(z) \in [0,1)$ and $y(z) := y(\alpha(z),\theta(z))$ such that

$$I(z) = h(\alpha(z),\theta(z)) = I(y(z)) \tag{32}$$

and

$$\theta(y(z)) = \theta(z). \tag{33}$$

In addition, inverting $h(\alpha,\theta)$ with respect to its first argument, we obtain

$$\alpha(z) = h^{-1}(I(z),\theta(z)) \tag{34}$$

where $h^{-1}(I,\theta)$ is continuous and strictly increasing in I, and $h^{-1}(0,\theta) = 0$. Note that if $n(z) = 1$, then $z = \bar{z}$ and $I(z) = 0$. In this case, we may still assume that (32)-(34) hold, by setting $\alpha(z) = 0$ and $y(z) = y(0,\theta(z)) = z$.

Now for $g = 1,2$, consider any $x^g \in \mathcal{X}$ and define $\alpha(x^g)$ and $y^g := y(\alpha(x^g),\theta(x^g))$ as above. Then (32) and (33) ensure

$$n(y^g) = n(x^g);\ \mu(y^g) = \mu(x^g);\ \text{and } I(y^g) = I(x^g). \tag{35}$$

It follows from (29) and (31) that

$$\begin{aligned} I(x^1,x^2) &= I(y^1,y^2) = I(y(\alpha(x^1),\theta(x^1)),y(\alpha(x^2),\theta(x^2))) \\ &= H(\alpha(x^1),\theta(x^1),\alpha(x^2),\theta(x^2)) \end{aligned}$$

for some function $H(\alpha_1,\theta_1,\alpha_2,\theta_2)$ which is continuous in α_1 and α_2. Substituting for $\alpha(x^g)$ we obtain

$$\begin{aligned} I(x^1,x^2) &= H(h^{-1}(I(x^1),\theta(x^1)),\ \theta(x^1),\ h^{-1}(I(x^2),\theta(x^2)),\ \theta(x^2)) \\ &= A(I(x^1),\ \theta(x^1),\ I(x^2),\ \theta(x^2)) \\ &= A(I(x^1),\mu(x^1),n(x^1),I(x^2),\mu(x^2),n(x^2)) \end{aligned} \tag{36}$$

for all $x^1,x^2 \in \mathcal{X}$, where $A(I_1,\mu_1,n_1,I_2,\mu_2,n_2)$ is continuous in I_1 and I_2. But (36) corresponds to the aggregation condition (23), so we can apply the results of Shorrocks (1984). In particular, adding replication and scale invariance to the list of properties of $I(\cdot)$ yields

<u>Theorem 1</u> An index $I(\cdot)$ satisfies assumptions (1)-(6) and (22) if and only if for some scalar c and some continuous, increasing function $F(\cdot)$ such that $F(0) = 0$,

$$F[I(x)] = \frac{1}{n(x)}\,\frac{1}{c(c-1)}\sum_{i=1}^{n(x)}\left[\left(\frac{x_i}{\mu(x)}\right)^c - 1\right] \qquad \text{for all } x \in \mathcal{X}. \tag{37}$$

The conclusion to be drawn is that the Subgroup Consistency Axiom alone provides most of the justification for use of the Generalised Entropy indices. If an inequality measure is not a monotonic transformation of one of the Generalised Entropy family, it must either violate one of the basic properties (1)-(6), or else admit the possibility that an increase in inequality within every single subgroup leads, *ceteris paribus*, to a reduction in overall inequality. Relatively little extra is required to proceed from (37) to the entropy measures (16). The adding-up condition (19) is sufficient, since from (37) we obtain

$$F[I(x,y)] = F[I(\bar{x},y)] + F[I(x,\bar{y})] - F[I(\bar{x},\bar{y})] \qquad \text{for all } x,y \in \mathcal{X},$$

and using (19) to substitute for I(x,y) yields a Cauchy equation of the form

$$F[u+v+w] = F[u] + F[v] + F[w],$$

which has the solution $F[u] = \alpha u$ for some scalar α. We may therefore state

Corollary 1 An index $I(\cdot)$ satisfies assumptions (1)-(6), (19) and (22) if and only if $I(x) = \alpha E(x)$ for some scalar $\alpha < 0$ and some $E(x)$ satisfying (16).

It follows that the Generalised Entropy family is completely characterised by the basic properties (1)-(6) and a consistent response to both subgroup inequality movements and alternative interpretations of the contribution of subgroup inequality.

4. Component Aggregation

Another major topic of interest in inequality analysis concerns the way that different components of income contribute to the inequality of total income. For example, we may want to assess the extent to which overall inequality is due to earnings or investment income, or the extent to which it is mitigated by tax and transfer payments. We may also wish to consider how changes in average earnings or the rate of interest are likely to affect total income inequality. (See, for example, Fei *et al* (1978) and Pyatt *et al* (1980)). These questions have not been studied as much as those relating to subgroup aggregation and, as a consequence, a number of methodological problems remain unresolved. But the issues raised are similar to those discussed in the previous section: what are the general principles that should guide the contributions assigned to income components? And do these principles suggest that certain forms of inequality measures are better suited to the problem in hand?

In this section we consider a fixed population of $n \geqq 2$ individuals, and let x_i^k indicate the income of person i from source k. Then, if there are K mutually exclusive and exhaustive sources of income,

$$x := (x_1, \ldots, x_n) = \Sigma_k (x_1^k, \ldots, x_n^k) = \Sigma_k x^k.$$

where x and x^k represent the distribution of total income and the distribution of income from source k, respectively. The questions to be considered concern the relationship between total income inequality I(x) and the characteristics of the component distributions x^k, and are perhaps best discussed in the context of a specific inequality measure. The variance σ^2 provides a convenient benchmark. For this index yields the equation

$$\sigma^2(x) = \Sigma_k \operatorname{cov}(x^k, x) \tag{38}$$

and, if the x^k happen to be mutually independent,

$$\sigma^2(x) = \Sigma_k \sigma^2(x^k). \tag{39}$$

Faced with equation (39) and asked to assess the contribution S_k made to total inequality $\sigma^2(x)$ by incomes from source k, it is difficult to avoid the conclusion that

$$S_k = \sigma^2(x^k). \tag{40}$$

The obvious appeal of this assignment can be traced to its attractive properties. To begin with

$$\Sigma_k S_k = I(x), \tag{41}$$

so the contributions S_k collectively exhaust the total amount of inequality that needs to be "explained". In addition S_k corresponds to a variety of different natural interpretations that might be given to the "contribution of source k incomes". For example, we might interpret the phrase to mean: (A) the inequality due to source k incomes alone

$$S_k^A = I(x^k); \tag{42}$$

or else (B) the reduction in inequality that would result if this source of income was eliminated

$$S_k^B = I(x) - I(x-x^k). \tag{43}$$

We may also regard the contribution of x^k to be (C) the inequality that would be observed if this was the only source of income differences, and all other incomes were allocated evenly

$$S_k^C = I(x^k+\bar{x}-\bar{x}^k); \tag{44}$$

or (D) the reduction in inequality that would follow from eliminating differences in source k incomes

$$S_k^D = I(x) - I(x-x^k+\bar{x}^k). \tag{45}$$

It is easy to confirm that if $I(x) = \sigma^2(x)$ and if the x^k are uncorrelated, then

$$S_k^A = S_k^B = S_k^C = S_k^D = \sigma^2(x^k).$$

Thus, in the circumstances described, all four interpretations support the assignment rule provided by (40).

Encouraged by this degree of agreement, we may, in the spirit of the previous section, explore whether an <u>exhaustive</u> (in the sense of (41)) and <u>interpretive</u> (in the sense of (42)-(45)) assignment can be extended to other inequality measures, and to component distributions that are not independent. To do so, we need consider only the case when K = 2. Then (41) together with either (42) or (43) produce the aggregation condition

$$I(x^1+x^2) = I(x^1) + I(x^2), \tag{46}$$

while (41) combined with (44) or (45) yields

$$I(x^1+x^2) = I(\bar{x}^1+x^2) + I(x^1+\bar{x}^2). \tag{47}$$

By first setting $x^1 = \bar{x}^1$ in (46), and then setting $x^2 = \bar{x}^2$, it can be seen that (47) subsumes (46). We therefore focus attention on the weaker condition (47).

Now if x^1 and x^2 are uncorrelated, (47) holds for indices other than the variance: for example, the square of the coefficient of variation, $\sigma^2(x)/\mu(x)$. (Although even this index violates the stricter requirement (46)). However, once the independence condition is relaxed, no inequality measure continues to satisfy (47).

Theorem 2 No index satisfies assumptions (1)-(4) and (47) for all $x^1, x^2 \in \mathcal{X}_n$.

Proof Consider any $\Delta \in (0,1)$ and define $x^1, x^2 \in \mathcal{X}_n$ by $x^1 = (1-\Delta,1+\Delta,1,\ldots,1)$ and $x^2 = (1+\Delta,1-\Delta,1,\ldots,1)$. Then $I(x^1+x^2) = I(\bar{x}^1+\bar{x}^2) = 0$, by (3); and $I(x^1+\bar{x}^2) = I(\bar{x}^1+x^2) > I(\bar{x}^1+\bar{x}^2)$ using symmetry (1) and the principle of transfers (2). Therefore

$$I(x^1+\bar{x}^2) + I(\bar{x}^1+x^2) \;>\; 2I(\bar{x}^1+\bar{x}^2) = 0 = I(x^1+x^2),$$

contradicting (47). □

Thus we may conclude that no exhaustive allocation rule is generally compatible with any one of the contribution interpretations corresponding to (42)-(45). In this respect the component aggregation problem has a less satisfactory outcome than the subgroup aggregation issue.

Once the search for interpretive significance has been abandoned, we can examine other criteria for discriminating among the various ways of defining the source contributions S_k. The decomposition given by (40) in the context of the variance index and independent components can still provide assistance here, by suggesting attractive properties that can be preserved in more general environments. For instance, the assignment rule (40) is a continuous function of the component distribution x^k and satisfies the condition

$$S_k = S(x^k,x), \tag{48}$$

so the different sources are treated in a symmetric (or anonymous) way, and the contribution allocated to component k does not depend on how the income $x-x^k$ is divided among the other income categories. The rule given by (40) also satisfies

$$S(x^j+x^k,x) = S(x^j,x) + S(x^k,x), \tag{49}$$

so the contribution of any set of components will be the same whether the components are aggregated before or after the assignment rule is applied. If we assume that $S(x^k,x)$ is a continuous function of x^k and that (49) holds for all x^j, $x^k \in \mathcal{X}_n$, the solution to the Cauchy equation (Aczel (1966), page 348), immediately yields

$$S(x^k,x) = \sum_{i=1}^{n} a_i(x)x^k. \tag{50}$$

In addition, if the adding-up condition (41) applies

$$S(x,x) = \sum_{i=1}^{n} a_i(x)x_i = I(x). \tag{51}$$

Equations (50) and (51) constrain the set of potential assignment rules, but the set remains large, due to the various ways in which the $a_i(x)$ can be defined. Shorrocks (1982) considers additional restrictions on the form of $S(x^k,x)$, of which one is the requirement

$$S(x, x+\Pi x) = S(\Pi x, x+\Pi x) \tag{52}$$

for all $x \in \mathcal{X}_n$ and all permutation matrices Π of dimension n. In (52), total income arises from two components whose distributions are permutations of each other. The symmetric situation of the two components suggests that the two sources should be assigned the same contribution, as indicated by (52). Further support is provided by the fact that every one of the interpretations (42)-(45) agree that $S_1 = S_2$ when $x^2 = \Pi x^1$ and $x = x^1+x^2$.

As shown in Shorrocks (1982, Theorem 3 and footnote 9), conditions (50) and (52), together with the basic inequality properties (1)-(4), imply

$$S(x^k,x) = \left[\frac{\text{cov}(x^k,x)}{\sigma^2(x)} + \alpha(x)\ \Sigma_i\beta_i(x)x_i^k\right] I(x), \tag{53}$$

where $\alpha(x)$ is any arbitrary continuous function, and $\beta = (\beta_1,..,\beta_n)$ satisfies $\beta.x = 0$ and is orthogonal to the (n-2)-dimensional vector space $\{y \mid y.x=0;\ \Sigma_i y_i=0\}$. These constraints on β mean that $\beta_i(x) = \gamma(x)x_i + \delta(x)$ for some real valued functions $\gamma(x)$ and $\delta(x)$. Since in addition $\Sigma_i\ \beta_i(x)x_i = 0$, we may deduce

$$0 = \gamma(x)\Sigma_i x_i^2 + \delta(x)\Sigma_i x_i = n\gamma(x)[\sigma^2(x) + \mu(x)^2] + n\delta(x)\mu(x),$$

and hence

$$\beta_i(x) = \gamma(x)\left[\ x_i - \frac{\sigma^2(x)}{\mu(x)} - \mu(x)\ \right]. \tag{54}$$

Substituting (54) into (53) then yields

$$\frac{S(x^k,x)}{I(x)} = \lambda(x)\frac{\mu(x^k)}{\mu(x)} + [1-\lambda(x)]\ \frac{\mathrm{cov}(x^k,x)}{\sigma^2(x)}, \tag{55}$$

where $\lambda(x) = -n\sigma^2(x)\alpha(x)\gamma(x)$. So the contribution of each source, expressed as a proportion of total inequality, is a simple combination of the factor share $\mu(x^k)/\mu(x)$ and the "natural" rule that would follow from the variance equation (38).

The decomposition rule (55) is still not unique, since the parameter $\lambda(x)$ remains unconstrained. However, this degree of freedom can be removed by assuming

$$S(\bar{x}^k,x) = 0 \qquad \forall\ x^k \in \mathcal{X}_n, \tag{56}$$

so that a component which is distributed equally makes no contribution to the inequality of total income. (This condition holds for each of the "interpretations" (A), (C) and (D) considered earlier in (42), (44) and (45)). Combining (55) and (56), we obtain $\lambda(x)=0$, and hence the unique rule derived in Shorrocks (1982)

$$\frac{S(x^k,x)}{I(x)} = \frac{\mathrm{Cov}(x^k,x)}{\sigma^2(x)}\ . \tag{57}$$

Notice in particular that this expression will generate identical proportional contributions to inequality whichever inequality index is used.

5. Summary and Conclusions

The principal properties of inequality measures, as captured in the symmetry, Pigou-Dalton, normalisation and continuity conditions (1)-(4), admit a wide variety of potential indices. Even adding the replication and scale invariance properties (5) and (6) allows far too many indices for most practical applications. They cannot all be given equal status, therefore, and a need arises for further criteria to guide the selection process.

This paper has considered different ways of providing these criteria, and the consequences that follow. One possibility is an explicit link with social welfare functions, which forms the basis of the "ethical" approach to inequality measurement. But, as has been demonstrated, every potential inequality index is consistent with some social welfare function, so "ethical" content itself does not help to narrow down the choice of index. Alternatively, consideration of the contexts in which inequality measures are often applied directs attention to the aggregation properties of the indices, particularly those concerned with the relation between overall inequality and the characteristics of population subgroups and income components. Section 3 examined the subgroup aggregation issue, and focussed on two fundamental properties: the "adding-up" condition (19) which is desirable if consistent answers are to be given to different interpretations of the same question; and the very appealing "Subgroup Consistency" Axiom (22), which is needed if overall inequality is to respond in a sensible way to changes in inequality within subgroups. Both of these properties generate a strong separability requirement of the index, which is violated by the Gini coefficient, for example. When (19) and (22) are added to the properties (1)-(6), only positive scalar multiples of the Generalised Entropy family (16) are admitted.

A similar type of analysis performed for aggregation over income components yields less clear-cut answers, since it is difficult to see how total inequality can be allocated between the income components in a way that corresponds to any reasonable interpretation of the component contributions. Certainly, the most obvious interpretations do not allow a decomposition into component contributions that is consistent with any index satisfying assumptions (1)-(4). Once the search for "interpretive" significance is abandoned, satisfactory contributions can be defined. But since they can be applied to any potential inequality measure, it is not immediately apparent that the component aggregation issue suggests any criteria for discriminating among alternative index forms.

References

Aczel, J.: Lectures on Functional Equations and Their Applications. New York: Academic Press, 1966.

Atkinson, A. B. "On the Measurement of Inequality", *Journal of Economic Theory*, 2 (1970), 244-263.

Blackorby, C. and D. Donaldson: "Measures of Relative Equality and Their Meaning in Terms of Social Welfare", *Journal of Economic Theory*, 18 (1978), 59-80.

Blackorby, C. and D. Donaldson: "A Theoretical Treatment of Ethical Indices of Absolute Inequality", *International Economic Review*, 21 (1980), 107-136.

Blackorby, C., D. Donaldson and M. Auersperg: "A New Procedure for the Measurement of Inequality Within and Among Population Subgroups", *Canadian Journal of Economics*, 14 (1981),665-685.

Bourguignon, F.: "Decomposable Income Inequality Measures", *Econometrica*, 47 (1979), 901-920.

Cowell, F. A.: "On the Structure of Additive Inequality Measures", *Review of Economic Studies*, 47 (1980), 521-531.

Cowell, F. A. and K. Kuga: "Additivity and the Entropy Concept: An Axiomatic Approach to Inequality Measurement", *Journal of Economic Theory*, 25 (1981), 131-143.

Das, T. and A. Parikh: "Decomposition of Inequality Measures and a Comparative Analysis", *Empirical Economics*, 7 (1982), 23-48.

Dasgupta, P., A. Sen and D. Starrett: "Notes on the Measurement of Inequality", *Journal of Economic Theory*, 6 (1973), 180-187.

Ebert, U.: "On the Decomposition of Inequality: Partitions into Non-overlapping Subgroups", mimeo, 1985.

Fei, J. C. H., G. Ranis and S. W. Y. Kuo: "Growth and the Family Distribution of Income by Factor Components", *Quarterly Journal of Economics*, 92 (1978), 17-53.

Fields, G. S. and J. C. H. Fei: "On Inequality Comparisons", *Econometrica*, 46 (1978), 303-316.

Foster, J. E.: "Inequality Measurement", in H. P. Young (ed.) *Fair Allocation*. Providence, Rhode Island: American Mathematical Society, 1985.

Kolm, S.-Ch.: "The Optimum Production of Social Justice", in J. Margolis and H. Guitton (eds.) *Public Economics.*- London: Macmillan, 1969.

Kolm, S.-Ch.: "Unequal Inequalities, I", *Journal of Economic Theory*, 12 (1976a), 416-442.

Kolm, S.-Ch.: "Unequal Inequalities, II", *Journal of Economic Theory*, 13 (1976b), 82-111.

Mookherjee, D. and A. F. Shorrocks: "A Decomposition Analysis of the Trend in U.K. Income Inequality", *Economic Journal*, 92 (1982), 886-902.

Pyatt, G.: "On the Interpretation and Disaggregation of Gini Coefficients", *Economic Journal*, 86 (1976), 243-255.

Pyatt, G., C. Chen and J. Fei: "The Distribution of Income by Factor Components", *Quarterly Journal of Economics*, 94 (1980), 451-474.

Sen, A. K.: *On Economic Inequality.* Oxford: Clarendon Press, 1973.

Shorrocks, A. F.: "The Class of Additively Decomposable Inequality Measures" *Econometrica*, 48 (1980), 613-625.

Shorrocks, A. F.: "Inequality Decomposition by Factor Components", *Econometrica*, 50 (1982), 193-211.

Shorrocks, A. F.: "Inequality Decomposition by Population Subgroups", *Econometrica*, 52 (1984), 1369-1385.

Theil, H.: *Economics and Information Theory.* Amsterdam: North Holland Publishing Co., 1967.

Toyoda, T.: "Decomposability of Inequality Measures", *Economic Studies Quarterly*, 31 (1980), 207-216.

On the Construction of an Index of Bequest Behavior

Martin Straub and Alois Wenig
Fernuniversität Gesamthochschule Hagen
FB Wirtschaftswissenschaft
Postfach 9 40
D-5800 Hagen

1. Introduction

Most economists would probably agree that both "too much" and "not enough" inequality in the distribution of income and wealth is undesirable. A large disparity in economic means may produce social tensions while overall equality makes economic incentives and efficiency disappear.

There have been many attempts to measure the degree of inequality in income and property by appropriate index numbers (see e.g. BÜRK and GEHRIG [1984], EICHHORN [1984], and KOLM [1976]. The major questions associated with this measurement problem have been addressed in the literature and acceptable solutions have been suggested. Not much attention, however, has so far been paid to the construction of index numbers which are indicators of the causes of distributional changes. In economic theory the following sources of wealth redistribution have been identified: differences in savings ratios, wage differentials, taxes, differences in the individual returns on capital, marriages, bequests and inheritances, and others (see e.g. ATKINSON [1974], BLINDER [1973], STIGLITZ [1969], and THUROW [1975]). In this paper we shall concentrate on bequest which is crucial to the long run distribution of wealth. The importance of bequest rules practiced in a society for the development of economic inequality can hardly be underrated as our analysis will show. We attempt to quantify the very complex pattern of individual bequest decisions by constructing basically two index numbers. Their numerical values provide information about the strength of the forces toward economic inequality occasioned by bequest and inheritance.

Measurement in Economics
ed. by W. Eichhorn

There are two different approaches to the construction of index numbers. One way is the postulation of a set of axioms from which the functional form of the index formula can be derived. This axiomatic approach requires information about the "economic logic" of the data to be represented by the index. If the principles of defining an index number for a given set of data are not known a priori then the only alternative is the construction of a model. The variables and parameters of this model must show how the various data are interrelated in the economic context under consideration. Then a variable or a parameter of a model can be interpreted as an index number if it is a function only of data that describe a particular economic phenomenon (e. g. bequest behavior) and if all other variables or parameters of the model do not hinge on this very set of data. The model we are going to analyse in the next section meets this requirement; each parameter and variable depends only on one subset of data and all the subsets of data that define a parameter or a variable in this model are mutually exclusive.

2. The Model

2.1 The Sequence of Generations and the Structure of Families

We consider an economy with many agents, the number of which is large enough to allow for the application of the Law of Large Numbers. Every agent is assumed to live in a family which consists of a father, a mother, and i children. We assume that every family has at least one child. Furthermore, let k denote the maximum number of children per family in this society so that $1 \leq i \leq k$. In the final section we discuss briefly how the case of families with no children could be dealt with in our model.

The economic life span of a family is a period of unity length. A family of generation t begins with a marriage of a boy and a girl who are respectively a son and a daughter of a family of generation $t - 1$. Upon their marriage husband and wife pool their wealth inherited from their parents. The marriage of all couples of generation t takes place at exactly the same point in time $t - 1$. From time $t - 1$ to time t every family raises children, accumulates additional wealth, pays various kinds of taxes, and eventually bequeathes its terminal wealth to its children at time t. These children form the new families of generation t + 1, etc.

We define p_i by the ratio

$$p_i = \frac{\text{number of families with i children}}{\text{total number of families}}$$

i.e. p_i is the probability of a randomly chosen family to have i children. Obviously, we have $\sum_{i=1}^{k} p_i = 1$. The sex structure of an individual family can be described by a vector $(c_1, \ldots, c_j, \ldots, c_i)$ with $c_j \in \{0,1\}$ where $c_j = 0$ and $c_j = 1$ respectively represent a boy and a girl. We define $C_i = \{c = (c_1, \ldots, c_j, \ldots, c_i) | c_j \in \{0,1\}\}$; an ele-element $c \in C_i$ is called a family structure. The probability of a randomly chosen family with the structure $c \in C_i$ is $p_i 2^{-i}$ because there are 2^i different i-dimensional vectors whose components are either 0 or 1 and because we assume that every structure of a family with i children has the same probability to occur. It should be noted that it is possible to attach a time index t to our parameters p_i without changing the basic results of our model. Obviously, we assume that every family has at least one child (i.e. $p_o = 0$). The model and its results would not be changed substantially if we had allowed for families with no children whose wealth is randomly distributed to the individuals of the next generation.

2.2 The Impact of Marriages on the Distribution of Wealth

Let X_t denote the inherited wealth of a randomly chosen family of generation t in the beginning of their economic life at time t-1. Furthermore, we define the two random variables U_t and V_t which respectively represent the inherited wealth of a randomly chosen boy or girl at time t-1 prior to their marriage. Obviously, we have

(1) $$X_t = U_t + V_t$$

because couples pool their inherited estates upon their marriages. Thus

(2) $$\sigma^2(X_t) = \sigma^2(U_t) + \sigma^2(V_t) + 2\,\mathrm{Cov}(U_t, V_t)$$

$$= \sigma^2(U_t) + \sigma^2(V_t) + 2\rho_t\sigma(U_t)\sigma(V_t)$$

where $\sigma^2(\ )$ denotes the variance, $\sigma(\ )$ the standard deviation, Cov $(\ ,\ )$ the covariance, and ρ_t the correlation coefficient of the two random variables U_t and V_t. In what follows we assume that Cov $(U_t, V_t) = 0$, i.e. $\rho_t = 0$. This means that the inherited wealth of a husband is stochastically independent of his wife's inherited estate. At the expense of tediously complicating our calculations we could, however, also allow for a positive ρ_t. This would not affect our results in principle but it would change the index formulas we suggest to describe bequest behaviour. In the final section we will briefly discuss the impact of a positive ρ_t. Under our assumption of $\rho_t = 0$ equation (2) can be replaced by

$$(2') \qquad \sigma^2(X_t) = \sigma^2(U_t) + \sigma^2(V_t) .$$

The inequality in the distribution of wealth of generation t (at time t-1 immediatley "after" the couples get married) can be measured by the coefficient of variation

$$(3) \qquad \gamma(X_t) = \frac{\sigma(X_t)}{x_t}$$

where x_t is the expected value of X_t. The purpose of our analysis is the construction of indices that measure the impact of bequest behaviour on $\gamma(X_t)$.

2.3 The Redistribution of Wealth During the Economic Life of a Generation

The theory of wealth distribution distinguishes between intragenerational and intergenerational redistribution. Reshuffling wealth across generations due to bequest (or inheritance respectively) is the major source of intergenerational wealth transfer. As for intragenerational wealth transfers we have already assumed that mating occurs at random so that the inherited wealth of a husband and his spouse are stochastically independent variables. All determinants of intragenerational redistribution other than marriages are incorporated in a random variable R_t which transfers initial wealth X_t of a family of generation t into terminal wealth Y_t of a family of this generation:

$$(4) \qquad Y_t = R_t X_t$$

R_t reflects differences in savings behavior, taxation, wage differentials, and other causes of wealth transfer.

We assume that the distribution of R_t is exogenously given and that $R_t > 0$, $r_t = E(R_t) \gtrless 1$, $\sigma^2(R_t) \geq 0$, and $Cov(R_t, X_t) = 0$. Under these assumptions we have

$$(5) \qquad y_t = r_t x_t$$

and

$$(6) \qquad \sigma^2(Y_t) = r_t^2\sigma^2(X_t) + \sigma^2(R_t)\sigma^2(X_t) + x_t^2\sigma^2(R_t).$$

From (6) we have

$$(7) \qquad \gamma^2(Y_t) = [1 + \gamma^2(R_t)]\gamma^2(X_t) + \gamma^2(R_t)$$

where $\gamma(\ \ )$ denotes again the coefficient of variation of the respective variables. The random variable R_t could be used by policy makers to reduce the inequality in the distribution of wealth. They would have to find and adopt tax schemes which lower the variance of R_t without diminishing the average rate of capital accumulation r_t.

2.4 The Pattern of Bequest Behaviour

The estates U_{t+1} and V_{t+1} of respectively men and women of generation t+1 randomly selected at time t are inherited from families of generation t whose economic life ends at time t and whose terminal wealth is given by the random variable Y_t. The transformation of Y_t into U_{t+1} and V_{t+1} is carried out by a complex pattern of bequest rules which we would finally like to concisely represent by a small number of indices.

In order to describe the whole pattern of bequest behaviour we define the following set of coefficients:

$A_{ij}(c)$ = the share the j-th child of a family with structure $c \in C_i$ inherits in his or her parents total bequest.

$A_{ij}(c)$ is assumed to be a random coefficient with $a_{ij}(c) = E(A_{ij}(c))$ and $s_{ij}(c) = \sigma^2(A_{ij}(c))$, $c \in C_i$. We assume that the bequest coefficients $A_{ij}(c)$ are independent for different families. Within the same family the shares of all children must, of course, always add up to unity. Marriage between the children of the same family does not occur. Therefore the bequest coefficients of a man and his wife are independent. To model these independencies let $A^t_{ij}(c)$ be independent repetitions of $A_{ij}(c)$ for each $i \in \{1, \ldots, k\}$, $c \in C_i$. $\{i,j,c,t\}$ denotes the subset of outcomes for which the chosen individual is the j-th child of a family with i children and with structure $c \in C_i$. Thus $A^t_{ij}(c) 1_{\{i,j,c,t\}}$ is the share of such a child in such a family if such a child in such a family is chosen.

3. A Basic Theorem on the Redistribution of Wealth Across Generations

Define the random variables

$$A^o_t = \sum_{i=1}^{k} \sum_{j=1}^{i} \sum_{\substack{c \in C_i \\ c_j = 0}} A^t_{ij}(c) \cdot 1_{\{i,j,c,t\}} \tag{8}$$

and

$$A^1_t = \sum_{i=1}^{k} \sum_{j=1}^{i} \sum_{\substack{c \in C_i \\ c_j = 1}} A^t_{ij}(c) \cdot 1_{\{i,j,c,t\}} \tag{9}$$

In (8) the random experiment consists of choosing men only and every man has the same probability to be chosen. In equation (9) the equivalent applies for women. Then

$$U_{t+1} = A^o_t Y_t \tag{10}$$

and

$$V_{t+1} = A^1_t Y_t \tag{11}$$

Since A_t^o, A_t^1, Y_t as well as A_1^o, A_2^o, ..., A_1^1, A_2^1, ... , and Y_1, Y_2, ... are independent we have

(12) $$E(U_{t+1}) = I_o y_t$$

$$E(V_{t+1}) = I_1 y_t$$

(13) $$\sigma^2(U_{t+1}) = I_o^2\, \sigma^2(Y_t) + J_o\, \sigma^2(Y_t) + J_o y_t{}^2$$

$$\sigma^2(V_{t+1}) = I_1^2\, \sigma^2(Y_t) + J_1\, \sigma^2(Y_t) + J_1 y_t^2$$

where

(14) $$I_o = E(A_t^o) = \sum_{i=1}^{k} \frac{p_i 2^{-i+1}}{K} \sum_{j=1}^{i} \sum_{\substack{c\in C_i \\ c_j=0}} a_{ij}(c)$$

(15) $$I_1 = E(A_t^1) = \sum_{i=1}^{k} \frac{p_i 2^{-i+1}}{K} \sum_{j=1}^{i} \sum_{\substack{c\in C_i \\ c_j=1}} a_{ij}(c)$$

(16) $$K = \sum_{i=1}^{k} ip_i$$

(17) $$J_o = \sigma^2(A_t^o) = E((A_t^o)^2) - (E\, A_t^o)^2 =$$

$$= \sum_{i=1}^{k} \frac{p_i 2^{-i+1}}{K} \sum_{j=1}^{i} \sum_{\substack{c\in C_i \\ c_j=0}} E(A_{ij}^2(c)) - I_o^2$$

$$= \sum_{i=1}^{k} \frac{p_i 2^{-i+1}}{K} \sum_{j=1}^{i} \sum_{\substack{c\in C_i \\ c_j=0}} \{s_{ij}(c) + a_{ij}^2(c)\} - I_o^2$$

$$(18) \qquad J_1 = \sigma^2(A_t^1) = E((A_t^1)^2) - (E\,A_t^1)^2 =$$

$$= \sum_{i=1}^{k} \frac{p_i 2^{-i+1}}{K} \sum_{j=1}^{i} \sum_{\substack{c \in C_i \\ c_j=1}} E(A_{ij}^2(c)) - I_1^2$$

$$= \sum_{i=1}^{k} \frac{p_i 2^{-i+1}}{K} \sum_{j=1}^{i} \sum_{\substack{c \in C_i \\ c_j=1}} \{s_{ij}(c) + a_{ij}^2(c)\} - I_1^2$$

The factor $\frac{p_i 2^{-i+1}}{K}$ in equations (14) and (15) is the probability of $\{i,j,c\}$ in the random experiment associated with (8) and (9) respectively.

$$P(i,j,c) = \frac{ip_i}{K} \cdot \frac{1}{i} \cdot 2^{-i+1} = \frac{p_i 2^{-i+1}}{K} .$$

The first factor $\frac{ip_i}{K}$ is the probability of a child to be a descendant of a family with i children. The second factor $\frac{1}{i}$ gives the probability of being the j-th child. Since $|C_i| = 2^i$ the probability of $c \in C_i$ to occur is 2^{-i}. $K = \sum_{i=1}^{k} ip_i$ is the average number of children per family. Therefore, the number of families increases from period to period by the factor $\frac{K}{2}$. Hence the average wealth y_t of a family at the end of period t translates into $x_{t+1} = \frac{y_t}{\frac{K}{2}} = \frac{2\,y_t}{K}$ which is the average wealth of a family in the beginning of period t+1.

Because of (2'), (7), and (13) we have

$$(19) \qquad \gamma^2(x_{t+1}) = \frac{\sigma^2(x_{t+1})}{x_{t+1}^2} = \frac{\sigma^2(U_{t+1}) + \sigma^2(V_{t+1})}{4y_t^2} K^2 =$$

$$= \frac{(I_o^2 + I_1^2 + J)\sigma^2(Y_t) + J\,y_t^2}{4y_t^2} K^2$$

$$= \frac{1}{4}(I_o^2 + I_1^2 + J)K^2\gamma^2(X_t) + \frac{1}{4} J K^2$$

$$= \frac{1}{4}(I_o^2 + I_1^2 + J)(1 + \gamma^2(R_t))K^2\gamma^2(X_t)$$

$$+ \frac{1}{4}(I_o^2 + I_1^2 + J)K^2\gamma^2(R_t) + \frac{1}{4} J K^2$$

where

(20) $$J = J_o + J_1$$

Summarizing our results we get the following

Theorem

The square of the coefficient of variation of the distribution of wealth, $\gamma^2(X_t)$, is recursively given by

(21) $$\gamma^2(X_{t+1}) = G_t\gamma^2(X_t) + H_t$$

where

(22) $$G_t = \frac{1}{4}(I_o^2 + I_1^2 + J)K^2(1 + \gamma^2(R_t))$$

(23) $$H_t = \frac{1}{4}(I_o^2 + I_1^2 + J)K^2\gamma^2(R_t) + \frac{1}{4} J K^2$$

I_o, I_1, and J are defined by equations (14), (15), and (20) respectively.

4. The Indices of Bequest Behavior

4.1 The Definition of Bequest Indices

The difference equation (21) shows that the development over time of distributive inequality depends crucially on the coefficients G_t and

H_t. If $G_t > 1$ for all future periods t then $\gamma^2(X_t)$, and hence $\gamma(X_t)$, both grow beyond any limit. On the other hand, since H_t is positive and must, in addition, be assumed to be bounded from above $\gamma^2(X_t)$ is also bounded for all future periods provided that $G_t < 1$. Finally, suppose $\gamma^2(R_t)$ to be constant over time then both $G_t = G$ and $H_t = H$ are also constant over time and $\gamma^2(X_t)$ converges with

$$\lim_{t\to\infty} \gamma^2(X_t) = \frac{H}{1-G} \quad \text{if } G < 1.$$

In general, we observe that the long run inequality of wealth increases or decreases as the coefficients G_t and H_t rise or fall respectively. The coefficient G_t is the product of two terms: $(1 + \gamma^2(R_t))$ and $\frac{1}{4}(I_o^2 + I_1^2 + J)K^2$. The first term measures the intragenerational redistribution of wealth due to different lifetime rates of return R_t on the wealth generation t inherits from generation t-1. The impact of those redistributional forces is exogenous to our analysis and so is the coefficient of variation $\gamma(R_t)$. We note, however, that $(1 + \gamma^2(R_t))$ is multiplicatively separable from $\frac{1}{4}(I_o^2 + I_1^2 + J)K^2$. This second term depends only on the fertility probabilites $p_1, \ldots, p_k$ and on the coefficients $a_{ij}(c) = E(A_{ij}(c))$ and $s_{ij}(c) = \sigma^2(A_{ij}(c))$ which describe certain properties of bequest behavior. Thus we suggest to interpret the term $\frac{1}{4}(I_o^2 + I_1^2 + J)K^2$ as an index of bequest behavior. In particular, we define the following three indices

$$B_1 = \frac{1}{4}(I_o^2 + I_1^2)K^2 \tag{24}$$

$$B_2 = \frac{1}{4}J\,K^2 \tag{25}$$

and

$$B = B_1 + B_2 = \frac{1}{4}(I_o^2 + I_1^2 + J)K^2 \tag{(26}$$

The index B appears in both coefficients, G_t and H_t, and in H_t, too, it is multiplicatively separable from $\gamma^2(R_t)$. The value of B is crucial to the development of $\gamma^2(X_t)$ over time. An increase in B tends to raise G_t and H_t and thus implies a tendency to more inequality in the distribution of wealth.

The index B_2 is the second additive term of the coefficient H_t (see (23)). B_2 plays a role by itself in determining the value of H_t. B and B_2 are, however, not independent of each other. From (17) and (18) we have

$$(27)\qquad B = \left(\frac{K}{2}\right)^2 \sum_{i=1}^{k} \sum_{j=1}^{i} \sum_{c \in C_i} \frac{p_i 2^{-i+1}}{K} (s_{ij}(c) + a_{ij}^2(c))$$

and

$$(28)\qquad B_2 = \left(\frac{K}{2}\right)^2 \{\sum_{i=1}^{k} \sum_{j=1}^{i} \sum_{c \in C_i} \frac{p_i 2^{-i+1}}{K} (s_{ij}(c) + a_{ij}^2(c)) - - I_o^2 - I_1^2\}$$

Since both, I_o and I_1, are weighted sums of the $a_{ij}(c)$ a change in these coefficients affects B and B_2 in a different way. In section 4.3. we will discuss the interrelation between B and B_2 in more detail.

Using the indices B, B_1, and B_2 the difference equation (21) can now be written as follows

$$(21^*)\qquad \gamma^2(X_{t+1}) = B(1 + \gamma^2(R_t))\gamma^2(X_t) + B\gamma^2(R_t) + B_2$$

$$= B(1 + \gamma^2(R_t)\ (1 + \gamma^2(X_t)) - B_1$$

The next section 4.2. is concerned with the index B. Since $\gamma^2(R_t) \geqq 0$ the coefficient G_t can only be smaller than unity if and only if $B < 1$. For $B \geqq 1$ distributive inequality grows beyond any limit. It is thus of particular interest to find out what numerical values the index B can attain.

4.2 Maximal and Minimal Values of the Index B

In the following two lemmas we discuss which values B can attain if we vary the bequest rules $A_{ij}(c)$ and the fertility probabilities p_i. We consider only the maximum and the minimum of B. Since B is a continous function of $A_{ij}(c)$ and p_i it can attain any intermediate values. Before stating the first lemma we define a bequest rule which we call primogeniture. This rule is given by

$$\bar{A}_{ij}(c) = \begin{cases} 1 & \text{for } j = \bar{j}(i,c) \\ 0 & \text{for } j = \bar{j}(i,c) \end{cases} \tag{29}$$

where $\bar{j}(i,c) \in \{1, \ldots, k\}$ is arbitrarily chosen and can also be a random coefficient.

Lemma 1

(a) For any given fertility probabilities $p_1, \ldots, p_k$ primogeniture maximizes the value of B and we have

$$\max_{\{A_{ij}(c)\}} B(A_{ij}(c)) = B(\bar{A}_{ij}(c)) = \frac{K}{2} .$$

(b) Maximizing B with respect to both the bequest rules $A_{ij}(c)$ and the fertility parameters $p_1, \ldots, p_k$ yields

$$\max_{\{p_i\}, \{A_{ij}(c)\}} B(A_{ij}(c); p_1, \ldots, p_k) = B(\bar{A}_{ij}(c); 0, \ldots, 0,1) = \frac{k}{2} ,$$

i.e. B attains its maximum if the bequest rule is primogeniture and if all families have the maximal number k of children (i.e. $p_k = 1$, which implies that all families have the same number of children).

<u>Proof.</u>

From the definition of B we have

$$B = \frac{K^2}{4} \; (I_o^2 + I_1^2 + J) = \frac{K^2}{4} \sum_{i=1}^{k} \; \frac{p_i 2^{-i+1}}{K} \sum_{j=1}^{i} \; \sum_{c \in C_i} \; E(A_{ij}^2(c))$$

(30)

$$= \frac{K}{2} \sum_{i=1}^{k} p_i 2^{-i} \sum_{c \in C_i} E(\sum_{j=1}^{i} A_{ij}^2(c))$$

The $A_{ij}(c)$ are subject to the following restrictions

(31) $0 \leqq A_{ij}(c) \leqq 1, \; \sum_{j=1}^{i} A_{ij}(c) = 1$

Given i and $c \in C_i$ we maximize $E(\sum_{j=1}^{1} A_{ij}^2(c))$ with respect to the vector of random variables $(A_{i1}(o), \ldots, A_{ii}(c))$. Obviously, $\sum_{j=1}^{i} A_{ij}^2(c)$ is largest if $A_{ij}(c) = 1$ for some j and $A_{ij}(c) = 0$ otherwise. Thus the maximizing bequest rule is primogeniture i.e. $A_{ij}(c) = \bar{A}_{ij}(c)$. Because $E(\sum_{j=1}^{i} \bar{A}_{ij}^2(c)) = 1$ we get

$$\max_{\{A_{ij}(c)\}} B(A_{ij}(c)) = B(\bar{A}_{ij}(c)) = \frac{K}{2} \sum_{i=1}^{k} p_i 2^{-i} \sum_{c \in C_i} 1 = \frac{K}{2}$$

This proves the first part of the Lemma.
Since the average number K of children is maximized if every family has k children ($p_k = 1$) we have

$$\max_{\{p_1,\ldots,p_k\}} K = \max_{\{p_1,\ldots,p_k\}} \{\sum_{i=1}^{k} ip_i\} = k.$$

From this it follows

$$\max_{\{p_i\},\; \{A_{ij}(c)\}} B(A_{ij}(c);\; p_1, \ldots, p_k) = \frac{k}{2}$$

which proves the second part of the Lemma. Q.E.D.

Preparing our next lemma we define a parameter L:

$$(32) \qquad L := \sum_{i=1}^{k} \frac{p_i}{i} .$$

L is the average share a family bequeathes to its children (which may not be confused with the average share a child inherits in his or her parents' legacy). Furthermore, we define the following bequest rule $\tilde{A}_j(c)$:

$$(33) \qquad \tilde{A}_{ij}(c) = \frac{1}{i}, \qquad j = 1, \ldots, i$$

We call this the equality rule.

Lemma 2

(a) For any given fertility probabilities $p_1, \ldots, p_k$ the equality rule minimizes the value of B and we have

$$\min \quad B(A_{ij}(c)) = B(\tilde{A}_{ij}(c)) = \frac{L \cdot K}{2} = \frac{1}{2} \sum_{m,n=1}^{k} \frac{m}{n} p_m p_n .$$

(b) Minimizing B with respect to both the bequest rules $A_{ij}(c)$ and the fertility parameters $p_1, \ldots, p_k$ yields

$$\min_{\{p_i\}, \{A_{ij}(c)\}} B(A_{ij}(c); p_1, \ldots, p_k) =$$

$$= B(\tilde{A}_{ij}(c); 0, \ldots, 0,1,0,\ldots,0) = \frac{1}{2} ,$$

The minimum is attained if all families have the same number i^* of children where i^* can be any number between 1 and k.

Proof

Given i and $c \in C_i$ we minimize $E(\sum_{j=1}^{k} A_{ij}^2(c))$ with respect to the vector of random variables $(A_{i1}(c), \ldots, A_{ii}(c))$. The constraints (31) in the proof of lemma 1 still apply. $\sum_{j=1}^{k} A_{ij}^2(c)$ is smallest if $A_{ij}(c) = \frac{1}{i}$ for every j. Thus the equality rule $\tilde{A}_{ij}(c)$ minimizes B. Because $E(\sum_{j=1}^{i} \tilde{A}_{ij}(c)) = \frac{1}{i}$ we get

$$\min \qquad B(A_{ij}(c)) = B(\tilde{A}_{ij}(c)) = \frac{K}{2} \sum_{i=1}^{k} p_i 2^{-i} \sum_{c \in C_i} \frac{1}{i} =$$

$$= \frac{K}{2} \sum_{i=1}^{k} \frac{p_i}{i} = \frac{L \cdot K}{2} .$$

From

$$L \cdot K = \{\sum_{i=1}^{k} \frac{p_i}{i}\} \; \{\sum_{i=1}^{k} ip_i\}$$

we have

$$\frac{L \cdot K}{2} = \frac{1}{2} \sum_{m,n=1}^{k} \frac{m}{n} p_m p_n .$$

This proves the first part of the lemma.

To prove the second part we define

$$M: = \min \{ \sum_{m,n=1}^{k} \frac{m}{n} p_m p_n ; \sum_{j=1}^{k} p_j = 1\}$$

and remark

$$(34) \qquad \min \{ \sum_{m,n=1}^{k} \frac{m}{n} p_m p_n ; \sum_{j=1}^{k} p_j = c\} = c^2 M \quad (c>0).$$

Furthermore because of

$$0 \le \sum_{j=1}^{k-1} \frac{(k-j)^2}{kj} p_j = \sum_{j=1}^{k-1} \frac{k^2 - kj + j^2 - kj}{kj} p_j$$

$$= k \sum_{j=1}^{k-1} \{\frac{1}{j} - \frac{1}{k}\} p_j + \frac{1}{k} \sum_{j=1}^{k-1} \{j-k\} p_j$$

we have

$$(35) \qquad 2(1-p_k) = 2\sum_{j=1}^{k-1} p_j \leq k\sum_{j=1}^{k-1}\frac{p_j}{j} + \frac{1}{k}\sum_{j=1}^{k-1} jp_j .$$

Now we proceed by induction along k. The case k = 1 is trivial and we go from k-1 to k:

$$\sum_{m,n=1}^{k}\frac{m}{n}p_m p_n = \sum_{m,n=1}^{k-1}\frac{m}{n}p_m p_n + p_k\{k\sum_{j=1}^{k-1}\frac{p_j}{j} + \frac{1}{k}\sum_{j=1}^{k-1} jp_j + p_k\}$$

$$(36) \qquad \geq (1-p_k)^2 + p_k^2 + p_k\{k\sum_{j=1}^{k-1}\frac{p_j}{j} + \frac{1}{k}\sum_{j=1}^{k-1} jp_j\}$$

$$= 1 - 2p_k(1-p_k) + p_k\{k\sum_{j=1}^{k-1}\frac{p_j}{j} + \frac{1}{k}\sum_{j=1}^{k-1} jp_j\} \geq 1.$$

Here we have used the hypothesis of induction and (34) for the first inequality and (35) for the second one. Thus LK ≥ 1 is proved. Because of part (a) of the lemma it suffices to show that LK = 1 is attained if and only if all families have the same number i^* of children. This is proved by induction, too. The case k = 1 is trivial. We proceed from k - 1 to k. If $p_k = 0$ we have the case k - 1 and nothing must be shown. Thus let $p_k \neq 0$. Then LK = 1 implies that all inequalities of (36) must be equations. Therefore, (35) must also be an equation and $p_1 = \dots = p_{k-1} = 0$ so that $p_k = 1$. This proves part (b) of the lemma.

Q.E.D.

4.3 The Domain of the Coefficient H_t

In the last section we discussed which values B - and therefore G_t - can attain. Now we are going to ask what the domain of the values of H_t is. As before the question can be reduced to the problem of finding the maximum and the minimum of H_t respectively. First we answer the question of the maximum.

For the use in the next lemma we define a bequest rule to be sex independent if it implies $I_o = I_1$ $(= \frac{1}{K})$, i.e. the expected shares in their parents' bequests are the same for boys and for girls.

Lemma 3

Let $\gamma(R_t)$ be exogenously given. Then:

a) For any given fertility properties $p_1, \ldots, p_k$ sex independent primogeniture is the unique bequest rule that maximizes H_t and we have

$$\max_{\{A_{ij}(c)\}} H_t(A_{ij}(c)) = \frac{K}{2}(1+\gamma^2(R_t)) - \frac{1}{2} .$$

b) Maximizing H_t with respect to both the bequest rules $A_{ij}(c)$ and the fertility parameters $p_1, \ldots, p_k$ yields

$$\max_{\{p_i\},\ \{A_{ij}(c)\}} H_t(A_{ij}(c);\ p_1,\ \ldots,\ p_k) = \frac{k}{2}(1 + \gamma^2(R_t)) - \frac{1}{2}$$

and H_t attains its maximum if and only if the bequest rule is sex independent primogeniture and if all families have the maximal number of children ($p_k = 1$).

Proof

$$H_t = \frac{1}{4}(I_o^2 + I_1^2 + J)K^2\gamma^2(R_t) + \frac{1}{4} JK^2$$

$$= B\gamma^2(R_t) + B_2$$

$$= B(1 + \gamma^2(R_t)) - B_1$$

$B_1 = \frac{1}{4}(I_o^2 + I_1^2)K^2$ attains its minimum for $I_o = I_1 = \frac{1}{K}$, i.e. for any sex independent bequest rule. By Lemma 1, (a) maximizing B with respect to all bequest rules proves part (a) of the lemma.

Part (b) is an immediate consequence of Lemma 1, (b). Q.E.D.

The next lemma gives the minimum value of H_t in the case of a deterministic lifetime rate of return R_t.

Lemma 4

Let R_t be non random i.e. $\gamma(R_t) = 0$. Then minimizing H_t with respect to both the bequest rules $A_{ij}(c)$ and the fertility parameters $p_1, \ldots, p_k$ yields

$$\min_{\{p_i\}, \{A_{ij}(c)\}} H_t(A_{ij}(c); p_1, \ldots, p_k) = 0,$$

and the minimum is attained if the equality rule applies and if, moreover, all families have the same number i^* of children. i^* can be any number between 1 and k.

Proof

For $\gamma(R_t) = 0$ we have $H_t = B - B_1$. The equality rule implies $B_1 = \frac{1}{2}$ because for sex independence $I_o = I_1 = \frac{1}{K}$ holds.

From Lemma 2, (b) $B = \frac{1}{2}$ follows. Therefore $H_t = 0$.

On the other hand

$$H_t = \frac{1}{4}(I_o^2 + I_1^2 + J)K^2 - \frac{1}{4}(I_o^2 + I_1^2)K^2 = \frac{1}{4} JK^2 \geq 0.$$

Therefore $H_t = 0$ is the minimum. Q.E.D.

5. Economic Interpretation of the Results and Extensions of the Model

The results of the preceding four lemmas are not counter-intuitive. The indices B and B_2 which measure the impact of bequest rules on the distribution of wealth are minimized if the parents treat their children equally and they are maximized if one child inherits the whole estate while his or her brothers and sisters get away empty-handed. The fertility parameters $p_1, \ldots, p_k$, too, play an important role. Small fertility differentials work as an amplifier of a prevailing tendency towards both more equality or more inequality because the four lemmas show that the two coefficients G_t and H_t attain their maximum maximorum as well as their minimum minimorum if all families have the same number of children. Fertility differentials per se can, however, also be a major source of inequality as a subsequent example to Lemma 2, part (a) will show (see also STRAUB and WENIG [1984]). This example, as well as the others in this section, are meant to interpret the lemmas of the preceding paragraphs and should illustrate in more detail how both bequest and fertility affect the distribution of individual wealth.

Let us first consider the case that every family has the same number of children, say i^* (i.e. $p_i{}^* = 1$). Suppose all parents apply the equality rule so that $A_{ij}(c) = \tilde{A}_{ij}(c) = \frac{1}{i^*}$. Since the equality rule is sex independent we have $I_o = I_1 = \frac{1}{K} = \frac{1}{i^*}$. Therefore $LK = \frac{1}{2}$ and we obtain $B_2 = B - B_1 = \frac{LK}{2} - \frac{1}{4}(I_o^2 + I_1^2)K^2 = \frac{1}{2} - \frac{1}{2} = 0$. From this it follows that $H_t = B\gamma^2(R_t)$ and the difference equation (21) becomes

$$(21') \qquad \gamma^2(X_{t+1}) = \frac{1}{2}(1 + \gamma^2(R_t))\gamma^2(X_t) + \frac{1}{2}\gamma^2(R_t)$$

If $\gamma(R_t) \leq c$ for some $c < 1$ then there exists an upper bound Γ such that $\gamma(X_t) \leq \Gamma$ for all t. Thus there is a limit to distributive inequality provided that intragenerational processes of wealth accumulation and redistribution allows for a sufficiently small coefficient of variation $\gamma(R_t)$ of the lifetime rate of return. Let R_t be independent repetitions of a random variable R so that $\{R_t\}$ is stationary. Then $\gamma(R) < 1$ implies

$$\lim_{t\to\infty} \gamma^2(X_t) = \frac{\gamma^2(R)}{1-\gamma^2(R)} .$$

We note that a solution of (21') depends only on the sequence $\gamma(R_t)$ and not, for example, on the rate of growth $\frac{K}{2} - 1$ of the population. If $\gamma(R_t) = 0$ then everybody has the same lifetime rate of return and the equality rule together with an equal number of children per family suffice to wash out all initial differences in the distribution of wealth. In this case we have

$$\lim_{t\to\infty} \gamma(X_t) = 0$$

so that the economy approaches a perfectly egalitarian state.

Quite the opposite results hold in those cases in which primogeniture is the dominant bequest rule. Even if everybody gets the same lifetime rate of return (i.e. $\gamma(R_t) = 0$) sex independent primogeniture and $p_{i*} = 1$ together imply that economic inequality must grow beyond any limit provided that the population does not decline (which means $i* \geq 2$). This follows from

$$(21'') \qquad \gamma^2(X_{t+1}) = \frac{i*}{2}\,\gamma^2(X_t) + (\frac{i*}{2} - \frac{1}{2})$$

which is an immediate consequence of Lemma 3, (a). If and only if every family has just one child then $\gamma(X_t)$, again, approaches 0 and the distribution of wealth becomes more and more equal. Except for $i* = 1$ primogeniture, therefore, turns out to produce a very strong tendency towards inequality.

Now we turn to an example which sheds some light on Lemma 2, part (a). In order to isolate the influence of fertility differentials from the impact of bequest decisions we allow for different numbers of children per family (i.e. $p_i < 1$ for every $i \in \{1, \ldots, k\}$) while we assume that parents bequeath their estates according to the equality rule.

From our first example we know already that this bequest rule is a powerful force towards more distributive equality provided that fertility differentials are small. Lemma 2, (a) tells us that

$A_{ij}(c) = \tilde{A}_{ij}(c) = \frac{1}{i}$ implies $B = \frac{L \cdot K}{2} = \frac{1}{2} \sum_{m,n=1}^{k} \frac{m}{n} p_m p_n$ and we have

$B_2 = B - \frac{1}{4}(I_o^2 + I_1^2)K^2 = \frac{LK}{2} - \frac{1}{2}$ because $I_o = I_1 = \frac{1}{K}$ due to the sex independence of the bequest rule. The difference equation (21) then writes

$$(21''') \qquad \gamma^2(X_{t+1}) = \frac{LK}{2}\,(1 + \gamma^2(R_t))\gamma^2(X_t) + \frac{LK}{2}\,(1 + \gamma^2(R_t)) - \frac{1}{2}$$

To illustrate which values $B = \frac{LK}{2}$ may attain we consider two cases:

a) $p_1 = p_2 = \ldots = p_k = \frac{1}{k}$ which means that every number of children per family has the same probability. Then

$$B = \frac{1}{2}\frac{1}{k^2}\sum_{m,n=1}^{k}\frac{m}{n} = \frac{1}{2}\frac{1}{k^2}\frac{k(k+1)}{2}\sum_{n=1}^{k}\frac{1}{n} = \frac{1}{4}(1+\frac{1}{k})\sum_{n=1}^{k}\frac{1}{n}$$

For k = 3, for example, we have $B = \frac{11}{18} < 1$. Thus in the stationary case with $\gamma(R) < \frac{7}{11}$, $\gamma(X_t)$ converges and we get

$$\lim_{t\to\infty}\gamma^2(X_t) = \frac{2 + 11\gamma^2(R)}{7 - 11\gamma^2(R)}$$

b) $p_1 = p_k = \frac{1}{2}$ which means that half of the population has only one child while the other half has the maximal number of children. In this case $B = \frac{1}{2}(\frac{1}{k} + k)$ so that k = 3 implies $B = \frac{5}{3} > 1$ and $\gamma(X_t)$ diverges.

$\frac{LK}{2}$ can be considered as a measure of fertility differentials. Even the equality rule as a bequest rule which occasions a strong tendency towards distributive equality is obviously not able to counter-balance large differences in fertility. These differences are alone able to generate an ever increasing trend to more distributive inequality.

All four lemmas of the preceding section refer to the two border-line cases of bequest behavior, primogeniture and equality rule. Our last example deals with a situation where the bequest rule lies somewhere between these two extremes.

Let every family have two children ($p_2 = 1$). The bequest rule is defined as follows:

$$A_{2j}(c) = \left\{\begin{matrix} 1 & \text{for} & j = 1 \\ 0 & \text{for} & j = 2 \end{matrix}\right\} \text{ if } c_1 = 0$$

$$A_{2j}(c) = \left\{\begin{matrix} d & \text{for} & j = 1 \\ 1-d & \text{for} & j = 2 \end{matrix}\right\} \text{ if } c_1 = 1$$

where d is a parameter with $0 \leq d \leq 1$. This means that the first child inherits everything if it is a boy. In case the first child is a girl then she gets the share d while the second child gets 1 - d independently of his or her sex.

According to (17) and (18)

$$B = \frac{1}{4}(I_o^2 + I_1^2 + J)K^2$$

$$= \frac{2^{-2+1}}{2}\{1 + 1 + d^2 + d^2 + 0 + 0 + (1 - d)^2 + (1 - d)^2\}$$

$$= \frac{1}{4}(4 + 4d^2 - 4d) = 1 - 4d + 4d^2$$

For $d = 1$ we obtain $B = 1$. Then $\gamma(X_t)$ diverges for any $\gamma(R_t)$. For $d < 1$ we get $B < 1$ so that $\gamma(X_t)$ can converge if $\gamma(R_t)$ is constant over time and sufficiently small.

These examples may suffice to illustrate our lemmas and to show how the development of distributive inequality is affected by bequest decisions and differences in the number of children per family. Further examples could be analyzed and constructed on the basis of less extreme and thus more realistic bequest patterns. However, the general features of our model may not yet be realistic enough for immediate empirical applications. Extensions seem desirable with respect to the following points:

- Our assumption that the inherited wealth of a husband and his sponse are independent is unrealistic. There is probably a positive correlation between the inherited estates of the two partners in a marriage.

- The size of the wealth of a family may affect its lifetime rate of return so that there is a correlation between R_t and X_t. In our analysis we treat R_t and X_t as independent variables.

- In reality there are also families without children while $p_o > 0$ in our model.

In principle these three aspects could be dealt with by means of appropriate generalizations of our model.

Allowing for $p_o > 0$ would not cause a major problem for our analysis if we assumed that the wealth of families with no children is randomly distributed to the rest of the society. This would generate a tendency towards more equality provided that every individual has the same chance to get the same amount.

The introduction of a positive coefficient of correlation ρ_t between the inherited stocks of wealth of the two partners in a marriage would slightly complicate our mathematical analysis. In particular, it is not clear whether or not we could still define bequest indices which depend only on the bequest rules and the fertility parameters. Even if this were not possible it would be interesting to find out how, in this case, the coefficient of correlation ρ_t enters the basic difference equation which determines $\gamma(X_t)$ recursively. The respective formula would still be useful to study the impact of bequest rules, fertility, and marriage behavior on the distribution of wealth.

Similarly, the introduction of a correlation between the lifetime rate of return R_t and the wealth of a family X_t may make it impossible to define bequest indices. In addition, however, it is not clear in this case whether the correlation between R_t and X_t is positive or negative. Very large estates as well as very small estates may have a relatively small yield whereas the rate of return may be maximal for intermediate values of X_t.

Empirical applications of our model or of more general versions require information about the fertility parameters $p_o, p_1, \ldots, p_k$ and the bequest coefficients $A_{ij}(c)$. The p_i's are, in general, available from published statistical tables. The coefficients $A_{ij}(c)$ may be obtained by drawing samples. For each type of family with i children and structure $c \in C_i$ a sufficiently large survey is required because the random vectors $(A_{i1}(c), \ldots, A_{ii}(c))$ are independent.

Summary

We have analyzed a model of intergenerational wealth transfer in which bequest behavior and individual differences in the number of children per family are the major determinants of the development of the distribution of wealth. In this model the complex patterns of family structures and bequest decisions are measured by two parameters which are independent of all other data. These two parameters alone determine the impact of bequest decisions on the development of distributive inequality. Therefore, we suggest to interpret these parameters as indices of bequest behaviour. The higher the values of the two indices the stronger is the tendency towards inequality. We have discussed the conditions under which the tendency towards inequality is maximized or minimized.

References

A.B. ATKINSON: The Economics of Inequality. Oxford 1975.

A.S. BLINDER: A Model of Inherited Wealth. Quarterly Journal of Economics. Vol. 87, No. 4, p. 608-626.

R. BÜRK and W. GEHRIG: Indices of Income Inequality and Societal Income. An Axiomatic Approach. In: Theory and Applications of Economic Indices. Edited by W. Eichhorn, R. Henn, O. Opitz, R.W. Shephard. Würzburg 1978, p. 309-358.

W. EICHHORN: What is an Economic Index? An Attempt of an Answer. In: Theory and Applications of Economic Indices. Edited by W. Eichhorn, R. Henn, O. Opitz, R.W. Shephard. Würzburg 1978, p. 3-40.

W. EICHHORN and J. VOELLER: Theory of the Price Index. Berlin-Heidelberg-New York 1976.

S.C. KOLM: Unequal Inequalities I. Journal of Economic Theory. Vol. 12, No. 3, June 1976, p. 416-442.

S.C. KOLM: Unequal Inequalities II. Journal of Economic Theory. Vol. 13, No. 1, August 1976, p. 82-111.

J.E. STIGLITZ: Distribution of Income and Wealth Among Individuals. Econometrica, Vol. 37, 1969, p. 382-397.

M. STRAUB and A. WENIG: Human Fertility and the Distribution of Wealth. In: Economic Consequences of Population Change in Industrialized Countries. Edited by G. Steinmann. Berlin-Heidelberg-New York-Tokyo 1984, p. 68-86.

L.C. THUROW: Generating Inequality - Mechanismus of Distribution in the US Economy. New York 1975.

Part VII Taxation

Risk-Taking under Progressive Taxation: Three Partial Effects

Günter Bamberg
Lehrstuhl für Statistik
Universität Augsburg
Memminger Straße 14
D-8900 Augsburg

Wolfram F. Richter
Lehrstuhl für Volkswirtschaftslehre II
FB Wirtschafts- und Sozialwissenschaften
Universität Dortmund
Postfach 500 500
D-4600 Dortmund 50

1. Introduction

The opinion is widely spread that taxation in general, and income taxation in particular, reduces the individual propensity to take risk. There are even sporadic statements of professional economists supporting such a view. Cf. e.g. M. Friedman (1962, p. 173). It is therefore an important theoretical insight that, by way of contrast, income taxation may *encourage* risk-taking. This proposition is due to Domar and Musgrave (1944) who assumed a proportional tax with full loss offset to show the effect. Domar and Musgrave's pioneering article has stimulated a considerable number of papers to clarify the effect of taxation on risk-taking for various frameworks. On the whole the conclusion is that the effect is highly ambiguous. Its direction heavily depends on the kind of assumptions being made about the investor's risk aversion and general tax provisions. Atkinson and Stiglitz (1980, Lecture Four) present a comprehensive analysis of various model specifications. Recent contributions consequently tend to prove indeterminacy of the effect as a generic feature instead of proving determinacy for special cases. Cf. Bamberg and Richter (1984), Bamberg

Measurement in Economics
ed. by W. Eichhorn

(1984), Buchholz (1985).

The analysis is generally conducted in a model of portfolio choice where financial investment decisions have to be made between two assets, a safe and a risky one. The "mean-variance" framework of early papers (Tobin, 1957/58; M.K. Richter, 1959/60) has later been succeeded by the more general Arrowian framework of expected utility maximization (Mossin, 1968; Stiglitz, 1969; Ahsan, 1974; Atkinson and Stiglitz, 1980; Koskela and Kanniainen, 1984).

The following analysis is off the mainstream in one important respect. We shall study the effect of taxation on the expected *utility* from alternative investments rather than the effect that taxation has on the *demand* for risky assets. We thus drop the portfolio model and any explicit demand analysis. This greatly simplifies the presentation and allows us to discuss arbitrary (though sufficiently differentiable) tax functions. The model specification was originally suggested by Feldstein (1969) and resumed by Schneider 1980 and Bamberg and Richter (1984).

The somewhat surprising result will be that even such a simple analysis of risk-taking requires to decompose the total effect of taxation into three partial ones. Their respective strength is measured by three income elasticities, namely, the investor's relative risk aversion and two local measures of tax progression. Theorem 1 of section 2 derives an explicit algebraic formula for decomposing the total effect. As the partial effects tend to be of opposite sign their combination produces ambiguity in general. Only if special assumptions concerning risk attitude and tax progression are made will the effect of taxation become determinate. Section 3 is devoted to an analysis of such special cases. Sections 4 and 5 take the viewpoint of some tax reform. In section 6 theorem 2 of section 4 is then applied to the German tax reform of 1986/88. This reform is one of the rare exceptions producing an unambiguous total effect. As we are going to demonstrate risk-taking should decrease as a result of this reform, at least in some broad medium income range.

2. The Effect of Taxation on Risk-Taking: A General Theorem

Let I be an interval in $\mathbb{R}_+ = \{Y \geq 0\}$ with non-empty interior $\mathcal{O} \subseteq I$. Let $\tilde{y}$ denote some random variable with values in $\mathcal{O}$. $\tilde{y}$ is interpreted as the stochastic return to some risky investment. Because $\mathcal{O} \subseteq I \subseteq \mathbb{R}_+$ losses do not occur by assumption. In case of full offset our results may however be extended to cases with negative returns. E stands for the expectation operator and $E\tilde{y} = \bar{y}$ for expected return.

Let $U:\mathbb{R}_+ \to \mathbb{R}$ be a von Neumann-Morgenstern utility function, twice continuously differentiable on $\mathbb{R}_{++}$ with $U'(Y) > 0$ for all $Y > 0$. $y_U = y_U(\tilde{y})$ is implicitly defined by

$$U(y_U) = EU(\tilde{y})$$

and interpreted as the *certainty equivalent*. In a world with no taxation the investor characterized by U would be indifferent between the riskless return y_U and the risky alternative $\tilde{y}$. $E\tilde{y} - y_U$ is a *risk premium*.

Let us now introduce taxation into the decision maker's world. Let $T:I \to \mathbb{R}$ be twice continuously differentiable in $\mathcal{O}$ holding $T(Y) < Y$ and $T'(Y) < 1$ for all $Y \in \mathcal{O}$. Interpret $T(Y)$ as tax liability and

$R(Y) := Y - T(Y)$ as residual income.

We say that T [*strictly*] *increases* U's *propensity to take risk (on* $\mathcal{O}$ *)* if for all [non-degenerate] random variables $\tilde{y}$ with values in $\mathcal{O}$

$$U(R(y_U)) \leq [<] \; EU(R(\tilde{y})) \; . \tag{1}$$

The idea is the following. Without taxation U is indifferent between the certain y_U and the uncertain $\tilde{y}$. When taxation is introduced U receives $R(y_U)$ and $R(\tilde{y})$, respectively, after tax. The implicit assumption is that there is no tax shifting so that U has to incur the full tax burden. If $EU(R(\tilde{y}))$ exceeds $U(R(y_U))$ then risk-taking is encouraged. In case of reversed inequality signs in (1) we speak of a [strict] decrease in U's propensity to take risk.

The question is: Under what conditions is risk-taking increased or decreased? The somewhat surprising result is that the highly stylized, partial analytical reduction of the problem still requires examining *three partial effects* for a full answer. The strength of the respective effects is measured by the following income elasticities $\eta_X(Y) = YX'(Y)/X(Y)$:

the *proportional inequality aversion* $\alpha(Y,T) = -\eta_{R'}(Y)$,

the *residual progression* $\rho(Y,T) = \eta_R(Y)$, and

the *relative risk aversion* $\alpha(Y,U) = -\eta_{U'}(Y)$.

The intuition is the following. Convex taxation, i.e. a monotone increasing marginal tax rate T' , imposes an excess burden on uncertain income: $ET(\tilde{y}) \geq T(E(\tilde{y}))$ ["Jensen's inequality"]. There are various ways to measure the excess burden. $ET(\tilde{y}) - T(E(\tilde{y})) = R(E(\tilde{y})) - ER(\tilde{y})$ would be a measure in units after tax. We can else choose $\bar{y} - R^{-1}(ER(\tilde{y}))$ as one of two obvious symmmetric expressions to measure the excess burden in units before tax. $\alpha(Y,T)$ is just a local measure for $[\bar{y} - R^{-1}(ER(\tilde{y}))]/\bar{y}$. Cf. Richter and Hampe (1984).

We may expect that risk-taking decreases when $\alpha(Y,T)$ becomes larger. The effect is hence of *negative* sign. For the sake of convenience we call this second order effect the *Jensen effect*.

On the other hand, progressive taxation, i.e. a strictly monotone increasing average tax rate $T(Y)/Y$, reduces income uncertainty. $R(\tilde{y})$ is more equally distributed in the sense of Lorenz than $\tilde{y}$. As Jakobson (1976) and Kakwani (1977) have shown, $\rho(Y,T)$ is a local measure of this levelling, first order effect, which we call the *risk-reducing effect*. We may expect a *positive* sign, i.e. risk-taking will increase when ρ-progression gets stronger (which by sign convention means smaller ρ-values).

Combining these two effects we may venture a conjecture. Linear progressive tax schedules, $T(Y) = bY-a$ with $a > 0$, $b < 1$ are best to encourage risk-taking. Furthermore, the encouragement is strongest for small ρ-values, i.e. for large $a/(1-b)$. Whether risk-taking definitely increases or not however depends on the investors risk aversion. That leads us to the third effect, the so-called *income effect*.

Non-trivial taxation, $T \neq 0$, has a pure income, zero order effect. It locally varies the investor's risk aversion. The sign of this last effect depends on $\frac{d}{dY}\alpha(Y,U)$ and is hence indeterminate in general. Risk-taking will however tend to increase if $\alpha(Y,U) \geq \alpha(R(Y),U)$ holds for all Y . The latter is the case if $T \geq 0$ and the Arrowian assumption of a monotone increasing relative risk aversion is met.

The literature in the portfolio-choice tradition focuses on proportional taxation. Ahsan (1974) goes beyond that by analyzing linear taxation. The consideration of non-linear progressive taxes seems to be the exception [e.g. Buchholz (1985)]. Note that the Jensen effect disappears under linear taxation and the risk-reducing one additionally disappears under proportional taxation. The income effect is governed by the relative risk aversion which thus takes the place of the wealth elasticity of the demand for risky investments in models of portfolio choice. The connection is the following theorem of Arrow (1965): The wealth elasticity of demand for the risky asset in a two-asset model of portfolio choice is less [greater] than unity if the relative risk aversion is strictly monotone increasing [decreasing].

Fellingham and Wolfson (1978, p. 342) developed a clear intuition about the three partial effects that taxation has on risk-taking. The following theorem makes their intuition precise and shows how the total effect decomposes algebraically.

Theorem 1:

T [strictly] increases U's propensity to take risk iff

$$\alpha(Y,U) \geq \alpha(R(Y),U)\rho(Y,T) + \alpha(Y,T) \qquad \text{for all } Y \in \mathcal{O} \tag{2}$$

[and $>$ for at least one Y in every subinterval].

The assertion holds in either the strong form (indicated in brackets) or the weak form (with the bracketed material omitted). Furthermore, "increases" may be replaced by "decreases" if the inequality sign in (2) is reversed. Note that the question whether risk-taking is increased or not locally depends only on the "curvature" of T and U and not on the distribution of risks.

The *proof* follows directly from Pratt's (1964) theorem 1. Just set $V(Y) := U(R(Y))$ and note that $V' > 0$ on $\mathcal{Y}$ by assumption. Then (1) reads

$$V(y_U) \leq [<] \; EV(\tilde{y})$$

where the right-hand equals $V(y_V)$ by definition. Hence (1) for all [non-degenerate] $\tilde{y}$ is equivalent to

$$y_U(\tilde{y}) \leq [<] \; y_V(\tilde{y}) \qquad \text{for all [non-degenerate] } \tilde{y}$$

which, by Pratt's theorem is equivalent to

$$\alpha(Y,U) \geq \alpha(Y,V)$$

for all $Y \in \mathcal{Y}$ [with $>$ for at least one Y in every subinterval]. It therefore remains to show

$$\alpha(Y,V) = \alpha(R(Y),U)\rho(Y,T) + \alpha(Y,T) \; . \qquad (3)$$

Note that $V(Y) = U(R(Y))$ implies

$$V'(Y) = U'(R(Y))T'(Y) \quad \text{and}$$
$$V''(Y) = U''(R(Y))[R'(Y)]^2 + U'(R(Y))R''(Y) \; ,$$

hence

$$\frac{V''(Y)}{V'(Y)} = \frac{U''(R(Y))}{U'(R(Y))}R(Y)\frac{R'(Y)}{R(Y)} + \frac{R''(Y)}{R'(Y)} \; ,$$

i.e. (3). q.e.d.

3. Analysis of Some Special Cases

Let us evaluate (2) for special cases.

We speak of *risk neutrality* if U is linear, $U(Y) = a + bY$ $\Leftrightarrow$ $\alpha(Y,U) = 0$. The combination of risk neutrality and convexity of T, $\alpha(Y,T) \geq 0$ for all Y, leaves us with a pure Jensen effect and hence an unambiguous total effect. (2) holds with reversed inequality signs. [Cf. e.g. Bamberg and Richter (1984, theorem 1) and Fellingham and Wolfson (1978)].

Corollary 2: In case of risk neutrality risk-taking strictly decreases whenever the tax is strictly convex. On the other hand, risk-taking is unaffected by linear taxation.

Since progressive tax schedules need not be convex, risk-taking may well increase for progressive T and risk-neutral U. Cf. Schneider (1980) and Fellingham and Wolfson (1984).

Consider proportional taxation next. $T(Y) = bY$, $Y \in I$, yields a pure income effect and (2) reduces to $\alpha(Y,U) \geq \alpha((1-b)Y,U)$. Increasing monotonicity of $\alpha(Y,U)$ is a widely accepted behavioural assumption giving the income effect a positive sign. If it is met we obtain Domar and Musgrave's (1944) classical result:

Corollary 3: If the relative risk aversion of U is [strictly] monotone increasing then risk-taking [strictly] increases under proportional taxation.

In case of some monotone decreasing $\alpha(Y,U)$ risk-taking is clearly decreased. This possibility was recognized by Feldstein (1969). [The effect of *proportional* taxation on risk-taking is discussed, among others, by Tobin (1958), M.K. Richter (1960), Mossin (1968), Stiglitz (1969), Allingham (1972), Haegert and Kramm (1975), Atkinson and Stiglitz (1980).]

Corollary 3 does not extend straightforwardly to linear taxes. The difficulty is that $R(Y)$ may exceed Y for low income Y so that increasing monotonicity of relative risk aversion does not ensure global unambiguity of the income effect. If however $I \subseteq [a/b,\infty)$ where $T(Y) = bY - a$, $a > 0$, $b < 1$ then we obtain

Corollary 4: If the relative risk aversion of U is positive and monotone increasing then risk-taking strictly increases on $\mathfrak{T} \subseteq I \subseteq [a/b,\infty)$ under linear progressive taxation $T(Y) = bY - a$.

Proof: By assumption $R(Y) < Y$ for $Y \in I$. Hence $\alpha(Y,U) \geq \alpha(R(Y),U) > 0$. Furthermore $\alpha(Y,T) = 0$ and $\rho(Y,T) < 1$, implying strict inequality in (2) .

U is called [*strictly*] *risk averse* at $Y > 0$ if $\alpha(Y,U) \geq [>] \ 0$.

For corollaries 5 - 7 we restrict consideration to isoelastic utility functions, thus neutralizing the income effect. Let $U = U_\varepsilon$ where

$$U_\varepsilon(Y) = \begin{cases} c \log Y + d & \text{for } \varepsilon=1 \\ c \dfrac{Y^{1-\varepsilon}}{1-\varepsilon} + d & \text{for } \varepsilon \neq 1 . \end{cases}$$

Because $\alpha(Y,U_\varepsilon) = \varepsilon$, (2) can be written

$$\varepsilon(1 - \rho(Y,T)) \geq [>] \ \alpha(Y,T) \ . \qquad (2')$$

The next result deals with a situation governed by a pure risk-reducing effect.

Corollary 5: If $U = U_\varepsilon$ is isoelastic with elasticity $\varepsilon > 0$ then a linear progressive tax strictly increases risk-taking.

For residually isoelastic $T(Y) = Y - bY^a$, (2') simplifies further:

$$\varepsilon(1 - a) \geq [>] \ 1 - a \ .$$

For progressive T , $a < 1$, this is equivalent to

$$\alpha(Y,U_\varepsilon) \geq [>] \ 1 = \alpha(Y,\log) \ .$$

We hence obtain a corollary originally suggested by Feldstein (1969):

Corollary 6: Let $U = U_\varepsilon$ and $T(Y) = Y - bY^a$ with $a < 1$. T increases risk-taking if and only if U_ε is more risk averse than log (i.e. iff $\varepsilon \geq 1$) .

Note that in this special case the *degree* of progression is irrelevant to whether risk-taking is increased or not. Only U's attitude towards risk matters. See Figure 1, below.

The next corollary is to sustain the intuition that *any* progressive tax increases risk-taking if only risk-aversion is sufficiently strong. The corollary thus contrasts with corollary 2.

Let I be *compact*. Let T be arbitrary but progressive in the local sense, $\rho(Y,T) < 1$ for *all* $Y \in I$. Then define

$$\sup_{Y \in I} \frac{\alpha(Y,T)}{1-\rho(Y,T)} =: \varepsilon_T < \infty .$$

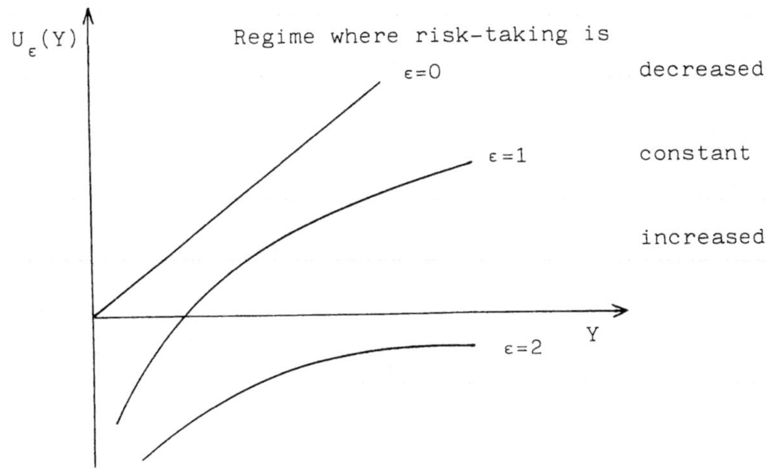

Figure 1: The effect of residually isoelastic progressive taxation on risk-taking when utility functions are isoelastic

Corollary 7: Risk-taking increases for all U_ε with $\varepsilon \geq \varepsilon_T$.

The proof follows from dividing (2) by $1 - \rho$.

By a similar argument we could easily show that risk-taking unambiguously increases if U displays constant absolute risk aversion, $-U''/U' = \gamma$, and if, furthermore, γ is sufficiently large.

4. The Effect of Tax Reform on Risk-Taking: A Theorem

Theorem 1 and all subsequent corollaries analyze risk-taking in reaction to a new tax. The discussion easily extends to the comparison of two alternative tax schedules T_1 and T_2 . This is the tax reform viewpoint. Denote $R_i(Y) = Y - T_i(Y)$, $U_i(Y) := U(R_i(Y))$ and define y_{U_i} by

$$U_i(y_{U_i}) = EU_i(\tilde{y}) .$$

Let us say that T_2 *increases risk-taking of* U *in comparison to* T_1 if for all random variables $\tilde{y}$ with values in $\mathcal{O}$

$$U(R_2(y_{U_1})) \leq EU(R_2(\tilde{y}))$$

Theorem 2:

T_2 increases risk-taking of U in comparison to T_1 iff for all $Y \in \mathcal{O}$

$$\left.\begin{array}{l} \alpha(R_1(Y),U)\rho(Y,T_1) + \alpha(Y,T_1) \\ \geq \alpha(R_2(Y),U)\rho(Y,T_2) + \alpha(Y,T_2) . \end{array}\right\} \quad (4)$$

The proof parallels the one of theorem 1.

5. Analysis of Special Cases

We shall give various applications of theorem 2. The first corollary is related to Ahsan's (1974) proposition III.1(b).

Corollary 8: If relative risk aversion of U is non-negative and monotone increasing, then an increase in the marginal tax rate in a system of linear progressive tax leads to increased risk-taking.

Proof: Set $T_i(Y) = b_iY - a$, $1 > b_2 \geq b_1$, $a \geq 0$. Then $\alpha(Y,T_i) = 0$ and $\rho(Y,T_1) \geq \rho(Y,T_2) > 0$. Furthermore, $R_1(Y) = (1-b_1)Y + a \geq (1-b_2)Y + a = R_2(Y)$ such that $\alpha(R_1(Y),U) \geq \alpha(R_2(Y),U) \geq 0$. Putting the pieces together yields (4). q.e.d.

Residual progression of some linear tax $T(Y) = bY - a$ can be increased by an increase of both the marginal tax rate b and the tax credit a. The effect on risk-taking is the same under the plausible Arrowian assumption of a monotone decreasing *absolute* risk aversion. The next corollary shows this for general T_1.

Corollary 9: $T_2(Y) = T_1(Y) - a$ with $a > 0$ increases risk-taking of U in comparison to T_1 if the absolute risk aversion $\alpha(Y,U)/Y$ is monotone decreasing.

Proof: We have to show

$$\alpha(R_1(Y),U)\rho(Y,T_1) \geq \alpha(R_2(Y),U)\rho(Y,T_2) \quad \text{which is equivalent to}$$

$$-\frac{U''(R_1(Y))}{U'(R_1(Y))} YR_1'(Y) \geq -\frac{U''(R_2(Y))}{U'(R_2(Y))} YR_2'(Y) \qquad \text{or}$$

$$-\left.\frac{U''}{U'}\right|_{R_1(Y)} \geq -\left.\frac{U''}{U'}\right|_{R_1(Y)+a} .$$

The latter holds whenever the absolute risk aversion is monotone decreasing. q.e.d.

The above corollary obviously holds, too, if "increases" and "decreasing" are replaced by "decreases" and "increasing". Following Arrow (1965) a decreasing absolute risk aversion is however considered to be a behaviourally more convincing assumption.

An exemplary tax reform producing a pure income effect and hence a clear-cut total effect on risk taking is the following:

$$R_2(Y) = bR_1(Y) \quad \Longleftrightarrow$$

$$T_2(Y) = T_1(Y) + (1-b)R_1 \quad \text{with} \quad b > 1 \,.$$

Because of $\rho(Y,T_1) = \rho(Y,T_2) > 0$, $\alpha(Y,T_1) = \alpha(Y,T_2)$ and $R_2(Y) > R_1(Y)$ we obtain

Corollary 10: T_2 decreases risk-taking of U in comparison to T_1 if the relative risk aversion of U is monotone increasing.

One would like to state similar results for other popular tax reforms such as

$$T_2(Y) = bT_1(Y) \,, \quad b > 1 \,, \quad \text{and}$$

$$T_2(Y) = T_1(Y+a) \,, \quad a > 0 \,.$$

Unfortunately, the total effect on risk-taking is highly ambiguous in these cases. The reason can be made plausible by the following observations. Whenever $T_1'(Y) > T_1(Y)/Y$ and $T_1''(Y) > 0$ then $\rho(Y,T_2) < \rho(Y,T_1)$ and $\alpha(Y,T_2) > \alpha(Y,T_1) > 0$ is obtained in case of $T_2 = bT_1$. T_2 is hence more progressive than T_1 in both the ρ- and the α-sense. Since both partial effects are of opposite sign with regard to risk-taking little can be said about the total effect. The case is different if $\alpha(Y,T_2) = \alpha(Y,T_1) = 0$. But then we are back in the situation of corollary 8. The case of $T_2(Y) = T_1(Y+a)$ tends to be even more indeterminate. Here all three effects may produce potential ambiguity. Without further assumptions concerning the sign of $\frac{d}{dY}\rho(Y,T_1)$ and $\frac{d}{dY}\alpha(Y,T_1)$ we even do not know whether T_2 increases progression in the ρ- or α-sense. We therefore refrain from analyzing this tax reform in any more detail.

6. The German Tax Reform: A Very Special Case

The overall conclusion is that a tax reform tends to produce counteracting partial effects in the general case. The case of an unambiguous total effect is nothing but a rare exception. Surprisingly enough, the German tax reform of 1986/88 is such an exception. The proof of this assertion shall close this paper and provide a last application of condition (4). (This section draws on W.F. Richter (1985).)

Let T_{81} denote the German income tax function having been effective since 1981. In 1985 the Parliament passed a tax reform providing a new formula T_{88} for the years 1988 onwards! (We shall disregard the introduction of an interim solution T_{86} for the years 1986 and 1987.) We now maintain that, assuming a monotone increasing relative risk aversion, T_{88} will definitely *decrease* risk-taking in comparison to T_{81} in some broad medium income range. Note that such a statement is an ordinal one. We do not say anything about the extent. The assertion concerns the direction only. Nevertheless, it will hardly be in conformity with implicit political objectives of the reformers.

The proof of our assertion is based on Figures 2 to 4. Figure 2 shows $T_{88}(Y) \leq T_{81}(Y)$ for all $Y \in \mathbb{R}_+$. Assuming a monotone increasing relative risk aversion we obtain $\alpha(R_{88}(Y),U) \geq \alpha(R_{81}(Y),U)$, so that risk-taking is decreased by the income effect. Figure 3 shows $\rho(Y,T_{88}) \geq \rho(Y,T_{81})$ for all $Y \in [19{,}000;\ 103{,}000]$. Inequality of residual income therefore increases under T_{88} which decreases the propensity to take risk. Finally according to Figure 4 $\alpha(Y,T_{88}) \geq \alpha(Y,T_{81})$ for all $Y \in [48{,}000;\ 79{,}000]$ and all $Y \in [82{,}000;\ \infty)$. The sign reversal in the interval $(79{,}000;\ 82{,}000)$ is thereby so insignificant that it may safely be ignored. Again, an increased Jensen effect tends to decrease risk-taking. The assertion now follows by setting $\mathfrak{S} := (48,000; 103,000)$.

7. Summary

The total effect of progressive taxation on risk-taking falls into three partial ones: the income, Jensen, and risk-reducing effects. Their strength is measured by the investor's relative risk aversion and by two local measures of tax progression, the proportional inequality aversion and the residual income progression. An explicit formula states how the total effect decomposes algebraically in the general case. Many important results of the literature relevant to the subject may be recovered by specialization.

References

Ahsan, S.M. (1974), Progression and risk taking, Oxford Economic Papers 26, 318-328

Allingham, M.G. (1972), Risk-taking and taxation, Zeitschrift für Nationalökonomie 32, 203-224

Arrow, K.J. (1965), Aspects of the theory of risk-bearing, Yrjö Jahnssonin Säätiö, Helsinki

Atkinson, A.B. and J.E. Stiglitz (1980), Lectures on public economics, McGraw-Hill, Maidenhaid

Bamberg, G. (1984), Auswirkungen progressiver Steuertarife auf die Bereitschaft zur Risikoübernahme, in: Aktuelle Probleme der Marktwirtschaft in gesamt- und einzelwirtschaftlicher Sicht, R. Blum and M. Steiner (eds.), Duncker & Humblot, Berlin, 265-277

Bamberg, G. and W.F. Richter (1984), The effects of progressive taxation on risk-taking, Zeitschrift für Nationalökonomie 44, 93-102

Buchholz, W. (1985), Die Wirkung progressiver Steuern auf die Vorteilhaftigkeit riskanter Investitionen, Zeitschrift für betriebswirtschaftliche Forschung 37, 882-890

Domar, E.D. and R.A. Musgrave (1944), Proportional income taxation and risk-taking, Quarterly Journal of Economics 58, 388-422.

Feldstein, M.S. (1969), The effects of taxation on risk-taking, Journal of Political Economy 77, 755-764

Fellingham, J.C. and M.A. Wolfson (1978), The effects of alternative income tax structures on risk-taking in capital markets, National Tax Journal 31, 339-347

Fellingham, J.C. and M.A. Wolfson (1984), Progressive income taxes and the demand for risky assets, National Tax Journal 37, 127-129

Friedman, M. (1962), Capitalism and freedom, the Univ. of Chicago Press, Chicago

Haegert, L. and R. Kramm (1975), Der Einfluß von Steuern auf die Vorteilhaftigkeit von Investitionen mit unterschiedlichem Risiko, Zeitschrift für betriebswirtschaftliche Forschung 27, 69-83

Jakobsson, U. (1976), On the measurement of the degree of progression, Journal of Public Economics 5, 161-168

Kakwani, N.C. (1977), Applications of Lorenz curves in economic analysis, Econometrica 45, 719-727

Koskela, E. and V. Kanniainen (1984), Changing the tax base and risk-taking, Oxford Economic Papers 36, 162-174

Mossin, J. (1968), Taxation and risk-taking: an expected utility approach, Economica 35, 74-82

Pratt, J.W. (1964), Risk aversion in the small and in the large, Econometrica 32, 122-136

Richter, M.K. (1959/60), Cardinal utility, portfolio selection, and taxation, Review of Economic Studies 27, 152-166

Richter, W.F. (1985), Modelltheoretische Analyse der Steuertarifreform 1986/88 und ihrer dämpfenden Wirkung auf die Risikobereitschaft im mittleren Einkommensbereich, Zeitschrift für betriebswirtschaftliche Forschung 37, 1070-1077

Richter, W.F. and J.F. Hampe (1984), Measuring the gain from splitting under income taxation, Methods of Operations Research 51, 384-400

Schneider, D. (1980), The effects of progressive and proportional income taxation on risk-taking, National Tax Journal XXXIII, 67-76

Stiglitz, J.E. (1969), The effect of income, wealth, and capital gains taxation on risk-taking, Quarterly Journal of Economics 83, 263-283

Tobin, J. (1957/58), Liquidity preference as behavior towards risk, Review of Economic Studies 25, 65-86

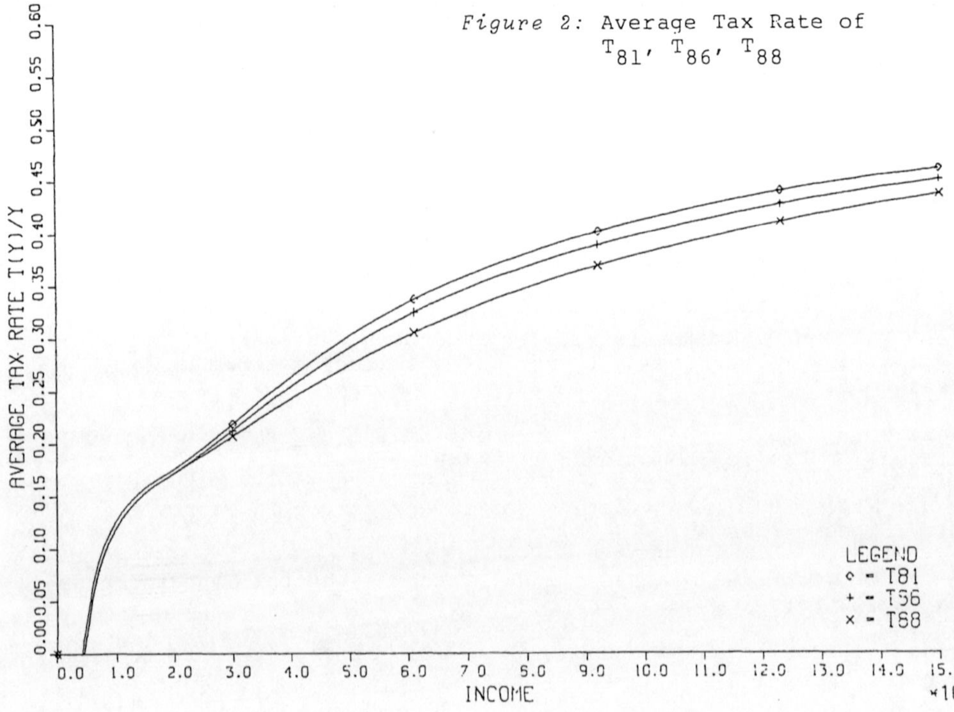

Figure 2: Average Tax Rate of T_{81}, T_{86}, T_{88}

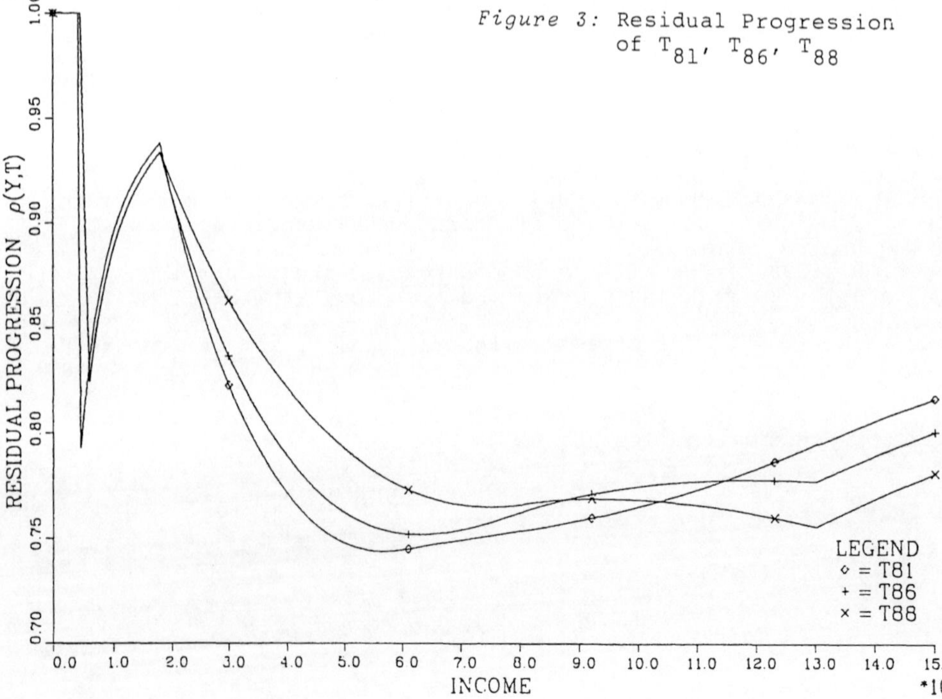

Figure 3: Residual Progression of T_{81}, T_{86}, T_{88}

Figure 4: Proportional Inequality Aversion of T_{81}, T_{86}, T_{88}

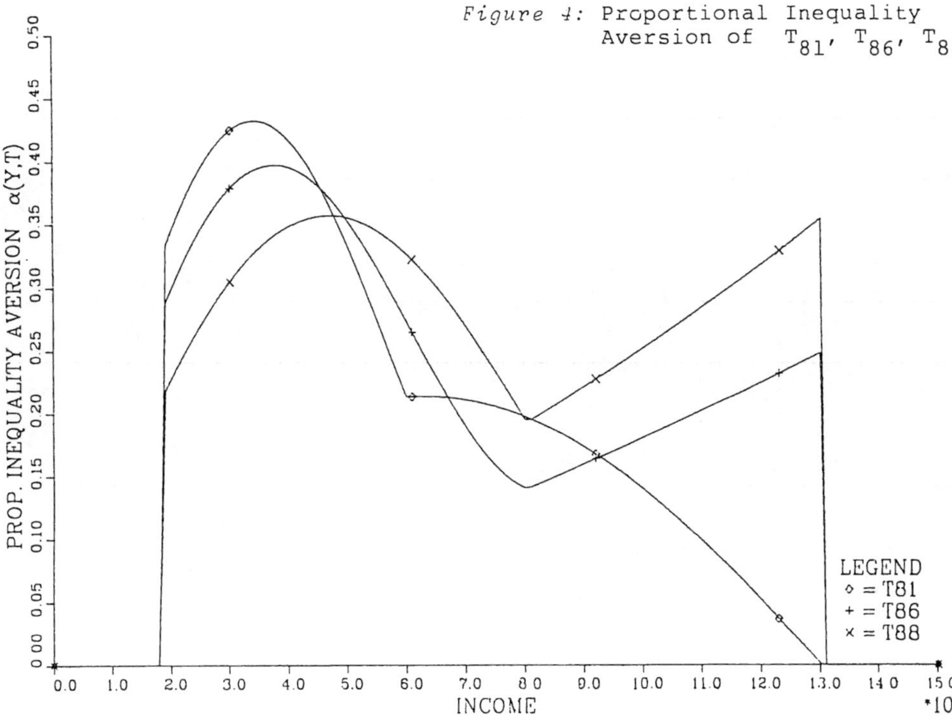

Measuring the Burden of Taxation: An Index Number Approach*

Bernd Genser
Department of Economics and Statistics
University of Konstanz
D-7750 Konstanz, Box 5560

Measuring the burden which taxes impose upon a representative citizen has been both an issue of public finance theory and of fiscal policy analysis for a long time. Nevertheless official national and international statistics offer rather crude tax/income ratios (based on summary figures of budget data and/or national account statistics or on imputed figures of specific benchmark households) only. Standardized measures of the tax burden, similar to indices used in price, wage, or production statistics are still lacking although such measures should serve as more reliable quantitative indicators to judge tax policy programmes which dominate todays political discussions.

This paper offers a guideline to establish tax burden indices concentrating on commodity taxes in the first sections but tackles the measurement of direct household taxes too. Having shown elsewhere (Genser 1985, 1985a) that simple summary measures, viz. aggregate elasticities, may be rather misleading to illustrate changes in the burden of Austrian consumer taxes I introduce a Laspeyres consumer tax index and a related consumer tax quota in section 1. Both measures can be calculated from disaggregated price index data. To overcome the bias of a Laspeyres index economic tax burden indices are defined in section 2, which may be extended to include the tax burden caused by the deadweight loss of distorting consumer taxes. In section 3 the consumer tax index concept is modified further integrating income tax and social insurance contributions thus catching the burden of direct and indirect household taxes simultaneously. These direct taxes can also be included in an economic household outlay index (section 4). Some additional remarks on the usefulness of tax burden indices conclude the paper.

*For helpful remarks on a preliminary version of the paper I owe thanks to two anonymous referees and to Michael Gilroy (Univ. of Konstanz)

Measurement in Economics
ed. by W. Eichhorn

1. The consumer tax index

Commodity taxes are a part of consumer prices and thus are included within the costs of living. Changing commodity tax rates give rise to economic adjustment processes and the resulting price changes can be measured by a cost of living index.

Usually the variety of influences on consumer prices will not allow to identify the tax induced component of price movements. Within an economic model the tax effects on consumer prices can be studied by splitting up consumer prices p into a producer price component π and a consumer tax component t.

$$p(x) = t + \pi(x) \tag{1}$$

The structure of the underlying technology determines how tax rate changes influence consumer prices via producer price adjustments besides the direct tax effect.

Nevertheless it is always possible to identify the tax component of any consumer price equilibrium ex post and thus a broad variety of consumer tax indices might be defined in formal analogy to different types of consumer price indices. If the investigator is free to choose a certain index concept his selection will depend on a list of desirable properties which such an index should fulfill. For price indices the Fisher tests (Fisher 1922, Eichhorn/Voeller 1976) or recent attempts to base certain types of index numbers on the theory of functional equations (Eichhorn 1978) offer an apt survey. A catalogue of basic as well as desirable properties for consumer tax indices is listed in Genser (1985). Some of these properties, which should be helpful to judge a consumer tax index concept, are referred to below.

To calculate a consumer tax index for Austria numerically all potential candidates for indices had to be omitted which would have needed data not yet available. In this context a Laspeyres fix weight consumer tax index has proved most promising as this index is closely related to the official consumer price index and makes use of the data fund of monthly consumer price statistics.

The current Austrian consumer price index CPI is defined by means of prices p_i and quantities q_i of 582 commodity items, the superscript o

Fig. 1: Consumer Tax Index and Consumer Price Index (annual growth rates)

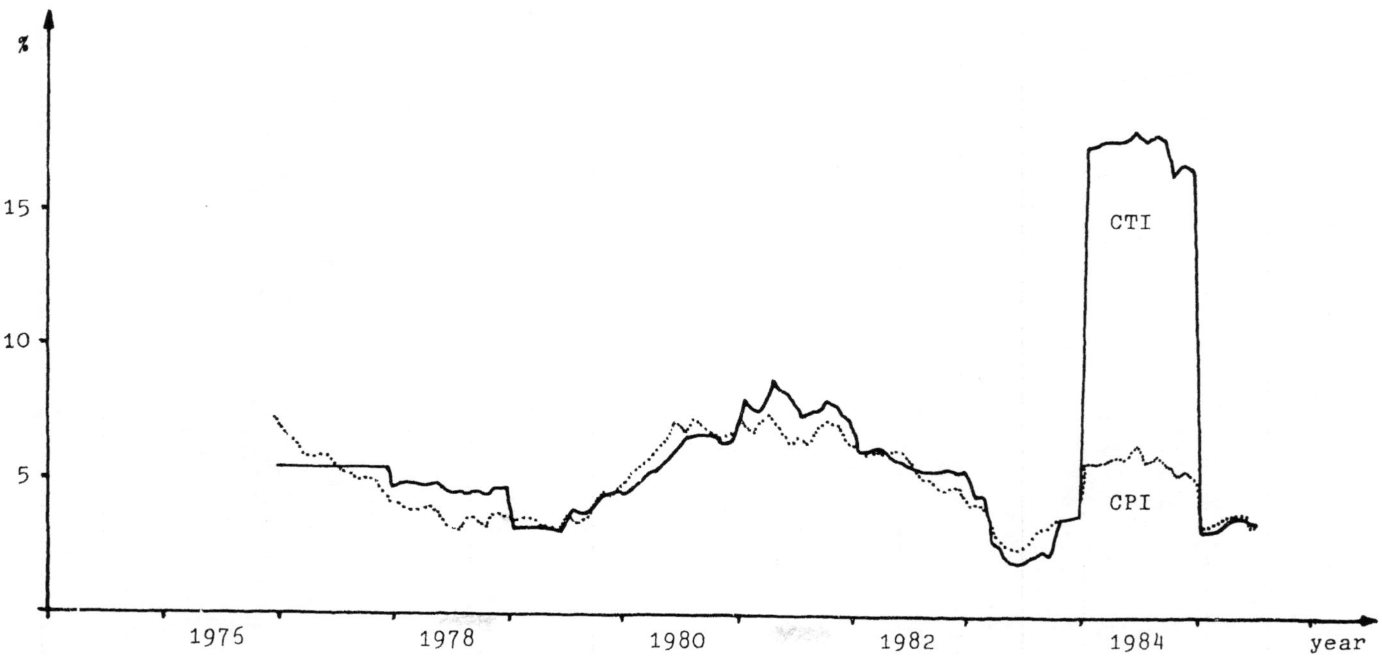

refers to the base period 1976.

$$CPI = \sum p_i q_i^o / \sum p_i^o q_i^o = \sum [p_i^o q_i^o / \sum p_j{}^o q_j{}^o] \cdot [p_i / p_i^o] = \sum w_i RP_i \qquad (2)$$

To catch the price movements across the whole nation relative price changes are reported instead of commodity prices and the CPI is calculated monthly as the weighted average of the national means of relative commodity price changes RP_i, the weights w_i being the expenditure shares of the commodity items in the base period consumer basket (ÖStZ 1976).

In analogy to (2) a consumer tax index CTI can be defined which making use of the same transformations reads as

$$CTI = \sum t_i q_i^o / \sum t_i^o q_i^o = \sum w_i [t_i / p_i^o] / \sum w_i [t_i^o / p_i^o] =$$
$$= \sum w_i RP_i [t_i / p_i] / \sum w_i [t_i^o / p_i^o] \qquad (3)$$

with t_i the unit tax component included in the consumer price p_i of commodity i.

For a numerical calculation of the CTI according to (3) weights w_i and relative prices RP_i can be used from the monthly price statistics. As most of the commodity taxes are ad valorem taxes most tax ratios needed in (3) are determined directly by tax laws. Only for some unit taxes (petrol tax, beer tax, alcohol monopoly duty) actual tax and price data are necessary to calculate the consumer tax index. A monthly time series of an Austrian CTI has been calculated (Genser 1985a) which includes ten major commodity taxes (value-added tax, tobacco tax, petrol taxes, alcohol tax, motor vehicle tax, insurance tax, beverage tax, beer tax, alcohol monopoly duty). The time profile of annual growth rates is shown in fig. 1. The change in the relative tax burden can be illustrated by comparing the monthly figures of the CTI with the CPI, which measures the relative increase of the costs for the whole commodity basket.

The graphical analysis shows very clearly the "upward shift of the commodity tax burden in 1978, 1981 and 1984, when VAT rates were increased, but it also catches minor tax reliefs caused by inflationary erosion of unit taxes, especially the petrol tax and the motor vehicle excise tax in 1980 and 1981, and the consequences of inhomogeneous price movements, which lower the tax burden if the prices of highly taxed "luxuries" rise less than those of lowly taxed "necessities" (or vice versa).

Besides this advantage of relying on official price data the consumer tax index (3) also fulfills important basic properties (monotonicity, homogeneity, identity, dimensionality and permutation invariance) and it satisfies the time reversal test, the circularity test, the determinateness test, and the decomposability test (cf. Genser 1985). The only well-known desideratum the CTI fails to pass is Fisher's factor reversal test or its less restrictive version, the product test. But opposite to the case of the price/quantity index symmetry the failure of the "quantity index of tax bases" defined by (3) implicitly

$$CTB = (\sum t_i q_i / \sum t_i^o q_i^o / CTI = \sum t_i q_i / \sum t_i q_i^o \qquad (4)$$

to pass the same tests as CTI, viz. the time reversal and the circularity test, thus violating the product test does not seem very harmful if one considers the minor economic relevance of such a tax base index.

Changes in the relative tax burden may be quantified by means of a consumer tax quota which measures consumer taxes as a share of overall commodity expenditures.

$$CTQ = \sum t_i q_i^o / \sum p_i q_i^o = CTI \cdot \sum t_i^o q_i^o / [CPI \cdot \sum p_i^o q_i^o] = CTQ^o \cdot CTI/CPI \qquad (5)$$

The standardized consumer tax quota turns out to be simply the base year quota adjusted by the ratio of consumer tax index and consumer price index. Formula (5) also offers a rather convenient factorization of the CTI

$$CTI = (CTQ/CTQ^o) \cdot CPI \qquad (6)$$

splitting up the growth factor of standardized tax load into a "tax quota index" catching the change in the average tax rate between base and current period and into the pure inflationary trend CPI.

The quantitative analysis may be refined by disaggregating the consumer tax index into subindices of selected commodity subgroups or of single commodity taxes making use of the decomposition property of CTI. A further step of empirical analysis should dismiss the single represen-

Fig. 2: Value-added tax/expenditure ratio for different household expenditure levels

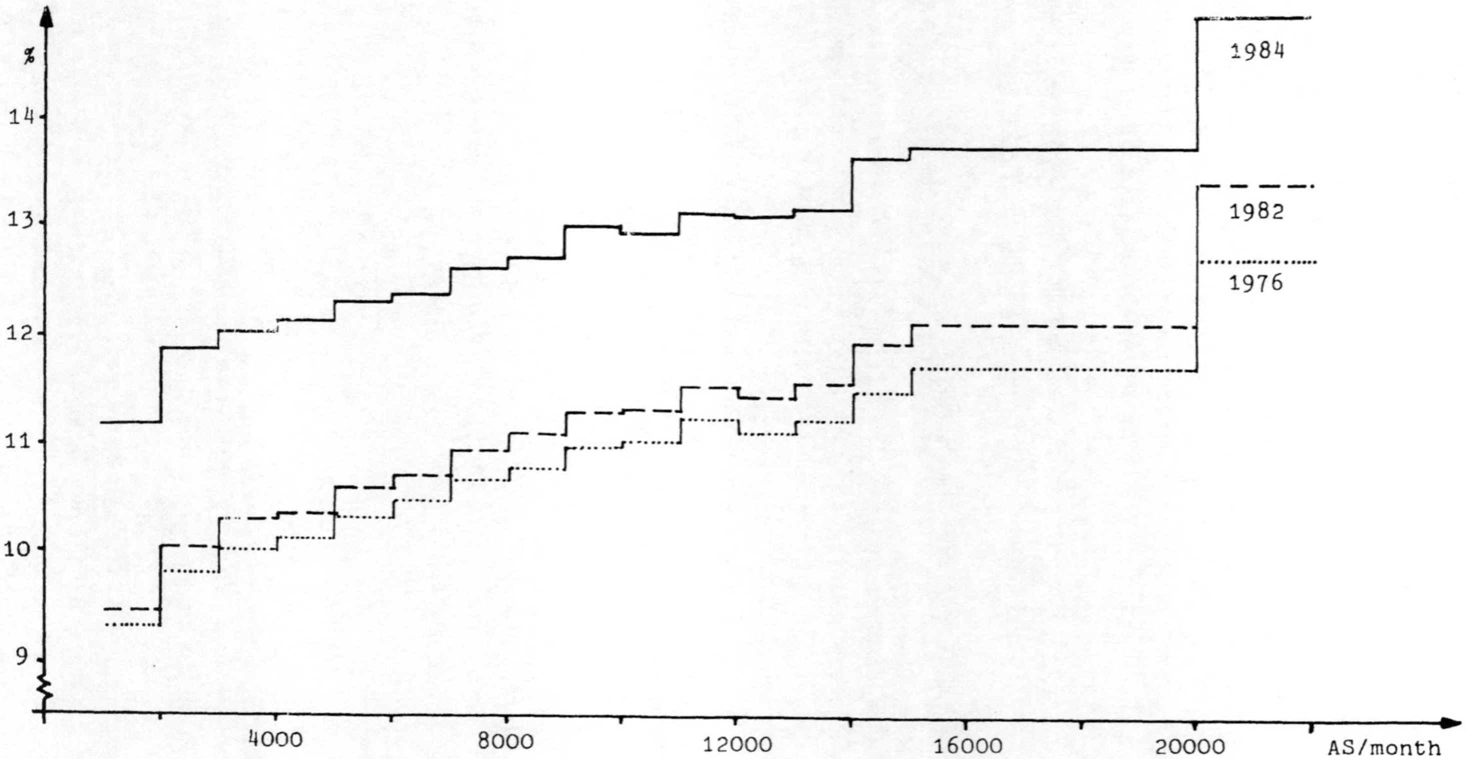

tative household concept and distinguish various household classes. A breakdown of households with respect to household income offers insight into the formal incidence of commodity taxes and allows an empirical test of the regressivity hypothesis of indirect taxes. A first quantitative analysis indicates that the graduation of the Austrian value-added tax is likely to produce a progressive structure of commodity taxes with respect to household budgets (fig. 2). Although reliable data on household saving are lacking progressivity with respect to household income would only prevail if saving elasticities were rather close to one.

2. Economic consumer tax indices

Whereas fixed weight indices are very attractive from a statistical viewpoint, they suffer from a severe conceptional shortcoming by economic standards. By fixing weights, as for the Laspeyres price index, substitutional adjustments made by economic agents are ignored by definition. Thus also the information on changes in the tax burden mirrored in the CTI is biased. From an empirical point of view one might be tempted to shut one's eyes to this problem of the CTI, as long as the same faultiness arises with the CPI which is widely recognized as the economic indicator of inflation and one of the most important policy targets.

Nevertheless this pragmatic view of an empirical investigator does not render superfluous attempts to elaborate the concept of a "true consumer tax index". To catch economic behavior such an index must be based in the economic framework of rational household decisions. Again the formal analogy to economic price indices provides a useful guideline.

2.1 The Konyus consumer tax index

The Konyus price index, perhaps still better known as the "true cost of living index", is most conveniently defined by

$$CPI^{K} = e(p,u(q^{*}))/e(p^{o},u(q^{*})) \tag{7}$$

$e(p,u(q^{*}))$ is the expenditure function which measures the minimal budget allowing the rational consumer to realize a welfare level $u^{*}=$

$u(q^*)$, fixed by an arbitrarily chosen reference commodity bundle q^*, when the commodity price vector is p. The Konyus index CPI^K is the ratio of these two minimal budgets and by this compares the two price situations p^o and p.

Due to its definition the expenditure function has a lot of convenient properties, viz. monotonicity in p and in u, linear homogeneity in p, concavity in p, continuity in p (cf. Diewert 1982). If we additionally assume differentiability in p we can apply the Euler Theorem for homogeneous functions and we arrive at a representation of the expenditure function with the help of the Hicksian compensated demand functions $q_i^c(p,u^*)$ (Shephard-Lemma)

$$\sum p_i[\partial e(p,u^*)/\partial p_i] = e(p,u^*) = \sum p_i \cdot q_i^c(p,u^*) \qquad (8)$$

The Konyus price index can therefore be written equivalently as

$$CPI^K(p^o,p,u^*) = [pq^c(p,u^*)]/[p^oq^c(p^o,u^*)] \qquad (9)$$

where we have changed to vector notation and scalar products to simplify the formulae.

Concentrating on the consumer tax components included in consumer prices, given a commodity tax system, a Konyus consumer tax index may be defined

$$CTI^K(t^o,p^o,t,p,u^*) = [tq^c(p,u^*)]/[t^oq^c(p^o,u^*)] \qquad (10)$$

Index (10) allows one to compare the tax payments of a rational, utility maximizing consumer who adjusts his commodity bundle to changes in both the commodity tax and the commodity price vector and at the same time is fully income compensated to reach the reference utility level u^* at best.

Whereas the Konyus price index can be shown to fulfill a series of desirable properties, eg. the tests mentioned in the previous section (cf. Diewert 1981, Genser 1985), the Konyus commodity tax index seems less attractive. Major desiderata, eg. homogeneity, proportionality, dimensionality, do no longer hold for CTI^K. Nevertheless the Konyus consumer tax index may be proved to inherit the time reversibility and the circularity property from the Konyus price index, as well as the invariance of utility level property for homothetic preferences.

As regards bounds for CTI^K the mean value property of the price index cannot be reestablished, but similar interval bounds may be shown to hold, shifting the extreme tax rate ratios by some "Laspeyres tax base index". For the lower bound of CTI^K we get

$$CTI^K = tq^c(p,u^*)/t^oq^c(p^o,u^*) = (\sum(t_i/t_i^o)t_i^oq^c(p,u^*))/t^oq^c(p^o,u^*) \geq$$
$$\min\{t_i/t_i^o\} \cdot t^oq^c(p,u^*)/t^oq^c(p^o,u^*) = \min\{t_i/t_i^o\}\ TBI \qquad (11)$$

Combined with an analogous upper bound CTI is bounded by

$$\max\{t_i/t_i^o\}\cdot TBI \geq CTI^K \geq \min\{t_i/t_i^o\}TBI \qquad (12)$$

In a similar way inequalities can be found which resemble the well known Laspeyres and Paasche bounds of the Konyus index, but modified by a factor catching the maximum variation of compensated commodity changes

$$t^1q^c(p^1,u^o)/t^oq^c(p^o,u^o) \leq CTI^L\cdot\max\{q_i^c(p^1,u^o)/q_i^c(p^o,u^o\}$$

$$t^1q^c(p^1,u^1)/t^oq^c(p^o,u^1) \geq CTI^P\cdot\max\{q_i^c(p^1,u^1)/q_i^c(p^o,u^1)\}$$

For homothetic preferences the two inequalities can be combined yielding a transformed interval of Laspeyres and Paasche bounds for the Konyus commodity tax index.

The Konyus consumer tax index and the Konyus price index can be linked by a standardized tax quota which measures the share of consumer taxes included in the minimum budget for the utility compensated commodity basket.

$$CTQ^K(t,p,u^*) = [tq^c(p,u^*)]\ /[pq^c(p,u^*)] = CTQ^{K,o}\cdot CTI^K/CPI^K \qquad (14)$$

Reshuffling (14) allows to split up the Konyus commodity tax index into a "Konyus tax quota index" and the true inflationary trend CPI in analogy to formula (6). If the expenditure function and thus also the compensated demands were known, then by imputation of consumer tax rates both the Konyus consumer tax index and the corresponding consumer tax quota may be calculated as well.

2.2 The price increment index

The Konyus consumer tax index catches the loss in private purchasing power due to the payment of taxes. But it is well known that commodity taxes usually do not only shift purchasing power to the public sector but additionally reduce it due to a deadweight efficiency loss. This welfare reduction of taxation imposes an excess burden on the consumer which should be taken into account if the total economic burden of a tax system is considered.

Formally commodity taxes cause an excess burden, if it is possible to withdraw a lump-sum tax which is larger than the amount of commodity taxes without reducing the consumer's welfare level, viz. if the strict inequality sign holds in the net expenditure relation.

$$e(p-t,u^*) \leq e(p,u^*) - tq^c(p,u^*) \tag{14}$$

In extending the burden consideration all the loss in purchasing power connected with the existence of commodity taxes can be regarded simultaneously. I have defined an absolute price increment of taxation $d(t,p,u^*)$ as the rise of the minimal budget which is necessary to realize a reference welfare level u^* if commodity taxes t exist opposed to the fictitious no tax case.

$$d(t,p,u^*) = e(p,u^*) - e(p-t,u^*) \geq tq^c(p,u^*) \tag{15}$$

A comparison of two commodity tax structures differing because of a change in commodity taxes can be made by looking at their absolute price increments. The ratio of two price increments may be called price increment index

$$PII^\kappa(t^o,t,p^o,p,u^*) = d(t,p,u^*)/d(t^o,p^o,u^*) \tag{16}$$

where the superscript κ again refers to the embedding of (16) in the Konyus conceptional framework. PII^κ measures the relative increase of additional financial means necessary to realize the fixed welfare level u^* if commodity taxes are changed. This incremental budget flows partly to the fiscal authority as commodity tax, the rest is an income compensation for the deadweight loss due to efficiency distortions. Evidently, the price increment index will coincide with the Konyus price index if no excess burden occurs, viz. the inequality sign in (15) holds thus indicating that a commodity tax system is non-distorting and equivalent to a lump sum tax.

Again a burden quota can be defined connecting PII^K with the true cost of living index

$$PIQ^K(t,p,u^*) = d(t,p,u^*)/e(p,u^*) = PIQ^{K,O} \cdot PII^K/CPI^K \qquad (17)$$

The relative price increment of commodity taxes PIQ^K indicates the share of the minimal budget which does not contribute to individual welfare but is absorbed by tax payments and efficiency losses.

To arrive at numerical calculations for economic consumer tax indices information on complete consumer demand systems is necessary. To demonstrate the differences between consumer tax indices Genser (1985) has considered the special case of fuel taxation in Austria. Fuel is subject to two mineral oil taxes (since 1982 integrated) based on the weight of the fuels and to two ad-valorem taxes, the value-added tax and a special duty on mineral-oil. Within a two commodity world it is possible to arrive at explicit solutions for the expenditure function by integrating the system of Roy-Ville identities if Marshallian demand functions are given (cf. Hausman 1981). Annual growth rates of the Laspeyres, the Konyus and the price increment index for Austrian fuel taxes are shown in Table 1.

Basically, the Laspeyres index shows smaller rates of growth in periods of stable petrol prices, when economic indices reflect an increase in compensated fuel demand, whereas it shows higher rates than the economic indices, when petrol prices were rising during the second oil shock. In quantitative terms the differences are rather small, as might have been suspected, because of the low price elasticity for fuel demand. Thus, the Laspeyres and Konyus indices do not deviate very much as compensated and Marshallian demands are only slightly different. The excess burden of major fuel tax changes remains small too and does not cause differences between the Konyus and the price increment index.

Table 1: Fuel tax indices and total fuel taxes (annual growth rates)

	CTI^L	CTI^K	PII	Fuel Taxes
1977	1.9	3.1	2.8	6.7
1978	0.0	0.8	0.6	4.2
1979	9.0	7.8	8.2	11.8
1980	8.7	6.7	6.8	2.7
1981	19.4	16.0	17.0	16.4
1982	2.7	3.0	2.8	5.0
1983	-0.8	0.5	0.2	3.2
average 76/83	5.7	5.3	5.35	7.0

Source: Genser (1985)

3. Integration of direct taxes in statistical tax and price indices

The structure of the Laspeyres index offers the possibility to extend a tax index stepwise if one wants to include further taxes. Thus also direct household taxes (income taxes, social insurance contributions) can be integrated into a generalized index covering both commodity and income taxes. A generalized tax index can be defined simply by extending the quantity vector q^o by factor supplies s^o covering the tax bases of direct taxes and the tax rate vector t by the rates for direct taxes r.

$$GTI = (tq^o + rs^o)/(t^oq^o + r^os^o) \tag{18}$$

An index of this type is calculated in Canada. The Fraser Institute has been publishing an annual Canadian Consumer Tax Index since 1976 (Pipes/Walker 1982) to illustrate the growing tax burden on the average Canadian consumer.

If one is interested in direct taxes primarily then a comparison of tax burdens can also be made by using a generalized cost of living index, which includes household outlays on direct taxes in addition to consumption expenditures

$$TPI = (pq^o + rs^o)/(p^oq^o + r^os^o) \tag{19}$$

The TPI quantifies the increase in household gross income necessary to buy the fixed commodity basket at current prices as well as to pay current direct taxes connected with a fixed factor supply. A monthly "Tax and Price Index" was first published in England in 1979 (CSO 1979). This index has been developed to deflate gross household income more properly than usual price deflators do, as real purchasing power is influenced by changes of both consumer prices and direct household taxes.

To calculate indices like (18) and (19) numerically requires a consistent data base on the relevant determinants of direct household taxes. Besides this statistical problem there is a methodical difficulty, too. Whereas the fixed commodity basket q^o reflects the commodity tax base of a non-growing economy, the fixed supply of labour is well in accordance with empirical evidence and thus s^o reflects an adequate wage tax base of a growing economy. The TPI will therefore overemphasize direct taxes as opposed to commodity taxes. A bias of that type as well as some problems of data collection can be avoided by integrating direct household taxes into a household outlay index.

3.1 Household outlay index

The household outlay index (HOI) does not look at actual bases of income taxes but postulates an immediate relation between consumer expenditures and gross income which allows a consumer to cover these expenditures after having paid his income taxes. The HOI compares two gross budget levels which are necessary to keep a reference consumption level, taking into account changing prices and payment of direct taxes. A Laspeyres-type HOI is defined by

$$HOI = (pq^o + t(y))/(p^o q^o + t^o(y^o)) \qquad (20)$$

where y and y^o are gross income levels sufficient to buy consumer goods q^o as well as to pay direct household taxes

$$y = pq^o + t(y) \qquad (21)$$

For a numerical calculation of HOI one certainly needs information about relevant income tax characteristics of the average consumer but no wage rates and other income data. Imputation of monthly figures is

Fig. 3: Household Outlay Index, Consumer Price Index and Contractual Wage Index
(annual growth rates)

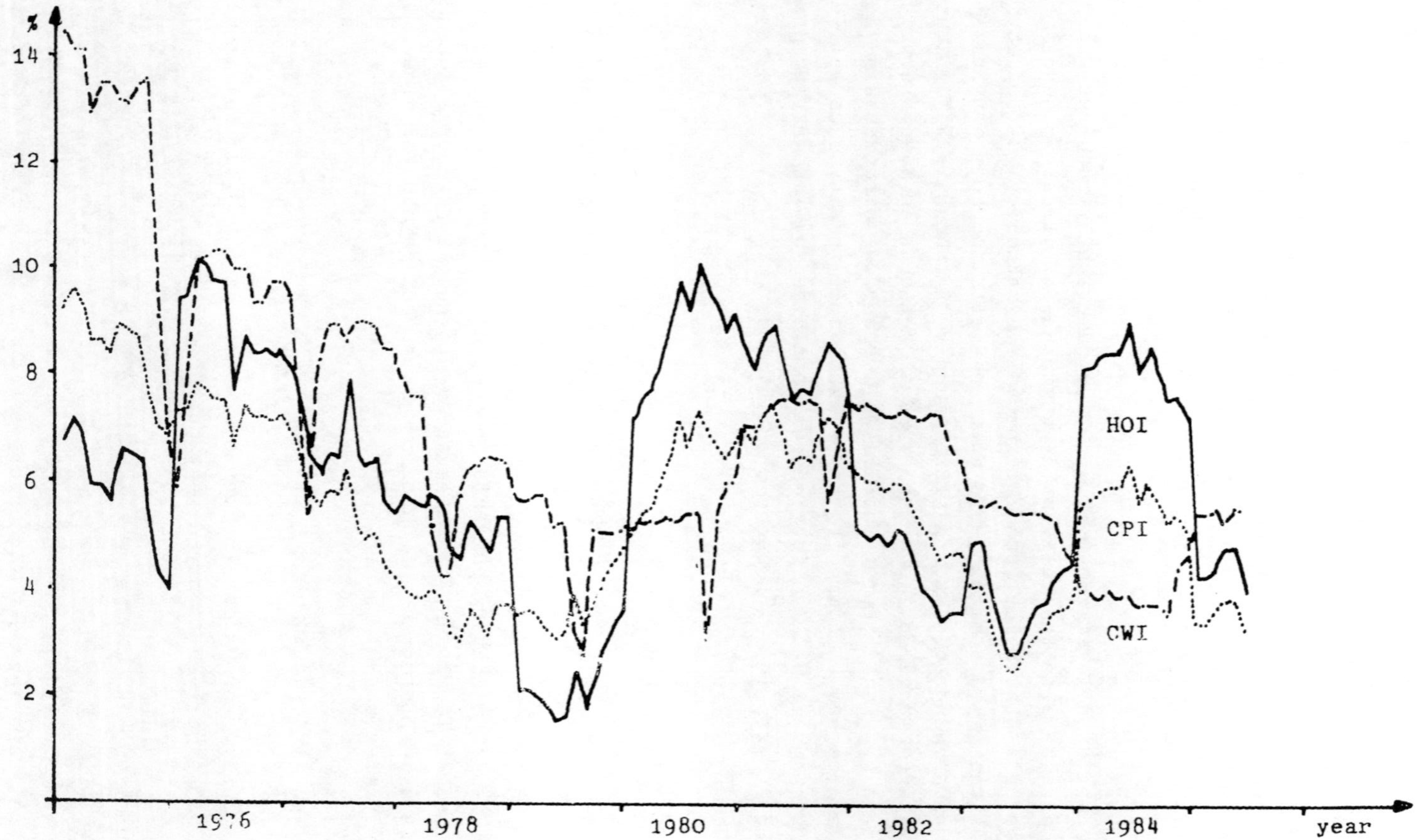

not trivial as progressivity effects and the annualization of income tax liability must be considered to produce a monthly series of HOI for Austria (Genser 1983). A HOI series for white collar workers in Austria (fig. 3) shows quite markedly the fiscal drag of the Austrian income tax which in 1980, 1981, and again in 1984 has led to a loss in net purchasing power although real gross income has grown. On the other hand income tax adjustments show considerable purchasing power gains in 1975, 1979, and 1982. In these years the rise in real income falls short of actual consumer gains, whereas all the other years are characterized by net purchasing power gains less than real income gains.

Along similar lines a Gross Earnings Deflator has been developed for England (Kay/Morris 1984). Monthly data have been published since 1979. Gillingham/Greenlees (1983) have recently used a HOI concept for US data on an annual base.

4. Integration of direct taxes in an economic household outlay index

Critical remarks on the neglection of commodity substitution are justified for the HOI as well as for any other Laspeyres index. By endogenizing commodity demand in (21) one arrives at a gross expenditure function which can be defined implicitly

$$g(p,u) = e(p,u) + t(g(p,u)) \tag{22}$$

Comparing the gross expenditure levels of two tax/price situations leads to the Konyus household outlay index which is defined as

$$HOI^K(t^o,t,p^o,p,u^*) = g(p,u^*)/g(p^o,u^*) \tag{23}$$

As regards index (23) it does not seem convincing to allow for substitution on the commodity side but at the same time to neglect possible consumer reactions on the labour supply side. If consumer decisions are considered within a model of endogenous work/leisure choice, the traditional view of the price index problem has to be changed. Disregarding direct taxes for the moment efficient allocations within a work/leisure model are characterized by an indirect utility function which includes the wage rate w as a further price parameter.

$$v(p,w,y) = \max_{q,f} \{u(q,f) \mid pq \leq w\cdot(1-f) \text{ with } s+f = 1\} \tag{24}$$

In (24) leisure f enters the utility function and is normalized as usual to add up to unity together with labour supply s. Solving the indirect utility function v(p,w,y) with respect to y for a given utility level u^* we may define a modified expenditure function as the solution of the dual minimum problem

$$e(p,w,u^*) = \min \{pq - w(1-f) \mid u(q,f) \geq u^*\} \tag{25}$$

But it is evident that defining a Konyus index with the help of expenditure function (25)

$$CPI^K(p^o,w^o,p,w,u^*) = e(p,w,u^*)/e(p^o,w^o,u^*) \tag{26}$$

will not result in a useful price index. By definition, expenditure function (25) catches only a residual component of the consumer budget, the lump-sum income in excess or short of compensated labour income to cover compensated consumer demand. This lump-sum income may well become zero or negative thus also the price index (26) may be undefined or negative.

Nevertheless a "useful" price index can be regained if the expenditure function is extended. We may define a "full expenditure function" which includes fictitious household outlays on leisure, the opportunity costs of reduced labour income,

$$e^F(p,w,u^*) = \min_{q,f}\{pq + wf \mid u(q,f) \geq u^*\} = w + e(p,w,u^*) > 0 \tag{27}$$

e^F must be positive by definition and e^F and e emanate from the same optimal consumption plan because the minimum problems (25) and (27) only differ in a scale shifting of the object function. Thus e and e^F describe the same efficient household decision. A Konyus type price index

$$CPI^F(p^o,w^o,p,w,u^*) = e^F(p,w,u^*)/e^F(p^o,w^o,u^*) \tag{28}$$

is always well defined and it measures the growth of the minimal "full expenditure budget" that allows the rational household to realize the reference utility level u^* after price and wage rate changes.

Following the lines of the household outlay index integration of direct taxes is straightforward. Besides outlays on commodities and leisure also direct taxes have to be paid. Nevertheless we have to consider that leisure is untaxed within existing income tax schemes and a "gross full expenditure function" must take care of this tax rule.

$$g^F(p,w,u^*;t) = \min_{q,f}\{g \mid u(q,f) \geq u^* \wedge g = pq+wf+t(g-wf)\} \qquad (29)$$

t is the income tax function which is applied to any tax base "gross full expenditure less fictitious outlays on leisure" to calculate tax liability. The "full household outlay index"

$$HOI^F = g^F(p,w,u^*;t)/g^F(p^o,w^o,u^*;t^o) \qquad (30)$$

compares the rise in gross budget needs of the representative household to cover expenditures on market commodities plus direct taxes to stay equally well off when prices, wages, and/or tax codes change.

Looking at the marginal conditions characterizing the Hicksian demands solving (29) we see immediately that g^F describes an efficient household decision which basically will deviate from that described by e^F, when income taxes are ignored. This is of course due to the fact that exempting leisure from taxation creates a distortion in relative prices which will cause excess burden losses if substitutional adjustments are made. However, the optimal plans yielding e^F and g^F will coïncide, if leisure is taxed too and thus income taxation is lump-sum. It can be shown further that although taking into account income taxes changes some of the well known duality results (homogeneity and symmetry properties), g^F is still monotonically increasing in prices, wages, and utility (cf. Baye/Black 1986, 47f.).

The full household outlay function g^F includes both consumer outlays on commodity taxes payed as a share of market prices and on income taxes which have been introduced explicitly in (29). Following the lines of commodity tax measurement in section 2 now again "true economic tax burden indices" and "standardized tax quotas" can be defined consistently for any tax or group of taxes desired by imputation of the respective tax amounts contained in g^F.

As regards progressivity analyses of the income tax an approach may be adopted which compares the current standardized tax load with a ficticious proportional income tax schedule determined by the average tax rate of some base period. For this special case of taxing income at a fixed tax rate τ the full household outlay function can be shown to be linearly homogeneous in its price variables

$$\begin{aligned} g^F(\lambda p,\lambda w,u^*;\tau) &= \min_{q,f}\{g\,|\,u(q,f)\geq u^*\wedge g = \lambda pq + \lambda wf + \tau(g-\lambda wf)\} = \\ &= \min_{q,f}\{\lambda\cdot\tilde{g}\,|\,u(q,f)\geq u^*\wedge g/\lambda = \tilde{g} = pq + wf + \tau(\tilde{g}-wf)\} = \\ &= \lambda g^F(p,w,u^*;\tau) \end{aligned} \quad (31)$$

a condition which ceases to hold for progressive or regressive tax codes. Nevertheless the proportionality benchmark case does not rule out the distorting effects of the income tax. If one compares the full household outlay function with a suitable expenditure function for a fictitious no tax case one is able to catch the efficiency loss due to the excess burden and to quantify the total burden of a distorting tax or tax system.

5. Concluding remarks

A natural way to improve the situation of lacking standardized measures of tax burden has been the introduction of an index concept. Statistical tax indices may be defined and calculated numerically in close relation to statistical price indices.

Like their price analogues statistical tax burden indices are biased, which calls for the development of economic tax burden indices. Although making use of the duality approach allows to define rather attractive economic indices, which even allow to quantify the burden due to the deadweight loss of welfare caused by distortionary taxes, economic tax burden indices do not possess certain convenient properties of cost of living indices. The situation even worsens if a progressive income tax is considered within a work/leisure model besides commodity taxes. Modified expenditure functions lose some of their important and convenient properties, but still allow to arrive at consistent measures of the joint burden of direct and indirect household taxes.

The question how closely true economic burden measures are approximated by statistical indices, which can be calculated using the existing data base, cannot be solved analytically. Nevertheless the instruments used to define the indices fit into the framework of applied general equilibrium models, which have recently been developed for some countries (cf. Shoven/Whalley 1984) and are being developed for some others. These models should offer further insight whether tax burden indices calculated from empirical data will be able to answer relevant questions, which can only be posed within a fully specified general equilibrium model at the moment.

References

Baye, Michael / Black, Dan (1986): Consumer Behavior, Cost of Living Measures, and the Income Tax. Springer, Berlin.

Central Statistical Office (1979): The Tax and Price Index - Sources and Methods. Economic Trends 310 (August), 81-89.

Diewert, Erwin (1981): The Economic Theory of Index Numbers: A Survey. In: A. Deaton (ed.): The Theory and Measurement of Consumer Behaviour. Cambridge University Press, 163-208.

Diewert, Erwin (1982): Duality Approaches to Microeconomic Theory. In: K. Arrow / M. Intriligator (eds.): Handbook of Mathematical Economics. Vol. 2, North Holland, Amsterdam, 535-599.

Eichhorn, Wolfgang (1978): Functional Equations in Economics. Addison-Wesley, Reading.

Eichhorn, Wolfgang / Voeller, Joachim (1976): Theory of the Price Index. Fisher's Test Approach and Generalisations. Springer, Berlin.

Fisher, Irving (1922): The Making of Index Numbers. Riverside Press, Cambridge (3rd ed.).

Genser, Bernd (1983): Household Outlay Index. A Measure of Real Purchasing Power and Tax Progressivity. Empirica 10, 205-214.

Genser, Bernd (1985): Steuerlastindizes. Theorie und empirische Evidenz. Springer, Berlin.

Genser, Bernd (1985a): Die Messung der Konsumsteuerbelastung. Forschungsbericht 8501, L.Boltzmann Institut für ökonomische Analysen, Wien.

Gillingham, Robert / Greenlees, John (1983): Incorporation of Direct Taxes into a Consumer Price Index. In: E. Diewert / C. Montmarquette (eds.): Price Level Measurement. Statistics Canada, Ottawa, 619-654.

Hausman, Jerry (1981): Exact Consumer's Surplus and Deadweight Loss. American Economic Review 71, 662-676.

Kay, John / Morris, Nick (1984): The Gross Earnings Deflator. Economic Journal 94, 357-369.

Pipes, Sally / Walker, Michael (1982): Tax Facts 3: The Canadian Consumer Tax Index and You. Fraser Institute, Vancouver.

Shoven, John / Whalley, John (1984): Applied General-Equilibrium Models of Taxation and International Trade: An Introduction and Survey. Journal of Economic Literature 22, 1007-1051.

Net Fiscal Incidence Progressivity: Some Approaches to Measurement

Peter J. Lambert
Economics Department
University of York
Heslington, York YO1 5DD, GB

I: INTRODUCTION

There is strong political interest in measuring the progressivity of the net fiscal system, and, correspondingly, a growing body of literature which examines the question. Several diverse approaches can now be discerned: see Kienzle (1981, 1982), Bridges (1984), Blackorby and Donaldson (1984), Kay and King (1984), Lambert (1985a) and Lambert and Pfähler (1986). In this paper we seek to unify these strands of the relatively young literature on *net fiscal incidence progressivity*; and to propose new measures designed to overcome some of the problems already apparent.

II: INCOME TAX PROGRESSION

We begin by surveying briefly some approaches to the measurement of *income tax progressivity*; this provides a framework and starting point for the extension to the net fiscal system.

It is commonly understood that an income tax schedule is progressive if the average rate of tax rises with income along the income scale. (See, however, Pfingsten (1987: this volume) for a different definition). Three well-appreciated consequences of this conventional definition of structural progression are that, given a distribution of pre-tax income, *(i)* revenue is elastic to equi-proportionate growth in all individual incomes; *(ii)* tax payments are more unequally distributed than pre-tax incomes; and *(iii)* post-tax incomes are more equally distributed than pre-tax incomes. We may call these effects, *(i)*, *(ii)* and *(iii)* respectively, the *revenue responsiveness effect*, the *departure from proportionality effect* and the *redistributive effect* of progressive income taxation.

Furthermore, these three effects have natural relationships with certain common measures of the structural progression of the income tax schedule.

Measurement in Economics
ed. by W. Eichhorn

Thus if *average rate progression* increases at every income level, revenue becomes more responsive to equi-proportionate growth in pre-tax incomes; if *liability progression* increases at every income level, the concentration curve for tax payments shifts outwards; and if *residual progression* increases at every income level, the concentration curve of post-tax income shifts inwards.

A proof of the revenue responsiveness proposition may be found in Hutton and Lambert (1979); and of the departure from proportionality and redistributive effect results, in Jakobsson (1976), Kakwani (1977b) or, most recently, under minimal assumptions, in Eichhorn, Funke and Richter (1984).

These important results identify income tax progression with revenue responsiveness, departure from proportionality and redistributive effect; they also validate the respective measures of structural progression.

Of course, average rate progression, liability progression and residual progression induce only *partial orderings* on the class of income tax schedules; but they provide a key to extending the domain in which progressivity comparisons can be made.

A *progressivity index (index of effective tax progression)* encapsulates the entire tax schedule and income distribution in a single number. Such an index induces a *complete ordering* upon the set of (tax schedule, income distribution) pairs.

Of course, the usefulness to the economist, policymaker or practitioner of such an index clearly must depend upon the properties of the induced ordering. Changes in the income distribution, as well as in the tax schedule, cause movements in a progressivity index, and it is important for international comparisons of progressivity, and for interpreting time series, that the separate rôles of both the tax schedule and income distribution in determining such an index be recognized.

A natural, *minimal requirement* for a progressivity index is:

> *If the tax schedule is adjusted in such a way that a measure of structural progression increases at every income level, and if the (pre-tax) income distribution does not change, then effective progression should increase.*

We call this minimal requirement "**MR**" in what follows. Since the different measures of structural progression rank tax schedules differently, the requirement **MR** has to be applied selectively.

Progressivity indices satisfying the minimal requirement **MR** clearly can be constructed from measures of revenue responsiveness, of non-proportionality in the distribution of the tax burden and of redistributive effect.

Thus it is shown in Hutton and Lambert (1979) that *average rate responsiveness* to equi-proportionate growth in pre-tax incomes satisfies **MR** with respect to average rate progression. This measures the excess of the effective marginal rate of tax over the average tax rate[1].

It is also worth recording that Kay and Morris' (1984) *gross earnings deflator* (GED) satisfies **MR** with respect to residual progression. The GED is, in fact, a tax and price index which "computes the average of the (variable) growth in gross incomes required to produce an equi-proportionate growth of net incomes" (*ibid*, page 358). It can also be interpreted as a revenue responsiveness measure: see Lambert (1984).

There are several well-known indices based upon the distributive consequences of progression taxation.

The Kakwani (1977a) index of deviation from proportionality measures (twice) the area between the concentration curves for pre-tax income and tax payments:

$$\pi^{K} = C^{tax} - C^{pre} \qquad (1)$$

where C^{pre} is the Gini coefficient for pre-tax income, and C^{tax} is the analogous coefficient for tax payment concentration. π^{K} satisfies **MR** with respect to liability progression.

So does the Suits (1977) progressivity index, say π^{S}, which is closely allied to that of Kakwani (being defined similarly, but in terms of *relative* concentration curves). See Formby, Seaks and Smith (1981), or Pfähler (1983), for a comparison of these two *area* measures.

A *length* measure of departure from proportionality is given in Pfähler (1983). Let $t(x)$ be the tax liability of an income x. Provided only that $t(x)/x$ is continuous and increasing, there exists one income level x° which experiences an average rate of tax $t(x^{\circ})/x^{\circ}$ equal to the overall average tax rate, say $\bar{t}$, and

$$x \gtreqless x^{\circ} \Leftrightarrow t(x)/x \gtreqless \bar{t} \qquad (2)$$

Now let p° be the rank of income x° in the pre-tax income distribution. Pfähler (1983) calls p° the *proportional shares coefficient* for the {tax schedule, income distribution} pair, and defines an index of deviation from proportionality, say π^{P1}, as the vertical distance apart of the concentration curves for pre-tax income and tax payments

(1) Some authors have used *revenue elasticity* with respect to equi-proportionate pre-tax income growth as an indicator of the progressivity of an income tax: see, for example, Cassidy (1970) and Snowbarger and Kirk (1973). But this does not satisfy **MR** with respect to any known measure of structural progression. See Hutton and Lambert (1979).

at percentile p°. This index in fact measures the *maximum* vertical separation of the two concentration curves (equally, of the relative concentration curves used to define the Suits index), and it satisfies **MR** with respect to liability progression[2].

Just as the progressivity indices π^K, π^S and π^{P1} are measures of the *deviation from proportionality* effect of progression taxation, so there are corresponding progressivity indices based upon the *redistributive effect*.

Consider therefore

$$\pi^{RS} = C^{pre} - C^{post} \tag{3}$$

which measures (twice) the area between the concentration curves for pre-tax and post-tax income, i.e. the reduction in the Gini coefficient achieved by the tax. π^{RS} was used by Reynolds and Smolensky (1977) for the US tax system, hence our notation, and has been analyzed in detail in Lambert (1985a). A somewhat *ad hoc* variant of this index is that of Pechman and Okner (1974):

$$\pi^{PO} = [C^{pre} - C^{post}]/C^{pre} \tag{4}$$

An area measure given in Pfähler (1983), π^{PF} say, differs from π^{RS} in the same way that the Suits index differs from the Kakwani index, being defined in terms of *relative* concentration curves for pre-tax and post-tax income.

The Pfähler length measure π^{P1} of departure from proportionality also has a redistributive effect analogue, π^{P2}, which evaluates the distance apart of the concentration curves for pre-tax income and post-tax income at percentile p°. This index has similar properties to π^{P1}.

All of these redistributive effect indices satisfy **MR** with respect to residual progression.

A most significant relationship exists between the departure from proportionality indices π^K, π^S, π^{P1} and corresponding redistributive effect indices π^{RS}, π^{PF}, π^{P2} outlined above. It is that *redistributive effect can be decomposed into average tax rate and departure from proportionality components:*

$$\pi^{RS} = [\bar{t}/(1-\bar{t})]\pi^K \tag{5}$$

$$\pi^{PF} = [\bar{t}/(1-\bar{t})]\pi^S \tag{6}$$

$$\pi^{P2} = [\bar{t}/(1-\bar{t})]\pi^{P1} \tag{7}$$

For proofs, see Kakwani (1977), Pfähler (1983) and Lambert (1985a).

There are, in the literature, also some measures of redistributive

---

(2) It may also be interpreted as the proportion of the total tax burden shifted by the progressive tax t(x) to high income recipients (x>x°) from low income recipients (x<x°) as compared with equal-yield distributionally-neutral taxation.

effect based upon the Atkinson (1970) index of inequality, which satisfy **MR** with respect to residual progression[3].

Let J be the Atkinson index of inequality. Kiefer (1985) proposes as a progressivity index

$$\pi^{KI} = J^{pre} - J^{post} \tag{8}$$

thus measuring redistributive effect by the reduction in the Atkinson index (recall that π^{RS} measures it by the reduction in the Gini coefficient). Blackorby and Donaldson (1984) propose a similar index:

$$\pi^{BD} = [J^{pre} - J^{post}]/[1-J^{pre}] \tag{9}$$

An important distiction between the Kiefer and Blackorby and Donaldson indices can be seen from the rankings they imply of {tax schedule, income distribution} pairs 1 and 2 for which $J_1 > J_2$. The index π^{KI} ranks these as equally progressive if $t_1(x)$ and $t_2(x)$ make equal improvements in the Atkinson index; whilst π^{BD} ranks 1 the more progressive in these circumstances, since it effects the given improvement on a *more unequal* pre-tax income distribution. This distinction is the very opposite of that which exists between the Gini-based indices $\pi^{RS} = C^{pre} - C^{post}$ and $\pi^{PO} = [C^{pre} - C^{post}]/C^{pre}$.

III: THE PROGRESSIVITY OF THE NET FISCAL SYSTEM

Our main purpose in thus reviewing measures of *income tax progressivity* is to set the scenario within which we may explore in a unified context extensions to the net fiscal system.

We may easily extend measures of income tax progressivity to *all taxes*, by employing suitable incidence assumptions for taxes not levied directly upon individual income. By also taking into account the incidence of the *benefits* of government expenditures, we arrive at individuals' *net tax payments*. The question arises, how progressive is the net fiscal system?

We begin by offering some observations about the possible use of *revenue responsiveness*, though interest in measuring net fiscal incidence progressivity has, to date, focussed largely upon extensions of the *departure from proportionality* and *redistributive effect* approaches to measuring tax progressivity.

We have not seen any studies of the *responsiveness of net tax revenue* to income growth. This would seem an important empirical

---

(3) if constant inequality aversion is assumed. However, the proposal of Kay and King (1984, page 222) does not satisfy **MR** with respect to any known measure of structural progression.

question and potentially a useful basis for the measurement of effective progressivity. In the UK at least, the tax and benefit systems are well-separated, administered under different criteria and on different income bases. But if *all* government expenditure benefits can be assigned to individual income levels, then net revenue may be identically zero (government budget in balance) - or negative if there is a deficit. It is not clear how the (one-period) net benefits of deficit spending should be computed: this is an area for further consideration.

Since net tax is necessarily negative for some income recipients, and positive for others, and may be zero, positive or negative in total, the "concentration of net tax" is a problematic concept, and measuring disproportionality in it is so *a fortiori* - notwithstanding some *ad hoc* attempts by Kienzle (1981, 1982) and Bridges (1984) to extend the tax progressivity indices π^K and π^S to the net fiscal system(4).

The difficulties inherent in the use of concentration to measure departure from proportionality will become more apparent when we have examined redistributive effect. After doing that, we will present a new, concentration-free methodology for the measurement of departure from proportionality, which not only obviates the problems besetting other approaches but also yields indices which enjoy relationships with redistributive effect like those in (5)-(7) above.

No theoretical problems exist for measuring the concentration of final (or "post-fisc") income; indeed, redistributive effect is the basis of several sound, existing approaches to quantifying the impact of the net fiscal system.

We survey all of these, and in addition present a parametric family of new measures of net fiscal incidence progressivity, having distinctive properties which should be of significant interest to both practitioner and policymaker, in what now follows.

Let us use the labels *original*, *posttax*, *postben* and *final* for income before taxes and benefits; after taxes only; after benefits only; and after both taxes and benefits.

We may readily extend the tax index $\pi^{RS} = \pi_T^{RS}$ to measure the redistributive effect of government expenditure benefits alone, and to the net fiscal system, simply by using the appropriate concentration curves. Thus, let

$$\pi_E^{RS} = C^{original} - C^{postben} \quad (10)$$

$$\pi_N^{RS} = C^{original} - C^{final} \quad (11)$$

---

(4) See Lambert and Pfähler (1986) for full details.

(see Lambert (1985a)). The extensions of π^{PF} and π^{P2} are entirely similar: see Lambert and Pfähler (1986). In fact, for each of these indices, π^{RS}, π^{PF}, π^{P2}, net fiscal incidence progressivity π_N is related to the separate measures of progressivity of taxes and government expenditure benefits, by an equation of the form:

$$\pi_N = [(1-\bar{t})\pi_T + (1+\bar{e})\pi_E]/(1-\bar{t}+\bar{e}) \tag{12}$$

where $\bar{e}$ is the overall average rate of government expenditure benefit. Net fiscal incidence progressivity is thus a weighted *sum* (but not a weighted *average*) of the corresponding indices for the progressivity of taxes and expenditure benefits applied separately to original income.

It is clear from (12) that taxes may be regressive on original income ($\pi_T<0$) and benefits progressive on original income ($\pi_E>0$), yet the net system more progressive than benefits alone ($\pi_N>\pi_E$). This happens when regressive taxes are progressive with respect to the less unequally distributed post-benefit income. Regressive taxes have been found to reinforce progressive government expenditure benefits in precisely this way for both the UK *and* US data examined in Lambert (1985a).

The inequality that reveals such an interaction of taxes and benefits is, from (12):

$$\pi_N > \pi_E \Leftrightarrow \pi_T > -[\bar{t}/(1-\bar{t})]\pi_E \tag{13}$$

This simple criterion does not demand that taxes and government expenditure benefits be jointly assigned to income levels, to be operational.

The tax progressivity indices π^{KI} and π^{BD} also have obvious extensions to the net fiscal system:

$$\pi_N^{KI} = J^{original} - J^{final} \tag{14}$$

$$\pi_N^{BD} = [J^{original} - J^{final}]/[1-J^{original}] \tag{15}$$

See Blackorby and Donaldson (1984) for the latter.

Blackorby and Donaldson (1984) derive a multiplicative decomposition of their net progressivity index into tax and benefit components, by evaluating the redistributive impact of benefits on *post-tax income*:

$$\pi_E^{BD} = [J^{posttax}-J^{final}]/[1-J^{posttax}] \tag{16}$$

Then we have

$$[1 + \pi_N^{BD}] = [1 + \pi_E^{BD}][1 + \pi_T^{BD}] \tag{17}$$

However, estimation of π_N^{BD} requires that taxes and benefits be *jointly assigned* to levels of original income; and it is not immediately obvious how these π^{BD}-measures make accessible the observation that regressive taxes can reinforce progressive government expenditure benefits.

A variant of the Blackorby and Donaldson approach helps to clarify this situation, and at the same time exposes one of the weaknesses of defining redistributive impact for taxes and benefits with respect to different income bases: the component measures, and the decomposition, are not unique.

Thus, let π_E^{*BD} denote the progressivity of government expenditure benefits with respect to original income:

$$\pi_E^{*BD} = [J^{original} - J^{postben}]/[1-J^{original}] \qquad (18)$$

and π_T^{*BD} the progressivity of taxes with respect to post-benefit income:

$$\pi_T^{*BD} = [J^{postben} - J^{final}]/[1-J^{postben}] \qquad (19)$$

(instead of the other way around). Then a different decomposition of net progressivity π_N^{BD} emerges:

$$[1 + \pi_N^{BD}] = [1 + \pi_E^{*BD}][1 + \pi_T^{*BD}] \qquad (20)$$

Both π_N^{BD} and π_E^{*BD} measure progressivity with respect to original income, and net redistributive effect will exceed the redistributive effect of benefits alone ($\pi_N^{BD} > \pi_E^{*BD}$) if taxes which are regressive on original income ($\pi_T^{BD} < 0$) are progressive on post-benefit income ($\pi_T^{*BD} > 0$).

IV: THE PROGRESSIVITY OF THE NET FISCAL SYSTEM - SOME NEW RESULTS

The Atkinson index has, of course, distinct normative advantages over the Gini coefficient. By using the Atkinson-based progressivity indices just reviewed, the policymaker may specify the inequality aversion parameter, or a range of values for it, and examine the robustness of progressivity comparisons to the degree of inequality aversion supposed. The concentration-based indices of net redistributive effect, π^{RS}, π^{PF} and π^{P2} reviewed earlier, do not admit of such a feature - but, against this, they do (as we have observed) yield well-defined decompositions which make accessible certain empirically significant observations about the interaction of taxes and benefits from separated data.

We shall now present an extension of the index π_N^{RS} which combines *all* of the advantageous features just described.

Following this, we will look again at the measurement of departure from proportionality. We shall define a new measure of departure from proportionality, for net taxes, and obtain a decomposition of net redistributive effect (as earlier defined) into net average tax rate and departure from proportionality components. This will parallel the decompositions that obtained for income tax progressivity in equations

(5)-(7). We thereby recover *for the net fiscal system* the ability to make meaningful observations about the distribution of the (net) tax burden, and about the complementary nature of departure from proportionality and redistributive effect[5].

We begin by briefly describing a family of inequality indices, the *S-Gini coefficients* of Donaldson and Weymark (1980), which generalize the Gini coefficient by incorporating a parameter which can be varied to introduce alternative distributional judgements.

Let $g(p)$ be the concentration curve for a distribution of income, $0 \leq p \leq 1$; then the Gini coefficient for that distribution is

$$G = 1 - 2 \int_0^1 g(p)dp \qquad (21)$$

Yitzhaki (1983) has shown that Donaldson and Weymark's S-Gini coefficients may be defined, one for each value of a parameter $v>1$, by:

$$G(v) = 1 - v(v-1) \int_0^1 (1-p)^{v-2} g(p)dp \qquad (22)$$

$G(2)$ is the familiar Gini coefficient; as $v \rightarrow 1$ the index $G(v)$ approaches unity (representing "inequality-neutrality", *ibid*, page 620); as $v \rightarrow \infty$ the ranking of distributions implied by $G(v)$ approaches that determined by the minimal income earner ("maxmin"). The rôle of v in determining a complete ordering by $G(v)$ of the set of income distributions is similar in some other significant respects, too, to the rôle of the inequality aversion parameter defining the Atkinson index: see both Yitzhaki, *ibid*, pages 622-626, where a strong case is made for regarding v as an inequality aversion parameter, and Donaldson and Weymark (1980), pages 74 *et seq*.

The S-Gini coefficients readily yield concentration-based indices of redistributive effect; and they put a distributional judgement parameter at the disposal of the analyst.

In terms of concentration curves, the progressivity index π^{RS} defined in equation (3) may be expressed as:

$$\pi^{RS} = 2 \int_0^1 [g^{post}(p) - g^{pre}(p)]dp \qquad (23)$$

Parametric indices $\pi_T(v)$, $\pi_E(v)$ and $\pi_N(v)$ are immediately suggested, based on the natural extension $\pi(v)$ of π^{RS} as given in (3) and (23):

$$\pi(v) = G^{pre}(v) - G^{post}(v)$$
$$= v(v-1) \int_0^1 (1-p)^{v-2}[g^{post}(p) - g^{pre}(p)]dp \qquad (24)$$

The index $\pi_T(v)$ of the redistributive effect of taxes, so generated, generalizes π_T^{RS} and satisfies the requirement **MR** with respect to residual progression. Also, as with π_N^{RS}, the net index $\pi_N(v)$ is a weighted sum:

$$\pi_N(v) = [(1-\bar{t})\pi_T(v) + (1+\bar{e})\pi_E(v)]/(1-\bar{t}+\bar{e}) \qquad (25)$$

---

(5) See Pfähler (1987: this volume) for an interpretation of these two aspects as *distinct*, rather than *complementary*, policy concerns.

of the separate indices for taxes and government expenditure benefits (compare (22) with (21), and follow Lambert (1985a), Appendix, inserting the term $(1-p)^{v-2}$ in the relevant integrands). Hence the criterion

$$\pi_N(v) > \pi_E(v) \Leftrightarrow \pi_T(v) > -[\bar{t}/(1-\bar{t})]\pi_E(v) \qquad (26)$$

obtains, making this important empirical observation accessible from separate data on taxes and benefits.

Finally, as for the indices of redistributive effect based upon the Atkinson inequality index, the analyst may select the value of v, or a range of values for v to check the robustness of the implied progressivity rankings to different distributional judgements. As $v \to \infty$ the indices $\pi_T(v)$, $\pi_E(v)$, $\pi_N(v)$ register concern increasingly with the tax/benefit position of the worst-off members of society, whilst as $v \to 1$ all individuals' positions assume equal importance. These are attractive properties for policy purposes, and clearly an early empirical application is merited.

We now turn to departure from proportionality

Let $\bar{s} = \bar{t} - \bar{e} \gtrless 0$ be the average net tax rate. Suppose that an index D of departure from proportionality could be devised enjoying a relationship like that in (5)-(7) with some index R of (net) redistributive effect:

$$R = [\bar{s}/(1-\bar{s})].D \qquad (27)$$

Suppose further that the government budget is balanced but that not all government expenditure benefits have been assigned to individuals. Then $\bar{s}>0$ and, we may assume, both R and D are positive. Now suppose that, by some means, successively more of the benefits of government expenditure are assigned to income levels; then $\bar{s} \to 0$ whilst R approaches a finite limit, namely the measure of *true* redistributive effect. It is immediate from (27) that $D \to \infty$. This demonstrates nicely the problem in extending the indices π^K, π^S and π^{P1}, and their relationship with redistributive effect as in (5)-(7), to the net fiscal system.

But we can retrieve the situation. Let s(x) be the net tax liability of an income x. Assuming only that s(x)/x is continuous and increasing, then as in (2) we have:

$$x \gtrless x^{\circ} \Leftrightarrow s(x) \gtrless \bar{s}x \qquad (28)$$

where x° is a benchmark income below which individuals pay less than would be their due under an equal-yield proportional tax. At all income levels x, the actual departure from proportionality is $[\bar{s}x - s(x)]$, counted positively for low incomes. If F(x) is the distribution function for original income, then for any $p = F(y) \in [0,1]$,

$$S(p) = \int_0^y [\bar{s}x - s(x)]dF(x) \qquad (29)$$

is the aggregate of this departure from proportionality across incomes up to rank p. Clearly S(p) increases to its maximum value at $p^\circ = F(x^\circ)$, and then falls to zero at p=1. If the curve S(p) shifts upwards, then departure from proportionality increases unambiguously throughout the net tax schedule: see Figure 1.

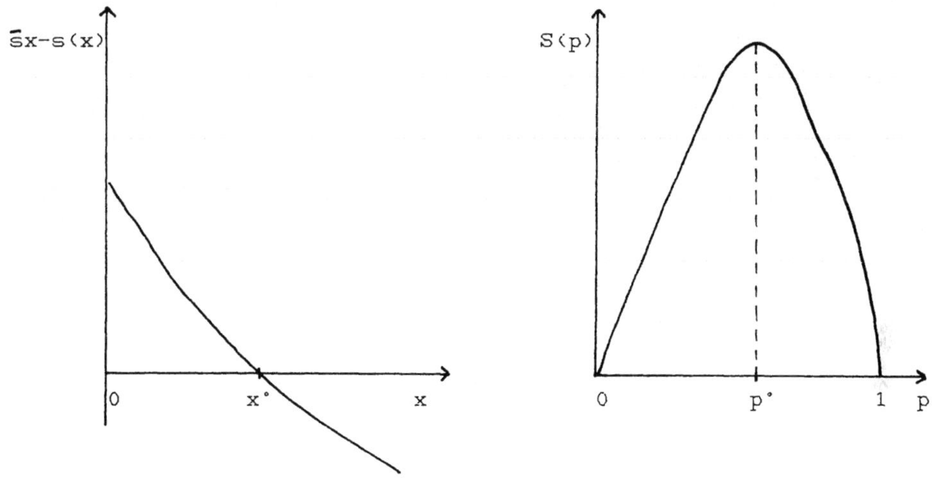

Figure 1

We may therefore define area and length measures of departure from proportionality using the curve S(p) (which, in contrast to the concentration curve $g^{net tax}(p)$, does not become undefined or infinite if $\bar{s}=0$). Specifically, let

$$D_A = 2\int_0^1 S(p)dp/\mu \qquad (30)$$

and

$$D_L = S(p^\circ)/\mu \qquad (31)$$

where μ is mean income. Because of the relationship

$$\mu(1-\bar{s})[g^{final}(p) - g^{original}(p)] = \int_0^y [\bar{s}x - s(x)]dF(x) = S(p) \qquad (32)$$

(see Lambert (1985a), Appendix, equation B) it is immediate that

$$\pi_N^{RS} = [1/(1-\bar{s})].D_A \qquad (33)$$

$$\pi_N^{P2} = [1/(1-\bar{s})].D_L \qquad (34)$$

Thus we recover, for these measures of net departure from proportionality, multiplicative decompositions into average net tax rate and net redistributive effect components.

(The normalization which ensures these results - division of S(p) by μ - not only makes the D-measures unit free but also purges the decompositions of an effect from income growth).

In fact we can derive a parametric family of measures of net departure from proportionality; these extend D_A and are related to the new redistributive effect indices $\pi(v)$. Letting

$$D_A(v) = v(v-1) \int_0^1 (1-p)^{v-2} S(p)dp/\mu \tag{35}$$

we find that

$$\pi_N(v) = [1/(1-\bar{s})].D_A(v) \tag{36}$$

(multiply both sides of equation (32) by $(1-p)^{v-2}$ and integrate). The numerical properties of these measures, as v varies, could be determined by simulation: this is an area for future work.

A final point worthy of note concerns the range within which the new measures of departure from proportionality are defined. It is clear enough that the length measure D_L, the area measure D_A and the parametric measures $D_A(v)$ of departure from proportionality are not confined to the interval [0,1] (whereas all of the redistributive effect measures we have considered are, for a progressive net tax schedule). This would be a desirable property to build in by further normalization.

Our final observation is that, if the area measure D_A is normalized by division by its maximum possible value given the net tax yield $\bar{s}$, then the (otherwise somewhat *ad hoc*) Pechman and Okner (1974) index of net redistributive effect is recovered:

$$D_A/[D_A]_{max} = \pi_N^{PO} \tag{37}$$

This follows from the fact that the maximum value of D_A, given $\bar{s}$, occurs when all individuals are left with equal final incomes.

(If $s_m(x) = x - \mu(1-\bar{s})$, so that the yield of $s_m(x)$ is the same as that of $s(x)$, then obviously $[\pi_N^{RS}]_m = [\pi_N^{RS}]_{max} = C^{original}$; and therefore, from (33), $[D_A]_m = [D_A]_{max} = (1-\bar{s})C^{original}$. Equation (37) follows immediately from equation (4)).

V: CONCLUSION

In this paper we have identified three pervading and indentifying aspects of progressive income taxation: the responsiveness of aggregate revenue to income growth; the departure from proportionality in the income tax burden; and the redistribution of income that is entailed by the tax.

We motivated an examination of approaches to the measurement of effective income tax progression by observing that increases in three well-known measures of structural progression variously imply increased revenue responsiveness, departure from proportionality in the tax burden and redistributive effect, given the pre-tax income distribution[6].

Next we enunciated a minimal requirement **MR** for the measurement of effective progression; and we used revenue responsiveness, departure from proportionality and redistributive effect to define progressivity indices.

We discussed the extensions of some of these indices to the net fiscal system, and highlighted some of the drawbacks and inadequacies thus entailed. Finally we proposed parametric families of new indices of net fiscal incidence progressivity, which meet the earlier criticisms and have important and distinctive properties of interest to the policymaker.

In thus structuring the paper, we have surveyed much of the existing literature on progressivity measurement. In so doing, we have brought together a number of ways of saying "tax system 1 is more progressive than tax system 2". But we have certainly not exhausted all possible answers to the question, "what as economists do we want such a statement to mean?"

Further exploration must surely address this question from an axiomatic base.

VI: ACKNOWLEDGEMENT

I have benefitted greatly in the preparation of this paper from discussions with Charles Blackorby, John Kay, Wilhelm Pfähler, Ian Preston and John Weymark.

VII: REFERENCES

Atkinson, A.B. (1970). On the measurement of inequality. *Journal of Economic Theory*, vol. 2, pp. 244-263.

Blackorby, C. and D. Donaldson (1984). Ethical social index numbers and the measurement of effective tax/benefit progressivity. *Canadian Journal of Economics*, vol. 17, pp. 683-694.

Bridges, B. (1984). Post-fisc distributions of income: comment. *Public Finance Quarterly*, vol. 12, pp. 231-240.

---

(6) It must be recorded that, throughout, we have neglected the effect of tax schedule changes upon the size distribution of original income. This is, however, customary: the given distribution of original income stands as a reference distribution for the purposes of evaluating the progressivity of different tax schedules. See Lambert (1985b) for a study of redistributive effect in which the distribution of original income is made *endogenous* to the tax-benefit schedule.

Cassidy, H.J. (1970). Is a progressive tax stabilizing? *National Tax Journal*, vol. 23, pp. 194-204.

Donaldson, D. and J.A. Weymark (1980). A single parameter generalization of the Gini indices of inequality. *Journal of Economic Theory*, vol. 22, pp. 67-86.

Eichhorn, W., H. Funke and W.F. Richter (1984). Tax progression and inequality of income distribution. *Journal of Mathematical Economics*, vol. 13, pp. 127-131.

Formby, J.P., T.G. Seaks and W.J. Smith (1981). A comparison of two new measures of tax progressivity. *Economic Journal*, vol. 91, pp. 1015-1019.

Hutton, J.P. and P.J. Lambert (1979). Income tax progressivity and revenue growth. *Economics Letters*, vol. 3, pp. 377-380.

Jakobsson, U. (1976). On the measurement of the degree of progression. *Journal of Public Economics*, vol. 5, pp. 161-168.

Kakwani, N.C. (1977a). Measurement of tax progressivity: an international comparison. *Economic Journal*, vol. 87, pp. 71-80.

Kakwani, N.C. (1977b). Applications of Lorenz curves in economic analysis. *Econometrica*, vol. 45, pp. 719-727.

Kay, J.A. and M.A. King (1984). *The British Tax System* (3rd edition). Oxford: University Press.

Kay, J.A. and C.N. Morris (1984). The gross earnings deflator. *Economic Journal*, vol. 94, pp. 357-369.

Kiefer, D.W. (1985). Distributional tax progressivity measurement. *National Tax Journal*, vol. 37, pp. 497-513.

Kienzle, E.C. (1981). Measurement of the progressivity of public expenditures and net fiscal incidence. *Southern Economic Journal*, vol. 48, pp. 197-203.

Kienzle, E.C. (1982). Post-fisc distributions of income: measuring progressivity with application to the United States. *Public Finance Quarterly*, vol. 10, pp. 355-368.

Lambert, P.J. (1984). Non-equiproportionate income growth, inequality and the income tax. *Public Finance/Finances Publiques*, vol. 39, pp. 104-118.

Lambert, P.J. (1985a). The redistributive effect of taxes and benefits. *Scottish Journal of Political Economy*, vol. 32, pp. 39-54.

Lambert, P.J. (1985b). Endogenizing the income distribution: the redistributive effect, and Laffer effects, of a progressive tax-benefit system. *European Journal of Political Economy*, vol. 1, pp. 3-20.

Lambert, P.J. and W. Pfähler (1986). On aggregate measures of the net redistributive impact of taxation and government expenditure. *Institute for Fiscal Studies Working Paper No. 87*.

Pechman, J.A. and B. Okner (1974). *Who Bears the Tax Burden?* Washington D.C.: Brookings Institution.

Pfähler, W. (1983). Measuring redistributional effects of tax progressivity by Lorenz curves. *Jahrbücher für Nationalökonomie und Statistik*, vol. 198, pp. 237-249.

Pfähler, W. (1987). Distributional equity and measurement of tax progressivity. *This Proceedings*.

Pfingsten, A. (1987). Measures of tax progression - an axiomatic approach. *This Proceedings*.

Reynolds, M. and E. Smolensky (1977). *Public Expenditures, Taxes, and the Distribution of Income: The United States, 1950, 1961, 1970*. New York: Academic Press.

Snowbarger, M. and J. Kirk (1973). A cross-sectional model of built-in flexibility, 1954-1969. *National Tax Journal*, vol. 26, pp. 241-249.

Suits, D. (1977). Measurement of tax progressivity. *American Economic Review*, vol. 67, pp. 747-752.

Yitzhaki, S. (1983). On an extension of the Gini index. *International Economic Review*, vol. 24, pp. 617-628.

Distributional Equity and Measurement of Tax Progressivity[1]

Wilhelm Pfähler
Wissenschaftliche Hochschule für Unternehmensführung
(The Koblenz School of Corporate Management)
Zwickauer Straße 23, D-5400 Koblenz, FRG

Abstract: Current literature shows revived interest in global (aggregate, summary) measures of tax progressivity. This paper deals with tax progressivity in a budget policy framework. The main question is whether or not, respectively when, redistributive effects of taxation can unequivocally be attributed to one of two distinct distributional objectives namely the fair distribution of public goods taxes and the fair distribution of (market) incomes. Since such an unequivocal separation of distributional issues is generally not possible in real world tax and transfer systems, the aggregate approach to measurement of tax progressivity is of limited value in assisting and controlling the design of a fair tax and transfer policy.

I. Introduction

Current literature in applied public finance shows revived interest in global (summary, aggregate) measures of tax progressivity as well as of its redistributive effect and of the net fiscal incidence (including cash transfers). In contrast to a longstanding tradition in applied public finance which has focused on empirical data generated by local measures of the progressivity of the statuary or effective tax schedule, this aggregate approach to measurement aims at representing the data by global indices. Furthermore, this aggregate approach takes into account the distribution of pre-fisc income along the tax scale and thus transforms the local tax scale analysis into an analysis of the global redistributive impact effects, or incidence, of the tax schedule.

---

[1] This paper was written during my stay as Visiting Professor at Georgetown-University Washington, D.C. and has also been discussed in a tax progressivity workshop of the IFS (London) in July 1985.

Measurement in Economics
ed. by W. Eichhorn

The aggregate approach is presently pursued in two different ways.[2] The first is based on usual concentration, or Lorenz, curves which plot the cumulative portion of total taxes (transfers, post-fisc income) falling on various cumulative portions of the population of pre-fisc income recipients. This approach was initiated by Dalton (1922) and Musgrave and Thin(1948) and is, for instance, pursued in Pechman and Okner(1974), Khetan and Podder(1976), Kakwani(1977), Reynold and Smolensky(1977), and Lambert(1985).

The second approach rests upon relative concentration curves which plot the cumulative portions of total taxes (transfers, post-fisc income) falling on cumulative portions of total pre-fisc income rather than income recipients . This second approach was initiated by Hainsworth(1964) and is, for instance, pursued by Suits (1977), Kienzle(1981), Bridges(1984), Pfähler(1983,1985a), and Lambert and Pfähler(1986a).

In nearly all of the literature on this aggregate approach to measurement little or no thought has been given to the questions of

- why one should be interested in these aggregate measures, and
- whether this interest is served by these measures.

This paper explicitly addresses these crucial questions in some detail. There is always an obvious and easy answer to these questions: The application of these measures presumably contributes to the body of positive (or descriptive) knowledge on the economic world we live in. However, in contrast to this common purview in the literature, this paper focuses on the need of these measures (or their underlying concentraction curves) in order to operationally specify equity objectives of budget policy and/or to evaluate and control the achievement of these objectives by current tax and transfer policies. It is from this normative, or budget policy, perspective that this paper reconsiders the meaning and relevance of global impact measures of tax progressivity.

The plan and the summary of the paper are as follows: In section II we introduce and, in turn, analyze budget-policies aiming at two distinct subgoals of distributional equity. The first policy focuses

---

[2] For a comparison of these two different ways see Formby, Seaks and Smith(1981,1984), Pfähler(1983), Kiefer(1984) and Lambert (1985b). A generalization and evaluation of the aggregate approach to measurement is contained in Pfähler (1987).

on an equitable distribution of taxes to finance public good expenditures ("iustitia distributiva"). The second is aimed at an equitable distribution of (market) incomes ("iustitia commutativa"). With each equity objective, there is an associated ideal tax (transfer) instrument which is progressive and which causes redistributive effects. Ideally, these two equity goals should be pursued by a dual system consisting of (1) taxes to equitably finance public good expenditures and (2) redistributive taxes and transfers to attain an equitable distribution of income. Two variants of such an ideal dual system of taxes and transfers will be presented. The redistributive effects of these variants can be subdivided into elements that are unequivocally attributed to one of the two equity objectives. In other words, an ideal dual system allows for a target-oriented design, control and measurement of public policy aimed at distributional equity.

Unfortunately, in real world politics, we do not find (and may even not want) an ideal dual system of taxes and transfers. We rather observe two-part systems. One part consists of taxes which are not separated into or earmarked as public good taxes and redistributive taxes. The other part are redistributive transfers. As shown in section III, it is generally impossible to unequivocally attribute the redistributive effects of a two-part system to either one of the two equity objectives. However, there are exceptions to this rule: One is a flat-rate tax system (with a constant marginal tax rate above a threshold). The other exception is a consensual judgment that a public good taxes should be strictly proportional. Neither exception is met in real world politics, although the income tax of England and the upcoming income tax of the United States closely approximate a flat-rate tax. Consequently, the measurement of tax and transfer progressivity and its redistributive effects, as it is currently pursued in the literature, is not capable of assisting in the design, control and reform of budget poliy aimed at distributional equity. This is the main conclusion of the paper in sec. IV.

II. Distributional Equity and Redistributive Effects in Theory

The central objectives of a government budget policy are allocative efficiency and distributional equity and, as welfare theory of public expenditures and taxation tells us, both objectives are, in general, inextricably intertwined (see Samuelson, 1954, and Diamond, 1975) . However, in all the literature on the measurement of tax progressivity and its redistributive effects, separability is tacitly assumed (i.e. it is assumed that the distribution of market income and the efficient supply of public goods are inedependent of each other and independent of tax and transfer measures).[3]

Following this assumption, the allocative branch may independently determine the required pattern and level of public good expenditures and, hence, the required revenue to finance these expenditures. It is then up to the distributive branch to separately determine how the cost of these goods and services should be shared in justice by the public in order to achieve an equitable distribution of taxes to finance public goods. In addition, and quite separately, the distributive branch may also wish to correct the distribution of market incomes generated from the production of private and public goods. For that purpose, it has to determine the equitable distribution of income and the means to achieve it.

A. Equitable distribution of public goods taxes: Objective, instrument, and redistributive effects

Let us first have a closer look at the policy aimed at achieving an equitable distribution of taxes to finance publicly provided good. The size of this public good budget is assumed to be predeterminded by a separate allocative decision.

What normatively acceptable and politically operational specification would characterize this distributional objective? Due to the free rider problem involved, one has to refrain from defining this objective in utility terms (like the benefit-recieved or ability-to-pay principle).[4] Among the (vertical) equity concepts which are defined in money terms, the concept of increasing relative tax distances between equidistant pre-tax income levels has earned prominent recognition.[5] This, in turn, implies that equal relative tax distances, or, equiva-

---

[3] For an exception with an endogenous pre-fisc income distribution see Lambert(1985c).

[4] The usual caveat of the lack of a cardinal concept of utility is of secondary importance.

[5] Other equity concepts are, for example, increasing absolute tax distances or increasing marginal tax distances.

lently, the prevailing relative pre-tax income distances, serve as a reference system for vertical equity or redistributional nonneutrality of taxes.

This can be translated easily into the empirically operational concept of Lorenz dominance: Equal relative tax distances are secured by a strictly proportional, or redistributionally neutral, public good tax $T^{Gn}(x) = gx$.[6] Applied to any fixed size and distribution of pre-tax income, this tax leads to a proportional tax distribution. Its concentration curve $L_T Gn = h_T Gn(p)$ coincides with the Lorenz curve of pre-tax income $L_x = h_x(p)$ (where $p = F(x)$ is the distribution of pre-tax income). Increasing relative tax differentials, in turn, are induced by a progressive tax $T^G(x)$ as defined by liability progression $LP(x) = d\log T^G(x)/d\log x > 1 \; \forall x$. If a LP-progressive tax is applied to any fixed size and distribution of pre-tax income, the concentration curve of the resulting tax distribution $L_T G = h_T G(p)$ is (strictly) lorenzinferior to the concentration curve of a proportional tax, i.e. $L_x = L_T Gn > L_T G \; \forall \; p \in (0,1)$ iff $LP(x) > 1 \; \forall x (0,\infty)$.[7]

In order to properly define a Lorenz dominance relationship, however, one should secure an <u>equal size</u> of the distributions compared. In comparing a proportional with a progressive tax, an equal size of the resulting tax distributions is secured if the proportional tax rate g in $T^{Gn}(x)$ equals the total tax ratio $g = \bar{T}^G/\bar{x}$ which emerges from the progressive public good tax $T^G(x)$ under a given size and distribution of pre-tax income ($\bar{T}$ and $\bar{x}$ denote the arithmetic means of taxes and pre-tax income, respectively).[8]

Thus, an equitable distribution of public good taxes can be operationally specified by means of Lorenz-inferiority to a proportional

---

6 For the concept of increasing absolute tax distances, a head tax, which preserves equal absolute tax distances, is the redistributionally neutral tax. For the concept of increasing marginal tax distances, the redistributionally neutral tax is a linear- progressive, or flat rate, tax preserving equal marginal tax distances.

7 This Lorenz dominance relationship follows from results obtained by Jacobsson(1976) and, under minimal requirements, by Eichhorn, Funke and Richter(1984).

8 The condition for revenue-equivalence is formally given as:

$$\int_0^\infty T^G(x)dF(x) = \bar{T}^G = \int_0^\infty gx dF(x) \quad \text{iff} \quad g = \bar{T}^G/\bar{x}$$

distribution of equal size. By invoking Atkinson's(1970) theorem, this Lorenz dominance relationship yields a partial ordinal (welfare) ranking of the equity of non-intersecting tax distributions of equal size.[9] In particular, Lorenz domination between tax distributions of equal size implies and is implied by Lorenz domination between the corresponding after-tax income distributions of equal size, as shown in Pfähler and Lambert(1986b)

A progressive tax, in relation to a revenue-equivalent proportional tax, shifts part of the total tax burden from low to high pre-tax income recipients.[10] This redistributive effect shall be called the pure tax redistribution effect of tax progressivity. It is of primary normative interest if one is concerned with the issue of an equitable distribution of the public good tax burden. Clearly, the tax redistribution effect also induces an (after-tax)income redistribution effect in relation to the situation of a revenue-equivalent proportional tax. Since by shifting part of the tax burden from low to high pre-tax income recipients, the progressive tax simultaneously shifts part of the total after-tax income from high to low income recipients.[11] However, at this point it is important to realize that this (after-tax) income redistribution effect is an inevitable by-product or a side-effect of the (pure) tax redistribution effect. This side-effect is not of primary concern in determining the equity of public goods taxes. Moreover, it should also not be attributed to or confused with a policy aiming at an equitable distribution of income (see below).

Suppose, for example, the government wishes to expand the public good budget without changing the prevailing distribution of public good taxes. It then simply has to scale-up all tax bills. This, in turn, will change the prevailing post-tax income distribution. The concentration curve for post-tax income shifts inwards.[12] But this income redistribution effect is simply a side-effect of the normative

---

[9] A complete ordering would comprise intersecting tax concentration curves. See more on this in Lambert and Pfähler(1986b).

[10] In particular, $T^G(x) = t^G(x)x \lesseqgtr gx$ for $x \lesseqgtr x_g := t^{-1}(g)$ where x_g denotes the redistributive break-even income of public good taxation.

[11] In particular, if $V^G(x) = x - T^G(x)$ denotes after-(public good-) tax income, then $V^G(x) \gtreqless (1-g)x \;\forall\; x \lesseqgtr x_g$.

[12] See for details, for example, Pfähler(1984).

decision to preserve the tax distribution while expanding the public good budget.

Both effects the pure tax redistribution effect and the induced income redistribution effect are, of course, intimately interrelated. The tax redistribution effect may be measured by the term $(L_T Gn - L_T G) = (L_x - L_T G)$ which is positive for a progressive tax - demonstrating increasing relative tax distances. Denote after-tax incomes as $V^{Gn}(x) = x - T^{Gn}(x)$ and $V^G(x) = x - T^G(x)$. Then the income redistribution effect may be measured by the term $(L_V Gn - L_V G) = (L_x - L_V G)$ which is negative - demonstrating the narrowing of relative income distances under progressive taxation. The (Lorenz curve) relationship between the tax and income redistribution effect of public good taxation is immediate:[13]

$$L_x - L_V G = - \frac{g}{1-g} \cdot (L_x - L_T G) \tag{1}$$

i.e. both redistribution effects are linked via the tax level effect which is measured by the total net tax ratio $g/(1-g) = \bar{T}^G/\bar{V}^G$. Consequently, both redistribution effects have different invariance properties. It is possible to change one without changing the other (see Kakwani,1977; and Pfähler,1984).

Eq. (1) represents itself a global multi-value measure of the (after-tax) income redistribution effect of public good taxation. Integration with respect to cumulative portions of income recipients (p) leads to the global single-value measure of the Musgrave/Thin-Kakwani-line. Integration with respect to cumulative portions of pre-tax income (L_x) , in contrast, leads to the global single-value measures of the Hainsworth-Suits-Pfähler-Lambert-line.[14]

---

[13] This follows from substitution of $V^G(x) = V^G(F^{-1}(p))$ by $V^G(x) = x - T^G(F^{-1}(p))$ in

$$L_{VG} = h(p) = (1/\bar{V}^G) \int_0^p V^G(F^{-1}(u))du$$

[14] For details see Pfähler(1987).

B. Equitable distribution of (market) income: Objective, instrument, and redistributive effects

Let us now turn to the second distributional objective, the equitable distribution of (market) income. As above, the concept of an equitable distribution of income has to be portrayed in terms of a normatively acceptable and politically operational characteristic which, in turn, lends itself to the specification of a reference system for redistributional non-neutrality. Traditionally, two such reference systems have been considered: One based on equal absolute income distances and one based on equal relative income distances.

If, for normative reasons, one adopts the concept of relative inequality, then any purely redistributive tax and transfer system which reduces the prevailing relative pre-tax income distances is RP-progressive (where $RP(x) = d\log(x-R)/d\log x < 1$ denotes residual income progression) and causes a pure income redistribution effect. This income redistribution effect is of primary normative concern for a policy aimed at an equitable distribution of income.

An ideal purely redistributive tax and transfer system can be designed, for example, as

$$R(x-x_R) = T^R(x-x_R) - E(x-x_R) \lesseqgtr 0 \;\forall\; x \lesseqgtr x_R \tag{2a}$$

where redistributive transfers (or negative taxes) $E(.)$ for pre-tax incomes below a redistributional break-even income x_R are financed by redistributive taxes $T^R(.)$ on incomes above x_R such that no resources are transferred to the government (i.e. $\vec{R} = \vec{T}^R - \vec{E} = 0$).

If this redistributive system is decomposed into a two-part system of redistributive taxes and transfers, one can identify four more redistributive effects. Let $V^R(x) = x-R(x-x_R)$ denote income after redistribution (or final income), $V^{TR}(x) = x-T^R(x-x_R)$ income after redistributive taxes, $V^{ER}(x) = x+E(x-x_R)$ income after redistributive transfers, and let $e = \vec{E}/\overline{x} = \vec{T}^R/\overline{x} = g^R$ be the total redistributive transfer or tax ratio. Then the pure income redistribution effect, $L_x - L_VR$, can be looked at as a weighted sum (but not weighted average) of two partial income redistribution effects: One results from the transfer side of the redistribution system, $L_x - L_VER$, and the other from the tax side, $L_x - L_VTR$, i.e.

$$L_x - L_V R = \frac{1+e}{1+e-g^R}(L_x - L_V ER) + \frac{1-g^R}{1+e-g^R}(L_x - L_V TR) \qquad (2b)$$

where

$$L_x - L_V E = \frac{e}{1+e}(L_x - L_E) \quad \text{and} \qquad (2c)$$

$$L_x - L_V TR = \frac{g^R}{1-g^R}(L_x - L_T R)$$

According to eqt. (2c), the partial income redistribution effects result from a respective level effect and a transfer or tax redistribution effect - in relation to revenue-equivalent proportional transfers or taxes. All these additional redistributive effects in eqts. (2b)-(2c) are means to achieve the primary pure income redistribution effect $L_x - L_V R$. Finally, integration of eqts. (2b)-(2c) leads, again, to global single-value measures of the various redistributive effects.

C. Decomposable dual tax and transfer system for distributional equity

A policy aimed at distributional equity would ideally require a dual system of budget measures consisting of (1) a tax (system) to equitably finance the cost of publicly provided goods (as determined by a separate allocative decision), and (2) a redistributive tax and transfer scheme to achieve an equitable distribution of (market) income. Such an ideal dual system would allow for

- the pursual of a strictly target-oriented design and reform of tax and expenditure policies and
- a target-oriented control and evaluation of these policies by means of measuring their redistributive effects.

This is due to the fact that such an ideal dual system lends itself to a decomposition of its entire income redistribution effect into elements that can be unequivocally attributed to either one of the aforementioned distributional objectives.

An ideal dual system can be designed either as a parallel or as a sequential system of redistributive taxes and transfers and of public good taxes. First consider an ideal parallel system which is fully harmonized with respect to the income concept, break-even income, tax unit, etc., i.e.

$$Q(x) = R(x-x_R) + T^G(x-x_R) \lesseqgtr 0 \quad \forall\, x \lesseqgtr x_R. \tag{3a}$$

where $\vec{Q}/\vec{x} = \vec{R}/\vec{x} + \vec{T}^G/\vec{x} = \vec{T}^G/\vec{x} = g$.

The target-oriented decomposition of the entire redistribution effect of this system is obtained as (for $V = x-Q$, $V^R = x-R$, and $V^G = x-T^G$)

$$L_x - L_V = \frac{1}{1-g}(L_x - L_{V^R}) - \frac{g}{1-g}(L_x - L_{T^G}) \tag{3b}$$

$$= \frac{1}{1-g}(L_x - L_{V^R}) + (L_x - L_{V^G})$$

I.e. the total income redistribution effect L_x-L_V is a weighted average of (i) the pure income redistribution effect $L_x-L_{V^R}$, which is required for an equitable distribution of income, and (ii) the pure tax redistribution effect $L_x-L_{T^G}$, which is necessary for an equitable distribution of public good taxes.[15]

An ideal sequential system of redistributive taxes and transfers and of subsequent public good taxes, which are now based on fairly distributed incomes, is theoretically more appealing since it implies a "true" separation of distributional issues. In case of full harmonization, such an ideal sequential system is defined as

$$W(x) = R(x-x_R) + T^G(V^R(x)) \lesseqgtr 0 \quad \forall\, x \lesseqgtr x_W \tag{4a}$$

where $V^R(x) = x-R(x-x_R)$, and where $\vec{W}/\vec{x} = \vec{R}/\vec{x} + \vec{T}^G/\vec{x} = \vec{T}^G/\vec{x} = g$.

The entire income redistribution effect of this sequential system can be decomposed as

$$L_x - L_V = (L_x - L_{V^R}) - \frac{g}{1-g}(L_{V^R} - L_{T^G}) \tag{4b}$$

$$= (L_x - L_{V^R}) + (L_{V^R} - L_V)$$

---

15 Note that $1/(1-g) - g/(1-g) = 1$. The pure income redistribution effect can, of course, be further subdivided along the lines outlined in eq. (2c).

and is now a weighted sum (but not a weighted average) of the pure income redistribution effect, $L_x - L_V R$, and the pure tax redistribution effect, $L_V R - L_T G$.[16]

Note, however, that the measurement of the <u>entire income redistribution effect</u> $L_x - L_V$ of a tax and transfer system always involves a <u>comparison of distributions of different sizes</u> (since $\bar{x} > \bar{V} = \bar{x} - \bar{T}^G$). Consequently, an ordinal (welfare) ranking of the entire income redistribution effects of different years or countries is not without severe ambiguities. In particular, Atkinson's(1970) theorem <u>cannot</u> be invoked in cases of unequal-mean comparisons.

III. Tax and Transfer Policy and Redistributive Effects in Practice

So far, we have depicted an "ideal" world in which distributional issues (equity objectives) are treated sepatately and in which tax and transfer instruments are implemented in a target-oriented way. Unfortunately, in practice, all western countries apply a <u>two-part system</u> of taxes and transfers which is <u>not</u> divided with respect to the two distributional objectives but rather along the lines of tax and transfer instruments.

Specifically, in practice we find on the one side an integrated system T(.) of public good taxes and redistributive taxes and, on the other side, a (usually very complex and non-harmonized) system of redistributive transfers E(.). For example,

$$S(x) = T(x-x_T) - E(x-x_E) \lesseqgtr 0 \quad \forall\, x \lesseqgtr x_I \tag{5a}$$

where, in general, $x_T < x_I < x_E$ and where $\bar{S}/\bar{x} = \bar{T}/\bar{x} - \bar{E}/\bar{x} = g^* - e = g$. With a fully harmonized system the break-even income x_E for transfers, and x_T for taxes would coincide with the break-even income x_I of the entire system, i.e. $x_T = x_E = x_I$.

The income redistribution effect of such a two-part tax and transfer system is often called the "net fiscal incidence". It can, of course, be decomposed into two redistributive effects on income. The first is caused by transfers and the second caused by taxes (see for

---

[16] Note that $1 - g/(1-g) < 1$.

details Lambert and Pfähler, 1986a). If one assumes a sequential application of transfers and subsequent taxes, one obtains the following decomposition (for $V(.) = x+E(.)-T(.) = V^{ER}(.)-T(.) = E(.) + V^{T}(.)$)

$$L_x - L_V = (L_x - L_V ER) + (L_V ER - L_V) \qquad (5b)$$

$$= (e/(1+e))(L_x - L_E) - (g^*/(1-g^*))(L_V ER - L_T)$$

where $g^* = \bar{T}/\bar{x} = (\bar{T}^G+\bar{E})/\bar{x}$ is the total tax ratio required to finance public goods and redistributive transfers. If, in contrast, one assumes a parallel policy of levying taxes and granting transfer one obtains the following decomposition:

$$L_x - L_V = \frac{1+e}{1+e-g^*}(L_x - L_V ER) + \frac{1-g^*}{1+e-g^*}(L_x - L_V T) \qquad (5c)$$

$$= \frac{e}{1+e-g^*}(L_x - L_E) \quad \frac{g^*}{1+e-g^*}(L_x - L_T)$$

where $1+e-g^* = \bar{V}/\bar{x}$ is the total net tax ratio.[17]

Neither redistributive effect in eqts. (5b)-(5c), in general, can be unequivocally associated with an equitable distribution of public goods taxes and/or an equitable distribution of (market) income. Thus, the measurement of "net fiscal incidence", in general, cannot assist a target-oriented design, control or evaluation of a policy aimed at two distinct objectives of distributional equity. This is because the income redistribution effect resulting from integrated public good and redistributive taxes (i.e. $L_V ER-L_V$ in eq.(5b) or $L_x - L_V T$ in eq.(5c)), in general, cannot be further subdivided into two redistributive effects: one which is unequicocally associated with public good taxes and one with redistributive taxes sufficient to finance redistributive transfers. This would require an unique division of the integrated tax scale $T(.)$ into a public goods tax part $T^G(.)$ and a redistributive tax part $T^R(.)$ such that $\bar{T}^R = \bar{E}$.

There exist (as far as I see) only two conditions which allow for such a unique division. The first is the normative premise that, for equity reasons, a public good tax should be strictly proportional. Progression and its implied redistributive effects can then be exclu-

---

17 Note that $(1+e) + (1-g^*) \neq 1$ and $e - g^* < 0$.

sively attributed to the objective of an equitable distribution of (market) income. The public and scholarly majority, however, does not share this normative view. Yet, I feel, that most of the literature on the measurement of tax progressivity and of its redistributive effect has this normative assumption as an implicit base. A higher income redistribution effect is usually connoted with a stronger sentiment for income redistribution, although it may simply result from a tax reform which either aimed at higher tax receipts (by scaling-up taxes) or at a more equitable distribution of the tax burden.

The second condition allowing for a unique division of the tax scale is the normative premise that, for equity reasons, a public good tax should be a linearly-progressive, or flat-rate, tax (with a constant marginal tax rate above a threshold), i.e. $T(x-x_I) = m\cdot(x-x_I)$. Such a linearly-progressive tax scale can be split uniquely into the tax scale $T(x-x_T) = (m^G+m^R)\cdot(x-x_I)$. This is due to the fact that the constant marginal tax rates m^G and m^R of the public good tax and the redistributive tax, respectively, can (for any given total tax ratio g^* and break-even income x_I) be solved as

$$m^G = \frac{T^G}{x(1-L_{xI}) - x_I(1-F_{xI})} = m - m^R, \tag{6}$$

where L_{xI} denotes the cumulative portion of pre-fisc income falling on the cumulative portion F_{xI} of income recipients with pre-fisc income less than or equal to the threshhold x_I. None of the OECD countries has a linearly-progressive income tax. Presently, the English income tax is the closest approximation of a flat-rate tax. The US-income tax, which is currently under revision, will soon approximate a flate-rate tax even more closely.

IV. Conclusion

In light of the analysis above, the current measurement of tax progressivity and of its redistributive effects can be criticized on various grounds. First, and above all, the confinement on the tax side alone (not including redistributive transfers and other attributable public expenditures) is of little or no interest from a budget policy perspective. Secondly, in interpreting the measured values of global tax progressivity and its redistributive effect on income much more care should be taken with respect to the meaning and relevance of these statistical values. Any income redistribution effect observed is, in part, due to the desire to equitably distribute the cost of public goods and has, as such, nothing to do with the desire for an equitable distribution of income. Unfortunately, there is no way to unequivocally delineate that part of income distribution. Thirdly, once it is recognized that the empirical findings do not lend themselves to a target-oriented control, reform and/or evaluation of tax and transfer policies, it is no longer obvious what the merits of these empirical studies are - except, perhaps, augmenting the body of descriptive knowledge.

Since the current, non-decomposable two-part tax and transfer system did not emerge from deliberate policy formation but from historical piece-meal reform, one might think of shifting the system in the future towards an ideal, decomposable dual system. For instance, one might pursue a piece-meal strategy towards a linearly-progressive, or flat-rate, tax and towards earmarking new taxes or tax hikes for redistributive or allocative purposes.

Finally, measuring the income redistribution effect (or net fiscal incidence) of an entire non-decomposable tax and transfer system always involves comparisons of distributions of different sizes. From a welfare perspective, this causes the problem of assesing the trade-off between size and shares. The literature on net fiscal incidence does not yet account for this trade-off.

References

Atkinson, A.B. (1970), On the measurement of inequality, Journal of Economic Theory, 2, 244-263.

Dalton, H. (1922), Principles of Public Finance, 4th ed. 1954, London.

Diamond, P. (1975), A many person Ramsey tax rule, Journal of Public Economics, 4, 335-342.

Eichhorn, W., Funke, H. and Richter, W.F.(1984), Tax progression and inequality of income distribution, Journal of Mathematical Economics, 13, 127-131.

Formby, J.P., Seaks, T.G. and Smith, W.J. (1981), A comparison of two new measures of tax progressivity, Economic Journal, 91, 1o15-1o19.

Formby, J.P., Seaks, T.G. and Smith, W.J. (1984), Difficulties in the measurement and comparison of tax progressivity: The case of North America, Public Finance/Finances Publiques, 39, 297-313.

Hainsworth, G.B.(1964), The Lorenz curve as a general tool of economic analysis, Economic Record, 4o, 426-441.

Jacobsson, U. (1976), On the measurement of the degree of progression, Journal of Public Economics, 5, 161-168.

Kakwani, N.C. (1977), Measurement of tax progressivity: an international comparison, Economic Journal, 87, 71-80.

Kiefer, D.W. (1984), Distributional tax progressivity indexes, National Tax Journal, 37, 497-513.

Kienzle, E.C. (1981), Measurement of the progressivity of public expenditure and net fiscal incidence, Southern Economic Journal, 48, 197-2o3.

Lambert, P. (1985a), On the redistributive effects of taxes and benefits, Scottish Journal of Political Economy, 32, 39-54.

Lambert, P.(1985b), Net fiscal incidence progressivity: some approaches to measurement, Proceedings of the 4th Karlsruhe International Symposium on Measurement in Economics, forthcoming.

Lambert, P.(1985c),Endogenizing the income distribution: The redistributive effect, and Laffer effects, of a progressive tax-benefit system, Europäische Zeitschrift für Politische Ökonomie/European Journal of Political Economy, 1, 3-2o.

Lambert, P. and Pfähler, W. (1986a), On Aggregate measures of the net redistributive impact of taxation and public expenditure, Ifs working papers, no. 87. London.

Lambert, P. and Pfähler, W. (1986b), Intersecting tax concentration curves and the measurement of tax progressivity, mimeo.

Musgrave, R.A. and Thin, T. (1948), Income tax progression, 1929-1948, Journal of Political Economy, 56, 498-514.

Pfähler, W. (1983), Measuring redistributional effects of tax progressivity by Lorenz curves, Jahrbücher für Nationalökonomie und Statistik, 198, 237-249.

Pfähler, W. (1984), 'Linear' income tax cuts: distributional effects, social preferences, and revenue elasticities, Journal of Public Economics, 24, 381-388.

Pfähler, W. (1985), Relative concentration curve: Functional form and measures of non-proportionality, Bulletin of Economic Research, 37, 201-211.

Pfähler, W. (1987), Redistributive effects of tax progressivity: Evaluating a general class of aggregate measures, Public Finance/ Finances Publiques, forthcoming.

Samuelson, P.A. (1954), The pure theory of public expenditure, Review of Economics and Statistics, 36, 387-389.

Suits, D. (1977), Measurement of tax progressivity, American Economic Review, 67, 747-752.

Measures of Tax Progression – An Axiomatic Approach

Andreas Pfingsten

Institut für Wirtschaftstheorie und Operations Research

Universität Karlsruhe, D-7500 Karlsruhe, FRG

Abstract

Two basic axioms for distributionally based local measures of tax progression are presented. A class of indices with these and further desirable properties is suggested. The measures are applied in constructing tax functions with constant progressivity over the whole income scale.

1. Introduction

In the literature on price or inequality measurement, for example, it is by now standard practice (e.g., Diewert [1983], Eichhorn/Voeller [1983], and Eichhorn/Gehrig [1982]) to use indices which are derived from more or less plausible requirements, often heroically called axioms. Even those scholars who do argue that certain requirements are far from being natural are seldom reluctant to admit a noticeable advantage of axiomatic approaches in general compared to using measures suggested somewhat ad hoc: usually the properties of indices applied emerge much more clearly.

Measures of tax progression in contrary, see the seminal paper of Musgrave/Thin [1948] as the classic example, have in most cases been proposed because of their intuitive appeal rather than being derived from first principles. Consequently, an axiomatic approach towards the measurement of tax progression should be useful, first, to improve the understanding of known indices, and second, to generate new measures with desirable properties not inherent in any of the previous suggestions.

Measurement in Economics
ed. by W. Eichhorn

In this paper, we present two axioms which each reasonable *local measure of progression* (measuring progressivity at certain income levels) should satisfy. Then a class of measures that meet this requirement is introduced and, in addition, the measures are shown to have further nice properties. These measures are finally used to construct tax functions with constant progressivity through out the income scale. For limitations of space we will not discuss *global* measures of (effective) progression in this paper (see Musgrave/Thin [1948], Kakwani [1977], Pfingsten [1986a], Poddar/Genser [1986], and many others).

Our progressivity measures are based on redistributional considerations. This according to Jakobsson [1976, p.162], Atkinson/ Stiglitz [1980, p.37], and Blackorby/Donaldson [1984] is quite acceptable. However, Khetan/Poddar [1976], Kakwani [1977], and Poddar/Genser [1986], among others, point out the different (and partially complementary) content of measures of redistribution on the one hand and measures of progressivity on the other. A nice equivalence of certain notions of progressivity and inequality reduction is shown by Eichhorn et al. [1984]. Yet the reader should consult the excellent survey by Lambert [1987] and the references cited therein to see that deviation from proportionality and revenue responsiveness (i.e., tax elasticity with respect to pre-tax income), respectively, are other starting points for progressivity measurement which are appealing, too.

2. Basic properties for progressivity measures

The tax functions $T:\mathbb{R}_{++}\to\mathbb{R}$ we use in this paper are assumed to be continuously differentiable. They map positive pre-tax incomes into tax liabilities (possibly negative) and satisfy the condition

$$T(x) < x \qquad \text{for all } x\in\mathbb{R}_{++}, \tag{2.1}$$

i.e., all post-tax incomes are positive. Such tax functions are called *admissible*. The average tax rate function $t:\mathbb{R}_{++}\to(-\infty,1)$ then is defined by

$$t(x) \equiv T(x) \,/\, x \,. \tag{2.2}$$

and it is obvious from condition (2.1) that the average tax rate indeed must be less than one everywhere. The marginal tax rate $T'(x)$ is not restricted although for practical applications one would probably want it to be strictly less than one in order to guarantee that post-tax income is an increasing function of pre-tax income.

Notice, the definition and determination of pre-tax income is not examined in this paper. It is certainly desirable to include (dis-) incentive effects of taxation in the analysis (see Lambert [1985]), but that is beyond the scope of the present approach.

When constructing a local measure of tax progression S, indicating the degree of progression of a tax function T at a pre-tax income level x, one first must decide from which data to calculate progressivity. Possible choices are, for example, pre-tax income x, tax liability $T(x)$, marginal tax rate $T'(x)$, average tax rate $t(x)$, slope $t'(x)$ of the average tax rate, or $t''(x)$, the second-order derivative of the average tax rate.

A rather general notion of progressivity (see Atkinson/Stiglitz [1980] or Jakobsson [1976] as just two examples) states that a tax function should be called progressive if the average tax rate increases with pre-tax income, i.e., if the average rate progression

$$\Pi(x|T) := \frac{d\ T(x)/x}{dx} = \frac{T'(x)\cdot x - T(x)}{x^2} \tag{2.3}$$

is positive. In accordance with this progressivity index our measures will be based on the tax function T and its first-order derivative but not on the average tax rate function: yet the reader should be aware that since income x is used as another variable, this is, because of identity (2.2), simply a matter of convenience. In Pfingsten [1987] a similar analysis is based on the average tax rate function t only, and the results are quite parallel. Summing up, progressivity of the tax function T at pre-tax income x will be calculated as $S[x,T(x),T'(x)]$.

(By ignoring second-order derivatives we do not want to deny the importance of the contribution by Richter [1984] who derives an intertemporal progressivity measure using T''. But here we are more interested in static effects.)

The technique applied in formulating our axioms is as follows: Two tax functions are compared at some income level. Their properties suggest immediately which ranking according to progressivity at this income level should result from a reasonable progressivity measure. This is then formalized.

The first axiom we propose is *strict monotonicity* in the marginal tax rate: if, at some income level x, two tax functions have the same value then the steeper one should be assigned the higher degree of progression there.

It is obvious that this property is consistent with the general notion of progressivity mentioned above, since with fixed positive pre-tax income x and fixed tax liability T(x) the average rate progression is increasing in the marginal tax rate T'(x).

The second axiom, called *μ-compatibility* , is an application of a value judgement on inequality. An inequality concept represented by a certain value μ ($0 \leq \mu \leq 1$) has the property of saying each (post-tax) income distribution $Y_\lambda \in \mathbb{R}^n_{++}$:

$$Y_\lambda = Z + \lambda \cdot [\mu \cdot Z + (1-\mu) \cdot \underline{1}], \tag{2.4}$$

where $Z \in \mathbb{R}^n_{++}$ and $\underline{1}$ is a vector of n ones (in income units), is *inequality-equivalent* to the (post-tax) income distribution Z. λ is a scaling parameter determining total income. Special inequality concepts are the well-known relative ($\mu=1$) and absolute ($\mu=0$) inequality concepts (see Kolm [1976]).

Suppose now, two tax functions T_1 and T_2, respectively their corresponding post-tax income functions N_1 and N_2 (where $N_i(x) \equiv x - T_i(x)$), have the following property for the concept represented by some chosen μ: For each pre-tax income distribution X the post-tax income distribution resulting from T_2 has the same degree of inequality as the one resulting from T_1, or to be more precise, for each $X \in \mathbb{R}^n_{++}$ the post-tax income distributions $\underline{N}_1(X)$ and $\underline{N}_2(X)$ are inequality-equivalent. Then it seems sensible to require that, at each income level, the degree of progression assigned to T_1 should equal that assigned to T_2.

The preceding consideration is based on an appealing though certainly debatable presumption, namely that inequality-equivalent distributions of post-tax incomes are generated by progressivity-equivalent tax functions. This view is shared by, e.g., Blackorby/Donaldson [1984] while Poddar/Genser [1986] and others favour the look at tax distributions.

If for all pre-tax income distributions $X \in \mathbb{R}^n_{++}$ the post-tax income distributions $\underline{N}_1(X)$ and $\underline{N}_2(X)$ are inequality-equivalent, i.e. satisfy for some $\lambda(X)$

$$\underline{N}_2(X) = \underline{N}_1(X) + \lambda(X) \cdot [\mu \cdot \underline{N}_1(X) + (1-\mu) \cdot \underline{1}], \tag{2.5}$$

then it follows easily (Pfingsten [1986b, p.392]) that there exists some $\overline{\lambda}$ such that

$$N_2(x) \equiv N_1(x) + \overline{\lambda} \cdot [\mu \cdot N_1(x) + (1-\mu)] \tag{2.6}$$

and hence

$$T_2(x) \equiv (1+\lambda \cdot \mu) \cdot T_1(x) - \lambda \cdot \mu \cdot x - \lambda \cdot (1-\mu) \tag{2.7}$$

Noting that the derivatives then are such that

$$T_2'(x) \equiv (1+\lambda \cdot \mu) \cdot T_1'(x) - \lambda \cdot \mu, \tag{2.8}$$

we are ready to define formally what we mean by a measure of progression:

<u>Definition 1</u>

Let $T: \mathbb{R}_{++} \to \mathbb{R}$ be an admissible tax function.

Then a *local measure of tax progression* of the tax function T at the income level x for the inequality concept represented by μ $(0 \leq \mu \leq 1)$ is a function

$$S_\mu: \mathbb{R}_{++} \times \mathbb{R}^2 \to \mathbb{R}$$
$$[x, T(x), T'(x)] \to S_\mu[x, T(x), T'(x)]$$

which satisfies the following two axioms for all triples $(a,b,c) \in \mathbb{R}_{++} \times \mathbb{R}^2$ such that $a>b$:

(A1) Strict Monotonicity

$$S_\mu(a,b,c) < S_\mu(a,b,c+\lambda) \quad \text{for all } \lambda \in \mathbb{R}_{++}. \tag{2.9}$$

(A2) μ-Compatibility

$$\left.\begin{array}{l} S_\mu(a,b,c) = \\ S_\mu[a,(1+\lambda\cdot\mu)\cdot b-\lambda\cdot\mu\cdot a-\lambda\cdot(1-\mu),(1+\lambda\cdot\mu)\cdot c-\lambda\cdot\mu] \end{array}\right\} \tag{2.10}$$

$$\text{for all } \lambda > -\frac{a-b}{\mu\cdot(a-b)+(1-\mu)}. \tag{2.11}$$

Note that the lower bound for λ, i.e., condition (2.11), is necessary to guarantee positivity of post-tax income on the right-hand-side of equation (2.10). Notice further that equation (2.10) can be rewritten

$$S_\mu(a,b,c) = S_\mu\left[a,b-\lambda\cdot[\mu\cdot(a-b)+(1-\mu)],c-\lambda\cdot\mu\cdot(1-c)\right] \tag{2.12}$$

which often simplifies notation and proofs.

3. A class of suitable progressivity measures

As it turns out, Definition 1 restricts the functions that can be called measures of progression to a certain class:

<u>Theorem 1</u>

A function $S_\mu:\mathbb{R}_{++}\times\mathbb{R}^2\to\mathbb{R}$ satisfies axioms (A1) and (A2) for all $(a,b,c)\in\mathbb{R}_{++}\times\mathbb{R}^2$ such that $a>b$ if and only if

$$S_\mu(a,b,c) = F_\mu\left[a,\frac{\mu\cdot(a\cdot c-b)+(1-\mu)\cdot c}{\mu\cdot(a-b)+(1-\mu)}\right] \tag{3.1}$$

where $F_\mu:\mathbb{R}_{++}\times\mathbb{R}\to\mathbb{R}$ is strictly increasing in the second argument.

Proof

For necessity note that by choosing

$$\lambda = \frac{b}{\mu\cdot(a-b) + (1-\mu)} > -\frac{a-b}{\mu\cdot(a-b) + (1-\mu)} \tag{3.2}$$

equation (2.12) becomes

$$S_\mu(a,b,c) = S_\mu\left[a,\ 0,\ c - \frac{b}{\mu\cdot(a-b) + (1-\mu)}\cdot\mu\cdot(1-c)\right] \tag{3.3}$$

or, equivalently,

$$S_\mu(a,b,c) = S_\mu\left[a,\ 0,\frac{\mu\cdot(a\cdot c-b) + (1-\mu)\cdot c}{\mu\cdot(a-b) + (1-\mu)}\right]. \tag{3.4}$$

To prove sufficiency, first check that axiom (A2) holds because

$$S_\mu(a,b,c) =$$

$$\frac{\mu\cdot[a\cdot(c-\lambda\cdot\mu\cdot(1-c))-(b-\lambda\cdot(\mu\cdot(a-b)+(1-\mu)))]+(1-\mu)\cdot[c-\lambda\cdot\mu\cdot(1-c)]}{\mu\cdot[a-(b-\lambda\cdot(\mu\cdot(a-b)+(1-\mu)))]+(1-\mu)}$$

$$= \frac{\mu\cdot[a\cdot(1+\lambda\cdot\mu)\cdot c-(1+\lambda\cdot\mu)\cdot b]+(1-\mu)\cdot(1+\lambda\cdot\mu)\cdot c}{\mu\cdot[(1+\lambda\cdot\mu)\cdot a-(1+\lambda\cdot\mu)\cdot b+\lambda\cdot(1-\mu)]+(1-\mu)} \tag{3.5}$$

$$= \frac{\mu\cdot(1+\lambda\cdot\mu)\cdot(a\cdot c-b)+(1-\mu)\cdot(1+\lambda\cdot\mu)\cdot c}{\mu\cdot(1+\lambda\cdot\mu)\cdot(a-b)+(1-\mu)\cdot(1+\lambda\cdot\mu)} = \frac{\mu\cdot(a\cdot c-b)+(1-\mu)\cdot c}{\mu\cdot(a-b)+(1-\mu)} .$$

The inequalities

$$\mu\cdot a + (1-\mu) > 0 \quad \text{and} \quad \mu\cdot(a-b) + (1-\mu) > 0 \tag{3.6}$$

imply that the monotonicity axiom (A1) is satisfied. ∎

In a more readable way we can express equation (3.1) as

$$S_\mu[x,T(x),T'(x)] = F_\mu[x,P_\mu(x|T)], \tag{3.7}$$

where we have used

$$P_{\mu}(x|T) := \frac{\mu \cdot [x \cdot T'(x) - T(x)] + (1-\mu) \cdot T'(x)}{\mu \cdot [x - T(x)] + (1-\mu)} . \qquad (3.8)$$

The argument of the function $P_{\mu}(x|T)$ should be read as "at pre-tax income x, given the tax function T". P_{μ} is a very simple member of the class defined by axioms (A1) and (A2). It will henceforth be used as our measure of progression. Thus we say that $P_{\mu}(x|T)$ is the *degree of progression of a tax function* T *at pre-tax income* x *with respect to* μ.

The two special cases $\mu=0$ and $\mu=1$ deserve attention. For the concept of absolute inequality ($\mu=0$), P_{μ} reduces to the marginal tax rate:

$$P_0(x|T) = T'(x) . \qquad (3.9)$$

For relative inequality we obtain one minus the residual income progression, i.e.,

$$P_1(x|T) = \frac{x \cdot T'(x) - T(x)}{x - T(x)} = 1 - \frac{x \cdot [1 - T'(x)]}{x - T(x)} \qquad (3.10)$$

$$= 1 - RIP(x|T) .$$

We can state our notion of progressivity now precisely:

<u>Definition 2</u>

Let $T:\mathbb{R}_{++}\rightarrow\mathbb{R}$ be an admissible tax function.

Then T is called *weakly progressive* at income x for the inequality concept represented by μ if and only if $P_{\mu}(x|T)$ is nonnegative, and it is called *strictly progressive* if and only if $P_{\mu}(x|T)$ is positive.

4. Further desiderata for progressivity measures

Apart form the basic requirements discussed above there are further properties which, although not indispensable, still are to some degree desirable. Some of these will be discussed in this section.

First, there is a normalization property: if a tax function is <u>not</u> redistributive then the progressivity should be equal to zero. Such tax functions, called *inequality-preserving* in Pfingsten [1986b], generate post-tax income distributions which are inequality-equivalent to the pre-tax income distribution. By letting $T_\mu := T_2$ and $T_1(x) \equiv 0$ it is easily seen from identity (2.7) that they are given, for an inequality concept represented by μ $(0 \leqq \mu \leqq 1)$, by

$$T_\mu(x) \equiv -\lambda \cdot \mu \cdot x - \lambda \cdot (1-\mu), \tag{4.1}$$

where certain restrictions on the tax yield parameter λ apply. Because of

$$T'_\mu(x) \equiv - \lambda \cdot \mu . \tag{4.2}$$

and hence

$$\left. \begin{aligned} P_\mu(x|T_\mu) &= \frac{\mu \cdot x \cdot \left[-\lambda \cdot \mu - [-\lambda \cdot \mu \cdot x - \lambda \cdot (1-\mu)]/x\right] + (1-\mu) \cdot (-\lambda \cdot \mu)}{\mu \cdot x \cdot \left[1 - [-\lambda \cdot \mu \cdot x - \lambda \cdot (1-\mu)]/x\right] + (1-\mu)} \\ &= \frac{\mu \cdot x \cdot [\lambda \cdot (1-\mu)/x] - \lambda \cdot \mu \cdot (1-\mu)}{\mu \cdot x \cdot [1 + \lambda \cdot \mu + \lambda \cdot (1-\mu)/x] + (1-\mu)} = 0 , \end{aligned} \right\} \tag{4.3}$$

we obtain:

<u>Lemma 1</u>

> If an admissible tax function T is inequality-preserving with respect to μ $(0 \leqq \mu \leqq 1)$ then
>
> $$P_\mu(x|T) = 0 \quad \text{for all } x \in \mathbb{R}_{++}. \tag{4.4}$$

It should be noted that a proportional tax function

$$T_\tau(x) \equiv \tau \cdot x \qquad (0 < \tau < 1) \tag{4.5}$$

is assigned a progressivity of degree zero only for $\mu=1$, the (relative) Lorenz concept, but positive values otherwise: this is the case because for the other inequality concepts a proportional tax is redistributive.

The second property, also a normalization, is motivated by observing that perfect equality in post-tax incomes is the maximum redistribution achievable without rank reversals on the income scale. Thus if the tax function generates equal post-tax incomes irrespective of the pre-tax incomes, then the index should equal one.

If for all pre-tax incomes the post-tax incomes are equal, to some fixed $y \in \mathbb{R}_{++}$ say, then the tax function must be perfectly equalizing:

$$T_y(x) \equiv x - y \ . \tag{4.6}$$

Observing that marginal tax rate in this case equals one and further noting

$$P_\mu(x|T_y) = \frac{\mu \cdot x \cdot [1-(x-y)/x] + (1-\mu) \cdot 1}{\mu \cdot x \cdot [1-(x-y)/x] + (1-\mu)} = 1 \ , \tag{4.7}$$

we can state:

<u>Lemma 2</u>

If an admissible tax function T is perfectly equalizing then

$$P_\mu(x|T) = 1 \qquad \text{for all } x \in \mathbb{R}_{++} \text{ and for all } \mu: 0 \leqq \mu \leqq 1. \tag{4.8}$$

A third desideratum: the progressivity of the sum of two tax functions should equal the sum of the degrees of progression of the two single tax functions. This property (an admittedly strong aggregation requirement) is desirable since splitting an overall tax function into two parts, into a federal tax and a local tax, for example, should not matter. It may be called *additivity*.

However, this property does only hold for $\mu=0$ (the sum of the marginal tax rates of two tax functions equals the marginal tax rate of the sum of two tax functions). Corollary VI.9.2 in Pfingsten [1986a,p.53] states that our axioms (A1) and (A2) for $0<\mu\leqq 1$ are not compatible with the additivity property.

5. Tax functions with constant progressivity

If all pre-tax incomes in an economy increase over some period of time, though not necessarily with the same rate, and if the tax function is not adjusted, then a well-known problem shows up: under a progressive tax schedule, progressive in the sense that the average tax rate increases with income, the ratio of post-tax to pre-tax income decreases and government's share in total income increases. It is often said that this situation is one of "hidden" increases in the degree of progression, although the notion of progressivity underlying this statement is seldom specified.

A solution to this problem was perfect indexation. With our inequality concept based on real incomes (and taxes), however, we cannot easily accomodate this. Yet with our precise definition of progressivity in general and of the degree of progression in particular, we can provide a different way to (at least partially) solve this problem. If we have a progressive tax function T such that, for a certain μ, $P_\mu(x|T)$ takes the same value p for all x, then as long as P_μ is accepted as measure of progression, for each individual the degree of progression p will be left unchanged no matter how his or her income changes. (When keeping progressivity constant this way we cannot in general preserve the post-tax/pre-tax income ratios at the same time.) More formally, we define:

<u>Definition 3</u>

An admissible tax function T is a *constant progressivity tax function with respect to* μ $(0 \leq \mu \leq 1)$ if and only if there exists some p $(0 \leq p \leq 1)$ such that

$$P_\mu(x|T) = p \qquad \text{for all } x \in \mathbb{R}_{++} \tag{5.1}$$

and p is the *degree of progression of* T *with respect to* μ.

For different pairs (μ, p) different functional forms for the tax function will arise. Inserting definition (3.8) into condition (5.1) yields

$$\frac{\mu\cdot[x\cdot T'(x)-T(x)]+(1-\mu)\cdot T'(x)}{\mu\cdot[\,x-T(x)\,]+(1-\mu)} = p \quad \text{for all } x\in\mathbb{R}_{++} \tag{5.2}$$

and upon rearranging terms finally

$$T'(x) - (1-p)\cdot\frac{\mu}{(1-\mu+\mu\cdot x)}\cdot T(x) \equiv p\,. \tag{5.3}$$

Solving this ordinary, first-order, linear differential equation as in Pfingsten [1986a,pp.64] gives rise to the following theorem which we state without proof:

<u>Theorem 2</u>

The only constant progressivity tax functions are:

$$T_{\mu,p}(x) = \begin{cases} x - c & (c>0) \text{ for } 0\leqq\mu\leqq 1, p=1, \\ p\cdot x - c_0 & (c_0\geqq 0) \text{ for } \mu=0,\ 0\leqq p<1, \\ x + \dfrac{1-\mu}{\mu} - c_\mu\cdot(1-\mu+\mu\cdot x)^{1-p} & \left(c_\mu\geqq\dfrac{(1-\mu)^p}{\mu}\right) \text{ for } 0<\mu<1,\ 0\leqq p<1, \\ x - c_1\cdot x^{1-p} & (c_1>0) \text{ for } \mu=1,\ 0\leqq p<1. \end{cases} \tag{5.4}$$

The degree of progression of $T_{\mu,p}$ with respect to μ is p.

For p=1, these are the tax functions generating equal post-tax incomes which already appeared in identity (4.6) above. For μ=0, we have the famous linear (or rather: quasilinear) tax schedules predominantly used in the optimal taxation literature. For μ=1, finally, the tax functions are *residually iso-elastic* (see Richter [1984, p.150]) or *lorenzgerecht* (see Genser [1980, p.111]).

Note that using such tax functions enables policy makers, at least in principle, to design a tax schedule resulting from three independent considerations: first, choose a value judgement on inequality μ, second, decide about the desired progressivity p, (i.e., the desired redistributional objective), and third, determine c_μ from the government's revenue requirement. This seems to be an important application of our distributionally based measures of tax progression.

References

Atkinson, A.B. and J.E. Stiglitz (1980):
Lectures on public economics.
Mc Graw-Hill, New York.

Blackorby, C. and D. Donaldson (1984):
Ethical social index numbers and the measurement of effective tax/benefit progressivity.
Canadian Journal of Economics (17), 683-694.

Diewert, W.E. (1983):
The theory of the cost of living index and the measurement of welfare
change.
In: W.E. Diewert (ed.), Price Level Measurement,
Statistics Canada, Ottawa, 163-233.

Eichhorn, W., Funke, H. and W.F. Richter (1984):
Tax progression and inequality of income distribution.
Journal of Mathematical Economics (13), 127-131.

Eichhorn, W. and W. Gehrig (1982):
Measurement of inequality in economics.
In: B. Korte (ed.), Modern applied mathematics: optimization and operations research, North-Holland, Amsterdam, 657-693.

Eichhorn, W. and J. Voeller (1983):
Axiomatic foundation of price indexes and purchasing power parities.
In: W.E. Diewert (ed.), Price Level Measurement,
Statistics Canada, Ottawa, 411-450.

Genser, B. (1980):
Lorenzgerechte Besteuerung.
Österreichische Akademie der Wissenschaften, Wien.

Jakobsson, U. (1976):
On the measurement of the degree of progression.
Journal of Public Economics (5), 161-168.

Kakwani, N.C. (1977):
Measurement of tax progressivity: an international comparison.
Economic Journal (87), 71-80.

Khetan, C.P. and S.N. Poddar (1976):
Measurement of income tax progression in a growing economy: the Canadian experience.
Canadian Journal of Economics (9), 613-629.

Kolm, S.C. (1976):
Unequal inequalities: I.
Journal of Economic Theory (12), 416-442.

Lambert, P.J. (1985):
Endogenizing the income distribution: the redistributive effect, and Laffer effects, of a progressive tax-benefit system.
European Journal of Political Economy (1), 3-20.

Lambert, P.J. (1987):
Net fiscal incidence progressivity: some approaches to measurement.
This volume.

Musgrave, R.A. and T. Thin (1948):
Income tax progression, 1929-48.
Journal of Political Economy (56), 498-514.

Pfingsten, A. (1986a):
The measurement of tax progression.
Studies in Contemporary Economics (20),
Springer, Berlin-Heidelberg-New York.

Pfingsten, A. (1986b):
Distributionally-neutral tax changes for different inequality concepts.
Journal of Public Economics (30), 385-393.

Pfingsten, A. (1987):
Axiomatically based local measures of tax progression.
Bulletin of Economic Research (39), forthcoming.

Poddar, S.N. and B. Genser (1986):
Measurement of effective tax progression.
Discussion paper I/224, Konstanz.

Richter, W.F. (1984):
Saving, taxation, and income inequality.
In: D. Bös, M. Rose and C. Seidl (eds.), Beiträge zur neueren Steuertheorie, Studies in Contemporary Economics (7),
Springer, Berlin-Heidelberg-New York, 139-161.

The author is indebted to two anonymous referees whose suggestions were very fruitful. It is solely his fault if neither all their comments nor additional remarks provided by (other) participants of Wolfgang Eichhorn's stimulating conference are incorporated.

Equal Sacrifice in Taxation*

H.P. Young
University of Maryland
School of Public Affairs
College Park
Maryland 20742, USA

1. Introduction.

A traditional justification for progressive taxation is that it causes all taxpayers to sacrifice equally. The equal sacrifice doctrine can be traced back to J. S. Mill, who argued for it as a principle of distributive justice: " As a government ought to make no distinction of persons or classes in the strength of their claims on it, whatever sacrifices it requires from them should be made to bear as nearly as possible with the same pressure upon all . . . Equality of taxation, therefore, as a maxim of politics, means equality of sacrifice." [Mill, 1848, Bk. V, Ch. II]. Of course, equal sacrifice by itself does not necessarily imply progressive taxation. If the marginal utility of income (or wealth) decreases the richer one is, then a given amount of tax falls more lightly on the richer than on the poorer. So equal loss of utility implies that the richer should pay more in tax than the poorer. But that is the extent of the matter; it does not require that the richer pay a higher proportion of their income (or wealth) in taxes. As Samuelson showed, the latter only holds if the marginal utility of income is sufficiently elastic, that is, if $xU''(x)/U'(x) \leq -1$. [Samuelson, 1947, p.227].

Today equal sacrifice is not very fashionable as a basis for tax policy, not because it lacks intuitive appeal, but because it seems to rely so heavily on interpersonal welfare comparisons. To apply the equal sacrifice approach in a real case, a specific form for the utility function would have to be agreed upon, and as a practical matter the same function would have

----

* This work was supported by the National Science Foundation under Grant SES 831 9530.

Measurement in Economics
ed. by W. Eichhorn

to be assumed to hold for all taxpayers. These assumptions seem to be completely unwarranted; one might as easily assume the tax distribution itself. Nevertheless, arguments based on equal sacrifice are " latent in much of modern discussion and thought," as Samuelson put it [id., p.227].

In this paper we shall show that the equal sacrifice approach can be justified on entirely different grounds than interpersonal comparisons of utility. In fact, no utility function for income need be postulated at all. Instead, we shall insist that a tax system be reasonably consistent in the the way that it treats related tax problems. Are groups with similar income distributions treated similarly? If taxes go up, does everyone share in the increase? Is the increase shared in an equitable manner? Is earning more income advantageous? These four properties imply that a tax method acts *as if* it equalizes sacrifice relative to some idealized. utility function. That is, they imply the existence of a utility function relative to which everyone suffers the same loss of welfare. One can even say a good deal about the form of this utility function if one assumes a further property -- namely, that equal sacrifice is maintained when tax schedules are re-indexed. In this case the utility function must be one of the standard functions from the theory of risk-bearing -- namely a logarithmic or simple power function [Arrow, 1971]. The tax schedules implied by this class of functions are quite interesting and seem not to have been studied before except in isolated cases.

The paper is intended to be a survey only; details of proofs and a more extensive motivation of the axioms may be found in [Young, 1987a,b,c].

2. Tax methods.

Let x be some index of ability to pay, such as taxable income or wealth. To be specific we shall speak of 'taxable income'. We do not enter here into a discussion of how taxable income is or ought to be defined; that is, of what constitutes the proper *basis* of taxation. This topic has been amply treated in the public finance literature. For now, x will stand for some monetary measure of ability to pay. A *tax schedule* is a function of form $t = f(x)$, where $x > 0$ represents the level of taxable income and t is the tax owed on x. We shall assume that $f(x)$ is nonnegative and bounded above by x. Thus no one is subsidized, and everyone is taxed within his means.

A tax schedule $f(x)$ is *strictly progressive* if $f(x)/x$ is strictly increasing in x, it is *flat* if $f(x)/x$ is constant, and it is *strictly regressive* if $f(x)/x$ is strictly decreasing in x. The term *progressive* applies to schedules for which $f(x)/x$ is nondecreasing.

A single tax schedule is inflexible as a tool of fiscal policy, because for any given distribution of taxable incomes it raises only one amount of tax. In practice one is interested in a tax method (e. g., a family of schedules) that can be applied to any given distribution of incomes, and raise any required amount of tax, as circumstances dictate. Let $\mathbf{x} = (x_1, x_2, \ldots, x_n) > 0$ be any finite distribution of taxable incomes, where x_i is the taxable income of individual i. The 'names' of the individuals will be chosen from the set of positive integers N. A *tax problem* is a pair $(\mathbf{x}, T)$ such that $\mathbf{x} \in R^I$ for some finite $I \subset N$, $\mathbf{x} > 0$, and $0 \leq T \leq \Sigma_I x_i$. A *method of taxation* is a function $F(\mathbf{x}, T)$ defined for all tax problems, such that $\mathbf{t} = F(\mathbf{x}, T) \in R^I$, $\Sigma_I t_i = T$, and $0 \leq \mathbf{t} \leq \mathbf{x}$.

Two properties of tax methods will be assumed throughout the following discussion. The first is that F is *symmetric* in the sense that persons with equal taxable incomes pay equal taxes :

$$\forall (\mathbf{x}, T)\ \forall i,j\ [\ \mathbf{t} = F(\mathbf{x}, T)\ \&\ x_i = x_j \Rightarrow t_i = t_j\ ]. \tag{1}$$

The second standing assumtion is that F is *continuous* on every subdomain $\{ (\mathbf{x}, T) : \mathbf{x} \in R^I_{++},\ 0 \leq T \leq \Sigma x_i \}$.

3. Consistency.

A general principle of fair allocation states that *an equitable allocation among a group of individuals should be equitable when restricted to each subgroup of those individuals.* Alternatively, one could say that an allocation that is globally fair should also be locally fair. This *consistency* principle plays a central role in a remarkable variety of problems where a resource or cost is to be distributed among a group of agents according to their individual characteristics [Young, 1987b]. In the context of taxation, consistency states that the way a given amount of tax is shared among a group of individuals should depend only on their *own* taxable incomes. In other words, a method F is *consistent* if for every finite set I of individuals, every $x \in R^I_{++}$ and $0 \le T \le \Sigma x_i$,

$$t = F(x, T) \Rightarrow \forall J \subseteq I \, [\, t_J = F(x_J, \Sigma_J t_i) \,]. \qquad (2)$$

This idea is so natural that it is likely to be taken for granted. Indeed, it is implicit in the very notion of a tax schedule. For, if a group of individuals pays taxes according to a fixed tax schedule $f(x)$, then it is certainly true that the distribution of tax within each subgroup of individuals depends only on their own taxable incomes.

We claim now that consistency, together with a monotonicity condition, implies that a tax method must be based on some generalized concept of equal sacrifice. Define a *sacrifice relation* as a transitive, complete, binary relation $\geq$ on the set of all pairs $\{ (x, t): x > 0, 0 \le t \le x \}$. The statement $(x, t) \geq (x', t')$ means that paying an amount t on a taxable income of x causes at least as much sacrifice as paying an amount t' on a taxable income of x'. The statement $(x, t) \sim (x', t')$ means that the pair (x, t) causes the same sacrifice as does (x', t'). We assume that sacrifice increases with t; that is, for every given x and $0 \le t < t' \le x$, $(x, t') > (x, t)$. We also assume that $\geq$ can be represented by a continuous, real-valued, order-preserving function $\phi(x, t)$. This will be true if, in addition to the above assumptions, $\geq$ is closed [Debreu, 1954]

A method F is a *generalized equal sacrifice method* relative to $\succeq$ if for all finite $I \subset N$, all $\mathbf{x} \in R^I_{++}$ and $0 \leq T \leq \Sigma x_i$;

$$t = F(\mathbf{x}, T) \Leftrightarrow \Sigma t_i = T \;\&\; \forall i,j \in I\,[\,(x_i, t_i) \sim (x_j, t_j)\,];$$

equivalently,

$$t = F(\mathbf{x}, T) \Leftrightarrow \Sigma t_i = T \;\&\; \exists \lambda \;\; \forall i \in I\,[\,\phi(x_i, t_i) = \lambda\,]. \qquad (3)$$

It is immediate by definition that every generalized equal sacrifice method is consistent. It is also clear that every generalized equal sacrifice method is *strictly monotonic* in the sense that everyone bears some share of a tax increase:

$$0 \leq T < T' \leq \Sigma x_i \Rightarrow F(\mathbf{x}, T) < F(\mathbf{x}, T'). \qquad (4)$$

Indeed, when T increases *someone* must pay more tax, hence if all sacrifice equally all must pay more tax. These two conditions are necessary and sufficient to be a generalized equal sacrifice method. The following theorem is proved in Young [1987b].

Theorem 1. *A method of taxation is consistent and strictly monotonic if and only if it is a generalized equal sacrifice method.*

It turns out that many classical tax methods are essentially of this type. The reason is the following. Typically, a tax method is expressed in the form of a 'parametric' tax schedule, that is, a function $t = f(x, \lambda)$, where x is the level of taxable income and λ is some parameter whose value is determined by the total amount of tax to be levied. For example, the *flat tax* can be written $t = \lambda x$ where λ is the tax rate. A family of strictly progressive tax schedules first proposed by A. J. Cohen Stuart [1889], and later discussed by Edgeworth [1919], is $t = x - x^{1-\lambda}$ where λ is some power between zero and one. Another classical tax proposal, due to G. Cassel [1901], is the parametric schedule: $t = x^2/(x + 1/\lambda)$, where λ is a positive real number that varies depending on the amount of tax to be raised.

Each of these proposals is an instance of the following general idea. A *parametric tax schedule* is a continuous function $f(x, \lambda)$, which is defined for all scalar $x > 0$ and all λ in some closed interval $[a, b]$ of the extended reals, such that, for every $x > 0$, f is weakly monotone increasing in λ and $f(x, a) = 0$, $f(x, b) = x$. The *parametric method* based on f is defined as follows:

$$t = F(x, T) \iff \Sigma t_i = T \ \& \ \exists\lambda \ \forall i \ [t_i = f(x_i, \lambda)] \tag{5}$$

The value of the parameter λ is determined by the total tax T that is to be levied. There always exists such a λ, because f is continuous and weakly monotone increasing in λ, and $0 = \Sigma f(x_i, a) \le T \le \Sigma f(x_i, b) = \Sigma x_i$. Furthermore, there is a unique t satisfying (5), though not necessarily a unique λ. The reason is that if $\Sigma f(x_i, \lambda) = \Sigma f(x_i, \lambda') = T$ and $\lambda \le \lambda'$, then by monotonicity $t_i = f(x_i, \lambda) = f(x_i, \lambda')$ for all i. Of course, if f is strictly monotone in λ then the value of λ will also be uniquely determined.

It is immediate that every parametric method is consistent, just as every single tax schedule is consistent. Conversely, it may be proved that every consistent (symmetric and continuous) method must be parametric [Young, 1987b].

Suppose now that F is a strictly monotonic parametric method. This means that it has a representation f that is strictly monotone increasing in λ. Invert f to obtain the function ϕ as follows:

$$\phi(x, t) = \lambda \iff f(x, \lambda) = t. \tag{6}$$

Let us now view ϕ as a cardinal measure of sacrifice. Then F is a generalized equal sacrifice method relative to ϕ. For if $t = F(x, T)$, then by (5) and (6), $\phi(x_i, t_i) = \lambda$ for some constant λ and all i. This says that all individuals sacrifice equally relative to ϕ.

We illustrate with several examples. The flat tax $t = \lambda x$ has the inverse $\phi(x, t) = t/x$, so in this case the level of sacrifice is simply the tax rate. The inverse of the Cohen Stuart tax is $\phi(x, t) = [\ln x - \ln(x - t)]/\ln x$. Here the level of sacrifice may be interpreted as the rate of loss in utility relative to the classical utility function for income $U(x) = \ln x$. The inverse of the Cassel tax is $\phi(x, t) = t/x(x - t) = 1/(x - t) - 1/x$. This can be interpreted as the absolute loss in utility relative to the utility function $U(x) = -1/x$, which is increasing, strictly concave, and has a coefficient of relative risk aversion equal to 2.

4. The composition of taxes.

Strict monotonicity says that a tax increase should be be felt to some degree by everyone; no one with positive ability to pay should escape entirely. But it does not say *how* the increase should be shared. In this section we suggest a natural answer. Let $\mathbf{t} = F(\mathbf{x}, T)$ and suppose that $T < T'$. Think of the amount $T' - T$ as a new tax added on top of the old (e. g., a surtax). The natural basis for allocating the new tax is the taxpayers' current ability to pay, that is, their current after-tax incomes. Therefore, if we were to apply the method F to the problem $(\mathbf{x} - \mathbf{t}, T' - T)$, we would conclude that $T' - T$ should be shared as $\mathbf{t}^* = F(\mathbf{x} - \mathbf{t}, T' - T)$. The idea is that every increment of tax should be assessed relative to what taxpayers currently have, using the method F. A natural requirement is that assessing taxes incrementally in this manner should lead to the same result as levying the full amount of tax in one shot. F satisfies the *composition principle* if for all problems $(\mathbf{x}, T)$ and $(\mathbf{x}, T')$ where $T < T'$:

$$\mathbf{t} = F(\mathbf{x}, T) < \mathbf{x} \Rightarrow F(\mathbf{x}, T') - F(\mathbf{x}, T) = F(\mathbf{x} - \mathbf{t}, T' - T). \qquad (7)$$

Note that consistency and composition imply monotonicity, but not necessarily strict monotonicity. (In fact; consistency alone implies monotonicity [Young, 1987b].)

There is another type of monotonicity that is relevant to taxation--namely, monotonicity in incomes. If i has a greater taxable income than j, then it is natural to require that i's after-tax income be greater than j's. If this were not true, then the incentive to increase income would be jeopardized. A method F is *strictly order-preserving* if

$$\forall(x, T)\ \forall i,j\ [\ t = F(x, T)\ \&\ x_i > x_j \Rightarrow x_i - t_i > x_j - t_j\ ]. \qquad (8)$$

5. An axiomatic characterization of equal sacrifice methods.

Let U(x) be some hypothetical utility function, which we assume to be strictly increasing and continuous in x. The two most customary interpretations of equal sacrifice are equal absolute and equal rate of sacrifice. *Equal absolute sacrifice* means that in paying taxes everyone gives up the same amount of utility, that is, $U(x_i) - U(x_i - t_i)$ is a constant for all taxpayers i. F is an *equal absolute sacrifice method* relative to U(x) if for all problems (x, T)

$$t = F(x, T) \Leftrightarrow \Sigma t_i = T\ \&\ \exists\lambda\ \forall i\ [\ U(x_i) - U(x_i - t_i) = \lambda\ ]. \qquad (9)$$

Equal rate of sacrifice means that everyone gives up the same percentage of their utility in paying taxes, that is, $U(x_i)/U(x_i - t_i)$ is a constant for all i. (In this case we assume that U(x) is everywhere positive.) F is an *equal rate of sacrifice method* relative to U(x) if for all problems

$$t = F(x, T) \Leftrightarrow \Sigma t_i = T \ \& \ \exists r \ \forall i \ [\ U(x_i)/U(x_i - t_i) = r\ ]. \qquad (10)$$

Observe that if (10) holds, then F is an equal absolute sacrifice method relative to ln U(x). Conversely, if F satisfies (9), then F is an equal rate of sacrifice method relative to $e^{U(x)}$. Hence we may speak of an *equal sacrifice method* F without danger of confusion; the only essential difference between the two cases is the form of the utility function.

Every equal sacrifice method has the following properties. First, it is strictly monotonic. Second, it is strictly order-preserving. Indeed, since the utility of income is strictly increasing and everyone suffers the same loss in utility, then all taxpayers are shifted down the utility curve by a constant amount. Hence their ordering by income is the same before and after taxes. Third, every equal sacrifice method satisfies composition. For suppose that everyone suffers the same loss in utility when **t** is the tax on **x**. Then $U(x_i) - U(x_i - t_i) = \lambda$ is a constant for all i. A general tax increase causes all to sacrifice at some higher level $\lambda' = U(x_i) - U(x_i - t'_i)$. Thus the incremental tax **t' − t** imposes an *additional* equal sacrifice on all, relative to their after-tax incomes **x − t**. In other words, every increment of tax is assessed according to the same principle as the whole amount of tax is assessed. So every equal sacrifice method satisfies composition. What is not so obvious is that composition, together with the other properties, implies the existence of a utility function relative to which all sacrifice equally [Young, 1987c].

Theorem 2. *A strictly monotonic, strictly order-preserving taxation method* F *satisfies consistency and composition if and only if it is an equal sacrifice method relative to some continuous, strictly increasing utility function* U(x).

In the next section we show that with one further assumption we can say more about the form that this utility function must take.

6. Scale invariant methods.

A method of taxation is *scale invariant* if it is homogeneous of degree one

$$\forall \theta > 0 \ \ \forall (\mathbf{x}, T) \ [F(\theta \mathbf{x}, \theta T) = \theta F(\mathbf{x}, T)]. \qquad (11)$$

Scale invariance says that the relative distribution of taxes depends only on the relative distribution of incomes and the relative size of the tax burden. As such it is a kind of fairness principle. It is motivated by the common observation that people tend to evaluate how fairly they are treated by looking at where they stand *relative* to others, not where they stand relative to some absolute benchmark (like a theoretically defined 'subsistence level').

An 'empirical' argument for scale invariance is its implicit use in the re-indexing of tax schedules. For example, suppose that real incomes shift upward by a factor $\theta > 1$. Under a fixed, strictly progressive tax schedule $f(x)$, all taxpayers are shifted into higher tax brackets. Hence the total real tax take increases by a factor *larger* than θ. If the tax system is to remain relatively revenue neutral -- in the sense that total taxes remain a fixed percentage of total real incomes--then the tax schedule must be altered. A standard approach is to re-index the schedule by the factor θ, that is, to create the new tax schedule $f^*(x) = \theta f(x/\theta)$. A similar problem arises in inflationary times. If a fixed schedule remains in place while the value of money erodes, then in real terms the schedule is being re-indexed. Most people would probably accept that re-indexing is 'fair', i. e., that it is a reasonable way to adjust the distribution of taxes when all incomes (and the tax burden) shift by some uniform proportion.

Now let us examine what re-indexing implies in conjunction with equal sacrifice. Suppose that: (i) a tax schedule imposes equal sacrifice relative to some utility function $U(x)$; (ii) the condition (though not necessarily the level) of equal sacrifice is maintained under re-indexing of the schedule. Then $U(x)$ must be a positive linear transformation of $\ln x$ or $(-1/p)x^{-p}$ for some $p > 0$. That is, equal sacrifice is preserved under re-indexing if and only if the utility function has constant relative risk aversion, and the coefficient of risk aversion must be at least unity [Young, 1987a]. This result has interesting consequences for the form of the tax function.

Theorem 3. *An equal sacrifice method F is scale-invariant if and only if it equalizes absolute sacrifice relative to a utility function of form* $\ln x$ *or* $(-1/p)x^{-p}$. *In the former case F is the flat tax, and in the latter case it is a parametric method of form*

$$t = x - [\, x^{-p} + \lambda^{-p} \,]^{-1/p} \qquad p > 0. \tag{12}$$

Cassel's method is the special case of (12) when $p = 1$.

Note that all of the methods characterized in Theorem 3 are progressive (i.e., flat or strictly progressive). Hence we obtain the following corollary [Young, 1987a], which gives yet another answer to the classical question: when does equal sacrifice imply progressive taxation?

Corollary. *Every scale-invariant, equal sacrifice method is progressive.*

References

1. K. J. Arrow, 1971, *Essays in the Theory of Risk-Bearing.* Chicago Markham.

2. G. Cassel, 1901, The theory of progressive taxation, *Economic ·Journal 11* , 481-491.

3. A. J. Cohen Stuart, 1889, On progressive taxation, in R.A. Musgrave and A. T. Peacock (eds.), *Classics in the Theory of Public Finance.* New York: MacMillan, 1958.

4. G. Debreu, 1954, Representation of a preference ordering by a numerical function, in P. Newman (ed.), *Readings in Mathematical Economics, Vol. 1: Value Theory.* Baltimore, Md. : The Johns Hopkins Press, 1968.

5. F. Y. Edgeworth, 1919, Methods of graduating taxes on income and capital, *Economic Journal 29,* 138-153.

6. J. S. Mill, 1848, *Principles of Political Economy..* W. J. Ashley, (ed.), London: Longmans Green, 1917.

7. P. A. Samuelson, 1947, *Foundations of Economic Analysis.* Cambridge, Mass. : Harvard University Press.

8. H. P. Young, 1987a, Progressive Taxation and the Equal Sacrifice Principle, *Journal of Public Economics 32,* 203-214.

9. H. P. Young, 1987b, On dividing an amount according to individual claims or liabilities, *Mathematics of Operations Research 12* .

10. H. P. Young, 1987c, Taxation and Bankruptcy. *Journal of Economic Theory* , forthcoming.

Part VIII Aggregation

Consistent Commodity Aggregates In Market Demand Equations*

Charles Blackorby
Department of Economics
University of British Columbia
Vancouver, B.C.
V6T 1Y2, Canada

and

William Schworm†
April 1987

1. Introduction

In both theoretical and empirical research on consumer demands for commodities, economists face choices concerning the aggregation of commodities. All sets of data available for applied demand analysis, for example, have some degree of commodity aggregation. Frequently, consumption and price data are presented only for very broad categories of commodities. The researcher confronted with such data must make difficult decisions with little guidance from theory about the process which generated the data.

In theoretical model building, economists are continually confronted with the trade-off between more qualitative results and less aggregation. A single consumer economy with two commodities has more qualitative properties than an Arrow-Debreu general equilibrium model. Of course, the hope is that insights gleaned from the highly aggregated models will provide an understanding of more complex environments. These hopes, however, are all too often unfounded.

In this paper, we investigate the conditions under which there exists a commodity aggregate in an economy. If an economy consisted of a single consumer only, then the conditions for commodity aggregation would be the standard separability restrictions. For a discussion of this case and references, see Blackorby, Primont, and Russell (1978). If, on the other hand, an economy is composed of many households acting independently, then the conditions for a commodity aggregate are quite different. Although this problem does not seem to have received much attention, related problems on the production side of the economy have been studied, e.g., Green (1964), Fisher (1968), Gorman (1984), Daal and Merkies (1984), Blackorby and Schworm (1984b). We draw heavily on this literature.

* This research has been supported by the SSHRC with a research grant and by leave fellowships to both authors. A substantial portion of the work was done while we were at CORE, Université Catholique de Louvain. We are grateful to both SSHRC and CORE for their support. We thank Margaret Slade and Jacques Thisse for comments and Russell Davidson for pointing out errors in a previous draft.

† University of British Columbia, Vancouver, B.C.

Measurement in Economics
ed. by W. Eichhorn

We posit a static, competitive economy with H households. Each household has a system of demand equations derived from utility maximization which is denoted by

$$\overset{*}{X}_h(Y_h, P), \tag{1.1}$$

where Y_h is money income and P is a vector of commodity prices. The demand system for the economy is the sum of the household demands:

$$\overset{*}{X}(Y_1, \ldots, Y_H, P) = \sum_h \overset{*}{X}_h(Y_h, P). \tag{1.2}$$

The commodity aggregation problem is *under what conditions can the system of demands in* (1.2) *be meaningfully reduced to a smaller number of demand equations for commodity aggregates.* The answer to this question depends on the prior restrictions which are imposed on the market demand system (1.2). In this paper, we investigate and compare four alternative assumptions about the structure of the market demand systems.

Our principle result is that the conditions for commodity aggregation for a single consumer do not suffice for commodity aggregation in a market system of demand equations. The aggregation of consumers required to obtain market demands affects the restrictions for commodity aggregation *regardless of the procedure used to aggregate across consumers.* If the relationship between the market demands and the individual household demands is ignored, then incorrect or incomplete conditions are obtained for the existence of commodity aggregates.

In section 3 of this paper, we assume the market demands (1.2) satisfy only those restrictions implied by the utility maximization of each household. As has been shown in a literature surveyed by Shafer and Sonnenschein (1982), these restrictions are minimal. If there are more households than commodities, the market demands must be continuous, homogeneous, and satisfy Walras Law but they inherit no integrability properties from the household demands. In this context, we derive necessary and sufficient conditions for commodity aggregation. We show that, in order for a commodity aggregate to exist, there must be a quasi-homothetic aggregator function. The existence of such an aggregator function induces an ordering over a subset of commodities so that the market demand equations satisfy some integrability conditions.

In section 4, we assume that the economy has a representative consumer with preferences that rationalize the system of market demands (1.2). The assumption of a representative consumer not only implies that the market demands satisfy the Slutsky integrability conditions but also implies that the demands are affine in a measure of aggregate economy income (See Gorman (1953)). Imposing commodity aggregation in this case, of course, implies substantially stronger restrictions than those obtained in section 3.

In section 5, we investigate an alternative method of rationalizing the system of market demands. We assume a planner allocates commodities to maximize a social welfare function. This determines a social utility function that rationalizes the market demands and insures that the market demands satisfy the Slutsky integrability conditions. If the commodity aggregate does not depend on the ethical judgements implicit in the social welfare function, then commodity aggregation implies that the preferences of each household must satisfy the same conditions as those derived in section 3. Social welfare maximization does not relax the commodity aggregation restrictions. The market demands consistent with commodity aggregation, however, are more restrictive than those obtained in section 3 since they must satisfy all the integrability conditions.

In section 6, we ask that market demands depend on a small number of income aggregates. This follows the research recently pursued by Gorman (1981), Jorgenson, Stoker, and Lau (1982), Jorgenson, Slesnick, and Stoker (1983), and Lau (1977, 1982). In this case, the market demands are not rationalizable by any preferences, in general, and so the demands satisfy weaker conditions than in sections 4 and 5. Again, in this case, commodity aggregation implies restrictions substantially stronger than those suggested by the separability conditions for a single consumer.

Section 2 contains the technical assumptions. Some concluding remarks are presented in section 7. The appendix contains the proofs of the Theorems.

2. Technical Assumptions

We consider a competitive economy in a static environment composed of H price-taking households each of whom has well-behaved preferences. The preferences of household h are represented by $U_h : \Theta \rightarrow \mathbf{R}$ where $\Theta \subset \mathbf{R}_+^N$ is closed convex and does not contain the origin. Each U_h is assumed to satisfy the following conditions:

R_1: for all $X_h \in \operatorname{int}\Theta$

(i) U_h is twice continuously differentiable,

(ii) $\nabla_x U_h(X_h) \gg 0_N$, and

(iii) $y \neq 0_N$ and $y^T \nabla_x U_h(X_h) = 0$ implies that $y^T \nabla_{xx}^2 U_h(X_h) y < 0$

where y^T denotes the transpose of y.

An alternative representation of the preferences is given by the expenditure function of each household, C_h, defined by

$$C_h(u_h, P) = \min_X \{ P \cdot X \mid U_h(X_h) \geq u_h \}, \tag{2.1}$$

for u_h in the range of U_h, $X_h \in \Theta$. The regularity conditions for C_h that are dual to R_1 are given by the following:

$\bar{R}_1$: for any $u_h = U_h(X_h)$ and $P = \nabla_x U_h(X_h)/X_h^T \nabla_x U_h(X_h)$ for $X_h \in \text{int}\Theta$,

(i) C_h is twice continuously differentiable,

(ii) $\nabla_p C_h(u_h, P) \gg 0$,

(iii) $\nabla_u C_h(u_h, P) > 0$, and

(iv) $y \neq 0_N$ and $y^T P = 0$ implies that $y^T \nabla^2_{PP} C_h(u_h, P) y < 0$.

A proof that R_1 and $\bar{R}_1$ are equivalent can be found in Blackorby and Diewert (1979), Theorem 9. The functions, U_h and C_h, are said to be differentially strictly pseudoconcave. These strong regularity conditions facilitate the proofs of the main Theorems in the paper which rely on the continuity of the Hessian of C_h in both u_h and P.

We also use the indirect utility function of each household which is given by

$$u_h = V_h(Y_h, P) \leftrightarrow Y_h = C_h(u_h, P). \tag{2.2}$$

It can be shown that V_h is differentially strictly pseudoconvex (Theorem 7 in Blackorby and Diewert (1979)).

There is an additional assumption we use which is not a standard assumption on preferences but which is necessary to eliminate examples which we believe to be uninteresting. It is designed to insure that the compensated demand for each commodity depends on utility for some value of P. We state the assumption as follows:

R_2: There exists at least one point (u_h, P) such that $\frac{\partial^2}{\partial u \partial P_i} C_h(u_h, P) \neq 0$ for $i = 1, \ldots, N$ and $h = 1, \ldots, H$.

The cost functions which are eliminated by this assumption can be written as

$$C_h(u_h, P) = \bar{C}_h(u_h, P^1) + \hat{C}_h(P) \tag{2.3}$$

where $P = (P^1, P^2)$ is a partition of the price vector. The dual utility function is

$$U_h(X_h) = \max_{(y^1, z^1)} \left\{ \bar{U}_h(y^1) \mid \hat{U}_h(z^1, X^2) = 0,\ y^1 + z^1 = X^1 \right\} \tag{2.4}$$

where $\bar{U}_h$ is dual to $\bar{C}_h$ and $\hat{U}_h$ is dual to $\hat{C}_h$ in (2.3), and $X = (X^1, X^2)$, is a partition of the commodity vector. The commodities, X^2, can only be used to satisfy the constraint of achieving zero utility given by $\hat{U}_h(z^1, X^2) = 0$ in (2.4). These commodities cannot be used to increase utility through the function $\bar{U}_h$. This class of cases appears to us to be uninteresting in the current context; however, the interested reader can find a discussion of the excluded cases in Blackorby and Schworm (1984b) for production theory where these cases are more natural; utility vectors become capital stock vectors.

We summarize our assumptions by

$$R = R_1 \cup R_2.$$

3. Commodity Aggregation in an Economy Without Income Aggregation

In this section, we present the conditions for commodity aggregation in an economy *without income aggregates.* In particular, we do not assume the existence of a representative consumer or the existence of sufficient statistics of the income distribution.

The economy consists of a set of consumers $h = 1, \ldots, H$ with preferences, satisfying condition R, that can be characterized by the better-than-sets,

$$B_h(u_h) = \{ X_h \mid U_h(X_h) \geq u_h \}. \tag{3.1}$$

For a given vector of utilities for consumers $u = (u_1, \ldots, u_H)$, the economy commodity vectors that can provide this vector of utilities are given by the Scitovsky sets (see Scitovsky (1942), and de Graaf (1957)):

$$B(u) = \sum_h B_h(u_h) = \left\{ X \mid U_h(X_h) \geq u_h,\ h = 1, \ldots, H,\ \sum_h X_h \leq X \right\}. \tag{3.2}$$

If $X \in B(u)$ then there exists an allocation $(X_1, \ldots, X_H)$ such that $\sum_h X_h \leq X$ and each consumer achieves utility level, u_h for $h = 1, \ldots, H$. If X is on the boundary of $B(u)$, then only an efficient allocation of X among consumers can produce the utility vector, u.

Let $I = (1, \ldots, N)$ be an index set that counts commodities and write a partition of I as $\hat{I} = (I^1, I^2)$. Denote the dimension of I^1 by n^1 and that of I^2 by n^2 so that $N = n^1 + n^2$. The corresponding partition of the commodity vector is denoted by $X = (X^1, X^2)$.

Definition: *There is a commodity aggregate for group 2 if and only if there exists a continuous increasing function* $\mathbf{X} : \Theta^2 \rightarrow \mathbf{R}_+$ *where* Θ^2 *is the projection of* Θ *into* $\mathbf{R}_+^{n^2}$, *and a family of aggregate Scitovsky sets* $\mathbf{B}(u) \subset \mathbf{R}_+^k$ *where* $k = n^1 + 1$ *such that*

$$X \in B(u) \leftrightarrow (X^1, \mathbf{X}(X^2)) \in \mathbf{B}(u) \tag{3.3}$$

for all u *such that* u_h *is in the range of* U_h.

A commodity aggregate exists if the set of commodities that produces a given vector of utilities can be described by the vector $(X^1, \mathbf{x}^2)$ which has lower dimensionality. Therefore a planner attempting to achieve a utility vector u need only use information on the quantities of X^1 and the aggregate $\mathbf{x}^2$ since $\mathbf{x}^2$ contains the relevant information about X^2.

For some purposes it is easier to work with the utility possibility set than the Scitovsky set. The utility possibility set $W(X)$ is defined by

$$u \in W(X) \leftrightarrow X \in B(u) \tag{3.4}$$

for $W(X) \subset \mathbf{R}^H$ (Samuelson (1950)).

In this characterization, a commodity aggregate of group two exists if there exist $\mathbf{X}$ and $\mathbf{W}$ such that

$$\mathbf{W}(X^1, \mathbf{X}(X^2)) = W(X) \tag{3.5}$$

for all $X \in \Theta$.

In the statements of the commodity aggregation requirement in (3.3) and (3.5), there is no reference to the allocation of goods among consumers. In particular, there is no assumption that commodities are efficiently distributed among consumers. However, utility vectors on the boundary of $W(X)$ are only achieved if goods are efficiently allocated among consumers. Similarly, utility vectors on the boundary of $\mathbf{W}(X^1, \mathbf{x}^2)$ are only attained if $(X^1, \mathbf{x}^2)$ are efficiently allocated among consumers. Since the boundaries of these two sets must be the same for consistent commodity aggregation, there is a close connection between efficient allocations of goods and commodity aggregation. The following definition of commodity aggregation is equivalent to the conditions (3.3) and (3.5) but emphasises the efficiency aspect.

Define,

$$\begin{aligned} \overset{*}{u}_1 &= \mathbf{U}(u_2, \ldots, u_H, X) \\ &= \max_{(X_1, \ldots, X_H)} \left\{ U_1(X_1) \mid U_h(X_h) \geq u_h,\ h = 2, \ldots, H;\ \sum_h X_h \leq X \right\} \end{aligned} \tag{3.6}$$

so that $\mathbf{U}(u_2, \ldots, u_H, X)$ is the maximum utility household one can achieve given the utility of all other households, and given the economy's endowment of commodities. The function $\mathbf{U}$ characterizes the boundary of B or W, and it is explicit in the definition of $\mathbf{U}$ that commodities are efficiently allocated to consumers. Commodity aggregation can be defined in terms of $\mathbf{U}$ as follows.

A commodity aggregate for X^2 exists if there exist continuous increasing functions, $\mathbf{X}$ and $\bar{\mathbf{U}}$, such that

$$\mathbf{U}(u_2, \ldots, u_H, X) = \bar{\mathbf{U}}(u_2, \ldots, u_H, X^1, \mathbf{X}(X^2)) \tag{3.7}$$

for all u_h in the range of U_h and $X \in \Theta$. This is easily seen to be equivalent to (3.3) and (3.5).

To state the necessary and sufficient conditions for commodity aggregation, it is convenient to use the support function of the Scitovsky set which is defined by

$$C(u, P) = \min_X \{ P \cdot X \mid X \in B(u) \}. \tag{3.8}$$

Since $C(u, P)$ is the minimum expenditure needed to achieve the utility vector $u = (u_1, \ldots, u_H)$, we refer to it as the *Scitovsky expenditure function.*

If there is a commodity aggregate in the economy, then the Scitovsky expenditure function has a special property that can be described as follows. Define the conditional Scitovsky expenditure function $\mathbf{C}^1$ by

$$\mathbf{C}^1(u, P^1, \mathbf{x}^2) = \min_{X^1} \{ P^1 \cdot X^1 \mid (X^1, \mathbf{x}^2) \in \mathbf{B}(u) \} \tag{3.9}$$

and the expenditure function dual to the commodity aggregate by

$$\mathbf{C}^2(P^2, \mathbf{x}^2) = \min_{X^2} \{ P^2 \cdot X^2 \mid \mathbf{X}(X^2) \geq \mathbf{x}^2 \}. \tag{3.10}$$

$\mathbf{C}^1$ is the minimum cost of achieving utility vector, u, at prices P^1 given that the quantity of the aggregate commodity is $\mathbf{x}^2$. $\mathbf{C}^2$ is the minimum cost of obtaining $\mathbf{x}^2$ of the aggregate commodity at prices P^2. A commodity aggregate exists in the economy if and only if the Scitovsky expenditure function can be written as

$$C(u, P) = \min_{\mathbf{x}^2} \{ \mathbf{C}^1(u, P^1, \mathbf{x}^2) + \mathbf{C}^2(P^2, \mathbf{x}^2) \}. \tag{3.11}$$

That is, the cost, of achieving utility vector, u, at prices P is the sum of the cost of achieving u at prices P^1 given $\mathbf{x}^2$ and the cost of achieving $\mathbf{x}^2$ given prices P^2 when $\mathbf{x}^2$ is chosen to minimize the sum.

If an economy consisted of a single household, then condition (3.11) would be the end of the matter. This condition exhausts the implications of commodity aggregation for a single household. Since, however, numerous independent consumers comprise an economy additional restrictions are implied by commodity aggregation. The additional restrictions follow from the fact that the Scitovsky expenditure function is additive in u:

$$C(u, P) = \sum_h C_h(u_h, P). \tag{3.12}$$

Therefore, an economy commodity aggregate exists if the Scitovsky expenditure function satisfies (3.11) and (3.12). This is equivalent to the requirement that an economy has a Scitovsky set $B(u)$ that satisfies both (3.2) and (3.3).

The following theorem states the restrictions on the expenditure functions that are necessary and sufficient for an economy commodity aggregate.

Theorem 3.1: *Assume R. There is an economy commodity aggregate of X^2, that is (3.2) and (3.3) hold (or equivalently (3.11) and (3.12)), if and only if for $h = 1, \ldots, H$*

$$C_h(u_h, P) = \min_{\mathbf{x}_h^2} \{ \mathbf{C}_h^1(u_h, P^1, \mathbf{x}_h^2) + \mathbf{C}_h^2(P^2, \mathbf{x}_h^2) \} - \delta_h(P), \tag{3.13}$$

where

$$\mathbf{C}_h^2(P^2, \mathbf{x}_h^2) = \bar{\mathbf{C}}^2(P^2)\mathbf{x}_h^2 + \hat{\mathbf{C}}_h^2(P^2) \tag{3.14}$$

and

$$\sum_h \delta_h(P) = (H-1)\min_{\mathrm{x}} \{ \bar{\mathrm{C}}^1(P^1,\mathrm{x}) + \bar{\mathrm{C}}^2(p^2)\mathrm{x} \}. \tag{3.15}$$

In this case,

$$\mathrm{C}^2(P^2,\mathrm{x}^2) = \bar{\mathrm{C}}^2(P^2)\mathrm{x}^2 + \hat{\mathrm{C}}^2(P^2) \tag{3.16}$$

where $\hat{\mathrm{C}}^2(P^2) = \sum_h \hat{\mathrm{C}}^2_h(P^2)$ *and the Scitovsky expenditure function can be written as*

$$C(u,P) = \bar{\mathrm{C}}^1(u,P^1,\bar{\mathrm{C}}^2(P^2)) + \hat{\mathrm{C}}^2(P^2). \tag{3.17}$$

Proof: see the appendix.

Condition (3.13) implies that except for the additive term, δ_h, each consumer has a commodity aggregate for X^2. The terms, δ_h, allow each household not to have an aggregate but these terms must sum to a term which resembles a utility-free household with a commodity aggregate. Therefore, all characteristics of the market demands would be unchanged if each δ_h is zero. Since the characteristics of the economy are unaffected by whether or not these terms are zero, we treat them cursorily in the paper. Note that if we required commodity aggregation to hold for variable numbers of households, then this would force each δ_h to be zero and every household would have an aggregate.

The cost of obtaining the commodity aggregate for each household must be described by a cost function with the form described in (3.14). That is $\mathrm{C}^2_h(P^2,\mathrm{x}^2_h)$ must be affine in x^2_h and the marginal cost of x^2_h,

$$\frac{\partial \mathrm{C}^2_h(P^2,\mathrm{x}^2_h)}{\partial \mathrm{x}^2_h} = \bar{\mathrm{C}}^2(P^2) \tag{3.18}$$

must be the same for all consumers. The common marginal cost of x^2 given in (3.18) serves as a *price index* that efficiently allocates the commodity aggregate among the consumers in the economy. Notice that no restrictions are placed on the conditional cost function, C^1, other than its existence.

The Scitovsky expenditure function of an economy with commodity aggregation is described by equations (3.11) and (3.16). The cost of obtaining the commodity aggregate in the economy must be an affine function of the aggregate. The restrictions in (3.11) and (3.16) imply that the Scitovsky expenditure function can be written as in (3.17). It is the sum of two different expenditure functions one of which depends only on P^2 and the other of which is homothetically separable in P^2.

In general the aggregate demand system of this economy satisfies only homogeneity and adding-up conditions and none of the integrability conditions. However, imposing commodity aggregation actually makes the conditional aggregate demand system for sector two integrable. This is easily seen from (3.16) as there is a conditional representative household for this sector.

The compensated demands for the economy are the minimizers in (3.8). If the economy has a commodity aggregate, then these compensated demands can be computed in a two-stage procedure that reveals their structure. First, notice that Theorem 3.1 does not restrict $\mathbf{C}^1$ as defined in (3.9). Therefore, the demands for X^1 conditional on $(u, P^1, \mathbf{x}^2)$ have no special properties. The demands for X^2 given $(u, P^2, \mathbf{x}^2)$ can be obtained from (3.16) as

$$X^2 = \bar{\Lambda}^2(P^2)\mathbf{x}^2 + \hat{\Lambda}^2(P^2). \tag{3.19}$$

The compensated demand for $\mathbf{x}^2$ can be obtained by solving

$$C(u, P) = \min_{\mathbf{x}^2} \left\{ \mathbf{C}^1(u, P^1, \mathbf{x}^2) + \bar{\mathbf{C}}^2(P^2)\mathbf{x}^2 + \hat{\mathbf{C}}^2(P^2) \right\} \tag{3.20}$$

where

$$\mathbf{C}^1(u, P^1, \mathbf{x}^2) = \min_{(\mathbf{x}_1^2, \ldots, \mathbf{x}_H^2)} \left\{ \sum_h \mathbf{C}_h^1(u_h, P^1, \mathbf{x}_h^2) \mid \sum_h \mathbf{x}_h^2 \leq \mathbf{x}^2 \right\} \tag{3.21}$$

for

$$\overset{*}{\mathbf{x}}{}^2 = \Lambda(u, P^1, \bar{\mathbf{C}}^2(P^2))$$

therefore, we have

$$\overset{*}{X}{}^1 = \Lambda^1\left(u, P^1, \Lambda(u, P^1, \bar{\mathbf{C}}^2(P^2))\right) \tag{3.22}$$

$$\overset{*}{X}{}^2 = \bar{\Lambda}^2(P^2)\Lambda(u, P^1, \bar{\mathbf{C}}^2(P^2)) + \hat{\Lambda}^2(P^2) \tag{3.23}$$

as the compensated demands for an economy with a commodity aggregate for X^2.

The following theorem presents the conditions for an economy commodity aggregate in terms of the utility functions of the consumers in the economy.

Theorem 3.2: *Assume R and assume that each household has a commodity aggregate so that the cost function of each household can be written as in (3.13) with $\delta_h(P) = 0$, $h = 1, \ldots, H$. There is an economy-commodity-aggregate for X^2 if and only if for $h = 1, \ldots, H$*

$$U_h(X_h) = \bar{U}_h(X_h^1, \mathbf{X}_h(X_h^2)) \tag{3.24}$$

and

$$\mathbf{X}_h(X_h^2) = \max_{(Y_h^2, Z_h^2)} \left\{ \bar{\mathbf{X}}^2(Y_h^2) \mid \hat{\mathbf{X}}_h^2(Z_h^2) = 0, Y_h^2 + Z_h^2 = X_h^2 \right\} \tag{3.25}$$

where $\bar{\mathbf{X}}^2$ is positively linearly homogeneous.

Proof: see the appendix.

Condition (3.24) states that X_h^2 is separable from X_h^1 in U_h for each consumer. This separability structure is just the requirement that each household have a commodity aggregate. Condition (3.25) represents the structure of the commodity aggregator function that is dual to $\mathbf{C}_h^2$ in (3.14). Each household has a fixed cost of the group 2 commodities which is household specific. Sufficient amounts of X_h^2 must be allocated to satisfy the constraint that $\hat{\mathbf{X}}_h^2(\cdot) = 0$. Once this constraint is satisfied, group 2 commodities are allocated to producing the commodity aggregate with an aggregator function that is the same for all households and is linearly homogeneous. The commodities, X_h^2, are allocated between the constraint and the production of $\mathbf{X}_h(\cdot)$ in order to maximize the amount of the aggregate, $\mathbf{x}_h^2$, obtained.

An important special case of the conditions for the existence of a commodity aggregate is homothetic separability with each consumer having the same aggregator function. An interesting example of non-homothetic aggregators is provided by a Stone-Geary aggregator function where the translated origin can be household-specific but all other parameters must be the same for all households.

Expenditure functions that can be expressed as in (3.14) with dual utility functions given by (3.25), will occur repeatedly in the following so it is useful to have a name for them. Following Gorman (1976), we will say a function is quasi-homothetic if it has a dual cost function expressible as in (3.14) and hence can be written as in (3.25). We will say that a household's utility function is quasi-homothetically separable if it is separable and the aggregator function is quasi-homothetic. In addition, if all households have preferences given by (3.11) and (3.14) or (3.24) and (3.25), we will call the preferences quasi-homothetically separable and similar, i.e., common marginal cost functions.

One interesting consequence of commodity aggregation is that it allows a decentralization in efficient resource allocation. Consider the group 2 aggregator functions, $\mathbf{X}_h$, $h = 1, \ldots, H$, as utility functions for group 2 goods. Then, an efficient allocation of X^2 to consumers can be defined for any distribution of the aggregate, $\mathbf{X}_h^2$, $h = 1, \ldots, H$ by the following:

$$\max_{(X_1^2, \ldots, X_H^2)} \left\{ \mathbf{X}_1(X_1^2) \mid \mathbf{X}_h(X_h^2) \geq \mathbf{x}_h, \; h = 2, \ldots, H, \; \sum_h X_h^2 \leq X^2 \right\} \tag{3.26}$$

Therefore, conditional on a distribution of $\{\mathbf{x}_h^2\}_{h=2}^H$, there is an efficient distribution, $(X_1^2, \ldots, X_H^2)$, which is independent of X^1 and the aggregate utility functions, $\bar{U}_1, \ldots, \bar{U}_H$, defined in (3.24).

Second, an efficient allocation of $(X^1, \mathbf{x}^2)$ can be achieved independently of X^2 and the aggregator functions, $\mathbf{X}_h$ for $h = 1, \ldots, H$, by the optimization problem:

$$\max_{\left\{ \substack{X_1^1, \ldots, X_H^1 \\ \mathbf{x}_1^2, \ldots, \mathbf{x}_H^2} \right\}} \left\{ \bar{U}_1(X_1^1, \mathbf{x}_1^2) \mid \bar{U}_h(X_h^1, \mathbf{x}_h^2) \geq u_h, \; h = 2, \ldots, H, \right.$$

$$\sum_h X_h^1 \leq X^1, \sum_h \mathbf{x}_h^2 \leq \mathbf{x}^2 \Big\}. \tag{3.27}$$

Therefore, there is a two-stage procedure for achieving an efficient allocation of resources each stage of which uses only a subset of the characteristics of the economy.

4. Commodity Aggregation with a Representative Consumer

In the previous section, no restrictions (other than regularity conditions) were imposed on preferences to simplify the structure of the Scitovsky set or the utility possibilities set. In both empirical and theoretical research, however, it is commonplace to assume that the demand system of the economy is generated by a single utility maximizing agent. In this and the following section we examine the implications of two different rationalizations of this single agent assumption in conjunction with commodity aggregation.

A representative household for the economy exists if the Scitovsky sets for the economy can be characterised in terms of an aggregate utility measure. That is, there exists a real-valued, continuous, increasing aggregator function, ϕ, (whose domain is the Cartesian product of the ranges of $\{U_h\}_{h=1}^H$) and a mapping, $\tilde{\mathbf{B}}$, such that the Scitovsky sets can be written

$$B(u) = \tilde{\mathbf{B}}(\phi(u)). \tag{4.1}$$

This is equivalent to writing the Scitovsky expenditure function as

$$C(u, P) = \sum_h C_h(u_h, P) = \tilde{\mathbf{C}}(\phi(u), P) \tag{4.2}$$

where $\tilde{\mathbf{C}}$ satisfies the conditions, $\bar{R}_1$, of an expenditure function. Therefore, $\tilde{\mathbf{C}}$ is the representative consumer's expenditure function and provides a dual representation of the representative consumer's preferences.

Since $\tilde{\mathbf{C}}(\phi(u), P) = \sum_h C_h(u_h, P) = \sum_h Y_h$, the indirect utility function of the representative consumer can be written as

$$\phi(u) = \mathbf{V}(P, \sum_h Y_h) \tag{4.3}$$

so that there is an aggregate income measure for the economy given by the sum of the households' incomes.

The economy demands for commodities are the sum of the individual household demands. Equations (4.2) and (4.3) immediately show that the sum of the compensated demands and the sum of the uncompensated demands can be written in terms of an aggregate utility and income measure, respectively, and can be rationalized by the representative consumer's preferences. That is,

$$\nabla_P \tilde{\mathbf{C}}(\phi(u), P) = \tilde{X}(\phi(u), P) = \sum_h \tilde{X}_h(u_h, P) \tag{4.4}$$

and

$$\nabla_P \mathbf{V}(P, \sum_h Y_h) / \left(\partial \mathbf{V}(P, \sum_h Y_h)/\partial Y \right) = X\left(\sum_h Y_h, P \right) = \sum_h X_h(Y_h, P). \tag{4.5}$$

Therefore, the aggregate demands satisfy all of the properties of systems of consumer demand equations. Asking for economy demands to depend on an aggregate income or utility measure is equivalent to requiring the existence of a representative consumer for whom the economy demands are optimal choices.

The necessary and sufficient conditions for the existence of a representative consumer have been derived by Gorman (1953). There exists a representative consumer in the sense that any one of the conditions (4.1) through (4.5) holds if and only if the cost function for each consumer can be expressed as

$$C_h(u_h, P) = \bar{\mathbf{C}}(P)\phi_h(u_h) + \hat{\mathbf{C}}_h(P) \tag{4.6}$$

for $h = 1, \ldots, H$. In this case, the economy cost function is

$$\mathbf{C}(\phi(u), P) = \bar{\mathbf{C}}(P) \sum_h \phi_h(u_h) + \sum_h \hat{\mathbf{C}}_h(P) \tag{4.7}$$

and the compensated economy demands are

$$X\left(\sum_h \phi_h(u_h), P \right) = \nabla_P \bar{\mathbf{C}}(P) \sum_h \phi_h(u_h) + \sum_h \nabla_P \hat{\mathbf{C}}_h(P). \tag{4.8}$$

The indirect utility functions that are necessary and sufficient for the existence of a representative consumer are obtained by inverting (4.6) to yield

$$V_h(Y_h, P) = \bar{\mathbf{V}}(P) Y_h + \hat{\mathbf{V}}_h(P) \tag{4.9}$$

for $h = 1, \ldots, H$. The economy indirect utility function is

$$\mathbf{V}(\sum_h Y_h, P) = \bar{\mathbf{V}}(P) \sum_h Y_h + \sum_h \hat{\mathbf{V}}_h(P) \tag{4.10}$$

so that the uncompensated demands are

$$X\left(\sum_h Y_h, P \right) = \frac{\nabla_P \bar{\mathbf{V}}(P)}{\bar{\mathbf{V}}(P)} \sum_h Y_h + \frac{\sum_h \nabla_P \hat{\mathbf{V}}_h(P)}{\bar{\mathbf{V}}(P)}. \tag{4.11}$$

For there to exist a representative consumer, the cost function for each consumer in the economy must be affine in utility with a common marginal cost of utility. Therefore, consumers have quasi-homothetic and similar preferences. This implies that each consumer has linear Engel curves and the slope of the Engel curve is the same for all consumers for each price vector, P.

These restrictions on the households in the economy imply that the representative consumer must have quasi-homothetic preferences. When we require in addition that the representative consumer has a commodity aggregate, the restrictions become even more severe.

The representative consumer has a commodity aggregate if and only if the economy cost function can be written in the following form

$$\mathrm{C}(\phi(u), P) = \min_{\mathbf{x}^2} \{ \mathrm{C}^1(\phi(u), P^1, \mathbf{x}^2) + \mathrm{C}^2(P^2, \mathbf{x}^2) \} \tag{4.12}$$

where C^1 and C^2 are conditional cost functions and C satisfies (4.2). The conditions under which (4.2) and (4.12) can be satisfied are stated in the following Theorem.

Theorem 4.1: *Assume R. There exists a representative consumer with a commodity aggregate for sector two, if and only if for $h = 1, \ldots, H$*

$$C_h(u_h, P) = \min_{\mathbf{x}_h^2} \{ \mathrm{C}_h^1(u_h, P^1, \mathbf{x}_h^2) + \mathrm{C}_h^2(P^2, \mathbf{x}_h^2) \} - \delta_h(P) \tag{4.13}$$

where

$$\mathrm{C}_h^1(u_h, P^1, \mathbf{x}_h^2) = \max_{\mathbf{y}_h, \mathbf{z}_h} \left\{ \bar{\mathrm{C}}^1(\phi_h(u_h), P^1, \mathbf{y}_h) + \hat{\mathrm{C}}_h^1(P^1, \mathbf{z}_h) \mid \mathbf{y}_h + \mathbf{z}_h \leq \mathbf{x}_h^2 \right\} \tag{4.14}$$

and $\bar{\mathrm{C}}^1$ is linearly homogeneous in $(\phi_h(u_h), \mathbf{y}_h)$, and

$$\mathrm{C}_h^2(P^2, \mathbf{x}_h^2) = \bar{\mathrm{C}}^2(P^2)\mathbf{x}_h^2 + \hat{\mathrm{C}}_h^2(P^2) \tag{4.15}$$

so that

$$C_h(u_h, P) = \bar{\mathrm{C}}(P^1, \bar{\mathrm{C}}^2(P^2))\phi_h(u_h) + \hat{\mathrm{C}}_h(P^1, \bar{\mathrm{C}}^2(P^2)) + \hat{\mathrm{C}}_h^2(P^2) - \delta_h(P), \tag{4.16}$$

and $\sum_h \delta_h(P)$ as in (3.15). In this case,

$$\mathrm{C}(\phi(u), P) = \bar{\mathrm{C}}(P^1, \bar{\mathrm{C}}^2(P^2)) \sum_h \phi_h(u_h) + \sum_h \hat{\mathrm{C}}_h(P^1, \bar{\mathrm{C}}^2(P^2)) + \sum_h \hat{\mathrm{C}}_h^2(P^2). \tag{4.17}$$

Proof: see the appendix.

In order for there to exist an economy-wide commodity aggregate, each consumer must have a commodity aggregate (except for an additive function which sums to a utility-free household with a commodity aggregate) as stated in (4.13). Also, as stated in (4.15), each consumer must have a marginal price index, $\bar{\mathbf{C}}^2(P^2)$, of the group 2 commodities that is the same for all consumers. Finally, to insure there is a representative consumer, the expenditure function of each consumer must be affine in transformed utility with a common marginal cost of transformed utility as described in (4.16). This requires that the conditional cost function, $\mathbf{C}^1$, be expressible as in (4.14).

By comparing (4.16) with (4.6), one can see the effect of aggregating commodities for a representative consumer. As required for the existence of a representative consumer, the household's cost function in (4.16) is affine in (a transform of) utility. In addition, the prices of the group 2 goods, P^2 , must be homothetically separable from P^1 in the marginal cost of utility. In this case, the representative consumer's preferences with a commodity aggregate are characterized by the expenditure function in (4.17) which is the sum of the consumers' expenditure functions in (4.16).

In the following Theorem, we characterize the utility functions of the consumers that are dual to the expenditure functions in Theorem 4.1 and, hence, necessary and sufficient for the existence of a representative consumer with a commodity aggregate.

Theorem 4.2: *Maintaining the assumptions of Theorem 3.2, there exists a representative consumer with a commodity aggregate for X^2 where $\delta_h = 0$ if and only if for $h = 1, \ldots, H$*

$$U_h(X_h) = \bar{U}_h(X_h^1, \mathbf{X}_h(X_h^2)) \tag{4.18}$$

where

$$\bar{U}_h(X_h^1, \mathbf{x}_h^2) = \max_{\left\{ \substack{Y_h, Z_h \\ \mathbf{y}_h, \mathbf{z}_h} \right\}} \{ \psi_h(\bar{\mathbf{U}}(Y_h, \mathbf{y}_h)) \mid \hat{\mathbf{U}}_h(Z_h, \mathbf{z}_h) = 0, Y_h + Z_h \leq X_h^1, \mathbf{y}_h + \mathbf{z}_h \leq \mathbf{x}_h^2 \} \tag{4.19}$$

where $\bar{\mathbf{U}}$ is linearly homogeneous and

$$\mathbf{X}_h(X_h^2) = \max_{(Y_h, Z_h)} \left\{ \bar{\mathbf{X}}^2(Y_h) \mid \hat{\mathbf{X}}_h^2(Z_h) = 0, Y_h + Z_h \leq X_h^2 \right\} \tag{4.20}$$

where $\bar{\mathbf{X}}^2$ is linearly homogeneous.

Proof: see the appendix.

The interpretation of these conditions follows directly from the interpretation of the restrictions on the cost functions. Condition (4.18) insures that each consumer has a commodity aggregate. Condition (4.20) insures that the aggregator functions are quasi-homothetic and similar. Condition (4.19) insures that the utility function, $\bar{U}_h$, defined on X_h^1 and the commodity aggregate, x_h^2, is quasi-homothetic and similar so that preferences can be aggregated across consumers to provide a representative consumer.

It is informative to notice the similarity in the structure of (4.19) and (4.20). This follows from the decentralized allocation that is feasible when the economy has a commodity aggregate. One can think of the economy as beginning with an endowment of X^2 and allocating it to consumers in an efficient fashion. If one thinks of each consumer's aggregate, x_h^2, as utility obtained from X^2, then demands for X^2 satisfy the usual properties of demands and one can ask for a representative consumer that rationalizes these demands. This is equivalent to asking for aggregate preferences that represent the aggregation of the aggregator functions, $\mathbf{X}_1, \ldots, \mathbf{X}_H$. The Gorman restriction for there to exist an aggregate are the cost function restrictions in (4.15) and the dual restrictions given by (4.20). These consumer restrictions on the aggregator functions are equivalent to the restrictions implied by commodity aggregation.

The existence of a representative aggregator function, $\mathbf{X}$, and the endowment, X^2, determines an economy endowment, x^2. The second stage in the allocation process is to efficiently allocate, (X^1, x^2) among consumers. The demands of consumers generate economy demands for (X^1, x^2). For there to be a representative consumer with preferences for (X^1, x^2), the utility functions, $\bar{U}_1, \ldots, \bar{U}_H$ must aggregate. The cost function restrictions for a representative consumer with commodities (X^1, x^2) are given in (4.6) while the primal restrictions are in (4.19).

Although (4.19) and (4.20) can be viewed as requirements for the existence of a representative household, (4.20) can also be viewed as the requirement for a commodity aggregate. In fact, given the existence of a representative household, if sector two is merely separable from its complement in the direct utility function of each household, then an economy commodity aggregate exists as stated in

Theorem 4.3: *If there is a representative consumer and if each household has a commodity aggregate, then there is an economy commodity aggregate.*

Proof: obvious from Theorem 4.1 and the discussion above.

The existence of an economy commodity aggregate requires that each consumer have a commodity aggregate and that their aggregator functions be similar. The existence of a representative consumer eliminates the similarity requirement because similarity is already implied by the existence of the representative consumer.

5. Commodity Aggregation With Demands Which Maximize Social Welfare

In this section we address an alternative rationalization of single agent economies. Suppose there is a planner whose preferences can be represented by a Bergson-Samuelson social welfare function. The planner has the ability to levy lump sum taxes and subsidies to maximise the social welfare function. If consumers respond parametrically to the lump sum transfers, there exists a social utility function defined on the aggregate amounts of the commodities consumed by the society. This social utility function has been interpretated as representing the preferences of a single consumer in the economy.

We assume that the planner's preferences are represented by a Bergson-Samuelson social welfare function

$$s = S(u_1, \ldots, u_H) = \sum_h \alpha_h \phi_h(u_h) \tag{5.1}$$

where each ϕ_h is increasing and concave and the social weights are positive, $\alpha = (\alpha_1, \ldots, \alpha_H) \gg 0$. We use the additive formulation only to be able to demonstrate precisely the role which the ethical judgement plays in this problem.

The planner maximizes social utility subject to the utility possibilities in the economy:

$$s = \mathbf{S}(\alpha, X) = \max_{\{X_1, \ldots, X_H\}} \left\{ S(u) \mid u_h = U_h(X_h),\ h = 1, \ldots, H,\ \sum_h X_h = X \right\} \tag{5.2}$$

The social utility function $\mathbf{S}$ associates with a vector of commodities, X, the maximum social welfare which is possible. We assume $\mathbf{S}$ is quasiconcave; sufficient conditions to guarantee this are well-known (see Samuelson (1956), Gorman (1959), Negishi (1963), Chipman and Moore (1979)).

Dual to the social utility function is a social expenditure function, D, defined by

$$D(s, \alpha, P) = \min_X \{ P \cdot X \mid \mathbf{S}(\alpha, X) \geq s \}. \tag{5.3}$$

Aggregate compensated demands can be derived from D by Shephard's Lemma as

$$\tilde{X}(s, \alpha, P) = \nabla_P D(s, \alpha, P). \tag{5.4}$$

An alternative derivation of D is useful for understanding the relationship between these aggregate compensated demands and the compensated demands of the households themselves. Recalling the definition of the household's expenditure function and using (5.2), the optimization problem in (5.3) can be written as

$$D(s, \alpha, P) = \min_{\{u_1, \ldots, u_H\}} \left\{ \sum_h C_h(u_h, P) \mid S(u) \geq s \right\} \tag{5.5}$$

so that

$$D(s,\alpha,P)=\sum_h C_h(\overset{*}{u}_h,P) \tag{5.6}$$

where $\overset{*}{u}$ is the set of minimisers in (5.5). Using Shephard's Lemma, (5.6) implies

$$\tilde{X}(s,\alpha,P)=\sum_h \tilde{X}_h(\overset{*}{u}_h,P) \tag{5.7}$$

where $\tilde{X}_h$ is the compensated demand system of household h. The demands generated by the social expenditure function are the sum of the consumers' compensated demands which, therefore, can be said to be rationalized by the social utility function (see Chipman and Moore (1979, Theorem 3.4) and Pollak (1981, section 2)).

There are several possible definitions of a commodity aggregate in a social utility function. A commodity aggregate would be most useful if its existence and construction did not depend upon the particular preferences of the planner. We formalize this in the following definition.

Definition. The social utility function has a commodity aggregate for X^2 if there exist continuous, increasing real-valued functions $\mathbf{X}$ and $\bar{\mathbf{S}}$ such that

$$\mathbf{S}(\alpha,X)=\bar{\mathbf{S}}(\alpha,X^1,\mathbf{X}(X^2)). \tag{5.8}$$

for all X in the domain of $\mathbf{S}$ and for all $\alpha \gg 0$.

The relationship between the social utility function and the utility possibilities set, $W(X)$, is given by the following:

$$\mathbf{S}(\alpha,X)=\max_{\{u_1,\ldots,u_H\}}\left\{\sum_h \alpha_h\phi_h(u_h)\mid u\in W(X)\right\}. \tag{5.9}$$

where the relation between the Scitovsky set $B(u)$ and the utility possibility set, $W(X)$, is given by

$$u\in W(X)\leftrightarrow X\in B(u). \tag{5.10}$$

The duality between the the social utility function and the utility possibility set expressed in (5.9) implies the following theorem.

Theorem 5.1*: *Assume R. There is a commodity aggregate for X^2 in the social utility function if and only if there is a commodity aggregate for X^2 in the utility possibility frontier and hence in the Scitovsky sets, that is,*

$$\begin{aligned}\mathbf{S}(\alpha,X)=\bar{\mathbf{S}}(\alpha,X^1,\mathbf{X}(X^2))&\leftrightarrow W(X)=\mathbf{W}(X^1,\mathbf{X}(X^2))\\ &\leftrightarrow\{X\in B(u)\leftrightarrow(X^1,\mathbf{X}(X^2))\in\mathbf{B}(u)\}.\end{aligned} \tag{5.11}$$

Proof: see the appendix.

* We thank Russell Davidson for pointing out an error in a previous version of this Theorem.

The implications of the above theorem are somewhat surprising: a commodity aggregate in the social utility function implies that there is a commodity aggregate in the utility possibilities set and the Scitovsky set. Therefore, each household in the economy satisfies the conditions in Theorems 3.1 and 3.2. Each household has a utility function with a quasi-homothetic and similar aggregator function. The expenditure function dual to the aggregator function is affine in the commodity aggregate and the marginal cost of the commodity aggregate is the same for all households. Since these restrictions on the household expenditure functions are sufficient, there are no restrictions on the social welfare function implied by commodity aggregation.

Theorem 5.1 shows that if a social utility function is separable, then each household has a utility function that satisfies properties stronger than separability. This additional structure imposed on the preferences of the households in turn implies that the social expenditure and social utility functions must satisfy restrictions in addition to that of separability. We state this as

Theorem 5.2: *Assume R. Then,*

$$\mathbf{S}(\alpha, X) = \bar{\mathbf{S}}(\alpha, X^1, \mathbf{X}(X^2)) \tag{5.12}$$

if and only if $\mathbf{X}$ *is quasi- homothetic, i.e.,*

$$\mathbf{X}(X^2) = \max_{\{Y^2, Z^2\}} \left\{ \bar{\mathbf{X}}(Y^2) \mid \hat{\mathbf{X}}(Z^2) = 0, Y^2 + Z^2 = X^2 \right\}, \tag{5.13}$$

where $\bar{\mathbf{X}}$ *is linearly homogeneous, or equivalently, the expenditure function dual to* $\mathbf{X}$ *is affine, i.e.,*

$$\begin{aligned} \mathbf{C}^2(P^2, \mathbf{x}^2) &= \min_{X^2} \{ P^2 \cdot X^2 \mid \mathbf{X}(X^2) \geq \mathbf{x}^2 \} \\ &= \bar{\mathbf{C}}^2(P^2)\mathbf{x}^2 + \hat{\mathbf{C}}^2(P^2). \end{aligned} \tag{5.14}$$

Proof: see the appendix.

The import of Theorem 5.2 is that a separable function such as $\bar{\mathbf{S}}$ whose aggregator $\mathbf{X}$ is *not* quasi-homothetic *cannot* serve as a social utility function. That is, the function cannot be constructed as $\mathbf{S}$ in (5.2) for any social welfare function, S, and consumer utility functions, U_h, $h = 1, \ldots, H$. Therefore, the commodity aggregation restrictions that suffice for single consumer preferences are not sufficient for commodity aggregation in a social utility function.

6. Commodity Aggregation With Multiple Income Aggregates

In general, market demand systems depend on the income of each household in the economy. If there is a representative consumer, then market demands depend only on the sum of the households' incomes. Intermediate situations can occur in which market demands depend on several aggregate income measures. These situations are interesting, although there is no representative consumer, because they allow a reduction in the number of independent parameters affecting market demands. In this section, we investigate commodity aggregation in such market demand functions.

We assume that market demand functions can be written in the following form

$$X(Y_1,\ldots,Y_H,P)=\sum_h X_h(Y_h,P)=\bar{X}(\mathbf{Y}_1(Y_1,\ldots,Y_H),\ldots,\mathbf{Y}_L(Y_1,\ldots,Y_H),P) \tag{6.1}$$

where $L<H$ and $\mathbf{Y}_1,\ldots,\mathbf{Y}_L$ are functionally independent.

Lau (1977, 1982) has shown that (6.1) is satisfied for arbitrary functions, X_h, (not necessarily demand functions) if and only if for each household, $h=1,\ldots,H$,

$$X_h(Y_h,P)=\sum_{\ell=1}^{L} A^\ell(P)\phi_h^\ell(Y_h)+A_h^0(P) \tag{6.2}$$

in which case, market demands can be written as

$$X(Y_1,\ldots,Y_H,P)=\sum_{\ell=1}^{L} A^\ell(P)\sum_h \phi_h^\ell(Y_h)+A^0(P) \tag{6.3}$$

where $A^0=\sum_h A_h^0$.

Gorman (1981) has shown that if (6.2) is the solution to a consumer's utility maximization problem then the $N\times(L+1)$ matrix

$$A=[A^0,A^1,\ldots,A^L] \tag{6.4}$$

has rank at most 3 and in the case where the rank is 3 the income functions can be written as

$$\phi_h^\ell(Y_h)=\mathbf{K}_{h\ell}Y_h(\ln Y_h)^{r_\ell}, \tag{6.5}$$

each r_ℓ an integer; or

$$\phi_h^\ell(Y_h)=\mathbf{K}_{h\ell}Y_h^{r_\ell+1}; \tag{6.6}$$

or

$$\phi_h^\ell(Y_h)=\mathbf{K}_{h\ell}Y_h\sin(r_\ell\log Y_h), \tag{6.7}$$

each $r_\ell\geq 0$ or

$$\phi_h^\ell(Y_h)=\mathbf{K}_{h\ell}Y_h\cos(r_\ell\log Y_h), \tag{6.8}$$

each $r_\ell\geq 0$ where r_ℓ, $\ell=1,\ldots,L$ are real numbers and $r_1=0$.

As a consequence, if household demands satisfy (6.1), then they can be written as

$$X_h(Y_h, P) = A_h^0(P) + A^1(P)Y_h + A^2(P)\sum_{\ell} \alpha^{\ell}(P)\phi_h^{\ell}(Y_h) \tag{6.9}$$

where $A_h^0(P)$, $A^1(P)$, and $A^2(P)$ are each $N \times 1$ vectors and $\alpha^{\ell}(P)$ for $\ell = 1, \ldots, L$ are scalars and the ϕ_h^{ℓ} for $\ell = 1, \ldots, L$ and $h = 1, \ldots, H$ satisfy (6.5) to (6.8). In this case, the economy demand functions are expressed as

$$X(Y_1, \ldots, Y_H, P) = A^0(P) + A^1(P)\sum_h Y_h + A^2(P)\sum_{\ell} \alpha^{\ell}(P)\sum_h \phi_h^{\ell}(Y_h). \tag{6.10}$$

In addition, Gorman (1981) has shown that if consumer demands are expressible as in (6.2), then the consumer's expenditure function can be written as

$$C_h(u_h, P) = \tilde{C}_h\left(u_h, \alpha_h(P), \beta_h(P), \gamma_h(P)\right) \tag{6.11}$$

where α, β and γ are functionally independent. That is, the expenditure function can depend on at most three price indices each of which can depend on all prices.

We have shown in section 3, that an economy has a commodity aggregate for X^2 if and only if every household's expenditure function can be written as in Theorem 3.1. A necessary condition for the existence of multiple income aggregates in an economy's demands is that each household's expenditure function have the form given in (6.11). Combining these results provides a necessary condition for an economy to have both a commodity aggregate with multiple income aggregates which we state in the following theorem.

Theorem 6.1: *If an economy has a commodity aggregate as defined by (3.3) or (3.5) and if the economy's demands can be written as in (6.1), then each household's expenditure function, given $\delta_h = 0$, can be expressed as follows*

$$C_h(u_h, P) = \tilde{C}_h(u_h, \alpha_h(P), \beta_h(P), \gamma_h(P)) \tag{6.12}$$

where

$$\alpha_h(P) = \bar{\alpha}_h(P^1, \bar{C}^2(P^2))$$
$$\beta_h(P) = \bar{\beta}_h(P^1, \bar{C}^2(P^2)),$$

and

$$\gamma_h(P) = \bar{\gamma}_h(P^1, \bar{C}^2(P^2)) + \hat{\gamma}_h(P^2)$$

for $h = 1, \ldots, H$.

Proof: see the appendix.

The existence of multiple income aggregates implies that each household's expenditure function can be written as a function of three price aggregates, $\alpha_h(P)$, $\beta_h(P)$ and $\gamma_h(P)$. Commodity aggregation for each household implies, in addition, that P^2 be homothetically separable from P^1 in at least two of the price aggregates and that P^2 be quasi-homothetically separable in the third price aggregate. In addition, the price aggregate for P^2 given by $\bar{C}^2(P^2)$ must be the same in α_h, β_h and γ_h and must be the same for every household. This price index is the marginal cost function for the commodity aggregate.

The following corollary presents an interesting special case of the preceding theorem.

Corollary 6.1 *Suppose $\frac{\partial}{\partial u}\tilde{C}_h(u_h, \alpha_h, \beta_h, \gamma_h)$ is a nonconstant function of α_h, β_h and γ_h. Then, in addition to (6.12) to (6.12),*

$$\gamma_h(P) = \bar{\gamma}_h(P^1, \bar{C}^2(P^2)) \tag{6.13}$$

so that

$$C_h(u_h, P) = \tilde{C}_h(u_h, \alpha_h(P), \beta_h(P), \gamma_h(P)) = \hat{C}_h(u_h, P^1, \bar{C}^2(P^2)). \tag{6.14}$$

This corollary shows that if marginal expenditure for a household depends on all three price aggregates, then P^2 is homothetically separable from (u_h, P^1) in each household's expenditure function and the P^2 aggregator function is the same for all households.

As in section 3, the existence of a commodity aggregate for X^2 implies that the demands for X^2 conditional on the aggregate quantity, $\mathbf{x}^2 = \mathbf{X}(X^2)$, are integrable. Therefore, this conditional subsystem of demands can be rationalized by a conditional group 2 cost function. This fact plus the structure of the demands necessary for the existence of multiple income aggregates implies the result in the following theorem.

Theorem 6.2: *Market demand equations that satisfy (6.1) have a commodity aggregate for X^2 if and only if*

$$\overset{*}{X}{}^2 = \bar{\Gamma}(P^2)Y^2 + \hat{\Gamma}(P^2) \tag{6.15}$$

where

$$Y^2 = B^0(P) + B^1(P)\sum_h Y_h^2 + B^2(P)\sum_\ell \alpha^\ell(P)\sum_h \phi_h^\ell(Y_h). \tag{6.16}$$

Proof: see the appendix.

Condition (6.15) states the market demand for group 2 commodities as a function of group 2 prices, P^2, and group 2 expenditure, Y^2. Group 2 expenditure is the sum of each consumer's expenditures on group 2 commodities. This conditional demand system for group 2 commodities is affine in group 2 expenditures. Group 2 expenditures can be directly computed from (6.10) and is given in (6.16) with obvious redefinitions of variables. The structure of Y^2 given in (6.16), therefore, follows immediately from the requirement of multiple income aggregates. The structure of the conditional demand in (6.15) is a consequence of commodity aggregation. Combining the two yields necessary and sufficient conditions for commodity aggregation with multiple income aggregates. Although the demands for X^1 also have special structure, it is implied by (6.15) and the conditions for integrability.

7. Conclusions

In this conclusion we would like to emphasize a general feature of our results that extends to a much larger class of problems than those considered in this paper. We begin in this paper with a general characterization of the preferences in the economy such as the Scitovsky set or the Scitovsky expenditure function. In this context, we ask for the conditions under which there exists a commodity aggregate. If we were to mistakenly assume that the Scitovsky expenditure function is a general function with no special properties, then the necessary and sufficient conditions for a commodity aggregate would be standard separability conditions. These conditions are that there exist functions $\mathbf{C}^1$ and $\mathbf{C}^2$ such that

$$C(u,P) = \min_{\mathbf{x}^2} \{ \mathbf{C}^1(u,P^1,\mathbf{x}^2) + \mathbf{C}^2(P^2,\mathbf{x}^2) \} \tag{7.1}$$

(repeating (3.11)). The Scitovsky expenditure function, however, satisfies the very strong property that it is the sum of household expenditure functions

$$C(u,P) = \sum_h C_h(u_h,P). \tag{7.2}$$

The true restrictions for commodity aggregation are obtained by combining the structure on C given in (7.1) with that given in (7.2). This implies that the Scitovsky expenditure function can be written as

$$\begin{aligned} C(u,P) &= \sum_h \bar{\mathbf{C}}_h^1(u_h,P^1,\bar{\mathbf{C}}^2(P^2)) + \hat{\mathbf{C}}^2(P^2) \\ &= \sum_h \max_{\mathbf{x}_h^2} \{ \mathbf{C}_h^1(u_h,P^1,\mathbf{x}_h^2) + \bar{\mathbf{C}}^2(P^2)\mathbf{x}_h^2 \} + \sum_h \hat{\mathbf{C}}_h^2(P^2) \end{aligned} \tag{7.3}$$

which is substantially more restrictive than (7.1). Therefore, *if the properties implied by the construction of the Scitovsky expenditure function are ignored one would obtain necessary but not sufficient conditions for commodity aggregation.*

The implication is even stronger if one assumes the economy has a representative consumer. In this case, there is a preference ordering that rationalizes market demands but it cannot be a general preference ordering. A representative consumer must have quasi-homothetic preferences. A model that has a representative consumer without quasi-homothetic preferences is internally inconsistent. The commodity aggregation restrictions for a representative consumer are that the Scitovsky expenditure function can be written as

$$C(u,P)=\bar{\mathrm{C}}^1(P^1,\bar{\mathrm{C}}^2(P^2))\sum_h \phi_h(u_h)+\hat{\mathrm{C}}(P^1,\bar{C}^2(P^2))+\hat{\mathrm{C}}^2(P^2). \tag{7.4}$$

Of course, this is a much stronger restriction than is required for a commodity aggregate for a single consumer.

The same point can be made in our other two problems. A planner that maximizes social welfare faces a constraint that is derived by summing over consumers. Market demands with multiple income aggregates are sums of consumer demands which also have multiple measures of income. These relationships between the aggregate economy and the individual households are essential for determining the conditions for commodity aggregation.

The general point we are making is that any analysis of economy demand behavior must recognize that it is an aggregate of the behavior of many individual households. If the implications of this relationship are ignored, then sufficient conditions for special properties of aggregate demands cannot be derived. Therefore, *the common practice of treating an economy as having a single consumer with general preferences cannot be rationalized by any aggregation procedures.*

Appendix

▪ Proof of Theorem 3.1

Commodity aggregation implies that

$$C(u,P)=\min_{\mathbf{x}^2}\{\,\mathrm{C}^1(u,P^1,\mathbf{x}^2)+\mathrm{C}^2(P^2,\mathbf{x}^2)\,\} \tag{A.1}$$

where

$$C(u,P)=\sum_h C_h(u_h,P). \tag{A.2}$$

Let

$$\overset{*}{\mathbf{x}}{}^2=\overset{*}{\mathbf{X}}{}^2(u,P) \tag{A.3}$$

be the minimizer in (A.1). Using (A.1) – (A.3) yields

$$\mathbf{C}^1(u, P^1, \overset{*}{\mathbf{x}}^2) + \mathbf{C}^2(P^2, \overset{*}{\mathbf{x}}^2) = \sum_h C_h(u_h, P). \tag{A.4}$$

Differentiating (A.4) with respect to P_i, $i \in I^1$ and P_k, $k \in I^2$ and using the Envelope Theorem yields

$$\frac{\partial}{\partial P_i}\mathbf{C}^1(u, P^1, \overset{*}{\mathbf{x}}^2) = \sum_h \frac{\partial}{\partial P_i} C_h(u_h, P), \quad i \in I^1. \tag{A.5}$$

$$\frac{\partial}{\partial P_k}\mathbf{C}^2(P^2, \overset{*}{\mathbf{x}}^2) = \sum_h \frac{\partial}{\partial P_k} C_h(u_h, P), \quad k \in I^2. \tag{A.6}$$

Since $\mathbf{C}^2$ is increasing in x, there is at least one derivative of $\mathbf{C}^2$ in (A.6) that is increasing in $\overset{*}{\mathbf{x}}^2$. Suppose (without loss of generality) that the Nth derivative is increasing in $\overset{*}{\mathbf{x}}^2$. Then, solve (A.6) for $k = N$ to get

$$\overset{*}{\mathbf{x}}^2 = \overset{*}{\mathbf{X}}^2(u, P) = \phi(P^2, \sum_h \frac{\partial}{\partial P_N} C_h(u_h, P)) \tag{A.7}$$

and substitute into the system of equations (A.6) to obtain

$$\frac{\partial}{\partial P_k}\mathbf{C}^2\left(P^2, \phi(P^2, \sum_h \phi_h(u_h, P))\right) = \sum_h \frac{\partial}{\partial P_k} C_h(u_h, P) \tag{A.8}$$

where

$$\phi_h(u_h, P) = \frac{\partial}{\partial P_N} C_h(u_h, P). \tag{A.9}$$

Now define $\tilde{\mathbf{C}}^2$ by

$$\frac{\partial}{\partial P_k}\tilde{\mathbf{C}}^2\left(P^2, \sum_h \phi_h(u_h, P)\right) = \frac{\partial}{\partial P_k}\mathbf{C}^2\left(P^2, \phi(P^2, \sum_h \phi_h(u_h, P))\right) \tag{A.10}$$

so that by Eulers' Theorem,

$$\tilde{\mathbf{C}}^2\left(P^2, \sum_h \phi_h(u_h, P)\right) = \sum_{k \in I^2} P_k \frac{\partial}{\partial P_k}\tilde{\mathbf{C}}^2\left(P^2, \sum_h \phi_h(u_h, P)\right). \tag{A.11}$$

Similarly, define $\tilde{\mathbf{C}}_h$ by

$$\frac{\partial}{\partial P_k}\tilde{\mathbf{C}}_h\left(P, \phi_h(u_h, P)\right) = \frac{\partial}{\partial P_k} C_h(u_h, P) \tag{A.12}$$

and define $\tilde{C}_h^2$ by

$$\tilde{C}_h^2\,(\,P, \phi_h(u_h, P)\,) = \sum_{k\in I^2} P_k \frac{\partial}{\partial P_k} \tilde{C}_h\,(\,P, \phi_h(u_h, P)\,)\,. \tag{A.13}$$

Then, (A.8) and the definitions of $\tilde{C}^2$ and $\tilde{C}_h^2$ imply that

$$\tilde{C}^2(P^2, \sum_h \phi_h(u_h, P)) = \sum_h \tilde{C}_h^2(P, \phi_h(u_h, P)). \tag{A.14}$$

Since $\phi_h(u_h, P)$ depends on u_h by assumption R_2, each $\phi_h(u_h, P)$ can be varied independently of all other $\phi_g(u_g, P)$ for $g \neq h$. Therefore, (A.14) is a Pexider equation and the only continuous solution is the following (see Eichhorn (1978)):

$$C^2(P^2, \overset{*}{x}^2) = \bar{C}^2(P^2)\overset{*}{x}^2 + \hat{C}^2(P^2) \tag{A.15}$$

and

$$\tilde{C}_h^2(P, \phi_h(u_h, P)) = C_h^2(P^2, \overset{*}{x}_h^2) = \bar{C}^2(P^2)\overset{*}{x}_h^2 + \hat{C}_h^2(P^2) \tag{A.16}$$

where

$$\hat{C}^2(P^2) = \sum_h \hat{C}_h^2(P^2). \tag{A.17}$$

This completes the necessity proof for the structure of the economy. We turn to the households. Choose an arbitrary vector $\bar{u}$ in the range of $\{U_h\}$, and define new functions as follows:

$$\bar{C}^1(P^1, x) = C^1(\bar{u}, P^1, x), \tag{A.18}$$

$$\tilde{C}^1(u - \bar{u}, P^1, x) = C^1(u, P^1, x) - \bar{C}^1(P^1, x), \tag{A.19}$$

$$\bar{C}_h(P) = C_h(\bar{u}_h, P), \tag{A.20}$$

and

$$\tilde{C}_h(u_h - \bar{u}_h, P) = C_h(u_h, P) - \bar{C}_h(P) \tag{A.21}$$

so that

$$\begin{aligned} C(u, P) &= \min_x \left\{ \tilde{C}^1(u - \bar{u}, P^1, x) + \bar{C}^1(P^1, x) + \bar{C}^2(P^2)x + \hat{C}^2(P^2) \right\} \\ &= \sum_h \left\{ \tilde{C}_h(u_h - \bar{u}_h, P) + \bar{C}_h(P) \right\} \end{aligned} \tag{A.22}$$

Letting $u = \bar{u}$, we obtain

$$C(\bar{u}, P) = \min_x \left\{ \bar{C}^1(P^1, x) + \bar{C}^2(P^2)x + \hat{C}^2(P^2) \right\} = \sum_h \bar{C}_h(P) \tag{A.23}$$

since $\tilde{\mathbf{C}}^1(0, P^1, \mathbf{x}) \equiv \tilde{C}_h(0, P) \equiv 0$ by the construction of these functions. Letting $u_h \neq \bar{u}_h$ while $u_g = \bar{u}_g\ \forall g \neq h$, we obtain

$$\min_{\mathbf{x}} \left\{ \tilde{\mathbf{C}}^1_h(u_h - \bar{u}_h, P^1, \mathbf{x}_h) + \bar{\mathbf{C}}^1(P^1, \mathbf{x}_h) + \bar{\mathbf{C}}^2(P^2)\mathbf{x}_h + \hat{\mathbf{C}}^2(P^2) \right\}$$
$$= \tilde{C}_h(u_h - \bar{u}_h, P) + \sum_h \bar{C}_h(P) \tag{A.24}$$

where $\tilde{\mathbf{C}}^1_h$ is defined as a projection of $\tilde{\mathbf{C}}^1$ as follows:

$$\tilde{\mathbf{C}}^1_h(u_h - \bar{u}_h, P^1, \mathbf{x}_h) = \tilde{\mathbf{C}}^1(0, \ldots, u_h - \bar{u}_h, \ldots, 0, P^1, \mathbf{x}_h). \tag{A.25}$$

Therefore, each household's cost function can be expressed as follows:

$$\begin{aligned} C_h(u_h, P) &= \tilde{C}_h(u_h - \bar{u}_h, P) + \bar{C}_h(P) \\ &= \min_{\mathbf{x}_h} \left\{ \tilde{\mathbf{C}}^1_h(u_h - \bar{u}_h, P^1, \mathbf{x}_h) + \bar{\mathbf{C}}^1(P^1, \mathbf{x}_h) + \bar{\mathbf{C}}^2(P^2)\mathbf{x}_h + \hat{\mathbf{C}}^2_h(P^2) \right\} - \delta_h(P) \\ &= \min_{\mathbf{x}_h} \left\{ \mathbf{C}^1_h(u_h, P^1, \mathbf{x}_h) + \bar{\mathbf{C}}^2(P^2)\mathbf{x}_h + \hat{\mathbf{C}}^2_h(P^2) \right\} - \delta_h(P) \end{aligned} \tag{A.26}$$

where

$$\mathbf{C}^1_h(u_h, P^1, \mathbf{x}_h) = \tilde{C}^1_h(u_h - \bar{u}_h, P^1, \mathbf{x}_h) + \bar{\mathbf{C}}^1(P^1, \mathbf{x}_h) \tag{A.27}$$

and

$$\delta_h(P) = \sum_{g \neq h} \left\{ \bar{C}_g(P) - \hat{\mathbf{C}}^2_g(P^2) \right\}. \tag{A.28}$$

Then, using (A.23) we obtain that

$$\sum_h \delta_h(P) = (H - 1) \min_{\mathbf{x}} \left\{ \bar{\mathbf{C}}^1(P^1, \mathbf{x}) + \bar{\mathbf{C}}^2(P^2)\mathbf{x} \right\}. \tag{A.29}$$

This completes the proof of necessity.

Sufficiency follows by noting that if each household has a cost function as in (3.13) and (3.14) with (3.15) satisfied, then both (A.5) and (A.6) are satisfied and, therefore, (A.1) and (A.2) hold. This completes the proof of sufficiency. ||

▪ Proof of Theorem 3.2

It follows from (3.13), (3.14) and Theorem 2 part I, Blackorby and Schworm (1984b). ||

▪ Proof of Theorem 4.1

From Theorem 3.1

$$C_h(u_h, P) = \max_{\mathbf{x}^2_h} \left\{ \mathbf{C}^1_h(u_h, P^1, \mathbf{x}^2_h) + \bar{\mathbf{C}}^2(P^2)\mathbf{x}^2_h \right\} + \hat{\mathbf{C}}^2_h(P^2) - \delta_h(P), \tag{A.30}$$

where $\sum_h \delta_h(P)$ can be written as in (3.15). From (4.6), we have

$$C_h(u_h, P) = \bar{\mathbf{C}}(P)\phi_h(u_h) + \hat{\mathbf{C}}_h(P). \tag{A.31}$$

Using (A.30) and (A.31) and the proof of Theorem 3 in Blackorby and Schworm (1984a) yield (4.14) where $\bar{\mathbf{C}}^1$ is linearly homogeneous in $\phi_h(u_h)$ and y_h. ||

▪ Proof of Theorem 4.2

Use Theorem 4.1 and then Theorem 2 part I in Blackorby and Schworm (1984b) to obtain (4.19) and (4.20). ||

▪ Proof of Theorem 5.1

The social utility function is related to the utility possibility set by the following optimization problem

$$\mathbf{S}(\alpha, X) = \max_{(u^1,\ldots,u^H)} \left\{ \sum_h \alpha_h u_h \mid u \in W(X) \right\} \tag{A.32}$$

where the utility functions of the consumers have been normalized so that the social welfare function is additive in u. The utility possibility set, $W(X)$, can be constructed from the social utility function by the following operation

$$W(X) = \left\{ u \mid \sum_h \alpha_h u_h \leq \mathbf{S}(\alpha, X),\ \forall \alpha \geq 0 \right\} \tag{A.33}$$

for each $X \in \Theta$.

Suppose there is a commodity aggregate in the utility possibility set so that

$$W(X) = \mathbf{W}(X^1, \mathbf{X}^2(X^2))$$

for all X. Then, substituting into (A.32) yields

$$\mathbf{S}(\alpha, X) = \bar{\mathbf{S}}(\alpha, X^1, \mathbf{X}^2(X^2)) = \max_{(u^1,\ldots,u^H)} \left\{ \sum_h \alpha_h u_h \mid u \in W(X^1, \mathbf{X}^2(X^2)) \right\}.$$

The converse is proved by noting that (A.33) implies that

$$W(X) = \mathbf{W}(X^1, \mathbf{X}^2(X^2)) = \left\{ u \mid \sum_h \alpha_h u_h \leq \bar{\mathbf{S}}(\alpha, X^1, \mathbf{X}^2(X^2)) \right\}$$

for each $X \in \Theta$. ||

▪ Proof of Theorem 5.2

The proof is identical to the proof of (3.25) in Theorem 3.2. ||

Proof of Theorem 6.1

Dropping the household subscript we prove that if

$$C(u,P) = \tilde{C}(u,\alpha(P),\beta(P)) = \min_{x}\{\,C^1(u,P^1,x) + C^2(P^2,x)\,\} \tag{A.34}$$

then

$$\alpha(P) = \bar{\alpha}(P^1,\bar{C}^2(P^2)) \tag{A.35}$$

and

$$\beta(P) = \bar{\beta}(P^1,\bar{C}^2(P^2)) + \hat{\beta}(P^2) \tag{A.36}$$

and that if the marginal cost depends upon α and β that $\hat{\beta}$ is zero; note that this is more than is required for the Theorem as we are only assuming separability and not quasi-homothetic separability.

Let $\overset{*}{x} = \overset{*}{X}(u,P)$ be the solution to (A.34) where $\overset{*}{X}$ is not a constant function of u (as a result of R). Then, suppressing the arguments of functions,

$$\tilde{C}_u = C^1_u \tag{A.37}$$

$$\tilde{C}_u\alpha_i + \tilde{C}_\beta\beta_i = C^1_i,\ i \in I^1 \tag{A.38}$$

and

$$\tilde{C}_\alpha\alpha_k + \tilde{C}_\beta\beta_k = C^2_k,\ k \in I^2. \tag{A.39}$$

First consider (A.37) and suppose that α and β are not ordinally equivalent to $\overset{*}{X}$ in P^2. In this case we can recover $\tilde{C}_u$ simply by moving through P^2 and C^1_u itself is independent of P^1, a contradiction. Hence we can write

$$\alpha(P) = \tilde{\alpha}(P^1,\xi(P)) \tag{A.40}$$

$$\beta(P) = \tilde{\beta}(P^1,\xi(P)) \tag{A.41}$$

and

$$\overset{*}{X}(u,P) = \bar{X}(u,P^1,\xi(P)). \tag{A.42}$$

Substituting (A.40) to (A.42) into (A.34) and recompute (A.38) to get

$$\tilde{C}_\alpha\left[\,\tilde{\alpha}_i + \tilde{\alpha}_\xi\xi_i\,\right] + \tilde{C}_\beta\left[\tilde{\beta}_i + \tilde{\beta}_\xi\xi_i\right] = C^1_i\left(u,p^1,\bar{X}(u,P^1,\xi(P))\right). \tag{A.43}$$

This implies that

$$\xi_i(P) =^1 (P^1,\xi(P)),\ i \in I^1. \tag{A.44}$$

Taking the derivative with respect to k, $k \in I^2$ in (A.44) reveals that I^2 is separable from I^1 in ξ. Hence α and β can be rewritten as required. Note that we could go on to prove that I^2 is separable from I^1 in C^2 and hence homothetic separability.

Next, suppose that $\tilde{C}_u$ is independent of β. By repeating the argument with respect to α we get (A.40) and (A.42) again. Recompute (A.38) to get

$$\tilde{C}_\alpha \left[\alpha_i + \alpha_\xi \xi_i \right] + \tilde{C}_\beta \beta_i = C_i^1 \left(u, P^1, \bar{\mathrm{X}}(u, P^1, \xi(P)) \right). \qquad (A.45)$$

Repeating the argument leading from (A.44) shows that α satisfies (A.35) and

$$\beta_i(P) = \tilde{\beta}_i(P^1, \varsigma(P^2)),\ i \in I^1 \qquad (A.46)$$

and

$$\beta(P) = \tilde{\beta}(P^1, \varsigma(P^2)) + \hat{\beta}(P^2) \qquad (A.47)$$

which completes the argument when there are only two aggregates. The case of three proceeds in the same way. ||

■ Proof of Theorem 6.2

Theorem 3.1 yields (6.15) where

$$Y^2 = \sum_h Y_h^2 = \bar{\mathrm{C}}^2(P^2) \sum_h \overset{*}{\mathrm{x}}{}_h^2 + \sum_h \hat{\mathrm{C}}_h^2(P^2) \qquad (A.48)$$

and Y_h^2 is easily computed from (6.9). ||

REFERENCES

Blackorby, C. and W.E. Diewert, "Expenditure Functions, Local Duality, and Second Order Approximations", *Econometrica*, **47**, 1979, 579-601.

Blackorby, C., D. Primont, and R. Russell, *Duality, Separability, and Functional Structure: Theory and Economic Applications*, North-Holland, New York, Amsterdam, 1978.

Blackorby, C. and W. Schworm, "The Structure of Economies with Aggregate Measures of Capital: A Complete Characterization", *Review of Economic Studies*, **51**, 1984a, 633-650.

Blackorby, C. and W. Schworm, "Consistent Aggregation in Competitive Economies", CORE Discussion Paper 8446, Université Catholique de Louvain, 1984b.

Chipman, J. and J. Moore, "On Social Welfare Functions and the Aggregation of Preferences", *Journal of Economic Theory*, **21**, 1979, 111-139.

Chipman, J. and J. Moore, "Social Utility and the Gains from Trade", *Journal of International Economics*, **2**, 1972, 157-172.

Daal, J. Van and A.Q.M. Merkies, *Aggregation in Economic Research: From Individual to Macro Relations*, D. Reidel, Dordrecht, Boston, Lancaster, 1984.

Eichhorn, W., *Functional Equations in Economics*, Addison-Wesley, 1978.

Gorman, W.M., "Community Preference Fields", *Econometrica*, **21**, 1953, 63-80.

Gorman, W.M., "Are Social Indifference Curves Convex?", *Quarterly Journal of Economics*, **73**, 1959, 485-496.

Gorman, W.M., "Tricks with Utility Functions", in *Essays in Economic Analysis: Proceeding of the 1975 AUTE Conference* (M.J. Artis and A.R. Nobay, eds.) Cambridge, Cambridge University Press, 1976.

Gorman, W.M., "Some Engel Curves", in *Essays in the Theory and Measurement of Consumer Behavior: in Honour of Sir Richard Stone* (A. Deaton, ed.) Cambridge, Cambridge University Press, 1981.

Gorman, W.M., *Aggregation in the Long and the Short Run*, unpublished manuscript, Nuffield College, Oxford, 1984.

Graaf, J. de V., *Theoretical Welfare Economics*, London, Cambridge University Press, 1957.

Green, H.A.J., *Aggregation in Economic Analysis: An Introductory Survey*, Princeton University Press, Princeton, 1964.

Fisher, F., "Embodied Technology and the Existence of Output and Labour Aggregates", *Review of Economic Studies*, **35**, 1968, 391-412.

Jorgenson, D., L. Lau, and T. Stoker, "The Transcendantal Logarithmic Model of Aggregate Consumer Behavior", *Advances in Econometrics*, **1**, JAI Press, 1982, 97-238.

Jorgenson, D., D. Slesnick, and T. Stoker, "Exact Aggregation over Individuals and Commodities", Discussion Paper 1005, Harvard Institute for Economic Research, Harvard University, 1983.

Lau, L., "Existence Conditions for Aggregate Demand Functions", Technical Report No. 248, IMSS Stanford, 1977 (revised 1980, 1982).

Lau, L., "A Note on the Fundamental Theorem of Exact Aggregation", *Economics Letters*, **9**, 1982, 119-126.

Negishi, T., "On Social Welfare Functions", *Quarterly Journal of Economics*, **77**, 1963, 156-158.

Samuelson, P., "Evaluation of Real National Income", *Oxford Economic Papers, N.S.*, **1**, 1950, 1-29.

Samuelson, P., "Social Indifference Curves", *Quarterly Journal of Economics*, **70**, 1956, 1-22.

Scitovsky, T., "A Reconsideration of the Theory of Tariffs", *Review of Economic Studies*, **9**, 1942, 89-110.

Shafer, W. and H. Sonnenschein, "Market Demand and Excess Demand Functions", in *Handbook of Mathematical Economics II*, (K. Arrow and M. Intriligator, eds.), North-Holland, Amsterdam, New York, 1982.

The Problem of Aggregation of Individual Economic Relations; Consistency and Representativity in a Historical Perspective

J. van Daal
Erasmus University Rotterdam
Faculteit der Economische
Wetenschappen
Postbus 1738
3000 DR Rotterdam

A.H.Q.M. Merkies
Vrije Universiteit Amsterdam
Interfaculteit an Acuariele
Wetenschappen en Econometrie
an Boelelaan 1081
Amsterdam

SUMMARY

It was already fairly late in the development of economic theory that aggregation of individual economic relations into macro relations was recognized as a serious problem. This is illustrated in this paper by pointing to the more or less incidental way in which aggregation problems are mentioned and solved in the older literature till the famous Econometrica debate in the late forties. In particular, we try to disentangle the notions of consistency and representativity.

1. INTRODUCTION

The problem of consistent aggregation to be dealt with in this paper can be described as follows. Assume that for each member of a certain group of J individuals the magnitude of some variable (e.g. consumption, output, investment) depends, according to some theory, on the magnitudes of certain explanatory variables (prices, interest rates, incomes, inputs of labour and capital, et cetera). For each $j = 1, \ldots, J$ this can be written as

(1) $$y_j = f_j(x_{j1}, x_{j2}, \ldots, x_{jM}),$$

where y_j is the magnitude of the variable to be explained for j and where the x_{jm} denote the magnitudes for j of the explanatory variable of kind m (= 1, ..., M). The problem of consistent aggregation of relationship (1) over all J individuals (or, rather, individual decision units) is now whether there are aggregation formulae yielding aggregates $y, x_1, x_2, \ldots, x_M$ of the respective kinds of variables such that, for all values of these variables within a certain domain D, there exists a macro relation F such that

(2) $$y = F(x_1, x_2, \ldots, x_M).$$ [1)]

In cases where one is interested in macro relations such as (2) but where the real

Measurement in Economics
ed. by W. Eichhorn

(logical, theoretical) relations are at the micro level, one has to pay attention to this aggregation problem. Although Cournot (1838) already touched on it, it was only some forty years ago that it was explicitly recognised as a serious problem. This will be illustrated in the next section from work of some famous economists as Cournot, Jevons, Walras, Marshall, Edgeworth, Cobb and Douglas and Tinbergen; the section has to be considered as a more or less personally flavoured historical account. In section 3 we deal with the famous Econometrica debate (1946-1948) on aggregation. Two notions played an important rôle in this debate. The first notion is that of consistency, dealing with the mathematical problem of the existence of aggregates and macro relations such as described above; the second one is that of representativity (whether or not together with consistency), dealing with the question whether the macro relation can be considered as the description of the behaviour of some (fictitious) representative agent acting more or less in the same way as individuals do. These two notions are the subject of sections 4 and 5, respectively.

The remainder of this section is devoted to some further remarks on consistency and representativity. If the only restriction on the domain D, mentioned above, of the micro variables x_{jm} is such that these variables have to have economically meaningful values (no negative quantities, e.g.) then we speak of global consistency; another term for the same notion is unconditional consistency. A weaker concept is that of local consistency or conditional consistency, meaning consistency in the sense above for only the variables x_{jm} from some sub-domain D' of D. D' may consist, e.g., of only those micro variables that satisfy certain optimum criteria, or that are distributed over the individuals in some special way. In general, the conditions for local consistency are less stringent than for global consistency. With respect to representativity we can also distinguish several degrees. The strongest form is total representativity or analogy. In that case all the functions f_j and F in (1) and (2) have the same mathematical origin. This may mean that they all have the same form (log-linear, e.g.); it may, however, also be that they are assummed to have a deeper mathematical explanation, e.g., all stemming from some optimization procedure such as profit maximization (micro as well as macro). Less exigent is the notion of partial representativity or representativity with respect to some specific aspect. An example of this is the case where the derivatives of all the functions f_j and F with respect to some variable (the mth one, say) have the same sign; another example is homogeneity of some degree of all the f_j and of F. Both forms of representativity can be combined with both forms of consistency, of course. This classification is very rough and far from complete but it will be sufficient for the purpose of this paper, viz. providing a quick view of how economists aggregated over individuals from the past till now and how they reflected on aggregation. We restricted ourselves to the more simple, less advanced cases with the only aim of describing what has happened. A deep analysis of the question why this happened lies outside the scope of this paper.

2. THE PERIOD TILL 1945

2.1 Consistency of aggregation in our global sense means that knowledge of the macro function and the aggregate explanatory variables gives us the same information on the aggregate dependent variable(s) as does knowledge of all micro relations together with all micro explanatory variables. Something like this could have been in Cournot's mind when he wrote in section[2] 21 of his Recherches sur les Principes Mathématiques de la theorie des Richesses (1838): 'Admettons donc que le débit ou la demande annuelle est, pour chaque denrée, une fonction particulière F(p) du prix p de cette denrée. Connaître la forme de cette fonction, ce serait connaître ce que nous appelons la loi de la demande ou du débit. Elle dépend évidemment du mode d'utilité de la chose, de la nature des services qu'elle peut rendre ou des jouissances qu'elle procure, des habitudes et des moeurs de chaque peuple, de la richesse moyenne et de l'échelle suivant laquelle la richesse est répartie.'(Cournot's italics). The reader may recognise some "cetera" of the ceteris paribus condition. Alternatively, however, we may assume that the aggregates as the habits and morals of the society and aggregate wealth (and income) as well as the income distribution are hidden in the symbol F and that they will become apparent as soon as F is specified. Both views seem to apply.
The latter idea might be to the point in the subsequent section 22 where Cournot tries to argue that the function F is continuous in p. He does so through a hardly convincing appeal on something like a law of large numbers: 'Mais plus le marché s'étendra [i.e., the number of demanders increases], plus les combinaisons des besoins, des fortunes ou même des caprices, seront variées parmi les consommateurs, plus la fonction F(p) approchera de varier avec p d'une manière continue.' (emphasis added). This reasoning is only acceptable, however, if there are among the individual demand functions, which are not necessarily continuous in Cournot's view, decreasing as well as increasing functions of p. It may be that the word "caprices" in the last quotation is meant in this sense, but if all (or almost all) individual demand functions are decreasing then, in general, the discontinuities may just reinforce each other. Hence, after all, Cournot could not escape making the assumption that the aggregate demand function is continuous[3], as he actually did in the opening sentence of section 22. The decreasingness of F as a function of p is so evident for Cournot that he does not argue it; this too, however, is not without problems as we know now (see Hildenbrand (1983)).

The ceteris paribus idea appears to prevail in most parts of the Recherches. In the chapters IV to X, on market behaviour, it is tacitly present. In chapter XI, entitled "Du revenu social", it is even explicitly stated; now the prices of other goods are also mentioned. In section 74 Cournot remarks, with regret, that the ceteris paribus condition, in his opinion, is necessary because the complete solution of an economic system, with all its interdependencies, 'surpasserait les forces de l'analyse mathématique et de nos méthodes pratiques de calcul, quand même toutes les valeurs des constantes pourraient être numériquement assignées.' See on this point also Theocharis (1983, pp.138-140).

Cournot's Recherches remained for more than thirty years nearly completely unnoticed possibly due to the fact that "political economy" was considered as a "general" science the results of which had to be understood also by non-economists such as lawyers, merchants, bankers and politicians, who usually did not have much mathematical training. It was Jevons who brought Cournot's Recherches to the attention of the English economists. In the preface to the second edition (1879) of his book The Theory of Political Economy (1st ed. 1871) Jevons writes: 'It is strange that it should have remained for me among Englishmen to discover its value.'

2.2 Though his approach is quite different, Jevons seems to be guilty of the same kind of ambiguity as Cournot with respect to the discrepancy between the behaviour of individuals on the one hand, and the "regularity" of aggregates on the other, as we shall see below. Jevons does not derive or use demand functions. His "pièce de résistance" is his treatment of the subject of exchange. In chapter IV of his Theory he derives his "Theory of exchange": the exchange ratio of two goods (i.e., the reciprocal of their price ratio) is the reciprocal of the ratio of the marginal utilities after the exchange is completed. The exchangers in this proces are so-called "trading bodies"; see the section entitled "Definition of Trading Body" in chapter IV. A trading body can be any group of individuals from only one person to 'the whole inhabitants of a continent.' Where Cournot aggregates the results of utility maximization (i.e., the individual demand functions), Jevons aggregates, before maximizing the utility, the individuals into a (big) group and assumes that this group, the trading body, as a whole, behaves itself again as an individual[4]. Both Jevons and Cournot tried to show that differences in powers, wants, habits and possessions cancel against each other[5]. In the introductory chapter I, section "Measurement of Feelings and Motives", Jevons states his general starting-point: 'I must here point out that, though the theory presumes to investigate the condition of a mind, and bases upon this investigation the whole of economics[6], practically it is an aggregate of individuals which will be treated. The general forms of the laws of economics are the same in the case of individuals and the nations; and, in reality, it is a law operating in the case of multitudes of individuals which gives rise to the aggregate represented in the transactions of a nation.' Here we have an early example of anology; see also subsection 5.2 below. Of course, these somewhat obscure ideas met with a lot of discussion and criticism.

A serious citicism is the seeming incompatibility of perfect competition with the presence of only two agents in a market, viz. the demanding trading body and the supplying one; in other (modern) words: the core consists of more than one point and, therefore, the contract between the two trading bodies is possibly indeterminate. It appears that Jevons is not unaware of this (see, e.g. the section entitled "Problems in the Theory of Exchange" in his chapter IV) but it is Edgeworth who is Jevons' advocate in this respect. In Appendix V of his <u>Mathematical Psychics</u> (1881) Edgeworth writes: 'His [i.e. Jevons'] couple of dealers are, I take it, a sort of typical couple, clothed with the property of "Indifference" (...). Each (...) is a "representative particular"; an individual only is presented, but there is presupposed a class of competitors in the background.' And he continues: 'exchange is indeterminate, if <u>either</u> (1) one of the trading bodies (<u>quâ</u> individual or <u>quâ</u> union) or (2) the commodity supplied by one of the dealers, be <u>indivisible or not perfectly divisible</u>.' (Edgeworth' italics). Nevertheless Edgeworth, too, admits that Jevons should have been more explicit on this point. Walras (1889 and further, section 163 of (1926)) criticized the fact that Jevons apparently considered 'le probleme (...) comme résolu avec le cas de deux échangeurs.' According to Walras, Jevons left reality by considering 'moyennes fictives', i.e. trading bodies. Apparently, however, he (Walras) was not aware as Edgeworth was of the necessity of imposing some extra condition (here perfect competion) in order to prevent indeterminateness; Edgeworth touched the heart of the problem of indeterminateness while Walras intuitively sensed it. Further, we mention Marshall (1920, III.III.6) who rejects the possibility of a price as measuring final (= marginal) utility to a trading body.

Marshall has also to be mentioned because he introduced the notion of the representative firm; in Book IV, Chapter XIII, section 2 of his <u>Principles of Economics</u> (8th ed., 1920 (1st ed. 1890)). The representative firm is not strictly an aggregate in the sense of the preceding section, i.e. it is not a firm with as input some kind of average of the inputs of all the firms of the industry in question and as output an average of all outputs. It is neither a marginal firm, nor an extremely succesful firm; it is just a firm between these extreme ones. Marshall's analysis of industries (an important part of his work) is carried out in terms of an analysis of the representative firm. In particular, the "normal supply price" of that firm (that is, the expenses of production, including gross earnings of management, per unit of output) is such that as the market supply price equals this price (i) the representative firm's output remains constant, (ii) some (marginal) firms are "falling" and decrease their outputs (iii) other (successful) firms are "rising" and increase their outputs, and (iv) aggregate output remains constant. All this is in the more or less short run (V.III.4). It is conceivable that the notion of representativity has, among others, its roots in Marshall's representative firm; but it must be noted that his term 'representative' has not much to do with our notion of representativity. Pigou (1938, II.XI,3 and App. III.I.2), e.g., borrows the conception of the representative firm under the name "equilibrium firm". Anyway, the notion has already a long life in spite of its obscurity. In this connection the following quotation of Schumpeter (1954, p.997, n.14) is interesting: 'Marshall's authority as a teacher secured mechanical acceptance of the concept. But it received neither the criticism nor the development it deserves.'

2.3 The position of Walras and Pareto with respect to their preconsiderations and their afterthoughts on the problem of aggregation is manifestly enigmatic: Walras aggregates without any comment in his general equilibrium analysis, whereas Pareto, without comments either, painfully abstains from aggregating in discussing general economic equilibrium; nevertheless the latter admits that he continues, in this respect, the work of the former. This, however, does not alter the fact that what they actually do is quite clear.

For each consumer Walras carefully derives, from utility maximization[7], demand and supply functions of consumption goods (les produits) and production factors (les services), respectively; these are functions of the prices of the respective goods and factors; see, e.g. the 20th lesson, section 201 of his Eléments d'Economie Politique Pure (Edition définitive, 1926). For instance, in his notation, an individual's supply of factor t is a function of the prices p_t, p_p, p_k, ... of factors t, p, k, ... and of the prices p_b, p_c, p_d, ... of goods b, c, d, ... (good a being the numéraire), written as

$$(3) \qquad o_t = f_t(p_t, p_p, p_k, \ldots, p_b, p_c, p_d, \ldots)$$

and that individual's demand function for b is likewise

$$(4) \qquad d_b = f_b(p_t, p_p, p_k, \ldots, p_b, p_c, p_d, \ldots);$$

the demand for good a is not written in the form (4), but in a form that is derived from the budget restriction of the individual in question.

In the subsequent section 202 Walras writes 'Et maintenant, en désignant par O_t, O_p, O_k ..., les offres totales des services, soit les excédents des o_t, o_p, o_k ... positifs sur les o_t, o_p, o_k ... négatifs, par D_a, D_b, D_c, D_d ... les demandes totales des produits, par F_t, F_p, F_k ... F_b, F_c, F_d ... les sommes des fonctions f_t, f_p, f_k ... f_b, f_c, f_d ... on aurait déjà, (...), le système suivant de n équations d'offre totale des services:

$$O_t = F_t(p_t, p_p, p_k \ldots p_b, p_c, p_d \ldots),$$

$$(\cdot \quad \cdot \quad \cdot) \qquad [1]$$

et le système suivant de m équations de demande totale des produits:

$$D_b = F_b(p_t, p_p, p_k \cdots p_b, p_c, p_d \cdots)$$

$$(\cdot \quad \cdot \quad \cdot) \qquad [2]$$

$$D_a = O_t p_t + O_p p_p + O_h p_h + \cdots - (D_b p_b + D_c p_c + D_d p_d + \cdots);$$

soit en tout n + m équations.' (emphasis added). These n + m equations are combined with technical and market behaviour equations of the firms into Walras' well-known model of general economic equilibrium (section 206); see also Van Daal, Henderiks and Vorst (1985). The whole sentence just cited has 21 lines in Walras' book, which is in no sense an exception in his works. The reader would expect some comments on Walras' bold example of aggregation, but throughout the whole book any such comment is lacking; he only repeats Cournot's argument (see above) in discussing the continuity of the functions O and D (section 52, where the simple case of two goods to be exchanged against each other is treated). Apparently, Walras saw no problem in arriving at the equations of the systems [1] and [2] (Walras' numbering) of the quotation above; this impression is further enhanced by the fact that nor the earlier editions of his Eléments, neither his correspondence (Jaffé (1965)) give further clues. Neither [1] nor [2] contain any explicit reference to initial endowments or individual preferences, even not in an aggregate sence; this is just as in the case of Cournot. That Walras allows for individual preferences to be different follows from his assertion "la rareté [marginal utility] est subjective..." (Eléments, section 101) and from his marginal utility curves that differ per individual(Eléments, figures 5 and 6). Furthermore, it follows from Walras' analysis (Eléments, section 201, for instance) that the individuals' initial endowments are also hidden somewhere in the functions F. Nevertheless, here we have the first explicit and comprehensive (to say the least) description in mathematical form of what happens if consumers and firms "meet" each other in the various markets of an economy under circumstances of perfect competition. The only contemperaneous author (as far as we know) who explicitly points to Walras' specific way of arriving at collective demand and supply functions is Edgeworth; he does this with the appreciation Walras deserves (Edgeworth (1881, p.42)). In Van Daal and Walker (1987) more attention is paid to aggregation problems in the work of Walras.

As mentioned above, Pareto, in analyzing general economic equilibrium, does not aggregate at all over the consumers, neither in his Cours d'Economie Politique (1896, note 100), nor in his Manuel d'Economie Politique (1909, Appendix, section 85), nor in his article "Economie Mathématique" (1911, section 31); these publications are the most important sources of (the development of) Pareto's ideas on general economic equilibrium and, in particular, of its mathematical formulation. All individuals remain identifiable in Pareto's general equilibrium models which have, therefore, a large number of equations, viz. the number of individuals times the number of first-order conditions (the budget restrictions and the equalities of the ratios of prices and corresponding marginal utilities) in addition to the technical equations (cost minimization) and those stemming from market behaviour (price taking and/or price setting) of the firms. In this sense Pareto's models are forerunners of the models of Arrow and Debreu and their successors[8]. It is a challenge to find out why Pareto developed his models as he did. One reason may have been that for his purpose, i.e., demonstrating consistency in general economic equilibrium models, he did not need aggregation. It remains a moot question, however, why he did not explain why he abstained from following Walras on this point.

2.4 An aggregate that did appear in Pareto's mathematical economics is total welfare of a whole community. Starting from an apparently cardinal utility concept, Pareto discussed shortly (and obscurely) the problem of maximization of this concept in a given economy; see Pareto (1909, Appendix, section 89 and 1911, section 28). In fact, Pareto considers in this kind of analysis, the economy as if it consists of only one consumption unit, apart from the firms. This is more or less in line with the ideas that lie behind Jevons' trading body.

With respect to total welfare also Edgeworth (1881) is noteworthy. He is more explicit on the subject. In a note in the beginning of his section entitled "Utilitarian Calculus" he considers total utility as a triple integral over 'Number of enjoyers × duration of enjoyment × degree thereof' (p.57). Two pages further he states in an axiom the measurability of utility as well as commensurability between different individuals.

2.5 During the period between both world wars aggregation over individuals was still not generally recognized as a problem[9]. It was passed over in silence. A notorious example of this is the study by Cobb and Douglas (1928) in which the famous Cobb-Douglas production function is introduced and estimated on time series (1899-1922) of indices for output (P), labour (L) and capital (C) for the American economy as a whole. The latter is considered as one big profit maximizing firm whose production function fits remarkably well the equation[10] $P = 1.015\ L^{3/4}C^{1/4}$; see also Schumpeter (1954, pp.1030,1042) for comments on so-called social production functions.

The same is the case with the macro models built by Tinbergen (1936 and 1939). Professor Tinbergen explained to us that his models were so extremely simple from the point of view of economic theory ('merely linear common sense macro relations') that aggregation over individuals was hardly relevant; the mathematical and statistical problems asked all attention. Moreover, the final aim of his work was (and has always been) to contribute to the solution of real economic problems. So his main interest was in models that "work" anyhow, i.e. that explain numerically the economic phenomena in their interdependence.

Other macroeconomic work in that period (non-econometric classical models as well as models devised by Keynes(ians)) started usually by formulating a macro theory simply stating the relationship between a few (mostly monetary) aggregates with at most some lip service to the microeconomic theories of individual behaviour of households and firms. It cannot be denied that this method seems to be the most sensible if one wishes to get at macro results without the risk of running ashore somewhere between the micro starting-point and the macro end. Moreover, the models were not precise in an econometric sense. Their main aim was to describe, qualitatively, general tendencies. Therefore, it is clear that most of the relations showed (or pretended to show) at most some kind of "representativity" as far as micro behaviour was considered.

2.6 The idea of macro analysis in the sense just above was not new. Quesnay (1759) already gave utterance to it in his Tableau Economique. We permit ourselves a little digression in describing it. In the tableau streams of total money expenditures and receipts between the classes of farmers ("classe productive"), landlords, and other workers ("classe sterile") are depicted for one time period of a stationary economy. Quesnay assumes that at the beginning of the period the landlords spend one half of total, cumulated rent of the preceding period (constituting their only income) on agricultural products and the other half on products of the classe sterile; during the period they are assumed not to spend anymore. The classe sterile spends also one half of its receipts to agricultural products; the other half is spent in the class itself. Further, Quesnay assumes the farmers to be "productive" in the sense that they succeed (by farming) in doubling their receipts from the other classes. Half of each doubled amount is paid as rent to the landlords, whereas the other half is halfly spent for 'consommation de production fournies par cette même classe, & l'autre moitié en entretien de vêtements, utensiles, instruments, & c. qu'il paye à la classe des dêpenses sterils.' (Quesnay (1759, p.ii). This process of producing and spending peters out just at the end of the period, leaving the landlords with the same total amount of rent as that with which they started, after which a new period begins. The tableau is perhaps the first economic application of a geometric series (with ratio 2). More important for our subject, however, is that Quesnay's exposition is rather obscure in the sense that he mixes micro and macro considerations. Clearly, he has in mind some prototype of a macroeconomic flow model; this can be inferred from the fact that in his numerical example the landlords' total income is about national income of France at that time. In describing the model, however, he sometimes gives the impression that he discusses the behaviour of only one landlord and one single tenant; in other places he describes the individuals as identical per class which gives him the possibility of simply adding individual amounts.

Ricardo (1821) paid likewise attention to individual (entrepreneurial) behaviour. He also let the social totals of individual quantities live their own life eventually, after having started his analysis from the individual firm. See, for instance, his chapter 6 in The Principles of Political Economy and Taxation where he explains the decrease of the profit rate as population increases. He did not refer back too much to the individuals' acts in making clear the argument of that difficult chapter. It can be argued that there is a whole chain of authors from the latter two to Keynes and further, who worked in the same line; see, e.g., Schumpeter (1954, pp.987-8).

3. THE ECONOMETRICA DEBATE

3.1 The beginning of the after-war period is characterised by three circumstances that are important for the subject of this paper: (i) more statistical data were gathered and became available, (ii) more and better econometric techniques were devised and (iii) research facilities (organizational as well as in man-power) increased considerably, in particular in the United States; see Roll (1973, pp.523ff.). This made possible a quantitative and qualitative progress of econometric work, microeconomic as well as macroeconomic. As a consequence, a first explicit statement of the problem of aggregation over individuals could not fail to appear. It was L.R. Klein who in 1946 in an article in Econometrica, entitled "Macroeconomics and the Theory of Rational Behavior," opened the discussion. He started by remarking that 'Many of the newly constructed mathematical models of economic systems, especially the business-cycle theories, are very loosely related to the behaviour of individual households or firms which must form the basis of all the theories of economic behaviour.' (p.93; emphasis added). As an example he mentions that 'the demand equations for factors of production in the economy as a whole are derived from the assumption that entrepreneurs collectively attempt to maximize some aggregate profit; whereas the usually accepted assumption is that the individual firm attempts to maximize its own profit.' (p.93).

In his aim to dot the i's and cross the t's in (mathematical) macroeconomics he suggested the aggregates to have to satisfy two criteria. The first one looks like what we called consistency in the introduction of this paper. He expressed it as follows (p.94): 'For example we have for the firm in microeconomics,

$$(5)^{11)} \qquad F_\alpha(x_{1\alpha}, \ldots, x_{m\alpha}; n_{1\alpha}, \ldots, n_{r\alpha}; z_{1\alpha}, \ldots, z_{s\alpha}) = 0,$$

$$\alpha = 1, 2, \ldots, A.$$

This relation states that the αth firm produces the m commodities $\{x_{i\alpha}\}$ through the input of the services of r kinds of labor $\{n_{i\alpha}\}$ and of s kinds of capital $\{z_{i\alpha}\}$. We now demand that there exist a function, in macroeconomics,

$$(6)^{11)} \qquad F(X, N, Z) = 0$$

which states that the entire community of firms produces the aggregate X through the input of the services of [aggregate] labor N and [aggregate] capital Z.' As far as we know, this was the first time that a requirement of consistency in aggregation was stated in an explicit and mathematically precise form. Walras cannot be given that honour because he only considered sums as aggregates and took the existence of his functions F for granted, irrespective of the form of his functions f; see subsection 2.3. Note that Klein specified his macro function in advance after which he had no more freedom to choose the mathematical form of his aggregates. Klein's problem in macroeconomics was how to find mathematical expressions for the aggregates X, N and Z such that not only the _technological_ macro relation (6) is fulfilled but that, in addition, a second criterion is satisfied, viz. that of _representativity_, or better, _analogy_. This means here that the marginal productivity equations for perfect competition hold in the aggregate:

$$(7) \qquad \frac{\partial X}{\partial N} = \frac{W}{P}$$

and

$$(8) \qquad \frac{\partial X}{\partial Z} = \frac{Q}{P},$$

where W, the wage aggregate, depends on the wages w_j ($j = 1, \ldots, r$) of the different types j of labour and where P and Q are output price and capital service price aggregates, respectively, depending on the prices p_i ($i = 1, \ldots, m$) of commodities i and prices q_t of the different types of capital services t (= 1, ..., s), respectively. For reasons of simplicity Klein assumed in his example that perfect competition prevails at the micro level. This means:

$$(9) \qquad \frac{\partial x_{i\alpha}}{\partial n_{j\alpha}} = \frac{w_j}{p_i}$$

and

$$(10) \qquad \frac{\partial x_{i\alpha}}{\partial z_{t\alpha}} = \frac{q_t}{p_i}$$

for $\alpha = 1, \ldots, A$, $i = 1, \ldots, m$, $j = 1, \ldots, r$ and $t = 1, \ldots, s$. This in itself is not sufficient for the choice of (7) and (8). Where Klein himself justifies this choice by the fact that his macro model is simple and manageable, we presume that, in addition, at the same time he attempted to reconcile the generally adopted practice of considering the behaviour of groups of individual decision units as similar to the behaviour of the individuals themselves, with mathematical rigour. In spite of his own criticism quoted above, he, too, was convinced, at that time, of the usefulness of this strong kind of representativity as a tool of economic analysis. Furthermore, he was of the opinion that linking the macro relation F explicitly with the micro production functions F_α was the only method to aggregate technological circumstances without spoiling them with other features, in particular those rooting in the behaviour of the economic units; moreover, his relation F was, in his opinion most suited for analysing consequences of technological change. So the micro models consisting of the relations (5), (9) and (10) and the macro model (6), (7) and (8) are completely analogous. In other words, the micro model(s) as well as the macro model are given; this was not new in macroeconomic analysis at that time (we shall discuss this further in section 5). The new element of Klein's article was the requirement of consistency of aggregation. The consequence of this is that, then, all degrees of freedom are exhausted which means that the mathematical form of the aggregates X, N and Z as functions of the $\{x_{i\alpha}\}$, $\{n_{j\alpha}\}$ and $\{z_{t\alpha}\}$, respectively, completely depends on the form of the given micro and macro models[12)] and, therefore, as a rule, will not be of a well-known type such as a sum or an unweighted arithmetic average. In the case of Cobb-Douglas micro and macro production functions, for instance, the aggregates are geometric averages.

3.2 The reactions were immediate. In the same Econometrica volume of 1946 there were articles by Pu and May and a reaction by Klein; a year later a second article by May appeared and in 1948 Nataf's famous study was published[13)]; they will be referred to by capital letters as indicated in footnote 13. Several points were touched upon. First, the mathematical shape of the aggregates as being mostly highly unusual (Pu). Second, the reasonability of imposing the macro relations a priori (Pu, May). Third, the possibility of alternatives; they stemmed from questions as: which kinds of relations do we aggregate and to what extent (Pu, May)? Fourth, the conditions for consistent aggregation (Nataf).

In C (pp.299-300) Pu considers Klein's Cobb-Douglas aggregates as constructions that 'certainly have no connection whatsoever with the economic variables which we are actually interested in, the total volume of employment and the total quantity of capital' and he qualifies them as 'monsters that are completely void of any economic significance.' We believe that Klein (D, pp. 310-311) made a good point in remarking that there is nothing 'sacred' about a sum and that it is not the first task of scientific theorists to make things familiar to the layman; very properly he states: 'Any macroeconomic theory which will enable us to make people happier through an analysis of the interrelationships between aggregates of income, employment, output, etc., is a good theory regardless of the specific form of the aggregates.'

The second point, that of imposing the macro function a priori, is certainly something that can be considered as a typical trait of economic scientists. There is among them a widespread belief that economic complexes behave in the same way as do the individual parts that constitute the complex in question. We will discuss this opinion in more detail in section 5 when discussing representativity. Pu and May were unambiguously against it. Both are of the opinion that a macro theory should be the result of looking for relations between (well-known) aggregates of features of micro elements on the basis of a theory of the behaviour of these elements. In other words, given the micro functions and aggregates we try to find the macro relation. May (D, p.59) gives as an example that Boyle's law in physics on the relation between volume (V) and pressure (P) of a gaseous mass of a given temperature, PV = constant, is a macro theory that is not in the least similar to the (micro) laws of behaviour of the gaseous particles. He adds: 'In any case, since the economy is hardly less complicated than a gas, it seems rash to insist in advance on the exact character of the aggregate implications of micromodels.' Klein, however, had to impose macro relations a priori because, apparently, he was highly attached to his "purely technological" macro production function (6) as a part of the macro model; we saw this already above. In order to complete the macro model, he had to impose further relations on his aggregates (D, p.305). Moreover, he was very doubtful about the possibility of deriving a relatively simple macro theory relating aggregates of the types supplied by statistical offices, given the micro theory (D, p.311). So it seemed wise to keep matters in his own hand by postulating the macro model in the hope that the implied aggregates become such that they can reasonably well be approximated by published ones.

3.3 The third point deals with alternatives to the problem of aggregation rather than with criticisms on Klein's procedure itself. Pu (C, pp.300–301) argues that Klein's apparent insistence on aggregates that are independent of the distribution of the micro quantities over the individuals is too strong because the micro quantities are, according to the theory, distributed in a particular way, other distributions being not relevant. This means that only the variables of some subset of the whole domain of explanatory variables have to be aggregated which weakens the requirement of global consistency to that of local consistency. As an example[14)] he discusses firms α (= 1, ..., A) with production functions $x_\alpha = f_\alpha(n_\alpha, z_\alpha)$, where the notation is taken from Klein (A, see above). As aggregates he simply takes $N = \Sigma_\alpha n_\alpha$, $Z = \Sigma_\alpha z_\alpha$ and $X = \Sigma_\alpha x_\alpha$. The pattern of distribution of the n_α and the z_α is determined by the marginal-productivity equations

$$(11)\qquad \frac{\partial x_\alpha}{\partial n_\alpha} = \frac{\partial x_\beta}{\partial n_\beta}, \qquad \frac{\partial x_\alpha}{\partial z_\alpha} = \frac{\partial x_\beta}{\partial z_\beta}$$

for $\alpha, \beta = 1, \ldots, A$. The micro production functions together with the definitions of N and Z and the relations (11) form 3A independent equations in 3A + 2 unknowns. Hence all x_α, n_α and z_α can be solved in terms of N and Z. Putting the solutions for x_α in $X = \Sigma_\alpha x_\alpha = \Sigma_\alpha f_\alpha(n_\alpha, z_\alpha)$ leads to an aggregate relation

$$(12)\qquad X = F(N, Z)$$

which in its optimum has the same (macro) marginal productivities as the micro relations have in their optima. It can not be denied that (12) is a production function in the sense that it relates macro output to macro inputs, given the technological and behavioural as well as possible other characteristics that prevail in the economy in question. Klein does not react on Pu's suggestion leading to (12). He insists on the importance of analyzing technological change which is, in his opinion, only possible by using his aggregate production function[15]. Theil (1954, p.13), however, generalizes Pu's idea (for linear relations) in introducing his "auxiliary equations" which are (in the notation used above) simply equations expressing the n_α and the z_α in the aggregates N and Z. The solution of n_α and z_α in N and Z as derived from, a.o., (11) form an example of a system of auxiliary equations, but, according to Theil, such a system does not necessarily have an economic meaning and hence Theil does not further elaborate Pu's idea. Green in his much citated Aggregation in Economic Analysis (1964) works out the idea (only citing May, however) in his chapter 6 entitled "Degrees of Freedom Restricted: Optimal Conditions of Exchange and Production" and he discusses the matter in the subsequent chapter; see also Van Daal and Merkies (1984, ch.2)

Another alternative to Klein's approach is first reducing the micro model to a set of relations such that each endogenous variable is expressed in the exogenous ones and, subsequently, aggregating these reduced form equations choosing the form of the aggregate a priori (see the second point above). May as well as Pu advocate this and we met this approach already in Cournot's Recherches (see also footnote 4); note that we have then again a case of global consistency. In Klein's example we then have to aggregate the following supply and demand equations that result from optimizing behaviour:

$$(13)\qquad x_{1\alpha} = x_{1\alpha}(p_{1\alpha}, \ldots, p_{m\alpha}; w_{1\alpha}, \ldots, w_{r\alpha}; q_{1\alpha}, \ldots, q_{s\alpha}),$$

$$(14)\qquad n_{j\alpha} = n_{j\alpha}(p_{1\alpha}, \ldots, p_{m\alpha}; w_{1\alpha}, \ldots, w_{r\alpha}; q_{1\alpha}, \ldots, q_{s\alpha}),$$

$$(15) \qquad z_{t\alpha} = z_{t\alpha}(p_{1\alpha}, \ldots, p_{m\alpha}; w_{1\alpha}, \ldots, w_{r\alpha}; q_{1\alpha}, \ldots, q_{s\alpha})$$

for $i = 1, \ldots, m$, $j = 1, \ldots, r$ and $t = 1, \ldots, s$ over $\alpha = 1, \ldots, A$. Klein chooses to combine all $x_{i\alpha}$ for $i = 1, \ldots, m$ into only one aggregate X of output and similarly for the $n_{j\alpha}$ and the $z_{t\alpha}$, but that is not necessary, of course.

May (E, p.58) gives an example of this procedure by studying the macro consequences of technological change. He finds that a technological change in the two sectors of his micro model such that output increases in both industries with the same percentage λ, turns out to result in an increase of output in the aggregate one-sector model with more than λ per cent. This shows once more that analogy reasoning à la Klein has its dangers. Furthermore, it may be possible that some parameters in the macro model (however aggregated from the micro model) are exlusively corresponding to micro parameters that express technological features. In such a case the analysis of the consequences of technological change is straightforward. Hence, in our opinion Klein's anxiety in this point is somewhat too extreme.

It is striking that Klein, when it comes to the (empirical) point, in his famous <u>Economic Fluctuations in the United States, 1921-1941</u> (1950, pp.13-14) aggregates in the way described just above which means that he aggregates relations that are the result of optimization processes performed by households and firms, e.g. consumption and investment functions. It may be that this change of attitude can be justified by recalling the well-known adage "different models for different purposes" (here models for theory versus models for practice). Anyway, we are denied empirical illustration of his ideas set out in A and D. On the other hand, Klein (1950, pp.58-80) has provided us with the Klein I model, which, apart from being a toy for every econometrician, is a nice example of explicit global aggregation of micro consumption, investment and wage functions.

The fourth point of the debate came somewhat later on the scene (1948). It deals with the technical question on the possibilities of consistent aggregation. Nataf (F) discovered that for globally consistent aggregation it is necessary and sufficient that all functions (the micro, macro and aggregation functions) are additively separable. This is the subject of the next section. Conditions for local consistency cannot be given in general because such conditions depend on how the sub-domain D' of D is defined.

3.4 We end this section with some remarks. The Econometrica debate on aggregation, in spite of its importance, seems only known to a few specialists. The scholar texts and the textbooks on the history of economic science do not refer to it at all with only one noteworthy exception as far as we know; see Blaug (1978, pp.491-494). Although the debate remains absent in most textbooks on economics and econometrics, they usually deal with the problem of aggregation itself in more or less detail. The attention it receives goes from only a few lines to a separate chapter; see e.g., chapter 20 in Allen's Mathematical Economics, chapter 4 of Theil (1975), chapter 3 of Barnett (1981) and chapter 3 of Pearce (1964). Monographs on aggregation are scarce. The first one that appeared is by Theil (1954); it is confined to linear aggregation in the sense that the aggregates are sums and that the relations to be aggregated are linear. Green's Aggregation in Economic Analysis (1964) is much more general; it is a somewhat esoteric but, nevertheless, frequently cited book. There are even quite a lot of researchers that apparently are of the opinion that citing Green (1964) gives them an excuse for their failure of not solving themselves their own aggregation problems properly. Other monographs on aggregation are Pokropp (1972) and the one recently written by the present authors (1984).

4. GLOBAL CONSISTENCY: NATAF'S THEOREM

4.1 Though coming last into the discussion, the consistency problem is in fact the "question préalable" in the debate on aggregation. This matter has to preceed all other questions as it concerns the mere possibility of consistent aggregation; here lies a striking analogy with the history of the attempts to prove the existence of equilibrium states in general equilibrium analysis (see Weintraub 1985, ch 6). It must be acknowledged that Klein, indeed, made the first step. He remarked that his aggregates X, N and Z as functions of the $\{x_{i\alpha}\}$, $\{n_{j\alpha}\}$ and $\{z_{t\alpha}\}$, respectively, are not independent of each other because all these micro variables have to satisfy the micro production functions. Requiring, furthermore, the existence of an aggregate production function $F(X, N, Z) = 0$ means a rank condition on the matrix whose columns are the gradients of X, N and Z with respect to a set of independent micro variables; it does not matter which set, see, e.g., Burkill and Burkill (1970, pp.230 ff.) or any other advanced textbook on mathematical analysis. From this rank condition Klein derives a system of differential equations (A, p.99) that the aggregates X, N and Z have to satisfy, given the micro relations. His Cobb-Douglas aggregates indeed satisfy this system, but that does not contribute to making more transparent that system.

It was Nataf who provided us with this transparency in solving Klein's system of partial differential equations; his results are reported on page 243 of F. It turns out that Klein's micro production functions have to be of the form

$$\theta_\alpha(x_{1\alpha}, \ldots, x_{m\alpha}) = \chi_\alpha\{H_\alpha(n_{1\alpha}, \ldots, n_{r\alpha}) + I_\alpha(z_{1\alpha}, \ldots, z_{s\alpha})\} \tag{13}$$

for all $\alpha = 1, \ldots, A$, where θ_α, χ_α, H_α en I_α are unspecified functions of m, one, r and s variables, respectively. Aggregation, now, is simple. We define the aggregate X by

$$(14) \qquad X = \sum_{\alpha=1}^{A} \chi_\alpha^{-1}(\theta_\alpha),$$

where we assume the χ_α to be invertible and omit from now on the micro arguments of the functions. Furthermore, we define

$$(15) \qquad N = \sum_{\alpha=1}^{A} H_\alpha, \qquad Z = \sum_{\alpha=1}^{A} I_\alpha.$$

From (13), (14) and (15) one simply derives the macro relation

$$(16) \qquad X = N + Z.$$

Nataf's solution of the consistency problem clearly demonstrates the two elements of this aggregation problem. The first one is an aggregation over goods and factors within each firm's production function: for each α the $\{x_{i\alpha}\}$ are aggregated into θ_α, whereas the $\{n_{i\alpha}\}$ and the $\{z_{i\alpha}\}$ boil down into H_α and Z_α, respectively. The second element is the aggregation over individuals resulting in (16), the subject of this paper; the θ_α, N_α and Z_α are now considered as single goods and factors. The remainder of this section is devoted to the latter kind of aggregation.

4.2 We start with reformulating the problem for micro functions with an arbitrary number M of variables that each apart have to be aggregated over the individual decision units. Note that it is completely irrelevant whether the functions involved are production functions, demand functions, supply functions or whatever. In the notation of (1) and (2) of section 1, we have J micro relations f_j, one for each individual, with arguments x_{jm}, where $m = 1, \ldots, M$ and M denotes the number of explanatory variables. We now ask ourselves whether there exist aggregation formulae g_m that aggregate the x_{jm} over j into the aggregate x_m, hence

$$(17) \qquad x_m = g_m(x_{1m}, \ldots, x_{Jm}),$$

for all $m = 1, \ldots, M$ as well as an aggregation rule G aggregating the micro dependent variables into the aggregate y, in other words

$$(18) \qquad y = G(y_1, \ldots, y_J),$$

such that there exists a <u>macro function</u> F with

$$(19) \qquad y = F(x_1, \ldots, x_M),$$

or, putting all things into one relation,

$$(20) \qquad F\{g_1(x_{11}, \ldots, x_{J1}), \ldots, g_M(x_{1M}, \ldots, x_{JM})\} =$$

$$= G\{(f_1(x_{11}, \ldots, x_{1M}), \ldots, f_J(x_{J1}, \ldots, x_{JM})\} =$$

$$= H(x_{11}, \ldots, x_{jm}, \ldots, x_{JM}) = y.$$

The function H of all JM micro variables is called the "<u>atomistic macro function</u>." Relation (20) can be illustrated by means of the following scheme:

$$
(21) \qquad
\begin{array}{ccccccccc}
x_{11}, & \ldots, & x_{1m}, & \ldots, & x_{1M} & \overset{f_1}{\rightarrow} & y_1 \\
\cdot & & \cdot & & \cdot & & \cdot \\
\cdot & & \cdot & & \cdot & & \cdot \\
\cdot & & \cdot & & \cdot & & \cdot \\
x_{j1}, & \ldots, & x_{jm}, & \ldots, & x_{jM} & \overset{f_j}{\rightarrow} & y_j \\
\cdot & & \cdot & & \cdot & & \cdot \\
\cdot & & \cdot & & \cdot & & \cdot \\
\cdot & & \cdot & & \cdot & & \cdot \\
x_{J1}, & \ldots, & x_{Jm}, & \ldots, & x_{JM} & \overset{f_J}{\rightarrow} & y_J \\
\downarrow g_1 & & \downarrow g_m & & \downarrow g_M & & \downarrow G \\
x_1, & \ldots, & x_m, & \ldots, & x_M & \overset{F}{\rightarrow} & y \; ;
\end{array}
$$

see also Pokropp (1972, p.31) and Van Daal and Merkies (1984, ch.1).

It is immediately clear that if we put plusses (+) between all the micro variables and between all the macro variables x_m and y_j of scheme (21) and equality signs instead of arrows, we have a very simple example of consistent aggregation. Likewise, consistent aggregation is possible if we replace in this example all variables by transformations of them, i.e. if we have micro functions that are <u>additively separable</u>, i.e.

$$(22) \qquad y_j = k_j\{\phi_{j1}(x_{j1}) + \ldots + \phi_{jM}(x_{jM})\}$$

where the k_j are invertable functions of only one variable, and if the aggregation formulae look like

$$(23) \qquad x_m = h_m\{\phi_{1m}(x_{1m}) + \ldots + \phi_{Jm}(x_{Jm})\}$$

$(m = 1, \ldots, M)$ and

(24) $$y = N\{k_1^{-1}(y_1) + \dots + k_J^{-1}(y_J)\}.$$

Scheme (21) then takes the form:

(25) $$\begin{array}{ccccc} \phi_{11}(x_{11}) + \dots + \phi_{1M}(x_{1M}) & = & k_1^{-1}(y_1) \\ + \qquad\qquad\quad + & & + \\ \vdots \qquad\qquad\quad \vdots & & \vdots \\ + \qquad\qquad\quad + & & + \\ \phi_{J1}(x_{J1}) + \dots + \phi_{JM}(x_{JM}) & = & k_J^{-1}(y_J) \\ \| \qquad\qquad\quad \| & & \| \\ h_1^{-1}(x_1) + \dots + h_M^{-1}(x_M) & = & N^{-1}(y). \end{array}$$

In the latter scheme all micro, macro and aggregation functions are additively separable. It can be proved that this is not only sufficient but also necessary for consistency; we call this Nataf's theorem. Nataf proved this already for Klein's case $M = 2$. It is not very practical to use Nataf's technique for arbitrary values of M, because that would mean the analysis of the consequences of requiring that a $JM \times (M+1)$ -matrix of $M + 1$ gradient vectors has rank M.[16] Therefore, another strategy of proof of the necessity of the scheme (25) has to be adopted. A short outline of this follows now; see also Van Daal and Merkies (1981 and 1984, ch.1).

Our proof, as others', leans heavily on two separation lemmas that go back to an article of 1945 in Janpanese by M. Sono (see Sono (1961)) and to Leontief (1947). The first lemma states that a function f which maps a vector $(z_1, \dots, z_N)' \in \mathbb{R}^N$ into the real line, is additively separable if and only if for all $i, j = 1, \dots, N$ the ratios $(\partial f/\partial x_i)/(\partial f/\partial x_j)$ depend only on x_i and x_j. The second lemma deals with what we call partial weak separability of a function. The function f is said to be partially weakly separable with respect to a subset S of its variables, say (for notational convenience), the first K (< N), if there are functions ϕ and ψ such that $f(z_1, \dots, z_N)$ can be written as $\phi\{\psi(z_1, \dots, z_K), z_{K+1}, \dots, z_N\}$ for all $z_1, \dots, z_N$ from the domain of f.[17] The second lemma states that a function f is partially weakly separable with respect to S if and only if for all i and j from S the ratios $(\partial f/\partial x_i)/(\partial f/\partial x_j)$ depend only on variables from S. New proofs for these two lemmas, that are much simpler than the existing ones, are provided by the present authors (1984, ch.1, Appendix B). The following two corollaries of these two lemmas appear to be useful: (i) if f is partially weakly separable with respect to each pair (i,j) for $i, j = 1, \dots, N$ then f is additively separable, (ii) if f is partially weakly separable with respect to S_1 and S_2, where $S_1 \cap S_2 \neq \emptyset$, then f is partially weakly separable with respect to $S_1 \cap S_2$, as well as $S_1 \cup S_2$. These truths are easily verified; see also Gorman (1968) and Blackorby, Primont and Russel

(1978).

Now we can prove the necessity of (25). First, the additive separability of the atomistic macro function H of (20) can be proved as follows. Given that (20) holds good, H is apparently partially weakly separable with respect to each "row" and each "column" of variables x_{jm} of the scheme (21) and hence, by the second corollary, it is, in particular, partially weakly separable with respect to each collection of variables x_{jm} of one or two rows and one column of such variables, or of one or two such columns and one row of the scheme. Consequently, H is partially weakly separable with respect to each set $(x_{jm}, x_{j'm'})$ of variables because such a set can always be found as the intersection of two collections as mentioned above[18]. Because of the first corollary, H is additively separable. Second, the additive separability of the other functions can now easily be proved.

4.3 The proof above requires differentiability, with non-zero first derivatives, of all the functions involved (to be precise, the functions have to be twice continuously differentiable because we needed that for the proofs of the lemmas). This implies strict monotonicity of all these functions; see Mak (1986) and the litterature mentioned there for more general conditions for separability. Green (1964, pp. 36 ff.) was the first who proved Nataf's theorem for arbitrary M. He assumed that all functions in question be thrice differentiable[19] and started with proving the additive separability of the functions F and G of our scheme (20) from which the additive separability of the f_j and the g_m functions follows. In fact, he left undone the proof of the atomistic macro function's additive separability. Green's proof contains some elements that can also be found in Nataf's. It is likewise very much complicated. Gorman (1968) dropped the assumption of differentiability of the functions involved but imposed monotonicity ("increasingness" in the case of production functions) and continuity instead. With these assumptions he succeeded in proving Nataf's theorem. Pokropp showed that the continuity of the micro functions to be aggregated is also inessential, provided that they are "separable" in a generalized sense; see Pokropp (1972, p.33 ff). Somermeyer and Van Daal (1978) presented an alternative proof in terms of finite differences, without assuming continuity either.

5. REPRESENTATIVITY

5.1 A macro relation is said to display representativity with respect to some aspect if that relation can <u>for that aspect</u> be considered as expressing some (fictive) representative agent's behaviour as being similar to the behavior (real or assumed) of the individual agents in question. See, for instance, (7) and (8) above. The strongest kind of representativity we met already in discussing Klein's <u>Econometrica</u>

articles A and D; namely complete analogy between the micro and the macro model. Klein may know himself backed up by one of the most influential authors since the thirties in the person of J.R. Hicks. The latter author writes in both editions of his Value and Capital (1946 (1939), XX.1): 'The transition [from micro to macro level] is made by using the simple principle (...) that the behaviour of a group of individuals, or group of firms, obeys the same laws as the behaviour of a single unit.' Until now, many economists are apparently convinced of the truth of this quotation. Note that representativity and consistency are separate notions that need not to coincide. One can, of course, investigate whether there is representativity (analogy) given consistency, i.e. within the framework of scheme (20). In that case analogy means that F and all the functions f_j in (20) have to be of the same type. Alternatively, however, representativity can also be presupposed without explicit requirement of consistency. The latter approach prevails in macroeconomics. At best one takes for granted (or one hopes) that not bothering about consistency is rather harmless; the following cases are examples of this approach.

In growth models analogy reasoning is the order of the day. In contradistinction to the problem of aggregating over sectors, aggregation over individuals is hardly seen as a problem. Mostly aggregate profit functions, in the form of $F(K, L) - WL - QK$ for the one-sector case, are posited and maximized over the whole economy. Famous examples are Solow's seminal article (1957) on technical change and factor productivity, Allen's textbook (1967) on macroeconomics and Burmeister and Dobell's, technically advanced, book (1970) on economic growth. Also in empirical econometric model building analogy reasoning is frequently used. To stay near home, we only mention two Dutch models that until recently were in use for practical purposes, namely Driehuis' quarterly model (1972) and Den Hartog and Tjan's vintage model (1980). The lists can be extended ad libitum with similar examples.

Furthermore, we encounter analogy reasonings in demand analysis (for consumption goods as well as for production factors). Sometimes a microeconomic demand system is simply confronted with macro data without any justification at all (e.g. Phlips (1983, p.101)). Sometimes the existence of a representative consumer, whose consumption and income are just the average amounts over the whole economy, is taken for granted. If in the latter case an estimated demand system does not pass all the tests on the integrability conditions, the representative consumer is considered not to "behave rationally"; it happens that, then, even all his real brothers and sisters of flesh and blood are likewise accused of the same irrationality; see, e.g., Christensen, Jorgenson and Lau (1975, p.381)[20]. In this respect we must also mention the recently developed methods of non-parametric demand analysis: aggregate consumption data are subjected to revealed-preference tests as if these data are related to one single person; see e.g. Afriat (1967, 1973, 1977), Maks (1980, pp.29-32) and Varian (1982, p.965).

5.2 The question that arises is: how came economists to reasoning by analogy? One of the first authors who was very definite on the subject of analogy is Jevons, as we have seen above where we discussed his trading body. He defends his analogy approach in economic analysis by means of an analogy reasoning of a higher order, so to speak. To make this clear, we have to refer to Jevons' Principles of Science (first edition 1874, second edition 1877). In chapter XVI of that book, entitled "The method of means" he develops the notion of a "fictitious mean". Such a mean is an average that, though not always really existing, 'is of the highest scientific importance, as enabling us to conceive in a single result a multitude of details.' As an example he mentions the point of gravitation of a gravitating body. The behaviour of the aggregate consisting of all the "particles" of the body, i.e. the behaviour of the whole body, 'will be exactly represented by the behaviour of this heavy point.' Two or more bodies, whether connected or separate, may also be conceived as having one centre of gravity. So the whole entity of all points of the bodies acts as if it were only one point (with respect to gravitating behaviour, of course). This example and others were for Jevons sufficient to construct by analogy the fiction of his trading body. Nevertheless, as said above, it remains an analogy reasoning on analogy reasoning: what can be said of physical sciences can likewise be said of the science of economics according to Jevons. Parenthetically, we remark that in science there are just as well examples where Jevons' fictitious mean does not exist. We already mentioned Boyle's law to stress the risks of analogy reasoning. Moreover, as Boyle's law and its generalizations work in practice, we see that Jevons' method of the fictitious mean is unnecessarily restrictive for deriving macro laws.

Consequently, the quotation from Hicks in the beginning of this section is not appearing out of the blue; Hicks, however, takes his arguments from economics itself. In section II.5 of Value and Capital he makes plausible that 'Market demand has almost exactly the same properties as individual demand.' He argues that for each individual the effect of a price change can be decomposed into a substitution effect and an income effect. Substitution effects (as far as regarding changes of the quantity of a good in response to its own price) are either all negative or all positive; hence the group effect, being the sum of the individual effects, is likewise negative or positive. The individual income effects, however, are not quite reliable in direction according to theory; the group income effect will usually be negligible, Hicks remarks, if the group as a whole spends a small proportion of its total income upon the commodity in question. That is all. It seems that there is some contradiction between Hicks' expositions regarding the similarity between individual and group demand behaviour as stated in Value and Capital and his proof in A Revision of Demand Theory (1956, pp.55-57), of the possibility of "irrational" community behaviour resulting from individual rationality: one can always construct

examples of individually rational decisions (i.e., optimal points on budget hyperplanes) such that after a change of prices and/or incomes the new individually optimal points are such that the two aggregate decision points (before and after the change of prices and/or incomes) do not pass the revealed preference tests in spite of the fact that all individual components of these aggregate points do pass the tests. This is, of course, simply a consequence of Arrow's "Possibility Theorem" stating the impossibility, in general, of rational group behaviour as an aggregation result of rational individual behaviour (Arrow (1963, pp.59,97)). It can be argued, however, that the above inconsistency may disappear if the determinants of the individuals' preference schemes do not differ too much, i.e. if we mitigate Arrow's "condition of the unrestricted domain"[21].
Because of the symmetry between producer theory and consumer theory, it is not amazing that Hicks states that a group of firms, operating in the same market, 'must obey the same laws as the single firm' (section VIII.3). Here there is a complication viz. that firms may leave or enter the industry in question. Hicks, however, argues that it is implausible that this complicates matters such that the direction of the total change, due to a change in (relative) prices, is affected. The difference between consumers and producers with respect to entry or leaving is, in fact, only a gradual one; it takes time for new consumers to enter a market, because before entering they have to be born, but new firms can be founded overnight.

Another attempt to justify analogy reasoning stems from Dresch (1938). He proves that, under conditions of perfect competition, aggregates of micro inputs and outputs of the form of Divisia indices indeed obey relations that are analogues of the micro (marginal) equilibrium conditions for profit maximization. He does not prove, however, that there exists an acceptable macro production function that links these Divisia aggregates without violating the macro equilibrium conditions. In our opinion, this is in general impossible.

A successful attempt to derive micro and macro models that are analogous to each other and at the same time consistent (in aggregation) with each other is Muellbauer's (1975, 1976) work on representative consumer models. It appears that a representative consumer only exists if the individual consumers' preference schemes are very similar, namely such that they result in demand equations that express all budget shares, as linear functions of a Box-Cox transformation η of income[22] plus a term which averages out to zero over all individuals, the intercepts and coefficients of the linear functions being functions of prices that can differ per commodity but not per individual. The representative individual's demand system, then expresses community's budget shares as the same linear functions as above of "representative income" which is some generalized harmonic mean of the individual incomes the form of which depends on η. Hence Muellbauer's representative consumer

is by no means a "mean" person. See also Pearce (1964, ch.3), however, for an alternative approach; he introduces an "average" consumer as the representative at the cost of assuming constancy of the income distribution over time.
Muellbauer's results, however, indicate clearly that the requirement of representativity, in addition to consistency, is unnecessarily restrictive as it is possible to derive macro models that are the result of consistent aggregation of micro models over individuals and that have Muellbauers representative consumer models as special cases; see on this point the present authors (1984, section 7.3).

The restrictiveness implied by the similarity of Muellbauer's households' preference schemes can be avoided if we assume that all households' preferences are homothetic (without being identical). Under this assumption and if the income distribution is fixed, total market demand can also be considered as generated by some homothetic preference scheme. This result, originally due to Eisenberg (1961), with Antonelli (1886) and Gorman (1953) as predecessors, initiated in important line of rather abstract research; see also Shafer and Sonnenschein (1982). Anyway, representativity of the market demand functions can only be achieved at the cost of seriously restrictive assumptions on micro behaviour.

5.3 Altogether, it remains a matter of taste, or of sheer necessity, whether one adopts analogy reasoning. In this respect we have to bear in mind that the behaviour of an individual decision unit such as a household or a firm is itself already the result of a considerable process of aggregation; going from that unit's behaviour to group behaviour is perhaps a relatively small step in the whole way of aggregation of the smallest "cells" of the individuals to the whole group. May's example of Boyle's law is, therefore, not quite fair; he compared two extremes, namely the behaviour of the highly aggregated whole gaseous mass as expressed in terms of the aggregates temperature, volume and tension on the one hand and, on the other hand, the gas molecules with their impulses, a case of extreme disaggregation, which is much simpler than most economic examples as he himself admits. Moreover, Boyle's law and its refinements, the laws of Gay-Lussac and Van der Waals, are discovered in first instance as macro laws in an empirical way. Similarly, macroeconomic relationships can be (and have been) found and verified (or falsified) in an empirical way without too much appeal on micro behaviour in the first instance. We already mentioned Tinbergen's models (1936, 1939) as good examples of such procedures: simple economic reasoning (such as, e.g., income and consumption are positively related) combined with carefully selected units of measurements of variables mostly running in relative changes. In this respect it is interesting to ascertain that Klein apparently left his ideas on strict representativity to become more and more eclectic over time; see Lindbeck (1985, p.45).

5.4 This brings us to a less extreme notion of representativity viz. the similarity between micro and macro theories with respect to some aspects only. A well-known example is the case of absence of money illusion in consumption behaviour: the individuals are supposed not to react in real terms on a simultaneous change in the same proportion of prices, wages and monetary variables such as income and wealth. This means that an individual's consumption function must be such that real consumption is a zero-homogeneous function of prices, wages, income and wealth. For that reason one sometimes imposes the same zero-homogeneity on the macro consumption function. A well-known example is Branson and Klevorick's (1969) macro consumption function. Using U.S. quarterly series from 1955-I to 1965-IV they estimated a log-linear macro consumption function which significantly turned out not to be zero-homogeneous in the sense mentioned above. This was for them reason enough to conclude that consumers suffer from money illusion. Apart from the question about the fundamental possibility anyway of deriving micro conclusions from macro results, one can in this case easily show that the macro consumption function's deviation of zero-homogeneity could be an "aggregation bias" arising from aggregating micro consumption functions each showing complete absence of money illusion but having parameter sets that can differ per individual; see, e.g., Van Daal (1980).

5.5 We end this section by discussing whether we do need representativity in some form. If it is the case that a macro model can be considered as the result of consistent aggregation of micro models over individuals then, in our opinion, the additional requirement of some kind of representativity is superfluous. It can even be argued that, then, requiring representativity is harmful in the sense that a false impression is raised about the individuals' behaviour from macro data only. We saw this already above where we discussed Christensen, Jorgenson and Lau's (1975, pp.381) claim that their results 'make possible an unambiguous rejection of the theory of demand.'

If the macro model is not the result of consistent aggregation of the micro models, then representativity can be imposed if one beliefs to have reason for that; it happened more then once that, then, even useful models were found. It is obvious, however, that the device of representativity for building macro models is not without danger if followed blindly. Being aware of what one is doing and a good intuition are prerequisites for avoiding mistakes.

6. CONCLUDING REMARKS

Macro theories can be derived as such, or alternatively, they may be founded upon analogy reasoning or upon explicit aggregation from microeconomics. In the development of economic doctrines there has not always been a clear distinction between the notions of consistency and representativity in discussing a macro model's connection with micro theory. We have shown how these concepts have been mixed in the older literature and how the requirements for consistent aggregation have arisen from the debate in Econometrica. The concept of representativity still needs further to be clarified; a recent attempt in this respect is Schlicht (1985). In particular its apparent popularity should be further analysed. In our opinion it is completely superfluous if a macro model is the result of consistent aggregation of individuals' micro models. Although the micro models' realism could be questioned, the introduction of representativity, does not help to make its aggregate, i.e. the macro model, more realistic. Good examples of a consistently aggregated macro model, which does not reflect some representative's behaviour, are Somermeyer and Bannink's (1972, chapters 5 and 7) macro consumption model and Jorgenson, Lau and Stoker's (1982) market demand system.

The reverse may be different. If a model is directly stated at the macro level and one is interested in general statements only, e.g. in welfare theory, it may be appropriate to introduce a representative (or, at least, "typical") consumer and/or producer (perhaps to the extreme analogy). In such a case, however, there remains a need for showing that this "representative's behaviour" is consistent with actual individual behaviour. To charge simply the "representative" with some particular behaviour, only helps in the sense that it shows that there is at least one possibility, viz. that where there is only one individual, with the indicated behaviour.

ACKNOWLEDGMENTS

The authors thank W. Eichhorn (Karlsruhe), J. Muysken (Maastricht), J. van Yzeren (Eindhoven) and two referees for useful comments.

NOTES

1) In (1) and (2) the functions all have the same number M of arguments; this, however, is not essential from a mathematical point of view as, e.g. all x_{j1} and x_{j2} can be combined into one single aggregate. From an economic point of view, however, it does make much difference because, then, aggregation over different goods is also in order. Furthermore, for the sake of convenience, we take the y_j and y as scalars.
2) If possible we indicate the places in the older literature by means of sections, lessons or something like that, in order to facilitate checking in translations or reprints.
3) And, therefore, in his opinion, differentiable in p. Cournot needed this for

discussing profit maximization. Note that at that time it was not yet generally known that continuity is not sufficient for differentiability; Weierstrasz' and Riemann's examples of everywhere continuous but nowhere differentiable functions still had to be devised. See, e.g. Cajori (1980, p. 425) who mentions 1861 as the year in which it was Weierstrasz who found for the first time such a function.

4) This contradistinction is just one of the points in the Econometrica debate to be discussed in the next section.

5) Both use the term "caprices" in discussing individual behaviour.

6) Jevons was one of the first who spoke of "economics" instead of "political economy" (preface second edition).

7) Both Walras and Jevons considered marginal utility of a good to depend only on the quantity of that good. Edgeworth (1881), Fisher (1892) and Pareto (albeit not already in his Cours; see, however, Manuel, p.593) assumed more general utility functions.

8) In fact, Pareto was not the first precursor of Arrow and Debreu in this respect. Fisher, in his doctor's thesis (1925 (1892), Part I, Chapters IV, V, VI), developed similar models. Pareto refers to Fisher's dissertation in note 59 of his Cours.

9) The problem of aggregation over goods was already widely investigated at that time. We mention the work on price and quantity indices by Fisher (1912, 1922), Frisch (1936), Konüs (1924), Leontief (1936), Bowley (1928), Divisia (1925/26, 1928); as professor Tinbergen pointed out to us this problem was highly topical at the meetings of the Econometric Society in the thirties, in contrast to aggregation over individuals.

10) We estimated the equation $\ln(P/C) = a + g \ln(L/C)$ on Cobb and Douglas' data and found OLS estimates $\hat{g} = .749$ and $\hat{a} = .0145$ (= ln 1.0147); for $\hat{g}$ we found a t-value of 18.1. It is evident that Cobb (who was responsible for the concerning part of the article) did the same, but he does not say anything about it.

11) The numbering is ours; Klein's numbers are (1) and (2), respectively.

12) Of course, the mathematically rather arbitrary choice of the aggregates and their arguments contributes to the above mentioned absense of freedom.

13) The precise titles of all the articles in the debate are:

A. L.R. Klein, "Macroeconomics and the Theory of Rational Behavior," Econometrica, 15 (1946), pp.93-108;

B. K. May, "The Aggregation Problem for a One-Industry Model," Econometrica, 15 (1946), pp.285-298;

C. S.S. Pu, "A Note on Macroeconomics," Econometrica, 15 (1946), pp.299-302;

D. L.R. Klein, "Remarks on the Theory of Aggregation," Econometrica, 15 (1946), pp.303-313;

E. K. May, "Technological Change and Aggregation," Econometrica, 16 (1947), pp.51-63;

F. A. Nataf, "Sur la Possibilité de Construction de Certains Macromodèles," Econometrica, 17 (1948), pp.232-244.

14) May, in fact, gives an example in the same line in which two kinds of labour are combined into only one aggregate.

15) May (D, p.63) argues that there are no purely technological (micro) production functions at the firm level. He mentions time schedules, worker morale and management habits as non-technological elements. We can add to this that, moreover, these element can differ per firm. If in such a case the micro production functions are of the Cobb-Douglas type with common degree of homogeneity and the aggregates are taken as unweighted geometrical averages, then the macro production function can be distorted in the sense that, in fact, its degree of homogeneity differs from that of the micro relations; see, e.g., Van Daal (1980).

16) In Nataf's case the rank requirement resulted in the vanishing of a number of 3 × 3 determinants with many zeroes. From this Klein's (A, p.99) system of differential equations could easily be derived.

17) In our monograph (1984) we use the term "quasi-separability" (p.28) but now we are of the opinion that the present term is more in line with related terms in the literature.

18) This can be illustrated as follows (—— = collection 1, - - - = collection 2):

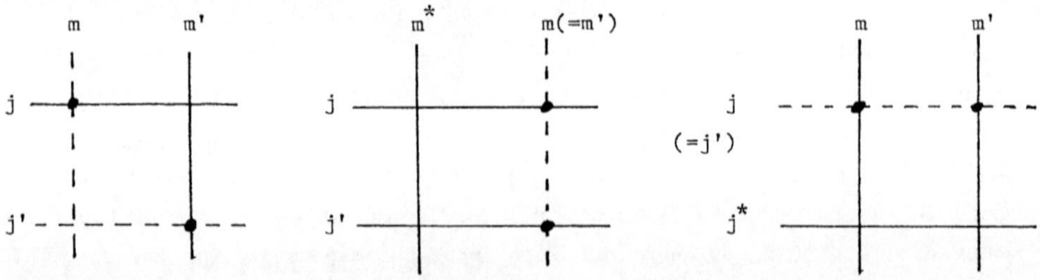

19) Some details of Green's proof, however, can be changed such that only the existence of continuous non-zero first derivatives is sufficient for his proof; this makes the conditions just as severe as Nataf had to impose.

20) In January 1983 at the occasion of a conference in Rotterdam (Econometric Institute, Erasmus University) Professor Jorgenson admitted, during a very successful lecture on the econometrics of general economic equilibrium, that this assertion was too bold. A better conclusion, he said, would have been that there exists no representative consumer (as mentioned above).

21) An example of such a mitigation is the case of "single-peaked" preferences for all individuals: for each individual the alternatives can be ordered in preference according to some one-dimensional criterion in a unimodal way (Arrow (1963, pp.75-77)); see Van Daal and Merkies (1984, p.117) for a suggestion to generalize this concept.

22) If y denotes income the Box-Cox transformation $\eta(y)$ is defined as $(y^a - 1)/a$ if

a $\neq$ 0 and as log y if a = 0; a is a parameter to be chosen or to be estimated.

REFERENCES

S.N. Afriat, "The Construction of a Utility Function from Expenditure Data," International Economic Review, 8 (1967), pp.67-77.

S.N. Afriat, "On a System of Inequalities in Demand Analysis: An Extension of the Classical Method," International Economic Review, 14 (1973), pp.460-472.

S.N. Afriat, The Price Index, Cambridge (U.K.): Cambridge University Press, 1977.

R.G.D. Allen, Mathematical Economics, second edition, London: MacMillan, 1964.

R.G.D. Allen, Macro-Economic Theory, London: MacMillan, 1967.

G.B. Antonelli, Sulla Teoria Matematica della Economia Politica, Pisa: Nella Tipografia del Folchetto, 1886.

K.J. Arrow, Social Choice and Individual Values, second edition, New York: Wiley, 1963.

W.A. Barnett, Consumer Demand and Labor Supply, Amsterdam: North-Holland, 1981.

C. Blackorby, D. Primont and R.R. Russell, Duality, Separability and Functional Structure, Amsterdam: North-Holland Publishing Company, 1978.

M. Blaug, Economic Theory in Retrospect, third edition, Cambridge (U.K.): Cambridge University Press, 1978.

A.L. Bowley, "Notes on Index Numbers," Economic Journal, 38 (1928), pp. 216-237.

W.H. Branson and A.K. Klevorick, "Money Illusion and the Aggregate Consumption Function," American Economic Review, 59 (1969), pp.832-849.

J.C. Burkill and H. Burkill, A Second Course in Mathematical Analysis, Cambridge (U.K.): Cambridge University Press, 1970.

E. Burmeister and A.R. Dobell, Mathematical Theories of Economic Growth, New York: The MacMillan Company, 1970.

F. Cajori, A History of Mathematics, third edition, New York: Chelsea, 1980.

L.R. Christensen, D.W. Jorgenson and L.J. Lau, "Transcendental Logarithmic Utility Functions," American Economic Review, 65 (1975), pp.367-383.

C.W. Cobb and P.H. Douglas, "A Theory of Production," The American Economic Review, 18 (1928), Supplement, pp.139-165.

A. Cournot, Recherches sur les Principes Mathématiques de la Théorie des Richesses, Paris: Hachette, 1838 (reprint, Paris: Marcel Rivière & Cie, 1938).

J. van Daal, "Money Illusion and Aggregation Bias," De Economist, 128 (1980), pp.86-93.

J. van Daal and A.H.Q.M. Merkies, "A Simple Proof of Nataf's Theorem on Consistent Aggregation," Economics Letters, 7 (1981), pp.441-446.

J. van Daal and A.H.Q.M. Merkies, Aggregation in Economic Research, Dordrecht/Boston: Reidel, 1984.

J. van Daal, R.E.D. Henderiks and A.C.F. Vorst, "On Walras' Model of General Economic Equilibrium," Zeitschrift für Nationalökonomie, 45 (1985), pp.219-244.

J. van Daal and D.A. Walker, "The problem of Aggregation in Walrasian General Equilibrium Theory," Report 8701/A, Econometric Institute, Erasmus University Rotterdam, 1987.

F. Divisia, "L'indice Monêtaire et la Theorie de la Monnaie," Revue d'Economie Politique, 29 (1925), pp.842-861, 980-1008, 1121-1151 and 30 (1926), pp. 49-81.

F. Divisia, Economie Rationelle, Paris: Dunod, 1928.

F.W. Dresch, "Index Numbers and the General Economic Equilibrium," Bulletin of the American Mathematical Society, 44 (1938), pp.134-141.

W. Driehuis, Fluctuations and Growth in a Near Full Employment Economy; A Quarterly Econometric Analysis of the Netherlands, Rotterdam: Rotterdam University Press, 1972.

F.Y. Edgeworth, Mathematical Psychics, London: C. Kegan Paul & Co., 1881.

B. Eisenberg, "Aggregation of Utility Functions," Management Science, 7 (1961), pp. 337-350

I. Fisher, Mathematical Investigation in the Theory of Value and Prices (1892), reprint, New Haven: Yale University Press, 1925.

I. Fisher, The Purchasing Power of Money, New York: MacMillan, 1912.

I. Fisher, The Making of Index Numbers, Boston: Houghton Miffin, 1922.

R. Frisch, "Annual Survey of General Economic Theory: The Problem of Index Numbers," Econometrica, 4 (1936), pp.1-39.
W.M. Gorman, "Community Preference Fields," Econometrica, 21 (1953), pp. 63-80.
W.M. Gorman, "The Structure of Utility Functions," Review of Economic Studies, 35 (1968), pp.367-390.
H.A.J. Green, Aggregation in Economic Analysis, Princeton: Princeton University Press, 1964.
H. den Hartog and H.S. Tjan, "A Clay-Clay Vintage Model Approach for Sectors of Industry in the Netherlands," De Economist, 128 (1980), pp.129-188.
J.R. Hicks, Value and Capital, second edition, Oxford: Clarendon Press, 1946.
J.R. Hicks, A Revision of Demand Theory, Oxford: Clarendon Press, 1956.
W. Hildenbrand, "On the 'Law of Demand'," Econometrica, 51 (1983), pp.997-1020.
W. Jaffé, ed., Correspondence of Léon Walras and Related Papers, 3 vols., Amsterdam: North-Holland, 1965.
W.S. Jevons, Principles of Science, second edition (1877), reprint, London: MacMillan, 1913.
W.S. Jevons, The Theory of Political Economy, second edition (1879), reprinted in Pelican Books, Harmondsworth: Penguin Books Ltd, 1970.
D.W. Jorgenson, L.J. Lau and T.M. Stoker, "The Transcendental Logarithmic Model of Consumer Behaviour," Advances in Economics, 1(1982), pp. 97-238.
L.R. Klein, "Macroeconomics and the Theory of Rational Behavior," Econometrica, 15 (1946), pp.93-108.
L.R. Klein, "Remarks on the Theory of Aggregation," Econometrica, 15 (1946), pp.303-313.
L.R. Klein, Economic Fluctuations in the United States, 1921-1941, New York: Wiley, 1950.
A.A. Konüs, "The Problem of the True Index of the Cost of Living," translated from Russian (1924), Econometrica, 7 (1939), pp.10-29.
W.W. Leontief, "Composite Commodities and the Problem of Index Numbers," Econometrica, 4 (1936), pp.39-59.
W.W. Leontief, "Introduction to a Theory of the Internal Structure of Functional Relationships," Econometrica, 15 (1947), pp.361-373.
A. Lindbeck, "The Price in Economics Science in Memory of Alfred Nobel," Journal of Economic Literature, 23 (1985), pp.37-56.
K.T. Mak, "On Separability: Functional Structure, " Journal of Economic Theory, 40 (1986), pp. 150-282.
J.A.H. Maks, Empirical Preference Orderings and Applied Demand Analysis, doctor's thesis, University of Groningen, 1980.
A. Marshall, Principles of Economics, 8th edition, London: MacMillan, 1920.
K. May, "The Aggregation Problem for a One-Industry Model," Econometrica, 15 (1946), pp.285-298.
K. May, "Technological Change and Aggregation," Econometrica, 16 (1947), pp.51-63.
J. Muellbauer, "Aggregation, Income Distribution and Consumer Demand," Review of Economic Studies, 62 (1975), pp.525-543.
J. Muellbauer, "Community Preferences and the Representative Consumer," Econometrica, 44 (1976), pp.979-1000.
A. Nataf, "Sur la Possibilité de Construction de Certains Macromodèles," Econometrica, 17 (1948), pp.232-244.
V. Pareto, Cours d'Economie Politique, 2 vols., Lausanne: F. Rouge, 1896-7.
V. Pareto, Manuel d'Economie Politique, Paris: Pichon et Durand-Auzias, 1909.
V. Pareto, "Economie Mathématique," dans Encyclopédie des sciences mathématiques, Paris: Gauthier-Villars, 1911, t.I, vol. IV, fasc. IV, pp.591-640.
I.F. Pearce, A Contribution to Demand Analysis, Oxford: Clarendon Press, 1964.
L. Philips, Applied Consumption Analysis, second edition, Amsterdam: North-Holland, 1983.
A.C. Pigou, The Economics of Welfare, fourth edition, Lonon: MacMillan, 1938.
F. Pokropp, Aggregation von Produktionsfunctionen, Berlin: Springer, 1972.
S.S. Pu, "A Note on Macroeconomics," Econometrica 15 (1946), pp.299-302.
F. Quesnay, Tableau Economique, reprint of the third edition (1759), edited by M. Kuczynski, Berlin: Akademie-Verlag, 1965.
D. Ricardo, The Principles of Political Economy and Taxation, 3rd edition (1821), reprinted in Everyman's Library, London: Dent, 1973.

E. Roll, A History of Economic Thought, New and revised edition, London: Faber and Faber, 1973.

E. Schlicht, Isolation and aggregation in Economics, Berlin/Heidelberg: Springer, 1985.

J.A. Schumpeter, History of Economic Analysis, London: George Allen & Unwin Ltd, 1954.

W. Shafer and H. Sonnenschein, "Market Demand and Excess Demand Functions," chapter 14 of K.J. Arrow and M.D. Intriligator (eds.), Handbook of Mathematical Economics, Amsterdam: North-Holland Publishing Company, 1982.

R.M. Solow, "Technical Progress and Productivity Change," Review of Economics and Statistics, 39 (1957), pp.312-320.

W.H. Somermeyer and R. Bannink, A Consumption-Savings Model and its Applications, Amsterdam: North-Holland, 1972.

W.H. Somermeyer and J. van Daal, "Consistent Aggregation - An Alternative Derivation and a Generalization of Nataf's Theorem," Zeitschrift für Nationalökonomie, 38 (1978), pp. 287-303.

M. Sono, "The Effect of Price Changes on the Demand and Supply of Separable Goods," International Economic Review, 2 (1961), pp. 239-271.

H. Theil, Linear Aggregation of Economic Relations, Amsterdam: North-Holland, 1954.

H. Theil, Theory and Measurement of Consumer Demand, Volume I, Amsterdam: North-Holland, 1975.

R. Theocharis, Early Developments in Mathematical Economics, second edition, London and Basinkstoke: MacMillan, 1983.

J. Tinbergen, "An Economic Policy for 1936," translated from Dutch (1936) in Selected Papers, edited by L.H. Klaassen, L.M. Koyck and H.J. Witteveen, Amsterdam: North-Holland, 1959, pp.37-84.

J. Tinbergen, Statistical Testing of Business-Cycle Theory, vol. I and II, Geneva: League of Nations, 1939.

H.R. Varian, "The Nonparametric Approach to Demand Analysis," Econometrica, 50 (1982), pp.945-974.

L. Walras, Eléments d'Economie Politique Pure ou Théorie de la Richesse Sociale, édition définitive, Paris: Pichon et Durand-Auzias, 1926. (First edition 1874-1877, second edition 1889, third edition 1896, fourth edition 1900, English translation (by W. Jaffé) 1954).

E.R. Weintraub, General Equilibrium Analysis: Studies in Appraisal, Cambridge: Cambridge University Press, 1985.

Aggregation and Efficiency[1]

Rolf Färe
Southern Illinois University
Carbondale, IL 62901, USA

C.A. Knox Lovell
University of North Carolina
Chapel Hill, NC 27514, USA

1. Introduction

Economic theory is typically developed in dimensions higher than those in which it is tested empirically. For example, producer theory is by now well developed for the general m-output, n-input case, although until recently empirical applications of the theory were restricted largely to the scalar output, two-input case. Even now, limitations imposed by data availability and computing resources restrict the empirical application of the theory to "small" numbers of inputs and outputs. The question naturally arises, therefore, whether one's stories about economic phenomena of interest are sensitive to the degree of aggregation of the underlying data.

The question of sensitivity of results to aggregation of variables ultimately involves the separability of certain functions describing the production process. Examples abound. Berndt and Christensen (1973) tested for the existence of a consistent capital aggregate, depending on structures and equipment subaggregates, by testing for the separability of a production function for U.S. manufacturing. They also tested for the existence of a consistent labor aggregate, depending on blue-collar and white-collar labor subaggregates, by testing for the separability in a different input partition of a production function for U.S. manufacturing (Berndt and Christensen (1974)). Their testing procedure has drawn commentary from Blackorby, Primont and Russell (1977), Denny and Fuss (1977), and Woodland (1978). In these and a great many other studies the focus has been on the role played by functional separability in determining whether variable aggregation would distort various indexes of the structure of technology.

[1]This problem was originally brought to our attention by Douglas Blair, to whom we are grateful for not providing the solution as well. We also wish to acknowledge the helpful comments of Charles Blackorby, Bill Schworm, Wolfgang Eichhorn and three insightful readers.

Measurement in Economics
ed. by W. Eichhorn

The purpose of this paper is to carry this line of inquiry one step further. We seek to examine the relationship between variable aggregation and the measurement of efficiency of production, efficiency being measured relative to a technology whose structure may be distorted by the aggregation process. Specifically, we inquire whether various indexes of productive efficiency are invariant with respect to input aggregation. The indexes we employ are a radial Debreu(1951)-Farrell (1957) index of technical efficiency, an index of cost efficiency, and the implied index of allocative efficiency. In the scalar output case it turns out that all three efficiency indexes satisfy this invariance property if the production function is homothetically separable. Much more useful from an empirical standpoint is the result that, for any number of outputs, all three efficiency indexes satisfy this invariance property if the cost function satisfies a certain separability property. There are of course other justifications for variable aggregation. For example, the Hicks aggregation theorem asserts in our context that if the prices of a group of inputs move proportionately, then that group can be treated as a single input. See Diewert (1980) for details, as well as for an "approximate" version of the Hicks aggregation theorem. In this paper we ignore price proportionality as a justification for aggregation, and focus our attention on functional separability as a justification.

2. The Technology

In order to investigate the effect of aggregation on the measurement of productive efficiency, it is first necessary to provide a characterization of the underlying production technology. Following Shephard (1970), the technology by which inputs $x = (x_1,...,x_n) \in R^n_+$ are transformed into outputs $u = (u_1,...,u_m) \in R^m_+$ is described in terms of the input correspondence

$$u \rightarrow L(u) \subseteq R^n_+, \ L(u) = \{x \in R^n_+: \text{at least output } u \text{ is produced}\}. \quad [2.1]$$

The input correspondence is assumed to satisfy axioms sufficiently strong for Proposition 1 to apply.

In the event that the production unit produces only a single output $u \in R_+$, the technology can be characterized by the scalar-valued production function $\phi: R^n_+ \rightarrow R_+$, which is defined in terms of the input correspondence as

$$\phi(x) = \max \{u: x \in L(u)\}. \quad [2.2]$$

The input correspondence also can be used to introduce the input distance function that provides an alternative characterization of technology. The input distance function is defined as

$$D_I(u,x) = \max\{\lambda: x/\lambda \in L(u)\}, \qquad [2.3]$$

and $D_I(u,x) \geq 1 \iff x \in L(u)$. The subscript "I" on the distance function and on the efficiency indexes F, O and A below indicates that they are input-based, rather than output-based, functions. The input distance function in turn can be used to obtain yet another characterization of technology, the cost function. In fact, the input distance function is dual to the cost function

$$Q(u,p) = \min\{px: D_I(u,x) \geq 1\}, \qquad [2.4]$$

where $p \in R^n_{++}$ is a vector of input prices.

The ability of the production unit to conserve on input usage in the production of its chosen outputs is measured by an index of technical efficiency. One such index, a radial measure of technical efficiency proposed by Debreu (1951) and Farrell (1957), is given by

$$F_I(u,x) = \min\{\lambda: \lambda x \in L(u)\} = D_I(u,x)^{-1}. \qquad [2.5]$$

This particular index of technical efficiency is selected for three reasons. First and foremost, it is a radial index that can be expressed as the reciprocal of the input distance function. This relationship plays an important role in establishing the link between separability and aggregation. Second, as Russell (1985, 1987) has noted, this index satisfies certain desirable properties under a range of axioms on the structure of technology. Third, this index is the most widely used index of technical efficiency in empirical work.

The ability of the production unit to conserve on cost in the production of its chosen outputs at given input prices is measured by a cost efficiency index of the general form

$$O_I(u,x,p) = Q(u,p)/px. \qquad [2.6]$$

Cost inefficiency not attributable to technical inefficiency must be due to allocative inefficiency, or to the selection of an input mix that is inappropriate for the outputs the production unit is producing and the input prices it faces. Consequently, from [2.5] and [2.6], the corresponding allocative efficiency index is given by

$$A_I(u,x,p) = O_I(u,x,p)/F_I(u,x). \qquad [2.7]$$

3. Aggregation and Efficiency

At issue is whether aggregation of inputs has any effect on the three indexes of input efficiency. To that end the input quantity vector and the input price vector are partitioned into $k < n$ mutually exclusive and exhaustive subvectors so that

$$x = (x^1,\ldots,x^r,\ldots,x^k),$$

$$p = (p^1,\ldots,p^r,\ldots,p^k).$$

From these subvectors economic input quantity indexes $X^r(x^r)$, $r = 1,\ldots,k$, and economic input price indexes $P^r(p^r)$, $r = 1,\ldots,k$, are constructed to be homogeneous of degree +1 and to satisfy $px = \sum_{r=1}^{k} P^r(p^r)X^r(x^r)$, where p^r and and x^r are conjugate duals (Blackorby, Primont and Russell (1978; 28)). Note that the non-existence result of Eichhorn (1978, Theorem 7.3.2, p. 144) and Eichhorn and Voeller (1976, Theorem 4.3.3, p. 74), which applies to axiomatic indexes defined for all nonnegative prices and quantities, does not apply to these economic indexes defined for conjugate dual prices and quantities. Hence there do exist such quantity and price indexes. The distinction between economic indexes and axiomatic (or mechanical, or statistical) indexes is eludicated by Blackorby (1983).

The following proposition contains the first two of three ingredients required to establish a relationship between input aggregation and efficiency measurement. These ingredients are (i) the duality relationships among the production, cost and distance functions, (ii) the restrictions imposed on these relationships by homothetic separability of the production function, and (iii) the inverse relationship between the distance function and the index of technical efficiency.

Proposition 1 (Blackorby, Primont and Russell (1978, Theorem 4.4, p. 123)): Let $m = 1$ and assume that ϕ is continuous, monotonic and quasi-concave. Then the following structures are equivalent:

(i) ϕ is homothetically separable, i.e.,

$$\phi(x) = \hat{\phi}(\phi^1(x^1),\ldots,\phi^r(x^r),\ldots,\phi^k(x^k)),$$

where $\hat{\phi}$ is monotonic and each ϕ^r is homothetic;

(ii) Q is separable, i.e.,

$$Q(u,p) = \hat{Q}(u,Q^1(p^1),\ldots,Q^r(p^r),\ldots,Q^k(p^k)),$$

where $\hat{Q}$ is monotonic and each Q^r is homogeneous of degree +1;

(iii) D_i is separable, i.e.,

$$D_I(u,x) = \hat{D}_I(u,D_I^1(x^1),\ldots,D_I^r(x^r),\ldots,D_I^k(x^k)),$$

where $\hat{D}_I$ is monotonic and each D_I^r is homogeneous of degree +1.

Proposition 1 establishes the equivalence of homothetic separability of ϕ, separability of Q in u and input price indexes, and separability of D_I in u and input quantity indexes. A proof is available in Blackorby, Primont and Russell (1978). The missing ingredient, the inverse relationship between F_I and D_I stated in equation [2.5], is used in the next proposition. This is the main result, for it establishes the relationship between input aggregation and the measurement of technical efficiency.

<u>Proposition 2</u>: Let m = 1, and let ϕ be continuous, monotonic and quasi-concave. Then there exist input quantity indexes $F_I^r(x^r)$, r = 1,...,k, with $F_I(u,x) = \hat{F}_I(u,F_I^1(x^1),\ldots,F_I^r(x^r),\ldots,F_I^k(x^k))$ if, and only if, $\phi(x) = \hat{\phi}(\phi^1(x^1),\ldots,\phi^r(x^r),\ldots,\phi^k(x^k))$ where $\hat{\phi}$ is monotonic, each ϕ^r is homogeneous of degree +1, and it is possible to choose $F_I^r(x^r) = \phi^r(x^r)$.

Proof: (<=)
$$\begin{aligned} F_I(u,x) &= \min\{\lambda: \phi(\lambda x) \geq u\} \\ &= \min\{\lambda: \hat{\phi}(\phi^1(\lambda x^1),\ldots,\phi^r(\lambda x^r),\ldots,\phi^k(\lambda x^k)) \geq u\} \\ &= \min\{\lambda: \hat{\phi}(\lambda\phi^1(x^1),\ldots,\lambda\phi^r(x^r),\ldots,\lambda\phi^k(x^k)) \geq u\} \\ &= \hat{F}_I(u,F_I^1(x^1),\ldots,F_I^r(x^r),\ldots,F_I^k(x^k)) \text{ with } F_I^r(x^r) = \phi^r(x^r). \end{aligned}$$

(=>)
$$\begin{aligned} \phi(\lambda x) &= \max\{u: (F_I(u,\lambda x))^{-1} \geq 1\} \\ &= \max\{u: (F_I(u,F_I^1(\lambda x^1),\ldots,F_I^r(\lambda x^r),\ldots,F_I^k(\lambda x^k)))^{-1} \geq 1\} \\ &= \max\{u: (\hat{F}_I(u,\lambda F_I^1(x^1),\ldots,\lambda F_I^r(x^r),\ldots,\lambda F_I^k(x^k)))^{-1} \geq 1\} \\ &= \hat{\phi}(\lambda\phi_I^1(x^1),\ldots,\lambda\phi_I^r(x^r),\ldots,\lambda\phi_I^k(x^k)) \end{aligned}$$

$$= \hat{\phi}(\phi_I^1(\lambda x^1),\ldots,\phi_I^r(\lambda x^r),\ldots,\phi_I^k(\lambda x^k)).$$

QED

Proposition 2 asserts that the radial index of technical efficiency has the same value using n inputs or using $k < n$ input quantity indexes homogeneous of degree +1 if, and only if, the production function is homothetically separable in these quantity indexes. (Recall that the homothetic quantity indexes ϕ^r in the homothetically separable production function can always be normalized to be homogeneous of degree +1 as demonstrated in Blackorby, Primont and Russell (1978, Lemma 3.3, p. 86)).

Proposition 2 uses only primal information on inputs and output. However the cost of using only primal information is the restriction to a single output. It is possible to relax that restriction, at the cost of requiring both primal and dual information. The reciprocal relationship between $F_I(u,x)$ and $D_I(u,x)$ extends to multiple outputs, as does the duality relationship between $D_I(u,x)$ and $Q(u,p)$, as demonstrated by Shephard (1970). Since the proof of Proposition 1 does not involve output, parts (ii) and (iii) of Proposition 1 also extend to multiple outputs. Combining these results, it follows directly that, for any number of outputs, $F_I(u,x) = \hat{F}_I(u,F_I^1(x^1),\ldots,F_I^r(x^r),\ldots,F_I^k(x^k))$ if, and only if, $Q(u,p) = \hat{Q}(u,Q^1(p^1),\ldots,Q^r(p^r),\ldots,Q^k(p^k))$. That is, for $m \geq 1$ the radial index of technical efficiency has the same value using n inputs or using $k < n$ input quantity indexes if, and only if, the cost function is separable in outputs and the corresponding input price indexes.

Finally, it is easy to show that these invariance results also apply to the measures of cost efficiency and allocative efficiency. If $px = \sum_{r=1}^{k} Q^r(p^r)F^r(x^r)$, where $Q^r(p^r) = P^r(p^r)$ and $F^r(x^r) = X^r(x^r)$, $r = 1,\ldots,k$, with both $Q^r(p^r)$ and $F^r(x^r)$ homogeneous of degree +1, then

$$O_I(u,x,p) = \frac{\hat{Q}(u,Q^1(p^1),\ldots,Q^r(p^r),\ldots,Q^k(p^k))}{\sum_{r=1}^{k} Q^r(p^r)F^r(x^r)}$$

$$= \hat{O}_I(u,F^1(x^1),\ldots,F^r(x^r),\ldots,F^k(x^k),Q^1(p^1),\ldots,Q^r(p^r),\ldots,Q^k(p^k))$$

and

$$A_I(u,x,p) = \frac{\hat{O}_I(u,F^1(x^1),\ldots,F^r(x^r),\ldots,F^k(x^k),Q^1(p^1),\ldots,Q^r(p^r),\ldots,Q^k(p^k))}{\hat{F}_I(u,F^1(x^1),\ldots,F^r(x^r),\ldots,F^k(x^k))}$$

$$= \hat{A}_I(u,F^1(x^1),\ldots,F^r(x^r),\ldots,F^k(x^k),Q^1(p^1),\ldots,Q^r(p^r),\ldots,Q^k(p^k)).$$

Consequently all three measures of productive efficiency are invariant with respect to input aggregation if, and only if, the cost function is separable in outputs and the corresponding input price aggregates.

3. Concluding Remarks

Separability of a cost function is equivalent to separability of the dual distance function. The distance function is the inverse of the radial Debreu-Farrell index of technical efficiency. A previously unnoticed, and potentially useful, consequence of these relationships is that technical, allocative and cost indexes of productive efficiency are invariant with respect to input aggregation if, and only if, the cost function is separable.

As long as technical efficiency is measured radially, this result extends symmetrically to the measurement of output efficiency. Thus it can be shown that technical, allocative and revenue indexes of productive efficiency are invariant with respect to output aggregation if, and only if, the revenue function is separable.

However it appears that these results may not go through when the technical efficiency index is nonradial, since these results utilize the reciprocal relationship between the (input or output) distance function and the (input or output) index of technical efficiency. This link is broken when the technical efficiency index is nonradial. Consequently these results may not apply to efficiency measurement based on the Russell measure of Färe and Lovell (1978) or the Russell-extended Farrell measure of Zieschang (1984). Nor, unfortunately, do they appear to apply to the hyperbolic graph efficiency measures proposed by Färe, Grosskopf and Lovell (1985) to treat inputs and outputs symmetrically.

This last conclusion suggests a promising complementary line of research. Given a certain technology, we find the radial Debreu-Farrell efficiency index, and perhaps only this efficiency index, to be invariant with respect to variable aggregation. Following a suggestion of Bol (1986), it may be worthwhile to reverse the direction of inquiry by starting with a certain efficiency index and seeking the technologies for which the index is invariant with respect to aggregation. This would provide a basis for comparison of radial and non-radial efficiency indexes by revealing the technologies for which each is invariant with respect to variable aggregation.

References

Berndt, E.R., and L.R. Christensen (1973), "The Translog Function and the Substitution of Equipment, Structures, and Labor in U.S. Manufacturing, 1929-1968," Journal of Econometrics 1:1 (March), 81-114.

Berndt, E.R., and L.R. Christensen (1974), "Testing For the Existence of a Consistent Aggregate Index of Labor Inputs," American Economic Review 64:3 (June), 391-404.

Blackorby, C. (1983), "Comments," in Price Level Measurement, ed. W. E. Diewert and C. Montmarquette. Ottawa: Statistics Canada.

Blackorby, C., D. Primont and R.R. Russell (1977), "On Testing Separability Restrictions With Flexible Functional Forms," Journal of Econometrics 5:2 (March), 195-209.

Blackorby, C., D. Primont and R.R. Russell (1978), Duality, Separability, and Functional Structure: Theory and Economic Applications. New York: North-Holland.

Bol, G. (1986), "On Technical Efficiency Measures: A Remark," Journal of Economic Theory 38:2 (April), 380-85.

Debreu, G. (1951), "The Coefficient of Resource Utilization," Econometrica 19:3 (July), 273-92.

Denny, M. and M. Fuss (1977), "The Use of Approximation Analysis to Test For Separability and the Existence of Consistent Aggregates," American Economic Review 67:3 (June), 404-18.

Diewert, W.E. (1980), "Aggregation Problems in the Measurement of Capital," in The Measurement of Capital, ed. D. Usher. Chicago: The University of Chicago Press for The National Bureau of Economic Research.

Eichhorn, W. (1978), Functional Equations in Economics. Reading, MA: Addison-Wesley Publishing Company.

Eichhorn, W., and J. Voeller (1976), Theory of the Price Index. Berlin, Heidelberg, New York: Springer-Verlag.

Färe, R., S. Grosskopf and C.A.K. Lovell (1985), The Measurement of Efficiency of Production. Boston: Kluwer-Nijhoff.

Färe, R., and C.A.K. Lovell (1978), "Measuring the Technical Efficiency of Production," Journal of Economic Theory 19:1 (October), 150-62.

Farrell, M.J. (1957), "The Measurement of Productive Efficiency," Journal of the Royal Statistical Society, Series A, General, 120, Part 3, 253-81.

Russell, R. R. (1985), "Measures of Technical Efficiency," Journal of Economic Theory 35:1 (February), 109-26.

Russell, R. R. (1987), "On the Axiomatic Approach to the Measurement of Technical Efficiency," this volume.

Shephard, R.W. (1970), Theory of Cost and Production Functions. Princeton:

Princeton University Press.

Woodland, A.D. (1978), "On Testing Weak Separability," Journal of Econometrics 8:3 (December), 383-98.

Zieschang, K. (1984), "An Extended Farrell Technical Efficiency Measure," Journal of Economic Theory 33:2 (August), 387-96.

Separability and the Existence of Aggregates

King-tim Mak
College of Business Administration
University of Illinois at Chicago
Chicago, Illinois 60680, U.S.A.

1. INTRODUCTION.

If a continuous real-valued function Φ in n variables $x_1,\ldots,x_n$ has the representation

(1.1) $\Phi(x_1,\ldots,x_n) = F(f(x_1,\ldots,x_k), x_{k+1},\ldots,x_n)$

where F and f are continuous real-valued functions, then the function Φ is said to be (continuously) *separable* in the subset of variables $x_1,\ldots,x_k$. The concept of separability is intimately tied with the concept of aggregation and indices: If Φ is a function which gives the interrelationship among n economic quantities $x_1,\ldots,x_n$, then a function f may serve as an aggregate for the quantities $x_1,\ldots,x_k$ when and only when (1.1) holds; moreover, f may qualify as a quantity index for $x_1,\ldots,x_k$ if it has certain desired properties such as monotonicity (see Eichhorn [4] for a methodological definition of economic indices).

As a contribution to the theory of aggregation and indices, this paper analyzes the conditions under which a continuous function is separable in a subset of variables. In doing so, it adds to our understanding of when aggregation is possible and when quantity indices may be constructed.

The above definition of separability does not require either the function F or f in (1.1) to be monotone. It therefore includes the familiar formulations of strict and nonstrict separability as special cases [Φ is said to be *strictly separable* (resp. *nonstrictly separable*) in $x_1,\ldots,x_k$ if (1.1) holds and F is strictly increasing (resp. nondecreasing) in f]. Removing the monotonicity of F in f is useful for economic modelling. For instance, it allows us to use calorie-count as a quantity index for food consumption even though beyond a certain range utility is likely to be decreasing rather than increasing in calorie intake. It is likewise useful for aggregating inputs into factors of production when too much inputs might lead to congestion and thus decrease in output. Later on we shall see that

Measurement in Economics
ed. by W. Eichhorn

sometimes only nonmonotone aggregates may be constructed. All in all, freeing the concept of separability from the restriction of monotonicity should make it an even more powerful tool for economic analysis.

The plan of the paper is as follows. Section 2 discusses how similarity among the conditional functions $\Phi(\cdot, x_{k+1}, \ldots, x_n)$ might lead to separability, and introduces a suitable concept of similarity. Section 3 analyzes the topological implication of this concept of similarity. The result obtained is then used in Section 4 to derive a necessary and sufficient condition for the existence of quantity indices; and in Section 5 a sufficient condition for the existence of aggregates is derived. Section 6 discusses in general the construction of aggregates.

The substance of this paper is a mathematical analysis of separability. It is hoped, however, that readers more interested in applications will find the ideas involved appealing and potentially useful for empirical work.

ASSUMPTION AND NOTATION. We assume $1 < k < n$ and write x for $(x_1, \ldots, x_k)$ and y for $(x_{k+1}, \ldots, x_n)$. Representation (1.1) then reads: $\Phi(x,y) = F(f(x),y)$.

The domain of the continuous function Φ is assumed to be the unit hypercube $[0,1]^n$. The domains X for x and Y for y are respectively the hypercubes $[0,1]^k$ and $[0,1]^{n-k}$. Other domains for x and y will serve just as well as long as they are compact connected subsets of Euclidean spaces.

2. SIMILARITY AND SEPARABILITY

In order for Φ to be separable in x as in (1.1), the conditional functions $\Phi(\cdot,y)$, all $y \in Y$, must be quite similar. At the very least, if x' and x'' were to have the same aggregate measure then $\Phi(x',y)$ and $\Phi(x'',y)$ must be the same for all y. In this section, we discuss how similarity among the conditional functions might lead to separability and introduce a concept of similarity suitable for establishing separability without monotonicity.

For a continuous function Φ on $X \times Y$, conditioned on $y \in Y$, the *conditional isoquant* of level μ is

$$Q(\mu|y) = \{x \in X | \Phi(x,y) = \mu\}$$

Since the continuous function Φ is not necessarily monotone, a conditional isoquant is a closed but in general not a connected subset of X. We shall call a closed connected set a *continuum*, and a maximal connected subset of a set a *component* of the set. Thus, a conditional isoquant in general is composed of components of disjoint continua which may very well have nonempty interiors.

Define a binary relation $\sim$ on X as follows: $x' \sim x''$ if and only if for all $y \in Y$ both x' and x'' belong to the same isoquant component of the conditional function $\Phi(\cdot,y)$. The relation $\sim$ is clearly symmetric, reflexive, and transitive. It is therefore an equivalence relation and partitions X into equivalence classes. Denote by $\mathcal{K}$ the space of equivalence classes: $\mathcal{K} = \{K_\alpha\}$. Call the equivalence classes K_α *isocomponents*. Since, conditioned on all y, elements of an isocomponent K_α always have the same Φ function values, if an aggregate is to be constructed, all the elements of an isocomponent should have the same aggregate measure.

Our idea for constructing aggregates and showing separability goes as follows. Each isocomponent is a subset of X. In the space $\mathcal{K}$, however, each isocomponent is a point. If the conditional functions $\Phi(\cdot,y)$ are similar enough, then with an appropriately constructed topology the isocomponents could be linearly ordered in a continuous manner so that the space $\mathcal{K}$ becomes an arc. If this were possible, then using the homeomorphism between the arc and the unit interval it would be possible to construct a continuous function f such that $f(x') = f(x'')$ only if x' and x'' belong to the same isocomponent. Once such an f is determined, it would be easy to construct a continuous F such that $\Phi(x,y) = F(f(x),y)$ and thereby establish the separability of Φ in x.

EXAMPLE AND ILLUSTRATION. The following discussion illustrates the ideas above. Suppose $x = (x_1,x_2) \in [0,1]^2$, $y \in [0,1]$, and

$$\Phi(x_1,x_2,y) = \begin{cases} -(x_1+x_2) + 4y & \text{if } (x_1+x_2) \le 2y, \\ 2(x_1+x_2) - 2y & \text{if } (x_1+x_2) \ge 2y. \end{cases}$$

It is easily verified that the conditional isoquants of $\Phi(\cdot,y)$, all $y \in Y$, are unions of two lines of the form

$$\{x|x_1+x_2 = a\} \cup \{x|x_1+x_2 = b\}.$$

Because of the similarity in shape and slope among the conditional isoquants, the isocomponents are precisely the lines $K_\alpha = \{x|x_1+x_2 = \alpha\}$, $0 \leq \alpha \leq 2$. These isocomponents as points in the space $\mathcal{K}$ clearly may be linearly ordered in a continuous manner as points on an arc.

Consider another example. Suppose now

$$\Phi(x_1,x_2,y) = x_1 + yx_2.$$

Here, the conditional functions $\Phi(\cdot,y)$ for different y are completely different linear functions. Their conditional isoquants are so dissimilar that for each x in X the isocomponent that contains it is the singleton $\{x\}$. Since the space $\mathcal{K}$ of isocomponents is X itself, it is impossible to order the isocomponents linearly into an (1-dimensional) arc and carry out our scheme for constructing an aggregate.

It is also instructive to review here the known necessary and sufficient conditions for strict and nonstrict separability in the context of isocomponents. (A good exposition of the theory of strict and nonstrict separability may be found in Blackorby *et al* [2].) We know from Debreu [3], Gorman [5] and others that Φ is strictly separable in x if and only if

<S> for all x', x'', $\Phi(x',y^*) \geq \Phi(x'',y^*)$ for some y^*

$\Rightarrow \Phi(x',y) \geq \Phi(x'',y)$ for all y.

And we know from Mak [8] that Φ is nonstrictly separable in x if and only if

<NS> for all x', x'', $\Phi(x',y^*) > \Phi(x'',y^*)$ for some y^*

$\Rightarrow \Phi(x',y) \geq \Phi(x'',y)$ for all y.

For the moment, assume Φ is monotone in x; then each conditional isoquant of $\Phi(\cdot,y)$ has only one component. In this case, the ordering relationships in <S> and <NS> immediately ensure that the isocomponents may indeed be linearly ordered. The case where the conditional isoquants have more than one component is more delicate. The reason why aggregates still exist in this case will be clarified by the analysis in subsequent sections. □

We now introduce a useful concept of similarity. The justification for this particular formulation of similarity is threefold: (i) it is a necessary condition for separability as Theorem (2.1) below will show; (ii) it ensures that the isocomponents are well behaved; and (iii) it captures our intuition that the shape of the isoquants of similar conditional functions, in so far as delineated by their boundaries, should not differ by much.

$\langle S^* \rangle$ If conditioned on some y^* there is a connected subset of the boundary of an isoquant component containing both x' and x'', then conditioned on every y, $\Phi(x',y) = \Phi(x'',y)$ and x', x'' belong to the same isoquant component.

(2.1) THEOREM. If Φ is separable in x, then the similarity condition $\langle S^* \rangle$ holds.

PROOF. Suppose conditioned on some y^* both x' and x'' belong to a connected subset S of the boundary of a component Q of a conditional isoquant of $\Phi(\cdot,y^*)$. Suppose Φ is separable in x and has the representation (1.1) with some continuous F and f. To establish the theorem, we only have to show that f is constant over the connected boundary subset S. Assume the contrary. For simplicity, assume $f(x') < f(x'')$. Since $\Phi(\cdot,y^*)$ is constant over the connected set S, $F(\cdot,y^*)$ is constant over the interval $[f(x'), f(x'')]$. Since S is connected, there exists a boundary point $x^\circ \in S$ with $f(x') < f(x^\circ) < f(x'')$. Now x° has a neighborhood N whose image $f(N)$ is contained in the interval $[f(x'), f(x'')]$. Hence, x° cannot a boundary point of the component Q since $\Phi(\cdot,y^*) \equiv F(f(\cdot),y^*)$ is constant over one of its neighborhoods; a contradiction. □

Next we show the similarity condition $\langle S^* \rangle$ ensures that the isocomponents are well behaved. As defined, each isocomponent K_α is the intersection of all the conditional isoquant components that contain it. Being an intersection of closed sets, each K_α is closed. In general, the isocomponents need not be connected even though the conditional isoquant components are. We have, however, the following.

(2.2) PROPOSITION. If Φ satisfies the similarity condition $<S^*>$, then every isocomponent is closed and connected.

In the remainder of this section, we sketch the technical proof of Proposition (2.2) with the help of a few topological concepts and lemmas.

DEFINITION [7, p.162]. A topological space $\mathcal{X}$ is *unicoherent* if it is connected and for all closed connected subsets A and B such that $\mathcal{X} = A \cup B$ the intersection $A \cap B$ is connected.

(2.3) LEMMA [1, p.134]. The unit hypercube $[0,1]^k$ is unicoherent.

(2.4) LEMMA. A closed subset S of a unicoherent space $\mathcal{X}$ is connected if and only if for every component G of $\mathcal{X}$-S the set $\mathcal{X}$-G is connected.

PROOF. The "necessity" part of the lemma is true for general topological spaces [7, p.140]. We use the property of unicoherence to prove the "sufficiency".

Suppose the closed subset S is not connected. We have to show that at least one component G of $\mathcal{X}$-S is such that $\mathcal{X}$-G is not connected. Let $\mathcal{G} = \{G_\nu\}$ be the family of components of $\mathcal{X}$-S. Let $\mathcal{G}^1$ be a minimal subfamily of $\mathcal{G}$ such that $S \cup \mathcal{G}^1 = S \cup \{G_\nu | G_\nu \in \mathcal{G}^1\}$ is connected. Such a minimal subfamily exists by Zorn's Lemma. Let $\mathcal{G}^2 = \mathcal{G} - \mathcal{G}^1$.

Since each component G_ν is open, so is $\cup\{G_\nu | G_\nu \in \mathcal{G}^2\}$. Therefore, $S \cup \mathcal{G}^1 = \mathcal{X} - \cup\{G_\nu | G_\nu \in \mathcal{G}^2\}$ is closed in addition to being connected. Consider arbitrary $G \in \mathcal{G}^1$. Clearly, $(\mathcal{X}-G) \cup (S \cup \mathcal{G}^1) = \mathcal{X}$. Thus, if the closed set $\mathcal{X}$-G were connected, then by the unicoherence of $\mathcal{X}$, the intersection $(\mathcal{X}-G) \cap (S \cup \mathcal{G}^1) = (S \cup \mathcal{G}^1) - G$ would also be connected. This contradiction to the minimality of $\mathcal{G}^1$ establishes that $\mathcal{X}$-G is not connected. □

(2.5) LEMMA. Suppose Φ is a continuous function on X × Y. Conditioned respectively on arbitrary $y^1, y^2 \in Y$, let Q_1 and Q_2 be any two conditional isoquant components with $Q_1 \cap Q_2 \neq \emptyset$, and let G_1 and G_2 be respectively arbitrary components of X-Q_1 and X-Q_2. If Φ satisfies the similarity condition $<S^*>$, then G_1 and G_2 are either disjoint or nested.

PROOF. If G_1 and G_2 are disjoint, there is nothing to prove. Therefore, assume $G_1 \cap G_2 \neq \emptyset$. Suppose G_1 and G_2 are not nested; i.e., $G_1 - G_2$ and $G_2 - G_1$ are nonempty. We shall show that then Φ does not satisfy $<S^*>$.

Since G_1 and G_2 are connected sets and they intersect, $\overline{G_1 \cup G_2}$ is closed and connected. Since Q_1 and Q_2 are both closed and connected, by the "necessity" part of Lemma (2.4), $X-G_1$ and $X-G_2$ are both connected. Their intersection is nonempty since both contain $Q_1 \cap Q_2$. Hence, $\overline{(X-G_1) \cup (X-G_2)}$ is also closed and connected. The union of the two closed and connected sets is clearly the hypercube X. Thus, since X is unicoherent according to Lemma (2.3), their intersection $\overline{G_1 \cup G_2} \cap \overline{(X-G_1) \cup (X-G_2)}$ $= \overline{(G_1-G_2) \cup (G_2-G_1)}$ is connected.

For i=1,2, the boundary $\partial(G_i)$ of the component G_i of $X-Q_i$ is a subset of the boundary $\partial(Q_i)$ of Q_i. And the boundaries of G_1-G_2 and G_2-G_1 are composed of subsets of $\partial(G_1)$ and $\partial(G_2)$. Because G_1-G_2 and G_2-G_1 are both nonempty and the closure of their union is connected, it can be shown that there exist x' and x'' such that

(i) $x' \in \partial(G_1) \cap \partial(G_2) \subset Q_1 \cap Q_2$,

(ii) $x'' \in \partial(G_1) \cap G_2$,

(iii) x' and x'' are both contained in a connected subset of $\partial(G_1) \subset \partial(Q_1)$.

If Φ satisfies $<S^*>$, then (iii) implies $\Phi(x',y) = \Phi(x'',y)$ for all y. In particular, $\Phi(x',y^2) = \Phi(x'',y^2)$. But this is impossible since by (i) $x' \in Q_2$ while by (ii) $x'' \in G_2 \subset X-Q_2$. □

PROOF OF PROPOSITION (2.2). Consider arbitrary isocomponent K_α. We have seen that K_α is closed; we now show that it is connected. Because of Lemma (2.4), it suffices to show that for every component G of $X-K_\alpha$ the set X-G is connected.

For each $y \in Y$, let Q_y be the conditional isoquant component of $\Phi(\cdot,y)$ that contains K_α. Then, $K_\alpha = \cap_y Q_y = X - \cup_y (X-Q_y)$, and each component G of $X-K_\alpha$ is the union of all those components of $X-Q_y$ that it contains. Fix an arbitrary component G of $X-K_\alpha$. Write G_y for a component of $X-Q_y$. Then, $G = \cup\{G_y | G_y \subset G\}$. Since all the Q_y's contain K_α, by Lemma (2.5), the G_y's are either disjoint or nested. Using this fact together with the compactness of X and the connectedness of G, it can be shown that for every closed set $D \subset G$ there exists a G_y such that $D \subset G_y \subset G$. This means every open set B containing X-G contains $X-G_y$ for some G_y.

If the closed set X-G is not connected, then it is the union of two disjoint closed sets M and N. Since the hypercube X is a Hausdorff space, there are open neighborhoods B_M and B_N of M and N that are disjoint. Then for some G_y, the set $X-G_y$ is contained in the open set $B_M \cup B_N$ and therefore cannot be connected. But since Q_y is closed and connected, by Lemma (2.4), $X-G_y$ is connected for all components G_y of $X-Q_y$. This contradiction establishes that X-G is indeed connected. □

3. TOPOLOGICAL IMPLICATIONS OF SIMILARITY.

In this section we show that if the similarity condition <S*> is satisfied then, with an appropriate topology defined on it, the space $\mathcal{K}$ of isocomponents is a tree. The next two sections will consider how such a tree may be reduced to become an arc for the purpose of constructing quantity indices and aggregates. We begin by illustrating how the tree structure of $\mathcal{K}$ comes about.

(3.1) EXAMPLE. Suppose Φ is a utility function whose utility level $\Phi(x,y)$ associated with the consumption $x = (x_1,x_2) \in [0,1]^2$ and $y \in [0,1]$ depends on the proximity of x to two preferred consumption mixes $x^* = (1/4,1/2)$ and $x^{**} = (3/4,1/2)$.

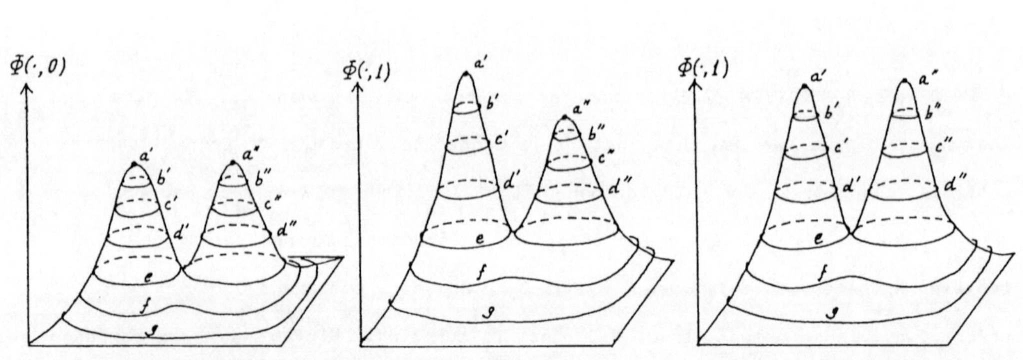

Figure 1.a Figure 1.b Figure 1.c

Version 1. Figures 1.a and 1.b give the graphs of the conditional utility functions $\Phi(\cdot,0)$ and $\Phi(\cdot,1)$. For $0 < y < 1$, $\Phi(\cdot,y)$ is given by the convex combination $(1-y)\Phi(\cdot,0) + y\Phi(\cdot,1)$. Note that as y increases the proximity of x to x^* contributes progressively more than the proximity of x to x^{**} to higher utility. The isoquant components of the conditional functions $\Phi(\cdot,y)$, however, retain the same shape. Thus, Φ satisfies the similarity condition $<S^*>$. The space $\mathcal{K}$ of isocomponents is given schematically in Figure 2.a. Regarding them as points in $\mathcal{K}$, the isocomponents a', b', c', etc. may be arranged as points on a Y-shaped tree as shown in Figure 2.b.

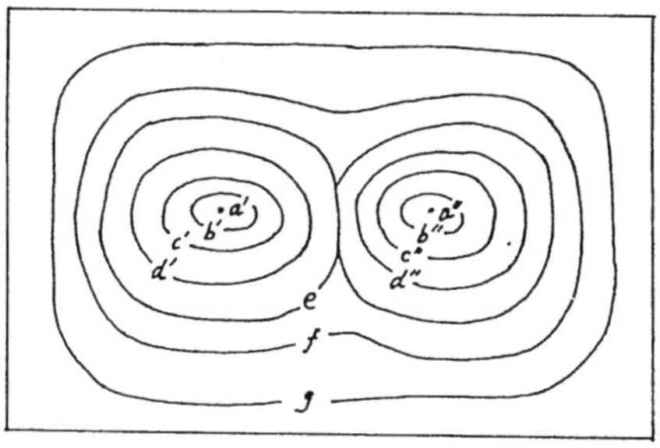

Figure 2.a

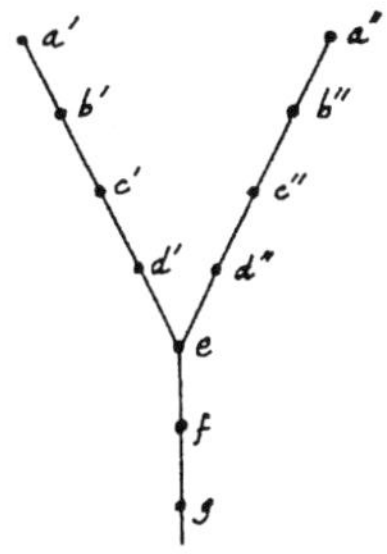

Figure 2.b

Version 2. Suppose the graph of the conditional utility function $\Phi(\cdot,1)$ is given by Figure 1.c instead of 1.b. For $0 < y < 1$, $\Phi(\cdot,y)$ is defined as before by convex combinations. It should be clear that in this version the space $\mathcal{K}$ of isocomponents may still be represented by the Y-shaped tree in Figure 2.b. In contrast to the previous version, here the proximity of x to x^* and to x^{**} contribute equally to higher utility as y increases. In fact, the utility function Φ is strictly separable in x. Now, for all y, the conditional utility function $\Phi(\cdot, y)$ takes the same values over the pairs of isocomponents a' and a'', b' and b'', etc. which lie on different branches of the Y-shaped tree. Thus, intuitively speaking, the separability of Φ and the existence of an aggregate for x is due to the fact that the two branches a'e and a''e may be "paired" and then "glued" together to make the tree a simple arc. □

We turn now to the formal proof that <S*> implies $\mathcal{K}$ has the tree structure. The arguments we will use are modifications of Arnol'ds' analysis of the tree structure of continuous functions [1, Appendix].

First, we introduce a metric on $\mathcal{K}$. For K_1, $K_2 \in \mathcal{K}$, $y \in Y$, and continuum $M \subset X$ containing both K_1 and K_2, let the *oscillation* of the conditional function $\Phi(\cdot,y)$ over M be denoted

$$\phi(M;y) = \max_{x \in M} \Phi(x,y) - \min_{x \in M} \Phi(x,y).$$

Taking infimum over all continua containing K_1 and K_2, define

$$\rho(K_1,K_2) = \operatorname*{Inf}_{K_1 \cup K_2 \subset M} [\operatorname*{Sup}_{y \in Y} \phi(M;y)].$$

(3.2) LEMMA. If <S*> holds, then ρ is a metric on $\mathcal{K}$.

PROOF. If <S*> holds, then according to Proposition (2.2) each isocomponent is a closed and connected set; i.e., a continuum.

Clearly, $\rho(K_1,K_2) = \rho(K_2,K_1) \geq 0$.

If $K_1 = K_2$, then with $M = K_1 = K_2$ we have $\Phi(\cdot,y)$ constant over M for all y. Therefore, $\rho(K_1,K_2) = 0$ if $K_1 = K_2$. To show the converse, note that $K_1 \neq K_2$ implies that for arbitrary $x^1 \in K_1$ and $x^2 \in K_2$ either (a) $\Phi(x^1,y) \neq \Phi(x^2,y)$ for some y, or (b) $\Phi(x^1,y) = \Phi(x^2,y)$ for all y, but for some y the points x^1 and x^2 belong to different isoquant components of $\Phi(\cdot,y)$. Thus every continuum M containing $K_1 \cup K_2$ contains an x° with $\Phi(x^\circ,y) \neq \Phi(x^1,y)$ for some y. Hence, $\rho(K_1,K_2) > 0$ if $K_1 \neq K_2$. That is, $\rho(K_1,K_2) = 0$ only if $K_1 = K_2$.

For isocomponents K_1, K_2, K_3, and continua M containing K_1 and K_3, N containing K_3 and K_2, it is clear that $M \cup N$ contains K_1 and K_2 and $\phi(M;y) + \phi(N;y) \geq \phi(M \cup N;y)$ for all $y \in Y$. From this inequality follows quite readily the triangle inequality $\rho(K_1,K_3) + \rho(K_3,K_2) \geq \rho(K_1,K_2)$. □

Associate to each $x \in X$ the unique isocomponent $K \in \mathcal{K}$ that contains it. Call this mapping i.

(3.3) LEMMA. If $<S^*>$ holds then with the metric ρ defined on $\mathcal{K}$, the mapping $i:X \to \mathcal{K}$ is continuous.

PROOF. Since the function Φ on $X \times Y$ is continuous and Y is compact, the following is true: for every $\epsilon > 0$ and $x \in X$ there exists an open ball $B_\delta(x) \subset X$ with radius δ and center x such that for all $y \in Y$ the oscillation of the conditional function $\Phi(\cdot,y)$ over $B_\delta(x)$ is less than ϵ. To show the mapping i is continuous at a point $x' \in X$, for given $\epsilon > 0$ pick an open ball $B_\delta(x')$ with the property above. A point x'' in $B_\delta(x')$ is joined to x' by an arc, say C, which lies completely within $B_\delta(x')$. For each $y \in Y$ the oscillation of $\Phi(\cdot,y)$ over the continuum $i(x') \cup C \cup i(x'')$ is simply the oscillation over C and is thus less than ϵ. Hence $\rho(i(x'),i(x'')) < \epsilon$. □

Formally, we define a *tree* to be a locally connected compact connected Hausdorff space which contains no simple closed curve [7, p.300]. We are now ready to state and prove the main result of this section.

(3.4) THEOREM. If a continuous function Φ on $X \times Y$ satisfies the similarity condition $<S^*>$, and if the conditional functions $\Phi(\cdot,y)$, $y \in Y$, are not all constant, then the space $\mathcal{K}$ of isocomponents is a tree.

PROOF. If for every $y \in Y$ the conditional functions $\Phi(\cdot, y)$ on X is constant, then $\mathcal{K}$ consists of a single point, namely X. We ignore this trivial case.

To show that $\mathcal{K}$ is a tree when $<S^*>$ holds, first note that the continuous mapping $i:X \to \mathcal{K}$ is monotone. This is so because for each $K \in \mathcal{K}$ the inverse image $i^{-1}(K)$ is the connected subset $K \subset X$ (cf. Proposition (2.2)). Next, note that the hypercube X is locally connected, unicoherent, compact, connected, and Hausdorff. Since these properties are invariant under continuous monotone mappings [7, p.255, p.434, p.438], the space $\mathcal{K}$ also has all these properties. Since every 1-dimensional topological space with these properties is a tree [7, p.442], to establish the theorem, we only have to show that condition $<S^*>$ implies $\mathcal{K}$ has dimension one. The arguments needed is provided by the two lemmas below. First, let us recall the inductive definition of the dimensions of topological spaces:

DEFINITION [6, p.273]. Let $\dim_p\mathfrak{X}$ denote the dimension of a topological space $\mathfrak{X}$ at the point p. The dimension $\dim\mathfrak{X}$ of $\mathfrak{X}$ is an integer defined inductively by the following three conditions:

1) $\dim\mathfrak{X} = -1$ if and only if $\mathfrak{X}$ is empty;
2) if $\mathfrak{X} \neq \emptyset$, then $\dim\mathfrak{X} = \operatorname{Sup}\{\dim_p\mathfrak{X} \mid p \in \mathfrak{X}\}$;
3) $\dim_p\mathfrak{X} \leq n+1$ if and only if p has arbitrarily small neighborhoods whose boundaries have dimension $\leq n$.

(3.5) LEMMA. If an isocomponent K is contained in an open set $G \subset X$, then for some $\delta > 0$ every isocomponent K' with $\rho(K,K') < \delta$ is also contained in G.

PROOF. If the lemma were not true, then there would exist isocomponents K_n with $\rho(K,K_n) < 1/n$ and each K_n contains a point x^n outside G. By the definition of the metric ρ, for each n there is a continuum M_n containing both K and K_n and over which the oscillation of all the conditional functions $\Phi(\cdot,y)$ are less than 2/n. The lower topological limit $\operatorname{Li}(M_n)$ of the continua M_n is nonempty since they all contain K. Hence, the upper topological limit $\operatorname{Ls}(M_n)$ is connected [7, p.171]. Since X-G is compact, the points x^n converges to a limit $x^\circ \in X-G$. Clearly, $\operatorname{Ls}(M_n)$ contains both K and x°.

Consider an arbitrary point x in $\operatorname{Ls}(M_n)$. No matter how large n is, every neighborhood of x meets an M_m with $m > n$; thus, for all y the value of the conditional function $\Phi(\cdot,y)$ at x differs by less than 2/n that over K. Hence, for all y, $\Phi(\cdot,y)$ is constant over the connected set $\operatorname{Ls}(M_n)$. This means $\operatorname{Ls}(M_n)$, which contains both K and x°, is a subset of some isocomponent. But this contradicts the fact that x° is outside G and must belong to an isocomponent other than K. □

(3.6) LEMMA. If the similarity condition <S^*> holds, then for each $K \in \mathcal{K}$ there exists a neighborhood U of K as small as we please (i.e., for arbitrary open set $E \subset \mathcal{K}$ which contains K there exists an open set $U \subset \mathcal{K}$ such that $K \in U \subset E$) whose boundary has dimension zero.

PROOF. Consider an arbitrary $K^\circ \in \mathcal{K}$. For each $y \in Y$ let $\mu(y)$ be the value of $\Phi(\cdot,y)$ over K°. Because Φ and the function $y \to \mu(y)$ are continuous and Y is compact, the function θ specified by

$$\theta(x) = \sup_{y \in Y} |\Phi(x,y) - \mu(y)|, \qquad x \in X,$$

is well-defined and continuous. For $\epsilon > 0$, let V_ϵ be the open set $\{x \in X | \theta(x) < \epsilon\}$. It is clear that the function θ has value ϵ on the boundary $\partial(V_\epsilon)$ of V_ϵ. We note here that $\partial(V_\epsilon)$ may be composed of components ∂^1, ∂^2, etc. (see Figure 3.a) and

$$(3.7) \qquad x \in V_\epsilon \iff i(x) \subset V_\epsilon$$

Let U_ϵ be the image of V_ϵ under the mapping $i: X \to \mathcal{K}$. We shall show that the U_ϵ's have the desired property.

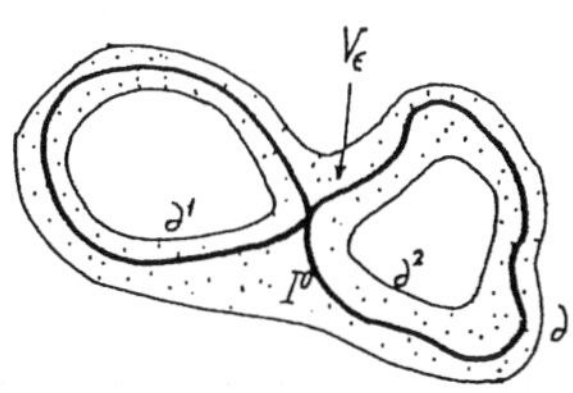

Figure 3.a

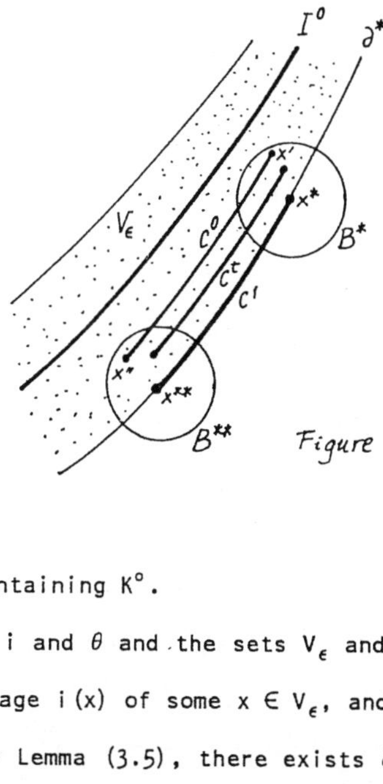

Figure 3.b

Result (A). U_ϵ is an open subset of $\mathcal{K}$ containing $K°$.

Proof. By the definition of the mappings i and θ and the sets V_ϵ and U_ϵ, $K° \in U_\epsilon$. Consider arbitrary $K \in U_\epsilon$. It is the image $i(x)$ of some $x \in V_\epsilon$, and therefore (cf. (3.7)) contained in the open set V_ϵ. By Lemma (3.5), there exists $\delta > 0$ such that $\rho(K,K') < \delta$ implies $K' \subset V_\epsilon$. Now, $K' \subset V_\epsilon$ means K' is the image $i(x')$ for some $x' \in V_\epsilon$ and therefore $K' \in U_\epsilon$. Thus, U_ϵ is an open subset of $\mathcal{K}$. □

Result (B). If K is a boundary point of U_ϵ, then $K = i(x)$ for some boundary point x of V_ϵ.

Proof. If an isocomponent K lies completely in the open set V_ϵ or in the open set $X - \overline{V_\epsilon}$, then because of Lemma (3.5), K cannot be a boundary point of U_ϵ.

Therefore, each boundary point K of U_ϵ contains a boundary point x of V_ϵ and $i(x) = K$ by the definition of the mapping i. □

Result (C). If condition <S^*> holds, then each component ∂^* of the boundary $\partial(V_\epsilon)$ is contained in exactly one isocomponent K^*.

Proof. Consider an arbitrary component ∂^* of the boundary $\partial(V_\epsilon)$. As noted earlier, $\theta(x) = \epsilon$ for all $x \in \partial^*$. Fix an arbitrary $x^* \in \partial^*$. The supremum in the definition of $\theta(x^*)$ is attained at some $y^* \in Y$. Assume w.l.o.g that $\Phi(x^*,y^*) = \mu(y^*) + \epsilon$.

We shall show that the conditional function $\Phi(\cdot,y^*)$ is constant over ∂^*. Assume not. Then, there exists $x^{**} \in \partial^*$ with

$$\mu^{**} = \Phi(x^{**}, y^*) < \Phi(x^*, y^*) = \mu^*.$$

Let $\delta = (\mu^* - \mu^{**})/4$. Since $\Phi(\cdot,y^*)$ is continuous, there exist open balls B^* and B^{**} centered at x^* and x^{**} such that

$$x \in B^* \Rightarrow |\Phi(x,y^*) - \Phi(x^*,y^*)| < \delta,$$
$$x \in B^{**} \Rightarrow |\Phi(x,y^*) - \Phi(x^{**},y^*)| < \delta.$$

Since both x^* and x^{**} are boundary points of V_ϵ, we may pick and fix an $x' \in V_\epsilon \cap B^*$ and an $x'' \in V_\epsilon \cap B^{**}$.

Since ∂^* is locally connected, there exists an arc C^1 in ∂^* which joins x^* to x^{**} (cf. [7, p.253-4]). Similarly, there exists an arc C^0 in V_ϵ which joins x' to x''. Let $h:[0,1] \times [0,1] \to X$ be a homotopy between the arcs C^0 and C^1 (see Figure 3.b) so specified that

(a) $h(0,\cdot)$ yields an arc in B^* which joins x' to x^*,

(b) $h(1,\cdot)$ yields an arc in B^{**} which joins x'' to x^{**},

(c) $h(\cdot,0)$ and $h(\cdot,1)$ respectively yield the arcs C^0 in V_ϵ and C^1 in ∂^*,

(d) for each $t \in [0,1]$, $h(\cdot,t)$ yields an arc C^t with one endpoint in B^* and the other in B^{**}.

Since $\Phi(\cdot,y^*)$ is continuous, the image $\Phi(C^t,y^*)$ is an interval which, by the way δ was specified, properly contains the nontrivial interval $[\mu^{**}+\delta, \mu^*-\delta]$. Therefore, for an arbitary $\mu \in [\mu^{**}+\delta, \mu^{*}-\delta]$ we may use the homotopy h to identify two points $x^0 \in C^0$ and $x^1 \in C^1$ both of which belong to the same component of the conditional isoquant of $\Phi(\cdot, y^*)$ with level μ. Indeed, we may pick x^0 and x^1 so that they belong to the same connected boundary of the component. By the similarity condition $\langle S^* \rangle$, the x^0 and x^1 thus identified belong to the same isocomponent. But x^0 is in the open set V_ϵ while x^1 being in ∂^* is outside V_ϵ. This contradicts (3.7); therefore $\Phi(\cdot,y^*)$ is indeed constant over ∂^*.

That $\Phi(\cdot,y^*)$ has the constant value $\mu(y^*)+\epsilon$ on the boundary component ∂^* of V_ϵ implies ∂^* is a connected subset of the boundary of an isoquant component of $\Phi(\cdot, y^*)$. Consequently, applying $\langle S^* \rangle$ again, we conclude that ∂^* is contained completely in an isocomponent. □

Result (D). The boundary of U_ϵ has dimension zero.

Proof. By Results (B) and (C), every boundary point K^* of U_ϵ is uniquely associated with a boundary component ∂^* of V_ϵ. Hence, there exists an open set $G \subset X$ (as small as we wish) which contains K^* and no other boundary point of U_ϵ. Thus, in view of Lemma (3.5), we may conclude that the boundary of U_ϵ has dimension zero. □

Lastly, we note that by making ϵ small the open neighborhood U_ϵ of K° can be made as small as we wish. This completes the proofs of both Lemma (3.6) and Theorem (3.4). □

4. EXISTENCE OF QUANTITY INDICES.

If Φ is separable in x with $\Phi(x,y) = F(f(x),y)$ and if the aggregate f is monotone nondecreasing, then we say f is a *quantity index* for x (relative to Φ). This definition of quantity indices is compatible with Eichhorn's [4] approach to defining economic indices and is consistent with common economic practice. In this section we use the result of the last section to give a necessary and sufficient condition for the existence of quantity indices. For this purpose, we introduce the concept of *branching index:*

The branching index of a point K of a tree $\mathcal{K}$ is defined as the number of disjoint components of $\mathcal{K}-\{K\}$. If $\mathcal{K}$ is the tree of isocomponents of a continuous function Φ which satisfies the similarity condition <S*>, then since the mapping $i:X \to \mathcal{K}$ is monotone, the branching index of each $K \in \mathcal{K}$ is precisely the number of components of the subset resulting from removing K from X. Refer back to the isocomponents in Figure 2.a and the tree in Figure 2.b. There, the branching index of isocomponent a' is 1, that of b' is 2, and that of e is 3.

Suppose f is a quantity index for x relative to Φ. Then, Φ satisfies <S*> according to Theorem (2.1). And for every $y \in Y$, the (disjoint) components of a conditional isoquant, of level μ say, of the conditional function $\Phi(\cdot,y) \equiv F(f(\cdot),y)$ all have the form

(4.1) $$\{x \in X | f(x) \in [\beta',\beta'']\},$$

where $[\beta',\beta'']$ is a maximal interval subset of $f(X)$ over which the continuous function $F(\cdot,y)$ has the constant value μ. Thus each isocomponent $K \in \mathcal{K}$, being the intersection of subsets of the form (4.1), has the form (4.1). Hence, removing an isocomponent K will separate X into two subsets, say

$$L(K) = \{x|f(x) < \beta'\}, \qquad U(K) = \{x|f(x) > \beta''\}.$$

Since f is monotone nondecreasing, both L(K) and U(K) are connected subsets of X. Further, L(K) is empty iff K contains the least element $0 = (0,\ldots,0)$ of the hypercube X and U(K) is empty iff K contains the greatest element $1 = (1,\ldots,1)$ of X. Thus, K separates X into at most two components. Equivalently, the branching index of K is at most 2. The monotonicity of f also implies that

(4.2.a) $0 \in L(K)$ if L(K) is nonempty,

(4.2.b) $1 \in U(K)$ if U(K) is nonempty,

(4.2.c) $x'' \geq x' \in K \cup U(K)$ implies $x'' \in K \cup U(K)$.

We have thus established the "necessity" part of the following theorem on the existence of quantity indices:

(4.3) THEOREM. Relative to a continuous function Φ on $X \times Y$ there exists a quantity index if and only if (i) Φ satisfies the similarity condition <S^*>, (ii) each isocomponent K separates X into at most two components, say L(K) and U(K), which satisfy condition (4.2).

SUFFICIENCY PROOF. By Theorem (3.4), (i) implies the space $\mathcal{K}$ of isocomponents is a tree. By (ii), each isocomponent has a branching index of at most 2. Therefore, $\mathcal{K}$ is actually an arc $\mathcal{A}$ which, according to (4.2.a-b), has endpoints K_0 and K_1 containing 0 and 1 respectively. Regard the arc $\mathcal{A}$ as joining K_0 to K_1 and let v be an order-preserving homeomorphism from $\mathcal{A}$ to [0, 1]. Define function f by composition: $f(x) = v(i(x))$, $x \in X$. Now, f is continuous since both i and v are continuous mappings. Condition (4.2) implies f is monotone nondecreasing. By definition, $f(x') = f(x'')$ only if conditioned on all y both x' and x'' belong to the same conditional isoquant component. Therefore, we may specify a function F so that $\Phi(x,y) = F(f(x),y)$ for all x and y. It is easy to verify that F is continuous. Thus, f is indeed a quantity index. □

5. A SUFFICIENT CONDITION FOR SEPARABILITY.

To see when aggregation of a vector x (not necessarily via a monotone quantity index) relative to a continuous function Φ is possible, we seek a sufficient condition for Φ to be separable in x. We saw in Example (3.1) how isocomponents might be "paired" so that different branches of the tree $\mathcal{K}$ might be "glued" together to make $\mathcal{K}$ become an arc. We now formalize the notion of "pairing" of isocomponents in order to use the "glued" arc to derive a sufficient condition for separability.

Two isocomponents $K', K'' \in \mathcal{K}$ are said to be *paired* if for all $y \in Y$ they are both contained in the same conditional isoquant of $\Phi(\cdot,y)$. We write $K' \gtrless K''$ if K' and K'' are paired. Now, $K' \gtrless K''$ if and only if $\Phi(x',y) = \Phi(x'',y)$ for all $y \in Y$, $x' \in K'$, and $x'' \in K''$. Thus, isocomponents K' and K'' are paired when and only when they are "synchronized" in regard to their effects on the function value of Φ.

(5.1) THEOREM. Φ is separable in x if Φ satisfies the similarity condition $<S^*>$ and if the space $\mathcal{K}$ of isocomponents contains an arc $\mathcal{A}$ with the properties that (i) no two isocomponents in $\mathcal{A}$ are paired, and (ii) for each K' outside $\mathcal{A}$ there is exactly one K'' in $\mathcal{A}$ paired with K'.

PROOF. Suppose Φ satisfies the similarity condition $<S^*>$. Then, according to Theorem (3.4), $\mathcal{K}$ is a tree. Let $\mathcal{A} \subset \mathcal{K}$ be an arc with properties (i) and (ii). To show Φ is separable in x, we have to construct continuous functions F and f so that Φ has the representation (1.1). We shall need the following result which follows directly from the continuity of Φ and the definitions of isocomponents and their pairedness.

Result (E). If two sequences $\{K_n'\}$ and $\{K_n''\}$ of isocomponents converges to K' and K'' respectively and $K_n' \gtrless K_n''$ for all n, then $K' \gtrless K''$.

Let $v: \mathcal{A} \to [0, 1]$ be a homeomorphism between the arc $\mathcal{A}$ and the unit interval. Extend v to become a function on $\mathcal{K}$: For $K' \notin \mathcal{A}$ let $v(K') = v(K'')$ where K'' is the unique isocomponent in $\mathcal{A}$ paired with K'.

Result (F). $v(K') = v(K'')$ if and only if $K' \gtrless K''$.

Proof. Since $\gtrless$ is a transitive relation, by (i) and (ii), $K' \gtrless K''$ if and only if for some $K^* \in \mathcal{A}$, $K' \gtrless K^*$ and $K'' \gtrless K^*$. It then follows from the definition of v that $v(K') = v(K'')$ if and only if $K' \gtrless K''$. □

Result (G). The function $v: \mathcal{K} \to [0, 1]$ defined above is continuous.

Proof. Let $\{K_n\} \subset \mathcal{K}$ be a sequence converging to K. We are to show that the sequence $\{v(K_n)\}$ converges to v(K). Let $\{J_n\} \subset \mathcal{A}$ be a sequence such that $J_n = K_n$ if $K_n \in \mathcal{A}$ and if $K_n \notin \mathcal{A}$ then J_n is the unique isocomponent in $\mathcal{A}$ paired with K_n.

As constructed, $J_n \gtrless K_n$ and hence $v(J_n) = v(K_n)$ for all n. The sequence $\{J_n\}$ converges. This is because if $\{J_n\}$ has two distinct accumulation points, say J^* and J^{**}, then by Result (E) isocomponent K would be paired with both J^* and J^{**} and consequently, in contradiction to (i), the two distinct points J^* and J^{**} in $\mathcal{A}$ would be paired. Let J be the limit point of $\{J_n\}$. By Result (E), $K \gtrless J$. If $K \in \mathcal{A}$, then $v(K) = v(J)$ since K = J by (i). If $K \notin \mathcal{A}$, then by (ii) and the definition of v we still have $v(K) = v(J)$. Now $\{v(J_n)\}$ converges to $v(J)$ since v on $\mathscr{A}$ is a homeomorphism and is therefore continuous. Thus, recalling that $\{v(K_n)\}$ is identical to $\{v(J_n)\}$, we see that the sequence $\{v(K_n)\}$ converging to $v(K)$. □

Define by composition the function $f(x) = v(i(x))$ for all $x \in X$. Since both i and v are continuous, f is continuous on X. Further, because v is constructed so that $v(K') = v(K'')$ if and only if $K' \gtrless K''$, we have $f(x') = f(x'')$ if and only if for all $y \in Y$ both x' and x'' belong to the same conditional isoquant (but not necessarily the same component) of the conditional function $\Phi(\cdot, y)$.

Consider an arbitrary $y \in Y$. By construction, f takes the same value over two different isocomponents K' and K'' only if the conditional function $\Phi(\cdot, y)$ likewise has the same value over K' and K''. Therefore there exists a transform F_y such that $\Phi(x,y) = F_y(f(x))$ for all $x \in X$. Considering all $y \in Y$ at the same time, we may rewrite the identity as: $\Phi(x, y) = F(f(x), y)$ for all $x \in X$ and $y \in Y$. Using the compactness of X and Y and the continuity of Φ and f, it is straightforward to show that F is a continuous function. Therefore, Φ is indeed separable in x. □

6. CONCLUDING REMARKS.

We end this paper with some remarks on the construction of aggregates and the relevance of Theorems (4.3) and (5.1) thereof.

If every isocomponent has a branching index of at most 2, then the space $\mathscr{K}$ is an arc and the existence of an aggregate is ensured. If in addition condition (4.2) holds, then by Theorem (4.3) we can actually construct a quantity index for x.

If the branching index of some isocomponent is larger than 2, then the space is truly a tree. We then have the problem of finding an aggregate that would assign values to isocomponents on different branches of $\mathscr{K}$ in a continuous manner. Now, a continuous aggregate exists if we can, using the pairedness of isocomponents, glue distinct branches of $\mathscr{K}$ together to give an arc. This is not likely to be possible (recall version 1 of Example (3.1)) as any lack of "synchronization" of isocomponents in regard to their effect on Φ will destroy pairedness.

Even when aggregation is not immediately ruled out by the lack of synchronization, the construction of an aggreagate appears to be rather difficult. Let us consider how aggregate measures are to be specified for two paired isocomponents. Knowing only the function Φ, any two paired isocomponents would appear completely equivalent to us. It therefore seems natural to seek an aggregate f that satisfies the following condition:

(6.1) $K' \gtrless K'' \Rightarrow f(x') = f(x'')$ for all $x' \in K'$, $x'' \in K''$.

Conditions (i) and (ii) of Theorem (5.1) on the pairing of isocomponents are essentially regularity conditions on Φ which gaurantee that we may indeed choose an aggregate f that satisfies (6.1). However, because Φ need not be monotone, condition (6.1) is not always appropriate as the following example demonstrates.

(6.2) EXAMPLE. Suppose $x = (x_1, x_2) \in [0,1]^2$, $y \in [0,1]$, and Φ has the form $\Phi(x_1, x_2, y) = F(x_1+x_2, y)$ with the isoquants of the function F given in Figure 4.

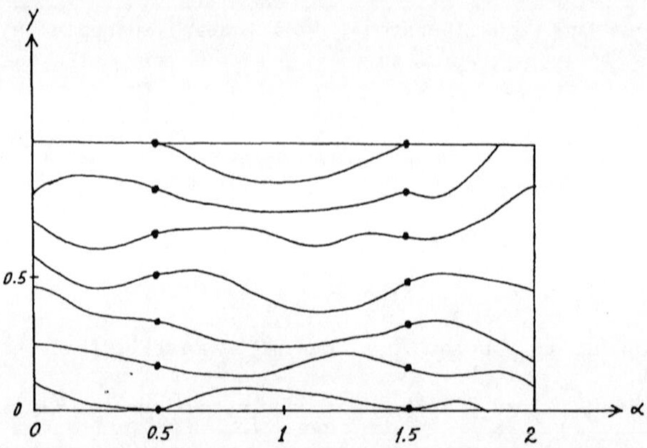

Figure 4

Without knowing that Φ actually has the representation (1.1) with $f(x_1, x_2) = x_1+x_2$, we nevertheless can deduce that the isocomponents of Φ are lines of the form

$$K(\alpha) = \{(x_1, x_2) \mid x_1+x_2 = \alpha\}, \quad 0 \le \alpha \le 2,$$

and the only isocomponents that are paired are $K' = K(0.5)$ and $K'' = K(1.5)$. In constructing an aggregate f for x, we must not set $f(K') = f(K'')$. Had we done so, then the continuity of f would force some isocomponents $K^* = K(\alpha^*)$ and $K^{**} = K(\alpha^{**})$, where $\alpha^*, \alpha^{**} \in (0.5, 1.5)$, to have $f(K^*) = f(K^{**})$; and we would end up with the contradiction that K^* and K^{**} are also paired. □

Thus, it appears that in order to have a general procedure for constructing aggregates, we somehow have to be able to decide, without the aid of monotonicity properties, which paired isocomponents are to have the same aggregate value and which not. It is not yet clear exactly how this may be done in general.

ACKNOWLEDGEMENT. I gratefully thank Professor W.M. Gorman for suggesting the topic of this paper. I would also like to thank Professor R.R. Russell for pointing out the restrictiveness of "synchronization", and thank Professors Y.O. Vartia, J.S. Chipman, P.P. Wakker, and two referees for helpful comments.

REFERENCES.

[1] V.I. ARNOL'D: Representation of Continuous Functions of Three Variables by the Superposition of Continuous Functions of Two Variables, *Amer. Math. Soc. Transl.* 28, 1963, 61-147.

[2] C. BLACKORBY/ D. PRIMONT/ R.R. RUSSELL: DUALITY, SEPARABILITY, AND FUNCTIONAL STRUCTURE, Elsevier North-Holland, New York, 1978.

[3] G. DEBREU: Topological Methods in Cardinal Utility Theory, in MATHEMATICAL METHODS IN THE SOCIAL SCIENCES, K. Arrow, S. Karlin, and P. Suppes (eds.), Stanford University Press, Standford, 1959, 17-26.

[4] W. EICHHORN: What is an Economic Index? An Attempt of an Answer, in THEORY AND APPLICATIONS OF ECONOMIC INDICES, W. Eichhorn, R. Henn, O. Opitz, and R.W. Shephard (eds.), Physica-verlag, Würzburg, 1978, 3-40.

[5] W.M. GORMAN: The Structure of Utility Functions, *Rev. Econ. Studies* 35, 1968, 367-390.

[6] K. KURATOWSKI: TOPOLOGY Vol. 1, new edition, Academic Press, New York and London, 1968.

[7] K. KURATOWSKI: TOPOLOGY Vol. 2, new edition, Academic Press, New York and London, 1968.

[8] K. MAK: On Separability: Functional Structure, *J. Econ. Theory* 40, 1986, 250-282.

Nataf's Theorem, Taylor's Expansion and Homogeneity in Consumer Demand

A.H.Q.M. Merkies
Vrije Universiteit Amsterdam
Interfaculteit an Acuariele
Wetenschappen en Econemetrie
an Boelelaan 1081
Amsterdam

J. van Daal
Erasmus University Rotterdam
Faculteit der Economische
Wetenschappen
Postbus 1738
3000 DR Rotterdam

1. Introduction

Macrorelations should obey Nataf's specification requirements to be decomposable into microrelations. Taylor expansions can command such obedience and indicate the omissions if approximations are used. This paper discusses in section 3 how additional restrictions such as equilibrium conditions can be incorporated in a Taylor framework to increase the variety of possible specifications. In section 4 it is shown how this variety shrinks if the condition of homogeneity must be satisfied. As such it may help to clarify some points of Gorman's (1981) general theorems on Engel curves. At the same time an inaccuracy in his paper is indicated.

2. Nataf's theorem and Taylor's expansion

2.1. Assume consumer j's demand function for some product is

$$D_j = D_j(x_{j1}, \ldots , x_{jM}) \tag{2.1}$$

where x_{jm} refers to the amount used of the mth input. The inputs may range from prices and income to all other determinants of j's demand such as his family composition, his environment or special marketing or tax factors. Aggregating over all J individuals leads to aggregate demand as a function of individual demands:

$$\bar{D} = G(D_1, \ldots ,D_J) \tag{2.2}$$

and aggregating over individual inputs leads to macro inputs as functions of individual inputs:

$$\bar{x}_m = g_m(x_{1m}, \ldots ,x_{Jm}) \quad m = 1,2,\ldots,M \tag{2.3}$$

Measurement in Economics
ed. by W. Eichhorn

According to Nataf's theorem - see Nataf (1948), Green (1964) or van Daal and Merkies (1984) [1] a market demand function

$$\bar{D} = \bar{D}(\bar{x}_1, \ldots, \bar{x}_M) \tag{2.4}$$

should be additively separable i.e. it is constrained to the specification

$$\bar{D} = \phi\left[\sum_j \sum_m \varphi_{jm}(x_{jm})\right] \tag{2.5}$$

to be consistently aggregated from (2.1) using (2.2) and (2.3). This means that if and only if (2.4) can be written in the form of (2.5) the conditions (2.1) to (2.4) can be satisfied simultaneously. If we write $w = \phi^{-1}(\bar{D})$ with ϕ an invertible function of one argument and $z_{jm} = \varphi_{jm}(x_{jm})$ formula (2.5) becomes

$$w = \sum_j \sum_m z_{jm} \tag{2.6}$$

i.e. in principle all specifications should be sums of (transformed) variables.

2.2. Nataf's theorem does not prevent the introduction of special determinants such as family composition or marketing factors in the market demand functions nor nonlinear price or income factors. The theorem only constrains these factors - as far as they differ individually - to be introduced in an additively separable form. As long as all individual demand functions are assumed to be sufficiently differentiable such separability can always be obtained through a Taylor expansion. The crucial element is that all individual functions can be linearized in the market (average) point $(\bar{x}_1, \ldots, \bar{x}_M)$. We will illustrate the implications below.

---

[1] As we will frequently refer to this book we will indicate it below by DM(1984).

First we present our notation (an accent (') denotes transposition):

$$x_{j\cdot} = (x_{j1}, \ldots, x_{jM}) \qquad j = 1, \ldots, J \qquad \text{(a)}$$

$$x_{\cdot m} = (x_{1m}, \ldots, x_{Jm})' \qquad m = 1, \ldots, M \qquad \text{(b)} \qquad (2.7)$$

$$\bar{x}. = (\bar{x}_1, \ldots, \bar{x}_m, \ldots, \bar{x}_M) \qquad \text{(c)}$$

$$\frac{\partial D_j}{\partial x_{j\cdot}} = \left[\frac{\partial D_j}{\partial x_{j1}}, \ldots, \frac{\partial D_j}{\partial x_{jM}}\right]' \qquad j = 1, \ldots, J \qquad (2.8)$$

A Taylor expansion of (2.1) gives

$$D_j = D_j(\bar{x}_1, \ldots, \bar{x}_M) + \left(\frac{\partial D_j}{\partial x_{j\cdot}}\right)_{x_{j\cdot} = \bar{x}.}' (x_{j\cdot} - \bar{x}.) + \tfrac{1}{2}(x_{j\cdot} - \bar{x}.)' \left[\frac{\partial^2 D}{\partial x_{j\cdot}\, x'_{j\cdot}}\right]_{x_{j\cdot} = \bar{x}.} (x_{j\cdot} - \bar{x}.) + \ldots \qquad (2.9)$$

To simplify our notation we write the micro gradient $\frac{\partial D_j}{\partial x_{j\cdot}}$ in the point $x_{j\cdot} = \bar{x}.$ as α_j and the Hessian in the point $x_{j\cdot} = \bar{x}.$ as A_j, so that (2.9) becomes

$$D_j = D_j(\bar{x}_1, \ldots, \bar{x}_M) + \alpha_j'(x_{j\cdot} - \bar{x}.) + \tfrac{1}{2}(x_{j\cdot} - \bar{x}.)' A_j (x_{j\cdot} - \bar{x}.) + \ldots \qquad (2.10)$$

To obtain market demand functions we add over individuals, divide by their number and allow for a transformation as permitted by (2.5) which gives

$$\bar{D} = \phi\left[\frac{1}{J}\sum_j D_j\right] = \phi\left[\frac{1}{J}\sum_j D_j(\bar{x}_1, \ldots, \bar{x}_M) + \frac{1}{J}\sum \alpha_j'(x_{j\cdot} - \bar{x}.) + \frac{1}{2J}\sum (x_{j\cdot} - \bar{x}.)' A_j (x_{j\cdot} - \bar{x}.) + \ldots\right] \qquad (2.11)$$

(2.10) and (2.11) are compact notations of individual and market demand respectively that facilitate the discussion of several problems involved in aggregation theory. This is shown in the section 3.

2.3. In empirical work aggregates are often determined by statistical offices etc. leaving no freedom for the researcher to choose his own functions G and g_m. This narrows the possibilities for consistent aggregation. Macro outputs are frequently given as simple averages which specifies (2.2) as

$$\bar{D} = \frac{1}{J}\sum_j D_j \tag{2.12}$$

This constrains the function ϕ to be the identity function and (2.11) becomes

$$\bar{D} = \frac{1}{J}\sum_j D_j(\bar{x}_1,\ldots,\bar{x}_M) + \frac{1}{J}\sum_j \alpha_j'(x_{j.}-\bar{x}_.) + \frac{1}{2J}\sum (x_{j.}-\bar{x}_.)'A_j(x_{j.}-\bar{x}_.) + \ldots \tag{2.13}$$

Macro inputs are for the same reason often specified as simple averages, which specifies (2.3) as

$$\bar{x}_m = \frac{1}{J}\sum_j x_{jm} \qquad m = 1,\ldots,M \tag{2.14}$$

In such case the second term of the righthand side of (2.13) can also be written as $\frac{1}{J}\sum_j(\alpha_j-\bar{\alpha})'(x_{j.}-\bar{x}_.)$ or as the sum of covariances between the input variables and their marginal effect on j's demand.

3. Simplifications and comparisons

3.1. In principle all market demand functions can be written in the form of (2.11) but often simplifications are possible. A first simplification is possible if the macro output can be defined as a simple average of micro outputs. We then have (2.12) and the specification of the demand function becomes (2.13). We have seen in section 2.3 that usually such specifications are required by the nature of the given data.

The second simplification is in the same line. If macro inputs can be (or have to be) defined as simple averages of micro inputs we have (2.14) but the specification of the demand function remains (2.13), albeit that the linear term has become a covariance.

There are other simplifications possible. For instance we may assume that all individuals have identical demand functions.

$$D_j = D(x_{j1}, \dots, x_{jM}) \qquad j = 1, \dots, J \tag{3.1}$$

which implies that $\alpha_j = \alpha$ and $A_j = A$ for all j. This is less restrictive as it may seem as differing parameters can always be treated as variables. With identical individuals and the two simplifications required by the data the market demand function becomes

$$\bar{D} = \bar{D}(\bar{x}_1, \dots, \bar{x}_M) + 1/(2J)\sum_j (x_{j\cdot}-\bar{x}_\cdot)'A(x_{j\cdot}-\bar{x}_\cdot) + \dots \tag{3.2}$$

Keller (1980) simply drops the higher terms of (3.2) and calls the quadratic term the aggregation bias, which he writes as 1/2 trace AC with

$$C = 1/J \sum_j (x_{j\cdot} - \bar{x}_\cdot)(x_{j\cdot} - \bar{x}_\cdot)' \tag{3.3}$$

This shows that unless A is diagonal covariances of variables x_{jm} and x_{jm*}, possibly interpreted as coefficients are involved again.

If the parameters α_j differ over individuals - which may be the case if parameters have not been introduced as variables or if the macro inputs are not simple averages- the linear term in (2.13) does not vanish. It depends upon the type of research whether the inclusion of such a linear term is useful.

3.2. Many equations can be derived as a special case of (2.11) or (2.13) . For instance market demand formula (3.6.17) of DM(1984), is given as

$$\bar{q}_k = \phi_k(\theta_k + \varphi_k \bar{C} + \sum_{n=1}^{N} \psi_{kn} w_n) \qquad (3.4)$$

where the index k refers to the type of commodity which index we have omitted sofar in this paper. DM(1984) introduces this function to argue that linear macro Engel curves are always compatible with Nataf's theorem provided that the (transformed) market demand function is completed with a number N of additional determinants w_n with coefficients ψ_n.

To discuss the issue in the present notation we start with the situation of (2.12) with identical individuals, i.e. we start from (3.2), but with a linear term. If income - indicated by y - is the only input this gives

$$\bar{D} = D(\bar{y}) + \psi_1 w_1 + \psi_2 w_2 + \ldots \qquad (3.5)$$

with

$$\psi_n = \frac{1}{n!}\left[\frac{\partial^n D}{\partial y_j^n}\right]_{y_j=\bar{y}} \qquad (3.6)$$

and

$$w_n = 1/J \sum_j (y_j - \bar{y})^n \qquad (3.7)$$

The w_n appear to be nothing else than the consecutive moments of the income distribution around $\bar{y}$. If $\bar{y}$ is the arithmetic average these are the central moments and hence $w_1 = 0$. If $\bar{y}$ is not equal to the mean a linear term is added.

In (3.4) the macro function is taken as linear in income and no other arguments are specified. We may generalize by specifying $D(\bar{y})$ as a non linear function of $\bar{y}$. It does not make any difference whether non linear terms are included in the average function $D(\bar{y})$ or in the additional terms $\psi_n w_n$ provided (3.5) remains satisfied. We may also allow for other inputs than income. DM(1984) does so in the discussion on differing individuals. These extensions simply fit into (3.2) -with or without a linear term- if we interpret individual differences as differences in inputs (e.g. number of children, location etc.) but keep the form of the demand functions identical.

If all macro inputs are simple averages the linear term vanishes and the additional terms $\psi_n w_n$ or $\chi_t w_r$ as we wrote them in our earlier work can simply be taken as the second and higher moments of the multivariate distribution of the inputs. These moments take the form of covariances (e.g. between income and the number of children or between the marginal income propensities and the number of children).

Further generalisations that allow for differing individuals can be obtained from (2.10) and (2.11) or (2.13) without introducing (3.1) but this gives only a different presentation of earlier results. For instance (2.10) may be written for only one input (income) as

$$D_j = D_j(\bar{y}) + \sum_{n=1}^{N} \psi_{jn} w_{jn} \qquad (3.8)$$

and (2.13) is simplified correspondingly.

For identical individual functions we have $D_j(\bar{y}) = D(\bar{y})$ and moreover $\psi_{jn} w_{jn} = \psi_n w_n$ and if macro inputs are simple averages we have

$$w_n = \frac{1}{J} \sum_j w_{jn} \qquad (3.9)$$

which leads to an aggregate of (3.8) that coincides with (3.5).

3.3. The most important simplification of (2.11) arises from equilibrium tendencies in the market. In the present context for instance this occurs if all consumers have to pay the same price. If p is a subvector of $x_{j.}$ containing all relevant prices we have $p_{j.} = \bar{p}.$ and clearly all prices vanish from the second term onwards in the right hand side of (2.10).

A further simplification of (2.11) appears if all individuals have equal (initial) inputs.

For some inputs, such as prices, such a situation may arise from market equilibrium. We will discuss this case first within the restriction of identical individuals. If (3.1) holds we do not need to specify the aggregation formulae (2.3) to conclude that the macro inputs coincide with the individual inputs i.e $x_{j.} = \bar{x}.$ for all $j = 1,\dots,J$. Hence with identical micro functions and equal inputs for everyone we have from (2.11)

$$g^{-1}(\bar{D}) = D(\bar{x}_1,\dots,\bar{x}_M) \qquad (3.10)$$

In the empirical case when also (2.12) holds we have perfect aggregation. It is of interest to see if we can extend this result to non-identical individuals. We will give one example. We allow the individual functions to vary but only such that they remain monotonic transformations of each other. In the words of DM(1984) the individual demand functions are similar but not equal. This means that instead of (3.1) we have

$$D_j = h_j(D(x_{j1}, \dots ,x_{jM})) \qquad (3.11)$$

where h_j is a function with one argument only. Let us write

$$f_j = h_j^{-1}(D_j) = D(x_{j1}, \dots ,x_{jM}) \qquad (3.12)$$

to make clear that for f_j the same conditions prevail as for the functions D_j before. We simply measure output in other units. The similarity of the problem enables us to write immediately

$$\bar{f} = 1/J \; \Sigma \; f_j = \bar{D}(\bar{x}_1, \dots , \bar{x}_M) \qquad (3.13)$$

if all inputs are common for each individual. Taking $\bar{f} = \phi^{-1}(\bar{D})$ as in (3.10) we may write (3.13) after substitution of (3.12) also as

$$\bar{D} = \phi\left[1/J \sum_j h_j^{-1}(D_j)\right] = \phi\left[\bar{D}(\bar{x}_1, \ldots, \bar{x}_M)\right] \tag{3.14}$$

which is equation (2.3.5) of DM(1984). Hence (3.14) is in accord with theorem 2.4 of DM(1984) saying:

Consistent aggregation [of production] in an economy that is always on its [production] frontier is possible [within certain lower bounds x^o_{jm} of the inputs] if and only if the (micro) [production] functions are similar-homothetic and strictly quasi-concave in the [restricted] domain of the inputs. See DM(1984) p. 78.

Our example is a special case of such an economy as we have excluded production (pure exchange) and given all consumers equal initial endowments. The extension to DM's theorem 2.4 shows that production - and differing endowments - may only be introduced on the condition that the production functions are homothetic.

4. Homogeneity

4.1. To reduce the number of possible specifications of market demand functions we may introduce restrictions from individual demand theory. Nataf's theorem requires each market demand equation to be of type (2.5) if one wishes it to meet conditions of consistent aggregation. The theorem also implies -see DM(1984) formula (1.2.1) on p. 23- that then the individual or micro demand functions must be

$$D_j = f_j[\sum_m \phi_{jm}(x_{jm})] \tag{4.1}$$

The specification of f_j is only of relevance in a discussion on the additivity constraint. As we will concentrate below on one equation it can be ignored.

We will assume that prices are equal for all consumers and there are no other determinants of individual demand than income. Under these assumptions (4.1) may be written as

$$D_j = \sum_{m=1}^{M} \theta_m(p)\eta_m(y_j) \qquad (4.2)$$

the so-called Gorman class of Engelcurves.

(4.2) is additively separable in functions of income if $\theta_m(p)$ does not depend upon income (and additively separable in prices if $\eta_m(y_j)$ does not depend upon prices). Note that (4.2) coincides with (3.8) if we equate the θ's with the ψ's and $\eta_m(y_j)$ with w_n but for the moment we will drop the assumption that (4.2) is generated by a Taylor expansion. Hence the $\eta_m(y_j)$ need not to be the contribution to the mth moment of the income distribution.

In the appendix to Chapter 3 of DM(1984) we analyzed a special case of (4.2) with M=3 viz. $\eta_1(y_j)=1$ and $\eta_2(y_j)=y_j$ and η_2 arbitrary giving

$$D_j = \theta_1(p) + \theta_2(p)y_j + \theta_3(p)\eta_3(y_j) \qquad (4.3)$$

We found that for (4.3) only three different specifications are compatible with the homogeneity condition. They are

$$D_j = R_1 + Q_1 y_j + P_1 y_j^h \qquad (a)$$

$$D_j = R_2 + Q_2 y_j + P_2 y_j \log y_j \qquad (b) \qquad (4.4)$$

$$D_j = R_3 + Q_3 y_j + P_3 \log y_j \qquad (c)$$

where the coefficients R_s, Q_s and P_s are functions of the prices. Note that a Taylor-expansion of any individual demand function can always generate (4.4a) if the expansion is around $y_j=0$ with all exponents of the terms $\psi_j y_j^n$ vanishing except for those with n=0, n=1 and n=h. It is clear that the same result may appear if the function is expanded around $\bar{y}$, all terms $(y_j-\bar{y})^n$ are elaborated and an appropriate choice of zero coefficients is inserted.

From such a generation of (4.4a) it is already clear that the coefficients of R_1, Q_1 and P_1 are functions of prices of degree 0, -1 and -h respectively. The additivity on budget constraint requires that the coefficients satisfy $\sum_k p_k R_{ks} = \sum_k p_k P_{ks} = 0$ and $\sum_k p_k Q_{ks}=1$ for s=1,2,3, where k refers to the type of commodity. If we would not have taken f_j as the identity function the requirements would have been a little more general as they allow each demand function D_{jk} to be transformed k-specific.

We also derived Slutsky requirements for the special case in which $R_s=0$. Specifications of (4.4) with $R_s=0$ are not compatible with the Slutsky restrictions unless there exist functions a and b of prices (both positive for all prices) and a concave expenditure function $c_j(u,p)$ of a particular form. These forms depend upon the specification chosen.

For (4.4a) they are

$$Q_1 = \frac{1}{b}\frac{\partial b}{\partial p_k} \qquad \text{(a)}$$

$$P_1 = \frac{1}{a^h}\left(\frac{\partial a}{\partial p_k} - \frac{a}{b}\frac{\partial b}{\partial p_k}\right) \qquad \text{(b)} \qquad (4.5)$$

$$C_j = \left(a^{1-h} + \frac{|1-h|}{1-h} u_j b^{1-h}\right)^{\frac{1}{1-h}} \qquad \text{(c)}$$

with $h \neq 1$ and u_j individual j's utility.

For (4.4b) they are

$$Q_2 = \frac{1}{a}\frac{\partial a}{\partial p_k} - \frac{1}{b}\frac{\log a}{\log b}\frac{\partial b}{\partial p_k} \qquad \text{(a)}$$

$$P_2 = \frac{1}{b \log b}\frac{\partial b}{\partial p_k} \qquad \text{(b)} \qquad (4.6)$$

$$C_j = \exp(\log a + u_j \log b) \qquad \text{(c)}$$

For (4.4c) they are

$$Q_3 = \frac{1}{b} \frac{\partial b}{\partial p_k} \qquad (a)$$

$$P_3 = 0 \qquad (b) \qquad (4.7)$$

$$C_j = a + b\, u_j \qquad (c)$$

where as before we have omitted the commodity index k attached to the coefficients Q and P.

4.2. In DM(1984) we made a conjecture that for M>3 apart from combinations of (4.4a)-(4.4c) other specifications might enter the scene, but we did not go beyond our special choice (4.3). The general case for (4.2) is analysed by Gorman (1981). Gorman states that rank r of the matrix

$$\begin{bmatrix} \theta_{11}(p) & \cdots & \cdots & \theta_{1M}(p) \\ \vdots & & \vdots & \vdots \\ \vdots & & \theta_{mk}(p) & \vdots \\ \vdots & & \vdots & \vdots \\ \theta_{k1}(p) & \cdots & \cdots & \theta_{kM}(p) \end{bmatrix} \qquad (4.8)$$

should obey the restriction $r \leq 3$. He also claims to present an exhaustive list of all possible specifications that satisfy the restrictions on demand theory. Gorman's conclusions are clearly presented in his paper, but this cannot be said for the way he achieves them. We must confess that so far we were not able to understand his derivations properly, but we are able to show that one of his conclusions is not correct. This may be a misprint but it seduced Deaton to make a wrong statement in the introduction of Deaton [1981] -the book in honour of Stone which also contains Gorman's paper-.

To clarify our point we will restrict ourselves to homogeneity and to individual demand. To save on notation we will drop the index j referring to the individual from now on.

4.3. The homogeneity condition on demand requires - of Deaton and Muellbauer (1980 p. 16) - that the sum of price elasticities and the income elasticity is zero or in symbols

$$\sum_i \frac{\partial \ln D}{\partial \ln p_i} + \frac{\partial \ln D}{\partial \ln y} = 0 \tag{4.9}$$

Application to (4.2) yields

$$\sum_m \frac{\eta_m \theta_m}{D} \sum_i \frac{\partial \ln \theta_m}{\partial \ln p_i} = - \sum_m \frac{\eta_m \theta_m}{D} \frac{\partial \ln \eta_m}{\partial \ln y}. \tag{4.10}$$

So the weighted income elasticities of the income components must be equal to the weighted sum of the price elasticities of the coefficients θ_m.

To know what functions $D(y)$ arise we first take (4.2) with only one term, i.e. $D = \theta_m(p)\,\eta_m(y)$. In that case (4.10) reduces to

$$\sum_i \frac{\partial \ln \theta_m}{\partial \ln p_i} = - \frac{\partial \ln \eta_m}{\partial \ln y} \tag{4.11}$$

Note that this follows immediately from (4.9) acknowledging that θ_m is independent of income and η_m independent of prices.

In (4.11) we have an equation in which the right hand side only depends upon income and the left hand side only upon prices. They must therefore both be equal to some constant. We will call this constant h without indicating its domain, which will be discussed later. This gives

$$\frac{d \ln \eta_m}{d \ln y} = h \tag{4.12}$$

This is a differential equation the solution of which is

$$\eta_m = A\, y^h \qquad h \neq 0 \tag{4.13}$$

Hence a possible solution for a homogenous demand function that is consistent with aggregation theory is

$$D = \theta_h(p)\,y^h \tag{4.14}$$

where the constant A is included in the function $\theta_h(p)$. From (4.11) it follows that $\theta_h(p)$ should be of degree -h in the prices.

With respect to M>1 we immediately notice that a linear combination of functions (4.14) each satisfying (4.12) is also homogenous provided that the coefficients are independent of prices and income. Applying this to (4.14) with for h the values 0, 1 and h respectively yields (4.4a) again. For $h \in N$ we are back to a polynomial specification.

4.4. The second and third equation of (4.4) already suggest that other specifications are available, but it seems we have exhausted all specifications arising from M=1. One possibility to generalize to M>1 is to assume that the nth derivative of all functions η vanishes except for one particular η_m. This is equivalent with the procedure adopted in DM (1984) to solve the specific case with M=3. In DM (1984) we first applied Euler on (4.2) in view of the homogeneity and consecutively we took derivatives. Here we follow the simpler approach by differentiating first. Applying the approach to (4.2) we get

$$D_n = \frac{\partial^n D}{\partial y^n} = \theta_m \phi_m \tag{4.15}$$

with

$$\phi_m = \frac{d^n \eta_m(y)}{dy^n} \tag{4.16}$$

One should realize that the n-th differential of a homogenous function is by definition also a homogenous function. Hence, if we establish the degree of θ_m afterwards we may state that if (4.2) is homogenous ϕ_m may be treated as η_m before. This gives

$$\frac{\partial \ln \phi_m}{\partial \ln y} = h \tag{4.17}$$

with solution

$$\phi_m = \frac{d^n \eta_m(y)}{dy^n} = A\ y^h \tag{4.18}$$

This is again a differential equation which for n=1 gives the solution

$$\begin{aligned} &\text{if } h \neq -1: \quad \eta_m(y) = \frac{A}{h+1}\, y^{h+1} + B \quad &(a) \\ &\text{if } h = -1: \quad\quad\quad\quad = A \ln y + B \quad &(b) \end{aligned} \tag{4.19}$$

The polynomial case is illustrative. If a polynomial is homogenous also its derivative -a polynomial with one term less- and its integral -a polynomial with one term more- are homogenous provided we adapt the coefficients to the required degree in the prices. But (4.19b) provides a new specification, which resulted from integrating (4.18) with h=-1. Note that (4.19) cannot be a homogenous function if B=0 unless of course also A=0. This explains why the specification $\eta_m = A \ln y$ was not found, when we studied the class M=1 as such. We may represent (4.19) concisely by

$$\eta_m^{(h)}(y) = A^*\left[\frac{y^{h+1}-1}{h+1}\right] + B^* \tag{4.20}$$

For h=-1 we have (4.19b) and for h≠-1 we have (4.19a) with $A^* = \frac{A}{h+1}$ and $B = B^* - \frac{A^*}{h+1}$.

In (4.20) we recognize the Box-Cox transformation of y used e.g. by Muellbauer (1975, 1976). Representation (4.20) suggests that (4.20) is not only valid for h=-1 and for instance for h=0 or h=-2 but also for intermediate positions. Hence we need not restrict the domain of h to $h\in\mathbb{Z}$ but we may extend it to $h\in\mathbb{R}$ but we will not go into it here.

Finally we notice again that a linear combination of functions now (4.13) and (4.19) each satisfying (4.12) and (4.17) respectively also generates homogenous functions if the weights are appropriate. For instance combining (4.13) for h=1 with (4.19b) yields (4.4c).

Continuing along this line we start from (4.18) with n=2. This gives the solution

$$\eta_m(y) = \frac{A}{h+1} y^{h+1} + By + C \qquad h \neq -2,\; h \neq -1 \qquad (a)$$

$$= A \ln y + By + C \qquad h = -2 \qquad (b) \qquad (4.21)$$

$$= Ay \ln y + By + C \qquad h = -1 \qquad (c)$$

which is m.m. equal to (4.4). So in (4.21c) we also have rediscovered (4.4b). Combination of functions shows that the terms ln y and y ln y can also appear together in one specification. Note that (4.21b) cannot be homogenous if B=0 unless A=0.

Combining (4.19a) and (4.19b) into (4.20) suggests that it is perhaps possible to find formulae -super Box-Cox transformations- that combine all specifications of (4.21). We have not found them yet. Another possibility is to combine Box-Cox transformations into a demand function

$$D = \Sigma \phi_m(p) \left[\frac{y^m - 1}{m}\right] \qquad (4.22)$$

which opens new fields if we do not restrict the domain of m to $\mathbb{Z}$.

4.5. Comparing (4.21) with (4.19) we observe that for higher n we only have to integrate the lower line to give the new specification. So for n=3 we add

$$\eta_m = Ay^2 \ln y + B y^2 + Cy + D \qquad (4.23)$$

with one restriction on the coefficients A and B. Extending this series for higher n generates terms that are either of type Ay^h or of type $Ay^h \ln y$ with $h \in \mathbb{N}$. In (4.20) we have seen that solutions of (4.18) are not only valid for

$h=-1$ and other $h\in Z$ but it seems that we may generalize for all $h\in\mathbb{R}$. In any case a class of formulae that satisfies constraints on consistent aggregation and on homogeneity is

$$D = \sum_{m\in \mathbb{N}} \theta_m(p) y^m + \sum_{h\in \mathbb{N}} \theta_h(p) y^h \ln y \qquad (4.24)$$

with one restriction upon the $\theta_h(p)$'s, which arises from the fact that the term $A\, y^h \ln y$ needs the possibility of being cancelled when differentiated. Comparison of (4.24) with the results obtained by Gorman (1981) reveals a difference. Instead of terms $y^h \ln y$ Gorman mentions terms $y \ln^h y$. We presume that this is a misprint. At least the terms $y^h \ln y$ that are not given by Gorman should be included. We fail to see where terms $\ln^h y$ with higher powers than $h=1$ might come from. Anyway, if such terms are not allowed, this is also true for

$$\ln D = A + B \ln y + C \ln^2 y \qquad (4.25)$$

which in our opinion does not satisfy Nataf and homogeneity simultaneously. This equation is used by Deaton in his introduction of Deaton [1981] to clarify Gorman's results.

4.6. Equation (4.24) is not yet the most general form. We may understand this if we realise that we can have admissable cases with two terms that are in itself inadmissable. We have seen them already in $D = A \ln y + B$ which is not allowed for $B = 0$ and $A \neq 0$. Another possibility arises for $M = 2$ where (4.15) to (4.17) are valid for both m but for different h and different n. An example is $n = 2$ for $m = 1$ and $n = 1$ for $m = 2$. A linear combination of them gives

$$\frac{d^2\eta}{\partial y^2} + w\frac{d\eta}{dy} + c = 0 \qquad (4.26)$$

This may lead to functions with terms like

$$\eta = Ae^{ay} \cos(wy-\varepsilon) \qquad (4.27)$$

Gorman has functions

$$\eta_m = y \sin m \ln y \tag{4.28a}$$

and

$$\eta_m = y \cos m \ln y \tag{4.28b}$$

We have not elaborated the point. We only notice the appearance of ln y instead of y in (4.28).

4.7. A final remark should be made on the aggregation of (4.24). It is clear that ignoring the dependency between the θ functions we may write

$$\bar{D} = \sum_{m \in \mathbb{N}} \theta_m(p)[\frac{1}{J} \sum_j y_j^m] + \sum_{h=0}^{H} \theta_h(p) [\frac{1}{J} \sum_j y_j^h \ln y]$$

or

$$\bar{D} = \sum_{m \in \mathbb{N}} \theta_m(p) g_m + \sum_{h=0}^{H} \theta_h(p) q_h \tag{4.29}$$

where both g_m and q_h are some kind of generalized "central" moment. It needs not be added that the degree of the functions θ(p) in the prices are to be derived from the degree in income of the connection term in income.

5. Final remark.

Although we have left the implications of Taylor's expansion in section 4, this will not indicate that all help that is offered by Taylor's expansion around Nataf's theorem is exhausted. For instance in the field of estimation which we have completely ignored here, Taylor approximations may be helpful.

References.

1. Deaton, A.S., Essays in the theory and measurement of consumer behaviour; in honour of Richard Stone, Cambridge University Press, 1981.

2. Deaton, A.S. and J. Muellbauer, Economics and consumer behaviour, Cambridge University Press, 1980.

3. Gorman, W.M., Some Engel Curves, Chapter 1 in: Deaton, A.S. (1981).

4. Green, H.A.J., Aggregation in economic analysis, an introductory survey, Princeton University Press, Princeton, 1964.

5. Keller, W.J., Aggregation of economic relations, A note, De Economist, 128 (1980), pp. 558-562.

6. Muellbauer, J., Aggregation, income distribution and consumer demand. Review of economic studies 62 (1975), pp. 525-543.

7. Muellbauer, J., Community Preferences and the Representative Consumer, Econometrica, 44 (1976), pp. 979-1000.

8. Nataf, A., Sur la possibilité de construction de certain macromodeles, Econometrica 16 (1948), pp. 232-244.

9. Van Daal, J. and A.H.Q.M. Merkies, Aggregation in economic research, D. Reidel Publ. Cy, Dordrecht, 1984.

Consistent Aggregation of a General Equilibrium Model

Arnis Vilks

Institut für Statistik und Ökonometrie
Universität Hamburg
Von-Melle-Park 5 , D - 2000 Hamburg 13

1. Introduction

While there are many results on topics such as aggregation of utility and of production functions, little attention has been paid to the problem of aggregating a complete general equilibrium model - where the economic behaviour of every firm and household with respect to every commodity is considered - into a similar model where only a few aggregate commodities are explicitly taken into account. This paper presents some definitions and results pertaining to this problem.

Throughout, the analysis will be confined to the most simple framework admitting a discussion of general equilibrium, namely, to static Walrasian theory on the excess demand function level. I.e., we assume that an economy can be described by a mapping

$$z: \mathbb{R}^n_{++} \longrightarrow \mathbb{R}^n ,$$

which attaches to each vector $p=(p_1,p_2,\ldots,p_n)$ of prices the vector $z(p)=(z_1(p),z_2(p),\ldots,z_n(p))$ of excess demands arising at prices p.

While in microeconomic theory the n commodities are thought of as being "completely specified physically, temporally, and spatially"[1], macroeconomists frequently employ models which are perfectly analogous to the micro ones, except that, however, the vast number of conceivable micro-commodities is replaced by only a few (typically 3 or 4) aggregate commodities, such as "the" consumption good, "labour", etc. In order that this practice be consistent with micro theory, yielding macro theory with the same type of explanatory power[2], one must be able, given a micro excess demand function z(.), to devise, along with definitions of aggregate prices and quantities, a macro excess demand function which depends on aggregate prices only. Moreover,

Measurement in Economics
ed. by W. Eichhorn

the zeros of the macro function must coincide with the aggregates of the zeros of z(.).

These requirements of consistency are made precise in Section 3 via the definition of an aggregate solution for a microeconomic excess demand function. It is then pointed out that, given the existence of an aggregate solution, central properties (gross substitutability, homogeneity, and continuity) of the micro excess demand function are either inherited by the corresponding macro model or can be made to hold by suitable choice of an aggregate solution.

Section 4 deals with the problem of existence of aggregate solutions. This is done by defining certain binary relations on the set $z(\mathbb{R}^n_{++})$ and imposing restrictions on these relations. A set of necessary conditions is presented which by a slight strengthening turns into a sufficient set of conditions.

Proofs of the theorems are given in Section 5.

2. Notation

Let A be a partition of $\{1,2,\ldots,n\}$, and I an element of A. Subvectors of $p\in\mathbb{R}^n$, and subfunctions of z(.) will then be denoted as follows:

$$Ip = (p_i)_{i\in I},$$

$$Iz(p) = (z_i(p))_{i\in I}.$$

Moreover, $I\in A$ will be used as a binary operator on $\mathbb{R}^n$ according to the definition:

$$pIq = r \quad \text{iff} \quad \begin{cases} r_i = p_i & \text{for all } i\notin I, \\ r_i = q_i & \text{for all } i\in I. \end{cases}$$

Vector-inequalities are denoted as follows:

$$p \geq q \quad \text{iff} \quad p_i \geq q_i \quad \text{for all } i,$$

$$p > q \quad \text{iff} \quad p \geq q \text{ and } p \neq q.$$

3. Aggregate Solutions and Properties of Macro-Models

Throughout the paper we will assume that $z(.)$ has the property

(CH) continuity and homogeneity of degree zero.

In order that consistent aggregation of $z(.)$ be possible, one must be able to specify, for each group of micro-commodities which is thought of as constituting one macro-commodity, how prices resp. quantities of this macro-commodity are to be measured. In addition, macro excess demands so defined must depend on the vector of macro prices only. We define[3]:

Definition 1. Let A be a partition of $\{1,2,...,n\}$ into N non-empty sets. A system $(p_I(.),Q_I(.),Z_I(.))_{I\in A}$ of 3N real-valued functions with appropriate domains of definition is called an aggregate solution for $z:\mathbb{R}^n_{++}\to\mathbb{R}^n$, w.r.t. A, iff for each $I\in A$, the following holds:

a) $Z_I((P_L(Lp))_{L\in A}) = Q_I(Iz(p))$, $\forall\, p\in\mathbb{R}^n_{++}$,

b) $P_I(.)$ is continuous and increasing,

c) $Q_I(.)$ is continuous and increasing.

While it is perfectly natural to require properties like b) and c) of the index functions $P_I(.)$, $Q_I(.)$, it is desirable to derive the properties of the macro excess demand function $Z(.)=(Z_I(.))_{I\in A}$ from properties of $z(.)$ and the index functions. A result of this type can be proved when $z(.)$ is assumed to have the property of gross substitutability.

Theorem 1. Let $z(.)$ satisfy (CH) and $(P_I(.),Q_I(.),Z_I(.))$ be an aggregate solution for $z(.)$. If $z(.)$ satisfies the assumption of (strict) gross substitutability (GS), then so does $Z(.)$.

(In accordance with common usage, (GS) is taken to mean the following:

(GS) If $p,q\in\mathbb{R}^n_{++}$ are such that $p_i > q_i$ and $p_k = q_k$ for all $k \neq i$, then: $z_i(p) < z_i(q)$, and $z_k(p) > z_k(q)$ for all $k \neq i$.

In the case of $Z(.)$, (GS) has to be defined analogously.)

Whereas on the micro level (GS) must be regarded as highly

restrictive[4] and therefore will not be assumed henceforth, we will, from now on, consider only such aggregate solutions, where the macro excess demand function $Z(.)$ satisfies (GS). In macro-economics, (GS) seems to be a natural - or at least usual - assumption, even when it is not supposed to hold on the micro level. If $Z(.)$ satisfies (GS), we will say, for short, that the aggregate solution itself satisfies (GS).

<u>Theorem 2</u>. If $z(.)$ satisfies (CH), and an aggregate solution satisfying (GS) exists, then there is an aggregate solution $(P_I(.),Q_I(.),Z_I(.))$ such that the $P_I(.)$'s are (positive) linear homogeneous and $Z(.)$ satisfies (GS) and (CH).

Homogeneity of degree zero means that one can chose one of the N macro commodities as a numéraire. Homogeneity and (GS) imply uniqueness of equilibrium[5] :

<u>Corollary 1</u>. Let the conditions of Theorem 2 be fulfilled and let $(P_I(.),Q_I(.),Z_I(.))$ be appropriately chosen. Then

$$Z_I(P_1^*,P_2^*,\dots,P_N^*) = Z_I(P_1^{**},P_2^{**},\dots,P_N^{**}) \quad \text{for all} \quad I \in A$$

implies that there is a $k \in \mathbb{R}_{++}$ such that

$$(P_1^*,P_2^*,\dots,P_N^*) = k \cdot (P_1^{**},P_2^{**},\dots,P_N^{**}).$$

However, there may be no zero of $Z(.)$, even if there is a zero of $z(.)$. In order that aggregating micro equilibrium prices gives us macro equilibrium prices, we require:

(E) $\quad z(p^*) = 0 \quad \text{implies} \quad Z((P_I(Ip^*))_{I \in A}) = 0$.

It is easily seen, however, that requiring (E) does not pose additional problems:

Let $(P_I(.),\overline{Q}_I(.),\overline{Z}_I(.))$ be an aggregate solution for $z(.)$, and let $z(p^*) = 0$. Then we can simply define

$$Q_I(Iz) = \overline{Q}_I(Iz) - \overline{Q}_I(Iz(p^*)),$$

$$Z_I(P_1,\dots,P_N) = \overline{Z}_I(P_1,\dots,P_N) - \overline{Z}_I((P_L(Lp^*))_{L \in A}),$$

and $(P_I(.),Q_I(.),Z_I(.))$ is an aggregate solution satisfying (E). Formally:

Corrollary 2. Let the conditions of Theorem 2 be fulfilled. Then an aggregate solution exists, which, in addition to linear homogeneity of the $P_I(.)$'s, (GS), and (CH), has property (E).

(Notice that, if z(.) has multiple equilibria, and an aggregate solution satisfying (GS) exists, all micro equilibrium price vectors must have the same aggregate values.)

In sum, then, existence of an aggregate solution satisfying (GS) allows us to describe a Walrasian economy z(.) by a similar, simplified macro-model Z(.). Appropriate measurement of aggregate prices and quantities could then legitimize macroeconomic arguments such as, e.g., "a rising wage-level deminishes excessdemand for labour". In order to determine macro prices compatible with micro equilibrium, one had to know only the macro excess demand functions.

We now turn to the question of existence.

4. Existence of Aggregate Solutions

What must be assumed about the micro model z(.), if it is maintained that an aggregate solution satisfying (GS) (w.r.t. a given aggregative structure A) exists ?

Consider any two excess demand vectors of group I:

$$x, y \in Iz(\mathbb{R}^n_{++}) .$$

It is obvious that an aggregate solution will exist only if it is always possible to decide unambiguously, whether x corresponds to a greater macro-excess demand for group I than y, or whether this is not the case. That is, for each group of commodities $I \in A$, there must be a partial order $\overset{I}{<}$ on the set of group I excess demand vectors $Iz(\mathbb{R}^n_{++})$ such that "$x \overset{I}{<} y$" may be interpreted as "x is, in the aggregate, less than y". Of course, the quantity index $Q_I(.)$ will have to be a numerical representation of this order. The Theorems 3 and 4 which will follow, suggest that this order may be formally defined as follows:

Definition 2.

$$x \overset{I}{<} y \quad \text{iff} \quad \exists p,q \in \mathbb{R}^n_{++},\ \exists\ K \in A : \quad Iz(p) < Iz(pKq),$$
$$x \leq Iz(qKp),\ Iz(q) \leq y .$$

I.e., relation $\overset{I}{<}$ holds for $x,y \in Iz(\mathbb{R}^n_{++})$, iff for some pair of price vectors p, pKq, which differ only in the K-th group components, and give rise to excess demands (in group I) which are comparable by "<", it is possible, by changing the prices outside group K, to get a pair of excess demands (in group I), the first one of which is (component-wise) not less than x, while the second is not greater than y. Loosely speaking, the relation holds between x and y, if they are indirectly "pressed apart" by excess demands arising at prices which differ only in one group's components.

Absence of the above relation will be denoted as follows:

$$x \overset{I}{\boldsymbol{>}} y \qquad \text{iff} \qquad \text{not} \quad x \overset{I}{<} y ,$$

while $\overset{I}{\boldsymbol{<}}$ and $\overset{I}{>}$ will, of course, denote the converse of $\overset{I}{\boldsymbol{>}}$ and $\overset{I}{<}$, respectively. (As the symbols are suggestive, it should be noted that $\overset{I}{<}$ may well fail to be an order.)

Using the relations just defined, it is possible to derive a number of necessary conditions for the existence of an aggregate solution satisfying (GS).

Theorem 3. If an aggregate solution for z(.) w.r.t. A exists, and satisfies (GS), then the following conditions must hold for all $I,K,L \in A$:

a) $\overset{I}{\boldsymbol{>}}$ is reflexive and complete;

b) $Ix > Iy$ implies $Ix \overset{I}{\boldsymbol{>}} Iy$,

c) $Kp > Kq$ implies $Iz(p) \overset{I}{\boldsymbol{>}} Iz(pKq)$ for $I \neq K$, and
$Kz(p) \overset{I}{\boldsymbol{<}} Kz(pKq)$;

d) if $Iz(p) \overset{I}{>} Iz(pKq)$, then

d1) $Iz(qKp) \overset{I}{\boldsymbol{>}} Iz(q)$,

d2) $Lz(p) \overset{L}{\boldsymbol{>}} Lz(pKq)$ for $I \neq L,\ K \neq I,\ K \neq L$,

d3) $Lz(p) \overset{L}{\boldsymbol{<}} Lz(pKq)$ for $I \neq L$, but $K=I$, or $K=L$.

Whereas the conditions of Theorem 3 are only necessary, Theorem 4 shows how they can be strengthened to result in a set of conditions which is sufficient.

Theorem 4. If, in the conditions of Theorem 3,
under a) "transitive and continuous" is added,
under b) and c) the weak relations ($\overset{I}{\succsim}$ and $\overset{K}{\precsim}$) are replaced by the corresponding strong ones ($\overset{I}{\succ}$ and $\overset{K}{\prec}$, respectively),
under d) the strong relation is replaced by the weak one, then the resulting set of conditions implies that an aggregate solution for z(.) w.r.t. A exists and satisfies (GS).

5. Proofs

Proof of Theorem 1. Let $(P_L(.),Q_L(.),Z_L(.))_{L\in A}$ be an aggregate solution for z(.) and let $p,q\in\mathbb{R}^n_{++}$ be such that for $I\in A$:

$$P_I(Ip) > P_I(Iq), \qquad \text{while}$$

$$P_K(Kp) = P_K(Kq) \qquad \text{for all } K\neq I.$$

By continuity and strict monotonicity of $P_I(.)$, there is a real number k>1, such that

$$P_I(Ip) = P_I(k\cdot Iq).$$

Then, by Definition 1a), c) and (GS), it follows that for $K\neq I$:

$$Z_K([P_L(Lp)]_{L\in A}) = Z_K([P_L(L(qIkq))]_{L\in A})$$

$$= Q_K(Kz(qIkq)) > Q_K(Kz(q)) = Z_K([P_L(Lq)]_{L\in A}),$$

and, exploiting homogeneity of z(.), it follows that

$$Z_I([P_L(Lp)]_{L\in A}) = Q_I(Iz(qIkq))$$

$$= Q_I(Iz((\tfrac{1}{k}\cdot q)Iq)) < Q_I(Iz(q)) = Z_I([P_L(Lq)]_{L\in A}).$$

Q.E.D.

<u>Proof of Theorem 2</u>. Let $(P_I(.), Q_I(.), Z_I(.))$ be an aggregate solution for $z(.)$ which satisfies (GS). First, we construct another aggregate solution $(\overline{P}_I(.), Q_I(.), \overline{Z}_I(.))$ such that the $\overline{P}_I(.)$'s are linear homogeneous.

Take $K \in A$, $a \in \mathbb{R}^n_{++}$, and define for each $I \in A$ a preordering $\overset{I}{\gtrsim}$ on $\mathbb{R}^{|I|}_{++}$ by:

$$Ip \overset{I}{\gtrsim} Iq \text{ iff } \begin{cases} Q_K(Kz(aIp)) \geq Q_K(Kz(aIq)) & \text{for } I \neq K, \\ Q_K(Kz(aIp)) \leq Q_K(Kz(aIq)) & \text{for } I = K. \end{cases}$$

The properties of these N preorderings are well known: Each $\overset{I}{\gtrsim}$ is represented by the corresponding $P_I(.)$ and, hence, $\overset{I}{\gtrsim}$ is increasing. Moreover, $\overset{I}{\gtrsim}$ is continuous. (Cf., e.g., BLACKORBY, PRIMONT, and RUSSELL (1978), pp. 59-60.) From Definition 1 and (GS) it follows that $\overset{I}{\gtrsim}$ does neither depend on K nor on a. This and homogeneity of $z(.)$ imply that $\overset{I}{\gtrsim}$ is homothetic (i.e., $Ip \overset{I}{\gtrsim} Iq$ implies $k \cdot Ip \overset{I}{\gtrsim} k \cdot Iq$ for all $k>0$). For $Q_K(Kz(aIp)) \geq Q_K(Kz(aIq))$ implies $Q_K(Kz(k \cdot (aIp))) \geq Q_K(Kz(k \cdot (aIq)))$ and, hence, $Q_K(Kz(aIkp)) \geq Q_K(Kz(aIkq))$. Following KATZNER (1970), pp. 24-25, we construct a linear homogeneous representation $\overline{P}_I(.)$ of $\overset{I}{\gtrsim}$ as follows. As $\overset{I}{\gtrsim}$ is increasing and continuously represented by $P_I(.)$, there is a mapping

$$m_I : \mathbb{R}^{|I|}_{++} \longrightarrow IE := \{ x \in \mathbb{R}^{|I|}_{++} \mid \exists k \in \mathbb{R}_{++} : x = k \cdot (1,1,\ldots,1) \},$$

such that $Ip \overset{I}{\sim} m_I(Ip)$. Now define $\overline{P}_I(.)$ as follows:

$$\overline{P}_I(Ip) = ||m_I(Ip)||.$$

Clearly, $\overline{P}_I(.)$ is a representation of $\overset{I}{\gtrsim}$. Moreover, it is linearly homogeneous, for homotheticity of $\overset{I}{\gtrsim}$ implies that

$$k \cdot Ip \overset{I}{\sim} k \cdot m_I(Ip),$$

whence, by linear homogeneity of the Euclidean norm and the fact that, for $x \in IE$, $m_I(x) = x$,

$$\overline{P}_I(k \cdot Ip) = ||m_I(k \cdot m_I(Ip))|| = k \cdot ||m_I(Ip)|| = k \cdot \overline{P}_I(Ip).$$

To prove that $\overline{P}_I(.)$ is continuous, notice that the restriction of $P_I(.)$ to IE is bicontinuous. Now, consider $O \subset IE$, open in IE. Bicontinuity of the restricted $P_I(.)$ implies that $P_I(O)$ is open in

$\mathbb{R}_{++}$. Continuity of $P_I(.)$ then implies that $P_I^{-1}(P_I(O))$ is open in $\mathbb{R}_{++}^{|I|}$. As $P_I^{-1}(P_I(O)) = m_I^{-1}(O)$, this proves continuity of $m_I(.)$ and, hence, of $\overline{P}_I(.)$.

To define the $\overline{Z}_I(.)$'s, observe that $P_L(Lp)=P_L(Lq)$ iff $\overline{P}_L(Lp)=\overline{P}_L(Lq)$. Hence, for each $I\in A$ a function $\overline{Z}_I(.)$ is well defined by

$$\overline{Z}_I((\overline{P}_L(Lp))_{L\in A}) = Z_I((P_L(Lp))_{L\in A}).$$

Of course, $(\overline{P}_I(.),Q_I(.),\overline{Z}_I(.))_{I\in A}$ is an aggregate solution for $z(.)$ and satisfies (GS).

It remains to prove that each $\overline{Z}_I(.)$ has the property (CH).

To prove continuity, consider a sequence (p^l) such that

$$\lim_{l\to\infty} ((\overline{P}_L(Lp^l))_{L\in A}) = (\overline{P}_L(Lp^*))_{L\in A} .$$

This implies that, for each $L\in A$, $\lim_{l\to\infty} m_L(Lp^l) = m_L(Lp^*)$.

Hence, by continuity of $Q_L(Lz(.))$ and Definition 1a) :

$$\lim_{l\to\infty} \overline{Z}_I((\overline{P}_L(Lp^l))_{L\in A}) = \lim_{l\to\infty} \overline{Z}_I((\overline{P}_L(m_L(Lp^l)))_{L\in A})$$

$$= \lim_{l\to\infty} Q_I(Iz((m_L(Lp^l))_{L\in A})) = Q_I(Iz((m_L(Lp^*))_{L\in A})$$

$$= \overline{Z}_I((\overline{P}_L(m_L(Lp^*)))_{L\in A}) = \overline{Z}_I((\overline{P}_L(Lp^*))_{L\in A}).$$

So the $\overline{Z}_I(.)$'s are continuous.

Finally, by linear homogeneity of the $\overline{P}_L(.)$'s and homogeneity of degree zero of $z(.)$:

$$\overline{Z}_I((k\cdot\overline{P}_L(Lp))_{L\in A}) = \overline{Z}_I((\overline{P}_L(k\cdot Lp))_{L\in A}) = Q_I(Iz(kp))$$

$$= Q_I(Iz(p)) = \overline{Z}_I((\overline{P}_L(Lp))_{L\in A}) ,$$

so the $\overline{Z}_I(.)$'s are homogeneous of degree zero. Q.E.D.

Theorem 3 is a simple consequence of the following

Lemma. Let $(P_I(.),Q_I(.),Z_I(.))$ be an aggregate solution satisfying (GS) and let the relations $\overset{I}{<}$ be defined according to Definition 2. Then

$$x \overset{I}{<} y \quad \text{implies } Q_I(x) < Q_I(y).$$

Proof. By definition, $x \overset{I}{<} y$ implies the existence of $a,b,p,q \in \mathbb{R}^n_{++}$, $K \in A$, such that

$$x \leq Iz(aKp), \quad Iz(aKq) \leq y, \quad Iz(bKp) < Iz(bKq).$$

By monotonicity of $Q_I(.)$, the latter inequality implies

$$Q_I(z(bKp)) < Q_I(z(bKq)),$$

which, by the properties of an aggregate solution, means that

$$Z_I((P_L(L(bKp)))_{L\in A}) < Z_I((P_L(L(bKq)))_{L\in A}) .$$

Hence, by (GS), $P_K(Kp) < P_K(Kq)$ if $I \neq K$, while $P_K(Kp) > P_K(Kq)$ if $I=K$. Again by (GS),

$$Z_I((P_L(L(aKp)))_{L\in A}) < Z_I((P_L(L(aKq)))_{L\in A}) ,$$

and, hence, $Q_I(Iz(aKp)) < Q_I(Iz(aKq))$.

Monotonicity of $Q_I(.)$ then implies $Q_I(x) < Q_I(y)$. Q.E.D.

Proof of Theorem 3. Making use of the above Lemma, the assumption that any of the conditions a) -d) is violated, can be readily seen to contradict the existence of an aggregate solution satisfying (GS). Consider, e.g., condition c). Assume that $Kp > Kq$ and, for an $I \neq K$, $IZ(p) \overset{I}{<} Iz(pKq)$. The Lemma implies $Q_I(Iz(p)) < Q_I(Iz(pKq))$, hence $Z_I((P_L(Lp))_{L\in A}) < Z_I((P_L(L(pKq)))_{L\in A})$. This, by (GS), implies $P_K(Kp) < P_K(Kq)$, which contradicts $Kp > Kq$.

Similarly, necessity of a),b),d), and the second part of c) can be proved. Q.E.D.

Proof of Theorem 4. Let a')-d') denote the conditions of Theorem 3, modified according to Theorem 4. Assume them to be fulfilled.

First, consider a fixed $I \in A$. By continuity of $Iz(.)$, the set $Iz(\mathbb{R}^n_{++})$ is connected. By a'), the Relation $\overset{I}{\gtrsim}$ is a continuous and complete preordering on this set and, hence, can be represented by a continuous real-valued function $Q_I(.)$. (Cf. DEBREU (1959), p. 56.) By b'), $Q_I(.)$ is increasing.
Now, consider the function $Q_I(Iz(.))$. It is continuous and, by c'), increasing (decreasing) in the i-th argument, if $i \notin I$ ($i \in I$). Moreover, by d'1), it is strictly separable in the partition A. Hence, it can be written in the form

$$Q_I(Iz(p)) = Z_I([P_K(Kp)]_{K \in A}),$$

where the $P_K(.)$'s are continuous and increasing, and $Z_I(.)$ is increasing (descreasing) in P_K if $K \neq I$ ($K=I$). (Cf. BLACKORBY, PRIMONT, and RUSSELL (1978), p. 108.)

As the same reasoning applies to each I, it remains to be shown that one and the same system of price indices $(P_K(.))_{K \in A}$ can be chosen for all I.

To show this, note that, with $Z_I(.)$ chosen appropriately, $P_K(.)$ may be any continuous representation of the preordering $\underset{K}{\overset{I}{R}}$ on the set $\mathbb{R}^{|K|}_{++}$, defined by

$$Kp \underset{K}{\overset{I}{R}} Kq \text{ iff } \begin{cases} Q_I(Iz(aKp)) \geq Q_I(Iz(aKq)) & \text{for } I \neq K \\ Q_I(Iz(aKp)) \leq Q_I(Iz(aKq)) & \text{for } I=K. \end{cases}$$

Now, assume $L \neq I$, $K \neq L$, and $K \neq I$. Then $Kp \underset{K}{\overset{I}{R}} Kq$ implies that

$Q_I(Iz(aKp)) \geq Q_I(Iz(aKq))$ and hence $Iz(aKp) \overset{I}{\gtrsim} Iz(aKq)$.
Then, by d'2), $Lz(aKp) \overset{L}{\gtrsim} Lz(aKq)$, hence $Q_L(Lz(aKp)) \geq Q_L(Lz(aKq))$, and, therefore, $Kp \underset{K}{\overset{L}{R}} Kq$. If $K=I$ or $K=L$, d'3) has to be applied analogously.

Thus, the preorderings $\overset{I}{\underset{K}{R}}$ and $\overset{L}{\underset{K}{R}}$ coincide and can be represented by the same $P_K(.)$. Q.E.D.

6. Concluding Remarks

Existence of an aggregate solution as defined above must be regarded as a minimal requirement for there to be a close analogy between detailed and aggregative models of general equilibrium. However, it is not more than that. At the risk of pointing at the obvious, we indicate briefly that, in itself, existence of aggregate solutions does not even suffice to make comparative statics on the macro level meaningful.

Let z(.) and z'(.) be two different economies, p, p' their respective equilibria in terms of a common numeraire, and let

$(P_I(.), Q_I(.), Z_I(.)), (P'_I(.), Q'_I(.), Z'_I(.))$ be

corresponding aggregate solutions, satisfying condition (E). If it now happens, e.g., that Ip>Ip', it seems that the corresponding inequality should hold unambiguously for aggregate equilibrium prices of group I.

Nevertheless it may be the case that $P_I(Ip) < P'_I(Ip')$.

In a sense, this type of problem is an inherent feature of the consistency approach to the aggregation problem. As consistency can only be achieved by choice of a "tailor-made" set of index functions, this approach makes the very definitions of the aggregates depend on the micro model. And when the micro model changes it is not only the macro model which has to change accordingly, but the meaning of the macro variables as well.[6)]

Footnotes

1) DEBREU (1959), p. 32.

2) When macro-models are only required to give "approximate" explanations, instead of deterministic or "causal" ones, other types of aggregation procedures are possible. Cf. VILKS (1984, 1986).

3) The term "aggregate solution" has been introduced by POKROPP in the context of aggregating production functions. Cf. POKROPP (1978).

4) Cf. ARROW and HAHN (1971), pp. 225-227.

5) This well-known fact can be easily proved by adapting an argument given by IRITANI (1981). Cf. VILKS (1984), pp. 64-65.

6) This was emphasized already by MAY (1947), pp. 58-63.

References

Arrow, K.J., F.H. Hahn (1971), General Competitive Analysis, Amsterdam, New York, Oxford.

Blackorby, Ch., D. Primont, R.R. Russell (1978), Duality, Separability, and Functional Structure, New York.

Debreu, G. (1959), Theory of Value, New Haven and London.

Iritani, J. (1981), On the Uniqueness of General Equilibrium, in: Review of Economic Studies 48.

Katzner, D.W. (1970), Static Demand Theory, London.

May, K. (1947), Technological Change and Aggregation, in: Econometrica 15.

Pokropp, F. (1978), The Functional Equation of Aggregation, in: Eichhorn, W., Functional Equations in Economics, London.

Vilks, A. (1984), Aggregation und Kausalität im Modell des allgemeinen Konkurrenzgleichgewichts, Göttingen.

Vilks, A. (1986), Approximate Aggregation of Excess Demand Functions, Unpublished.

Part IX Econometrics

The Concept of "Scale" and Related Topics in the Specification of Econometric Cost Functions: Theory and Application to Hospitals

Friedrich Breyer and Franz-Josef Wodopia
Universität Heidelberg
Alfred-Weber-Institut
Grabengasse 14
D-6900 Heidelberg

1. Introduction[1]

Analysing the cost structure of firms in a particular industry may serve several purposes, especially if the industry in question is subject to public regulation.

(1) By estimating the relationship between the costs per unit of output and the size of the plant (or, alternatively, the level of operation), inferences can be drawn on returns to scale and thus on optimal plant size. If the industry consists partly or entirely in publicly owned firms, this information can have important policy consequences.

(2) In particular if the output of the industry is a non-storable good, a "service" with stochastic demand, the regulator may want to split up total operating costs into a constant component that reflects the costs of providing the service as such and a variable component that depends upon the level of utilization of the plant. This division can, e.g., be of interest with regard to socially optimal pricing rules like "marginal cost pricing".

(3) While in both considerations above it is assumed that the firms in question produce their respective quantities of output at minimum costs, this is certainly not in general true if the market for the industry's product is regulated and the firms themselves have non-profit status. This is often the case with natural monopolies and, particularly, public utilities. In these cases, comparing the unit costs across firms, accounting for differences in scale of

[1] The authors are grateful to Shawna Grosskopf and C.A. Knox Lovell for helpful discussions and to Joachim Neipp and two anonymous referees for critical comments on an earlier draft of this paper.

Measurement in Economics
ed. by W. Eichhorn

operation, product quality, factor prices and other relevant determinants of costs, is an important step towards assessing and controlling the efficiency with which an individual firm operates.

The estimation of the cost structure of an industry with econometric techniques is especially important if the regulating agency wants to promote efficiency by setting appropriate price incentives. E.g., prices may be set equal to the "standard" costs of producing a certain product in plants with comparable characteristics rather than the actual costs of the individual regulated firm.

(4) Finally, the property rights structure of the firms may itself be the subject of public concern. Comparing the unit costs incurred by otherwise similar firms of different ownership type (private profit-oriented, private non-profit, public) and different organizational structure can serve the public in deciding on the nationalization or denationalization of industry or on the opening of regulated markets to commercial suppliers.

An econometric cost study tries to estimate the structural parameters of a mathematical function that is postulated to express the relationship between the costs incurred by a firm in a certain period (either in total or per unit of output) and various explanatory variables like quantity and quality of the firm's output, size of the plant, product mix (for multiproduct firms), factor prices and organizational structure. As there is usually no way of measuring the efficiency of operation independently of the incurred costs, efficiency can not be entered as an explanatory variable, but has to be inferred in retrospect from the residual of the cost estimation.

In this paper we are concerned, among other problems, with the question how to measure the theoretical construct "size of the plant" or "scale of operation" in a meaningful way in econometric cost studies. In Section 2 we present a general model of a firm's cost function and discuss the choice of scale indexes in this theoretical framework. Section 3 is devoted to the application to a particular industry, namely to hospitals. Using this example we are going to show what difficulties are encountered if a) the notion of "unit of output" is ambiguous, and b) the firm produces more than just a few different outputs. Section 4 gives a short summary.

2. The General Methodology

2.1 Theoretical and Empirical Cost Functions

Usually it is assumed that minimal variable costs are a function of the vector of produced quantities $y \in R^m$, the vector of prices of variable inputs $p_v \in R^k$ and a vector of fixed inputs $z \in R^r$ (see NADIRI 1982, p.454):

$$C_v = C_v\ (p_v, y, z). \qquad (2.1)$$

If the vector of prices of fixed inputs is denoted by p_z we can easily deduce the short-run total cost function from (2.1):

$$C_s = C_v\ (p_v, y, z) + p_z \cdot z. \qquad (2.2)$$

In the long run costs do not depend on z but on the prices of fixed factors, p_z, and these fulfill the envelope condition if cost minimizing behavior is assumed.

The application of the above type of cost functions is restricted, however, to cases in which there are no deviations from the cost-minimizing input combination. An alternative approach designed for empirical application is denoted "behavioral cost function" (EVANS 1971). Here, the assumption of cost minimization is replaced by the assumption that a different type of managerial behavior (which one, may be unknown to the researcher) prevails, which again makes costs a well-defined function of the exogenous variables.

This approach should be adopted if the performance of different firms, the individual degree of efficiency and the influence of individual decisions on costs are the objectives of analysis. As we are interested in measuring scale effects in such an analytical environment, we will apply an empirical cost equation containing the following regressors:

- output quantities represented by a vector y (especially different qualities of a heterogeneous output)
- factor prices
- output capacity, i.e. quantities of fixed factors.

The costs resulting from the estimation of such a cost equation, in the following denoted by C^{emp}, can then be interpreted as "standard costs", i.e. the costs incurred by a firm operating with an average degree of efficiency. The degree of efficiency of an individual firm can be read from the error term e, which measures the deviation of actual costs in the firm from the costs predicted by the estimation.

With the formulation of (2.2) the first econometric problem of cost studies becomes obvious: the estimated parameters of fixed factors have no single interpretation as either prices of fixed factors p_z or as parameters of the variable cost function C_v, which in turn are determinants of the opportunity costs of capital. To isolate these effects we should estimate in general only variable cost equations. To distinguish theoretical and empirical concepts in the following we will speak of "operating" costs instead of "variable" costs. This nomenclature has the following advantage. Even variable factors may have both a fixed and a variable component. We avoid this semantic contradiction by using the term operating costs,

$$C_o^{emp} = C_o^{emp}(p_v, y, z). \qquad (2.3)$$

2.2 Measurement of Returns to Scale

For the time being we restrict our considerations to a single-product firm with one output whose quantity is denoted by $Y \in R$, and a single fixed factor, measured by $Z \in R$. The empirical cost equation has then the following shape:

$$C_o^{emp} = C_o^{emp}(p_v, Y, Z). \qquad (2.4)$$

In Section 2.8 we shall extend the analysis to the multiproduct firm. In the introduction we mentioned the importance of measuring returns to scale and drawing inferences on the optimal plant size. Our first question is whether the size of a plant or the output reflects scale effects better. As the theoretical definition of returns to scale relates to the produced quantities, let us start with this measure. The output, however, also reflects changes in capacity utilization because it is a measure for actually used capacity whereas the plant size describes a potential. For this reason we have to be aware of the "regression fallacy"-problem. FRIEDMAN (1955) has shown that the dependency of the indicator for firm size on the utilization rate may lead to wrong interpretations of returns to scale. Suppose, e.g., that short-run fluctuations in capacity utilization have little impact on total operating costs. Then an increasing utilization rate leads to increasing output and decreasing average operation costs.

This negative correlation could be interpreted erroneously as indicating increasing returns to scale.

The second possible measure for returns to scale is the size of a plant. If we denote by D a time interval, e.g. 365 days, the output capacity of one year is given by Z·D. If we use the output capacity Z·D as an indicator of returns to scale, or - as D is a constant - only Z, we have to consider that firms often need part of their capacity as a reserve for stochastic fluctuations in demand. It is sometimes argued that this fraction will itself depend negatively on the firm size (see. e.g., CARR and FELDSTEIN, 1967, JOSKOW 1980). Corrections for reserve capacity are then necessary. If, however, there is a network of suppliers serving a given set of potential customers then reserve requirements refer to the set of suppliers as a whole rather than to the individual firm. There is little reason to suppose that smaller firms have to bear more than a proportional share of this combined reserve requirements. Therefore we think that Z is in general a better measure for scale than Y.

2.3 The Impact of Capacity Utilization on Costs

So far we have not yet considered the problem of a changing capacity utilization over time, especially daily, seasonal and other cyclical effects. Theoretically we could formulate a disaggregated model with respect to time. However, if available data are aggregated over time or if we want to concentrate also on long-run effects we cannot fully disaggregate over time. Then we have to solve the problem of finding an aggregate representation for a technology which is constant within one period but at the same time allows for varying utilization of fixed factors.

A very simple and often the only possibility to capture this problem is using average capacity utilization as a variable, which we denote by U. But a look at equation (2.4) shows that U in principle has already been included, when Y and Z are in the equation, since the three are interrelated for technical reasons. Take electricity generation as an example. Dividing the produced quantity of electricity (Y) by the maximal power of a plant (Z) yields the capacity utilization factor (U) of a plant. In this and many other applications we therefore have to be aware of the following identity:

$$Y = Z \cdot U. \qquad (2.5)$$

Introducing U as an additional argument into (2.4) thus will generate multicollinearity, which in turn leads to high standard errors and perhaps even to implausible signs of parameter estimates. A better procedure would be to estimate the modified version of (2.4) together with (2.5) as a simultaneous equation system.

2.4 The Shape of the Cost Function

In empirical studies cost functions are often specified as linear in all arguments. While linear functions are computationally easy to handle, this form is based on the implicit assumption of strong separability (additivity) in all regressors. Furthermore, linear cost functions are in general not linear- homogeneous in factor prices and therefore are incompatible with cost minimization. However, as we are concerned with behavioral cost functions, the latter is not a major objection (see also Section 2.6 below).

An alternative concept which allows for non-separable structures and in some cases also for testing for cost minimization is based on "flexible functional forms", which have the advantage that they can in most cases be interpreted as local second order Taylor-approximations of the true functional relationship. The forms suggested and empirically applied in the literature have the following shape, where $(x_1,\ldots,x_n)$ is the vector of arguments in the cost function:

$$g(C(x)) = a_0 + \sum_i a_i \cdot f_i(x_i) + \frac{1}{2} \sum_i \sum_j a_{ij} \cdot f_i(x_i) \cdot f_j(x_j) \qquad (2.6)$$

$(a_{ij} = a_{ji}$ for all i,j).

In the case of the translog form the functions g and f_i are logarithms, in order to receive the generalized Diewert form (see LAU 1974, p.184) we have to substitute $g(C)=C$ and $f_i(x_i)=\sqrt{x_i}$, and the quadratic form is characterized by $g(C)=C$ and $f_i(x_i)=x_i$ (BLACKORBY, PRIMONT and RUSSELL 1978, pp.290). Flexible functional forms require weaker implicit economic assumptions than other functional forms (see e.g. WODOPIA 1986, pp.129). On the other hand we have to deal with the symmetry restrictions $a_{ij}=a_{ji}$, and the number of parameters to be estimated incrases dramatically with the number of arguments in the vector x. Especially products of functions of economic variables are additional regressors. This in turn leads to fundamental problems in connection with the identity (2.5). An inclusion of all relevant variables, Y, Z, and U, at the same time will clearly result in perfect multicollinearity. E.g. with ln Y the translog function implicitly includes ln(Z·U) = ln Z + ln U, in the generalized Diewert form the term $\sqrt{Z}\cdot\sqrt{U}$ corresponds to $\sqrt{Y}$ and the quadratic form includes Z·U = Y directly.

We conclude that there is a discrepancy between the econometric problem of multicollinearity as a reason for the omission of one the variables of (2.5) and the modelling of non-separable structures. Which variable should be omitted is largely a matter of convenience. It will turn out that the choice of an appropriate dependent variable will have an impact on this question, too.

2.5 Total Costs versus Average Costs

There are mainly two types of econometric cost functions,[2]

- regressions on absolute magnitudes, and
- regressions on per-unit magnitudes.

The first approach uses total costs as dependent variable. This leads usually to high values of R^2. Nevertheless this does not imply that the economic model explains well the underlying technology. The observed correlation is often only a trivial one (KOLLER 1963, p.69) between costs, output and capacity. Further, regressions on absolute magnitudes will cause heteroskedastic errors because the residual is presumably correlated with firm size (BREYER 1986, p.10).

The problem of multicollinearity of output and capacity implying high standard errors and vague estimators is circumvented if the total cost equation is divided by output quantity and thus average costs, that is costs per unit of output, are used as regressand. Especially we note that the new error term e/Y is more likely to meet the OLS-assumption of homoskedastic errors.

2.6 Choice of Regressors

In the following we will confine our discussion to the quadratic form:

---

[2] The following considerations hold for linear functions as well as for flexible functional forms with g(C)=C.

$$g(C(x)) = a_0 + \sum_i a_i \cdot x_i + \frac{1}{2} \sum_i \sum_j a_{ij} \cdot x_i \cdot x_j \quad (2.7)$$

$(a_{ij} = a_{ji}$ for all i,j).

We know from Section 2.4 that one of the theoretically relevant variables Y, Z and U has to be omitted. There are two economically reasonable ways to do this. First a look at identity (2.5) suggests that Y is a derived variable that can be eliminated. This point of view is supported by the fact that capacity and utilization are the relevant variables to describe how a "fund factor" (see GEORGESCU-ROEGEN 1971, p.224) is used over time.

However, by using costs per unit of output as left-hand side variable the quadratic cost function (2.7) with arguments Z and U would contain the variables Z/Y (= 1/U), U/Y (= 1/Z), a constant, Z^2/Y (= Z/U) and U^2/Y (= U/Z). Some of these variables do not lend themselves to an easy interpretation. In addition it is not very expedient to have both Z/U and its inverse as regressors.

The second approach is used more frequently in the literature, because it corresponds closely to the theoretical function (2.1): Here Y and Z are used as original variables, and thus an average cost function corrsponding to (2.7) contains the terms Z/Y (= 1/U), a constant, Z, Z^2/Y (= Z/U) and Y. This approach is more convenient than the first one, because it is plausible that average costs depend on capacity, the relation of capacity to its utilization and output. Only 1/U seems superfluous and may be eliminated if muticollinearity does still present a problem.

Let us turn to the problem of how to enter factor prices into the cost function. Cost functions which are based on cost minimization must be positive linear-homogeneous in factor prices (PLH). Therefore a functional form should have this property for at least one combination of parameters if this behavioral assumption is made. As mentioned in Section 2.1 we are, however, interested in behavioral cost functions which are not derived from cost minimization and therefore do not have to be PLH. As a consequence we are allowed to apply linear cost functions and the quadratic form which has an interpretation as local second order Taylor-approximation but is not PLH.

Although factor prices play an important rôle in theoretical cost functions they are sometimes difficult to measure or are even inaccessible. Furthermore, in cross-section analysis they often do not differ across observations and may therefore reveal no great impact.

Let us assume that only one factor price P_v and the variables Y and Z have to be considered. Then (2.7) can be specialized to

$$C_o^{emp}(Y,Z,P_v) = a_0 + a_1 \cdot Y + a_2 \cdot Z + a_3 \cdot P_v + \frac{1}{2}a_{11} \cdot Y^2 + \frac{1}{2}a_{22} \cdot Z^2 + \frac{1}{2}a_{33} \cdot P_v^2 + a_{12} \cdot Y \cdot Z + a_{13} \cdot Y \cdot P_v + a_{23} \cdot Z \cdot P_v. \quad (2.8)$$

In Section 2.5 we argued that average costs should be used as regressand rather than total costs. Therefore we divide (2.8) by Y to get average costs:

$$C_a^{emp}(Y,Z,P_v) = \frac{a_0}{Y} + a_1 + a_2 \cdot \frac{Z}{Y} + a_3 \cdot \frac{P_v}{Y} + \frac{1}{2}a_{11} \cdot Y + \frac{1}{2}a_{22} \cdot \frac{Z^2}{Y} + \frac{1}{2}a_{33} \cdot \frac{P_v^2}{Y} + a_{12} \cdot Z + a_{13} \cdot P_v + a_{23} \cdot \frac{ZP_v}{Y}. \quad (2.9)$$

2.7 The Impact of Plant Size on Unit Costs

An interesting question is whether there is an optimal plant size, as far as operating costs per unit of output are concerned. For this purpose, the average cost function has to be differentiated with respect to Z. In doing this, however, it is not allowed to hold output Y constant because this would imply that arbitrarily large and therefore infeasible values of capacity utilization U are considered. In contrast, a useful approach is based on varying Y in proportion with Z so that U is held constant. We therefore substitute Y by Z·U (see (2.5)), reformulate (2.9) in order to express average costs as a function of U, Z and P_v and differentiate the modified equation (2.9) partially with respect to Z:

$$\frac{\partial C_a^{emp}(U,Z)}{\partial Z} = a_{12} + \frac{a_{11}}{2}U + \frac{a_{22}}{2} \cdot \frac{1}{U} - \frac{1}{UZ^2}(a_0 + a_3 \cdot P_v + \frac{a_{33}}{2}P_v^2) \quad (2.10)$$

If (2.10) is set equal to zero we receive the following necessary first order condition for optimal plant size:

$$Z^{opt} = \sqrt{\frac{2a_0 + 2a_3 \cdot P + a_{33} \cdot P_v^2}{a_{22} + 2a_{12} \cdot U + a_{11} \cdot U^2}} \tag{2.11}$$

In this case for every given capacity utilization we can calculate an optimal size of plant, as far as operating costs are concerned. The necessary condition is also sufficient for a minimum of average costs with respect to Z if the numerator of the square root in (2.11) is positive. If the same is true for the denominator, the solution is economically meaningful.

2.8 Multiproduct Cost Functions

The main additional problem brought about by the multi-product naature of most firms is that the number of parameters to be estimated rises rapidly with the number of different outputs that have to be distinguished. This is true in particular for flexible functional forms, where the number of parameters increases at least with the square of the number of original variables (see, e.g., CAVES, CHRISTENSEN and TRETHEWAY 1980), so it soon becomes unsuitable for estimation with a limited number of empirical observations. Therefore it is not surprising that the term "multi" in multi-product cost functions estimated so far mostly refers to a number between 2 and 5.

In order to gain additional degrees of freedom, researches often estimate cost share equations (for the individual inputs) along with the cost function since from Shephard's Lemma both are characterized by the same parameters (e.g. CAVES, CHRISTENSEN and SWANSON 1980). However, this produce is not applicable to behavioral cost functions, because Shephard's Lemma makes use of the cost minimization assumption, which is not valid here.

A further problem consists in the fact that in some cases the arguments of the multiproduct cost function are not directly observable. This holds in particular for the output vector $y_1,\ldots,y_n$. Therefore one has to define aggregation functions $m_s=m_s(y_s)$ on S nonempty disjoint subsets of the vector y, namely y_s (s=1,...,S) and to replace the left-hand side of (2.3) by

$$C_o^{emp} = C_o^{emp}(P_v, m_1(y_1), \ldots, m_S(y_S), z). \tag{2.12}$$

This partition is admissible if and only if the function $C_o^{emp}(.)$ is weakly separable with respect to the partition S. However, in practice we will often observe only proxy variables which describe the product-mix imperfectly, for example the sum of heterogenous components of the vector y_s. In general, the sum operator differs from the theoretical aggregation function m_s, so that outputs are not aggregated consistently. In Section 3 we are going to discuss the problem of finding appropriate vectors of proxy variables for the empirical application to hospitals.

3. Application to Hospitals

3.1. Measuring Output

If we apply the model developed in Section 2 to hospitals, an obvious measure of plant size Z is the number of beds, and the time dimension of service is measured in days, so that in cross-sectional studies covering one year, D takes on the value 365. The expression $Z \cdot D$, "available bed days per year", measures the capacity to deliver services in terms of patient days.

This, however, is not the whole story since at least two problems are involved in measuring plant size and output level.

The first problem is concerned with the choice of an appropriate output measure. An obvious measure that corresponds to the index of service capacity introduced above would be the number of patient days. If the symbol Y is interpreted accordingly, then Y is bounded from above by the number of available bed days, $Z \cdot D$. Furthermore, $U = Y/Z$ denotes the number of days per year in which the average hospital bed is filled, and the ratio $Q := U/D$ denotes the average occupancy rate of the hospital, i.e. the average proportion of beds that are occupied.

However, "patient days" as output has several serious drawbacks:

1. The final output of a hospital is the improvement in health status of the patients treated. Since this concept is very hard to operationalize, let alone to measure, an appropriate proxy has to be used. Of the available proxies, number of hospital admissions or cases X, and number of inpatient days Y, the former comes closer or the true output "improvement in health stauts", whereas days in hospital themselves can be considered as an input into the

treatment of patients (cases) along with other inputs like surgical procedures, x-rays or injections (see LAVE and LAVE 1978).

2. The number of cases treated in a particular hospital during a period of time is almost exclusively determined outside the hospital, especially by the morbidity of the relevant population and the decisions of ambulatory care physicians to refer patients to this hospital. In contrast, this does not hold for the number of patient days delivered. Once a patient has been admitted, the length of his stay is at the discretion of the in-hospital physicians who are in charge of his care.

   Therefore, Y as a product of number of cases X and average length of stay L is itself an endogenous quantity. If in econometric studies of hospital costs total costs are regressed on number of patient days and other explanatory factors, this introduces the danger of simultaneity bias, since hospital decision-makers may have expanded length of stay and thus total patient days in order to make up unecpected cost increases by generating additional revenues. So costs have influenced output rather than the reverse.

Both considerations suggest using the number of cases treated, X, as output measure, so that unit costs refer to the costs per admission. This procedure has the additional advantage that there is no longer a one-to-one correspondence between output quantity X and capacity utilization, U·Z, as long the mean length of stay L is variable. This can be inferred from the identity

$$U \cdot Z = Y = X \cdot L \tag{3.1}$$

Consequently, in applying the flexible functional form model postulated in equation (2.9) to the variables X and Z, the problem of multicollinearity is less serious than in the general case discussed above. Here the full second-order approximation of the theoretical per-unit cost equation is

$$\frac{C}{X} = \frac{a_0}{X} + a_1 + a_2 \cdot \frac{Z}{X} + a_3 \cdot \frac{P_v}{X} + \frac{1}{2} a_{11} \cdot X + \frac{1}{2} a_{22} \cdot \frac{Z^2}{X} + \frac{1}{2} a_{33} \cdot \frac{P_v^2}{X}$$
$$+ a_{12} \cdot Z + a_{13} \cdot P_v + a_{23} \cdot \frac{ZP_v}{X}. \tag{3.2}$$

Again, we notice that the term Z/X is connected with two pairs of other terms (viz. Z and X as well as Z and Z^2/X) through simple multiplicative identities. Hence this term should probably be omitted from the equation in order to reduce the degree of multicollineraity.

3.2 Specifying the Functional Form

The functional form in (3.2) can be compared with an ad-hoc specificatiion underlying the typical empirical cost estimation in the hospital cost literature (e.g. EVANS 1971, FELDSTEIN and SCHUTTINGA 1977, LAVE, LAVE and SILVERMAN 1972). This is of the type

$$\frac{C}{X} = b_1 + b_2 \cdot L + b_3 \cdot Q + b_4 \cdot Z + b_5 \cdot Z^2 + b_6 \cdot P_v. \qquad (3.3)$$

The two terms in Z are included in order to capture the effect of plant size on costs per case: A negative coefficient of Z and a positive coefficient of Z^2 would suggest that there is an "optimal" plant size where costs per case are minimized. In order to make the specification consistent with the flexible functional form given in (3.2), however, Z^2 should be divided by X.

Furthermore, it is not reasonable to include both mean length of stay L and average occupancy rate Q as separate regressors in addition to number of beds Z, because L, Q, and Z are interrelated through the identity

$$L \cdot X = D \cdot Z \cdot Q. \qquad (3.4)$$

Having all three variables in the equation would aggravate the problems of multicollinearity. Instead, (3.2) suggests using the ratio Z/X as a regressor, which is related to L and Q through

$$\frac{Z}{X} = \frac{1}{D} \cdot \frac{L}{Q}, \qquad (3.5)$$

where 1/D is a constant. So it is perfectly consistent with our flexible functional form approach to use the ratio of L and Q as a regressor in order to analyse the influence of (inverse) capacity utilization on unit costs.

3.3 The Multiproduct Nature of Hospital Production

The third problem encountered in applying our general model of the case of hospitals is the heterogeneity of output. The multiproduct nature of hospital production is seen most clearly when output is measured by the number of cases, i.e. the number of patients treated. From a medical viewpoint, each patient constitutes an individual case type due to his characteristics like type, stage and severity of illness, secondary diagnoses, age, and response to therapy. Even if patients with similar characteristics are grouped together, a large number of categories have to be introduced in order to achieve a sufficient degree of in-group homogeneity. With such a categorization, the patient mix variables, which measure the frequency distribution of patients across the various categories, become important determinants of hospital costs.

As we argued in Section 2.8, the number of parameters to be estimated varies dramatically with the inclusion of new variables if the flexible functional form approach is used. Therefore, in the application of this approach to a hospital cost function COWING and HOLTMANN (1983) employed a very crude classification of output (patients) in only five categories. In contrast, the traditional hospital cost studies used considerably finer classification systems with the number of categories ranging from 17 to several hundred.

Obviously, such large numbers of output variables would cause the flexible functional form approach to collapse. On the other hand, it is theoretically unsatisfactory to impose a linear relationship just to economize on degrees of freedom. A reasonable middle course would be using a specific functional form which can be regarded a good approximation to the true functional relationship between costs and their determinants.

Let $x(j)$ denote the number of cases in the j-th category $(j=1,...,n)$ and $m(j) = x(j)/X$ the corresponding proportion such that

$$\sum_{j=1}^{n} x(j) = X \qquad (3.6)$$

$$\sum_{j=1}^{n} m(j) = 1, \qquad (3.7)$$

then a possible specification for the costs per case equation is

$$\frac{C}{X} = \frac{a_0}{X} + a_1 + a_2 \cdot X + a_3 \cdot \frac{Z}{X} + a_4 \cdot \frac{Z^2}{X} + a_5 \cdot \frac{P_v}{X} + a_6 \cdot \frac{P_v^2}{X}$$

$$+ \sum_{j=1}^{n-1} b_j m(j) \tag{3.8}$$

The underlying idea is that the true total cost equation is approximated by a polynomial of degree two in the global variables capacity (Z), output (X) and factor price (P_v), and interaction effects are ignored. Dividing by X yields (3.8). The case-mix adjustment variables m(j) are entered only linearly in order to keep the number of parameters manageable. Here the last category m(n) is omitted to avoid linear dependence of the vector of m's with the constant term.

It remains to be seen in empirical applications whether this specification can explain real data well. In any event, the quadratic form allows for any type of behavior of costs with respect to scale both in terms of capacity and of output quantity and thus constitutes a progress over most of the specifications used so far in the applied literature.

4. Summary

The empirical methodology for estimating cost functions for firms in specific industries has considerably advanced during the last decades through the development of duality theory and of flexible functional forms. However, in actual applications certain modifications of these basic concepts may be necessitated by real-world characteristics such as deviations from cost-minimizing behavior, varying degrees of capacity utilization, or multiple-output production.

After discussing theoretical solutions to these problems in general we illustrated their possible application using the hospital industry as an example. The specification proposed in this paper differs markedly both from the ad-hoc forms prevailing in the hospital cost literature to date and from the basic flexible functional form model. Of course only the actual empirical application can show the relative usefulness of this model compared to others.

References

BLACKORBY, C., PRIMONT, D., and RUSSELL, R.R. (1978), Duality, Separability, and Functional Structure: Theory and Economic Applications (New York: North-Holland).

BREYER, F. (1986), "Krankenhaus-Kostenstudien: Ein methodischer Überblick", Zeitschrift für Betriebswirtschaft 56: 260-286.

CARR, W.J. and P.J. FELDSTEIN (1976), "The Relationship of Cost to Hospital Size", Inquiry 4: 45-65.

CAVES, D.W., L.R. CHRISTENSEN, and J.A. SWANSON (1980), "Productivity in U.S. Railroads, 1951-1974", Bell Journal of Economics 11: 166-181.

CAVES, D.W., L.R. CHRISTENSEN, and M.W. TRETHEWAY (1980), "Flexible Cost Functions for Multiproduct Firms", Review of Economics and Statistics 62: 477-481.

COWING, T.G. and A.G. HOLTMANN (1983), "Multiproduct Short-Run Hospital Cost Functions: Empirical Evidence and Policy Implications from Cross-Section Data", Southern Economic Journal 49: 637-653.

EVANS, R.G. (1971), "'Behavioral' Cost Functions for Hospitals", Canadian Journal of Economics 4: 198-215.

FELDSTEIN, M.S. and J. SCHUTTINGA (1977), "Hospital Costs in Massachusetts: A Methodological Study", Inquiry 14: 22-31.

FRIEDMAN, M. (1955), "Comment" on C.A. Smith, "Survey of the Empirical Evidence on Economies of Scale", in: G. Stigler (ed.): Business Concentration and Price Policy, Princeton.

GEORGESCU-ROEGEN, N. (1971), The Entropy Law and the Economic Process, Cambridge/Mass.

JOSKOW, P.L. (1980), "The Effects of Competition and Regulation on Hospital Bed Supply and the Reservation Quality of the Hospital", Bell Journal of Economics 11 (2): 421-447.

KOLLER, S. (1963), "Typisierung korrelativer Zusammenhänge", Metrika 6: 65-75.

LAU, L.J. (1974), "Comments" on W.E. DIEWERT, "Applications of Duality Theory", in: M.D. INTRILIGATOR and D.A. KENDRICK (Eds.), Frontiers of Quantitative Economics, Vol.II, Amsterdam: 176-199.

LAVE, J.R. and L.B. LAVE (1978), "Hospital Cost Function Analysis: Implications for Cost Controls", in: M. ZUBKOFF et al. (eds.), Hospital Cost Containment. New York: 538-571.

LAVE, J.R. and L.B. LAVE, and L.P. SILVERMAN (1972), "Hospital Cost Estimation Controlling for Case-Mix", Applied Economics 4: 165-180.

NADIRI, M.I. (1982), "Producers Theory", in ARROW, K.J. and INTRILIGATOR, M.D. (ed.), Handbook of Mathematical Economics II. New York: North-Holland.

WODOPIA, F.-J. (1986), Intertemporale Produktionsentscheidungen: Theorie und Anwendung auf die Elektrizitätswirtschaft. Mathematical Systems in Economics (Eds. W. EICHHORN et al.), Vol. 102, Frankfurt/M.

Theory and Measurement of Productivity and Cost Gaps: A Comparison for the Manufacturing Industry in U.S., Japan and Germany, 1960 - 1979

Klaus Conrad
Lehrstuhl für Volkswirtschaftslehre
insb. Mikroökonomie
Seminargebäude A5
D-6800 Mannheim 1

1. Introduction

The purpose of this study is the quantification of the hypothesis that in international competition in technology and efficiency the less developed countries chase the newly developed countries, these in turn chase Japan, and Japan has chased Western Europe and the United States. Since the U.S. and Western Europe seem to forfeit their role as the engine of innovations, they run the risk of getting surpassed by the former trailers like Japan and the newly developed countries. One reason for the catching-up process is that after World War II individual countries have experienced different growth rates in total factor productivity (TFP). Such differences accumulate over time and contribute to the reduction of prevailing productivity gaps in an international comparison. Besides this unexplained residual TFP there are also pure economic factors which contribute to a change in productivity gaps. Amongst those factors are an equalization of marginal productivities, of input and output prices and of factor intensities.

In this paper we attempt to measure and explain the development of differences in productivity relative to a base country for the manufacturing industry of the U.S., Japan and Germany. Our first objective is to provide a theoretical framework within which the change in total factor productivity, the change in the differences in levels of technologies and the sources of those changes can be analyzed. This framework, first developed by Jorgenson and Nishimizu (1978, 1979) is extended here to

* I thank Ralph Unger for computing assistance and i am indebted to Dale W. Jorgenson for providing the U.S. data and to M. Kuroda for the Japanese data.

Measurement in Economics
ed. by W. Eichhorn

the dual cost approach to reflect the efficiency aspect of the productivity gap in terms of a cost disadvantage. Our three country comparison is based on index numbers of the Törnqvist-type. As these economic indexes represent translog aggregator functions, our second objective is to employ the translog production and cost function in order to analyze the source of the changes in productivity and cost gaps.

In section 2 we present a brief discussion of the methodology developed by Jorgenson and Nishimizu (1978) in their bilateral comparison of aggregate output, input and productivity for the U.S. and Japan. This concept has been extended to multilateral comparisons by Caves, Christensen and Diewert (1982) and Denny and Fuss (1983), and has been implemented empirically by Christensen, Cummings and Jorgenson (1981) and Conrad and Jorgenson (1985). Our methodological novelty will be to introduce indexes of cost gaps as dual to the productivity gaps which are related to cost functions instead of production functions. In section 3 we briefly discuss the sources of data for outputs, input, and purchase power parities. We also introduce a Törnqvist index of purchasing power parities of inputs to obtain a purchasing power parity index of output. In section 4 we provide an empirical description of the development of productivity gaps and cost gaps for the manufacturing industry for the period 1960 - 1979. In section 5 we present the econometric model consistent with our choice of Törnqvist-index numbers, interpret the parameter estimates and discuss their signs and magnitudes. In section 6, finally, we summarize our results.

2. The Methodology of Measuring Productivity and Cost Gaps

For measuring productivity and cost gaps we employ a formal analytical framework which is based on the neoclassical theory of cost an production.[1)]

As a point of departure we assume long run equilibrium on the factor markets in spite of business cycles, slack capacity, price shocks and regulation. It is left for future research to weaken this strong assumption and to study the relevance of its implication. Following Jorgenson and Nishimizu (1978), our methodology is based on a constant returns to scale joint production function for a sectoral output of our three coun-

---

1) See Nelson (1981) for a recent review on research on productivity and differences

tries U.S. (U), Japan (J) and Germany (G):

(1) $x = F(v, D_J, D_U, t)$

where x is the sectoral output, v is the vector of inputs, t is time, and D_J and D_U are dummy variables equal to one for the corresponding country and zero otherwise. As we express levels of output, input and total factor productivity relative to Germany, we omit a dummy variable for Germany from the production function. The dummy variables capture the country-specific deviation from the joint production process as given in (1). If we want to derive the difference in the level of output between Germany and Japan at a given point of time, we differentiate (1) totally with respect to D_J (see Denny and Fuss (1983,b) for a justification):

(2) $$\frac{d\,x}{d\,D_J} = \sum_{i=1}^{n} \frac{\partial F}{\partial v_i} \frac{d\,v_i}{d\,D_J} + \frac{\partial F}{\partial D_J}$$

In terms of logarithmic derivatives (2) is equivalent to:

(3) $$\frac{d \ln x}{d\,D_J} = \sum_{i=1}^{n} \frac{\partial \ln x}{\partial \ln v_i} \frac{d \ln v_i}{d\,D_J} + \frac{\partial \ln x}{\partial D_J}$$

The difference in productivity between any country and Germany, say $w_{J,G}$ in case of Japan, is defined as follows:

(4) $$w_{J,G} \equiv \frac{\partial \ln x}{\partial D_J} = \frac{d \ln x}{d\,D_J} - \sum \frac{\partial \ln x}{\partial \ln v_i} \frac{d \ln v_i}{d\,D_J}$$

The difference in productivity of a sector between two countries, $w_{J,G}$, is the logarithmic difference in that sectors' output levels between countries, holding factor input and time constant. For calculating the difference in productivity we use (4) with weights depending on the assumptions made with respect to firms' behavior and price determination.

Under the assumption of perfect competition we obtain:

(5) $$\frac{\partial \ln x}{\partial \ln v_i} = \frac{q_i\, v_i}{p \cdot x} \equiv w_i \qquad i = 1, \ldots, n$$

where p and q_i ($i = 1, \ldots, n$) are the prices of output and inputs, respectively. In this case, the difference in productivity (4) can be calculated as:

$$(6) \quad w_{J,G} = \frac{d \ln x}{d D_J} - \sum_{i=1}^{n} w_i \frac{d \ln v_i}{d D_J}$$

The advantage of measuring differences in productivity by means of Divisia index (6) is that the production function need not be specified. Since measurement is based on discrete data points we approximate the continuous Divisia index by a discrete index. In order to make the resulting approximation error as small as possible we make sure that the index is "exact".[2] We use as a discrete approximation of the Divisia index the Törnqvist-index. This index number is exact if the underlying production function is of the flexible translog specification.

In this case (6) becomes an expression for differences in productivity referred to as <u>translog index of differences in productivity:</u>[3]

$$(7) \quad \bar{w}_{J,G} = \ln x(J) - \ln x(G) - \sum_i \bar{w}_i(\ln v_i(J) - \ln v_i(G))$$

where $\bar{w}_i$ is an average of the cost shares of both countries:

$$\bar{w}_i = \frac{1}{2}\,(w_i(J) + w_i(G)) \;.$$

$\bar{w}_{J,G}$ is the rate of change in output of the Japanese relative to the German industry. Therefore, if $\bar{w}_{J,G}$ is positive (negative) the Japanese are more (less) efficient in combining the German input quantities and the German sector has a productivity disadvantage (advantage).

Similarly to the translog index of differences in productivity we can define the translog index of productivity growth (Christensen and Jorgenson (1970)). For this reason we do not determine differences in output and productivity between two countries but between two points in time. Instead of (3) we obtain

---

2) See Diewert (1976), and Lau (1979) for exact indexes in the economic theory of index numbers.

3) The translog index of differences in productivity was introduced by Jorgenson and Nishimizu (1978).

$$\text{(8)} \quad \frac{d \ln x}{dt} = \Sigma_i \frac{\partial \ln x}{\partial \ln v_i} \cdot \frac{d \ln v_i}{dt} + \frac{\partial \ln x}{\partial t}$$

where $w_t := \frac{\partial \ln x}{\partial t}$ is the rate of productivity growth defined as the growth of output with respect to time, holding factor inputs and the country dummy variables constant. Similarly as above, the <u>translog index of productivity growth</u> between consecutive discrete data points for a given country is:

$$\text{(9)} \quad \bar{w}_t = \ln x(t) - \ln x(t-1) - \Sigma_i \bar{w}_i (\ln v_i(t) - \ln v_i(t-1))$$

where $\bar{w}_i = \frac{1}{2}(w_i(t) + w_i(t-1))$ is an average of the countries cost shares.

For making multilateral productivity comparisons we cannot use the bilateral index discussed above as those indexes are not base-country invariant. Bilateral indexes do not satisfy the circularity condition; i.e. all pairs of comparisons should pass the following circularity condition for the differences in productivity relative to the base country:

$$w_{J,G} = w_{J,U} + w_{U,G}$$

Caves, Christensen and Diewert (1982) have derived a translog multilateral index of productivity which satisfies the circularity condition and imposes no a priori restrictions on the structure of production. To achieve circularity they construct a hypothetical country H with output $\overline{\ln x}$, inputs $\overline{\ln v_i}$ and cost shares $\overline{w_i}$ where a bar indicates the average over all three countries. Using their approach the difference in productivity between any country C = J,U relative to Germany is:

$$\begin{aligned} \bar{w}_{C,G} &= \ln x(c) - \ln x(G) \\ \text{(10)} \qquad & - \frac{1}{2} \Sigma_i (w_i(C) + \bar{w}_i)(\ln v_i(C) - \overline{\ln v_i}) \\ & + \frac{1}{2} \Sigma_i (w_i(G) + \bar{w}_i)(\ln v_i(G) - \overline{\ln v_i}) \,. \end{aligned}$$

This expression for differences in productivity, the translog multilateral index of differences in productivity, is base-country invariant (circular), and specializes to the bilateral index in the two-country case.

Given a well-behaved joint production function we obtain by definition the corresponding joint cost function:

$$(11)\quad c = C(x,q,D_J,D_U,t) = \min_v \{q'v | x = F(v,D_J,D_U,t)\}$$

where the v_i's and x are measured in constant dollar values obtained from national data by the definition:

$$(12)\quad v_i = v_i^C \,/\, PPv_i^C,\ x = x^C \,/\, PPx^C$$

Here, v_i^C and x^C are the inputs or output quantities respectively, in constant national currency units of country C and PPv_i^C and PPx^C are the purchase power parities (PPP) for input i or output in national currency units per dollar; i.e. DM/$, Yen/$ or unity for C = U.S.. As price times quantity on dollar base should be equal to the nominal cost in national currency units we require as factor reversal test for q_i and p to be:

$$(13)\quad q_i = q_i^C \cdot PPv_i^C \quad,\quad p = p^C \cdot PPx$$

where q_i^C and p^C are price indexes from the national accounts of country C.

If we want to derive the difference in the level of cost between Germany and Japan at a given point of time, we differentiate (11) logarithmically with respect to D_J:

$$(14)\quad \frac{d \ln c}{d D_J} = \frac{\partial \ln c}{\partial \ln x}\,\frac{d \ln x}{D\, D_J} + \Sigma_i \frac{\partial \ln c}{\partial \ln q_i}\,\frac{d \ln q_i}{d D_J} + \frac{\partial \ln c}{\partial D_J}$$

Using Shephard's lemma we obtain:

$$(15)\quad \frac{\partial \ln c}{\partial \ln q_i} = \frac{q_i\, v}{c} \equiv w_i \qquad\qquad i = 1,\ldots, n\,.$$

To show that the following theorem holds for any degree of homogeneity, we assume for a moment C (·) to be homogenous of degree r in x; i.e. $\partial \ln c/\partial \ln x = r$. We can rewrite (14) to find the <u>difference in cost efficiency</u> of a sector between Japan and Germany:

$$(16)\quad W_{J,G} \equiv \frac{\partial \ln c}{\partial D_J} = \frac{d \ln c}{d D_J} - r\,\frac{d \ln x}{d D_J} - \Sigma_i w_i\,\frac{d \ln q_i}{d D_J}$$

The difference in cost efficiency between any country and Germany, $W_{J,G}$, is the logarithmic difference in that sectors' cost levels between countries, holding factor prices and time constant. The following theorem holds:

Theorem

Under perfect competition in the goods and factor markets in all countries C it is:

$$(17) \quad -\frac{\partial \ln C}{\partial D_C} = r \frac{\partial \ln x}{\partial D_C}, \quad \text{or} \quad -W_{C,G} = r\, w_{C,G}$$

where $r = 1/r_F$ with r_F as the degree of homogeneity of the production function F in (1). The proof is given in the appendix.

In our case with $r_F = 1$, a German productivity gap ($w_{C,G} > 0$) implies $W_{C,G} < 0$, that is a German cost inefficiency compared to country C. Given German output and factor prices at a certain point in time, a switch of the production process from Germany to country C entails a cost advantage.

We conclude from the theorem that the productivity gap can be calculated either by the Divisia index (6) or by the Divisia index (16). As a discrete approximation of the Divisia index we use again a Törnqvist index. This index number is exact, if the underlying cost function is a translog function. We refer to the expression

$$(18) \quad \bar{W}_{J,G} = \ln c(J) - \ln c(G) - \ln x(J) - \ln x(G) - \\ - \Sigma_i \bar{w}_i (\ln q_i(J) - \ln q_i(G))$$

as the translog index of differences in cost efficiency. Again we need not to estimate the parameters of the translog cost function in order to calculate the gap but for the econometric analysis in section 5 we know already the appropriate specification of the cost and production functions

Due to the linear homogeneity assumption we can write

$$(19) \quad c = x\, P(q, D_J, D_U, t) = x \cdot p$$

where $p = P(q, D_J, D_U, t)$ is the price or unit cost function. Now (18) reads:

$$(20)\quad \overline{W}_{J,G} = \ln p(J) - \ln p(G) - \Sigma_i\, \overline{w}_i(\ln q_i(J) - \ln q_i(G))$$

A translog multilateral index of differences in cost efficiency can be constructed along the lines which resulted in (10):

$$\overline{W}_{C,G} = \ln p(c) - \ln p(G)$$

$$(21)\quad - \frac{1}{2}\,(\Sigma w_i(C) + \overline{w}_i)(\ln q_i(C) - \overline{\ln q_i})$$

$$+ \frac{1}{2}\,(\Sigma w_i(G) + \overline{w}_i)(\ln q_i(G) - \overline{\ln q_i})$$

where a bar indicates the average over all three countries.

Finally, we can derive the rate of growth of the price of output, holding prices of all inputs and the dummy variables constant:

$$(22)\quad W_t = \frac{\partial \ln p}{\partial t} = \frac{d \ln p}{dt} - \Sigma\, w_i \frac{d \ln q_i}{dt}$$

It is a well known result (Ohta (1974)) with $r_F = 1$ that the negative of the rate of productivity growth is equal to the rate of growth of the price diminution; i.e.:

$$(23)\quad - w_t = W_t$$

The translog index of the price diminution for a given country is:

$$(24)\quad W_t = \ln p(t) - \ln p(t-1) - \Sigma_i\, \overline{w}_i(\ln q_i(t) - \ln q_i(t-1))$$

3. Data and Purchasing Power Parities

The starting point for the analysis of differences in the pattern of cost and production between countries is the production account for the manufacturing industry in each country. We employ an aggregated account of the sectoral production accounts developed for the United States by Gollop and Jorgenson (1980), for Japan by Kuroda (unpublished report), and for Germany by Conrad and Unger (1984). Leaving the details of the accounts to these studies, we now briefly summarize the main characteristics of the data base.

Price and quantity indexes of labor input for every sector in each country are measured on the basis of labor compensation and manhours worked, classified at least by workers, employees, and self-employed and family workers. Labor input for each country is the product of employment, average hours worked, and an index of educational attainment. Hourly wage rates are obtained by dividing labor compensation for employees, workers and self-employed in each country by the corresponding labor input. Price and quantity indexes of sectoral capital input in each country are measured on the basis of property compensation and capital stocks, estimated by asset types (structures, producers' durable equipments, inventory) within each sector. For each asset the flow of capital input is assumed proportional to the level of capital stocks in each sector. Under the assumption that the relative efficiency of the j-th capital goods declines geometrically with age, the rate of replacement, say δ_j, is a constant.

The dual to the perpetual inventory method, involving the prices p_I of investment goods and of capital services q_K, implies that the rental price q_{K_J} of the jth capital input can be expressed as

$$(25) \quad q_{K_J}(t) = p_{I_J}(t-1)\{i(t) - p_{I_J}(t)\} + \delta_j p_{I_J}(t)$$

where i(t) is the sectors' nominal rate of return on capital. Corrected by the rate of inflation $\dot{p}_I$ we obtain the own rate of return on capital. Price and quantity indexes of sectoral intermediate input in each country are measured on the basis of interindustry transaction matrices estimated annually for each country.

To achieve comparability in the levels of output, inputs and levels of total factor productivity requires data on the relative prices of output and inputs among all the countries included in the comparison. Such data must be based on direct observations of prices for comparable products.

We develop purchasing power parities (PPPs) based on the work of Kravis, Heston and Summers (1982). They provide PPPs for detailed components of aggregate consumption goods output and investment goods output for the year 1975 between the yen and the dollar, and between the DM and the dollar. We construct the PPPs for sectoral output and intermediate input by mapping the Kravis et al's classification system and our one output and 28 input industry classification system. To obtain relative price levels of capital and labor input for 1975 we follow Jorgenson and Nishimizu (1978) in constructing PPPs for labor and capital input for this base year 1975. We multiply the relative hourly wage rates for any two countries by the ratio of labor input per hour worked for the two countries. This ratio adjusts manhours worked in Germany and Japan in the base year to achieve equivalence with American and Japanese manhours (see Conrad and Jorgenson (1985)). To obtain PPPs for capital input in 1975, we take the ratio of the price of capital input in (25) for one country relative to that of the other one. Rewriting this ratio gives the following PPP for capital input in 1975:

$$(26)\quad \frac{q_{K,t}(C)}{q_{K,t}(US)} = \frac{p_{I,t}(C)}{p_{I,t}(US)} \frac{pr_{I,t}(C) \cdot \tilde{i}_t(C) + \delta(G)}{pr_{I,t}(US) \cdot \tilde{i}_t(US) + \delta(US)}$$

where $\tilde{i}_t$ is the own rate of return on capital as specified in (25) and $pr_{I,t}(C) \equiv p_{I,t-1}(C)/p_{I,t}(C)$. The first ratio on the right of (26) is the PPP for new investment goods given for 1975 in Kravis et.al. The second term is a correction term if own rates of return and of replacement differ among national industries.

As the PPPs by Kravis et.al. are not available as time series but only for 1970 and 1975, we use 1975 as the base year and construct relative price indexes for other years by chain-linking them to 1975. In symbols we calculate for C = G and J:

$$(27)\quad PPx^C = PPx^C(0)(p^C/p^{US})$$

where $PPx^C(0)$ is the PPP for manufacturing output in DM (C = G) or Yen (C = J) per dollar for 1975, and p^C is the national output deflator. Similarly, PPPs for labor (v_1 = L) and material (v_2 = M) are

$$(28)\quad PPv_i^C = PPv_i^C(0)\,(q_i^C/q_i^{US})\quad ,$$

where the meaning of the variables is analogous to (27).

The PPP formula (28) has not been extended to capital input due to the following problem. If there is a joint production or cost function which relates inputs to output or input prices to output prices respectively, should there also be a relation between PPPs of inputs and PPP of output? Such a relationship exists if we postulate that the national rates of change of total factor productivity (TFP) should be invariant with respect to the common currency (here dollars) chosen for the joint production or cost function. In other words, TFP calculated from the joint cost or production function should coincide with the national TFP calculated on the base of national currencies. This requires the following condition on the PPPs:

Invariance Postulate:

A necessary and sufficient condition for the national rate of change of TFP, i.e. w_t (\$) from (1), or of cost diminution, i.e. W_t(\$) from (11), to be equal to the corresponding rate w_t(C) or W_t(C) based on the production or cost function (1) or (11) under domestic currencies C (C = DM, Yen) is a Divisia index for the PPPs:

$$(29) \quad \frac{d \ln PPx}{dt} = r_F \, \Sigma \, w_i \, \frac{d \ln PPv_i}{dt}$$

where w_i are the cost shares and r_F is the degree of homogeneity of the production function. The proof ist given in the appendix.[4)]

We use the Törnqvist-index as a discrete approximation of (29) and refer to this expression for the rate of change of PPP of output as the translog index of PPP change

$$(30) \quad \ln PPx(t) - \ln PPx(t-1) = \Sigma \bar{w}_i (\ln PPv_i(t) - \ln PPv_i(t-1))$$

where $\bar{w}_i = (w_i(t) + w_i(t-1))/2$.
As mentioned before, the time series construction of PPPs in (27) and (28) has not been extended to capital. The reason for this is that we prefer to calculate the PPP for capital from (30) using the base year construction (26) and the changes in PPP for x from (27) and for labor (v_1 = L) and for material (v_2 = M) from (28). Due to the unreliability of the quality of data for the price of capital input we decided to choose the PPP for capital input as the residual.

---

4) For further remarks see Conrad (1985).

4. Descriptive empirical results

In Table 1 we present some economic indicators which provide information concerning the relative economic performance of the manufacturing sector in three countries.[5] For each of the three inter-country comparisons the first column shows the productivity gap over time. Columns 2 to 4 give an economic interpretation of the changes of PPPs over time in terms of relative marginal productivity of labor, capital and material, respectively. PPPs for output have been calculated from (27), for labor and material from (28), and the PPP for capital followed from the Invariance Postulate (29); i.e. as Törnqvist index (30). In order to interprete the PPPs in terms of marginal productivity we employ the necassary conditions for producer equilibrium:

$q_j = p \cdot F_{v_j}(v,D,t)$.

If we divide the necessary condition of the German industry by the necessary condition of the U.S. industry we obtain:

$$(31) \quad q_j^{G}/q_j^{US} = (p^{G}/p^{US}) \frac{F_{v_j}(v,D_J=0,D_{US}=0,t)}{F_{v_j}(v,D_J=0,D_{US}=1,t)}$$

If we then denote the ratio of the marginal productivities in (31) by RMP, we can interpret changes in PPPs by changes in relative marginal productivities:

$$(32) \quad RMP_j(C,US) = PPv_j^{C}/PPx^{US} \qquad C = J,G; \qquad j = 1(L),2(M),3(K)$$

If RMP_j is greater (less) than one, the marginal productivity of input j is higher (lower) in country C's industry than in the U.S. industry. For a Japan-Germany comparison the analog to (32) is:

$$(33) \quad RMP_j(G,J) = (PPv_j^{G}/PPv_j^{J})/(PPx^{G}/PPx)$$

If $RMP_j(G,J)$ is greater (less) than one, the marginal productivity of input j is higher (lower) in the German industry than in the Japanese one

Columns 5 to 8 present relative output and relative inputs. RXX is the inter-country ratio of output, RLL the ratio of labor, RKK the ratio of

---

[5] Results for 28 industries are presented in Conrad (1985).

capital and RMM the ratio of material. CAPINT measures the relative capital intensity as the ratio of KIL for two countries.

An U.S. - Germany comparison reveals a productivity disadvantage for German manufacturing industries (gap $w_{US,G} > 0$). In 1960, German resources used by the U.S. manufacturing industries would have increased output by 17 percent. In 1970 the U.S. productivity advantage was still 12 percent but in 1979 the German industries have completely caught-up. In terms of the dual interpretation ($W_{US,G} = - w_{US,G}$) given German output and input prices, the U.S. industry was able to produce the output at lower costs. Due to the U.S. efficiency costs would have been lower by 17 percent in 1960, 12 percent in 1970 and the same in 1979.

A value of less than one for relative marginal productivity of labor (Germany over U.S.) reveals that marginal productivity of labor (MPL) is still higher in the U.S. manufacturing industry than in the German one. In 1960, the U.S. MPL was three times as high as in Germany (RMPL = 0.33). The difference in the MPL became smaller over time but in 1979 the U.S. MPL was still 33 % higher than the German MPL (RMPL = 0.75). The capital shortage in Germany in the early sixties shows up in the high marginal productivity of capital (MPK) relative to the U.S.. In 1960 MPK was 2.8 times as high as in the U.S. and even in 1979 it is still higher than in the U.S. although we again observe a tendency of equalization. The marginal productivity of material (MPM) was about the same in the sixties and has increased in the U.S. relative to Germany in the seventies.

The German output ratio (RXX) has increased frome one quarter of the U.S. level to one third of the U.S. level. This improvement has been achieved with a declining labor ratio (RLL). RLL dropped from 0.77 to 0.28 in 1979. In the early sixties the ratio of capital (RKK) was lower than the ratio of output, but since 1973 (energy price hike) RKK exceeds the output ratio RXX. The relative capital intensity CAPINT reflects this development. The K/L ratio (Germany over U.S.) was rather low in the sixties and has improved remarkable in the seventies. This might be a result of obsolete capital in the U.S. industry due to the jumps in the price of energy (see the jump in CAPINT from 1973 to 1979).

A negative gap in the Japan-Germany comparison ($w_{J,G} < 0$) means a Japanese disadvantage in producing manufactured goods. German resources transfered to Japan would reduce output by 28 percent in 1960, but only by 8 percent in 1970. Since then Japan has nearly closed the gap leaving a

TABLE 1: Productivity gap, relative marginal productivities (RMP) and ratios of inputs and outputs

Year	GAP	RMPL	RMPK	RMPM	RXX	RLL	RKK	RMM	CAPINT
	U.S. - Germany								
1960	.17	.33	2.88	1.01	.25	.77	.15	.23	.19
1965	.17	.43	2.10	1.01	.24	.53	.23	.24	.43
1970	.12	.46	2.40	.95	.31	.50	.19	.34	.39
1975	.02	.62	1.34	.96	.33	.36	.42	.32	1.18
1979	.0	.75	1.26	.90	.33	.28	.46	.34	1.65
	Japan - Germany								
1960	-.28	2.13	1.0	1.03	1.52	.81	1.41	1.16	1.73
1965	-.23	1.82	.92	1.03	1.13	.79	.95	.91	1.21
1970	-.08	1.35	1.13	1.03	.76	.92	.54	.68	.59
1975	-.02	1.16	1.24	.99	.73	1.09	.43	.70	.40
1979	-.03	1.34	1.10	.96	.69	.81	.42	.68	.52
	Japan - U.S.								
1960	-.44	.16	2.87	.98	6.13	1.05	9.69	4.96	9.19
1965	-.40	.23	2.28	.97	4.66	1.48	4.17	3.79	2.82
1970	-.19	.34	2.12	.92	2.45	1.85	2.79	1.97	1.50
1975	-.04	.54	1.07	.96	2.25	3.05	1.03	2.20	.34
1979	-.04	.55	1.15	.95	2.08	2.91	.92	2.0	.32

GAP: $w_{U,G}$ or $w_{J,G} > 0$: German prod. gap; $w_{J,US} > 0$: U.S. prod. gap.

RMPL: Rel.marg.prod. of labor (of capital (RMPK), of material (RMPM)): Germ. over U.S.; Germ. over Japan or Japan over U.S. respectively.

RXX: Ratio of output (of labor input (RLL), of capital input (RKK), of material (RMM)): Germ. over U.S.; Germ. over Japan; U.S. over Japan.

CAPINT: Relative capital intensity: Germany K/L ratio over U.S. K/L ratio; German K/L ratio over Japan K/L; U.S. K/L ratio over Japan K/L.

small productivity advantage for German manufacturing industries. RMPL is always larger than one with marginal productivity of labor in Germany more than twice as high than in Japan in 1960. RMPL moves towards one but MPL in Germany remains higher than in Japan. However, MPK and MPM is roughly the same in both countries with a slightly higher MPK in German manufacturing. The output ratio RXX shows the impressing performance of the Japanese economy. The output of German manufacturing, once 150 percent of the Japanese column, dropped to 69 percent in 1979. In spite of this decline, the labor ratio RLL remained nearly unchanged by about 0.8 with even an increase in the seventies. The capital ratio RKK dropped faster than RXX showing a relative increase in the capital stock of Japanese manufacturing. The increase in Japanese labor productivity and capital stock shows up in the dramatic fall of relative capital intensity from 1.7 in 1960 to 0.52 in 1979.

A U.S. comparison shows the fast catching-up process of Japanese manufacturing industries. The Japanese disadvantage of 44 percent less output with the U.S. resources in 1960 has been reduced to 4 percent in 1975 and remains since then on that small gap. RMPL as MPL of Japan over U.S. has improved over time but U.S. labor productivity is still about twice as high as the Japanese one. Similar to the Germany-U.S. comparison, the shortage of capital in Japan in the sixties results in about the same series of RMPK over time, but with a stronger tendency for an equalization. MPM is higher in the Japan-U.S. comparison as well as in the Germany-U.S. comparison. The Japanese growth performance shows up in the fall of RXX from 6.1 in 1960 to 2.0 in 1979. What strikes most is that the labor ratio RLL has moved in the opposite direction of RXX. In 1960 U.S. manufacturing produced with the same labor input as Japan six times the output level of Japan. In 1979 the U.S. has produced with about three times the labor input of Japan only twice the output level of Japan. This excellent performance of Japan was due to the enormous increase in relative capital input (see RKK) and in capital intensity. In 1960 CAPINT in the U.S. was 9 times higher than in Japan but in 1979 CAPINT in Japan was three times higher than in the U.S. manufacturing industries.

5. Econometric analysis of productivity gaps

Given the above description of productivity gaps and their development over time, our next step is to carry out an econometric analysis in order to find the source of the changes in the gaps. Since the Törnqvist-index is exact if the production or cost function is translog we employ this flexible form for an econometric analysis. Also, as we prefer prices as explaining variables of productivity gaps, we choose the approach of a joint cost function as defined in (11).

Our simultaneous system of equations for the manufacturing industry consists of the cost-share equations (see (15)):

$$(34)\quad \frac{\partial \ln c}{\partial \ln q_i} = w_i , \qquad i = K,L,M$$

the equation for the rate of productivity growth (w_t), that is, the rate of growth of the price diminution (see (22)):

$$(35)\quad \frac{\partial \ln c}{\partial t} = W_t ,$$

and the equations for the difference in productivity or cost efficiency (see (16)):

$$(36)\quad \frac{\partial \ln c}{\partial D_J} = W_{J,BR} \qquad \frac{\partial \ln c}{\partial D_{US}} = W_{US,BR}$$

Using the translog cost function

$$(37)\quad \ln c = \ln x + \Sigma\, \alpha_i\, z_i + \frac{1}{2}\, \Sigma_i\, \Sigma_j\, \beta_{ij}\, z_i\, z_j$$

where $z = (\ln q_K, \ln q_L, \ln q_M, t, D_J, D_{US})$ and with i for K, L, M, t, D_J, D_{US}, the partial derivatives with respect to its variables result in the six equations (34) - (36). Restrictions on the parameter of the cost function due to linear homogeneity in prices and due to symmetry are:

$$(38)\quad \alpha_K + \alpha_L + \alpha_M = 1$$

$$(39)\quad \beta_{ij} = \beta_{ji} \qquad \text{for all } i, j.$$

$$(40)\quad \beta_{iK} + \beta_{iL} + \beta_{iM} = 0 \qquad \text{for all } i.$$

The specification (37) and the restrictions (38) - (40) imply the following explicit version of (34)-(36):

$$w_K = \alpha_K + \beta_{LK}\ln\frac{q_L}{q_K} + \beta_{MK}\ln\frac{q_M}{q_K} + \beta_{Kt}t + \beta_{KD_J}D_J + \beta_{KD_{US}}D_{US}$$

$$w_L = \alpha_L + \beta_{LL}\ln\frac{q_L}{q_K} + \beta_{LM}\ln\frac{q_M}{q_K} + \beta_{Lt}t + \beta_{LD_J}D_J + \beta_{LD_{US}}D_{US}$$

$$w_M = \alpha_M + \beta_{LM}\ln\frac{q_L}{q_K} + \beta_{MM}\ln\frac{q_M}{q_K} + \beta_{Mt}t + \beta_{MD_J}D_J + \beta_{MD_{US}}D_{US}$$

$$W_t = \alpha_t + \beta_{Lt}\ln\frac{q_L}{q_K} + \beta_{Mt}\ln\frac{q_M}{q_K} + \beta_{tt}t + \beta_{tD_J}D_J + \beta_{tD_{US}}D_{US}$$

$$W_{J,G} = \alpha_{D_J} + \beta_{LD_J}\ln\frac{q_L}{q_K} + \beta_{MD_J}\ln\frac{q_M}{q_K} + \beta_{tD_J}t + \beta_{D_JD_J}D_J + \beta_{D_JD_{US}}D_{US}$$

$$W_{US,G} = \alpha_{D_{US}} + \beta_{LD_{US}}\ln\frac{q_L}{q_K} + \beta_{MD_{US}}\ln\frac{q_M}{q_K} + \beta_{tD_{US}}t + \beta_{D_JD_{US}}D_J + \beta_{D_{US}D_{US}}D_{US}$$

Due to the circularity condition $W_{J,US} + W_{US,G} = W_{J,G}$ a regression equation for $W_{J,US}$ can be omitted; its parameters can be obtained from the parameters in the last two equations. For estimating the unknown parameters we add stochastic terms and employ the maximum likelihood method. Since the cost shares add to unity, their error terms add to zero. We remove the capital equation from the system and estimate the parameters of the equation for w_K from the parameter restrictions (38)-(40). There are 20 unknown parameters to be estimated. We have stacked the observations to a 3 x T vector (T = 20 yearly data) beginning with German data ($D_J = D_{US} = 0$ in the regressions), then with the Japanese data ($D_J = 1$, $D_{US} = 0$), and finally with the U.S. data ($D_J = 0$, $D_{US} = 1$). The productivity gap, linking data of two countries, is not available as time series for each country. Thus it has been stacked three times to give a vector of dimension 3 x T.

The joint technology in the three countries shows up in the common β-parameters for input prices and time. Therefore, the share elasticities with respect to factor prices and time do not differ between countries and are:[6)]

---

6) The Jorgenson (1986) for an interpretation of translog parameters

$$(41)\quad \frac{\partial\, w_i}{\partial\, \ln q_j} = \beta_{ij} \qquad\qquad \frac{\partial\, w_i}{\partial t} = \beta_{it} \quad (i,j = K,L,M)\ .$$

The α-parameters will be corrected however in their levels by the dummy parameters. From the equation W_t for TFP we realize for instance, that the change in total factor productivity differs by the parameters β_{tD_J} and $\beta_{tD_{US}}$, respectively, given equal relative input prices in the three countries. As we have normalized prices to be unity in 1970 and time to be zero in 1970, all α-parameters can be interpreted as average cost-shares, average change in TFP or average productivity gaps.

A standard interpretation of the parameters is in terms of price elasticities and elasticities of substitution. The partial elasticity of substitution is $\sigma_{ij} = (\beta_{ij} + w_i w_j)/w_i \cdot w_j, i \neq j$; if $\beta_{ij} > 0$, then $\sigma_{ij} > 1$. For the price elasticities we obtain $\varepsilon_{ij} = w_i \cdot \sigma_{ij}$ $(i \neq j)$ and $\varepsilon_{ii} = (\beta_{ii}/w_i) + w_i - 1$.

The parameter β_{it} measures the bias of technical change on the cost shares. By rewriting the cost share regression we obtain as the rate of change of an input with respect to the level of technology:

$$(42)\quad \varepsilon_{i,t} = \frac{\partial \ln v_i}{\partial t} = (\beta_{it}/w_i) + W_t \qquad\qquad i = K,L,M\ .$$

If technical change is input i using, i.e. $\beta_{it} > 0$, the overall reduction of input quantities by the rate W_t is reduced for input i by the rate β_{it}/w_i. If technical change is input i saving, i.e. $\beta_{it} < 0$, the quantity of input i can be reduced additionally by β_{it}/w_i percentage points.

Looked at the interpretation of the parameter β_{it} as $\partial W_t/\partial \ln q_i = \beta_{it}$, a proportional increase in the price q_i reduces the rate of change of TFP in case of input i using technical change ($W_t < 0$ increases in $\ln q_i$). Similarly, if technical change is input i saving, an increase in q_i results in a higher rate of cost reduction.

A similar interpretation can be given for the parameter β_{i,D_C}. It measures the difference in the cost share w_i between the German and country C's industry holding prices and time fixed. For an interpretation as a measure of the country bias of input i we derive from the cost share equation the measure:

$$(43) \quad \varepsilon_{i,D_C} = \frac{\partial \ln v_i}{\partial D_{C,G}} = (\beta_{iD_C}/w_i) + W_{C,G} \quad .$$

ε_{i,D_C} is the rate of change of input i if we switch cet.par. from the German industry to the industry in country C. If the country bias is input i saving ($\beta_{iD_C} < 0$), the overall difference in cost efficiency is lower for input i, namely by the rate β_{iD_C}/w_i. If a productivity advantage exists for the German industry ($W_{C,G} > 0$), the industry of country C requires more of all inputs at a rate $W_{C,G}$, however corrected by the bias factor. If the country bias is input i using, country C's industry requires even more of input i in addition to the rate $W_{C,G}$. If a productivity disadvantage exists for the German industry ($W_{C,G} < 0$), country C's industry needs less of all inputs at a rate $W_{C,G}$. In case the country bias is input i saving, country C needs even less of input i than the overall rate $W_{C,G}$.

Due to symmetry the parameter for the country bias permits to derive the change in the gap if input prices change world-wide:

$$(44) \quad \frac{\partial W_{C,G}}{\partial \ln q_i} = \beta_{i,D_C} \quad .$$

If the country bias is input i saving, i.e. $\beta_{i,D_C} < 0$, a proportional increase in the price of input i in all three countries leads to a reduction of country C's gap if $W_{C,G} > 0$.

Finally, also the parameter β_{t,D_C} permits a symmetric interpretation:

$$(45) \quad \frac{\partial W_t}{\partial D_C} = \beta_{t,D_C} = \frac{\partial W_{C,G}}{\partial t} \quad .$$

The first derivative gives the country bias of TFP. If $\beta_{t,D_C} < 0$, country C's rate of change of TFP is by β_{t,D_C} larger than Germany's W_t. The right hand side derivative expresses the fact that in this case country C's gap ($W_{C,G} > 0$) will be reduced by the rate β_{t,D_C} per year.

In table 2 we present the estimated parameters of our simultaneous system including the parameters for $W_{J,US}$ derived from the circularity condition, and the parameters for w_K, derived form the additivity restriction of the cost shares.

In table 2 we present the estimated parameters of our simultaneous system including the parameters for $W_{J,US}$ derived from the circularity condition, and the parameters for w_K, derived from the additivity restriction of the cost shares.

We first observe that the average cost share of labor is significantly lower in Japan ($\beta_{LD_J} < 0$) and higher in the U.S. ($\beta_{LD_U} > 0$); i.e. the elasticity of output with respect to labor is lower in Japan and higher in the U.S. manufacturing industry compared to the German industry. The direct share elasticity of labor β_{LL} is positive. A proportional increase in the price of labor implies that the real wage rate increases faster than labor productivity. This means that in all three countries the real wage rate has increased faster than the labor productivity.

Furthermore, an increase in the price of material decreases the cost share of labor; the same holds for an increase in the price of capital (not significant). The bias of technical change is labor-saving ($\beta_{LT} < 0$); keeping prices constant the cost share of labor declines over time. As $\beta_{MD_J} > 0$, the Japanese cost share of materials is higher than the German one; the same holds for the U.S. cost share of materials. Again, the direct share elasticity β_{MM} is significantly positive; the real price of material has increased more than material productivity. As $\beta_{Mt} > 0$, technical change is material using.

The average cost share of capital (α_K) is for the U.S. industry lower than in Germany and for the Japanese industry higher than in Germany. The direct share elasticity of capital β_{KK} is positive implying that the real price of capital has increased faster than capital productivity. Technical change is capital saving, but non-significantly.

The endogenous variable W_t is usually negative and measures the change in cost diminution; $-W_t = w_t$ is the rate of change of technical change. The average rate α_t in absolute terms is small, but higher in Japan, and even lower in the U.S. As technical change is labor saving (see $\beta_{LT} < 0$) and capital saving ($\beta_{Kt} < 0$), a proportional increase in the price of labor or capital will lead to a higher rate of cost diminution. As technical change is material using, a proportional increase in its price will dampen the rate of cost diminution. Since β_{tt} is significantly positive, we can detect a slowdown of the exogenous growth in TFP.

Since the productivity gap $w_{J,G}$ or cost efficiency gap $W_{J,G}$ ($= - w_{J,G}$)

have changed considerably over time, the average parameter α_{D_J} cannot convey the actual situation. If it is positive, it means that on the average total cost of production will increase by $\alpha_{D_J} \cdot 100$ percent if production of German manufacturing will be transfered to Japan given German input prices; Japan has a productivity disadvantage. As the Japan bias of labor is labor saving (all $\beta_{LD_J} < 0$), Japanese industries need more of all inputs by the rate $W_{J,G}$, but relatively less with respect to labor (see (44)). Therefore relatively high wages world-wide have favored the Japanese catching-up process because the disadvantage in terms of more inputs was comparatively less with respect to labor.

The Japan bias of material is material using (all $\beta_{MD} > 0$); the input structure of Japanese industries needs relatively more of material so that an increase in the price of material will slow down the Japanese catching-up process. As can be seen from Table 1, the two jumps in energy prices have stopped considerably the Japanese dynamics to close the gap. A similar argument holds for the price of capital and its ex-post increase due to high interest rates in the seventies. The negative cost efficiency bias β_{tD_J} favors a Japanese closing of the productivity gap due to the higher rate of TFP in Japan. The parameters $\beta_{D_JD_J}$ and $\beta_{D_JD_U}$ would be zero if relative input prices (corrected by the purchase power parities) are the same in all three countries. Those parameters are not significantly different from zero in our study. A test of a hypothesis of equal relative input prices can therefore not be rejected.

Since α_{D_U} is negative, it is cost reducing on the average to transfer German resources in production to the U.S.. The U.S. bias of labor is labor using so that an increase in the price of labor will reduce the German cost inefficiency (the same holds for material). However, the U.S. bias of capital is capital saving ($\beta_{KD_U} < 0$). The German manufacturing sector uses more inputs, especially capital, so that an increase in the price of capital will hamper a German catching-up process. Since β_{tD_U} is positive, technical change works for a German improvement of cost efficiency.

From the circularity condition it follows that the U.S. is the base country. Therefore a positive $\alpha_{J,US}$ indicates an U.S. cost advantage. Higher wages will reduce this cost advantage. Since Japan's additional use of all inputs is structured towards relatively less labor input, higher wages world-wide will improve its relative position to U.S. industries. However, a higher price of material or of capital will favor the U.S. cost efficiency lead. The higher change in productivity in Japanese

TABLE 2: Parameter estimates for the joint cost model

Parameters	α_L	β_{LL}	β_{LM}	β_{LK}	β_{Lt}	β_{LD_J}	β_{LD_U}
Cost share of labor	.23	.019	-.017	-.002*	-.0013	-.085	.045
	α_M	β_{LM}	β_{MM}	β_{MK}	β_{Mt}	β_{MD_J}	β_{MD_U}
Cost share of material	.61	-.017	.056	-.038	.0015	.061	.0097
	α_K	β_{LK}	β_{MK}	β_{KK}	β_{Kt}	β_{KD_J}	β_{KD_U}
Cost share of capital	.15	-.002*	-.038	.058	-.0001	.024	-.055
	α_t	β_{Lt}	β_{Mt}	β_{Kt}	β_{tt}	β_{tD_J}	β_{tD_U}
Technical change	-.007	-.0013	.0015	-.0001*	.0008	-.006	.0038
	α_{D_J}	β_{LD_J}	β_{MD_J}	β_{KD_J}	β_{tD_J}	$\beta_{D_J D_J}$	$\beta_{D_J D_U}$
Productivity gap 1), G-J.	.11	-.085	.061	.024	-.006	-.0014*	-.0063*
	α_{D_U}	β_{LD_U}	β_{MD_U}	β_{KD_U}	β_{tD_U}	$\beta_{D_U D_U}$	$\beta_{D_J D_U}$
Productivity gap 2), G-U.S.	-.13	.045	.0097	-.055	.0038	.03	-.0063*
	$\alpha_{J,US}$	$\beta_{LD_{JU}}$	$\beta_{MD_{JU}}$	$\beta_{KD_{JU}}$	$\beta_{tD_{JU}}$	$\beta_{D_{JU} D_{JU}}$	$\beta_{D_{UJ} D_{UJ}}$
Productivity gap 3), U.S.-J.	.24	-.13	.051	.079	-.0098	.0049	-.0363

*) not significant for a significance level of 5 %.

1) $W_{J,G} < 0$: German productivity gap 2) $W_{US,G} < 0$: German productivity gap

3) $W_{J.US} < 0$: U.S. productivity gap

crease internationally. As the U.S. cost share of capital is lower, U.S. capital productivity relative to the German one exceeds the relative real price of capital so that a higher price of capital helps to support the U.S. lead. Time as index of technology favors the German catching-up process. An U.S. - Japan comparison shows that higher prices for material and capital will stop the Japanese catching-up process, while higher wages and the level of technology (time) will support it. The reason for that is, that the U.S. material and capital productivity relative to the Japanese one is higher than the corresponding relative factor prices. This helps the U.S. to manage better an increase in those factor prices. But for labor, the U.S. labor productivity relative to the Japanese one is lower than the relative wage rate which helps Japan to cope better with higher wages. The general tendency of our econometric analysis is that higher wages help the Japanese manufacturing industries to catch-up, higher capital prices help the U.S. to defend its lead and higher prices for material help the German industries due to their advantage in the material productivity - price ratio.

Appendix

The proof of the theorem is similar to the one given by Ohta (1974) for the statement $-\partial \ln C/\partial t = r\, \partial \ln x/\partial t$ with $r = 1/r_F$. From (14) and (15) we obtain

$$\text{(A1)} \quad \frac{d \ln c}{d D} = r \frac{d \ln x}{d D} + \Sigma_i w_i \frac{d \ln q_i}{d D} + \frac{\partial \ln c}{\partial D}$$

with $w_i \equiv \dfrac{q_i v_i}{c}$.

Since $c = \Sigma_i q_i v_i$, we have:

$$\frac{d c}{d D} = \Sigma_i \frac{dq_i}{d D} v_i + \Sigma_i q_i \frac{dv_i}{d D}$$

or

$$\text{(A2)} \quad \frac{d \ln c}{d D} = \Sigma_i w_i \frac{d \ln q_i}{d D} + \Sigma_i w_i \frac{d \ln v_i}{d D}$$

From (A1) and (A2) we have:

$$\text{(A3)} \quad -\frac{\partial \ln c}{\partial D} = r \frac{d \ln x}{d D} - \Sigma\, w_i \frac{d \ln v_i}{d D}$$

From the production function approach in (2) we have:

$$\frac{d \ln x}{d D} = \Sigma\, F_{v_i} \frac{v_i}{x} \frac{d \ln v_i}{d D} + \frac{\partial \ln x}{\partial D}$$

or, because of $p \cdot F_{v_i} = q_i$ and $p = C_x$,

$$\frac{d \ln x}{d D} = \Sigma \frac{q_i\, v_i}{x \cdot C_x} \frac{d \ln v_i}{d D} + \frac{\partial \ln x}{\partial D} \quad .$$

Finally, using $x \cdot C_x = r \cdot c$,

$$\text{(A4)} \quad \frac{\partial \ln x}{\partial D} = \frac{d \ln x}{d D} - \frac{1}{r} \Sigma \frac{q_i\, v_i}{c} \frac{d \ln v_i}{d D}$$

Comparing (A3) and (A4) proofs the theorem as $r = 1/r_F$ holds without change in reasoning from Ohta. Q.e.d.

Proof of the invariance postulate:

From (8) or (A4) (with t instead of D) the rate of TFP in the common U.S. - currency for country C is:

$$\text{(A5)} \quad w_t(\$) = \frac{d \ln x}{dt} - \frac{1}{r} \Sigma w_i \frac{d \ln v_i}{dt}$$

Transforming the dollar figures into national currencies by using (12), (A5) becomes:

$$w_t(\$) = \frac{d \ln x^C}{dt} - \frac{1}{r} \Sigma w_i \frac{d \ln v_i^C}{dt} - \frac{d \ln PP_x^C}{dt}$$

(A6)

$$+ \frac{1}{r} \Sigma w_i \frac{d \ln PPv_i^C}{dt}$$

as $w_i^C = w_i$ because of $q_i v_i = q_i^C v_i^C$.

The first difference on the right is the rate of change of TFP, $w_t(C)$, in the country's own currency. It is equal to $w_t(\$)$, the country's rate on the common dollar currency, if the invariance postulate (29) holds ($\frac{1}{r} = r_F$).

Similarly, from (A1) (with t instead of D), we have:

$$\text{(A7)} \quad W_t(\$) \equiv \frac{d \ln c}{dt} - r \frac{d \ln x^C}{dt} - \Sigma w_i \frac{d \ln q_i^C}{dt}$$

$$+ r \frac{d \ln PPx^C}{dt} - \Sigma w_i \frac{d \ln PPv_i^C}{dt}$$

as cost c is invariant due to $q_i v_i = q_i^C v_i^C$.

Again, if the invariance postulate (29) holds then we get $W_t(\$) = W_t(C)$.

References

Caves, D. W., L. R. Christensen and W. E. Diewert, 1982, Multilateral comparisons of output, input and productivity using superlative index numbers, Economic Journal, 92, 73-86.

Christensen, L. R., D. Cummings and D. W. Jorgenson, 1981, Relative Productivity levels, 1947 - 1973: An international Comparison, European Economic Review, 61-94.

Christensen, L. R. and D. W. Jorgenson, 1970, U.S. real product and real factor input, 1929 - 1967, Review of Income and Wealth, 16, 19-50.

Conrad, K. and D. W. Jorgenson, 1985, Sectoral Productivity Gaps between the United States, Japan and Germany 1960 - 1979. In: Probleme und Perspektiven der weltwirtschaftlichen Entwicklung. Schriften des Vereins für Socialpolitik, Neue Folge Band 148, 335-347.

Conrad, K. and R. Unger, 1984, Dynamische Allokation von Produktionsfaktoren: Produktivitätsentwicklung und Produktionsfaktoren in 28 Produktbereichen, 1960 - 1978. Paper presented at the Symposium "Intertemporale Allokation", Universität Mannheim.

Conrad, K., 1985, Produktivitätslücken nach Wirtschaftszweigen im internationalen Vergleich; Beschreibung und ökonometrische Ursachenanalyse für die USA, Japan und die Bundesrepublik Deutschland, 1960 - 1979. Springer-Verlag, Heidelberg, New York.

Denny, M. and M. Fuss, 1983, Intertemporal Changes in the levels of regional labor productivity in Canadian Manufacturing. In Dogramaci, A. (ed.): Developments in Econometric Analysis of Productivity, Boston.

Denny, M. and M. Fuss, 1983 b, The Use of Discrete Variables in Superlative Index Number Comparisons, International Economic Review, 24,2,419-421.

Diewert, W. E., 1976, Exact and superlative index numbers, Journal of Econometrics, Vol. 4, 115-145.

Gollop, F. and D. W. Jorgenson, 1980, U.S. productivity growth by Industry, 1947 - 1973, in J. W. Kendrick and B. Vaccara (eds.), New Developments in Productivity Measurement and Analysis, Studies in Income and Wealth, 41, 17-136.

Jorgenson, D. W., 1986, Econometric Methods for Modeling Producer Behavior. In Z. Griliches and M. D. Intriligator (ed.), Handbook of Econometrics, Vol. III, North-Holland Publishing Co., 1842 - 1915.

Jorgenson, D. W. and M. Nishimizu, 1978, U.S. and Japanese Economic Growth, 1952 - 1974: An International Comparison, Economic Journal, 88, 707-726.

Jorgenson, D. W. and M. Nishimizu, 1979, Sectoral differences in levels of technology: An international comparison between the United States and Japan, 1955 - 1972. Paper presented at the North American Summer Meeting of the Econometric Society, Montreal, Canada, June 27-30.

Kravis, I. B., A. Heston and R. Summers, 1982, World Product and Income, International comparisons of real gross product, Baltimore and London.

Lau, L. J., 1979, On exact index numbers, The Review of Economics and Statistics, 73-82.

Nelson, R. R., 1981, Research on Productivity growth and productivity differences: Dead ends and new departures, Journal of Economic Literature, 19, 1029-1064.

Ohta, M., 1974, A Note on the Duality between Production and Cost Functions: Rate of Returns to Scale and Rate of Technical Progress, Economic Studies Quarterly, 25, 63-65.

Indices of Allocation Inefficiencies for Heterogeneous Labor

Georg Hasenkamp and Birgit Kracht-Müntz
Soziälökomomisches Seminar
der Universität Hamburg
Von-Melle-Park 5
D-2000 Hamburg 13

1. Introduction

Previous work on "aggregating" heterogeneous labor into one composite measure of labor (see e.g. Dougherty, 1972 and Bowles, 1970) starts out with a model which can be summarized as follows: The two (-or more) different "types" of labor, their quantities measured as x_1 and x_2, can be aggregated into the labor composite X by a function

$$X = g(x_1, x_2).^{1)} \tag{1}$$

This labor composite in turn becomes part of a general production function

$$Y = f(X,K), \tag{2}$$

where Y denotes output and K the (aggregate of) capital services. Substitution among the two different types of labor is implicitly assumed to be symmetric in the sense that x_1 can be substituted for x_2 and vice versa along a given isoquant for the aggregator function (1). [2)] Such an implicit assumption of symmetric substitution possibilities might even be correct on purely technical grounds. However, as we shall argue throughout this paper, institutional restrictions will (- in most countries according to our knowledge, not only in Germany) prevent a symmetric substitution between the different types of labor. The standard cliché of our time is the University educated teacher who cannot find employment within the intended profession, but who may job around as a

---

1) This (sub-) aggregator function is supposed to fulfill all the appropriate requirements - see e.g. the theoretical setting for aggregation in Blackorby, Primont, and Russell (1978, Chap. 3.3). We shall limit our discussion to only two types of labor even though the theory with n>2 types is virtually the same.

2) Differences in the "types" of labor can be classified along different lines - e.g. education, skill or the type of work performed. In the last case, the question of possible aggregation between specific types of labor (- blue/white collar work) and specific types of capital services might become a relevant question in production theory.

Measurement in Economics
ed. by W. Eichhorn

taxi-driver. On the other hand, a person "by profession" a taxi-driver could not - even if personally qualified - be employed as a teacher, due to institutional regulations and restrictions. In this paper we shall assume that the classification of the "two" different "types" of labor x_1 and x_2 is made according to "Abitur" and "No Abitur" - i.e., according to a graduation or not from a secondary school, where x_1 denotes labor classified under "No Abitur" and x_2 the labor with "Abitur". In a country like Germany, the "Abitur" is not only a prerequisite for admission to University education, but is also specified as a "must" for a wide range of professions. For example, the rank of an officer in the armed forces, the upper levels of the civil services, and most high rank positions in business and industry simply "require" the "Abitur".[1)]

How decisive the "Abitur" can be on the classification of types of labor will be illustrated by the differences in income: The average income earned by persons with "Abitur" is about 1.6 - times as large as the average income of persons without "Abitur".

Now, given the institutional prerequisite of "Abitur" for a certain type of labor, it becomes impossible to maintain symmetric substitution possibilities: A person with "Abitur" may actually be employed in a position where "Abitur" is <u>not</u> a prerequisite; the other way around, however, is not possible.

From now on we shall use the following notations and interpretations:

x_1^* = actually employed labor in positions where "Abitur" is <u>not</u> a prerequisite

x_2^* = actually employed labor in positions where "Abitur" is a prerequisite

$\bar{x}_1$ = number of employed labor without "Abitur"

$\bar{x}_2$ = number of employed labor with "Abitur"

q_1 = wage for x_1

q_2 = wage for x_2

---

1) Some of the "prerequisites" are formally specified by "law", others are stipulated more or less by tradition or convention. Thus, some exceptions to the rule are possible in the real life.

In the following diagram (I), actual employment is only possible along the line between the points A-B-C, or within the area O-A-B-C. An employment position along the dashed line B-D is not possible, due to the institutional restrictions.

Thus, quite apart from any technological contraints of a production or aggregator function, institutional restrictions impose another additional contraint on the actual employment situation. The confinement of actual employment to a point in the area O-A-B-C can then be seen as the additional contraints

$$x_1^* + x_2^* \leqq \bar{x}_1 + \bar{x}_2$$

and

$$x_2^* \leqq \bar{x}_2 \ .$$

In particular the contraint $x_2^* \leqq \bar{x}_2$ puts our problem into a similar theoretical setting as the quantity contraint problem of rationing in consumer demand theory as discussed e.g. by Deaton (1981), or as the case of return regulation in factor demand theory as dicussed e.g. by Atkinson and Halvorsen (1984) or by Toda (1976). In particular, the implications concerning cost-inefficiencies are very similar in these two related problems, as we shall point out below.

Diagram (I)

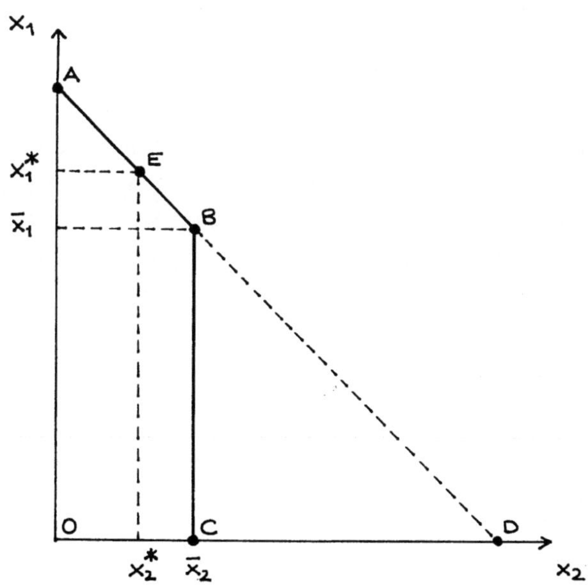

At a point like E, employment of the two types of labor is x_1^* and x_2^* respectively; there are $(\bar{x}_2 - x_2^*)$ persons with "Abitur" employed in a position where "Abitur" is not a prerequisite, so that $x_1^* = \bar{x}_1 + (\bar{x}_2 - x_2^*)$.

From the aggregator function (1) $X = g(x_1, x_2)$ we now impose a set of isoquants on diagram (I) to obtain the following diagram (II):

Diagram (II)

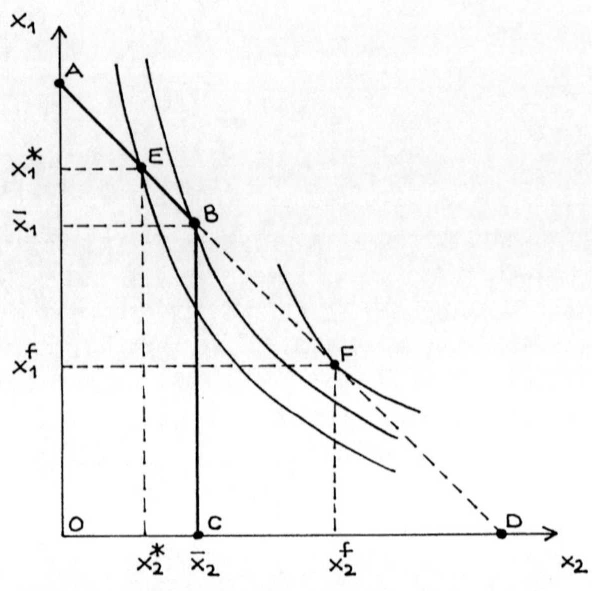

At both points E and B there exists full employment. However, the composite measure X (and hence output Y for given K also) is larger at B than at E. On the other hand, the technical rate of substitution (and hence the ratio of wages q_1 to q_2 corresponding to the two types of labor, given the condition of cost-minimization) will be larger at B than at E. The "maximum output" position at point F is not feasible, due to the institutional restriction $x_2 \leqq \bar{x}_2$.

This leads us right up to the interesting question of the optimum amount of (re-) education. If (re-) education were costless, so that the ratio of wages q_1/q_2 could be equal to unity, the optimal (re-) education policy would call for educating in addition $(\bar{x}_1 - x_1^f)$ persons up to a level of "Abitur", so that the total supply of labor with "Abitur" becomes x_2^f.[1)]

This, of course, implicitly assumes that the $(\bar{x}_1 - x_1^f)$ persons are personally qualified to be (re-) educated, which need not be true in the real life. However, (re-) education cannot be costless, so that the wage ratio must always fulfill the restriction $(q_1/q_2) < 1$, and hence a policy of "optimal" (re-) education calls for position on the line to the left of point F.

We shall argue that the actual employment position will be at a point like E; some persons with "Abitur" are employed in positions where "Abitur" is not required.[2)] But we should note that the point E is already determined without assuming a cost-minimization condition. As a matter of fact, as we shall argue, at a point E the conditions of cost-minimization - tangency of the iso-cost curve, which is determined by the wage ratio q_1/q_2 - is very unlikely to hold. The same institutional restrictions which prevent persons without "Abitur" from working among the x_2-working force, will also provide the conditions that enable those persons within the x_2- working force to receive a wage rate in excess of wage rate q_1 plus education cost. Just about all indicators from the real life economy tend to support this hypothesis, since the persons employed in the x_2- working force are also in the "higher rank" employment positions. Therefore, the possibilities of claiming a wage rate in excess of q_1 plus education cost are built right into the whole institutional setting.

In the diagram (III) below, the line segment a-b shall represent the iso-cost curve corresponding to the actual wage ratio. The line segment c-d represents an iso-cost curve corresponding to a hypothetical wage ratio, where the wage q_2 has been reduced to a level such that the point E also fulfills the minimum cost condition. Let the actual wages be q_1 and q_2, so that actual cost at point E is $q_1x_1^* + q_2x_2^* = C$.
The hypothetical (and lower) wage rate for the persons employed in the

1) It cannot be optimal to (re-) educate every person to the higher level of "Abitur", unless the two types of labor are perfect substitutes in the production process.
2) We shall use the symbols $\bar{x}_1$ and $\bar{x}_2$ for the actually employed, so that unemployment is not accounted for here. However, it is rather simple to distinguish the actually employed supply and the potential supply of labor by considering a line above the straight line A-D, which then represents the potential supply.

x_2- working force we write q_2^*, so that the hypothetical minimum cost for an employment situation at point E is $q_1x_1^* + q_2^*x_2^* = C^*$. The ratio C/C^* then provides an index of the cost inefficiency resulting from market imperfections induced by institutional restrictions in the labor market.

Diagram (III)

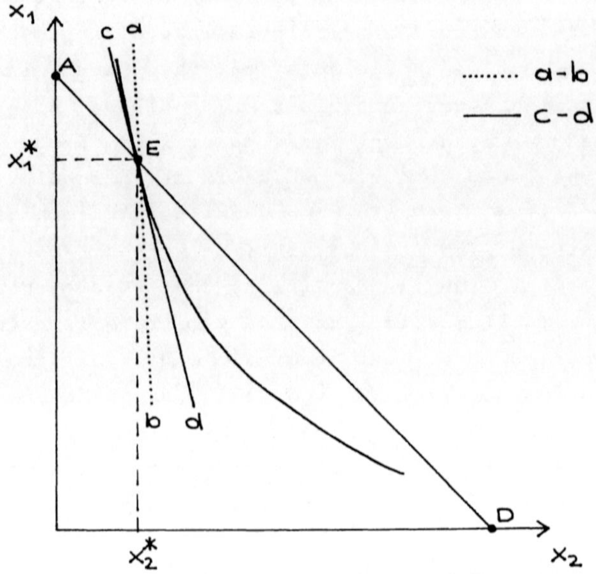

In essence the same theoretical setting concerning cost inefficiency results under factor regulation, where the hypothetical and not observed factor prices, which would make the observed factor quantities optimal under cost-minimization, are referred to as "shadow prices" by Toda (1976) and Atkinson and Halvorsen (1984). Their case of factor regulation amounts to a contraint $x_2^* = \bar{x}_2$ in our case. In a similar fashion, under quantity rationing in consumer demand Deaton (1981) refers to these hypothetical and not observed prices as "virtue prices".

In the next section 2 of this paper we will outline the framework under which we have pursued finding answers to the following questions that came up in a model as outlined above:

1. The index of cost inefficiency C/C^*.
2. The index of wage inefficiency q_2^*/q_2; this ratio indicates the proportion of actual wages which would make the actual employment situation a minimum cost situation.
3. The optimal (re-) education policy. This indicates the optimal partition of total labor into the two types of labor. This optimal partition depends on a given wage ratio q_1/q_2, but no cost considerations of (re-)education are accounted for here.
4. An index comparing the composite measure of labor under optimal (re-) education and under the actual employment situation. This is an index of allocation inefficiency.

In section 3 of this paper we shall then present the results of our empirical investigation with employment data from W.-Germany.

2. Theoretical Framework

Central in the empirical work is the specification of an analytic form for the aggregator function $g(x_1,x_2)$ of equation (1). We have limited our attention to the CES-type version

$$X = \alpha_o (\alpha_1^* x_1^{\beta^*} + \alpha_2^* x_2^{\beta^*})^{1/\beta^*}, \tag{3}$$

with the usual parameter restrictions $\alpha_o > 0$, $\alpha_1^* > 0$, $\alpha_2^* > 0$ and $-\infty < \beta^* < 1$ with $\beta^* \neq 0$. The special case of this function, the Cobb-Douglas version

$$X = \alpha_o x_1^{\alpha} x_2^{(1-\alpha)}, \tag{4}$$

with $\alpha_o > 0$ and $0 < \alpha < 1$, was considered separately.

(Since only two types of labor are involved, our selfimposed confinement to the CES-type function should not represent an unreasonable restriction.)

The dual cost functions to these aggregator functions follow as

$$C(q_1,q_2,X) = (X/\alpha_o) (\alpha q_1^{\beta} + (1-\alpha) q_2^{\beta})^{1/\beta}, \tag{3'}$$

with $\beta^* = \beta/(\beta-1)$, $\alpha_1^* = \alpha^{-1/(\beta-1)}$ and $\alpha_2^* = (1-\alpha)^{-1/(\beta-1)}$,

as well as

$$C(q_1,q_2,X) = (X/\alpha_o) q_1^{\alpha} q_2^{(1-\alpha)} \tag{4'}$$

respectively. The (long run) cost optimal demand functions would be

$$x_1^d = \partial C(q_1,q_2,X) / \partial q_1 = x_1^d(q_1,q_2,X) \tag{5}$$

and

$$x_2^d = \partial C(q_1,q_2,X) / \partial q_2 = x_2^d(q_1,q_2,X) \tag{6}$$

respectively. However, the condition that actual demand is entirely determined by this (long run) optimal demand will not be fulfilled by actual data. Therefore, we imposed a partial adjustment process for each type of labor demand.[1)]

The actual demand at time period t is then given by

$$x_1^*(t) = \gamma_1 x_1^*(t-1) + (1-\gamma_1)x_1^d(q_1(t),q_2(t),X(t)) \tag{7}$$

and

$$x_2^*(t) = \gamma_2 x_2^*(t-1) + (1-\gamma_2)x_2^d(q_1(t),q_2(t),X(t)) \ , \tag{8}$$

with each of the partial adjustment parameters γ_1 and γ_2 falling into the range between zero and unity.

The used data are W.-German quarterly employment data for the first quarter 1976 to the first quarter 1982 - i.e., for 25 observation points altogether.

These employment data only distinguish the number of employed persons with or without "Abitur", but not according to a correct classification of the type of labor performed. As illustrated in diagram (II), the points $\bar{x}_1$ and $\bar{x}_2$ correspond to the data classification of employed persons with or without "Abitur". But the points x_1^* and x_2^* correspond to the correct classification of labor according to their different types of employment, and as explained by the theory represented by equations (7) and (8). Thus, in order to make the data conform to the theoretical demand functions (7) and (8), a "correction" is required.
Let $\lambda(t)$ be the number of persons with "Abitur" employed in a position where "Abitur" is not required. The actual, available data are then related to the theoretical demand $x_1^*(t)$ and $x_2^*(t)$ of equations (7) and (8)

---

1) See e.g. Kmenta (1971, p. 476-477) for a theoretical foundation of a partial adjustment process as used in this paper.

as

$$\bar{x}_1(t) + \lambda(t) = x_1^*(t) = \gamma_1 x_1^*(t-1) + (1-\gamma_1)x_1^d(q_1(t),q_2(t),X(t)) \qquad (9)$$

and

$$\bar{x}_2(t) - \lambda(t) = x_2^*(t) = \gamma_2 x_2^*(t-1) + (1-\gamma_2)x_2^d(q_1(t),q_2(t),X(t)). \qquad (10)$$

For our empirical work, we have postulated that $\lambda(t)$ is proportional to the potential supply of persons in the labor market with "Abitur", say $\bar{\bar{x}}_2$, so that

$$\lambda(t) = \lambda\bar{\bar{x}}_2 , \qquad (11)$$

where λ is a parameter.

To complete our assumptions, we now add to the expressions (9) and (10) stochastic disturbances $\varepsilon_1(t)$ and $\varepsilon_2(t)$, both having zero means and a joint (normal) distribution with covariance matrix Ω, constant over time:

$$x_1(t) = \gamma_1 x_1^*(t-1) + (1-\gamma_1)x_1^d(q_1(t),q_2(t),X(t)) + \varepsilon_1(t) \qquad (12)$$

and

$$x_2(t) = \gamma_2 x_2^*(t-1) + (1-\gamma_2)x_2^d(q_1(t),q_2(t),X(t)) + \varepsilon_2(t) . \qquad (13)$$

The analytic versions of either CES or Cobb-Douglas result from using cost functions (3') or (4') for the determination of x_1^d and x_2^d , as it is specified by equations (5) and (6). We have used an estimation method as proposed by Malinvaud (1970, Chap.9), since both demand functions are non-linear in parameters and since parameter restrictions exist across a system of (those two) functions. In the next section 3 we then present both the Least-Squares (LS) and the Maximum-Likelihood (ML) estimation results with their corresponding implications.

An answer to the first two questions raised in the introduction, namely the indices of wage and cost inefficiency, requires a correction term for the wage rate q_2. After some extensive experimenting we have decided to choose the following form of correction:

$$q_2^*(t) = \delta(t)q_2(t) , \qquad (14)$$

with

$$\delta(t) = 1.0 - (\delta_o + \delta_1^u) , \tag{15}$$

where u is the unemployment rate (in percentage) of the persons with "Abitur". At the appropriate values for the parameters δ_o and δ_1, the term $\delta(t)$ varies between about 0.9 at the lowest unemployment rate of 2.2 % and 0.97 at the largest unemployment rate of about 4.6 %. The term $\delta(t)$ provides a direct answer to the index of wage inefficiency q_2^*/q_2. The index of cost inefficiency was being obtained by first estimating the demand functions (12) and (13) using a corrected wage rate, namely $q_2^*(t)$. Given the notation $\hat{x}_1(t)$ and $\hat{x}_2(t)$ for the fits, the minimum cost for each observation point t is then

$$C^*(t) = q_1(t)\,\hat{x}_1(t) + q_2^*(t)\,\hat{x}_2(t) , \tag{16}$$

and the actual, higher cost is

$$C(t) = q_1(t)\,\hat{x}_1(t) + q_2(t)\,\hat{x}_2(t) . \tag{17}$$

The answers to the question of optimal (re-) education have been formulated in "long run" only, as if total adjustment has already taken place. This, we think, is quite in accordance with the goals of any "optimal policy" procedure. Let $\bar{\bar{x}}_1(t)$ and $\bar{\bar{x}}_2(t)$ be the potential actual labor supply of each type, we then define $k(t) = \bar{\bar{x}}_1(t) + \bar{\bar{x}}_2(t)$. The total demand for each type of labor - disregarding any restriction on the availability of each type - is determined by the two (long-run) demand functions (5) and (6). The sum of demand for each type now has to satisfy

$$k(t) = x_1^d(q_1(t),q_2(t),X^p(t)) + x_2^d(q_1(t),q_2(t),X^p(t)) , \tag{18}$$

where k(t) is exogeneously given and $X^p(t)$ - the maximum possible value of aggregate labor - is implicitly determined in equation (18). The optimal value of each type of labor, namely the goal of an optimal (re-) education program, is then determined by substituting $X^p(t)$ into demand equations (5) and (6) to obtain

$$x_1^p(t) = x_1^d(q_1(t),q_2(t),X^p(t)) \tag{19}$$

$$x_2^p(t) = x_2^d(q_1(t),q_2(t),X^p(t)) . \tag{20}$$

The index of allocation inefficiency follows from a comparison of the actual value for X(t) with $X^p(t)$. This comparison is made using the actual wages $q_1(t)$ and $q_2(t)$ (- alternatively $q_2^*(t)$). These wage rates do not (- not even q_2^* -) reflect differences in the cost of (re-) education alone, but this point has not been pursued in this paper, since meaningful values for the additional cost of (re-) education are not readily available.

3. Empirical Results

In this section, the empirical results - both estimation results and the corresponding interpretations, namely the answers to the raised questions - are presented for both the CD and CES aggregator functions. For these, both the LS and ML estimates are presented in Table 1.

The standard errors are presented in parentheses below the estimates for the parameters. The "fit-measure" R_1^2 corresponds to the first labor demand function and R_2^2 to the second. The elasticity of substitution is computed as $\sigma = 1/(1-\beta^*)$. The parameters δ_o and δ_1 in the function $\delta(t)$ of equation (15) were set at the indicated values.

The function specified for $\delta(t)$ turned out to be very sensitive to alternate values of δ_o and δ_1, and since only 25 observation points are available, a simultaneous estimation of both the parameters (as presented in Table 1) and δ_o and δ_1 frequently led to a breakdown of the (non-linear) least-squares estimation program. Since we accepted the resulting values for $\delta(t)$ as plausible and reasonable, we considered this compromise as sensible. For the last reason given, we have also "set" the value for λ in $\lambda(t)$ of equations (12) and (13); however, λ was set by choosing that value which minimized the error-sum-of squares in the estimation procedure.

The results in Table 2 indicate a rather low loss of cost efficiency. In this Table 2 the additional cost resulting from the "wrong" market wage q_2 is expressed in percentage terms and is computed as $(C-C^*/C^*) \cdot 100$. For the presented "short run" cost situation this can be explained by the relatively large values of the adjustment parameters γ_1 and γ_2, which imply a rather inelastic reaction of actual employment to variations of relative wages. In Table 2 we also present the values for $\delta(t)$ along with the unemployment rate for x_2, namely AL2.

However, as soon as the "long run" implications of our estimation results are considered, the differences are more outstanding, as can be illustrated by the results in Tables 3 and 4. The results in Table 3 point out that the actual educational situation is far from optimal; this holds for both the CD and the CES versions. We note, however, that the actual educational situation has improved over time, since the ratios $x_2^p / \bar{\bar{x}}_2$ have fallen. The most dramatic implication is presented in Table 4, which contains the indices of allocation inefficiency. This loss compares the actual value of aggregate labor X to the one resulting under an optimal re-education of labor, given full employment. Here the differences between the implied results of the CD and CES versions become more dramatic. Given the precise estimate for β in the CES version, one should reject the CD version in favor of the CES version. But given the estimate for β, this implies a rather large value for the (technical) elasticity of substitution - or relatively "flat" isoquants. Hence, the loss in aggregate labor value should become less dramatic under optimal re-education, because of the implied easy technical substitution possibility between the two types of labor.

References

Atkinson,S.E. and Halvorsen,R.:"Parametric Efficiency Tests, Economies of Scale, and Input Demand in U.S. Electric Power Generation". International Economic Review 25, 1984, 647-662.

Blackorby,Ch., Primont,D., and Russell,R.R.: Duality, Separability, and Functional Structure: Theory and Applications. North-Holland, New York 1978

Bowles,S.: "Aggregation of Labor Inputs in the Economics of Growth and Planning: Experiments with a Two-Level CES Function". Journal of Political Economy 78, 1970, 68-81.

Deaton,A.S.: "Theoretical and Empirical Approaches to Consumer Demand under Rationing". Essays in the Theory and Measurement of Consumer Behavior. Cambridge 1981, 55-72.

Dougherty,C.R.S.: "Estimates of Labor Aggregation Functions". Journal of Political Economy 80, 1972, 1101-1119.

Kmenta,J.: Elements of Econometrics. New York 1971.

Malinvaud,E.: Statistical Methods of Econometrics. North Holland, Amsterdam 1970.

Toda,Y.: "Estimation of a Cost Function when the Cost is not a Minimum: The Case of Soviet Manufacturing Industries, 1958-1971". The Review of Economics and Statistics 58, 1976, 259-268

Table 1

Parameter Estimation Results

Parameter	CD $\lambda = 0.08$ $\delta_o = 0.03$ $\delta_1 = 0.3$		CES $\lambda = 0.08$ $\delta_o = 0.03$ $\delta_1 = 0.0$	
	LS	ML	LS	ML
γ_1	0.8415 (3.2355E-5)	0.8922 (4.3546E-3)	0.9192 (1.6911E-3)	0.9194 (1.8565E-1)
γ_2	0.9025 (6.6803E-3)	0.9121 (2.5534E-1)	0.8583 (6.2929E-4)	0.8991 (3.8491E-2)
α	0.7187 (5.9292E-4)	0.7292 (5.2479E-2)	0.6948 (1.1456E-3)	0.6371 (3.7992E-2)
k_o	0.4133 (4.1844E-4)	0.4308 (3.5484E-2)	1.2965 (7.0130E-4)	1.3571 (2.0006E-2)
β	(0.0)	(0.0)	-6.6338 (1.0444E-5)	-5.0139 (4.1870E-4)
β^*	0.0	0.0	0.8690	0.8337
σ	1.0	1.0	7.6338	6.0139
R_1^2	0.9582	0.9557	0.9336	0.9333
R_2^2	0.9994	0.9994	0.9997	0.9997

Table 2

Cost-Comparison

t	AL2 in %	CD			CES		
		$\delta(t)$	LS additional cost in %	ML additional cost in %	$\delta(t)$	LS additional cost in %	ML additional cost in %
1	2.83262	0.936972	0.636	0.638	0.97	0.303	0.304
2	2.80493	0.935852	0.649	0.650	0.97	0.304	0.304
3	2.77778	0.934718	0.662	0.663	0.97	0.304	0.304
4	2.75229	0.933618	0.674	0.675	0.97	0.304	0.305
5	2.72615	0.932455	0.687	0.688	0.97	0.305	0.305
6	2.65957	0.929321	0.719	0.719	0.97	0.304	0.304
7	2.67423	0.930033	0.711	0.711	0.97	0.304	0.304
8	2.60939	0.926788	0.744	0.744	0.97	0.303	0.303
9	2.58552	0.925528	0.757	0.756	0.97	0.303	0.303
10	2.52722	0.922294	0.794	0.793	0.97	0.304	0.304
11	2.47148	0.918983	0.841	0.839	0.97	0.308	0.308
12	2.45536	0.917983	0.863	0.862	0.97	0.313	0.313
13	2.40350	0.914631	0.911	0.910	0.97	0.317	0.317
14	2.35832	0.911537	0.957	0.955	0.97	0.321	0.321
15	2.28279	0.905971	1.041	1.040	0.97	0.329	0.329
16	2.24422	0.902928	1.098	1.097	0.97	0.336	0.336
17	2.17670	0.897247	1.188	1.187	0.97	0.344	0.344
18	2.41884	0.915645	0.994	0.994	0.97	0.352	0.352
19	2.62658	0.927673	0.852	0.852	0.97	0.352	0.352
20	2.83286	0.936982	0.743	0.743	0.97	0.353	0.353
21	3.06729	0.945101	0.647	0.648	0.97	0.353	0.353
22	3.46427	0.954562	0.536	0.536	0.97	0.353	0.353
23	3.82263	0.959972	0.475	0.475	0.97	0.355	0.355
24	4.23216	0.963875	0.431	0.431	0.97	0.358	0.358
25	4.57399	0.965942	0.408	0.409	0.97	0.359	0.360

Table 3

Ratios of optimal to actual educational levels

t	CD				CES			
	LS		ML		LS		ML	
	$x_2^p / \bar{\bar{x}}_2$	$x_1^p / \bar{\bar{x}}_1$	$x_2^p / \bar{\bar{x}}_2$	$x_1^p / \bar{\bar{x}}_1$	$x_2^p / \bar{\bar{x}}_2$	$x_1^p / \bar{\bar{x}}_1$	$x_2^p / \bar{\bar{x}}_2$	$x_1^p / \bar{\bar{x}}_1$
1	3.22264	0.787460	3.10318	0.798883	3.49654	0.761269	4.15768	0.698047
2	3.19497	0.788112	3.07653	0.799545	3.46651	0.761900	4.12197	0.698626
3	3.16795	0.788762	3.05051	0.800204	3.43719	0.762528	4.08711	0.699201
4	3.14240	0.789387	3.02591	0.800839	3.40948	0.763132	4.05415	0.699756
5	3.11627	0.790039	3.00075	0.801499	3.38112	0.763762	4.02044	0.700333
6	3.09074	0.790686	2.97616	0.802157	3.35342	0.764388	3.98750	0.700907
7	3.06433	0.791369	2.95073	0.802850	3.32477	0.765049	3.95343	0.701513
8	3.03976	0.792016	2.92708	0.803506	3.29811	0.765674	3.92173	0.702086
9	3.01542	0.792669	2.90364	0.804168	3.27170	0.766305	3.89033	0.702664
10	2.95420	0.794362	2.84469	0.805886	3.20528	0.767942	3.81135	0.704166
11	2.89557	0.796058	2.78824	0.807606	3.14167	0.769581	3.73571	0.705669
12	2.83948	0.797754	2.73422	0.809327	3.08081	0.771221	3.66334	0.707172
13	2.78575	0.799449	2.68248	0.811046	3.02252	0.772859	3.59402	0.708675
14	2.70369	0.802183	2.60346	0.813821	2.93348	0.775503	3.48815	0.711099
15	2.62764	0.804888	2.53023	0.816565	2.85096	0.778118	3.39003	0.713497
16	2.55556	0.807619	2.46082	0.819335	2.77276	0.780758	3.29704	0.715917
17	2.48856	0.810317	2.39631	0.822072	2.70007	0.783366	3.21061	0.718309
18	2.47995	0.810676	2.38802	0.822436	2.69072	0.783713	3.19949	0.718627
19	2.47143	0.811033	2.37981	0.822799	2.68148	0.784058	3.18850	0.718944
20	2.46360	0.811364	2.37228	0.823134	2.67299	0.784378	3.17841	0.719237
21	2.45527	0.811719	2.36426	0.823495	2.66395	0.784722	3.16766	0.719552
22	2.43616	0.812544	2.34585	0.824331	2.64321	0.785519	3.14300	0.720283
23	2.41814	0.813335	2.32850	0.825134	2.62366	0.786284	3.11975	0.720984
24	2.39971	0.814158	2.31076	0.825969	2.60367	0.787079	3.09598	0.721714
25	2.38250	0.814939	2.29419	0.826762	2.58500	0.787835	3.07378	0.722407

Table 4

Loss of aggregate labor value due to allocation inefficiency
(in percent)

t	CD		CES	
	LS	ML	LS	ML
1	17.730	16.478	5.3393	6.9326
2	17.535	16.298	5.3141	6.9087
3	17.355	16.134	5.3115	6.9047
4	17.170	15.964	5.3065	6.8953
5	16.995	15.805	5.3121	6.8938
6	16.396	15.221	4.9345	6.4911
7	16.196	15.045	4.9814	6.5167
8	15.990	14.866	5.0402	6.5476
9	15.788	14.689	5.1097	6.5823
10	15.751	14.676	5.2345	6.7073
11	15.340	14.275	5.1016	6.5607
12	14.954	13.899	4.9826	6.4264
13	14.571	13.527	4.8653	6.2927
14	13.979	12.945	4.5453	5.9476
15	13.435	12.414	4.3957	5.7697
16	12.921	11.910	4.2545	5.5985
17	12.415	11.418	4.1165	5.4294
18	12.581	11.576	4.5093	5.8194
19	12.754	11.752	4.7093	6.0227
20	12.910	11.913	4.9019	6.2182
21	13.075	12.085	5.1047	6.4238
22	13.325	12.341	5.4053	6.7225
23	13.593	12.621	5.7801	7.0949
24	13.865	12.904	6.1607	7.4727
25	14.126	13.179	6.5317	7.8411

On the Identification of Key Sectors: Critical Theoretical and Empirical Analysis of Key Sector Indices

Hartmut Kogelschatz
Institut für international vergleichende
Wirtschafts- und Sozialstatistik
Universität Heidelberg
Grabengasse 14

D-6900 Heidelberg, West Germany

1. Introduction

When investigating the inter-industry linkages of an economy the question arises: which sectors will for a given increase in their final demand induce comparatively large production, employment and income effects in the whole system? The answer is of particular interest for decisions upon the distribution of a government spending programme or a programme for developing countries.

The concept of key sectors has been proposed in the framework of input-output analysis and goes back to Hirschman (1958) and Rasmussen (1956). Various methods for identifying key sectors have been suggested associating an index number with each sector for its inter-industry linkages. Recent theoretical and empirical studies refer mainly to Rasmussen's ideas, in particular to his 'power of dispersion index'

$$U_j = \frac{L_j}{\frac{1}{n}\sum_{k=1}^{n} L_k} \quad \text{with } L_j = \sum_{i=1}^{n} l_{ij} \quad \text{(linkage index)}, \; j=1,\ldots,n. \qquad (1)$$

Cf. the discussions in the 'Quarterly Journal of Economics' (1973, 1976) and in 'Kyklos' (1975) as well as the contributions by Hazari (1970), Schintke (1976), and Katzenbeisser (1979). Here $(l_{ij})=L=(I-A)^{-1}$ denotes the Leontief-inverse of an nxn input matrix $A \geq 0$ in value terms, which is assumed to fulfil the Hawkins-Simon condition. The notion 'total linkage' is due to Yotopoulos/Nugent (1973, p.161). The linkage index L_j from which U_j differs by a norming factor captures the value of gross production in the whole economy induced per unit of final demand for commodities of sector j. The norming factor is given by the reciprocal of the average output increase resulting from spending an additional unit of final demand on each sector. The sectors with the largest values of U_j or L_j, resp., are in a favoured position to produce strong output stimuli for the whole economy and may therefore be called 'key sectors'. Rasmussen (1956, p.140) requires, in addition, a small coefficient of variation within column j of L. Hazari (1970) requires these conditions to hold also for the corresponding row. Since the

Measurement in Economics
ed. by W. Eichhorn

indices U_j and L_j yield the same ranking of sectors, attention is focused upon the linkage index L_j, which can be interpreted as multiplier of gross production value with respect to the additional final demand in sector j. The index L_j is referred to as key sector index (KSI) in the following.

Since the KSI's are assumed to give hints for efficient public investment decisions, it is worth investigating how these indices are influenced by price changes and by technological change such as process substitution and productivity improvement. These problems are analysed, as well as the question of how sensitive these indices are with respect to aggregation and to errors in the input matrix A. Since the values of L_j obtained from empirical IO tables lie very close together, even small changes may create a different ranking of sectors. Theoretical results by Kogelschatz/Goldstein (1978) on the sensitivity of the KSI are referred to and applied to empirical IO data for the Federal Republic of Germany. A considerable sensitivity of the KSI can be observed, so that KSI results should be used with caution by decision makers.

The key sector concept orginally formulated for output effects can be extended to employment and national income effects. These three multipliers are studied for three versions of the static open IO model with exogenous final demand, sectoral consumption functions, and investment functions. For the empirical German IO data the ranking of key sector indices is compared for these nine cases by computing Spearman's rank correlation coefficient. It is shown that the ranking of the output and employment indices varies considerably for different models (in particular, for the output), whereas the ranking of national income multipliers is invariant with respect to making consumption and investment endogenous. Since this invariance generally holds and since a high national income is a commonly accepted target, it is suggested that one should concentrate on these income multipliers for a short run analysis, despite of certain deficiencies.

I am indebted to W. Breinlinger and I. Busch for computational assistance and to the Stiftung Volkswagenwerk for supporting a related project.

2. Sensitivity Analysis in the Static Open Input-Output Model

2.1 The Data

The data base for the empirical investigation is the input matrix of West Germany for 1972 compiled by the German Institute of Economic Research (DIW). The input matrix with 14 sectors is condensed to 12

production sectors by deleting the sector 'state' and 'private households'. In table 1 these sectors are arranged in the rank order resulting from the Rasmussen index U_j and L_j.
In the following we investigate how the above mentioned changes and errors influence this ranking. These modifications will occur in the sector food, machinery, or energy, which are originally ranked as 1, 2, and 5, respectively; in the text the complete sector names are abbreviated by writing only the first name. Besides the two top-ranked sectors, sector 5 was selected, since energy is of particular interest in current discussions.
Changes in prices and proportional changes in technology are considered at prescribed levels of 5,10,20, and 30%; however, here only 10% and 30% increases are described.

2.2 Price Changes

Empirical input-output tables are based on values which are calculated by pricing technological quantities. When prices are changed, the new input matrix A is obtained from the original input matrix A by a similarity transformation with the diagonal matrix of the price change factors π_i. Possible factor substitution is not taken into account. The corresponding new Leontief inverse is obtained by applying the same similarity transformation to the former Leontief inverse.
A general price increase of all goods by the same percentage has no influence on the key sector index, whereas a change of relative prices does have an influence. For the special case of a price increase of only good k from p_k to $p_k' = \pi_k p_k$ with $\pi_k > 1$ we get

$$L_j' = L_j + (\pi_k - 1) \cdot l_{kj} > L_j \quad \text{for all } j \neq k \tag{2}$$

and for j=k

$$L_k' = \frac{1}{\pi_k} \cdot \sum_{i \neq k} l_{ik} + l_{kk} < L_k . \tag{3}$$

An increase in price k induces a decrease of the KSI of sector k, while the KSI of the other sectors increase proportionally to l_{kj}. Thus, the relative weight of the sector in which prices are increased declines, and the higher the price increase the greater the decline. The results of a price index increase in sector 1,2, or 5 by 10% or 30% are reported in table 2. An alteration of the ranks is indicated by an asterisk and L_j' is the new KSI value.
In the food sector a price increase of 10% has no influence on the

ranking. However, at a 30% increase this sector falls from rank 1 to rank 4 without influencing the ranking of the other sectors. In both the machinery and the energy sector already a price increase of 10% influences the ranking of other sectors. A 30% price increase induces an even greater index change, and more sectors change ranks. The machinery sector falls from rank 2 to rank 6 and the energy sector from rank 5 to 7.

2.3 Substitution of Production Processes

Each production process is represented by a column vector $a_{.j}$ in the input matrix A. A process substitution in sector k means a switch of the input vector $a_{.k}$ to the new input vector $a'_{.k} = a_{.k} + \Delta a_{.k}$. The resulting change in the KSI can be written as

$$\Delta L_j = c_k l_{kj} \quad \text{for all } j, \text{ where } c_k = (\sum_i L_i \, \Delta a_{ik})/(1 - l_{k.} \Delta a_{.k}). \tag{4}$$

Here and in the following $m_{.k}$ and $m_{k.}$ are the kth column and row vector, respectively, of a matrix M.

Consequently all indices change in the same direction because $l_{ij} \geq 0$. The sign of the numerator of c_k determines whether an increase or a decrease in the KSI results. Its size is proportional to l_{kj} and usually has a maximum in sector k, since $l_{kk} > l_{kj}$ for all j, if net value added is positive for every sector. The constant of proportionality c_k is a linear combination of the indices L_j. In the special case of a proportional process change ($\Delta a_{.k} = \gamma a_{.k}$ with $\gamma > -1$) the constant can be written as

$$c_k = \gamma(L_k - 1) \; / \; (1 - \gamma(l_{kk} - 1)); \tag{5}$$

thus it depends only upon the index L_k. With a more efficient process in sector k, i.e., a process which uses less of all inputs, all indices decrease and the index of sector k decreases the most. This leads to the following problem:

Suppose that sector k has been a key sector that has been supported by public investment. Then this sector could lose its favourable position when a more efficient process is introduced since its index declines the most. If an industry expects that a much smaller KSI value will result in fewer public orders, this could counteract technological progress.

In the empirical evaluation the special case of a proportional process change is considered, so the input coefficient vector $a_{.k}$ of sector k

is substituted by $a'_{.k} = (1+\gamma)\ a_{.k}$ with $\gamma < 0$, which means an increase in efficiency. The impact on the ranking of the sectors is given in table 3. An increase in efficiency of 10% in the food sector leads to a fall to rank 2, and an increase of 30% to a fall to rank 8. Also those sectors which are closely connected to the food sector (e.g. agriculture and services) change ranks. The same efficiency increases in the machinery sector induce a fall from rank 2 to rank 6 and rank 11. In the energy sector these efficiency increases do not result in such drastic changes. It falls from rank 5 to 7 and 11, respectively.
The ranking of the other sectors is not influenced by an efficiency change in the machinery and energy sector.

2.4 Change in Productivity

The productivity of factor k in sector j is given by the reciprocal value α_{kj} of the input coefficient a_{kj} provided $a_{kj} \neq 0$. A change in productivity of factor k in each sector is thus represented by a change of the k-th row vector $a_{k.}$ in the input matrix A. For the change in the indices L_j the following sensitivity result is given

$$\Delta L_j = c_k \Delta a_{k.} \Delta l_{.j} \quad \text{for all } j, \text{ where } c_k = L_k/(1-\Delta a_{k.} l_{.k}). \qquad (6)$$

Some indices can increase whereas others decrease, if the components of the vector $\Delta a_{k.}$ have different signs, which means that the productivity of factor k rises in some processes and falls in others. A change in the same direction, which is characteristic of process substitution, results when the productivity of factor k increases or decreases in all processes. The change in L_j is proportional to the scalar product $\Delta a_{k.} l_{.j}$, the proportionality constant being a multiple of L_k. In contrast to process substitution it cannot be generally said which index changes the most.
For the special case of proportional productivity change

$(\Delta a_{k.} = \gamma a_{k.}$ with $\gamma > -1)$ we get

$$\Delta L_j = c_k (l_{kj} - \delta_{kj}) \quad \text{for all } j, \text{ where } c_k = \gamma L_k/(1-\gamma(l_{kk}-1)), \qquad (7)$$

i.e., ΔL_j is proportional to l_{kj} for all $j \neq k$. This result is very similar to the corresponding result for a proportional process substitution.

The empirical evaluations are again done for the special case of proportional change (see table 4). At a 10% productivity increase of the factor food, the food sector remains at rank 1, however, at an increase of 30% it falls to rank 4. The ranking of the other sectors is influenced, as well. When the productivity of the factors in the machinery and energy sector is increased by 10%, then the rank of this sector falls down to 3 and 6, respectively, however, the ranking of the other sectors is not influenced. At a 30% increase both sectors fall back in ranking even more and the other sectors change ranks, as well.

2.5 Errors in Input Coefficients

Empirical input-ouput tables do have mistakes, which occur in the measurement, estimation and up-dating of data. The influence of an error on the KSI is considered only for the simple case in which only one input coefficient a_{ik} is incorrect and the error has the size Δa_{ik}. For the case of a process change the induced error in the indices L_j is

$$\Delta L_j = c_{ik} l_{kj} \text{ for all } j, \text{ where } c_{ik} = \Delta a_{ik} L_i / (1 - \Delta a_{ik} l_{ki}) \quad (8)$$

or as a first-order approximation

$$\Delta L_j \sim L_i l_{kj} \Delta a_{ik}. \quad (9)$$

All errors in the indices have the same sign as the error Δa_{ik} provided that $l_{kj} \neq 0$. The errors are proportional to l_{kj} and the proportionality constant is a multiple of the supplying sector's index L_i. The index L_k of the purchasing sector changes the most under the assumption mentioned in section 2.3, which is no constraint for empirical input matrices. A measurement error of -50%, which the input coefficients in the food sector take alternately, results in changes of the L_j - values and rank changes reported in table 5. Errors of this size may occur in input matrices since the compiling institutes have to do rough estimations in some cases. The greatest change is induced by a measurement error in the diagonal element (see equation 8): In our example the leading sector falls to rank 6, while sector 4 takes rank 2. Errors of this size in the other input coefficients of the food sector only in some cases result in minor rank alterations.

In the energy sector an error of -50% in the diagonal element leads to a fall from rank 5 to 11, while an error of +50% makes it the top-ranked sector. Errors in other input coefficients result only in minor ranking changes similar to the observation in the food sector.

2.6 Aggregation of Sectors

For most countries input-output tables are compiled with varying degree of aggregation, i.e., with different numbers of sectors; for example, for West Germany such tables are compiled with 56 and 14 sectors. Thus, the question arises if and how the ranking of the KSI is influenced by aggregation of sectors. Bharadwaj (1966, p. 316) points out that the sensitivity of the KSI with regard to aggregation has to be examined before much confidence is placed in these indices. By aggregation of sectors the nxn input matrix A is transformed to a smaller mxm matrix A. Here only the effect of an elementary aggregation of two sectors on the KSI is discussed. Obviously, any aggregation can be composed of such elementary aggregations. For simplicity we regard the consolidation of the last two sectors n-1 and n. The change in the KSI is given by

$$\Delta L_j = c_{n,n-1}(w_n l_{n-1,j} - (1-w_n) l_{nj}) \text{ for } j=1,\ldots,n-1, \tag{10}$$

where

$$c_{n,n-1} = (L_n - L_{n-1}) / [(1-w_n)(l_{nn} - l_{n,n-1}) - w_n(l_{n-1,n} - l_{n-1,n-1})]$$

and

$$w_n = x_n^o / (x_{n-1}^o + x_n^o) \text{ with } x^o = \text{output vector of the base period.}$$

The change of the KSI L_j is proportional to the weighted difference of the coefficients $l_{n-1,j}$ and l_{nj} of L. Some indices will rise, while others must decrease unless by chance $L_n = L_{n-1}$. The ranking can change, as well.

The empirical investigation of the influence of sector aggregation on the ranking was done by combining from two up to six sectors. All possible combinations of two sectors were considered, but not all groups of three to six sectors. In table 6 the effect of the aggregations of the food sector with all other sectors is reported. The aggregate remains at rank 1 when sector 1 is combined with sector 2 to 6; however, its rank falls as low as to rank 7 when sector 1 is merged with sector 12. In general, the new rank that results from an aggregation of two sectors lies between the two former ranks of the sectors. Thus the L_j - values (and the U_j - values) of the high-ranked sectors fall and those of the low-ranked sectors rise. Some other sectors also change ranks. These empirical results support Bharadwaj's critical comment.

2.7 Employment Effect, Change in Labour Productivity

While the linkage indices L_j considered so far comprise the gross production of the whole economy that is induced per unit of final demand for good j, similarly constructed indices $B_j = \sum_{i=1}^{n} b_{ij}$ capture the impact on total employment. Rasmussen (1956, p. 141f.) also mentions employment and import as possible targets for a definition of key industries. The so-called employment inverse B is obtained from L by a left multiplication with the diagonal matrix Λ of the reciprocal labour productivities λ_j. The elements b_{ij} indicate how many persons are employed in sector i per unit of final demand for good j. It is assumed that the economy runs at full capacity or a constant percentage of it. This seems to be not realistic in today's world of underutilized capacities. A proportional change of labour productivity λ_k in sector k to $\lambda_k' = \gamma\lambda_k$ $(\gamma>0)$ results in the following change of the indices B_j.

$$\Delta B_j = (1/\gamma-1)b_{kj} \text{ for all } j. \tag{11}$$

The changes are proportional to $b_{kj} \geq 0$ and thus have the same sign. The greatest change occurs usually in the index B_k of the sector with the altered labour productivity, since $b_{kk} \geq b_{kj}$ is implied by positive net values added (cf. section 2.3).

In table 7 the sectors are arranged according to the employment indices B_j; again the public sector and private households are not considered. By far the greatest employment effects are to be expected in agriculture. The food sector takes rank 2, while the machinery sector is at rank 9 and the energy sector at rank 12.

The change in the indices B_j is empirically investigated when the labour productivity in the sectors agriculture, food or trade (rank 3) and transportation (rank 4) increases by 10% or 30% (see table 7). With productivity increases of this size in agriculture, this sector remains at rank 1, while the food sector falls behind the trade sector. This is easily explained, because the B_j index value of agriculture is much higher than those of the other sectors lying rather close together. Moreover, there is a strong supply relationship from agriculture to the food sector. A productivity increase in the latter sector makes it rank behind the trade sector. In the trade sector a productivity increase of 10% has no influence on the order of the B_j-values; at an increase of 30% this sector falls from rank 3 to rank 9. A similar change in ranking can be observed in the transportation sector already at a 10% productivity increase in labour, which causes a fall from rank 4 to 7, and at a 30% increase with a fall to rank 9.

3. Introduction of Sectoral Consumption and Investment Functions

3.1 Theoretical Considerations

In the preceding analysis final demand has been exogenously given. In order to make part of final demand endogenous, sectoral consumption and investment functions have been introduced into the static open IO model. Schumann (1975) computes empirical output multipliers for given government spending programmes underlying such extended models. Similarly, Schnabl/Holub (1979) empirically compare KSI for the standard and the extended model. A theoretical derivation of the impact of partly endogenized final demand on the KSI is given below.

Sectoral consumption functions of the Keynes type are introduced into the formerly used static open IO model by

$$C_i = c_i Y + b_i \qquad i=1,\dots,n. \tag{12}$$

Here C_i, c_i, b_i and Y denote nominal consumption demand, marginal propensity to consume, autonomous consumption, and national income, resp.. Thus, the extended static open IOM results

$$(I - A - cv)x = f^a, \tag{13}$$

where v and f^a stand for the row vector of net value added coefficients and the column vector of autonomous final demand.
For a closed economy without government the solution is given by (cf. Kogelschatz (1977 , p. 106))

$$x = L(I + \frac{1}{s} ce)f^a = L^z f^a, \tag{14}$$

where s denotes the total marginal propensity to save and e a row vector of n ones. Here depreciation is assumed to be considered in the input coefficients. In addition, sectoral investment functions depending linearly on Y can be introduced (cf. Schumann (1975)). Formally, the results are not affected, however, the coefficients c_i have then to be interpreted as the sum of the marginal propensities to consume and to invest.
The relationship between the KSI L_j and the analogously constructed indices L_j^z of the extended model

$$L_j^z := \sum_{i=1}^{n} l_{ij}^z, \text{ where } L^z = (l_{ij}^z) = (I-A-cv)^{-1}, \tag{15}$$

is easily obtained from equation (14) as

$$L_j^z = L_j + \frac{1}{s} \sum_i c_i L_i \quad j=1,\dots,n. \tag{16}$$

This result also holds for the employment indices B_j^z of the extended model, if L is replaced by B. Obviously, the KSI L_j are augmented by a linear combination of the L_j-values. This constant can be interpreted as additional output induced by the endogenized consumption, when exogenous final demand for good j is increased by one unit. The ranking of the KSI is not affected, not even by a change in the marginal propensities to consume. Hence, the empirical sensitivity of the ranking needs not be examined. Bounds for the additive constant are given by

$$\frac{1-s}{s} \leq \frac{1-s}{s} \min_i L_i \leq \frac{1}{s} \Sigma c_i L_i = \frac{1-s}{s} \Sigma \frac{c_i}{1-s} L_i \leq \frac{1-s}{s} \max_i L_i . \tag{17}$$

For the empirical input matrix underlying this study we obtain with s assumed as 1/3, e.g.

$2 \cdot 1{,}46 = 2{,}92 \leq \frac{1}{s} \Sigma c_i L_i \leq 4{,}08 = 2 \cdot 2{,}04$,

which shows a considerable increase in the KSI of the extended model with sectoral consumption functions. Clearly, the new total output multiplier is greater than Keynes' simple investment multiplier, since the former comprises induced intermediate demand.

The preceding results (14) and (16) have to be modified, if depreciation is not taken into account in the input coefficients and/or if an open economy with government is considered. Empirical IO tables normally have an extra vector of depreciation. Under the usual assumption that depreciation D, import M, indirect taxes T_{ind}, and subsidies Z depend linearly on output x, (14) has to be replaced by the more general formula (cf. Kogelschatz (1977), p. 108))

$$x = L(I + \frac{1}{s + rLc} c(e - rL))f^a = L^z(r) f^a, \tag{18}$$

where r is a row vector of 'reduction' coefficients

$r_i := (D+M+T_{ind}-Z)_i / x_i$.

The corresponding equation for the KSI now reads

$$L_j^z(r) = L_j + \frac{1}{s+rLc} (\sum_{i=1}^{n} c_i L_i) \cdot (1 - \sum_{k=1}^{n} r_k l_{kj}) \quad j=1,\dots,n \tag{19}$$

and

$$\Delta L_j^z(r) = \Delta L_j^z \frac{s}{s+rLc} (1 - \Sigma_k r_k l_{kj}) = k(1-\hat{r}_j) \Delta L_j^z \leq \Delta L_j^z, \tag{20}$$

which implies $L_j \leq L_j^z(r) \leq L_j^z$.

The increment in the KSI values L_j is no longer a constant, but it is proportional to $(1-\hat{r}_j) := 1-(rL)_j = (vL)_j =: \hat{v}_j$, which is the net value added coefficient with respect to autonomous final demand f_j^a (instead of x_j in the definition of v_j). Hence, the rank order of the KSI can change, which is observed for empirical IO tables (cf. Schumann (1975), Schnabl/Holub (1979)). The first author also studies the empirical relationship between the Leontief inverses L and $L^z(r)$ with his data (cf. p. 393). This can be theoretically done by equation (18) which yields fixed proportions between the row and column vectors, resp., of the matrix $\Delta L^z(r)$. Those sectors with the greatest values of $\hat{v}_j$, which are supposed to have a high positive rank correlation coefficient with the smaller values of v_j, will probably improve in the ranking of the KSI, if they are not yet at the top. This statement, which is supported by empirical observations, has a simple economic explanation: final demand for those sectors yields the greatest increases in national income, hence, also in induced consumption and production. The constant of proportionality is given as product of a generalized income multiplier $1/(s+rLc)$ with respect to additional net value added $\hat{v}_j$ and the term $\Sigma c_i L_i$ which stands for total output induced by consumption per unit of income.

The employment indices for the extended model are derived from the representation of $L^z(r)$ as

$$B_j^z(r) = B_j + \frac{1}{s+\hat{r}c}(\Sigma_i c_i B_i)(1-\hat{r}_j) \qquad j=1,\dots,n, \tag{21}$$

which corresponds perfectly to the formula for the KSI $L_j^z(r)$. Hence, similar conclusions may be drawn. The targets total output or employment are used to be focused upon in the literature on key sectors, just as in the previous analysis.

However, another reasonable target would be national income Y. In which sector does a given amount of autonomous final demand have to be spent in order to obtain the greatest increase in Y? For a closed economy without government (and with depreciation considered in the input coefficients) the answer is that each sector is equally suitable; the income effect always is given by Keynes' investment multiplier (cf. Kogelschatz (1977), p. 112f.).

However, in an open economy with government (and/or depreciation not considered in the input coefficients) this result does not hold. In this general case, the national income multiplier $Y_j^z(r)$ with respect to a unit increase in autonomous final demand f_j^a for sector j can be derived as

$$Y_j^z(r) = (1-\hat{r}_j)\cdot(1 + \frac{1-s}{s+\hat{r}c}(1-\hat{r}_j)) \qquad j=1,\dots,n. \tag{22}$$

For a proof see Kogelschatz (1985). This result extends Keynes' foreign trade multiplier (without repercussions) to a multi-sector economy with intermediate production and sectoral consumption functions. The income impact depends on the sector in which additional money is spent. Its maximum is taken for sector j_o which has the greatest value of $\hat{v}_j$, which coincides with the greatest national income multiplier Y_j in the standard IO model without consumption functions. Furthermore, it can be seen that the ranking of income multipliers is the same in both models (repercussions are not taken into account).

Obviously, the multipliers for an open economy are also applicable for a change in autonomous export demand. For this case production and employment effects are used to be studied in the framework of the standard model which is likely to underestimate the impacts by neglecting the income propagation process induced by consumption.

3.2 Empirical Results

For the introduction of linear consumption and investment functions the parameters have to be estimated from time series. For simplicity we take the OLS estimates from Schumann (1975, p.391) computed for the period 1954-1967. As expected the estimates for consumption are more significant than those for investment. Though some of these estimates are unsatisfactory, similarly to Schumann (1975) we want to investigate the effects of partly endogenizing consumption (model version 1) and, in addition, investment (model version 2). Both versions are confronted with the standard IO model (version 0) with exogenous final demand only. The comparison refers to multipliers (and their ranking) with respect to total output, employment and income induced by additional autonomous final demand. Schumann (1975) compares the empirical matrix multipliers of the three versions and computes the associated total output multipliers for two government spending programmes.

Table 8a shows the KSI or output multiplier. The average gross production impact (induced by a unit of final demand uniformly distributed over all sectors) is given 1.77 (version 0), 3.02 (version 1) and 4.25 (version 2). This shows a considerable increase in the KSI when consumption and investment functions are introduced. The ranking tends to be reversed. A drastic example is given by the sectors food and transportation

Rank	version 0	version 1	version 2
Food	1	4	11
Transportation	11	5	2

These alterations are caused by differences in the coefficients r_j. (here: $r_1 \sim 0.26$; $r_{11} \sim 0.15$). The higher r_j the lower Y_j and hence induced consumption and investment demand. The rankings of the KSI for model versions i,j are compared by Spearman's rank correlation coefficients RC(Vi,Vj): RC(V0,V1)~ 0.32, RC(VO,V2)~-0.27, RC(V1,V2)~ 0.65. These coefficients point out that the ranking of KSI essentially depends on the underlying model and should be critically considered in decision processes.
The employment indices B_j reported in table 8b also show some great changes in the ranking, e.g.,

Rank	version 0	version 1	version 2
Food	2	5	9
Services	9	8	5

On the whole, the rank changes are more moderate, the RC-values lying between 0.7 and 0.91. By far the greatest employment effects are observed in agriculture, followed in versions 1 and 2 by trade, transportation, and construction. With respect to the KSI L_j these sectors are found at the end of the rank order for the standard model.

The income multipliers Y_j in table 8c are much smaller than the KSI L_j (about 1/3 on the average). The greatest impacts are observed for additional final demand in the transportation sector (with KSI rank 11 in the standard model) followed by construction, services, agriculture, and trade. These sectors (except for trade) are also leading in the ranking of the indices B_j and L_j if model version 2 is regarded. In version 0 these sectors are at the end of L_j-ranking. For version 2 the ranks of B_j and Y_j are highly correlated. Spearman's rank correlation coefficients for all model versions and all multipliers are listed in the following table:

RC	version 0	version 1	version 2
(L_j,B_j)	-.33	.29	.57
(L_j,Y_j)	-.8	.23	.76
(B_j,Y_j)	.38	.68	.87

It shows that endogenizing final demand makes the rankings of any two multipliers more similar. The RC-values for a given index considered for different models are reported in table 8.

The average multipliers are given by:

	version 0	version 1	version 2
$\bar{L}$	1.77	3.02	4.25
$\bar{B}\ 10^6$	28.15	47.12	66.97
$\bar{Y}$	.65	1.1	1.57

Furthermore, for model version 1 partial and proportional increases of 10% and 30% in the marginal propensities to consume and in the reduction coefficients $r_i = (D+M+(T_{ind}-Z))_i/x_i$ are investigated. The impact on the multipliers L_j, B_j, Y_j and their ranking is relatively small for partial changes in c_1, c_2 and c_5, which are considered here. However, a proportional change of all propensities to consume of 10% or 30% induces a change in the average multipliers $\bar{L}$, $\bar{B}$, $\bar{Y}$ by nearly the same percentages. The ranking of the L_j and B_j are affected to a considerable extent, which is reflected by rank correlation coefficients of .76 and .91 for a 30% increase of c. A proportional increase in the reduction coefficients, e.g., by higher taxes or imports, yields by far smaller changes in the multiplier values and their ranking. Partial increases in r_i, however, can disturb the ranking: e.g., $RC(L_j) = .8$ at a 30% increase of r_1, which makes the food sector fall from rank 4 to 11.
Similar changes in r_2 and r_5 have smaller effects on the 3 multipliers.

Finally, the national income multipliers Y_j are modified. If sectoral subsidies are constant and not proportional to output, then the formerly leading transportation sector, which receives the largest subsidies, takes rank 3 preceded by construction and services, and followed by machinery and trade. If the multipliers Y_j^m for the net national product at market prices are considered in order to take into account indirect taxes and subsidies, then the leading sectors are trade, construction, services, transportation, machinery, ranging between 1.46 and 1.36 for version 1 and between 2.05 and 1.95 for version 2. Agriculture does no longer stay in the leading group. The greatest indirect tax $(T_{ind}-Z)$ multipliers are observed in the sectors trade and food with values of .2 and .18. The higher the direct and indirect tax multipliers the lower are the final costs per unit of additional government expenditures.

In contrast to the national income multipliers the ranking of the NNP multipliers is not invariant to endogenizing final demand.

4. Critical Summary

The concept of key sectors can be formulated for different targets, e.g.,

gross production, national income and employment which are considered here. Which sectors play a central rôle for economic development depends on the target and on the underlying model.
In the familiar static open IO model with purely exogenous final demand, the preceding empirical investigations show that the ranking of output and employment multipliers is very sensitive to changes in prices and technology, as well as to errors in data and to aggregation. A sector inducing comparatively large output effects may show a relatively small impact on employment (e.g., machinery sector) and income (e.g., food sector).
When consumption and investment functions that depend linearly on income are introduced (model versions 1 and 2), their influence on the multipliers is different for a closed economy without government and an open economy with government. In a closed economy without public economic activity (and with depreciation considered in the input coefficients) the rankings of the output and employment multipliers are not affected by partly endogenizing consumption and investment. National income multipliers for version 1 and 2 are independent of the sector, where autonomous final demand is increased.

In an open economy with government (and/or depreciation not considered in the input coefficients) these statements do not hold. The rankings of the indices L_j and B_j are affected, indeed. The greatest changes are observed for the output multipliers L_j, smaller ones for the employment multipliers B_j. However, the ranking of income multipliers Y_j remains unchanged. This fact makes these multipliers especially useful for economic decisions, e.g., on the distributions of government spending programmes.
A trade-off between income and employment policy is not expected to prevail for the given data, since the ranking of employment multipliers is positively correlated with that of Y_j. For the multipliers B_j and Y_j the group of the 5 topranked sectors coincides in model version 2, this nearly also holds for Y_j^m with the exception of agriculture. These 5 sectors are found at the bottom of the L_j-ranking in the standard IO model usually considered for identifying key sectors in the literature. The KSI values L_j and their ranking are not very useful for decision making on government spending programmes unless capacity constraints, scarce resources or import possibilities have to be considered. Furthermore, they cannot be regarded as a guiding rule for development policy in developing countries, since dynamic aspects are missing. This also holds for other proposals for identifying key sectors which are derived from a static model.
A dynamic IO model usually is obtained by introducing investment functions according to the acceleration principle. However, actual development can-

not by explained by this model, since negative output is expected to occur. The dynamic model should be considered as a model of steady state growth (cf. Meyer/Schumann 1977). In this context the question arises how investment spending in different sectors influences the equilibria of growth.

References

Bharadwaj, K.R. (1966): A Note on Structural Interdependence and the Concept of Key Sector. Kyklos 19, p. 315-319.

Eichhorn, W. and J. Voeller (1976): Theory of the Price Index. Fisher's Test Approach and Generalizations. Lecture Notes in Economics and Mathematical Systems, Berlin-Heidelberg-New York.

Hazari, B.R. (1970): Empirical Identification of Key Sectors in the Indian Economy. The Review of Economics and Statistics 52, p.301-305

Hirschman, A.O. (1958):The Strategy of Economic Development. New Haven.

Katzenbeisser, W. (1979): Ein Vergleich von Methoden zur Bestimmung von Schlüsselsektoren. Jahrbücher für Nationalökonomie und Statistik 194, p. 279-297.

Kogelschatz, H. (1977): Strukturänderungen und Wachstumsgleichgewichte. Input-Output-Theoretische Untersuchungen. Mathematical Systems in Economics 38, Meisenheim.

Kogelschatz, H. and B. Goldstein (1978): On the Sensitivity of Key Sector Indices. In: Theory and Applications of Economic Indices. (Ed. by W. Eichhorn et al.), Würzburg, p. 389-400.

Kogelschatz, H. (1985): Income, Production and Employment Multipliers in Disaggregated Economies. Diskussionsbeiträge des Instituts für Statistik und Mathematische Wirtschaftstheorie, Univ. Karlsruhe.

Meyer, U. and J. Schumann (1977): Das dynamische Input-Output-Modell als Modell gleichgewichtigen Wachstums. Zeitschrift für die gesamte Staatswissenschaft 133, p. 1-37.

Pischner, R. and R. Stäglin (1975): Input-Output-Rechnung für die Bundesrepublik Deutschland 1972. DIW-Beiträge zur Strukturforschung, Heft 38, Berlin.

Rasmussen, P.N. (1956): Studies in Inter-Sectoral Relations. Kopenhagen-Amsterdam.

Schnabl, H. and H.W. Holub (1979): Qualitative und quantitative Aspekte der Input-Output-Analyse. Zeitschrift für die gesamte Staatswissenschaft 135, p. 657-678.

Schumann, J. (1975): Möglichkeiten und Bedeutung einer teilweise endogenen Erklärung des privaten Konsums und der privaten Investition im statischen offenen Input-Output-Modell. Jahrbücher für Nationalökonomie und Statistik 189, p. 378-409.

Stäglin, R. and R. Pischner (1976): Weiterentwicklung der Input-Output Rechnung als Instrument der Arbeitsmarktanalyse. Beiträge zur Arbeitsmarkt- und Berufsforschung der Bundesanstalt für Arbeit. Heft 13, Nürnberg.

Yotopoulos, P.A. and J.B. Nugent (1973): A Balanced-Growth Version of the Linkage-Hypothesis. A Test. The Quarterly Journal of Economics 87, p. 157-171.

Appendix

Table 1a

Classification of sectors[1] (ordered according to KSI values)

1 Food
2 Machinery-, steel-, vehicle construction
3 Chemicals
4 Iron, steel, NFM
5 Energy, mining
6 Electrical goods
7 Timber, paper, textiles
8 Agriculture
9 Construction
10 Other services
11 Transportation, communication
12 Trade, commerce

Table 1b

Key sector indices

Rank	Sector[2]	L_j	U_j
1	Nahrung	2.0407	1.1528
2	St,Ma,Fz	1.9164	1.0826
3	Chem, Ste	1.8799	1.0620
4	Eisen,Ne	1.8781	1.0609
5	Energ,BB	1.8460	1.0428
6	Elt, Ebm	1.8199	1.0281
7	Holz,Tex	1.7417	0.9839
8	Landw	1.6935	0.9567
9	Bau	1.6832	0.9508
10	Dienstl	1.6431	0.9282
11	Verkehr	1.6395	0.9262
12	Handel	1.4604	0.8250

1) see Pischner/Stäglin (1976), where the IO table is taken from.
2) Abbreviations in the computer prints.

Table 2: Changes in prices

FOOD			price increase of 10%			price increase of 30%		
Rank	Sector	L_j	L'_j	ΔL_j	Rank New	L'_j	ΔL_j	Rank New
1	Nahrung	2.0407	1.9760	-0.0647	1	1.8764	-0.1643	4•
2	St,Ma,Fz	1.9164	1.9182	0.0018	2	1.9220	0.0056	1•
3	Chem,Ste	1.8799	1.8831	0.0032	3	1.8895	0.0096	2•
4	Eisen,Ne	1.8781	1.8796	0.0015	4	1.8827	0.0046	3•
5	Energ,BB	1.8460	1.8473	0.0013	5	1.8498	0.0038	5
6	Elt,Ebm	1.8199	1.8217	0.0018	6	1.8254	0.0055	6
7	Holz,Tex	1.7417	1.7437	0.0020	7	1.7479	0.0062	7
8	Landw	1.6935	1.7083	0.0148	8	1.7378	0.0443	8
9	Bau	1.6832	1.6842	0.0010	9	1.6864	0.0032	9
10	Dienstl	1.6431	1.6539	0.0108	10	1.6754	0.0323	10
11	Verkehr	1.6395	1.6407	0.0012	11	1.6433	0.0038	11
12	Handel	1.4604	1.4618	0.0014	12	1.4648	0.0044	12
MACHINERY			price increase of 10%			price increase of 30%		
Rank	Sector	L_j	L'_j	ΔL_j	Rank New	L'_j	ΔL_j	Rank New
1	Nahrung	2.0407	2.0434	0.0027	1	2.0487	0.0080	1
2	St,Ma,Fz	1.9164	1.8534	-0.0630	4•	1.7564	-0.1600	6•
3	Chem,Ste	1.8799	1.8824	0.0025	3	1.8874	0.0075	3
4	Eisen,Ne	1.8781	1.8841	0.0060	2•	1.8960	0.0179	2•
5	Energ,BB	1.8460	1.8519	0.0059	5	1.8635	0.0175	4•
6	Elt,Ebm	1.8199	1.8234	0.0035	6	1.8306	0.0107	5•
7	Holz,Tex	1.7417	1.7434	0.0017	7	1.7468	0.0051	7
8	Landw	1.6935	1.7000	0.0065	8	1.7130	0.0195	8
9	Bau	1.6832	1.6883	0.0051	9	1.6986	0.0154	9
10	Dienstl	1.6431	1.6457	0.0026	10	1.6510	0.0079	11•
11	Verkehr	1.6395	1.6449	0.0054	11	1.6558	0.0163	10•
12	Handel	1.4604	1.4627	0.0023	12	1.4673	0.0069	12
ENERGY			price increase of 10%			price increase of 30%		
Rank	Sector	L_j	L'_j	ΔL_j	Rank New	L'_j	ΔL_j	Rank New
1	Nahrung	2.0407	2.0441	0.0034	1	2.0510	0.0103	1
2	St,Ma,Fz	1.9164	1.9208	0.0044	2	1.9296	0.0132	2
3	Chem,Ste	1.8799	1.8869	0.0070	4•	1.9010	0.0211	4•
4	Eisen,Ne	1.8781	1.8709	0.0128	3•	1.9167	0.0386	3•
5	Energ,BB	1.8460	1.8016	-0.0444	6•	1.7333	-0.1127	7•
6	Elt,Ebm	1.8199	1.8241	0.0042	5•	1.8325	0.0126	5•
7	Holz,Tex	1.7417	1.7449	0.0032	7	1.7513	0.0096	6•
8	Landw	1.6935	1.6988	0.0053	8	1.7094	0.0159	8
9	Bau	1.6832	1.6857	0.0025	9	1.6908	0.0076	9
10	Dienstl	1.6431	1.6464	0.0033	10	1.6531	0.0100	10
11	Verkehr	1.6395	1.6433	0.0038	11	1.6508	0.0113	11
12	Handel	1.4604	1.4619	0.0015	12	1.4649	0.0045	12

Table 3: Process substitution

FOOD			efficiency increase of 10%			efficiency increase of 30%		
Rank	Sector	L_j	L'_j	ΔL_j	Rank New	L'_j	ΔL_j	Rank New
1	Nahrung	2.0407	1.9068	-0.1339	2·	1.6630	-0.3777	8·
2	St,Ma,Fz	1.9164	1.9145	-0.0019	1·	1.9111	-0.0053	1·
3	Chem,Ste	1.8799	1.8767	-0.0032	3	1.8708	-0.0091	3
4	Eisen,Ne	1.8781	1.8765	-0.0016	4	1.8737	-0.0044	2·
5	Energ,BB	1.8460	1.8447	-0.0013	5	1.8424	-0.0036	4·
6	Elt,Ebm	1.8199	1.8180	-0.0019	6	1.8146	-0.0053	5·
7	Holz,Tex	1.7417	1.7396	-0.0021	7	1.7358	-0.0059	6·
8	Landw	1.6935	1.6786	-0.0149	9·	1.6515	-0.0420	9·
9	Bau	1.6832	1.6821	-0.0011	8·	1.6800	-0.0032	7·
10	Dienstl	1.6431	1.6323	-0.0108	11·	1.6126	-0.0305	11·
11	Verkehr	1.6395	1.6382	-0.0013	10·	1.6359	-0.0036	10·
12	Handel	1.4604	1.4589	-0.0015	12	1.4562	-0.0042	12

RC(10%)=0.979
RC(30%)=0.7762

MACHINERY			efficiency increase of 10%			efficiency increase of 30%		
Rank	Sector	L_j	L'_j	ΔL_j	Rank New	L'_j	ΔL_j	Rank New
1	Nahrung	2.0407	2.0383	-0.0024	1	2.0337	-0.0070	1
2	St,Ma,Fz	1.9164	1.8067	-0.1097	6·	1.6012	-0.3152	11·
3	Chem,Ste	1.8799	1.8777	-0.0022	2·	1.8735	-0.0064	2·
4	Eisen,Ne	1.8781	1.8727	-0.0054	3·	1.8626	-0.0155	3·
5	Energ,BB	1.8460	1.8408	-0.0052	4·	1.8310	-0.0150	4·
6	Elt,Ebm	1.8199	1.8166	-0.0033	5·	1.8106	-0.0093	5·
7	Holz,Tex	1.7417	1.7401	-0.0016	7	1.7373	-0.0044	6·
8	Landw	1.6935	1.6876	-0.0059	8	1.6767	-0.0168	7·
9	Bau	1.6832	1.6786	-0.0046	9	1.6699	-0.0133	8·
10	Dienstl	1.6431	1.6408	-0.0023	10	1.6364	-0.0067	9·
11	Verkehr	1.6395	1.6346	-0.0049	11	1.6255	-0.0140	10·
12	Handel	1.4604	1.4583	-0.0021	12	1.4544	-0.0060	12

RC(10%)=0.9301
RC(30%)=0.6853

ENERGY			efficiency increase of 10%			efficiency increase of 30%		
Rank	Sector	L_j	L'_j	ΔL_j	Rank New	L'_j	ΔL_j	Rank New
1	Nahrung	2.0407	2.0379	-0.0028	1	2.0328	-0.0079	1
2	St,Ma,Fz	1.9164	1.9128	-0.0036	2	1.9063	-0.0101	2
3	Chem,Ste	1.8799	1.8742	-0.0057	3	1.8638	-0.0161	3
4	Eisen,Ne	1.8781	1.8676	-0.0105	4	1.8486	-0.0295	4
5	Energ,BB	1.8460	1.7351	-0.1109	7·	1.5349	-0.3111	11·
6	Elt,Ebm	1.8199	1.8164	-0.0035	5·	1.8102	-0.0097	5·
7	Holz,Tex	1.7417	1.7391	-0.0026	6·	1.7343	-0.0074	6·
8	Landw	1.6935	1.6892	-0.0043	8	1.6813	-0.0122	7·
9	Bau	1.6832	1.6811	-0.0021	9	1.6773	-0.0059	8·
10	Dienstl	1.6431	1.6404	-0.0027	10	1.6355	-0.0076	9·
11	Verkehr	1.6395	1.6364	-0.0031	11	1.6308	-0.0087	10·
12	Handel	1.4604	1.4591	-0.0013	12	1.4569	-0.0035	12

RC(10%)=0.9790
RC(30%)=0.8531

Table 4: Changes in productivity

FOOD			productivity increase of 10%			productivity increase of 30%		
Rank	Sector	L_j	L'_j	ΔL_j	Rank New	L'_j	ΔL_j	Rank New
1	Nahrung	2.0407	1.9757	-0.0650	1	1.8574	-0.1833	4•
2	St,Ma,Fz	1.9164	1.9127	-0.0037	2	1.9061	-0.0103	1•
3	Chem,Ste	1.8799	1.8736	-0.0063	4•	1.8621	-0.0178	3
4	Eisen,Ne	1.8781	1.8750	-0.0031	3•	1.8659	-0.0086	2•
5	Energ,BB	1.8460	1.8435	-0.0025	5	1.8390	-0.0070	5
6	Elt,Ebm	1.8199	1.8162	-0.0037	6	1.8095	-0.0104	6
7	Holz,Tex	1.7417	1.7376	-0.0041	7	1.7301	-0.0116	7
8	Landw	1.6935	1.6643	-0.0292	9•	1.6111	-0.0824	10•
9	Bau	1.6832	1.6810	-0.0022	8•	1.6771	-0.0061	8•
10	Dienstl	1.6431	1.6219	-0.0212	11•	1.5832	-0.0599	11•
11	Verkehr	1.6395	1.6370	-0.0025	10•	1.6324	-0.0071	9•
12	Handel	1.4604	1.4574	-0.0030	12	1.4521	-0.0083	12

RC(10%)=0.9790
RC(30%)=0.9161

MACHINERY			productivity increase of 10%			productivity increase of 30%		
Rank	Sector	L_j	L'_j	ΔL_j	Rank New	L'_j	ΔL_j	Rank New
1	Nahrung	2.0407	2.0356	-0.0051	1	2.0262	-0.0145	1
2	St,Ma,Fz	1.9164	1.8746	-0.0418	3•	1.7961	-0.1203	6
3	Chem,Ste	1.8799	1.8752	-0.0047	2•	1.8664	-0.0135	2
4	Eisen,Ne	1.8781	1.8668	-0.0113	4	1.8456	-0.0323	3
5	Energ,BB	1.8460	1.8351	-0.0109	5	1.8145	-0.0315	4
6	Elt,Ebm	1.8199	1.8131	-0.0068	6	1.8005	-0.0194	5
7	Holz,Tex	1.7417	1.7385	-0.0032	7	1.7325	-0.0092	7
8	Landw	1.6935	1.6813	-0.0122	8	1.6584	-0.0351	8
9	Bau	1.6832	1.6735	-0.0097	9	1.6555	-0.0277	9
10	Dienstl	1.6431	1.6382	-0.0049	10	1.6290	-0.0141	10
11	Verkehr	1.6395	1.6293	-0.0102	11	1.6102	-0.0293	11
12	Handel	1.4604	1.4560	-0.0044	12	1.4479	-0.0125	12

RC(10%)=0.9930
RC(30%)=0.9301

ENERGY			productivity increase of 10%			productivity increase of 30%		
Rank	Sector	L_j	L'_j	ΔL_j	Rank New	L'_j	ΔL_j	Rank New
1	Nahrung	2.0407	2.0345	-0.0062	1	2.0235	-0.0172	1
2	St,Ma,Fz	1.9164	1.9085	-0.0079	2	1.8944	-0.0220	2
3	Chem,Ste	1.8799	1.8674	-0.0125	3	1.8447	-0.0352	3
4	Eisen,Ne	1.8781	1.8551	-0.0230	4	1.8137	-0.0644	4
5	Energ,BB	1.8460	1.7823	-0.0637	6•	1.6673	-0.1787	8•
6	Elt,Ebm	1.8199	1.8124	-0.0075	5•	1.7989	-0.0210	5•
7	Holz,Tex	1.7417	1.7360	-0.0057	7	1.7257	-0.0160	6•
8	Landw	1.6935	1.6840	-0.0095	8	1.6670	-0.0265	9•
9	Bau	1.6832	1.6786	-0.0046	9	1.6704	-0.0128	7•
10	Dienstl	1.6431	1.6372	-0.0059	10	1.6265	-0.0166	10
11	Verkehr	1.6395	1.6327	-0.0068	11	1.6206	-0.0189	11
12	Handel	1.4604	1.4577	-0.0027	12	1.4528	-0.0076	12

RC(10%)=0.9930
RC(30%)=0.9441

Table 5: Errors in input coefficients: Errors of -50% in the input coefficients in the food sector

Error in:		a_{11}		a_{21}		a_{31}		a_{41}		a_{51}		a_{61}	
Rank	Sector	ΔL_j	Rank New	ΔL_j	Rank New	ΔL_j	Rank New	ΔL_j	Rank New	ΔL_j	Rank New	ΔL_j	Rank New
1	Nahrung	-0.2615	6	-0.0002	1	-0.0010	1	-0.0001	1	-0.0001	1	-0.0002	1
2	St,Ma,Fz	-0.0037	1	-0.0058	2	-0.0014	2	-0.0006	2	-0.0001	2	-0.0006	2
3	Chem,Ste	-0.0063	3	-0.0001	3	-0.0158	4	-0.0001	3	-0.0001	3	-0.0002	3
4	Eisen,Ne	-0.0030	2	-0.0003	4	-0.0010	3	-0.0045	4	-0.0003	4	-0.0003	4
5	Energ,BB	-0.0025	4	-0.0003	5	-0.0011	5	-0.0002	5	-0.0026	5	-0.0003	5
6	Elt,Ebm	-0.0037	5	-0.0002	6	-0.0014	6	-0.0006	6	-0.0001	6	-0.0062	6
7	Holz,Tex	-0.0041	7	-0.0001	7	-0.0016	7	-0.0001	7	-0.0001	7	-0.0002	7
8	Landw	-0.0291	9	-0.0003	8	-0.0014	8	-0.0001	8	-0.0001	8	-0.0001	8
9	Bau	-0.0022	8	-0.0003	9	-0.0028	9	-0.0003	9	-0.0001	9	-0.0003	9
10	Dienstl	-0.0211	11	-0.0001	10	-0.0006	10	-0.0000	10	-0.0000	10	-0.0001	10
11	Verkehr	-0.0025	10	-0.0003	11	-0.0012	11	-0.0001	11	-0.0001	11	-0.0002	11
12	Handel	-0.0029	12	-0.0002	12	-0.0005	12	-0.0001	12	-0.0001	12	-0.0001	12

RC = .8741 RC = .9930

error in:		a_{71}		a_{81}		a_{91}		$a_{10,1}$		$a_{11,1}$		$a_{12,1}$	
Rank	Sector		Rank New		Rank New		Rank New		Rank New		Rank New		Rank New
1	Nahrung	-0.0003	1	-0.0276	1	-0.0000	1	-0.0058	1	-0.0001	1	-0.0003	1
2	St,Ma,Fz	-0.0003	2	-0.0007	2	-0.0000	2	-0.0051	2	-0.0001	2	-0.0003	2
3	Chem,Ste	-0.0004	3	-0.0013	3	-0.0000	3	-0.0068	4	-0.0001	3	-0.0003	3
4	Eisen,Ne	-0.0002	4	-0.0006	4	-0.0000	4	-0.0049	3	-0.0002	4	-0.0003	4
5	Energ,BB	-0.0002	5	-0.0006	5	-0.0000	5	-0.0043	5	-0.0001	5	-0.0001	5
6	Elt,Ebm	-0.0004	6	-0.0007	6	-0.0000	6	-0.0052	6	-0.0001	6	-0.0003	6
7	Holz,Tex	-0.0070	7	-0.0026	7	-0.0000	7	-0.0046	7	-0.0001	7	-0.0003	7
8	Landw	-0.0002	8	-0.1076	11	-0.0000	8	-0.0060	8	-0.0001	8	-0.0002	8
9	Bau	-0.0004	9	-0.0005	8	-0.0012	9	-0.0029	9	-0.0001	9	-0.0003	9
10	Dienstl	-0.0003	10	-0.0035	9	-0.0000	10	-0.0799	11	-0.0000	10	-0.0001	10
11	Verkehr	-0.0003	11	-0.0005	10	-0.0000	11	-0.0052	10	-0.0022	11	-0.0002	11
12	Handel	-0.0002	12	-0.0006	12	-0.0001	12	-0.0052	12	-0.0003	12	-0.0049	12

RC = .9580 RC = .09860

Table 6: Aggregation of 2 sectors: food sector and one other sector

			Sector 1 and 2		Sector 1 and 8		Sector 1 and 9	
Rank	Sector	L_j	ΔL_j	Rank New	ΔL_j	Rank New	ΔL_j	Rank New
1	Nahrung	2.0407	-0.0768	1•	-0.0572	1•	-0.1979	5•
2	St,Ma,Fz	1.9164	0.0475	1•	-0.0001	3•	-0.0015	1•
3	Chem,Ste	1.8799	-0.0009	4•	0.0003	4•	-0.0034	3
4	Eisen,Ne	1.8781	0.0014	3•	-0.0000	5•	-0.0010	2•
5	Energ,BB	1.8460	0.0016	5	0.0006	6•	0.0004	4•
6	Elt,Ebm	1.8199	0.0003	6	0.0000	7•	-0.0018	7•
7	Holz,Tex	1.7417	-0.0006	7	0.0052	8•	-0.0022	8•
8	Landw	1.6935	-0.0061	8	0.2900	1•	-0.0199	9•
9	Bau	1.6832	0.0014	9	0.0002	9	0.1596	5•
10	Dienstl	1.6431	-0.0052	11•	-0.0008	10	-0.0088	11•
11	Verkehr	1.6395	0.0014	10•	0.0001	11	0.0005	10•
12	Handel	1.4604	0.0000	12	0.0001	12	-0.0004	12
			RC=0.9825		RC=0.8077		RC=0.8497	

			Sector 1 and 5		Sector 1 and 11		Sector 1 and 12	
Rank	Sector	L_j	ΔL_j	Rank New	ΔL_j	Rank New	ΔL_j	Rank New
1	Nahrung	2.0407	-0.0606	1•	-0.1615	4•	-0.3361	7•
2	St,Ma,Fz	1.9164	0.0035	3•	0.0069	1•	0.0078	1•
3	Chem,Ste	1.8799	0.0054	5•	0.0123	2•	0.0060	3
4	Eisen,Ne	1.8781	0.0120	4	0.0118	3•	0.0084	2•
5	Energ,BB	1.8460	0.1341	1•	0.0089	6•	0.0041	4•
6	Elt,Ebm	1.8199	0.0032	6	0.0076	7•	0.0079	5•
7	Holz,Tex	1.7417	0.0021	7	0.0075	8•	0.0072	6•
8	Landw	1.6935	-0.0019	8	-0.0111	10•	-0.0287	10•
9	Bau	1.6832	0.0020	9	0.0090	9	0.0078	9
10	Dienstl	1.6431	-0.0019	11•	-0.0065	11•	-0.0218	12•
11	Verkehr	1.6395	0.0031	10•	0.2397	4•	0.0036	11
12	Handel	1.4604	0.0007	12	0.0201	12	0.2442	7•
			RC=0.9196		RC=0.7587		RC=0.7308	

Table 7: Employment Multipliers $B_j \cdot 10^6$, Increases in Labour Productivity [1)]

Agriculture

	0% - B =	10% increase: 10% - B=	dB=	30% increase: 30% - B =	dB=
Sektor 1	31.1094 (2)	29.9894 (3)	-1.1200	28.2664 (3)	-2.8430
Sektor 2	25.9625 (8)	25.9360 (3)	-.0265	25.8952 (8)	-.0673
Sektor 3	20.5050 (11)	20.4541 (11)	-.0509	20.3757 (11)	-.1293
Sektor 4	21.1921 (10)	21.1698 (10)	-.0223	21.1355 (10)	-.0566
Sektor 5	18.2689 (12)	18.2428 (12)	-.0261	18.2027 (12)	-.0662
Sektor 6	26.7631 (7)	26.7353 (7)	-.0278	26.6926 (7)	-.0705
Sektor 7	27.3088 (5)	27.2031 (5)	-.1056	27.0406 (5)	-.2682
Sektor 8	56.2290 (1)	51.8636 (1)	-4.3654	45.1476 (1)	-11.0814
Sektor 9	26.8083 (6)	26.7889 (6)	-.0194	26.7591 (6)	-.0491
Sektor 10	25.2696 (9)	25.1248 (9)	-.1448	24.9021 (9)	-.3675
Sektor 11	27.9210 (4)	27.9008 (4)	-.0202	27.8697 (4)	-.0513
Sektor 12	30.4156 (3)	30.3916 (2)	-.0240	30.3547 (2)	-.0609

$\overline{B}$ = 28.1461, CV = .3283 $\overline{B}$ = 27.6500, CV = .2939 $\overline{B}$ = 26.8868, CV = .2411

RC(VO,V1) = .993; RC(V1,V2) = 1.000; RC(VO,V2) = .993

Food

	0% - B =	10% increase: 10% - B=	dB=	30% increase: 30% - B =	dB=
Sektor 1	31.1094 (2)	29.9992 (3)	-1.1101	28.2914 (3)	-2.8180
Sektor 2	25.9625 (8)	25.9470 (8)	-.0155	25.9231 (8)	-.0394
Sektor 3	20.5050 (11)	20.4783 (11)	-.0266	20.4373 (11)	-.0676
Sektor 4	21.1921 (10)	21.1793 (10)	-.0128	21.1596 (10)	-.0324
Sektor 5	18.2689 (12)	18.2584 (12)	-.0105	18.2422 (12)	-.0267
Sektor 6	26.7631 (7)	26.7476 (7)	-.0155	26.7236 (7)	-.0394
Sektor 7	27.3088 (5)	27.2914 (5)	-.0174	27.2647 (5)	-.0441
Sektor 8	56.2290 (1)	56.1054 (1)	-.1236	55.9153 (1)	-.3136
Sektor 9	26.8083 (6)	26.7992 (6)	-.0091	26.7852 (6)	-.0231
Sektor 10	25.2696 (9)	25.1798 (9)	-.0898	25.0417 (9)	-.2280
Sektor 11	27.9210 (4)	27.9104 (4)	-.0106	27.8941 (4)	-.0269
Sektor 12	30.4156 (3)	30.4034 (2)	-.0123	30.3845 (2)	-.0312

$\overline{B}$ = 28.1461, CV = .3283 $\overline{B}$ = 28.0249, CV = .3279 $\overline{B}$ = 27.8386, CV = .3280

RC(VO,V1) = .993: RC(V1.V2) = 1.000; RC(VO,V2) = .993

Trade

	0% - B =	10% increase: 10% - B=	dB=	30% increase: 30% - B =	dB=
Sektor 1	31.1094 (2)	30.9803 (2)	-.1291	30.7816 (2)	-.3277
Sektor 2	25.9625 (8)	25.8457 (3)	-.1168	25.6660 (7)	-.2965
Sektor 3	20.5050 (11)	20.3724 (11)	-.1326	20.1685 (11)	-.3365
Sektor 4	21.1921 (10)	21.0777 (10)	-.1144	20.9018 (10)	-.2903
Sektor 5	18.2689 (12)	18.2012 (12)	-.0677	18.0970 (12)	-.1719
Sektor 6	26.7631 (7)	26.6448 (7)	-.1183	26.4629 (6)	-.3002
Sektor 7	27.3088 (5)	27.1922 (5)	-.1166	27.0128 (4)	-.2960
Sektor 8	56.2290 (1)	56.1344 (1)	-.0945	55.9890 (1)	-.2399
Sektor 9	26.8083 (6)	26.7099 (6)	-.0984	26.5585 (5)	-.2498
Sektor 10	25.2696 (9)	25.2099 (9)	-.0597	25.1180 (8)	-.1516
Sektor 11	27.9210 (4)	27.8572 (4)	-.0638	27.7590 (3)	-.1620
Sektor 12	30.4156 (3)	28.1367 (3)	-2.2789	24.6306 (9)	-5.7850

$\overline{B}$ = 28.1461, CV = .3283 $\overline{B}$ = 27.8635, CV = .3307 $\overline{B}$ = 27.4288, CV = .3374

RC(VO.V1) = 1.000; RC(V1,V2) = .8531; RC(VO,V2) = .8531

1) Labour coefficients $1/\lambda_i$ were taken from Stäglin/Pischner (1976).

Table 8: Multipliers L_j, B_j, Y_j in 3 Model Versions

Table 8a: Gross production multipliers L_j (Key sector indices)

V0:	L(1) =	2.0405 (1)	V1:	L(1) =	3.0603 (4)	V2:	L(1) =	4.0720 (11)
V0:	L(2) =	1.9163 (2)	V1:	L(2) =	3.2406 (1)	V2:	L(2) =	4.5545 (1)
V0:	L(3) =	1.8798 (3)	V1:	L(3) =	2.8850 (11)	V2:	L(3) =	3.8824 (12)
V0:	L(4) =	1.8780 (4)	V1:	L(4) =	3.0286 (7)	V2:	L(4) =	4.1701 (7)
V0:	L(5) =	1.8460 (5)	V1:	L(5) =	3.0052 (8)	V2:	L(5) =	4.1552 (8)
V0:	L(6) =	1.8199 (6)	V1:	L(6) =	3.0828 (2)	V2:	L(6) =	4.3357 (6)
V0:	L(7) =	1.7417 (7)	V1:	L(7) =	2.9457 (10)	V2:	L(7) =	4.1403 (9)
V0:	L(8) =	1.6935 (8)	V1:	L(8) =	3.0409 (6)	V2:	L(8) =	4.3777 (4)
V0:	L(9) =	1.6831 (9)	V1:	L(9) =	3.0634 (3)	V2:	L(9) =	4.4328 (3)
V0:	L(10) =	1.6432 (10)	V1:	L(10) =	2.9993 (9)	V2:	L(10) =	4.3448 (5)
V0:	L(11) =	1.6394 (11)	V1:	L(11) =	3.0561 (5)	V2:	L(11) =	4.4617 (2)
V0:	L(12) =	1.4604 (12)	V1:	L(12) =	2.7973 (12)	V2:	L(12) =	4.1238 (10)

$\bar{L}$ = 1.7702, CV = .0847 $\bar{L}$ = 3.0171, CV = .0347 $\bar{L}$ = 4.2543, CV = .0436

RC(VO,V1) = .3217; RC(V1,V2) = .6503; RC(VO,V2) = -.2797

Table 8b: Employment multipliers $B_j \cdot 10^6$

V0:	B(1) =	31.1094 (2)	V1:	B(1) =	47.2024 (5)	V2:	B(1) =	62.3577 (9)
V0:	B(2) =	25.9625 (8)	V1:	B(2) =	46.8613 (6)	V2:	B(2) =	67.1917 (6)
V0:	B(3) =	20.5050 (11)	V1:	B(3) =	36.3687 (12)	V2:	B(3) =	51.8010 (12)
V0:	B(4) =	21.1921 (10)	V1:	B(4) =	39.3495 (10)	V2:	B(4) =	57.0131 (10)
V0:	B(5) =	18.2689 (12)	V1:	B(5) =	36.5618 (11)	V2:	B(5) =	54.3572 (11)
V0:	B(6) =	26.7631 (7)	V1:	B(6) =	46.6925 (7)	V2:	B(6) =	66.0799 (7)
V0:	B(7) =	27.3088 (5)	V1:	B(7) =	46.3093 (9)	V2:	B(7) =	64.7931 (8)
V0:	B(8) =	56.2290 (1)	V1:	B(8) =	77.4926 (1)	V2:	B(8) =	98.1780 (1)
V0:	B(9) =	26.8083 (6)	V1:	B(9) =	48.5905 (4)	V2:	B(9) =	69.7805 (4)
V0:	B(10) =	25.2696 (9)	V1:	B(10) =	46.6705 (8)	V2:	B(10) =	67.4395 (5)
V0:	B(11) =	27.9210 (4)	V1:	B(11) =	50.2784 (3)	V2:	B(11) =	72.0278 (3)
V0:	B(12) =	30.4156 (3)	V1:	B(12) =	51.5139 (2)	V2:	B(12) =	72.0384 (2)

$\bar{B}$ = 28.1461, CV = .3283 $\bar{B}$ = 47.8243, CV = .2123 $\bar{B}$ = 66.9673, CV = .1694

RC(VO,V1) = .8671; RC(V1,V2) = .9091; RC(VO,V2) = .6993

Table 8c: National income multipliers Y_j

V0:	Y(1) =	.5287 (11)	V1:	Y(1) =	.9017 (11)	V2:	Y(1) =	1.2862 (11)
V0:	Y(2) =	.6866 (6)	V1:	Y(2) =	1.1710 (6)	V2:	Y(2) =	1.6702 (6)
V0:	Y(3) =	.5212 (12)	V1:	Y(3) =	.8888 (12)	V2:	Y(3) =	1.2678 (12)
V0:	Y(4) =	.5966 (10)	V1:	Y(4) =	1.0174 (10)	V2:	Y(4) =	1.4511 (10)
V0:	Y(5) =	.6010 (9)	V1:	Y(5) =	1.0250 (9)	V2:	Y(5) =	1.4620 (9)
V0:	Y(6) =	.6548 (7)	V1:	Y(6) =	1.1166 (7)	V2:	Y(6) =	1.5928 (7)
V0:	Y(7) =	.6243 (8)	V1:	Y(7) =	1.0646 (8)	V2:	Y(7) =	1.5185 (8)
V0:	Y(8) =	.6986 (4)	V1:	Y(8) =	1.1914 (4)	V2:	Y(8) =	1.6994 (4)
V0:	Y(9) =	.7157 (2)	V1:	Y(9) =	1.2205 (2)	V2:	Y(9) =	1.7409 (2)
V0:	Y(10) =	.7031 (3)	V1:	Y(10) =	1.1991 (3)	V2:	Y(10) =	1.7104 (3)
V0:	Y(11) =	.7346 (1)	V1:	Y(11) =	1.2527 (1)	V2:	Y(11) =	1.7868 (1)
V0:	Y(12) =	.6932 (5)	V1:	Y(12) =	1.1821 (5)	V2:	Y(12) =	1.6862 (5)

$\bar{Y}$ = .6465, CV = .1065 $\bar{Y}$ = 1.1026, CV = .1065 $\bar{Y}$ = 1.5727, CV = .1065

RC(VO,V1) = 1.0000; RC(V1,V2) = 1.0000; RC(VO,V2) = 1.0000

CV = Coefficient of variation, RC = Rank correlation coefficient

Testing Integrability Conditions in a Dynamic Framework

Shinichiro Nakamura
School of Politics and Economics
Waseda University
Nishiwaseda 1, Tokyo, 160 Japan

1. Introduction

Since the publication of Diewert (1976) we know that if a set of favorable conditions are satisfied a lot of measurement in economics can be done without laborious econometric estimation of parameters of flexible cost, production or profit functions. In the case of trans-log (TL) functions, for example, all we need is simply to compute the Toernqvist index. This exact index number approach has been intensively used in the measurement of changes in TFP levels over time and/or space (Christensen, Cummings and Jorgenson (1981), Caves, Christensen and Diewert (1982)).

An essential point in using this approach is whether the required conditions are indeed satisfied by the data. The most crucial of them is that the realized data do coincide with the theoretical optimal values (up to nonsystematic random errors). A natural question to be raised is whether this holds empirically. Empirical studies do not seem to provide a strong support to this. In fact econometric studies of demand models are full of negative test results reporting inconsistency with the data of integrability conditions (Barten (1969,75), Courakis (1975), Christensen, Jorgenson and Lau (19755), Griffin(1977), Halvorsen (1977), Pindyck (1979), Deaton and Muellbauer (1980)).

Still it may be too early to conclude that the demand theory has no empirical validity. In all these studies static demand models are directly applied to data. Implicit in this is the assumption of instantaneous adjustment of the pattern of demand to a change in exogenous variables . Since this is a fairly strong assumption, one might doubt the validity of test results which use it as a maintained hypothesis. In fact, Berndt, McCurdy and Rose (1980), Anderson and Blundell (1982,83,84), Veall and Zimmermann (1984), and Nakamura

Measurement in Economics
ed. by W. Eichhorn

(1985) found that integrability conditions turned out to be consistent with the data when tested in a dynamic framework without assuming the instantaneous adjustment, while they were rejected when imposed on the static model. In these studies the usual static assumption (of instantaneous adjustment) is replaced by a more general one that not the realized data itself but the stationary solution of the data generation process (DGP) coincides with the integrable static demand model. Results of these studies support the hypothesis that rejection of integrability conditions is due to the misspecification of the DGP.

In this paper I test integrability conditions for a system of demand functions derived from a multiproduct macro production model within a flexible dynamic framework. I consider a macro production model with three types of final outputs (consumption goods, investment goods, export of intermediate goods) and three types of primary inputs (labor services, capital services, import of intermediate gods). Explicit treatment in the macro production process of export and import of intermediate goods can be mentioned as a unique feature of the present model (see the US model of Burgess (1974,76), the Canadian model of Denny and Pinto (1978), and the German model of Conrad and Jorgenson (1977)).

The model consists of a TL multiple output cost function and an ARX (1,1) model as a representation of the DGP. Applying the model to West German quarterly data 1970 - 1980, I test hypotheses on the DGP, integrability conditions, and the structure of technology such as homogeneity and separability between inputs and outputs. Testing of integrability conditions at a macro level will be of interest in its own right since most current macro econometric models (including large scale ones) are more or less based on optimization behaviors at a macro model (see Ando (1981), Eckstein (1981)). Section 2 presents and discusses theoretical aspects of the model. Empirical results are reported and their implications discussed in Section 3. Section 4 gives concluding remarks.

2.The Model

We consider an economy producing three final outputs,(1) consumption goods,(2) investment goods, and (3)export of intermediate goods, using three primary inputs, (1)capital services, (2) labor services, and (3)import of intermediate goods. We denote the vector of positive finite output quantities by $y:=(y_1,y_2,y_3)'$, and the vector of positive finite input prices by $p:=(p_1,p_2,p_3)'$. We now assume that p is independent of the level of the inputs and outputs, and that the macro cost function is given by a translog (TL) function:

$$\ln C(p,y) = \pi_o + \Pi_p' \ln p + 1/2 \ln p'\Pi_{pp} \ln p + \ln p'\Pi_{py} \ln y$$

$$+ \Pi_y' \ln y + 1/2 \ln y'\Pi_{yy} \ln y \qquad (1)$$

where $\pi_o, \Pi_p, \Pi_{pp}, \Pi_{py}, \Pi_y$, and Π_{yy} are constant matrices of orders 1×1, 3×1, 3×3, 3×3, 3×1 and 3×3, respectively, $\Pi_{pp}=\Pi_{pp}'$, and $\Pi_{yy}=\Pi_{yy}'$. A cost function is homogeneous of degree one and concave in p. This implies for (1):

$$i'\Pi_p = 1, \ 1'\Pi_{pp} = i'\Pi_{py} = (0,0,0), \qquad (2a)$$

$$\theta'(\Pi_{pp} + U)\theta \leqq 0 \qquad (2b)$$

where i is a 3×1 unity vector, θ is an arbitrary 3×1 nonzero vector, and

$$U = \nabla_{\ln p}\ln C(p,y)[\nabla_{\ln p}\ln C(p,y)]' - \text{diag}\{\nabla_{\ln p}\ln C(p,y)\}.$$

Let w(t) be the realized value of expenditure shares for the three inputs at time t and $x(t):=(p(t)',y(t)')$. In the usual static modeling w(t) is assumed to be related to (1) (via Shephard's lemma) through

$$E[w(t) \mid x(t)] = \nabla_{\ln p}\ln C(x(t)) \qquad (3)$$

This implies instantaneous adjustment of w(t) to the optimal value corresponding to x(t) up to nonsystematic random errors in optimization. We replace this strong assumption on the data generation process (DGP) by a weaker one given by:

$$E[w(t) \mid x(s)=x^o, \forall s \leqq t\ ] = \nabla_{\ln p}\ln C(x^o) \qquad (4)$$

In short, we assume that the demand theory holds in the long run only. Note that (3) is a special case of (4).

We now compare (4) with another generalization of (3) made by Lau and Yotopoulos (1971), Toda (1976), and Lovell and Sickles (1982). Using the same notation as above this can be give by

$$E[w(t) \mid x(t)] = \nabla_{\ln p} \ln C(Vx(t)) \tag{5}$$

where V is an appropriately dimensioned diagonal matrix with positive diagonal elements. V represents systematic allocative as well as technical errors in optimization (see Lovell and Sickles (1982) for these errors in optimization). For V = I this reduces to (3). A remarkable difference between (4) and (5) is that the latter is a static one while the former is not. Thus (5) excludes any possibility of convergence over time to the optimal value of the realized data. Furthermore, the assumption of V being fixed is a rather strong one, although this approach is surely useful for analyzing several aspects of errors in optimization.

The adjustment model (4) allows the DGP to take a stationary ARMAX (p,q,s) model of any degrees. While this being the case in principle, the rather small size of the sample we are using in this paper allows the use of a simpler process only. In particular, we choose to represent the DGP by an ARX(1,1) model as follows:

$$w(t) = a_p + A_{pp} \ln p(t) + A_{py} \ln y(t) + \Gamma_{pp} \ln p(t-1) +$$

$$\Gamma_{py} \ln y(t-1) + B\, w(t-1) + u(t) \tag{6}$$

where a_p is a 3× 1 constant vector, $A_{pp}, A_{py}, \Gamma_{pp}, \Gamma_{py}$ and B are constant matrices of 3× 3, and u(t) is 3× 1 vector of random variables which are assumed to be i.i.d. with $E(u(t))=(0,0,0)'$ and $E[u(t)u(t)'] = \Omega$. We assume stochastic independence of u(t) from p(s) and y(s) for all $s \leqq t$. The above parameters are subject to the adding up condition:

$$i'a_p = 1 - \alpha,\ i'A_{pp} = i'A_{py} = i'\Gamma_{pp} = i'\Gamma_{py} = (0,0,0),$$
$$i'B = \alpha\, i,\ i'u(t) = 0, \text{ and } i'\Omega = (0,0,0) \tag{6a}$$

where α is a scalar. We further assume that the characteristic values of the 2× 2 matrix D given by

$$D := [b_{ij} - b_{i3}],\ i=1,2 \tag{7}$$

with b_{ij} being the (i,j)th element of B, are smaller than unity in modulus, and note that given our assumption on u(t) this condition is necessary and sufficient for stationarity of (6) (Berndt and Savin (1975, p.944)).

Inserting (1) and (6) into (4) and rearranging we can represent the DGP as:

$$w(t) = (I-B)\Pi_p + A_{pp}\,\Delta \ln p(t) + (I-B)\Pi_{pp} \ln p(t-1) +$$

$$A_{py}\,\Delta \ln y(t) + (I-B)\Pi_{py} \ln y(t-1) + B\,w(t-1) + u(t) \tag{8}$$

where Δ is the backward difference operator. This model includes well known dynamic models such as AR(1) residual term, partial adjustment, and static models as special cases (see Anderson and Blundell). A new item to be added in this paper is the distributed lag model which corresponds to the case of B=[0].

Because of the adding up property (8) is singular. This system can be made nonsingular by deleting one of its equations (recall that by assumption all elements of w(t) are nonzero). Utilizing the adding up conditions (2a) and (6a), and deleting the third equation, the resulting nonsingular system will be given by:

$$w(t)_{,3} = (I-D)\Pi_{p,3} + A_{pp,3}\,\Delta \ln p(t) + (I-D)\Pi_{pp,3} \ln p(t-1) +$$

$$A_{py,3}\,\Delta \ln y(t) + (I-D)\Pi_{py,3} \ln y(t-1) + D\,w(t-1)_{,3} + u(t)_{,3} \tag{9}$$

where z_3 refers to that the third row of the matrix z has been deleted, and D is given by (7). Because of its nonsingularity all parameters of (9) can be estimated by using the usual ML algorithm. In this connection we note that ML estimates of the parameters are independent of the equation deleted, and that while all the parameters of (9) are identifiable, the elements of G are in general not identifiable from those of D (Berndt and Savin (1975)). This point is worth noting in assessing implications on D of test results of hypothesis on G.

The main purpose of this paper is to test integrability conditions represented by symmetry and negativity of the Slutsky matrix for (9). These conditions are equivalent to the symmetry of Π_{pp} and condition (2b), respectively. We now consider the test procedure of (2b). A useful method for this purpose is to apply the Cholesky factorization (Lau,1978). Let L be a 3× 3 unit lower triangular matrix and F a 3× 3 diagonal matrix. Then, applying Cholesky factorization the matrix in the parentheses of (2b) can be represented by:

$$\Pi_{pp} + U = LFL'$$

$$= \begin{bmatrix} F_1 & F_1L_{21} & F_1L_{31} \\ F_1L_{21} & F_1L_{21}L_{21} + F_2 & F_1L_{21}L_{31} + F_2L_{32} \\ F_1L_{31} & F_1L_{21}L_{31} + F_2L_{32} & F_1L_{31}L_{31} + F_2L_{32}L_{32} + F_3 \end{bmatrix} \tag{10}$$

In terms of this representation (2b) holds if and only if the diagonal elements of F (Cholesky values) are nonpositive. Since the left hand side of (10) sums up to zero, it follows that $F_3 = 0$ and hence that (2b) holds if and only if the first two diagonal elements of F are nonpositive.

The main difficulty in using the representation (10) consists in that the matrix U is not a priori known because of the very reason that their elements are theoretical optimal shares and not the realized ones. In most econometric applications this problem has been set aside by setting U equal to zero. Needless to say this implies testing of negative semidefiniteness of the matrix Π_{pp} itself, i.e., global concavity of the model. Although this guarantees the model to be concave for all positive prices, it imposes strong restrictions on elasticities. In fact, imposition of this condition resulted in Jorgenson and Fraumeni (1983) to set 204 out of 360 second order parameters of the TL cost function equal to zero. This implies a substantial reduction in the flexibility of the TL function. We note here that in general the imposition of global concavity deprives flexible functional forms of their very flexibility, which was indeed the main reason of introducing them in economic analysis (see Barnett and Lee (1985)).

Instead of setting U equal to zero and imposing unduly strong restrictions on elasticities we choose to approximate its elements by mean values of the realized value shares. Thus we test (2b) locally at the mean sample point. Let U^o be the matrix U obtained in this way. Then (2b) at the sample mean can be tested by testing whether F_1 and F_2 are nonpositive in the following representation:

$$\Pi_{pp} = LFL' - U^{o} \tag{11}$$

Up to this point our analysis has been limited to the system of demand functions corresponding to (1). Of course, a similar procedure could be applied to a system of supply price functions. This, however, requires a stronger assumption of macro profit maximization in the long run. Since we are interested in testing the weaker condition of cost minimization, we choose to limit the scope of our analysis to the demand system only. This implies that our inference on the underlying technology has to be limited to that part of technology represented by Π_p, Π_{pp} and Π_{py}. This point is important in testing the homogeneity of technology with respect to inputs and outputs. In terms of (1) the underlying technology is homogeneous of degree λ in inputs and outputs if and only if $i'\Pi_y = 1/\lambda$, $i'\Pi_{yy} = i'\Pi_{py}' = (0,0,0)$. Since the equation system (9) does not involve Π_y and Π_{yy}, all what we can test by estimating the system is the last condition on Π_{py} only. In other words, we can test a necessary condition for the homogeneity of technology only.

In terms of (1) the underlying technology is homothetically separable between inputs and outputs if and only if $\Pi_{py} = [0]$ (Hall, 1973). Homothetic separability between inputs and outputs implies that the composition of inputs is independent of the composition of outputs. Since this condition is frequently assumed in macro production models, it will be of interest to test its consistency with the data. Finally we note that tests of hypotheses on the structure of technology make sense only if the estimated demand system is integrable, since otherwise it will contain no information on the structure of technology.

3. Empirical Results

We now apply the above model to seasonally unadjusted quarterly data for the West German private sector for 1970 to 1980 (for details of the data, see Data Appendix). In the usual static framework it is usual to estimate the cost function together with the corresponding demand system. In the present case of short run disequilibrium, however, there seems to exist no unambiguous relationship between the

Table 1: Hypotheses and its implications on parameters

Integrability:	
Symmetry	$\Pi_{pp}=\Pi_{pp}'$
Negativity	$F_1 \leqq 0,\ F_2 \leqq 0$
Technology:	
Homogeneity	$i'\Pi_{py} = (0,0,0)$
Homothetic Separability	$\Pi_{py,3} = [0]$
Dynamic Structures	
AR(1) residual	$A_{pp,3} = \Pi_{pp,3}'$, $A_{py,3} = \Pi_{py,3}$
Partial adjustment	$A_{pp,3} = (I-D)\Pi_{pp,3}$, $A_{py,3} = (I-D)\Pi_{py,3}$
Distributed lag	$D = [0]$
Static	$A_{pp,3} = \Pi_{pp,3}$, $A_{py,3} = \Pi_{py,3}$, $D = [0]$

realized cost and the theoretical cost. We therefore estimate the demand system (9) only, after having deleted the share equation for capital services. Although the quarterly data is used no adjustment of the data has been done for possible seasonal effects. The estimator is MLE implemented in TSP 4.0B.

The maintained hypothesis is the ARX(1,1) model without symmetry of Π_{pp}. We test hypothesis on the structure of DGP which are nested in the ARX(1,1) model, integrability conditions, and hypotheses on the structure of technology. Table 1 presents the hypotheses to be tested together with the corresponding parameter restrictions. We note that due to the unidentifiability of the matrix B restrictions involving the matrix D in Table 1 represent necessary conditions only. Hence, if a restriction on D is not rejected, this does not necessarily imply acceptance of the corresponding restrictions on G. For example, although G = [0] implies D = [0] the converse does not hold.

Table 2 presents summary statistics of the estimation results. Using the h statistic (Durbin, 1970) we cannot reject the null hypothesis of zero first order autocorrelation of residuals for the ARX(1,1) model with and without integrability conditions at the level of significance of 0.05. Furthermore the estimated ARX(1,1) model satisfied a sufficient condition for stationarity $|d_{1j}|+|d_{2j}|<1$, j=1,2 (Murata, 1977 p.96).

We first test hypotheses on dynamic structures. The test statistic is minus twice the logarithmic of the likelihood ratio which is well known to be asymptotically distributed as $\chi^2(r)$ with r being

Table2: Summary statistics of the estimation results*

Models	Number of parameters	ln L	d(L)	d(M)	h(L)	h(M)
1. ARX(1,1) without symmetry	30	358.40	1.98	1.81	n.d.	1.85
2. ARX(1,1) with symmetry	27	357.99	2.04	1.83	-.26	1.53
3. ARX(1,1) with symmetry and negativity	26	355.54	2.02	1.99	-.36	.69
4. 3. with homogeneity in outputs	24	354.29	2.14	1.92	-.60	.55
5. 3. with homothetic separability between inputs and outputs	20	344.40	2.01	2.29	-.04	.55
6. AR(1) without symmetry	18	325.07	1.90	2.19	.39	-.71
7. AR(1) with symmetry	15	315.64	1.37	2.12	2.61	-.44
8. Partial adjustment without symmetry	18	326.34	1.50	1.50	3.65	2.53
9. Partial adjustment without symmetry	15	316.86	1.36	1.49	3.69	3.17
10. Distributed lag without symmetry	26	348.97	1.59	1.29		
11. Distributed lag with symmetry	23	343.85	1.30	1.30		
12. Distributed lag with symmetry and negativity	22	336.97	1.34	1.05		
13. Static without symmetry	14	307.91	2.55	1.04		
14. Static with symmetry	11	295.77	2.47	1.03		

* ln L: logarithm of the maximum oh the likelihood function,
d: Durbin Watson statistic, L and M in the parentheses refer to the share functions for labor and imported intermediate goods, respectively. h: h statistic. n.d.: not defined (complex value).

Table 3: Test results of DGP

Maintained hypothesis: ARX(1,1) without symmetry

Dynamic structures	Degrees of freedom	Critical values	Test statistics
AR(1) residual	12	26.22	66.66
Partial adjustment	12	26.22	64.12
Distributed lag	4	13.28	18.86
Static	16	31.99	100.98

the number of restrictions to be tested. To keep the overall level of significance of the whole tests considered simultaneously at a reasonable level, the level of significance of 0.01 is used for each test. Table 3 presents the test results. We reject all hypotheses on the dynamic structure properly nested in the ARX(1,1) model. We note that imposition of less general dynamic structures tends to introduce autocorrelation of residuals indicating model misspecifications. In particular for the partial adjustment model the h statistic shows values which are significantly different from zero at the level of 0.01 indicating the presence of autocorrelation in the residuals. We conclude that the DGP which is less general than ARX(1,1) is inconsistent with the data, and note that similar findings have been made by Anderson and Blundell(1982,1983), Veall and Zimmermann (1984), and Nakamura (1985).

We next turn to test results of integrability conditions. Estimation of the ARX(1,1) model subject to symmetry and Cholesky factorization yields (-.1028,.0221) as estimates of the Cholesky values F_1 and F_2. We therefore impose (2b) by setting $F_2 = 0$. Test results of Table 4 show that for the ARX(1,1) model symmetry as well as concavity conditions (at the mean sample point) are not rejected even at the level of significance of 0.05. Imbedded in the ARX(1,1) model the demand model thus turned out to be consistent with the data.

For reference purposes Table 4 shows also test results of the symmetry condition subject to less general forms of DGP. Except for the distributed lag model symmetry is decisively rejected for all the less general DGP considered. Furthermore, for the distributed lag model concavity (at the mean sample point) is rejected. Since these forms of DGP have been found to be inconsistent with the data, rejection of integrability conditions appears to be due to missspecification of the DGP.

Table 4: Test results of integrability conditions

Models	Degrees of freedom	Critical values	Test statistics
ARX(1,1)			
symmetry	3	11.35	.82
symmetry and negativity	4	13.28	5.72
AR(1) residual			
symmetry	3	11.35	18.86
Partial adjustment			
symmetry	3	11.35	18.96
Distributed lag			
symmetry	3	11.35	10.24
symmetry and negativity	4	13.28	24.00
Static			
symmetry	3	11.35	24.28

We now turn to economic implications of the estimated model. Table 5 shows the estimates of the Allen Uzawa elasticities of substitution (AUES), σ_{ij}, and price elasticities of demand, e_{ij}, evaluated at the sample mean point. Several important conclusions emerge from Table 5: (1) the demand for labor (L), capital (K), and imported intermediate input (M) are responsive to a change in their own prices - the estimated own price elasticities e_{LL}, e_{KK} and e_{MM} are -.13,-.13 and -.22, respectively; (2) labor and imported input are slightly substitutable - the estimated σ_{LM} is .47, while the estimated cross price elasticities e_{LM} and e_{ML} are .05 and .34, respectively; (3) labor and capital are less substitutable than usually supposed - the estimated σ_{LK} is .49 while the estimated e_{LK} and e_{KL} are .08 and .35, respectively; (3) imported intermediate input and capital display substantial complementarity - the estimated σ_{MK} is -.26 while the estimated e_{MK} and e_{KM} are -.21 and -.14, respectively. Our finding of capital - imported intermediate input complementarity is consistent with that of Burgess for the US economy (Burgess considered all imports including final goods). Since the West German import of intermediate goods contains a substantial por tion of energy (the sample mean of the value share of energy and min ing products is .25) this result can be compared with the frequently observed capital - energy complementarity (see Berndt and Wood (1975, 79), and Nakamura (1984)).

Table 5: Estimates of Allen Uzawa Elasticities of Substitution and Price Elasticities of Demand (evaluated at mean shares)

input i	Elasticities of Substitution σ_{iL}	σ_{iM}	σ_{iK}	Price Elasticities e_{iL}	e_{iM}	e_{iK}
(L) labor services	-1.3812	.4742	.4901	-.1335	.0517	.0818
(M) import of intermediate goods	.4742	-1.2192	-1.2600	.3433	-.1329	-.2104
(K) capital services	.4901	-1.2600	-1.3022	.3548	-.1373	-.2175

Table 6: Test results of the structure of technology
Maintained hypothesis: ARX model with symmetry and negativity

Hypotheses	Degrees of freedom	Critical values	Test statistics
homogeneity	2	9.21	2.50
homothetic separability of outputs from inputs	6	16.81	22.28

We finally turn to test results of the hypotheses on the structure of technology reported in Table 6. Although (a necesary condition of) homogeneity is not rejected, homothetic separability between inputs and outputs is rejected. The demand for different inputs is not independent of the composition of outputs. This is indeed consistent with the finding of Burgess for the US economy and Denny and Pinto for the Canadian economy. It seems necessary to cast some doubt on the usual practice of specifying the macro technology by a single output model based on the separability assumption between inputs and outputs.

4. Concluding Remarks

In this paper I tested integrability conditions for a system of demand functions for labor, capital and imported intermediate input within a flexible dynamic framework for West German macro quarterly data 1970 - 1980. The system is based on a model of multiproduct technology with three final outputs and three primary inputs.

Since aggregated data is used, the failure of integrability may be due to improper aggregation as well as improper specification of DGP. the failure may also be due to improper specification of the underlying technology. Using the published macro data I limited the scope of this paper to the implication of dynamics on integrability only.

Estimation results indicate that although integrability conditions are not rejected when tested subject to the ARX (1,1) model, all the less general DGPs considered are inconsistent with the data. Similar findings were made also by Anderson, Blundell, Veal and Zimmermann. These results support the hypothesis that rejection of integrability conditions is due to misspecification of the DGP. A simple direct application to data of the static demand theory seems misleading. Thus we should be rather careful in applying the exact index number approach.

Data Appendix

The quarterly data used in this paper consist of quantities of labor services, capital services, import of intermediate goods, domestic output of consumption goods, investment goods, and export of intermediate goods as well as prices of labor services, capital services and import of intermediate goods for the West German private sector for the period 1970 - 1980. Investment goods include consumer's durables. Import of intermediate goods consists of goods which are not classified as investment or consumption goods. Export of intermediate goods is defined in an analogous way. We have extended the accounting framework of Conrad and Jorgenson (1975) on West German annual data to include import and export of intermediate goods. The data on prices of labor services and capital services were obtained by dividing total labor compensation and capital compensation by total hours worked and real capital stock taken from Mueller and Nakamura (1982), respectively.

References

Anderson,G.J. and R.W.Blundell (1982): Estimation and hypothesis testing in dynamic equation systems, Econometrica 50, 1559 - 1571

Anderson,G.J. and R.W.Blundell (1983): Testing restrictions in a flexible dynamic demand system, Review of Economic Studies 50,397-410

Anderson,G.J. and R.W.Blundell (1984): Consumer nondurables in the UK, Economic Journal 94, 35 - 44

Ando,A.(1981): On a theoretical and empirical basis of macroeconometric models, in J.Kmenta and J.B.Ramsey eds., Large Scale Macro Econometric Models, North Holland, Amsterdam, 329 - 368

Barnett,Y.A. and Y.W.Lee (1985): The global properties of the minflex Laurent, generalized Leontief, and translog flexible functional forms, Econometrica 53, 1421 - 1437

Barten,A.P. (1969): Maximum likelihood estimation of complete system of demand equations, European Economic Review 1, 7 - 73

Barten,A.P. (1975): The system of consumer demand functions approach, in M.D. Intriligator ed. Frontiers of Quantitative Economics 3A, North Holland, Amsterdam, 23 - 57

Berndt,E.R., T.H.McCurdy and D.E.Rose (1980) : On testing theories of financial intermediary portfolio selection, Review of Economic Studies 47, 861 - 873

Berndt,E.R. and N.E.Savin (1975) : Estimation and hypothesis testing in singular equation demand systems with autoregressive disturbances, Econometrica 43, 937 - 957

Berndt,E.R. and D.Wood (1975): Technology, prices and the derived demand for energy, Review of Economics and Statistics 52, 259 - 268

Berndt,E.R. and D.Wood (1979): Engineering and economic interpretation of energy - capital complementarity, American Economic Review 69, 342 - 354

Burgess,D.F. (1974): A cost minimization approach to import demand equations, Review of Economics and Statistics 56, 225 - 234

Burgess,D.F. (1976) : Tariffs and income distribution, Journal of Political Economy 84, 17 - 45

Caves,D.W., L.R.Christensen and W.E.Diewert (1982): Multilateral comparison of output, input and productivity using superlative index number, Economic Journal 92, 73 - 86

Christensen,LR., D.Cummings and D.W.Jorgenson (1981): Relative productivity levels, 1947 - 1973, an international comparison, European Economic Review 16, 61 - 94

Christensen,L.R., D.W.Jorgenson and L.J.Lau (1975) : Transcendental logarithmic utility functions, American Economic Review 65, 367 - 383

Conrad,K. and D.W.Jorgenson (1975) : Measuring performance in the private economy of the Federal Republic of Germany, 1950 - 1975, Mohr, Tuebingen

Conrad,K. and D.W.Jorgenson (1977) : Tests of a model of production for the Federal Republic of Germany, 1950 - 1973, European Economic Review 10, 51 - 75

Courakis,A.S. (1975): Testing theories of discount house portfolio selection, Review of Economic Studies 42, 643 - 648

Deaton,A.S. and J.Muellbauer (1980): An almost ideal demand system,American Economic Review 70, 312 - 326

Denny,M. and C.Pinto (1978): An aggregate model with multiproduct technologies, in M.Fuss and D.McFadden eds., Production Economics 2, North Holland, Amsterdam, 249 - 267

Diewert,E.W. (1976): Exact and superlative index numbers, Journal of Econometrics 4, 115 - 145

Durbin,J. (1970): Testing for serial correlation in least squares regression when some of the regressors are lagged dependent variables, Econometrica38, 410 - 421

Eckstein,O. (1981): Economic theory and econometric models, in J.Kmenta and J.B.Ramsey eds., Large Scale Macro Econometric Models North Holland, Amsterdam,,155 - 176

Griffin,J.M. (1977): Interfuel substitution possibilities, International Economic Review 18, 755 - 770

Hall,R.E. (1973): The specification of technology with several kinds of output, Journal of Political Economy 81, 878 - 892

Halvorsen,R. (1977): Energy substitution in U.S. manufacturing, Review of Economics and Statistics 59, 381 - 388

Jorgenson,D.W. and B.M.Fraumeni (1983): Relative prices and technical change, in W.Eichhorn et al. eds., Quantitative Studies of Production and Prices, Physica Verlag, Wuerzburg, 241 - 269

Lau,L.J. (1978): Testing and imposing monotonicity, convexity and quasi convexity constraints, in M.Fuss and D.McFadden eds., Production Economics 1, North Holland, Amsterdam, 409 - 454

Lau,L.J. and P.A.Yotopoulos (1971): A test of relative efficiency and application to Indian agriculture, American Economic Review 61, 94 - 109

Lovell,C.A.K. and R.C.Sickles (1982): Testing efficiency hypothesis in joint production, Review of Economics and Statistics 64, 51 - 58

Mueller,S. and S.Nakamura (1982): The Bonn quarterly macroeconomic model for the West German economy, Discussion Paper N.134, University of Bonn

Murata,Y. (1977): Mathematics for Stability and Optimization of Economic Systems, Academic Press, New York

Nakamura,S. (1984): An Interindustry Translog Model of Prices and Technical Change for the West German Economy, Springer Verlag, Berlin

Nakamura,S. (1985): A test of restrictions in a dynamic singular demand system, Zeitschrift fuer Nationaloekonomie 45, 313 - 330

Pindyck,R.S. (1979): Interfuel substitution and industrial demand for energy, Review of Economics and Statistics 61, 169 - 179

Toda,Y. (1976) : Estimation of a cost function when the cost is not minimum, Review of Economics and Statistics 58, 259 - 268

Veall,M.R. and K.Zimmermann (1984): A monthly dynamic consumer expenditure system for Germany with different kinds of households, Paper presented at the Econometric Society European Meeting, Madrid

Value-Added Total-Factor-Productivity Measurement: A Monte-Carlo Assessment

Margaret E. Slade
The University of British Columbia
and Universite Catholique de Louvain

I: INTRODUCTION

In this paper, Monte-Carlo methods are used to assess the specification errors that result when value-added total-factor productivity (TFP) indices are used to assess true rates of technical change.

Growth of total factor productivity and increases in economic well being of a society are intimately related. When society can produce more output from the same inputs, the inputs (labor and the owners of other factors) become wealthier. Assessing rates of growth of total factor productivity is therefore an important economic problem.

A common approach to the problem is to calculate changes in a total-factor-productivity index -- the rate of change of an index of outputs divided by an index of inputs. Ideally, one would like to include all outputs and inputs in the construction of these indices. Data constraints, however, can make such an exercise infeasible. In particular, the lack of data on intermediate inputs often forces researchers to construct value-added TFP indices.

A value-added TFP index corresponds to a value-added production function, where two inputs, labor and capital, produce net output or value added. All intermediate inputs are netted out of the calculation. Shifts in the value-added production function or its dual cost function are then investigated and equated with shifts in the economy's production possibilities -- the aggregate rate of technical change.

Many researchers have constructed value-added TFP indices to assess rates of technical change at the economy (Jorgenson and Griliches, 1967, Clark, 1979, and Baily, 1981), sectoral (Norsworthy, Harper, and Kunze, 1979, and Nadiri, 1980), and regional (Hulten and Schwab, 1984) levels for a single country (the United States in this

Measurement in Economics
ed. by W. Eichhorn

case). Others have used value-added indices to compare rates of technical change across countries (Jorgenson and Nishimuzu, 1978 and Christensen, Cummings, and Jorgenson, 1980). This is only a partial list of the many studies that analyse changes in value-added TFP over time, across geographic regions, and by economic sector.

In order for changes in value-added TFP indices to capture shifts in the production possibilities open to society, certain strong assumptions must be satisfied (see Section II).

1) An aggregate production function relating gross output to all inputs must exist and satisfy certain regularity conditions such as differentiability, concavity, and nondecreasingness in inputs.
2) A value-added production function relating net output to the services of capital and labor must exist. For this to be true, capital and labor must be separable from intermediate materials. It is shown in the next section that if technical change is not Hicks neutral, the separability required is of a particularly strong variety.
3) Technical change must affect only the value-added production function.

In this paper, assumption one is maintained and violations of two and three are investigated.

Assumptions two and three are not only testable, they have in fact often been tested. The result is uniform rejection. For example, starting with Berndt and Wood (1975) almost all researchers who have considered the issue have rejected the separability of capital and labor from intermediate inputs such as energy and raw materials. In addition, those who have estimated production or cost functions with nonneutral technical change (Jorgenson and Fraumeni, 1981, Moroney and Trapani, 1981, and Hazilla and Kopp, 1982) have found biased technical change that affects intermediate inputs as well as capital and labor.

Rather than abandon the calculation of value-added TFP indices, it is informative to assess the magnitudes and signs of the errors that are made when assumptions two and three are wrongly maintained. That is, knowing that these conditions are apt to be violated, we can ask if value-added TFP indices still provide reasonable approximations to true rates of technical change or if they are very misleading. This paper attempts such an assessment.

Because the process that generated real-world data is unknown, it is not possible to use such data to perform an assessment of specification errors. Monte-Carlo techniques, in contrast, do not suffer from this limitation. In fact an advantage of Monte-Carlo techniques is that the underlying technology is not only known with certainty, it can be designed to possess any characteristics of interest.

Monte-Carlo methods are used here to assess the specification errors that result from violations of assumptions two and three. The factors that are varied in the assessment include the elasticities of substitution between factors, the Hicks-neutral rate of technical change, the biased (materials using or saving) rate of technical change, and the trend in the price of the omitted intermediate factor.

To anticipate results, it is found that specification errors tend to be larger when substitution is easier, when technical change is materials using, and when the price of the omitted factor is falling. In addition, when there is a positive trend in materials price coupled with little netural technical change, the rate of change of a value-added TFP index often differs in sign from the true rate of technical change.

The organization of the paper is as follows. In the next section, the theoretical model is discussed. Section III describes the Monte-Carlo experiments -- the true technology, experimental design, and assessment of errors. Section IV contains the empirical results, and the final section summarizes and concludes. Appendices contain proofs and details concerning the construction of specific technologies.

II: THEORETICAL BACKGROUND

In what follows, it is assumed that an aggregate technology transforms a vector of homogeneous inputs X into an aggregate output Y. In addition, real value added VA is produced by two components of X, capital K and labor L. For simplicity it is assumed that X consists of only three inputs, K, L, and intermediate materials M. These relationships can be expressed as [1]

$$Y = F(K,L,M,t) = \tilde{F}(VA,M,t) \qquad (1)$$

where

$$VA = V(K,L,t)$$

and t represents time, a proxy for technical change.

F and V are assumed to be differentiable, concave, and nondecreasing in inputs for fixed t.

We are interested in when the temporal shift in the value added production function V_t/V equals the aggregate rate of technical change F_t/F. This leads to

Proposition 1: Under the above assumptions on F and V, $V_t/V = F_t/F$ if and only if the aggregate production function satisfies one of the following restrictions:

$$F(K,L,M,t) = V(K,L,t)h(M) \qquad (3)$$

or

$$F(K,L,M,t) = \bar{V}(g(K,L),t)\bar{H}(g(K,L),M). \qquad (4)$$

Proof: see the appendix.

With both restrictions on aggregate production, technical change affects only the value-added portion of the production function. With the second case, technical change must be Hicks-Neutral whereas with the first, nonneutral technical change is allowed but more than separability of K, L, and t from M is required. When the production function can be written as in equation 3 (i.e., when the production function decomposes multiplicatively) K,L, and t are said to be strictly independent of M.[2]

---

[1] If K and L are not separable from M, a value-added production function does not exist.

[2] For a discussion of strict independence and its implications, see Blackorby, Primont, and Russell (1978, pp. 165-171).

In what follows it is assumed that F and V are positively linearly homogeneous in inputs.[3] Regardless of whether restrictions 3 or 4 are satisfied, dual cost functions

$$CT = f(r,w,p,t)Y = rK^* + wL^* + pM^* \tag{5}$$

and

$$CV = g(r,w,t)VA = rK^* + wL^* \tag{6}$$

exist, where CT is total cost, CV is value-added cost, r, w, and p are the prices of K, L, and M respectively, and *'s denote minimized values.

If input and output markets are in competitive equilibrium and if costs are minimized, conventional TFP indices corresponding to 5 and 6 can be written as

$$\dot{TFP}^T/TFP^T = \dot{Y}/Y - (s_K^T \dot{K}/K + s_L^T \dot{L}/L + s_M^T \dot{M}/M) \tag{7}$$

and

$$\dot{TFP}^V/TFP^V = \dot{VA}/VA - (s_K^V \dot{K}/K + s_L^V \dot{L}/L), \tag{8}$$

where a dot over a variable denotes a time derivative and s_i^T (s_i^V) denotes factors i's share in total (value-added) cost, i = K,L,M (i = K,L).

If the aggregate production function satisfies restrictions 3 or 4 of proposition one, the rate of change of TFP calculated from the value-added relationship 8 will equal the true rate of technical change $\dot{TFP}^T/TFP^T$. When the restrictions are violated, the two indices can be calculated and compared. The specification error (the difference between the two) will in general depend on such factors as the degree of substitutability among inputs, the trend in the price of M, and the biased (M using or saving) rate of technical change. It is to assess these factors that we turn to the Monte-Carlo experiments.

---

[3] Linear homogeneity is not required for the analysis but it simplifies the calculations. If the cost funciton is to have the same separability structure as the production function, V must be homothetic.

III: THE MONTE-CARLO EXPERIMENTS

IIIa: The True Technology

In constructing the true technology, the idea is to work with a functional form that is sufficiently flexible to capture all the features that are of interest in the experiments. When this has been done, specific technologies can be created from the general function by specifying sufficient properties of the technology so as to completely determine the parameters of the function.

Here we work with a translog cost function (Christensen, Jorgenson, and Lau 1971). The translog is chosen because the Tornqvist (1936) TFP index, the index most commonly used by empirical researchers, is exact for this function (Diewert 1976). In this way, approximation errors are avoided and all errors can be attributed to misspecification.

The general functional form for the total-cost function is[4]

$$\ln CT = \alpha_1 \ln(r/p) + \alpha_2 \ln(w/p) + \ln p + \ln Y + \alpha_t t + 1/2\alpha_{11}(\ln(r/p))^2$$

$$+ 1/2\alpha_{22}(\ln(w/p))^2 + \alpha_{12} \ln(r/p)\ln(w/p) + \alpha_{2t} \ln(w/p)t, \quad (9)$$

$$CV = CT - p M, \quad (10)$$

where all variables are defined as in section II.

It should be noted that linear homogeneity in prices, symmetry of substitution effects, and adding up of cost shares have been imposed a priori in the specification of (9).[5] When specific cases have been constructed, curvature restrictions must be checked. That is, the constructed cost function should be concave in prices. Because prices are random variables, it is not possible to impose curvature at all possible data points. However, all functions constructed satisfy

---

[4] This cost function is not completely flexible but it captures the features of interest.

[5] For properties of cost functions, see Diewert (1981).

curvature restrictions at the means of the data series and at almost all generated price-quantity combinations.

The features of the technology that define the specific cases are

		Number of Restrictions
1)	The shares of capital and labor in total costs, s_i^T,	2
2)	The elasticities of substitution σ_{ij} between factor i and factor j, $i \neq j$,	3
3)	The Hicks-neutral rate of technical change, α_t, and	1
4)	The biased rate of technical change, α_{2t}.	1
	Total number of restrictions =	7

Relationships 1 - 4 constitute seven equations in seven unknowns. They can be solved numerically for the seven parameters of the cost function. Appendix B contains mathematical details and lists parameter estimates.

IIb: Experimental Design

Certain features of the technology and of the economic environment are held constant in all of the experiments. Prices r and w are lognormally distributed with mean of $\ln p_i = 0$ and standard error of $\ln p_i = .25$. ($p_i = r,w$). Gross output Y is held constant at one. In addition, mean factor shares of total cost are set at $s_K^T = .05$, $s_L^T = .25$, and $s_M^T = .70$. These are consistent with values observed in aggregate U.S. data (Berndt and Wood 1975, for example).

Specific experiments correspond to varying the following parameters:

1) The trend in material's price, β,

2) The Hicks-neutral rate of technical change, α_t,

3) The biased rate of technical change, α_{2t}, and

4) The substitutability of the technology.

In each case a "high" and a "low" value of a parameter is chosen. Values are selected so that they correspond to ones frequently found in real-world data. A priori restrictions 1 - 4 are imposed at the means of the data series.

High and low parameter values are selected as follows.

1) The trend in material's price:
p is generated so that lnp has a linear trend,

$$\ln p = \gamma + \beta t. \tag{11}$$

Low values correspond to a negative trend with $\gamma = .22$ and $\beta = -.02$ and high values correspond to a positive trend with $\gamma = -.22$ and $\beta = .02$. These trends are consistent with ones found in an aggregate energy and raw-materials price index by Slade (1982). The negative trend corresponds to the period 1920-1945 for that index, and the positive trend to the period 1945-1980.

2) The Hicks-neutral rate of technical change:
The low value of α_t is -.005 and the high value is -.02. The low value is consistent with econometric estimates of this parameter (Berndt and Kaled 1979 and Pindyck and Rotemberg 1983, for example) and the high value is consistent with TFP index-number estimates (Hulten and Schwab 1984, for example).

3) The biased rate of technical change:
It is very difficult to specify even the sign of this parameter a priori. For example, Berndt and Kaled (1979) find technical change to have been energy using and materials saving, leaving the sign of an aggregate of the two unknown. Low and high values of α_{2t} were (somewhat arbitrarily) chosen as -.0025 and +.0025, respectively. It should be noted that when $\alpha_{2t} < 0$, technical change is M using and L saving and when $\alpha_{2t} > 0$, it is M saving and L using.

4) Substitutability of the technology:
Three elasticities of substitution, σ_{KL}, σ_{KM}, and σ_{LM}, determine the substitutability of the technology. Low and high values are chosen to be 0.2, 0.2, and 0.4 and 2.0, 2.0, and 1.5, respectively. The

nonsubstitutable technology is thus close to fixed-coefficient whereas with the high elasticities, substitution possibilities are considerably richer than with a Cobb-Douglas technology.[6]

Table I summarizes the high and low values of all parameters.

A priori one expects approximation errors to be larger when the σ_{ij}'s are large. When p changes relative to r and w, if substitution is easy much of what is registered as technical change with a value-added TFP index will really be subsitution for the omitted factor.

The effects of varying β and α_{2t} are harder to predict a priori. If these parameters are large in absolute value, approximation errors should be larger. The effects of changes in the signs of these parameters, however, are ambiguous.

For each experiment, Tornqvist TFP indices are calculated for the total and value-added technologies. Tornqvist indices are discrete approximations to the continuous indices 7 and 8 and are defined by

$$\begin{aligned}\ln(TFP^T_t/TFP^T_{t-1}) &= \ln(Y_t/Y_{t-1}) - 1/2(s_{K\,t}^{T} + s_{K\,t-1}^{T})\ln(K_t/K_{t-1}) \\ &- 1/2(s_{L\,t}^{T} + s_{L\,t-1}^{T})\ln(L_t/L_{t-1}) \\ &- 1/2(s_{M\,t}^{T} + s_{M\,t-1}^{T})\ln(M_t/M_{t-1}) \qquad (12)\end{aligned}$$

and

$$\begin{aligned}\ln(TFP^V_t/TFP^V_{t-1}) &= \ln(VA_t/VA_{t-1}) \\ &- 1/2(s_{K\,t}^{V} + s_{K\,t-1}^{V})\ln(K_t/K_{t-1}) \\ &- 1/2(s_{L\,t}^{V} + s_{L\,t-1}^{V})\ln(L_t/L_{t-1}). \qquad (13)\end{aligned}$$

There are thus $2^3 = 8$ technologies to be considered. Each must be evaluated in two economic environments. Sixteen Monte-Carlo

---

[6] Complementarity is not tested. When there are only three inputs, the inputs tend to be substitutes (see Humphrey and Moroney, 1975, for example).

TABLE 1

VALUES OF PARAMETERS FOR DIFFERENT SIMULATIONS

Low		High
	Trend in p	
$\gamma = .22,\ \beta = -.02$		$\gamma = -.22,\ \beta = .02$
	Hicks-Neutral Technical Change	
$\alpha_t = -.005$		$\alpha_t = -.02$
	Biased Technical Change	
$\alpha_{2t} = -.0025$		$\alpha_{2t} = .0025$
	Substitutability:	
$\sigma_{KL} = 0.2$		$\sigma_{KL} = 2.0$
$\sigma_{KM} = 0.2$		$\sigma_{KM} = 2.0$
$\sigma_{LM} = 0.4$		$\sigma_{LM} = 1.5$

simulations are therefore run. For each experiment there are twenty one observations (twenty first differences). Finally, each experiment is replicated 50 times. Values shown in section IV are therefore averages over the replications and over the sample.

IIIc: Assessment of Errors

For each experiment and at each data point, the specification error is the difference between the true rate of technical change (12) and the value-added approximation (13). It is possible to view these errors in several ways.

First, magnitudes of errors are of interest; that is, we wish to assess the absolute value of the difference between the measures. Second, the direction of the error is of interest. For example, we wish to know if, on average, the value-added index over or underestimates the true index. Finally, sign reversals are of interest. For example, we are interested in knowing the circumstances under which the two measures are of opposite sign.

For a systematic assessment of errors due to misspecification, $|D\bar{I}F|$, the average value over the sample of the absolute value of the difference between the two indices, is calculated. In addition, the sign of the difference is recorded. Finally, sign reversals are noted. (Because the true index is always positive, sign reversals correspond to negative value-added indices). There are sixteen observations on each of these measurement errors.

Dummy variables equal to one if a parameter assumes its high value and equal to zero otherwise are created for each of the four parameters that distinguish the technologies and environments. $|D\bar{I}F|$ is then regressed on the dummy variables in order to find systematic associations between magnitudes of errors and characteristics of technologies. Signs of errors and sign reversals are also assessed by seeking regular patterns that can be associated with variations in the parameters.

IV: EMPIRICAL RESULTS

Table II shows the characteristics that distinguish the experiments and the average measurement errors for each of the sixteen

TABLE II

SPECIFICATION ERRORS

Experimental Parameters						Measurement Errors		
β	α_t	α_{2t}	α_{ij}	$\frac{\overline{\dot{TFP}}^T}{TFP^T}$	$\frac{\overline{\dot{TFP}}^V}{TFP^V}$	$\|DIF\|$	Sign	
H	L	H	L	.0050	-.0228	.0305	+	*
H	H	H	L	.0200	.0152	.0275	+	
H	H	L	L	.0200	.0220	.0240	-	
L	H	L	L	.0200	.1036	.0860	-	
L	L	L	L	.0050	.0714	.0673	-	
L	L	H	L	.0050	.0650	.0617	-	
H	L	L	L	.0050	-.0292	.0361	+	*
L	H	H	L	.0200	.0908	.0772	-	
L	H	L	H	.0200	.1027	.1668	-	
L	L	L	H	.0050	.0658	.1236	-	
L	L	H	H	.0050	.0561	.0801	-	
H	L	H	H	.0050	-.0277	.0635	+	*
H	H	H	H	.0200	.0087	.0861	+	
H	H	L	H	.0200	.0122	.1156	+	
L	H	H	H	.0200	.0872	.1564	-	
H	L	L	H	.0050	-.0302	.0784	+	*

simulations. In the table, H denotes a high value of a parameter and L a low value. $|\overline{DIF}|$ is the magnitude of the specification error, Sign shows the sign of the error (true minus value-added index), and a * stands for a sign reversal (negative value-added index). A $^{-}$ over a variable signifies that the variable has been averaged over the sample and over the replications.

To distinguish regular patterns in the specification errors shown in table II, first $|\overline{DIF}|$ was regressed on the dummy variables that distinguish the different technologies and environments. The result is

$$\widehat{|\overline{DIF}|} = \underset{}{0.68} - \underset{(-5.3)^{**}}{.045\, D_{\beta}} + \underset{(2.9)^{*}}{.025\, D_{\alpha t}} - \underset{(-2.2)^{*}}{.014\, D_{\alpha 2t}} + \underset{(6.8)^{**}}{.058\, D_{\sigma ij}}, \qquad (14)$$

$$R^2 = .89, \qquad F = 21.3^{**}.$$

t statistics are shown in parentheses under the estimated coefficients, * denotes significance at the 95 percent, and ** at the 99 percent confidence level.

As predicted, errors are larger when substitution is easier. In addition, they are larger when the price of the omitted factor is falling and when technical change is M using.

The second two effects were difficult to predict ex ante. Ex post, however, they can be rationalized. If the price of M is falling or if technical change is M using, materials are substituted for K and L over time. When relatively less K and L is used, and when input usage is falling in general ($\alpha_t < 0$), the two effects (neutral and biased change) have the same sign. As a consequence, measurement errors are larger.

A casual glance at table II reveals that, in general, value-added indices overestimate true rates of technical change. Nevertheless, value-added indices can be negative. Sign reversals occur when there is a positive trend in materials price coupled with a low rate of neutral technical change. When p is rising, more and more K and L are used in production. And when α_t is small, substitution of K and L for M overwhelms the neutral technical change (the fall in the use of all inputs) and appears as a decline in TFP.

For a systematic assessment of the direction of the errors, the value-added index was regressed on the true rate of technical change. The result is

$$(\widehat{\dot{TFP}^V/TFP^V}) = a + b\ (\dot{TFP}^T/TFP^T), \tag{15}$$

	a	b		
	.006	2.45		
	(.023)	(1.6)	R = .15,	F = 2.5.

Standard errors are shown under the estimated coefficients.

There exists a positive but statistically insignificant relationship between the two indices. In spite of its lack of significance, however, the estimated coefficient $\hat{b}$ is quite large. It is therefore worth analysing why this might be so. If we can believe the coefficient $\hat{b}$, the value-added index overstates the true index by a factor of approximately 2.5 (note that a is approximately zero). An explanation for this result is as follows.

Suppose that the conditions of proposition one are not satisfied and that r, w, and t are merely separable from p in CT.[7] Under these conditions, the total cost function can be written as

$$CT = f(r,w,p,t)Y = \tilde{f}(v(r,w,t),p)Y, \tag{16}$$

where v can be interpreted as the price index of value added.

By Shephard's lemma (1957)

$$VA = \partial CT/\partial v = \tilde{f}_v Y\ , \tag{17}$$

and value added's share in total cost is

$$s_v^T = (v \cdot VA)/CT. \tag{18}$$

---

[7] Because constant returns is assumed, the cost and production functions have the same separability structure. This assumption also implies that the rate of technical change calculated from the cost function is the same as that calculated from the production function (correcting for sign).

Taking logarithmic derivatives, we have

$$CT_t/CT = \partial \ln CT/\partial t = \partial \ln f/\partial t$$

$$= (\tilde{f}_v Y v_t)/(\tilde{f} Y) = s_v^T\ v_t/v. \tag{19}$$

Equation 19 shows that the true rate of technical change equals value added's share in total cost times the shift in the value-added cost function. If value added's share is approximately .70 as in our data, then the coefficient b should be approximately 1.5. We cannot reject the hypothesis that $\hat{b}$ = 1.5.

V: SUMMARY AND CONCLUSIONS

The Monte-Carlo assessment of value-added TFP indices helps to isolate and assess sources, magnitudes, and signs of specification errors. This information is valuable when interpreting the results of value-added TFP studies.

Approximations to underlying shifts in aggregate production or cost functions are seen to deteriorate when substitution between K and L and the omitted factor is easier, when the price of the omitted factor is falling, and when technical change is biased towards using more of the omitted factor. In addition, even though errors are larger in absolute value when the price of M is falling, sign reversals are more apt to occur when this price is rising, especially if neutral technical change is not very significant.

These general results can be used to determine when conclusions drawn from value-added TFP studies might be reliable. For example, it is often claimed that an abrupt slowdown in TFP growth occurred in 1972-74 (see, for example Lindbeck 1983). This period, however, was characterized by dramatic increases in raw-materials prices -- OPEC oil-price increases and the "commodity boom" for other basic inputs. Under these circumstances, value-added TFP indices tend to underestimate true rates of growth of productivity. Conversely, in normal periods value-addedd indices tend to overestimate the actual situation. A measured "slowdown" could therefore result merely from a dramatic change in relative prices.

If value-added TFP indices are to capture rates of technical change exactly, heroic assumptions on the structure of production must be satisfied. This does not mean, however, that value-added estimates are always poor. If relative-price changes are not large and if technical change is not very biased with respect to the use of an omitted factor, the true and calculated indices should at least move in the same direction. Simple index-number studies of very turbulent periods, however, should be viewed with skepticism.

The finding that, on average, value-added TFP indices overstate underlying shifts in the production or cost function might help to explain the discrepancy between econometrically estimated rates of technical change and those computed using index-number techniques. In general, econometric estimates are smaller than TFP estimates.

For example, Pindyck and Rotemberg (1983), who estimate a four-input cost function for aggregate U.S. manufacturing, find neutral rates of technical change between .2 and .5 percent per year.[8] In contrast, Hulten and Schwab (1984), who calculate value-added TFP indices for aggregate U.S. manufacturing, find neutral rates of technical change of approximately 1.7 percent.[9] Of course, there are other differences in the two approaches such as the treatment of returns to scale and of fixed factors. Nevertheless, the omission of intermediate inputs could at least partly explain the discrepancy.[10]

---

[8] With the Pindyck and Rotemberg model, the rate of technical change is for a variable-cost function. When only the capital stock is fixed, however, total and variable costs differ by about five percent. The presence of fixed factors alone, therefore, cannot account for the large difference in the estimates.

[9] The Hulten and Schwab estimate is based on a production function. Their assumption of constant returns, however, implies that a cost-function estimate would be the same.

[10] These are not the only examples. Berndt and Kaled (1979), using an econometric approach, find little evidence of technical change whereas Norsworthy et.al. (1979), who calculate value-added TFP indices, find much higher growth rates for aggregate U.S. manufacturing. The omission of intermediate inputs, however, does not account for the entire difference. For example, Hazilla and Kopp (1984) calculate index-number and econometric productivity measures from the same data set and find the index-number estimates to be 30 percent higher on average. Nevertheless, with the inclusion of intermediate inputs the discrepancy is substantially reduced.

A final caveat is that the study assesses only the Tornqvist direct quantity aggregator. This is the TFP index that is used in the vast majority of empirical research. Nevertheless, it would be interesting to see results for indirect quantity aggregators and for other superlative indices such as the Fisher ideal (Fisher 1922).

APPENDIX A
PROOF OF PROPOSITION ONE

Let $Y = F(K,L,M,t) = \tilde{F}(VA,M,t)$ and $VA = V(K,L,t)$ be the gross and value-added production functions respectively. F and V are assumed to be differentiable, concave, and nondecreasing in inputs for fixed t.

Proposition 1: $V_t/V = F_t/F$ if and only if F can be written as

$$V(K,L,t)h(M)$$

or

$$\bar{V}(g(K,L),t)\bar{H}(g(K,L),M).$$

Proof:

By assumption

$$F(K,L,M,t) = \tilde{F}(V(K,L,t),M,t). \tag{A0}$$

Suppose that

$$F_t/F = V_t/V. \tag{A1}$$

Integrating A1 we have

$$F(K,L,M,t) = V(K,L,t)H(K,L,M) \tag{A2}$$

From A0

$$F_K/F_L = \tilde{F}_V V_K/\tilde{F}_V V_L = V_K/V_L. \tag{A3}$$

By A2 and A3

$$(V_K H + H_K V)/(V_L H + H_L V) = V_K/V_L. \tag{A4}$$

Case i: $H_K = H_L = 0$.

Then $F(K,L,M,t) = V(K,L,t)h(M)$. (A5)*

Case ii: $H_L = 0$, $H_K \neq 0$.

A3 implies that

$$V_L V_K H + V_L H_K V = V_L V_K H \tag{A6}$$

which in turn implies that $H_K = 0$. Similarly, if $H_K = 0$, then $H_L = 0$.

Case iii: $H_L \neq 0$, $H_K \neq 0$.

A3 implies that

$$V_L V_K H + V_L H_K V = V_L V_K H + V_K H_L V$$

or

$$V_L/V_K = H_L/H_K. \tag{A7}$$

The left-hand side of A7 is independent of M and the right-hand side is independent of t. Therefore

$$V(K,L,t) = \bar{V}(g(K,L),t)$$

and

$$H(K,L,M) = \bar{H}(g(K,L),M). \tag{A8}$$

Substitution into A2 yields

$F(K,L,M,t) = \bar{V}(g(K,L),t)\bar{H}(g(K,L),M)$. (A9)*

Sufficiency of A5 and A9 is obvious.

APPENDIX B
THE SPECIFIC TECHNOLOGIES

The general functional form for all technologies is

$$\ln CT = \alpha_1 \ln(r/p) + \alpha_2 \ln(w/p) + \ln p + \ln Y + \alpha_t t + \frac{1}{2}\alpha_{11}(\ln(r/p))^2$$

$$+ \frac{1}{2}\alpha_{22}(\ln(w/p))^2 + \alpha_{12}\ln(r/p)\ln(w/p) + \alpha_{2t}\ln(w/p)t.$$

The restrictions listed in section IIIa are imposed at the means of all time series.

Restrictions 1 and 2: $s_K^T = c_1$ and $s_L^T = c_2$.

$$s_K^T = \partial \ln CT/\partial \ln r = \alpha_1 + \alpha_{11}\ln r + \alpha_{12}\ln w - (\alpha_{11} - \alpha_{12})\ln p$$

$$= \alpha_1 \quad \text{at the mean,}$$

implying that

$$\alpha_1 = c_1.$$

Similarly,

$$\alpha_2 = c_2.$$

Restrictions 3, 4, and 5: $\sigma_{KL} = c_3$ $\sigma_{KM} = c_4$ $\sigma_{LM} = c_5$.

$$\sigma_{KL} = (\alpha_{12} + s_K^T s_L^T)/(s_K^T s_L^T) = c_3$$

$$\alpha_{12} = s_K^T s_L^T(\sigma_{KL} - 1)$$

$$= c_1 c_2 (c_3 - 1).$$

TABLE B

SPECIFIC TECHNOLOGIES

	Parameters						
CT	α_1	α_2	α_{11}	α_{22}	α_{12}	α_t	α_{2t}
1	.05	.25	.038	.115	-.010	.005	-.0025
2	.05	.25	.038	.115	-.010	.005	.0025
3	.05	.25	.038	.115	-.010	.02	-.0025
4	.05	.25	.038	.115	-.010	.02	.0025
5	.05	.25	-.048	-.100	.013	.005	-.0025
6	.05	.25	-.048	-.100	.013	.005	.0025
7	.05	.25	-.048	-.100	.013	.02	-.0025
8	.05	.25	-.048	-.100	.013	.02	.0025

Characteristics of Technologies

CT	σ_{ij}	α_t	α_{2t}
1	L	L	L
2	L	L	H
3	L	H	L
4	L	H	H
5	H	L	L
6	H	L	H
7	H	H	L
8	H	H	H

Similarly,

$$\alpha_{13} = c_1(1 - c_1 - c_2)(c_4 - 1)$$

and

$$\alpha_{23} = c_2(1 - c_1 - c_2)(c_5 - 1),$$

where

$$\alpha_{13} = - \alpha_{11} - \alpha_{12} \quad \text{and} \quad \alpha_{23} = - \alpha_{12} - \alpha_{22}.$$

These relationships therefore determine α_{11}, α_{22}, and α_{12}.

Restrictions 6 and 7: $\alpha_t = c_6$ and $\alpha_{2t} = c_7$.

All parameters are now determined.

Table B shows parameter estimates and characteristics of the eight technologies.

REFERENCES CITED

Baily, N.M. (1981) "The Productivity-Growth Slowdown and Capital Accumulation," *American Economics Review*, Vol. 71, 326-331.

Berndt, E.R. and Kaled, M.S. (1979) "Parametric Productivity and Choice Among Flexible Functional Forms," *Journal of Political Economy*, Vol. 87, 1220-1245.

__________ and Wood, D.O. (1975) "Technology, Prices, and the Derived Demand for Energy," *Review of Economics and Statistics*, Vol. 57, 259-268.

Blackorby, C.E., Primont, D. and Russell, R.R. (1978) *Duality, Separability, and Functional Structure*, Amsterdam: North Holland.

Christensen, L.R., Cummings, D. and Jorgenson, D.W. (1980) "Economic Growth, 1947-73, An International Comparison," in J.W. Kendrick and B.W. Vaccara (eds.) *New Developments in Productivity Measurement and Analysis*, Chicago: University of Chicago Press.

__________ Jorgenson, D.W. and Lau, L.J. (1971) "Conjugate Duality and the Transcendental Logarithmic Production Function," *Econometrica*, Vol. 39, 255-256.

Clark, P.K. (1979) "Issues in the Analysis of Capital Formation and Productivity Growth" *Brookings Papers on Economic Activity*, Vol. 2, 423-431.

Diewert, W.E. (1976) "Exact and Superlative Index Numbers," *Journal of Econometrics*, Vol. 4, 115-145.

__________ (1981) "The Theory of Total Factor Productivity Measurement in Regulated Industries," in *Productivity Measurement in Regulated Industries*, T.G. Cowing and R.E. Stevenson (eds.) New York: Academic, 17-44.

Fisher, I. (1922) The Making of Index Numbers, Boston: Houghton Mifflin.

Hazilla, M. and Kopp, R.J. (1982) Substitution Between Energy and Other Factors of Production: U.S. Industrial Experience 1958-1974, EPRI EA Research Project 1475-1, Final Report.

______ (1984) "The Measurement of Sectoral Productivity: A Comparative Evaluation of Alternative Approaches," Resources for the Future Discussion Paper No. QE84-11, Washington, D.C.

Hulten, C.R. and Schwab, R.M. (1984) "Regional Productivity Growth in U.S. Manufacturing: 1951-1978," American Economic Review, Vol. 74, 152-162.

Humphrey, D.B. and Moroney, J.R. (1975) "Substitution among Capital, Labor, and Natural-Resource Products in American Manufacturing," Journal of Political Economy, Vol. 83, 57-82.

Jorgenson, D.W. and Fraumeni, B.M. (1981) "Substitution and Technical Change in Production," in Measuring and Modeling Natural Resource Substitution, E.R. Berndt and B. Field (eds.) Cambridge: M.I.T. Press.

______ and Griliches, Z. (1967) "The Explanation of Productivity Change," Review of Economic Studies, Vol. 34, 249-282.

______ and Nishimizu, M. (1978) "U.S. and Japanese Economic Growth 1952-1974: An International Comparison," Economic Journal, Vol. 88, 707-726.

Lindbeck, A. (1983) "The Recent Slowdown of Productivity Growth," Economic Journal, Vol. 93, 13-34.

Moroney, J.R. and Trapani, J.M. (1981) "Factor Demand and Substitution in Mineral Intensive Industries," Bell Journal of Economics, Vol. 12, 272-284.

Nadiri, M.I., (1980) "Sectoral Productivity Slowdown," American Economic Review, Vol. 70, 349-352.

Norsworthy, J.R., Harper, M.J., and Kunze, K. (1984) "The Slowdown in Productivity Growth: Analysis of Some Contributing Factors," Brookings Papers on Economic Activity, Vol. 2, 387-421.

Pindyck, R.S. and Rotemberg, J.J. (1983) "Dynamic Factor Demands and the Effects of Energy Price Shocks," American Economic Review, Vol. 73, 1066-1079.

Shephard, R.W. (1957) Cost and Production Functions, Princeton: Princeton University Press.

Slade, M.E. (1982) "Trends in Natural Resource Commodity Prices: An Analysis of the Time Domain," Journal of Environmental Economics and Management, Vol. 9, 122-137.

Tornqvist, L. (1936) "The Bank of Finland's Consumption Price Index," Bank of Finland Monthly Bulletin, No. 10, 1-8.

FSC
www.fsc.org
MIX
Papier | Fördert
gute Waldnutzung
FSC® C083411

Kolibri 360 GmbH
Ferdinand-Jühlke-Straße 7
99095 Erfurt, Deutschland
produktsicherheit@kolibri360.de